Tolley's Taxwise II 2023/24

Inheritance Tax
Taxation of Trusts and Estates

Disclaimer

In the preparation of this guide, every effort has been made to offer current, correct and clearly expressed information. However, the information in the text is intended to afford general guidelines only. This publication should not be regarded as offering a complete explanation of the tax matters referred to and is subject to changes in law and practice.

No responsibility for any loss occasioned to any person acting or refraining from action as a result of any material included in or omitted from this publication can be accepted by the authors or publishers. This work does not render legal, accounting or tax advice. Readers are encouraged to consult with professional advisers for advice concerning specific matters before making any decision.

Tolley's Taxwise II 2023/24

Inheritance Tax
Taxation of Trusts and Estates

Author: Donald Pearce-Crump BA (Hons) LLB CTA (Fellow) ATT

LexisNexis® UK & Worldwide

United Kingdom RELX (UK) Limited trading as LexisNexis®, 1–3 Strand, London WC2N 5JR

LNUK Global LexisNexis® encompasses authoritative legal publishing brands dating back to the 19th century including: Butterworths® in the United Kingdom, Canada and the Asia-Pacific region; Les Editions du Juris Classeur in France; and Matthew Bender® worldwide. Details of LexisNexis® locations worldwide can be found at www.lexisnexis.com

Published by LexisNexis®

A CIP Catalogue record for this book is available from the British Library.

ISBN for this volume: 9780754559122

Printed and bound by CPI Group (UK) Ltd, Croydon, CR0 4YY

Visit LexisNexis at www.lexisnexis.co.uk

About this book

For over 30 years Tolley's Taxwise II has provided practitioners with a practical means of keeping up to date with changing legislation relating to inheritance tax and trusts. This is achieved by way of worked examples, which have been updated annually and which, in this edition, illustrate the major changes introduced by Finance Act 2023 and Finance (No 2) Act 2023.

The publication is useful as a manual for staff, also acting as a training aid, as well as giving guidance as to the layout of computations. The examples are supplemented with explanatory notes explaining the law and practice relating to the issue illustrated.

The Taxwise publications are invaluable for students enabling them to apply their theoretical knowledge to practical examples of the types used by examiners in professional examinations.

COVERAGE

A selection of examples on inheritance tax, taxation of trusts and taxation of estates, based on the legislation current for 2023/24, complete with annotated solutions. Examples on the Law of Wills have been included in the final section of the book.

The examples are preceded by a summary on page (xvii) of the relevant provisions of Finance Act 2023, which received Royal Assent on 10 January 2023 and Finance (No 2) Act 2023, which received Royal Assent on 11 July 2023.

The book is not an exhaustive work of reference but it shows the treatment of the points that are most likely to be encountered.

The contents list starting on page (vii) shows the broad coverage of each example. In addition, there is a general index at the back of the book to assist in the location of specific points.

All statutory references in the inheritance tax sections of the book are to the Inheritance Tax Act 1984 unless otherwise stated.

References to TCGA 1992 are to the Taxation of Chargeable Gains Act 1992, ITTOIA 2005 are to the Income Tax (Trading and Other Income) Act 2005 and references to ITA 2007 are to the Income Tax Act 2007.

THE AUTHOR

Donald Pearce-Crump BA(Hons) LLB CTA (Fellow) ATT (Fellow) has been a tax lecturer and tutor for about 35 years. He runs a CTA training programme that was accredited by the Chartered Institute of Taxation (CIoT) for direct entry to the CTA exams (until the non-direct entry requirement was removed in 2019) and was instrumental in devising the Diploma in Tax Research and Communication (delivered by the City Law School). He works with CLT in relation to the tax training provided for the STEP Diploma and The STEP Advanced Certificate in UK Tax for International Clients. He is a visiting Fellow to the Business School at Bournemouth University. He is the author of the chapters on Deceased Estates and Investment Trust Companies in Tolley's 'Tax Planning'. He is the author of 'Payments made on the Termination of Employment' in Bloomsbury Tax Planning annual.

COMPANION PUBLICATION

Tolley's Taxwise I 2023/24 (covering Income Tax and National Insurance, Corporation Tax, Capital Gains Tax, Stamp Duty and VAT).

Contents

Abbreviations

AA 1870	Apportionment Act 1870
A & M trusts	Accumulation and maintenance trusts
art	Article
CA	Court of Appeal
CAA	Capital Allowances Act
c/f	compare
CFC	Controlled Foreign Company
ChD	Chancery Division
CIoT	Chartered Institute of Taxation
CGT	Capital Gains Tax
CGTA 1979	Capital Gains Tax Act 1979
CIR	Commissioners of Inland Revenue ('the Board')
CRCA	Commissioners for Revenue and Customs Act
CT	Corporation Tax
CTT	Capital Transfer Tax
CTTA 1984	Capital Transfer Act 1984
DoTAS	Disclosure of tax avoidance schemes
EC	European Communities
ECHR	European Court of Human Rights
ECJ	European Court of Justice
EEC	European Economic Community
EU	European Union
Ex D	Exchequer Division
FA	Finance Act
F(No 2)A	Finance No 2 Act
FII	Franked Investment Income
FY	Financial Year
HC(I)	High Court (Ireland)
HL	House of Lords
HMRC	Her Majesty's Revenue and Customs
ICTA	Income and Corporation Taxes Act 1988
IHT	Inheritance tax
IHTA 1984	Inheritance Tax Act 1984
IIP	Interest in possession
IPDI	Immediate post-death interest

ITA	Income Tax Act 2007
ITEPA 2003	Income Tax (Earnings and Pensions) Act 2003
ITTOIA 2005	Income Tax (Trading and Other Income) Act 2005
NIC	National insurance contribution
NPDI	Net pre-death income
NSB	National Savings Bank
pa	per annum
POA	Payments on account
POCA 2002	Proceeds of Crime Act 2002
RCC	Revenue and Customs Commissioners
s	Section
SA	Self-assessment
Sch	Schedule
SI	Statutory Instrument
SSCBA 1992	Social Security Contributions and Benefits Act 1992
SSI	Scottish Statutory Instrument
SP	Revenue Statement of Practice
Sp C	Special Commissioners
STC	Simon's Tax Cases
STC (SCD)	Simon's Tax Cases (Special Commissioners)
STEP	Society of Trusts and Estate Practitioners
TCGA 1992	Taxation of Chargeable Gains Act 1992
TMA 1970	Taxes Management Act 1970
TCIA 2013	Trusts (Capital and Income) Act 2013
TSI	Transitional serial interest
UKFTT	UK First-tier Tribunal
UKUT	UK Upper Tribunal
VAT	Value Added Tax
VATA 1994	Value Added Tax Act 1994
VE	Value of estate
VQTI	Vulnerable person's liability (see also Finance Act 2005 s 28)

Tax Rates and Thresholds

CAPITAL TRANSFER TAX – RATES FROM 13 MARCH 1975 TO 14 MARCH 1988

Nil-rate threshold	*From*	*To*
£15,000	13.03.1975	26.10.1977
£25,000	27.10.1977	25.03.1980
£50,000	26.03.1980	08.03.1982
£55,000	09.03.1982	14.03.1983
£60,000	15.03.1983	12.03.1984
£64,000	13.03.1984	05.04.1985
£67,000	06.04.1985	17.03.1986
£71,000	18.03.1986	16.03.1987
£90,000	17.03.1987	14.03.1988

INHERITANCE TAX – RATES FROM 15 MARCH 1988

Since 15 March 1988 there has been a single rate of inheritance tax of 40% (halved for some lifetime transfers), applicable where the gross cumulative chargeable transfers exceed a stipulated threshold. That threshold is set out in the table below. Since 6 April 2017 there is a separate threshold applicable to homes that are inherited by a deceased person's direct descendants. That threshold is not a fixed amount but is ascertained by reference to a statutory amount of £100,000 (2017/18), £125,000 (2018/19), £150,000 (2019/20) and £175,000 (2020/21).

Threshold	*Fixed by*	*Applicable to following transfers*
110,000	Finance Act 1988 s 136	Between 15 March 1988 and 5 April 1989
118,000	SI 1989/468	Between 6 April 1989 and 5 April 1990
128,000	SI 1990/680	Between 6 April 1990 and 5 April 1991
140,000	SI 1991/735	Between 6 April 1991 and 9 March 1992
150,000	F (No 2) A 1992 s 72, FA 1993 s 196, and FA 1994 s 246	Between 10 March 1992 and 5 April 1995
154,000	SI 1994/3011	Between 6 April 1995 and 5 April 1996
200,000	Finance Act 1996 s 183	Between 6 April 1996 and 5 April 1997
215,000	Finance Act 1997 s 93	Between 6 April 1997 and 5 April 1998
223,000	SI 1998/756	Between 6 April 1998 and 5 April 1999
231,000	SI 1999/596	Between 6 April 1999 and 5 April 2000
234,000	SI 2000/803	Between 6 April 2000 and 5 April 2001
242,000	SI 2001/639	Between 6 April 2001 and 5 April 2002
250,000	Finance Act 2002 s 118	Between 6 April 2002 and 5 April 2003
255,000	SI 2003/841	Between 6 April 2003 and 5 April 2004
263,000	SI 2004/771	Between 6 April 2004 and 5 April 2005
275,000	Finance Act 2005 s 98	Between 6 April 2005 and 5 April 2006
285,000	Finance Act 2005 s 98	Between 6 April 2006 and 5 April 2007
300,000	Finance Act 2005 s 98	Between 6 April 2007 and 5 April 2008
312,000	Finance Act 2006 s 155	Between 6 April 2008 and 5 April 2009
325,000	Finance Act 2006 s 155	Between 6 April 2009 and 5 April 2010
325,000	Finance Act 2010 s 8	Between 6 April 2010 and 5 April 2015
325,000	Finance (No 2) Act 2015 s 10	Between 6 April 2015 and 5 April 2021
325,000	Finance Act 2021 s 86	Between 6 April 2021 and 5 April 2028

INCOME TAX RATES FOR INDIVIDUALS

Earnings, pensions, taxable state benefits, self-employed profits and rental profits (ie non-savings non-dividend income) of non-Scottish taxpayers up to the basic rate limit of £37,700 (2023/24) are taxed first at the rate of 20% (basic rate). Such income and profits of Scottish taxpayers is charged to tax at 19% (on the first £2,162 of taxable income), 20% (on taxable income falling in the range £2,163 to £13,118) and 21% (on taxable income falling in the range £13,119 to £31,092).

The basic rate limit for Scottish taxpayers is £31,092 (2023/24). The definition of a Scottish taxpayer is based on the location of an individual's main place of residence. Although technically speaking income tax rates and limits for Welsh taxpayers (ie those having their main place of residence in Wales) may differ from those applying in England and Northern Ireland, in practice the rates and limits are the same in 2023/24.

Savings income (being, broadly speaking, bank and building society interest but defined further in ITA 2007 s 18) is regarded as the part of taxable income which is taxed next. There is a 0% starting rate for savings income only. The starting rate limit for 2023/24 is £5,000.

If taxable non-savings income (ie earnings, pensions etc as mentioned above) is more than this limit, then the 0% savings rate will not apply and savings income will be taxed in full at the savings basic rate of 20%. Scottish and Welsh taxpayers are entitled to a basic rate limit of £37,700 when taxing their savings income. However, if an individual has total taxable non-dividend income (which term includes savings income and non-savings income as listed above) of between £12,570 and £17,570, the 0% rate will apply to all of his savings income. From 6 April 2016 a new savings nil rate applies. From that date an individual has a savings allowance of £1,000, £500 or nil (determined according to the amount of his taxable income) and so much of his savings income as falls within his savings allowance is taxed at 0%. The savings nil rate applies in addition to the starting rate for savings.

Taxable non-savings non-dividend income over £37,700 (£31,092 for Scottish taxpayers) will be taxed at the 42% higher rate for Scottish taxpayers and at the 40% higher rate for Welsh and other UK taxpayers up to the higher rate limit of £125,140. Non-savings non-dividend income over £150,000 is taxed at the 46% top rate for Scottish taxpayers and the 45% additional rate for other UK taxpayers. Taxable savings income over £37,700 (for all UK taxpayers) will be taxed at the 40% savings higher rate up to the higher rate limit of £125,140. Savings income over £125,140 is taxed at the savings additional rate of 45%.

Dividends and other distributions (including those from share buy-backs) form the final part of taxable income. They are regarded as the top slice of an individual's taxable income and are taxed at the dividend nil rate of 0% to the extent that they fall within the individual's dividend allowance of £1,000 (£2,000 from 2018/19 to 2022/23), at the dividend ordinary rate of 8.75% to the extent that they then fall within the basic rate limit of £37,700 (for all UK taxpayers), at the dividend upper rate of 33.75% to the extent that they then fall between the basic rate limit and the higher rate limit of £125,140, and at the dividend additional rate of 39.35% to the extent they exceed the higher rate limit. With effect from 6 April 2016 dividends etc no longer carry tax a non-refundable credit.

An individual's personal allowance is withdrawn (gradually) where adjusted net income is in excess of £100,000 until the personal allowance is extinguished at an income level of £125,140 (in 2023/24). For income between £100,000 and £125,140 the effective marginal income tax rate is thus 60%.

INCOME TAX RATES FOR TRUSTS AND ESTATES

Special trust rates

The 'trust rate' (ITA 2007 s 9) applies to income of discretionary and accumulation trusts and to certain deemed income of other trusts. In 2023/24 the rate is 45% (ITA 2007 s 9(1)).

The 'dividend trust rate' applies to company dividends and other distributions (including share buy-backs) of discretionary and accumulation trusts. In addition it applies to share buy-back distributions received by all trusts. In 2023/24 the rate is 39.35% (ITA 2007 s 9(2)).

These special trust rates do not apply to the first £1,000 of trust income; instead that will be charged at the default basic rate of 20% or the dividend ordinary rate (ie 8.75%) as the case may be.

Trust income not liable at special rates and personal representatives

Trustees of other trusts and personal representatives of deceased estates are charged at the dividend ordinary rate of 8.75% on dividend income (except, as already stated, in the case of trustees, in relation to a distribution on a share buy-back), and the default basic rate of 20% on savings income and non-savings income. Trustees and personal representatives are not taxed at the default higher or additional rates or at the savings nil rate or the dividend nil rate.

Trusts with vulnerable beneficiaries

Trusts with vulnerable beneficiaries are able to elect irrevocably for the income and gains of the trust to be taxed as if the income belonged to the vulnerable beneficiary. See **Example F4**.

CAPITAL GAINS TAX RATES

Gains qualifying for business asset disposal relief (formerly known as entrepreneurs' relief) and investors' relief will be charged at a rate of 10%. The lifetime limit for business asset disposal relief is £1 million (£10 million before 11 March 2020) of qualifying gains and that for investors' relief is £10 million. The reliefs are discussed in more detail in **Examples A24** and **D3**.

Apart from the business asset disposal relief rate and the investors' relief rate, the rate of capital gains tax for an individual is, subject to what is said below, 10% or 18% (in respect of gains on residential property) (TCGA 1992 s 1H(2), (3)) and that is applied to his net chargeable gains for a year (ie after the annual exemption of £6,000 in 2023/24 (£12,300 in 2022/23)). However, if income tax is charged at the higher rate or the dividend upper rate in respect of any part of the taxable income (after personal allowances) of an individual for a tax year, the rate of capital gains tax in respect of the gains accruing to him in the year is 20% or 28% (in respect of gains on residential property) (TCGA 1992 s 1H(2), (3)). If no income tax is chargeable at the higher rate or the dividend upper rate in respect of an individual's income for a tax year, but the amount on which the individual is chargeable to CGT exceeds the unused part of his basic rate band of £37,700 (for all UK taxpayers), the rate of CGT on the excess is 20% or 28% as the case may be (TCGA 1992 s 1I(2)). In applying this rule, gains charged at the business asset disposal relief rate and the investors' relief rate are treated as the lowest part of the amount on which the individual is charged to CGT (TCGA 1992 s 1I(4), (5)).

Certain CGT reliefs allow a gain arising on a disposal of an asset to be deferred until sometime after the disposal. For instance, a gain can be reinvested in shares under the Enterprise Investment Scheme (EIS) and, subject to conditions, can be deferred until the EIS shares are disposed of. The CGT rates on a gain deferred in this way will be those in force at the time the deferral ends and the gain becomes liable to tax.

Personal representatives are entitled to the annual exemption, currently £6,000 for the tax year of death and the next two tax years. For 2023/24, gains not covered by the exemption are taxed at 20% and 28% (in respect of residential property) (TCGA 1992 s 1H(5), (6)). They are not entitled to business asset disposal relief or investors' relief.

For **trustees**, the CGT rate in 2023/24 is 20% and 28% (in respect of residential property) except in certain cases where business asset disposal relief or investors' relief applies when the rate is 10%. Trustees are entitled to an annual exemption (AE) of £3,000 in 2023/24, divided equally between UK trusts created by the same settlor after 6 June 1978, subject to a minimum AE in 2023/24 of £600 for each trust.

Finance Act 2023 measures relevant to this publication

Section in FA 2023	*Description of measures*
5	Basic rate limit and personal allowance for income tax fixed at £37,700 and £12,570 respectively for all tax years up to and including 2027–28.
6	Higher rate limit for income tax fixed at £125,140 for all tax years up to and including 2027–28.
7	The income tax dividend nil-rate reduced to £1,000 for 2023-24 and £500 for 2024–25 and subsequent tax years.
8	The capital gains tax annual exemption for individuals reduced to £6,000 for 2023–24 and £3,000 for 2024–25 and subsequent tax years. The provision increasing the annual exempt amount to reflect increases in CPI repealed. The limit for reporting capital gains on tax returns fixed at £50,000.
9	The inheritance tax nil-rate band (£325,000), residential nil-rate band (£175,000) and taper threshold for residential nil-rate band (£2 million) fixed for all tax years up to and including 2027–28.

Finance (No 2) Act 2023 measures relevant to this publication

Section in FA(No 2)A 2023	*Description of measures*
1	Income tax is charged for the tax year 2023–24.
2	The main rates of income tax for 2023–24 are set at 20% (basic rate), 40% (higher rate) and 45% (additional rate).
3	The default rates of income tax and the savings rates of income tax are set at 20% (default basic rate/savings basic rate), 40% (default higher rate/savings higher rate) and 45% (default additional rate/savings additional rate) respectively. The savings rates apply to the savings income of all UK taxpayers. The default rates apply to the non-savings, non-dividend income of taxpayers who are not subject to the main rates of income tax or the Scottish or Welsh rates of income tax (eg non-UK resident individuals). The Scottish Parliament (by way of Resolution) sets the Scottish rates of income tax for the non-savings, non-dividend income of Scottish taxpayers; the rates and thresholds for 2023–24 set by the Scottish Parliament are 19% on the first £2,162 of taxable income), 20% (on taxable income in the range £2,163 to £13,118), 21% (on taxable income in the range £13,119 to £31,092), 42% (on taxable income in the range £31,093 to £125,140) and at 47% on taxable income in excess of £125,140. The Welsh Assembly sets the Welsh rate income tax for the non-savings, non-dividend income of Welsh taxpayers; the rates and thresholds for 2023/24 for Welsh taxpayers match those for non-Scottish taxpayer in the rest of the UK.
4	The starting rate limit for savings income remains at £5,000 for 2023–24 and subsequent years of assessment.

Section in FA(No 2)A 2023	*Description of measures*
29 & Sch 2	This section introduces Schedule 2 which contains amendments to the rules on estates in administration and trusts. Part 1 makes technical amendments to the applicable rate for grossing up basic amounts of estate income, provides that income from stock dividends and release of close company loans are treated as bearing income tax at 0% and provides that estate income which derives from personal representatives' dividend income is treated, from 6 April 2023, as a residuary legatee's dividend income (thus mirroring the existing treatment of savings income). Part 2 introduces prospective provision (effective from 6 April 2024) for estates and trusts whose income is £500 or less to be taxed at 0% (with the limit for trusts to be reduced in certain circumstances where a settlor has created more than one trust). Estate income of legatees who receive income from estates to which this measure applies will be exempt from income tax. Part 3 abolishes, with effect from 6 April 2024, the provisions in ITA 2007 relating to accumulation and discretionary trusts' first slice income.
343	Definition of charity for UK tax purposes restricted to UK charities only.
347	Rights to reclaim the monetary value of a dormant asset in an authorised reclaim fund (set up under the UK's dormant assets scheme) will, from 6 June 2022, be treated for inheritance tax purposes as if they were the original asset where the original owner is alive at the time of transfer into the fund but subsequently dies before the asset is reclaimed.

Inheritance Tax — Personal and Estates — General

Question

(a) Outline the basic principles of inheritance tax.

(b) 'Disposition', 'transfer of value', 'chargeable transfer', 'potentially exempt transfer' and 'relevant property' are primary terms which need to be considered when determining whether an inheritance tax liability arises on a transaction. Explain the meaning of each term, demonstrating how the terms are linked together.

(c) Outline the exemptions from inheritance tax.

Answer

(a) Basic principles of inheritance tax

Introduction of inheritance tax

Inheritance tax (IHT) is a continuation of capital transfer tax which was originally introduced by FA 1975 and which had effect from 27 March 1974 for lifetime gifts, and from 13 March 1975 for transfers on death. The tax (and the legislation) was renamed IHT from 18 March 1986 when the approach to lifetime gifts was radically overhauled.

Charge to inheritance tax

The tax applies to individuals and trusts. In the case of an individual, IHT must be considered when he enters into transactions during his lifetime that result in a fall in the value of his overall wealth (ie his estate) and when he dies. Husbands and wives and civil partners are separate chargeable persons for IHT, each being able to take advantage of any available reliefs and exemptions.

In order to be within the charge to IHT an individual must be linked with the UK either by being domiciled in the UK or by owning property that is located in the UK. Consequently, if an individual is domiciled in the UK, he is liable to IHT on all his assets no matter where in the world they are located. If he is not domiciled in the UK, then he is liable to IHT only on those assets that are located in the UK. For more information on these matters, including situations where a person may be treated for IHT as domiciled in the UK (even though he may not be domiciled in any part of it under the common law), see **Example A5 part (a)**.

Lifetime transfers

Lifetime transfers that result in a fall in the value of an individual's estate are called 'transfers of value' and are prima facie within the charge to IHT. Transfers of value occur most obviously when an individual makes gifts of his property. Gifts (and other transfers of value) may be outside the scope of IHT or completely exempt from IHT (see **part (c)**). If they are not exempt, they are classified either as *chargeable lifetime transfers* or *potentially exempt transfers* (see **part (b)**).

Position on death

IHT also applies when an individual dies. On this occasion two matters have to be considered. First, the transfers that the individual has made during his lifetime in the seven years before his death are reconsidered and their liability to IHT is re-assessed. Secondly, all the property that he owns at the time of his death (ie his deceased estate) is charged to tax. The individual is deemed to make a transfer of his entire estate at the moment before he dies. In some cases, the deceased estate is regarded as containing property not in the direct ownership of the deceased, such as that owned by trustees in which the deceased has a qualifying interest in possession (see **Example C3**) and that owned by a donee in circumstances where the donor still enjoys the use of the property so that he is said to have a reservation of benefit in it (see **Example B4**).

Where the donor has avoided a pre-owned asset income tax charge by making an election under FA 2004 Sch 15 para 21 or para 22 then the asset concerned is treated for IHT as a gift with reservation and is similarly treated as forming part of his estate when he dies (see **Example B4**).

Inheritance tax – the occasions of charge

In general terms, it follows from the above outline that a charge to IHT may arise on three separate occasions:

- When an individual makes a transfer of his property during his lifetime ('lifetime' charge).
- On his death when his lifetime gifts are reconsidered ('supplementary' charge).
- On his death when the property that he owns is taxed ('estate' charge).

These occasions are considered in the order set out above. This is because the tax arising on a later transfer (including the deemed transfer of the deceased estate at death), depends on the timing and size of earlier transfers.

For example, where IHT is calculated on a chargeable lifetime transfer (the so-called 'lifetime' charge), it is necessary to take into account chargeable transfers that have been made in the previous seven years. Tax is calculated on the current transfer by reference to the total amount of chargeable transfers made in that period. If the aggregate of the values of the cumulated, earlier transfers and the present chargeable transfer exceeds the nil-rate threshold at which tax becomes payable, then the current transfer is charged at the rates applicable at the time it is made. See **Example A2 part** (**a**) for more details about the rates of IHT.

Similarly, when an individual dies, the value of his chargeable estate is added to the aggregate values of the chargeable transfers made in the seven years preceding his death to determine the tax liability arising in relation to his estate (the so-called 'estate' charge). Tax is charged to the extent that the combined values exceed the nil-rate threshold in force at the time of his death. Again see **Example A2 part** (**a**) below for a definition of the term 'nil-rate threshold'.

In addition, transfers made in the seven-year period before death that were potentially exempt now become chargeable because of the death, the so-called 'supplementary' charge). Transfers made in the same period before death that were chargeable when made (ie they were *chargeable lifetime transfers*), suffer an additional charge to tax. In charging both types of transfer on death, chargeable transfers made within the period of seven years before each particular transfer are taken into account even though the rates of tax used are those applicable at the date of death (if those rates produce a lower charge than the rates in force at the date of the transfer). Tax will only be payable to the extent that the aggregate value of the transfers, less any unused annual exemption at the time of the gift, exceed the general (ie non-residential) nil-rate threshold (and, where relevant, the residence nil-rate amount) in force at the date of death; and a taper relief is available in respect of tax on lifetime transfers made at least three years before death as indicated in **Example A2 part** (**a**) below. See **Example A2 part** (**b**) below for a discussion of the residence nil-rate band.

If a donor survives a *potentially exempt transfer* by seven years, it will not attract IHT unless the donor retains an interest in or benefits from the gifted property, in which case the seven year survivorship period only starts to run from the time the interest or benefit ceases (see **Example B5**).

Calculation of tax

Because the IHT nil-rate threshold (see **Example A2 part** (**a**)) is increased annually (unless Parliament decides otherwise – which it has for years up to and including 2020/21 (F(No 2)A 2015 s 10) and now to 2027/28 (FA 2021 s 86, as amended by FA 2023 s 9)) and because tax rates may also change, it should be borne in mind that the correct starting point for calculating tax on any occasion of charge is the cumulative chargeable transfers within the previous seven years. Those transfers are deemed to use up the nil-rate band before the current transfer. So the tax on the current transfer should be calculated using a cumulative tax figure for the earlier transfers based on the *current* scale of rates (or, if lower, the scale of rates at death, where tax or additional tax arises as a result of the donor's death within seven years). That cumulative tax figure for computation purposes will often not equate to the tax that has actually been paid, but it is the simplest way to make the tax calculation (see **Example A2 part** (**a**)).

Trusts

Where property is held in trust, the IHT treatment depends on the type of trust involved. The detailed provisions relating to trusts are dealt with in **Examples C1** to **C19**.

(i) If the settlement has an *interest in possession* (IIP) (see **Example C3**, broadly where one or more persons are entitled to the income of the settlement), and it is a qualifying IIP (again see **Example C3** in which this term is explained), the property in the settlement is deemed to belong to the person who is entitled to that interest and any liability will arise when that person's interest in the property comes to an end (eg where he makes a sale or gift of his interest, or his interest ceases by reason of a death, marriage, appointment or other reason) (see **Examples C4, C5** and **C6**). Like any other transfer in lifetime, however, the cessation of the life interest may be potentially exempt. This will apply where the trust property is transferred to an individual, or to a disabled trust. The transfer will only become a chargeable transfer if the life tenant who has given up his interest dies within the next seven years, the tax being computed by taking into account transfers within the seven years before the now chargeable transfer and calculating tax using the rates applicable at the date of death (see **Example A4 explanatory note 3**).

(ii) In most other cases – which includes discretionary trusts and many interest in possession trusts created since 22 March 2006 – the trust property will be subject to the 'relevant property' regime, in which case a charge to tax will occur on the tenth anniversary of the creation of the trust and at ten yearly intervals thereafter. The tax is charged on the value of the 'relevant property' in the trust, at 30% of the effective rate of tax on a notional chargeable transfer (see **Example C15 explanatory note 2**).

The lifetime rate of tax is used to calculate the effective rate, and the maximum possible charge is 30% of 20%, ie 6%.

As it would otherwise be possible to avoid an impending ten yearly charge to tax on a relevant property settlement by distributing assets between ten-year anniversaries, an 'exit charge' arises when property ceases to be relevant property. The tax on the amount leaving the settlement is charged at the appropriate fraction of 30% of an effective rate, the appropriate fraction depending on the number of complete quarters that have elapsed since the creation of the trust or the last ten year anniversary as the case may be. For more details see **Examples C10 to C13**.

A relevant property trust is any trust to the extent that the trust property is *not* within one of the following categories (the list is not exhaustive):

(a) excluded property (see **Example A5**);

(b) property held for charitable purposes only, whether for a limited time or otherwise;

(c) property held on accumulation and maintenance terms, in the restricted (and transitional) scope of that concept from 6 April 2008 (only applicable to trusts which have qualified continuously from immediately before 22 March 2006);

(d) property held on terms of a trust for bereaved minors (IHTA 1984 s 71A) or an age 18-to-25 trust (s 71D) (available only on the death of a parent of the beneficiary, and also where the trust is established under the terms of the Criminal Injuries Compensation Scheme or the Victims of Overseas Terrorism Compensation Scheme, except that an age 18-to-25 trust can apply from 6 April 2008 to a former accumulation and maintenance trust existing before 22 March 2006 where beneficiaries will become entitled to capital by age 25);

(e) property held on trust for disabled people settled before 10 March 1981;

(f) property held on terms of an approved maintenance fund for historic buildings;

(g) property held in registered pension schemes (but not benefits which, having become payable under a fund or scheme, become comprised in a settlement);

(h) property in which an IIP subsists which results in the beneficiary being treated as though he were beneficially entitled to the trust property itself. From 22 March 2006 this is restricted to the following categories of IIPs (called 'qualifying IIPs' for more details of which see **Example C3**):

(i) where the beneficiary has been beneficially entitled to the IIP since before 22 March 2006; or

(ii) an immediate post-death interest; or

(iii) a disabled person's interest; or

(iv) a transitional serial interest; or

(v) where the beneficiary became entitled to the IIP on or after 9 December 2009, at a time when he was domiciled in the UK, and did so under an arm's length transaction within s 10 (see s 5(1B));

(i) property in which a company has an IIP if the company purchased that interest at arm's length from an individual in whose hands it was an estate IIP and the company's business consists wholly or mainly of the acquisition of interests in settled property (s 59(2)).

(b) Dispositions, transfers of value, potentially exempt transfers and chargeable transfers

Chargeable transfers and transfers of value

IHTA 1984 Part I incorporates a number of sections in arriving at the definition of a *chargeable transfer*:

s 1: IHT shall be charged on the value transferred by a *chargeable transfer*.

s 2(1): A *chargeable transfer* is any *transfer of value* made by an individual other than an exempt transfer. (It is also provided in s 2(3) that references to chargeable transfers include references to occasions on which tax is payable by relevant property and other trusts under Part 3 Chapter 3 as explained in **part (a)** above.)

s 3(1): A *transfer of value* is any disposition made by a person (the transferor) as a result of which the value of his estate immediately after the disposition is less than it would be but for the disposition; and the amount by which it is less is the value transferred by the transfer. Unless otherwise provided, 'transfers of value' include events on which tax is chargeable (such as the transfer which an individual is treated as making when he dies or when a qualifying interest in possession comes to an end in lifetime) (s 3(4)).

s 3(2): Any diminution in the value of a person's estate brought about by the disposition by him of 'excluded property' is ignored.

The value charged by a *chargeable transfer* is therefore the difference between the value of the transferor's estate before and after the transfer, less any exemptions and ignoring disposals of excluded property (as to which see **Example A5**).

A person's estate is defined by s 5(1) as the aggregate of all the property to which he is beneficially entitled (certain items being excepted); however, the estate of a person immediately before his death does not include excluded property. 'Property' includes rights or interests of any description, but does not include 'settlement powers', ie powers over, or exercisable directly or indirectly in relation to, settled property or a settlement (s 272). The result is that a person's estate is comprised of virtually everything that he actually owns. As a general, basic principle, nothing is excluded from a person's estate, not even his 'excluded property' (except on his death). One must not be misled by the term 'excluded property'. It is a common error to assume that excluded property is 'excluded' from a person's estate, or from the scope of the tax altogether. This is not the case. 'Excluded property' is a subset of the property in a person's estate which is afforded special treatment when it itself is the subject-matter of a disposition.

Dispositions

A disposition has to be made by an individual in order for it to be said that he has made a transfer of value. The term *disposition* is not defined but case law has determined that the word has no special or technical meaning (*Ward v CIR* (1956)). It therefore covers any act by which a person deliberately divests himself of the beneficial ownership of his property. The legislation extends its meaning where there are associated operations (ss 268 and 272), deliberate failures to exercise rights (s 3(3)), and alterations of rights attaching to shares in a close company (s 98) (see **Example A20**). Certain dispositions are ignored by the IHT regime and so cannot give rise to transfers of value (see **Example A4**).

The most obvious example of a disposition that results in a transfer of value is a gift made by an individual. But transfers of value can occur in less obvious circumstances, as illustrated in *HMRC v Parry* [2018] STC 2324 where the Court of Appeal decided that a transfer of money from the deceased's company pension scheme to her personal pension scheme six weeks before her death constituted a transfer of value. The deceased and her husband had built up a successful company. She had a company pension which had been created as part of the settlement reached between her and her husband when they divorced. The deceased was diagnosed with a terminal illness and upon learning that on her death the funds in her company pension would, to the extent that they exceeded the death benefits payable, revert to the company (and hence potentially payable to her former husband as shareholder) she transferred the funds into a personal pension scheme in respect of which she nominated her two sons as beneficiaries of the death benefit. Before the transfer the sons would have benefitted from the company pension fund death benefits which, having been paid into the deceased's estate, would have been payable to them as beneficiaries of her estate. After the transfer they still took the death benefits from the private pension fund but under a letter of wishes and pursuant to the discretion of the pension fund trustees. The difference was that in the latter case the benefits would be paid free of IHT. The deceased died less than two months after the transfer.

HMRC argued that the pension transfer was a disposition (which was not disputed) and that disposition was also a transfer of value. This arose by reference to the right to the death benefit which before the transfer was under the deceased's control and payable to her estate. That right had value as the deceased was about to die shortly and hence her estate was so much the more valuable. After the transfer the death benefit was not payable to her estate or under her control but was, subject to the pension trustees' discretion which was likely to be exercised, payable to her sons. Hence her estate suffered a fall in value. The Court of Appeal agreed with HMRC's argument. On appeal to the Supreme Court (see case report at [2020] STC 1836), this point was not discussed in any detail as it was accepted by the taxpayer (the deceased executors) that there was a transfer of value unless IHTA 1984 s 10 (Dispositions not intended to confer gratuitous benefit – see **Example A4 part (a)**) applied. The Supreme Court held that it did apply and so concluded that there was no transfer of value in the case for that reason.

It will be noted in this regard that where an individual who is in normal health transfers a fund from one pension scheme to another, there is no transfer in value as the death benefits have no enhanced value so that any loss is negligible. By contrast if he is in ill health then the loss to the estate is significant. For these purposes HMRC adopt a two-year rule so that it will only investigate cases if death occurs within two years of transfer, provided at the time of transfer the individual was already in ill health and was aware of it.

Potentially exempt transfers

A potentially exempt transfer is a species of lifetime transfer that may be made by an individual. The concept is defined in s 3A, which was introduced by FA 1986, extended by F(No 2)A 1987 and restricted again by FA 2006. Any lifetime transfer of value which:

(1) is made by an individual on or after 18 March 1986, and

(2) would otherwise be a chargeable transfer, and

(3) is a 'gift' to another individual (as defined – see below)

is 'potentially exempt' from IHT.

A potentially exempt transfer is initially treated as an *exempt transfer* (s 3A(5)). However if the transferor dies during the next *seven* years the potentially exempt transfer becomes retrospectively a *chargeable transfer* (s 3A(4)). Any tax on the gift then arising is paid by the transferee.

To come within the definition of a 'gift' to another individual, the value transferred must be attributable to property that becomes part of that individual's estate, or as a result of which the individual's estate is increased. For transfers made before 22 March 2006, this included gifts to a trust in which the individual had an interest in possession. Since 22 March 2006, if the property is settled property immediately after the transfer (whether or not it was so immediately before the transfer) this condition can be fulfilled only if the property is then subject to a disabled person's interest.

A more unusual example of a gift in this context is where a person with an interest in trust property uses his own assets to buy a reversionary interest in the trust property (and, if his interest is not already in possession, the interest he buys is longer deferred than his own). Payment of the price for the reversionary interest in these circumstances is a transfer of value by virtue of s 55, since nothing comes into his estate in return for the price and it is not protected by s 10; but if he pays the price to another individual then the value transferred by that transfer is attributable to property – the price – which (even if paid outside the UK to a non-domiciliary) becomes comprised in the seller's estate and therefore qualifies the transfer as a 'gift' to another individual within s 3A(2). This unusual situation underlines the fact that the 'gift to another individual' condition doesn't actually require a gift in the usual sense of the word – the word is simply used as a label for a transfer of value that fits within s 3A(2).

Potentially exempt transfers which become chargeable transfers (because the transferor dies within the ensuing seven years) are charged to IHT at their value at the time of the transfer, but using the rates applicable at the time of death. Where such transfers have occurred more than *three* years before death any tax due on that particular transfer (but not tax due on the transferor's estate at death) is reduced by taper relief, as in **Example A2 part** (a). Even though the potentially exempt transfers have become chargeable transfers, no tax is payable (and taper relief is not therefore relevant) if when added to the chargeable transfers in the previous seven years they do not exceed the nil-rate threshold (and as the case may be, the residence nil-rate amount) in force at the date of death. The general (ie non-residential) nil-rate band available in respect of the death estate is, however, correspondingly reduced.

Relevant property

As explained in **part (a) above,** IHT charges arise in relation to relevant property trusts. Relevant property is, broadly speaking, settled property in which there is no qualifying interest in possession (see **Example C3**). Generally speaking, all settled property is relevant property unless it is excluded property or is held on the types of trust listed in **part (a) above.** For the charging mechanisms in relation to relevant property trusts see **Examples C10–C13.**

(c) Inheritance tax exempt transfers

Most lifetime transfers of value made by an individual other than into trust are *potentially exempt*, only becoming chargeable if the donor dies within seven years after the gift (s 3A).

There are however some transfers which are *completely exempt* when made (and such exemptions, once given, can never be taken away). The following transfers are exempt (although some of these exemptions apply only in lifetime, others in lifetime and on death):

(a) *Transfers between spouses and civil partners* (s 18).

This applies to all lifetime and death transfers between spouses except where the transferee spouse is foreign domiciled and the transferor spouse is UK domiciled, when, from 6 April 2013, transfers are only exempt to a cumulative total of an amount equal to the nil-rate band in force at the time of the transfer (£55,000 before 6 April 2013) (FA 2013 s 176(4)). To make the point clear, there is no limit on the exemption for transfers where both spouses/civil partners are domiciled in the UK, where neither spouse/civil partner is domiciled in the UK or where the transferee spouse/civil partner is domiciled in the UK and the transferor spouse/civil partner is not domiciled in the UK. See **Example A5 part** (a) for more detailed information about an individual's domicile and **Example A5 part** (c) about transfers to a spouse or civil partner not domiciled in the UK.

Where the transfer results in property being held in trust, with the transferor's spouse or civil partner having a qualifying interest in possession or deemed interest in possession (see **Example C3**), the exemption will apply on death.

In lifetime, the exemption will only apply in relation to a transfer that results in property being held in trust where the transferee spouse or civil partner is a disabled person so that the interest in possession (or deemed interest in possession) to which the property is subject is a disabled person's interest; otherwise the trust will be a relevant property trust and the transfer will be a chargeable transfer.

In the case of *Burden v UK* ([2008] STC 1305) two sisters in their eighties who had lived together all their lives complained that the legislation as to civil partnerships, which replicates as between same-sex couples the long-established 'prohibited degrees' of relationship which, for marriage, take their justification primarily from genetic reasons, infringed their human rights so that they should be able to qualify for the same tax treatment as those who had gone through the necessary civil ceremony. However this complaint was rejected, and they did not qualify for the exemption.

(b) *Annual exemption.*

For those lifetime transfers which are not completely exempt there is an annual exemption.

The first £3,000 of transfers in any tax year are exempt provided they are completed in the lifetime of the individual. Any unused portion of the exemption may be carried forward for one year only, for use in the following tax year after the exemption for that following year has been completely used.

The annual exemption is applied to lifetime transfers that are not completely exempt in strict chronological order. In the case of a lifetime transfer which does not give rise to an immediate charge, it is only the balance over and above any available exemptions, including any annual exemptions, which is a potentially exempt transfer, as illustrated in **Example A2 part (c)**. Also see the additional commentary on the annual exemption in **Example A5 explanatory note 9**.

(c) *Small gifts to same person* (s 20).

Any outright lifetime gifts to any one person in any one tax year are exempt up to the combined value of £250. If they exceed that value at all, this exemption is inapplicable as regards all gifts to that person in that year.

(d) *Normal expenditure out of income* (s 21).

To obtain exemption the gift must be made in lifetime only and must be:

(1) Part of the donor's normal expenditure.

(2) Made out of income (taking one year with another).

(3) Such as will not reduce the donor's available net income (after all other similar transfers) below that required to maintain his usual standard of living.

An example of such expenditure would be the payment of a regular life insurance or pension premium for the benefit of another. HMRC will normally look for a pattern of giving in relation to this exemption. There is no statutory limit on the value of the gift to which this exemption applies. (See **explanatory note 1** for further commentary.)

(e) *Gifts in consideration of marriage or civil partnership* (ss 22 and 57).

A gift made in lifetime only of up to £5,000 by a parent of a party to a marriage; of £2,500 by a lineal ancestor; of £2,500 by one party to the marriage to the other; or of £1,000 by any other person is exempt provided it is a lifetime gift made in consideration of the marriage. If the gift is to a marriage settlement, the settlement must exclude from benefit all persons other than the parties to the marriage, their issue or the spouses of such issue (see s 22(4) for the detail); it is not necessary for the settlement to confer any interest in possession. The limit applies to gifts by any one donor for any one marriage. For this exemption 'children' include step-children, adopted and illegitimate children.

The same rules apply in relation to gifts made in contemplation of persons entering into a civil partnership, and the reference in the preceding paragraph to spouses includes civil partners.

(f) *All gifts to charities or registered community amateur sports clubs* (s 23).

All such gifts are exempt whether in lifetime or on death, whether the gifts are made directly to the charity or club or held on trust for charitable purposes only or, in the case of a sports club, held for the purposes of the club or another registered club or an eligible sports governing body or a charity. Following the decision of the European Court in the *Pershe* case the government eventually conceded that gifts to charities elsewhere in the European Union (and other territories as specified in regulations – currently Norway and Iceland have been specified (see The Taxes (Definition of Charity) (Relevant Territories) Regulations 2010, SI 2010/1904) as has Lichtenstein (see The Taxes (Definition of Charity) (Relevant Territories) (Amendment) Regulations 2014, SI 2014/1807) will qualify for this exemption, but introduced the controversial 'fit and proper' persons requirement, in relation to those who have the general control and management of a charity, with a view to minimising the scope for abuse of charity reliefs (see FA 2010 s 30 and Sch 6). Charities registered in EU and the other overseas countries mentioned will cease to be charities for the purposes of inheritance tax from 1 April 2024 at the latest (F(No 2)A 2023 s 344). The definitions are set out in more detail in **Example B12**.

(g) *Gifts to political parties* (s 24).

Gifts to a qualifying political party (see **explanatory note 3**), whether in lifetime or on death, are wholly exempt.

(h) *Gifts for national purposes* (s 25 and Sch 3).

All such qualifying gifts are exempt whether in lifetime or on death.

(i) *Gifts to housing associations* (s 24A).

Gifts of land to registered housing associations are exempt whether in lifetime or on death.

(j) *Maintenance funds for heritage property* (s 27 and Sch 4).

On a claim being made, transfers into a settlement established for the maintenance, repair or preservation of heritage property are exempt provided a Treasury direction is made in respect of the property under Sch 4. The exemption applies in lifetime and on death. A claim must be made within two years of the date of transfer or such longer period as HMRC may allow.

(k) *Employee trusts* (s 28, s 28A).

Transfers by individuals of shares or securities in a company to a trust for the benefit of employees (Employee Benefit Trusts and Employee Ownership Trusts) of the company are exempt, provided detailed conditions are satisfied. In particular the exemption does not apply where the a trust permits any of the settled property to be applied at any time for the benefit of a person who is shareholder in a company whose shares are settled on the trust, or any person connected with him. Thus shareholders and those connected with them cannot be beneficiaries of the trust concerned. These prohibition tests, if they are to apply, must be met at the time of the transfer of the shares into the trust. If a person is connected with the shareholder at the time of settlement of the shares, the prohibition will apply and the transfer of the shares will not be exempt. The fact that persons may become not connected with the shareholder at a later date is irrelevant (*Barker v Baxendale Walker* [2017] ECWA Civ 2056).

As indicated in **part (b) above**, certain property that is not exempt is nonetheless left out of account because it is 'excluded property'. Certain other types of property, although not within the strict definition of the term 'excluded property' is also left out of account when calculating IHT – see **Example A5 part (b)**. Details of excluded property are also in **Example A5 part (b)**.

Abatement of exemptions applicable on death

Where an exempt beneficiary settles a claim against a deceased's estate out of his own resources the exemption is abated. This could occur, for example, where a claim is made for financial provision against an estate by a non-exempt beneficiary (eg a child or mistress of the deceased). If, instead of the estate meeting the claim, an exempt beneficiary meets the liability (eg spouse, charity etc) out of their separate resources then tax would be avoided, since that part of the estate passing to the exempt beneficiary rather than to the non-exempt beneficiary would not have attracted tax. Section 29A provides that any such value transferred by the exempt beneficiary is treated as a chargeable part of the deceased's estate.

Availability of exemptions to trusts

With the exception of (c), (d) and (k), the above exemptions are available to transfers out of trusts with a qualifying interest in possession, subject in the case of the annual and marriage exemptions to certain conditions (s 57 – see **Example C6 explanatory note 3**).

The exemptions are not available on distributions out of relevant property trusts since those distributions are not 'transfers of value' (although they are 'chargeable transfers'); but equivalent exemptions are provided in the case of distributions to employee trusts or charitable trusts – see **Example C10 explanatory note 11**.

Conditional exemption for heritage property (s 30)

On a claim being made within two years of a transfer and specified undertakings being given, exemption is granted, subject to conditions, for the transfer of property that is designated by the Treasury as of pre-eminent national, scientific, historic, artistic or scenic interest (eg works of art and historic buildings). This applies to transfers on death and to lifetime transfers where the property has been owned for six years or more by the transferor and/or his spouse, or where it passed to the transferor on the death of another. Tax may become chargeable if the property is disposed of or the conditions are no longer satisfied, though in the case of a disposal otherwise than on sale the conditional exemption may be renewed on the giving of further undertakings by the transferee – see **explanatory note 5**.

Explanatory Notes

Normal expenditure out of income

(1) 'Normal expenditure out of income' was considered in the case of *Bennett and Others v CIR* (1994). In that case the taxpayer was the life tenant of her late husband's Will Trust. She had sufficient income in her own right and instructed the trustees to pay to her three sons the income from the Will Trust. This they did, amounting to some £28,000 in February 1989 and then £180,000 in February 1990, a few days before Mrs Bennett died. The judge was satisfied that 'normality of expenditure' had been achieved. He said that the donor had had a single and continuing intention regarding the surplus trust income which intention was put into effect. This decision is likely to prove helpful in cases where a life assurance policy has been effected in trust, but the grantee of the policy died unexpectedly having only paid one or a very limited number of the regular premiums which would have been due had he survived. Lightman J said, in summary:

(i) 'normal expenditure' means expenditure which, when it took place, accorded with the settled pattern of expenditure adopted by the donor;

(ii) a settled pattern can be established either by examining the donor's expenditure over a period of time, or by showing that the donor has assumed a commitment, or adopted a firm resolution, regarding future expenditure and has thereafter complied with it;

(iii) there is no fixed minimum period during which expenditure has to be incurred. A single payment implementing the commitment or resolution may be sufficient;

(iv) where there is no commitment or resolution, a series of payments may be required;

(v) a pattern need not be immutable, but it must be intended to remain for a sufficient period (barring unforeseen circumstances). Thus 'death-bed' resolutions would be excluded;

(vi) the expenditure need not be fixed, nor need the recipient need be the same on each occasion. The amount of the gift may be fixed by a formula, eg a percentage of earnings, or by reference to an ascertainable liability, eg the cost of nursing home fees, and the donees may be a general class, eg family members or needy friends; and

(vii) tax planning does not disqualify the expenditure.

The test of 'normal expenditure' is easy enough to satisfy once a couple of gifts have been made and a pattern becomes discernible; in *Bennett* the judge said that a settled pattern can be established by examining a donor's expenditure over a period of time. The test is less easy to apply without the benefit of hindsight, but it is still possible for the exemption to apply to the initial gift(s) that subsequently become part of a settled pattern of giving. In *Bennett* it was said that a settled pattern can also be established by showing that the donor has assumed a commitment (such as their executing a deed of covenant or setting up a standing order on their bank account), or has adopted a firm resolution, regarding future expenditure and has thereafter complied with it. There is no fixed minimum period during which expenditure has to be incurred (although HMRC's view is that a period of three or four years is reasonable). Indeed, a single payment implementing the commitment or firm resolution may be sufficient to establish the requisite settled pattern, although the donor will be on more certain ground where the gifts continue over time in accordance with the initial commitment or resolution. HMRC do not rule out the application of the exemption of a single gift made close to an individual's death, but they do say that strong evidence must be provided that the gift was genuinely intended to be the first in a pattern and that there was a realistic expectation that further payments would be made (IHTM 14242).

The gift must be out of income. Income is not defined in the IHTA 1984 but should be determined for each year in accordance with normal accountancy rules. It is not necessarily the same as income for income tax purposes (so that capital receipts deemed to be income for income tax purposes will not qualify).

There was an unsurprising Special Commissioner's decision in *Nadin v IRC* [1997] STC (SCD) 107 that capital sums produced by sales of investments are not income. It should be noted that sums that are capital in nature but which are charged to income tax (or so chargeable but for an exemption) are not income for the purposes of this exemption. Hence the following amounts are not income: capital elements of annuities, premium bonds, the proceeds of a buy-back by a company of its owns shares, stock options and income tax free withdrawals from non-qualifying life assurance policies. The income that is the subject-matter of the gift must belong to the donor; care must be taken in the case of joint bank accounts where only a proportion of the balance on the account will belong to the donor.

The income of the year in which gifts were made is first considered to see if there is enough income available to make the gift. Income from earlier years does not retain its character as income indefinitely. At some point it becomes capital but there are no hard and fast rules about when this point is. If there is no evidence to the contrary, HMRC consider that income becomes capital after a period of two years (IHTM 14250). Each case will depend on its own facts but, in general, the longer the period of accumulation, the more likely it is that the income has become capital.

The gift has to be made out of income taking one year with another. The legislation accommodates the case where an individual's income fluctuates from year to year but overall they have enough income to make normal gifts and meet their standard of living on an ongoing basis. In these cases, the income and expenditure over a number of years may need to be considered to see if the income test is satisfied. Although income can be carried over from year to year in these circumstances, usually HMRC will investigate cases where a taxpayer wishes to carry forward more than two year's income (to ensure earlier income has not become capital).

HMRC Inheritance Tax stated in their Newsletter Volume 2.3 December 1997, in response to questions raised by the Private Trust Committee of the Association of Corporate Trustees:

> 'There is no rule of thumb. We basically judge each case on its merits. We do look very closely at the standard of living of the transferor. The test of "normality" requires a pattern of giving to be established. That is why it is not always possible to say that, at the time it is made, a particular gift is or is not exempt as "normal".'

In order to establish the pattern of giving, it is useful for an individual to have a gift memorandum in place detailing what percentage of their annual surplus income is the subject of a gift. Documentation evidencing a donor's income and expenditure, how much is surplus and their intention to make gifts should be drawn up annually. An extraordinary amount of expenditure in any one year should not affect the pattern of giving. Such documentation is useful in supporting a claim for the exemption and to this end form IHT403 could be completed each year for record purposes.

See further **Example A25** and **Example C15**.

Gifts in consideration of marriage or civil ceremony

(2) Whether a gift is in consideration of a marriage or civil ceremony is a question of fact. A gift made on the occasion of a marriage or civil ceremony or one made conditionally upon the marriage/civil ceremony taking place, whilst usually qualifying, is not automatically in consideration of marriage/civil ceremony. This is an involved legal point and reference to appropriate judicial decisions should be made if the point requires consideration in greater depth.

Gifts to political parties

(3) Exemption is not given for gifts to all political parties, but only to those where, at the last general election preceding the transfer:

(a) two members of that party were elected to the House of Commons, or

(b) one member of that party was elected to the House of Commons and no fewer than 150,000 votes were given to candidates of that party (s 24(2)).

In *A Banks v HMRC* [2019] UKFTT 617 the taxpayer made donations during 2014 and 2015 to the United Kingdom Independence Party (UKIP). He claimed that the donations were exempt under s 24(2) notwithstanding that UKIP had not succeeded in having any of its candidates elected as MPs at the 2010 general election. The FTT observed that UKIP secured a greater proportion of the popular vote at the 2010 general election than any other parties that did succeed in having candidates elected, at the time of the donations there were UKIP MPs but they had been elected at by-elections held after the 2010 general election, UKIP was a registered political party, in 2014 and 2015 UKIP was widely represented on local councils in the UK and that UK candidates had been elected to the European Parliament. The FTT found, as claimed by the taxpayer, that s 24 was incompatible with the European Convention on Human Rights (ECHR) as it did not strike a fair balance in the context of the provision of tax relief for the funding of political parties. The tax treatment of the donations amounted to discrimination on the grounds of his political opinions. Hence the taxpayer's human rights had been breached. However, as the FTT had no jurisdiction to rewrite s 24(2) (the making of the legislation compliant being a matter for Parliament alone), the taxpayer's claim to relief was dismissed.

The taxpayer renewed his argument before the Upper Tribunal [2020] STC 996 which found that there was no discrimination under the ECHR because there was no link between the legislation and the taxpayer's status as a member of UKIP. A donation to any political party could meet the conditions at any time depending on its electoral success. The legislation did not directly target UKIP specifically. Whether relief was available was simply political happenstance rather than evidencing anything of a systematic nature amounting to discrimination. The Tribunal held that the aim of s 24 was to provide tax relief on donations to political parties that are participating in a parliamentary democracy by being represented in the House of Commons, and that the legislation was proportionate because the condition in s 24 was rationally connected to that legitimate aim. The taxpayer's appeal therefore failed.

The taxpayer failed again in an appeal to the Court of Appeal [2021] EWCA Civ 1439 which affirmed the decision of the Upper Tribunal. The court held that s 24 did not discriminate against the taxpayer, either directly or indirectly, on the basis of his political opinions, and there was no breach of art 14 of the convention on that basis. The only statutory aim or purpose of s 24 that could safely be inferred from its terms was the provision of a fiscal incentive for the funding of political parties that had achieved a specified minimum level of representation in the UK Parliament at Westminster, and thereby to promote the functioning of parliamentary democracy in the UK. The qualifying conditions were deliberately intended to limit the availability of the exemption to cases where the party had an established presence in the House of Commons, measured in one or other of the ways specified, and thus in the functioning of parliamentary democracy in the UK through the Westminster Parliament. There was no causal link between the taxpayer's political views, manifested in his support for UKIP and the substantial donations that he made to that party, and the failure of the donations to qualify for exemption under s 24. The reason for the non-exemption of the donations made in the 2014–15 tax year had nothing to do with the taxpayer's political opinions. Section 24 applied in the same way to parties across the political spectrum, from the far right to the far left. The political views of the donor were completely irrelevant to the question whether or not the donation qualified for relief under the section. Nor could it be said that the qualifying conditions were in any way a proxy for discrimination against the taxpayer on the grounds of his political opinions. In relation to indirect discrimination in particular, it could not be inferred, as a matter of common sense or otherwise, that the requirements of s 24 had any particular disproportionate effect on supporters of UKIP in general, or the taxpayer in particular, as compared with their impact on supporters of any other political party that did not qualify for exemption at the material time. There was nothing about UKIP or its supporters that placed them in a different category from all other supporters of political parties who were denied exemption for their gifts by the criteria of s 24.

Gifts to housing associations

(4) Land is not defined for the purpose of the s 24A exemption on gifts to housing associations. It would appear therefore that buildings are included, since they are within the definition of land in the Interpretation Act 1978 Sch 1.

Heritage property

(5) The conditions under which exemption is available for heritage property and the circumstances in which IHT becomes payable are dealt with in **Example B9**.

Voidable transfers

(6) A transfer which is set aside by enactment or rule of law (eg bankruptcy) is not counted as a transfer for IHT purposes, and neither is the transfer back (s 150 – voidable transfers).

Dispositions that are not transfers of value

(7) This Example deals with transfers of value that are wholly or partly exempt. **Example A4** at **part (a)** illustrates that there are certain dispositions which are ignored for IHT purposes and so not treated as transfers of value at all.

Failure to exercise a right

(8) As indicated in **part (b)** of the Example, the failure to exercise a right is a disposition for IHT under s 3(3), unless it is shown that the failure was not deliberate. Such a disposition is treated as made at the latest time that the right could have been exercised – so if it is still exercisable then there will as yet have been no deemed disposition (see **Example A20 part (d)**).

In *HMRC v Parry* [2020] STC 1836 the Supreme Court explained that there was no mandate to import a temporal requirement into the subsection, requiring an immediate temporal link between the reduction in one estate and the increase in the other. There was a correlation of substance between the reduction and the increase, in that one resulted from the other, but they need not occur at precisely the same time. That was not to say that questions of timing would be irrelevant to a determination of whether the subsection was satisfied. As with all questions of causation, the evaluation of whether another person's estate was increased by the omission to exercise a right required consideration of all the facts and circumstances. Putting it another way, the omission had to be the operative cause of the increase. That was reinforced by the fact that s 3(3) required only that another person's estate was increased. It was not concerned with the identity of the other person.

Before 6 April 2011 an IHT charge could arise in a scheme member's lifetime under s 3(3) if he did not exercise his right to take pension benefits. The charge applied at the latest time when the right could be exercised, ie immediately before death. For example, if a scheme member did not take his pension when his life expectancy was seriously impaired and this resulted in an enhanced death benefit being paid to his beneficiaries then IHT could apply (see *HMRC v Parry* [2018] STC 2324 and [2020] STC 1836). But IHT was not charged in respect of these enhanced death benefits where the beneficiary was a spouse, civil partner or person who was financially dependent on the scheme member. Nor was IHT applied where a scheme member chose not to exercise a right at a time when this choice did not trigger a charge (for example, choosing not to take a pension when they were in good health) and did not subsequently vary that choice, even when a reduction in their life expectancy would in strictness trigger an IHT charge. In addition, payments arising in these circumstances which are made to charity were also be exempted from IHT. With effect from 6 April 2011, where a person who is a member of a registered pension scheme (or a qualifying non-UK pension scheme) omits to exercise pension rights under the pension scheme, s 3(3) does not apply in relation to the omission (IHTA 1984 s 12(2ZA), inserted by FA 2011 Sch 16 para 85). However, this exclusion did not apply to persons who elected to draw down all or part of their pensions thereby becoming entitled to those funds. Having become entitled, any failure by them to exercise their rights over the drawdown funds so that they left funds undrawn on their death meant that the rule on failure to exercise a right applied and an IHT charge could arise. This was on the basis that the exclusion in s 12(2ZA) applied only to the member's right to elect to crystallise the pension plan and so draw benefits. It did not apply to the member's rights actually to draw the funds once they had been designated as drawdown funds (although this omission has not been corrected retrospectively (see the next paragraph). For example, Jessica was aged 70 when she dies on 1 February 2017 holding rights in a pension plan from which she had drawn no benefits. While Jessica had omitted to exercise a right to have crystallised her plan, s 12(2ZA) protected her from an IHT in respect of her failure to exercise her right. By contrast, Alice, aged 75, crystallised her pension plan on 1 August 2015 taking a 25% tax-free lump sum. She designated the remaining fund as a drawdown fund but took no income. She died shortly afterwards on 2 December 2015. The protection of s 12(2ZA) did not apply to Alice as she was already in income drawdown at the time of her death.

From April 2015 changes were introduced to the pension tax rules that allow more people to flexibly access their money purchase pension funds from age 55. Such flexible access arrangements and an increase in drawdown arrangements mean that the IHT charge can apply to more people. FA 2016 s 93 effectively introduces an exemption so that an IHT charge will not arise where a person has failed to exercise their rights to draw designated funds from a drawdown pension fund or a flexi-access drawdown fund during their lifetime and so has left unused funds when they die. The 'exemption' takes effect retrospectively from 6 April 2011 in respect of drawdown pension funds and from 6 April 2015 in respect of flexi-access drawdown funds. This change to the law benefits Alice in the above illustration. See **Example A4 part (a)** for details on dispositions that are not transfers of value which now include pension drawdown funds not used up.

For a further discussion of the IHT treatment of pension schemes, see **Example B13**.

Fall in value of gift before donor's death

(9) For detailed notes on the relief where the value of a gift has fallen before the donor's death see **Example A14**.

Meaning of 'settlement'

(10) For IHT purposes a settlement is defined as any disposition or dispositions of property whereby the property is for the time being:

(a) held in trust for persons in succession, or for any person subject to a contingency (s 43(2)(a));

(b) held by trustees on trust to accumulate the whole or any part of any income of the property, or with power to make payments out of that income at the discretion of the trustees or some other person, with or without the power to accumulate surplus income (s 43(2)(b));

(c) charged or burdened (otherwise than for full consideration in money or money's worth) with the payment of any annuity or other periodical payment for a life or any other limited or terminable period (s 43(2)(c)).

A bare trust – for an individual absolutely entitled, even if presently a minor – is not a settlement.

Also treated as a settlement is a lease of property for the duration of a person's life or persons' lives (or for a period ascertainable, through the giving of notice or otherwise, only by reference to a death), unless the lease was granted for full consideration in money or money's worth (s 43(3)). See **Example C14** for a more detailed examination of leases of property for a person's life.

The words 'settlement' and 'trust' are usually regarded as being interchangeable, although as can be seen from the definition, 'settlement' has a wider coverage. Any reference in IHTA 1984 to a trustee, in relation to a settlement where there would otherwise be no trustees, is to any person in whom the settled property or its management is vested (s 45).

Classes of settlement

(11) For IHT purposes settlements may be considered to fall into four main classes:

(a) Settlements with a qualifying interest in possession (see **Example C3**).

(b) Relevant property settlements (whether or not an interest in possession subsists, if it is not a qualifying IIP or held by a reversionary interest company) (see **Example C14 explanatory note 2**).

(c) Privileged trusts for children and young persons, being bereaved minors' trusts, age 18-to-25 trusts, and any pre-2006 accumulation and maintenance trusts remaining as such (with beneficiaries due to become absolutely entitled by age 18) since 6 April 2008 (see **Example C3 explanatory note 1**).

(d) Certain other special types of settlement, eg trusts for the benefit of employees, protective trusts and charitable trusts.

The distinction between settlements in which there is a qualifying interest in possession and relevant property trusts is fundamental to an understanding of the operation of IHT in relation to settlements. The position is dealt with in detail in the section of this book dealing with settlements and trusts.

The IHT settlement provisions do not apply to registered pension schemes.

Review of inheritance tax

(12) The Office of Tax Simplification ('OTS') launched an inheritance tax consultation to inform its review of:

(a) the existing legislative framework; and

(b) the administrative processes through which taxpayers interact with HMRC in relation to IHT.

In response to the consultation, the Law Society has submitted recommendations, including the following:

- a streamlined, online process for the completion of IHT forms;
- a graduated tax rate or a return to the inflationary increase in the amount of the IHT nil rate threshold;
- increased annual exemption, taking more lifetime gifts out of scope of IHT;
- repeal of the residence nil rate band, replacing it with an increase in the standard nil rate band;
- removal of inconsistencies, particularly around business property relief and agricultural property relief; and
- re-extension of the bereaved minor trust regime and repeal of 18–25 trusts.

In the OTS's first report the key recommendation for the longer term is for a fully integrated digital system, which should include completing and submitting probate applications. A further seven recommendations cover short-term improvements.

The Office of Tax Simplification released a second report in July 2019 outlining recommendations to make considerable aspects of the design of inheritance tax simpler, more intuitive and easier to operate. Eleven recommendations are made as follows:

- Replace the annual exemption and the exemption for gifts in contemplation of marriage or civil partnership with a single personal gifts allowance; consider the amount of this allowance and reconsider the amount of the small gifts exemption; reform the exemption for normal expenditure out of income or replace it with a higher personal gift allowance (for a discussion of these reliefs see **Example A1 note (c)**);
- Reduce the seven-year PET transfer period to five years and abolish taper relief (for a discussion of the tax treatment of PETs see **Example A4** and **Example A6**);
- Remove the need to take account of gifts made outside the seven-year period when calculating the IHT due (the '14-year rule');
- Explore options for simplifying and clarifying the rules on payment of tax on lifetime gifts to individuals and the allocation of the NRB proportionately across all lifetime gifts and then the death estate rather than to the earliest gift first (for a discussion of the due dates of payment see **Example A7** and **Example A2** for a discussion of the NRB);
- Where an IHT relief or exemption applies on death, remove the capital gains uplift in base cost and instead provide that the recipient is treated as acquiring the assets at the historic base cost of the person who has died (see **Example D1 explanatory note 1**);
- Consider whether it continues to be appropriate for the level of trading activity for BPR (more than 50%) to be set at a lower level than that for gift holdover relief or business asset disposal relief (formerly known as entrepreneurs' relief) (which is over 80%); review the treatment of indirect non-controlling holdings in trading companies; consider the possible alignment of the IHT treatment of furnished holiday lettings with that of income tax and capital gains tax (for a discussion of BPR see **Example A21**);
- Review the treatment of limited liability companies (LLPs) to ensure they are treated appropriately for the purposes of the BPR trading requirement;
- HMRC to review its approach to the eligibility of farmhouses for APR in sensitive cases (eg where the owner leaves for medical treatment or to go into care) (for a discussion of APR see **Example A22**);
- HMRC to amend guidance to make it clear when a valuation of a business or a farm is required and whether any valuation needs to be formal or estimated;

- Ensure that death benefit payments from term life assurance is IHT free on the death of the life assured without the need to write them in trust; and

- Review the pre-owned assets rules and their interaction with other IHT anti-avoidance legislation (for a discussion of POAT see **Example B4**).

The government has not taken the recommendations forward at the current time.

Question

(a) Explain the rates at which inheritance tax is charged, the concept of the 'nil-rate band' and state briefly when a transfer of the nil-rate band is available.

(b) Explain when the residence nil-rate band is available and illustrate simply how it is calculated. State briefly when a downsizing addition may be made to the residence nil-rate band and its effect on the amount of the residence nil-rate band. State when a transfer of the residence nil-rate band is available.

(c) Explain how inheritance tax can become payable at death in respect of transfers of value already made in lifetime.

(d) Explain the 'grossing up' of a lifetime transfer.

Answer

(a) The rates of inheritance tax, the nil-rate band and its transfer

The rates of IHT applicable to chargeable transfers made by individuals differ depending on the occasion of charge (s 7 and Sch 1).

Rates for chargeable lifetime transfers

The rates at which tax is charged on chargeable lifetime transfers are half those applicable on death, so currently 0% and 20%. The 20% rate of tax applies to the value of the transfer (after taking into account the cumulative totals of chargeable transfers made in the previous seven years) that exceeds the nil-rate threshold in force at the time the chargeable transfer is made.

Rates of tax applicable when an individual dies

As already explained in **Example A1 part (a)**, where an individual dies two calculations are made, the first in relation to all lifetime transfers made in the seven years before his death and the second in relation to his deceased estate. The rates at which tax is charged in the first of these cases are currently 0% and 40%. The rates at which tax is charged in the second of these cases are also 0% and 40%, or, where the deceased has made substantial donations to charity in his will, the rates are 0% and 36% (see **Example B12**). In both cases, taking into account cumulated chargeable transfers (including potentially exempt transfers that have become chargeable by virtue of having been made less than seven years before the transferor's death), the 40% rate (or the 36% rate as the case may be) of tax applies to the value of the transfer or estate (after taking into account, in the case of an estate, the residence nil-rate band where relevant (see **part (b)** below) that exceeds the general (ie non-residential) nil-rate threshold in force at the time of death. Any tax paid at the rate of 20% on a chargeable lifetime transfer is credited against the tax now arising (but not so as to result in any repayment of tax).

Nil-rate of tax and the nil-rate band

For IHT purposes the general (ie non-residential) nil-rate band (which may be regarded as a 'general' nil-rate band, distinct from the residence nil-rate band (see **part (b)**) is the value (after taking into account cumulative transfers) of an estate (in excess of the residence nil-rate amount) or lifetime transfer to which the 0% rate of IHT applies. For example, if an estate (including any assets held in a qualifying interest in possession trust) and transfers of value made within seven years of death, is (after the application of the residence nil-rate amount where relevant) within the general nil-rate band, no IHT will be due on it. The general nil-rate threshold is the point at which the 0% rate gives way to the higher rates of IHT. (In this work the general nil-rate band is referred to simply as the nil-rate band.)

A simplified form of IHT reporting is available for 'excepted estates' (see **Example A23 part (d)**). One factor in determining whether the estate is an 'excepted estate' is its size relative to the general nil-rate band or 'IHT threshold'. Excepted estates are examined in more detail in **Example A23**.

The nil-rate band archive since March 1975

The table below shows the different nil-rate bands in use for transfers up to 2027/28:

From	To	Nil-rate band
13.03.1975	26.10.1977	£15,000
27.10.1977	25.03.1980	£25,000
26.03.1980	08.03.1982	£50,000
09.03.1982	14.03.1983	£55,000
15.03.1983	12.03.1984	£60,000

13.03.1984	05.04.1985	£64,000
06.04.1985	17.03.1986	£67,000
18.03.1986	16.03.1987	£71,000
17.03.1987	14.03.1988	£90,000
15.03.1988	05.04.1989	£110,000
06.04.1989	05.04.1990	£118,000
06.04.1990	05.04.1991	£128,000
06.04.1991	09.03.1992	£140,000
10.03.1992	05.04.1995	£150,000
06.04.1995	05.04.1996	£154,000
06.04.1996	05.04.1997	£200,000
06.04.1997	05.04.1998	£215,000
06.04.1998	05.04.1999	£223,000
06.04.1999	05.04.2000	£231,000
06.04.2000	05.04.2001	£234,000
06.04.2001	05.04.2002	£242,000
06.04.2002	05.04.2003	£250,000
06.04.2003	05.04.2004	£255,000
06.04.2004	05.04.2005	£263,000
06.04.2005	05.04.2006	£275,000
06.04.2006	05.04.2007	£285,000
06.04.2007	05.04.2008	£300,000
06.04.2008	05.04.2009	£312,000
06.04.2009	05.04.2028	£325,000

Transfer of the nil-rate band between spouses and civil partners

FA 2008 s 10 and Sch 4 (para 2 inserted ss 8A–8C into IHTA 1984) introduced legislation to allow a claim to be made to transfer any unused IHT general nil-rate band on a person's death to their surviving spouse or civil partner who dies on or after 9 October 2007. This applies where the IHT general nil-rate band of the first deceased spouse or civil partner was not fully used in calculating the IHT liability of their estate. When the surviving spouse or civil partner dies, the unused portion (as calculated in accordance with the appropriate rules) may be added to their own general nil-rate band. The claim must be made within 24 months from the end of the month in which the surviving spouse or civil partner dies. For a detailed explanation of the transfer of the general nil-rate band between spouses and civil partners, see **Example A3**.

(b) The residence nil-rate band and downsizing addition and the transfer of the residence nil-rate band

F(No 2)A 2015 s 9 introduced rules which enable an additional amount of the chargeable transfer which a person is deemed to make on his death (see **Example A1 part** (a)) to be charged at the rate of 0%. This is the individual's residence nil-rate amount (or, as it is commonly called, his residence nil-rate band (RNRB)).

In general terms, the objective of the RNRB is to charge the *chargeable* value (or a portion of that value) of an individual's home at the 0% rate of IHT where that home is passed on his death on or after 6 April 2017 to his direct descendants. Consequently with effect from 6 April 2017 there are two nil-rate bands for the purposes of IHT – the 'general' nil-rate band (as explained in **part** (a) above – and simply to be referred to as the nil-rate band) and the RNRB.

FA 2016 s 92 and Sch 15 has made further provision in relation to the RNRB by allowing an additional amount (known as a downsizing addition (DA)) to be taken into account in calculating an individual's RNRB. This recognises the fact that individuals who had downsized to a smaller property or who had sold their home when they moved into care might lose some or all of their entitlement to the RNRB. The downsizing provisions provide a way for any RNRB that might otherwise have been lost due to the disposal or downsizing to be reinstated, as long as their other assets are inherited by their direct descendants.

Application of the RNRB in calculating inheritance tax

The RNRB applies only for the purpose of calculating the amount of IHT arising in respect of the transfer that an individual is deemed to make of his estate when he dies (s 8D(1)). It is not, therefore, available in calculating the additional charge to IHT that arises as a result of an individual's death in respect of a gift of his home that he may have made within seven years before his death. The RNRB does however apply to an individual's entire chargeable estate; it is an extra nil-rate band and is *not* an exemption or relief in respect of the individual's home per se, applied directly to the chargeable value of the home.

In calculating the amount of IHT arising in respect of an individual's chargeable estate, the RNRB is taken into account first (ie the individual's home is treated as the first slice of his chargeable estate) (s 8D(3)). The remainder of his estate (which may include the value of his home in excess of his RNRB) is then considered. The value of the remainder as is equal to the general nil-rate band (eroded where relevant by the cumulative amount of chargeable transfers made in the seven years before death) is taxed at 0% and the balance is taxed at 40% or 36% as the case may be. In other words, the RNRB is to be applied in calculating the amount of IHT arising in respect of an estate before the application of the general nil-rate band. Moreover it is, unlike the general nil-rate band, never eroded by the cumulative amount of chargeable transfers made in the seven years before death (as explained in **part (c)**). Consequently, the residence nil-rate band is in the nature of an allowance although technically it is a 0% rate of tax. It is best reflected in computations as a first deduction against an individual's chargeable estate so that the amount of IHT on the balance of the estate is correctly calculated, taking into account cumulative transfers (if any) in the period of seven years before death (see the illustration of Edward in **part (c)** below).

Conditions for the application of the RNRB

In order for a RNRB to be available in computing the amount of IHT arising in respect of an estate, the following conditions have to be met in respect of an individual:

(a) he dies on or after 6 April 2017 (s 8D(1)),

(b) his estate immediately before his death includes a 'qualifying residential interest' (s 8E(1)(a)), and

(c) all or part of that interest is 'closely inherited' (s 8E(1)(b)).

Broadly speaking, the term 'qualifying residential interest' (QRI) is the term used by the legislation to describe an individual's home. The concept is explained in more detail in **explanatory note 2.** A home is 'closely inherited' where the individual who inherits it is a member of a defined class comprising (broadly speaking) the deceased's children, grandchildren and remoter descendants. The concept is explained in more detail in **explanatory note 3**.

The conditions for the availability of the RNRB (as set out above) are not listed as such in the legislation and the above statement of the conditions is a convenient way of bringing into a single place the rules that are scattered between the relevant statutory provisions. Strictly speaking the conditions are expressed statutorily as having to be satisfied in order to calculate an individual's RNRB rather than establishing his entitlement to a RNRB as such. This is a fine point of interpretation but it does explain the provisions of s 8F (which may be seen as a superfluous provision on an uninformed reading). If an individual's estate immediately before his death does not include a home or includes a home that is not closely inherited, then (subject to qualifying for any downsizing addition (DA) as discussed below) the individual's RNRB is nil (s 8F(1),(2)). It is not that he is not 'entitled' to a RNRB; rather he is 'entitled' to one (as it were) but the amount of it is nil. Every individual, therefore, 'has' a RNRB; it is just that in certain circumstances (as set out above) its amount is nil. Where this is the case, an amount (calculated as explained below) is available for carry-forward in the sense explained below and in **Example A3 part E** (ie it may be transferred to his surviving spouse or civil partner) (s 8F(3)).

An estate may also qualify for RNRB if the estate previously contained a home of the deceased but that residence was disposed of (or downsized from) on or after 8 July 2015, provided other assets in the deceased's estate are left to direct descendants. This is known as the downsizing addition (DA) and is explained further below. Hence the failure of the estate merely to meet condition (b) above is not necessarily fatal to there being an entitlement to a RNRB; before that conclusion is reached it must be asked whether DA may be available.

Summary of the calculation of an individual's RNRB

In order to calculate the amount of the RNRB that is due in respect of a particular estate, two steps have to be followed:

Step 1: Establish the maximum RNRB that could possibly apply to that particular estate. This will be one of two bespoke amounts, namely either the *default allowance* or the *adjusted allowance* (as explained below).

Step 2: Establish *the* RNRB that is to be used in computing an individual's IHT liability. This will be the *lower* of the maximum RNRB calculated under Step 1 and the chargeable value of the proportion of the deceased's home that is included in his estate and that is closely inherited. In other words, how much of the two bespoke amounts that is in fact used as the individual's actual RNRB in ultimately calculating his IHT liability depends upon the circumstances of the deceased immediately before his death.

If the value of the home used in Step 2 is less than the maximum RNRB established under Step 1 then it is possible that some extra RNRB may be available in the form of a downsizing addition (DA) (which is discussed below) or for there to be unused RNRB that could be transferred to the estate of a surviving spouse/civil partner (see **Example A3 part E**).

Step 1: The maximum amount of the RNRB

Unlike the (general) nil-rate band which is a fixed amount of £325,000 (for 2023/24 and has been since 6 April 2009), the maximum amount of an individual's RNRB is not a fixed number but is the lower of one of two bespoke amounts (called alternatively the 'default allowance' and the 'adjusted allowance'). Establishing which of the two bespoke amounts is applicable in any case may be regarded as the first step to be employed in calculating the amount of RNRB to which an estate is entitled and establishes what may be regarded as the maximum RNRB to which an estate is entitled in any case.

The two criteria

The first criterion by reference to which the bespoke amounts are calculated is called the 'residential enhancement' as set out in s 8D(5)(a). The residential enhancement is as follows:

(a) £100,000 for the tax year 2017/18,

(b) £125,000 for the tax year 2018/19,

(c) £150,000 for the tax year 2019/20, and

(d) £175,000 for the tax year 2020/21 and subsequent tax years (subject to its being indexed by reference to the consumer prices index unless Parliament decides otherwise (ss 8D(6),(7) which it has done until 2027/28 (FA 2021 s 86 as amended by FA 2023 s 9)).

The second criterion by reference to which the bespoke amounts are calculated is the 'taper threshold' applicable at the time of a person's death (TT) which is set at £2,000,000 for 2017/18 and subsequent years (s 8D(5)(b),(c)) (subject to its being indexed from 2020/21 by reference to the consumer prices index unless Parliament decides otherwise (s 8D(6),(7) which it has done until 2027/28 (FA 2021 s 86 as amended by FA 2023 S 9)).

The two bespoke amounts

From these two criteria are derived the two bespoke amounts mentioned earlier, one of which will be the maximum amount of RNRB to which an estate is entitled. The two bespoke amounts are:

(a) *The default allowance*: this is the amount of the residential enhancement at the individual's death together with his 'brought forward' allowance, if any (see **Example A3 part E**) (s 8D(5)(f)). So the default allowance comprises two component elements.

(b) *The adjusted allowance*: this is the amount of the individual's default allowance (comprising its two component elements) reduced by a further amount. In other words, his adjusted allowance is his 'abated default allowance' as it were. The amount of the reduction (ie the abatement) is equal to one-half of the difference between the value of the person's estate immediately before his death (see **explanatory note 4**) and the 'taper threshold' at the time at which the individual dies (which since 2017/18 has been £2,000,000 and will continue at this level until at least 2027/28 (FA 2021 s 86 as amended by FA 2023 s 9)). If the amount of the abatement is greater than the default allowance, then the adjusted allowance is nil (s 8D(5)(g)). For example, if an individual dies on 15 October 2023 owning an estate valued at £2,100,000, the amount of the abatement or reduction to be used in calculating his adjusted allowance is (£2,100,000 - £2,000,000)/2 = £50,000.

It is important to note that the abatement is calculated by reference to the person's estate immediately before his death, that is to say the aggregate of all his property to which he is beneficially entitled after deduction of any debts and liabilities that are taken into account in valuing the estate. The legislation refers to this amount as 'E' and is not to be confused with the chargeable value of an individual's estate (ie the amount ultimately charged to IHT after the deduction of exemptions and reliefs – which the legislation refers to as 'VT') (see the illustration in **explanatory note 4**).

It should be noted that the value of the default allowance or adjusted allowance does not depend on the value of the home that is closely inherited. It simply sets the maximum amount of the RNRB that a particular estate could possible qualify for. It also sets the maximum amount of unused RNRB that might be available to transfer to a surviving spouse or civil partner. The amount of the maximum RNRB that is actually used on calculating the IHT arising on the deceased estate is a matter for Step 2 of the process and is discussed next.

Step 2: The amount of the RNRB used in calculating IHT

As to whether all of an individual's default allowance or his adjusted allowance is used as his RNRB in calculating the IHT arising in respect of his chargeable estate (VT) depends upon the circumstances pertaining at his death – whether any home which forms part of his estate is closely inherited, what proportion of his home is so closely inherited and the chargeable value of that proportion (ie so much of VT as is attributable to the chargeable value of that proportion of the home). The proportion is explained more fully in **explanatory note 5**. Establishing how much of the two bespoke amounts may be used in any case to calculate IHT may be regarded as the second step to be employed in calculating the amount of RNRB to which an estate is entitled and establishes how much of an estate is charged at 0% and how much (if any) RNRB may be transferred to a surviving spouse/civil partner.

The amount of the RNRB that is used in calculating IHT arising in respect of a deceased estate is ascertained by reference to the chargeable value of the proportion of the home that has been closely inherited (which concept is termed as NV/100 in the legislation – see **explanatory notes 4 and 5**). It is important to note that it is the value of the deceased's home that has been included in his estate (ie the value of the home chargeable to inheritance tax) that is used in this context; this means its value *after* being adjusted under s 38 (Attribution of value to specific gifts (ie single and double grossing up)) and s 39 (Attribution of value to residuary gifts) and after deduction of agricultural property relief and business property relief after applying, if necessary, s 39A (Operation of ss 38 and 39 in cases of business or agricultural relief) (see **explanatory note 5**).

Examples

(1) Where an individual's estate is less than or equal to £2,000,000 (the taper threshold since 2017/18) and the value of the proportion of his home that has been closely inherited is less than or equal to the individual's *default allowance* (£100,000 for 2017/18, £125,000 for 2018/19, £150,000 for 2019/20 and £175,000 for 2020/21 until 2027/28), then the amount of the individual's RNRB is equal to the value of the proportion of the home that has been closely inherited (s 8E(2)). In such a case, the balance of the amount of the default allowance will pass to the deceased's spouse or civil partner (or as the legislation puts it, it is 'available for carry-forward' – see **Example A3 part E**).

Illustration

Amy dies on 3 May 2023 owning an estate valued at £1,000,000 which includes her home valued at £90,000. She is survived by her husband Mark. Her home is inherited by her step-daughter. Mark has agreed to move into another property. She is not entitled to a downsizing addition. The amount of Amy's RNRB is £90,000 (ie the chargeable value of the proportion (100%) of her home that is closely inherited) as her estate is less than £2,000,000 and the value of her home is less than £175,000 (her default allowance for 2023/24). The balance of her default allowance of £85,000 (£175,000 - £90,000) is passed to Mark.

If in her Will Amy had left her home to both Mark (her husband) and her step-daughter equally, then the amount of her RNRB that is used is limited to £45,000 (50% × £90,000) as that is the value of the proportion of her home that has been directly inherited. In this case the balance of her default allowance of £130,000 (£175,000 - £45,000) is passed to Mark.

(2) Where an individual's estate is less than or equal to £2,000,000 (the taper threshold since 2017/18) and the value of the proportion of his home that has been closely inherited is greater than the individual's *default allowance* (£175,000 for 2020/21 until 2027/28), then the amount of the individual's RNRB is equal to his default allowance (and no amount is available for carry-forward) (s 8E(3)).

Illustration

Brenda dies on 3 May 2023 owning an estate valued at £2,000,000 which includes her home valued at £250,000. She is survived by her husband Norman. Her home is inherited by her step-daughter. Norman has agreed to move into another property. She is not entitled to a downsizing addition. The amount of Brenda's RNRB is £175,000 (the amount of her default allowance for 2023/24) as her estate is equal to £2,000,000 and the chargeable value of the proportion (100%) of her home that is closely inherited is £250,000 which is more than £175,000 (her default allowance for 2023/24). No amount of Brenda's RNRB passes to Norman.

Where the estate is greater than the taper threshold (TT)

(3) Where an individual's estate is greater than £2,000,000 (the taper threshold since 2017/18) and the value of the proportion of his home that has been closely inherited is less than or equal to the individual's *adjusted allowance*, then the amount of the individual's RNRB is equal to the value of the of the proportion of the home that has been closely inherited (s 8E(4)). In such a case, the balance of the amount of the adjusted allowance will pass to the deceased's spouse or civil partner (or as the legislation puts it, it is 'available for carry-forward' – see **Example A3 part E**).

Illustration

Carol dies on 3 May 2023 owning an estate valued at £2,100,000 which includes her mobile home valued at £40,000. She is survived by her husband Oscar. Her home is inherited by her step-daughter. Oscar has agreed to move into another property. She is not entitled to a downsizing addition. As her estate is more than £2,000,000, in order to calculate Carol's RNRB her adjusted allowance first has to be ascertained. Her adjusted allowance is £175,000 - (£2,100,000 - £2,000,000)/2 = £125,000. The amount of Carol's RNRB is £40,000, the chargeable value of the proportion (100%) of her home that has been closely inherited as the value of her home is less than her adjusted allowance (of £125,000) for 2023/24. The balance of her adjusted allowance of £85,000 (£125,000 - £40,000) is passed to Oscar.

(4) Where an individual's estate is greater than £2,000,000 (the taper threshold since 2017/18) and the value of the of the proportion of his home that has been closely inherited is greater than the individual's *adjusted allowance*, then the amount of the individual's RNRB is equal to his adjusted allowance (and no amount is available for carry forward) (s 8E(5)).

Illustration

Deborah dies on 3 May 2023 owning an estate valued at £2,100,000 which includes her home valued at £225,000. She is survived by her husband Peter. Her home is inherited by her step-daughter. Peter has agreed to move into another property. She is not entitled to a downsizing addition. As her estate is more than £2,000,000, in order to calculate Deborah's RNRB her adjusted allowance first has to be ascertained. Her adjusted allowance is £175,000 - (£2,100,000 - £2,000,000)/2 = £125,000. The amount of Deborah's RNRB is £100,000 (the amount of her adjusted allowance for 2023/24) as the chargeable value of the proportion (100%) of her home that has been closely inherited (ie £225,000) is more than her adjusted allowance. No amount of Deborah's RNRB passes to Peter. Had Deborah's estate been valued at £2,500,000 her adjusted allowance would have been nil as the default allowance of £175,000 would have been less than the abatement of (£2,500,000 - £2,000,000)/2 = £250,000.

Further modification of the amount of the RNRB

In each of the above scenarios, the amount of a RNRB is subject to further modification where it exceeds the value of an individual's estate chargeable to IHT when he dies. The amount of the RNRB is restricted to the value of the chargeable estate so computed and the appropriate unused excess is available for transfer to a spouse or civil partner (ie it is available for carry-forward). The circumstances in which this rule may (rarely) apply are set out in **explanatory note 6.**

It will also be recalled that where an individual's estate immediately before his death does not include a home or includes a home that is not closely inherited, then the individual's RNRB is nil (s 8F(1),(2)). Where this is the case, an amount equal to his default allowance or adjusted allowance is available for carry-forward in the sense explained below and in **Example A3 part E** (ie it may be transferred to his surviving spouse or civil partner) (s 8F(3)).

Downsizing addition (DA)

The introduction of the RNRB may encourage older taxpayers to remain in homes bigger than they actually need. In order to counteract this, those who downsize or dispose of their homes on or after 8 July 2015 will be able effectively to keep the RNRB to which they were entitled when they downsized from or sold their former home and use it against the remaining value of their estate when they pass on a more modest home (if there is one) and other assets to an equivalent value to their direct descendants. So the downsizing provisions provide a way for any RNRB that might otherwise have been lost due to the disposal or downsizing of a former home to be reinstated as long as other assets are then closely inherited. So an individual is entitled to a downsizing addition (DA) in calculating his RNRB in one of the two cases – where he owns a home when he dies and where he does not as a result of transactions that took place on or after 8 July 2015. However, only one such transaction can be taken into account. Putting it another way, DA may be available where entitlement to a RNRB is zero or less than the maximum amount and there has been a former home.

It must be emphasised that, in order for the downsizing provisions to be in point, there must have been a home in the individual's estate on or after 8 July 2015 which has either been disposed of or downsized from before the date of his death. The provisions will not be in point where the home was disposed of before 8 July 2015 and never replaced. Also the downsizing rules are designed to replace the RNRB that has been lost due to the downsizing or disposal; they cannot apply for example to replace a RNRB because a home is not closely inherited (in which case there would have been no entitlement to RNRB in the first place). Finally it must be said that there is no automatic entitlement to a DA. The deceased's personal representatives must make a claim for the DA and nominate the disposal that they wish to be taken into account.

Entitlement to a downsizing addition

For the downsizing provisions to be in point there must have been a home in an individual's estate on or after 8 July 2015 which has either been downsized from or disposed of before the date of death. There are different rules regarding entitlement to DA in each of these cases.

In the first case where an individual owns a new home on his death, by virtue of s 8FA(1), an individual is entitled to a DA in calculating his RNRB where each of the following conditions is met. Broadly speaking, the conditions are that the deceased must have disposed of his 'old' home and the 'new' home subsequently acquired by him must have a lower value at the date of his death than the value of his old home. Specifically the conditions are:

(a)

(i) the individual's estate includes a home (the 'new' home) that is directly inherited and the maximum RNRB (ignoring any entitlement to DA) is calculated as the default allowance or adjusted allowance according to the circumstances set out in illustrations 1 and 3 above (ie under s 8E(2) or s 8E(4)) (s 8FA(2)(a)), or

(ii) the individual's estate includes a home that is not directly inherited and whose value is less than the maximum RNRB (ie the default or adjusted allowance) to which he would be entitled. The maximum RNRB (ignoring any entitlement to DA) is calculated as the default allowance or adjusted allowance according to the circumstances set out in illustrations 1 and 3 above (ie under s 8E(2) or s 8E(4)) (s 8FA(2)(b)).

(b) the value transferred by the transfer which he is deemed to make on his death is attributable not just to his (current) home but to other property as well (s 8FA(3)). In other words, there must be other *chargeable* property in the deceased individual's estate apart from his 'new' home. For example, if Alfred dies and leaves a half-share in his home to his son and the rest of his estate to his wife, the chargeable transfer on his death is attributable only to his home (the balance of the transfer being exempt) and so this condition is not met.

(c) he had a former home (more formally there is 'a qualifying former residential interest' (QFRI) in relation to the individual (s 8FA(4)). This means that the deceased must have disposed of his 'old' home in his lifetime and that disposal must have taken place on or after 8 July 2015.

(d) the value of the former home exceeds the value of the current home that is part of the transfer which he is deemed to make on his death (s 8FA(5)), This means that the 'old' home disposed of by the deceased in his lifetime must have been more valuable than the 'new' home which he owned on his death. For example, Richard sold his home for £250,000 in October 2022 and bought a flat for £90,000. He dies in January 2024 leaving an estate valued at £400,000 (including the flat then valued at £110,000). Under his Will Richard leaves £15,000 to charity and the residue of his estate to his son. The chargeable value of his new home on his death is £110,000 which is less than the value of his 'old' home of £250,000. Consequently this condition is met.

(e) at least some of his estate (other than his current home) is closely inherited (s 8FA(6)). This means that ignoring his current home, some of the remainder of his estate is closely inherited. Continuing the example in (d) above, assume that Richard leaves his flat and £75,000 of cash to his sister as specific legacies in addition to leaving £15,000 to charity and the residue of his estate to his son. Richard's estate is valued at £400,000 of which £110,000 is the value of the flat. The remainder of his estate is £290,000 of which Richard's son inherits £200,000. Hence this condition is met.

(f) a claim is made for the DA (s 8FA(7)). The personal representatives (or other persons liable to he tax chargeable) must make a claim for the DA within 2 years from the end of the month in which the death occurs, or (if it ends later) 3 months beginning with the date on which the personal representatives first begin to act (s 8L). In some cases HMRC may allow a late claim.

In the second case where an individual does not own a new home when he dies, he is nevertheless entitled to a DA in calculating his RNRB by virtue of s 8FB(1) if each of the following conditions is met:

(a) before he dies his estate does not include a home (s 8FB(2)),

(b) the value transferred (VT) by the transfer which he is deemed to make on his death is greater than nil (s 8FB(3)),

(c) he had a former home (more formally there is 'a qualifying former residential interest' (QFRI) in relation to the individual) (s 8FB(4)). This means his 'old' home must have been disposed of on or after 8 July 2015 and before the date of his death,

(d) at least some of his estate is closely inherited (s 8FB(5)), and

(e) a claim is made for the DA (s 8FB(6)). The personal representatives (or other persons liable to he tax chargeable) must make a claim for the DA within 2 years from the end of the month in which the death occurs, or (if it ends later) 3 months beginning with the date on which the personal representatives first begin to act (s 8L). In some cases HMRC may allow a late claim.

Calculation of the amount of a downsizing addition

In both of the above cases where an individual is entitled to a downsizing addition, the amount of the DA to which he is entitled is one of two amounts, namely the LRA (lost relievable amount) or the VTC (value of the chargeable estate which is in fact closely inherited or, as the case may be, the remainder of his chargeable estate which is in fact closely inherited). Broadly speaking, the LRA is the amount of the RNRB (in percentage terms) that has been 'lost' by the deceased as result of disposing or downsizing from his 'old' home. In short, the operation of the law (as set out in detail below) results in the amount of DA available being the lower of LRA and VTC. However, the amount of the DA cannot result in the RNRB exceeding the default allowance or adjusted allowance to which the individual would otherwise have been entitled to if he had not downsized from or disposed of his former home.

The amount of an individual's DA is equal to LRA (the 'lost relievable amount') if LRA < VTC (s 8FA(8)(a), s 8FB(7(a)). The amount of an individual's LRA is subject to complicated rules (see s 8FE) but the essence of the calculation is illustrated below. See **explanatory note 8** for a detailed discussion on the calculation of LRA (which differs according to whether the deceased owns a home on his death or not as the case may be) together with examples.

The amount of an individual's DA is equal to VTC in all other cases (ie where LRA ≥ VTC) (s 8FA(8)(b), s 8FB(7(b)).

Effect of being entitled to a downsizing addition

The effect of being entitled to a DA is that the DA is added to the amount of the RNRB to which an individual would otherwise be entitled when he dies (as calculated under s 8E or 8F as the case may be and illustrated above in examples (1) to (4)). The total of the two amounts gives the total RNRB to which the individual is then entitled (s 8FC, 8FD). In practical terms the DA may be seen as a third nil-rate band to be used in addition to the general nil-rate band and residence nil-rate band in calculating the tax due in respect of a deceased's estate.

Simple illustration

Antony, a single person, sold his family home for £240,000 in May 2023 and moved into a very small flat worth £90,000. His RNRB at the time of the sale was £175,000. By downsizing, Antony has lost £85,000 of the RNRB that would have been available to him had he died just before selling the more valuable property. This is Antony's 'lost relievable amount' (LRA). Antony dies in July 2024 when the flat is worth £100,000 and the rest of his estate is valued at £500,000. Antony's adopted son inherits all of his estate. The RNRB to which he is prima facie entitled is £100,000 (ie the value of his home as that is less than the default allowance of £175,000 applicable in 2024/25). However, Antony's personal representatives can claim a DA of £85,000, so that the RNRB applicable at the time of Antony's death is £185,000. This means that Antony's home and £85,000 worth of his other assets are taxed at 0% (before IHT is calculated in the normal way in respect of the rest of his other assets).

Claim for downsizing addition

The claim for DA must be made (or withdrawn) by the individual's personal representatives (or any other person liable for the tax chargeable on his death) within the same time periods as a claim made (or withdrawn) for the transfer of his RNRB (see next paragraph).

Transfer of the RNRB

A claim may be made to transfer an individual's unused RNRB on his death to his surviving spouse or civil partner. This applies where the individual's default allowance or adjusted allowance (as the case may be) was not fully used on his death (as illustrated in the cases of Amy and Carol above). A claim is also in point where, when an individual dies, he does not own a home or, if he does, his home is not closely inherited (s 8F). When, in turn, the surviving spouse or civil partner dies, the brought-forward allowance (as it is called) is added to their default allowance at the date of their death (s 8D(5)(f)) from which their RNRB is calculated (in accordance with the rules set out above and includes DA in appropriate cases). The claim must be made within 24 months from the end of the month in which the surviving spouse or civil partner dies (s 8L). For a detailed explanation of the transfer of the RNRB between spouses and civil partners, see **Example A3 part E**.

(c) Tax chargeable on lifetime transfers following transferor's death

As explained in **Example A1 parts (a)** and **(b)** above, on an individual's death, tax may become payable because a transfer which was potentially exempt becomes chargeable; and additional tax may become due on chargeable lifetime transfers made within seven years before death. Tax on these lifetime transfers is calculated by reference to the full (40%) rate in force at the time of the transfer or (if more beneficial, as it usually has been), at the time of death. The reduced (36%) rate of IHT can never apply in relation to these (or any) lifetimes transfers.

Four points have to be taken into account in calculating such tax:

(1) If, because of a change in rate, taper relief, or for any other reason, the tax calculated at death is less than that calculated at the time of the gift, no repayment of tax is due.

(2) Lifetime gifts which are reckoned at death are brought in at their value at the time of the gift, but if the value of a gift has fallen before death, its value at the time of death may sometimes be substituted (s 131).

(3) Taper relief reduces the tax on the gift, not the value of the gift, for the purpose of calculating the tax payable. So if the lifetime gift was below the nil-rate threshold at death, taper relief will be irrelevant. The percentages used for taper relief are as follows:

Years between transfer and death	*Percentage reduction*	*Percentage of full rate tax due*
3+ to 4	20	80
4+ to 5	40	60
5+ to 6	60	40
6+ to 7	80	20

(s 7(3)).

(4) If business property relief or agricultural property relief was available to reduce the value transferred by the lifetime gift, certain conditions must be satisfied if the benefit of those reliefs is still to be available in respect of the additional charge on death (see **Example A21 part A(c)**).

Even though tax is only payable on most lifetime gifts if the donor does not survive them by *seven years*, it will still be necessary to keep records for IHT purposes of lifetime chargeable transfers for up to 14 years.

Illustration

Edward, having used his available annual exemptions, makes a lifetime gift of £145,000 cash to a discretionary settlement on 31 May 2010. Although this is a chargeable transfer, no tax is payable since it is within the nil-rate band of £325,000.

Edward makes a lifetime gift of £196,000 cash to Christopher on 30 April 2017. No tax is payable at that time since the first £6,000 of the gift is covered by two years' annual exemptions of £3,000 each, and the balance of £190,000 is a potentially exempt transfer.

Edward dies on 31 March 2024, leaving an estate at death of £235,000. This includes his home valued at £75,000 which is inherited by his son.

The tax arising at death is calculated as follows:

On £190,000 of the gift on 30.4.2017, which was within seven years before death

Having been a potentially exempt transfer, the gift of £190,000 is now chargeable by reference to the rates of tax in force at 31 March 2024:

		Tax on scale at time of death on 31.3.24
	£	£
Gift within previous seven years (31 May 2010)	145,000	–
Gift on 30 April 2017 (196,000 – 6,000 exempt, see **part (a)**)	190,000	4,000*
	335,000	4000*
(* 335,000 – 325,000 = 10,000 @ 40%)		
Tax on £190,000 potentially exempt transfer now chargeable		4,000
Tax after taper relief payable by donee (Christopher) (20% of full rate for surviving 6 years but not 7)		800
On estate at death 31 March 2024		
Gift within previous seven years (30 April 2017)	190,000	–
Estate at death (£235,000 - £75,000 (RNRB))	160,000	10,000*
	350,000	10,000*
(* 350,000 – 325,000 = 25,000 @ 40%)		
Tax payable on estate at death		£10,000*

The gift of £145,000 to the discretionary settlement was made more than seven years before death (almost 14 years in fact), but because of the seven-year cumulation period it has to be taken into account in calculating the tax on the gift to Christopher on 30 April 2017 which has become chargeable having been made within seven years after the gift to the trust and within seven years before Edward's death. The tax chargeable on the gift to Christopher is therefore calculated at the rates applicable to transfers between £145,000 and £335,000. (Had the gift of £145,000 been *potentially exempt*, it would have become totally exempt on 31 May 2017, and would not have been taken into account in calculating the tax on the potentially exempt transfer of £190,000 that became chargeable because of Edward's death.)

The gift to the discretionary settlement is excluded from the seven-year cumulation period after it was made, that is at 31 May 2017, so that it does not enter into the cumulative total at death on 31 March 2024. The tax on the death estate is calculated (after taking into account the residence nil-rate band of £75,000 – see below) at the rates applicable to transfers between £190,000 and £350,000. The £190,000 (which is the amount of the cumulated transfers) is deemed to use up the general nil-rate band first and so in the death estate calculation, the tax on the gift of £190,000 is shown as nil (whereas the tax actually chargeable, before taper relief, is £4,000). This is because the tax on the earlier cumulative transfers is a notional figure, based on the rates in force at death, in order to give the correct starting point for the calculation of tax on the death estate itself (see **Example A1 part (a)**).

Edward's estate of £235,000 is less than £2,000,000 (the taper threshold since 2017/18) and the value of the proportion (100%) of his home (£75,000) that has been inherited by his son is less than his *default allowance* (£175,000 for 2023/24). So the amount of Edward's RNRB is equal to the value of the proportion of his home that has been inherited by his son (ie £75,000) (s 8E(2)). The RNRB is treated as a deduction from his total chargeable estate at death. The balance of the amount of his default allowance (£50,000) will pass to his widow or civil partner.

(d) 'Grossing up' of a lifetime transfer

'Grossing up' a lifetime transfer applies where the donor pays the IHT arising on the making of a lifetime chargeable transfer. The value of the donor's estate is reduced not only by the disposition itself by also by the tax liability which he satisfies (see s 5(6)), and the IHT is calculated by reference to the reduction in the value of the donor's estate.

Illustration

Mr Smith has already made chargeable transfers of £325,000 and has used up all his available exemptions. He makes a chargeable transfer of £8,000 to a discretionary settlement on 1 May 2023 and agrees to pay the IHT. The rate of tax on lifetime gifts over £325,000 is one half of 40%, ie 20% so that the £8,000 received by the settlement must represent 80% of the gross gift, so the gross gift is 100/80ths of the net gift = £10,000.

The calculation is as follows:

		Gross	*Tax*	*Net*
		£	£	£
Cumulative chargeable transfers to date		325,000	Nil	325,000
1 May 2023	Gift to discretionary settlement			
	Net			8,000
	Grossed up			
$\frac{100}{80} \times 8{,}000$		10,000	2,000	
Cumulative chargeable transfers carried forward		335,000	2,000*	333,000
(*335,000 – 325,000 = 10,000 @ 20%)				

If Mr Smith's previous transfers had been £319,000 instead of £325,000, the position would have been:

		Gross	*Tax*	*Net*
		£	£	£
Cumulative chargeable transfers to date		319,000	Nil	319,000
1 May 2023	Gift to settlement within nil rate band	6,000	Nil	6,000
	Remaining net gift			2,000
	Grossed up			
$\frac{100}{80} \times 2{,}000$		2,500	500	
Cumulative chargeable transfers carried forward		327,500	500*	327,000
(*327,500 – 325,000 = 2,500 @ 20%)				

A potentially exempt transfer never has to be grossed up. This is because the transferor is never personally liable for the tax. If tax is payable it is because of the death of the transferor within seven years of his having made the transfer (ie under the 'supplementary' charge). In that event the donee is primarily responsible for the tax.

Explanatory Notes

Taper relief

(1) It should be noted that even though transfers may immediately or subsequently be chargeable transfers, no tax is payable until the cumulative total exceeds the general nil-rate threshold. Any transfers within that nil-rate band do not attract any tax, later transfers above the threshold bearing the whole of the tax payable (subject to taper relief if available). Since the transfers within the general nil-rate band never attract any tax, the taper relief that applies when a donor survives a gift by more than three years but less than seven is irrelevant on those transfers.

Illustration

A wealthy married couple who have made no previous gifts want to know how much cash they could give away on 4 April 2024 without any possibility of IHT ever being payable on the gifts, and assuming that neither the normal income expenditure exemption nor any specific exemptions are available.

Each spouse could give £331,000, making a total of £662,000. £6,000 each would be covered by the current and previous years' annual exemptions, leaving potentially exempt, or immediately chargeable (at 0%), transfers of £325,000 each. These transfers would be covered by the general nil-rate band however soon their deaths occurred afterwards; but tax at 40% (ignoring RNRB) would be payable on the whole of their respective chargeable estates at death, since the general nil-rate band would have been used up by the lifetime gifts.

If they survived for seven years, they could in the meantime each make annual gifts amounting to the £3,000 annual exemption plus any intervening increase in the general nil-rate band and after the seven years they could then make further gifts equal to the then general nil-rate band each (after allowing for any 'topping-up' gifts which were not yet seven years ago), because their initial gifts would then be more than seven years before the fresh gifts and therefore no longer part of their respective IHT accumulations. Taper relief would not be relevant no matter how long they survived, since all gifts would be either exempt or covered by the general nil-rate band. Again tax at the full or reduced rate would be paid on the whole of their chargeable death estates, since the general nil-rate band would have been fully used against lifetime gifts.

The residence nil-rate band (RNRB)

(2) One of the conditions that has to be met in order for an individual's RNRB to be calculated is that his estate immediately before his death must include a home (as it may be referred to colloquially) or, formally in legislative terms, a 'qualifying residential interest' (QRI) (s 8E(1)(a)). A QRI is defined in turn by reference to an individual's 'residential property interest' (RPI), that is to say an interest in a dwelling-house which has been the individual's residence at a time when his estate included that, or any other interest, in the dwelling-house (s 8H(2)).

The interest enjoyed by the individual at the time when he resided in the home need not be the same as the interest owned by him at death – for example the individual may have been entitled to a leasehold estate during his occupation of the dwelling-house but at the time of his death this may have been enlarged to a freehold interest. Also the individual who owns the interest in the dwelling-house when he dies need no longer be living there when he dies so long as the dwelling-house was his home at some time during his period of ownership. For example an individual owns both a house and a flat (which is rented out) when he dies. At the time of his death he is living in the house, but the flat was his home before he acquired the house. The flat is still an RPI. Whether the RNRB is calculated by reference to the flat is a different question; as explained below, the flat would need to be nominated as the property interest by reference to which the RNRB is calculated. There is no minimum period of ownership for a home to be a QRI. However, only one home can qualify for RNRB.

An individual will have a QRI in one of two cases:

(a) first, where his estate immediately before his death includes RPIs in just one dwelling-house (s 8H(3));

(b) secondly where his estate immediately before his death includes RPIs in each of two or more dwelling-houses and his personal representatives nominate one (and only one) of those dwelling-houses (s 8H(4)).

The RPI in question must be part of the individual's estate at his death. This means that it cannot be excluded property because it would not then form part of his estate. However, an individual will be regarded as having an RPI where the RPI is settled and the individual was beneficially entitled to a qualifying interest in possession in it. It is possible for an individual to have more than one RPI in the same dwelling-house. For example, he may own one-half of the dwelling-house absolutely and have a qualifying interest in possession in the other half. These are two separate RPIs in the same dwelling-house but they are combined into a single RPI for these purposes.

It will be noticed how closely the definition of an RPI is modelled on the only or main residence relief for capital gains tax purposes. The interpretation of the concepts on which the relief is based will therefore be persuasive in the interpretation of an RPI (and this is intimated by HMRC in IHTM46030). The following discussion of the meaning of an RPI draws heavily, therefore, on how the concepts employed to define an RPI are understood in the context of the capital gains relief.

An interest in a dwelling-house

The definition of an RPI refers not just to a dwelling-house but to an interest in a dwelling-house. This recognises the technicalities of land law and the fictions of IHT that determine the constitution of an individual's estate. It means that an individual must have an estate or interest in the dwelling-house. This covers both freehold and leasehold estates and the undivided shares owned by tenants in common and the severable shares of joint tenants. However, a mere licence to occupy is not included and an individual who occupies a dwelling-house under licence does not have an interest in the dwelling-house for the purposes of the definition. (A licence is a permission to reside in a property which may be contractual or gratuitous. For instance, staying in a hotel or in lodgings are examples of residence under contractual licence. Staying with family or friends is an example of residence under gratuitous licence.) If at any time a dwelling-house was settled property and the deceased was beneficially entitled to a qualifying interest in possession in it, then the deceased will be treated as having an interest in the dwelling-house (s 49). The same may be said of the case where an individual's estate comprises an interest in a dwelling-house on account of the gift with reservation of property rules (FA 1986 s 102(3)).

A dwelling-house that is a residence

The definition of an RPI refers not just to a dwelling-house but a dwelling-house that has been a residence. The former concept (dwelling-house) describes an edifice; the latter (residence) describes something different, namely the use to which the edifice has been put.

A dwelling-house – primary meanings

In the first instance the focus of the definition is on a dwelling-house that is to say a structure. The legislation does not define the term 'dwelling-house'. There are no cases directly in point, so we look at a dictionary definition. The new shorter Oxford English Dictionary defines a dwelling-house as 'a place of residence; a habitation, a house'. This confirms that any structure or edifice can be a dwelling-house for these purposes. So, the expression 'dwelling-house' includes a flat, as well as a house and presumably includes any building, or structure, which could be occupied as a home. Such a structure does not have to be wholly used as a residence; but the whole structure is the dwelling-house. Is a caravan (ie a chattel, or tangible moveable property) a dwelling-house? In the context of capital gains tax, case law gives the answer: 'it depends on the facts of the individual case'. In *Makins v Elson* (1976) 51 TC 437, it was held that a caravan was indeed a dwelling-house. In that case the seminal feature of the caravan was that it had been jacked up and rested on supports (ie its wheels were off the ground) and it had been connected to the electricity and water mains and had a telephone line connected. This contrasts with the case of *Moore v Thompson* [1986] STC 170 where it was held that a caravan was not a dwelling-house. In that case the caravan was not connected to any utility services, although calor gas was used for cooking and heating. No evidence was found as to whether the caravan rested on its wheels or was jacked up. The General Commissioners held on these facts that the caravan was not a dwelling-house and the High Court did not disturb this finding as being unreasonable. What the cases show is that the degree of immobility of the chattel (the caravan) and its connection with the basic utilities are important factors in determining whether it is a dwelling-house. Static caravans should typically therefore qualify as dwelling-houses. What about house boats? A taxpayer could establish a permanent residence in a house boat and successfully argue that it is covered by the exemption on the same footing as that in the *Makins* case.

The definition of an RPI refers to a dwelling-house and so the question arises whether a dwelling-house can comprise of more than one edifice. The question has been answered (again in the context of the capital gains tax only or main residence relief) by the Court of Appeal in the case of *Batey v Wakefield* [1982] STC 521. Fox LJ stated that in its ordinary usage the word 'dwelling-house' can comprise several buildings not physically joined together. The learned Lord Justice then went on to define the test that needed to be applied in order to determine which of two or more buildings comprised a dwelling-house, but his test was rendered nugatory by the later case of *Lewis v Lady Rook* [1992] STC 171. In the Lewis case Balcombe LJ stated that in determining whether a cottage formed part of the dwelling-house in that case, the correct test to apply was whether the cottage was within the curtilage of, and appurtenant to, the main house so as to be part of the entity which, together with the main house, constituted the dwelling-house occupied by the taxpayer as a residence. So both cases must be taken together to establish the answer to this question. However, the latter case has introduced a general land law concept into revenue law and it is necessary to explore the meaning of the concept of 'curtilage'.

When is one building within the curtilage of another? The definition of curtilage in the Oxford English Dictionary is 'small court, yard, garth or piece of ground attached to a dwelling-house and forming one enclosure with it'. The concept of curtilage embraces a relatively small area. A discussion of the concept has been the subject-matter of a large number of non-tax cases. In the Leasehold Reform Act 1967 case of *Methuen-Campbell v Walters* [1979] 1 QBD 525, quoted with approval in Lewis, the Court held that: 'For one corporeal hereditament to fall within the curtilage of another, the former must be so intimately associated with the latter as to lead to the conclusion that the former in truth forms part and parcel of the latter, that they constitute an integral whole'. In *AG v Calderdale BC* [1982] 46 P&CR 399 Stephenson LJ identifies three factors in determining whether a structure was in the curtilage of an existing building and focuses on the integral whole rather than the smallness of the area. This case was marginalised in the House of Lords however. In *Debenhams v Westminster City Council* [1987] AC 396 the House of Lords said that the concept envisaged is that of principal and accessory. It did not comment on the size of the curtilage at all. In *Dyer v Dorset County Council* [1989] 1 QB 346 curtilage was defined as a small area about a building. The case went further to say that considerations of function, history, ownership and physical layout were all material, but that the essential concept of size had also to be taken into account. In *Secretary of State for the Environment, Transport and the Regions and another v Skerritts of Nottingham Ltd* [2000] 1 All ER 245 it was held by the Court of Appeal that the curtilage of a substantial listed building was likely to extend to what were or had been, in the terms of ownership and function, ancillary buildings. It was further stated that of course, 'physical layout' came into the matter as well. In the nature of things, the curtilage within which a mansion's satellite buildings were found was bound to be relatively limited, but the concept of smallness was in that context so completely relative as to be almost meaningless and unhelpful as a criterion. It said that on a review of all the foregoing authorities (*Dyer* being marginalised) that the notion of smallness is not inherent in the concept of curtilage. In *Morris v Wrexham County Borough Council* [2001] All ER (D) 02 it was held that in determining whether building A was within the curtilage of building B, the test was whether the two buildings were sufficiently close and accessible to one another and whether, in terms of function, building A is ancillary to building B. This requires one to look at factors such as physical proximity of A, the access between the A and B, and the use to which A is put by the occupier of B. A recent discussion of the meaning of the curtilage of a building may be found in *Blackbushe Airport Ltd v Secretary of State for Environment, Food and Rural Affairs* [2021] EWCA Civ 398. The court approved the definition of the concept as set out in *Methuen-Campbell* and reviewed many of the authorities quoted above. It confirmed that the correct question to ask is whether land falls within the curtilage of a building, not whether land together with a building fall within, or comprise, a unit devoted to the same or equivalent function or purpose, or whether a building forms part and parcel of some unit which includes that land. Land must form part and parcel of a building, not part and parcel with the building. On the facts of the case, it was found that the extensive operational area of a working airport did not fall within the curtilage of the terminal building.

HMRC's view of the concept of curtilage (which is based primarily on the *Methuen-Campbell* case is set out at CG64245. HMRC start with the dictionary definition and say that it has been adopted by the Courts in non-tax cases and emphasis is placed on the smallness of the area comprised in the curtilage. Buildings standing around a court yard together with the main house will be within the curtilage of the main house. Where more dispersed groups of buildings have a clear relationship with each other they will fall within a single curtilage if they constitute an integral whole. Whether one building is part and parcel of another will depend primarily on whether there is a close geographical relationship between them. Furthermore, because the test is to identify an integral whole, a wall or fence separating two buildings will normally be sufficient to establish that they are not within the same curtilage. Similarly, a public road or stretch of tidal water will set a limit to the curtilage of the building. Buildings which are within the curtilage of a main house will normally pass automatically on a conveyance of that house without having to be specifically mentioned. There is a distinction between the curtilage of a main house and the curtilage of an estate as a whole and the fact that a whole estate may be contained within a single boundary does not mean that the buildings on the estate should be regarded as within the curtilage of the main house.

A dwelling-house – extended meaning

Section 8H(5) extends the concept of a dwelling-house to include any land (without limit on area) occupied and enjoyed with the dwelling-house as its garden or grounds, excluding however any trees or underwood which are the subject to an woodland's election under s 125. Despite there being no limit on size, it must be noted that not all land around a dwelling-house automatically comes within the concept of a dwelling-house; it has to meet the other conditions listed, primarily that it must be garden or grounds. Land is not defined in the IHTA 1984 (other than to exclude estates, interests or rights by way of mortgage or other security – s 272) but the reference to land in s 8H(5)(a) seems to limit land to bare land without buildings. The phrase 'garden or grounds' is not defined in the statute, nor is there judicial authority on the meaning of the phrase. The word must carry its everyday meaning and whether a piece of land can be regarded as the garden of a residence is a question of fact. HMRC take the following dictionary definition as their starting point for determining what is a garden: 'a piece of ground, usually partly grassed and adjoining a private house, used for growing flowers, fruit or vegetables and as a place of recreation' (HMRC capital gains tax manual, CG64360). The 'grounds' go beyond the garden. In general, HMRC accepts that land surrounding the residence and in the same ownership constitutes the grounds of the dwelling-house, unless it is used for some other purpose. HMRC is unlikely to regard land which is used for some other purpose (for example agriculture, trade or business) as part of the garden or grounds. Also, land which is under development is likely to be excluded from being the grounds of a dwelling-house. Land which has traditionally been part of the grounds of the dwelling-house but which is unused or overgrown is not excluded, nor are paddocks or orchards if there is no significant business use. Land which is physically separated from the dwelling-house may cause problems. Land which can be shown objectively, on the facts, to be naturally and traditionally the garden of the dwelling-house, so that it would normally be offered to a prospective purchaser as part of the dwelling-house, will be accepted. An example of this is where, as in some villages, it is common for a garden to be across the street from the dwelling-house. The separation itself would not be regarded as a reason for excluding the land from the concept of a dwelling-house. It must be stressed that these cases will be rare and if land is separated from the dwelling-house by other land which is not in the same ownership as the residence, it will usually not be part of the garden or grounds. For example, land bought some distance from the dwelling-house due to an inadequate garden at the residence and which is cultivated and regarded as part of the garden may not be included in the concept of a dwelling-house.

The garden and grounds must be occupied and enjoyed with the dwelling-house at the time of the individual's death. Influenced by the case of *Varty v Lynes* [1976] STC 508 if an individual disposes his house and part of his garden without disposing of the rest of the garden and then dies, it is unlikely that the extant garden will be included in the concept of a dwelling-house as, at that time, it does not add to the enjoyment of the dwelling-house. The phrase 'occupation and enjoyment' is understood by reference to the legal meaning of the words used. Occupation means possession of the land while enjoyment means possession without contested claims from third parties.

A residence

The definition of an RPI requires that a dwelling-house must have been an individual's residence. When is an edifice a residence? This requires one to consider the use to which the edifice is put. In some early cases in the context of the capital gains only or main residence relief, the word residence was interpreted as meaning 'home' (*Sansom v Peay* 52 TC 1). In *Frost v Feltham* 55 TC 1 Nourse J said a residence is a place where someone lives. This question was addressed in *Goodwin v Curtis* [1998] STC 475. It was held by the Court of Appeal that a dwelling-house is a residence when there is evidence that the residence at a property showed some degree of permanence, some degree of continuity or some expectation of continuity. It must be more than temporary occupation of the dwelling-house in order to amount to its being a residence because temporary occupation at an address does not make an individual resident there. The nature, quality, length and circumstances of occupation have to be taken into account in order to establish whether occupation per se matures into residence. Short-term occupation is not therefore fatal provided short term occupation is not evidence of temporary occupation. In the *Goodwin* case the taxpayer had purchased a derelict farmhouse and refurbished it. He entered into a contract for its sale and between exchange and completion moved into the premises hoping to benefit from the exemption through his occupation. He failed! Outside the field of Revenue Law the term has had clearer definition. Under the Representation of the People Act 1948 entitlement to vote in Parliamentary elections is given to persons resident in a constituency on a qualifying date. In *Fox v Stirk, Ricketts v Registration Officer for the City of Cambridge* [1970] 3 All ER 7 the Court of Appeal considered whether students should be regarded as resident in the constituency of the University they attended. Lord Denning MR stated three principles about an individual's residence. The first principle is that a man can have two residences. He can have a flat in London and a house in the country. He is resident in both. The second principle is that temporary presence at an address does not make a man resident there. A guest who comes for the weekend is not resident. A short stay visitor is not resident. The third principle is that temporary absence does not deprive a person of his residence. If he happens to be away for a holiday or away for the weekend or in hospital, he does not lose his residence on that account. Lord Widgery commented that '[t]his conception of residence is of the place where a man is based or where he continues to live, the place where he sleeps and shelters and has his home'. These dicta are of course persuasive but what the authorities show that occupation is a necessary precondition for residence. One then has regard to the quality of that occupation.

In IHTM46031 HMRC give the example of an elderly person who has recently moved into their new home and has barely finished unpacking when they are taken ill and have to move to a nursing home. HMRC would consider the person to have established their residence in the new home. By contrast someone who stays in a property for a number of weeks living out of a suitcase would not have established their residence in that property.

However, s 8H(6) provides for the situation where a taxpayer cannot occupy a dwelling-house because he resides in job-related accommodation but in due course he intends to occupy the dwelling-house in question as his only or main residence. Non-occupation of the dwelling-house in this circumstance is deemed to be occupation and that is sufficient for the purposes of meeting the definition of residence in the context of the definition of an RPI. Indeed it will be noted that a dwelling-house which is in fact never subsequently occupied is deemed to be occupied so long as, while in job-related accommodation the individual had the requisite *intention*. By virtue of s 8F(7) accommodation is job-related for this purpose where:

(a) it is provided for him by reason of his employment, or for his spouse or civil partner by reason of the spouse's or civil partner's employment where (i) it is necessary for the proper performance of the duties of the employment that the employee should reside in that accommodation, (ii) where the accommodation is provided for the better performance of the duties of the employment, and it is one of the kinds of employment in the case of which it is customary for employers to provide living accommodation for employees or (iii) where, there being a special threat to the employee's security, special security arrangements are in force and the employee resides in the accommodation as part of those arrangements; or

(b) under a contract entered into at arm's length and requiring him or his spouse or civil partner to carry on a particular trade, profession or vocation, he or his spouse or civil partner is bound (i) to carry on that trade, profession or vocation on premises or other land provided by another person (whether under a tenancy or otherwise); and (ii) to live either on those premises or on other premises provided by that other person.

If the living accommodation is provided by a company and the employee is a director of that or an associated company, paragraph (a)(i) or (ii) above shall not apply unless (a) the company of which the employee is a director is one in which he or she has no material interest; and (b) either the employment is as a full-time working director, or the company is non-profit making, that is to say, it does not carry on a trade nor do its functions consist wholly or mainly in the holding of investments or other property, or the company is a charitable company. Paragraph (b) above does not apply if the living accommodation concerned is in whole or in part provided by a company in which the borrower or his spouse or civil partner has a material interest; or any person or persons together with whom the borrower or his spouse or civil partner carries on a trade or business in partnership. For the purposes of the above rules a company is an associated company of another if one of them has control of the other or both are under the control of the same person; and 'employment', 'director', 'full-time working director', 'material interest' and 'control', in relation to a body corporate, have the meanings given by ITEPA 2003, Pt 3, Chap 2.

Time when a dwelling-house is a residence

An individual's estate must include a QRI (ie a home) immediately before his death in order to be able to calculate his RNRB (s 8E(1)). This requires the RPI to exist at that time and so the dwelling-house must be a residence at that time. If at the time of death the dwelling-house it is no longer the individual's residence, then a RNRB cannot be calculated in respect of it. If at that time the individual owns two dwelling-houses that are residences, then his personal representatives must nominate which dwelling-house is to be the RPI which founds his QRI. For example, consider a taxpayer who dies in 2023/24 owning a flat in Edinburgh (worth £500,000) and a cottage in Fife (worth £300,000). Under his Will he leaves the Edinburgh property to his son (subject to it bearing its own tax) and the Fife property to his daughter (subject to it bearing its own tax). The residue of his estate (valued at £700,000) is to be divided between his son and daughter equally. The taxpayer is a widower having inherited his late wife's property when she died a few years ago. The executors claim for the transfer of the wife's NRB and RNRB to the taxpayer'. They should also elect for the RNRB (of £350,000) by reference to the Edinburgh flat because the Fife cottage will not use the RNRB in full.

Location of the dwelling-house

There is no requirement in the legislation that the dwelling-house has to be located in the UK. But it does have to be within the scope of IHT for a RNRB to operate in relation to it. This in turn depends upon the domicile status of the deceased who owned the dwelling-house at the time of his death.

(3) The other condition that has to be met in order for an individual's RNRB to be calculated is that his home (or formally, his QRI), or a proportion of it must be closely inherited. In order for a QRI to be closely inherited, it has to be inherited and that inheritance must be by qualifying individuals.

Inherited

A home (formally a QRI) which forms part of the estate of a person who has died (D) is 'inherited' by a person (B) from D in *any* of the following cases:

(a) there is a disposition of the home to B. The disposition may be effected under D's will (as a specific legacy or as part of the residue of the estate), or on D's intestacy, as D's surviving joint tenant by right of survivorship or otherwise (eg under forced heirship rules, under a nomination or under a donatio mortis causa) (s 8J(2)).

All that is required under this head is that there is a disposition of the home to B. One needs to identify an act on the part of D of alienating or relinquishing the home to B. This does not mean necessarily that B has to acquire the home (although of course he may do so). It is HMRC's view (see IHTM46033) that for there to be a disposition of the home to B, B has to become beneficially entitled to it on the death of D. This may be little misleading as they go on to state that the actual residence does not have to end up in the hands of the B; if D's personal representatives sell the residence as part of the administration of the estate and pass the sale proceeds to B, there will have been a disposition of the home to B. Equally, where D dies owning a home and D's will directs his personal representatives to sell his the home with the sale proceeds being paid to B, again the home would be regarded as inherited under a disposition of it to B. Similarly where, under his will, D leaves his home to B and B directs D's personal representatives to sell the home and distribute the proceeds to B, B nevertheless inherits the home. HMRC then go on to state, by contrast, that if D's will has a condition that B has to reach a certain age before he can inherit D's home (ie the home is held in trust subject to a contingency), B does not inherit the home because B does not inherit it 'on' the death of D. What HMRC seem to be signifying is that there must be an unconditional disposition of the home in order for B to inherit it. B will not be regarded as inheriting the home under this head if it becomes comprised in a settlement on D's death or immediately before D's death the home was settled property in which D was beneficially entitled to an interest in possession and it remains settled property on his death.

The disposition may occur following the variation of a deceased person's will (s 142) or where an appointment of D's home which has become trust property is made under s 144. Similarly where an order is made under the Inheritance (Provision for Family and Dependants) Act 1975 that satisfies IHTA 1984 s 146 there may be disposition of a home to B (if that is what the court order provides).

An appropriation of property is not a disposition of it. Where a home is merely appropriated to B by D's personal representatives under administrative powers given expressly in D's will or by the Administration of Estates Act s 41 on D's intestacy, there is no disposition of the home. For example, D dies and under his will he leaves his estate (which includes his home) as to one half on life interest trust for his mother and as to the other half absolutely to B (his son). Only one half of the home is treated as inherited by B (there being a disposition to B of a one-half interest in the home. If using their administrative powers D's personal representatives appropriate the home in its entirety to B in satisfaction of his half share of the estate, although the home now passes absolutely to the son, it does so by virtue of the personal representative's powers and not under D's will. It remains the case that B has inherited only one-half of D's home.

(b) B becomes beneficially entitled on D's death to a qualifying IIP (see **Example C3**) in the home, which IIP is an immediate post death interest (IPDI) or a disabled person's interest (DPI) but not a transitional serial interest (TSI) (s 8J(4)(a)). It will be noted that B does not inherit the home where it is settled on discretionary trust of which B is in the class of beneficiaries. However, if an appointment is made out of the trust within two years of the settlor's death to B as a qualifying beneficiary, then B will be regarded as having inherited the home under head (a) above (s 144).

(c) B is the beneficiary of a bereaved minor's trust or an 18–25 trust (see **Example C15**) which is established on the death of D and the home is settled on such a trust at the time of D's death for B's benefit (s 8J(4)(b)).

(d) B becomes beneficially entitled to the home on D's death in the case where immediately before D's death the home was settled property in which D was beneficially entitled to any IIP (s 8J(5)). For example, X dies leaving his home on life interest trust for his spouse (D) with remainders over to B1 (their child). When D dies, the home passes under the terms of the trust to B1. D's life interest was an IPDI and so a qualifying IIP and so B1 (his child) will inherit the home.

(e) B is the person to whom a disposal of the home was made by D by way of gift inter vivos, but in the case where the home forms part of D's estate immediately before his death as a result of the home being a gift with reservation of benefit (s 8J(6)).

Qualifying individuals

In order for a home to be closely inherited it has to be inherited (in one of the circumstances set out above) by one of the following individuals (referred to in this note as a 'qualifying individual'):

(a) L: a lineal descendant of D as defined (see below) (s 8K(1)(a));

(b) S: the spouse or civil partner of L at the time of D's death (s 8K(1(b));

(c) W: the spouse or civil partner of L where L had predeceased D or had died at the same time as D provided also that W has not in the period beginning with L's death and ending with D's death become the spouse or civil partner of another person (s 8K(1)(c)).

The following persons fall into the first of the above categories and are regarded as the lineal descendants of D:

(a) a biological lineal descendant (child, grandchild, great-grandchild etc) of D. This means that property passing to a deceased person's parents, siblings, nephews nieces, cousins or other non-lineal descendants of D is not 'closely inherited';

(b) a step child of D and a step-child of D's lineal descendants (s 8K(3));

(c) the natural child of D in the case where that child has been adopted (as defined in s 8K(9)) and would otherwise be regarded only as the child of his adoptive parent (s 8K(4));

(d) a foster child of D (where D is a foster parent as defined in s 8K(10));

(e) the ward of D where D acts in the capacity of guardian (appointed under the Children Act 1989 or under corresponding law having effect in Scotland or Northern Ireland or any other territory) where the guardianship commenced whilst the ward was under the age of 18 years (s 8K(6)); and

(f) the ward of D where D acts in the capacity as special guardian (appointed under the Children Act 1989 or under corresponding law having effect in Scotland or Northern Ireland or any other territory) where the special guardianship commenced whilst the ward was under the age of 18 years (s 8K(7)).

Where under the list of D's lineal descendants as defined, a person L is to be treated as a child of D, L's lineal descendants are treated as lineal descendants of D regardless of when they were born (s 8K(8)).

Examples

John dies intestate and his estate, including his home, is divided under the intestacy rule between his three nieces and nephews. The home is not closely inherited as his nieces and nephews are not qualifying individuals.

Pamela dies and leaves her home to her late son's widow who has not remarried at the time of Pamela's death. The widow is a qualifying individual (W) and the home is closely inherited. The widow would not be a qualifying individual if she had remarried before Pamela's death.

Jane marries Edward at a time when Edward has two sons from his previous marriage. They have no children of their own. Following Edward's death, Jane dies and leaves her home to Charlotte who is the daughter of Edward's elder son. Charlotte was born before Jane married Edward. Charlotte is a qualifying person (L) and the home is closely inherited. Edward's sons become Jane's step-children upon her marriage to Edward and they remain so following Edward's death. Charlotte is a lineal descendant of Jane in that she is Jane's step-grandchild (and so it does not matter that she was born before she acquired that status on the marriage of Jane and Edward).

Paul is the adopted child of Timothy and Belinda. Following their death Paul inherits the family home. Paul is a qualifying person (L) and the home is directly inherited. A few years later Paul inherits the home of his natural mother, Millicent. Paul is also a qualifying person (L) in relation to Millicent and her home is also closely inherited.

Sam was 14 years old when James was appointed has his guardian under the Children Act 1989. Sam married Glenda when he was aged 25 but died a few years later. In his will James leaves his home to Glenda and dies after Glenda marries Chris. The home is not closely inherited as Glenda is not a qualifying person on James's death. She would have been a qualifying person (W) had she not remarried as she would have been the widow of a lineal descendant of James (ie Sam who became his ward when he was under 18).

Angela dies leaving her home on life interest trust to her spouse Barry with remainders over to their children Charlie and Daniel in equal shares absolutely. Charlie dies before Barry. When Barry dies, the home passes under the terms of the trust as to one half to Daniel who is a qualifying person (L) and so is directly inherited as to that extent. When Charlie died her reversionary interest in the home will have passed under her Will or intestacy. If that disposition was to a lineal descendant of Barry (or Charlie's spouse or civil partner), that person too will have been a qualifying person (L or W as the case may be).

(4) A distinction must be drawn between the value of an individual's estate immediately before his death (referred to as E in s 8D(5)(d)) and the value transferred by the chargeable transfer which he is deemed to make on his death (referred to as VT in s 8D(5)(e)).

E is the value of the deceased person's chargeable estate at the time of his death calculated as the aggregate value of the property comprised in the estate but after deducting labilities that may be taken into account (see **Example A12 part C**) but including also the value of assets passing by survivorship, gifts in which the deceased person had a reservation of benefit and any assets held in trust in which the deceased person enjoyed a qualifying IIP (see **Example A8 explanatory note 1**).

VT, on the other hand, is the value of the deceased person's chargeable estate at the time of his death calculated in the normal way, that is to say after deducting exempt legacies, liabilities that may be taken into account and other reliefs that reduce the value of an estate (eg business property relief) but including the value of assets passing by survivorship, gifts in which the deceased person had a reservation of benefit and any assets held in trust in which the deceased person enjoyed a qualifying IIP.

Both E and VT may be affected by a person's domicile, in that if he is not domiciled in the UK then his foreign-sited assets (and other excluded property) will not be counted as part of his estate (s 5(1)(b)). Also, where, under the terms of a double taxation agreement, an asset is not subject to inheritance tax, it will be left out of account in quantifying both E and VT.

For example, William dies in November 2023 owning assets worth £2,150,000 (including a qualifying interest in possession valued at £50,000) and agricultural property valued at £50,000 which attracts 100% APR. He owes debts of £20,000 at the time of his death. Under his will he leaves £100,000 to charity. The value (E) of William's estate is £2,150,000 - £20,000 = £2,130,000. By contrast the chargeable value (VT) of his estate on which inheritance tax is charged is £2,130,000 - £50,000 - £100,000 = £1,980,000, that is the value of his estate after the APR and the exempt legacy. The maximum amount of RNRB to which William is entitled is his default allowance of £175,000 - (2,130,000 - £2,000,000)/2 = £110,000. The RNRB is ascertained by reference to the amount of 'E' and not 'VT'.

(5) The proportion of an individual's home that is directly inherited is referred to in the legislation as N% (where N is a number greater than 0 and less than or equal to 100). For example, if any individual's home is inherited equally by his son and his nephew, N% would be 50%. From this is derived the percentage NV/100 which is N% of the value of the chargeable transfer made on death as is attributable to the QRI (s 8E(1)(b) and rider). In other words NV/100 is ascertained by reference to VT (see **explanatory note 16**) and it is ensured that the value attributable to a person's home (ie his QRI) is its value after being adjusted under s 38 (Attribution of value to specific gifts (ie single and double grossing up)) and s 39 (Attribution of value to residuary gifts) (see **Examples A16** to **A19**) and after deduction of agricultural property relief (see **Example A22**) and business property relief (see **Example A21**) after applying, if necessary, s 39A (Operation of ss 38 and 39 in cases of business or agricultural relief) (see **Examples A16** and **A18**).

Illustration

Jing dies on 6 April 2023 owning a home whose unencumbered value is £300,000. A mortgage of £100,000 is secured on the home and it qualifies for agricultural property relief of 100%. Her home is inherited by her daughter. The other property in Jing's free estate (E) is valued at £180,000 against which liabilities of £20,000 may be deducted. Jing also enjoys a qualifying interest in possession in a trust whose assets are valued at £10,000. The value of Jing's estate is (£300,000 - £100,000) + (£180,000 - £20,000) + £10,000 = £370,000. The value transferred by the chargeable transfer (VT) which she is deemed to make on her death is (£300,000 - £100,000 - £200,000(APR)) + (£180,000 - £20,000) + £10,000 = £170,000. For the purposes of calculating Jing's RNRB, NV/100 is 100% of the value of the chargeable transfer made on death as is attributable to the value of her home (ie 100% × (£300,000 - £100,000 - £200,000(APR)) = 0%). Therefore, by virtue of s 8E(2), Jing's RNRB is nil and the whole of her default allowance of £175,000 (the 2023/24 amount) passes to her widower or surviving civil partner (if she has one).

(6) In each of the illustrations in **part (b)**, the amount of the RNRB is subject to further modification where it exceeds the value of an individual's chargeable estate when he dies. Although this seems odd, it could arise where the value of the home is greater than the net value of the estate after liabilities and other reliefs have been deducted. The amount of the RNRB is restricted to the value of the chargeable estate and the unused excess is available for transfer to a spouse or civil partner (ie it is available for carry-forward).

Illustration

Fiona dies on 3 May 2023 owning an estate valued at £1,000,000 which includes her home valued at £90,000 (after deducting a mortgage of £10,000 secured on the home). In valuing her estate for the purposes of IHT BPR of £950,000 is taken into account. She is survived by her husband Ralph (who is independently wealthy). Her home is inherited by her step-daughter; the rest of her estate is inherited by her son from a previous marriage. Ralph has agreed to move into another property. The amount of Fiona's RNRB is prima facie £90,000 (ie the value of her home) as her estate is less than £2,000,000 and the value of her home is less than £175,000 (her default allowance for 2023/24). However, the value of her chargeable estate is £1,000,000 - £950,000 (BPR) = £50,000. Consequently her RNRB (prima facie of £90,000) is reduced to £50,000 and the balance of her default allowance of £125,000 is passed to Ralph.

(7) Where a taxpayer's estate exceeds £2,000,000 consideration should be given as to whether it may be reduced in order to prevent the tapering of the RNRB. Whilst the RNRB gives some benefit to those who die with assets worth more than £2,000,000, the effect of tapering is to create a 60% rate of tax above the threshold (TT). A number of mechanisms may be considered to reduce a taxpayer's estate to (or below) the thresholder. Married couples (or those in a civil partnership) may arrange for transfers between them to equalise their respective estates. A nil-rate band discretionary trust in the will of the first party to die can take £325,000 out of the survivor's estate and so help preserve the RNRB. This is the best planning for any assets that attract business property relief (see **Example A21**) or agricultural property relief (see **Example A22**) owned by the first to die. It may also be beneficial for the first party to die to use their RNRB rather than letting it be carried forward to the survivor (see **Example A3**). This will be the case if the survivor will die definitely owning property worth more than £2,000,000. Alternatively it may make the difference between the survivor's estate being above or below the critical threshold. A nil-rate band discretionary trust is almost always worthwhile if either spouse or civil partner has previously been widowed. This can give the couple £1,500,000 of allowances between them. If both spouses/civil partners were widowed before marrying, £2,000,000 of allowances in total might be unlocked.

For example, if one of the parties to a marriage or civil partnership has already died, a reduction in the size of the estate of the deceased may be possible by taking advantage of s 142 (see **Example B6 explanatory note 5**) or s 144 to redirect the assets of their estate (see **Example C11 explanatory note 11**). To use the deceased's RNRB over part of the home where the survivor is still living and occupying it, consider giving children an immediate post-death interest in possession (IDPI) (see **Example C3**) in a fraction of the home. Although unmarried couples cannot transfer RNRB between their estates or obtain any RNRB of gifts to each other's children, if the first to die has children of their own (or even stepchildren from a previous marriage/civil partnership), consider giving those children and IPDI in part of a property where the survivor continues to live. The surviving spouse or civil partner may also consider making a lifetime gift of their property to reduce the size of their estate. For example, consider a widow with the potential to benefit from £1,000,000 of the own and transferred RNB and RNRB. She owns a flat worth £700,000 and investments with large unrealised gains of £2,000,000. If she dies owing these assets, her estate will not benefit from her RNRB and TRNRB as it be fully tapered. A lifetime gift of £700,000 worth of investments could unlock the maximum £350,000 RNRB (saving IHT of as much as £140,000) even though the lifetime gift may not escape IHT on its own value. If such a gift is not possible (because of capital gains tax), the widow could reduce her estate to £2,000,000 by giving away her flat (paying a market rent to ensure there is no gift with reservation of benefit – see **Example B1**); downsizing allowance would preserve the effect of having a RNRB.

(8) This note discusses in detail the concept of a qualifying former residential interest (QFRI) in the context of DA. For DA to be in point there must have been a QFRI, that is a residential property interest in a person's estate on or after 8 July 2015 which has either been disposed of or downsized from before the date of death. The QFRI ('former home') must have been in the person's estate immediately before the disposal and the disposal must take place on or after 8 July 2015, after the former home first became the person's residence and before the person dies (s 8H(4F)). There can only ever be one QFRI for DA purposes. Although a person may have moved home a number of times since 8 July 2015 or may have disposed of more than one former home, only one of these may be taken into account for DA. A former home that has been disposed of is not automatically a QFRI. The deceased's personal representatives must nominate the dwelling-house which they want to take into account.

Although one tends to think of a QFRI as ownership of a whole dwelling-house, in fact it is more accurate to address oneself to an interest in the dwelling-house. Where only one interest has been disposed of in a nominated dwelling-house, that single interest is the QFRI. Where more than one interest in the same dwelling-house is disposed of on the same day (as may be the case where an individual owns one-half of a home absolutely and has a QIIP in the other half), all of those disposals combine to be a single interest in the nominated dwelling-house. Where more than one interest in the same dwelling-house is disposed of on different days, the deceased's personal representatives have to nominate which interest is to be taken into account. For example, if a deceased person made gifts of 5% of their home to each of 4 children on the same day, the QFRI would be 20% of the home gifted. However, if the gifts took place on four consecutive days, the personal representatives would have to nominate which of those separate disposals is to be taken into account as the QFRI which would then be only 5% of the home gifted.

Where the disposal of a QFRI takes place pursuant to contract which is completed by a conveyance, the disposal occurs at the time when the interest is conveyed.

Where an interest in a former home is held in trust, then strictly speaking it would be the trustees of the trust that dispose of the interest rather than the person who subsequently dies (as required for an interest in former home to be a QFRI). To address this issue s 8H treats the disposal by the trustees as a disposal by the deceased where the deceased has a QIIP in the settled property which consists of an interest in a dwelling-house that is his residence. Where the trustees of the settlement dispose of the interest in the dwelling-house to someone other than the beneficiary, or there is a coming to an end of the beneficiary's interest in their lifetime, this will be treated as a disposal by the beneficiary if the person's IIP subsisted throughout the period from the time he became entitled to it up to the time of disposal and the interest in the dwelling-house is the settled property immediately before the disposal.

In practical terms, the following would qualify as disposals by the deceased:

(i) The trustees sell a dwelling-house in the trust and buy a less valuable one.

(ii) The trustees sell a dwelling-house in the trust and do not replace it.

(iii) The trustees bring the deceased's interest in possession in the trust which includes a dwelling-house to an end in the deceased's lifetime.

(iv) The deceased brings their interest in possession in the trust which includes a dwelling-house to an end in their lifetime.

In cases where an individual's estate is treated as including a dwelling-house under the gift with reservation rules, in the context of the DA rules, the initial gift of the home by the deceased is not treated as a disposal, but if the reservation comes to an end during the deceased's lifetime, then that is treated as a disposal (s 8H(4D)).

(9) This note discusses in detail the calculation of the 'lost relievable amount' in the context of DA.

Low value home owned at the date of death

Where an individual has downsized to a lower value property, the calculation of the DA is set out in s 8FE(9). Take the following steps to calculate the LRA (lost relievable amount):

Calculate the RNRB that would have been available when the disposal of the old home took place. This is the person's 'former allowance' and is made up of the residential enhancement at the date of the former home's disposal plus any transferred RNRB which is available at the date of death. If the disposal occurred between:

Step 1: a) 8 July 2015 and 5 April 2018 this figure is £100,000,
b) 6 April 2018 and 5 April 2019 this figure is £125,000,
c) 6 April 2019 and 5 April 2020 this figure is £150,000, and
d) 6 April 2020 and 5 April 2021 and all later tax years this figure is £175,000.

Step 2: Express the chargeable value of the person's former home as a percentage of his former allowance, but the percentage is limited to 100%.

Step 3: Express the chargeable value of the person's current home as a percentage of the default or adjusted allowance available at the date of his death, but the percentage is limited to 100%.

Step 4: Calculate P% by subtracting the percentage given by Step 3 from the percentage given by Step 2 (taking the difference as 0% if the result is negative).

Step 5: The LRA is P% of the individual's RNRB on his death.

For example, consider Moritz who in May 2023 downsized from a large house worth £600,000 to a small flat which was valued at £105,000 on his death in September 2025. He left the flat to his son and the rest of his estate worth £200,000 to his two daughters. Moritz is not entitled to any transferred RNRB on his death.

First calculate the LRA:

Step 1: Moritz's former allowance is £175,000, being the residential enhancement for the date of disposal of his house (2023/24).

Step 2: The chargeable value of Moritz's former home (£600,000) as a percentage of his former allowance (£175,000) is 342.88% (£600,000/£175,000 × 100%) but this is limited to 100%.

Step 3: The chargeable value of Moritz's current home (£105,000) as a percentage of his default allowance of £175,000 at the date of his death in 2025/26 is 60% (£105,000/£175,000 × 100%).

Step 4: P% = 100% - 60% = 40%.

Step 5: The LRA is £70,000 = 40% × £175,000 (ie the lower of the residential enhancement and the chargeable value of his home at the time of his death).

Now calculate the amount of the RNRB available. This means that the amount of the RNRB which is used in calculating the tax arising in respect of Moritz's estate is £105,000 (being the lower of the residential enhancement (£175,000) and the chargeable value of his home at the time of his death (£105,000)). In addition the amount of the DA which is so used is £70,000 (being the lower of the LRA (£70,000) and the amount of his other assets that are directly inherited (£200,000)). Strictly speaking the DA is added to his RNRB giving him a total RNRB of £175,000. (If instead Moritz had left £20,000 of his other assets to his daughters, his DA would have been limited to £20,000).

Secondly consider Margaret who in August 2023 downsized from a large house worth £450,000 to a smaller house which was valued at £200,000 on her death in December 2025. The house was left to her grand-niece. Of the balance of her estate of £800,000, £600,000 was left to her grandchildren. Margaret is not entitled to any transferred RNRB on her death.

First calculate the LRA:

Step 1: Margaret's former allowance is £175,000, being the residential enhancement for the date of disposal of her house (2023/24).

Step 2: The chargeable value of Margaret's former home (£450,000) as a percentage of her former allowance (£175,000) is 257.14% (£450,000/£175,000 × 100%) but this is limited to 100%.

Step 3: The chargeable value of Margaret's current home (£200,000) as a percentage of her default allowance of £175,000 at the date of his death in 2025/26 is 114.286% (£200,000/£175,000 × 100%) but this is limited to 100%.

Step 4: P% = 100% - 100% = 0%.

Step 5: The LRA is £Nil = 0% × £175,000 (ie the lower of the residential enhancement and the chargeable value of her home at the time of her death).

As the percentage at Step 4 is 0%, there is no lost RNRB and so no DA. In fact as no RNRB is available on Margaret's death (her home is not closely inherited as it is left to her grand-niece) there can be no DA either.

Thirdly, consider Neville who in January 2024 downsized from a large house worth £400,000 to a small flat which was valued at £105,000 on his death in September 2025. He left the flat in equal shares to his son and his wife and the rest of his estate worth £150,000 to his step-daughter. Neville is not entitled to any transferred RNRB on his death.

First calculate the LRA:

Step 1: Neville's former allowance is £175,000, being the residential enhancement for the date of disposal of his house (2023/24).

Step 2: The chargeable value of Neville's former home (£400,000) as a percentage of his former allowance (£175,000) is 228.57% (£400,000/£175,000 × 100%) but this is limited to 100%.

Step 3: The chargeable value of Neville's current home (£105,000) as a percentage of his default allowance of £175,000 at the date of his death in 2025/26 is 60% (£105,000/£175,000 × 100%).

Step 4: P% = 100% - 60% = 40%.

Step 5: The LRA is £70,000 = 40% × £175,000 (ie the lower of the residential enhancement and the chargeable value of his home at the time of his death).

Now calculate the amount of the RNRB available. This means that the amount of the RNRB which is used in calculating the tax arising in respect of Neville's estate is £52,500 (being the lower of the residential enhancement (£175,000) and the chargeable value of the proportion of his home at the time of his death that is left to his son (£105,000/2 = £52,500)). In addition the amount of the DA which is so used is £70,000 (being the lower of the LRA (£70,000) and the amount of his other assets that are directly inherited (£150,000)). Strictly speaking the DA is added to his RNRB giving him a total RNRB of £122,500. (If instead Neville had left £20,000 of his other assets to his step-daughter, his DA would have been limited to £20,000, giving a total RNRB for the estate of £72,500 (£52,000 + £20,000). This means that the balance of the RNRB of £102,500 (£175,000 - £72,500) available to be transferred to Neville's wife.)

Finally, consider Henry and Albert (who are civil partners) who in March 2018 downsized from a large house worth £300,000 which they owned jointly to a smaller house. Albert dies in December 2024 leaving his half-share of the smaller house, valued at £122,500 to Henry and other assets in his estate worth £80,000 to their adopted son.

First calculate the LRA:

Step 1: Albert's former allowance is £100,000 (as the downsizing occurred in the period 8 July 2015 to 5 April 2018).

Step 2: The chargeable value of Albert's interest in his former home (£150,000) as a percentage of his former allowance (£100,000) is 150% (£150,000/£100,000 × 100%) but this is limited to 100%.

Step 3: The chargeable value of Albert's interest in the current home (£122,500) as a percentage of his default allowance of £175,000 at the date of his death in 2024/25 is 70% (£122,500/£175,000 × 100%).

Step 4: P% = 100% - 70% = 30%.

Step 5: The LRA is £52,500 = 30% × £175,000 (ie the lower of the residential enhancement and the chargeable value of his home at the time of his death).

Now calculate the amount of the RNRB available. As the smaller home is left to Henry (Albert's civil partner) the RNRB available on Albert's death is £Nil. In addition the amount of the DA which is available on calculating the tax arising on Albert's estate is £52,500 (being the lower of the LRA (£52,500) and the amount of his other assets that are directly inherited (£80,000)). Strictly speaking the DA is added to his RNRB giving a total RNRB of £52,500. Albert's estate had a default allowance of £175,000 of which £52,500 has been used. There is unused RNRB of £122,500 which is available for transfer to Henry. (If instead Albert had left £10,000 of his other assets to his adopted son, his DA would have been limited to £10,000, giving a total RNRB for the estate of £10,000. This means that the balance of the RNRB of £165,000 (£175,000 - £10,000) is available to be transferred to Henry.)

No value home owned at the date of death

Where an individual has disposed of his home in his lifetime and there is no home in their estate when he dies, the calculation of the DA is set out in s 8FE(10). Take the following steps to calculate the LRA (lost relievable amount):

Step 1: Calculate the RNRB that would have been available when the disposal of the old home took place. This is the person's 'former allowance' and is made up of the residential enhancement at the date of the former home's disposal plus any transferred RNRB which is available at the date of death. If the disposal occurred between 8 July 2015 and 5 April 2018 this figure is £100,000.

Step 2: Express the chargeable value of the person's former home as a percentage (X%) of his former allowance, but the percentage is limited to 100%.

Step 3: The LRA is X% of the individual's default or adjusted allowance on his death.

For example, consider Juliet who sold her former for £342,000 in October 2023 to go into residential care. She died in 2026 owning an estate worth £500,000. She left half of her estate to her son and the balance to her nephew. She is not entitled to any transferred RNRB on her death.

First calculate the LRA:

Step 1: Juliet's former allowance is £175,000, being the residential enhancement for the date of disposal of her house (2023/24).

Step 2: The chargeable value of Juliet's former home (£342,000) as a percentage of her former allowance (£175,000) is 195.43% (£342,000/£175,000 × 100%) but this is limited to 100%.

Step 3: The LRA is £175,000 = 100% × £175,000.

Now calculate the amount of the RNRB available. This means that the amount of the RNRB which is used in calculating the tax arising in respect of Juliet's estate is £Nil as she does not own a home when she dies. However, the amount of the DA which is used in calculating the tax on her estate is £175,000 (being the lower of the LRA (£175,000) and the amount of her other assets that are directly inherited (£250,000)). Strictly speaking the DA is added to her RNRB giving her a total RNRB of £175,000. (If instead Juliet had left £100,000 to her son and the rest of her estate to her nephew, her DA would have been limited to £100,000).

Secondly, consider Janet who sold her former for £105,000 in May 2024 to move in with her daughter. She died in January 2026 owning an estate worth £600,000 all of which she left to her daughter. She is not entitled to any transferred RNRB on her death.

First calculate the LRA:

Step 1: Juliet's former allowance is £175,000, being the residential enhancement in force on the date of disposal of her house (2024/25).

Step 2: The chargeable value of Juliet's former home (£105,000) as a percentage of her former allowance (£175,000) is 60% (£105,000/£175,000 × 100%).

Step 3: The LRA is £105,000 = 60% × £175,000

Now calculate the amount of the RNRB available. This means that the amount of the RNRB which is used in calculating the tax arising in respect of Janet's estate is £Nil as she does not own a home when she dies. However, the amount of the DA which is used in calculating the tax on her estate is £105,000 (being the lower of the LRA (£105,000) and the amount of her other assets that are directly inherited (£600,000)). Strictly speaking the DA is added to her RNRB giving her a total RNRB of £105,000.

Annual exemption

(10) The treatment of the annual exemption outlined in **part (c)** of the Example appears to conflict with s 19(3A), which provides that if a potentially exempt transfer becomes a chargeable transfer because of the donor's death within seven years, any annual exemption which has not been used then becomes available, and is given against the earliest transfer if there is more than one. An annual exemption which has already been given on chargeable transfers in the same year is not to be disturbed, even if some or all of the potentially exempt transfers that have become chargeable were made before the transfers against which the annual exemption had been utilised. But potentially exempt transfers that become chargeable take priority over chargeable transfers in a later tax year, so that where an unused annual exemption had been carried forward and used in the following tax year, the exemption is to be given instead against the potentially exempt transfers, and the tax on the transfers which originally used it has to be recomputed.

These provisions of s 19(3A) are, however, redundant when considered in the light of the definition of 'potentially exempt transfer' in s 3A, namely that a potentially exempt transfer is a transfer that would be a chargeable transfer but for s 3A. Any part of a transfer covered by the annual exemption is an exempt transfer, and therefore would not be a chargeable transfer apart from s 3A. It follows that if a potentially exempt transfer becomes chargeable there cannot possibly be any available annual exemption to use against it. Despite the fact that a drafting error makes s 19(3A) meaningless, no action has been taken to correct it.

The capital gains tax gifts holdover relief provisions of TCGA 1992 s 260 are available against a lifetime gift that is to any extent a chargeable transfer at the time, even if a slice of it is covered by the IHT annual exemption. The relief cannot be claimed retrospectively in relation to a potentially exempt transfer that becomes chargeable as a result of the transferor's death. Capital gains tax gifts relief is dealt with in the companion to this book, **Tolley's Taxwise I 2023/24. See Example A21 part A(c)** for the interaction between the annual exemption and business and agricultural property relief.

Question

A

Explain the conditions that must be met in order for unused nil-rate band to be transferred between spouses and civil partners.

B

Explain the consequences of unused nil-rate band being transferred between spouses and civil partners.

C

You have been asked by a board of examiners to submit a series of short questions and answers concerning the computation of the amount of unused nil-rate band that may be transferred between spouses and civil partners. They will consider using your questions when setting the inheritance tax paper of the examination over the next couple of years. You have drafted the following questions; prepare answers to them.

(i) Rupert died on 23 October 2006. His free estate was valued at £150,000. He enjoyed an interest in possession in a trust settled by his father before 22 March 2006; the remainderman of the trust was Rupert's son Michael. The trust assets were valued at £100,000 at the time of his death. Under his will he left £50,000 to his daughter Elizabeth and the rest of his free estate to his wife Mary. Rupert had made two lifetime transfers. He had given £106,000 to his son two years before his death and in 1998/99 had settled £206,000 on a discretionary trust in favour of his nephew Harry. Mary dies in 2029 (having made no lifetime transfers). Assume that at the time of her death the nil-rate band is £350,000 and that all appropriate claims have been correctly made.

Calculate the amount of the nil-rate band to which Mary is entitled when she dies.

(ii)

(a) Sidney, who was married to Jane (a person of substantial independent means), died in December 1973 owning estate valued at £10,000 which he left under his will to his wife. They had no children. Jane married John in 1992. She died in June 2012 owning estate valued at £90,000 which was left to charity. She had made no lifetime transfers. John himself dies in 2029 and his estate is fully chargeable. Assume that at the time of his death the nil-rate band is £350,000 and that he has made no lifetime transfers. Assume also that separate claims under IHTA 1984 s 8A are made by Jane's personal representatives and by John's personal representatives.

Calculate the amount of the nil-rate band to which John is entitled when he dies.

(b) Compare this to the amount of the nil-rate band to which Jane would have been entitled on her death had she survived to 2029 and John had died in August 2012 having made no lifetime transfers and leaving chargeable estate of £225,000.

(iii) Priscilla (who is UK domiciled and who had made no lifetime gifts) died in October 2007 leaving an estate worth £200,000 to her civil partner Helga who is domiciled in Austria. Helga dies in December 2023 (having made no lifetime transfers) and under her will she settles on a discretionary trust 'such sum from my UK bank account as I could leave immediately before my death without IHT becoming payable'.

Calculate the amount of the nil-rate band to which Helga is entitled when she dies, and explain how much money is acquired by the trustees on Helga's death.

D

The rules on the transfer of unused nil-rate band operate in a special way where a charge to inheritance tax arising on the death of an individual is deferred because of woodlands relief or the rules on conditionally exempt transfers. Explain how the rules operate in these cases and calculate the amount of nil-rate band to which Julia is entitled when she dies in December 2023 leaving her estate to her children in the following scenario:

(i) Hector who died in August 2002 leaving estate of £550,000, and who had made no relevant lifetime transfers, is survived by his wife Julia. He left non-commercial woodlands to his children as a specific legacy; the growing timber was valued at £125,000 and the land itself at £50,000. In respect of the trees, a claim under IHTA 1984 s 125 was made for deferral of tax. The residue of his estate was left to Julia. Before Julia's death in December 2023 the timber on the woodlands was all felled and sold in March 2006 for £200,000. The costs of felling and selling the timber amounted to £25,000.

(ii) Explain how your answer would have differed if the timber had been felled and sold in 2029 for £350,000 (after deductible expenses) and when she died in December 2023 Julia had left an estate worth £450,000? Assume that the nil-rate band in force in 2029 is £350,000.

E

Prepare notes for a lecture that you will give to your colleagues at a lunchtime technical meeting explaining:

(i) the conditions that must be met in order for unused residence nil-rate band to be transferred between spouses and civil partners,

(ii) the amount of the residence nil-rate band that may be transferred, and

(iii) the consequences of such a transfer.

Answer

A. Conditions to be met for the transfer of unused nil-rate band

The conditions that have to be met in order for unused nil-rate band to be transferred between spouses and civil partners are as follows:

(a) a person (who will be referred to as the 'deceased person') dies at any time;

(b) immediately before his death he had a spouse or civil partner (who will be referred to as the 'survivor');

(c) the survivor dies on or after 9 October 2007;

(d) the deceased person had unused nil-rate band on his death; and

(e) a claim is made within the relevant time limit.

Death of the deceased person

The object of the legislation is, broadly speaking, to transfer a deceased person's unused nil-rate band to his or her surviving spouse or civil partner who is then able to use it on his or her subsequent death to calculate the inheritance tax arising in relation to his or her estate. Although the rules came into effect on 9 October 2007 (FA 2008 Sch 4 para 9), it does not matter when the deceased person died. He may already have been dead on that day or he may die subsequently.

In either case, it does not matter how the deceased person suffered death, be it through natural causes, accident, on account of illness or otherwise. Also it does not matter whether the deceased person died testate or intestate. Where the High Court has made a declaration under s 2 of the Presumption of Death Act 2013 in respect of a missing person to whom the Act applies, the declaration is conclusive proof of the person's presumed death (s 3(1)) and is effective for all purposes including the ending of a marriage or civil partnership to which the person is a party (s 3(2)). Thus where a missing person is presumed to be dead, he will be treated as a 'deceased person' for the purposes of the inheritance tax provisions relating to the transfer of unused nil-rate band, The Act came into force on 1 October 2014 (The Presumption of Death Act 2013 (Commencement and Transitional and Saving Provision) Order 2014 SI 2014/1810 art 2).

Status of the deceased person before his death

Immediately before his death the deceased person must be married to the survivor or in a civil partnership with the survivor (IHTA 1984 s 8A(1)(a)). The marriage or civil partnership must be a valid marriage or civil partnership and recognised by the law of a territory comprised in the United Kingdom (as explained further in **explanatory note 1**). If at the date of the deceased person's death he is separated from the survivor, then he will still be the spouse or civil partner of the survivor and condition (b) above will be met.

In the case of civil partnerships, for UK law purposes a person cannot have been a civil partner at any time before 5 December 2005 when the Civil Partnership Act 2004 (CPA 2004) came into force. Therefore, the parties must have entered into the partnership in the UK (or abroad) on or after 5 December 2005 in accordance with the formalities set out in CPA 2004. Since civil partnerships have been recognised by the law from 5 December 2005 only, the deceased person must have died on or after 5 December 2005. Civil partnerships that were validly entered into abroad before 5 December 2005 are treated as having been formed on that date (CPA 2004 s 215(3)). The Civil Partnership (Opposite-sex couples) Regulations, SI 2019/1458 extend the option, in England and Wales, of entering into a civil partnership to opposite-sex couples with effect from 2 December 2019. The Civil Partnership (Scotland) Act 2020 makes similar provision in Scotland and was brought fully into effect on 1 June 2021 (Civil Partnership (Scotland) Act 2020 (Commencement No 3, Savings and Transitional Provisions) Regulations 2021 (SSI 2021/23). The Northern Ireland (Executive Formation etc) Act 2019 makes similar provision in Northern Ireland and was brought into force on 13 January 2020 by the Marriage (Same-sex Couples) and Civil Partnership (Opposite-sex Couples) (Northern Ireland) Regulations 2019 (SI 2019/1514).

It clearly follows from the above discussion that, where the marriage or civil partnership of the deceased person has been dissolved at the time of his death (or was never validly entered into in the first place), then the former spouse or civil partner who survives the death of the deceased person will not be able to claim that the unused nil-rate band of the deceased person be transferred to him.

Existence of unused nil-rate band

At the time when the deceased person dies he must have unused nil-rate band (IHTA 1984 s 8A(1)(b)). Section 8A(2) provides that a person has unused nil-rate band on death if:

M > VT

M is the maximum amount transferrable at 0% and, after giving effect to the deceased's residence nil-rate band, is computed as follows:

- take the nil-rate band in force at the date of the deceased person's death (increased, as the case may be, by reference to any unused nil-rate band of a former deceased spouse or civil partner of the deceased person);
- reduce the above amount by the cumulative chargeable transfers made by the deceased person in the seven years before his death; this means that the value of the deceased person's estate is not taken into account in working out the amount of M.

VT is the value of the deceased person's chargeable estate at the time of his death calculated in the normal way, that is to say after deducting exempt legacies, liabilities that may be taken into account and other reliefs that reduce the value of an estate (eg business property relief) but including the value of assets passing by survivorship, gifts in which the deceased person had a reservation of benefit and any assets held in trust in which the deceased person enjoyed a qualifying IIP. This means, in particular, that the amount of a deceased person's chargeable estate may be affected by his domicile, in that if he is not domiciled in the UK then his foreign-sited assets (and other excluded property) will not be counted as part of his estate (s 5(1)(b)). Also, where, under the terms of a double taxation agreement, an asset is not subject to inheritance tax, it will be left out of account in quantifying the deceased person's chargeable estate. By contrast, however, where an inheritance tax liability that arises in respect of the deceased person's estate is reduced by double tax relief or quick succession relief, it is most likely to mean that his estate was fully chargeable and his nil-rate band entirely used up. (Also see **explanatory note 3** as to other circumstances in which the deceased person's nil-rate band may be used up, whether wholly or in part.) Excess tax relief cannot be turned into unused nil-rate band.

Where spouses or civil partners die in circumstances where it cannot be known which of them survived the other, then the commorientes rules (discussed in **Example B6**) need to be considered in establishing whether the deceased person had unused nil-rate band at the time of his death.

Claim

In order for the estate of the survivor to benefit from the transfer of the unused nil-rate band of the deceased person, a claim has to be made on the death of the survivor by either his or her personal representatives or (if no claim is made by them) by any other person liable to the tax chargeable on the survivor's death (s 8B(1)).

Claims by personal representatives

The claim to transfer unused nil-rate band must be made by the personal representatives of the survivor after he dies (and not when the first spouse or civil partner dies). They will need to fill in a claim form IHT402 available online, or from the helpline on 0300 123 1072 (deceased estate helpline or 0300 200 3300 Bereavement helpline), and send it to HMRC together with a copy of the documents requested.

The form IHT402 is a request for information about the estate of the deceased person and is necessary to calculate the amount of the nil-rate band that was unused at the time of his death. A calculation can then be made to determine the extent to which the nil-rate band available to the survivor may be increased so that the revised nil-rate band can be used to calculate the inheritance tax payable on the survivor's estate.

The form should be sent to HMRC at the same time as form IHT400 for the estate of the survivor together with the documents listed in IHTM43006, namely a copy of the grant of representation (Confirmation in Scotland), the death certificate of the deceased person, a copy of his will, his marriage certificate and copies of any other documents that affect the devolution of his estate (eg a Deed of Variation). Where there is difficulty in obtaining these documents, and the time limit for making a claim is approaching, then HMRC will allow a provisional claim to be made.

A claim made by the personal representatives of the survivor must be made within the period of two years from the end of the month in which the survivor dies or (if it is later) the period of three months beginning with the date on which the personal representatives first begin to act, although HMRC may allow a longer period within which a claim may be made (s 8B(3)). For example, if a person dies on 13 October 2022 and his personal representatives start to act on 2 November 2022, a claim must be made by them by the later of 31 October 2024 and 1 February 2023. A claim made within the periods mentioned above may be withdrawn no later than one month after the end of the period concerned (s 8B(4)). In the above Example, the claim may be withdrawn on or before 30 November 2024. As to when personal representatives start to act is a question of fact. An administrator can begin to act only after letters of administration have been granted, whereas an executor can start to act before the grant of probate. Where an executor acts in such a way as to indicate that he intends to take on the office of executor and would thus be prevented from renouncing probate (eg by bringing or defending an action in his capacity of executor, carrying on the deceased's business or demanding debts due to the deceased), then he will start to act from that time.

Late claims by personal representatives are likely to be in point where there is a dispute that needs to be settled before their identity is established. HMRC will admit a late claim in this case where it can be shown that the personal representatives have been actively pursuing matters to resolve the problem. Late claims will also be accepted by HMRC where the claimant can show that an event beyond his control prevented a making of a claim in the permitted period; examples of such events are listed in IHTM43009. However, if a claimant was able to manage the rest of his private or business affairs during the period in question, HMRC are unlikely to accept that he was genuinely prevented, as personal representative, from making the claim on time.

It will be noted that no specific action need be taken on the first death. The transfer of unused nil-rate band is capable of occurring only on the death of the survivor, so there is no need to agree the amount of nil-rate band that is transferable on the death of the deceased person. However, it is best practice to preserve certain records that will be needed on the death of the survivor to establish the amount of the deceased person's unused nil-rate band and for which the personal representatives of the survivor may call. These records are set out in **explanatory note 2**.

The personal representatives of the survivor will be able to obtain copies of some of the documents required from public records bodies:

- Service (for England and Wales, www.gov.uk/government/organisations/hm-courts-and- tribunals-service, for Scotland www.scotcourts.gov.uk, and for Northern Ireland www.courtsni.gov.uk); and
- copies of death certificates and marriage certificates are available from the General Register Office (for England & Wales www.gro.gov.uk, for Scotland www.gro-scotland.gov.uk, and for Northern Ireland www.groni.gov.uk).

These will give the value of the deceased person's estate that was declared for probate/confirmation and will also provide information about who inherited the assets that passed under the deceased person's will or intestacy. However, it will not provide any information about other assets that are chargeable when someone dies (as listed in **explanatory note 2**).

The personal representatives of the survivor will need to make enquiries of those who inherited the estate of the deceased person to see if they can recall whether or not he had made any lifetime transfers or whether there may have been other assets not passing under his will or intestacy, or discovered subsequent to the grant of probate or letters of administration that were chargeable on his death. Similarly they may ask the same questions of the deceased person's personal representatives themselves (who can typically be identified from the probate/letters of administration). Getting hold of a copy of the estate accounts will obviously be a great help, wherever such were prepared. If values are known, they should be included on the claim form; if values are not known, the personal representatives should complete the claim form to the best of their ability and explain the position to HMRC when they make their claim. If there is no evidence that any other assets were chargeable, the personal representatives can make their claim based on the information they have from the documents already mentioned. Such persons should also be asked to confirm details of any deed of variation, or other transfer (eg under s 143 (Compliance with testator's request)), following the death of the deceased person, since in many situations these can take place without needing to be notified to the personal representatives of the deceased person.

With regard to agreeing values of assets such as houses or household goods and whether a relief such as agricultural or business property relief applies, it will only be necessary to agree values where such assets passed to chargeable beneficiaries on the deceased person's death (ie someone other than the survivor or charity); the same point will apply to lifetime transfers by the deceased person. This will be done when the survivor dies, but only where it is necessary to do so because the amount of the unused nil-rate band may affect the amount of IHT to pay on the survivor's death. Similarly, if a farm is left to, say, a son and the personal representatives of the deceased person consider that agricultural property relief is due against the whole property, the extent to which the relief is due will be established, if it is necessary, on the death of the survivor.

If the gross value of the estate of the survivor is below the IHT nil-rate band that applies when he dies, no claim need be made for transfer of the unused nil-rate band of the deceased person.

The personal representatives of the deceased person's estate may be liable for penalties where a claim to transfer unused nil-rate band to the survivor is based on an incorrect amount because of errors made negligently by them when they delivered their account to HMRC. For more information on the charging of penalties, see **Example A7**.

Claims by persons other than personal representatives

If no claim for the transfer of the unused nil-rate band of a deceased person is made by the personal representatives of the survivor (or they withdraw their claim), then a claim may be made by another person liable to tax chargeable on the survivor's death within such period as HMRC may allow (s 8B(2)). This situation may arise where the survivor left all his property to charity but was the beneficiary of a qualifying IIP which gave rise to IHT on his death. In this case the claim would be made by the trustees of the trust. Such persons cannot usually make a claim until two years have passed from the end of the month in which the survivor died, although HMRC will allow a provisional claim where it is obvious that no claim will be made by the survivor's personal representatives. Claims made by persons other than the survivor's personal representatives must be made on form IHT216 (which may be downloaded from the HMRC website only at www.gov.uk/government/publications/inheritance-tax-claim-to-transfer-unused-inheritance-tax-nil-rate-band-iht216).

B. Consequences of the transfer of unused nil-rate band between spouses and civil partners

Effect on nil-rate band of survivor

Where a valid claim to transfer unused nil-rate band is made, the nil-rate band that is available when the surviving spouse or civil partner dies will be increased by a percentage which is worked out by reference to the nil-rate band unused on the death of the deceased person (s 8A(3), (4)).

In order to work out the percentage (which by HMRC practice is taken to four places of decimals – see IHTM43020) apply the formula:

$$\frac{E}{NRBMD} \times 100$$

E is the difference between M and VT (as defined above) (ie E = M – VT)

NRBMD is nil-rate band in force at the time of the deceased person's death (s 8A(7))

For example, if on the death of the deceased person his chargeable estate (VT) is £162,500 and the nil-rate band (M) is £325,000, the percentage derived from the application of the above formula would be 50% (ie [(325,000 – 162,500) ÷ 325,000]). If the statutory nil-rate band when the survivor dies is, say, £400,000, then that would be increased by 50% (ie £200,000) so that a nil-rate band of £600,000 would be used to calculate the amount of IHT arising on the survivor's death. It will be noticed that it is not simply a case of transferring the amount of the unused nil-rate band of the deceased person to the survivor and adding it to the nil-rate band in force at the time of the survivor's death.

However, the percentage increase in the survivor's nil-rate band is limited to 100% so that the nil-rate band available to the survivor's estate can never be more than twice the amount of the nil-rate band in force when the survivor dies (s 8A(5)).

A reason why the percentage increase may exceed 100% is because the rules can apply in relation to the survivor by reference to the death of more than one deceased person who had unused nil-rate band on death (s 8A(6)(b)). Where this is the case a separate claim form must be completed for each deceased person who died before the survivor. For example, Martin dies on 14 April 2013 with an estate of £250,000, leaving £130,000 to his son Thomas and the remainder to his spouse Pamela. The nil-rate band when Martin dies is £325,000 so 60% of his nil-rate band is unused. Pamela later marries Will who dies on 14 May 2015 and also leaves 60% of his nil-rate band unused. Pamela dies on 14 June 2029 with an estate of £750,000 when the nil-rate band is £350,000. Pamela's nil-rate band is increased to reflect the transfer from Martin and Will, but the amount of increase (ostensibly 60% + 60%) is limited to 100% of the nil-rate band in force at the time. So Pamela's nil-rate band is £700,000, leaving £50,000 chargeable to IHT on her death.

Another reason why the percentage increase may exceed 100% is because of a succession of nil-rate band transfers (ie where the unused nil-rate band of a person (A) is passed to his survivor (B) which increased nil-rate band is passed, when he dies in turn, to his survivor (C)). This scenario is illustrated below in **part C(ii)** of this Example. (This compares with the situation in the paragraph above where Pamela was the survivor of both Martin and Will from each of whom she claimed the respective unused nil-rate band.)

It will be noted that the unused nil-rate band that is transferred to a survivor cannot be used in respect of any lifetime tax arising in respect of chargeable lifetime transfers made by him; it may only be used in respect of the tax arising when he dies (be this the additional or supplementary charge arising on lifetime gifts made in the seven years before his death, or the estate charge arising on his deceased estate).

Effect on excepted estates

The increased nil-rate band available to the survivor may be taken into account when determining whether or not his estate is an excepted estate, provided his death occurs on or after 6 April 2010. See **Example A23** for more detail on this matter.

Effect on the amount of a gift under a will

The increased nil-rate band available to the survivor may affect the amount of a gift he makes under his will. This is illustrated in the case of *Woodland Trust v Loring* [2014] EWCA Civ 1314. The deceased executed a will in 2001 which provided for a legacy to her children and grandchildren of 'such amount as is at the date of my death the amount of my unused nil-rate band for inheritance tax'. The residue of her estate was left to the Woodland Trust, a charity. When the deceased died her estate was valued at approximately £680,000; her executors claimed under s 8A that her nil-rate band of £325,000 be increased to include her husband's unused nil-rate band with the result that the legacy to her children amounted to £650,000 which meant that the charity received only £30,000. The charity brought an action claiming that it was entitled to £355,000 on the basis that the proper interpretation of the deceased's will meant that, despite the claim made by her executors, the deceased's nil-rate band (and hence the amount of the family's legacy) should be limited to £325,000.

Although the Court of Appeal acknowledged that the charity's arguments based on the subjective wording of the will and the state of the testator's knowledge at the time she executed the will were strong, it held that the deceased had understood that the size of the legacy at the date of her death could be different to that at the date of her will and that the implicit purpose of the deceased's will was to give as much as possible to her family without incurring inheritance tax and to give the rest to charity. Consequently, giving effect to the purposes and values which were expressed or implicit in the wording of the will, the court dismissed the charity's appeal.

See **explanatory note 5** for further commentary on the matter of drafting a will appropriately to give effect to a testator's intention.

Effect on capital gains tax valuations

TCGA 1992 s 274 provides that where the value of an asset in a deceased estate has been ascertained for IHT purposes, that value also has effect for CGT purposes. The person who inherits the asset inherits it with a base cost equal to the amount ascertained for the purposes of IHT.

However, it will not always be necessary to ascertain for IHT purposes the value of an asset at the time of the death of the deceased. This means that when the asset is subsequently disposed of by the person who has inherited it, its market value at the time of its acquisition will need to be established in order to work out his gain.

If after the disposal of the asset, a claim is then made to transfer the unused nil-rate band of the deceased person, the IHT value of the asset might need to be established in order to work out the percentage of the nil-rate band that was not used by the deceased person in his death.

In this case, if the value of the asset differs from that previously agreed for CGT purposes, s 274 would ordinarily give grounds for requiring that the CGT base cost of the asset be adjusted and the gain on the disposal of the asset be recalculated on the basis of the value agreed for IHT purposes. However, that is prevented by FA 2008 Sch 4 para 8.

C. Examples

C(i) *Mary's nil-rate band on her death*

Transfers made by Rupert in his lifetime

			£	£
1998/99	Gift to discretionary trust			206,000
	Less: Annual exemptions	1998/99	3,000	
		1997/98	3,000	(6,000)
	Chargeable transfer			200,000
2004/05	Gift to Michael			106,000
	Less: Annual exemption	2004/05		(3,000)
		2003/04		(3,000)
	Potentially exempt transfer			100,000

Tax arising on lifetime transfers made seven years before Rupert's death in October 2006

	Gross £	Tax on 2006/07 scale £
Cumulative transfers in seven years before 2004/05		
1998/99 — discretionary trust	200,000	–
2004/05 — gift to Michael	100,000	6,000*
	300,000	6,000*

(* 300,000 – 285,000 = 15,000 @ 40%)

Tax arising on Rupert's estate

	Gross £	*Tax on 2006/07 scale* £
Cumulative transfers in seven years before death		
2004/05 – Gift to Michael	100,000	–
Free Estate chargeable on death	150,000	
Settled Estate chargeable on death	100,000	
Less: Exempt – legacy to wife	(100,000)	
	250,000	Nil*

*Value of chargeable estate is less than the nil-rate band of £285,000

When Mary dies in 2029 her personal representatives make a claim so that Rupert's unused nil-rate band is transferred to her. In order to work out the amount of the nil-rate band on her death, the following calculations are carried out:

In relation to Rupert's death:

M = £285,000 - £100,000 = £185,000 (ie nil-rate band net of Rupert's gift to his son in October 2004)

VT = £250,000 - £100,000 = £150,000 (ie Rupert's estate net of legacy to wife)

As M > VT, there is unused nil-rate band of £35,000 (185,000 – 150,000) on Rupert's death.

E = M – VT = £35,000

NRBMD = £285,000

The percentage of the nil-rate band available to transfer to Mary is:

$$\frac{\text{E}}{\text{NRBMD}} \times 100 = \frac{35,000}{285,000} \times 100 = 12.281\%$$

When Mary dies in 2029 the statutory nil-rate band in force is £350,000.

This will be increased by the above percentage to £350,000 + (350,000 × 12.281%) = £392,983.

So when Mary dies the nil-rate band that she is entitled to is £392,983.

See **explanatory note 3** for further commentary on this Example.

C(ii)(a) *John's nil-rate band on his death*

Tax arising when Sidney dies in December 1973

	Gross £	*Estate Duty* £
Free Estate chargeable on death	10,000	
Less: Exempt – legacy to wife	(10,000)	
	Nil	Nil*

*Value of estate is less than the nil-rate band of £15,000

When Jane dies in June 2012 her personal representatives make a claim so that Sidney's unused nil-rate band is transferred to her. (Although the facts of the question state that a claim is made by them, this is actually not necessary as Jane's estate is exempt from IHT in any event and, in practice, therefore they are unlikely to incur the expense of making such a claim.) Yet given the fact in the question that a claim is made, in order to work out the amount of the nil-rate band on Jane's death, the following calculations are carried out:

In relation to Sidney's death:

M = £15,000

VT = £Nil

As M > VT, there is unused nil-rate band of £15,000 (15,000 – Nil) on Sidney's death.

E = M – VT = £15,000

NRBMD = £15,000

The percentage of the nil-rate band available to transfer to Jane is:

$$\frac{E}{NRBMD} \times 100 = \frac{15,000}{15,000} \times 100 = 100\%$$

When Jane dies in June 2012 the statutory nil-rate band in force is £325,000.
This will be increased by the above percentage to £325,000 + (325,000 × 100%) = £650,000.
So when Jane dies the nil-rate band that she is entitled to is £650,000.

Tax arising when Jane dies in June 2012

	Gross	Tax on 2012/13 scale
	£	£
Free Estate chargeable on death	90,000	
Less: Exempt – legacy to charity	(90,000)	
	Nil	Nil*

*Value of estate is less than the nil-rate band of £325,000

When John dies in 2029 his personal representatives make a claim so that Jane's unused nil-rate band is transferred to him. In order to work out the amount of the nil-rate band on his death, the following calculations are carried out:

In relation to Jane's death:

M = £650,000

VT = £Nil

As M > VT, there is unused nil-rate band of £650,000 (650,000 – Nil) on Jane's death.

E = M – VT = £650,000

NRBMD = £325,000

The percentage of the nil-rate band available to transfer to Jane is prima facie:

$$\frac{E}{NRBMD} \times 100 = \frac{650,000}{325,000} \times 100 = 200\%$$

When John dies in 2029 the statutory nil-rate band in force is £350,000.
This will be increased by the above percentage to £350,000 + (350,000 × 200%) = £1,050,000. However, this will be capped at £700,000 (twice the nil-rate band of £350,000 in force when he dies).
So when John dies the nil-rate band that he is entitled to is £700,000.
See **explanatory note 4** for further commentary on this Example.

C(ii)(b) *Jane's nil-rate band on her death*

By contrast, if John had died in 2012 leaving chargeable estate of £225,000 and Jane had died in 2029, her personal representatives make a claim so that Sidney's and John's unused nil-rate bands are transferred to her. In order to work out the amount of the nil-rate band on John's death, the following calculations are carried out:

In relation to John's death:
M = £325,000
VT = £225,000

As M > VT, there is unused nil-rate band of £100,000 (325,000 – 225,000) on John's death.
E = M – VT = £100,000
NRBMD = £325,000
The percentage of the nil-rate band available to transfer to Jane is:

$$\frac{E}{NRBMD} \times 100 = \frac{100,000}{325,000} \times 100 = 30.7692\%$$

When Jane dies in 2029 the nil-rate band in force is £350,000.
This will be increased by the above percentage to £350,000 + (350,000 × 30.7692) = £107,692.
As Jane's executors have made two claims, the total amount of nil-rate band to which Jane is prima facie entitled on her death is £350,000 + (350,000 × 100%) + (350,000 × 30.7692) = £350,000 + £350,000 + £107,692 = £807,692 which is capped at £700,000 (twice the nil-rate band of £350,000 in force when she dies).
So when Jane dies the nil-rate band that she is entitled to is £700,000.
See **explanatory note 4** for further commentary on this Example.

C(iii) *Helga's nil-rate band on her death*

Tax arising when Priscilla dies in 2007

	Gross	*Tax on 2007/08 scale*
	£	£
Free Estate chargeable on death	200,000	
Less: Exempt – legacy to non-domiciled civil partner	(55,000)	
	145,000	Nil*

*Value of estate is less than the statutory nil-rate band of £300,000

When Helga dies in December 2023 her personal representatives make a claim so that Priscilla's unused nil-rate band is transferred to her. In order to work out the amount of the nil-rate band on her death, the following calculations are carried out:

In relation to Priscilla's death:
M = £300,000
VT = £145,000

As M > VT, there is unused nil-rate band of £155,000 (300,000 – 145,000) on Priscilla's death.
E = M – VT = £155,000
NRBMD = £300,000
The percentage of the nil-rate band available to transfer to Helga is:

$$\frac{E}{NRBMD} \times 100 = \frac{155,000}{300,000} \times 100 = 51.6667\%$$

When Helga dies in December 2023 the nil-rate band in force is £325,000 (unaffected by her domicile status).
This will be increased by the above percentage to £325,000 + (325,000 × 51.6667%) = £492,916.

So when Helga dies the nil-rate band that she is entitled to is £492,916.

In HMRC's opinion, the amount received by the trust on Helga's death is, under the terms of her will, £325,000. They argue that her will is drafted in such a way that it does not provide for an amount equal to the enhanced nil-rate band to be transferred to the trust. The authors do not agree with HMRC's interpretation of the clause and are of the opinion that the amount received by the trust on Helga's death is, under the terms of her will, £492,916.

See **explanatory note 5** for further commentary on this Example. Also see the discussion of *The Woodland Trust v Loring* [2014] EWCA Civ 1314 in **part B** above.

D. Deferred charges to inheritance tax

Two special rules apply in relation to the transfer of unused nil-rate band where the conditions for such a transfer are met (see **part A** of this Example) and after the death of the deceased person an amount becomes liable to inheritance tax ('the deferred charge') on the occurrence of a chargeable event under the conditionally exempt transfer rules (see **Example B9**) or under the rules applying to woodlands relief (see **Examples B11** and **B12**) (s 8C(1)). In these cases, generally speaking, the deferred charge is computed by treating the amount arising on a chargeable event as if it were the top slice of the value of the deceased person's estate. Tax is then calculated by reference to the nil-rate band in force at the time of the chargeable event (if tax rates have decreased since the time of the deceased person's death).

Deferred charge arises before death of the survivor

The first special rule applies where the deferred charge to tax arises before the death of the survivor. In this case, the amount of the nil-rate band which is capable of being transferred to the survivor will be less on account of the deferred charge being calculated by reference to the estate of the deceased person. So, by virtue of s 8C(2), the percentage used to increase the nil-rate band that is in force on the survivor's death is ascertained according to the following formula, rather than the formula set out in **part B** of this Example above. The formula is:

$$\left(\frac{E}{NRBMD} - \frac{TA}{NRBME}\right) \times 100$$

where:

E is the difference between M and VT (as defined above) (ie E = M – VT)

NRBMD is the statutory nil-rate band in force at the time of the deceased person's death (s 8A(7))

TA is the amount on which tax is charged on the chargeable event

NRBME is the statutory nil-rate band in force at the time of the chargeable event

The effect of this formula is to reduce proportionately the percentage that would have been calculated in the absence of a chargeable event, to reflect the chargeable event that occurs. As already intimated, this is necessary because the tax on the amount that falls into charge on a chargeable event is calculated by reference to the inheritance tax position of the deceased person and so more of his nil-rate band is necessarily used up in this process. In short, there is less nil-rate band to transfer to the survivor.

Where more than one chargeable event occurs before the death of the survivor, the above calculation is carried out for each event, the fraction (TA ÷ NRBME) in the formula is increased to the aggregate of (TA ÷ NRBME) for each of the events (s 8C(3)). These rules are illustrated in **part D(i)** below.

Deferred charge arises after death of the survivor

The second special rule applies where the deferred charge to tax arises after the death of the survivor. In this case, the survivor's estate will already possibly have benefited from a transfer of the deceased person's nil-rate band. The rule is set out in s 8C(4)(5) and its effect is not to disturb the IHT position of the survivor (to whom the deceased person's unused nil-rate band has already been transferred) but to reduce the nil-rate band available at the time of the chargeable event to the extent that the nil-rate band transferred to the survivor has been used by him so that his estate is charged to tax at the rate of 0%. It is as if the survivor claimed only so much of the deceased person's nil-rate band as to ensure his estate was taxed at 0%. These rules are illustrated in **part D(ii)** below. In other words, s 8C(4), (5) provide for an appropriate reduction in the amount of the deceased person's nil-rate band (as determined on the scale of rates in force at the time of the chargeable event) that is used for calculating the deferred charge. The amount of the reduction reflects the amount of that up-rated nil-rate band that was needed to keep the survivor's estate free of tax (or the whole of it if the survivor's estate was liable to tax at a positive rate even after the transfer of the deceased person's nil-rate band). The amount of nil-rate band that remains to be used in calculating the deferred charge is ascertained as follows:

- Step 1: take the amount of the nil-rate band to which the survivor was entitled on his death and divide it into two elements: the amount of the statutory nil-rate band in force at the time of his death (the first element) and the amount by which the statutory nil-rate band was increased as a result of the transfer of the deceased person's (or several deceased persons') unused nil-rate band to the survivor (the second element).

- Step 2: take the amount of the survivor's chargeable estate and from it subtract the first element found at Step 1.

- Step 3: Follow either (a) or (b) below:

  (a) If the result of Step 2 is less than the second element found at Step 1 (ie if the survivor's chargeable estate did not fully utilise the nil-rate band available after effecting a transfer of the deceased person's unused nil-rate band), then proceed to Step 4A and then to Step 5A.

  (b) If the result of Step 2 is greater than the second element found at Step 1, then take the second element as the result of Step 3 and proceed to Step 4B and then to Step 5B.

- Step 4A: reduce the nil-rate band in force at the date of the death of the deceased person or the happening of the chargeable event (as the case may be) by the amount found under Step 2.

- Step 5A: the nil-rate band available for working out the tax to be charged on the chargeable event is the amount found under Step 4A.

- Step 4B: reduce the nil-rate band in force at the date of the death of the deceased person or the happening of the chargeable event (as the case may be) by the amount found at Step 3(b).

- Step 5B: the nil-rate band available for working out the tax to be charged on the chargeable event is the amount found under Step 4B.

Answer to example

D(i) Julia dies after sale of timber

When Hector died in August 2002 (when the statutory nil-rate band was £250,000), the growing timber of £125,000 was left out of account in valuing his estate and calculating the inheritance tax payable on his death. So his estate was valued at £425,000 of which £50,000 was chargeable, the rest being exempt under the spouse exemption.

So in relation to Hector's death:

M = £250,000

VT = £50,000

As M > VT, there is unused nil-rate band of £200,000 (250,000 – 50,000) on Hector's death.

E = M – VT = £200,000

NRBMD = £250,000

Before taking account of the sale of timber, the percentage of the nil-rate band prospectively available to transfer to Julia would have been:

$$\frac{E}{NRBMD} \times 100 = \frac{200,000}{250,000} \times 100 = 80\%$$

In March 2006 when the felled timber was sold for £175,000 (after deductible expenses), the statutory nil-rate band then in force was £275,000. The sale proceeds are added to Hector's chargeable estate to calculate the IHT arising. His chargeable estate is increased to £225,000. Even though no tax arises in respect of the chargeable event (£225,000 being less than the nil-rate band of £275,000 in force in 2005/06 when the disposal of the woodlands occurs), Hector's unused nil-rate band must be reduced and an adjustment is therefore needed to the 80% figure provisionally calculated previously.

The adjustment is calculated according to the formula in s 8C(2):

$$(\frac{E}{NRBMD} - \frac{TA}{NRBME}) \times 100 = (\frac{200,000}{250,000} - \frac{175,000}{275,000}) \times 100 = 16\%$$

When Julia dies in December 2023, the statutory nil-rate band in force is £325,000.

This will be increased by the above, adjusted, percentage to £325,000 + (325,000 × 16%) = £377,000.

So when Julia dies the nil-rate band that she is entitled to is £377,000.

See **explanatory note 6** for further commentary on this Example.

D(ii) Julia dies before sale of timber

If Julia dies in December 2023 leaving chargeable estate of £450,000 and the timber is sold for £350,000 (after deductible expenses) in 2029, then the calculation proceeds as follows:

- Step 1: The nil-rate band in force at the time of Julia's death is £325,000 (the first element). The amount by which the nil-rate band in force on Julia's death is increased is (£325,000 × 80%) = £260,000 (the second element).
- Step 2: Julia's chargeable estate minus the first element from Step 1 is £450,000 – £325,000 = £125,000.
- Step 3: The result of Step 2 (£125,000) is less than the second element found at Step 1 (£260,000). So following option (a) at Step 3 proceed to steps 4A and 5A.
- Step 4A: The nil-rate band in force on the sale of the woodlands (£350,000) is reduced by the result from Step 2 (£125,000), ie £350,000 – £125,000 = £225,000.
- Step 5A: The nil-rate band to be used in working out the tax on the chargeable event is £225,000.

On the chargeable event the net sale price of the timber of £350,000 is added to Hector's chargeable estate of £50,000 and from this is deducted the result of Step 5A so that the tax due on the sale of the timber is (£400,000 – £225,000) × 40% = £70,000 (and as no tax was payable originally on Hector's estate, this amount is not further reduced).

On the chargeable event the net sale price of the timber of £350,000 is added to Hector's chargeable estate of £50,000 and from this is deducted the result of Step 5A so that the tax due on the sale of the timber is (£400,000 – £225,000) × 40% = £70,000 (and as no tax was payable originally on Hector's estate, this amount is not further reduced).

See **explanatory note 7** for further commentary on this Example and see **Example B11** for further commentary on woodlands relief.

E. Transfer of unused residence nil-rate band between spouses and civil partners

It was explained in **Example A2 part (b)** that a claim may be made to transfer an individual's residence nil-rate band (RNRB) or, as the case may be, his unused RNRB to his surviving spouse or civil partner (known as 'P' in the terms of the legislation and in the rest of this Example). The amount of the RNRB so transferred is called P's 'brought-forward allowance' and is available for use on P's own death.

(i) *Conditions for the transfer*

Although, strictly speaking, there is no single provision of the Act that sets out the conditions that have to be met for P to have a brought-forward allowance, a number of conditions can be carved out of the statutory provisions as they stand. It may therefore be said that P may be entitled to a brought-forward allowance where:

(a) P dies on or after 6 April 2017,

(b) P was the spouse or civil partner of another person (the 'related person') who died before P and who was P's spouse or civil partners at that time (ss 8G(1),(2)), and

(c) a claim is made for the brought-forward allowance under s 8L (s 8G(3)).

The other person (ie the related person)

The other person who died before P is known as a 'related person' in the terms of the legislation (and will be referred to as D in the rest of this Example). It does not matter when D (the related person) died – it may be before 6 April 2017, the date on which the legislation in respect of the RNRB otherwise becomes effective. It may be that P has survived two or more marriages or civil partnerships so that there may be two or more persons who are related persons in relation to P (to be called D1, D2 etc as the case may be). In relation to each of D, D1, D2 etc, the amount of his RNRB or unused RNRB at the time of his death is said to be available for carry-forward. In such a case P may have two or more brought-forward allowances. It does not matter when D, D1, D2 etc died. He may already have been dead on 6 April 2017 or may die after that day. As is the case for the transfer of the (general) nil-rate band, it does not matter how D, D1, D2 etc died whether by accident, from natural causes or otherwise (see **part A**).

Status of the related person before his death

Immediately before his death, D, D1, D2 etc must have been married to or in a civil partnership with P. The same rules apply here as apply for the transfer of the (general) nil-rate band (see **part A**).

Claim

In order for P to benefit from the transfer of the unused RNRB of D, D1, and D2 etc, a claim has to be made on the death of P by either his personal representatives or (if no claim is made by them) by any other person liable for the tax chargeable on P's death (s 8L(1)). Although there is no prescribed form, a claim for brought-forward allowance may be made using schedule IHT436 to form IHT400. The information and documents that should be kept on the death of the deceased person, in order more easily to facilitate a future claim made by the survivor's personal representatives for the transfer of the deceased person's unused residence nil-rate band to the survivor, include an audit trail (probably based on changes in the land register) from the first death to show the transfer of title into the sole name of the survivor, the date and place of the parties' marriage/their entering into the civil partnership and the relevant certificates and any IHT reference numbers.

Claim by personal representatives of P

The claim for brought-forward allowance for P may be made under s 8L(1)(a) by P's personal representatives after he dies (and not when D, D1, D2 etc dies). A claim must be made by the personal representatives within the period of two years from the end of the month in which P dies or (if it ends later) the period of 3 months beginning with the date on which the personal representatives act as such, or such longer period as HMRC may allow (s 8L(2)). For example, if P dies on 16 October 2024 and his personal representatives start to act on 13 November 2024, a claim must be made by them by the later of 31 October 2026 and 12 February 2025. A claim made within the permitted period may be withdrawn no later than one month after the end of the period concerned (s 8L(3)). In the above example, a claim may be withdrawn on or before 30 November 2026. The same rules here apply in relation to late claims as they do in relation to late claims to transfer the (general) nil-rate band (see **part A**).

Claims by persons other than personal representatives of P

If no claim for brought-forward allowance for P is made by the his personal representatives (or they withdraw a claim), then a claim may be made by another person liable to tax chargeable on P's death within such period as HMRC may allow (s 8L(1)(b)). A claim so made may be withdrawn no later than one month after the end of the period concerned (s 8L(3)). This situation may arise in the same circumstances as it arose in respect of claims made for the transfer of the general nil-rate band (see **part A**).

Claims following a series of deaths

In the case of a series of deaths and a claim was not made on the death of P for brought-forward allowance and the failure to make the claim has affected the IHT liability on the later death of another person (called A in the legislation), a claim for the brought-forward allowance of P may be made by the personal representatives of A provided that the claim makes no difference to the amount of IHT payable on the death of P or any other person apart from A (s 8L(4),(5)(a)). The time within which A's personal representatives may make the claim is two years from the end of the month in which A dies or (if it ends later) the period of 3 months beginning with the date on which A's personal representatives act as such, or such longer period as HMRC may allow (s 8L(6)). If no claim for the brought-forward allowance of P is made by A's personal representatives (or they withdraw a claim), then a claim may be made by another person liable to tax chargeable on A's death within such period as HMRC may allow (s 8L(5)(b), (6). A claim made within either of the permitted periods may be withdrawn no later than one month after the end of the period concerned (s 8L(7)).

(ii) *The amount that may be transferred*

P's brought forward allowance is Nil if no claim is made for it under s 8L (s 8G(3)(rider)). However, if such a claim is made, P's brought-forward allowance(s) is calculated by taking the following three steps:

(1) Identify the amounts available for carry-forward from the death of D, D1, D2 etc (s 8G(3)(a)). This will entail applying the rules set out and illustrated in **Example A2 part (b)** examples (1) and (3) for D, D1 D2 etc. An amount of brought-forward allowance is also available where D, D1, D2 etc dies not owning a home or, where he does own a home, the home is not closely inherited (s 8F). Those rules can be applied only where D, D1, D2 etc dies on or after 6 April 2017. The amounts available for carry-forward will include any downsizing addition (DA) to which D, D1, D2 etc was entitled (as DA will have been added to his RNRB and taken into account in working out how much it was unused).

Where D, D1, D2 etc died before 6 April 2017 his amount available for carry-forward is taken as £100,000 (s 8G(4)(a)). However, in this case, where the value of D's, D1's, D2's etc estate immediately before his death (RPE) was greater than £2,000,000, the amount available for carry forward is reduced (but not below nil) by an abatement amount equal to (RPE – £2,000,000)/2.

In short therefore, the circumstances in which there is unused RNRB is where D, D1, D2 etc did not have a qualifying residence, if he did have such a residence it was not left to a direct descendant, the value of the residence was less than the value of the RNRB, or he died before 6 April 2017.

(2) Express each amount available for carry forward as a percentage of the residential enhancement at the respective dates of D's death, D1's death, D2's death etc (s 8G(3)(b)). A residential enhancement exists only in relation to a death occuring on or after 6 April 2017. Where D, D1, D2 etc died before 6 April 2017 the residential enhancement at the date of his death is taken as £100,000 and 100% of it will be available for carry-forward (s 8G(4)(b)).

(3) Add together the percentages calculated under Step 2 (s 8G(3)(c)).

The amount of P's brought-forward allowance is determined under s 8G(4) as one of the following amounts:

(a) Where the amount calculated at Step 3 is equal to or less than 100% (X%), P's brought forward allowance is X% of the residential enhancement applicable at P's death.

(b) Where the amount calculated at Step 3 exceeds 100%, P's brought-forward allowance is the amount of the residential enhancement applicable at P's death.

Consequently, P cannot get more than one RNRB as his brought-forward allowance. This mirrors the rule for the transferrable (general) nil-rate band.

Illustration

Amy died on 3 May 2019 owning an estate valued at £1,000,000 which included her home valued at £90,000. She is survived by her husband Mark. Her home is inherited by the daughter from her first marriage. Mark has agreed to move into another property. The amount of Amy's RNRB is £90,000 that is the value of her home as her estate is less than £2,000,000 and the value of her home is less than £150,000 (her default allowance for 2019/20). The balance of her default allowance is passed to Mark. The amount carried-forward is calculated by reference to the unused amount of her default allowance of 60,000 (£150,000 - £90,000).

Mark dies on 31 August 2025. Amy's carry-forward amount expressed as a percentage of the residential enhancement applicable at her death is £60,000/£150,000 × 100% = 40%. The amount of Mark's brought-forward amount is 40% × £175,000 = £70,000 (£175,000 being the residential enhancement at the date of Mark's death in 2025/26).

Illustration

Ethel died on 3 May 2019 owning an estate valued at £1,000,000 which includes her home valued at £90,000. She is survived by her husband Neal. Her home is inherited by her niece. Neal has agreed to move into another property. The amount of Ethel's RNRB is nil as her home is not closely inherited (s 8F(1)(2)). Ethel's default allowance is the residential enhance at the date of her death (ie £150,000). This is the amount by reference to which Neal's brought-forward amount will be calculated (s 8F(3)).

Neal dies on 31 August 2025. Ethel's carry-forward amount expressed as a percentage of the residential enhancement applicable at her death is £150,000/£150,000 × 100% = 100%. The amount of Neal's brought-forward amount is 100% × £175,000 = £175,000 (£175,000 being the residential enhancement at the date of Neal's death in 2025/26).

Illustration

Timothy died in 2015 and left his estate, value at £950,000 to his wife Erica who died in July 2025 leaving her estate (which is valued at less than £2 million and includes her home worth £400,000) in turn to her daughter. As Timothy's death is before 6 April 2017 and his estate is less than £2,000,000, the amount available for carry forward to Erica's estate is calculated by reference to £100,000 and 100% of that amount is so available. If Erica's personal representatives make a claim for brought-forward allowance from Timothy, the maximum RNRB in 2025/26 available to her estate (her default allowance) is £350,000 (£175,000 + (100% × £175,000)).

Illustration

Peter's wife, Lynne, died in September 2019. She owned an estate worth £2,100,000 including a share of a flat valued at £30,000. Lynne had previously occupied the flat as her home and she left her share in it to her daughter. Lynne left £100,000 to her sister and the rest of her estate to Peter. The maximum RNRB available in 2019/20 in respect of Lynne's estate is £150,000 - (£2,100,000 - £2,000,000)/2 = £100,000 of which £30,000 was used in respect of the bequest of the interest in her flat to her daughter. The unused amount of her RNRB is £70,000 which represents 46.6667% of the (statutory) residential enhancement of 2019/20 (ie £70,000/£150,000). Peter dies in June 2024 owning an estate of less than £2,000,000 including a home which is left to his daughter. If his personal representatives make a claim for brought-forward allowance from Lynne, the maximum RNRB in 2024/25 available to his estate (his default allowance) is £256,667 (£175,000 + (46.6667% × £175,000)).

Illustration

Joyce had been pre-deceased by two husbands (James and Alfred) when she died in 2026. James had died in 2015 and Alfred died in May 2024. Under his will, Alfred left his flat valued at £50,000 to his daughter. Both husbands died owning property valued at less than £2,000,000.

On James's death before April 2017 the percentage of residential enhancement unused is 100%. On Alfred's death the maximum RNRB to which his estate was entitled was £175,000, £50,000 of which was used. This means that 71% of the residential enhancement is unused (ie £125,000/£175,000). The total of these two percentages is 171% (and so is limited to 100%).

If Joyce's personal representatives make the requisite claim and she dies owning an estate of £2,100,000, the maximum RNRB when she dies (her adjusted allowance) is £300,000 (that is [£175,000 + (£175,000 x 100%)] - [(£2,100,000 - £2,000,000)/2]).

(iii) *The consequences of the transfer*

P's brought-forward allowance is added to the residential enhancement that applies at the time of his own death. The total amount of these two component elements determines P's default allowance at the date of his death (s 8D(5)(f)). It is by reference to this amount that P's RNRB is calculated in accordance with the rules set out in **Example A2 part (b)**. So in the above examples, Mark's and Neal's default allowances are £245,000 and £350,000 respectively.

Explanatory Notes

(1) In order for a marriage to be valid and recognised by the law of a territory comprised in the United Kingdom, the parties must have the capacity to marry (as determined by the law of their ante-nuptial domicile) and the marriage itself must be celebrated in accordance with the form required by the law of the country where the marriage was celebrated. So, for example, if a marriage is celebrated in England and Wales between two persons who are domiciled there, they must be over 16 years of age, be free to marry and the ceremony (whether civil or religious) must conform to the requirements of the law in England and Wales (*Holland (Executor of Holland deceased) v IRC* (2003)). A couple whose marriage is recognised by Scots Law as being a marriage by cohabitation and repute are validly married for the purposes of the rules on the transfer of unused nil-rate band. This form of marriage was abolished with prospective effect by the Family Law (Scotland) Act 2006 s 3 with effect from 4 May 2006. This means that such marriages constituted before that date continue to be valid marriages. For the avoidance of doubt, there is no such thing as a 'common law' marriage under the law of England and Wales. A couple in the UK who enter into an Islamic religious marriage (the *nikah* ceremony) will also have to go through a UK civil ceremony in order for their marriage to be recognised. Where a person validly contracts a polygamous marriage abroad, then this too will be recognised as a valid marriage.

The Marriage (Same Sex Couples) Act 2013 ('the 2013 Act') took effect from 13 March 2014. The Act, which applies only in England and Wales, enables same sex couples to marry and provides that such marriages are the same as marriages between a man and a woman. Section 11(1) of the 2013 Act provides that in the law of England and Wales, marriage has the same effect in relation to same sex couples as it has in relation to opposite sex couples. Section 11(2) of the 2013 Act provides that the law of England and Wales (including all England and Wales legislation whenever passed or made) has effect in accordance with subsection (1). Paragraphs 1 to 3 of Schedule 3 to the 2013 Act provide that, in existing English and Welsh legislation, a reference to a marriage is to be read as including a reference to the marriage of a same sex couple, a reference to a married couple is to be read as including a reference to a married same sex couple, and a reference to a person who is married is to be read as including a reference to a person who is married to a person of the same sex. Paragraph 1(2) of Schedule 3 provides that related references such as a reference to a person whose marriage has ended are to be read in the same way. In addition, Schedule 3 to the 2013 Act provides that references to persons who are not married but living together as if they are married are to be read as including references to a same sex couple who are not married but living together as a married couple; and that a reference to a person who is living with another person as if they were married is to be read as including a reference to a person who is living with another person of the same sex as if they were married.

The 2013 Act does not remove the availability of civil partnerships for same sex couples (but there is provision for those in a civil partnership to convert that relationship to a marriage if they choose to do so). Overseas marriages of opposite sex couples which are valid as to capacity and form according to the relevant law are recognised under the law of England and Wales. New and existing overseas marriages of same sex couples which are valid as to capacity and form according to the relevant law will be recognised under the law of England and Wales from 13 March 2014 (The Marriage (Same Sex Couples) Act 2013 (Commencement No 2 and Transitional Provision) Order 2014 (SI 2014/93) art 4).

The Marriage and Civil Partnership (Scotland) Act 2014 provides for the marriage of same sex couples in Scotland. Such marriages are recognised under Scots Law from 16 December 2014 (The Marriage and Civil Partnership (Scotland) Act 2014 and Civil Partnership Act 2004 (Consequential Provisions and Modifications) Order 2014 (SI 2014/3229) art 1). English same sex marriages were, before that date, treated as civil partnerships in Scotland (Marriage (Same Sex Couples) Act 2013 (Consequential and Contrary Provisions and Scotland) Order 2014 (SI 2014/560) art 5).

The Northern Ireland (Executive Formation etc) Act 2019 provides for the marriage of same sex couples in Northern Ireland. Such marriages are recognised under Northern Ireland Law from 13 January 2020 (Marriage (Same-sex Couples) and Civil Partnership (Opposite-sex Couples) (Northern Ireland) Regulations 2019 (SI 2019/1514)). English, Welsh and Scottish same sex marriages were, before that date, treated as civil partnerships in Northern Ireland (Marriage (Same Sex) Couples Act 2013 Sch 2 para 2, Marriage and Civil Partnership (Scotland) Act 2014 and Civil Partnership Act 2004 (Consequential Provisions and Modifications) Order 2014 (SI 2004/3229), Art 6).

(2) The information and documents that should be kept on the death of the deceased person, in order more easily to facilitate a future claim made by the survivor's personal representatives for the transfer of the deceased person's unused nil-rate band to the survivor, include:

(i) a copy of the HMRC return (form IHT205 or IHT400; in Scotland, forms C1 and C5);

(ii) a copy of his death certificate, marriage or civil partnership certificate, his will (if any) and details of inter vivos gifts (including gifts with reservation of benefit);

(iii) a copy of any documents, such as a Deed of Variation, executed after his death, that change who benefits from their estate;

(iv) any valuation(s) of assets that pass under his will or intestacy other than to the survivor;

(v) any evidence to support the availability of relief (such as agricultural or business property relief) where the agricultural or business property pass to someone other than to the survivor.

But there can be other assets that are chargeable when someone dies such as:

(i) assets owned by the deceased person jointly with another person;

(ii) assets held in trust from which the deceased person was entitled to benefit and which are treated as forming part of his estate on death;

(iii) any lifetime gifts made by the deceased person in the seven years before his death;

(iv) any gifts made by the deceased person where he did not give up possession and use of the assets, or where he retained a right to use the asset through an arrangement (a gift with reservation of benefit); and

(v) before 6 April 2011, where the deceased person was over 75, any alternatively secured pension fund from which he received a pension.

If any of these apply to the estate of the deceased person, the personal representatives of the deceased person should pass on whatever information they hold about these assets as well, for example:

(i) details of the assets concerned and evidence of their values;

(ii) details about any exemptions and/or relief taken into account in arriving at the chargeable values.

(3) Although in this case assets were left to the spouse of the deceased person, it is not necessary that this happen in order for unused nil-rate band to arise on the death of the deceased person. He could have unused nil-rate band for any reason (eg he left an exempt legacy to a charity).

Unused nil-rate band might also be available on the death of the deceased person even though tax was also due at that time. This can happen where tax is paid on a failed PET by reason of an earlier chargeable transfer which cumulates with the PET but which may not cumulate with the deceased person's estate. So, where the deceased person dies with a cumulative total of lifetime transfers, the nil-rate band is used against those transfers first. This reduces the amount of nil-rate band that is available against the death estate and, in turn, that reduces the amount that may be available for transfer.

It is only where a positive amount of IHT is payable on some part of the deceased person's estate (in the meaning of that expression for IHT purposes) that no unused nil-rate band will be available for transfer to the survivor.

Also see IHTM43041 for an explanation of the effect of legitim under Scots Law on calculating the amount of unused nil-rate band that may be transferred to a survivor.

(4) **Part C(ii)(a)** of the Example illustrates the position where the survivor (John) has been married to (or in a civil partnership with) a person (Jane) who was herself the survivor of an earlier marriage (or civil partnership). If Jane was entitled to unused nil-rate band from that earlier marriage (or civil partnership), the amount of any nil-rate band available for transfer on the death of Jane to John is calculated by reference to the nil-rate band in force on Jane's death as increased by the proportion of the nil-rate band unused from Jane's earlier marriage (or civil partnership). This means that on Jane's death, it must have been possible for her personal representatives to have made a claim had that been necessary which in turn means that Jane's death must have occurred on or after 9 October 2007.

If a claim to transfer unused nil-rate band on Jane's death was possible (ie she died on or after 9 October 2007) but not appropriate (eg because her estate qualified as an excepted estate) (and indeed in this Example it was not appropriate for a claim to have been made albeit not for the reason just stated), then that may reduce the amount of unused nil-rate band available for transfer when John dies. Section 8B(2) avoids the problems that would otherwise exist if Jane's personal representatives, to save unnecessary expense, chose not to make a claim on her death by allowing the personal representatives of John to include in their own claim a claim in respect of Jane's death, provided it will not affect the tax payable on Jane's death.

Part C(ii)(a) of the Example also shows that the rules on unused nil-rate band can apply where the deceased person died before the introduction of inheritance tax. It does not matter that they died when Capital Transfer Tax or Estate Duty was in force. FA 2008 Sch 4 paras 10 and 11 contain technical provisions to enable the rules in ss 8–8C to apply where the first death occurred under these respective regimes (also see IHTM43060). Although there was no spouse exemption for Estate Duty before 1969, those provisions can result in an amount that is treated as unused nil-rate band if the amount chargeable to Estate Duty on the deceased person's death was below the level at which a positive rate of Estate Duty became chargeable.

Part C(ii)(b) of the Example illustrates the position where the survivor (Jane) has been married (or in a civil partnership) more than once and has survived both or all of her former spouses or civil partners. The amount of unused nil-rate band at each previous death can be carried forward to the survivor's death, subject to the overall cap at 100% of the nil-rate band current at the survivor's death.

(5) This Example illustrates the care that must be exercised when drafting the will of a survivor if his intention is to make a bequest that is equal to his nil-rate band as increased by the proportion of the nil-rate band unused by his deceased spouse or civil partner (called the enhanced nil-rate band of the survivor). The drafting of nil-rate band legacies should now *always* make clear which solution is intended (with clear instructions on the matter being taken).

Although it is always for the courts to construe the effect of a will (and not HMRC), in IHTM43065 HMRC give the following examples of clauses that result in a legacy equal in amount to the enhanced nil-rate band of the survivor and those that do not:

- 'I give free of tax to my trustees such sum as at my death equals the maximum amount which could be given to them by this will without inheritance tax becoming payable in respect of my estate' will enable an amount equal to the enhanced nil-rate band to be transferred to the trustees.

- 'I give free of tax to my trustees an amount equal to the upper limit of the nil per cent rate band in the table of rates in Schedule 1' will also result in an amount equal only to the amount of the nil-rate band in force at the time the survivor dies being transferred to the trustees.

- 'To my trustees an amount equal to the nil rate band in force at my death' will again result in an amount equal only to the amount of the nil-rate band in force at the time the survivor dies being transferred to the trustees.
- 'To my trustees such sum as I could leave immediately before my death without IHT becoming payable' will not enable an amount equal to the enhanced nil-rate band to be transferred the trustees. The amount that will be transferred to them will be equal only to the amount of the nil-rate band in force at the time the survivor dies because any nil-rate band that may transferred is not available immediately before his death.

The author agrees with the stated conclusion in the first three bullet points, but not the fourth. One has to construe the will as a whole, and two factors lead to the view that this clause will enable an amount equal to the enhanced nil-rate band to be transferred to the trustees. First, that in referring to 'immediately before my death' the draftsman of the will may well have had in mind the fact that the IHT transfer of value on death is deemed to take place immediately before his death, so he is talking about one and the same thing as 'the charge to tax on the death of the survivor' in s 8A(3). Secondly that he uses the word 'leave', not 'give', and 'leaving' something to someone clearly connotes doing so on death not by lifetime gift. It is suggested that this example is an object lesson in not relying on the HMRC manuals/guidance especially on matters that are not directly of tax law.

The interpretation of a clause in a will similar to that in bullet point four was the subject of the case of *The Woodland Trust v Loring* [2014] EWCA Civ 1314 discussed in **part B** of this Example. In construing a will it is the duty of the court to give effect to the testator's intention by looking at the circumstances at the date he executed it. In the words of James LJ in *Boyes v Cook* (1880) 14 Ch D 'you may place yourself . . . in his arm-chair, and consider the circumstances by which he was surrounded when he made his will to assist you in arriving at his intention'. Among those circumstances are the facts known or assumed by the deceased at the time the document was executed (*Marley v Rawlings* [2014] UKSC 2). The relevant background includes not only the factual background but also the legal background, and the latter takes into account changes in the law following execution of the document. In *Debenhams Retail plc v Sun Alliance and London Assurance Co Ltd* [2005] EWCA Civ 868 it was held that a court has 'to promote the purposes and values which are expressed or implicit in the wording, and to reach an interpretation which applies the [document's] wording to the changed circumstances in the manner most consistent with them'.

Where they have not already done so, all individuals with nil-rate band legacies in extant pre-2007 wills should be advised to review their wills (and the wording used in them) with a view (a) to checking that the operation of the words used, as to the amount of the legacy, does still match up with what they would intend in the changed fiscal circumstances, and (b) to deciding whether a nil-rate band legacy is still wanted at all (as to which see **Example C11 explanatory note 9**).

(6) Where there is more than one recapture charge before the survivor dies, the calculation in s 8C(2) is performed for each charge and the nil-rate band available for transfer to the survivor is reduced by each successive amount (s 8C(3)). The calculation should be performed from scratch, so that in the context of the calculation in **part D**(i) of the Example, if the TA ÷ NRBME calculation for a second recapture charge was 20%, the percentage to be used to ascertain the amount of the nil-rate band to transfer to Julia on her death would become (80% – (64% + 20%)). This would result in the whole of Hector's unused nil-rate band having being absorbed, with no amount therefore remaining available in computing the tax payable on the chargeable event.

(7) **Part D**(ii) of the Example illustrates the case where part only of the deceased person's nil-rate band is needed to keep the survivor's estate in a non-tax paying position. If all of that nil-rate band is needed by the survivor for this purpose, the calculation of the deferred charge to tax would be as follows. Using the same example as before, but assuming that Julia died leaving estate worth £700,000, the computation would be as follows:

Step 1: The nil-rate band in force at the time of Julia's death is £325,000 (first element). The amount by which the nil-rate band in force on Julia's death is increased by (£325,000 × 80%) = £260,000 (second element).

Step 2: Julia's chargeable estate minus the first element from Step 1 is £700,000 – £325,000 = £375,000.

Step 3: The result of Step 2 (£375,000) is greater than the second element found at Step 1 (£260,000). So following option (b) at Step 3 proceed to Steps 4B and 5B taking the latter amount (£260,000) as the result of this step.

Step 4B: The nil-rate band in force on the sale of the woodlands (£350,000) is reduced by the result from Step 3 (£260,000), ie £350,000 – £260,000 = £90,000.

Step 5B: The nil-rate band to be used in working out the tax on the chargeable event is £90,000.

On the chargeable event the net sale price of the timber of £350,000 is added to Hector's chargeable estate of £50,000 and from this is deducted the result of Step 5B so that the tax due in the sale of the timber is (£400,000 – £90,000) × 40% = £124,000.

Question

(a) Consider whether the following 'dispositions' are 'transfers of value':

(i) Payment of school fees for the education of the transferor's son.

(ii) Payment of school fees for the education of the transferor's grandson.

(iii) Payments to a sister of the transferor for her maintenance.

(iv) Waivers of entitlements to a bonus as sales director of a family company, and to a dividend on a holding of shares therein.

(v) Payment by a sole trader of £30,000 compensation for loss of office to a former employee.

(vi) The making of a loan of £50,000 to a friend.

(b) Charles, a widower, made the following gifts (after all exemptions other than the annual exemption):

(i) 10 July 2009: £66,000 to grandson.

(ii) 20 May 2013: £310,000 to a discretionary settlement – on condition that the trustees paid the inheritance tax due.

(iii) 12 June 2014: £37,000 to nephew.

(iv) 20 October 2016: £208,000 to a discretionary settlement – on condition that the trustees paid the inheritance tax due.

(v) 1 January 2018: £273,000 to a discretionary trust (the terms of which qualify it for treatment as a disabled trust) for the maintenance of his godson.

On 8 August 2023 Charles died leaving an estate of £400,000 comprising property which was in his direct and sole ownership. By his will he left £200,000 to the Save the Children Fund and the balance to his daughter absolutely. The residue included Charles's home which he has not replaced since before 8 July 2015; at the time of his death its unencumbered value was £150,000 and the outstanding mortgage was £30,000. As Charles has always believed strongly that tax should be paid on inherited wealth, he has left instructions for his executors to make an election to ensure that the 36% rate of tax does not apply to his estate.

Calculate the inheritance tax payable on each of the gifts in lifetime and on death, and on the death estate.

Answer

(a) Dispositions that are not transfers of value

A disposition made by a person that results in a fall in the value of his estate is a transfer of value for the purposes of inheritance tax (see **Example A1 part (b)**). However, certain dispositions are not transfers of value even though the estate of the person making them may fall in value. The types of disposition that fall into this category as disregarded dispositions are:

(1) A disposition which is not intended to confer any gratuitous benefit and which is made in a transaction on arm's length terms (IHTA 1984 s 10).

In *HMRC v Parry* [2020] STC 1836 the Supreme Court explained that in interpreting IHTA 1984 s 10, the question was not simply whether a gratuitous benefit was conferred on any person, but the search was for what the disponor intended, and in particular for whether the disponor had intended to confer any gratuitous benefit on any person. The disponor's actual intention in making the disposition was, therefore, in point. That militated against an over-technical interpretation of what was meant by 'confer any gratuitous benefit'. The words 'confer' and 'benefit' had to be given their ordinary meaning, and the dictionary definitions showed that they imported the idea of granting or bestowing some advantage on the recipient. It was not appropriate to speak of a disposition having been intended to confer any gratuitous benefit if the recipient of the benefit was intended to receive no more than he would have had in any event. It was necessary, therefore, to ask whether the disponor was intending, by the overall effect of the disposition, to put the recipient in a better position, or putting things broadly, to ask whether the disposition was being used to improve someone's position on a gratuitous basis. The exercise was not, however, simply a matter of asking the disponor whether or not he or she intended to confer benefit. It was not possible to consider whether a disposition was intended to improve someone's position without taking into account what rights the recipient had, in law, before and after the disposition. That legal context would permit a more rigorous evaluation of whether the requisite absence of intention had been shown. But that legal analysis of the rights was a factor in the evaluation, not the be-all and end-all of the consideration.

(2) Expenditure for family maintenance (s 11). This covers dispositions made:

(a) in favour of the transferor's spouse (or former spouse) for the maintenance of that spouse (or former spouse) made during the marriage and on its dissolution or annulment (s 11(1) and (6)). The same rules apply to civil partnerships.

(b) in favour of a child for his maintenance, education or training for a period ending not later than the tax year in which he becomes 18 years of age or, after attaining that age, ceases to undergo full-time education or training if the child is:

(i) A child, step-child or adopted child of the transferor or his spouse (or civil partner (or former civil partner)) (s 11(1), (6)).

(ii) An illegitimate child of the transferor (s 11(4)).

(iii) A child who is not in the care of a parent (but dispositions to such a child for a period ending after the year in which he reaches age 18 will not be disregarded unless the child was in the care of the transferor for substantial periods before he became 18) (s 11(2)).

(c) for the reasonable care or maintenance of a dependent relative (s 11(3)).

The term 'dependent relative' is defined in s 11(6) as the transferor's own relatives (or those of his spouse or civil partner) who are incapacitated by old age or infirmity from maintaining themselves, or his mother or father (or the mother or father of his spouse or civil partner). In light of this amended definition ESC F12 (Disposition for maintenance of unmarried mother) is now obsolete and HMRC withdrew it on 6 April 2015 (see HMRC document entitled Extra-Statutory Concessions as at 6 April 2017).

(3) A waiver or repayment of remuneration (s 14), and a waiver of dividends made within twelve months before any right to the dividend has accrued (s 15).

(4) Expenditure which is allowable as a deduction in computing a person's profits or gains for income or corporation tax (s 12).

(5) A failure during lifetime to exercise rights to drawdown designated funds from a drawdown pension fund or a flexi-access fund so that there are unused funds on death (s 12A). This means that the value of a deceased estate is not reduced by the omission to draw down all the funds (see **Example A1 explanatory note 8**).

(6) Transfers to qualifying employee trusts by close companies, subject to tight conditions (s 13).

(7) Dispositions by close companies to employee-ownership trusts (s 13A).

(8) A grant of an agricultural tenancy for full consideration (s 16).

(9) Deeds of variation or disclaimer within s 142 and certain other post-death adjustments (s 17).

The position in the six situations given is therefore:

(i) *School fees for education of transferor's son*

School fees paid for the education of the transferor's son will not be a disposition (and hence a transfer of value) provided the son is under 18 or still in full-time education or training. This being the case there is no need to consider the application of any exemption in relation to the payments (eg that they were paid out of income and therefore may be exempt as normal expenditure out of income (see **Example A1 part (c)**).

(ii) *School fees for education of transferor's grandson*

The payment will be a disposition that may give rise to a transfer of value unless the grandson is under 18 and is not in the care of a parent (which includes adoptive and step-parents); or the grandson is over 18, is not in the care of a parent *and* has been in the care of the grandparent for substantial periods before reaching the age of 18. (This excludes from this treatment the support, in education after 18, of a grandchild where the parents with whom he has been living both die before he has completed his education.) If the payments are dispositions then the transfers occasioned by them may be exempt if the payments qualify for the normal expenditure out of income exemption (see **Example A1 part (c)**).

(iii) *Gifts for maintenance of sister*

Gifts to the transferor's sister for her maintenance will be a disposition that gives rise to a transfer of value unless the sister, by reason of old age or infirmity, is incapable of maintaining herself *and* the amounts paid are reasonable for her care or maintenance. The payments may also not be dispositions giving rise to transfers of value if the sister is in the same position as the transferor's grandson in **(ii) above**, that is to say she is not in the care of a parent and is either under 18 years of age or, if over 18, has been in the care of the transferor for substantial periods before reaching age 18 and in that event is still in full time education or training. If the payments are dispositions then the transfers occasioned by them may be exempt if the payments qualify for the normal expenditure out of income exemption (see **Example A1 part (c)**).

(iv) *Waiver of remuneration and dividends*

The waiver of remuneration is a disposition that does not give rise to a transfer of value, and neither does the dividend waiver provided it has been waived within twelve months before any right to it has accrued.

(v) *Compensation for loss of office*

So long as the compensation payment is allowed as a deduction in computing the sole trader's profits, it will not be a disposition that gives rise to a transfer of value.

(vi) *Loan to a friend*

If a person lends money or other property for a prolonged period or denies himself the opportunity to recall that money or property, the right to demand the return of the money or property is then worth less in his hands than it would be if he has unfettered use of the money or property (as he did before he lent it). So, for example, if the £50,000 is lent free of interest for a fixed term of ten years and after making the loan the lender requires the cash, the only way to obtain it is for him to assign the debt (ie his right to eventual repayment) for consideration to someone else. But how much could he sell the debt for? Not £50,000, because the assignee will want a commercial return which he will obtain by paying sufficiently below £50,000 to compensate for having to wait for the remainder of the ten years before the capital sum becomes payable to him. A transfer of value will thus be made by the lender when he lends the money (ie makes a disposition) in these circumstances on the difference between the amount lent and the discounted present value of the future right to repayment.

If, however, the loan is repayable on demand or on reasonable notice, especially but not necessarily if it is at a commercial rate of interest, and there is no question about the borrower's ability to repay it, then there will be no diminution in the value of the lender's estate (his right to repayment being of the same value as the sum lent). A transfer of value will not arise because the disposition (ie the transfer of the money to the borrower) will not result in a fall in value of the lender's estate.

If the various conditions stated above were not satisfied, the payments would be dispositions giving rise to transfers of value against which the disponor's current and previous years' annual exemptions (or other exemptions) may be used if available.

To the extent that the amounts in (iii) and (v) are not covered by the annual exemption (or in the case of (iii) are not normal expenditure out of income), they will be potentially exempt transfers and therefore only brought into account if the donor dies within the next seven years of making them.

If the school fees under (i) and (ii) are not within the 'family maintenance' category, it is possible that the transfers could be regarded as chargeable transfers of value (subject to any available exemptions such as for normal expenditure out of income) rather than potentially exempt transfers. This is because for a transfer to an individual to be potentially exempt, property must become comprised in the transferee's estate or, so far as property does not become comprised in the estate of another person, the transferee's estate must be increased by the transfer (s 3A(2)), which would not occur in these two instances. Rather the transfer results in an increase in the amount of money owned by the school. If this represents a risk it can be avoided by paying the money in the first instance to, or to a bare trustee for, the person whose education is being funded, with a view to that person (or trustee) then actually paying the school fees. Similarly, any transfer of value arising out of the loan at (vi) would be a chargeable transfer rather than a potentially exempt transfer unless the estate of the borrower could be regarded as increased by the value of the right to have the loan on favourable terms.

(b) Charles — inheritance tax position on lifetime gifts and on estate at death

Tax payable in lifetime

					Gross accumulation	*Tax*
					£	£
10 July 2009 —	gift to grandson			66,000		
	Less: Annual exemptions	2009/10	3,000			
		2008/09	3,000	(6,000)		
Potentially exempt transfer				60,000		
20 May 2013 —	gift to discretionary settlement			310,000		
	Less: Annual exemptions	2013/14	3,000			
		2012/13	3,000	(6,000)		
Lifetime chargeable transfer (one-half rates)					304,000	0*
(* 304,000 – 325,000 (2013/14 threshold) = Nil @ 20%)						
12 June 2014 —	gift to nephew			37,000		
	Less: Annual exemption	2014/15		(3,000)		
Potentially exempt transfer				34,000		

					Tax on 2016/17 scale
				304,000	Nil
20 Oct 2016 —	gift to discretionary settlement		208,000		
	Less: Annual exemptions	2016/17	(3,000)		
		2015/16	(3,000)		
Lifetime chargeable transfer (one half rates)				202,000	36,200*
				506,000	36,200*

(* 506,000 – 325,000 (2016/17 threshold) = 181,000 @ 20%)

Inheritance tax payable by trustees £36,200.

1 Jan 2018 —	gift to disabled person's trust		273,000	
	Less: Annual exemption	2017/18	(3,000)	
Potentially exempt transfer			270,000	
20 May 2020 —	exclude transfer seven years earlier			(304,000)
				202,000

On death of Charles — 8 August 2023

			Gross £	*Tax (using 2023/24 rates)* £
Transfers within seven years before death i.e. 9 August 2016 to 8 August 2022:				
20 October 2016 — gift to discretionary settlement				
Cumulative *chargeable* transfers within previous seven years (ie 21 October 2009 — 20 October 2016 — see **explanatory note 3**)			304,000	Nil
Chargeable transfer (full rates)			202,000	72,400*
			506,000	72,400*
(* 506,000 – 325,000 = 181,000 @ 40%)				
1 January 2018 — gift to disabled person's trust				
Cumulative *chargeable* transfers within previous seven years (ie 2 January 2011 – 1 January 2018)			506,000	72,400
Chargeable transfer			270,000	108,000
			776,000	180,400*
(776,000 – 325,000 = 451,000 @ 40%)				
8 August 2023 – date of death				
Cumulative chargeable transfers within previous seven years (ie 9 August 2016 – 8 August 2023) (202,000 + 270,000)			472,000	58,800*
Estate on death		400,000		
Less:	Exempt – Legacy to charity	(200,000)	200,000	32,000
			672,000	
Less:	Residence nil-rate band (see **explanatory note (5)**)		(120,000)	
			552,000	90,800**

(* 472,000 – 325,000 = 147,000 @ 40%)

(** 552,000 – 325,000 = 227,000 @ 40%) – see **explanatory note (6)**)

Inheritance tax payable — lifetime

		£
(i)	Grandson	Nil
(ii)	Trustees of 2013 discretionary settlement	800
(iii)	Nephew	Nil
(iv)	Trustees of 2016 discretionary settlement	36,200
(v)	Trustees of 2018 disabled person's trust	Nil

Inheritance tax payable — death

	£	£
By grandson, trustees of 2013 discretionary settlement and nephew (excluded as gifts were made more than seven years before death, but without giving rise to refund in favour of trustees in respect of lifetime tax paid)		Nil
By trustees of 2016 discretionary settlement		
Tax at full death rates	72,400	
Tax after taper relief 20% (6–7 years)	14,480	
Less: Paid on lifetime transfer	(36,200)	Nil
(No repayment will be made to the trustees)		
By trustees of 2018 disabled person's trust		
Tax at full death rates	108,000	
Tax after taper relief 40% (5–6 years)		43,200
By personal representatives		32,000
Total		75,200

Explanatory Notes

Dispositions for family maintenance: inheritance tax treatment

(1) The distinction between school fees paid for the education of the transferor's son and his grandson illustrates how carefully the wording of a section has to be considered, particularly since the heading (called the side note) of a section is often widely descriptive, in this case being 'dispositions for maintenance of family' (s 11). Broadly speaking, dispositions for the maintenance of one's own children are not transfers of value if the child is either under 18 or still in full time education. Dispositions for the maintenance of another child are transfers of value and may be charged to inheritance tax (in the absence of other exemptions) unless the child is *not* in the care of a parent and, if over 18, was in the care of the transferor for substantial periods before reaching age 18 and is still in full time education or training.

In *Phizackerley v HMRC* (2007) the Special Commissioner stated that whether a payment was for the maintenance of another depended upon all the facts and circumstances in which the payment was made. Although the term 'maintenance' did not mean just enough to enable a person to get by, neither did it mean anything which might be regarded as reasonably desirable for his general benefit or welfare. The ordinary meaning of maintenance had a flavour of meeting recurring expenses. It was wide enough to cover the transfer of a house or part interest in a house but only if it relieved the recipient from income expenditure, for example on rent. It did not cover the case where a person, in order to give his wife or spouse security of tenure, transferred his house into joint names. When a husband put a house in the joint names of himself and his wife during their marriage it was not within the ordinary meaning of the term maintenance. In view of the subsequent decision in *McKelvey v HMRC* (2008) this must be taken as referring to the transfer of a house for the transferee to live in, since the Special Commissioner in *McKelvey* allowed relief, to a limit of what he considered reasonable provision for care or maintenance, in respect of the transfer of two let houses from which the transferee derived rent.

Potentially exempt transfers to grandson and nephew: inheritance tax treatment

(2) The gifts to grandson and nephew in **part (b)** are made after 17 March 1986 and are outright gifts by one individual to another individual. They are, therefore, potentially exempt transfers in so far as they exceed the available annual exemptions (and other exemptions that may be available).

Since the transferor (Charles) did not die within seven years after making these gifts, the potentially exempt transfers become exempt transfers (s 3A(4)). Consequently, no inheritance tax liability arises in respect of them and they are not taken into account in the figure of cumulative chargeable transfers. For more detailed notes see **Example A6 explanatory note 6.**

Calculation of inheritance tax: cumulation of transfers

(3) When calculating the tax on a transfer, the tax on the brought forward figure (ie the cumulative chargeable transfers made in the period of seven years before the transfer being considered) is always recalculated using the rates currently in force. The recalculated amount may, or may not, represent the tax that was actually paid on the earlier transfers. But this amount gives the correct starting point for calculating the tax on the current transfer (which is treated as falling in the nil-rate band to the extent only that the nil-rate band has not been used up by the cumulative amounts brought forward). This is particularly important where the cumulative transfers are below the nil-rate threshold applicable at the date of the current transfer, because the current transfer (if it is chargeable) will fall to be charged partly at the nil rate and partly at the higher rate. Where the cumulative transfers exceed the nil-rate threshold applicable at the date of the current transfer, the current transfer (if it is chargeable) will be charged to inheritance tax at the higher rate applicable (ie 20% or 40% as the case may be – see **Example A2 part (a)** for an explanation of the rates at which inheritance tax is charged). The recalculated amount does not charge previous transfers to tax again, but gives effect to the progressive nature of inheritance tax and the cumulation principle on which the tax is based. Where the cumulative transfers exceed the nil-rate threshold applicable at the date of the current transfer it is not strictly necessary to calculate the tax on the cumulative brought forward amount; it is sufficient to observe that the nil-rate band has been exhausted by the cumulative total and to calculate the tax on the current transfer at 20% or 40% as the case may be. In this Example the strict position is shown but elsewhere in the book the shorter method is often adopted (see **Example A9**).

(4) In the Example, when calculating the additional (or supplementary) charge to inheritance tax on Charles's death in relation to the gift to the discretionary trust on 20 October 2016, the cumulative chargeable transfers within seven years before that date exclude the gifts to the grandson and the nephew on 10 July 2009 and 12 June 2014 respectively (both being potentially exempt transfers that have became exempt as Charles has survived for more than seven years after making them), but include the 20 May 2013 transfer (being a chargeable transfer which, although more than seven years before Charles's death, occurred in the seven years before the 20 October 2016 transfer which attracts the additional charge to tax).

The cumulative chargeable transfers to be considered when working out the additional charge to tax in respect of the 1 January 2018 transfer include both the 20 May 2013 and 20 October 2016 gifts to the discretionary trust.

When calculating the estate charge to inheritance tax on Charles's death, both the 20 October 2016 chargeable transfer and the 1 January 2018 potentially exempt transfer (now chargeable) are the cumulative chargeable transfers to be taken into account.

Inheritance tax residence nil-rate band (RNRB)

(5) Charles's estate benefits from a RNRB as he dies after 6 April 2018 owning a home which is closely inherited by passing under a disposition under his will to his son (his direct descendant). As his estate does not exceed the taper threshold of £2,000,000, the amount of the RNRB prima facie available is £175,000 (the default

allowance for 2023/24). The actual amount of RNRB used in calculating the inheritance tax arising in respect of Charles's estate is limited to the chargeable value of the proportion of his home that is closely inherited. In this case, the chargeable value of Charles's home is its encumbered value of £120,000 (£150,000 - £30,000) and as the whole home is closely inherited this figure acts as the limit on the amount of RNRB available. The limit operates in Charles's case and so the amount of the RNRB used in calculating the IHT arising on his estate is £120,000. See **Example A2 part (b)** for a detailed discussion on the RNRB.

The rate of inheritance tax

(6) The rate at which tax is charged on an estate is 40%. This is reduced to 36% where the deceased has, by his will, left 10% or more of his net estate to charity (IHTA 1984 Sch 1A inserted by FA 2013 s 209 and Sch 33). However, the executors may make an election under Sch 1A para 8 to opt out of the lower rate of tax so that they are treated as if the charitable donation had failed the 10% test. Following Charles's wishes it is assumed that the executors make this election so that his estate is charged at 40%. The election must be made in writing within 2 years of Charles's death (ie by 8 August 2025). See **Example B12** for a detailed discussion of the reduced rate of inheritance tax.

Question

(a) Explain the roles that domicile and the location of property play in the context of the charge to inheritance tax, setting out the rules that determine an individual's domicile and the place where property is located.

(b) Explain the meaning and inheritance tax treatment of excluded property for both domiciled and non-domiciled individuals.

(c) Explain the inheritance tax treatment of transfers to a spouse or civil partner not domiciled in the UK.

(d) Briefly explain how relief is obtained in the UK for inheritance tax levied by overseas countries.

(e) John who was born in England to English parents and who has lived all his life in Cheshire, was on holiday in Kenya in 2016 when he met Natasha. Natasha was born in Kenya, her parents having settled there twenty years previously. John and Natasha were married on 5 August 2018 and, although they settled in John's home town, Natasha intends to return to Kenya should John predecease her. They have no children. John died unexpectedly on 4 June 2023 at which date his assets (net of deductible liabilities) were valued at:

Quoted investments	£56,000
Cash at bank	£10,000
House in Cheshire	£2,000,000

John had purchased the house in Cheshire before 8 July 2015. By his will John gave the residue of his estate to Natasha absolutely.

John, who had not made any chargeable transfers before 4 June 2016, made a gift to Natasha of £758,500 on 2 August 2018 in contemplation of their marriage on 5 August 2018. At the time of John's death, Natasha owned a residential investment property in Nairobi valued at £2,500,000 which she had purchased on 5 December 2022 funded partly from John's lifetime gift and partly from a gift of money from her parents. Natasha has never lived in that property.

Calculate the inheritance tax arising on John's death and comment on whether Natasha should then make a lifetime election to be treated as domiciled in the UK.

Answer

(a) Domicile and the location of property

Effects of domicile on inheritance tax

Domicile is a concept of the common law whose origins have nothing to do with taxation. It is essentially a private international law concept used to establish where an individual has his permanent legal home. An individual's domicile determines the system of personal law which applies where an individual has connections with more than one jurisdiction. Personal law is that part of the law which governs such matters as marriage, divorce, legitimacy, and succession to property. Whenever a question arises in the UK courts about these matters, it must be determined according to the law of the domicile of the person concerned and not by English, Scots or Northern Ireland law (unless the individual is domiciled in one of those territories). The law governing such disputes will normally be the legal system of a country (a political entity), but it may be that of an individual state within a country if it has its own legal system. Such countries include the United States, Canada and Australia; even the UK has three separate legal jurisdictions for domicile purposes (England and Wales; Scotland; and Northern Ireland). Strictly speaking an individual is domiciled in England and Wales, or Scotland, or Northern Ireland rather than being domiciled in the UK. It is, however, a convenient shorthand to refer to an individual being domiciled in the UK or having a UK domicile and this label is used here (as indeed it is in IHTA 1984 itself).

Domicile is also employed in a tax context to determine an individual's territorial connection with the UK and hence his liability to UK tax in general, and inheritance tax in particular. This is appropriate since domicile governs his personal affairs including the transfer of property (which is the focus of UK inheritance tax). Moreover, as inheritance tax is a cumulative tax, the effectiveness of the tax depends upon a link of the greatest possible strength being used to attach a person to the UK and domicile provides such a link, the bonds of domicile being very difficult to break. The inheritance tax regime uses the common law of domicile as the basis of imposing the charge to tax; it also goes further however and employs the concepts of deemed domicile and elective domicile in so doing.

Whether a lifetime disposition by a person gives rise to a liability to UK inheritance tax may depend on whether the person is domiciled, or deemed to be domiciled, in the UK at the time he makes it. Likewise, whether a charge to inheritance tax arises on a person's death, depends upon his domicile when he dies. In short a UK domiciled individual is within the charge to inheritance tax on his worldwide property whereas a non-UK domiciled individual is liable to inheritance tax only in respect of his property that is located in the UK.

In the UK, the rules for ascertaining a person's domicile according to the law of England and Wales (and also that of Northern Ireland) are different from those that apply under Scots Law. Before the types of domicile are described, the five basic principles of domicile may be stated as follows:

(a) No one, at any time, is without a domicile.

(b) No one can simultaneously have more than one domicile.

(c) Domicile must relate to a territory subject to a single system of law, whether or not the limits of that territory coincide with national boundaries.

(d) A change of domicile may never be presumed; it must always be proved on a balance of probabilities by the person that asserts the change.

(e) Domicile must be determined in accordance with English (or Scots or Northern Ireland) law (as the case may be).

Domicile of origin (English Law)

A child's 'domicile of origin' is the domicile of the child's father at the time when the child is born (if the parents were married at that time). If the child's parents were not married at that time, the child will take the domicile of his mother at the time of his birth. This may not necessarily be the actual country of birth. For example, if Jack is born in Germany while his father is working there, but the father's permanent home is in England, Jack's domicile of origin is in England and Wales.

Domicile of dependency (English Law)

Until a person can change it by acquiring a domicile of choice, his domicile will be the same as that of the person on whom he is legally dependent. If that person's domicile changes, the dependant person automatically acquires the same domicile in place of his existing domicile at that time (eg his domicile of origin may be displaced by the new domicile). This is known as a domicile of dependency. This rule applies to children under the age of 16 years.

Until 1 January 1974 a wife's domicile automatically followed that of her husband, again as a domicile of dependency. When this rule was abolished on that date, those already married retained the previous domicile of dependency for the time being as though it was a domicile of choice, but became capable of changing their domicile like any other independent adult.

Domicile of choice (English Law)

Persons can legally acquire a new domicile, a domicile of choice, from the age of 16. To do so, they must be physically present in a country, and in addition provide irrefutable evidence that they intend to live there permanently or indefinitely.

The fact of living in another country for a long time, although an important factor, does not prove that an individual has the requisite intention to acquire a new domicile, and as might be expected, there is a substantial body of case law on this topic. Generally speaking, 'there is no act, no circumstance in a man's life, however trivial it may be itself, which ought to be left out of account of consideration in trying the question whether there was an intention to change the domicile' (*Drevon v Drevon* (1864)). Some of the circumstances which are taken into account in order to determine whether a person has the necessary intention include the place where his personal belongings are kept, the contents of his will, the exercise of political rights, his naturalisation as a citizen and his social and religious associations. No one factor, is determinative. However, for inheritance tax purposes retaining overseas electoral voting rights will not be taken into account in determining an individual's domicile (FA 1996 s 200).

Domicile under Scots Law

Before 5 May 2006, the rules determining the domicile of a person under Scots law were the same as those that applied under English law. With effect from 4 May 2006, the rules of domicile under Scots Law are set out in the Family Law (Scotland) Act 2006 s 22 (SSI 2006/212).

For so long as a child is under the age of 16, his domicile will be that of his parents provided they are domiciled in the same country as each other and the child has a home with one or with both of them. If his parents do not share the same domicile as each other, the child will be domiciled in the country with which he has for the time being the closest connection. As a result of this enactment, the old rules of domicile of dependency no longer apply in Scotland. However, as a matter of law, it is not settled how the rules governing the acquisition of a domicile of origin now apply in Scotland although it is considered that a child acquires a domicile of origin on his birth under Scots Common Law (according to rules which are identical to those that apply in England and Wales) and that domicile of origin is immediately displaced by the rules introduced by the Family Law (Scotland) Act 2006 described above.

However, the Family Law (Scotland) Act 2006 has not altered the law governing the acquisition of a domicile of choice under Scots Law and so the law that applies for this purpose under English law continues to apply in Scotland.

Deemed domicile for inheritance tax

There is a concept of 'deemed domicile' for inheritance tax which applies throughout the United Kingdom. The rules were altered with effect from 6 April 2017 by F(No 2)A 2017 s 30.

As the rules existed before 6 April 2017 (the 'old rules'), even if a person was not domiciled in the UK under common law he was treated as if he were domiciled in the UK at the time of a transfer (or on death as the case may be) if:

- he was domiciled in the UK at any time within the three years immediately before the transfer (or date of death) (IHTA 1984 s 267(1)(a)), or
- he was resident in the UK in at least 17 of the 20 *tax years* ending with the year in which he makes the transfer (or dies) (s 267(1)(b)). This rule could therefore sometimes have applied little more than 15 years after a person first became UK resident, if that was late in a tax year (see the example of Imran below).

With effect from 6 April 2017 (F(No 2)A 2017 s 30(9)), even if a person is not domiciled in the UK under common law he will be treated as if he is domiciled in the UK at the time of a transfer (or on death as the case may be) if:

- he was domiciled in the UK at any time within the three years immediately before the transfer (or date of death) (IHTA 1984 s 267(1)(a)),
- he is a formerly domiciled resident for the tax year in which the time of transfer or death falls (s 267(1)(aa)), or
- he was resident in the UK in for least 15 of the 20 *tax years* preceding the tax year in which he makes the transfer (or dies) and for at least one of the four tax years ending with the tax year in which he makes the transfer (or dies) (s 267(1)(b)).

In the context of the second of the above tests that applies from 6 April 2017, an individual is a 'formerly domiciled resident' in relation to a tax year if he was born in the UK, his domicile of origin was in the UK, he was resident in the UK in that tax year and he was resident in the UK for at least one of the two tax years immediately preceding that tax year (s 272). This rule will not apply to an individual who has a UK domicile of origin but who was born abroad.

As compared with the corresponding old rule, the third of the above tests that applies from 6 April 2017 reduces the time for which an individual has to be UK resident in order to be treated as being deemed UK domiciled. However, the rule is somewhat narrower in its operation as it requires residence in at least one of the four tax years ending with the tax year in which a transfer is made or he dies. This means that a person will not be deemed domiciled in the UK in a tax year where he has been non-UK resident for the previous four consecutive tax years even though he would otherwise satisfy the tests. Subject to this restriction, this rule can still sometimes apply little more than 13 years after a person first became UK resident, if that was late in a tax year. The third test is also subject to a transitional provision that ensures that a person who is not resident before 2017/18 will not be subject to the 15-year rule provided he never becomes resident in the UK ever again (F(No 2)A 2017 s 30(10)).

A person is regarded as resident in a tax year for the purposes of the 17-year and 15-year rules (and in order for him to have the status of a 'formerly domiciled resident') if he is resident in the UK for income tax purposes in that year (but in HMRC's view without regard to the provision of any double tax agreement by virtue of which his residence status is determined) (IHTA 1984 s 267(4)).

When applying the above rules, a person's elective domicile (see below) is ignored in determining whether he is, or at any time was, domiciled in the UK (s 267(5)). For example, the first deemed domicile rule (the 3-year rule) will not apply to a person who was domiciled in the UK within the three years immediately before the transfer (or the date of death) only because he had made an election under s 276ZA to be so domiciled.

The deemed domicile rules do not apply to the various forms of UK government investment whose IHT status as excluded property turns (or used to turn) on the owner's domicile (see items (vii) and (viii) in **part (a)** below). Otherwise, a person will, for inheritance tax, be domiciled outside the UK if he does not have a domicile in any part of the UK under the common law and is not caught by the deemed domicile rules.

Generally, if an individual is domiciled in some part of the UK, or is deemed to be domiciled in the UK, inheritance tax applies to his assets wherever they are situated. Also, inheritance tax applies to settled property situated outside the UK where the settlor was domiciled, or deemed to be domiciled, in the UK when the property was settled.

Examples: old rules

Imran is domiciled under the common law in Qatar (his domicile of origin). He became resident in the UK for tax purposes on 1 April 2000 (but without forming any intention to settle there permanently). He leaves the UK permanently on 10 April 2016 (becoming not resident in the UK for income tax purposes on that date) and dies on 19 September 2016. Imran is treated for the purposes of IHT as domiciled in the UK when he dies and is liable to UK inheritance tax on all the property he owns no matter where in the world it is located. This is the case even though in the common law Imran has never lost his domicile of origin in Qatar and is domiciled there when he dies. As regards IHT, the period of twenty tax years ending with the date of Imran's death on 19 September 2016 (which falls in 2016/17) began with the year 1996/97. In that period Imran has been UK resident in each of the years 1999/00 through to 2016/17. So he has been resident (in law) in the UK for 17 tax years of the 20 tax years ending with 2016/17 (even though he has been physically present (in fact) for little over 15 calendar years).

James who has a domicile of origin in England, leaves the UK for good on 31 December 2013 in order to settle and make a new life for himself in Australia. He arrives in Queensland, Australia on 1 January 2014. James dies on 10 August 2015. As James arrived in Queensland on 1 January 2014 with the intention of settling there permanently he acquired a domicile of choice there under the common law on that date. However, as he was domiciled in England immediately preceding his arrival in Australia he remains domiciled in the UK for the purposes of IHT until midnight on 31 December 2016. As James dies on 10 August 2015, he is domiciled in the UK at the time of his death as he has been domiciled in England within 3 years preceding that date. Consequently he is liable to UK inheritance tax on all the property he owns, no matter where in the world it is located. This is the case even though in the common law James has a domicile of choice in Queensland, Australia at the time of his death.

Michael has a domicile of origin in Northern Ireland. In 1999 he moved to Spain to settle and make a new life for himself. He acquired a domicile of choice there on his arrival. Michael became worried about the economic situation in Spain and decided to settle in a country that enjoys a more stable environment. He left Spain on 1 April 2015 and arrived in Canada on 2 April 2015. Michael died on 6 April 2016. When his flight left Spain, Michael abandoned his domicile of choice in Spain as he was no longer present in Spain with the intention of remaining there indefinitely. But, not having yet arrived in Canada, he had not yet acquired a domicile of choice there. Since he could not be without a domicile during the flight, his Northern Ireland domicile of origin revived under the common law. As he was domiciled in Northern Ireland immediately preceding his arrival in Canada Michael remains domiciled in the UK for the purposes of IHT until midnight on 31 March 2018 (under the 3-year rule). When Michael dies on 6 April 2016 he is domiciled in the UK for IHT purposes and so is liable to UK inheritance tax on all the property he owns, no matter where in the world it is located. This is so even though he abandoned the UK as a home somewhat 15 years previously and he dies at a time when he has a domicile of choice under the common law in Canada.

Judith has a UK domicile of origin and has been resident here all her life. She emigrates to Lichtenstein and arrives there on 1 January 2017. She has not since been resident in the UK. When Judith arrives in Lichtenstein with the intention of remaining there indefinitely, she acquires a domicile of choice in Lichtenstein under the common law. However, as she was domiciled in the UK immediately preceding her arrival in Lichtenstein, for the purposes of the 3-year rule she remains domiciled in the UK until midnight on 31 December 2019 and under that rule ceases to be domiciled in the UK from the start of 1 January 2020. However, before this is taken as the definitive position of Judith's status for inheritance purposes, the 17-year rule must also be considered. In her case the period of twenty tax years which applies for the purposes of the 17-year rule ends with the tax year 2019/20. From 2020/21 Judith will not have been UK resident in the 17-year period ending with that year. Despite her acquiring a domicile of choice under the common law in Lichtenstein on 1 January 2017, Judith is treated for the purposes of IHT as ceasing to be domiciled in the UK (and so no longer within the charge to UK inheritance tax on her foreign-sited property) from 6 April 2020 only. This interaction of the two deemed domiciled rules must not be overlooked and the interaction is still applicable under the rules that came into effect on 6 April 2017. Judith's position is determined under the old rules because she is subject to the transitional rule in F(No 2)A 2017 s 30(10), never having returned to the UK since her departure.

Examples: current rules

Irfan is domiciled under the common law in Saudi Arabia (his domicile of origin). He was resident in the UK in 2003/04 and again from 2007/08 to 2020/21 (inclusive), leaving the UK permanently on 5 April 2021. During his time in the UK, at no point did he form the intention to settle there permanently. Irfan dies on 29 September 2022. Imran is treated for the purposes of IHT as domiciled in the UK when he dies and is liable to UK inheritance tax on all the property he owns no matter where in the world it is located. This is the case even though in the common law Irfan has never lost his domicile of origin in Saudi Arabia and is domiciled there when he dies. As regards IHT, the period of twenty tax years ending before the tax year in which the date of Irfan's death on 29 September 2023 falls (ie 2023/24) began with the tax year 2003/04. In the period 2003/04 to 2022/23 (inclusive) Irfan has been UK resident for 15 tax years, This includes 2020/21 which is one of the four tax years falling in the period 2020/21 to 2023/24 inclusive.

George who has a domicile of origin in England, leaves the UK for good on 31 December 2021 in order to settle and make a new life for himself in Canada. He arrives in Manitoba, Canada on 1 January 2022. George dies on 29 August 2022. As George arrived in Manitoba on 1 January 2022 with the intention of settling there permanently he acquired a domicile of choice there under the common law on that date. However, as he was domiciled in England immediately preceding his arrival in Canada he remains domiciled in the UK for the purposes of IHT until midnight on 31 December 2024. As James dies on 29 August 2023, he is domiciled in the UK at the time of his death as he has been domiciled in England within three years preceding that date. Consequently he is liable to UK inheritance tax on all the property he owns, no matter where in the world it is located. This is the case even though in the common law James has a domicile of choice in Manitoba, Canada at the time of his death.

Charlotte was born in the UK in 1966 and has a UK domicile of origin. Since her birth she lived in the UK but then left the UK permanently in July 1996 and went to live in Austria. She has made but a handful of short visits to the UK since then. Her employer required her to work in the UK and she was seconded to the London on 9 June 2022 for three years. Charlotte died unexpectedly on 14 July 2023. Despite not having been resident in the UK for over 20 years, she dies deemed domiciled in the UK and is liable to IHT on all the property she owns no matter where in the world it is located. This is because, for 2023/24 (the tax year of her death), Charlotte has the status of a 'former domiciled resident'. She was born in the UK, had a UK domicile of origin, was resident in the UK for income tax purposes in the year in which she died (ie 2023/24) and was so resident for 2022/23 (one of the two tax years immediately preceding 2023/24).

Elective domicile for inheritance tax

Introduction

Finance Act 2013 makes provision for an individual (who satisfies certain conditions – a qualifying individual) to have (what is not a legislative term but what is referred to as) an elective domicile in the UK for inheritance tax purposes. IHTA 1984 ss 267ZA and 267ZB give effect to the rules relating to this type of domicile. An individual may have an elective domicile only for the purposes of inheritance tax; his domicile status for the purposes of income tax and capital gains tax (and hence his ability to be taxed on the remittance basis) remains unaffected by any election made in respect of inheritance tax.

The making of an election to be domiciled in the UK is closely allied to the operation of the spouse/civil partner exemption which is limited where a transfer is made by a UK domiciled spouse/civil partner to a spouse/civil partner who is domiciled abroad (see **part (c)** of the Example).

In understanding the application of the rules on elective domicile, a distinction needs to be drawn between *making* an election and the *taking effect* of an election. An election may be made on or after 17 July 2013 by either a qualifying individual or his personal representatives (ie the election may be made by either person); an election takes effect on or after 6 April 2013 only in respect of the qualifying individual (irrespective of whether he or his personal representatives made the election).

An election cannot be revoked once it has been made (s 267ZB(9)) although it may lapse and cease to have effect. If a person who made an election is not resident in the UK for income tax purpose for a period of four successive tax years beginning at any time after the election is made, the election ceases to have effect at the end of that period (s 267ZB(10)). It would appear that the election can be renewed by a person who is not resident in the UK.

Understanding the rules is made easier if one has in mind a simple scenario. Consider a person Q who wishes to make an election to be domiciled in the UK; we shall describe the rules by reference to him and his spouse/civil partner S. In very broad outline Q who is not domiciled in the UK and who is married to (or in a civil partnership with) S who is domiciled in the UK, may elect to be treated as UK domiciled. However, as will be seen the rules go wider. If Q has become UK domiciled, he will be able to make an election to cover an earlier period when he was not so domiciled; and similarly, if Q's marriage to/civil partnership with S has been dissolved a retrospective election may be made to cover a period when he was married/in a civil partnership with S (a UK domiciled person). So an election may still be made by a UK domiciled individual for a past period when he was not so domiciled and an election may also be made by an individual previously married or in a civil partnership to make a retrospective election following divorce or dissolution.

Ascertaining a person's domicile

It will be appreciated from this general introduction that the rules on elective domicile require one to consider the actual domicile status of Q. However, an individual (Q) need only have regard to his actual domicile status in the common law when considering whether it is possible for him to acquire an elective domicile. The rules on deemed domicile play no part in determining that question (s 267ZA(8)). However, the deemed domicile rules may apply to determine the domicile of S (ie the spouse/civil partner) in the application of the rules on elective domicile. For example, consider Florence who has a domicile of origin in Zimbabwe and who, without forming the requisite intention to remain in the UK indefinitely, has been resident here continuously for more than 15 tax years. Florence is not domiciled in the UK under the common law but is deemed to be domiciled here under the 15-year rule for the purposes of inheritance tax. Nevertheless, Florence is treated as not domiciled in the UK when applying the elective domicile rules.

Making an election: the qualifying individual Q himself

Q may make an election after 16 July 2013 to be treated for the purposes of inheritance tax as domiciled in the UK (and not elsewhere) (s 267ZA(1)).

An election may be made by Q after 16 July 2013 only if one of two conditions is met. The conditions are:

- Condition A: that at any time on or after 6 April 2013 and during the period of 7 years ending with the date on which the election is made, Q was alive, was married to/in a civil partnership with S and S was domiciled in the UK (s 267ZA(3)).

- Condition B: that S dies and at any time on or after 6 April 2013 and within the period of 7 years ending with the date of death, S was domiciled in the UK and was the spouse or civil partner of Q (s 276ZA(4)).

An election made where Condition A is satisfied is called a lifetime election; an election made where Condition B is met is called a death election (s 267ZB(1)).

As regards Condition A, Q and S will typically both be alive and married/in a civil union when Q makes the election. However, Q may still make an election in more complicated circumstances. Q does not necessarily need to be married or in a civil partnership at the time the election is made and neither does he have to be non-UK domiciled at that time (although of course the election will take effect for a time when he was not so domiciled – but that is not a condition for his being able to make an election). All that is required is that at any time on or after 6 April 2013 and during the 7 years before the making of the election Q was married to (or in a civil partnership with) S; hence the election can be made by Q if he is divorced from S (or if Q's civil partnership with S has been dissolved) provided Q and S were married/in a civil partnership at some time after 6 April 2013 and during the 7-year period stated. Hence Q cannot make an election if he was divorced from S (or his civil partnership with S was dissolved) before 6 April 2013. A divorce or dissolution takes effect when a court hands down a decree absolute to that effect. Necessarily Q must be married/in a civil partnership after 5 April 2013 in order to make an election and if this condition is met then for the time being he will also be so married/in a civil partnership at some time during the 7-year period so stated. The seven-year period that may be counted in satisfying this condition may have started before 6 April 2013. For example, in May 2012 Julian who was domiciled in the UK transferred £200,000 to his civil partner Michael who is not domiciled in the UK. Of this transfer £55,000 is exempt (s 18(2)) and £145,000 is a PET. If Julian and Michael's partnership is dissolved in January 2013, Michael cannot, after 16 July 2013, make an election to be domiciled in the UK at the time Julian made his gift as he (Michael) was not in a civil partnership with Julian on or after 6 April 2013. Hence the transfer between them can never be treated as wholly exempt.

Q will rely on Condition B where he is a widower but the condition will only be met if S died after 6 April 2013 and at any time after 6 April 2013 at any time and during the period of 7 years ending with his death he was domiciled in the UK and married to (in a civil partnership with) Q. For example, Q (who is not domiciled in the UK) and S (who became domiciled under the deemed domicile rules on 6 April 2013) are married and S dies on 31 May 2023. Q is able (as it is after 16 July 2013) to make an election to be domiciled in the UK at an earlier time.

Making an election: the personal representatives of the qualifying individual Q

Q's personal representatives may likewise make an election following Q's death for Q to be treated for the purposes of inheritance tax as domiciled in the UK (and not elsewhere) at some time before his death (s 267ZA(2)). The ability for personal representatives to make an election depends only on Condition B being satisfied. Hence personal representatives may only make a death election. Practically speaking, personal representatives will only need to consider making an election where Q is a widower at the time of his own death; the election cannot be made by the personal representatives of Q where S survives. The personal representatives will also only need to consider making an election where transfers between Q and S were made at a time when the full spouse exemption under s 18 was not available.

So Q's executors will rely on Condition B where he has died as a widower after 6 April 2013 but the condition will only be met if S also died after 6 April 2013 and at any time after 6 April 2013 and during the period of 7 years ending with S's death he was domiciled in the UK and married to (in a civil partnership with) Q. For example, Q and S are married and not divorced on 6 April 2013 and have been married for many years. S (who is domiciled in the UK) dies on 30 April 2023 and Q dies a month later at a time when he is not domiciled in the UK. Q's executors are able (as it is after 16 July 2013) to make an election for Q to be domiciled in the UK at an earlier time.

The effect of an election and the date it takes effect

An election once made, will take effect from a given date. From that date Q will be treated as domiciled in the UK and not elsewhere. It is clear that Q will not have been so domiciled at the time the election takes effect and for the period it is effective (although he may not necessarily have to be non-UK domiciled when he *makes* the election as explained above). This means that any transfers made between Q and S from the date stated in the election will qualify for the full spouse exemption.

A lifetime or death election is treated as having taken effect on a date specified in the notice of election (see below) (s 267ZB(3)).

The date so specified (and hence from which Q is treated as domiciled in the UK) must meet a number of conditions. The conditions to be met differ for lifetime and death elections.

In the case of a lifetime election all of the following conditions must be met:

- the date specified must fall on or after 6 April 2013 (s 267ZB(4)(a)). This means that Q cannot be treated as domiciled from a time before 6 April 2013; the earliest he can be treated as UK domiciled by election is on and after 6 April 2013;
- the date specified must fall at any time within the period of 7 years ending with the date of the election (s 276ZB(4)(b)(i)). This means that the election can be retrospective but not to a time before 7 years before the date of the election (and not before 6 April 2013 in any event);
- on the date specified for the election to take effect Q must have been married to or in a civil partnership with S and S was domiciled in the UK (s 276ZA(4)(c), (5)(a)). Q does not need to have been married to or in a civil partnership with S and S does not have to be domiciled in the UK when Q makes the election, but Q and S have to be married/in a civil partner and S has to be UK domiciled on the date the election takes effect.

In the case of a death election all of the following conditions must be met:

- the date specified must fall on or after 6 April 2013 (s 267ZB(4)(a)) (as is the case for a lifetime election);
- the date specified must fall within the period of 7 years ending with the date on which S dies (s 276ZB(4)(b)(ii)) (as is the case for a lifetime election);
- on the date specified for the election to take effect Q was married to, or in a civil partnership with, S and S was domiciled in the UK (s 276ZA(4)(c), (5)(b)). Although S (and, if Q's personal representatives are making an election, Q as well) will have died before Q makes the election, both Q and S must be alive on the date the election (retrospectively but not before 6 April 2013) takes effect, both must be married on that date and S must be UK domiciled on that date.

Where an election (whether a lifetime or death election) is made, takes effect retrospectively and a transfer made between the earlier date and the date on which the election is made becomes chargeable as a result of the election being made, then the legislation modifies the dates on which an account of the transfer must be delivered and the date of payment of any tax arising. The due date for the delivery of an account in respect of the now chargeable transfer is 12 months from the end of the month in which the election is made (s 276ZB(7),(8)(a)). For the payment of the tax and the date from which interest is charged, the now chargeable transfer is treated as if it were made at the date of the election (s 276ZB(7),(8)(b)). (See the example of Imogen in (**explanatory note 3**) below.)

Form of the election

An election to be domiciled in the UK must be made by notice in writing to HMRC (s 276ZB(2)) and as already stated cannot be revoked once it has been made (s 276ZB(9)). There is no prescribed form for the election but HMRC have signified at IHTM13043 that it must contain:

- the full name and address of the person making it or about whom the personal representatives are making an election;

- the date of birth of the person and, if relevant, his date of death;
- the full name of the person's spouse or civil partner who is UK domiciled; and
- the date from which the election is to take effect (as described above).

Disclosure of elections

HMRC acknowledge (at IHTM13045) that if a person who has made an election has died, it is possible that their personal representatives may want to know whether or not a lifetime election has been made (as it could have an impact on the tax liability that arises on the death). HMRC will accede to such requests but only if they are made in writing (ie not over the telephone) and the personal representatives provide evidence that they are the persons entitled to apply for a grant of representation. This may be shown by including a copy of the deceased's will (in the case of executors) or by including evidence of an application of letters of administration (or that they are entitled to apply) with the letter (in the case of administrators).

Purposes within the scope of IHT for which an elective domicile does not apply

An election to be domiciled in the UK does not apply when considering an individual's domicile in the following cases (ie his elective domicile is ignored in the following cases):

- in connection with the various forms of UK government investment whose IHT status as excluded property turns (or used to turn) on the owner's domicile (see items **(vii)** and **(viii)** in **part (a)**) (s 276ZA(5));

- when interpreting or applying Estate Duty Conventions and certain Double Taxation Agreements which determine the domicile of an individual (namely those with France, Italy, India or Pakistan) (s 267ZA(6), (7)).

Location of assets

If a person is domiciled abroad, inheritance tax applies only to their assets located in the UK; their property located abroad will be excluded property, as will some specific items of property even though they are located in the UK (see **part (b)**).

The location of assets is subject to common law as amended by any special provisions in a double taxation agreement. The normal UK rules for the more common types of asset are that:

- rights or interests in or over immovable property and chattels are situated where the property is located;
- registered shares or securities are situated where they are registered;
- coins and bank notes are situated wherever they happen to be at the time of the transfer;
- bearer securities are situated where the certificate of title is located at the time of the transfer. On or after 26 March 2015, UK companies may no longer issue bearer shares and any such shares issued before that date must, by 26 December 2015, be converted into registered shares or cancelled (Small Business, Enterprise and Employment Act 2015, s 84 and Sch 4);
- goodwill is situated where the business, to which it is attached, is carried on;
- an interest in a partnership is situated in the country whose law governs the partnership agreement;
- debts are situated where the debtor resides (including from January 2013 (according to HMRC practice as stated in IHTM27079) specialty debts – ie those debts created or recorded under a deed or a debt incurred under statute; before that date HMRC treated specialty debts as being situated where the deed was physically located (as appears to be correct according to the case law – see *Gurney v Rawlins (1863)*; *Commissioner of Stamps v Hope (1891)* thus enabling such debts easily to be treated as excluded property). In its Trusts and Estates Newsletter dated December 2018 HMRC has updated its guidance on the location of specialty debts and IHTM27079 sets out the following rules. Where the debt is solely secured on land or other tangible property situated in the UK the situs of the debt will also be in the UK. HMRC considers the situs of the debt follows the genuine interest of the creditor in the secured property, not merely the personal obligation of the debtor to repay (which may be situated elsewhere, for example where the debtor is resident). Where the debt

is not secured the view of the Courts is that the situs of the debt is usually where the relevant deed or instrument evidencing the debt is found. HMRC will generally adopt this approach to unsecured specialty debts. However, it is possible to exploit this approach artificially by, for example, removing the document from the UK to avoid an IHT charge. Where the creditor and debtor are both resident in the UK but the deed evidencing the debt has been removed from the UK, it may be possible for HMRC to argue that the debt is nevertheless situated in the UK for the purposes of the IHT charge;

- bank accounts are situated at the branch where the account is kept;
- HMRC's view is that exchange tokens (cryptoassets) are located where the individual who beneficially owns them is resident. Therefore, even if the exchange tokens of a UK resident are held in a digital wallet outside the UK, they will be subject to IHT on the beneficial owner's death.

The above situs rules which apply for the purposes of IHT should not be conflated with those in TCGA 1992 ss 274–275C which apply only for the purposes of capital gains tax.

(b) Excluded property

'Excluded property' is defined in IHTA 1984 ss 6 and 48. The latter section deals with settled property and the former deals with non-settled property (ie that owned both at law and in equity by a person).

The following types of property are excluded property:

(i) Property owned by an individual domiciled outside the UK that is situated outside the UK (s 6(1)).

With effect from 6 April 2017 (F(No 2)A 2017 Sch 10 para 9), this rule is modified so that it does not apply in relation to overseas property owned by such a person (IHTA 1984 Sch A1 para 1) comprising certain shares in a close company, certain interests in partnerships and certain loans where the value of the shares, interest or loan is attributable directly or indirectly to UK residential property (IHTA 1984 Sch A1 paras 2 and 3). Consequently the charge to inheritance tax is extended to UK residential property that is held or financially supported by or through overseas structures by individuals who are domiciled outside the UK. For this purpose, residential property means UK land that consists of a dwelling, where the land includes a dwelling (to the extent that it does so as determined on a just and reasonable basis), and an interest in land that subsists under a contract for an off-plan purchase (Sch A1 para 8).

Shares in a close company and an interest in a partnership (as defined in Sch A1 paras 9 and 10 – see **explanatory note** 5) (provided it is, when counted together with the holdings or interests of connected persons, at least a 5% holding or interest) will not be excluded property where the value of the shares or partnership interest is directly or indirectly attributable to UK residential property (Sch A1, paras 2(1)–(4)). In determining the value of the shares or interest that is attributable to a UK residential property, the liabilities of the company or partnership are to be attributed to all the property it holds on a rateable basis (Sch A1, para 2(5)). This means that where a company or partnership holds a UK residential property as well as other property, any liabilities of that company or partnership will be attributed to each property in proportion to its value. It will be noted that the rule also extends to UK residential property owned indirectly through other close companies and partnerships.

The rights of a creditor under an overseas loan are not excluded property where the loan has been used by an individual, partnership or trustees to finance directly or indirectly the acquisition (maintenance or enhancement) of UK residential property or the acquisition of shares in or an interest in a close company or partnership and the acquisition (maintenance or enhancement) by that company or partnership is of UK residential property or property (eg close company shares) to which Sch A1 para 2 applies (Sch A1, paras 3(a) and 4). This exclusionary rule on loans also applies to a loan made to acquire any property which is then sold and the proceeds used to acquire UK residential property or the proceeds from such a sale are used to make (or repay) a loan to purchase UK residential property (Sch A1 para 4(2)). Furthermore, this exclusionary rule also applies to any overseas property used as security, collateral or guarantees for such loans but only up to the amount of the loan (Sch A1 para 3(b)). It will be noted that an overseas loan to a close company is not expressly mentioned but is within the scope of this rule because the creditor will be a participator of the close company and therefore the holder of an interest in the company. A loan ceases to be within these exclusionary rules where the UK residential property which the loan financed is disposed of (Sch A1 para 4(4)). An example of the operation of the new rule as it applies to loans is given in **explanatory note** 5.

Where the shares in a company, the interest in a partnership or the creditor rights of a loan (which have been described above) are sold on or after 6 April 2017, the proceeds of sale are not treated as excluded property for a two-year period starting with the date of disposal of the property concerned (Sch A1 para 5). Where the proceeds are held in a qualifying foreign currency bank account (see below), likewise the bank account is also not left out of account for IHT purposes for the same two-year period (Sch A1, para 5(2)(b)). The proceeds will become excluded property again at the end of this two-year period. The two-year rule also applies to amounts repaid on or after 6 April 2017 in respect of a loan used as described above. An example of the operation of the new two-year rule is given in **explanatory note 5**. The two-year rule does not apply if the company itself sells the property; in that case the shares immediately revert to being excluded property (see **explanatory note 5**).

It must be appreciated that on 6 April 2017 an immediate change occurs to the tax position of an individual who already owns UK residential property through an offshore structure on that date. Consider for example, Anushka who is not UK domiciled and never has been. She owns the entire share capital of a Guernsey company whose sole asset is a freehold house in Manchester, valued at £2 million. Before 6 April 2017 the shares would have been excluded property because they are not located in the UK and Anushka is not domiciled in the UK. There would not have been a charge to IHT, for example, if she had died before that date. From 6 April 2017 the shares are no longer excluded property and, were Anushka were to die after that date, the shares would have formed part of her estate and would have been valued at £2 million as the value of the shares is wholly attributable to the UK residential property. If the Guernsey company had, in addition to the house in Manchester, other, non-UK residential property assets, valued at say £1 million (so that it is valued in total at £3 million), then the value of the company's shares in Anushka's estate would still be £2 million. The shares are still excluded property in so far their value is attributable to property that is not UK residential property. If the Guernsey company owns shares in another overseas company that owns the house in Manchester, then the new rule still applies.

(ii) Settled property situated outside the UK where the settlor was domiciled outside the UK at the time the settlement was made – so called excluded property trusts (s 48(3)). In relation to transfers made on or after 22 July 2020 (the date when the Royal Assent is given to the Finance Act 2020), this rule is changed to read: 'Settled property situated outside the UK where the settlor was domiciled outside the UK at the time property became comprised in the settlement', and this change is treated as always having had effect (FA 2020 s 73(11)). Accumulated income is treated as becoming comprised in the settlement when the property from which it arose first became comprised in the settlement.

With effect from 6 April 2017, this rule is modified for trustees of an excluded property trust as it is for individuals (IHTA 1984 s 48(3) is made subject to Sch A1) so that it does not apply in relation to overseas property comprising certain shares in a close company, certain interests in partnerships and certain loans where the value of the property is attributable to UK residential property (Sch A1 paras 2 and 3). Consequently, the charge to inheritance tax is extended to UK residential property that is held or financially supported by or through overseas structures by the trustees of excluded property trusts. The same rules as apply to individuals in respect of shares in a close company and interests in partnerships, the sale proceeds of such shares and interests and creditor rights under a loan (and the repayment of such a loan), apply also to trustees of excluded property trusts.

With effect from 6 April 2017 the rule regarding excluded property trusts is further modified where in any tax year the settlor of property comprised in a settlement was a formerly domiciled resident in that year. An individual is a 'formerly domiciled resident' in relation to a tax year if he was born in the UK, his domicile of origin was in the UK, he was resident in the UK in that tax year and he was resident in the UK for at least one of the two tax years immediately preceding that tax year (s 272) (see **part (a)** of this Example). This modification means that settled property loses its excluded property status in a tax year where the individual is resident in that tax year provided he has the status of being a 'formerly domiciled resident' in the year in which he is so resident (s 48(3E)).

(iii) A holding in an authorised unit trust (AUT) and a share in an open-ended investment company (OEICs) if held:

- by an individual domiciled outside the UK (s 6(1A)), or
- in a trust made by a settlor domiciled outside the UK at the time the settlement was made (s 48(3A)). In relation to transfers made on or after 22 July 2020 (the date of Royal Assent to the Finance Act

2020), this rule is changed to read: 'in a trust made by the settlor domiciled outside the UK at the time property became comprised in the settlement', and this change is treated as always having had effect (FA 2020 s 73(11)). This rule is modified from 6 April 2017. Where the settlor of such property comprised in a settlement is not domiciled in the UK at the time the settlement was made (or property first became comprised in it as the case may be), the property is not excluded property at any time in a tax year if the settlor was a formerly domiciled resident in that year (s 48(3B)). This means that such settled property loses its excluded property status in a tax year where the individual is resident in that tax year provided he has the status of being a 'formerly domiciled resident' in the year in which he is so resident.

(iv) Reversionary interests in settled property (other than in a deemed settlement arising from a lease for life (see **explanatory note 2** and **Example C14 explanatory note 3**) (s 48(1)–(2)). The following reversionary interests are, however, not excluded property:

- where the interest has at any time been owned by the settlor of the settled property or his spouse or civil partner (but not where the settlement was made before 16 April 1976, or where the current owner acquired the interest before 10 March 1981); and
- where the interest has at any time been owned by someone who acquired it for a consideration in money or money's worth;

but even those exceptions do not apply to the extent that the settled property is situated outside the UK or comprises holdings in AUTs or OEICs, so long as the owner of the reversionary interest is domiciled outside the UK and no UK domiciled individual has owned an interest in possession which was acquired on or after 9 December 2005 for consideration in money or money's worth (s 48(3)–(3B)).

(v) A relevant decoration or award provided it has never been disposed of for a consideration in money or money's worth (s 6(1B)). In relation to transfers made on or after 3 December 2014, this provision applies to decorations or similar awards falling within one of the following six categories – those designed to be worn to denote membership of an Order specified at any time in the Order of Wear (see The Gazette, dated 11 January 2019) or an Order of a foreign country, those specified at any time in the Order of Wear, those awarded for valour or gallant conduct, those awarded for a person being or having been a member of or employed or engaged in connection with the armed forces of any country, those awarded for a person who is in or has been in or connected with the emergency services (as defined) or those awarded by any country for or in connection with public service or achievement in public life (FA 2015 s 74). Before 3 December 2014 only decorations or other awards given for valour or gallant conduct were treated as excluded property.

(vi) FOTRA securities first issued before 30 April 1996 if the owner is neither domiciled nor resident in the UK (although there are, after 9 March 2015, no longer any such securities still in existence) (s 6(2)). For FOTRA securities first issued after 29 April 1996 new conditions apply which mean that domicile is not relevant. An individual needs to be not resident in the UK in order for the security to be excluded property. From 6 April 1998 the new conditions apply to all British Government Securities, except, until 9 March 2015 when it was repaid, 3½% War Loan 1952 or later. Before 6 April 2013 references to residence were references to ordinary residence (FA 2013 Sch 44 para 114).

(vii) National savings certificates, war savings certificates, premium savings bonds, deposits with the National Savings Bank and a certified SAYE savings arrangements provided the owner is domiciled in the Channel Islands or the Isle of Man (s 6(3)). The deemed domicile provisions do not apply in the context of this provision (s 267(2)) and neither do the elective domicile provisions (s 267ZA(5)). However these holdings are not excluded property in the hands of a person domiciled further afield.

(viii) Visiting armed forces – emoluments and tangible movable property of members of visiting forces (other than British Citizens, British Overseas Territories Citizens or British Overseas Citizens or British Nationals (Overseas)) and certain staff of allied headquarters. For inheritance tax purposes, HMRC will not take periods spent on duty in the UK into account in deciding whether a transferor is resident, domiciled or deemed to be domiciled here (ss 6(4) and 155(1)).

Excluded property is, generally speaking, outside the scope of inheritance tax, because inheritance tax is not charged on a lifetime disposal of such property nor on such property passing at death (ss 3(2) and 5(1)). A charge to tax in respect of a lifetime transfer of non-excluded property can, however, be affected by excluded property, because excluded property is taken into account when measuring the value of an estate before and after a transfer of non-excluded property. Consider, for example, the case of a person who owns shares in a non-UK incorporated company in his own right, and also has a qualifying interest in possession in shares in the company under a settlement made by a non-UK domiciled settlor. If the two holdings together constitute a controlling interest, and a transfer is made of the shares held directly so that the combined holding is reduced to a minority holding, the loss to the donor's estate will be calculated by reference to the combined holding. This is because a person's estate is comprised of virtually everything that he actually owns. As a general, basic principle, nothing is excluded from a person's estate, not even his 'excluded property' (except on his death). One must not be misled by the term 'excluded property'. It is a common error to assume that excluded property is 'excluded' from a person's estate, or from the scope of the tax altogether. This is not the case. 'Excluded property' is a subset of the property in a person's estate which is afforded special treatment only when it itself is the subject-matter of a disposition.

Excluded property held in a settlement (which is not a protected settlement) at its outset can also affect the calculation of relevant property ten-yearly and exit charges that arise before 18 November 2015 (see **Example C11 explanatory notes 2** and **6**, and **Example C19**), because it is not left out of account in establishing the value of the settled property immediately after it became comprised in the settlement. With regard to points (ii), (iii) and presumably (i) (in relation to trust property invested in non-sterling bank accounts), HMRC take the view that a separate settlement is made when property is put into an existing settlement (s 44(2)). This means that even if a settlement of foreign property had been made when the settlor was not UK domiciled, foreign property derived from any further property added to the settlement at a time when the settlor was UK domiciled would not be excluded property (Tax Bulletin February 1997).

Certain other property, although not within the strict definition of 'excluded property', is also outside the scope of inheritance tax as follows:

- Works of art which are physically present in the UK on the death of a foreign owner because they have been brought into the UK solely for public exhibition, cleaning or restoration are not counted as part of his UK estate if normally kept overseas (s 5(1)(b) as amended by SI 2009/730).
- Cash options under approved annuity schemes (s 152).
- Pension payments and gratuities – certain pension payments and gratuities are treated as being paid abroad so that any amounts due in respect of them to the estate of a deceased pensioner who dies whilst domiciled abroad will be excluded property. Additionally there are special rules about pensions paid to former employees of former colonial governments: on the death of a former employee any pension or gratuity payable under the Government of India Act 1935 s 273, or an equivalent scheme under the Overseas Pensions Act 1973 s 2, is exempt from inheritance tax on the pensioner's death irrespective of his domicile (but the pension is not excluded property as such, so cannot be disposed of in lifetime without inheritance tax consequences). For these rules see s 153.
- Property passing on the death on or after 19 March 2014 of an individual who, being an 'emergency responder', died from an injury sustained, accident occurring or disease contracted or aggravated, when he was responding to 'emergency circumstances' (s 153A). Neither does inheritance tax or additional inheritance tax arise in relation to PETs and chargeable lifetime transfers (as the case may be) made within the period of seven years before the death of such a person. 'Emergency circumstances' means circumstances which are present or imminent and are causing or likely to cause the death or serious illness of or serious injury to a person or animal or the worsening of such illness or injury. Also included are such circumstances causing serious harm to the environment (including the life and health of plants and animals), serious harm to any building or other property, or a worsening of such harm. An 'emergency responder' is a member of the fire or fire and rescue services, search or rescue services, medical, ambulance or paramedical services, services for the transportation of organs, blood, medical equipment or medical personnel, a constable or person employed for police purposes, or a person employed by the government of a territory, an international organisation or a charity in connection with the provision of humanitarian assistance. In short, the provision applies to emergency service personnel and humanitarian aid workers. It does not matter whether the individual was paid or unpaid. It is HMRC's view that doctors, nurses, paramedics, ambulance drivers and others providing medical services in response to the coronavirus emergency qualify as responding to emergency circumstances as an emergency provider. Within social care, employees of publicly funded care homes and home care or those employed by a charity providing services in response to the emergency also qualify.
- Property passing on the death of an individual who, being a member of the armed forces of the Crown or a civilian subject to service discipline, died as a result of wounds inflicted, accident occurring, or disease

contracted or aggravated, on active military service against an enemy, on other service of a warlike nature, or responding to emergency circumstances (as defined above) in the course of his duties (s 154). In relation to deaths occurring on or after 19 March 2014, inheritance tax or additional inheritance tax does not arise in relation to PETs and chargeable lifetime transfers (as the case may be) made within the period of seven years before the death of such a person. The exclusion of such property from tax is very old and can be traced back to The Stamp Act 1694. In the context of the exclusion of property from IHT, death does not have to occur on the battlefield in order for the property of the individual to be left out of account. The disregard applies in respect of an individual dying at any time and at any age if the cause of death can be linked to an injury or illness contracted when acting as a member of the armed forces or a civilian subject to service discipline. The rules apply therefore where a death can be linked to injury or illness suffered many years earlier. In *Barty-King v Ministry of Defence* [1979] STC 218 the court rejected the argument that there had to be a direct causal link between a wound or injury received on active service and the death. In that case the deceased died of cancer 23 years after sustaining a wound on active service. The wound had resulted in recurrent attacks of septicaemia which lowered his resistance to cancer, accelerated his death and masked the timely diagnosis and treatment of the disease. The court held that the question to ask was whether, applying common sense, the wound caused the death. It does not have to be the only cause or a direct cause in the sense of having a direct pathological case or physiological connection. The answer depends upon the evidence available.

- Property passing on the death on or after 19 March 2014 of an individual who is a constable or service person and who died from an injury sustained or disease contracted or aggravated in circumstances where he was deliberately targeted by reason of his status as a constable or service person (s 155A). Neither does inheritance tax or additional inheritance tax arise in relation to PETs and chargeable lifetime transfers (as the case may be) made within the period of seven years before the death of such a person. A 'service person' means a person who is a member of the armed forces of the Crown or a civilian subject to service disciple. It does not matter whether the deceased was acting in the course of his duties as a constable or service person when the injury was sustained or the disease was contracted. This provision will not, however, apply where the individual's death occurs as a result of responding to emergency circumstances which would be covered under s 153A or as a result of being on active service which would be covered under s 154.
- Balances on non-sterling accounts with a bank are excluded from inheritance tax on death if they are held:
  - by an individual not domiciled or resident (or before 6 April 2013 ordinarily resident) in the UK, or
  - as settled property where such an individual has an interest in possession, if the trustees are not domiciled or resident (or before 6 April 2013 ordinarily resident) in the UK and the settlor was not domiciled in the UK when the settlement was made (s 157). In relation to transfers made on or after 22 July 2020 (the date of Royal Assent to the Finance Act 2020), this rule is changed to read: 'as settled property where such an individual has an interest in possession, if the trustees are not domiciled or resident (or before 6 April 2013 ordinarily resident) in the UK and the settlor was not domiciled in the UK when property became comprised in the settlement', and this change is treated as always having had effect (FA 2020 s 73(11)). (The interest in possession need not be a qualifying interest in possession – see **Example C3** for this purpose.)
- Following the enactment of the Taxation of Pensions Act 2014, in respect of deaths occurring after 5 April 2015, funds in a pension scheme can be passed on to a deceased's beneficiaries outside his estate for inheritance tax purposes, as a pension fund. However, if an individual withdraws his accumulated fund from the pension, it will become part of his estate and subject to inheritance tax as any other property owned directly by him.

In relation to some property, the IHT arising on that property is allowed as a credit against the IHT arising on an individual's deceased estate. In effect therefore that property is left out of account for IHT. This treatment applies in relation to deaths occurring on or after 1 January 2015 to 'qualifying payments' made at any time to an individual or his personal representatives (s 153ZA). A payment is a qualifying payment if it falls within one of the following categories:

- Payments from the ten schemes listed in Part 1 of Sch 5A (Compensation payments from defined funds) made to a person, or the personal representatives of a person who was a victim of Nazi persecution or the spouse or civil partner of such a victim. The schemes are operated by the governments of Germany, Switzerland,

Austria and the Netherlands. In particular fixed payments of €2,500 from the Child Survivor Fund established by the German government in 2015 are included in the list.

- Payments listed in Part 2 of Sch 5A (Payments of a fixed amount made from the Far Eastern Prisoners of War Ex Gratia Scheme).
- Payments listed in regulations made by the Treasury made a person, or the personal representatives of a person who was held as a prisoner of war or civilian internee during the Second World War, or the spouse or civil partner of such a person.

Persons who died before 1 January 2015 were dealt with under HMRC concession F20 which provides that ex gratia compensation payments of up to £10,000 made by the government to British survivors of Japanese imprisonment or their spouses, and various other modest amounts paid by European bodies to slave labourers and other World War 2 victims or their spouses, or payments of such compensation made to the person's personal representatives, are left out of account in calculating the value of a person's estate for inheritance tax.

Similar rules providing for an exemption from IHT apply to payments under the Windrush Compensation Scheme (in respect of deaths occurring on or after 1 January 2019), the Troubles Permanent Disability Payment Scheme (in respect of deaths occurring on or after 29 May 2020) and other payments that may be made in regulations (in respect of deaths occurring on or after the date specified in the regulations so made) (FA 2020 s 102, Sch 15). In relation to payments made under or in connection with the Windrush Compensation Scheme, the relief for does not apply to payments made after the death of the primary recipient to anyone other than the recipient's personal representatives (FA 2020 s 102, Sch 15 para 5(4)).

Overturned historical conviction compensation payments (made after 22 July 2021) and infected blood scheme compensation payments (made after 28 October 2022) are, by virtue of The Post Office Horizon Compensation and Infected Blood Compensation Payment Schemes (Tax Exemptions and Reliefs) Regulations 2023, SI 2023/184 (effective from 16 March 2023), retrospectively brought within FA 2020 Sch 15 and are effectively exempt from IHT (by reducing the tax chargeable on the value transferred by the transfer made on the person's death to zero). Overturned Historical Conviction compensation payments are made by Post Office Limited to people who have had a conviction quashed because it involved evidence from the Horizon system.

As regards the computation of inheritance tax, special rules apply in relation to the deduction of liabilities incurred in respect of excluded property and, with from 17 July 2014, balances on non-sterling accounts with a bank (see **Example A12 part (c)**).

(c) Transfers to a spouse or civil partner not domiciled in the UK

The spouse/civil partner exemption from inheritance tax is restricted to a total of the 'exemption limit':

- where the deceased/donor spouse/civil partner is domiciled in the UK, and
- the transferee spouse/civil partner is not domiciled in the UK.

The 'exemption limit' is an amount equal to the (general) nil-rate threshold in force at the time of the transfer (or death) concerned (s 18(2), (2A)). This rule applies in relation to transfers made or deaths occurring on or after 6 April 2013 (FA 2003 s 176(4)) (which restores the law in this respect to the position it was in before 9 March 1982 when the exemption limit was linked to the amount of the nil-rate threshold). For transfers made or deaths occurring before 6 April 2013 the amount of the exemption was limited to £55,000. The limit on exempt transfers addresses the risk that an individual whose domicile is outside the UK, could remove assets abroad following an exempt transfer from his UK-domiciled spouse or civil partner to escape any inheritance tax on their subsequent transfer.

For the purpose of the exemption, a person's domicile is ascertained in accordance with **part (a)** of the Example (which includes the application of the rules on deemed domicile and elective domicile).

It must be emphasised that the exemption limit is a lifetime limit as regards the transferor; it does not renew itself (although it can be used in addition to the transferor's available nil-rate band which is applied after the exemption). Therefore, if a UK domiciled spouse makes a lifetime gift to a non-UK domiciled spouse that uses up the exemption, any further gift to the same (or other) non-UK domiciled spouse will enjoy no spouse exemption and will be treated as a PET. The gift with reservation rules may be engaged in relation to the PET if the donor spouse enjoys any benefit in the property transferred (see **Example B1**).

As regards the transfer of the nil-rate band (see **Example A3**), this restriction may mean that bequests to the surviving spouse or civil partner will use up some of the nil-rate band available on the non-domiciled individual's death; but any amount unused remains available for transfer and can be claimed by the personal representatives of the surviving spouse or civil partner when they die.

For example, Mr and Mrs Hill live in the UK. Mr Hill is UK domiciled but his wife is and always has been domiciled in Fiji. Mr Hill owns a house in Cornwall which he purchased before 8 July 2015; as his wife likes the area, he decides to gift the house to her as a birthday present on 15 August 2023. The property is worth £645,000 at the time of the gift. Had Mrs Hill been UK domiciled the whole gift would have been an exempt transfer, but under s 18(2) only £325,000 of the gift is exempt and the remaining £320,000 is a potentially exempt transfer. Mr Hill will need to live for a further seven years if the gift is to become exempt from IHT. If Mr Hill were to die on 1 November 2025 (ie within seven years of having made the gift), Mrs Hill might consider at that time making an election (before 31 October 2027) to be treated as domiciled in the UK from 15 August 2023 so that the gift to her of the house in Cornwall is treated as wholly exempt resulting in her not having to pay the tax arising on the failed PET (see **part (a)** of this Example). No question arises in respect of Mr Hill's death of his being entitled to a residence nil-rate band in respect of the house as it has been the subject-matter of a lifetime gift by him.

In February 2005, Mr Cliff, who was domiciled in the UK, transferred £200,000 to Mrs Cliff, who was not domiciled in the UK. Of this transfer, £55,000 was exempt under s 18(2), and £145,000 was a potentially exempt transfer and assumed to be exempt when made. If Mr Cliff had died in July 2012 and had left all of his property to Mrs Cliff, who remained domiciled outside the UK, then, even though Mr Cliff had survived for seven years after making the transfer (so that the PET of £145,000 was exempt from tax), the limited exemption under s 18(2) had all been used and was not available in respect of the transfer of his estate to Mrs Cliff on his death. By contrast, if Mr Cliff dies in July 2023, the amount of his estate devolving on his wife that may be treated as exempt is £125,000 (that is the exemption limit in force when he dies (£325,000) less the amount transferred to Mrs Cliff in February 2005 (namely, £200,000)).

In 2012 Mr Brink transfers a UK property worth £500,000 to Mrs Brink. Both are domiciled outside the UK. Exemption under s 18(1) is available in full. In 2023/24 it is established that Mr Brink is deemed to be domiciled in the UK and in that tax year gives £100,000 to Mrs Brink who remains domiciled outside the UK. The limited exemption under s 18(2) is not then available because the amount of exemption already conferred under s 18 as a whole exceeds the exemption limit in force when the gift is made (namely £325,000). The previous transfer in 2012 is taken into account in 2023/24 even though both spouses were not UK domiciled at the time of the earlier transfer (when the inter-spouse exemption applied without limit). Mrs Brink could elect (it being after 16 July 2013) to be treated as domiciled in the UK from 6 April 2013 (see **part (a)** of this Example) so that the £100,000 gift from Mr Brink is wholly exempt (but the consequence of this is that her worldwide estate will (subject to the application of any double tax agreement – see **part (d)**) be within the charge to UK inheritance tax).

Julia, who is UK domiciled, gives her civil partner, Lauren (who is also UK domiciled), £500,000 in 2018. In 2021 Julia and Lauren have their partnership dissolved. In January 2023 Julia marries Klaudia who is not UK domiciled. Julia dies unexpectedly in December 2023 and leaves all her property to Klaudia. No spouse exemption is available on Julia's death because her lifetime, limited spouse exemption has been used in respect of the gift to Lauren five years earlier.

(d) Relief from UK inheritance tax for inheritance tax levied by overseas countries

Relief from UK inheritance tax for inheritance tax levied in overseas countries may be obtained under a double tax agreement or by way of UK unilateral relief.

The UK has a number of bilateral treaties for taxes on estates, gifts and inheritances.

For the purpose of the agreement, the treaties typically permit:

- The country in which the transferor is (or in the case of a death, was) domiciled, to tax all property wherever it is, and the other country to tax only specified types of property, such as immovable property, in its territory. The treaty in question will contain provisions to explain what is meant by 'domicile' under each country's domestic law and which is to be treated as the country of domicile for the purpose of the treaty if both countries regard the individual as domiciled there under their respective domestic laws. In this context, an election by an individual to be treated as domiciled in the UK under s 257ZA(1) is to be ignored when interpreting or applying Estate Duty Conventions and certain Double Taxation Agreements which determine the domicile of an individual (s 267ZA(6), (7)).

- Where the person is taxed in both countries there are rules for deciding which country gives credit for the other's tax. Where, exceptionally, the relief given by a treaty would be less than that given by unilateral relief, the person receives the benefit of unilateral relief.

If a transfer or estate is liable to inheritance tax and also to a similar tax imposed by another country with which the UK does not have an agreement, an individual may be able to get relief under the unilateral relief provisions (see s 159).

Credit is given against inheritance tax for the tax charged by another country on assets situated in that country. For this purpose, UK law determines the location of an asset (see the rules discussed above). If the tax that is charged on the asset by the other country exceeds the UK inheritance tax on that asset, the credit is limited to the amount of UK inheritance tax (s 159(2)).

Credit is also given where both the UK and another country impose tax on assets that are situated:

- in a third country, or
- both in the UK under UK law and in the other country under that country's law.

In these cases the credit is a proportion of the tax. The amount of the credit is computed by the formula:

$$\frac{A}{(A+B)} \times C$$

where A is the inheritance tax, B is the overseas tax and C is whichever of A or B is the smaller (s 159(3)).

If the UK and two or more other countries charge the same asset to tax – the above applies but with modifications.

Example 1

Kirsty is domiciled in Xanadu, but is also treated as domiciled in the UK. She makes a gift of property situated in Shangrila.

UK inheritance tax (A) £1,500,

Xanadu inheritance tax (B) £500,

C is the smaller of A and B £500,

The amount to be set against UK inheritance tax is:

$$\frac{£1,500}{(£1,500+£1,500)} \times £500=£375$$

Balance of UK tax due is £1,125.

Example 2

Jamie is domiciled in Shangrila but holds shares in a Xanadu company, which maintains a duplicate share register in the UK. Under UK law the shares are regarded as situated in the UK, but Xanadu law regards them as situated in Xanadu. Jamie dies (but his estate is not liable to Shangrilan tax).

UK inheritance tax (A) £500,

Xanadu inheritance tax (B) £2,000,

C is the smaller of A and B £500,

The amount to be set against UK inheritance tax is:

$$\frac{£500}{(£500+£2,000)} \times £1,000 = £200$$

Balance of UK tax due is £300.

(e) Inheritance tax payable on John's death – 4 June 2023

	Gross	*Tax on 2023/24 Scale*
Gifts within seven years before death:	£	£
Accumulation before only such gift	Nil	Nil
2 August 2018		
Gift to Natasha	758,500	
Less: marriage exemption	(2,500)	
Less:		
Annual exemption 2018/19	(3,000)	
Annual exemption 2017/18	(3,000)	
	750,000	170,000*

*(£750,000 – £325,000) = 425,000 @ 40%

Estate of John deceased

	Date of death 4 June 2023	
	£	£
Quoted investments		56,000
Cash at bank		10,000
Home in Cheshire		2,000,000
Less: spouse exemption		(325,000)
Chargeable estate		1,741,000
Cumulative transfers in seven years before death	750,000	170,000
Chargeable estate and tax thereon	1,741,000	696,400
	2,491,000	866,400**

** (£2,491,000 – £325,000) = £2,166,000 @ 40%

The total amount of inheritance tax arising on John's death is £866,400, £170,000 is payable by Natasha in respect of the lifetime gift to her on 2 August 2018 and £696,400 is payable by John's executors. It is clear that there are insufficient liquid funds in John's estate to pay the tax owed by the executors and it could be that the home in Cheshire may have to be sold to discharge the liability.

In order to reduce the tax payable in respect of John's estate, Natasha may consider making an election to be treated as domiciled in the UK.

If the election were to apply to Natasha from 4 June 2023, the date of John's death, then an inheritance tax liability of £170,000 arises as follows:

Estate of John deceased

		Date of death 4 June 2023
	£	£
Quoted investments		56,000
Cash at bank		10,000
Home in Cheshire		2,000,000
		2,066,000
Less: spouse exemption		(2,066,000)
Chargeable to inheritance tax on death		Nil
Cumulative transfers in seven years before death	750,000	170,000
Chargeable estate and tax thereon	Nil	Nil
	750,000	170,000*

* (£750,000 – £325,000) = £425,000 @ 40%

The total amount of inheritance tax payable on John's death is therefore £170,000 which, as before, is payable by Natasha. By Natasha making an election to be domiciled in the UK a saving of £696,400 of inheritance tax can be made.

However, before this advice is offered, the full effect of the election must be considered. The effect of the election is to bring Natasha's Kenyan property (which whilst she was non-UK domiciled was excluded property) within the charge to UK inheritance tax so that, in a worse-case scenario, should she die soon after John, the inheritance tax arising on her estate will be as follows (it being assumed that she has made no lifetime gifts and that she dies when the nil-rate threshold still stands at £325,000 and that the property she owns comprises her legacy from John and her Kenyan property and the property has not appreciated in value since the time of John's death):

Estate of Natasha deceased

	Date of death
	£
Quoted investments	56,000
Cash at bank	10,000
Home in Cheshire	2,000,000
Home in Kenya	2,500,000
Chargeable estate	4,566,000
Tax payable	1,696,400**

** (£4,566,000 – £325,000) = £4,241,000 @ 40%

If Natasha makes the election, the total amount of inheritance tax payable on both John's and Natasha's death is therefore £1,866,400, comprising £170,000 payable on John's death and £1,696,400 payable on Natasha's death.

However, if Natasha does not make the election to be domiciled in the UK, then her Kenyan property remains excluded property so that should she die soon after John, the inheritance tax arising on her estate will be as follows (it again being assumed that she has made no lifetime gifts and that she dies when the nil-rate threshold still stands at £325,000 and that the property she owns comprises her legacy from John and her Kenyan property and the assets have not appreciated in value since the time of John's death):

Estate of Natasha deceased

	Date of death
	£
Quoted investments	56,000
Cash at bank	10,000
Home in Cheshire	2,000,000
Chargeable estate	2,066,000
Tax payable	696,400
** (£2,066,000 – £325,000) = £1,741,000 @ 40%	

A summary of the tax payable under each scenario is as follows:

	Tax payable on John's death	*Tax payable on Natasha's death*	*Total tax payable*
	£	£	£
Without election	866,400	696,400	1,562,800
With election	170,000	1,696,400	1,866,400

An increased amount of tax of £303,600 is payable were Natasha to make an election to be treated as UK domiciled from the time of John's death. The increase is in part attributable to Natasha's Kenyan property losing its excluded property status on account of her becoming UK domiciled. On this simple basis she is best advised not to make the election. In order to fund the inheritance tax arising on John's death she may be able to take a loan secured on the Cheshire home. The loan would go to reduce the value of the home on her subsequent death, reducing the amount of inheritance tax then arising by £278,560.

However, the above advice is based on a worse-case scenario in that it has been assumed that Natasha will die very soon after John. It could very well be that Natasha is in robust good health and will move back to Kenya after John's death. Assuming she returns to Kenya before 5 April 2024 and provided she survives beyond 5 April 2028 (ie for more than 4 successive tax years after ceasing to be resident in the UK), then any election she had made to be domiciled in the UK will lapse (with no retrospective effect). If this were to be the case, the tax payable on John's death is £170,000 and her Kenyan property will again be regarded as excluded property. Should her death then supervene, she will be chargeable to UK inheritance only on her UK sited property, giving rise to a charge to tax of £696,400 subject to quick succession relief (assuming that the nil-rate band has not increased in value and that the aggregate value of the UK sited property has not appreciated in value). Without taking any further planning measures, the overall tax burden is therefore £866,400, the same position that pertained on John's death without her having made an election.

The charge to tax on her UK sited property could however be entirely avoided if that property were liquidated and the funds taken to Kenya, thereby converting the whole of that property into excluded property. In this case the tax payable on John's death would be only the £170,000 arising on the failed PET to Natasha on 2 August 2018. It would be necessary to quantify the potential capital gain arising on the sale of the property and the availability of any reliefs. With effect from 6 April 2015, non-resident persons are charged to UK tax on gains accruing on UK residential property (see **explanatory note 4**). If the above scenario could be played out, Natasha could be best advised to make the election to be treated as domiciled in the UK at the time of John's death (which, being a death election, must be made before 4 June 2025 which is after Natasha's return to Kenya).

Explanatory Notes

Overseas aspects of inheritance tax

(1) For further illustration of the overseas aspects of inheritance tax see **Example B7**. **Example B7** also illustrates excluded property held by a non-UK domiciled person. For a more detailed example on double taxation relief see **Example B8**. **Example A12(c)** discusses the inheritance tax treatment of liabilities relating to excluded property and foreign currency bank accounts.

Reversionary interest – inheritance tax treatment

(2) A 'reversionary interest' is defined in s 47 as a future interest under a settlement, whether vested or contingent. Where, for example, property is settled on A for life, then to B absolutely, B (sometimes called the remainderman) has a reversionary interest in the settled property.

If a reversionary interest in settled property has been purchased, or is owned by the settlor or the spouse or civil partner of the settlor, then it will not be excluded property (see item (iv) in **part (b)** of the Example); but from 9 December 2010 an additional anti-avoidance rule is introduced in cases where the reversionary interest is owned by such a person (relevant reversioner), whereby, if the settled property is relevant property and the reversionary interest comes to an end by reason of the relevant reversioner becoming entitled to an interest in possession in it, then the relevant reversioner is deemed to have made a disposition of the reversionary interest at that time. The resultant transfer of value cannot be a potentially exempt transfer (s 81A). It is unclear whether this rule will be interpreted as catching the more usual case where the reversionary interest does not come to an end but merely ceases to be reversionary.

For the treatment of reversionary interests see **Example C9**.

The inheritance tax position of John and Natasha

(3) For an explanation of the calculation of inheritance tax arising on an individual's death see **Examples A6** and **A8**.

The marriage exemption is available in respect of the gift John makes to Natasha on 2 August 2018 as it is made in contemplation of their marriage on 5 August 2018 (see **Example A1 explanatory note 2**). As John and Natasha are not married at the time the gift is made, the amount of the gift is not counted as part of the amount of the limited spouse exemption available where a UK domiciled spouse transfers property to his non-UK domiciled spouse (see **part (c)** of this Example). Natasha appears to have retained her Kenyan domiciled of origin despite having moved to live in the UK after her marriage to John as she intends to return to Kenya should he predecease her. She is not a 'formerly domiciled resident' as she was not born in the UK.

Although Natasha may make an election after John's death to be treated as UK domiciled from the start of 4 June 2023 (the date of his death), she cannot further backdate the election to 2 August 2018 in the hope of taking advantage of the unlimited spouse exemption (and avoiding the tax payable of £170,000) because, although an election can take effect from a time after 6 April 2013, Natasha was not married to John on 2 August 2018.

In calculating the inheritance tax payable on Natasha's death, only her nil-rate band is available to her; John has no unused nil-rate band that could be claimed by her executors (see **Example A3**).

If Natasha were to return to Kenya and liquidate her UK sited property whilst non UK resident, she may be liable to capital gains tax as there is a disposal of UK sited residential property after 5 April 2015 by a non-UK resident individual (TCGA 1992 s 1A(3)(b)). For more detail on this see the companion volume **Tolley's Taxwise I 2023/24** (**Example F2** (Non-residents) and **L8** (Private residences)).

Effect of elective domicile on inheritance tax planning

(4) The making of an election by an individual to be treated as domiciled in the UK may have both positive and negative tax outcomes and these need to be considered carefully when making an election. Whether an

individual should make an election to be domiciled in the UK will depend upon his or her personal circumstances and those of his or her spouse or civil partner.

For an instance of where an election with retrospective effect may be beneficial, see the case of Mr and Mrs Hill and Mr and Mrs Brink in **part (c)** of this Example.

An instance of where an election with retrospective effect may be less beneficial is in relation to a transfer of what would have been excluded property at the time the transfer occurred. For example, in June 2025 Imogen (who was born overseas and is not UK domiciled) settles overseas property on an overseas discretionary trust. At the time when she made the transfer no inheritance tax liability would have arisen as the property transferred would have been excluded property. If for whatever reason Imogen is entitled to and indeed makes (say in October 2027) a lifetime election to be treated as UK domiciled from a time before 2028 when she settled the trust, then her transfer to the trust will now become a chargeable transfer. Imogen has 12 months from the end of October 2027 to deliver an account of the transfer to HMRC (IHTA 1984 s 267ZB(7), (8)(a)). The transfer is also treated as having occurred when the election was made in October 2027 in order to work out the date of payment of any tax due and to work out any interest arising on unpaid tax (s 267ZB(7), (8)(b)). As a result of making the election, any overseas property in Imogen's estate when she comes to die will also be chargeable property rather than excluded property. Had Imogen not backdated the election to a time before 2025 when she settled the trust, then that transfer would not have been affected by her making the election.

As a general proposition, an election will probably be beneficial where the UK domiciled spouse or civil partner is the wealthier party in the relationship. Conversely, where most of the wealth is owned by the non-UK domiciled spouse and is held abroad, an election might not be advisable (as is illustrated by **part (e)** of this Example). The decision will never, however, be a simple one and is likely to involve a host of factors.

For example, Mr Beach who is UK domiciled and who has never made any lifetime gifts, owns UK-sited property worth £4 million. His wife, who is and always has been domiciled abroad under the common law, owns property in Hungary that is worth £2 million. None of the property owned by them entitles them to a residence nil-rate band. Mr Beach dies on 1 May 2023 leaving all of his property to his wife. The amount of inheritance tax arising on his death would be £4,000,000 – £325,000 (spouse exemption) – £325,000 (nil-rate band) = £3,350,000 × 40% = £1,340,000. Mrs Beach would inherit UK-sited property valued at £4,000,000 – £1,340,000 = £2,660,000. Assuming that Mrs Beach dies six years later on 1 May 2029 at a time when she is neither domiciled (still) in the UK under the common law nor deemed to be domiciled here, her liability to inheritance tax in respect of the UK property will be £2,660,000 – £325,000 (nil-rate band) = £2,335,000 × 40% = £934,000. The total tax payable on both deaths amounts to £2,274,000 but the property in Hungary remains outside the charge to UK inheritance tax. By contrast, if Mrs Beach had elected (by 30 April 2025 as it is a death election) to be treated as domiciled in the UK, no tax would have arisen on the death of Mr Beach and the inheritance tax arising in 2029 in respect of her own death, assuming the nil-rate band is £325,000 and that her executors make an election to transfer Mr Beach's unused nil-rate band, will be £6,000,000 – £650,000 = £5,350,000 × 40% = £2,140,000. The overall inheritance tax burden is lower for having made the election (despite Mrs Beach's Hungarian-sited property being charged to inheritance tax as a result). (In this example if Mrs Beach had not made the requisite election within two years of her husband's death, her own personal representatives could have made the election on her behalf after her death in 2029. This too is a death election and has to be made by them on or before 30 April 2031.)

What would have been the position if when she dies, Mrs Beach is deemed to be domiciled in the UK (despite still being domiciled abroad in the common law)? If no election had been made by her to be domiciled in the UK, the tax arising on her husband's death would remain at £1,340,000. The tax due in respect of her own estate (which would now include the Hungarian-sited property) would be £4,660,000 – £325,000 (nil-rate band) = £4,335,000 × 40% = £1,734,000. Thus the total tax arising in respect of both deaths is £3,074,000. It would clearly be beneficial for Mrs Beach's executors to elect for her to be domiciled in the UK. If they do so she will be UK domiciled under the election just before her husband died. This means no tax will be payable on his estate and the tax arising in respect of her death will again be £2,140,000. Presumably the tax that was paid on her husband's death of £1,340,000 will be refunded to her estate so that it passes together with the rest of her property (after the tax on her own estate has been paid) under her will or according to the law of intestacy (which would be the law of her common law domicile in respect of movable property or the law of the country in which immovable property is situated).

Part (e) of this example illustrates the case where a death election by a surviving spouse is not prima facie beneficial. However, the outcome for John and Natasha could have been improved prior to his death had Natasha taken advice on 5 December 2022 when she had acquired her Kenyan property. Had she transferred the property into an overseas trust at that time (so that the trust was an excluded property trust) the protection of the property from inheritance tax would not have been disturbed by her making an election to be treated as UK domiciled from the time of John's death on 4 June 2023. Consequently tax of £170,000 would have arisen on John's death and the tax arising on her death (in the worse-case scenario described and on the basis of the assumptions stated) would have been £696,400 (as the Kenyan property would not be counted as part of her estate despite her having made the election). The total tax payable would therefore have been £866,400 (the position she would have been in had she made the election, returned to and survived beyond 5 April 2028 still owning the UK sited property. Although a capital gain may arise on the disposal of the Kenyan property to the trust, this could be sheltered from UK tax by Natasha making a claim for the remittance basis of taxation. For more detail on the remittance basis of taxation see the companion volume **Tolley's Taxwise I 2023/24 Example F4.**

Inheritance tax excluded property status of enveloped UK dwellings and related finance

(5) **Part (b)** of this Example describes the excluded property rules. In particular, the rights of a creditor under an overseas loan are not excluded property where the loan has been used by an individual, partnership or trustees to finance the acquisition (maintenance or enhancement) of UK residential property or the acquisition of shares in or an interest in a close company or partnership and the acquisition (maintenance or enhancement) by that company or partnership is of a UK residential property (Sch A1, para 3). For example, Carlos is not domiciled in the UK. He lends £1 million to his son Ferdinand and he uses the money to purchase a £1.1 million house in Cambridge. If Carlos dies, then the value of the loan will form part of his estate for the purposes of UK IHT even if the loan is a non-UK sited asset. If Ferdinand has no other assets in the UK or elsewhere, his net estate is initially £100,000 (£1.1 million less the £1 million loan). A loan for the purposes of this rule also includes money or other assets held or otherwise made available as security, collateral or guarantee (valued at the lower of the value of the loan or the security, collateral or guarantee). So if the loan to Ferdinand has been made by a bank which had received a right over £2 million of Carlos' assets, then those assets (the collateral for the loan) is not excluded property, the taxable value of those assets is capped at £1 million, the value of the loan. If the owner of the UK property disposes of it, then the loan immediately ceases to be excluded property as would be the case were Ferdinand to sell the house which means that Carlos will no longer have an asset within the charge to UK IHT.

It was explained in the Example that overseas property comprising certain shares in a close company, certain interests in partnerships and certain loans (as just discussed) is not excluded property where the value of the shares, partnership interest or loan is attributable to UK residential property (IHTA 1984 Sch A1). Consequently, the charge to inheritance tax is extended to UK residential property that is held or financially supported by or through overseas structures by individuals (or trustees) who are domiciled outside the UK. Where such shares, interests or creditor rights (n the case of a loan) are sold (or the loan is repaid), the proceeds of sale (or amounts repaid) are not treated as excluded property for a two-year period starting with the date of disposal of the property concerned (Sch A1 para 5). For example, Alice is neither resident nor domiciled in the UK. She owns shares in an overseas close company that owns UK residential property. Those shares are not excluded property but within the charge to UK IHT. In 31 January 2023 Alice sells her shares for £1 million (their market value) and the proceeds are deposited in her Jersey bank account. She later invests the proceeds in some land in Portugal. In November 2023 she gifts the Portuguese land to her children when it is worth £1.2 million. The land is not excluded property because it is derived from the proceeds of the disposal of her shares in the overseas close company and the disposal was made less than two years before the gift. The gift is a PET valued at £1 million (before exemptions). At the end of the two-year period following the sale of the close company shares (ie from 31 January 2025), the Portuguese land becomes excluded property again; there is no IHT charge on that occasion. It will be noted that, as explained in the preceding paragraph) this rule does not apply where the UK land itself is sold and the loan repaid.

In the context of the above rules, a company is a close company if it is defined as such for the purposes of Corporation Tax (or would be so defined if UK resident), namely a company under the control of five or fewer participators or any number of its directors who are also participators. A participator is as defined in CTA 2010 s 454 and broadly speaking comprises a company's shareholders and loan creditors (IHTA 1984 Sch A1 para 9). Similarly, for the purposes of the above rules a partnership means an 1890 partnership, a 1907 limited partnership, an LLP or a firm or entity of a similar character to such entities formed under the law of an overseas country or territory (Sch A1 para 10).

There was a short-term transitional rule for chargeable events affected by these new measures. The relevant date for the delivery of an IHT account (see **Example A23**) and the due date for interest (see **Example A7**) will be the later of the statutory date and the end of the month following the Royal Assent to F(No 2)A 2017. Royal Assent was given to that Act on 16 November 2017, so that if there was a chargeable event after 5 April 2017 or in May 2017 and the due date for payment of inheritance tax was 31 October 2017 or 30 November 2017, then the due date was extended to 31 December 2017 (F(No 2)A 2017 Sch 10 paras 10 and 11).

From 6 April 2017 there is a new targeted anti-avoidance rule for arrangements entered into for the sole or main purpose of avoiding or minimising the effect of the modified rules on excluded property (Sch A1 para 6). Furthermore nothing in any double tax treaty will prevent a person from being liable for IHT under the new measures where no tax similar to IHT is charged in the overseas jurisdiction or there is such a tax but its effective rate is 0% (Sch A1 para 7).

Question

Mr C T Tax made the following lifetime gifts:

20 November 2016	£327,000 to a discretionary trust
11 January 2018	£53,000 to his sister, Ann
3 May 2020	£86,000 to his daughter, Joan
4 April 2021	£90,000 to his son, Ben

Mr C T Tax died on 2 April 2024 leaving an estate of £640,000 equally to Ben and Joan. He had lived in rented accommodation all his life and so did not own a home at the time of his death.

(i) Compute the tax payable by reason of the death of Mr C T Tax.

(ii) Would the tax payable be different if Mr C T Tax had not made gifts to his children in 2020 and 2021 totalling £176,000 but had left an estate of £816,000 instead of £640,000?

(iii) Show the tax payable in lifetime and on death if the circumstances were as in (i) except that instead of giving £90,000 to Ben on 4 April 2020, Mr C T Tax transferred £90,000 to a discretionary trust (the trustees paying the tax) on:

(a) 4 March 2021; or

(b) 6 April 2022.

Answer

(i) Inheritance tax position of Mr C T Tax

Tax payable in lifetime

			£	£
20 Nov 2016	gift to discretionary trust			327,000
	Less: Annual exemptions	2016/17	3,000	
		2015/16	3,000	(6,000)
	Chargeable transfer			321,000
	Tax payable by trustees (on 2016/17 scale)			
	321,000 is within the nil-rate band of £325,000		Nil	
11 Jan 2018	gift to Ann			53,000
	Less: Annual exemption	2017/18		(3,000)
	Potentially exempt transfer			50,000
3 May 2020	gift to Joan			86,000
	Less: Annual exemptions	2020/21	3,000	
		2019/20	3,000	(6,000)
	Potentially exempt transfer			80,000
4 April 2021	gift to Ben — potentially exempt transfer			90,000

On death of Mr C T Tax 2 April 2024 the transfers made since 3 April 2017 (which were potentially exempt transfers) now become chargeable transfers:

	Gross £	*Tax on 2023/24 scale* £
Cumulative transfers in seven years before gifts to Ann, Joan and Ben		
20 November 2016 — discretionary trust	321,000	Nil
11 January 2018 — gift to Ann	50,000	18,400*
	371,000	18,400*
(* 371,000 – 325,000 = 46,000 @ 40%)		
3 May 2020 — gift to Joan	80,000	32,000
	451,000	50,400**
(** 451,000 – 325,000 = 126,000 @ 40%)		
4 April 2021 — gift to Ben	90,000	36,000
	541,000	86,400***
(*** 541,000 – 325,000 = 216,000 @ 40%)		
20 November 2023		
Deduct transfer made more than seven years previously (ie prior to 21 November 2016)	(321,000)	
Cumulative transfers in seven years before death (ie 3 April 2017 to 2 April 2024)	222,000	Nil
Estate chargeable on death	640,000	214,000****
	860,000	214,000****

(**** 860,000 – 325,000 = 535,000 @ 40%)

	£
Inheritance tax payable:	
By Ann on gift made 11 January 2018: As gift is made more than 6 but not more than 7 years before death tax payable is 20% × 18,400	3,680
By Joan on gift made 3 May 2020:	
As gift is made more than 3 but not more than 4 years before death tax payable is 80% × £32,000 =	25,600
By Ben on gift made 4 April 2021:	
As gift is within 3 years of death there is no reduction in the tax payable	36,000
By Estate	214,000
Tax payable by reason of death of Mr C T Tax	279,280

(ii) If no lifetime gifts made to children — position on death of Mr C T Tax 2 April 2024

	Gross £	*Tax* £
Cumulative transfers in seven years before death		
(ie 3 April 2017 – 2 April 2024)		
11 January 2018	50,000	Nil
Estate chargeable on death	816,000	216,400*
	866,000	216,400*
(* 866,000 – 325,000 = 541,000 @ 40%)		
Tax with gifts to children (**part (i)**)		279,280
Less: Tax without gifts to children — estate	216,400	
Tax on gift to Ann — as above	3,680	(220,080)
Reduction in tax if lifetime gifts to children are not made		£59,200

(iii) Inheritance tax position of Mr C T Tax with gift to discretionary trust instead of to Ben

(a) *Gift to discretionary trust on 4 March 2021*

Tax payable in lifetime

		Gross £	*Tax on 2016/17 scale* £
20 November 2016 —	chargeable transfer	321,000	Nil
11 January 2018 and 3 May 2020 —	potentially exempt transfers valued at £50,000 and £80,000 as before		

			Tax on 2020/21 Scale
			£
Cumulative transfers before gift to discretionary trust on 4 March 2021		321,000	Nil
4 March 2021 —	gift to discretionary trust	90,000	17,200*
		411,000	17,200*

(* 411,000 – 325,000 = 86,000 @ 20%)
Tax payable by trustees £17,200

On death of Mr C T Tax 2 April 2024

		Gross	*Tax (using rates at 2 April 2024)*
		£	£
Cumulative transfers in seven years prior to gift to Ann		321,000	Nil
11 January 2018 —	gift to Ann	50,000	18,400*
		371,000	18,400*
(* 371,000 – 325,000 = 46,000 @ 40%)			
3 May 2020 —	gift to Joan	80,000	32,000
		451,000	50,400**
(** 451,000 – 325,000 = 126,000 @ 40%)			
4 March 2021 —	gift to discretionary trust	90,000	36,000
		541,000	86,400***
(*** 541,000 – 325,000 = 216,000 @ 40%)			
20 November 2023			
Deduct transfer made more than seven years previously		(321,000)	
		220,000	Nil
Estate chargeable on death		640,000	214,000****
		860,000	214,000****
(**** 860,000 – 325,000 = 535,000 @ 40%)			
Inheritance tax payable by Ann on gift made 11 January 2018 20% × 18,400 (taper relief as before)			3,680
Inheritance tax payable by Joan on gift made 3 May 2020 80% × £32,000 (taper relief as before)			25,600
Additional inheritance tax payable by trustees — as gift is made more than 3 but not more than 4 years before death tax payable is 80% × 36,000:		28,800	
	Less: paid in lifetime	(17,200)	11,600
Tax on estate			214,000
Tax payable by reason of the death of Mr C T Tax			£254,880

(b) *Gift to discretionary trust on 6 April 2022*

Tax payable in lifetime

			Gross £	Tax on 2016/17 scale £
20 November 2016 —	chargeable transfer as before		321,000	Nil
11 January 2018 and 3 May 2020 —	potentially exempt transfers valued at £50,000 and £80,000 as before			
Cumulative transfers before gift to discretionary trust on 6 April 2022 (c/f)			321,000	Nil

			Gross £	Tax on 2022/23 scale £
Cumulative transfers before gift to discretionary trust on 6 April 2022 (b/f)			321,000	Nil
6 April 2022 — gift to discretionary trust		90,000		
Less: Annual exemptions	2022/23	(3,000)		
	2021/22	(3,000)	84,000	16,000*
			405,000	16,000*

(* 405,000 – 325,000 (using 2022/23 scale) = 80,000 @ 20%)
Tax payable by trustees £16,000

On death of Mr C T Tax 2 April 2024

	Gross £	Tax on 2023/24 scale £
Cumulative transfers in seven years prior to gift to Ann (as above)	321,000	Nil
11 January 2018 — gift to Ann	50,000	18,400*
	371,000	18,400*
(* 371,000 – 325,000 = 46,000 @ 40%)		
3 May 2020 — gift to Joan	80,000	32,000
	451,000	50,400**
(** 451,000 – 325,000 = 126,000 @ 40%)		
6 April 2022 — gift to discretionary settlement	84,000	33,600
	535,000	84,000***
(*** 535,000 – 325,000 = 210,000 @ 40%)		
20 November 2023		
Deduct transfer more than seven years previously (ie prior to 21 November 2016)	(321,000)	
Cumulative transfers in seven years before death	214,000	–

		Gross £	Tax on 2023/24 scale £
Estate chargeable on death		640,000	211,600****
		854,000	211,600****
(**** 854,000 – 325,000 = 529,000 @ 40%)			
Inheritance tax payable by Ann on gift made 11 January 2018 20% × 18,400 (taper relief as before)			3,680
Inheritance tax payable by Joan on gift made 3 May 2020 80% × £32,000 (taper relief as before)			25,600
Additional inheritance tax payable by trustees on gift made 6 April 2022 (no taper relief because within 3 years before death):			
Tax on death scale	33,600		
Less: paid in lifetime	(16,000)		17,600
Tax payable by estate			211,600
Tax payable by reason of death of Mr C T Tax			£258,480

The tax payable on the estate plus the additional tax payable on the gifts made within seven years before death in each of the four scenarios is:

(i)	(ii)	(iii)(a)	(iii)(b)
£279,280	£220,080	£254,880	£258,480

The reduction of £59,200 in the total tax payable in (ii) as compared with (i) is due to the tax saved because there have been no gifts to the children, as reduced by the extra tax payable because of the increased value of the estate. Also see **explanatory note 6.**

Tax saved because no gifts to children (25,600 + 36,000)	61,600
Less: additional tax payable on estate (216,400 – 214,000)	(2,400)
Difference in tax payable as between (i) and (ii)	£59,200

The reduction of £24,400 in the total tax payable on death in (iii)(a) as compared with (i) is due to the gift to the discretionary trust of £90,000 on 4 March 2021 (in place of the gift to Ben on 4 April 2021 taking place a month later). As such it is made more than three but less than four years before death (which was not the case in respect of the gift to Ben) and hence the tax payable is reduced by taper relief:

Additional tax on gift to Ben	36,000
Less: additional tax on gift to discretionary trust	(11,600)
Difference in tax payable as between (i) and (iii)(a)	£24,400

As regards the transfers in (iii)(a), this represents the taper reduction of £7,200 (36,000 × 20%), plus the reduction attributable to the tax paid on the lifetime transfer of £17,200 (ie £7,200 + £17,200) = £24,400).

The increase of £3,600 in the tax payable in (iii)(b) as compared with (iii)(a) is due to a number of factors. A summary of the tax payable under each scenario is as follows:

	(a)	(b)	Difference
	£	£	
Ann	3,680	3,680	Nil
Joan	25,600	25,600	Nil
Trustees	28,800	33,600	4,800
Estate	214,000	211,600	(2,400)
Total tax payable	272,080	274,480	2,400
Less: Paid in lifetime by trustees	(17,200)	(16,000)	1,200
Due on death	254,880	258,480	3,600

The lower amount of lifetime tax paid in (iii)(b) of £1,200 is because of the availability of the 2021/22 and 2022/23 annual exemptions representing a tax saving of £6,000 × 20% = £1,200.

The reduction of £2,400 in the estate charge in (iii)(b) is because the cumulative lifetime transfers in that scenario are lower by £6,000 by reason of the availability of the 2021/22 and 2022/23 annual exemptions, representing a tax saving of £6,000 × 40% = £2,400.

In summary, therefore, the increase in the tax payable of £3,600 in (iii)(b) arises because of the following in relation to that scenario:

Increase in tax due to loss of taper relief on transfer to trust, (since gift in (iii)(b) now less than three years before death)	4,800
Increase in tax on death due to the lower amount of tax paid on the lifetime transfer in (iii)(b) (17,200 – 16,000)	1,200
	6,000
Less: reduction in estate charge (214,000 – 211,600)	(2,400)
	£3,600

It can be seen, therefore, that the inheritance tax liability can vary depending on the timing of lifetime gifts. C T Tax has made transfers of the same values in each of the **Examples** (i), (iii)(a) and (iii)(b), but total tax payable in respect of them is different in each case.

Explanatory Notes

Inheritance tax: potentially exempt transfers to sister and children

(1) As the transfers to the sister and to the children are gifts by one individual to another they are potentially exempt transfers, and are valued after deducting available annual exemptions from the earliest gift in any tax year. No tax is payable at the time the gifts are made because they are treated for the time being as exempt transfers (s 3A(5)). See **Example A1** for a discussion of the meaning of a potentially exempt transfer.

Inheritance tax liability arising on death

(2) On the death of Mr C T Tax a liability arises both on his estate at death and also on transfers made within seven years before his death.

The additional charge to tax on lifetime chargeable transfers is calculated using the rates in force on the date of death. Any tax paid on a gift during lifetime will be set off against the additional tax due in respect of that transfer on death. However, if the tax already paid exceeds that now due no refund will arise. Any additional tax due as a result of the death is payable primarily by the donee (see **Example A6**).

Transfers which were potentially exempt in lifetime become chargeable if the donor dies within seven years after the lifetime transfer. Each is chargeable on its value when made, but at the rates in force at the time of death (but only if this is lower than the rates in force at the date of the gift).

Inheritance tax: taper relief on lifetime transfers

(3) Where the period between a gift (whether chargeable or a potentially exempt transfer) and death exceeds three years, then the tax calculated at the time of death is reduced as follows:

Years between transfer and death	*Percentage reduction*	*Percentage of full rate tax due*
3+ to 4	20	80
4+ to 5	40	60
5+ to 6	60	40
6+ to 7	80	20

Thus, in **part** (i) of the Example the taxable payable on the gift to Ann will attract an 80% reduction as the gift is made more than six but less than seven years before the donor's death. The tax payable on the gift to Joan will attract a 20% reduction as the gift was more than three but less than four years before the donor's death. The tax payable on the gift to Ben will attract no reduction as his gift was within three years of the donor's death.

Calculating inheritance tax on potentially exempt transfers that become chargeable

(4) When computing the tax on potentially exempt transfers which have become chargeable it is necessary to take into account other *chargeable* transfers made within *seven years before those potentially exempt transfers* even though those earlier chargeable transfers themselves may not be subject to any additional tax on death because they were made more than seven years before the donor's death. Thus when computing the tax on the gifts in January 2018, May 2020 and April 2021 the cumulative chargeable transfers include the gift into settlement in November 2016. However, when computing the tax due on the death estate, the November 2016 chargeable transfer is excluded since it was made more than seven years prior to the donor's death. The November 2016 transfer (had it been of sufficient amount) is not subject to the additional charge to tax because Mr C T Tax survived making it by seven years.

Inheritance tax: use of annual exemption in relation to chargeable/potentially exempt transfers

(5) **Part (iii)** of the Example illustrates the application of the provisions relating to the annual exemption where there are both chargeable lifetime transfers and potentially exempt transfers within the same year. The detailed notes are in **Example A1**. The annual exemption is given against transfers in strict chronological order. Thus the gift to Joan on 3 May 2020 (which is otherwise potentially exempt) takes the benefit of the annual exemptions (even though no tax will be payable in respect of it if C T Tax survives for more than seven years of making it). No exemptions are accordingly available to reduce the chargeable lifetime transfer on 4 March 2021 in **part** (iii)(a) and tax of £17,200 is immediately payable by the trustees. By contrast, if the gifts in (iii)(a) to Joan on 3 May 2020 and to the discretionary trust on 4 March 2021 had occurred in reverse order then the annual exemptions of 2019/20 and 2020/21 totalling £6,000 would reduce the value of the chargeable transfer to the trust to £84,000 and the tax immediately payable to £16,000. This benefit would have been retained if C T Tax had lived for more than seven years of making the gifts in that order. In the Example death occurs within that period so that the annual exemptions reduce the value of the transfer on which Joan is chargeable and so have not been wasted by being used against a potentially exempt transfer that never becomes chargeable.

Inheritance tax calculation: cumulation with earlier chargeable transfers

(6) It is not always appreciated that making gifts within seven years before death rather than leaving a correspondingly greater amount at death can *increase* the overall tax liability. This occurs because of the need, in calculating the additional tax payable on a gift when the donor dies, to include *chargeable* transfers made within the seven years before the gift. (Potentially exempt transfers are never taken into account in these circumstances unless the donor dies within seven years after making them, in which case they become chargeable transfers.) Thus a period of up to fourteen years might need to be taken into account to calculate the inheritance tax liability arising on a death in respect of lifetime gifts. By contrast, the earlier transfers (ie

those made in years 8–14 before death) are eliminated after seven years and are therefore never included in calculating the liability on the estate itself. The additional charge on lifetime gifts is often mitigated by the taper relief provisions set out at **note 3** above and the amount chargeable is reduced by use of lifetime exemptions. However, as shown in **parts (i)** and **(ii)** of this Example, those reductions are often insufficient to mitigate against the effect of having to include the gifts made in years 8–14 before death. In the context of this Example, the additional tax payable by reason of the lifetime transfers to the children in **part (i)** is as follows:

	£
Additional tax payable on lifetime gifts to Joan and Ben (£80,000 + £90,000) × 40%	68,000
Less: reduction of additional tax by benefit of taper relief on gift to Joan (£32,000 – £25,600)	(6,400)
Less: reduction of tax payable on estate because of reduction in amount of gifts cumulated with the estate (6,000 × 40%)	(2,400)
Additional tax liability in **Example (i)**	£59,200

The additional tax payable on lifetime transfers to Joan and Ben is calculated wholly at 40% because the gifts of £321,000 and £50,000 on 20 November 2016 and 11 January 2018 (totalling £371,000) which are cumulated with the gifts to Joan and Ben together exceed the nil-rate band of £325,000 and so no part of the gifts to Joan and Ben is taxed at 0%.

The reduction in the amount of the gifts to be cumulated with the estate is attributable to the 2020/21 and 2019/20 annual exemptions of £6,000 that reduce the value of the gift to Joan.

This problem only arises when gifts that were chargeable in lifetime are taken into account in calculating the tax on potentially exempt transfers that become chargeable on the donor's death. If, for example, C T Tax's transfer on 20 November 2016 had been a potentially exempt transfer, the transfers to Ann, Joan and Ben would still have become chargeable transfers, but the potentially exempt transfer on 20 November 2016 made more than seven years before C T Tax's death, would then have been totally exempt and would not have entered into the cumulative total taken into account in charging these later gifts.

Taken on its own, this factor might suggest that, when planning lifetime gifts that include both potentially exempt transfers and immediately chargeable transfers, the potentially exempt transfers should be made first. However, if the immediately chargeable transfers involve (as they usually will) putting property into a relevant property trust, there is another factor which points in the opposite direction, possibly more strongly. This is that, if the donor dies within seven years after the potentially exempt transfers, and they have been made before the gift into trust, the permanent cumulative total that will affect inheritance tax charges under the relevant property regime for the whole life of the trust will be increased by the amount of the potentially exempt transfers that have thus become chargeable. So the normal rule of thumb will be to make chargeable transfers before potentially exempt transfers (see **Example C11 explanatory note 8**). The problem highlighted in this Example will for this reason be more relevant to the planning of gifts when a chargeable lifetime transfer has been made some time ago but not yet quite seven years ago: in those circumstances there may well be good reason to defer any sizeable potentially exempt transfers until the previous chargeable transfer has dropped out of cumulation altogether, ie until more than seven years have passed since it was made.

Interaction of inheritance tax with capital gains tax

(7) Where a gift is made of a chargeable asset for capital gains tax purposes, that tax needs to be considered in addition to inheritance tax. Capital gains tax is not payable on death, and the base values of the deceased's assets are automatically uplifted to their market value at the date of his death (TCGA 1992 s 62). The market value of an asset is the price which it might reasonably be expected to fetch on a sale in the open market (s 272(1)). However, where the value of an asset has been *ascertained* at the time of a person's death for the purposes of charging inheritance tax on his death estate, the value so ascertained is taken as the market value of the asset at the date of the person's death (s 274). Thus if an IHT value has been ascertained for an asset and it is higher than its open market value (as defined in s 272), then that higher amount will be taken as the base cost of the asset in the hands of the person on whom the asset devolves (see **Example A26 explanatory note 1** for a more detailed explanation). If an election has been made in respect of an asset to avoid a pre-owned asset income tax charge then the asset is included within the estate at death for inheritance tax. However, that election does not apply for capital gains tax, and the value of the asset concerned will continue to be its value at the time of transfer (normally open market value at date of original gift) (s 18; see

Example B4 explanatory note 13). Similarly, if a gift with reservation falls to be charged to inheritance tax on death, its base cost for capital gains tax purposes will be its value at the date of the gift.

On gifts made in lifetime, capital gains tax may be payable unless the gain is deferred under the gifts holdover relief provisions – either the business gifts relief of s 165 or the relief under s 260 for gifts that are *immediately* liable to inheritance tax (such as gifts to relevant property trusts). Consequently, capital gains tax may be paid on a potentially exempt transfer, and if the donor dies within seven years the gift will also be liable to inheritance tax (unless covered by reliefs or exemptions). There is no direct relief against inheritance tax for the capital gains tax paid, although the donor's chargeable estate at death will have been reduced by the capital gains tax paid or owing.

If the capital gains tax gifts holdover relief *is* available, and the potentially exempt transfer becomes liable to inheritance tax, any inheritance tax payable is deducted in computing the donee's gain when he eventually disposes of the asset (s 165(10)). The same rule applies in relation to the inheritance tax on a gift to which capital gains holdover relief under s 260 applied because the gift was immediately chargeable to inheritance tax (s 260(7)). The inheritance tax taken into account in each case to reduce the capital gain is the amount finally payable, after any adjustments following death.

For detailed coverage on capital gains tax see the companion to this book, **Tolley's Taxwise I 2023/24.**

Question

(a) When is inheritance tax due to be paid:

(i) on chargeable lifetime transfers?

(ii) when it arises because of death?

(b) Who is accountable for the inheritance tax arising on:

(i) chargeable lifetime transfers?

(ii) potentially exempt transfers which become chargeable at death?

(iii) the estate at death?

(iv) settled property in which the deceased enjoyed a life interest?

(c) What penalties can be charged for incorrect returns and understatement of IHT due, late filing, and late payment?

(d) What are the time limits for making assessments and claims?

Answer

(a) Due date of payment of inheritance tax

Payment of inheritance tax may sometimes be made by instalments, but otherwise the due date is as follows (IHTA 1984 s 226):

(i)	Lifetime chargeable transfers between 6 April and 30 September	30 April in following year
	Lifetime chargeable transfers between 1 October and 5 April	6 months after end of month in which transfer was made
(ii)	Death, including tax on what were previously potentially exempt transfers and additional tax on chargeable lifetime transfers	6 months after end of month in which death occurred

The personal representatives must, however, pay any tax for which they are liable when they deliver their account in connection with their application for a grant of probate or administration, even if this is earlier than the due date shown above. This will be before they have access to the funds. However certain financial institutions may be prepared to release the funds of the deceased before probate is granted by way of an electronic transfer to HMRC against an inheritance tax reference (see **explanatory note 13**).

The same rules apply to charges in relation to settled property other than on the death of a beneficiary with a qualifying interest in possession, which count as chargeable transfers under s 2(3).

Interest on unpaid inheritance tax has changed may times recently following the changes made by the Bank of England. A table of rates is set out in **explanatory note 1**.

(b) Liability for payment of inheritance tax

(i) *Chargeable lifetime transfers*

On chargeable lifetime transfers of property not already comprised in a settlement, primary liability for payment of tax rests with the *donor* except in the case of any extra tax payable on death which is primarily the responsibility of the *donee*. The personal representatives are only liable if the additional tax exceeds the value of the asset in the hands of the recipient, or if the tax is not paid by the recipient (s 204).

The donor and donee may, however, agree between them who is to pay the tax, and if the donor is to pay the tax the transfer has to be grossed up, because the extent to which the donor's estate is depleted is the transfer to the donee plus the tax paid (see **Example A8**). If the donee pays the tax grossing up is not necessary.

Grossing up does not apply on a potentially exempt transfer since tax is not payable in the donor's lifetime.

A return for inheritance tax because of a chargeable transfer in lifetime has to indicate who is to pay the tax.

In the case of lifetime transfers of property comprised in a settlement, the primary liability is that of the trustees.

(ii) *Potentially exempt transfers which become chargeable*

The liability on potentially exempt transfers which become chargeable at death is primarily that of the donees. The donee is also primarily responsible where property subject to reservation of an interest by the deceased becomes liable to tax on death.

(iii) *Estate at death*

The personal representatives are liable to pay the tax on property which is not immediately before death included in a settlement, or owned jointly by the deceased and others as joint tenants (usually called the 'free estate'). It is no defence to this obligation that the personal representatives have distributed the estate to a beneficiary who has undertaken to pay the estate's taxes (and who fails to do so) (Harris as Personal Representative of *Helena McDonald (deceased) v HMRC* [2018] UKFTT 204).

They are also liable to pay the tax on UK land which is included in a settlement but which devolves on them in their capacity as personal representatives.

In England and Wales this is limited to settlements governed by the Settled Land Act 1925 when the settlement comes to an end on the death of the tenant for life.

Property owned by the deceased and others as joint tenants is not dealt with by the personal representatives because it becomes the property of the other owner(s) and any tax attributable to the value of that property is payable by the person(s) in whom it is vested (s 200(1)(c)).

See **explanatory note 10** as to who bears the tax.

(iv) *Settled property in which deceased had interest in possession*

In all cases of inheritance tax charges on settled property other than the special situation in (iii) above, the liability rests with the trustees of the settlement. Whether an inheritance tax charge arises on the death of the interest in possession beneficiary, however, depends on whether:

- his interest is a qualifying interest in possession (see **Example C3**), in which case the trust fund will be aggregated with his estate and charged on his death; or
- the trust fund is relevant property, in which case an exit charge under s 65 will only arise if the death brings the settlement to an end or (exceptionally) an interest in possession arises for a person who was a disabled person when the property was originally settled (see **Example C10** and **Example C11**, and again **Example C3**); or
- the trust fund is within the age 18-to-25 trusts regime (s 71D) and the beneficiary is over age 18 (but by definition under age 25), in which case there is an exit charge under s 71E; or
- the beneficiary had an interest in possession despite being still under age 18 and the trust fund is (wholly exceptionally) within the bereaved minors' trusts regime (s 71A), the age 18-to-25 trusts regime (s 71D) or the much-restricted A & M trusts regime for pre-2006 A & M trusts (s 71), in which case no charge will arise.

Other persons liable for payment

In addition to the persons mentioned above, certain other people may be liable to pay inheritance tax in respect of a lifetime transfer, but usually only where tax remains unpaid after the due date.

This is because of s 199, which is headed 'Dispositions by transferor' and imposes a liability on:

(1) The transferor.

(2) Any person whose estate is increased by the transfer.

(3) In respect of tax attributable to the value of any property, any person in whom the property is vested, whether beneficially or otherwise, at any time after the transfer or who is beneficially entitled to an interest in possession in the property.

(4) Where property has become settled property, any person for whose benefit any of the property or income from it is applied.

Where more than one person is liable for the same tax then each of them may be called upon for the whole amount (s 205).

Section 199 poses a problem for personal representatives, because the deceased's estate is liable for tax on potentially exempt transfers in the seven years before death (even though the liability would not arise if the tax was paid, as it ought to be, by the donee), and the personal representatives may not be able to trace all such transfers. HMRC have, however, stated that they would not usually pursue the personal representatives for any such unpaid tax if, after making full enquiries and doing all in their power to disclose all lifetime transfers to HMRC, the personal representatives had obtained a certificate of discharge and distributed the estate before a chargeable lifetime transfer came to light (see IHTM30044).

Similarly wide extensions to liability, mirroring broadly **points** (3) and (4) above, are contained in s 200 relating to a person's estate on death and s 201 relating to other charges on settled property.

(c) Penalties

Penalties for errors

Any person(s) for inheritance tax purposes who understates their tax liability, whether deliberately or by failing to take reasonable care in completing returns, will be subject to the penalty regime introduced in FA 2008 ss 122, 123 and Sch 40. This legislation extended the provisions enacted in FA 2007 Sch 24. The penalty will be determined by the amount of tax understated, the nature of the behaviour giving rise to the understatement and the extent of disclosure by the taxpayer.

Penalties for failure to notify have effect for failure to meet notification obligations that arise on or after 1 April 2009.

For incorrect returns, the rules apply for return periods which commenced on or after 1 April 2009 where the return filing date is on or after 1 April 2010.

HMRC have now set out their guidance on the above provisions. There is now one penalty regime for inaccuracies in tax returns and other tax documents for most taxes. Consequently, if the liable person takes 'reasonable care' they will not suffer a penalty, even if they do make a mistake. Finance Act 2008 Sch 40 contained provisions to extend this regime to inheritance tax.

The commencement order for Sch 40 has been published and the revised penalty regime applies to inheritance tax for all chargeable events that occur on or after 1 April 2009. The provisions of IHTA 1984 ss 247(1) and (2) will continue to apply to events before that date.

So, for events on or after this date, the liable person(s) may be charged a penalty if they do not take 'reasonable care' in preparing their inheritance tax account or excepted estate return. There may also be a penalty if the liable person(s) subsequently discovers an inaccuracy but does not take reasonable steps to notify HMRC.

The test is now of 'reasonable care' rather than 'negligence'. HMRC considers the personal representatives will have taken reasonable care where they:

- follow the guidance provided about filling in forms such as the IHT400 and IHT205/207/C5;
- make suitable enquiries of asset holders and other people (as suggested in the guidance) to establish the extent of the deceased's estate;
- ensure correct instructions are given to valuers when valuing assets;
- seek advice about anything they are unsure of;
- follow up inconsistencies in information they receive from asset holders, valuers and other people;
- identify any estimated values included on the form.

Where the personal representatives leave all this in the hands of an agent, HMRC expects them to check through the form before signing it and to question anything that does not accord with what they know about the deceased. Simply signing an account completed by an agent is not taking reasonable care.

Where inheritance tax is payable other than on death, HMRC expects the transferor (or trustees) to deliver a full and complete return of the transaction concerned, and to have sought professional advice as necessary. Again, simply signing an account completed by an agent is not taking reasonable care.

The penalty regime identifies three levels of behaviour that give rise to an inaccuracy in an account or return that may give rise to a penalty. These behaviours are:

- careless;
- deliberate;
- deliberate and concealed.

The less serious the reason for the inaccuracy, the smaller the penalty.

In addition, HMRC will have regard to the nature of disclosure of the inaccuracy – whether it was prompted or unprompted. The legislation sets out a minimum penalty for each combination of behaviours.

Behaviour	*Disclosure*	*Minimum penalty*	*Maximum penalty*
Careless	Unprompted	0%	30%
	Prompted	15%	30%
Deliberate	Unprompted	20%	70%
	Prompted	35%	70%
Deliberate and concealed	Unprompted	30%	100%
	Prompted	50%	100%

FA 2015 Sch 20 increases the amount of the penalties where errors relate to offshore matters and offshore transfers, including inaccurate returns involving an omitted offshore asset or offshore transfer; the legislation takes effect in relation to errors in documents relating to transfers of value made on or after 1 April 2016 (Finance Act 2015, Schedule 20 (Appointed Days) Order 2016 SI 2016/456, art 3). The above penalties are increased by either 0%, 50% or 100% (depending on the territory concerned). Statutory limits for reductions for disclosure are increased by the same percentages. From 1 April 2017, the offshore penalty regime also applies to domestic offences where the proceeds are hidden offshore. From a date to be appointed the territory classification system will be updated to reflect the countries that adopt the new global standard of automatic tax information exchange and there will be four levels of penalty instead of three.

There is the potential for a penalty to be charged where a document given to HMRC contains an inaccuracy in connection with a deduction, exemption or relief taken against the estate or transfer. This includes the information given on the relevant supplementary pages to the account and makes explicit what was implicit in the inheritance tax legislation.

The legislation also permits a penalty to be charged where an inaccuracy in the liable person's document was attributable to another person. The penalty is 100% of potential lost revenue but is subject to reduction for disclosure as set out above. This is particularly relevant to inheritance tax where the personal representatives will inevitably be relying on other people to provide them with information about the deceased's estate. Such a penalty was levied on the beneficiary of a deceased estate in *Hutchings v HMRC* [2015] UKFTT 9 where he had deliberately and intentionally failed to declare that he had received a lifetime gift within the period of seven years before the deceased's death both at a meeting with the executors (where the question was put) and in response to a subsequent letter sent by them to the beneficiaries. The result of not giving the information was that the executors submitted an inaccurate IHT account resulting in an underpayment of tax. HMRC did not charge the executors a penalty as the evidence showed that the incorrect return was not due to a careless or deliberate error on their part (the blame fell on the beneficiary who had deliberately failed to provide the required information).

Where it can be shown that the other person deliberately withheld information or supplied false information to the liable person, with the intention that the inheritance tax account or return would contain an inaccuracy, a penalty may be charged on that other person. But that will not necessarily mean that the personal representative themselves may not also be chargeable to a penalty. If the withheld or false information gives rise to inconsistencies in the information they have received about the estate and they do not question those inconsistencies, the liable person may still be charged a penalty for failing to take reasonable care as well.

If after discussion with the taxpayer, HMRC is unable to agree that a penalty should be charged, or the amount of a reduction, a penalty assessment will be issued. It is this document against which the liable person can appeal, and they will then be subject to processes that apply (also from 1 April 2009) within the tribunal system (see **explanatory note 14**).

In addition FA 2008 Sch 36 para 39 applies to a person who fails to comply with an information notice or deliberately obstructs an officer during an inspection authorised by a First-tier tribunal – the penalty is £300 and continues at £60 per day (para 40) for each day on which the failure or obstruction continues.

Penalties for late filing of returns

The current rules

The current rules for late filing penalties are in IHTA 1984 s 245 and are as follows:

- a £100 penalty immediately after the due date for filing (whether or not the tax has been paid) and a further penalty not exceeding £60 for every day after the day on which the failure has been declared by the tribunal and the day before the day on which the return is delivered;
- a further £100 penalty if the return is more than six months late; and
- a maximum penalty of £3,000 if the return is more than a year late.

The two £100 penalties are capped by the amount of tax due. The £3,000 penalty is not limited to the amount of tax due.

The revised rules

FA 2009 s 106 and Sch 55 introduced a revised penalty regime for late filing of tax returns for income tax and inheritance tax. The provisions have not yet come into force for the purposes of inheritance tax. Taxpayers have a right of appeal against all penalties and no penalty can be charged if a taxpayer has a reasonable excuse for their failure.

The Schedule details the returns to which an annual or occasional penalty applies and provides that a failure to submit a return listed in the Schedule will result in the following penalties.

Schedule 55 also sets out the conditions for charging daily penalties where the delay in filing a return is prolonged. These are:

a penalty of £100 (para 3).

a penalty will be payable of £10 for each day (annual obligations only) that the failure to submit a return continues for a period of up to 90 days beginning with the date specified in the notice (para 4(2));

a penalty will be payable if a return is still outstanding six months after the filing date and there would have been a liability to tax shown in the return (para 5(1)); such penalty will be the greater of £300 or 5% of the liability to tax shown in the return (para 5(2));

a penalty will be payable if a return is still outstanding twelve months after the filing date and there would have been a liability to tax shown in the return (para 6(1));

a penalty will be payable where, by failing to make the return, a person withholds information which would enable or assist HMRC to assess the person's liability to tax (para 6(2));

in any other case, the penalty is to be the greater of £300 or 5% of the liability shown in the return (para 6(3)).

Reductions for disclosure (paras 14 and 15)

Where there has been information withheld by failure to make a return, there may be reductions for disclosure in certain penalties where the taxpayer discloses relevant information.

Schedule 55 defines what is meant by disclosure of relevant information. It sets out three distinct elements, all of which are required for the maximum reduction:

(1) admission – telling HMRC that information has been withheld;

(2) taking active steps – giving HMRC reasonable help in assessing any tax unpaid as a result of the information being withheld; and

(3) access – allowing HMRC access to records to check the extent of any liability.

There are two types of disclosure:

- unprompted – where the taxpayer has no reason to believe that HMRC have discovered or are about to discover the relevant information;
- prompted – all other disclosures.

Schedule 55 provides definitions regarding:

- quality of disclosure in terms of timing (how promptly the disclosure was made);
- nature (the level of evidence provided and degree of access to test the disclosure); and
- extent (how complete the disclosure may be).

HMRC cannot reduce the penalty under this paragraph to below the minimum amount set under Sch 55 para 14.

Special reduction (para 16(1))

Paragraph 16(1) gives HMRC a power to reduce any penalty under Sch 55 including the minimum amount penalty where they think it right because of special circumstances.

Interaction with other penalties and late payment surcharges (para 17)

Schedule 55 sets out which penalties HMRC should charge if a taxpayer is liable to more than one penalty which is determined by reference to the same tax liability (which could, for example, include late payment surcharges, penalties for incorrect returns etc), subject to some exclusions. Tax-geared penalties under this Schedule cannot exceed 100% of the relevant liability to tax.

All penalties must be paid before the end of the period of 30 days beginning with the day on which the notification of the penalty is issued.

The assessment of any penalty must be made on or before the later of two dates:

- the first date is the last day of the two-year period beginning with the filing date;
- the second date is the last day of the period of twelve months beginning with the end of the appeal period for the assessment of the amount of tax shown on the return, or, where there is no such assessment, the date on which the amount of tax is ascertained.

Appeals

Schedule 55 gives appeal rights against decisions by HMRC to impose a penalty and of the amount of the penalty (para 20).

A person is not required to pay a penalty before an appeal against the assessment of the penalty is determined (para 21(2)).

Reasonable excuse (para 23)

No penalty arises in relation to any failure if the person satisfies HMRC or (on appeal) the tribunal that there is a reasonable excuse for the failure (para 23(1)).

Schedule 55 para 23(2) contains provisions about what is precluded from being a reasonable excuse.

Penalty for failure to pay tax on time

The current rules

Penalties for late payment where the obligation to make payment is annual or occasional include:

- penalties of 5% of the amount of tax unpaid, generally one month after the payment due date (or at the filing date of the relevant return for CT and IHT);
- further penalties of 5% of any amounts of tax still unpaid at six and twelve months; and
- suspension of late payment penalties where the taxpayer agrees a time to pay arrangement (where a tax debt is paid over time) with HMRC.

The revised rules

Finance Act 2009 s 107 and Sch 56 introduced a revised penalty regime for most taxes including late payment of income tax and inheritance tax. The provisions have yet to come into force for the purposes of inheritance tax. Taxpayers have a right of appeal against all penalties and no penalty can be charged if a taxpayer has a reasonable excuse for their failure.

The penalties to be charged are:

- A penalty of 5% of the amount of tax unpaid (para 3(2)). This penalty is incurred if a taxpayer fails to pay the tax in full by the due date (the 'penalty date').
- Where tax is unpaid at the end of the period of five months after the penalty date, an additional penalty of 5% of the remaining unpaid tax (para 3(3)).
- Where tax is unpaid at the end of the period of eleven months after the penalty date, an additional penalty of 5% of the remaining unpaid tax (para 3(4)).

Schedule 56 provides for a reduction in penalty where there are special circumstances (para 9(1)).

This will occur when:

(a) the taxpayer fails to pay an amount of tax;

(b) before the date before the taxpayer becomes liable to any penalty under the Schedule, they make a request to HMRC that the amount of tax be deferred (commonly referred to as a time-to-pay arrangement); and

(c) HMRC agrees to defer that payment (even if the agreement comes after the penalty is incurred).

If the taxpayer breaks the agreement and HMRC serves a notice specifying to which penalties they would become liable, they become liable to that penalty from the date of the notice. This provision effectively enables HMRC on issue of a notice to reinstate a liability.

Appeals (para 13)

Schedule 56 para 13 gives appeal rights against decisions by HMRC to impose a penalty and of the amount of the penalty.

Reasonable excuse (para 16)

No penalty arises in relation to any failure under Sch 56 if the person satisfied HMRC or (on appeal) the tribunal that there is a reasonable excuse for the failure. The Schedule contains provisions about what is precluded from being a reasonable excuse.

Suspension of penalties

Under FA 2009 s 108 taxpayers who enter into agreements with HMRC to defer payment of taxes are not liable to certain surcharges or penalties that would otherwise be due because of late payment. Section 108 includes a power to impose the surcharge or penalty if the taxpayer does not keep to the terms of the agreement. The change becomes effective for deferral agreements reached on or after 24 November 2008.

(d) Time limits for making assessments and claims

Introduction

There are new time limits for the making of assessments and claims for the purposes of inheritance tax. The new rules took effect from 1 April 2011, with a transitional saving for proceedings by HMRC in the case of a loss of tax brought about deliberately where the chargeable transfer in question took place on or before 31 March 2011 (SI 2010/867 which brings into force Finance Act 2009 s 99 and Sch 51).

The revised rules

FA 2009 s 99 and Sch 51 amend IHTA 1984 by introducing changes to time limits that apply to inheritance tax claims and assessments.

Schedule 51 para 6 inserts s 131(2ZA) into IHTA. It introduces a new time limit of four years from the transferor's death for a claim under s 131(2)(b) of IHTA (Transfers within seven years before death).

Schedule 51 para 11(2) amends s 240(2) of IHTA (Underpayments). This reduces the period allowed for HMRC to bring proceedings to recover additional tax under s 240(2) of IHTA (ie in a case where an account has been delivered) from six to four years.

Section 240(3) of IHTA is also amended by Sch 51 para 11(3):

- It confirms that the time limit remains at six years where the underpayment has been brought about carelessly (s 4).
- The time limit is increased to 20 years where the loss of tax is brought about deliberately (s 5) and the time limit applies in cases where no account has been delivered, and there is no deliberate loss of tax (s 6).
- There is a 20-year time limit on proceedings to recover additional tax in such cases (s 7). The rules include settlors of trusts in certain cases (s 8).

Section 240A (Underpayments: supplementary) is inserted into IHTA by Sch 51 para 12:

- The section supplements the revised time limits in s 240 of IHTA (s 1).
- Section 240A provides that a loss of tax is brought about carelessly by any person if the person fails to take reasonable care to avoid bringing about that loss (s 2). This corresponds with the definition of careless at FA 2007 Sch 24 para 3(1)(a).
- Where information is provided to HMRC by someone who later discovers that the information was inaccurate but does not take reasonable steps to inform HMRC, any loss of tax brought about by this is to be treated as having been brought about carelessly (s 3). This corresponds with the definition in FA 2007 Sch 24 para 3(2).
- Under s 240A, where a loss of tax is brought about by a deliberate inaccuracy in a document, it is to be treated as brought about deliberately. This is to ensure that in cases where a penalty is due for deliberate inaccuracy under FA 2007 Sch 24 para 3, the corresponding increase in time limit also occurs.

IHTA s 241(1) is also amended by Sch 51 para 13 by reducing the period in which repayment of an excess tax payment may be claimed from six to four years. Claims for overpayment relief must be in writing.

A penalty may be levied for a failure to notify HMRC of an error in assessment within 30 days. The penalty is 30% of potential lost revenue, but there are reductions related to the quality of disclosure. For unprompted disclosure the minimum penalty is 0% and for prompted disclosure the minimum penalty if 30%. In December 2017 HMRC announced a restriction on quality of disclosure penalty reductions where taxpayers take a 'significant period (normally 3 years) to correct or disclose the inaccuracy. They will restrict the penalty range by 10% above the minimum before working out the reductions.

Explanatory Notes

Rates of interest on unpaid and overpaid inheritance tax

(1) As stated in part (a) of the Example, the rates of interest on unpaid inheritance tax and overpaid inheritance tax are as follows:

	Unpaid Tax	Overpaid Tax
From 7 April 2020	2.60%	0.5%
From 7 January 2022	2.75%	0.5%
From 21 February 2022	3.00%	0.5%
From 5 April 2022	3.25%	0.5%
From 24 May 2022	3.50%	0.5%
From 5 July 2022	3.75%	0.5%
From 23 August 2022	4.25%	0.75%
From 11 October 2022	4.75%	1.25%
From 22 November 2022	5.50%	2.00%
From 6 January 2023	6.00%	2.25%
From 21 February 2023	6.50%	3.00%
From 13 April 2023	6.75%	3.25%
From 31 May 2023	7.00%	3.50%
From 11 July 2023	7.50%	4.00%
From 22 August 2023	7.75%	4.25%

In making interest calculations, HMRC Capital Taxes use a denominator of 366 for interest on overdue tax and 365 for interest on overpaid tax, whether or not a leap year is involved (March 1997 CTO Newsletter). In both cases this gives a slight advantage to the taxpayer.

The official rate of interest on pre-owned assets is 2.5% for 2019/20, 2.25% for 2020/21 and 2% for 2021/22 and 2% for 2023/24.

Rates of interest on overpayments of tax generally

(2) Finance Act 2009 s 103 established a single rate of interest applied by HMRC on overpayments across all taxes, duties and penalties. The regulations would also provide for a single rate of interest to apply to late payments across all taxes, duties and penalties.

Section 103 also provides the power to arrive at the prevailing rates of interest using formulae. The proposal is for HMRC to calculate interest by reference to the Bank of England base rate.

The legislation includes the power for regulations to be made that set different rates for different taxes, if appropriate.

The most recent interest rates detailed in explanatory note 1 above reflect these new rules.

Tax treatment of interest on overdue and overpaid tax

(3) Interest charged on overdue tax does not qualify for tax relief, nor is interest received on an overpayment taxable (IHTA 1984 ss 233(3) and 235). HMRC have issued a statement of practice (SP 6/95) indicating that they do not automatically initiate an assessment that would lead to a repayment of tax if the amount involved is £25 or less, although the repayment will be made if claimed.

Where payments are made before HMRC Capital Taxes notify the amount due, if their calculation shows a balance of tax due of less than £20 it will not be collected and if less than £10 is overpaid it will not be repaid unless claimed by the taxpayer (HMRC Inheritance Tax: Customer Guide (online version only)). Payments in advance do not attract interest, which only runs from the date that tax is due for payment (see **Example A10** for an illustration).

Late payment interest on sums due to HMRC

(4) Finance Act 2009 s 101 introduced the rules for applying late payment interest to any sum due to HMRC but paid late. Schedule 53 sets out the special provisions concerning the amounts, start date and end dates for charging late payment interest as well as further provisions to clarify the effect of interest on certain reliefs.

Section 101 is intended to apply a simple and consistent interest charge to late payments across all taxes and duties. Late payment interest will apply, for the majority of payments due to HMRC and made late, from the payment due date until the date that payment is received. The interest charged will be simple interest, and will not generally be deductible in computing profits or income.

Section 101 sets out the method for applying late payment interest to any sum due to HMRC but paid late. The formulae follow FA 2008 s 127(1), which was designed to facilitate recovery action for sums owed to HMRC.

Repayment interest payable by HMRC

Finance Act 2009 s 102 and Sch 54 sets out the general rules for applying repayment interest on sums to be repaid by HMRC. HMRC will pay interest on repayments from the date the tax was due to be paid or, if later, the date the payment was actually received, to the date the repayment is made.

Schedule 54 also includes the exceptions to the general rules set out in s 102 regarding repayment interest and covers how repayment interest will operate in particular situations.

Conditionally exempt transfers for inheritance tax

(5) Where tax has not been paid because a transfer was conditionally exempt (works of art and historic buildings etc), or because of the deferral relief for woodlands, and it later becomes payable on those objects, buildings or woodlands, the due date is six months after the end of the month in which the event by reason of which it is chargeable occurs (IHTA 1984 s 226(4)), following which interest then runs (s 233). (See **Example B9** for an example of a conditionally exempt transfer and **Example B11** for an example on woodlands relief.)

Different tax payment dates in relation to one transaction

(6) It should be noted that tax can be due at different times in respect of one transaction. If, for example, a chargeable transfer was made to a discretionary trust on 1 May 2023, the tax would be payable on the lifetime transfer on 30 April 2024. Any additional tax payable as a result of the subsequent death of the donor would be due six months after the end of the month in which the donor died. Therefore if the donor died on 21 May 2023 the additional tax would be payable on 30 November 2023, some five months before the date for payment of the original liability.

Inheritance tax: payment by instalments

(7) Tax may be paid by equal yearly instalments over ten years on qualifying assets in respect of transfers on death; chargeable lifetime transfers if the donee pays the tax; and transfers of settled property where the property concerned continues to be comprised in the settlement (eg termination of a qualifying interest in possession without the property leaving the settlement; or ten yearly charges on relevant property trusts) (s 227). The first instalment is due for payment on death transfers and on additional liabilities arising because

of the death of the donor six months after the end of the month in which the death occurred. The first instalment on lifetime chargeable transfers is due on the normal due date as indicated in **part (a)(i)** of the Example.

The instalment option applies to the following assets:

(a) Land of any description, wherever situated.

(b) Shares which gave the transferor control immediately prior to the transfer.

(c) Unquoted shares and securities (unquoted being defined as not listed on a recognised stock exchange (ss 227(1AA) and 228(5)):

(i) where tax cannot be paid without undue hardship (s 228(1)(c)); or

(ii) for shares only, where they are valued in excess of £20,000 and either the nominal value of the shares is not less than 10% of the nominal value of all the shares of the company at that time or, if the shares are ordinary shares, their nominal value is not less than 10% of the nominal value of all ordinary shares in the company at that time (s 228(3)); or

(iii) where the tax payable on the shares or securities, together with the tax on the other instalment assets, amounts to 20% or more of the tax payable by the same person on the same transfer (s 228(2)). This applies only to transfers on death.

(d) A business or an interest in a business.

(e) Timber, when a chargeable transfer is made following its being left out of account on a previous death (s 229).

The facility to pay by instalments is only available on potentially exempt transfers which become chargeable transfers if the transferee still owns the qualifying property at the time of the transferor's death, (or, for transfers of property qualifying for business or agricultural relief replacement property).

The instalment option on unquoted shares is not available for tax payable in consequence of the donor's death, unless the shares are still unquoted when the donor dies (or if earlier, when the donee dies) (s 228(3A)). This applies to both controlling and non-controlling holdings.

Unquoted shares include those dealt in on the Alternative Investment Market, ISDX Markets Group and NASDAQ Europe.

See **Example C10 explanatory note 12**, in relation to the instalment option and the ten yearly charge on a relevant property settlement. Also see **Example A11** and **Example A22** for a further example on the instalment option.

(8) In the case of land, except land that forms part of a business (as distinct from land owned by partners or directors and occupied by their business) or land that qualifies for agricultural property relief, interest is charged on the *total* amount of tax for the time being remaining unpaid, the interest being added to each instalment as it falls due. Interest is also charged on any instalment that is paid late.

In the case of land that forms part of a business, land qualifying for agricultural property relief and all other assets in (b) to (e) of **explanatory note 7** above (excluding shares in an investment company) interest is not charged unless an instalment is paid late, in which case the interest is charged only on the late instalment and not on the full amount of the deferred tax (s 234).

Sale of instalment property: payment of inheritance tax

(9) If instalment property is sold, the outstanding tax becomes payable immediately (s 227(4)). This explains why a lifetime transferor cannot pay tax on his chargeable transfer by instalments, because he cannot direct the actions of the transferee. If instalment property were comprised in a potentially exempt transfer and then disposed of by the donee, the instalment option would not be available to the donee if a charge to inheritance tax subsequently arose because of the donor's death within seven years.

Incidence of inheritance tax

(10) The question of who is liable to pay inheritance tax is complex and is dealt with in IHTA 1984 ss 199 to 214. HMRC have powers to collect tax from a wide range of persons, but in most cases tax would be paid by the persons indicated in **part (b)** of the Example. Additionally, where property is counted as part an estate under the reservation of benefit rules, the persons primarily liable for the payment of the tax are, broadly speaking, those in whom the property is vested. Personal representatives only become liable for that tax if the tax remains unpaid 12 months after the end of the month in which the death occurs (s 204(9)).

Where tax is unpaid there is normally a HMRC charge on the property concerned, however, this cannot take priority over an existing valid charge (s 237). No HMRC charge may be imposed on personal or movable property vested in personal representatives (other than settled property in which the deceased had a qualifying interest in possession). The HMRC charge can also apply in relation to outstanding tax and interest on assets from which heritage reliefs have been withdrawn.

The person who is liable to pay inheritance tax because of death is not necessarily the person who ultimately bears the tax out of his own resources. Tax on death is borne as follows:

Tax relating to a qualifying interest in possession of the deceased in settled property is borne by the trust funds and thus reduces the value of the funds for the person who becomes entitled to them, or to an interest in them.

Tax relating to property nominated to others during the lifetime of the deceased or held jointly by the deceased and others as joint tenants, is payable out of that property, and hence borne by the nominees or joint tenants.

Tax (and interest on it) on all other property in the UK (both real and personal) that vests in the deceased's personal representatives, other than property which was comprised in a settlement immediately before the death, is a testamentary expense and, in the absence of specific provisions in the will, payable out of the residue of the estate and thus borne by the residuary legatees (s 211). This is most important in relation to the drafting of wills and if it is intended that any particular asset should bear its own tax, this should be expressly provided in the terms of the will.

The tax on property situated abroad is a charge on that property.

Where the personal representatives are liable for and pay tax (and interest) which is not a testamentary expense under the above rule, the amount paid is, where occasion requires, to be repaid to them by the person in whom is vested the property to whose value the tax was attributable (s 211(3)).

Income tax relief re loan to pay inheritance tax

(11) Income tax relief is available in respect of interest paid for a period of up to one year on a loan raised by personal representatives to pay inheritance tax in order to obtain probate. Any excess interest over income of the estate in the tax year of payment may be carried back against the income of the estate in the preceding tax year(s) and any remaining excess is carried forward against future income of the estate (ITA 2007 s 405).

Obtaining an IHT reference number

(12) Before a personal representative can make the first payment of inheritance tax they must obtain an inheritance tax reference number and payslip. They can do this by applying for an IHT reference online or by using the Form IHT422 application for an inheritance tax reference. The application for a reference should be made at least three weeks before the expected date of any payment and be sent to HM Revenue & Customs, Trusts & Estates Inheritance Tax, Ferrers House, PO Box 38, Castle Meadow Road, Nottingham, NG2 1BB.

HMRC will send a note of the reference number and a pre-referenced payslip by post which should be used to pay the tax. The payslip can be used only for payments regarding a particular estate.

Before 6 April 2017, personal representatives could alternatively apply for an IHT reference number on-line at www.gov.uk/government/organisations/hm-revenue-customs/contact/inheritance-tax-payments. From that date personal representatives will no longer be able to apply on-line; they will have to submit Form IHT422 (see HMRC Trusts and Estates Newsletter: December 2016).

Electronic transfer of inheritance tax from participating financial institutions

(13) Most banks and building societies are able to accept instructions from personal representatives to make a payment of inheritance tax, by electronic transfer, before probate is obtained. They will need to complete Form IHT423 Direct Payment Scheme for each bank or building society making the transfer of funds.

If personal representatives wish to use this facility they must first apply for an IHT reference number (see above), which is to be entered on the application to the bank. When the personal representatives are ready to apply for probate (or letters of administration) they will send the Form IHT 423 to the bank/building society. They in turn will transfer funds to HMRC electronically. HMRC will provide the personal representatives with a receipt which must be presented to the Court Service to obtain the grant.

Reviews of HMRC decisions and appeals

(14) The system of tax appeals changed fundamentally from 1 April 2009, and was accompanied by (optional) statutory provisions for a review by HMRC of their decisions prior to an appeal being taken forward. The legislation for inheritance tax is in ss 222–224 as amended (including new ss 223A–223I). For details see **Example A23 explanatory notes 6 and 7.**

Other penalties

(15) For both trusts and estate practitioners, FA 2015 Sch 21 introduced from 27 March 2015 an 'offshore asset move' penalty for moving hidden offshore assets from one territory with the Territory Classification System to another, the main purpose of one of the main purposes of which was to prevent or delay discovery by HMRC. This penalty is 50% of the amount of the underlying offshore penalty regime penalty.

(16) For both trusts and estate practitioners, FA 2016 Sch 20 introduced from 1 January 2017 (SI 2016/1249) penalties for deliberate enablers of offshore evasion or compliance. A person who has enabled another person (Q) to commit a relevant offence in relation to income tax, capital gains tax or inheritance tax or to engage in conduct which makes Q liable for a penalty for an inaccurate return, failure to notify chargeability, failure to make a return on time or for an offshore asset move is liable to a penalty under FA 2016 Sch 20. The amount of the penalty in relation to an offshore asset move penalty is the higher of 50% of the potential lost revenue in respect of the original tax non-compliance and £3,000. In relation to the other penalties listed above, the amount of the penalty under FA 2016 Sch 20 is the higher of 100% of potential lost revenue and £3,000. Reductions are available in respect of the penalty for disclosure.

(17) For both trusts and estate practitioners, FA 2016 Sch 22 introduced from 1 April 2017 (SI 2017/277) asset-based penalties for offshore penalties and failures in relation to inheritance tax. A person to whom an IHT penalty (for an inaccurate return, failure to notify chargeability, or failure to make a return on time) already applies for a deliberate failure in relation to an offshore matter or transfer for a tax year in which the potential lost revenue exceeds £25,000, is liable to a penalty under FA 2016 Sch 22. The amount of the penalty is the lower of 10% of the value of the asset and 10 times the offshore potential lost revenue (as defined). Reductions are available in respect of the penalty for disclosure.

Further reading

(18) The compliance matters covered in this Example are also the subject of an article entitled 'A Higher Burden' by S McKie and C McKie in *Taxation*, dated 6 February 2020. An article by Charles Bradley in *Tax Adviser* for June 2022 explores the anomalies that arise in charging penalties in the context of inheritance tax.

Question

You have been asked by the chairman of your company for advice on the inheritance tax position on the death of his father.

The following information is available:

(1) The chairman's father died on 1 March 2024.

(2) His estate comprised:

(a) Freehold house and land valued for probate at £500,000. This property was owned jointly by the deceased and his wife (who survived him) as beneficial joint tenants. The house, which cost £450,000, had been purchased on 1 August 2022 following the sale of their former home (purchased in the 2000s) for £575,000.

(b) Stocks and shares:

(i) £100,000 6% bonds valued @ 92–96.

Interest is payable half-yearly on 30 June and 31 December.

(ii) £20,000 4% stock valued @ 86–88 ex dividend.

Interest is payable on 31 March.

(c)	Bank deposit account	£23,305
	Accrued interest	£800
	Assume no income tax is due on interest	
(d)	Proceeds of an insurance policy	£27,990
(e)	Personal chattels	£20,000

(3) He had for the past twenty-two years been the life tenant of a trust fund, the assets of which amounted to £216,000, including gross accrued non-dividend savings income to 1 March 2024 of £1,000 (taxable at 20%). The trust funds are payable to the chairman on the death of his father.

(4) Household debts (which were paid by his executors) and funeral expenses amounted to £2,675.

(5) By his will the deceased bequeathed legacies of £5,000 to each of two grandchildren, a legacy of £5,000 and the personal chattels to his widow and the residue to your chairman.

(6) There had been no lifetime transfers.

Prepare a statement showing the amount of inheritance tax payable, who is accountable for the payment, and upon whom the burden falls.

Answer

Estate of Chairman's Father

			Date of death 1 March 2024		
			£	£	£
Property jointly owned with spouse					
Freehold house – half share – related property valuation				250,000	
Less: devolving on widow by survivorship (s 18)				(250,000)	Nil
Free estate					
£100,000 6% bonds		@ 93		93,000	
£20,000 4% stock		@ 86½% ex dividend	17,300		
Add: interest 31 March 2024			800	18,100	
Bank deposit account, including accrued interest				24,105	
Proceeds of insurance policy				27,990	
Personal chattels				20,000	
Accrued income from trust fund to 1 March 2024 (£1,000 less 20%)				800	
				183,995	
Less:	household debts and funeral expenses			(2,675)	
				181,320	
Less:	spouse exemption				
	Legacy		5,000		
	personal chattels		20,000	(25,000)	156,320
Settled property					
Trust fund				216,000	
Less:	gross accrued income			(1,000)	215,000
					371,320

Inheritance tax due on death (2023/24 scale)

Inheritance tax payable on (371,320 – 325,000) = 46,320 @ 40% £18,528

Estate rate

$$= \frac{18{,}528}{371{,}320} \times 100 = 4.9898\%$$

Payable by executors	156,320	@ 4.9898%	7,800
Payable by trustees of trust fund	215,000	@ 4.9898%	10,728
	£371,320		£18,528

The tax payable by the executors will fall on the residue of the estate, so that the two grandchildren will receive their £5,000 legacies in full, with the chairman receiving the balance of residue after legacies and inheritance tax.

The tax payable by the trustees will reduce the trust fund remaining for the chairman.

Explanatory Notes

Meaning of estate for inheritance tax

(1) IHTA 1984 s 5 defines what is meant by a person's estate. Section 5(1) provides that a person's estate is the aggregate of all of the property to which he is beneficially entitled. The term 'property' is not per se defined in the inheritance tax legislation and so encompasses everything that is capable of ownership – both realty and personalty (the latter term encompassing in turn leasehold interest in land, all tangible moveable property and all intangible property). Section 272 confirms that the term includes rights and interests of any description but excludes a settlement power.

A person is treated as being beneficially entitled to settled property in which a qualifying interest in possession subsists (see **Example C3**) and such property is therefore counted as part of the person's estate (s 49). Furthermore, a person who has a general power (ie a power or authority enabling the person by whom it is exercisable to appoint or dispose of property as he thinks fit) which enables him (or would if he were sui juris enable him) to dispose of any property other than settled property, or to charge money on any property other than settled property, shall be treated as beneficially entitled to the property or money and therefore counted as part of his estate (s 5(2)).

Despite the very wide meaning given to the concept of a person's estate, certain property is omitted from a person's estate. The main type of property so omitted is excluded property (see **Example A5(A)** for a discussion of the types of property that are not counted as part of a person's estate).

Inheritance tax: quoted securities — valuation, sale within twelve months of death

(2) UK quoted securities are valued cum div at a price one-quarter up on the difference between the buying and selling quoted market prices. Thus the 6% bonds at 92–96 are valued at 92 + (¼ × (96 - 92)) = 93. If the midpoint between the highest and lowest recorded bargains gives a lower figure, then this is used instead. This rule (which is set out in IHTM18093) is adopted from TCGA 1992 s 272(3) as it applied before 6 April 2015. HMRC has confirmed that this rule will continue to apply for valuing quoted shares for inheritance tax despite changes to the capital gains tax valuation rule that apply from 6 April 2015. For capital gains tax purposes quoted shares are valued at a price one-half up on the difference between the lowest and highest closing prices of the day (except that where there is an ascertained value for shares forming part of a death estate for the purposes of inheritance tax, the capital gains tax value follows the inheritance tax value (s 274)) (Market Value of Shares, Securities and Strips Regulations 2015 (SI 2015/616)).

Where securities are quoted ex div then it is necessary to add the amount of the next dividend (exclusive of the tax credit for dividends received before 6 April 2016) or interest payment (after deduction of tax at the basic rate if applicable. From 6 April 2016 banks, building societies and the National Savings Bank are no longer required to deduct basic tax at source from interest. From 6 April 2017 this is extended to a number of other lending platforms) as additional property in the estate.

Relief may be claimed if quoted securities are sold for less than their value at death within twelve months after death. All securities sold have to be aggregated to determine whether there is any relief. In arriving at the aggregate sale proceeds the sale values are taken *before* deducting any expenses of sale. The relief is restricted if any purchase of quoted securities takes place in the period beginning at the date of death and ending two months after the date of the last sale within the twelve month period after death (IHTA 1984 ss 178–189). See **Example A13** for a detailed illustration.

Life interest in settlement — accrued income for inheritance tax

(3) Accrued income of a life interest in a trust fund belongs to the free estate of the deceased life tenant and not to the succeeding beneficiaries, the trustees having a liability to pay the accrued income net of the appropriate rate of tax to the estate of the deceased life tenant (the appropriate rate being the rate of dividend ordinary rate on dividend income (8.75%) and the basic rate (20%) on other income). This applies whether or not the life interest is a qualifying interest in possession such that the trust capital is taxed as part of the life tenant's estate (see **Example C3**). In the present case the chairman has been entitled to his life tenancy from before 22 March 2006.

Joint tenancy and tenancy in common in the context of inheritance tax

(4) Assets held in joint names (whatever the marital etc status of the co-owners) are presumed to be held on a beneficial joint tenancy unless the evidence leads to a contrary conclusion.

The characteristic of a beneficial joint tenancy is that there are no separate shares which can be disposed of, so that on the death of a beneficial joint tenant his share automatically merges with that of the survivor. It therefore follows that the intestacy rules do not apply to the distribution of such assets, nor do they pass under the deceased's will nor do they vest in his personal representatives.

If co-owners do not jointly own property under a beneficial joint tenancy, the property is owned under a beneficial tenancy in common. This means that there are separate shares which do not merge on death and which can therefore be dealt with independently by will or under the rules of intestacy.

Had the chairman's father and mother owned the house in this Example as beneficial tenants in common, his will would have covered the disposition of his share, and for it to have been exempt it would have had to be devised to his widow as distinct from accruing to her by survivorship (as in the case of the beneficial joint tenancy indicated in the Example).

(5) Had the house been owned by say the chairman's father and his uncle, the position would have been:

(a) If held as beneficial tenants in common, the will would cover the disposition of the share and it does not automatically go to the survivor.

The share would be exempt if devised/bequeathed to a spouse or a charity (for example) but otherwise would be chargeable.

(b) If held under a beneficial joint tenancy, the share of the deceased would automatically merge with the survivor's share. The share would accordingly be chargeable on the death of the chairman's father since clearly its devolution to the uncle would not be exempt.

In both cases, however, the value of the share in the property would be reduced by reason of there being a co-owner with a say in decisions such as sale.

(6) However, where the property is held jointly by husband and wife or civil partners, whether as beneficial joint tenants or beneficial tenants in common, the related property provisions do not permit any such reduction in the value of a share in the property, because the legislation provides that the whole is first valued and then divided pro rata between the part owners. Having said that, if, say, a married couple and one of their children own a property jointly, the co-ownership discount referred to in **explanatory note 5** would already have been applied in establishing the value of the 'whole' of what the husband and wife own, and it would be that value which then falls to be attributed to each of them in proportion to their respective interests. For the detailed provisions on related property see **Example A12**.

(7) As indicated in **explanatory note 5**, property of which the deceased was a co-owner may or may not be liable to inheritance tax.

Further, it may or may not form part of the deceased's estate for the purposes of applying for a grant of probate or administration and in administering the estate (see **Examples G1 to G3**).

If it is held under a beneficial joint tenancy with accrual to the survivor, it does not form part of the deceased's free estate for succession purposes (although it is part of his 'estate' as defined for inheritance tax purposes, and so may be liable to tax depending on who the other joint tenant is) and is not therefore comprised in the probate summary in the HMRC account.

This is one reason why the value of published estates often does not accord with what the public expects to see; the values of assets devolving under a beneficial joint tenancy are simply not included in the total. Similarly, settled property will generally not vest in the personal representatives (but see **Example A7 part (B)(iii)**) and will not be included in the published value of an estate.

(8) In the administration of an estate all that is required in relation to assets held in joint names on a beneficial joint tenancy is the registration of the death, for example by a building society or bank in the case of joint

accounts, or the placing of a death certificate with the title deeds (or the production of it to the Land Registry) in the case of properties, the share in the asset itself having accrued by survivorship.

A share of an asset held as a beneficial tenant in common does form part of a deceased estate, will appear in the probate summary in the HMRC account and will have to be dealt with by the personal representative as distinct from accruing by survivorship (see **Examples G1** to **G3**).

Inheritance tax position of surviving spouse where private residence owned as tenants in common

(9) As indicated in **explanatory note 4**, where a home is held by husband and wife (or civil partners) as beneficial tenants in common, the will of the deceased will deal with that person's share, and in order to avoid wasting the inheritance tax nil-rate band of the first to die, it was common (until the introduction of the transferable nil-rate band in 2007) for the share to be left other than to the survivor. In order to protect the survivor's right to remain in the home, however, it used to be common for older wills to provide for the surviving spouse (or civil partner) to be allowed to remain in the property free of charge, the share then passing on their death, say, to the children. Such a provision was held in *CIR v Lloyd's Private Banking Ltd* to create an interest in possession in favour of the survivor, so that the whole property became chargeable on the second death. The negative effects of this decision are largely eliminated by the rules relating to the transfer of unused nil-rate band between spouses and civil partners (see **Example A3** which also deals with the transfer of unused residence nil-rate band between spouses and civil partners).

Position of co-habiting couples co-owning property in the context of inheritance tax

(10) It is possible that there can be beneficial co-ownership of property even where the title to the property is in the name of only one person. So care needs to be taken where unmarried couples share a house that is purchased in the name of only one of them. If it is intended that the ownership of the property is to be regarded as shared, the purchaser could make a written declaration that the property is held on trust for himself and the co-habitant as joint tenants in equal beneficial shares. The tax treatment will then be as indicated in **explanatory note 5** above, so that on the first death the survivor will acquire the deceased's share. Such a declaration would not represent a transfer of value by the purchaser to the extent that the other person had contributed to the cost. Any amount not so covered would be a potentially exempt transfer. This will be the case even where the couple marry, or become civil partners, soon afterwards (see for instance **Example C17**): there is no backdating of the spouse exemption.

In the absence of such a declaration the legal position is complex and HMRC may argue that, even if the co-habitant has made substantial direct or indirect contributions to the cost of the property (for example by sharing mortgage payments, cost of alterations and household bills generally), the whole property is chargeable on the death of the legal owner (see also **Example A12 part A** regarding the valuation of the share of a co-habitant). The position is no less fraught following the decision of the House of Lords in *Stack v Dowden* [2007] 2 AC 432 where it was held that each party is entitled to that share of the property which the court considers fair having regard to the whole course of dealing between them in relation to the property, taking account of all conduct which throws light on the question what shares were intended including the arrangements which they make to meet the outgoings which have to be met if they are to live in the property as their home. The most authoritative modern guidance as to the proper approach in such a case is set out in the Supreme Court's judgment in *Jones v Kernott* [2011] AC 996. The following are the principles applicable in a case where a family home is bought in the joint names of a cohabiting couple who are both responsible for any mortgage but without any express declaration of their beneficial interests:

(i) The starting point is that equity follows the law and they are joint tenants both at law and in equity.

(ii) That presumption can be displaced by showing that the parties had a different common intention at the time they acquired the home or that they later formed the common intention that their respective shares would change.

(iii) Their common intention is to be deduced objectively from their conduct. The relevant intention of each party is the intention which was reasonably understood by the other party to be manifested by that party's words and conduct even though he did not consciously formulate that intention in his own mind or even acted with some different intention which he did communicate to the other party (*Gissing v Gissing* [1971] AC 886).

(iv) In those cases where it is clear either that the parties did not intend joint tenancy at the outset or had changed their original intention, but it is not possible to ascertain by direct evidence or by inference what their actual intention was as to the shares in which they would own the property, the answer is that each is entitled to that share which the court considers fair having regard to the whole course of dealing between them in relation to the property (*Oxley v Hiscock* [2005] Fam 211). The whole course of dealing in relation to the property should be given a broad meaning, enabling a similar range of factors to be taken into account as may be relevant to ascertaining the parties' actual intentions.

(v) Each case will turn on its own facts. Financial contributions are relevant but there are many other factors which may enable the court to decide what shares were intended or fair.

In the case of a family home that is put into the name of one party only, The Supreme Court stated that the starting point is different. The first issue is whether it was intended that the other party have any beneficial interest in the property at all. If he does, the second issue is what that interest is. There is no presumption of joint beneficial ownership. But their common intention has once again to be deduced objectively from their conduct. If the evidence shows a common intention to share beneficial ownership but does not show what shares were intended, the court will have to proceed as at (iv) and (v) above.

While the search is primarily to ascertain the parties' actual shared intentions, whether express or to be implied from their conduct, there are at least two exceptions. The first is where the classic resulting trust presumption applies (which is rare in a domestic context but might arise where domestic partners were also business partners – see *Stack v Dowden*). The second which will arise more frequently is where it is clear that the beneficial interests are to be shared, but it is impossible to divine a common intention as to the proportions in which they are to be shared. In these two cases the court is driven to impute an intention to the parties which they may never have had. (For an example of the application of the second exception see *Graham-York v York* [2015] EWCA Civ 72.)

Ascertaining property in an estate for inheritance tax – claims to compensation

(11) In their *Trusts and Estates Newsletter* dated April 2013 HMRC points out in particular that a right to pursue a claim for compensation is an item of property and therefore an asset of a person's estate. They explain that there are many situations where a claim to compensation may arise, such as a claim that is specific to an individual (eg where they have received poor financial advice) or where a more widespread issue has arisen (eg a financial institution is instigating its own investigations into a larger body of transactions). Guidance on the treatment of compensation payments is set out in IHTM10261. Where personal representatives are aware of a potential claim at the date of a person's death, they should record the existence of the claim on form IHT400 and provide as much information about the claim as they can. They should include a reasoned estimate of the open market value of the claim (see **Example A12**) where they are able to do so.

Ascertaining property in an estate for inheritance tax – dormant assets

(12) Where an amount standing to the credit of an individual in a bank or building society account that is dormant or the individual is otherwise within the dormant assets scheme (see the Dormant Bank and Building Society Accounts Act 2008 and the Dormant Assets Act 2022), the amount or asset will be transferred to an authorised reclaim fund (or a charity). The individual will at that time acquire a right to the monetary value of the asset that has been transferred. By virtue of Inheritance Tax Act 1984 s 159A, with effect from 6 June 2022, the right to the reclaim is treated as if it were the same asset that was originally transferred into the reclaim fund, acquired as the original asset was acquired and having the same characteristic as that asset. This measure will typically apply where the original owner was alive at the time of transfer but subsequently dies before the asset has been claimed. So, if the original asset were exempt from IHT, the right to reclaim it (which will form part of the individual's estate) will also be exempt.

Calculation of inheritance tax

(13) In the Example, the specific gifts to the widow (cash and chattels) are exempt under s 18 and are therefore deducted from the free estate before the inheritance tax calculation is made.

(14) As no lifetime transfers had been made by the deceased the scale rates apply to the taxable value of the estate without aggregation with any earlier transfers, giving an estate rate of 4.9898%. The tax is then payable by the executors and by the trustees of the settled property on presentation of the probate papers (s 226(2)).

Interest is payable from 30 September 2024 (being six months after the end of the month in which the death occurred (s 233(1)).

(15) Had the trust funds in which the chairman's father had a life interest devolved on his death to his widow, either for her lifetime (as a transitional serial interest under s 49D, the chairman's life interest dating from before 22 March 2006) or absolutely, they would have been left out of the inheritance tax calculation on his death because of the spouse exemption. There would then have been no tax payable on the father's death, since the £156,320 free estate would have been below the £325,000 limit of the nil-rate band.

Inheritance tax residence nil-rate band and downsizing addition

(16) In the context of the Example, no RNRB is available on the chairman's father's death in respect of the freehold house owned by him (together with his wife as beneficial joint tenants) as his interest in the home passes by right of survivorship to his wife and so is not directly inherited by a lineal descendant. However, there is a carried forward amount of RNRB which may pass to the wife and this is calculated by reference to £175,000 (being, since the father's estate is less than £2,000,000, the lower of the residential enhancement of £175,000 for 2023/24 and the value of the home in the father's estate of £250,000).

On the father's death downsizing addition is not available as although his estate includes a home (which replaced a more expensive home owned on 8 July 2015) that is not closely inherited, its value (£250,000) is not less than the maximum RNRB (ie the default or adjusted allowance) to which he would be entitled (being a maximum of £175,000) (s 8FA(2)(b)).

For a detailed discussion of the residence nil-rate band and the downsizing addition, see **Example A2 part (b)**.

Question

Christopher died on 20 March 2024 when his estate comprised the following assets which were valued at:

Quoted investments	£156,000
Cash at bank	£5,312
Life policies on his own life, producing	£47,500

Christopher had lived in rented accommodation all his life and so did not own a home at the time of his death. Outstanding liabilities at 20 March 2024 for household and personal goods (which were paid by his executors) were £4,464 and the funeral expenses amounted to £1,748. The quoted investments were sold by the executors on 28 September 2024 for £150,000, less expenses of sale of £2,500 giving net proceeds of £147,500.

By his will Christopher gave the residue of his estate to his daughter absolutely.

Christopher had not made any chargeable transfers before 5 April 2017 but since then he had made the following cash gifts:

2017	26	April	UK registered charity	£110,000
2017	2	June	Discretionary trust	£333,000
2018	24	December	Daughter	£63,000
2019	20	February	Godson (on the occasion of his marriage)	£1,600
2022	24	December	Daughter	£90,000
2023	2	June	Discretionary trust	£77,500

Christopher had agreed to pay any tax due on the lifetime gifts.

Compute:

(a) The original amounts of tax payable on the lifetime gifts, stating the due dates for payment.

(b) The additional amount of tax payable on the gifts following Christopher's death, showing who is liable for the tax, and stating the due date for payment.

(c) The amount of inheritance tax payable by the executors, stating the due date for payment.

Answer

Inheritance tax payable in Christopher's lifetime

				Gross	Tax on 2017/18 scale	Net
		£	£	£	£	£
26 April 2017						
Gift to charity			110,000			
Less:	Exempt transfer (s 23)		(110,000)	Nil	Nil	Nil
2 June 2017 (**explanatory note 1**)						
Settlement on discretionary trust			333,000			
Less:	Annual exemptions					
	2017/18	3,000				
	2016/17	3,000	(6,000)			
Net transfer, grossed up			327,000	327,500	500	327,000
24 December 2018						
Gift to daughter —			63,000			
Less:	Annual exemption 2018/19		(3,000)			
Potentially exempt transfer			60,000			
20 February 2019						
Gift to godson			1,600			
Less:	Marriage exemption (s 22)		(1,000)			
Potentially exempt transfer			600			
24 December 2022						
Gift to daughter			90,000			
Less:	Annual exemptions					
	2022/23	3,000				
	2021/22	3,000	(6,000)			
Potentially exempt transfer			84,000			
					Tax on 2023/24 scale	
2 June 2023 (**explanatory note 1**)						
Chargeable transfers within previous seven years				327,500	500	327,000
Settlement on discretionary trust			77,500			
Less:	Annual exemption 2023/24		(3,000)			
			74,500			
Net transfer, grossed up						
	(*420,625 – 325,000 = 95,625 @ 20%)			93,125	18,825*	74,500
				420,625	19,125*	401,500

On Christopher's death – 20 March 2024

	Gross	Tax on 2022/23 scale
	£	£
Gifts within seven years before death:		
Accumulation before first such gift	Nil	Nil
2 June 2017		
Settlement on discretionary trust	327,500	1,000*
(*327,500 – 325,000 = 2,500 @ 40%)		
24 December 2018		
Gift to daughter	60,000	24,000
(**387,500 – 325,000 = 62,500 @ 40%)	387,500	25,000*
20 February 2019		
Gift to godson	600	240
	388,100	25,240
24 December 2022		
Gift to daughter	84,000	33,600
	472,100	58,840
2 June 2023		
Settlement on discretionary trust	93,125	37,250
Cumulative transfers in seven years prior to death	565,225	96,090

Estate of Christopher deceased

	Date of death 20 March 2024	
	£	£
Quoted investments		156,000
Cash at bank		5,312
Life policies		47,500
		208,812
Less: Liabilities	4,464	
Funeral expenses	1,748	
Lifetime inheritance tax re settlement 2 June 2023	18,625	(24,837)
Value on death		183,975
Less: Loss on sale of quoted securities		
Probate value	156,000	
Proceeds (before expenses)	150,000	(6,000)
Chargeable to inheritance tax on death		177,975
Cumulative transfers in seven years before death	565,225	96,090
Chargeable estate and tax thereon	177,975	71,190
	743,200	167,280

Summary

(a) The original amounts of inheritance tax payable on chargeable lifetime gifts were as follows:

Gift	*Tax payable*	*Due date*
2 June 2017	£500	30 April 2018
2 June 2034	£18,625	30 April 2024

(b) The additional amounts of inheritance tax payable by reason of the death of Christopher are:

By discretionary trust

Amounts payable by trustees re transfers to discretionary trust made on:

2 June 2017—	On death	1,000	
	Tax after taper relief as gift is made more than 6 but less than 7 years before death – 1,000 x 20%	200	
	Paid on original transfer	(500)	Nil
(No amount repayable)			Nil
2 June 2023 —	On death	37,250	
	Payable on original transfer	18,625	18,625
			£18,625

By daughter

24 December 2018	Gift	24,000	
Tax after taper relief as gift is made more than 5 but not more than 6 years before death – 24,000 × 40%			9,600
24 December 2022	Gift		33,600
			£43,200

By godson

20 February 2019	Gift	240	
Tax after taper relief as above — 240 × 40%			£96

The tax is payable in each case on 30 September 2024 (ie six months after the end of the month in which the death occurred).

(c) The amount of inheritance tax payable by the executors is £71,190. It is payable on 30 September 2024 (ie six months after the end of the month in which the death occurred), or if earlier, upon the application for a grant of probate.

Interest runs from 30 September 2024 (ie six months after the end of the month in which the death occurred).

If tax had been paid on the estate before relief was claimed for the shares sold at a loss (amounting to £6,000 @ 40% = £2,400), the amount paid would have been £73,590 and the £2,400 reduction due to the fall in value of the shares would be repaid with interest from 30 September 2024 (or the date of payment if later) once the claim for fall in value relief was made.

Explanatory Notes

Inheritance tax: grossing up lifetime gifts to discretionary trust

(1) The gift to the discretionary trust on 2 June 2017 is a chargeable lifetime transfer liable to inheritance tax at one half of the full rate (IHTA 1984 s 7(2)). As Christopher has agreed to pay the tax on the transfer the net chargeable gift must be grossed up using the 2017/18 lifetime rate. The net transfer of £327,000 exceeds the nil-rate band of £325,000 by £2,000 which is grossed up using the 20% lifetime rate. The calculation is therefore:

	Net	Gross
	£	£
Nil band	325,000	325,000
Net amount within 20% rate band is	2,000	
Grossed up		
$2,000 \times \frac{100}{80}$		2,500
	327,000	327,500

The second transfer to the discretionary trust on 2 June 2023 must also be grossed up. Tax on the cumulative transfers brought forward is recomputed on the 2023/24 scale to give the starting point for later transfers. As the cumulative total of £327,500 exceeds the 2023/24 nil-rate band of £325,000, the second transfer to the discretionary trust of £74,500 does not fall within the nil-rate band but is wholly within the 20% band, the gross equivalent of which is:

	Net	Gross
	£	£
Nil band	325,000	325,000
Net amount within 20% rate band	74,500	
Grossed up		
$74,500 \times \frac{100}{80}$		93,125
	399,500	418,125

The gross chargeable transfer is therefore £93,125.

Inheritance tax: potentially exempt transfers

(2) The other gifts are all potentially exempt transfers. They are reduced by the marriage exemption on the gift to the godson on 20 February 2019 and the annual exemptions on the gift to the daughter on 24 December 2023 for the purposes of any future charge to inheritance tax (see **Example A2 part (c)**).

Inheritance tax: re-computation of tax following Christopher's death

(3) On the taxpayer's death, gifts within seven years before death must be reconsidered and the tax recomputed using the rates applicable at the date of death (s 7). If the original gift required grossing up, the grossed up gift as calculated when made during lifetime is used in the second calculation. The tax payable is the difference between that now calculated and the amount previously paid (Sch 2 para 2). If the amount previously paid exceeds the revised amount due at the date of death, no refund of tax is made.

Inheritance tax: Valuation of quoted securities sold at a loss after death

(4) Quoted securities sold within the twelve months following death by the person liable to account for the inheritance tax thereon must be aggregated and if the resulting sale proceeds are lower than the probate value of those securities a claim may be made for the loss to be deducted from the probate value (ss 178–189). For this purpose proceeds means sale value *before* deducting any expenses of sale. For detailed notes see **Example A10** and for a detailed illustration see **Example A13**.

Due date of payment of inheritance tax

(5) Inheritance tax is payable on chargeable lifetime transfers six months after the end of the month in which the transfer was made, or at the end of April in the following tax year if this is later (s 226(1)).

Inheritance tax on the estate at death (other than tax payable by instalments, as to which see **Example A11**) is payable six months after the end of the month in which death occurred (s 226(1)). It may be payable earlier than this if and when the deceased's personal representatives make delivery of the HMRC account (s 226(2)). The account is submitted in conjunction with the application for a grant of probate or administration, which is usually made within twelve months after death. Interest runs from six months after the end of the month in which death occurred (s 233(1)).

Inheritance tax on potentially exempt transfers that become chargeable and the additional inheritance tax on chargeable lifetime transfers made within seven years before death is payable by the transferee six months after the end of the month in which the death occurred (s 226(1), (3)).

The due date of payment of the tax and the liability for the tax, interest and penalties are discussed in detail in **Example A7**.

Question

(a) On 31 May 2023 Nigel, a bachelor, died leaving a net estate included in the application for probate at £364,250. Application for probate was made on 2 March 2024 and inheritance tax of £15,700 was paid on that date. Interest of £107 was also paid. Nigel's sister, Jane, inherited the residue of his estate in accordance with the provisions of his will.

(b) The executors subsequently became aware that certain assets valued at £12,500 had been omitted from the HMRC Account completed at the time the application for probate was made.

(c) Before his death the deceased had contracted for certain alterations to be made to the house in which he resided. The work was completed on 10 June 2023 and the valuation for probate which was subsequently made had taken the improved condition of the house into account. The contractors were now requesting payment of their final account amounting to £9,500, which had not been deducted from the value of the estate for probate purposes, since it was not clear at that time whether all alterations had been paid for by progress payments. The executors paid the contractors on 8 July 2024 in accordance with the terms of the contract (namely within 30 days of presentation of their invoice).

(d) Prior to his death the deceased had made an unsecured loan of £8,000 to the company XZ Ltd, which loan had been included in the value of the estate for probate at its face value. On 1 May 2023 the company had gone into liquidation and it was now clear that nothing would be available for the unsecured creditors.

(e) In order to pay the cash legacies the executors had to sell all the deceased's quoted securities. They did this on 1 April 2024 as follows:

(i) 2,000 £1 shares in CD plc, quoted at death at 219p–223p with recorded bargains of 219p, 220p and 222p, were sold at 190p.

(ii) 4,000 £1 shares in DE plc, quoted at death at 109p–116p with recorded bargains of 109p, 109½p and 111p, were sold at 87½p.

(iii) 12,000 6% preference shares in DE plc, quoted at death at 53p–61p with no recorded bargains, were sold at 60p.

Advise the executors how they should proceed, and calculate the inheritance tax and interest payable or repayable if the position were finalised on 2 September 2024, assuming that the rates of interest on underpaid and overpaid inheritance tax remain in force throughout, namely at the time of writing, 7.75% (effective from 22 August 2023) and 4.25% (effective from 22 August 2023) respectively.

Answer

The executors should submit a corrective account which should include the omitted assets and other amendments (IHTA 1984 s 217).

Quoted securities (see explanatory note 1)

Where quoted securities are sold by the persons liable to account for the inheritance tax thereon within twelve months after death at an aggregate value that is lower than probate value, relief may be claimed for the loss. In arriving at the aggregate value the sale values taken into account are the gross proceeds *before* deducting selling expenses. In this case the position is:

	Death Value		*Realised Value*	
2,000 shares in CD plc	@ 220p	4,400	@ 190p	3,800
4,000 shares in DE plc	@ 110p	4,400	@ 87½p	3,500
12,000 6% preference shares in DE plc	@ 55p	6,600	@ 60p	7,200
		£15,400		£14,500

A reduction of £900 (£15,400 – £14,500) is available on a claim being made (ss 178–189).

Alterations to the house

The deceased had placed the contract for the work to be done and therefore he or his estate is liable for the cost, the value of his house having reflected the work done or to be done in performance of the contract and that increased value being included in the net estate. A deduction is taken for the costs because the amount owing has been paid by Nigel's executors after his death (s 175A(1)).

Unsecured loan to XZ Ltd

The loan must be valued at the price it would have realised on a sale on the open market at the time of death (s 160). The market value at the date of death in the circumstances outlined will be nil. Since the value included in the net estate was £8,000, a reduction of £8,000 will be made. The valuation is not affected by an event *after* death. Here the liquidation had commenced *before* death but the proper value *as at death* has been ascertained later.

After making the appropriate adjustments the revised inheritance tax will be:

Value per account submitted at the time of the application for probate			364,250
Omitted assets			12,500
			376,750
Less:	Loss on quoted securities	900	
	Additional debt paid	9,500	
	Reduction in value of loan to XZ Ltd	8,000	(18,400)
Adjusted estate			358,350
Inheritance tax at 2023/24 death rates			
	(358,350 – 325,000 = 33,350 @ 40%)		13,340
Less: Amount paid			(15,700)
Repayment due			2,360
Interest overpaid in relation to refund (1 December 2023 to 1 March 2024)			
92 days @ 7.75% × £2,360			46
Inheritance tax overpaid			2,360

Interest overpaid	46
	2,406
Interest thereon (185 days @ 4.25% 2 March 2024 to 2 September 2024)	51
Total repayable	£2,557

Explanatory Notes

Inheritance tax: valuation of quoted securities

(1) Quoted securities are valued at cum div prices at the lower of:

(a) ¼ up from the lower of the closing prices.

(b) The midpoint of recorded bargains.

(This rule which is derived from TCGA 1992 s 272(3) as that section applied before 6 April 2015, is applied, as a matter of practice, for IHT valuation purposes (see IHTM18093).)

X's estate therefore includes the following values:

				Lower
Value of CD plc shares				
(a) ¼ (223 – 219) = 1	+ 219	=	220	220p
(b) ½ (219 + 222)		=	220.5	
Value of DE plc shares				
(a) ¼ (116 – 109) = 1.75	+ 109	=	110.75	
(b) ½ (109 + 111)		=	110	110p
Value of DE plc preference shares				
(a) ¼ (61 – 53) = 2	+ 53	=		55p
(b) N/A				

Inheritance tax: quoted securities – Valuation, sale within twelve months of death

(2) The relief for a fall in value of quoted securities sold in the twelve months following death (see **Example A8, explanatory note 1**) is not available if the person who claimed the relief purchases further quoted securities of a value equal to or greater than the proceeds of sale within the period beginning with the date of death and ending two months after the date of the last sale in that twelve month period. If the reinvestment is not equal in amount to all of the sale proceeds, the relief is withdrawn proportionately (IHTA 1984 s 180). For an illustration see **Example A13**.

(3) *All* sales of quoted securities, whether at a loss or at a profit, which take place in the period of twelve months following the death must be included in the computation for relief (s 179).

(4) The provisions giving relief where securities are sold at a loss within twelve months after death also apply to securities for which quotation is suspended, or which are cancelled, within that period. For details see **Example A13.**

Interest on overpaid inheritance tax

(5) The repayment of inheritance tax, including the interest overpaid (calculating the overpayment at the late payment rate(s) used to calculate the original interest charge in favour of HMRC), carries interest against HMRC from the due date (or the date of payment if later) to that of repayment, at the repayment rate(s) (s 235 and see FA 1989 s 187 and SI 2010/1879) (see **Example A6 explanatory note 1**).

(6) The original tax and interest will have been calculated as follows:

Net estate per original probate application	£364,250
Tax on (364,250 – 325,000) = £39,250 @ 40%	£15,700
Interest at 7.75% pa from 1 December 2023 to 1 March 2024 (92 days)	£306

Inheritance tax: provisional figures in HMRC Account

(7) Personal representatives need to take care when including provisional figures in the HMRC Account, because HMRC are taking a harsher attitude to penalties where asset values are understated – see **Example A23 explanatory note 9.**

Inheritance tax: notification of corrections to HMRC Account and calculation of tax

(8) In order to reduce the amount of correspondence that is sent dealing with minor amendments to IHT400s, HMRC announced in their *Trusts and Estates Newsletter* for April 2014, that, from 1 May 2014 and in certain cases, personal representatives do not need to contact HMRC every time that they find out about a new amendment to the value of an estate. Rather all amendments are notified at once (on form C4 Corrective Account (or C4(S) Corrective Inventory used in Scotland)) when the personal representatives believe they have the final amendments to the value of the estate or 18 months has passed since the date of death (whichever is earlier). Personal representatives do not need to inform HMRC that they are taking advantage of this practice (if indeed they decide to do so – it is not compulsory for them to do so).

This facility is, however, not available to personal representatives in the following cases:

- where HMRC has informed the personal representatives that they are starting a compliance check (in which case the personal representatives must report any amendments at that time);
- where the deceased's estate includes a qualifying interest in possession or a gift with reservation of benefit;
- where there is an overall change in the value of the estate of more than £50,000 (before any exemptions and reliefs);
- where the amendments relate to changes in the value of land or buildings or unlisted shares;
- where the amendments relate to a claim for loss on the sale of land or shares; or
- where assets have been sold on which tax is being paid by instalments.

If the estate has not been settled within 18 months, personal representatives need to start informing HMRC about amendments as they arise, again.

Interest is still charged on any unpaid tax where personal representatives decide to save up amendments and report them all at once. A payment on account can be made to stop interest accruing in such circumstances.

HMRC has stated that as long as the estate and amendments follow the criteria for saving up amendments the taxpayer or agent will not be at any greater risk to penalties than they would be if they had told about the amendments within six months of discovering them (which is the statutory time limit for notifying HMRC of corrections) (IHTM31023).

HMRC announced in their *Trusts and Estates Newsletter* for August 2016 that they expect agents to calculate the amount of any inheritance tax due as a result of changes to the value in an estate unless it is complex (in which case HRMC will perform the calculation). Complex estates are those where:

- grossing up applies because there are legacies that are free of tax and part of the estate is exempt;
- inheritance tax is due at the reduced rate of 36% on one or more components of the estate because at least 10% passes to charity;

- successive charges relief or double taxation relief applies.

Payments on account should still be made to reduce or stop any potential interest charges arising.

The 2011 UK–Swiss Tax Agreement

(9) FA 2012 s 218 and Sch 36 gave legislative effect to the UK–Swiss tax agreement that came into force 1 January 2013. Under the agreement, bank accounts (and other financial assets) held by UK residents in Switzerland were subject to a one-off deduction of between 21% and 41% of the value of the assets (which was paid to HMRC) to settle past tax liabilities as long as the accounts were open on 31 December 2010 and were still open on 31 May 2013. The levy settled past income tax, capital gains tax, inheritance tax and VAT liabilities. The levy did not apply if the account holder instructs the bank to disclose details of the account to HMRC.

In their *Trusts and Estates Newsletter* of April 2014, HMRC confirm that where beneficiaries or executors of an estate have paid the one-off charge, the asset in respect of which the charge was paid still continues to form part of the deceased person's estate. Whilst the inheritance tax attributable to the Swiss asset is covered by the one-off charge, being part of the deceased's estate may result in the asset affecting the tax payable in respect of the free estate or other aggregable property (such as settled property) (eg by the Swiss asset using the nil-rate band). Executors that have not declared relevant Swiss assets on Form IHT400 or IHT205 must take corrective action.

(10) In their *Trusts and Estates Newsletter* of April 2022, HMRC has requested that the C4 corrective account not be used to report a decrease in the value of listed shares and land where the decrease has resulted from a sale of the assets. In this case post-mortem relief should be claimed using Forms IHT35 and IHT38 respectively. The C$ corrective account should be used only to report amendments to the value of assets and liabilities retuned on the IHT400 where it is discovered that the probate value was incorrect and to report assets and liabilities not previously returned on the IHT400. For more information on post-mortem relief for land and listed shares, see **Example A12** and **Example A13** respectively.

The reduced rate of inheritance tax

(11) Schedule 1A provides for a reduction in the rate of inheritance tax from 40% to 36% where 10% or more of a deceased person's net estate (after deducting exemptions and the nil-rate band) is left to charity. Whilst some estates will qualify for the reduced rate from the outset, others may qualify at a later stage as a result of changes to the estate. This may be the case where changes are made to the values of the property in the estate which result in one or more components of the estate then meet the 10% test. Similarly where an estate first met the 10% tests and subsequent changes are made to the values of the property in the estate, it should be checked to see whether it still passes the 10% test. Executors should be advised to make these checks when they submit corrective and supplementary accounts. For a detailed explanation of the reduced rate of inheritance tax see **Example B12.**

Question

Smith, who had been in partnership with his son for many years, died on 5 April 2024. He had made a lifetime gift on 12 November 2018 of £207,000. He had subsequently made gifts to use his annual exemptions but had made no other transfers of value.

The value of his estate at the date of his death was agreed as follows:

	£
Stocks and shares	10,000
Cash at bank	2,000
Furniture and effects	4,000
Interest as a partner in partnership of Smith & Son	200,000
His house, 5 Side Street purchased before 8 July 2015	363,000
Let UK agricultural land (owned and let on same lease for 33 years)	173,000
His outstanding debts were:	
General household bills (paid by his executors)	7,250
Income tax and capital gains tax	11,000

His funeral expenses amounted to £2,750.

Under his will his whole estate passed to his son absolutely.

Where possible the inheritance tax in connection with his death is being paid by instalments. The first instalment and the inheritance tax not payable by instalments was paid on 1 January 2025. The second instalment was paid on 1 January 2026.

Calculate the inheritance tax and interest payable on those two dates, assuming that the rate of interest on underpaid inheritance tax, namely, at the time of writing, 7.75% effective since 22 August 2024, remains in force throughout.

Answer

Estate of Smith deceased

						Date of death 5 April 2024
Non-instalment option property						£
Stocks and shares						10,000
Cash at bank						2,000
Furniture and effects						4,000
						16,000
Less:	Funeral expenses				2,750	
	General household bills				7,250	
	Income tax and capital gains tax				11,000	(21,000)
Amount to be deducted from instalment option personalty						(5,000)
Instalment option property						
Freehold house						363,000
Let agricultural land					173,000	
Less:	agricultural property relief 50%				(86,500)	86,500
Personalty – Interest as a partner in partnership of Smith & Son					200,000	
Less:	balance of debts as above				(5,000)	
(see **explanatory notes 3 and 4**)						
					195,000	
Less:	business property relief 100%				(195,000)	Nil
Chargeable to inheritance tax at death						449,500

						Tax on 2023/24 scale
					£	£
November 2018 — Gift				207,000		
Less: Annual exemptions		2018/19	3,000			Nil
		2017/18	3,000	(6,000)	201,000	
Chargeable estate					449,500	60,200*
Less: residence nil-rate band (see **explanatory note (6)**)					(175,000)	
					475,500	60,200*

(* 475,500 – 325,000 = 150,500 @ 40%)

Tax on estate at death is therefore:	£60,200
Part attributable to house (see **explanatory note (6)**)	
$\frac{363,000}{449,500} \times 60,200$	48,615
Part attributable to agricultural land	
$\frac{86,500}{449,500} \times 60,200$	11,585
	£60,200

The tax may be paid by ten equal annual instalments in each case. Interest on the tax relating to the house is charged on the *total* amount for the time being remaining unpaid, the interest being added to each instalment as it falls due, and interest is also charged on the instalment if it is paid late. In respect of land qualifying for agricultural relief, interest is payable only on the amount of the instalment if it is paid late.

The amounts of tax and interest payable are therefore:

	£	£
On 1 January 2025		
Re agricultural land:		
Instalment due 31 October 2024	1,159	
Interest thereon from 31 October 2024 to 31 December 2024		
£1,159 × 7.75% × 62/366	15	1,174
Re house:		
Instalment due 31 October 2024	4,861	
Interest thereon from 31 October 2024 to 31 December 2024		
£4,861 × 3.75% × 62/366	64	4,925
Total tax and interest due		6,099
On 1 January 2026		
Re agricultural land:		
Instalment due 31 October 2025	1,159	
Interest thereon from 31 October 2025 to 31 December 2025		
£1,159 × 7.75% × 62/366	15	1,174
Re house:		
Instalment due 31 October 2025	4,861	
Interest thereon from 31 October 2025 to 31 December 2025		
£4,861 × 7.75% × 62/366	64	
Interest on unpaid tax of (£48,615 less 1st instalment of £4,861 ie £43,754) from 31 October 2024 to 31 October 2025		
£43,754 × 7.75% × 1 year	3,391	8,316
Total tax and interest due		9,490

Explanatory Notes

Re-computation of inheritance tax following donor's death

(1) Where gifts are made within seven years before the donor's death, tax has to be recomputed (or, in the case of potentially exempt transfers, computed) on the death scale in force at the date of death. Any additional tax arising is payable by the donee (but no tax is repayable should the tax at the current rates be less than the tax originally paid on chargeable lifetime transfers).

Payment of inheritance tax by instalments

(2) Tax may be paid by equal yearly instalments over ten years on certain assets where they are transferred on death. The instalment facility is also available for chargeable lifetime transfers where the donee pays the tax, and, so long as the assets are still owned by the donee, in respect of additional tax or tax on potentially exempt transfers that becomes payable on death. The detailed notes on the assets qualifying for this treatment are in **Example A7 explanatory note 7**. Smith's instalment assets are his freehold house and agricultural land. His partnership interest would also have qualified but as it attracts 100% business property relief no tax is payable in respect of that asset.

Inheritance tax: debts payable out of estate

(3) Where the rules in IHTA 1984 ss 162A–162C (see **Example A12**) do not apply to govern the treatment of a debt (as here), debts payable out of a deceased's estate are deducted primarily from personalty (ie property other than freehold land and buildings) unless charged against specific property, in which case the deduction is against that property (s 162(4)). It could be argued that the liabilities should be deducted pro-rata against the non-instalment personalty (£16,000 in this Example) and the instalment personalty (£200,000 in this Example). Since the instalment personalty in the Example qualifies for 100% business property relief, the effect would be to increase the chargeable estate by the proportion of the debts set against that property. It is understood that in practice it is accepted that the debts reduce non-instalment option personalty before instalment option personalty.

Inheritance tax: business property relief

(4) Business property relief is given at the rate of 100% or 50% on relevant business property (for detailed notes see **Example A21**). In the case of a business or an interest in a business the value is defined as the value of the assets used in the business (including goodwill) reduced by the liabilities incurred for the purpose of the business (s 110). Even if any of the tax liabilities in this Example relate to the business, they will not have been incurred for the purpose of the business and do not affect the value of the business property. Section 104 provides, however, that business property relief is given on such part of the value transferred as is attributable to relevant business property. In this Example the excess of liabilities over non-instalment option personalty reduces the value transferred in respect of the partnership interest. The excess of £5,000 therefore reduces the amount on which 100% business property relief is given.

Inheritance tax: agricultural property relief

(5) Agricultural property relief on agricultural property let before 1 September 1995 is at the rate of 50% (subject to special transitional provisions for certain property owned since before 10 March 1981 and let within a farming family). See **Example A22** for details.

Inheritance tax: residence nil-rate band (RNRB)

(6) Smith's estate benefits from a RNRB as he dies after 6 April 2017 owning a home which is closely inherited by passing under a disposition under his will to his son (his direct descendant). His estate (after deduction of expenses but before APR and BPR) is £731,000 (£449,500 + £86,500 + £195,000). As his estate does not exceed the taper threshold of £2,000,000, the amount of the RNRB prima facie available is £175,000 (the default allowance for 2023/24). The actual amount of RNRB used in calculating the inheritance tax arising in respect of Smith's estate is limited to the chargeable value of the proportion of his home that is closely inherited. In this case, the chargeable value of Smith's home is £363,000 and as the whole home is closely inherited this figure acts as the limit on the amount of RNRB available. The limit does not operate in Charles's case and so the amount of the RNRB used in calculating the IHT arising on his estate is £175,000. See **Example A2 part (b)** for a detailed discussion on the RNRB.

The RNRB applies to Smith's entire chargeable estate; it is an extra nil-rate band and is not an exemption or relief in respect of Smith's home per se, applied directly to the chargeable value of the home. In calculating the amount of IHT arising in respect of Smith's chargeable estate, the RNRB is taken into account first (ie the individual's home is treated as the first slice of his chargeable estate) (s 8D(3)). The remainder of his estate (which will include the value of his home in excess of his RNRB) is then considered. The value of the remainder as is equal to the general nil-rate band (eroded where relevant by the cumulative amount of chargeable transfers made in the seven years before death) is taxed at 0% and the balance is taxed at 40%. It is the tax so calculated that is then attributable to Smith's instalment and non-instalment property according to the chargeable value of the individual items of property. In particular, the tax of £60,200 chargeable on Smith's estate that is attributable to his home is found by taking the taxable value of his home (ie £363,000) (s 227(1)). That value is not reduced by the RNRB because, as already stated, it does not operate as an exemption or relief in respect of Smith's home per se but as a rate of tax applicable to his whole estate.

Interest on overdue inheritance tax

(7) Where tax is not paid on the due date, interest is payable thereon, currently (at the time of writing) at 7.75% from 22 August 2023, in respect of transfers made on death and on the tax or additional tax payable on gifts

within the previous seven years. The detailed provisions and previous rates of interest are in **Example A7.** HMRC use a denominator of 366 when calculating interest due on overdue tax, as shown in the Example (and a denominator of 365 when calculating interest payable on overpaid tax) – see **Example A7 explanatory notes 1** and **2.**

(8) Although land is one of the assets qualifying for the instalment treatment as indicated in **explanatory note 2** above, interest is charged not only on the amount of any instalment paid late but also on the *total* amount of tax remaining unpaid, the interest being added to each instalment as it falls due (s 227(3)). (This does not apply to land that forms part of a business or qualifies for agricultural property relief (s 234).) Thus in the Example, in the case of the first instalment of tax due in relation to the freehold house, interest is charged on the late paid instalment only. In the case of the second such instalment due, interest is charged not only on the overdue instalment but also on the balance of tax outstanding after deducting the first instalment. As regards the latter, interest is calculated for the period between the due date of the first instalment and the due date of the second (ie a period of one year) (see IHTM 30362). So, the amount on which interest will be calculated at 31 October 2026 is £38,893, being the previous balance of £43,754 less the second instalment of £4,861. Further interest on the tax due in relation to the freehold house will arise on the due date of the third instalment and if the third instalment is paid late, and so on.

Reduced rate of inheritance tax for substantial charitable gifts

(9) Schedule 1A provides for a reduction in the rate of inheritance tax from 40% to 36% where 10% or more of a deceased person's net estate (after deducting exemptions and the nil-rate band) is left to charity. Where this is the case and there is also instalment and non-instalment property in the component of the estate qualifying for the reduced rate, the tax payable at the reduced rate will be apportioned between the two types of property in the same way as if the property were charged to tax at the rate of 40% (as in this Example). See **Example B12** for a discussion of the rules providing for the reduced rate of inheritance tax.

Question

A.

Inheritance tax is charged on the value transferred by a chargeable transfer.

How is property valued for this purpose, and how is the value affected if the property is 'related property'?

Comment upon the rules of valuation applicable to the following property:

(a) Unquoted securities.

(b) Farm cottages and farmhouses.

and the effect on that valuation of:

(i) A special purchaser.

(ii) Capital gains tax.

B.

A testator who was a widower died in November 2023 leaving a freehold residential property, Blackacre to his nephew. The value as at the date of his death is agreed by the executors with HMRC as being £700,000 and inheritance tax is paid on that basis.

What effect will there be, if any, on the inheritance tax payable in respect of Blackacre if eighteen months after his death the executors sell Blackacre for (i) £650,000 or (ii) £750,000?

C.

Explain how liabilities are taken into account in calculating inheritance tax. In the light of your explanation calculate Nigel's chargeable estate when he dies in March 2024, domiciled in the UK. At the time of his death he owned shares in an unquoted trading company worth £2,000,000, a storage unit worth £700,000, a family home worth £1,500,000, a cottage in Bavaria worth £300,000 and other UK assets worth £400,000. He owed credit card debts of £100,000 at the time of his death; they were paid off by his executors. He also owed £1,500,000 in loans taken out as follows: £800,000 in January 2013 to acquire the shares in the unquoted trading company, £500,000 in June 2018 to acquire the storage unit and £200,000 in July 2018 to acquire the cottage. The first two loans are secured on the family home. Under his will, Nigel's son will inherit all of his father's assets.

Answer

A. Valuation of property

The amount on which inheritance tax is charged on a lifetime chargeable transfer is the difference between the value of the transferor's estate before and after the transfer less any exemptions and ignoring disposals of excluded property (IHTA 1984 ss 1, 2, 3). On death the chargeable amount is the value of the deceased's estate (other than excluded property) immediately before his death less any exemptions due (s 4). In arriving at the value of the transferor's estate (or that of the deceased as the case may be), the property comprised in the estate requires valuation. Part VI of IHTA 1984 sets out the rules for valuing property for the purposes of inheritance tax.

The value of property is the price which it ought reasonably to be expected to fetch if sold on the open market at the time of the transfer or of the death as the case may be. The value is not, however, to be reduced on the ground that the whole property is to be placed on the market at one time (s 160). The sale is an entirely hypothetical one and so it is irrelevant that in the circumstances the property cannot in fact be sold in the open market. The parties to the sale are also hypothetical and the characteristics and circumstances of the person who actually owns the property are ignored in applying the above test. The open market referred to is also hypothetical although it is assumed that the sale will be advertised to all prospective purchasers who are assumed to be informed of all information that would have been available to a real purchaser.

With regard to open market value, it has been held by the Land Tribunal in the case of *Walton (exor of Walton decd) v CIR* (1994), that the interest of a partner in a non-assignable agricultural tenancy should be valued according to the extent to which the partnership profits were enhanced as a result of not paying a full market rent, rather than by reference to the vacant possession value compared with the tenanted value. The case of *Watkins (exor of Watkins decd) v RCC* (2011) concerned the valuation of a retained interest in the income stream of a discounted gift trust. Although a hypothetical market had to be envisaged, HMRC put forward a valuation based on an established methodology for valuing interest derived from an existing trust. The taxpayer argued that other types of sale were possible and that all reasonable and practicable hypotheses had to be taken into account. The First-tier Tribunal held that the executors could prove no existing open market for the income stream to be valued or any similar type of entitlement and that the hypotheses put forward by them served no purpose in establishing the characteristics of the hypothetical market. As the executors were unable to disprove the valuation adopted by HMRC their appeal was dismissed. In *Estate of Thomas (deceased) v HMRC* [2020] UKUT 6, the Lands Chamber of the Upper Tribunal, expert witnesses used two valuation approaches for ascertaining the s 160 value of land owned by the deceased when he died. They used a market comparison (based on comparables) and a residual valuation (potential profit less costs) to arrive at the land's market value. The tribunal placed little weight on the latter approach but was also not convinced by the former. Rather it consider all the evidence to determine the best price which the land ought reasonably to be expected to fetch if sold on the open market. The emphasis in land valuation is to ascertain that price. For further discussion on the open market value rule in s 160 see **explanatory note 1**.

HMRC Brief 22/2013 (dated 7 August 2013) sets out HMRC's view on how to calculate the value subject to inheritance tax for a discounted gift scheme held in a relevant property trust when the ten year anniversary arises for the trust (see **Example C10**). The Brief also sets out updated guidance on how the transfer value is to be calculated when a discounted gift scheme is effected including providing clarification and revisions to the assumption underlying the valuation.

In their *Trusts and Estates Newsletter* for August 2013, HMRC explain that the open market value of a right to pursue a claim for compensation at the date of an individual's death depends on several factors, but is fundamentally down to what is known, or capable of being known, at the date of death about the amount of compensation that might reasonably be anticipated based on the information available, the likelihood of the claim being successful, the likely costs that would be expected to be incurred in obtaining a successful outcome, and the time delay between the date of death and the date when the compensation might reasonably be expected to be made. The right to pursue a claim can be available whether or not the individual entitled to make the claim was aware of this, provided that the information was capable of being known at the relevant date. The open market value of the right to pursue the claim becomes more valuable as the outcome becomes more certain, so particular events can trigger a substantial increase in value.

Valuation on death

The valuation of property on death is dealt with in ss 171–177. These sections provide that the value of property shall be that immediately prior to death, but taking into account changes in the value of the estate resulting from the death (other than changes relating to life interests or property passing by survivorship). However, allowances are to be made for reasonable funeral expenses (s 172) and for expenses incurred in administering or realising property situated outside the United Kingdom not exceeding five per cent of the value of that property, where the expense is incurred because of the situation of the property (s 173). Thus the deduction is limited to the additional cost of administering the property because it is situated outside the United Kingdom.

In some circumstances where the value of property has fallen between the date of a gift and the donor's death, the lower value may be taken into account to compute the tax or additional tax payable by the donee. The value in the accumulation for later transfers, including that on death, is not, however, altered (s 131(1), (2)).

Where a death estate includes quoted securities and they are sold, cancelled or the quotation is suspended within twelve months after the date of death, then a claim may be made for relief for the fall in value under ss 178–189 (see **Example A13**). Similarly if the estate includes land which is sold within four years after death, ss 190–198 apply as detailed in **part B** below.

When valuing assets in a deceased's estate, care must be taken to ensure that all parts of an asset included in the estate are aggregated when considering its value, eg if the deceased owned a half share of a house personally and had an estate life interest in the other half then the value to be used will be that of the whole, allocated equally between the free estate and the settled property.

By comparison, if the deceased owned a half-share of a house personally and the other half is owned by a co-habitant then the value of the deceased's share should be reduced by a discount, typically 15%, to reflect the fact that any purchaser would have to share the house with the co-habitant (*Wright & Another v CIR* (1982)). See **Example A8 explanatory note 10** for a discussion on how to establish whether co-habitants do actually share the ownership of the property.

Valuation of lifetime transfers

Similar valuation rules apply in relation to lifetime transfers, except where a transfer is of settled property in which the transferor has a qualifying interest in possession (see **Example C3**). In that event s 52(1) provides that the value transferred is treated as being equal to the value of the property in which the life interest subsists. Where a life tenant also owns property of a similar kind (eg shares in the same company) in his own right, the value of the settled property is valued independently if the transfer relates to the settled property. If therefore someone owned shares both directly and as a life tenant, and the combined holding gave a controlling interest, a lifetime gift of the shares owned directly that reduced the combined holding to a minority holding would be valued so as to reflect the loss of control. By contrast, a transfer of the life interest would be valued only in terms of the life interest shares, even though the life tenant's estate had fallen in value by a greater amount.

Related property

Special rules apply to calculate the value of an asset to which the related property rules apply (s 161). These rules do not apply if the asset is sold within three years after death and relief is claimed under s 176 (see **explanatory note 4**).

The related property rules provide that property is related to the property in a person's estate if it is:

(a) Property belonging to his spouse or civil partner.

(b) Property which was the subject of an exempt transfer by the taxpayer or his spouse (or civil partner) to a charity, political party, national heritage body or housing association after 15 April 1976 and which is owned by that body *or* which has been owned by that body at any time in the five years preceding the transfer (or death).

If property valued using the related property rules ('the related value') produces a higher value than when valued without applying those rules (its 'unrelated value'), the value of the property in the transferor's estate will be:

$$\frac{\text{Value of that property at unrelated value}}{\text{Value of that property and the related property at unrelated value}} \times \text{Related value of total}$$

For example, Eleanor died owning (as a tenant in common with her civil partner Samantha) a plot of land of 1,000 acres. At the time of her death, Eleanor's 70% share was valued at £1,250,000 and Samantha's 30% share was valued at £450,000. The market value of the whole plot of 1,000 acres was £2,000,000. The value of Eleanor's interest in the land to be included in her estate for the purposes of inheritance tax is:

$$\frac{£2,000,000 \times £1,250,000}{(£1,250,000 + £450,000)} = £1,470,588$$

This related property value (of £1,470,588) is used in computing the value of Eleanor's estate instead of the unrelated value (of £1,250,000) as it is the higher of the two.

In arriving at this proportion for shares or debentures of the same class, the respective unrelated values are deemed to be proportional to the number of shares held (s 161(4)).

For example, the shareholders of Related Ltd are Mr R 40%, Mrs R 25%, Others 35%.

A 65% shareholding is valued at £58,500

A 40% shareholding is valued at £24,000

A 25% shareholding is valued at £15,000

The inheritance tax values of the shares held by Mr & Mrs R will be:

$$\text{Mr R} \frac{40}{65} \times £58,500 \text{ for a } 65\,\% \text{ holding} = £36,000$$

$$\text{Mrs R} \frac{25}{65} \times £58,500 \text{ for a } 65\,\% \text{ holding} = £22,500$$

since these are higher than £24,000 (for a 40% holding) and £15,000 (for a 25% holding) respectively.

It will be noted that the calculation that applies to value shares contrasts with that used to value land. The related value of the land is *not* taken simply as Eleanor's 70% share of the market value of the whole plot (ie 70% × £2,000,000 = £1,400,000).

Consider as a further example a gift of 1,000 unquoted company shares by George to his sister Charlotte. Before the gift George owned 6,000 shares and a registered charity owned the remaining 4,000 shares. The charity had recently acquired its shares from George's wife. The shareholdings were valued as follows:

£800,000 for a 100% holding

£700,000 for a 90% shareholding

£420,000 for a 60% shareholding

£250,000 for a 50% shareholding.

Calculate the value of George's gift for the purposes of inheritance tax.

Before the gift, George's shareholding is valued at:

Applying the related property rules 6,000/10,000 × £800,000 = £480,000

Without applying those rules £420,000

After the gift, George's shareholding is valued at:

Applying the related property rules 5,000/9,000 × £700,000 = £388,889

Without applying those rules £250,000

In each case, George's holding is higher when applying the related property rules and so the value of his gift for IHT purposes is £91,111 (£480,000 - £388,889). This is so despite the fact that is gift is valued at £170,000 (£480,000 - £250,000) without the application of those rules.

Excluded property is a component part of an individual's estate (see **Example A1 part (b)**) and for the purposes of the related property rules, it is important to remember that excluded property can be related property. So, for example, where a husband owns excluded property (because he is domiciled overseas and the property is situated abroad), for example, shares in company incorporated abroad, his share will be taken into account in valuing his wife's shares (where she is UK domiciled and owns shares in the same company).

Unquoted securities

Section 168 refers to *unquoted shares and securities* and states that their valuation is to be made on the basis that a prospective purchaser has available all the information which a prudent purchaser might reasonably require in an arm's length transaction.

Farm cottages and farmhouses

Section 169 deals with *farm cottages* occupied by agricultural employees. In valuing agricultural property which includes cottages, no account is to be taken of any value attributable to the fact that the cottages are suitable for residential purposes of persons who are not employed solely for agricultural purposes in connection with that agricultural property. If the cottage is occupied by a retired employee or the retired employee's widow(er) it is deemed to be occupied by an employee provided it is occupied under a statutorily protected tenancy or under a lease granted to the employee (and surviving spouse) for life as part of his contract of employment (ESC F16).

It should be noted that only the agricultural value of a farmhouse qualifies for agricultural property relief, not its full market value, which will often be much higher (see **Example A22 explanatory note 4**).

A special purchaser

A problem arises when the property to be valued could be the subject of a bid by a *special purchaser*. For example, a piece of land with a normal value of £100,000 might be worth more to an adjoining landowner because of the value that it would add to his own holding. Although he might be prepared to bid up to, say £170,000, he would, in fact, only usually make the bid necessary to obtain the land. That might well be very little more than its normal market value. The value of such property will therefore be between its normal value and the highest price that a special purchaser would pay.

Capital gains tax

If the gift of an asset gives rise to a liability to *capital gains tax* and the *donee* bears that tax, then the value transferred for inheritance tax is reduced by the capital gains tax paid (IHTA 1984 s 165).

Capital gains tax may be held over on the disposal of certain property otherwise than under a bargain at arm's length if a claim is made under the provisions of TCGA 1992 s 165 or s 260. In this event the inheritance tax value is not altered, but any inheritance tax payable, either immediately or as a result of the donor's death within seven years, is deducted in computing the chargeable gain arising when the donee eventually disposes of the asset (but not so as to create or increase a loss) (ss 165(10), 260(7)).

Note however that, if the disposal was a potentially exempt transfer, this deduction in respect of inheritance tax, for capital gains tax purposes, is available only if the gain was held over under s 165 (business and agricultural assets), because the deduction in the case of s 260 is restricted to disposals within s 260(2)(a) which expressly excludes potentially exempt transfers. Hold-over relief under s 165 is not available if it could be claimed under s 260 (s 165(3)(d)); but if a claim under s 260 is precluded because the disposal is a potentially exempt transfer then a claim under s 165 will be possible provided the asset is of an appropriate type. If the nature of the asset is not such as to attract hold-over relief under s 165 then no off-set is available between capital gains tax and inheritance tax if the potentially exempt transfer proves to be chargeable by reason of the donor's death within seven years.

B. Blackacre — sale after death above or below probate value of £700,000

Sale below probate value

If Blackacre is sold for less than its probate value within three years of the testator's death, then relief is available under IHTA 1984 s 191 for the reduction in value provided a claim is made. The reduction is the difference between the land's value at death and its gross sale price (no account being taken of the incidental costs of sale). Should Blackacre be sold in the fourth year immediately following the death of the testator, then it would be treated as having been sold within the three-year period mentioned above (but only if its sale value would be less than its value on death) (s 197A)).

If the reduction so computed is less than £1,000 (or 5% of the value of the land at death if lower) then no adjustment will be made for that disposal (s 191(2)).

The relief can only be claimed if the land was sold to an unconnected person by the 'appropriate person', ie the person liable to pay the inheritance tax on the land at death (eg personal representative or trustee of settlement). Should a claim lie to the appropriate person, the merits of making one need to be considered before it is submitted (see **explanatory note** 7).

In arriving at the *sale value* there are provisions to substitute for the *sale price*, the best consideration which could reasonably have been obtained at the time of sale.

If a claim for relief is made, all sales of land within the *three* years after death (ie including those at a profit but ignoring those covered by the de minimis rule above) must be taken into account. Sales at a profit in the *fourth* year are not taken into account, but those at a *loss* must be considered.

With effect from 1 April 2011, a claim under s 191 must be made by the appropriate person within the period of four years after the end of the three-year period following the date of the deceased's death (even where a sale of land in the fourth year is being considered under s 197A) (s 191(1A) introduced by FA 2009 Sch 51 para 10 and brought into effect by SI 2010/867 reg 2(2)).

Sale above probate value

If land included in a deceased estate increases in value no additional inheritance tax is payable on the increase provided no claim for a reduction in value of other properties has been made (but capital gains tax at 28% as residential property (see **Example C15 part B paragraph** (4)) *is* payable subject to any exemptions and reliefs available to the executors). Such a sale may, however, influence the agreement of a value on death (see **explanatory note** 7).

Therefore, if the executors sell Blackacre for £650,000 on the open market eighteen months after the date of death, and the estate does not sell any other land, a claim under s 191 should be made, reducing the value of the estate by £50,000. If the property were sold in similar circumstances for £750,000 the executors would be liable for capital gains tax on a gross gain of £50,000, reduced by the capital gains tax annual exemption.

C. Liabilities

The rules governing the deduction of liabilities in the computation of inheritance tax have, following the enactment of FA 2013 and FA 2014, become more complex. The scheme of rules that applies to deaths, transfers and relevant property trust charges that occur on or after 17 July 2013 is as follows: there are a number of general rules that apply regarding the treatment of liabilities (see ss 5, 162 and 175A); there is also a set of special rules on liabilities in relation to excluded property and property (called 'relievable property') qualifying for business property relief, agricultural property relief and/or woodlands relief. In respect of transfers and deaths that occur on or after 17 July 2014 (the date of enactment of FA 2014), the set of special rules is extended to include liabilities attributable to financing non-residents' foreign currency accounts.

The effect of the overall scheme of rules on the deduction of liabilities in the context of inheritance tax is to prevent a tax advantage being gained by obtaining a deduction for a liability that is not repaid after death or acquiring an asset which is not chargeable to inheritance tax, but otherwise, generally speaking, to ensure that inheritance tax is charged on the net value of a deceased estate after deducting liabilities.

General rules

Statement of rules

In determining the value of an individual's estate at any time (ie before and after he makes a transfer, or his estate when he dies), a liability of his at that time shall reduce the amount of his estate but only if (s 5(3), (5)):

- it is imposed by law (eg income tax and capital gains tax owing), or
- he acquired some property, service or other consideration for incurring the liability. This means that the deceased must have acquired something of value as a result of incurring the debt (eg buying clothes on a credit card, utility bills, and care home fees). This means that any debts created under a moral obligation (eg promising to make a gift) or that are legally unenforceable (eg gambling debts) cannot be counted in determining the value of an individual's estate. However, statute barred debts (debts that are no longer enforceable owing to the passing of time) may be so taken into account.

The liability is to be valued at the time when it is to be taken into account in valuing a transfer (and not the time at which it falls to be discharged – ie paid) (s 162(3)).

These general rules on liabilities must be applied together with the following rules:

- when valuing an individual's estate immediately after a transfer, his liability for IHT due on the transfer may be deducted (but not his liability for any other tax resulting from the transfer; also no allowance is made for the fact that the tax will not be due immediately (ss 5(4), 162(3));
- if the individual has the right to be reimbursed for any liability, then the liability may be deducted only to the extent that reimbursement cannot reasonably be expected to be obtained (s 162(1));
- a liability which is secured or charged on any particular item of property must, so far as possible, reduce the value of that property (s 162(4)) (see **Example A17**);
- where the liability is due to a person resident outside the UK and the liability is neither to be discharged in the UK nor is secured or charged on property in the UK, it must, so far as possible, reduce the value of property outside the UK (s 162(5));
- where the individual is in business as a sole trader or in partnership, any business debts should be deducted firstly against business property (s 110(b)).

Apart from the liabilities on secured property and overseas property, liabilities are generally deducted from the total value of all chargeable assets held at the same title (eg assets in the deceased's free estate are not available to trustees to settled trust debts). They are, generally speaking, deducted first from property that does not qualify for the instalment option of paying IHT (see **Example A11**). So for example, an unsecured overdraft might be set against cash and chattels before it is set against the residential property in the estate.

Whereas the above rules apply for the purposes of inheritance tax generally, the following rules on liabilities apply only in valuing an individual's deceased estate. The following liabilities may be deducted for that purpose:

- any liability to income tax in respect of an offshore income gain which arises because of the deemed disposal of the individual's interest in the fund because of his death;
- any liability to income tax in respect of a deeply discounted security which arises because of the deemed disposal of the security on the individual's death.

Where a liability to IHT reduces the value of an individual's deceased estate but the tax does not get paid out of the estate, the value of the estate must be treated as increased by the amount of the tax (s 174).

HRMC allows Canadian income tax due on death as a deduction from a person's estate. Under Canadian income tax law, a deceased person is treated as having disposed of all their property immediately before death and income tax is charged on any resulting gain. As the income tax charge may not arise until death has occurred, strictly it does not count as a deduction in arriving at the value of the estate immediately before death. The concession allows the Canadian income tax charge as a deduction for IHT purposes in line with the IHT treatment of other income tax charged which are repayable out of the estate (see IHTM 28102).

Although they are not debts as such, reasonable funeral expenses and associated costs involved with obtaining foreign probate and realising foreign assets (limited to 5% of the value of the foreign asset) are also allowable deductions in determining the value of an estate on death. However, UK estate administration costs and the costs of UK probate are not so deductible.

Discharge of liabilities after death

In relation to a death occurring on or after 17 July 2013 additional rules apply to deal with the repayment of liabilities after death. First, in arriving at the value of a deceased estate, a deduction for a liability will only be allowable to the extent that the liability has been repaid on or after death out of the assets in the estate or from excluded property owned by the person immediately before death, provided the deduction is not disallowed by some other rule (s 175A(1)). It must be noted that the liability must be paid out of the assets in the deceased person's estate which according to s 5 means all the property to which he is beneficially entitled (certain items being excepted); but for the purposes only of determining whether a liability has been discharged the normal meaning of estate is extended to include excluded property owned by the deceased. It is important to note here that the excluded property must be owned by the deceased so that the property of an excluded property trust in which the deceased had an interest is not property owned by the deceased.

Prior to the introduction of the disguised remuneration rules, it was common planning for employee benefit trusts (and similar third party structures) to make loans to beneficiaries which were left outstanding indefinitely and which were often waived after the individual's death. The above rules will require these sorts of loans to be repaid in order for the liability to be deducted in calculating the IHT liability on the individual's estate.

Strictly the legislation requires that, although no time limit is specified for the repayment of a debt, it must be repaid in the course of the administration of the deceased estate in order to be allowable. This means that because it will often be impossible to settle liabilities before a grant of probate (because for example they need to raise funds from the sale of other assets in the estate (which they cannot do without a grant of probate)), executors will have to pay inheritance tax based on the deceased's gross estate and then submit corrective accounts in order for the correct amount of inheritance tax to be calculated (which could lead to hardship if the estate is insufficiently liquid) (see **Example A10**). However, it is HMRC practice not to insist on the application of the strict letter of the law in all cases. IHTM28030 acknowledges that as the majority of liabilities taken as deductions against an estate will be arm's length, the starting assumption is that all liabilities will be repaid. So, unless the personal representatives are aware beforehand that a liability is not going to be repaid and is not otherwise allowable as a deduction, they may include all the deceased's liabilities when filling in the IHT400. HMRC officials are advised that there is no need to make any enquiries to establish that liabilities which are clearly commercial and at arm's length have been repaid as it is more than likely that the creditor will want to recover money owed. Examples of such liabilities include utility and credit card bills, council tax, payments due to HMRC, care fees, professional fees, overpaid pension and payments for goods and services. If, however, an arm's length liability for which a deduction is included is not actually repaid in the course of administration of the estate, then a corrective account must be submitted to HMRC.

It would appear that liabilities which are not arm's length (eg amounts owed to family members, family trusts or companies, or liabilities deducted in connection with avoidance schemes) may also, in the first instance, be treated as having been repaid when IHT400 is first submitted. However, in such cases HMRC then require personal representatives subsequently to prove that the money has been repaid. They may produce as evidence a copy of the letter enclosing a cheque made out to the creditor or confirmation of receipt of the payment by the creditor. Moreover there must be evidence that the amount has been repaid out of the deceased's estate or from excluded property owned by him at the date of his death. So personal representatives might provide copies of their bank statements to prove this or a copy of the ledger entry from the appropriate solicitor's client account.

The concessionary practice does not extend however to liabilities that personal representatives do not have to repay during the normal administration of an estate. Deductions for such debts (provided they are not within the class of innocent debts provided for in s 175A(2) – see below) cannot be taken into account when form IHT400 is first submitted. If the debt is subsequently repaid, then a deduction is allowed and tax repaid, provided the claim for repayment is made within 4 years (s 241).

The strict letter of the law also requires that in order for a liability to be deducted in valuing a deceased estate it has to be paid out of the assets of the deceased's estate (or from excluded property owned by him). IHTM28027 acknowledges that there may be cases where an estate has very little by way of liquid assets from which a liability can be repaid so that personal representatives may need to borrow money actually to repay debts. Where this happens, with the result that the estate is charged with repaying that new debt, HMRC accepts that the liability owed by the deceased has been repaid out of his estate. The source of such a loan is not relevant in the context of this concession. HMRC give the following example at IHTM28027. Kevin's estate of valued at £750,000, £700,000 of which is attributable to his home. A mortgage of £100,000 is secured against the house. The executors borrow £100,000 to repay the mortgage and secure the new loan on the house so that the beneficiary receives the property encumbered with the new debt. HMRC treat the liability (ie the mortgage) as having been discharged out of Kevin's estate. They will not enquire into the source of the funds lent to the executors. Provided the mortgage has actually been repaid from funds charged against the estate, the deduction may be allowed as this has the same effect as the liability being discharged out of the estate had there been sufficient liquid assets. It is possible that a beneficiary of the estate may be able to make a loan to the estate from the proceeds of an insurance policy held in trust outside the estate for the purposes of repaying the mortgage. Again HMRC will not be concerned as to the source of the funds in applying this concession. Unfortunately the situation described in this example may give rise to an SDLT problem where the home is situated in the UK. As the beneficiary acquires property together with the assumption of existing debt, chargeable consideration arises for the purposes of SDLT equal to the amount of the debt (FA 2003 Sch 4 para 8). Although in the above example the amount of the debt of £100,000 falls in the SDLT nil-rate band, if the amount were greater SDLT could become chargeable. FA 2003 Sch 3 para 3A provides that where the personal representatives distribute property which is subject to secured debt, there is an exemption from the SDLT charge if the only consideration given by the beneficiary is the assumption of that secured debt (which is defined as 'debt that, immediately after the death of the deceased person, is secured on the property'). In the case of Kevin above, the new debt taken out by the executors cannot be described as debt that, immediately after the death of the deceased person, is secured on the property. If the executors had transferred the home subject to the original mortgage, the SDLT exemption would apply but there would be no deduction for the debt for inheritance tax purposes. This tension between inheritance tax and SDLT is a real problem.

There is a class of what may be called innocent debts that, although not discharged after the deceased's death out of his estate, may yet still be deductible in computing the value of his estate (IHTA 1984 s 175A(2)). An innocent debt is one:

- where it is shown that there is a real commercial reason for not paying the liability (or part of it);
- the purpose of leaving the liability (or part of it) unpaid is not so as to obtain a tax advantage; and
- the liability (or part) is not otherwise prevented (by the IHTA 1984) from being deducted.

For example, it may be the case that where the deceased's business is being taken over by his beneficiaries (rather than being wound up by his executors) that a bank is agreeable to any lending and overdraft facilities to continue and to be taken over by the beneficiaries. In such a case, the deceased's business debts will be deductible as an innocent debt even though they have not been discharged by the deceased's executors. Similarly, consider the case of Edmund whose estate includes a house valued at £1m. There is a commercial mortgage of £200,000 from a family trust charged against the property. Edmund leaves his house to his son. The trustees are content that the house can be transferred to the son who has entered into legal arrangements with the trustees to assume liability for the mortgage. Again, although the liability has not been repaid, the arrangements are commercial and there is no tax advantage arising from the son taking over the mortgage; hence the debt of £200,000 may be allowed as a deduction from Edmund's estate.

It will be noted that in the context of the relaxation of the prohibition rule for innocent debts, when the liability has not been repaid as part of arrangements that seek to secure a tax advantage, it is the failure to repay the liability which has to give rise to the tax advantage, rather than looking only at whether the liability was part of any arrangements. In the context of this rule on innocent debt, it is deemed that there is a real commercial reason for a liability not being paid where it is shown that the liability is to a person dealing at arm's length (or that an arm's length creditor would not require the liability to be repaid) (s 175A(3)). There may be other occasions proved on the facts of a case where a debt may be regarded as an innocent debt. Tax (in the term 'tax advantage') includes income tax and capital gains tax (s 175A(6)), and advantage means a relief from tax (or increased relief from tax), a repayment of tax (or an increased repayment from tax), the avoidance, reduction or delay of a charge to tax or an assessment to tax, or the avoidance of a possible assessment to tax or determination in respect of tax (IHTA 1984 s 175A(5)).

Incidental effects of rule on discharge of liabilities after death

For the purposes of the IHT exemption for transfers between spouses or civil partners, where a liability is not repaid and is disallowed in arriving at the value of a deceased person's estate, the increase in value of the estate of the deceased's spouse or civil partner is treated as the full value without any deduction for the disallowed liability (s 175A(4)). For example, Mary makes a loan of £25,000 to her mother to help with living expenses and the amount is secured on the mother's house valued at £500,000. On the mother's death, the property passes to her husband (ie Mary's father) and the loan is not repaid. As an arm's length creditor would be unlikely to leave the loan outstanding, the debt owed by the mother of £25,000 is not deductible in valuing her estate so that the value of the house remains at £500,000 (rather than being valued at £475,000). For the purposes of the spouse exemption, the liability is also ignored so that the amount of the mother's estate that is exempt on account of that exemption is £500,000 (even though the husband (Mary's father) acquires an asset worth £500,000 but encumbered by a mortgage of £25,000).

Also, the rule on the repayment of liabilities does not apply for the purposes of the ten year anniversary charge that arises in relation to relevant property trusts.

Special rules on excluded property, foreign currency bank accounts and relievable property

Special rules apply in relation to the deduction of liabilities where the liabilities concerned relate to excluded property, balances on non-residents' foreign currency accounts and property qualifying for business property relief, agricultural property relief and/or woodlands relief (collectively called relievable property). Apart from the rules that apply to foreign currency accounts, the special rules apply to settled relevant property as well as property owned personally by an individual. HMRC has stated that these new special rules will only affect individuals entering into avoidance schemes involving debts to reduce artificially the value of an estate (HMRC Budget 2013 Note). However, the changes may also affect standard arrangements and planning to mitigate an individuals' (or trust's) exposure in the absence of an abusive tax avoidance motive.

Excluded property

The rules on the deductibility of liabilities incurred in respect of excluded property apply in relation to transfers of value, deaths and relevant property trust charges arising on or after 17 July 2013 regardless of when the liability was incurred (FA 2013 Sch 36 para 5(1)).

Where a liability has been incurred directly or indirectly to acquire, maintain (ie keep in good order) or enhance (ie improve or augment) any excluded property, the liability may not be deducted in calculating inheritance tax unless one of the three statutory exceptions to this rule is met (s 162A(1)). It will be noted that the rule disallowing a deduction for liabilities incurred in respect of excluded property goes beyond merely borrowing to acquire the excluded property.

For example, consider the case of the trustees of a discretionary trust settled by a non-domiciled individual where the trust property comprises overseas property and UK property valued at £2.5m. The trustees borrow £2m and charge it against the UK property. They use half the money to buy shares in an overseas company and they deposit the balance in an overseas bank account. The liability of £2m is not deductible as the money borrowed was used to acquire excluded property (namely the overseas company shares and the money on deposit overseas).

By way of further example, take the case of Fabien who wants to invest £1.5m in his overseas business. In order to achieve this aim he sells his UK home for £2m; he buys a new home for £½m and invests the balance of the monies in his business. Should Fabien die, his net estate is £½m. By contrast, consider Jacques who has the same objective. Instead of selling his UK house for £2m, he borrows £1.5m secured on the property. He invests the borrowed funds in the overseas business. Although economically speaking Jacques has a net estate of £½m, for inheritance tax purposes he is not able to deduct the borrowing with the result that his estate is valued at £2m. These two examples reflect the operation of the rules which seek to charge tax having regard to the reality of a taxpayer's position rather than having regard to the position in which he finds himself due to any deliberate manipulation of the value of excluded property.

The three statutory exceptions to the blanket rule preventing the deduction of liabilities relating to excluded property are as follows:

- *Sale of excluded property and proceeds chargeable to IHT*: where the excluded property has been disposed of for full consideration, a deduction may be taken for the liability of an amount equal to the consideration as is subject to tax and has not been used to acquire, maintain or enhance the excluded property, or to repay a liability that itself would not be allowable (s 162A(2)). So the liability may be deducted if the excluded property has been sold for full value and the proceeds form part of the individual's estate so that they are chargeable to inheritance tax (ie the proceeds are not themselves excluded property). In the case of the trustees in the above example, were they to transfer the funds in the overseas bank account to a UK bank account, they will have disposed of the excluded property comprising the overseas bank account and replaced it with an asset (a UK bank account) that is within the charge to inheritance tax. £1m of the amount borrowed may be deducted from the value of the trust's UK property when the trust is next charged to inheritance tax in respect of its relevant property.

- *Excluded property no longer excluded*: where the excluded property has not been disposed of, a deduction may be taken for an amount equal to the value of such of the excluded property as has not been disposed of and which is no longer excluded property (s 162A(3)). This rule is directed at cases where property, whilst still owned by the taxpayer, ceases to be excluded property and becomes chargeable to IHT before the question of whether to take the liability into account arises. The deduction may be allowed to the extent that the property has not been disposed of and is subject to tax. For example, Philippe who is not domiciled in the UK borrows £3m abroad to buy a property abroad. The interest on the loan is added to the principal. Philippe becomes domiciled in the UK and subsequently dies when the property is worth £5m and the amount due on the loan is £5.5m. The loan was used to acquire excluded property and prima facie is not deductible in computing the inheritance tax arising on Philippe's estate; however, since the property is subject to inheritance tax on Philippe's death, the liability may be deducted up to the value of the property (ie £5m) in computing his inheritance tax liability. The remaining £½m may not be deducted however.

- *Excluded property has genuinely fallen in value*: where the excluded property has not been disposed of, is still excluded property and any remaining liability exceeds the value of the property, a deduction for the excess may be made but only so far as the remaining liability is not due to one of (what may be called) offensive reasons (s 162A(4), (7)). So where excluded property has not been sold, was acquired with borrowings and has fallen in value through no fault of the taxpayer, a deduction is allowed up to the value of the excluded property and any excess borrowing is also deductible unless the excess has arisen because one of the three offensive reasons.

  The offensive reasons referred to above are (a) arrangements whose purpose is to obtain an inheritance tax advantage (eg where arrangements artificially depress value of assets to create an excess liability), or (b) an increase in the amount of the liability due to interest accruals or otherwise (eg the increase is worked out by reference to some formula), or (c) a disposal of the property.

  For example, Jens who is not domiciled in the UK borrows £1m which is charged in his UK assets worth £1.7m and uses the money to acquire a villa in Germany. The market value of the property falls to £700,000 on account of a downturn in the economy. The £1m is not a deductible amount on first principles, but as the fall in value of the excluded property is not due to a tax advantaged arrangement, an increase in the value of the liability or a disposal of the excluded property, £300,000 (£1m less the £700,000 value of the German villa) is allowed as a deduction and reduces the chargeable value of the UK assets to £1.4m.

  By contrast consider the case of the trustees of an excluded property trust which includes UK property worth £2m, borrow £1.5m which they charge on the UK property. They use the funds to acquire more property overseas. At the next ten year anniversary of the trust the loan stands at £1.8m as the interest on the loan has been added to capital and the value of the excluded property is £1.6m. No relief is available for the excess value of the liability over the asset to be taken into account as the increase in the loan over the value of the excluded asset is due to an increase in the value of the liability. The whole liability of £1.8m is disallowed.

There is also a rule dealing with the position where an individual has taken out a loan to acquire, maintain or enhance property that was not excluded property at the time of the loan but which has subsequently become excluded property whilst still in the ownership of the borrower (s 162A(5)). In this case, the liability is only deductible to the extent that it exceeds the value of the property that has become excluded property unless the excess is due to one of the offensive reasons cited above (s 162A(6)). For example, Eugenio who is domiciled outside the UK borrows £1m to invest in precious gemstones which he keeps in the UK. He subsequently transfers the gemstones to a safe deposit box in France. On his death the gemstones are worth £1m but as the interest on the loan has been added to capital, Eugenio now owes £1.25m. Only the excess of the debt over the value of the asset (ie £250,000) is potentially deductible in computing Eugenio's liability to inheritance on his UK estate. However as the excess liability is due to an increase in the loan due to the accrual of interest (an offensive reason), none of the excess (ie none of the £250,000) is so deductible. By contrast, Roberto who is not domiciled in the UK borrows £750,000 to buy two antique, solid silver candlesticks which he keeps in his Manchester flat. He subsequently takes one of the candlesticks (when both are worth £450,000 each) to his home in Brazil (so that the candlestick becomes excluded property). Roberto subsequently dies when the loan is still outstanding and the values of the antiques have not altered. The excess of the liability over the excluded property is £300,000 and this is allowed as a deduction in computing the value of Roberto's estate chargeable to IHT.

Non-residents' foreign currency bank accounts

The rules on the deductibility of liabilities incurred in respect of balances held on non-residents' foreign currency accounts apply in relation to deaths arising on or after 17 July 2014 (the date of enactment of FA 2014) regardless of when the liability was incurred (FA 2014 Sch 21 para 3(8)). These rules block a loophole left after the enactment of the special rules relating to excluded property enacted by FA 2013. Funds in a non-resident individual's foreign bank account are not excluded property per se but are left out of account in valuing the individual's estate on his death.

Where a liability incurred on or after that date is attributable (wholly or partly) to financing (directly or indirectly) a balance on any qualifying foreign currency account, then, the liability is to be left out of account under s 157 in determining the person' estate immediately before his death to the extent that, in the first instance, it is equal to or less than the amount of the balance (s 162AA(1), (2)). If the liability exceeds the balance held on the account then it may be deductible under s 157 in determining the person' estate immediately before his death but only so far as the excess does not arise as a result on arrangements the main purpose, or one of the main purposes of which is to secure a tax advantage or an increase in the amount of the liability (whether due to the accrual of interest or otherwise) (s 162AA(2), (3), (4)). A qualifying foreign currency account is a foreign currency account with a bank (as defined in ITA 2007 s 991) that is held in the name of the deceased individual himself or the trustees of a trust where the bank account forms part of the settled property in which the individual is beneficially entitled to an interest in possession (provided that the settlor of the trust was not domiciled in the UK when he made the settlement and the trustees are not domiciled or resident in the UK immediately before the beneficiary's death) (IHTA 1984 s 157(1), (3), (5)). Interestingly the interest in possession in this case does not have to be a qualifying IIP (see **Example C3**) (although it is thought that s 157 can have no practical application unless the interest in possession is a qualifying IIP).

Section 157 provides that balances on UK bank accounts denominated in a foreign currency held by an individual who is not domiciled and not resident in the UK immediately before death will not be taken into account in determining the value of that individual's estate. By virtue of these special rules, where he had borrowed money which was held on that account or had a liability that indirectly financed the funds in that accounts, that liability may only be allowed as a deduction to the extent that it exceeds the balance held on the account but only if the excess has not arisen as a result of tax avoidance arrangements or due to manipulation of the value of the liability (as defined).

For example, consider Dorothy who is not domiciled and not resident in the UK. She borrows £500,000 in 2010 and places it in a US dollar account with a UK bank. If Dorothy (never having made any lifetime gifts) had died on 31 December 2013 owning UK sited assets of £500,000 she would have paid no inheritance tax. The balance standing to her credit on her US dollar is left out of account under s 157 in valuing her estate and the debt of £500,000 is set against her chargeable estate of £500,000 to reduce it to nil. By contrast if Dorothy dies on 31 December 2023, her US dollar account continues to be left out of account in valuing her estate but she will be unable to set the debt against her chargeable estate of £500,000. An inheritance tax liability of (£500,000 - £325,000) @ 40% = £175,000 arises.

Relievable property

The rules on the deductibility of liabilities incurred in respect of relievable property apply in relation to transfers of value, deaths and relevant property trust charges arising on or after 17 July 2013 but only in relation to those liabilities incurred on or after 6 April 2013; liabilities incurred before that date are not subject to the special rules about to be described (FA 2013 Sch 36 para 5(2)). A liability is to be treated as incurred when an agreement is made or the date an agreement is varied if the variation enables a liability to be incurred under it (FA 2013 Sch 36 para 5(2), (3)). So the protection afforded by this grandfathering rule is not available where a pre-6 April 2013 agreement is varied so that a liability could be incurred under it; in this case the liability is treated as incurred on the date of the variation of the agreement (and hence after 5 April 2013). In contrast to the case of relievable property, it will be noted that liabilities in respect of excluded property are not grandfathered; this means that liabilities in existence before 17 July 2013 fall within the special rule relating to excluded property discussed above.

Where a liability incurred on or after 6 April 2013 has been incurred to acquire, maintain (ie keep in good order) or enhance (ie improve or augment) property which qualifies for business property relief (BPR), or to acquire, or maintain or enhance the agricultural value of property that qualifies for agricultural property relief (APR), then, the liability is deductible only to the extent that it reduces the value of the property concerned to nil (IHTA s 162B(1), (2), (3), (4)). This is so even if the liability is actually secured against the other assets of the estate (s 162(4)) or even if the liability is otherwise required to be taken into account in relation to overseas property (s 162(5)). These rules also apply to occasions when inheritance tax is charged on relevant property trusts (s 162B(9)).

For example, consider Gareth who borrows £500,000 which is charged on his house, in order to buy shares quoted on AIM (ie the shares are relevant business property – see **Example A21 part A**). At the date of his death, the AIM shares are worth £600,000 and the rest of his estate is valued at £1.5m. The loan is repaid by Gareth's executors. The liability first reduces the value of the AIM shares to £100,000; BPR then further reduces the chargeable amount to nil. As the liability has been taken into account in valuing the AIM shares, it cannot be used to reduce the value of the house against which it is secured. The chargeable estate is £1.5m.

Consider also the case of Stuart who borrows £800,000 which he uses to buy a farm. On his death his estate is valued at £2m of which the farm is worth £1m with an agricultural value of £750,000. The loan is repaid by his executors. The loan has been used to acquire assets that are both agricultural property (that is the farm itself – see **Example A22**) and relevant business property (that is the farming business – see **Example A21 part A**). IHTA 1984 s 114 provides that were both APR and BPR can apply, APR is given in priority to BPR. Under s 162B(4) the agricultural value of the agricultural property is reduced by the loan to nil leaving no value qualifying for APR. The remaining £50,000 liability reduces the value of the farming business to £200,000 which is then reduced to nil by BPR. The chargeable estate is therefore £1m.

In the case of a business that is relevant business property, where the liability has already been taken into account in arriving at the net value of a business under s 110(b), the rule in s 162B has no effect (s 162B(2)). For example, Dion, who runs a business selling paintings, borrows £100,000 to buy a shop. The loan is unsecured and is shown in the accounts as a liability of the business. The liability has been taken into account in valuing the business before BPR is considered; the liability is not taken into account again under s 162B.

Where a liability has been incurred to acquire land, trees or underwood that qualify for woodlands relief, or to plant the trees or underwood, or to enhance or maintain the value of those trees or underwood, and the value of a person's estate immediately before death contains land on which trees or underwood are growing but the value of the trees or underwood is left out of account on account of a claim to woodlands relief (see **Example B11**), the liability reduces the value of the trees or underwood so that the claim applies only in relation to their net value which is then left out of account (s 162B(5), (6)).

For example, Annika borrows £200,000 to buy woodland and this amount is secured on a life assurance policy of which she is the beneficiary. At the date of her death the value of the trees and underwood is £225,000 and a claim is made for that amount to be excluded from her chargeable estate. The loan is repaid by her executors. As the loan has been used to acquire the woodland, £200,000 first reduces the value of the trees and woodland in her estate (even though the loan has been secured on another asset) so that the claim only lies in respect of the £25,000 net value of the trees and underwood. Only £25,000 has been left out of her estate because of woodlands relief.

In the three cases of relievable property, the following two additional rules also apply:

- to the extent that a liability has been taken into account in determining the value of a chargeable transfer, the liability is not then taken into account again in relation to a subsequent transfer by the same transferor (s 162B(7)). This rule addresses the situation where relievable property is given away in an earlier lifetime transfer and ensures that once a liability has been taken into account, it cannot be taken into account against another transfer by the same transferor. In order for this rule to apply the liability must reduce the value transferred by a chargeable transfer (a chargeable lifetime transfer or a failed PET). If a transferor survives seven years after making a PET (so that it becomes absolutely exempt), the liability may still be deducted from the transferor's estate on death as it will not have been taken into account by an earlier transfer.

  For example, Glenna who has an estate of £3m (the value of which does not change) borrows £1m to buy a farm and the loan is secured against her holiday home. Three years later she gives the farm to her daughter when it is worth £1.2m but Glenna remains liable for repaying the loan. The value of the PET made by Glenna (ignoring annual exemptions) is £1.2m less the borrowing of £1m less APR of £200,000 (ie nil). If Glenna dies two years after making the gift the £1m liability cannot be taken into account again in valuing her holiday home and so her chargeable estate remains at £3m.

- the above rule is not taken into account for the purposes of a ten-year anniversary charge so that a liability can be taken into account again for subsequent ten year anniversary charges (s 162B(8)). So while the assets acquired with the borrowed money remain in the trust, the liability can be taken into account at each ten year charge. But once the assets cease to be relevant property, so that the liability is taken into account in computing the exit charge, then if the liability remains with the trustees it will be prevented under s 162B(7) from being taken into account against any further charges.

These special rules on the relief for liabilities will apply typically to entrepreneurs who borrow to invest in their businesses but secure the borrowings on other assets. The individuals concerned will have to deduct the borrowing from the business assets for inheritance tax purposes and not from the estate as a whole. It is only after the borrowings have been so deducted that business property relief, agricultural property relief and/or woodlands relief (as the case may be) further reduces the value of the property concerned (see **Example A14**).

It is not clear in the application of this special rule whether the property acquired (maintained or enhanced) with borrowings must be relievable property at the time it is acquired (maintained or enhanced) or whether it is the status of the property when a tax charge rises that is relevant. There is also no legislative guidance on how liabilities should be split where the borrowing has been used to acquire property that is part relievable property and part not; it is not clear whether the liability should be pro-rated by reference to the acquisition values of the two elements or their values at the date of transfer. The proportions of these may be different or there may, in fact, have been no relievable element at the time of acquisition. It is HMRC practice to apportion the liability at the date of acquisition in order to provide certainty of approach (IHTM28021).

Priority rules: mixture of excluded property, non-residents' foreign currency bank accounts, relievable property and other property

There are three priority rules that come into play where liabilities relate to a mixture of excluded property, non-residents' foreign currency bank accounts, relievable property and other UK property.

First, a priority rule applies to deal with the deduction in determining the value of an estate on death of a liability that has been incurred to acquire, maintain or enhance a mixture of excluded property, relievable property and/or other property and/or where a liability is attributable to financing a non-resident's foreign currency bank account where the liability has been partially repaid before it is taken into account for the purposes of a deduction (s 162C(1)). The repayment is first applied to any part of the liability that was not attributable to excluded or relievable property or the funds held on the foreign currency bank account, then to any part used to finance relievable property, then to any part attributable to financing funds held on the foreign currency bank account and finally to any part used to finance excluded property (s 162C(1A)). The result is the part of the liability that may be allowable as a deduction under the general rules is treated as paid off first. This is a worst case scenario for the taxpayer.

Secondly, a priority rule applies to deal with the deduction otherwise than in determining the value of an estate on death of a liability that has been incurred to acquire, maintain or enhance a mixture of excluded property, relievable property and/or other property and/or where a liability is attributable to financing a non-resident's foreign currency bank account where the liability has been partially repaid before it is taken into account for the purposes of a deduction (s 162C(1)). The repayment is first applied to any part of the liability that was not attributable to excluded or relievable property, then to any part used to finance relievable property and finally to any part used to finance excluded property (s 162C(2)). The result is the part of the liability that may be allowable as a deduction under the general rules and/or that is attributable to financing funds held on the foreign currency bank account is treated as paid off first. This too is a worst case scenario for the taxpayer.

For example, on 2 August 2013, Henrico who was domiciled abroad settled €2.4m on trust (ie an excluded property trust). The trustees immediately used all of the money to purchase a house in the UK worth £2m. Subsequently the trustees borrowed £1.5m and charged it against the house. They use the loan to acquire a flat in St Lucia (ie excluded property) for £900,000, shares in UK unquoted trading companies (ie relevant business property qualifying for BPR) for £350,000 and shares in UK quoted investment companies for £250,000. Just before the ten year anniversary of the trust on 2 August 2023, the trustees repay £700,000 of the loan leaving £800,000 still owing. Under s 126C(2), the amount repaid of £700,000 is first matched to the amount of the original loan used to acquire the UK quoted shares (£250,000), then to the amount of the original loan used to acquire the UK unquoted shares (£350,000) and lastly to the amount of the original loan used to acquire the flat in St Lucia. Consequently, it may be said that no money was borrowed to acquire the UK quoted shares, no money was borrowed to acquire the UK unquoted shares and that £800,000 (£900,000 – £100,000 (the £100,000 being part of the repayment of £700,000 that was not matched to the UK quoted and unquoted shares)) was borrowed to acquire the flat in St Lucia. (It is precisely £800,000 that the trustees still owe out of the £1.5m originally borrowed.) On 1 August 2023 it is anticipated that the value of the UK house will be £2.5m, the flat in St Lucia will be £1m, the UK unquoted shares will be £400,000 and the UK quoted shares will be £300,000. Hence the amount charged to inheritance tax on the ten year anniversary of the trust on 2 August 2023 will be £2.8m, comprising £300,000 of UK quoted shares, £0 of UK unquoted shares (their value being reduced entirely by BPR) and £2.5m relating to the UK house. The flat in St Lucia is excluded property and so, not being relevant property, is not taken into account in the levying IHT on the trustees on the ten-year anniversary of the trust. The £800,000 borrowing relates wholly to the excluded property of the trust and so cannot reduce the value of the relevant property charged to IHT (s 162A). For more detail on how relevant property trusts are charged to inheritance tax, see **Examples C11, C12** and **C13.**

Thirdly, there is a priority rule where a liability is attributable to a mixture of excluded property, the financing a non-resident's foreign currency bank account, relievable property and/or other property and has only been partially repaid after death. The part of the liability that is attributable to excluded property is taken to be repaid first, followed by any part attributable to financing the bank account, followed in turn by any part attributable to relievable property, and finally to any remaining part (s 175A(7)).

For example, Frederick who is not domiciled in the UK, borrows £1.5m from an excluded property trust and charges the liability against his UK chargeable property worth £2m. He uses the loan to buy £600,000 of excluded property, £500,000 of property qualifying for business property relief, £100,000 on a foreign currency bank account and £300,000 of chargeable UK property. On his death (at a time when he not resident in the UK), Frederick's executors repay the £1.5m loan. Assuming that none of the exceptions to the general rules applies and the values of the assets in his estate have not changed. The debt of £1.5m is dealt with as follows:

- the £600,000 used to acquire excluded property is disallowed (s 162A) even though it has been repaid by Frederick's executors after his death out of his estate;
- the £100,000 placed on the foreign currency bank account is disallowed (s 162AA) even though, again, it has been repaid by Frederick's executors after his death out of his estate;
- the £500,000 used to buy the agricultural property reduces the value of that property to nil (and so no APR is available) (s 162B);
- the £300,000 used to acquire chargeable UK assets goes to reduce the value of his UK chargeable estate of £2.3m to £2m (s 175A).

If the executors had paid only £750,000 of the liability from the deceased's estate after his death, the full debt of £1.5m is dealt with as follows:

- the first £600,000 used to acquire excluded property is disallowed (s 162A; s 175A(7)(a));
- the next £100,000 used to finance the foreign currency bank account (s 162 AA; s 197A(7)(aa));
- the final £50,000 is taken to have discharged part of the debt of £500,000 incurred to acquire the agricultural property. This reduces the value of the agricultural property to £450,000 but this is recued to nil by APR (assuming APR at the rate of 100% is available) (s 162B; s 175A(7)(b));
- the UK chargeable estate is valued at £2.3m.

Nigel's chargeable estate

Nigel's chargeable estate at the time of his death in March 2024 is as follows:

Date of death March 2024

		£	£
Shares in unquoted trading company		2,000,000	
Less:	100% business property relief (note(a))	(2,000,000)	Nil
Storage Unit		700,000	
Less:	Loan to buy storage unit (note (b))	(500,000)	
Less:	50% business property relief	(100,000)	100,000
Family home		1,500,000	
Less:	Loan to buy shares in unquoted trading company (note (a))	(800,000)	700,000
Cottage in Bavaria			300,000
Other assets		400,000	
Less:	Loan to buy cottage (note (c))	(200,000)	
	Credit card debts	(100,000)	100,000
Total estate on which inheritance tax is payable			1,200,000

The deductions for the loans in the computation of Nigel's chargeable estate are explained as follows:

(a) The loan to buy the shares in the unquoted trading company (which is relevant business property) was taken out before 6 April 2013 and is therefore deductible in valuing the asset on which it is secured.

(b) The loan to buy the storage unit (which is relevant business property) was taken out after 5 April 2013 and reduces the value of that property before business property relief is taken.

(c) The cottage in Bavaria is not excluded property as Nigel is domiciled in the UK. As the loan to acquire it is unsecured it is deducted from the estate generally.

For an explanation as to how these deductions affect the amount of the residence nil-rate band available in respect of Nigel's estate, see **explanatory note 8**.

Explanatory Notes

Inheritance tax: open market value

(1) The 'open market value' rule is the general valuation rule applicable to property comprised in both lifetime and death transfers. There are, however, a number of special rules relating to particular assets, some of which are dealt with in the Example.

The special rules relating to valuation of quoted securities on death are dealt with in **Examples A8, A10** and **A13**. The provisions for claiming relief for a fall in value of a lifetime gift before the donor's death are dealt with in **Example A14**. Also see **Example A26 explanatory note 1** for differences in valuation for capital gains tax and inheritance tax purposes.

But the general rule is that the value of property for IHT is the price the property might reasonably fetch if sold in the open market at the time of the transfer (s 160). This statutory price is not reduced as it would be in practice if all the relevant property were placed on the market on the valuation date, which in a normal market might depress the price.

The use of the 'open market price' value is imposed by statute even though in reality an 'open market' may not exist. In *Baird's Executors v IRC* [1991] it was decided that even though there may not actually be a commercial market for a tenancy, the tenancy is not valueless and the existence of such a market had to be assumed. The statute creates a fictional market rather like an auction, although occasionally sales by private treaty may give the best guide where there has been a sale at about the same time of similar property. It is assumed there has been adequate publicity before any sale and it is also assumed the property is offered for sale to the whole world so that any purchaser has an equal chance of buying.

What is valued is the interest of the transferor at the relevant time, but restrictions that would prevent or hamper a sale in reality are considered in turn. It is generally assumed that any purchaser would be subject to the same restrictions and that the price they pay would take those restrictions into account if imposed on them.

In *Gray (surviving executor of Lady Fox) v IRC* [1994] STC 360 the deceased owned a large agricultural estate and was one of the partners who farmed it under an agricultural tenancy. She was entitled to 92.5% of the partnership profits. The Court of Appeal approved a valuation of the tenancy based on the investment value of the land, disregarding the partnership share.

The planning status of the land is relevant to its value, whether or not planning permission has actually been applied for or obtained. The 'hope value' of the land will affect its valuation.

Valuation of life policies for inheritance tax

(2) The usual market value rule applies to the valuation of life policies (whether on the life of the transferor or of someone else) and for this purpose it will be necessary to consider not only the surrender value of the policy (if applicable) but also the actuarial value in the sense of what sum the policy will produce and how long (taking account of the life expectancy, health etc of the life assured) a putative buyer would have to wait to receive that sum. However, two other points may be relevant:

(a) Except for transfers on death (or transfers where the policy does not leave the transferor's estate) the sum of the premiums paid to date must in many cases be substituted if it is higher than the market value ascertained on the above principles (s 167). This does not however apply to term policies or survivorship policies, provided (in broad terms) that in the case of policies for a term of more than three years (whether initially or by exercise of a policy option) premiums are payable at least annually and in regular amounts and for at least two thirds of the term of the policy.

(b) In the case of a transfer on death, if the death results in the policy maturing and the proceeds being payable, the value to be taken will be the amount of the proceeds, as being one instance of a change in value resulting from the death (s 171).

Inheritance tax: associated operations

(3) The valuation to be placed on a particular asset will be affected if it is disposed of as part of a series of associated transactions (see **Example A20**).

Inheritance tax: related property

(4) Where property in a death estate has been valued under the related property rules, and the property is sold within three years after the death, a claim may be made under s 176 for the value of the property immediately before the death to be re-determined as if the related property rules did not apply. This does *not* mean substituting the *sale proceeds* for the probate value.

A claim may only be made if:

(a) The property is sold either by the personal representatives or the person in whom the property is vested.

(b) The sale is at arm's length for a freely negotiated price and not made in conjunction with a sale of any of the related property.

(c) The vendor and purchaser are unconnected.

(d) The vendor does not have a right to reacquire the property.

Valuation at death for inheritance tax

(5) Although the value of property at death is deemed to be its value immediately prior to death, the valuation may anticipate the effect of the death, but not the effect of the sale of the assets. For example, the value of unquoted shares in a company would be affected by the death of the sole director who ran the business and this could be taken into account. But if someone had a large holding of shares, the availability of which affected the market and caused the price to drop, the drop in price could not be taken into account in arriving at the death valuation, since the drop would be attributable to the *sale* not to the *death*.

(6) Where an estate at death includes a building society account on which demutualisation profits in the form of a cash bonus and/or shares will arise, but the date when the benefits will be received is not determined at the date of death, the value of the rights in the demutualisation will be taken into account in the death valuation, but it will be discounted to reflect the degree of uncertainty or delay at the time of death.

Sale of land after death and its effect on inheritance tax

(7) Valuation adjustments have to be made where the legal interest in land sold within four years after death is not the same as that held at death, and such adjustments also have to be made in connection with leases, exchanges and compulsory purchase (ss 192–198).

In order to qualify for relief under s 191, the sale of the land must actually take place. In the case of *Jones v CIR* (1997), contracts had been exchanged within the (then) three year period, but the sale did not take place and the intended purchaser forfeited his deposit. It was held that s 191 relief was not available.

HMRC Inheritance Tax will not consider a claim under s 191 where there is no chargeable transfer and as a consequence there is no appropriate person. This would arise where, for instance, 100% agricultural property relief would be due. This was confirmed in the case of *Stonor & Mills (Dickinson's Executors) v CIR* (2001), where the executors sold land within three years of death at figures considerably in excess of the probate values. They tried to use s 191 to increase the IHT value of the land (with a view to their using this as an ascertained value under TCGA 1992 s 274 so as to give an increased base cost and so eliminate their capital gain). However, no inheritance tax was payable on the estate because of the nil-rate band and the charities exemption The executors' attempt to have the values revised under s 191 failed because the Special Commissioners upheld the Revenue's view that there was no 'appropriate person' who could make a claim because no one was liable to pay any IHT on the estate.

Although HMRC were successful in the *Stonor* case, this argument would not be available to them if some tax, albeit of a small amount, were due apart from the intended s 191 claim. However, with CGT at 28% (on residential property disposals) and 20% otherwise and IHT on the increase in value at 40% it would not be worthwhile making such a claim (without other sales at an equal or greater loss as against probate value) if there were no reliefs etc in point; but if the asset passed partly to the surviving spouse and partly to chargeable beneficiaries, or if it attracted APR or BPR in relation to a sizeable part of its value, then a s 191 claim might yet be worthwhile.

Inheritance tax residence nil-rate band (RNRB)

(8) The RNRB has been discussed in full in **Example A2 part (b)**. As explained there in working out how much RNRB is given effect to in computing the IHT liability arising in respect of his estate when he dies, regard must be had to . . . the size of his estate (E) so that if it exceeds the taper threshold of £2,000,000 (since 2017/18) the RNRB to which the estate is entitled is the tapered default allowance (the so-called 'adjusted allowance'). E is the value of the deceased person's chargeable estate at the time of his death calculated as the aggregate value of the property comprised in the estate but after deducting labilities that may be taken into account but including also the value of assets passing by survivorship, gifts in which the deceased person had a reservation of benefit and any assets held in trust in which the deceased person enjoyed a qualifying IIP. The liabilities taken into account are those described in **part C** of this Example. E is to be distinguished from VT which is the value of the deceased's chargeable estate at the time of his death after exemptions and other reliefs. So in the case of Nigel's estate VT is £1,200,000 whereas E is £3,300,000 (ie BPR and APR are ignored). This means that his adjusted allowance would be £175,000 – (£3,300,000 - £2,000,000)/2 = Nil and no RNRB would be given effect to in calculating the IHT payable in respect of his chargeable estate of £1,200,000 on his death.

Interaction of inheritance tax and capital gains tax gifts holdover relief

(9) If an asset is transferred in lifetime and a gifts holdover election for capital gains tax is made under TCGA 1992 s 165 or s 260, any inheritance tax paid in respect of the chargeable lifetime transfer is allowed as a deduction in computing the chargeable gain when the donee disposes of the asset. This will also apply if the transfer is a potentially exempt transfer for inheritance tax purposes and a death occurs within seven years, causing inheritance tax then to be payable (but, as explained at the end of the answer to **part A** of the Example, only in the case of a gifts holdover election under s 165). The inclusion of inheritance tax as an allowable cost cannot have the effect of creating an allowable loss. See **Example A6 explanatory note 7** for further details (full details of when a chargeable capital gain may be held over under TCGA 1992 s 165 or s 260 are in companion book **Tolley's Taxwise I 2023/24**).

Question

When Antony, a widower, died on 7 April 2023 his own assets included a policy on his own life which produced £21,600. As soon as the proceeds of the policy were available his executors invested the whole sum in a new issue of 28,000 shares in AB plc, doing so in July 2023.

He owned at death:

5,000	50p	ords in AB plc quoted at 75–79 with bargains done at 75, 75½ and 78
5,000	£1	ords in CD plc quoted at 121–129 with bargains done at 121 and 123
20,000	£1	ords in EF plc quoted at 240–242 but with no recorded bargains
15,000	£1	ords in GH plc quoted at 252–256 with a single bargain at 252
10,000	£1	ords in IJ plc quoted at 4–6 with no recorded bargains
1,000	50p	ords in KL plc quoted at 92–96 with bargains at 93 and 95

His executors made the following sales:

1 February 2023:	5,000	shares in CD plc sold for £7,500 gross
3 March 2024:	20,000	shares in EF plc sold for £40,550 gross
23 March 2024:	15,000	shares in GH plc sold to the residuary beneficiary Y for £37,000 gross
12 April 2024:	33,000	shares in AB plc sold for £26,400 gross

Antony had also been entitled to receive equally with his brother the income from a settled fund set up under the will of his father in 2005. The trust assets at the date of Antony's death were:

8,000	50p	ords in AB plc
12,000	£1	ords in EF plc
20,000	£1	ords in MN plc quoted at 251–256 with bargains done at 251, 251½ and 253

On 5 May 2023 the trustees sold half the shares in EF plc (6,000 shares) for £13,800 gross which they used to pay the inheritance tax in respect of half the trust fund in connection with Antony's death. They then retired and appointed new trustees. There was a dispute about the devolution of Antony's half share of the trust fund and the new trustees sold half the shares in AB plc on 24 February 2024 (4,000 shares) for £3,120 gross which they used to pay the cost of Counsel's Opinions etc. It is agreed that Antony's son Gregory is entitled to Antony's half share of the trust fund absolutely and the new trustees accordingly transferred to him half of the shares in MN plc plus the remaining cash capital in hand. On 15 March 2024 Gregory sold for £27,000 gross, the 10,000 shares in MN plc which were transferred to him.

In each sale or purchase, the expenses incidental to that sale or purchase may be taken to be equal to 1% of the gross sale or purchase price.

On 23 November 2023 IJ plc went into liquidation and the shares were subsequently cancelled without payment of dividend.

The Stock Exchange suspended the shares in KL plc on 5 March 2024, the market value of the 1,000 shares on 7 April 2024 being £400.

Appropriate claims for relief are made.

HMRC point out that at the time of the sale by the executors of the 15,000 shares in GH plc to the residuary beneficiary, such shares were quoted at 253–256, with a single recorded bargain at 253.

Calculate the original and revised values for taxation purposes placed on each holding of shares as at the date of death of Antony.

Answer

(1) Valuation of Antony's own shares

Date of death 7 April 2023				£	£
5,000	50p	ord in AB plc	@ 76	3,800	
5,000	£1	ord in CD plc	@ 122	6,100	
20,000	£1	ord in EF plc	@ 240½	48,100	
15,000	£1	ord in GH plc	@ 252	37,800	
10,000	£1	ord in IJ plc	@ 4½	450	
1,000	50p	ord in KL plc	@ 93	930	97,180

Less relief for loss on shares sold, cancelled or suspended within one year after death:

AB plc —	Sold more than one year after death (12 April 2024)		Nil	
CD plc —	Sale price (1 February 2024)	7,500		
	Probate value	6,100	1,400	
EF plc —	Sale price (3 March 2024)	40,550		
	Probate value	48,100	(7,550)	
GH plc —	'Best price' (23 March 2024)	37,950		
	Probate value	37,800	150	
KL plc —	Suspended security — market value	400		
	Probate value	930	(530)	
Reduction in value			£(6,530)	
Acquisition of 'qualifying investments' —			£	
	Shares in AB plc purchased by executors		21,600	
Total value of disposals within year —				
	(£7,500 + £40,550 + £37,950 + £400)		86,400	
Reduction in value on death is therefore restricted by				
	$\frac{21,600}{86,400}$			ie ¼
Less: claim for reduction in probate value ¾ × 6,530				(4,898)
				92,282

The value of each holding on death then becomes:

Shares in	AB plc	3,800
	CD plc (£ 6,100 + ¾ of £1,400)	7,150
	EF plc (£48,100 – ¾ of £7,550)	42,438
	GH plc (£37,800 + ¾ of £150)	37,912
	IJ plc (see **explanatory note 4**)	450
	KL plc (£930 – ¾ of £530)	532
		£92,282

(2) Valuation of trust fund (in which Antony has a one-half interest)

Date of death 7 April 2023					£	£
	8,000	50p	ord in AB plc	@ 76	6,080	
	12,000	£1	ord in EF plc	@ 240½	28,860	
	20,000	£1	ord in MN plc	@ 252	50,400	£85,340

Relief for loss on shares sold within one year after death:

			£	£
EF plc	Sale price (5 May 2023)		13,800	
	Probate value			
		6,000 @ 240½	14,430	(630)
AB plc	Sale price (24 February 2024)		3,120	
	Probate value			
		4,000 @ 76	3,040	80
MN plc	Sale by beneficiary cannot affect position			Nil
Reduction in value				(550)

Value of shares taxable on death of Antony			
	½ of £85,340		42,670
Less:	Reduction in value		
	½ of £550		(275)
			£42,395
The value of each holding on death then becomes:			
Shares in	AB plc	½ of (£6,080 + £80)	3,080
	EF plc	½ of (£28,860 – £630)	14,115
	MN plc	½ of £50,400	25,200
			£42,395

Explanatory Notes

Inheritance tax: treatment of quoted securities

(1) The notes to **Examples A8** and **A10** relating to shares sold within twelve months after death apply also to this Example, but the problems of partial reinvestment and a partial interest in trust property are also considered here.

(2) Listed shares and securities are valued at the lower of:

(a) The lower closing price plus one-quarter of the difference between the lower and higher closing prices; or

(b) Halfway between the highest and lowest recorded bargains for the day of valuation.

(This rule, derived from TCGA 1992 s 272(3), is applied from 6 April 2015, as a matter of practice, for IHT valuation purposes.)

The respective valuations are therefore:

Own Shares	*Closing Prices*	*Bargains*		*Lower*
AB plc	75 + ¼ (79 – 75) = 76	$\frac{75 + 78}{2}$	= 76½	76
CD plc	121 + ¼ (129 – 121) = 123	$\frac{121 + 123}{2}$	= 122	122
EF plc	240 + ¼ (242 – 240) = 240½	None		240½
GH plc	252 + ¼ (256 – 252) = 253	252		252
IJ plc	4 + ¼ (6 – 4) = 4½	None		4½
KL plc	92 + ¼ (96 – 92) = 93	$\frac{93 + 95}{2}$	= 94	93
Trust Shares				
MN plc	251 + ¼ (256 – 251) = 252¼	$\frac{251 + 253}{2}$	= 252	252

Where a death occurs on a Sunday or other day for which no prices are available, the price of each individual shareholding may be taken for either the first day before or after the death for which prices are available. Units in an approved unit trust are valued at the manager's buying price (ie the lower of the two prices quoted). If no prices were published on the date of death the last published prices before death should be used.

Inheritance tax: sales within twelve months after death

(3) When qualifying investments are sold at an overall loss within twelve months after death, IHTA 1984 s 179 enables the 'appropriate person', ie the personal representatives or trustees accounting for the tax, to claim a reduction in the value of those investments at the time of death. 'Qualifying investments' means quoted shares or securities, or holdings in authorised unit trusts. 'Quoted securities' means securities listed on a recognised stock exchange or dealt in on the Unlisted Securities Market (ss 178(1) & 272). Securities on the Alternative Investment Market (AIM), ISDX Markets Group and NASDAQ Europe are therefore unquoted for inheritance tax purposes.

To compute the reduction, if any, *all* qualifying investments sold within one year after death by the appropriate person are taken into account (s 179(1)(a)). The total sale proceeds (or if higher, the best consideration which could reasonably have been obtained for them at the time of sale), are in effect substituted for their probate value at death (s 179(1)(b)). No allowance is made for expenses incurred in disposing of the investments (s 178(5)).

Thus the sale of shares in AB plc by the executors is ignored as it occurred more than twelve months after death.

Actual selling prices before expenses are in effect substituted for the probate value of the holdings in CD plc and EF plc (subject to **explanatory notes 5 and 6**).

The shares in GH plc were sold to the residuary beneficiary for £37,000 but if they had been sold on the Stock Exchange they would probably have made 15,000 × 253 = £37,950.

HMRC would normally use the same valuation rules as for date of death ie the lower of

Closing Prices	*Bargains*	*Lower*
253 + ¼ (256 – 253) = 253¾	253	253

A claim cannot be restricted to disposals with losses; all disposals must be included in the computation.

Inheritance tax: shares cancelled or in which dealings suspended

(4) If dealings in quoted shares (or other qualifying investments) are suspended as at the first anniversary of death, and the then market value is lower than the value at death, the security may be deemed to have been sold at its market value twelve months after death (s 186B). The shares in KL plc are therefore deemed to have given rise to a notional loss of £530. In practice it will be difficult to arrive at a market value for shares, in which dealings are suspended. No guidance has been given as to how such a market value is to be arrived at.

Under s 186A, if a qualifying investment is cancelled within twelve months after death, it may be treated as sold twelve months after death for £1. Shares are sometimes cancelled in company reorganisations, but the apparent intention of s 186A is to deal with company liquidations. Cancellation does not, however, take place when liquidation commences, but at the time the liquidation is completed. It would be rare for a company whose shares had a significant value on death to go into liquidation and for the liquidation to be completed within the required twelve month period. It appears, therefore, that s 186A does not meet its objective. One possible solution where shares have a significant value at death but then become worthless, is to undertake a deed of variation to direct the shares to an exempt beneficiary, such as a charity. Their value will not then be included in the chargeable estate.

It has been assumed that the liquidation of IJ plc in the Example was not completed before 7 April 2023.

Inheritance tax: sales of quoted shares post mortem followed by reinvestment

(5) To prevent the appropriate person selling investments and reacquiring them shortly afterwards s 180 provides that, if any qualifying investments are acquired by him in his capacity as the appropriate person within a period beginning on the date of death and ending two months after the date of the last sale (or deemed sale) to qualify for relief, then the claim shall be reduced by the proportion which the purchase prices of all such qualifying purchases bears to the aggregate sale prices used in the claim.

In this Example the executors had invested £21,600 in quoted securities during the relevant period. The total relief is therefore reduced by the proportion which that investment bears to the sale values of securities disposed of or deemed to be disposed of within twelve months after death (ie CD plc + EF plc + GH plc + KL plc = £86,400) giving actual relief of:

$$£6,530 - \left(\frac{21,600}{86,400} \times 6,530\right) = £4,898$$

The purchase does not have to be made out of the proceeds of sale of the investments sold. Any purchase of qualifying investments made during the period commencing with the date of death and ending two months after the date of the last sale, whether before or after the sale, and irrespective of the source of the purchase money, reduces the amount of relief available.

(6) The relevant proportion of any gain or loss arising is then added to or subtracted from the probate value at death of each security included in the claim to give the revised value for inheritance tax. That revised value of the shares is also deemed to be their market value at the date of death for capital gains tax (s 187).

Thus the value of the shares in AB plc is unaltered because they are not sold within twelve months after death and therefore not included in the s 179 claim;

The value of the shares in CD plc is increased by ¾ of the gain on sale, £1,400;

The value of the shares in EF plc is reduced by ¾ of the loss on sale, £7,550;

The value of the shares in GH plc is increased by ¾ of the notional gain of £150 on disposal, notwithstanding the fact that the actual proceeds showed a loss;

The value of the shares in IJ plc remains unaltered because they were not cancelled within twelve months after death;

The value of the shares in KL plc is reduced by ¾ of the notional loss on suspension, £530.

Inheritance tax: shares forming trust property in which deceased had a part interest

(7) As the trust assets have not been appropriated into separate funds for Antony and his brother, the entirety of the trust fund has to be valued at the death of Antony (s 186) but only one half of that valuation (representing his life interest) is included in the computation of tax due. This has the effect of treating a part of the securities disposed of as belonging to the non-taxable part of the trust and therefore restricts the relief that may be claimed. In this Example one-half of the trust fund is taxable and therefore only one-half of the computed reduction in value may be claimed.

(8) The trustees of a settled fund are treated as a single and continuing body of persons (s 178(4)) and therefore the computation includes the sales of shares by the old and new trustees.

However, the beneficiary Gregory is not the same person as the trustees and is not himself accountable for the tax on the death even though he ultimately bears the burden of its payment (by receiving less funds from the trust). Therefore, the disposal by Gregory as beneficiary of shares in MN plc transferred to him by the trustees is not a disposal by the 'appropriate person' and is not therefore included in the calculation of any relief.

Inheritance tax: post mortem relief on shares – investments not known of until more than twelve months after death

(9) The relevant sale must take place within twelve months of the date of death for relief for any loss to be available. In the case of *Executors of CE Lee v IRC* (2002) the documents relating to the investment were not found until more than twelve months after death. The shares had lost value. The value for inheritance tax was market value at date of death. Relief for loss in value was not available.

Question

Pilling, who had been a widower since 2001, died on 3 September 2023. He was survived by a son and daughter – twins born in 1964. Mrs Pilling had an estate of £225,000 and there is no available nil-rate band to carry forward to be utilised on Pilling's death.

For many years up to 5 April 2016, Pilling had made regular gifts, fully using the annual exemption for inheritance tax, but he had not made any chargeable transfers.

Pilling had made the following gifts after 5 April 2016:

15 June 2017	To nephew £216,400 in securities.
15 April 2018	10,000 £1 shares in Black plc, a listed company, to his niece. The shares were worth £13.00 each at the date of the gift. On 3 December 2018 Black plc was taken over by White plc and in exchange for her Black plc shares, Pilling's niece was given 15,000 White plc shares of 25p each, those shares being worth £7.00. At Pilling's death they were worth £2.80 each.
25 December 2018	Motor car worth £12,600 to his nephew. Two days before Pilling's death the car was totally destroyed by fire. The insurance compensation was £5,000.
4 July 2020	Cash gift of £63,000 to his grandson in consideration of his marriage, which took place on that date.

At the time of his death Pilling owned 3,200 ordinary shares in Briggs and Pilling Ltd; he had subscribed for these shares when the company was formed in 1967 and they were valued at £55 per share on his death. The company has an issued capital of 5,000 ordinary shares and is engaged in demolition contracting. Pilling had borrowed £3,200 at no interest to acquire the shares; the loan was repaid by Pilling's executors after his death.

His other assets comprised quoted investments and personal chattels with a total value of £240,700. He had a bank overdraft of £29,900 arising from personal expenditure which was repaid by his executors and his funeral expenses were £1,100. He had lived in rented accommodation since the death of his wife and so did not own a home at the time of his death.

By his will, which was made immediately after the death of his wife in 2001, Pilling left his shares in Briggs and Pilling Ltd to his son, with the residue of his estate divided equally between his son and his daughter.

Pilling's son accepts that because he will receive the legacy of the shares in Briggs and Pilling Ltd, his sister or her family should have a larger share in the residue of the estate. In November 2023 they ask you for advice on dealing with their father's estate in the most efficient way in relation to inheritance tax. The son is married with two children whose ages are 13 and 10; the daughter is a widow whose only child is Pilling's grandson who was married on 4 July 2020.

(a) Calculate the inheritance tax payable as a result of Pilling's death, stating the due date of payment.

(b) List the points that you would bring to the attention of Pilling's son and daughter in connection with altering the terms of Pilling's will.

Answer

(a) Inheritance tax payable as a result of Pilling's death on 3 September 2023

Lifetime transfers

					Gross	*Tax on 2023/24 scale*
	Potentially exempt transfers now chargeable:			£	£	£
15 June 2017	Nephew — securities			216,400		
	Less:	Annual exemptions	2017/18	(3,000)		
			2016/17	(3,000)	210,400	Nil
15 April 2018	Niece — shares			130,000		
	Less:	Annual exemption 2018/19		(3,000)	127,000	4,960*
	*(337,400 – 325,000 = 12,400 @ 40% = £4,960)				337,400	4,960*
25 December 2018	Nephew — car				12,600	5,040**
4 July 2020	Grandson			63,000		
	Less:	Marriage exemption		(2,500)		
		Annual exemptions	2020/21	(3,000)		
			2019/20	(3,000)	54,500	21,800
					404,500	

* On a claim by the niece, tax on her gift may be recomputed as follows:

Value of gift		130,000
Less: Value on death (15,000 @ £2.80)		(42,000)
Reduce transfer by		£88,000
Giving chargeable transfer of (127,000 – 88,000) =	£39,000	

When this is added to the chargeable transfers brought forward of £210,400, the total is £249,400, which is below the nil-rate threshold, so that the inheritance tax payable by the niece is reduced to nil.

** Taper relief will be available to the nephew on the gift on 25 December 2018, because it was made between four and five years before death. Inheritance tax payable will therefore be 60% × £5,040 = £3,024. The fall in value relief in respect of the niece's shares has no effect on the cumulative total of £337,400 by reference to which tax on the gift to the nephew (and on Pilling's death) is calculated.

		£	*Due date*
Tax payable on PETs which became chargeable because of Pilling's death within 7 years:			
15 June 2017	By nephew	Nil	
15 April 2018	By niece (after claim re fall in value)	Nil	
25 December 2018	By nephew (after taper relief)	3,024	31 March 2023
4 July 2020	By grandson	21,800	31 March 2023

Pilling's estate at death

		Date of death 3 September 2023
		£
Shares in Briggs and Pilling Ltd 3,200 @ £55	176,000	
Less: 100% business property relief	(176,000)	Nil
Quoted investments and personal chattels		240,700
		240,700
Less: Debts and funeral expenses (29,900 + 3,200 + 1,100)		(34,200)
Chargeable estate at death		206,500

As the loan to purchase the shares in Briggs and Pilling Ltd (which qualify for business property relief) was taken out before 6 April 2013 it is unaffected by the rules governing relief for liabilities relating to relievable (ie BPR) property (s 162B(1), (2) as read with FA 2013 Sch 36 para 5(2)) (see **Example A12**(c)). Hence the loan is not set against the value of shares before BPR is given in respect of them, but goes (since the loan was repaid after his death – s 175A) to reduce the value of Pilling's total estate.

Since the lifetime transfers exceed the nil-rate band (the fall in value relief being ignored when computing the cumulative total by reference to which the estate charge is computed), the tax payable by the personal representatives is £206,500 @ 40%, ie £82,600. The due date for payment is 31 March 2024, or when they deliver their account with their application for probate if earlier.

(b) Points to be brought to the attention of Pilling's son and daughter in connection with altering the terms of Pilling's will

(1) Pilling's son and daughter may vary the way in which the estate is distributed, provided they do so in writing within two years after the date of his death and make the appropriate statement as to the instrument having effect for inheritance tax purposes – IHTA 1984 s 142. The son must sign the instrument of variation; signature by the daughter is not necessary if she is not giving up any of her existing entitlement under the will. The personal representatives will not be required to sign the instrument of variation either since the variation will not result in any additional tax being payable by them. The variation will be treated for inheritance tax as if the changed dispositions had applied at the date of death (see **explanatory note 7**).

(2) The variation is also effective for capital gains tax purposes (provided a statement to that effect is included within the deed – TCGA 1992 s 62(6) and (7)). As a result, the ultimate beneficiaries who receive any chargeable assets directly from the personal representatives will be treated as having acquired them at market value at the date of Pilling's death.

(3) For income tax purposes, any income arising on the assets before the variation takes effect and which was taxable on the original beneficiary under the will is still treated as belonging to him and taxed at his/her tax rates. If that person is assessed to higher-rate or additional-rate tax on the income, it may be thought appropriate for the tax to be paid by whoever receives the income; this needs careful drafting to avoid the payment being treated as inadmissible consideration which disqualifies the deed of variation from being effective for tax purposes.

(4) If Pilling's son and daughter already have adequate income, they may wish to provide in the instrument of variation that some or all of Pilling's estate is transferred direct to their children. In the case of Pilling's infant grandchildren, the funds are likely to be held in trust until they reach age 18. If, however, Pilling's son gives up some or all of his entitlement in favour of his own infant children this will be treated as a parental settlement. Any funds that are applied for the benefit of his children while they are infants will be treated as Pilling's son's income, up to a limit of the income arising from the assets in that same period. This will not be the case where the funds are transferred to a settlement that provides for the income to be accumulated. There will be no such problems in relation to Pilling's daughter, since her son is married, nor in relation to any transfer by Pilling's son to his nephew.

Explanatory Notes

Inheritance tax: relief for fall in value of gift before death

(1) If the value of a gift has fallen between the date of gift and the date of death (when the additional charge to tax arises), a claim may be made for the tax to be computed as if the value transferred by the gift were reduced by the reduction in value of the asset. The re-computation does not affect the amount of the chargeable transfer taken into account in the figure of cumulative transfers for the purpose of computing the tax on any later chargeable transfers or the estate on death. The relief does not apply to wasting chattels, and hence the car's value is not reduced in this Example (IHTA 1984 s 131). If the asset is shares and there is a reorganisation or takeover prior to death, the original shares and the new holding are treated as the same property (s 135).

(2) A claim for the relief must be made by the person liable to pay the tax. So, following a claim by Pilling's niece, the value of the shares given to her is reduced by £88,000 in computing the tax payable.

(3) These provisions also apply where an asset has been sold prior to death by the transferee or his spouse, provided it was a bona fide sale at arm's length to an unconnected person (s 131(3)). In this case the relief applies to the difference between the value transferred by the gift and the sale proceeds.

(4) If the property to which the claim for reduction of value relates qualifies for business property relief (or agricultural property relief) then that relief is also in effect reduced proportionately. This will only have practical relevance where the relief is less than 100% (see **Example A21** and **Example A22**).

(5) If the original gift was a chargeable lifetime transfer on which the donor paid the tax, the *original* amount of tax must be added to the amount of the transfer before the fall in value relief is taken. In other words, the tax on the previous lifetime transfer is added to the recomputed transfer as illustrated in the next example.

Cumulative transfers assumed to exceed nil-rate band

		Gross	*Tax*	*Net*
		£	£	£
Net gift of 10,000 shares worth £4 each to discretionary trust				40,000
Grossed up $\left(\times \frac{100}{80}\right)$		50,000	10,000 (½ rate)	
Shares worth £3 each on death within seven years				
Recomputed gift 10,000 @ £3	30,000			
Add tax on original gift	10,000	40,000	16,000 (full rate)	

Additional tax payable because of the donor's death within seven years after the gift is £6,000 (£16,000 – £10,000), subject to any available taper relief.

Inheritance tax: increase in value of gift before death

(6) If the value of a gift has *increased* between the date of the gift and the date of the donor's death, the death scale is nonetheless applied only to the amount of the original transfer of value.

Inheritance tax: deeds of variation

(7) Deeds of variation do not have to be sent to HMRC Inheritance Tax unless the variation results in additional tax becoming payable. If that is the case, the beneficiaries and personal representatives must send a copy of the variation to HMRC Inheritance Tax within six months of its execution and notify them of the amount of additional tax payable (s 218A). See **Example B6** for further details, in particular **explanatory note 5**.

Cross references

(8) For further notes on exemptions, see **Example A1**; on business property relief, see **Example A21**; on dates of payment, see **Example A7** and on the treatment of liabilities in relation to the instalment option and business property relief, see **Example A11** and **Example A12**(c).

Question

A.

Thomas died on 20 December 2023. He and his wife had lived in rented accommodation all their lives.

He left an estate valued at £400,000 after payment of all debts and funeral expenses. By his will he gave £256,000 to his son Dick, with the residue of his estate to his wife.

Thomas had, on 31 December 2020, made a gift of £255,000 to Dick. This was the only gift made by Thomas since 2016.

(i) Calculate the inheritance tax payable in consequence of Thomas's death.

(ii) Calculate the inheritance tax payable in consequence of Thomas's death if his estate of £400,000 included a family home valued at £256,000 (which was owned by him alone) and that he gave his home to his son Dick (instead of the pecuniary legacy); his wife who, on account of her age, moved into sheltered accommodation.

B.

Sanjay (a bachelor with no direct descendants) died on 26 February 2024 leaving an estate valued at £1 million after deduction of liabilities. He had made no lifetime transfers. None of the property that he owned at the time of his death was owned jointly with any other person. Neither did Sanjay have any interests in any settled property. Under his will he gave his lifelong friend a pecuniary legacy totalling £245,000 free of tax. The residue of his estate was left to his sister Rajinda, after the payment of a donation of 10% to a charity that is registered in Norway and that was set up to help the families of the victims of the shootings that had occurred in the country in 2011. The charity had received many donations, some from UK taxpayers under Gift Aid. The charity had claimed tax back from HMRC accordingly.

Calculate the amount of inheritance tax payable by Sanjay's executors.

Answer

A(i). Thomas

Lifetime transfer

				£
31 December 2020				
Gift to Dick				255,000
Less: Annual exemptions	2020/21		3,000	
	2019/20		3,000	6,000
Potentially exempt transfer				249,000

Inheritance tax payable on death of Thomas 20 December 2023

	Gross	Tax on 2023/24 scale
	£	£
By Dick		
31 December 2020		
Gift — potentially exempt transfer now chargeable	249,000	Nil

By Estate

Tax is payable on the grossed up equivalent of the £256,000 pecuniary legacy to Dick when added to an inheritance tax accumulation of £249,000 using the 2023/24 scale:

		Gross	Net
	£	£	£
Cumulative transfers in seven years before death		249,000	Nil
Chargeable estate			
Pecuniary legacy (see working note)	376,000		
Residue	24,000		
		400,000	120,000*
		649,000	
Less: exempt transfer to spouse		(24,000)	
Chargeable amount		625,000	
Tax payable by estate			120,000*

*(£625,000 – 325,000) = £300,000 @ 40%

The estate will accordingly be divided as follows:

	£	£
Gross estate		400,000
To HMRC — payment of inheritance tax		120,000
To Dick — pecuniary legacy		256,000
To Wife (exempt transfer)		
(ie) £400,000 estate – £256,000 to Dick	144,000	

Less:	Tax on Dick's legacy	120,000	24,000
			400,000

Working Note

The cumulative net transfers to be taken into account in ascertaining the gross taxable value of the pecuniary legacy comprise the value of the transfers made in the seven years before Thomas' death (£249,000) and the amount of the legacy itself (£256,000), that is £505,000. As the lifetime gifts are treated as using up the nil-rate band of £325,000 first, this means that of the net pecuniary legacy of £256,000, £76,000 (£325,000 - £249,000) falls within the balance of the nil-rate. The 40% rate of tax applies to the excess of £180,000 (£256,000 - £76,000), giving a gross equivalent for that part of the specific legacy of:

$$\frac{100}{60} \times £155,000 = £258,333$$

Hence the taxable value of Thomas' chargeable estate that is attributable to the pecuniary legacy is £376,000 (£76,000 + £300,000). This is the amount used to calculate the chargeable value of his estate in order to calculate the amount of tax due.

A(ii). Thomas

Lifetime transfer

				£
31 December 2020				
Gift to Dick				255,000
Less: Annual exemptions		2020/21	3,000	
		2019/20	3,000	6,000
Potentially exempt transfer				249,000

Inheritance tax payable on death of Thomas 20 December 2023

	Gross	Tax on 2023/24 scale
	£	£
By Dick		
31 December 2020		
Gift — potentially exempt transfer now chargeable	249,000	Nil

By Estate

Tax is payable on the grossed up equivalent of the £256,000 specific legacy to Dick when added to an inheritance tax accumulation of £249,000 using the 2023/24 scale:

		Gross	Net
	£	£	£
Cumulative transfers in seven years before death		249,000	Nil
Chargeable estate			
Specific legacy of home (see working note)	259,333		
Residue	140,667		
		400,000	
		649,000	

Less: exempt transfer to spouse	(140,667)
Chargeable amount	508,333
Less: RNRB (see **explanatory note 5**)	(175,000)
Balance of chargeable amount	333,333

Tax payable by estate	£3,333*

*(£333,333 – 325,000) = £8,333 @ 40%

The estate will accordingly be divided as follows:

	£	£
Gross estate		400,000
To HMRC — payment of inheritance tax		3,333
To Dick — specific legacy of home		256,000
To Wife (exempt transfer)		
(ie) £400,000 estate – £256,000 to Dick	144,000	
Less: Tax on Dick's legacy	3,333	140,667
		400,000

Working Note

The cumulative net transfers to be taken into account in ascertaining the gross taxable value of the specific legacy comprise the value of the transfers made in the seven years before Thomas's death (£249,000) and the amount of the legacy itself (£256,000), that is £505,000. Thomas' estate benefits from the residence nil-rate band of £175,000 (in 2023/24) (see **explanatory note** 5) and so the total amount of his estate in respect of which tax is computed at 0% is £500,000 (£325,000 + £175,000). As the lifetime gifts are treated as using up the nil-rate bands first, this means that of the net specific legacy of £256,000, £251,000 falls within the balance of the nil-rate (£500,000 - £249,000). The 40% rate of tax applies to the excess of £5,000, giving a gross equivalent for that part of the specific legacy of:

$$\frac{100}{60} \times £5{,}000 = £8{,}333$$

Hence the taxable value of Thomas' chargeable estate that is attributable to the specific legacy comprised of his home is £259,333 (£251,000 + £8,333). This is the amount used to calculate the chargeable value of his estate in order to calculate amount of tax due.

B. Sanjay

Inheritance tax payable on death of Sanjay on 26 February 2024

The residue of Sanjay's estate is £1,000,000 – £245,000 = £755,000 and so the amount donated to charity appears to be £75,500. This seems to result in £924,500 being charged to inheritance tax. However, as there are specific legacies that are free of tax, they must be grossed up with the result that the residue (and hence the share passing to charity) will be reduced by the tax paid. The legacies will ultimately be grossed up at 36% if the charitable legacy passes the 10% test (see Step 4 of the method statement followed below as explained fully in **Example B12**).

In order to see whether the legacy passes that test apply the rule in IHTA 1984 Sch 1A para 6(1) which provides that, where the grossing up rules in s 38(3) apply, for the purpose of calculating the donated amount and the baseline amount, gross up the specific gifts at the lower rate of inheritance tax of 36%. Given that Sanjay's estate comprises only a general component, in order to calculate the donated amount, the grossing up calculation is as follows:

Chargeable estate (as above):	£924,500
Tax on estate (924,500 – 325,000) @36%	£215,820
Estate rate: 215,820/924,500 × 100% = 23.3445%	
Gross up specific gifts at estate rate: £245,000 × 100/(100 – 23.3445)	£319,611
Residue of estate after grossing up (1,000,000 – 319,611)	£680,389
The donated amount becomes 10% × £680,389 = £68,039	
Chargeable estate is now £1,000,000 – £68,039	£931,961

Choice of rate of inheritance tax

- Step 1: Calculate the chargeable amount of the general component comprised in Sanjay's estate. The chargeable amount is the value of pecuniary legacies (grossed up) together with the chargeable residue which in this case is £319,611 + £612,350 = £931,961.
- Step 2: Deduct from the chargeable amount of the general component determined under Step 1, the appropriate proportion of the available nil-rate band applicable to the general component. The nil-rate band of £325,000 available on Sanjay's death reduces the chargeable amount of the general component to £606,961 (931,961 – 325,000). This is the result of Step 2.
- Step 3: Add to the amount of the general component determined under Step 2, the charitable donation made and restate the chargeable amount of the general component of the estate. This amount is the 'baseline amount' of the general component, ie £606,961 + 68,039 = £675,000.
- Step 4: Perform the 10% test – that is, compare with 10% of the baseline amount for the general component, the 'donated amount' (ie the charitable donation) in respect of the component. The donated amount made from a component must be at least 10% of the baseline amount of that component if the 10% test is to be satisfied.

  In Sanjay's case the donated amount is £68,039 and 10% of the baseline amount of the general component is £67,500. The test is whether the donated amount is at least 10% of the relevant component. Here, as the donated amount of £68,039 is greater than £67,500, the 10% test is met.
- Step 5: As the 10% test is met in relation to the general component, tax is charged on the chargeable amount of the general component of Sanjay's estate at 36%.

Tax payable

The tax payable (and borne) by the executors of Sanjay's estate is £931,961 × 36% = £335,506 which means that his estate is distributed as follows:

		£	£
Gross estate			1,000,000
To HMRC — payment of inheritance tax			335,506
To Sanjay's friend			245,000
To charity (exempt transfer)			68,039
To Rajinder			
(ie) (£1,000,000 estate – £245,000 to friend — £68,039 to charity)		686,961	
Less:	Tax on chargeable residue and friend's legacy	335,506	351,455
			1,000,000

Explanatory Notes

Potentially exempt transfer on 31 December 2020

(1) The gift made on 31 December 2020, in so far as it exceeded the available annual exemptions, was a potentially exempt transfer that became a chargeable transfer on the death of Thomas (IHTA 1984 s 19). It is then chargeable using the rates applicable at death. The lifetime gift attracts the nil rate band before the estate at death and accordingly no tax is due on that gift. If a liability had arisen it would be payable by the transferee.

Specific and pecuniary legacies and their effect on inheritance tax

(2) On death, the residue left to the wife is exempt (s 18) but it cannot be ascertained until the tax payable by the estate has been calculated. Tax is payable on the pecuniary/specific legacy and since the legatee receives the actual amount of the legacy, the tax payable is found by grossing it up (ss 36–42).

(3) In part A(i) of this Example, the amount received by the widow is much less than she at first sight appears entitled to:

Estate	400,000
Dick's pecuniary legacy	256,000
Apparent entitlement	£144,000

but in fact she gets:

Estate		400,000
Dick's pecuniary legacy	256,000	
after tax of	120,000	376,000
		£24,000

(4) Contrast the above with the position if the will had left a pecuniary legacy of £256,000 to the widow and the residue (£144,000) to Dick. Then the taxable estate would be:

Value on death at 20 December 2023	400,000
Less: Exempt legacy – wife	256,000
Chargeable to inheritance tax on death	£144,000

Inheritance tax due on death		2023/24 *scale*
	£	£
Chargeable transfers accumulation at death	249,000	Nil
Chargeable estate	144,000	27,200*
	393,000	27,200*

(* 393,000 – 325,000 = 68,000 @ 40%)

The estate would then be divided:

	£	£
Gross estate		400,000
To HMRC – payment of inheritance tax		27,200
To Wife		256,000

To Dick		144,000	
Less:	Tax on residue	27,200	116,800
			400,000

The widow is better off by more than Dick is worse off, HMRC being the loser:

	Legacy to Dick Residue to widow	*Legacy to widow Residue to Dick*	*Difference* £
Dick	256,000	116,800	(139,200)
Widow	24,000	256,000	232,000
HMRC	120,000	27,200	(92,800)
	£400,000	£400,000	

There is nothing to prevent the widow making a personal gift to Dick from her own resources, covered in part by available exemptions and the amount reckonable being a potentially exempt transfer. If, however, a claim was made by Dick against the estate for an increased share of the estate and that claim was settled by Thomas's widow out of her own assets rather than out of assets from the estate, then s 29A would operate to treat that amount as being a payment out of the estate, reducing accordingly the exempt amount to the widow (claims under the Inheritance (Provision for Family and Dependants) Act 1975 that are settled out of the estate are already treated as if they were effected by the will (s 146)).

The inheritance tax residence nil-rate band (RNRB)

(5) In **part A(ii)** of the Example, Thomas' estate benefits from a RNRB as he dies after 6 April 2017 owning a home which is closely inherited by passing under a disposition under his will to his son (his direct descendant). As his estate does not exceed the taper threshold of £2,000,000, the amount of the RNRB prima facie available is £175,000 (the default allowance for 2023/24). The actual amount of RNRB used in calculating the inheritance tax arising in respect of Thomas's estate is limited to the chargeable value of the proportion of his home that is closely inherited. In this case, the chargeable value of Thomas' home is its grossed up value of £259,333 (not its prima facie value of £256,000) and as the whole home is closely inherited this figure acts as the limit on the amount of RNRB available. The limit does not operate in Thomas' case and so the amount of the RNRB used in calculating the IHT arising on his estate is £175,000. See **Example A2 part (b)** for a detailed discussion on the RNRB, especially, in the context of this Example, **explanatory note 5.**

The lower rate of inheritance tax

(6) FA 2012 s 209 and Sch 33 introduced Sch 1A to IHTA 1984 which provides for a lower rate of inheritance tax (namely 36%) to be charged on a deceased person's estate where 10% or more of his net estate has been left to a charity or a registered community amateur sports club. The new rate takes effect for deaths occurring on or after 6 April 2012 (FA 2012 Sch 32 para 10(1)). The application of the lower rate of tax has been set out fully in **Example B12.**

(7) In this Example, the application of the new rate is considered in the context of the grossing up of specific legacies given free of tax. There is a special rule in IHTA 1984 Sch 1A para 6(1) that provides that in quantifying the donated amount (and also the baseline amount), the specific gifts are grossed up at the lower rate. If the 10% test is then met, the inheritance tax itself (to be charged (in part at least) at the rate of 36%) is calculated using the specific legacy grossed up at 36%. (This will not entail a separate calculation to gross up the specific gifts as they will already have been grossed up at 36%.)

But if the 10% test is not met (so that the estate cannot benefit from the lower rate of tax), then the specific gifts will need to be grossed up at the rate of 40% and the tax on the estate recalculated at that rate in the usual way (see **part A** of this Example). This second calculation will not, of course, disturb the choice of rate calculation which, applying the special rule in Sch 1A para 6(1) in relation to the donated and baseline amounts, determined that the 40% rate of tax applied. It is important to realise that there are two distinct stages:

(a) the choice of rate calculation (to work out whether the 10% test is met);

(b) the calculation of tax in respect of the chargeable estate, applying the appropriate rate of inheritance tax.

(8) Where an election is made to merge components (see **Example B12 explanatory notes 27–33**), the merger takes place only for the purposes of establishing whether the combined, notional component qualifies for the lower rate of inheritance tax. So the value of each component is computed (using the special 36% grossing up rule described above as appropriate), then they are merged and then the 10% test is carried out.

(9) Where a legacy to charity is worded in such a way that the amount of the legacy must meet the 10% test then the problem of having to recalculate the tax using the 40% rate of tax will not arise (see **Example B12 explanatory note 37**).

(10) The donation to the charity registered in Norway qualifies for exemption under s 23. Such a charity satisfies the new definition of a charity applicable from 1 April 2010 (see **Example A1 part (c)** and **Example B12 explanatory note 15**). Having made claims before 15 March 2023 against HMRC for the repayment of income tax on donations under gift aid (ie having asserted its status as a charity), it will cease to qualify as a charity for the purposes of inheritance tax from 1 April 2024 (F(No 2)A 2023 s 344(2)(e), (10)).

(11) The reason why the special valuation rule has been introduced to determine the donated and baseline amounts (and hence the satisfaction, or otherwise, of the 10% test) is because of the fact that the determination of the amount transferred to charity out of residue is affected by the amount of the residue (which bears the tax on the specific gifts). If specific gifts were grossed up at 40%, that would increase the amount of tax borne by the residue and so lower the amount of the donation to charity that could be made. Considering an estate comprised only of the general component, this would mean that the baseline amount of the component would increase, the donated amount would decrease and the result would be that the component might fail the 10% merely on account of the grossing up. The special rule in Sch 1A para 6(1) obviates this problem.

(12) The grossing up of a legacy may result in an estate becoming prima facie insolvent. To avoid this problem the grossed up amount is reduced to the value of the estate and so the value of the estate is then used to calculate the baseline amount and apply the 10% test (see IHTM 12088).

Question

A.

Samuel Smith died on 31 March 2024 leaving net estate valued as follows:

	£
His half share in the business of S and D Smith carried on in partnership for many years (his brother, David Smith, owning the other half share)	400,000
An office building occupied by S and D Smith (in respect of which there are no liabilities)	430,000
Bank and building society accounts	34,600
Quoted securities	95,300
Half share in the matrimonial home (acquired on 7 July 2016) and contents, valued at £545,000, being held by himself and Mrs Smith (who survived him) as joint tenants	272,500
Life assurance policies on his own life — amount receivable	132,400
A house in France (there are no additional costs of administration because of the situation overseas)	140,800

The house in France had never been occupied as a residence and had only ever been let to holiday makers. No additional services had ever been provided to them as part of their letting of the home.

Samuel made bequests of £100 to each of three grandchildren and £5,000 to his daughter on her reaching the age of twenty-five or her earlier marriage.

He left £18,000 to a registered social landlord that operates in the town (in England) in which Samuel had lived and £100 to a political party. The registered social landlord is not registered as a charity with the Charity Commission.

He left his widow a legacy of £150,000.

The house in France was left to his daughter with the stipulation that she bore any inheritance tax applicable to it.

His share in the partnership business together with the office building occupied by the partnership was left to his son with the stipulation that he bore any tax thereon.

The residue of the estate was left equally to his son and daughter. He had made no lifetime transfers.

(a) Calculate the inheritance tax payable and show by whom it would be borne.

(b) Explain the position regarding capital gains tax on the assets comprised in the estate.

B.

Clive Foster who was domiciled in the UK also died on 31 March 2024. He had made no lifetime transfers but left estate valued as follows:

	£
Family home and possessions	400,000
Holiday home in Barbados	300,000
Bank and building society accounts	800,000
Shares in Archibald Ltd, an unquoted trading company owning no excepted assets; Clive had owned the shares for over 20 years	500,000

He made bequests of the family home and possessions and £100,0000 in cash to his wife Lin and the residue of his estate to his son Stuart.

(a) Calculate (with explanations) the inheritance tax payable as a result of Clive's death.

(b) If he had made the £100,000 cash legacy to the RSPB (a registered, UK national charity) instead of Lin, his wife, re-calculate (with explanations) the inheritance tax payable as a result of Clive's death.

Answer

A.

(a) *S Smith deceased*

			Date of death 31 March 2024 £	£
Share in matrimonial home and contents			272,500	
Less:	Exempt because of devolution on widow		(272,500)	Nil
House in France (see **explanatory notes 4 and 5**)				140,800
Half share in S and D Smith			400,000	
Less:	100% business property relief		(400,000)	Nil
Office building occupied by S and D Smith			430,000	
Less:	50% business property relief		(215,000)	215,000
Residuary estate				
Bank and building society accounts			34,600	
Quoted securities			95,300	
Life assurance policy proceeds			132,400	
			262,300	
Less:	Exempt legacies			
	Gift to registered social landlord	18,000		
	Gift to political party	100		
	Legacy to widow	150,000	168,100	94,200
Total estate on which inheritance tax is payable				450,000

Comprising:

Estate before reliefs and exemptions (*after* jointly owned assets which pass directly to widow)		1,233,100
Less:	Business property relief	(615,000)
		618,100
Less:	Exempt legacies	(168,100)
		£450,000
Tax payable on estate (450,000 – 325,000) = £125,000 @ 40%		£50,000

No residence nil-rate band is available in calculating the tax as the family home is not closely inherited passing as it passes to his wife, Mrs Smith, rather than being inherited by his children (see **Example A2 part (b)** and, in particular, **explanatory note 3**).

Which would be borne as follows:		*Tax*	*Borne by*
Matrimonial home		Nil	
House in France	$\frac{140,800}{450,000} \times 50,000$	15,644	Daughter

Office Building	$\frac{215,000}{450,000} \times 50,000$	23,889	Son
Residue	$\frac{94,200}{450,000} \times 50,000$	10,467	Son and daughter out of residue
		£50,000	

The tax on the house in France and on the office building could be paid by instalments over ten years so long as the daughter and son retained the assets, but subject to payment of interest on the outstanding tax for the time being – even in the case of the business premises, which are not covered by the interest-free rule in IHTA 1984 s 234(1) (see **Example A6**).

(b) *Capital gains tax position on death*

There is no capital gains tax charge on death (but note the income tax charge, referential to the capital gains tax rules, on any offshore income gains deemed to be realised on an individual's death under SI 2009/3001 art 34 made under FA 2008 ss 41, 42 (see now Taxation (International and Other Provisions) Act 2010 ss 354–363A and Sch 9 paras 33, 34). The legatees or devisees who receive chargeable assets acquire them for capital gains tax purposes at their probate value (ie their market value at the date of the deceased's death), so that the increase in value during the ownership of the deceased escapes capital gains tax.

B.

(a) *Clive Foster – no bequests to charity*

The key difference between the bequests made by Samuel Smith (in part A) and Clive Foster is that whereas Samuel left business property (ie his half-share in the partnership business and the office building occupied by the partnership) as a specific gift to his son, Clive left business property (ie the shares in Archibald Ltd) as part of the residue of his estate (which has devolved on his son). Given also that there are other specific gifts, in Clive's case, the application of the rules in IHTA 1984 s 39A is invoked which provide as follows:

(a) where under a will there is a specific gift of business property (BP) or agricultural property (AP), the BPR and APR reduces the value of the particular asset comprised in the gift for the purposes of computing inheritance tax (as is illustrated in **part A** of the Example). Put formally, the value of any specific gifts of relevant business property or agricultural property shall be taken to be their value as reduced by BPR and APR (s 39A(2)).

(b) where under a will BP or AP is not left as a specific gift (but, by implication, as part of the residue of the estate), then, for the purposes of computing inheritance tax, the value of any specific gift of property under the will that is not BP or AP is nevertheless reduced by part of the BPR or APR applicable to the gifts in the residue (thereby increasing their values). Put formally, the value of any specific gift not falling within s 39A(2), shall be taken to be the 'appropriate fraction' of their value (s 39A(3)).

Stating it succinctly, therefore, where BP or AP is left under a will as part of the residue of an estate, then the BPR or APR is split pro-rata between all the gifts in the estate! To put it in the terms of the Act, the value of the specific gifts is taken to be the 'appropriate fraction' of their value. In other words, the value of a specific gift of property that is not BP or AP is reduced (and this is the position that pertains to the estate of Clive Foster).

The value of the specific gifts of property that are not BP or AP is ascertained using the following formula (s 39A(4)):

$$\text{Specific gift} \times \frac{\text{Assets transferred (net of BPR/APR) less specific gifts of business/agricultural property (net of BPR/APR)}}{\text{Assets transferred (before BPR/APR) less specific gifts of business/agricultural property (before BPR/APR)}}$$

A16.5 LEGACIES AND OTHER SPECIFIC GIFTS INVOLVING BUSINESS AND AGRICULTURAL PROPERTY

A 'specific gift' is any gift other than a gift of residue or of a share in residue (s 42). The concept therefore covers both specific legacies of particular property and general (ie pecuniary) legacies. It would also cover property passing by survivorship and settled property which devolves under the terms of a settlement in which the deceased had a qualifying interest in possession.

The value of the specific gift so reduced is then used in computing the inheritance tax payable in respect of the deceased estate. In the case of Clive Foster the computation proceeds as follows:

Estate on death

	Date of death 31 March 2024		
	£	£	£
Family home and possessions	400,000		
Bank and building society accounts	100,000	500,000	
Less: Exempt legacy to widow		(400,000)	
Exempt legacy to widow		(100,000)	Nil
Residuary estate			
Shares in Archibald Ltd		500,000	
Less: 100% business property relief		(500,000)	Nil
Bank and building society accounts (balance)		700,000	
Holiday home in Barbados		300,000	
			1,000,000
Total estate on which inheritance tax is payable			1,000,000

Preliminary stage: allocation of business property relief to specific gifts and residue

		Before BPR	*After BPR*
Total free estate		2,000,000	1,500,000
Allocate a pro-rata share of			
BPR to other specific gifts (using fraction 1,500,000 /2,000,000)			
Pecuniary legacy to widow		100,000	75,000
Family home and possessions to widow	gross × $\frac{3}{4}$	400,000	300,000
		500,000	375,000

Summary of specific gifts and allocation of BPR

			Before BPR	*After BPR*
Total free estate			2,000,000	1,500,000
Specific gifts from free estate				
Pecuniary legacy to widow	100,000	75,000		
Family home and possessions to widow	400,000	300,000		
Total specific gifts			500,000	375,000
Residue of free estate (after BPR of £500,000/(£500,000 – £125,000)			1,500,000	1,125,000
			2,000,000	1,500,000

Estate on death restated

		Date of death 31 March 2024	
		£	£
Estate before reliefs and exemptions			2,000,000
Less:	exempt legacies	375,000	
Less:	business property relief	500,000	(875,000)
Total estate on which inheritance tax is payable			1,125,000

Tax payable on estate: (1,125,000 – 325,000) = 800,000 @ 40% = £320,000

No residence nil-rate band is available in calculating the tax as the family home is not closely inherited passing as it does to Clive's wife, Linne, rather than being inherited by his son (see **Example A2 part (b)** and, in particular, **explanatory note 15**). However, had the home been inherited by his son Stuart by way of a specific gift, then a RNRB would have been available in calculating the death estate. The value of Clive's estate at the time of his death (before exemptions and reliefs) would be £2,000,000 exactly and so the amount of RNRB prima facie available would be £175,000 (the default allowance for 2023/24). Assuming a nil value for the possessions, the amount of the RNRB used in calculating the IHT arising would be the lower of the available RNRB of £175,000 and the chargeable value of the proportion (100%) of the home that is inherited by Stuart – namely £300,000 (after the application of s 39A) and not £400,000 (its value before the application of s 39A). The tax would therefore have been reduced by £175,000 x 40% = £70,000.

(b) *Clive Foster – bequests to charity*

As Clive has made a gift to charity in his will, the question that arises is whether his estate is charged to inheritance tax at the lower rate of 36%. In order to ascertain the answer to this question, first the business property relief is allocated to the specific gifts and the residue (applying s 39A), and then the method statement for the choice of the rate of inheritance tax (as set out in **Example B12**) applies except that at Step 4 of the method statement, s 39A does *not* apply to a specific gift of property to charity for the purposes of ascertaining the 'donated amount'; s 39A does however apply to a specific gift of property to charity at Step 3 of the method statement for the purposes of calculating the baseline amount (Sch 1A para 6(2)). The computation therefore proceeds as follows:

Estate on death

		Date of death 31 March 2024		
		£	£	£
Family home and possessions		400,000		
Bank and building society accounts		100,000	500,000	
Less:	Exempt legacy to widow		(400,000)	
	Exempt legacy to RSPB		(100,000)	Nil
Residuary estate				
Shares in Archibald Ltd			(500,000)	
Less:	100% business property relief		500,000	Nil
Bank and building society accounts			700,000	
Holiday home in Barbados			300,000	
				1,000,000
Total estate on which inheritance tax is payable				1,000,000

Preliminary stage: allocation of business property relief to specific gifts and residue

		Before BPR	*After BPR*
Total free estate		2,000,000	1,500,000
Allocate a pro-rata share of			
BPR to other specific gifts (using fraction 1,500,000 /2,000,000)			
Pecuniary legacy to charity		100,000	75,000
Family home and possessions to widow	gross × $\frac{3}{4}$	400,000	300,000
		500,000	375,000

Summary of specific gifts and allocation of BPR

	Before BPR	After BPR		
Total free estate			2,000,000	1,500,000
Specific gifts from free estate				
Pecuniary legacy to charity	100,000	75,000		
Family home and possessions to widow	400,000	300,000		
Total specific gifts			500,000	375,000
Residue of free estate (after BPR of £500,000/(£500,000 – £125,000)			1,500,000	1,125,000
			2,000,000	1,500,000

Choice of rate of inheritance tax

Having allocated business property relief to the specific gifts and residue and using the amounts thereby ascertained, test whether the reduced rate of inheritance tax applies (following the method statement set out in **Example B12** (adapted to the facts of the Example where the deceased estate comprises only a general component)):

- Step 1: Calculate the chargeable amount of the general component comprised in Clive's estate. The chargeable amount is the value of the bequest to the wife, the legacy to the charity and the chargeable residue which in this case is £1,125,000.

- Step 2: Deduct from the chargeable amount of the general component determined under Step 1, the appropriate proportion of the available nil-rate band applicable to the general component. The nil-rate band of £325,000 available on Clive's death reduces the chargeable amount of the general component to £800,000 (1,125,000 – 325,000). This is the result of Step 2.

- Step 3: Add to the amount of the general component determined under Step 2, any charitable donation made (taking into account the application of s 39A) and restate the chargeable amount of the general component of the estate. This amount is the 'baseline amount' of the general component, ie 800,000 + 75,000 = £875,000.

- Step 4: Perform the 10% test – that is, compare with 10% of the baseline amount for the general component, the 'donated amount' (ie the charitable donation before the application of s 39A to it) in respect of the component. The donated amount made from a component must be at least 10% of the baseline amount of that component if the 10% test is to be satisfied.

  In Clive's case the donated amount is £100,000 and 10% of the baseline amount of the general component is 10% × £875,000 = £87,500. The test is whether the donated amount is at least 10% of the relevant component. Here, as the donated amount of £100,000 is greater than £87,500, the 10% test is met.

- Step 5: As the 10% test is met in relation to the general component, tax is charged on the chargeable amount of the general component of Clive's estate at 36%.

The computation of the inheritance tax due on Clive's estate may now be completed.

Estate on death restated

			Date of death 31 March 2024
		£	£
Estate before reliefs and exemptions			2,000,000
Less:	Exempt legacy to wife	300,000	
	Exempt legacy to RSPB	75,000	
Less:	business property relief	500,000	(875,000)
Total estate on which inheritance tax is payable			1,125,000

Tax payable on estate: (1,125,000 – 325,000) = 800,000 @ 36% = £288,000

No residence nil-rate band is available in calculating the tax as the family home is not closely inherited passing as it does to Clive's wife, Linne, rather than being inherited by his son (see **Example A2 part (b)** and, in particular, **explanatory note 15**).

Explanatory Notes

Joint tenancies and tenancies in common: inheritance tax treatment

(1) For details of joint tenancies (and tenancies in common), see the explanatory notes to **Example A8**. Since Smith's matrimonial residence and contents are jointly owned with his wife as joint tenants, they automatically accrue to his widow who survives him, and are thus left out of the calculation of the chargeable estate for inheritance tax because of the spouse exemption.

Had the house been held under a tenancy in common, then husband and wife would each be entitled to a separate share, which would have formed part of the residue of the estate which devolved on the son and daughter, Smith's one half share of the value then being included in the calculation of the chargeable estate.

Life insurance: inheritance tax treatment

(2) **Part A** of the Example illustrates that life insurance on one's own life swells the chargeable estate where the proceeds are payable to the estate. A preferable alternative is where the policy is taken out by the taxpayer on his own life but a trust is created in favour of his children, so that the proceeds of the policy eventually fall into the trust fund as distinct from the estate.

Any gifts will have occurred yearly as the taxpayer has maintained the policy by paying the premiums. They will usually be exempt from inheritance tax as payments out of the donor's income (s 21). The proceeds are payable to the trustees; if it is a bare trust, the money is passed on to the beneficiaries without any inheritance tax liability, since the beneficiaries have always had a right to the capital of the trust fund (which has now become cash instead of a life policy). If it is a different form of trust the relevant inheritance tax rules will apply.

Alternatively the children of a taxpayer could themselves take out and maintain a policy on the life of their parent on a 'life of another' basis with the same inheritance tax advantages.

(3) Another advantage of life policies not belonging to the estate is that the beneficiaries have cash without waiting for the grant of probate. The policy monies do not belong to the deceased and their receipt does not depend upon the grant of probate. They are paid upon proof of death – the death certificate. This is often a useful way of putting the dependants in funds for family necessities, or to pay inheritance tax, as well as mitigating the inheritance tax charge.

Foreign property and domicile in the context of inheritance tax

(4) Property situated abroad does not escape inheritance tax unless the taxpayer is also domiciled abroad. Domicile is a complex legal concept and differs from nationality or residence; but it also has a specially extended meaning for inheritance tax (see **Example A5 part (a)**).

(5) Where property is situated abroad, an allowance of up to a maximum of 5% of the value of the property may be claimed in respect of the additional expenses incurred in administering or realising that property because it is situated overseas (s 173).

Inheritance tax treatment of specific gifts and gifts of residue where there are exempt beneficiaries

(6) Detailed notes on business and agricultural property relief are in **Example A21**. In particular, Samuel's house in France that had only ever been let to holiday makers to whom no additional services had ever been provided part of their letting of the home would not have qualified as relevant business property.

In **part A** of this Example the interests in the partnership business and related office building were left specifically to the son and thus did not attract any exemption from inheritance tax, as they would have done if left, for example, to a surviving spouse or to a charity. There are various ways in which a deceased may have dealt with business or agricultural property in his will, and the effect is as follows (s 39A):

(a)	Business or agricultural property left specifically to a non-exempt beneficiary (as it was to the son in this Example)	BPR/APR reduces the value of the business/agricultural property, reducing the tax accordingly, and it is not affected by any exempt legacies.
(b)	Business or agricultural property left specifically to an exempt beneficiary, such as to a spouse (or as part of residue to an exempt beneficiary)	BPR/APR wasted, since no tax payable on the property in any event.
(c)	Business or agricultural property left as part of residue that goes wholly to a non-exempt beneficiary, where there are no pecuniary or other specific gifts to exempt beneficiaries	BPR/APR reduces the value of the residue, reducing the tax accordingly.
(d)	Business or agricultural property left as part of residue to a non-exempt beneficiary where there are pecuniary or other specific gifts to exempt beneficiaries, or where the residue is left partly to an exempt beneficiary (eg half to son, half to spouse)	BPR/APR is applied rateably to the exempt and non-exempt parts of the estate, and is thus wasted to the extent that it is attributed to exempt legacies or exempt residue.

For the technical way in which this is expressed in the legislation and the complications where part of the residue is exempt from tax and part is chargeable, see **part B** of this Example and **Example A18**. Wills should not be drawn up so as to trigger the operation of s 39A as it dilutes the availability of BPR and APR in the estate (see **part B** of this Example). Deeds of variation may be used to reverse the effect of s 39A where a will has not been drawn up appropriately.

(7) The exempt legacies in **part A** of this Example, which are pecuniary legacies rather than legacies of specific property but which are still specific gifts for inheritance tax purposes, are paid out of assets not subject to business property relief and the business property relief is therefore fully available.

If the will had merely left the legacies as stated with the residue to the son and daughter, without specifically leaving the partnership share and office building to the son, then the relief for business property would be spread rateably between the exempt and non-exempt parts of the estate, that relating to the exempt part then being wasted as follows:

$$\text{Maximum business property relief } (615{,}000) \times \frac{\text{Exempt estate } (168{,}100)}{\text{Total estate } (1{,}233{,}100)} = £83{,}839$$

The full business property relief would still be deducted from the business property in ascertaining what tax relates to that property from an instalment option point of view (see **explanatory note 10**), the reduction in relief being regarded as reducing the exempt legacies. The estate liable to inheritance tax would become:

Estate before reliefs and exemptions as before				1,233,100
Less:	Business property relief			(615,000)
				618,100
Less:	Exempt legacies		168,100	
	Restricted by reference to business property relief		83,839	(84,261)
				£533,839
Comprising:				
	House in France			140,800
	Residue as before		262,300	
	Business property	830,000		
	Less: 100%/50% business property relief	(615,000)	215,000	
			477,300	
Less:	Exempt legacies		(84,261)	393,039
				£533,839
Tax payable would be (533,839 – 325,000) = £208,839 @ 40%				£83,536

Which would be borne as follows:

Daughter	$\frac{140,800}{533,839} \times 83,536$	22,033
Residuary legatees	$\frac{393,039}{533,839} \times 83,536$	61,503
		£83,536

(8) Similarly if the partnership share and office building formed part of the residue and the matrimonial home had been held as tenants in common in equal shares rather than beneficial joint tenancy, but Samuel Smith's half share had been left as a specific gift to the widow, the position would be:

Estate before exemptions and reliefs as before	1,233,100
Add matrimonial home half share	272,500
	£1,505,600

Maximum business property relief is restricted by:

$$615,000 \times \frac{\text{Exempt estate}(168,100 + 272,500)}{\text{Total estate}} = \frac{440,600}{1,505,600} = £179,974$$

The estate liable to inheritance tax becomes:

Estate					1,505,600
Less:	Business property relief				(615,000)
					890,600
Less:	Exempt legacies			440,600	
	Restricted by reference to business property relief			179,974	(260,626)
					£629,974
Comprising:					
	House in France				140,800
	Matrimonial home			272,500	
	Residue as before		262,300		
	Business property	830,000			
	Less: 100%/50% business property relief	(615,000)	215,000		
			477,300		
	Less: Exempt legacies		(260,626)	216,674	489,174
					£629,974

Tax payable would be (629,974 – 325,000) = £304,974 @ 40% £121,990

Which would be borne as follows:

Daughter	$\frac{140,800}{629,974} \times 121,990$	27,265
Residuary legatees	$\frac{489,174}{629,974} \times 121,990$	94,725
		£121,990

(9) The above shows that on S Smith's estate the increase in the inheritance tax payable if the business property is part of the residue is as follows:

	If exempt legacies were £168,100	If exempt legacies were £440,600
Tax payable	83,536	121,990
Compared with tax payable as per **part (a)** of Example	(50,000)	(50,000)
	£33,536	£71,990

Although the exempt legacies are the *cause* of the higher tax, they do not themselves *bear* any of it. It is borne rateably by the residuary estate and by the specific legacies that bear their own tax under the terms of the will, as shown in **explanatory notes 7** and **8**.

(10) In **explanatory note 7**, the tax of £61,503 borne by the residuary legatees would relate to the respective parts of residue as follows:

Business property	$\frac{215,000}{477,300} \times 61,503$	27,704
Remainder of residue	$\frac{262,300}{477,300} \times 61,503$	33,799
		£61,503

In **explanatory note 8**, the tax of £94,725 borne by the residuary legatees would relate to the respective parts of residue as follows:

Business property	$\frac{215,000}{477,300} \times 94,725$	42,669
Remainder of residue	$\frac{262,300}{477,300} \times 94,725$	52,056
		£94,725

The tax relating to the business property could be paid by instalments if the conditions were satisfied, but see the note as to interest at the end of **part (A)** of the Example (see **Example A7 explanatory note 9**).

(11) The reduced rate of inheritance tax of 36% that applies to an estate where the deceased has made certain charitable legacies under his will has no application in **part A** of this Example because the gift to the registered social landlord is exempt under s 24A rather than s 23. Since the registered local landlord is, on the facts of the question, not also a charity (being as it is not registered with the Charity Commission), the gift cannot come within s 23 on that account. See **Example B12** for a detailed discussion of the definition of a charity for the purposes of inheritance tax.

(12) Part B of this Example illustrates how the reduced rate of inheritance tax applies in the case of a situation where s 39A applies. The explanation to the computation explains how the 'donated amount' at Step 4 of the method statement for choosing the reduced rate is valued without reference to s 39A. This benefits the taxpayer as s 39A operates to reduce the value of specific gifts left to charity. Without specific provision, this may mean that a component of his estate would fail the 10% test, because the value of the gift is reduced to an amount that is less than 10% of the baseline amount. To avoid this outcome, the donated amount is taken as the amount of the specific gift to charity before s 39A is applied to it. Where the 10% test is failed, the chargeable estate will be the same, but tax is charged at 40%.

Question

Mr Algernon, who has always lived in rented accommodation, died on 3 May 2023. His estate contained the following:

	Value at date of death
	£
Proceeds from insurance policy	300,000
Quoted shares	775,000
Bank account	898,000
Other possessions	40,000

Mr Algernon's will which was executed in 2005 required that:

(1) his daughter Jane receive £337,000 free of all taxes;

(2) his son John receive £400,000 (comprising cash and shares) bearing its own taxes;

(3) his wife receive one-half of the residue, the other half to pass into a trust for his grandchildren, and the division into equal shares to be made before deduction of inheritance tax thereon.

Mr Algernon had made no lifetime transfers.

Advise the trustees as to the amount of funds they can expect from Mr Algernon's estate.

Answer

Death of Mr Algernon 3 May 2023 — calculation of inheritance tax

Insurance policy	300,000
Quoted shares	775,000
Bank account	898,000
Other possessions	40,000
Gross estate	2,013,000

Stage 1

Gross up specific gifts which do not bear their own tax as though they alone were chargeable to inheritance tax on death:

	£
Legacy to daughter (see **explanatory note 5**)	337,000
Tax thereon	8,000
Gross gift	345,000

Stage 2

Using the gross gift as calculated in Stage 1, divide the estate between exempt and non-exempt parts:

	Exempt	*Non-Exempt*	
	£	£	£
Gross estate			2,013,000
Gross legacy to daughter		345,000	
Legacy to John bearing its own tax		400,000	
Residue (£1,268,000)			
Wife	634,000		
Trust		634,000	
	634,000	1,379,000	2,013,000

Stage 3

Calculate the inheritance tax on the non-exempt estate at Stage 2:

1,379,000 – 325,000 = £1,054,000 @ 40% = £421,600

Stage 4

Using the tax computed at Stage 3, re-compute the grossing up of specific gifts not bearing their own tax:

$$\text{Legacy to daughter } 337{,}000 \times \frac{1{,}379{,}000}{1{,}379{,}000 - 421{,}600} = £485{,}401$$

Stage 5

Using the revised gross gifts from Stage 4, re-divide the estate between exempt and non-exempt parts:

	Exempt	*Non-Exempt*	
	£	£	£
Gross estate			2,013,000
Legacy to daughter as in Stage 4		485,401	
Legacy to John		400,000	
Residue (£1,127,599)			
Wife	563,800		
Trust		563,799	
	563,800	1,449,200	2,013,000

Stage 6

Calculate the inheritance tax on the revised non-exempt part of the estate and calculate the effective rate of tax:

1,449,200 – 325,000 = £1,124,200 @ 40% = £449,680

$$\frac{449{,}680}{1{,}449{,}200} \times 100 = 31.0295\% \text{ effective rate}$$

Stage 7

The residue of the estate is therefore as follows:	£	£	£
Gross estate			2,013,000
Less: Inheritance tax payable			(449,680)
			1,563,320
Less: Legacy to daughter		337,000	
Legacy to John	400,000		
Less IHT thereon at 31.0295%	(124,118)		
Net Legacy		275,882	
Net legacy John/Daughter			(612,882)
Residue			950,438

However none of the charge to inheritance tax is to fall on the exempt part due to the spouse.

The estate is therefore distributed as follows:	£	£	£
Daughter			337,000
John			275,882
			612,882

Tax on legacies at 31.0295% (per Stage 6) at grossed up value (per Stage 4) 485,401 + 400,000 = £885,401 × 31.0295%		274,735	
Residue before tax (2,013,000 – (612,882 + 274,735))	1,125,383		
Half to widow (1,125,383 @ 50%)			562,691
Half to Trust (1,125,383 @ 50%)	562,692		
Less: Tax @ 31.0295% on £563,799 (per Stage 5)	(174,944)	174,944	
Trust share of residue net of tax*	387,748		387,748
Inheritance tax		449,679	449,679
Gross estate			2,013,000

*The trustees may therefore expect to receive £387,748.

Explanatory Notes

Incidence of inheritance tax on deceased's estate

(1) The calculation of the inheritance tax and the distribution of the estate is not straightforward where on a person's death part of the estate is the subject of an exempt transfer (in this case to the surviving spouse) and part is chargeable.

(2) The ultimate incidence of tax on a deceased's estate is as follows:

Tax relating to a qualifying interest in possession of the deceased in settled property (including where the settlement ends on the death) is payable out of the trust funds.

Tax relating to nominated and jointly held property of the deceased, and property subject to a reservation, is payable out of that property.

The tax on property situated abroad is a charge on that property.

In the absence of specific provisions in the will, tax on all other property, both real and personal, wherever situated in the UK, is a testamentary expense payable out of the residue of the estate.

However, under IHTA 1984 s 200 the deceased's personal representatives are liable for all the inheritance tax chargeable on the death transfer with the exception of property that was comprised in a settlement immediately before the death (but including land in the UK which, even though so comprised, devolves on or vests in the personal representatives on the death), and – subject to the instalment option – they are obliged to pay that tax on delivering their inheritance tax account (s 226(2)). To the extent that the tax is not a testamentary expense, the personal representatives then have a statutory right to recover it from the persons in whom the property in question is vested (s 211, and see **Example A7 explanatory note 10**).

Partially exempt legacies: burden of inheritance tax

(3) Thus, although the widow's share of the estate is exempt, the tax on specific legacies must come out of the residue (unless the will specifically provides that the legacy is to bear its own tax).

If the residue then remaining is left partly to the widow (exempt) and partly by way of chargeable transfer (not exempt), the tax on the residue must be borne in accordance with the will. This is subject to s 41, which provides that, notwithstanding the terms of the will, none of the tax on a particular gift (whether specific or residuary) is to fall on that gift if that gift is exempt.

Re Benham and Re Ratcliffe

In the case of *Re Benham's Will Trusts* (1995) it was held that the plain intention of the deceased's will was that each beneficiary should *receive* the *same amount* and that this was not inconsistent with s 41. Consequently the non-exempt shares of residue had to be grossed up so that the after tax amounts were equal. This had the effect of increasing both the tax charged on the estate and the shares of non-exempt residuary beneficiaries at the expense of exempt beneficiaries, which was contrary to the accepted practice and was not the view taken by the Capital Taxes Office. In 1999 a different High Court judge came to the opposite conclusion in the case of *Re Ratcliffe (deceased)*. He referred to the *Benham* approach as the 'net division' approach and the previously accepted approach as the 'gross division' approach, and held that the 'gross division' approach was correct on the facts of the case. The case was not taken to appeal, but is generally regarded as overriding the *Benham* decision except where the particular facts in point are very close to those arising in *Benham*. Even so, it would be sensible to review the wording of wills where there is partly exempt residue, to ensure that it is clear whether the division of residue is to take place before or after deducting the tax on that residue.

Stages in tax calculation; double grossing up

(4) The procedure is straightforward where lifetime transfers exceed the general nil-rate threshold, because all grossing calculations are at the same rate, ie 100/60 (see **explanatory note** 7). However, where the cumulative lifetime transfers are less than the general nil-rate threshold the method of calculation is complex (ss 36 to 42).

Where, as in this example, the lifetime transfers are less than the general nil-rate threshold, there are seven stages in the calculation, the first six of which are notional calculations used in order to ascertain the effective rate of inheritance tax on the estate.

The stages are as follows:

(i) Gross up specific gifts which do not bear their own tax as though they were the only chargeable transfers made at death (s 38(1) and (3)).

(ii) Using the grossed up gifts arrived at in (i) divide the estate between exempt and non-exempt parts.

(iii) Compute tax on the *notional* non-exempt part of the estate determined at (2).

(iv) Once again gross up specific gifts which do not bear their own tax but using the tax arrived at in (iii) (ss 38(4) and (5)). This now replaces the outcome of (i).

(v) Using the revised gross gifts in (iv) re-divide the estate between exempt and non-exempt parts.

(vi) Compute tax on the non-exempt part determined in (v) and calculate the effective rate of tax (s 38(1)).

(vii) Distribute the estate in such a way that the tax, if any, on the gifts in the will not bearing their own tax comes out of the whole of the residue, and the tax on the residue falls on the part of the residue that is not exempt (s 41).

(5) The grossing up calculation in Stage 1 of the example on the legacy to the daughter is as follows:

Cumulative net transfers of £337,000 exceed £325,000 by £12,000. This is grossed up using the 40% tax rate thus:

	Gross £	*Tax* £	*Net* £
	325,000	Nil	325,000
Gross equivalent $\frac{100}{60} \times 12{,}000$	20,000		12,000
and tax thereon (20,000 @ 40%)		8,000	
	345,000	8,000	337,000

(6) The calculation of tax on the trustees' share of the residue is based upon their notional share of residue ie £563,799 per Stage 5 not their actual share of £562,692 at Stage 7. This method is used by HMRC Inheritance Tax. Views have been expressed that the tax should be based upon the actual share of residue (ie £562,692 @ 31. 0295% = £174,600 compared with £174,944 as computed). This does not appear to follow the requirement that none of the tax as computed is to fall on the spouse or other exempt transfers. Instead it re-computes the tax yet again.

Calculation if lifetime transfers exceed general nil-rate threshold

(7) If Mr Algernon had made cumulative lifetime transfers of £325,000, the seven stage calculation would not be necessary and the position would be as follows:

	Gross	*Tax*	*Net*
	£	£	£
Inheritance tax accumulation at death on 2023/24 scale	325,000	Nil	325,000
Legacy to daughter grossed up 337,000 × 100/60	561,667	224,667	337,000
Legacy to John	400,000	160,000	240,000
Leaving residue of 2,013,000 – (561,667 + 400,000) = £1,051,333, of which half, ie £525,666, is exempt, so that non-exempt residue is	525,667	210,267	315,400
	1,812,334	594,934	1,217,400

The estate would therefore be distributed as follows:

Daughter — legacy			337,000
John — legacy			240,000
Widow's share of residue			525,666
Trust's share of residue		525,667	
Less tax @ 40%		(210,267)	315,400
Inheritance tax:			
On legacies —	daughter	224,667	
	John	160,000	
On Trust's share of residue		210,267	
Total tax			594,934
			£2,013,000

The same procedure would apply if the lifetime transfers had been of any amount in excess of £325,000.

Further examples

(8) For further illustrations of the treatment of partially exempt legacies, including the provisions in relation to settled property, business property and agricultural property relief and intestacy, see **Examples A18** and **A19**. For an illustration of the treatment of partially exempt legacies where the estate concerned is subject to single grossing up and also qualifies for the reduced rate of inheritance tax of 36%, see **explanatory note 10** below and **Example A15**.

Grandchildren's trust: inheritance tax treatment

(9) As Mr Algernon's will was executed in 2005, it is likely that the grandchildren's trust would have been an accumulation and maintenance settlement in accordance with IHTA 1984 s 71 (as that section applied at that time). Had Mr Algernon died before 22 March 2006, this would have allowed the income to have been accumulated until the grandchildren reached the age of 25 at the latest without the trust fund becoming relevant property (and so subject to the ten-yearly and exit charges regime). However, the trust terms would have to have been amended before 6 April 2008 to make it compliant with the amendments made to s 71 by FA 2006 (ie to have allowed the income to have been accumulated until the grandchildren reached the age of

18 at which time they would have had to become absolutely entitled to the trust property) if the trust were to retain its status as an accumulation and maintenance settlement so as not to fall within the relevant property regime. Alternatively the trust terms could have been amended to so that the trust became and 18-25 trust but in that case a modest tax charge would have arisen (at the latest) when the beneficiaries turned 25 and became absolutely entitled to the trust property. See **Example C16** for details of the accumulation and maintenance trust regime and the treatment of those trusts from 22 March 2006.

However, since Mr Algernon died after 21 March 2006, any trust for his grandchildren would constitute relevant property except in so far as it conferred an immediate post-death interest in possession within s 49A or a disabled person's interest within s 89B.

The reduced rate of inheritance tax and double grossing

(10) FA 2012 s 209 and Sch 33 introduced Sch 1A to IHTA 1984 which provides for a lower rate of inheritance tax (namely 36%) to be charged on a deceased person's estate where 10% or more of the net estate has been left to a charity or a registered community amateur sports club. The lower rate takes effect for deaths occurring on or after 6 April 2012 (FA 2012 Sch 32 para 10(1)). The application of the lower rate of tax has been set out fully in **Example B12.**

(11) The issue that needs to be addressed is how the lower rate applies in the context of a double grossing up computation. There is a special rule in IHTA 1984 Sch 1A para 6(1) that provides that in quantifying the donated amount (and also the baseline amount), the specific gifts are grossed up at the lower rate. If the 10% test is then met, the inheritance tax itself (to be charged (in part at least) at the rate of 36%) is calculated using the specific legacy grossed up at 36%. (This will not entail a separate calculation to gross up the specific gifts as they will already have been grossed up at 36%.)

But if the 10% test is not met (so that the estate cannot benefit from the lower rate of tax), then the specific gifts will need to be grossed up at the rate of 40% and the tax on the estate recalculated at that rate in the usual way (see **main part** of this Example). This second calculation will not, of course, disturb the choice of rate calculation which, applying the special rule in Sch 1A para 6(1) in relation to the donated and baseline amounts, determined that the 40% rate of tax applied. It is important to realise that there are two distinct stages:

(a) the choice of rate calculation (to work out whether the 10% test is met);

(b) the calculation of tax in respect of the chargeable estate, applying the appropriate rate of inheritance tax.

The reasoning behind the introduction of this special valuation rule is explained in **Example A15 explanatory note 10.**

(12) In the case of Mr Algernon, part of the residue of his estate was exempt from tax because it was left under his will to his wife. However, if that part of the residue had instead been left to charity, it needs to be considered whether the lower rate of inheritance tax of 36% may then apply. To make this decision in the context of this question, at Stage 1 of the computation the grossing up of the specific gifts which do not bear their own tax is carried out using the 36% rate and the non-exempt part of the estate is computed at Stage 2 using that amount from Stage 1. In this case the calculation would be as follows:

Stage 1

Gross up specific gifts which do not bear their own tax as though they alone were chargeable to inheritance tax on death. Following the process described in **explanatory note 5**, the cumulative net transfers of £337,000 exceed £325,000 by £12,000. This is grossed up using the 36% tax rate so that the gross equivalent of £12,000 is £12,000 × 100/64 = £18,750 and the tax on that amount is £18,750 × 36% = £6,750. Hence the gross gift is:

	£
Legacy to daughter	337,000
Tax thereon	6,750
Gross gift	343,750

Stage 2

Using the gross gift as calculated in Stage 1, divide the estate between exempt and non-exempt parts:

	Exempt	*Non-Exempt*	
	£	£	£
Gross estate			2,013,000
Gross legacy to daughter		343,750	
Legacy to John bearing its own tax		400,000	
Residue of 1,269,250 (£2,013,000 – (343,7520 + 400,000))			
Charity (1,269,250 @ 50%)	634,625		
Trust (1,269,250 @ 50%)		634,625	
Total	634,625	1,378,375	2,013,000

Choice of rate of inheritance tax

Having completed Stage 2 of the computation and using the figures ascertained from Stage 2, test whether the lower rate of inheritance tax applies (following the method statement set out in **Example B12** (adapted to the facts of the Example where the deceased estate comprises only a general component)):

- Step 1: Calculate the chargeable amount of the general component comprised in Mr Algernon's estate. The chargeable amount is the value of the legacy to the daughter (grossed up), the legacy to John and the chargeable residue which in this case is £1,378,375 (see above).
- Step 2: Deduct from the chargeable amount of the general component determined under Step 1, the appropriate proportion of the available nil-rate band applicable to the general component. The nil-rate band of £325,000 available on Mr Algernon's death reduces the chargeable amount of the general component to £1,053,375 (1,378,375 – 325,000).
- Step 3: Add to the amount of the general component determined under Step 2 (£1,053,375), any charitable donation made (£634,625) and restate the chargeable amount of the general component of the estate. This amount is the 'baseline amount' of the general component, ie £1,053,375 + £634,625 = £1,688,000.
- Step 4: Perform the 10% test – that is, compare with 10% of the baseline amount for the general component, the 'donated amount' (ie the charitable donation) in respect of the component. The donated amount made from a component must be at least 10% of the baseline amount of that component if the 10% test is to be satisfied.

  In Mr Algernon's case the donated amount is £634,625 and 10% of the baseline amount of the general component is 10% × £1,688,000 = £168,800. The test is whether the donated amount is at least 10% of the relevant component. Here, as the donated amount of £634,625 is greater than £168,800, the 10% test is met.

- Step 5: As the 10% test is met in relation to the general component, tax is charged on the chargeable amount of the general component of Mr Algernon's estate at 36%.

  So the double grossing procedure continues to Stage 3 using the 36% rate (as set out below). If the test at Step 4 were failed, then the 40% rate of tax would apply and the double grossing up procedure would recommence at Stage 1 and use the 40% (as in the main Example). (Where a legacy to charity is worded in such a way that the amount of the legacy must meet the 10% test then the problem of having to recalculate the tax using the 40% rate of tax will not arise (see **Example B12, explanatory note 37**)).

Stage 3

Calculate the inheritance tax on the non-exempt estate at Stage 2:

£1,378,375 – £325,000 = £1,053,375 @ 36% = £379,215

Stage 4

Using the tax computed at Stage 3, re-compute the grossing up of specific gifts not bearing their own tax:

$$\text{Legacy to daughter } 337{,}000 \times \frac{1{,}378{,}375}{1{,}378{,}375 - 379{,}215} = £464{,}902$$

Stage 5

Using the revised gross gifts from Stage 4, re-divide the estate between exempt and non-exempt parts:

	Exempt	*Non-Exempt*	
	£	£	£
Gross estate			2,013,000
Legacy to daughter as in Stage 4		464,902	
Legacy to John		400,000	
Residue £1,148,098 (2,013,000 – (464,902 + 400,000))			
Charity (1,148,098 @ 50%)	574,049		
Trust (1,148,098 @ 50%)		574,049	
Total	574,049	1,438,951	2,013,000

Stage 6

Calculate the inheritance tax on the revised non-exempt part of the estate and calculate the effective rate of tax:

1,438,951 – 325,000 = £1,113,951 @ 36% = £401,022

$$\frac{401{,}022}{1{,}438{,}951} \times 100 = 27.8691\% \textit{ effective rate}$$

Stage 7

The residue of the estate is therefore as follows:	£	£	£
Gross estate			2,013,000
Less: Inheritance tax payable			(401,022)
			1,611,978
Less: Legacy to daughter		337,000	
Legacy to John	400,000		
Less IHT thereon at 27.8691%	(111,476)		
Net legacy to John		288,524	
Total legacies			(625,524)
Residue			986,454

However none of the charge to inheritance tax is to fall on the exempt part due to the charity.

The estate is therefore distributed as follows:	£	£	£
Daughter			337,000
John			288,524
			625,524
Tax on legacies at 27.8691% (per Stage 6) at grossed up value (per Stage 4) 464,902 + 400,000 = £864,902 × 27.8691%		241,040	
Residue before tax (2,013,000 – (625,524 + 241,040)	1,146,436		
Half to charity			573,218
Half to Trust	573,218		
Less: Tax @ 27.8691% on £574,049 (per Stage 5)	(159,982)	159,982	
Net legacy			413,236
Inheritance tax		401,022	401,022
Gross estate			2,013,000

The trustees may therefore expect to receive £413,236.

The residence nil-rate band (RNRB) and double grossing

(13) In the Example, Mr Algernon did not own a home when he died. However, if he had and it was (in whole or in part) inherited by his children (or either one of them), the RNRB would need to be considered in computing the IHT payable by his estate (and hence its subsequent division).

So how would the computation in this Example have proceeded had the facts remained as previously stated except that Thomas died owning a home (acquired before 8 July 2015) worth £487,000, his Will required that his daughter Jane receive the home free of all taxes (instead of her pecuniary legacy), and his bank account contained £398,000?

The double grossing procedure would then, in the authors' opinion, proceed as follows:

Stage 1

Gross up specific gifts which do not bear their own tax as though they alone were chargeable to inheritance tax on death. In this case then, in addition to the general nil-rate band, the residence nil-rate band available on the specific gift of the home given to Mr Algernon's daughter would be his default allowance of £150,000 (see **Example A2 part (b)**). Consequently the result of Stage 1 would (taking into account **explanatory note 5 above**) be:

	£
Legacy to daughter	487,000
Tax thereon (487,000 - 325,000 - 150,000) × 40/60	8,000
Gross gift	495,000

Stage 2

Using the gross gift as calculated in Stage 1, divide the estate between exempt and non-exempt parts:

	Exempt	*Non-Exempt*	
	£	£	£
Gross estate			2,000,000
Gross legacy to daughter		495,000	
Legacy to John bearing its own tax		400,000	
Residue (£1,105,000)			
Wife	552,500		

	Exempt	*Non-Exempt*	
	£	£	£
Trust		552,500	
Total	552,500	1,447,500	2,000,000

Stage 3

Calculate the inheritance tax on the notional non-exempt estate at Stage 2. Again the residence nil-rate band would be £175,000 (as the notional estate is less than the RNRB taper threshold of £2,000,000):

1,447,500 – 325,000 – 175,000 = £947,500 @ 40% = £379,000

Stage 4

Using the tax computed at Stage 3, re-compute the grossing up of specific gifts not bearing their own tax as though they alone were chargeable to inheritance tax on death. In this case then, in addition to the general nil-rate band, the residence nil-rate band available on the specific gift of the home given to Mr Algernon's daughter would be his default allowance of £150,000. Consequently the result of Stage 4 would be:

$$\text{Legacy to daughter } 487{,}000 \times \frac{1{,}447{,}000}{(1{,}447{,}000 - 379{,}000)} = £658{,}821$$

Stage 5

Using the revised gross gifts from Stage 4, re-divide the estate between exempt and non-exempt parts:

	Exempt	*Non-Exempt*	
	£	£	£
Gross estate			2,000,000
Legacy to daughter as in Stage 4		657,821	
Legacy to John		400,000	
Residue (£934,027)			
Wife	470,589		
Trust		470,589	
	470,589	1,529,410	2,000,000

Stage 6

Calculate the inheritance tax on the revised non-exempt part of the estate and calculate the effective rate of tax. Again the residence nil-rate band would be £175,000:

1,529,410 – 325,000 – 175,000 = £1,029,410 @ 40% = £411,764

$$\frac{411{,}764}{1{,}529{,}410} \times 100 = 26.9231\% \textit{ effective rate}$$

Stage 7

The residue of the estate is therefore as follows:	£	£	£
Gross estate			2,000,000
Less: Inheritance tax payable			(411,764)
			1,588,236
Less: Legacy to daughter		487,000	
Legacy to John	400,000		
Less IHT thereon at 26.9231%	(107,692)		
Net legacy		292,308	
Net legacies John/Daughter			(779,308)
Residue			808,928

However none of the charge to inheritance tax is to fall on the exempt part due to the spouse.

The estate is therefore distributed as follows:	£	£	£
Daughter			487,000
John			292,308
			779,308
Tax on legacies at 26.9231% (per Stage 6) at grossed up value (per Stage 4) 658,821 + 400,000 = £1,058,821 × 26.9231%		285,067	
Residue before tax (2,000,000 – (779,308 + 294,271)	935,625		
Half to widow (935,625 @ 50%)			467,813
Half to Trust (935,625 @ 50%)	467,812		
Less: Tax @ 26.9231% on £467,812(per Stage 5)	(125,949)	125,949	
Trust share of residue net of tax*	341,863		341,863
Inheritance tax		411,016	411,016
Gross estate			2,000,000

*The trustees may therefore expect to receive £341,862.

Question

On 1 January 2019 X, who had made no previous lifetime transfers, gave £123,000 to his daughter D and on 1 November 2019, £81,500 each to his daughter E and his son S.

On 1 June 2023 X died leaving an estate which, after payment of all personal debts and funeral expenses, was valued at £300,000, after deduction of business property relief of £150,000. X had never owned a residential property.

By his will he left business property valued at £120,000 (before business property relief of £60,000) equally to his daughter E and his wife W free of tax, £25,000 to the Conservative Party, a pecuniary legacy of £40,000 to his son S and the residue of his estate equally (before inheritance tax thereon) to W and three children D, S and E. The residue of the estate comprises only cash.

X was entitled for life to the income of the residuary estate of his father (and had been so since his father's death in 2003) with remainder to his son S. The assets of that settlement were valued at £100,000 on 1 June 2023 and did not qualify for BPR/APR.

Calculate the inheritance tax payable on X's death.

Answer

X — inheritance tax cumulation

1 January 2019		£
Gift to D		123,000
Less: Annual exemptions 2018/19	3,000	
2017/18	3,000	
		(6,000)
Potentially exempt transfer		117,000
1 November 2019		
Gift to E		81,500
Gift to S		81,500
		163,000
Less: Annual exemption 2019/20 (split equally)		(3,000)
Potentially exempt transfers		160,000

On death of X — 1 June 2023

	Gross	*Tax on 2023/24 scale*
	£	£
PET to D — 1 January 2019	117,000	Nil
PETs to E and S — 1 November 2019	160,000	Nil
Inheritance tax cumulation at death	277,000	Nil

No tax payable on lifetime transfers since below nil-rate threshold (but correspondingly no tapering relief).

Estate on Death

Free estate	450,000	
Less: Business property relief	(150,000)	
		300,000
Settled property		100,000
		£400,000

A18.3 PARTIALLY EXEMPT RESIDUE (AFFECTED BY TRUST FUNDS, BUSINESS PROPERTY RELIEF (BPR) AND AGRICULTURAL PROPERTY RELIEF (APR))

Preliminary Stage: Allocation of business property relief to specific gifts, and residue, for grossing calculations

		Before BPR		*After BPR*
Total free estate		450,000		300,000
First allocate BPR on specific gifts of business property to that property				
Business property to wife — W	60,000		30,000	
Business property to daughter — E	60,000		30,000	
		(120,000)		(60,000)
Remainder of estate		330,000		240,000
Then allocate a pro rata share of remaining BPR (net/gross – × 240,000 / 330,000) to other specific gifts				
Pecuniary legacy to Conservative Party $\text{gross} \times \frac{240,000}{330,000}$		25,000		18,182
Pecuniary legacy to son — S		40,000		29,091
		65,000		47,273

Summary of specific gifts and allocation of BPR

		Before BPR		*After BPR*
Total free estate		450,000		300,000
Specific gifts from free estate				
Business property to wife — W	60,000		30,000	
Business property to daughter — E	60,000		30,000	
Pecuniary legacy to Conservative Party	25,000		18,182	
Pecuniary legacy to son — S	40,000		29,091	
Total specific gifts		185,000		107,273
Residue of free estate (receives balance of BPR)		265,000		192,727
Total free estate		450,000		300,000

Division of estate to compute exempt transfers

Stage 1

Gross up non-exempt specific gifts that do not bear their own tax, at net of BPR values, as though they alone were chargeable to IHT on death:

Half of business property (after BPR) to E	30,000
Legacy to S (after BPR)	29,091
	£59,091

	Gross £	*Tax* £	*Net* £
Inheritance tax accumulation at death	277,000	Nil	277,000
Specific gifts	66,485	7,394	59,091
	343,485	7,394	336,091*

* Grossed up

Net		*Gross*
325,000		325,000
11,091	× 100/60	18,485
£336,091		£343,485

Stage 2

Using notional gross gift as calculated in Stage 1, divide estate, net of business property relief, between exempt and non-exempt parts:

		Exempt £	*Non-exempt* £	*Total* £
Business property to wife W (as prelim. stage)		30,000		30,000
Business property to E	$\frac{30,000}{59,091} \times 66,485$		33,754	33,754
Legacy to S	$\frac{29,091}{59,091} \times 66,485$		32,731	32,731
Legacy to Conservative Party	(as prelim. stage)	18,182		18,182
Total specific gifts		48,182	66,485	114,667
Residue —	Balance			185,333
	Wife (¼)	46,333		
	Children (¾)		139,000	
		94,515	205,485	300,000

Stage 3

Calculate the notional inheritance tax payable on non-exempt estate at Stage 2:

	Gross £	*Tax* £
Accumulation at death	277,000	Nil
Non-exempt estate	205,485	62,994*
	482,485	62,994*

(* 482,485 – 325,000 = 157,485 @ 40%)

Stage 4

Using the tax computed at Stage 3, re-compute the grossing up of specific gifts not bearing their own tax:

$$£59,091 \times \frac{205,485}{(205,485 - 62,994)} = £85,215$$

Stage 5

Using the revised gross gifts from Stage 4, re-divide the estate between exempt and non-exempt parts:

		Exempt	Non-exempt	Total
		£	£	£
Business property				
to wife W	Specific gift after BPR	30,000		30,000
to daughter E	$\frac{30,000}{59,091} \times 85,215$		43,263	43,263
Pecuniary legacies				
to son S	$\frac{29,091}{59,091} \times 85,215$		41,952	41,952
to Conservative Party	specific gift after BPR	18,182		18,182
		48,182	85,215	133,397
Residue				166,603
	Wife (¼)	41,651		
	Children (¾)		124,952	
		89,833	210,167	300,000

Stage 6

Calculate the inheritance tax on the revised non-exempt part of the estate and calculate the effective rate of tax:

		Gross	Tax
		£	£
Accumulation at death		277,000	Nil
Non-exempt estate as stage 5	210,167		
Settled property	100,000	310,167	104,867*
		587,167	104,867*

(* 587,167 – 325,000 = 262,167 @ 40%)

Effective rate $\frac{104,867}{310,167} \times 100 = 33.81\%$

Inheritance tax payable by

Personal representatives	210,167	× 33.81% =	71,057
Trustees of settled property	100,000	× 33.81% =	33,810
	£310,167		£104,867

Stage 7

Distribution of free estate:

Estate at death				450,000
Less:	Inheritance tax			(71,057)
				378,943
Less:	Exempt specific gifts			
	To	Wife	60,000	
		Conservative Party	25,000	(85,000)
				293,943
Less:	Non-exempt specific gifts (not bearing their own tax)			
	To	E	60,000	
		S	40,000	(100,000)
Net residue				£193,943

Distribution of net residue so that no inheritance tax relates to widow

Legacies to E and S (at grossed up value stages 4 and 5) at final effective rate of 33.81%

Tax thereon = £85,215 × 33.81% = £28,811

Estate on death			450,000
Exempt legacies	— wife	60,000	
	— Conservative Party	25,000	
Legacies not bearing own tax			
	— E	60,000	
	— S	40,000	
	— tax thereon	28,811	(213,811)
Residue before tax			£236,189
Net residue as at stage (7) above			193,943
One quarter of residue before tax to widow ¼ × 236,189			(59,047)
Balance equally to children:			£134,896
D			£44,965
S			£44,965
E			£44,966

Summary of division of estate and trust funds

		£	£
To Son S from trustees of settled property		100,000	
Less:	Inheritance tax thereon (stage 6)	(33,810)	66,190
To Conservative Party	Legacy		25,000
To E	specific gift of business property	60,000	
	share of residue (stage 7)	44,966	104,966
To S	Legacy	40,000	
	share of residue (stage 7)	44,965	84,965
To D	share of residue (stage 7)		44,965

To wife	specific gift of business property	60,000	
	share of residue (stage 7)	59,047	119,047
Inheritance tax (including that on settled property) (stage 6)			104,867
			£550,000

Explanatory Notes

Inheritance tax treatment of same-day transfers

(1) The first step is to compute the inheritance tax accumulation at death.

(2) Where two or more transfers are made on the same day they are treated except in certain special circumstances as one transfer and the effective rate of tax on the total transfer is applied to the individual transfers (IHTA 1984 s 266(2)).

Inheritance tax treatment of a qualifying interest in possession in settled property

(3) Settled property in which the donor had a qualifying IIP is treated as belonging to the donor absolutely for inheritance tax purposes, although the tax relating to the settlement is payable by the trustees of the settlement (ss 49 and 200(1)(b)). An interest in possession to which the beneficiary had been entitled since before 22 March 2006 (known as a qualifying interest) continues to be treated in this way despite the changes wrought by FA 2006.

Inheritance tax treatment of partially exempt legacies and business and agricultural property relief

(4) In order to compute the tax payable on death the rules for partially exempt transfers must be applied (ss 36–42). These are detailed in **Example A17**.

Where an estate is entitled to business property relief or agricultural property relief and there are specific gifts then special rules apply in computing the inheritance tax payable detailed, as follows:

(a) Specific gifts of relevant business property or agricultural property are taken at their value reduced by BPR or APR (s 39A(2)).

(b) Specific gifts other than in (a) above are taken at the appropriate fraction of their value (s 39A(3)), that is:

$$\text{Specific gift} \times \frac{\text{Assets transferred (net of BPR/APR) less specific gifts of business/agricultural property (net of BPR/APR)}}{\text{Assets transferred (before BPR/APR) less specific gifts of business/agricultural property (before BPR/APR)}}$$

A specific gift is any gift other than a gift of residue or of a share in residue (s 42). It therefore covers both specific legacies of particular property and general (ie pecuniary) legacies. It would also cover settled property which devolves under the terms of the settlement (and not under the terms of the life tenant's will by way of general power of appointment, which would be unusual).

Where specific gifts are tax-free then the grossing up rules are applied to the value so reduced, as shown at Stage 1.

Inheritance tax treatment of gifts out of different funds

(5) Section 40 provides that where gifts take effect separately out of different funds (for example where a deceased has a free estate and a qualifying life interest in a settlement, and gifts are made out of the free estate), the partial exemption rules in ss 36–39A are to be applied separately to the gifts taking effect out of each of those funds. The rate of tax used to gross up the gifts is arrived at by looking at each fund separately

and in isolation. In this Example, therefore, the tax on the non-exempt estate at stage (3) that is used to re-gross the specific gifts is arrived at by taking into account only the free estate and not the settled property.

Inheritance tax treatment of pecuniary legacies

(6) Where a will provides a pecuniary legacy (a gift of cash like the legacy of £40,000 to S), then the legatee receives the amount stated and any inheritance tax relating to that legacy is borne by the residue of the estate unless the will provides that the legatee is to bear the tax (s 211). For further notes on this point see **Example A5 explanatory note 10.**

Re Benham and Re Ratcliffe

(7) Where a will provides that the residuary shares are computed on the residue after deduction of inheritance tax, there were conflicting views in *Re Benham* and *Re Ratcliffe* on how the shares of residue should be calculated. It is now generally regarded as settled that the established approach in dealing with partly exempt estates is correct unless the will is very clear in specifying that the shares are fixed *after* deducting inheritance tax – see **Example A17 explanatory note 3.**

The lower rate of inheritance tax

(8) FA 2013 s 209 and Sch 33 introduced Sch 1A to IHTA 1984 which provides for a lower rate of inheritance tax (namely 36%) to be charged on a deceased person's estate where 10% or more of his net estate has been left to a charity or a registered community amateur sports club. The lower rate takes effect for deaths occurring on or after 6 April 2013 (FA 2013 Sch 32 para 10(1)). The application of the lower rate of tax has been set out fully in **Example B12.**

(9) Where an estate component includes property that qualifies for business property relief and/or agricultural property relief and the estate is also partially exempt because assets pass to charity (either as a specific legacy or as part of the residue of the estate), it is still necessary to apply IHTA 1984 s 39A to allocate the business property relief and/or agricultural property relief and the charities exemption correctly. This section has the effect of reducing the value of specific gifts to charity. This may, in turn, have the effect of resulting in the failure of the 10% test so that the estate cannot qualify for the lower rate of inheritance tax of 36%. In order to avoid this unwarranted effect on the amount of the charitable legacy (the donated amount), there is a special rule in Sch 1A para 6(2). This is to the effect that the rule in s 39A reducing the value of a specific gift to charity does not apply for the purpose of calculating the 'donated amount' (so that the charitable legacy is taken as its unreduced value). The rule in s 39A continues to apply in the usual way however when calculating the 'baseline amount' in the method statement in respect of the component of the estate under consideration. These rules apply only to specific gifts to charity and not to any other specific gift which is reduced or relieved in the normal way. A detailed calculation of the application of this rule is contained in **Example A16(B)**. For an example where both double grossing up and the rule in s 39A apply in determining whether the 10% baseline test is met, see IHTM 45032. In that example after s 39A has been applied, Stages 1 and 2 of the double grossing up procedure are carried out assuming in the first instance that the lower 36% rate of tax applies. Then, using the figures ascertained from Stage 2, the choice of rate procedure is applied. If the lower rate of 36% indeed applies, the grossing up procedure continues to Stage 3. If it is found that the lower rate of 36% does not apply to the estate, it is necessary to start the grossing up procedure again by returning to Stage 1 and use the full rate grossing up calculation.

Question

Jones, who was domiciled in England and Wales, died intestate on 10 June 2023 and was survived by his wife and two adult children. He and his family have always lived in rented accommodation.

He had made no chargeable lifetime transfers.

His estate according to the account accompanying the application for a grant of administration consisted of:

5,000	£1 shares in A plc quoted at 1088–1092 with recorded bargains at 1088, 1089, 1090 and 1091
10,000	£1 shares in B plc quoted at 295–297 with a sole recorded bargain at 295
8,000	50p shares in C plc quoted at 60–69 with bargains at 61, 61½, 62 and 63
10,000	shares in the Fantasian Bank valued at £70,000

	£
Cash at bank	87,569
Policy on his life, insuring	270,000
Salary accrued due to date of death (net)	2,275
Rents from his father's will trust (net of basic rate income tax)	
accrued due	645
apportionment to date of death	621
Furniture and effects	10,500
His debts were shown as:	
Funeral expenses	1,650
General household bills (electricity, gas, etc)	220
Daughter, under a deed of covenant dated 1 January 2002 binding his legal personal representatives to pay her on his death	5,000

Under the will of his father who had died in 1996 he also had a life interest in a commercial property, No 12 High Street, valued at £200,000, which passed on his death to his children equally absolutely. The rent due to Jones at death is indicated above.

A grant of administration was obtained on 15 March 2024 when inheritance tax amounting to £2,630 and £41 interest was paid by the intended administrators on the basis of the above information.

The administrators subsequently discover:

(1) Jones is entitled to a pecuniary legacy of £10,000 free of tax under the will of his brother who died on 4 August 2022. Inheritance tax amounting to £13,000 had been paid on the brother's (fully taxable) estate valued at £100,000.

(2) There was an outstanding income tax liability of £750.

(3) There were bonuses totalling £47,250 attaching to the life policy.

(4) The value of the shares in the Fantasian Bank is agreed at £70,000, but death duties amounting to the sterling equivalent of £7,000 and £420 interest had to be paid locally because the shares were registered in Fantasia. The additional cost of employing a local agent to make title to the shares, including agreeing the value with the local fiscal authorities, amounted to a sterling equivalent of £4,150.

(5) The remaining values were agreed with HMRC.

A corrective account is lodged and the final adjustment to the inheritance tax payable is made on 5 November 2024, the trustees also paying any tax and interest attributable to the trust funds on that day.

Given that the 'statutory legacy' payable to the spouse on an intestacy when the intestate leaves issue is £270,000 with the spouse also taking the personal chattels and one half of the residue absolutely, whilst the other half of the residue devolves on the issue:

(a) Calculate the inheritance tax and interest paid by or repaid to the administrators on 5 November 2024.

(b) Show the distribution of the free estate and trust funds upon Jones's death and the allocation of the tax payable.

The rate of interest on tax overdue is, at the time of writing, 7.75% from 22 August 2023. The rate payable on tax refunded is 4.25% (from 22 August 2023); assume that these rates remain in force throughout 2024/25.

Answer

(a) Estate of Jones (after submission of corrective account)

		Date of Death 10 June 2023 £	£
Free estate			
Quoted shares:			
5,000 £1 shares in A plc	@ 1089	54,450	
10,000 £1 shares in B plc	@ 295	29,500	
8,000 50p shares in C plc	@ 62	4,960	88,910
Cash at bank			87,569
Policy on life		270,000	
Bonuses thereon		47,250	317,250
Salary due			2,275
Rents accrued due to date of death (after basic rate income tax) (645 + 621)			1,266
Furniture and effects			10,500
Legacy due from un-administered estate of brother			10,000
Property abroad			
10,000 shares in the Fantasian Bank		70,000	
Less: Costs of administration (£4,150 but restricted to maximum 5%)		(3,500)	66,500
			584,270
Less: Funeral expenses		1,650	
General household debts paid		220	
Income tax		750	
Covenanted debt — no deduction possible since no consideration was given		Nil	(2,620)
			581,650
Settled property			
Father's will trust			200,000
Total estate for inheritance tax			781,650

The statutory legacy of £270,000 plus furniture and effects of £10,500 and one half of the residue for the widow are exempt transfers. To determine the amount of the residue to be transferred to the widow it is technically necessary to apply the 'double grossing up' rules that apply to partially exempt residue (though on the figures this has no practical impact).

Division of estate to compute exempt transfer

(1) Gross up specific gifts not bearing own tax:

Covenanted gift to daughter	£5,000
As there were no lifetime transfers and the value of the gift is below £325,000, its grossed up value is	£5,000

(2) Divide estate between exempt and non-exempt parts, using notional gross gifts:

		Exempt	Non-exempt	Total
Specific gift			5,000	5,000
To Wife	Statutory legacy	270,000		270,000
	Furniture etc	10,500		10,500
	½ of residue	148,075		148,075
To Children	½ of residue		148,075	148,075
		£428,575	£153,075	£581,650

(3) Inheritance tax payable on non-exempt estate:

	Gross	Tax
Inheritance tax accumulation at death	Nil	Nil
Non-exempt free estate	£153,075	£Nil

As the value of the non-exempt free estate (ie excluding settled property) is less than £325,000, it is not necessary to re-gross up the specific gift, or to re-divide the free estate. The inheritance tax payable is therefore:

		Gross	Tax
Non-exempt free estate	£153,075		
Settled property	£200,000	£353,075	£11,230*

(* 353,075 – 325,000 = 28,075 @ 40%)

			£
Inheritance tax on chargeable estate			11,230
Less: Quick succession relief			
$100\,\%\text{ of }\dfrac{10{,}000}{100{,}000}\times £\,13{,}000$			(1,300)
			9,930
Less: Relief for overseas tax — re Fantasia Bank shares. (Amount paid £7,000 but restricted to the UK inheritance tax attributable to that property.)			
$\dfrac{66,500}{781,650}\times 9,930$			(845)
			9,085
Revised Tax payable by administrators			
$\dfrac{153{,}075}{353{,}075}\times 9{,}930 = 4,305 - 845$			3,460
Less: already paid on 15.3.2024			(2,630)
Additional tax payable			830
Interest on £3,460 at 7.75% from 1.1.2024 to 15.3.2024 = 75 days		55	
Interest on £830 at 7.75% from 15.3.2024 to 5.11.2024 = 236 days		41	
		96	
Less: interest paid at time of grant		(41)	55

	Gross	Tax
Total payable by the administrators 5.11.2024		885
Tax payable by the trustees of father's will trust		
$\frac{200,000}{353,075} \times 9,930 =$		5,625
Interest on £5,625 at 7.75% from 1.1.2024 to 5.11.2024 = 310 days		369
Total payable by the trustees 5.11.2024		£5,994

(b) Distribution of funds and allocation of tax payable

		£	£
Daughter —	specific gift (covenanted payment)		5,000
Widow —	Cash (statutory legacy)	270,000	
	Chattels	10,500	280,500
Widow —	½ of residue as at (a) (2)		148,075
Children —	½ of residue as at (a) (2)	148,075	
	Less: inheritance tax payable	(3,460)	144,615
Inheritance tax payable by administrators			3,460
			581,650
Inheritance tax payable by trustees of father's will trust			5,625

The interest payable on overdue tax will be dealt with through the income accounts of the estate and the trust.

Explanatory Notes

Partially exempt legacies for inheritance tax — intestacy

(1) The notes to **Examples A17 and A18** also apply to this Example. The Example highlights the fact that an intestacy will often create partially exempt residue, though there will only rarely be specific non-exempt gifts payable out of the free estate. In this example the impact would have been greater if lifetime chargeable transfers had exceeded the available nil-rate band. See in particular **Example A18 explanatory note 5** regarding the treatment to be adopted where a partly exempt estate consists of free estate and a qualifying interest in settled property. The rules relating to distribution on intestacy in England and Wales are set out at **explanatory note 6** below. For further details on:

Corrective and supplementary accounts	see **Example A10**
Administration of foreign assets	see **Example A16**
Quick succession relief	see **Example B3**
Double taxation relief	see **Example B8** and **Example A4(c)**

Valuation of quoted shares for inheritance tax purposes

(2) Quoted shares are valued at the lower of:

(a) One quarter up on lower quoted closing price

(b) Midpoint of bargain prices

This rule, which is derived from TCGA 1992 s 272(3) as that section applied before 6 April 2015, is applied as a matter of practice for IHT valuation purposes (see IHTM18093). The Market Value of Shares, Securities and Strips Regulation 2015 (SI 2015/616) which amended the valuation rules for CGT with effect from 6 April 2015 did not extend to IHT. So the shares in this Example are valued as follows:

	Closing Price	*Bargains*	*Lower*
Shares in A plc	1088 + ¼ (1092 – 1088) = 1089	$\frac{1088 + 1091}{2}$ = 1089½	1089
B plc	295 + ¼ (297 – 295) = 295½	295	295
C plc	60 + ¼ (69 – 60) = 62¼	$\frac{61 + 63}{2} = 62$	62

Covenanted gift: treatment of a specific gift for inheritance tax

(3) The non-deductible covenanted sum is treated as a specific gift (s 38(6)) and thus does not bear its own tax.

Double tax relief: inheritance tax

(4) Double tax relief is available where an equivalent estate tax is charged both abroad and in the UK. For detailed notes see **Example B8 explanatory note 6**. The relief is given as a reduction of the tax on the relevant property (s 159). In this Example therefore the relief reduces the tax on the non-settled part of the estate – unlike quick succession relief (see **Example B3 explanatory note 4** and **Example C4**), it is not diluted by reducing the overall charge that is then divided proportionally between the free estate and the trust fund.

The additional costs of administering or realising assets abroad may be deducted if shown to be attributable to the situation of the property, up to a maximum of 5% of the value of the property (s 173).

Intestacy rules for dividing estates

(5) When a person dies without leaving a will, or leaves a will that does not fully dispose of his estate, then the rules of intestacy apply to the estate not disposed of by will. These rules determine to whom the estate is to be distributed. The inheritance tax rules then determine the amount of tax to be paid, with the amounts allocated to the spouse being exempt transfers. Section 211 provides that the tax payable is to be borne by the residue of the estate as a general testamentary expense. This is subject to s 41, which provides that none of the tax on residue is to fall on any part of the residue that is exempt. Thus, in this Example, although the widow's share of the estate is exempt, the tax, if any, on specific legacies must come out of residue and the tax on the residue must be borne wholly by the chargeable part of the estate. The rules for calculating the tax are set out in ss 38 to 42.

(6) The rules of intestacy for England and Wales are to be found in Administration of Estates Act 1925 ss 46–47, as amended by the Family Provision Act 1966, Civil Partnership Act 2004 and Inheritance and Trustees' Powers Act 2014. The fixed sums payable to the surviving spouse are provided for by Family Provision (Intestate Succession) Order 2009 (SI 2009/135) in respect of deaths on or after 1 February 2009.

In respect of deaths occurring before 1 October 2014, the rules provide that the estate is to be distributed as set out below.

Those surviving	*Those entitled to the estate*
Spouse/civil partner — no issue, parent, brother, sister or issue thereof	Spouse/civil partner absolutely
Spouse/civil partner and issue	Spouse/civil partner takes: (i) Personal chattels (ii) £250,000 (iii) Life interest in ½ of residue Issue share other ½ of residue (on statutory trust to 18) and take spouse/civil partner's life interest share on his (her) death.
Spouse/civil partner, no issue but parent(s)	Spouse/civil partner takes: (i) Personal chattels (ii) £450,000 (iii) ½ of residue absolutely Parent(s) share ½ of residue absolutely.
Spouse/civil partner, no issue or parents but brothers or sisters of the whole blood (or issue thereof)	Spouse/civil partner takes: (i) Personal chattels (ii) £450,000 (iii) ½ of residue absolutely Brothers and sisters (or their issue) share ½ of residue absolutely
No spouse/civil partner but issue	Issue take all absolutely (held on statutory trust if under 18)
No spouse/civil partner or issue but	
Parent(s)	Take absolutely
Brothers and sisters of the whole blood (or issue thereof)	Take absolutely
Brothers and sisters of the half blood (or issue thereof)	Take absolutely
Grandparents	Take absolutely
Uncles and aunts (whole blood) (or issue thereof)	Take absolutely
Uncles and aunts (half blood) (or issue thereof)	Take absolutely
(Each category takes the whole estate to the exclusion of any later category.)	
No relatives mentioned above	The Crown, The Duchy of Lancaster, The Duchy of Cornwall

In respect of deaths occurring on or after 1 October 2014 and before 6 February 2020, the second, third and fourth entries in the above table are amended by The Inheritance and Trustees' Powers Act 2014 which received the Royal Assent on 14 May 2014 and came into force on 1 October 2014 (The Inheritance and Trustees' Powers Act 2014 (Commencement) Order 2014 (SI 2014/2039). The Act alters the destination of property owned by a person who at the time of his death was married or in a civil partnership. If the person dies whilst his spouse/civil partner and his parents or siblings are still alive, then his residuary estate will now pass to his spouse/civil partner absolutely rather than partly to his parents or siblings as set out in the table above. Furthermore, if the person is survived by his spouse/civil partner and issue, the surviving spouse's/civil partner's share of residue is no longer held on trust but passes to the surviving spouse/civil partner absolutely.

Consequently, the first four entries in the above table read as follows (the rest of table remaining unaltered):

Those surviving	*Those entitled to the estate*
Spouse/civil partner — no issue, parent, brother, sister or issue thereof	Spouse/civil partner absolutely
Spouse/civil partner and issue	Spouse/civil partner takes: (i) Personal chattels (ii) £250,000 (iii) ½ of residue absolutely Issue share other ½ of residue (on statutory trust to 18).
Spouse/civil partner, no issue but parent(s)	Spouse/civil partner absolutely
Spouse/civil partner, no issue or parents but brothers or sisters of the whole blood (or issue thereof)	Spouse/civil partner absolutely

In respect of deaths occurring on or after 6 February 2020, the amount of £250,000 in the second of the above entries is increased to £270,000 (Administration of Estates Act 1925 (Fixed Net Sum) Order 2020 (SI 2020/33) so that the amended first four entries (as amended) in the main table read as follows:

Those surviving	*Those entitled to the estate*
Spouse/civil partner — no issue, parent, brother, sister or issue thereof	Spouse/civil partner absolutely
Spouse/civil partner and issue	Spouse/civil partner takes: (i) Personal chattels (ii) £270,000 (iii) ½ of residue absolutely Issue share other ½ of residue (on statutory trust to 18).
Spouse/civil partner, no issue but parent(s)	Spouse/civil partner absolutely
Spouse/civil partner, no issue or parents but brothers or sisters of the whole blood (or issue thereof)	Spouse/civil partner absolutely

From 1 January 1996 a spouse (and since 5 December 2005, a civil partner) does not inherit under the intestacy rules unless he/she survives the deceased by at least 28 days.

With effect from 1 February 2012, under the Estates of Deceased Persons (Forfeiture Rule and the Law of Succession) Act 2011 ('the 2011 Act'), an individual may, in certain circumstances, inherit on the intestacy of a remoter ancestor where the intervening generation(s) has not died. The 2011 Act only applies to deaths occurring after its commencement (ie 1 February 2012) and it extends to England and Wales only (s 4(4), (5) of the 2011 Act).

The Act amends the law of succession in England and Wales where a person disclaims an inheritance or is disqualified from receiving an inheritance under the Forfeiture Act s 1 (the so-called forfeiture rule). That rule precludes a person who has unlawfully killed another, or has unlawfully aided, abetted, counselled or procured the death of that other, from acquiring a benefit in consequence of the killing (eg receiving an inheritance from the deceased). The rule does not however apply where an offender's murder conviction has been quashed (*Challen v Challen and another* [2020] EWHC 1330). In that case the High Court exercised its discretion under s 2 of the Act to modify the forfeiture rule in a case where a wife had suffered years of coercive control at the hands of her husband whom she unlawfully killed. The wife's murder conviction was quashed and she was found guilty of manslaughter. The court decided in the exercise of its discretion that the wife could inherit her deceased husband's estate (and so the transfer was exempt). In pursuing her claim for the court to exercise its discretion, she had no wish to deprive her sons of their inheritance and was motivated by a wish for them to benefit from the substantial tax saving that relief from forfeiture would generate.

In the case of *Re DWS (deceased)* [2001] Ch 568 (CA), a person (P) had killed both of his parents neither of whom left a will. The court had to decide who was entitled to inherit P's father's estate under the English intestacy rules. P was not allowed to inherit because of the forfeiture rule. P's child, the grandchild of P's victim, could not inherit either in place of P under the intestacy rules because P was still alive. Instead the victim's estate passed to his late sister's estate.

A similar outcome would have ensued in other cases, namely:

- in the circumstances of the above case, had P's victims died having made wills and P had forfeited an inheritance under the will;
- where a person disclaims an inheritance under a will or on intestacy (eg where on an intestacy the person who disclaims is the only child of the deceased, the inheritance will by-pass the child's descendants because grandchildren may only inherit from their grandparent if their parent dies before the grandparent. The inheritance passes to the deceased's other blood relatives);
- where a minor, who is entitled to inherit an interest in the estate of an intestate but who dies unmarried and without entering a civil partnership before the age of 8, the children of that minor person are unable to inherit their parent's interest in that estate.

The Act legislates to remove all of the above anomalies so that on the death of a person's remoter ancestor, that person may inherit under the will or intestacy of the remoter ancestor even though the intervening generation(s) is still alive. In particular, in the case of an intestacy s 1 of the 2011 Act (Disclaimer or forfeiture on intestacy) inserts a new s 46A into the Administration of Estates Act 1925 (AEA 1925). It provides as follows:

- Section 46A(1) AEA 1925 specifies that the new section applies where a person ('X') disclaims an inheritance or is disqualified from inheriting from another person because of the forfeiture rule.
- Section 46A(2) AEA 1925 provides that for the purpose of deciding who should inherit X's interest in the deceased's estate in these situations, X should be deemed to have died immediately before the intestate. This overcomes the requirement in AEA 1925 s 47(1) that a child cannot inherit in place of his or her parent if that parent is still alive. The effect of the new section is that if a person disclaims or is disqualified under the forfeiture rule, the inheritance to which he or she is no longer entitled will go to the next person listed in the order of priority in AEA 1925 s 46, even though the person who disclaimed or suffered the forfeiture is still alive.
- Section 46A(3) AEA 1925 provides that the rule introduced by the section give way to any order made by a court under the Forfeiture Act 1925 s 2 (which gives a court the power to modify the effect of the forfeiture rule where the offender has not been convicted of murder (eg by allowing the killer to inherit all or part of the estate)).

Section 1(3) of the 2011 Act makes a consequential amendment to AEA 1926 s 47(1) which defines the statutory trusts for descendants on intestacy. Before amendment it provided that no grandchild or descendant may inherit if his or her parent is still alive when the intestate dies. This is now inconsistent with AEA 1926 s 46A and so a suitable amendment is made to AEA 1925 s 47(1) to make it subject to AEA 1925 s 46A.

Section 1(4) of the 2011 Act makes a consequential amendment to AEA 1925 s 47 by inserting AEA 1925 s 47(4A) stating that AEA 1925 ss 47(2) and 47(4) are also subject to AEA 1926 s 46A. The former subsection used to provide that, where no descendant of the intestate attains a vested interest by reaching the age of 18 or marrying or entering a civil partnership under that age, the estate is to be distributed as if the intestate had died without issue. The latter subsection applied a similar rule to the statutory trusts for siblings or issues of siblings.

The effect of the change in law is that in the case of *Re DWS* discussed above, P's child would now inherit his grandfather's estate and if P were under 18, the statutory trust arising under the Administration of Estates Act 1925 ss 46 and 47 would qualify as a bereaved minor's trust (BMT) under IHTA s 71A. See **Example C17, part A** for the qualifying conditions and the Inheritance Tax treatment of a BMT (bereaved minor's trust).

It should also be noted that in respect of deaths occurring on or after 1 October 2014, the Inheritance and Trustees' Powers Act 2014 has amended the definition of the term 'chattel' has been redefined as tangible movable property, other than such property which:

- consists of money or securities for money,

- was used at the date of death of the intestate solely or mainly for business purposes, or
- was held at the date of death of the intestate solely as an investment.

(7) The rules of intestacy applying to the distribution of an estate in Scotland are provided for in The Succession (Scotland) Act 1964 and are as follows:

1. Prior rights

After debts and other liabilities have been met, a widow, widower or a surviving civil partner has certain 'prior rights of a surviving spouse or civil partner' in the deceased person's estate, where no will has been left.

He or she is entitled to the dwelling house of the deceased in which the surviving spouse or civil partner was resident at the time of the deceased's death, plus up to the value of £24,000 (increased to £29,000 with effect from 1 February 2012) any furnishings and furniture of that house. (In certain cases, eg where the house is a farmhouse or part of a shop, or where the house is worth more than £300,000 (increased to £473,000 with effect from 1 February 2012) the entitlement is not to the house itself, but to its value up to £300,000 (increased to £473,000 with effect from 1 February 2012).)

The surviving spouse or civil partner is also entitled to the first £42,000 (increased to £50,000 with effect from 1 February 2012) out of the estate if the deceased left children or descendants of children or to the first £75,000 (increased to £89,000 with effect from 1 February 2012) if the deceased left no children or descendants.

Prior rights are a first claim on the estate, before legal rights (see below).

The increases in the above amounts were given effect by The Prior Rights of Surviving Spouse and Civil Partner (Scotland) Order 2011 SSI 2011/436 art 2 in relation to the estate of any person dying on or after 1 February 2012.

2. Legal rights

A surviving spouse or civil partner and children are entitled to certain 'legal right' out of the deceased person's moveable estate. In Scots law, heritable property means land and buildings, while moveable property includes such things as money, shares, cars, furniture and jewellery.

The surviving spouse or civil partner is entitled to *one-third* of the deceased's moveable estate if the deceased left children or descendants of children, or to *one-half* of it if the deceased left no such children or descendants.

The children are collectively entitled to *one-third* of the deceased's moveable estate if the deceased left a spouse or civil partner, or to *one-half* of it if the deceased left no spouse or civil partner. Each child has an equal claim. Where a child would have had a claim had he (she) not died before his (her) parent, his (her) descendants may claim his (her) share by the principle known as representation.

3. Other rights on intestacy

After any prior rights and legal rights have been satisfied, the remainder of the intestate estate, both heritable and moveable, devolves (without distinction between heritable and moveable estate) in the following order, any surviving relative in an earlier group taking precedence, thereby precluding any surviving relatives in a later group from succeeding to any part of the estate, *viz:*

(a) Children take the whole.

(b) Either or both parents and brothers and sisters – half to parent or parents and half to brothers and sisters.

(c) Brothers and sisters take the whole.

(d) Either or both parents take the whole.

(e) Husband or wife or civil partner – surviving spouse or civil partner takes the whole.

(f) Uncles or aunts (on either parent's side) take the whole.

(g) Grandparent or grandparents (on either side) take the whole.

(h) Brothers and sisters of any grandparents (on either side) take the whole.

(i) Ancestors of intestate remoter than grandparents, on both paternal and maternal sides generation by generation successively take the whole, but if no ancestors survive in any generation their brothers and sisters come before ancestors of the next more remote generation.

(j) Finally, the Crown, failing any relatives in the foregoing categories, takes the whole.

The application of the foregoing order of succession is subject to three general principles:

(i) There is no preference for male persons, or in regard to age. For instance, brothers do not rank before sisters, or elder brothers before younger (except in relation to succession to such things as titles and coats of arms).

(ii) There is representation in all branches of succession, ie where any relative who would, if alive, have been entitled to succeed to the whole or any part of the intestate estate has predeceased leaving children, such children take equally among them the share which their deceased parent would have received if in life. If, however, the persons taking by representation are all in the same degree of relationship to the deceased, each individual takes an equal share.

(iii) In the case of collaterals, ie brothers and sisters of the deceased or of an ancestor of the deceased, both those of the full blood and those of the half blood are entitled to succeed, but collaterals of the full blood have preference: if there are no collaterals of the full blood, the collaterals of the half blood rank without distinction as between those related through the father or mother.

4. Adopted children

The position of adopted children is the same as that of natural children for the purposes of succession. Thus an adopted child has the same rights of succession in relation to its adoptive parent's estate as a natural child, and adoptive parents have the same rights of succession that they would have, had they been natural parents of the child.

5. The cohabitant's claim

Section 29 of the Family Law (Scotland) Act 2006 ('the 2006 Act') allows a cohabitant to ask the court for a share of his or her cohabitant's estate. A cohabitant is defined in the 2006 Act as either one of a couple who are (or were) living together as if they were husband and wife or civil partners.

Certain factors are relevant in determining whether a person is a cohabitant, including the length of time they lived together and the nature of the relationship during that time (2006 Act, s 25). For example, the court might look at what sort of arrangements the couple made about money, such as whether they had a joint bank account and whether they supported one another financially.

When the court is trying to decide whether to make an award, s 29 provides it must take into account factors including:

- the size and the nature of the available estate;
- any benefit the cohabitant has received as a result of the death from somewhere other than the available estate (eg a payment under a life insurance policy or a survivor's pension);
- the nature and extent of other rights to, and claims on, the available estate.

6. Changes to the intestacy rules in England and Wales

The changes to the intestacy rules described in **explanatory note (6)** above do not apply in Scotland.

7. Proposals for change to the intestacy rules in Scotland

Where a deceased person leaves a spouse or civil partner (but no children) the Scottish Law Commission (SLC) report in 2009 on succession (Scot Law Com No 215) has recommended that the spouse or civil partner should inherit the whole estate. This is a change to the current law where the spouse or civil partner might have to share the estate with the deceased's parents and siblings. Where the person who has died leaves a spouse or civil partner and children, the report recommends that the spouse or civil partner should inherit the whole estate up to the value of a 'threshold sum'. The report then recommends that the remainder of the estate should be shared equally between the deceased person's children. In 2009, the SLC recommended that the threshold sum should be £300,000 but the Scottish Government is consulting on a range of figures for this sum, between £335,000 and £650,000. Where the deceased person leaves children (but no spouse or civil partner) the report recommends that the children should inherit the whole estate. This reflects the current law. The report also contains proposals for the abolition of the distinction between heritable and moveable property. All of these proposed changes are not contained in the Succession (Scotland) Act 2016 which received the Royal Assent on 3 March 2016 and so, for the time being, remain merely proposals for the reform of the intestacy law of Scotland.

The Scottish Government consulted on these proposed changes but has decided to make no changes to the law for the time being. In a statement dated 18 October 2018, in relation to the proposal to change the intestacy rules it stated: 'The "simplified" approach put forward by the SLC was clearly not as straightforward as suggested and public views in relation to how an intestate estate should be divided where there is both a spouse and children varied significantly. As such, the Scottish Government concluded that they will consult further on these proposals and, in the meantime, there will be no change here. However, the position is more straightforward where the deceased is only survived by either a spouse or civil partner, or only by their issue. In these circumstances, the Scottish Government agreed with the proposals a) and b) above (namely that the surviving spouse or issue should inherit the whole estate) and confirmed they will be implemented in future succession legislation.' In relation to the proposal to abolish the distinction between heritable and moveable property it stated: 'Views here were divided but the majority (59%) of respondents disagreed with this proposal. As such, there are no plans to remove this distinction and the Scottish Government will consult further on intestate succession generally. This was thought to be among the areas most likely to change. The confirmation of the present rules again provides welcome certainty.'

Question

In order to reduce the potential liability to inheritance tax on his accumulated wealth, Henry, aged 80, who has made cash gifts every year to use up his annual exemption, proposes the following:

(a) To sell one of a pair of antique objects to his daughter at its market value of £40,000, and then in a year's time to give her the other of equal value.

The value of the pair is £130,000.

(b) To sell 2% of his holding of 51% of the shares in Henry Ltd, a property investment company, to John, an unconnected friend, for its market value, then to give the remaining 49% of the shares to his son, Simon, who already holds 35% of the shares.

The market value of the shares in Henry Ltd is:

51%	holding	£800,000
49%	holding	£500,000
15–20%	holding	£100,000
2%	holding	£5,000

(c) If the scheme in (b) above is unsuitable, Henry proposes giving 2% of his shares to 'Age UK', a registered charity, then to give the remaining 49% of the shares to Simon.

(d) A further suggestion is that next winter while Henry is on a cruise around the world Henry Ltd should make a rights issue of four shares for every one share held. Henry will not be back until after the issue has been made and will not be able to take up his entitlement.

Advise him of the inheritance tax effect of each of the above proposals.

Answer

(a) Pair of antiques — sale followed by gift to daughter

There are two problems in relation to Henry's proposed sale and gift of the two antique objects.

The first is whether the sale at full value to his daughter will itself escape being treated as a transfer of value at that time, since although she would be paying full price for the object, his estate would actually fall by £50,000 (£130,000 – £80,000 (comprising the cash received of £40,000 and the value of the remaining object of £40,000)). A sale at full value is not a transfer of value if it was not intended to confer a gratuitous benefit on anyone and was either made at arm's length (which this transaction is not) or was such as might be expected to have been made at arm's length (IHTA 1984 s 10 – see **Example A5 part (a)**). Since the daughter would be paying the full market price, which is the same amount as a stranger would have paid, the transaction might arguably not be treated as a transfer of value at that time; this would turn on whether Henry could show that his disposition was not intended to confer any gratuitous benefit on any person, as to which Henry's stated intention to give the second object to the same person in the following year (which would have the effect of increasing the value to her of the object for which she was paying £40,000) might well present him with a problem. If he failed in that argument, he would have made a transfer of value of £50,000 at the time of the sale, and then a further transfer of value of £40,000 at the time of the later gift of the second object.

But even if he succeeded in that argument, and there was no transfer of value at the first stage, when Henry later gives his daughter the other object, HMRC may use the associated operations rules in s 268 to treat the two events as one. There would then be a potentially exempt transfer on the second occasion of £90,000 (£130,000 – £40,000 cash received) which would become a chargeable transfer if Henry dies within seven years of the gift of the second object.

If he had not already used his annual exemptions each year, Henry might be better off losing (or not pursuing) the argument on gratuitous intent, since he would then have transfers of value in two successive tax years with the ability to set up to three years' annual exemptions against them in total. As things are, unless he were realistically confident of succeeding in avoiding any transfer of value on the first occasion, it would have been better for Henry to sell the *pair* of objects to his daughter for £40,000 in the first place, because the potentially exempt transfer of £90,000 would then have been made one year earlier and the seven year survivorship period would have started at that time.

(b) Shares – sale followed by gift to son

Again HMRC may seek to use the associated operations rules in s 268 in determining the inheritance tax position on the gift of shares to Simon. The reason they might do so is as follows; no inheritance tax implications arise on the sale of shares to John, because, viewed in isolation, this is a commercial transaction at arm's length and so not a transfer of value. Also, the gift of shares to Simon is a potentially exempt transfer and inheritance tax will become payable only on Henry's death within seven years on a transfer of £500,000 (the value of a 49% holding). In other words, by entering into the transactions in the way he proposes, there is a likelihood that no inheritance tax is payable despite a fall in value of Henry's estate on account of his making disposals of property.

By contrast, if Henry had merely gifted a 49% holding of shares to Simon, the gift, although potentially exempt, would have been valued as the difference between a 51% holding (£800,000) and a 2% holding (£5,000), ie at £795,000. HMRC can be expected to look inter alia for any evidence that the gift was conceived of before the sale had been completed.

If HMRC applied s 268 the value transferred by this composite transfer would be as follows:

	£
Value of 51% before first of associated operations	800,000
Value of 0% after second of associated operations	Nil
	800,000
Less: Cash received (on the sale of the 2% holding)	(5,000)

	£
Value transferred (potentially exempt transfer)	795,000

(c) Shares — gift to charity followed by gift to son

If Henry adopts the alternative proposal of giving 2% of the shares to 'Age UK', the related property rules will be applied. These are contained in s 161. The rules provide (inter alia) that where property is transferred to a charity, political party, national heritage body or housing association by the taxpayer or his spouse/civil partner, such property is related to any other property of the taxpayer and his spouse/civil partner.

It should be noted that the property will continue to be related until five years after it is disposed of by the charity, political party, national heritage body or housing association.

The value of appropriate parts of the related property is proportionate to the value of all related property, if this produces a higher value than the value of the appropriate part on its own (see **Example A11(a)** for a more detailed explanation of these rules).

Consequently the value transferred by Henry will be:

2% to charity — exempt transfer			
49% to son — value before transfer			
Own holding		49%	
Related holding		2%	
	Value of	51% =	£800,000
Henry's 49% holding is therefore worth	$\frac{49}{51} \times £800{,}000 =$		768,627
Value of Henry's holding after transfer			Nil
Value of transfer (which is a potentially exempt transfer)			£768,627

The above computation would apply unless Henry deferred the gift of shares to Simon until five years after 'Age UK' had disposed of its shares. If the transfer took place after that time the potentially exempt transfer would be:

Value transferred (49% holding — assuming no change in values)	£500,000

Care will need to be taken over any pre-emption rights in Henry Limited's Articles of Association, if 'Age UK' seeks to dispose of the shares given to it. Any failure by Henry (or for that matter Simon) to exercise pre-emption rights given to other shareholders by the Articles could itself give rise to a deemed disposition by them under s 3(3) (see **(d) below**), and any such disposition by Henry may well be taken with his original gift to 'Age UK' as associated operations. Any resultant loss to his estate would then itself constitute a transfer of value by him.

(d) Failure to take up rights shares

Henry's proposal concerning the rights issue is covered by s 3(3), which provides that the deliberate omission to exercise a right is a disposition (and in turn capable, depending on its results, of being a transfer of value).

The issue of rights shares in the circumstances outlined would be caught by this subsection.

The value transferred would be:

Value of estate before omission (51%)				800,000
Less: Value of estate after omission:	*Original Shares*	*Rights Shares*	*Totals*	
Henry	51	Nil	51	
Son	35	140	175	
Others	14	56	70	
Totals	100	196	296	
Value of $\frac{51}{296} = 17.23\%$ *holding*				(100,000)
Value transferred (potentially exempt transfer)				700,000

Because s 3(3) treats the deliberate omission to exercise a right as a disposition, this would constitute an actual transfer of value and s 3A would apply treating the transfer as potentially exempt.

Explanatory Notes

Associated operations for inheritance tax

(1) The associated operations rules are contained in s 268. Certain other provisions may also be in point when considering matters on which the associated operations rules might have a bearing, viz:

- Related property – s 161 (see **explanatory note** 8).
- Omission to exercise a right – s 3(3) (see **part (d)** of the Example and **Example A1 explanatory note 10**).
- Alteration of capital – s 98 (see **explanatory note** 8).
- Annuity purchased in conjunction with life policy – s 263 (see **explanatory note** 4).

(2) One cannot be certain whether HMRC will seek to use the associated operations rules in any particular case, but s 268 defines associated operations, extremely widely, as being:

(i) Two or more operations of any kind affecting the same property (s 286(1)(a) – first limb).

(ii) Two or more operations, one of which affects some property and the other (or others) of which affects property that represents, whether directly or indirectly, that property or income arising from that property, or any property representing accumulations of such income (s 268(1)(a) – second limb).

(iii) Any two operations of which one is effected with reference to the other, or with a view to enabling the other to be effected, or facilitating its being effected and any further operation having a like relation to any of those two and so on (s 268(1)(b)).

The operations might be effected by the same person or different persons and might or might not be simultaneous (s 268(1)).

An 'operation' includes an omission (s 268(1)).

(3) Where a transfer of value is made by associated operations carried out at different times, it is treated as made at the time of the last of them (s 268(3)). But where one or more of the earlier operations also constitutes a

transfer of value made by the same transferor, the value transferred by the earlier transfers is treated as reducing the value transferred by all the operations taken together, except to the extent that the earlier transfers were exempt transfers because of the spouse/civil partner exemption (s 18) but all operations taken together were not so exempt (s 268(3)).

(4) Another context in which the IHTA 1984 relies on the definition of associated operations to produce a deemed transfer of value is where:

- a policy of life insurance is issued or substituted for a pre-27 March 1974 policy (or a pre-27 March 1974 policy is varied),
- an annuity on the same person's life is issued (before, after or at the same time as the life policy), and
- the benefit of the policy is vested in someone other than the person who purchased the annuity.

If these conditions are satisfied then, under s 263, the person who purchased the annuity will be held to have made a transfer of value at the date the life policy became vested as above, *unless* it is shown that the purchase of the annuity and the making of the insurance were *not* associated operations. (The burden of proof in that respect is thus on the taxpayer; but HMRC will accept that the policy and annuity were not associated operations if the life policy was issued on full medical evidence of the life assured's health and would have been issued on the same terms if the annuity had not been purchased – Statement of Practice E4.) This deemed transfer of value excludes any other transfer of value which the person might have made as a result of the vesting of the policy, or as a result of the vesting and the purchase being associated operations. Section 263(2) sets out how to calculate the value transferred by this deemed transfer of value.

If the taxpayer succeeds in showing that the two elements were not associated operations then the payment of the premiums on the life policy may in principle attract the normal income expenditure exemption (s 21, see **Example A1 part (v)(c)** and **Example C15**); but it must be remembered that the annuity receipts under a purchased life annuity are only partly income for income tax purposes – a substantial part of each payment will typically be a return of capital – and the part that is excluded from the income tax charge is expressly excluded from being considered as part of the transferor's income for the purpose of the normal income expenditure exemption (s 21(3)). The exemption is wholly denied if the taxpayer is unable to show that the policy and annuity were not associated operations: s 21(2).

Inheritance tax associated operations: series of settlements

(5) The taxpayer was successful in the Court of Appeal, in the case of *Rysaffe Trustee Co (CI) Ltd v IRC* (2003), in contending that the associated operations provisions did not apply where five separate identical settlements were created on five separate dates within the same month (see **Example C13 explanatory note 12**). A subsequent decision of a Special Commissioner (*Smith v IRC* (2007)) distinguished the *Rysaffe* decision where three annuities and three life assurance policies were issued on the same date: in that case the associated operations provisions did apply. This shows that whether there are associated operations is a question of fact.

Inheritance tax: interaction of associated operations and related property provisions

(6) HMRC Inheritance Tax have indicated (in correspondence with Butterworths Tolley (as it was then known) – see *Taxation* 15 February 1996) how the related property and associated operations provisions interact where assets are transferred in stages, with some being routed via a spouse (or, now also a civil partner). The example used to illustrate the advice concerns a set of four antique chairs, of which two are given by husband to wife, and each then gives one to their son in successive years. The related property rules will value each of the first transfers to the son at half of the value of the set of four less half the value of a set of two, and each of the second transfers at half the value of a set of two, thus bringing into account the total value of the set of four, half being a transfer by the husband and the other half a transfer by the wife.

If the associated operations rules were invoked at the time the son became the owner of the set, the transfers by the wife would be treated as made by the husband (although, in such a case, it is not clear whether the wife would therefore be treated as not having made a transfer in her own right). The overall effect would be the same in terms of the value transferred, but the whole of the transfer would affect the husband's tax position.

See **Example B4** for other illustrations of associated operations.

Inheritance tax associated operations: grant of a lease

(7) The grant of a lease for full consideration in money or money's worth is not associated with any operation effected more than three years after the grant (s 268(2)).

By granting a lease, even for full value, a property owner restricts his rights over the property subject to the lease. If he were then to make a gift of those rights (ie the right to receive the rent under the lease and the freehold reversion) the full value of both rights might be less than that of the unencumbered freehold. He might therefore first grant a lease followed by a gift of the reversion, instead of giving the freehold out of which the donee could grant the lease.

The associated operations rules will not apply if the gift is more than three years after the grant of the lease.

Inheritance tax: alteration of share or loan capital of a close company

(8) In **part (d)** of this Example, if the unquoted share or loan capital of a close company is altered (or there is any alteration in the rights attaching to such shares or debentures) instead of a rights issue being made that is available equally to all shareholders, then s 98 applies. This provides that such a change is to be treated as a disposition made by the participators. Such a transfer cannot be a potentially exempt transfer (s 98(3)).

Where there are deferred shares, HMRC take the view that an alteration of rights within s 98(1)(b) takes place when the deferred shares come to rank equally, or become merged, with shares of another class.

Business property relief for inheritance tax

(9) Business property relief is not available in relation to the shares in Henry Ltd because it is a company that invests in land and buildings (s 105(3)).

Gifts with reservation etc for inheritance tax

(10) In addition to the associated operations legislation donors must also be fully aware of the rules relating to gifts with reservation and the treatment of certain debts. These are illustrated in **Examples B1, B2 and B3**.

Failure to take up rights for inheritance tax

(11) For further discussion on the failure to take up rights see **Example A1 explanatory note 8 and Example A4** part (a).

Question

A.

Relief from inheritance tax is available on 'relevant business property'.

(a) What is relevant business property?

(b) What types of business do not qualify for this relief?

(c) What is the nature of the relief and at what rates is it given?

B.

On 19 July 2018 Stanley (who had never made a lifetime gift before) gave Elizabeth (his granddaughter) the whole of his shares in Printers Ltd, a trading company, together with the freehold of the land and buildings occupied by the company, but which he owned personally.

On the same day Peter (who has made chargeable transfers within the previous seven years amounting to £180,000 and has fully utilised his exemptions for 2018/19 and 2017/18) gave Elizabeth (his daughter and granddaughter of Stanley) his shareholding in Printers Ltd.

Prior to the above transfers the shareholdings in Printers Ltd (which had remained unchanged for many years) were:

		Shares
Stanley		4,000
Phyllis	(Stanley's wife)	4,000
Peter	(Stanley's son)	1,000
Barbara	(Peter's sister)	900
Elizabeth	(Peter's daughter)	100
		10,000

and the agreed values for inheritance tax purposes were:

100% holding	£1,600,000	51% holding	£900,000
80% holding	£1,400,000	40% holding	£300,000
60% holding	£1,000,000	10% holding	£40,000

The value of the land and buildings transferred by Stanley was agreed at £800,000.

On 13 November 2023 Stanley died. Elizabeth still owned the property and shares at that date.

(a) Compute the inheritance tax payable by Elizabeth on the lifetime gift;

(b) Assuming that the instalment option will be elected for, state the date on which the first instalment is due, and the amount payable on that day;

(c) Explain under what circumstances interest will be payable on the instalments (without calculating the amount of any interest).

Answer

A. Business property relief

(a) *Relevant business property*

Relevant business property means (IHTA 1984 s 105):

(i) A sole trader's business (including professions and vocations), or a partnership share.

(ii) Unquoted *securities* of a company which, together with any unquoted *shares* of the company give the transferor control immediately before the transfer (control being established by taking into account related property).

(iii) *Any* unquoted *shares* in a company.

(iv) Quoted shares and/or securities of a company which give the transferor control immediately before the transfer (again, control being established by taking into account related property).

(v) Land, buildings, plant or machinery which immediately before the transfer were used wholly or mainly for the purposes of a business carried on by a company of which the transferor then had control, or by a partnership of which he was then a partner. (It will be noted that there is no need for a formal lease of the premises in question and neither is there a requirement to pay rent; all that is needed is for the property to be used in the business concerned. However, this category applies only to land, buildings, machinery or plant and does not extend to goodwill or other intangibles or intellectual property rights held outside the business.)

(vi) Any land or buildings, machinery or plant which, immediately before the transfer, was used wholly or mainly for the purposes of a business carried on by the transferor and was settled property in which he was then beneficially entitled to an interest in possession.

It is often perceived that partnerships are transparent for tax purposes. However, this is not the case for the purposes of inheritance tax. As general partnerships formed in accordance with the Partnership Act 1890 are not transparent, the asset that is included in the estate of a deceased partner (and which may be relevant business property) is the interest in the partnership itself and not the underlying assets of the business. On account of s 267A the interest of a member of an LLP is treated in the same way; that section provides that for the purposes of inheritance tax property to which an LLP is entitled is treated as property to which members are entitled *as partners*. These two words of the section deem the LLP members to hold property in the same way as partners of an 1890 partnership so that the asset that is included in the estate of a deceased member of an LLP is the interest in the LLP and not the assets owned by the LLP.

Quoted shares and securities are defined as shares and securities listed on a recognised stock exchange (ss 105(1ZA), 113A(3B)). Shares or securities on the Alternative Investment Market (AIM), ISDX Markets Group and NASDAQ Europe are treated as unlisted and therefore qualify as unquoted under (ii) and (iii) above unless quoted simultaneously on a recognised exchange. It is not unusual for shares to be quoted on AIM and also on a recognised overseas stock exchange in which case those shares will not be treated as unquoted shares for the purposes of business property relief. Any inheritance tax payable on such shares cannot be paid by instalments either – see **part B** of this Example. Where owners of AIM shares become aware that the company is seeking a listing on a recognised stock exchange but wish to preserve their entitlement to BPR they should perhaps seek to dispose of their shares before the listing takes place and reinvest the net proceeds of sale in the shares of another qualifying company (or other qualifying replacement asset). On the date of acquisition, the replacement asset will be deemed to have been owned for the period that the AIM shares were held for the purposes of the two-year rule (see below).

In the case of *CIR v Mallender and others (exors of Drury-Lowe decd)* (2001), it was held that an asset (which in this case was land) used as security for a guarantee was not itself used in the business and was not therefore part of the relevant business property.

The relevant business property concerned must have been owned by the transferor throughout the two years immediately preceding the transfer (s 106) or be property replacing relevant business property where the combined period of ownership of the original and replacement property is at least two years out of the last five years (but relief is then granted only on the lower of the value of the original or replacement property) (s 107). Property acquired as a result of death is deemed to have been owned from the date of death, or for property acquired by the surviving spouse, from the date the deceased spouse acquired it (s 108). The two year rule does not apply where the property was eligible for business property relief on an earlier transfer and either the earlier transfer or the subsequent transfer was made on the death of the transferor (s 109). Where a person starts up a new business, however, (rather than inherits it) and then dies within two years, business property relief is not available.

If unquoted shares in trading companies (for example on AIM) are sold and the net proceeds of sale are reinvested in other shares qualifying for BPR, then the new shares will be treated as replacement property under s 107(1).

(b) *Non-qualifying businesses*

A business, or an interest in a business, or shares in or securities of a company, are not relevant business property if the business, or as the case may be, the business of the company, consists wholly or mainly of (what may be called the following 'offensive' businesses):

(i) Dealing in securities, stocks or shares (except for market makers and discount houses both in the UK and, on and after 31 December 2012, in any EEA state).

(ii) Dealing in land or buildings.

(iii) Making or holding investments (see **explanatory note** 20 re land which is let or subject to a grazing licence) (s 105(3)).

However, the shares in or securities of a company whose business consists wholly or mainly of being a holding company of one or more companies whose businesses in turn are not offensive businesses in the context of s 105(3) are not themselves disqualified from being relevant business property (s 105(4)). It is not clear whether this 'look through' applies to a chain of holding companies (although it is thought that it does). So a company's shares qualify for business property relief if more than 50% of its activities consist in its being the holding of trading subsidiaries (ie subsidiaries whose own businesses do not consists wholly or mainly of dealing in securities, stocks or shares, land or buildings or making or holding investments). HMRC treat the following activities as indicative of the business of a holding company:

(a) holding shares in subsidiaries;

(b) co-ordinating the activities of those subsidiaries by means of voting control and the ability to control the boards of the subsidiaries;

(c) provision of loan and other finance to those subsidiaries;

(d) providing strategic direction and oversight of the activities of the subsidiaries and ensuring the subsidiaries work together to achieve a common aim;

(e) monitoring the financial performance of subsidiaries, providing a treasury function and co-ordinating guarantees and cross-group collateral;

(f) providing a structure to allow ring-fencing of the activities of subsidiaries, nurturing new higher-risk activities, and reorganising the businesses of subsidiaries as they change and grow; and

(g) managing relations with shareholders on behalf of all subsidiaries.

If these activities predominate and the group subsidiaries themselves are not investment companies, the business property relief will normally be available for the shares in the holding company. A problem however arises where a holding company carries on a mixture of activities. For example if its activities as a whole, analysed by reference to turnover, profits and management time as approximately 40% trading, 20% investment and 40% acting as the holding company of a trading group then business property relief would not be available. The company does not mainly carry on a trade and neither does it mainly carry on the activities of a holding company. It does not pass the test in s 105(4) and its business is not mainly that of a trading company.

Where an LLP takes the place of a holding company, then s 105(4) does not however apply and BPR is likely to be denied in relation to an interest in an LLP holding shares in trading companies. This follows from the non-transparent nature of an LLP (and partnerships in general) in the context of inheritance tax (see above). This is a very complex topic which is beyond the scope of the book but interested readers are referred to Parts A and B of the ICAEW's Tax Guide 1/14 issued jointly in January 2014 by the CIoT, STEP and the ICAEW Tax Faculty. A summary of the guide is accessible at www.taxadvisermagazine.com/article/llps-focus.

The inheritance tax legislation does not define an investment business but some guidance may be obtained from *Cook v Medway Housing Society Ltd* (1997) in which Lightman J defined investment as the laying out of moneys in anticipation of profitable capital or income return. He commented further than in determining what is the business of a company it is necessary to have regard to the quality, purpose and nature of the company and its activities and this includes the full circumstances in which the relevant assets are acquired and retained. It is relevant to have regard to the actual activities carried on at the relevant date but these have to be viewed with regard also to the taxpayer's past history or future plans lest they give only a partial or incomplete picture. The critical question said Lightman J is whether the holding of assets to provide a profitable return is merely incidental to the carrying on of some other business or is the very business carried on by the taxpayer. It is useful to ask whether the holding of the land is incidental to the carrying on of the business.

Ascertaining whether a business is an offensive business in the context of inheritance tax has been the subject of much case law. *George & Anor (Exors of Stedman dec'd) v IRC* (2004) concerned a claim for business property relief by the executors where the deceased owned 85% of the shares in a company carrying on the business of running a caravan park. The Inland Revenue (as HMRC was known at the time) contended the business of the company was making or holding investments. The Court of Appeal allowed the executors' claim on the ground that making or holding investments was only one (and not the main) component of a composite business (see **explanatory note 20**). The business was an active family business and there was no principle why it should be excluded from business property relief merely because it involved the use of land. Carnwarth LJ identified a number of principles regarding the application of s 105(3):

(i) The decision in any case is a question of fact.

(ii) The treatment of the business in question for the purposes of other taxes (eg income tax and corporation tax) is not determinative of the matter and is unlikely to be helpful.

(iii) There can be a spectrum at the one end of which the business could be that of investment but at the other end of which the facts would point away from a finding of fact that a similar activity was an investment.

(iv) The business should be considered in the round and that there was no decisive factor which would indicate whether a business consisted wholly or mainly of the making of the holding or making of investments.

The earlier Special Commissioners' case of *Farmer & Giles (Farmer's Executors) v CIR* (1999) had held that in determining whether a business comprises the making or holding of investments the whole business should be considered 'in the round'. This includes considering the turnover and profits derived from its activities, and the value of assets used in the business and investment activities. It could also include considering time spent by the owners, employees and others on the respective parts of the business. It would appear that if a single set of accounts is prepared for the whole business, there is unified management and if the majority of the above tests point to business, then there is a business that does not consist wholly or mainly of the making of investments. In SVM 111150, HMRC state that the wholly or mainly test is looked at over a reasonable period to allow for temporary fluctuations in activity and performance.

In *Phillips v RCC* (2006) the deceased owned shares in a company that lent money to property investment companies that were in the common ownership and control of the deceased either alone or with her husband and children. The Special Commissioner observed that it could not be said that the making of loans is always the making of an investment or that it never is. At one end of the spectrum of lending could be investment in bonds or debentures but at the other end of the spectrum could be the making of informal unsecured loans which activity amounts to no more than money lending. It was therefore necessary to have reference to all the facts in the round to determine the nature of a business. On the facts of the case it was held that the lending company did not make or hold investments but it had made informal loans to its related companies as a money lender. The loans it made were not assets acquired or held by the company for the purpose of making profits but were made for the purpose of providing a benefit to the other companies. The loans were not investments for their own sake but the provision of a finance facility to the other companies. The company did not acquire any interest in the other companies or their property; all it was entitled to was the interest payable on the loans. The Special Commissioner dismissed HMRC's argument that the loans were investments because the companies to which the loans were made were themselves investment companies; also he observed that if a loan is not an investment it cannot be made into an investment by the fact that the company to which the loan was made was in common ownership and control. Neither did the terms on which the loans were made (that they were not made on the same terms as loans made by a third party) convert the business of making loans to the making or holding of investments.

In *Brander (representative of James (deceased), Fourth Earl of Balfour) v RCC (2010)*, the Upper Tribunal summarised the relevant case law as follows:

(i) In deciding what the term 'the business of holding investments' means, the test which the decision-maker applies is that of an intelligent businessman who would be concerned with the use to which the asset was being put and the way in which it was being turned to account.

(ii) The question whether a business consisted wholly or mainly of making or holding investments is a question of fact for the decision-maker.

(iii) The decision-maker is required to look at the business in the round and, in the light of the overall picture, to form a view as to the relative importance to the business as a whole of the investment and non-investment activities in that business.

(iv) This exercise involves looking at the business over a period of time.

(v) In so doing, the decision-maker can have regard to various factors, such as the overall context of the business, the turnover and profitability of various activities, the activities of employees and other persons engaged to assist the business, the acreage of the land dedicated to each activity and the capital value of that acreage. Not one of these factors is conclusive as the exercise involves looking at the business in the round. It also appears that while the decision-maker must consider all relevant factors in relation to a particular business, there will be circumstances in which a factor, which is relevant to one business, is not relevant to another.

(vi) The fact that the owner of an investment engages in activities to manage and maintain his investment does not of itself take the business out of the investment category.

(vii) In looking at the question in the round it is not appropriate in every case to compartmentalise the business and attribute management and maintenance activity either to investment or to non-investment as an ancillary activity.

The facts of the case itself are very complex and involved a mixed settled estate in Scotland. The First-tier Tribunal found that the entire estate had been run by the deceased for his own benefit and to preserve the estate for his future heirs, regarding himself as carrying on a single business (with only passive involvement by the trustees of the trust of which the deceased was a life tenant). In this the deceased was either a life tenant (life renter in Scots Law), a sole trader or a partner in a partnership. Although the trust had been a separate entity from the deceased which had certain administrative and accounting implications, this did not mean there were two separate businesses. The preponderance of the activity of the single business was one of trade rather than investment (although part of the business activity had been the letting of land and buildings). The Upper Tribunal did not disturb the conclusion reached by the judge on the facts.

In *The Trustees of David Zetland Settlement v RCC* (2013) the First-tier Tribunal again denied business property relief in a case where, considering the nature of the services provided to tenants by the landlord of short-term lets of commercial offices and looking at the business in the round (by taking into account the income and profit raised from the non-investment activities and the staff involved in them), it was held that the services amounted to nothing more than being ancillary to the core business of the generation of income from rentals and the exploitation of property rights in the sense that they were primarily concerned with increasing the rents from the building. The Tribunal acknowledged that the business concerned was not simply the receipt of rent from let property. There was also the provision of certain services and facilities to tenants (including the hire of conference rooms and the provision of project management services, the provision of hospitality, cleaning, internet service, catering, cafe, mail room, bicycle parking, security and reception facilities, and the provision of a porter, a gymnasium and a hairdresser). But those activities did not elevate the business from mere ownership or mere investment into a business that was not excluded from business property relief. The tribunal considered the various leading cases and concluded that it was appropriate to look back over five years in order to get a flavour of the business, that the business should be looked at in the round with no one factor being determinative and that when looking at the income and profits from rent when compared with the income and profits from additional services, it was important to apply a qualitative rather than a quantitative test.

John Best v HMRC (2014) was another case in which the taxpayer failed to meet the stringent requirements required to avoid being disqualified from entitlement to business property relief under s 105(3). In that case the deceased owned shares in a company that owned and managed a business centre which comprised land and buildings occupied for office and light industrial use. Businesses occupying the business centre under licences benefited from the services of a receptionist and could also (for an additional fee) hire the services of a forklift truck. Taking into account the nature and extent of the additional services and their contribution to the business both qualitatively and quantitatively, the First-tier Tribunal concluded that the non-investment services provided by the company did not predominate when considering the activities of the company as a whole. Most of the income from additional services related to re-charges for electricity, telephone and postage and the income from the other additional services was very modest when compared with the licence fee income.

The case is useful in that the judge (having regard to the *George* and *McCall* cases set out above), summarised as follows the principles derived from them for resolution of cases of this type (namely whether a business consists wholly or mainly in the holding of investments):

(1) The various activities involved in operating a business relating to the exploitation of land may be allocated between 'investment' and 'non-investment' activities.

(2) In the light of that allocation the question is whether the investment element of the business is predominant (see *George* at [11]).

(3) The ultimate issue concerns the relative importance of non-investment activities to the business as a whole (see *George* at [51].

(4) There is a wide spectrum involved in such businesses. At one end is the granting of a tenancy together with activities sufficient to make it a business. At the other end is the running of a hotel or shop on the land. The holding of land as an investment may be the very business carried on or it may be merely incidental to the business. It may also be one of a number of principal components of a composite business (see *George* at [12] and [16]).

(5) It is necessary to look at the business in the round. The relative income and profitability of the various activities is relevant but not determinative (see *George* at [13]).

(6) The exception in section 105(3) IHTA 1984 is not confined to purely passive property investment (see *George* at [18]).

(7) Property 'management' is part of the business of holding property as an investment, including finding occupiers and maintaining the property as an investment. However that term does not extend to additional services or facilities provided to occupiers and it is irrelevant whether the provision of such additional services is included in the lease. The characterisation of such services depends on the nature and purpose of the activity and not on the terms of the lease (see *George* at [27] and [28]). (In the later case of *Pawson* –see **explanatory note 12** – the Upper Tribunal went on to say in this regard that where the business is one of letting a building, the provision of additional services or facilities to the occupants is unlikely to be material because they will not be enough to prevent the business remaining 'mainly' one of holding the property as an investment. In the normal property letting business, the provision of additional services or facilities of a non-investment nature will either be incidental to the business of holding the property as an investment, or at least will not predominate to such an extent that the business ceases to be mainly one of holding the property as an investment.)

(8) The test to be applied is that of an intelligent businessman, concerned with the use to which the asset was being put and the way in which it was being turned to account (see *McCall* at [11]).

(9) The test involves a question of fact and degree as to where a particular business falls within the spectrum (see *McCall* at [18]).

In *Green v HMRC* [2015] UKFTT 236 the tribunal held that the taxpayer's furnished holiday letting business did not qualify for business property relief. The property was located on the north Norfolk coast and was marketed on the basis of its location. The business was marketed via a website and brochures. The taxpayer booked the accommodation via the website, correspondence and telephone. The price paid by guests included the use of linen and towels, electricity, various kitchen equipment and other household furniture and Wi-Fi. A welcome pack was provided, the property was cleaned between occupancy by guests, and a caretaker was available in emergencies. There was also expenditure on repairs and maintenance; the property was liable for business rates and the business paid an accountant and a secretary. However, the guests did their own laundry and cooking, cleaned the cooker, microwave, cooking equipment and eating utensils before departure, changed light bulbs, set the heating thermostat and rarely contacted the caretaker who was available only for property-related emergencies. Starting from the proposition set down in the Upper Tribunal in *Pawson* that the owning and holding of land in order to obtain an income from it is generally to be characterised as an investment activity, the tribunal analysed the taxpayer's business in detail by looking at the additional services which the taxpayer offered guests. The activities that fell on the investment side of the line were marketing, pricing, booking, dealing with complaints and requests, insurance, repairs and maintenance. The business rates were part of the cost of managing the investment. On the non-investment side of the line were electricity provision, the welcome pack and the provision of linen, towels, furniture, equipment, Wi-Fi and cleaning. The tribunal held that the extra services provided by the taxpayer were minor and ancillary to the provision of the accommodation and that consequently the taxpayer carried on a business that was mainly the holding or making of investments. That conclusion was further supported by the accounts of the business which showed that property management costs accounted for at least 60% of the business's expenditure. The price charged to guests was largely attributable to the location of the property, the season and to supply and demand. It was not credible that over 50% of the price paid was for the additional, non-investment services.

A similar conclusion was reached in the *Executors of M Ross v HMRC* [2017] UKFTT 507. Mrs Ross was a partner in a partnership which operated holiday letting cottages and in connection with the letting provided many services to the guests. The tribunal acknowledged that a high level of services was provided to guests and these services were more extensive than those considered in any previous case. That sounded encouraging. However, it was irrelevant because, in the view of the tribunal, business property relief would not be available 'however high the standard of services which were provided and whatever the level of expenditure incurred on those services'. The tribunal denied relief on the grounds that the business of the partnership consisted mainly of investment in property. The fact that the business was run on sound business lines and with much effort, was considered not to be relevant.

In *The Personal Representatives of the Estate of MW Vigne (Deceased) v RCC* [2017] UKFTT 632 the deceased had carried on a DIY livery business, providing grazing and some stabling for horses. Additional services were provided including the provision of food for the horses in the winter, checking them daily, the removal of manure and deworming. HMRC had denied business property relief on the business on the basis that there were insufficient activities or expenses of a business nature, characterising the activities carried on by the deceased as a business of mainly holding investments, even while accepting that the operation of a livery business necessitated the provision of services as well as land. However, the First-tier Tribunal held that the relief was due finding that Customers demanded more from Mrs Vigne's livery business than the right to allow the horses to graze on the field in return for their money. They expected the livery to take on a significant degree of responsibility. This included keeping the fields free from manure, ensuring the horses were in good health and organising follow-up services – vets and farriers – if necessary. They would have also expected the people who performed these duties to be well qualified because they were paying for knowledge and experience that they may not have had themselves. The wellbeing of the horses ultimately lay with the livery. If the main priority of the livery's business consisted of holding investments, it is unlikely it would have been willing to take on such a responsibility. Hence it was concluded that the deceased's business offered significantly more than the mere right to occupy a parcel of land. The point in this case is that livery businesses and riding schools may qualify for relief but, in common with the caravan park cases, it will depend on who does what. Livery may range from full livery, when the landowner runs the equine equivalent of a hotel, to the grass livery for which the landowner provides grazing and a supply of water but nothing else. The former will be a business that qualifies for 100% relief; the latter is a property business that, standing alone, will be disqualified for relief by s 105(3). However, relief might be due when a DIY livery is part of a larger hybrid business of farming and letting property in which the letting does not predominate.

HMRC's appeal to the Upper Tribunal in the *Vigne* case was unsuccessful as the First-tier Tribunal had neither applied the wrong test nor misapplied the correct test [2018] UKUT 357. The Upper Tribunal's decision is important however in its clarification of the judgment in *Pawson*. HMRC had relied in *Vigne* on the *Pawson* decision and had submitted that any business involving the exploitation of land should as a matter to law, be assumed to wholly or mainly a business of investment unless the taxpayer could establish otherwise. The tribunal considered that this overstated the position. The Upper Tribunal in *Pawson* had said only that such an assumption applies to the owning and holding of land in order to obtain an income from it (a much more restricted proposition). Indeed the Court of Appeal in *Pawson* had said that there was no presumption that has to be rebutted that a business, which consists of the exploitation of land for profit, is an investment business. Rather the business has to be looked at in the round. In *Vigne*, the Upper Tribunal could find no fault with the approach of the First-tier Tribunal's approach which was to start by asking the question whether the taxpayer was carrying on a business, wholly or mainly of holding investments. It is not correct to start with the preconceived idea that in any given situation, the business is wholly or mainly one of holding investments and then to ask whether there are factors that result in that preliminary view being altered. The proper starting point was to make no assumption but to establish the facts and then to determine whether they indicate that the business is one of holding investments.

In *Personal Representatives Graham (Deceased) v RCC* [2018] UKFTT 306 the taxpayer operated four self-catering holiday flats and occasional bed and breakfast accommodation from part of the family home. Guests had use of a solar-heated outdoor pool, extensive well-maintained gardens, a sauna, games room, laundry and barbeque area. A separate guest lounge with books was also available. As well as bed linen and towels, each flat was supplied with fresh flowers, homemade goods, toiletries and cleaning materials. A golf buggy and bicycles could also be hired. On arrival guests were provided with refreshments and a welcome pack. The owners were on hand to help with taking in shopping, organising birthday and other celebrations and suggestions on walks and other activities. The flats were cleaned between lettings and there was regular maintenance of the pool, garden and other facilities. Time was also spent advertising for tenants, collecting payments and general maintenance. A claim for BPR was successful and it was the nature of the service which resulted in this outcome. The deceased had lavished personal care upon the guests. The totality of the services and the hours required to provide them enabled the Tribunal to draw the distinction between a normal letting business and the situation in Graham which was more akin to a family run hotel than a second home let out in the holidays. The judge in the case commented that only an exceptional letting business qualifies for BPR. He said that the services provided in the case just predominated. HMRC were refused leave to appeal.

In the case of *Executors of the late S Cox* (2020) the deceased owned four of five apartments in a manor house. He used three as holiday lets and lived in the other. He ran the lettings business as a sole trader and employed his wife to assist him. The executors claimed business property relief on the basis that the business was a commercial lettings business of furnished holiday accommodation. The activities of the business were categorised as follows:

- Investment activities such as the provision of accommodation, parking spaces, laundry facilities, repairs and maintenance of the buildings, gardens and grounds, and all administration dealing with bookings and advertising.
- Incidental or ancillary activities including the provision of electricity and water, appliances and furniture, kitchen and eating equipment, kitchen basics such as tea and coffee, consumables such as washing up liquid and toilet paper; cleaning the apartments, laundry of bed linen and towels and welcoming guests.
- Non-investment activities such as the provision of books, DVDs, information leaflets, use of tennis or badminton racquets, crab lines, frisbees or buckets and spades.

The judge in the First-tier Tribunal considered the ancillary activities were an integral part of the provision of the accommodation, so should be considered as part of the business of holding the property as an investment. The non-investment activities were so insignificant in scale as to be negligible. There was no evidence that extra services such as dog sitting, child minding, transport, breakfast and supper were rendered to guests with any regularity. Indeed they appeared to be 'ad hoc' in nature. It was concluded that business property relief was not available in relation to the lettings business which was one of mainly holding the property as an investment and the additional services provided were not enough to prevent it from being so.

In *Firth v HMRC* [2022] UKFTT 219 the taxpayers' case was that a business carried on by a company was as a boutique hotel. The tribunal took into account a variety of factors in determining whether the business' non-investment activities were more significant from its investment activity of holding land. The former included the provision of a welcome pack to guests, cleaning services as requested, linen, shower gel, furniture, white goods, DVD players/TVs, wi-fi, food and the ability to purchase extra packages such as flowers, chocolates, birthday cakes and prosecco. However, other activities (such as marketing, benchmarking letting rates, preparing the apartments for guests, dealing with complaints and requests, maintenance and repair of properties) were all characterised as investment activities, designed to maximise the taxpayers' return for their investment in the properties themselves. The FTT found that, although some aparthotels could be categorised as a service business with an ancillary business in land, on the facts of the case the non-investment activities of the business were ancillary to the investment in land.

Accordingly, the taxpayers' interest in the business was not relevant business property and so did not qualify for BPR. In an article entitled 'Where is the concierge?' (*Taxation* 22 September 2022), the author discusses the decision in detail, setting out the facts in detail and explaining why the business did not qualify for BPR.

In an article entitled 'Horses for Courses' (I 13 December 2018) the authors have usefully attempted to reconcile the recent cases on BPR an area which is very fact sensitive. They suggest that the difference is between the cases is where customers of a business want the services of the business (where BPR would be available) and those who want the land where the services provided in connection with the land are merely ancillary (where BPR is not available). So in *Ross* (where BPR was denied) the business's first and main focus was to attract customers to make use of the property; it then used the services provided to make the property more attractive. No matter how many services were offered, what the customers wanted was the right to occupy the property and the intention of the business was to provide them with that. By contrast in *Graham* (where BPR was not denied), the business was focused on delivering an experience and package to the client. The customers wanted more than just to occupy the land. Likewise in *Vigne* the service was the livery and this was the core of the business, notwithstanding the use of the land. HMRC's Manuals (at IHTM25280) seems to base itself on this distinction where it refers to services provided as an end in themselves and services that are purely ancillary to the main intention of the renter which is occupation of the land.

(c) *Nature and amount of relief*

The relief applies to transfers of value in lifetime and on death and to the exit and 10 yearly charges on relevant property trusts, the value of the transfer attributable to relevant business property being reduced by 100% in respect of (i) to (iii) in **part** A(a) of this Example above and 50% in respect of (iv) to (vi) in **part** A(a) of this Example above (s 104). With effect from 17 July 2013, where a liability has been incurred on or after 6 April 2013 to acquire, or maintain or enhance property which qualifies for business property relief, the liability is deductible only to the extent that it reduces the value of the property concerned to nil (s 162B(1), (2)). These rules also apply to occasions when inheritance tax is charged on relevant property trusts (s 162B(9)). So, for example, a loan taken out after 5 April 2013 to acquire business property and secured on other property owned by the individual (such as a life assurance policy) will reduce the value of the business property before business property relief is applied. (For more detail on the deductibility of liabilities incurred in relation to property qualifying for business property relief, see **Example A12 part (c)**.)

The relief is applied automatically without the need for a claim and is given after applying agricultural property relief (where relevant – see **Example A22 part (a)**) and before applying any other exemption (eg annual exemptions, as indicated below).

The meaning of 'the value transferred [being] attributable to the value of . . . relevant business property' was examined in *HMRC v Trustees of Nelson Dance Family Settlement* (2009). There the transferor settled part of the land used in a farming business that he carried on personally, and business property relief was claimed on the development value of the land so far as it exceeded the agricultural value that attracted agricultural property relief. It was common ground that the subject matter of his transfer of value was not the business that he had carried on, merely part of the assets of that business. It was held that although in one sense the value transferred was attributable to the value of the land as such, in another sense it was attributable to the value of the business because the value of the business was taken into account in ascertaining the loss to the donor. Section 104 did not require a choice to be made between the two senses and it was sufficient to be able to characterise the transfer in the second sense. Consequently the transfer of the land qualified for business property relief. But see below if the donor's death occurs within seven years afterwards.

Meaning of control

Control means control of voting on all questions affecting the company as a whole (s 269(1)). In considering which shares give control care must be taken with shares that only have votes in special circumstances (eg preference shares entitled to votes when the preference dividends are in arrears). When voting rights relate only to the question of winding-up, or to questions primarily affecting shares of a particular class, then such rights are ignored (s 269(4)). Otherwise the rights are included in determining control. For example, say an unquoted company has a total issued share capital of £100, consisting of 25 ordinary shares of £1 held by A, and 75 preference shares of £1 held by B, the preference shares having votes when the preference dividends are in arrears and on reduction of capital. Neither A nor B *controls* the votes on *all* questions affecting the company as a whole, so neither would qualify for business property relief on any land etc. owned personally and used by the company. If the voting rights on the preference shares related only to winding-up, A would then control the company and would be entitled to the 50% relief on land etc. owned personally. B's position would be unchanged.

Death of donor within seven years

For lifetime gifts made after 17 March 1986, whether chargeable at the time or potentially exempt, where the death of the donor occurs within seven years, the fact that business property relief was applicable at the date of the lifetime transfer will not of itself suffice to obtain the relief when calculating the tax/additional tax arising as a result of the death. The relief is only preserved for that purpose if:

(1) the original property (or qualifying replacement property – see below) has been owned by the transferee throughout the period beginning with the date of the lifetime transfer and ending with the death of the transferor (s 113A(3)(a)), and

(2) immediately before the death of the donor the original property (or qualifying replacement property) is relevant business property in the hands of the transferee (ignoring the two year period of ownership rule).

This second condition does not need to be satisfied, however,

(i) in relation to shares or securities that were quoted at the time of the original transfer (s 113A(3A)(a)) (ie it does not matter that when the donor dies the donee does not own a controlling holding of quoted shares in order to be entitled to business property relief), or

(ii) in relation to shares that were unquoted at the time of the transfer, provided they are still unquoted when the donor dies (s 113A(3A)(b)).

If the transferee dies before the donor then the property must meet the above conditions in (1) and (2) at the date of his death rather than the date of the donor's death (s 113A(4)).

Proportionate relief is available where only part of the property is owned at the date of death (s 113A(5)).

See **explanatory note 14** for a discussion of the application of this rule in **part B** of this Example.
Note that these conditions would seem to be incapable of being satisfied in circumstances such as those of the *Nelson Dance* case above. In that case the relevant business property (ie the business) to whose value the value transferred was attributable was not itself in fact transferred; only land forming part of the assets of the business was transferred and the value of that transfer was attributable (inter alia) to the value of the transferor's business itself under the loss to donor principle. The 'original property' in s 113A is defined as the property which was relevant business property in relation to the lifetime transfer (which in the context of the case was the business itself). The transferee in the *Nelson Dance* case would never own the business itself. So business property relief is likely to be unavailable for the purpose of calculating the additional tax due by reason of the death of the transferor, even if the donee retains the land that was transferred.

To the extent that the original transfer was covered by annual exemptions, whether the transfer was chargeable at the time or potentially exempt, it is considered that a clawback of business property relief occasioned by the death of the donor within seven years does not affect those exemptions. See **Example B5 explanatory note 2**, and the illustration in that Example.

It should be noted that if business property relief is not available in calculating the additional tax resulting from the donor's death within seven years after an immediately *chargeable* lifetime transfer, it is only that tax calculation that is affected. The donor's total of cumulative transfers is not altered (s 113A(2)), and the relief is not retrospectively withdrawn in relation to the tax payable at lifetime rates on the original transfer. By contrast, where the lifetime transfer was a potentially exempt transfer, s 113A(1) provides for the relief not to be allowed if the conditions set out above are not satisfied, and this affects the figure for cumulative transfers as much as the tax due on the (failed) potentially exempt transfer itself.

Example

In July 2023, a donor who has already fully used his (general) nil-rate band settles (other than on a disabled person's interest) a building worth £337,000 which is used for business purposes by a company of which he has control. The transfer qualifies for 50% business property relief. The value of the transfer of £337,000 is reduced by 50% business property relief to £168,500, which is further reduced by two years' annual exemptions to £162,500. This is charged at the 20% lifetime rate as the nil-rate band has already been exhausted; the settlor pays the tax of £40,625 arising. If the donor dies within seven years and the trustees have in the meantime disposed of the property, the additional charge by reason of the donor's death will be calculated as though the chargeable transfer had not been reduced by business property relief. (The relief would be retained to the extent that the transfer of value was exempt at the time under the annual exemptions – so that the £6,000 of reduced value which was exempt, equating to £12,000 of unreduced value, would retain the relief: s 113A(2) affects only 'the value transferred by any chargeable transfer, other than a potentially exempt transfer'.) The recalculated charge would thus be by reference to a chargeable transfer of £325,000 (£337,000 – £12,000); assuming that the nil-rate band had not in the meantime increased far enough to exceed the previous transfers, and that no taper relief was due, the additional charge would thus be £130,000 (£325,000 × 40%), less the £32,500 paid at lifetime rates. However, the amount of the chargeable transfer relating to the building, to be aggregated with any subsequent transfers and with his estate, will remain at £162,500.

By comparison, if the donor had instead gifted the same building to his son in July 2023 it would have been a potentially exempt transfer so far as not covered by the annual exemptions. The calculation at the time of the potentially exempt transfer would be the same as with the transfer into trust above, namely value transferred after 50% business property relief of £168,500, of which £6,000 is exempt (two years' annual exemptions) and the remaining £162,500 is potentially exempt. If on the donor's death within seven years the transfer had still qualified for business property relief, those figures would stand (s 113A would not call for any re-evaluation); the donor's chargeable transfer (failed potentially exempt transfer) taken into account as part of his cumulative total would be £162,500, and the tax to be borne by the donee would be based on that figure. However, if on the donor's death within seven years the circumstances were such that business property relief no longer applied (ie his son having since disposed of the property, or even having retained it but not himself having control of the company that uses it), the relief would be lost to the extent that the transfer had been potentially exempt. (Again it would be retained in excess of that, ie in relation to the £12,000 of unreduced value, or £6,000 of reduced value, that was exempt: s 113A(1) affects only 'the value transferred by a potentially exempt transfer'.) The son's liability will therefore be liable to tax on £325,000 (337,000 – 12,000) as above; but the difference from the lifetime chargeable transfer is that in this case the cumulative amount to be aggregated with subsequent transfers and with the donor's estate will also be £325,000. This different treatment arises because s 113A(1), dealing with potentially exempt transfers, deals with the tax charged as a whole, whereas the operation of s 113A(2) is restricted to the calculation of 'the additional tax chargeable by reason of the death'.

Qualifying replacement property

Provision is made for property that replaces all or part of the original property to satisfy the continuing ownership test up to the donor's (or donee's) death provided the replacement property also qualifies as business property, and provided the whole of the proceeds of the original property are used in purchasing the replacement property within three years after the disposal of the original property, or such longer period as HMRC may allow (s 113B(1)). HMRC interpret 'the whole of the consideration' as meaning the sale proceeds net of any professional costs of the sale and net of any capital gains tax payable on the disposal (IHTM25369). Replacement shares or property must not be acquired in advance of the disposal of the original property, or at least a binding contract for such disposal (see s 113B(7)). Non-agricultural business property that is replaced by agricultural property which is a farming business is also qualifying replacement property.

Excepted assets

For the purpose of calculating business property relief, the value of the relevant business property excludes *excepted assets*, ie assets which were neither used wholly or mainly for the purposes of a business throughout the two years preceding the transfer, nor required at the time of the transfer for future use for those purposes (s 112(2)). See the Special Commissioners' case of *Barclays Bank Trust Co Ltd* (1998 SpC 158) for the denial of relief to the extent that there were substantial cash balances held within a company. However, excess cash that is surplus to immediate business needs will not be treated as an excepted asset where it is required for future business use (or as the Special Commissioner put it: 'I do not accept that "future" means at any time in the future nor that "was required" includes the possibility that the money might be required should an opportunity arise to make use of the money in two, three or seven years' time for the purposes of the business. In my opinion and I so hold that "required" implies some imperative that the money will fall to be used upon a given project or for some palpable business purpose.'

HMRC state (at IHTM25352 and SVM111220) that whether this test is satisfied is a question of evidence in the circumstances of the particular case. One has to have regard to the nature and previous history of the business and such evidence as may be produced (which may incidentally affect the open market value of the business) as to prospective development and capital outlay. Also the business's trading cycles must be taken into account in applying the excepted asset test – for example the accounts for a farming business may show large cash assets after the sale of a harvest or livestock and before the purchase of next year's seed or stock. In such a case the cash balance is unlikely to be treated as an excepted asset (IHTM25342).

However, HMRC are of the view that the holding of funds as an excess buffer to weather a downturn in the economic climate is not a sufficient reason for them not to be classed as an excepted asset (see Part C of the ICAEW's Tax Guide 1/14 issued jointly in January 2015 by the CIoT, STEP and the ICAEW Tax Faculty accessible at www.tax.org.uk/taxpolicy/Topics/InheritanceTax/TaxGuide_IHT_BPR_LLP).

B. Instalment option

(a) Inheritance tax payable by Elizabeth as donee of lifetime transfers:

On death of Stanley 13 November 2023

Potentially exempt transfers 19 July 2018, now chargeable transfers (see **explanatory notes 13 and 14**):

	Gross	*Tax*
	£	£
Shares in Printers Ltd (100% business property relief)	Nil	Nil
Land and buildings (see **explanatory note 13**)	394,000	27,600*
(* 394,000 – 325,000 = 69,000 @ 40%)		

Tax payable (after taper relief) is 40% of £27,600 = £11,040, which is payable over 10 annual instalments.

Peter — inheritance tax accumulation

	Gross	*Tax*
	£	£
Previous transfers	180,000	Nil

19 July 2018 — potentially exempt transfer £40,000 less 100% business property relief £40,000 = nil. (No tax payable even if Peter dies within seven years and business property relief is not then available, since cumulative transfers total (of £180,000 plus £40,000) is within nil-rate band. See **explanatory note 15**.)

(b) The first instalment of the tax of £11,040 in respect of the land and buildings, amounting to £1,104, is payable on 31 May 2024.

(c) Interest is payable on the tax in respect of land and buildings from 31 May 2024 to the date of the instalment, calculated on the full amount of tax for the time being unpaid. In addition interest is paid on the instalment from its due date to the actual date of payment of the instalment.

Explanatory Notes

Business property relief legislation

(1) The provisions relating to business property relief are contained in ss 103–114.

(2) The main provisions are dealt with in the Example, other points of importance being covered in the following notes.

Inheritance tax business property relief: meaning of control

(3) Control of a company means the control of voting on all questions affecting the company as a whole, subject to what is said in **part A(c)** of the Example (s 269).

Shares or securities which are related property under s 161 are taken into account in determining whether a person controls a company (s 269(2)), except where related property is left out of account under s 176 because of a sale after death (ss 105(2), 122(2)) (see **Example A12** for the related property rules, **explanatory note 4** of that Example dealing with s 176). See **explanatory note 13** for a discussion of the application of this rule in **Part B** of this Example.

The voting powers attaching to shares or securities comprised in a settlement are deemed to be exercisable by the person beneficially entitled in possession to the shares or securities (broadly the person entitled to the income for the time being) (s 269(3)).

Business property relief is also available on the occasion of an exit charge and a ten yearly charge on a settlement without a qualifying interest in possession. For this purpose the trustees are deemed to be a transferor (ss 66, 103(1)(b), 115(1)(b)).

Inheritance tax business property relief: parcels of shares acquired over a period of time — matching provisions

(4) As indicated in the Example, an asset is not relevant business property unless it has been owned by the transferor throughout the two years before the transfer (or it is qualifying replacement property). As far as shares are concerned, they may have been acquired in separate parcels over a period of time and some of the acquisitions may have been only within the last two years. Shares are fungible assets. Assets are fungible if they are of the same type (ie each matches the same description such that one asset can be replaced with another). Shares of the same class in a company are typically fungible as each share is identical and the mere fact that each share is allocated a unique number in the company's share register does not detract from those shares being treated as fungible (ie they cannot be identified separately). Also certificates bearing the name of the holder do not detract from the fungible nature of the shares as they merely represent the shares. So the entire share issues makes up one single asset with each of the securities being a fractional part of an undivided whole. The company owes only one set of obligations to the shareholders and a share represents an undivided fractional part of the issuing company. The consequence of this is that it is impossible to identify which part of a shareholding has been held for a qualifying period.

Unlike the capital gains position, there are no matching rules in the inheritance tax legislation, so that there is scope for uncertainty over which shares are contained in a transfer; it is impossible to identify which part of a shareholding has been held for a qualifying period. However, in the context of BPR, the issue is resolved by HMRC practice. At SVM111090 they write: 'Where the transferor acquired additional shares during the two years prior to the transfer and it is claimed that the shares transferred derived from the holding acquired earlier, [taxpayers] should be asked to provide the necessary evidence – such as a copy of the relevant entries in the register of transfers or of the relevant share certificates. However if, exceptionally, firm evidence does not exist (for example because, following a reorganisation of the share capital, a fresh certificate was issued to cover the whole of the transferor's holding) relief may be given to the extent that it would be available on the basis of a "first in – first out" assumption'. Firm evidence may also be established either by the separate parcels of shares having been originally registered in the names of different nominees or by the share certificates that are cancelled as a result of a gift being those acquired more than two years previously. The evidence to support any such claim would need to be carefully preserved.

In *Vinton and others v HMRC* (2008) shortly before the deceased's death she had acquired two parcels of shares; the first by way of a rights issue (ie a reorganisation of the company's share capital) and the second by way of a simple subscription. It was held that the shares acquired under the rights issue were identified with the shares that she had held for more than two years and so qualified for relief (s 107(4)). The second parcel had not been held for two years and so failed to qualify.

Binding contract for sale: effect on business property relief

(5) Property that is subject to a binding contract for sale (ie a contract that is or has become unconditional) at the time of a transfer is not relevant business unless:

(a) the sale is to a company that is to carry on the business, the consideration being wholly or mainly shares or securities in the company, or

(b) the property is shares or securities of a company and the sale is made for the purpose of reconstruction or amalgamation (s 113).

Where partners or company directors have entered into 'buy and sell' agreements whereby on their death their personal representatives are *obliged* to sell and the survivors *obliged* to buy the deceased's interest (funds often being provided by life assurance policies), such an agreement in HMRC's view constitutes a binding contract for sale and business property relief is not available (Statement of Practice 12/80). If, however, a double option agreement is entered into under which the surviving partners or shareholders have an option to buy and the deceased's personal representatives an option to sell, such options to be exercised within a stated period after the partner's death, this does not cause business property relief to be lost (IHTM 25292).

Other reliefs and exemptions: interaction with business property relief

(6) Business property relief is given before any exemptions since they apply to transfers of value (s 104(1)), such transfers being calculated before reliefs and exemptions (s 3(1)). In relation to potentially exempt transfers that become chargeable transfers, neither relief is available unless the relevant conditions are satisfied at the time of death, as indicated in the Example (s 113A(1)).

Gifts of business property subject to a reservation

(7) Where a gift of business property is subject to a reservation of benefit, then it has to satisfy two conditions to qualify for business property relief. First, the property must have been relevant business property at the time of the gift. Secondly, at the time of the charge to tax (on the death of the donor or earlier release of the reservation within seven years before the donor's death) the property must have qualified for the relief (tested by reference to a notional disposal of it by the donee) (FA 1986 Sch 20 para 8). Where the requirements for 100% relief are satisfied at both stages, the fact that a gift of qualifying property was subject to a reservation will not result in any extra tax charge on death.

In order to test the donee's entitlement to relief, there are provisions to enable him to satisfy the occupation/ownership requirements by reference to the occupation/ownership of the donor (FA 1986 Sch 20 para 8).

For the gifts with reservation provisions see **Example B1**.

Exempt and partially exempt estates: effect on business property relief

(8) Where business property forms part of an estate at death, the benefit of the business property relief will be lost if the property is left to an exempt beneficiary. Even if it is not left to an exempt beneficiary, part of the relief will be wasted where there are exempt legacies and the business property forms part of the residue of the estate, rather than being left as a specific gift. This is because the relief is then regarded as applying to the whole estate, including the exempt part of it, so that again relief is wasted to the extent that it is allocated to the exempt legacies (s 39A). For further notes on this point see **Example A16 explanatory notes 6 to 9.**

Gifts out of and into trusts: availability of business property relief

(9) Business property relief is available on transfers of trust property provided the conditions are satisfied. For life interest trusts, the person with a qualifying interest in possession (see **Example C3**) is treated as the beneficial owner of the property (s 49) and when the interest comes to an end, he is treated as having made a transfer at that time (s 52). In other cases (including where an interest in possession is not within s 49 and hence is not a qualifying interest in possession), the relief is available when relevant property is transferred out of the trust and on the occasion of the ten yearly charge, the trustees being treated as the transferor (ss 103, 113) (see **Example C13 explanatory note 5**).

Detailed notes on the inheritance tax treatment of trusts are contained in **Examples C1 to C19**. See **Examples C11 and C12** in particular for the treatment of business property.

Various points need to be borne in mind when placing business property or agricultural property into a trust, and the possible effects for the different types of trust need to be carefully considered.

(10) Before 22 March 2006, if property was placed into a life interest trust, the transfer was potentially exempt and would only become chargeable if the donor died within seven years after the transfer. If the property was business property, the relief was taken into account in arriving at the amount of the potentially exempt transfer. The property needed to remain 'owned' by the life tenant (whether by virtue of the life interest or following its release to him absolutely) for two years before any transfer (or deemed transfer) by him would qualify for relief. This still applies where a person becomes entitled to a qualifying interest in possession (typically an immediate post-death interest or a disabled person's interest, though only the latter can result from a lifetime transfer – see **Example C3**).

If the donor dies within seven years after transferring the property to the trust, so that the potentially exempt transfer becomes a chargeable transfer, the trustees still need to hold the property at that time in order for the relief to be available. (If the donor died within two years this would not prevent the relief being available provided the property was still held in the trust.) If the trust does not satisfy the conditions at the donor's death, the relief is not available against the now chargeable transfer, and the donor's 'clock' of cumulative transfers will include that chargeable transfer.

(11) Since 22 March 2006, the lifetime transfer of property into any trust other than one conferring a disabled person's interest is now an immediately chargeable transfer (at half of the rates of tax payable on death) after being reduced by business property relief where available. The trustees need to retain the property for two years before being entitled to relief on any appointments of the property out of the trust or on terms of a disabled person's interest; but any other appointment that results in the property remaining within the settlement can be made within that period without having to re-qualify for the relief. Furthermore, if there are any appointments of the property after that time but within ten years after the trust's creation, then although the relief is available on the transfer the *rate of tax* is based on the full value of the property when settled (see **Example C13 explanatory note 5**). This would not be a problem, however, if the property qualified in full for 100% relief, because the amount chargeable at that rate would be nil. If the donor dies within seven years after the transfer, the tax on the lifetime transfer is recalculated on the death scale, additional tax being payable accordingly. As with life interest trusts, the trustees still need to hold the property when the donor dies in order for the relief to remain available on the donor's transfer (and they would be entitled to the relief even if the donor died within two years provided the property was still held in the trust). If the trust does not satisfy the conditions for relief when the donor dies, the relief is not taken into account in calculating the additional tax on the lifetime transfer, but the amount of the donor's cumulative transfers would not be affected. Relief will not be available against the lifetime transfer to the trust because the trustees have disposed of the property between the time of the gift and the time of death.

Let property, including holiday lettings: availability of business property relief

(12) HMRC take the view that a property letting business (as defined for income tax purposes) will not usually qualify for business property relief, because it will be regarded as a business of making or holding investments (s 105(3)). This is supported by the Special Commissioners' decisions in *Exors of Moore dec'd* and *Exor of Burkinyoung dec'd* (1995). In both cases business property relief was denied, even though the taxpayers (or in the *Burkinyoung* case, the managing agents) carried out considerable work as part of the lettings (eg repairs, decoration and maintenance). The taxpayers were described as being merely busy landlords. In *The Trustees of David Zetland Settlement v RCC* [2013] UKFTT 284 the taxpayer again failed to qualify for business property relief.

Hotels, bed and breakfast and residential homes will usually qualify for relief because of the level of additional services provided. In the case of *short-term* holiday lettings (eg weekly or fortnightly), where the property owner or his agent is substantially involved with the holidaymakers during the holiday, it may be that, considering the type and level of additional services provided, business property relief will be available even if the lettings are for part of the year only (HMRC's Inheritance Tax Manual IHTM25278). It is all a matter of fact and degree. The matter was addressed in *Pawson v RCC* [2012] UKFTT 51. The deceased had owned and let a cottage to holiday makers. The first question to be decided was whether the exploitation of the cottage was a business at all, but the First-tier tribunal was satisfied that it was because on the evidence the operation of the property as a holiday cottage was a serious undertaking earnestly pursued, there was a reasonable continuity in the operation, the activity had a measure of substance (judged by its profitability – although a loss made on one year was due to substantial expenditure on refurbishment) and had been conducted in a regular manner and on sound business principles (despite its occasion use by family members). Having decided that the letting of the cottage was a business, attention was turned to whether it was merely a business of holding an investment. This question was answered in the negative on account of the level of services provided by the deceased in running her business. It was observed that the services were a significant part of the reason why the occupiers were prepared to pay what they paid for the package of benefits they received when they booked to use the property as a holiday destination. There was evidence that holiday makers paid a premium compared to longer-term tenants because of the value of the services provided. The provision of services that resulted in the holiday lettings qualifying for business property relief were:

- Provision of telephone and television.
- Cleaning of premises before each letting.
- Maintenance of the garden for recreation.
- Property was fully furnished and heated.
- Provision of utilities (eg gas and electricity) – and the hot water was turned on before visitors arrived.
- Provision of a fully equipped kitchen.
- A cleaner/caretaker inspected the property regularly and bought cleaning materials for the cottage. Repairs were made as required.
- Supply (and change) of clean bed linen.

The First-tier Tribunal concluded, applying the test in *George v Stedman's Executors* [2004] STC 163, that an intelligent businessman would not regard the ownership of a holiday letting property as an investment as such and would regard it as involving far too active an operation for it to come under that heading. Having to find new occupants and provide the relevant services were not the equivalent of owning a property as an investment and in reality the property was a business asset being used to provide a service. The decision of the First-tier Tribunal was reversed however on appeal to the Upper Tribunal ([2013] UKUT 50) on the ground that it had applied the wrong test in law in concluding that the business carried on at the cottage had not been mainly one of holding it as an investment. It held that the relevant test was not the degree or level of activity but rather the nature of the activities carried out and that, on the basis of its finding of fact, the only conclusion that was open to the First-tier Tribunal to draw had been that the business carried on at the cottage had remained one which had been mainly that of holding the property as an investment. The services provided had all been of a fairly standard nature and they had all been aimed at maximising the income which could be obtained from the short term holiday letting of the property. Looking at the business in the round the Upper Tribunal concluded that there had been nothing to distinguish it from any other actively managed furnished letting business of a holiday property and certainly no basis for concluding that the services comprised in the total package had preponderated to such an extent that the business ceased to be one which had been mainly of an investment nature. Although the First-tier Tribunal had sought to apply the correct test of how an intelligent businessman, assumed to be fully instructed in the relevant law, would regard the business, it had failed to explain how such a person could conclude that the service elements had outweighed the investment elements to such an extent that the 'mainly' test had no longer been satisfied.

The Upper Tribunal identified three important points from the Court of Appeal's decision in George to help decide cases such as these:

(a) The general proposition that property management forms part of the business of holding property as an investment, and included under that heading maintenance of the property as an investment as well as the activity of finding tenants and arranging leases or licences.

(b) A distinction between such management activities on the one hand and the provision of addition services or facilities to the tenants or occupants, whether they are separately charged for or included in the lease and covered by the tenant on the other hand. The characterisation of such services depends on the nature and purpose of the activity, and not on the terms of the lease or licence.

(c) Where the business is one of letting a building, the provision of additional services or facilities is unlikely to be material because they will not be enough to prevent the business being 'mainly' one of holding the property as an investment. The implication is that in any normal property letting business, the provision of additional services or facilities of a non-investment nature will either be incidental to the business of holding the property as an investment or at least will not predominate to such an extent that the business ceases to be mainly one of holding the property as an investment.

In addition it noted the observation of the High Court in the McCall case that a landowner who derives income from land or a building will be treated as having a business of holding an investment notwithstanding that in order to obtain the income he carries out incidental maintenance and management work, finds tenants and grants leases.

The *Pawson* decision does not mean that a furnished holiday letting business can never qualify for business property relief. But it does set the bar very high so that it will be exceptional if such a business does qualify. The services provided by the deceased in the *Pawson* case may have been fewer than those offered by other modern holiday lettings. Other services that might be offered in any case to strengthen an argument that the letting of holiday accommodation qualifies for business property relief might include the following (from the article 'Business property relief on furnished holiday letting' written by Matthew Hutton that appeared in the April 2012 issue of *Tax Adviser*, the journal of the Chartered Institute of Taxation and the Association of Taxation Technicians, published by LexisNexis):

- Making up of beds during occupation.
- Provision of sports facilities (eg a tennis court, swimming pool).
- Advice on local attractions.
- Supply of complementary food and drinks and flowers on arrival.
- Supply newspapers and other reading material.
- Taking delivery of groceries ordered in advance of arrival.
- Arranging for babysitting.
- Reservation of tables at local restaurants.
- Arranging transfers to airport/station.
- Disposal of rubbish.

The difficulty of qualifying for business property relief in the context of furnished holiday lettings after the *Pawson* case is illustrated in the decision of the First-tier Tribunal in *The Executors of the Estate of Marjorie Ross (Deceased)* [2017] UKFTT 507. In that case, despite the high level of services provided by the deceased in respect of her holiday lettings, the main character of her business remained one of investment in land so that her estate was not entitled to business property relief. The Judge in the case usefully provided the following summary of the main principles derived from case law:

(a) The owning and holding of land to earn rental income is generally to be treated as an investment activity.

(b) The holding of land can include non-investment activities.

(c) The test under IHTA 1984, s105 requires a considered of whether those non-investment activities are more significant than the investment activities.

(d) The question of whether a business is mainly an investment business is a question of fact and degree.

(e) The question of whether something is an investment activity is not limited to passive investment activities such as long leases managed by managing agents.

(f) The holding of land may be incidental to the running of a business (as in a hotel or holiday camp) or may be the essence of the business.

(g) Accounting evidence and the profits or expenses allocated to the investment and non-investment activities of the business is one factor but is not the decisive factor.

(h) Additional services provided to a rental property are 'unlikely to be material' and in a normal property rental business additional services will either be incidental or will not be sufficient to prevent the business being one of mainly holding investments.

(i) The characterisation of any additional services provided depends on the nature and purpose of the activity and not on the terms of any lease.

(j) To come to a conclusion the business must be looked at in the round.

(k) The test to be applied is that of an intelligent business person concerned with the use to which an asset is put and the way it is turned to account.

In a decision of the *Special Commissioners (Furness v CIR)* (1999), it was held that a caravan park business qualified for business property relief. Although there were both static and touring caravans, the larger part of the business's profits came other than from renting out caravan pitches, and the activities of the owner and his staff were greatly in excess of what one would expect in a business concerned wholly or mainly with the making or holding of investments.

The opposite decision was, however, reached in *Weston (exor of Weston dec'd) v CIR* (2000), where the Court confirmed the Special Commissioner's decision that the greater part of a caravan park's profits came from pitch fees and bank interest rather than caravan sales, so that the business was mainly one of making or holding investments. The same conclusion was reached by the High Court in *IRC v George & Anor (Exors of Stedman dec'd)* (2002) where the main activities were the letting of sites for 167 residential mobile homes; storage of touring caravans; letting of a shop and warehouse and fields let on grazing licences. This outweighed the ancillary activities of a country club and an insurance agency, so the business was mainly one of making or holding investments. However, that decision was subsequently overturned by the Court of Appeal which reinstated the Special Commissioner's finding that the company was mainly trading.

The criteria set out in the *Farmer & Giles* case mentioned in **part A(b)** of the Example provide a good basis on which to judge whether a business consists mainly of making or holding investments. See however *McCall & anor (PRs of McClean dec'd) v HMRC* (2008), where land was subject to a grazing agreement. The Court of Appeal in Northern Ireland held that the Special Commissioner had not erred in law when holding that the landowner's business did not consist of growing grass on the land for consumption by the grazier's livestock, but rather of exploiting the land as an investment, so that business property relief was excluded by s 105(3).

Inheritance tax: related property and business property relief

(13) Using the related property rules (s 161) (see **Example A12**), Stanley's gift of shares on 19 July 2018 must be valued as a proportion of an 80% holding (ie his own plus his wife's holding), of which one-half relates to him. The combined holding also determines the size of the holding for the purposes of establishing whether Stanley controls Printers Ltd (s 269(2)). The rate of business property relief at 19 July 2018 was 100% on the shares and 50% on the land and buildings, so the original calculation was:

		£
	$\text{Value of shares (80 \%) } 1{,}400{,}000 \times \dfrac{4{,}000 \text{ shares}}{8{,}000 \text{ shares}} =$	700,000
Less:	Business property relief (100%)	(700,000)
Transfer of value		Nil

The transfer of value on the same day in respect of the land and buildings was:

				£
Value of property				800,000
Less:	Business property relief (50%)			(400,000)
				400,000
Less:	Annual exemptions	2018/19	3,000	
		2017/18	3,000	(6,000)
Chargeable transfer				394,000

For the position where business (or agricultural) property relief is withdrawn at death because the conditions are no longer satisfied see **Example B5 explanatory note 2.**

Inheritance tax: availability of business property relief

(14) When Stanley died in November 2023, his gift of shares to Elizabeth becomes subject to inheritance tax and she is liable for any tax arising. To qualify for 100% business property relief on the gift of the *shares*, Elizabeth merely needs, at the time of Stanley's death, still to own the shares that were transferred to her (s 113A) and so long as the company is still trading, the shares are relevant business property in Elizabeth's hands.

To get 50% business property relief on the gifted *land and buildings*, as well as owning them Elizabeth must also *control* Printers Ltd when Stanley dies (s 113A(3)).

The shares owned by Elizabeth following the gifts on 19 July 2018 and still held by her on 13 November 2023 are:

Original shareholding	100
Gift from Stanley	4,000
Gift from Peter	1,000
Total shares held	5,100

Consequently, she has control of Printers Ltd and is therefore entitled to business property relief on the land and buildings. The land and buildings would not have qualified for any relief had they not been transferred to Elizabeth. A trap typically exists where the trading premises of a business are owned by one spouse and it is the other spouse who owns the shares in question. Care needs to be exercised where shares are transferred between spouses perhaps to minimise income tax on dividends.

Because Stanley died more than five but less than six years after the date of his gift, taper relief is available so that 40% of the tax otherwise due from Elizabeth becomes payable.

(15) Peter's gift of his Printers Ltd shareholding to Elizabeth on 19 July 2018 qualified for 100% business property relief. The whole of the gift is a potentially exempt transfer. If he should die before 19 July 2024, the potentially exempt transfer will become chargeable, and the business property relief will only then be available if Elizabeth still owns the shares on his death, they are unquoted at that time, and the company is still trading. No tax would then be payable on Peter's gift since the cumulative transfers are within the nil-rate band. However, if 100% business property relief were not then available, the value of the gift would be taken into account in the cumulative total for a death within seven years.

Inheritance tax: instalment option for payment of tax

(16) Inheritance tax payable on certain assets on death (or on lifetime chargeable transfers where the transferee pays the inheritance tax) may be paid by ten equal annual instalments (ss 227 and 228). See **Examples A7** and **A11.**

The instalment option is available on potentially exempt transfers that become chargeable because of the donor's death within seven years provided the donee still owns the gifted property (or, for transfers of property qualifying for business property or agricultural property relief, replacement property) at the time of the donor's death (s 227(1A), (1C)).

Unquoted shares and securities (including shares which do not qualify for business property relief, eg shares in property investment companies) that do not represent a controlling holding only qualify as instalment assets if:

(a) the inheritance tax cannot be paid in one sum without undue hardship, or

(b) (for shares only) they are valued at more than £20,000 and their nominal value is at least 10% of the nominal value of all the company's shares (or if they are ordinary shares, 10% of the nominal value of the company's ordinary shares), or

(c) in the case of a transfer on death, the tax payable on the shares or securities, together with the tax on other instalment assets, amounts to 20% or more of the tax payable by the same person on the same transfer (s 228).

Furthermore the instalment option on unquoted shares is not available for tax payable as a consequence of the donor's death unless the shares are still unquoted when the donor dies (or if earlier, when the donee dies).

The gift of 10% of the shares in Printers Ltd by Peter to Elizabeth would not satisfy any of the conditions listed above so that if tax were to become chargeable the instalment option would not be available.

The instalment option is available as indicated in respect of Stanley's gift to Elizabeth of the land and buildings.

Inheritance tax business property relief and liabilities

(17) For a discussion as to the value of property qualifying for business property being reduced by the owner's liabilities see **Examples A12(c)**.

Question

Relief from inheritance tax is available for 'agricultural property'.

(a) Under what circumstances is a transferor entitled to inheritance tax relief when transferring agricultural property and what is the nature of the relief?

(b) Is the relief available to a transferor of shares or debentures in a farming company?

(c) Whiteacre is a farm of 200 acres which for the last ten years has been owned and farmed by Arthur personally with assistance from his son.

It has been proposed that Arthur should form a partnership with his son because of his advancing age, failing health and the necessity of providing for his wife when he dies.

Arthur would then grant a lease of the land at full rent to that partnership so that on his death the land will be valued at tenanted value.

The current agricultural value of the land is £2,000 per acre vacant possession and £1,400 per acre tenanted. Both are professional valuations.

Advise Arthur as to the viability of the above proposal, quantifying the value chargeable to inheritance tax on Whiteacre on his subsequent death.

(d) X owned 800 acres of freehold farmland known as Greenacre let to and farmed by the partnership of X himself, Mrs X and their son Y. The tenancy was granted in 1980 and the partnership has subsisted since before that time. There is no farmhouse on the farmland and the family live in rented accommodation near Greenacre.

In July 2023 X died leaving his interest in Greenacre to his son Y (subject to Y paying the inheritance tax thereon). It was valued (tenanted) at £479,000. X left the residue of his estate (including his interest in the partnership valued at £60,000) to his wife. He had not made any previous lifetime gifts.

After an accident on the farm Y, who was unmarried, died in September 2023.

Y's estate consisted of:

	£
Greenacre Farm (let to the farming partnership of himself and his mother)	479,000
Interest in the farming partnership	60,000
Other assets (cash and quoted shares)	89,000

Compute the inheritance tax payable:

(i) on the death of X;

(ii) on the death of Y assuming he had not made any lifetime transfers and that he left the whole of his estate to his mother.

Answer

Agricultural property relief

(a) *Availability of agricultural property relief*

Agricultural property relief (APR) is available on the transfer of agricultural property which is defined as:

- agricultural land or pasture;
- also woodland occupied with agricultural land or pasture and any building used in the intensive rearing of livestock or fish if the occupation of the woodland or building is ancillary to that of the agricultural land or pasture; and
- also such cottages, farm buildings and farmhouses, together with the land occupied with them, as are of a character appropriate to the property (ie the agricultural land or pasture) (s 115(2)).

The basic meaning of the term 'agriculture' is not defined in the legislation but a useful list of the activities that are recognised as agriculture are set out in IHTM 24061 as follows:

- cultivation to produce food for human and animal consumption;
- use of land to support livestock kept to produce food for human consumption such as meet or milk or other products such as wool;
- the keeping of such other animals as may be found on an ordinary farm, eg horses kept for farm work;
- land set aside for permanent or rotational fallow.

The agricultural property has to be situated in the UK, the Channel Islands, the Isle of Man or a state which, at the time of the transfer of value, is in the EEA (s 115(5)). With effect from 6 April 2024, the government proposes to introduce legislation to restrict APR to agricultural property in the UK only.

The cultivation of short rotation coppice (ie the harvesting of trees planted at high density at intervals of less than ten years) is regarded as agriculture, and therefore the land used for this purpose is agricultural land and ancillary buildings are farm buildings (FA 1995 s 154).

The breeding and rearing of horses on a stud farm and the grazing of horses in connection with those activities are treated as agriculture for the purposes of the relief, and any buildings used in connection with those activities are treated as farm buildings (s 115(4)).

Agricultural property relief is also available on land taken out of farming and dedicated to wildlife habitats under the Government Habitat Schemes, together with buildings used for the management of the land (s 124C).

Giving effect to agricultural property relief is very similar to business property relief, in that the agricultural value of agricultural property is reduced by (s 116(2)):

(i)	Where the transferor had the right to vacant possession immediately before the transfer or the right to obtain such possession within the next twelve months, extended to 24 months by HMRC Concession F17; or (also by Concession F17) the property is valued at an amount broadly equivalent to the vacant possession value.	100%
(ii)	Where the agricultural property transferred is let on a tenancy granted on or after 1 September 1995 (including successions to tenancies following the death of the previous tenant on or after that date – see **explanatory note 14**).	100%

(iii) Where the transferor has been beneficially entitled to his interest in the property since before 10 March 1981 and satisfies certain conditions (see **explanatory note 10**). 100%

(iv) Otherwise. 50%

The percentage deduction only applies to the agricultural value of the property transferred, ie its value on the assumption that the property was subject to a perpetual covenant prohibiting its use otherwise than as agricultural property (s 115(3)). In arriving at the agricultural value any loan secured on the agricultural property must be deducted from the open market value of the property, and the agricultural value attracting relief will then be the same proportion of the net value as would have been the case if there had been no such secured loan. For example, assume that agricultural land is worth £500,000 and that its agricultural value ignoring any encumbrance is £400,000. If a loan of £250,000 is secured on the land, the value on which agricultural property relief will be calculated is £200,000 ($^4/_5$ × (£500,000 – £250,000)).

With effect from 17 July 2013, it is not strictly necessary for a loan to be secured on the agricultural property in order for its agricultural value to be reduced before applying agricultural property relief. Where a liability has been incurred on or after 6 April 2013 to acquire, or maintain or enhance the agricultural value of, property that qualifies for agricultural property relief, the liability is deductible only to the extent that it reduces the value of the property concerned to nil (s 162B(3), (4)). These rules also apply to occasions when inheritance tax is charged on relevant property trusts (s 162B(9)). So, for example, a loan taken out after 5 April 2013 to acquire agricultural property and secured on other property owned by the individual (such as a life assurance policy) will reduce the agricultural value of the agricultural property before agricultural property relief is applied. (For more detail on the deductibility of liabilities incurred in relation to agricultural property qualifying for agricultural property relief see **Example A12 part (c).**)

Meaning of agricultural land or pasture – farmhouses

The third limb of the definition of agricultural property refers to certain buildings, including farmhouses. However, a farmhouse only qualifies for agricultural property relief if a number of strict conditions are met. In short, in order to obtain relief for any farmhouse (or cottage or other farm building), it is necessary to show that its occupation is ancillary to that of the agricultural land itself (*Starke (Brown's Exors) v CIR* (1994)).

First, the building concerned must be a farmhouse – that is a dwelling occupied by a farmer from which the farm business is managed. In *Rosser v IRC* (2003) the deceased had purchased a 41-acre farm and carried on a farming operation, living in the main house on the farm. In 1990 he retired from farming and gave 39 acres to his daughter who continued the farming operations. The deceased continued to live in the house and provided food and refreshments to the farm workers. It was held that the house was no longer a farmhouse from 1990 as from that time it had turned into a retirement home. Any incidental agricultural duties still carried on at the house were incidental to its prime function as a retirement home and were not sufficient to characterise the house as a farmhouse. In *Arnander v HMRC* (2006) the Special Commissioner held that a seven-bedroom Grade 2* listed manor house owned together with 187 acres of agricultural land failed to attract relief. In the final years of his life the deceased had entered into contract farming arrangements whereby he employed a land agent who was responsible for the farming activities. Although the deceased was the person in overall control of the agricultural business conducted on the land, he was not the farmer – that is the person who farmed the land on a day-to-day basis. This indicated the purpose of occupation of the house in which the deceased lived had changed and the house ceased to be the base from which the farm business was managed (the day to day management and all acts of farm husbandry being the sole responsibility of the contractors not the deceased). In *Arnander* the Special Commissioner made the following general comments on the meaning of the term 'farmhouse':

(i) the wording of the legislation makes it clear that the agricultural land is paramount: other things must be either ancillary or of a character appropriate to the land;

(ii) there is nothing to suggest that every farm must have a farmhouse; the reference in s 115(2) is to farmhouses generally;

(iii) a farmhouse is a dwelling for the farmer from which the farm is managed (*Rosser*) and the farmer of the land is the person who farms it on a day to day basis rather than the person who is in overall control of the agricultural business conducted on the farm (*Antrobus*);

(iv) the status of the occupier is not the test, rather it is the purpose of the occupation that is relevant;

(v) whether a building is a farmhouse is a matter of fact to be decided on the circumstances of each case and according to the ordinary ideas of what is appropriate in terms of size, content and layout in the context of the particular farm buildings and the area farmed.

A building is therefore likely to be a farmhouse where the owner-occupant or the tenant-occupant is a working farmer who directs the day-to-day farming activities but not where the tenant is the working farmer who directs the day-to-day farming activities but the occupant of the farmhouse is the landowner.

Secondly, the farmhouse must be of a character and size appropriate to the agricultural land or pasture and the requirements of the farming activities conducted on the agricultural land (*Exor of Higginson v IRC* (2002)). This means that the house and the farmland must form an integral agricultural unit in which the land must predominate and where the farmhouse must be ancillary to the land. In that case the deceased who was a farmer lived in a lodge set in a landed estate of 134 acres. The lodge had been built in the nineteenth century as a hunting lodge and was not a typical farmhouse. After his death the lodge was sold for over £1m; the value of the farmland at the time was considerably less. This led to the conclusion that the lodge was not of a character appropriate to the agricultural land as the lodge had predominated. The amount for which the house was sold indicated that the deceased had made a poor farming investment and that the house predominated the land. It was a house with farmland going with it (and not vice versa).

The case of *Lloyds TSB (personal representatives of Antrobus dec'd) v IRC* (2002) (SpC 336) summarises the five principles established in earlier authorities for deciding whether a farmhouse is of a character appropriate to the agricultural property. Those principles are:

(i) whether the house was appropriate by reference to its size, content and layout, with the farm buildings and the particular area of farmland being farmed;

(ii) whether the house was proportionate in size and nature to the requirements of the farming activities conducted on the agricultural land or pasture in question;

(iii) although it might not be possible to describe a farmhouse which satisfied the 'character appropriate' test, the principle was that you would know one when you saw it;

(iv) whether the educated rural layman would regard the property as a house with land, or a farm; and

(v) how long the house in question had been associated with the agricultural property and whether there was a history of agricultural production.

In the *Arnander* case, the Special Commissioner added a further factor: the relationship between the value of the farm (and especially the house) and the profitability of the land. In that case the return from agriculture (of a few thousand pounds) did not provide a living income for a person who paid over £3m for the whole estate and so would not attract demand from a commercial farmer. This factor counted towards the denial of relief. In the *Antrobus* case the taxpayer was successful in showing that the farmhouse in question satisfied the above criteria. Similarly in *Golding v RCC* (2012) it was shown that the farmhouse was of a character approximately 16 acres of agricultural land so that agricultural property relief was available.

Thirdly, the farmhouse must have been owned and occupied for the qualifying periods set out in s 117 (which is discussed further under the next head).

It is the second condition above (ie the need for the character and size of the farmhouse to be appropriate to the agricultural land) that is particularly difficult to satisfy. In *Hanson v HMRC* (2012) the deceased held a farmhouse on trust for himself for life with remainder on trust for his son. The deceased moved out of the farmhouse and into a residential property next to the house, his son and family taking up residence in the farmhouse from which the son ran the farming operations. Part of the farm land was owned in part by the deceased; the rest was owned by his son. The farmhouse was counted as part of the deceased's estate but HMRC refused agricultural property relief in respect of it on the grounds that there was insufficient land within the *ownership* of the deceased to say that the farmhouse was occupied with the farm (and hence of a character appropriate to it). It was held by the First-tier Tribunal that the farm land by reference to which the appropriate character of the building was judged had to be in the same *occupation* as the building, not that the buildings were in the same ownership as the farm land. In this case the farm land owned by the deceased's son could be also taken into account in determining that the farmhouse qualified for relief as being of a character appropriate to the farm property. The decision of the First-tier Tribunal was confirmed by the Upper Tribunal in 2013. An earlier decision of the Special Commissioner in *Rosser v IRC* (2003) which held that the link between the farmhouse and the property which it served had to be one of ownership (rather than occupation) was not followed. In that case the Inland Revenue (as HMRC was known at the time) had refused a claim to agricultural property relief on a house and barn owned by the deceased. The case was subsequently referred to the Special Commissioners who allowed the appeal in part – the barn was of a character appropriate to the property and was owned and occupied for the relevant period. Relief was granted on the barn but not the house. The agricultural value (qualifying for agricultural property relief) of a farmhouse which is an historic building in an attractive location providing a residence independently of its merits as a farmhouse may be much lower than the open market value of the property. This is illustrated in *Lloyds TSB Private Banking Plc v Peter Twiddy (Inland Revenue Capital Taxes)* (10 October 2005, unreported), where the agricultural value was agreed at 30% less than its market value.

Qualifying conditions as to occupation and ownership

The agricultural property must, under s 117, at the time of the transfer have been either:

(i) occupied by the transferor for the purposes of agriculture throughout the period of *two years* ending with the date of the transfer or have replaced other agricultural property which, together with the replacement property, was occupied for agricultural purposes for at least two years out of the last five years ending with the date of transfer, or

(ii) owned by the transferor throughout the period of *seven years* ending with the date of transfer and occupied for the purposes of agriculture by him or another throughout that period. In the case of replacement property this condition is satisfied if the other property and the replacement property were owned by him and occupied for the purposes of agriculture by himself or another for at least seven years out of the period of ten years ending with the date of transfer.

Neither the two-year rule in (i) nor the seven-year rule in (ii) applies where:

- the property was eligible for agricultural property relief on an earlier transfer by virtue of which it became the property of the transferor on a subsequent transfer,
- either the earlier transfer or the subsequent transfer was made on the death of the transferor, and
- the property is occupied for agricultural purposes by the second transferor (or by the personal representative of the first transferor) at the date of the subsequent transfer (s 121).

The requirement that buildings are occupied for agricultural purposes is satisfied if they are occupied by the farmer himself, by his agent or are occupied under tenancy by a person employed solely for agricultural purposes, or by retired farm workers or their widow(er)s, and such occupation is a statutorily protected tenancy or the lease was granted to the employee for life as part of his/her terms of employment ('vicarious occupation'). A person does not occupy property where it has been let to a person who is not an employee of the landlord. However, actual ownership is essential; a mere intention to occupy is not sufficient (*Harrold v IRC* (1996)).

In the context of a farmhouse, the ownership and occupation conditions in s 117 have been considered in a number of cases. In *RCC v Atkinson and another* (2011) the deceased acquired a farm which included a farmhouse. He later built a bungalow on the farm in which he subsequently lived. He farmed the land in partnership with his son (and after his son's death, his daughter-in-law), granting a tenancy of the farm to the partnership. In 2002 the deceased became ill and was eventually moved to a care home where he died in 2006. While the deceased was in the care home his daughter-in-law and grandson attended the bungalow a few times a week to collect post, deal with frost and access the water supply system. The deceased returned to the bungalow occasionally in the period between 2002 and 2006. In that period he also discussed the farming operation at least once a week. HMRC refused a claim to APR on the bungalow (on the grounds that it had not been occupied for the purposes of agriculture at the time of his death) and this was upheld by the Upper Tribunal. The Tribunal held that the phrase 'occupied for the purposes of agriculture' implied a requirement that there be an objective connection between the residential use of a building and an agricultural purpose. Temporary non-occupation did not negate occupation for the purposes of the Act, and the question whether vacancy of a building negated occupation for the purposes of the Act was a matter of fact and degree. In this case the bungalow had not been the deceased's residence for over four years before his death and during that period there ceased to be any possibility of the deceased returning there. The occasional attendance of members of his family did not render their occupation of the bungalow for the purposes of agriculture. Once the deceased ceased to live in the bungalow the purpose of its occupation for agriculture ceased to be fulfilled. The continued limited use of the bungalow in the four-year period was not, on the facts of the case, occupation for the purposes of agriculture.

In *Dixon v IRC* (2002) the deceased owned a 60% interest in a property consisting of a cottage, garden and orchard with a total area of 0.6 acres. The orchard annually produced a small crop of fruit which was sold in the local market for about £70. Hens were kept in the orchard and the garden for their eggs and poultry meat. Occasionally the deceased kept geese. The neighbour was allowed to graze his ewes and lambs in the orchard which was quite overgrown. It was held that the cottage was not occupied for the purposes of agriculture. Although fruit growing and the use of land for grazing could be agriculture, whether those activities were or were not agriculture for the purposes of inheritance tax was a matter of fact and degree. In the case the scale of the activities were consistent with the conclusion that the property was occupied for the purposes of a private residence and not for agriculture. So for APR it is thought that there needs to be a business (that is the intention to make a profit although it is not a requirement that a profit actually be made (*Golding*)).

An individual who occupies a farmhouse where the farmland concerned is pasture that is grazed by others may satisfy the ownership and occupation conditions in s 117. In order to do so he must ensure that he carries on some activity on the land that amounts to husbandry. He must pay attention to the nature of any grazing agreement he enters into and the activities he contracts to perform under that agreement. What the individual must be able to show is that he is in occupation of the pasture and that his occupation is for the purposes of husbandry. In *CIR v Forsyth-Grant* 25 TC 369 it was noted that the laying down of grass in suitable parks, the manuring of the land so as produce a good crop and the arranging for the seasonal eating-off the grass by cattle brought on to the land are operations of husbandry. Although the growth of grass on a grass park does not require cultivation in the same sense as grain crops, the occupier conducts an agricultural operation if he carries on activities that are necessary to promote its growth such as manuring. In *McCall & anor (PRs of McClean dec'd) v HMRC* (2008) the taxpayer did not qualify for agricultural property relief because the grass being grazed had not been sown or grown in the manner of a crop. There were no acts of husbandry commensurate with growing the grass as a crop and accordingly no occupation of the land for the purposes of husbandry. Under the grazing agreement used in that case, the landowner merely performed such acts of maintenance that were necessary to exploit the land for grazing. Only the grazier was allowed to fertilise the land so as to maximise the growth of the grass. (Business property relief was not available in that case either – see **explanatory note 12 in Example A20**.) Hence it is important in satisfying the conditions of s 117 to have regard to the nature of the grazing agreement. Where the agreement is merely a species of tenancy rather than seasonal lets of grazing, agricultural property relief is unlikely to be available (*Drummond v CIR* 32 TC 263; *Bennison v Roper* 46 TC 613). The grazing agreement should ensure that the landowner and not the grazier is responsible for growing the crop and for acts of husbandry in that connection (eg fertilising, seeding and weeding the pasture). The landowner should actually go on to the land to perform these operations as well as being responsible for maintaining boundaries and water supply. In other words, the contract should be a pasturage agreement and not a farm business tenancy for grazing. It should not affect the relief as to the type of animal that grazes the land, although in the case of *Wheatley's Executors v CIR* [1998] SSCD 60 grazing by horses was held not to be an agricultural purpose (although being a decision of the Special Commissioners the case does not create precedent and it may be that it was wrongly decided in any event) and in *Hemens v Whitsbury Farm and Stud Ltd* [1987] 1 All ER 430 it was noted that zebras and bison grazing land at a zoo was not an agricultural operation.

In *Charnley and others v HMRC* [2019] UKFTT 650, the taxpayer died owning a farm which comprised the house in which he lived, a yard, brick barn and outbuildings, 21.19 acres of bare agricultural land (permanent pasture) and a range of buildings and a yard let for the storage of commercial grass cutting equipment. He also owned other property which consisted of permanent pasture, some land and storage buildings and a residential property which was let. He did not own any livestock but he allowed farmers to graze their animals on his land under annual grazing licences. He checked the livestock daily and carried out the husbandry and maintenance of the land. He grew vegetables on his farm and bartered them in the local shop. He claimed the single farm payment. The taxpayer's executors claimed agricultural property relief and business property relief (although not on the let property). HMRC refused the claim for agricultural property relief on everything except the agricultural land (ie the land used for grazing) and the claim for business property relief on the grounds that the business was one of investment in land rather than farming. In its view the farmhouse was not eligible for relief because in the last two years of his life, the individual was no longer farming the land attached to the property, but had rented it out for livestock grazing and was just maintaining it. The executors appealed arguing that the land, farmhouse and buildings were agricultural property as they were occupied by the deceased for the purposes and it was wrong to break down the farm into various discrete elements rather than considering the overall nature of the farm. The FTT allowed the appeal. It found that despite the deceased's age and infirmity, he was still a farmer engaged in farming at the time of his death. It said that the activities carried out by the taxpayer were and always had been those of a farmer, working an active farm. He may have gradually ceased to rear animals but this was not enough to alter the true nature of his work. The deceased had always been a farmer and continued to be, albeit having to adapt on account of his increasing years and frailty. The modification of the activities was not done to let the land or prepare it for letting or to improve it so as to increase his income (which activities would have been closer to those of an investor or a business in the letting of land). In relation to the pasture let on grazing licences, he would move the animals depending on the state of the land through the seasons. He was still repairing fences, controlling weeds and carrying out other maintenance work. His vehicles and equipment, stored in the outbuildings, were used for and in connection with working the land. This was all a continuation of his lifetime activities. The land used to grow vegetables was not a mere vegetable patch (as HMRC claimed) as that failed to take account of the history of the farm and the evidence that crops had been grown in the past. The legislation did not lay down a minimum requirement for crops produced. The farmhouse was occupied by an active farmer and so used for the purposes of agriculture. The FTT was of the view that an intelligent businessman would view the asset as a farming business being turned to account by the day-to-day farming carried out by the taxpayer with the additional component of some investment income being received. It concluded that the farmhouse and other buildings were occupied for the purpose of agriculture and the business was that of farming and not wholly or mainly the holding of investments.

Where the transferor becomes entitled to the agricultural property on the death of another person he is treated, for the purpose of the occupation/ownership requirements in s 117, as having owned it from the date of that person's death, and as having occupied it from that date provided he does in fact occupy it from some later date. Further, if that person was his spouse/civil partner, their respective periods of occupation and/or ownership are aggregated to determine whether the transferor meets those requirements (s 120).

For lifetime gifts, whether chargeable at the time they are made or potentially exempt, where the death of the donor occurs within seven years, agricultural property relief is only available for the purpose of calculating the tax or additional tax arising as a result of the death if under s 124A:

(a) the original property (or qualifying replacement property) has been owned by the transferee throughout the period beginning with the date of the chargeable transfer and ending with the death of the transferor, and

(b) immediately before the death of the donor the original property (or qualifying replacement property) is agricultural property in the hands of the transferee (ignoring the two-year and seven-year ownership/occupation rules above).

If the transferee dies before the donor then the property must qualify at the date of his death rather than the date of the donor's death (s 124A(4)).

Proportionate relief is available where only part of the property is owned at the date of death (s 124A(5)).

Annual exemptions and effect of donor's death within seven years

Where, at the date of the donor's death within seven years of a lifetime gift, the agricultural property is no longer owned by the donee, or is no longer occupied for agricultural purposes, corresponding clawback provisions apply as for business property relief in relation to disallowing the relief for the purpose of calculating the additional tax due by reason of that death (including the differing effects on the transferor's cumulative total according to whether the lifetime transfer was a potentially exempt transfer or an immediately chargeable transfer, and the interaction of these provisions with the donor's annual exemption) (see **Example A21 part A(c)**).

Similar provision is made for property that replaces all or part of the original property to satisfy the continuing ownership test provided the replacement property also qualifies as agricultural property, and provided the whole of the proceeds of the original property are used in the purchase of the replacement property within three years after the disposal of the original property, or such longer period as HMRC may allow (s 124B).

Business property relief on non-agricultural value

Where agricultural property also satisfies the conditions for business property relief, business property relief is available in respect of any part of the value transferred that does not qualify for agricultural property relief (s 114(1)). Since agricultural property relief is given only on the agricultural value of the agricultural property then business property relief where applicable will be given on any excess over that value. However, where only the 50%

rate of agricultural property relief applies, the relief has still been allowed on the whole of the agricultural value, and it appears to be only the excess of the market value over the agricultural value that will be eligible for business property relief by virtue of this provision (although this interpretation of the law is not shared by all practitioners).

Where agricultural property is replaced by business property, then provided the agricultural property is qualifying property for business property relief, the period of ownership of the agricultural property (in its character as relevant business property) will be taken into account in deciding whether the conditions for business property relief are satisfied. But in the case of a farming business carried on by a sole trader the farm land as such will not have been relevant business property, and so will not attract this replacement rule.

(b) *Transfer of shares or debentures in farming company*

Agricultural property relief is available on the transfer of shares or debentures in a farming company, provided the holding gave the transferor control of the company immediately before the transfer and the agricultural property forms part of the company's assets (s 119). Relief is given only on that part of the value of the holding that reflects the agricultural value of the underlying property. The rate of relief is 100% where the company occupies the property or where the property is let on a tenancy granted on or after 1 September 1995, and 50% for property let before that date, and the two year/seven year rules in (i) and (ii) in **part** (a) above apply as if the company were the transferor. (For this purpose the company is treated as having occupied the property at any time when it was occupied by a person who subsequently controls the company.) Furthermore the shares or securities must have been owned by the transferor throughout the two-year or seven-year period as the case may be.

Business property relief is available on the non-agricultural value of a holding where the relevant conditions are satisfied at 100% on holdings in unquoted farming companies and at 50% on quoted controlling holdings.

Agricultural property relief, like business property relief, is given automatically without the need for a claim.

(c) *Mitigation of inheritance tax through lease of land*

The immediately perceived advantage of the proposal is that the value of the freehold interest in the agricultural land will be reduced from £400,000 (200 × £2,000) to £280,000 (200 × £1,400) on the granting of the tenancy. This act by itself will not have any inheritance tax consequences provided the grant is for full consideration in money or money's worth (s 16).

Furthermore, the rate of agricultural property relief on tenanted property for tenancies granted on or after 1 September 1995 is 100% (compared to 50% if the tenancy dates from before then) so that unless there are adverse changes in the agricultural property relief provisions, there will be no disadvantage in terms of the rate of relief available. Unless the conditions for agricultural relief were no longer satisfied at the time of Arthur's death, there would therefore be no net value chargeable to inheritance tax at that time. If the conditions were not satisfied, then provided the property remained tenanted, the proposal would achieve the objective of reducing the value of the property in the death estate.

(d) *Inheritance tax payable on the death of X in July 2023*

		Chargeable transfer £	*Tax* £
Inheritance tax accumulation prior to death		Nil	Nil
Estate on death			
Freehold property — Greenacre — to son			
Agricultural value (tenanted)	479,000		
Less: 100% agricultural property relief (**explanatory note 13**)	(479,000)	Nil	Nil
Residue of estate to spouse — exempt		Nil	Nil

Inheritance tax payable on the death of Y in September 2023

	£	£
Greenacre (tenanted since 1980)	479,000	
Less: 50% agricultural property relief (**explanatory note 12**)	(239,500)	239,500
Interest in farming partnership (**explanatory note 12**)	60,000	
Less: 100% business property relief	(60,000)	Nil
Other assets		89,000
		328,500
Tax thereon (no lifetime transfers)		
(328,500 – 325,000 = 3,500 @ 40%)		£1,400

Explanatory Notes

Agricultural property relief legislation

(1) The provisions relating to agricultural property relief are contained in ss 115–124C.

(2) The main provisions are dealt with in the Example, other points of importance being covered in the following notes.

(3) Agricultural property relief is also available on the occasion of an exit charge and a ten yearly charge on a relevant property settlement and on the occasion of an exit charge from an 18-25 trust. For this purpose the trustees are deemed to be a transferor (ss 66, 103(1)(b), 115(1)(b)).

Agricultural value of agricultural property

(4) The agricultural value of property is its value ascertained on the assumption that it is subject to a perpetual covenant prohibiting its use otherwise than as agricultural property (s 115(3)). The relief does not therefore extend to any value in excess of the agricultural value as defined. For example, if the value of some land were £100,000 (because it was hoped that permission would shortly be forthcoming for its use as a caravan site), but the value of the land on the basis that it must be used perpetually for agriculture was £10,000, agricultural property relief would be available only on the lower amount of £10,000. Depending on the circumstances, business property relief may be available on the excess value (see **part B(a)** of the Example).

Occupation of agricultural property by company

(5) Occupation of agricultural property by a company controlled by the transferor is treated as occupation by the transferor for the purpose of the minimum two year period of occupation or seven year period of ownership (s 119(1)). For the meaning of control see the discussion in **Example A21 explanatory note 3.**

Hence agricultural property owned by a controlling shareholder and occupied by his farming company qualifies for relief.

Binding contract for sale: effect on agricultural property relief

(6) Property that is subject to a binding contract for sale at the time of a transfer is not agricultural property unless:

(a) the sale is to a company that is to carry on the business, the consideration being wholly or mainly shares or securities in the company which will give the transferor control of the company, or

(b) the property is shares or securities of a company and the sale is made for the purpose of reconstruction or amalgamation (s 124).

Where partners or company directors have entered into 'buy and sell' agreements whereby on their death their personal representatives are *obliged* to sell and the survivors *obliged* to buy the deceased's interest (funds often being provided by life assurance policies), such an agreement in HMRC's view constitutes a binding contract for sale and agricultural property relief is not available (Statement of Practice 12/80). If, however, a double option agreement is entered into under which the surviving partners or shareholders have an option to buy and the deceased's personal representatives an option to sell, such options to be exercised within a stated period after the partner's death, this does not cause agricultural property relief to be lost.

Other reliefs and exemptions: interaction with agricultural property relief

(7) Agricultural property relief is given before any exemptions since they apply to transfers of value (s 115(1)), such transfers being calculated before reliefs and exemptions (s 3(1)). In relation to potentially exempt transfers that become chargeable transfers, relief is not available unless the relevant conditions are satisfied at the time of death (s 124A(1)).

Gifts of agricultural property subject to a reservation

(8) Where a gift of agricultural property is subject to a reservation of benefit, then it has to satisfy two conditions to qualify for agricultural property relief. First, the property must have been agricultural property at the time of the gift. Secondly, at the time of the charge to tax (on the death of the donor or earlier release of the reservation within seven years before the donor's death) the property must have qualified for the relief (tested by reference to a notional disposal of it by the donee) (FA 1986 Sch 20 para 8). Where the requirements for 100% relief are satisfied at both stages, the fact that a gift of qualifying property was subject to a reservation will not result in any extra tax charge on death.

In order to test the donee's entitlement to relief, there are provisions to enable him to satisfy the occupation/ownership requirements by reference to the occupation/ownership of the donor (FA 1986 Sch 20 para 8).

For the gifts with reservation provisions see **Example B1**.

Pre 10 March 1981 transfers of agricultural property and transitional relief

(9) For transfers of agricultural property prior to 10 March 1981, agricultural property relief was 50% of the agricultural value of the agricultural property after reduction for exempt transfers. The relief had to be claimed within two years of the transfer and was limited to relief on £250,000 or on 1,000 acres, whichever was the greater (counting rough grazing land as one-sixth of its actual area).

In order to be eligible to claim relief the transferor had broadly to be a working farmer, although relief could still be claimed after the farmer retired, provided the property had been occupied for agricultural purposes by his family throughout the period between his retirement and the date of the transfer, either under a lease or under some informal arrangement.

Relief was not available on let agricultural land except where it was let to a member of the family (as above) or where it was let to a farming partnership of which the transferor was a member or to a farming company controlled by the transferor.

As a transitional measure, where the transferor has been beneficially entitled to his interest in the property since before 10 March 1981, he is entitled to 100% agricultural property relief provided the following conditions are satisfied:

(a) He would have been entitled to claim the (then) 50% agricultural property relief had he disposed of his interest before that date, and

(b) His interest did not at any time between 10 March 1981 and the date of transfer carry a right to vacant possession and did not fail to carry such a right through any act or deliberate omission of his.

Where the former relief would have been limited by reference to value or acreage, the 100% relief is available up to the limit and any excess agricultural value attracts relief at 50%.

Where a transferor has acquired agricultural property on the death of his spouse/civil partner on or after 10 March 1981, the transitional 100% relief is available where the spouse/civil partner satisfied condition (a) above and both spouses/civil partners satisfy condition **(b) above.**

These transitional provisions thus enable relief to be claimed on the first subsequent transfer at the 100% rather than the 50% rate by retired farmers whose families have continued to work the farm and by partners or controlling shareholders who let land to the partnership or company.

The transitional relief will not be relevant where a tenancy commences (or is re-granted) on or after 1 September 1995, because relief is now available on such tenanted property at the 100% rate in any event. Had Arthur in **part B(c)** of the Example not been entitled to the 100% relief under the normal provisions, he would not have been able to claim the transitional relief because he had the right to vacant possession after 9 March 1981 and before the transfer (on his death) on which relief is to be claimed.

Formation of partnership: inheritance tax effect

(10) The formation of a partnership between Arthur and his son would not give rise to any current or potential liability to inheritance tax provided that any reduction in the value of the estate of either resulted from an agreement that was not intended to confer any gratuitous benefit and was such as would have occurred in an agreement made at arm's length between unconnected persons (s 10).

Grant of agricultural tenancy: inheritance tax effect

(11) The grant of the tenancy of Whiteacre by Arthur in **part B(c)** of the Example will not give rise to any liability to inheritance tax because of the exclusion provided by s 16 for agricultural tenancies if the grant is made for full consideration. It should be noted, however, that the rent receivable by Arthur will be investment income whereas previously the income was earned income, being embraced in the profits of a farming business carried on by Arthur personally. This will reduce the Class 4 national insurance contributions payable, but will affect the future earnings on which Arthur can claim income tax relief for personal pension premiums (but note that a personal pension premium of up to £3,600 a year may be paid with basic rate tax relief at source by someone who has no earnings). If the tenancy were not granted for full rent, a charge to inheritance tax could arise on the reduction in the value of Arthur's estate and the 'gift' could be 'with reservation' as Arthur would still have a benefit in the land and accordingly could be valued at vacant possession value at the date of Arthur's death.

See **Example A12 part A** regarding the valuation of tenanted agricultural property.

(12) On the death of X in **part B(d)** of the Example, Greenacre qualifies for 100% relief because the tenancy was granted before 10 March 1981 and all of the conditions mentioned in **explanatory note 9** are satisfied.

On the death of Y Greenacre qualifies for relief even though Y only owned it for three months because the minimum occupation/ownership rules do not apply on a succession where all of the following conditions of s 121 are satisfied:

(i) The value transferred by the earlier transfer qualified for relief.

(ii) The property became that of the later transferor as a result of such an earlier transfer and at the time of the subsequent transfer was *occupied* by the later transferor or the personal representative of the earlier transferor for the purposes of agriculture.

(iii) The property would have qualified for relief if the normal minimum ownership and occupation conditions had been met.

(iv) Either the earlier or later transfer was a transfer on death.

Alternatively Y would still have qualified under the two year occupation test as Y occupied the land as a tenant farmer in the farming partnership for two years even though his ownership did not commence until the death of his father.

The rate of relief on Y's death is only 50%, because the tenancy was granted before 1 September 1995 and Y does not satisfy the conditions for the transitional relief, having not become the owner of Greenacre until his father's death.

Although Y's death is within twelve months of X's death, quick succession relief is not relevant because no tax was payable on X's estate.

In the example we are told that X's interest in the partnership is valued at £60,000 at the time of his death. This seems to assume that the (AHA) farm tenancy has no value in the partnership's hands, which wouldn't ordinarily be the case. Any such value would attract 100% APR at the partners' level, and the balance of the partnership assets would qualify for BPR. The net effect at the end of the day is nil in tax terms.

(13) The availability of 100% agricultural relief in relation to tenanted property was extended by FA 1996. Where a tenant dies on or after 1 September 1995 and someone else succeeds to the tenancy, the new tenancy is deemed to commence on the date of the first tenant's death. Accordingly, if the landlord dies after the death of the first tenant, but before the succession by the second tenant, 100% agricultural property relief is available on the landlord's death. 100% relief is similarly available where a succession to a tenancy is triggered by a notice of retirement given by the retiring tenant to the landlord, and the succession takes effect after the landlord's death (on or after 1 September 1995) and within 30 months of the notice (s 116(5A), (5B) and (5D)). Since the passing of the Regulatory Reform (Agricultural Tenancies) (England and Wales) Order 2006 (SI 2006/2805), a pre-1995 tenancy can be replaced by a new tenancy which gives the tenant the same protection as the old style Agricultural Holdings Act tenancies. So an agricultural landlord can agree a new tenancy with a secure tenant and increase his inheritance tax relief from 50% to 100%.

Deed of variation: effect on inheritance tax

(14) The tax on the death of Y in **part B(d)** of the Example (£1,400) could be avoided by a deed of variation under which the executors of X and of Y (with the agreement of Mrs X as beneficiary of Y's estate) agreed to vary the terms of X's will so that the freehold property devolved to X's widow instead of to Y. This would save the whole of the tax on the death of Y since his estate would then only amount to £89,000 (£239,500 for the farm property no longer being in his estate) which is within the nil-rate band.

The respective executors should have no reservations about this variation, since the estate of Y has in any event been left to his mother, who would simply take the farm property on the death of her husband rather than of her son. See **Example B6** for details of deeds of variation. HMRC accept that the variation rules can still apply where the ultimate destination of the property remains unchanged as here (IHTM 35042).

Furthermore the income tax 'pre-owned' asset rules will not impose an income tax charge on Y as FA 2004 Sch 15 para 16 provides that a party to a deed of variation is not taxed as a former owner simply because of having an interest which they have now signed away (Y's Executor signing on behalf of Y).

Exempt and partially exempt estates: effect on agricultural property relief

(15) Where agricultural property forms part of an estate at death, the benefit of the agricultural property relief will be lost if the property is left to an exempt beneficiary. Even if it is not left to an exempt beneficiary, part of the relief will be wasted where there are exempt legacies and the agricultural property forms part of the residue of the estate, rather than being left as a specific gift. This is because the relief is then regarded as applying to the whole estate, including the exempt part of it, so that again relief is wasted to the extent that it is allocated to the exempt legacies (s 39A). For further notes on this point see **Example A16 explanatory notes 6** to **9**.

Gifts out of and into trusts: availability of agricultural property relief

(16) Agricultural property relief is available on transfers of trust property provided the conditions are satisfied. For life interest trusts, the person with a qualifying interest in possession (see **Example C3**) is treated as the beneficial owner of the property (s 49) and when the interest comes to an end, he is treated as having made a transfer at that time (s 52). In other cases (including where an interest in possession is not within s 49 and hence is not a qualifying interest in possession), the relief is available when relevant property is transferred out of the trust and on the occasion of the ten yearly charge, the trustees being treated as the transferor (s 113) (see **Example C13 explanatory note 5**).

Detailed notes on the inheritance tax treatment of trusts are contained in **Examples C1 to C19**. See **Example C11** in particular for the treatment of agricultural property.

Various points need to be borne in mind when placing agricultural property into a trust, and the possible effects for the different types of trust need to be carefully considered.

(17) Before 22 March 2006, if property was placed into a life interest trust, the transfer was potentially exempt and would only become chargeable if the donor died within seven years after the transfer. If the property was agricultural property, the relief was taken into account in arriving at the amount of the potentially exempt transfer. The property needed to remain 'owned' by the life tenant (whether by virtue of the life interest or following its release to him absolutely) for two years before any transfer (or deemed transfer) by him would qualify for relief. This still applies where a person becomes entitled to a qualifying interest in possession (typically an immediate post-death interest or a disabled person's interest, though only the latter can result from a lifetime transfer – see **Example C3**).

If the donor dies within seven years after transferring the property to the trust, so that the potentially exempt transfer becomes a chargeable transfer, the trustees still need to hold the property at that time in order for the relief to be available. (If the donor died within two years this would not prevent the relief being available provided the property was still held in the trust.) If the trust does not satisfy the conditions at the donor's death, the relief is not available against the now chargeable transfer, and the donor's 'clock' of cumulative transfers will include that chargeable transfer.

(18) Since 22 March 2006, the lifetime transfer of property into any trust except one conferring a disabled person's interest is now an immediately chargeable transfer (at half of the rates of tax payable on death) after being reduced by agricultural property relief where available. The trustees need to retain the property for two years (or seven years as applicable) before being entitled to relief on any appointments of the property out of the trust or on terms of a disabled person's interest; but any other appointment that results in the property remaining within the settlement can be made within that period without having to re-qualify for the relief. Furthermore, if there are any appointments of the property after that time but within ten years after the trust's creation, then although the relief is available on the transfer the *rate of tax* is based on the full value of the property when settled (see **Example C13 explanatory note 5**). This would not be a problem, however, if the property qualified in full for 100% relief, because the amount chargeable at that rate would be nil. If the donor dies within seven years after the transfer, the tax on the lifetime transfer is recalculated on the death scale, additional tax being payable accordingly. As with life interest trusts, the trustees still need to hold the property when the donor dies in order for the relief to remain available on the donor's transfer (and they would be entitled to the relief even if the donor died within two years provided the property was still held in the trust). If the trust does not satisfy the conditions for relief when the donor dies, the relief is not taken into account in calculating the additional tax on the lifetime transfer, but the amount of the donor's cumulative transfers would not be affected. Relief will not be available against the lifetime transfer to the trust because the trustees have disposed of the property between the time of the gift and the time of death.

Comparison of agricultural property relief with business property relief

(19) Agricultural property relief differs from business property relief in a number of respects:

(a) It applies only to agricultural land and to buildings occupied with that land; business property relief can apply to assets of all kinds used in a business to interests in partnerships to shares in companies.

(b) It applies only where the land and buildings have been occupied for the purpose of agriculture as well as owned for a minimum period; for business property relief only a minimum ownership period is needed.

(c) It takes only the agricultural value of land and buildings (as defined in **explanatory note** (4)) out of inheritance tax; business property relief applies to the full value of the assets that satisfy its conditions.

(20) However, it is usual for a claim for business property relief to be linked with a claim for agricultural property relief. The reliefs act in tandem and must be considered together – for example:

(a) Many assets of a farming business (eg farm vehicles, stock and cash) do not qualify for agricultural property relief but will often obtain business property relief.

(b) Woodland (which on its own does not qualify for agricultural property relief) may qualify for business property relief.

(c) Land and buildings no longer used for agricultural property may still qualify for business property relief (eg former farmworkers' cottages now let to third parties). The same may be true of buildings used for the intensive rearing of animals if no land is occupied with the buildings.

(d) Where the market value of farmland and associated buildings is more than their agricultural value (eg they have development potential or hope value), the excess may be eligible for business property relief.

(e) Where farmers and landowners have diversified their activities to increase the amount of income derived from their property such a installing wind turbines and photovoltaic electricity generating units. Such units and turbines used within the farming business would be eligible for business property relief and to units used to generate power that is sold to third parties as a separate trading activity.

Agricultural property relief and the residence nil-rate band

(21) The availability and operation of the residence nil-rate band (RNRB) is explained fully in **Example A2 part b**. In calculating the amount of a deceased individual's estate (E) for the purposes of computing the maximum amount of RNRB that it is entitled to (under Step 1 of the method statement set out therein), agricultural property relief is ignored. The amount of the RNRB that is to be used in computing IHT (under Step 2 of the method statement set out therein) is the lower of the maximum RNRB available to the deceased and the chargeable value of the proportion of the deceased's home that is included in his estate and that is closely inherited. It is the value of the deceased's home that has been included in his estate (VT) (ie the value of the home chargeable to inheritance tax) that is used in this context; this means its value after taking agricultural property relief into account (see **Example A2 explanatory note 5**).

Question

(a) In relation to inheritance tax there is a statutory duty laid on solicitors, accountants and other professional persons (except barristers) to make a return to the Board of HMRC when they have been acting in a professional capacity on behalf of a settlor in certain given circumstances.

When does that statutory duty arise and what are its limitations?

(b) A client who has undertaken to discharge any inheritance tax payable informs you that he has received a Notice of Determination from HMRC in which it is specified that the value of a holding of 2,500 shares in T Ltd (representing 25% of the equity) which he had transferred to a discretionary settlement, has been determined at £20 per share.

If your client considers that the value of the shares is not more than £5 each, what advice would you offer?

(c) As in (b) above, a client who has undertaken to discharge any inheritance tax payable informs you that he has received a Notice of Determination from HMRC in which it is specified that the value of a plot of land (Blackacre), transferred to the trustees of a discretionary settlement, should be £250,000.

If your client considers that the value of Blackacre is overstated in the Notice of Determination, what further advice would you offer?

(d) When and in what circumstances is it possible to obtain a grant of representation to a deceased person without first delivering to HMRC a full Inheritance Tax Account (Form IHT400)?

How is the legal personal representative protected against any subsequent claim from HMRC for inheritance tax in connection with the death when a grant has been issued in this way, and in what circumstances is such protection lost?

Can he still be called on to complete an HMRC Account?

(e) When and in what circumstances is it necessary to render an account of transfers of value made during the lifetime of the transferor or charges relating to a relevant property trust?

(f) Briefly describe the rules requiring trustees to register trusts with HMRC.

Answer

(a) Duty to make return to HMRC in relation to settlements

IHTA 1984 s 218 provides that where any person, other than a barrister, has in the course of his trade or profession been concerned with the making of a settlement where the settlor is domiciled in the UK and the trustees are not or will not be resident in the UK, he must within three months of the making of the settlement make a return to the Board of HMRC. The return must state the names and addresses of the settlor and of the trustees.

For this purpose the trustees are regarded as non-resident unless the general administration of the settlement is carried on in the UK and the trustees or a majority of them are also resident in the UK (s 218(3)).

A return is not required where the settlement is created by a will (which would include a settlement created by deed of variation by a beneficiary otherwise absolutely entitled under the will, because of the deeming effect of s 142(1)), or where such a return has already been made by another person, for example the trustees (s 218(2)).

(b) Notice of Determination relating to value of shares

The client should be advised to appeal in writing against the determination of the value of the shares specified in the notice. The appeal must be made within 30 days of service of the notice and must state the client's grounds of appeal, ie that the true value of the shares is not more than £5 each (s 222(1)).

The appeal is made in the first instance by notice in writing given to the Board of HMRC. The client may then choose to notify the appeal direct to the tribunal under ss 223A, 223D, or to require HMRC to review the matter in question (ss 223A, 223B).

There is no set time limit for taking either of those steps provided the notice of appeal has been given to HMRC within the 30-day period mentioned; but HMRC can themselves offer to review the matter in which case the client will have 30 days in which to accept the offer of a review (or to notify the appeal to the tribunal), failing which he will be bound by HMRC's view of the matter as stated in their offer unless the tribunal gives permission for late notification of the appeal (ss 223C, 223H).

If a review is carried out by HMRC (after being required to do so by the client, or after he has accepted their offer of a review) and the client is dissatisfied with its conclusion as notified to him by HMRC, the client has 30 days (or longer if he can get permission from the tribunal) in which then to notify the appeal to the tribunal.

See generally **explanatory note 6** for more detail in relation to the procedure for appeals and reviews.

(c) Notice of Determination relating to value of land

The client should be advised to appeal in writing against the determination of the value of Blackacre as described in **(b) above**. However, because the matter in dispute relates to the value of land in the United Kingdom, it may be notified at the appropriate stage to the 'appropriate tribunal' in the first instance (the Upper Tribunal (Lands Chamber) for land in England and Wales, or the Lands Tribunal for Scotland or the Lands Tribunal for Northern Ireland for land in those respective jurisdictions). Even if it is notified to the First-tier Tribunal, any dispute as to the value of land in the UK must anyway be determined on a reference to the 'appropriate tribunal' (ss 222(4A)–(4B)).

(d) Grant of representation to deceased's estate, exempt and excepted estates

In order to obtain a grant of representation, personal representatives complete a Probate Summary in the form of supplementary page IHT421 to the HMRC Inheritance Tax Account (Form IHT400). The HMRC account (with the probate summary) must be sent to HMRC Inheritance Tax and the inheritance tax on the non-instalment property (together with any instalments that have already fallen due in respect of instalment-option property) must be paid before the grant is issued. The probate registry will not issue the grant until they have received the probate summary stamped by HMRC to confirm the above duties have been discharged.

Excepted estates

The requirement for an HMRC account to be submitted is relaxed by regulations issued under the provisions of s 256(1). The regulations enable a grant of representation to be issued without the completion of an HMRC account in the case of excepted estates. The procedures are explained in HMRC's Customer Guide to Inheritance Tax.

In relation to deaths occurring before 1 January 2022, to apply for a grant of representation for an excepted estate the personal representative completes instead a Return of Estate Information, Form IHT205(2011) (Form C5 in Scotland) or Form IHT 207 for those domiciled abroad. The form is sent directly to the Probate Registry. This requirement has been removed for deaths on or after 1 January 2022, with the relevant IHT information being captured within the probate forms (or the online application process).

An estate is an excepted estate where the conditions set out below are satisfied, unless the deceased had made a gift with reservation of benefit which either continued until death or ceased within seven years before death.

There are three types of excepted estate set out in the Inheritance Tax (Delivery of Accounts) (Excepted Estates) Regulations 2004 (SI 2004/2543) (applicable from 1 November 2004 with respect to deaths on or after 6 April 2004) as amended with respect to deaths on or after 1 September 2006 by SI 2006/2141, for deaths on or after 6 April 2010 (or, as to certain provisions, 1 March 2011) by SI 2011/214 for deaths on or after 1 April 2014 by SI 2014/488, and for deaths on or after 1 January 2022 by SI 2021/1167. The three types of excepted estate are: low value excepted estates; exempt excepted estates and excepted estates of foreign domiciliaries. The description of the three types of excepted estate set out immediately below are those that apply in relation to deaths occurring on or after 1 January 2022 (see **explanatory note 6** for the relevant descriptions of excepted estate in relation to deaths occurring before that date).

(A) Low value excepted estates: under reg 4(2) the conditions are:

(i) the deceased was domiciled in the UK at the date of death;

(ii) the estate consists only of property passing under the deceased's will or intestacy or under a trust, nominated property, or joint property passing by survivorship;

(iii) where any trust assets were held in a single trust in which the deceased had an interest in possession, they had a value not exceeding £250,000;

(iv) not more than £100,000 of the estate represents the value of property situated outside the UK;

(v) the deceased died without having made any chargeable transfers in the seven years before his death except cash, quoted shares or quoted securities, or land and buildings (and contents), with a total gross value not exceeding £250,000. For the purpose of this test alone:

- business property relief and agricultural property relief are disregarded, and
- transfers totalling more than £3,000 in any tax year which are claimed to be exempt transfers by virtue of the normal expenditure out of income exemption must be counted as though they were chargeable transfers;

(vi) the gross value of the estate did not exceed the general nil-rate band in force at the date of death, or where the criteria set out below are met, the general nil-rate band together with the transferrable nil-rate band in force at the date of death. The residence nil-rate band has no application in the context of the excepted estates regulations. For this purpose, the gross value of an estate includes:

- exempt transfers to a spouse/civil partner, charities, political parties, housing associations, historic buildings maintenance funds and employee trusts within seven years of death; and
- chargeable transfers within seven years of death of cash, quoted shares or quoted securities, or land and buildings (and contents). In relation to valuing those chargeable transfers, business property relief and agricultural property relief is disregarded and transfers totalling more than £3,000 in any tax year which are claimed to be exempt transfers by virtue of the normal expenditure out of income exemption must be counted as though they were chargeable transfers.

(B) Exempt excepted estates: under reg 4(3) the conditions are:

(i) the deceased was domiciled in the UK at the date of death;

(ii) the estate consists only of property passing under the deceased's will or intestacy or under a trust, nominated property, or joint property passing by survivorship;

(iii) where any trust assets were held in a single trust in which the deceased had an interest in possession, they had a value not exceeding £1,000,000, and of those trust assets, not more than £250,000 was attributable to property other than property transferred on that person's death by a spouse, civil partner or charity transfer;

(iv) not more than £100,000 of the estate represents the value of property situated outside the UK;

(v) the deceased died without having made any chargeable transfers in the seven years before his death except cash, quoted shares or quoted securities, or land and buildings (and contents), with a total gross value not exceeding £250,000. For the purpose of this test alone:

- business property relief and agricultural property relief are disregarded, and
- transfers totalling more than £3,000 in any tax year which are claimed to be exempt transfers by virtue of the normal expenditure out of income exemption must be counted as though they were chargeable transfers;

(vi) the gross value of chargeable assets of the estate (before deducting liabilities, reliefs or exemptions), does not exceed £3,000,000. For this purpose, the gross value of an estate includes:

- exempt transfers to a spouse/civil partner, charities, political parties, housing associations, historic buildings maintenance funds and employee trusts within seven years of death, and
- chargeable transfers within seven years of death of cash, quoted shares or quoted securities, or land and buildings (and contents). In relation to valuing those chargeable transfers, business property relief and agricultural property relief is disregarded and transfers totalling more than £3,000 in any tax year which are claimed to be exempt transfers by virtue of the normal expenditure out of income exemption must be counted as though they were chargeable transfers;

(vii) the total value transferred on the deceased's death to a spouse, civil partner or charity is greater than nil; and

(viii) the net qualifying value of the estate does not exceed the general nil-rate band in force at the date of death or the general nil-rate band together with the transferrable nil-rate band in force at the date of death. The residence nil-rate band has no application in the context of the excepted estates regulations. For this purpose the net qualifying value of an estate is the gross value of the estate (as defined in (vi) above) after deduction of spouse/civil partner and charity exemptions together with the total liabilities of the estate. The total liabilities of the estate that may be deducted in calculating the net chargeable estate do not include those not discharged after death, those attributable to financing excluded property and those which are prevented from being taken into account by any other provisions.

(C) Excepted estates for foreign domiciliaries: Under reg 4(5) the conditions are:

(i) the deceased was never domiciled (or deemed domiciled) in the UK;

(ii) the deceased was neither entitled to shares in an overseas close company nor the creditor of an overseas sited loan, which assets are treated as non-excluded property under Sch A1 (companies owning or loans relating to UK residential property);

(iii) the deceased died without have made any chargeable transfers in the period of seven years before his death (noting that transfers totalling more than £3,000 in any tax year which are claimed to be exempt transfers by virtue of the normal expenditure out of income exemption must be counted as though they were chargeable transfers);

(iv) the estate consists only of cash or quoted shares which pass by will, intestacy or survivorship;

(v) the estate's gross value does not exceed £150,000.

In the context of A(vi) and B(viii) above, the general nil-rate band in force at the date of the deceased's death is increased by the amount of any transferable nil-rate band. However, this will be the case only where the following criteria are met (reg 5A):

- the deceased was the spouse or civil partner of another person immediately before the death of that other person (the 'first deceased person');
- the deceased had survived the first deceased person;
- the first deceased person died on or after 13 November 1974 (where he was the spouse of the deceased) or the first deceased person died on or after 5 December 2005 (where he was the civil partner of the deceased);
- a claim is made pursuant to IHTA 1984 s 8A by virtue of which the nil-rate band at the time of the deceased's death is treated as increased by the percentage computed under that section and the claim is made in respect of not more than one first deceased person;
- the first deceased person died domiciled in the UK;
- the value of the first deceased person's estate is attributable wholly to property passing under his will or intestacy or by survivorship in a beneficial joint tenancy;
- of that property not more than £100,000 represented value attributable to property which immediately before the first deceased person's death was situated outside the UK;
- the first deceased person died without having made any chargeable transfers during the period of seven years ending with his death (business property relief and agricultural property relief being ignored in determining whether he made a transfer of value; also, in relation to death on or after 1 March 2011, transfers made less than seven years prior to his death totalling more than £3,000 in any tax year which are claimed to be exempt transfers by virtue of the normal expenditure out of income exemption must be counted as though they were chargeable transfers); and
- the value transferred by any chargeable transfer made on the death of the first deceased person was not reduced by virtue of business property relief or agricultural property relief.

Where the excepted estates regulations apply so that no HMRC accounts has to be submitted, the person responsible for submitting the account must nevertheless provide the probate registry (or sheriff in Scotland or probate and matrimonial officer in Northern Ireland) (reg 7) with the information set out in regs 6 or 6A (the latter regulation applying to individuals who die domiciled abroad).

In relation to low value estates and excepted estates for UK domiciliaries, the information required is the full name and date of death of the deceased and, in relation to their estate, its IHT gross and net values (as defined above), its net qualifying value (as defined above) and a declaration that the estate is an excepted estate.

In relation to excepted estates of individuals domiciled abroad, the information required is the full name, date of death, marital/civil partnership status, occupation, domicile and address of the deceased, whether they have any surviving spouse/civil partner, parent or sibling, the number of their surviving children, step-children, adopted children or grandchildren and details (including value) of all cash and quoted shares or securities situated in the United Kingdom to which the deceased was beneficially entitled and the liabilities of the estate which fall to be discharged in the United Kingdom.

Reduced accounts

As explained above, the requirement for an HMRC account to be submitted is relaxed by regulations issued under the provisions of s 256(1) so that a grant of representation may be issued without the completion of an HMRC account in the case of excepted estates.

Also, where because of exemptions some or all of an estate is exempt, personal representatives are able to deliver a 'reduced' Inheritance Tax Account.

The qualification and procedure for reduced accounts can be found on page 5 of HMRC's 'Guide to Completing your Inheritance Tax Account (IHT400 Notes)'. In brief, the estate qualifies if:

(a) the deceased was UK domiciled;

(b) some, or all of the property passing by Will or intestacy, passes to an 'exempt beneficiary', viz either absolutely or on an interest in possession trust for a surviving spouse, or to become the property of an exempt body (eg the National Trust) or of a charity; and

(c) the gross value of property passing by Will or intestacy to chargeable beneficiaries, together with other property chargeable on death and any chargeable lifetime transfers, does not in total exceed the IHT nil-rate band (together with unused nil-rate band transferred to the deceased if a claim for the transfer has been made). This will include the deceased's share of any jointly owned assets, any assets chargeable under the reservation of benefit regime and any assets outside the UK which do not pass under the UK Will or intestacy.

Where the reduced account procedure applies, only certain parts of IHT400, as listed on page 6 of HMRC's guide, have to be completed, together with any schedules which apply to the assets for which the grant is required. Note in this connection that the gross value of an asset is the value before deducting liabilities, reliefs or exemptions.

Protection from liability to inheritance tax

After 60 days (the 'prescribed period') (35 days in Scotland) from the issue of the grant all persons potentially liable for inheritance tax in respect of the excepted estate are automatically discharged from liability and any charge for such tax on any property comprised in the estate is removed.

The protection is lost:

(1) in the case of fraud or failure to disclose material facts; or

(2) if it subsequently comes to light that there is further property which causes the excepted estate conditions not to be satisfied (eg the gross value exceeds £1,000,000, or other property exceeds the stipulated limits); or

(3) if within the 'prescribed period' a notice in writing is issued by HMRC to the personal representatives requiring delivery of an HMRC account.

If it is discovered at any time that the estate is not an excepted estate then the personal representative must deliver a Corrective Account (C4) to HMRC within six months of the discovery (see **Example A9**).

If an estate ceases to be an excepted estate because of a deed of variation then the personal representatives should deliver a full IHT400 so the estate can be properly considered (IHTM06034).

(e) Rendering an account of lifetime transfers of value or charges under a relevant property trust

Under section 216 persons liable to inheritance tax are required to submit an account in respect of *chargeable transfers* made in lifetime, or occasions of charge under the regime for relevant property trusts that occur before 6 April 2014 (using form IHT100 in both cases), before the end of twelve months from the end of the month in which the transfer is made or occasion occurs, unless:

(i) another liable person has already done so (s 216(5)); or

(ii) one of the exceptions in 1 to 3 below applies and HMRC have not served notice requiring the delivery of the account.

In relation to occasions of charge under the regime for relevant property trusts that occur on or after 6 April 2014, an account must be submitted before the end of six months from the end of the month in which the occasion concerned occurs.

Whilst a potentially exempt transfer is a transfer of value, it is not a chargeable transfer unless the transferor dies within seven years. Accordingly there is no requirement to notify HMRC Inheritance Tax on the making of such a transfer – still less on the making of an exempt transfer. On the death of the transferor the transferee is primarily liable for any inheritance tax on a potentially exempt transfer and is obliged to submit an account (using form IHT100) within twelve months from the end of the month in which the transferor died (s 216(6)). The personal representatives of the transferor have a secondary liability for any inheritance tax arising, and they are required under s 216 to give details of all chargeable transfers made by the deceased with the seven years before his death. If they cannot establish the exact value of any property, the account may contain a provisional figure, but they must undertake to deliver a further account as soon as the exact amount is ascertained.

Where, on the death of the donor, a person holds property subject to a reservation of benefit (or that person holds property in respect of which the reservation was released within seven years of the death of the donor) that person must deliver to the Board an account of such property within twelve months from the end of the month in which the donor died using form IHT100 (s 216(6)(ab)).

If someone who has submitted an account discovers that it is materially incorrect, he must submit an amended account within six months after the discovery of the defect (s 217).

In the same way as for excepted estates (see **(d) above**), several exceptions have been prescribed in relation to the obligation to deliver accounts other than on death, by regulations made by HMRC under s 256:

(1) **Excepted transfers**

A chargeable transfer made on or after 6 April 2007 is an excepted transfer under SI 2008/605 reg 4, if the value transferred (when added to the values transferred by previous chargeable transfers by the transferor within the preceding seven years):

(i) does not exceed the general nil-rate band for the time being (the residence nil-rate band has no application in the context of these regulations), and the value transferred is attributable only to cash and/or quoted shares or securities; or

(ii) does not exceed 80% of the general nil-rate band for the time being (the residence nil-rate band has no application in the context of these regulations), and the value transferred (before available exemptions and disregarding business and agricultural property reliefs) does not exceed the hitherto unused part of the general nil-rate band.

(2) **Excepted terminations**

The termination of qualifying interest in possession in settled property is an excepted termination under SI 2008/605 reg 5, if the value transferred in consequence of the termination (disregarding business and agricultural property reliefs):

(i) (when added to the values transferred by previous chargeable transfers by the transferor within the preceding seven years) does not exceed the general nil-rate band for the time being (the residence nil-rate band has no application in the context of these regulations), and the value of the property in which the interest subsisted is attributable only to cash and/or quoted shares or securities; or

(ii) (when added to the values transferred by previous chargeable transfers by the transferor within the preceding seven years) does not exceed 80% of the general nil-rate band for the time being (the residence nil-rate band has no application in the context of these regulations), and the value of the property in which the interest subsisted does not exceed the hitherto unused part of the transferor's general nil-rate band; or

(iii) does not exceed the amount of the transferor's available annual or marriage/civil partnership exemptions made available by him to the trustees by notice given to them within six months after the termination under s 57.

These provisions also apply to the termination of an interest in possession of a bereaved minor under a bereaved minor's trust within s 71A; but in practice a deemed transfer of value in such a case would be limited to the extremely rare case where the minor's interest in possession had subsisted since before 22 March 2006 and the beneficiary is still under age 18. The settled property does not form part of the minor's estate (s 49(1B)) but it appears to be envisaged that a deemed transfer of value under s 52 is still possible (even where a flat-rate exit charge under s 71B does not arise) if the interest comes to an end without the minor becoming absolutely entitled.

(3) **Excepted settlements**

A settlement is an excepted settlement for the purpose of any occasion of charge to inheritance tax arising under Part 3, Chapter 3 on or after 6 April 2007, under SI 2008/606 reg 4, if:

(i) no qualifying interest in possession subsists in the settlement immediately before the occasion of charge,

(ii) there are no related settlements (ie settlements created by the same settlor on the same day),

(iii) throughout the trust's existence the trustees have been UK resident (tested in terms of the general administration being ordinarily carried on in the UK and the trustees or a majority of them (and of each class of trustees if more than one) being UK resident), and

(iv) either:

(A) the assets have always comprised only cash of a value not exceeding £1,000 and the settlor has not added any capital to the trust after its creation (essentially covering pilot trusts) (reg 4(2)), or

(B) the settlor has at all times since making the settlement (until his death if he is no longer living) been domiciled in the UK, the charge arises under s 64 (ten-yearly charges for relevant property), s 65 (exit charges for relevant property) or s 71E ('good' exit charges for age 18-to-25 trusts), and the value transferred by the notional chargeable transfer used for ascertaining the rate of tax (disregarding all liabilities and reliefs) does not exceed 80% of the general nil-rate band for the time being (the residence nil-rate band has no application in the context of these regulations) (reg 4(3)–(8)).

In the case of an excepted termination or an excepted settlement (properly treated as such), and in the absence of fraud or a failure to disclose material facts, the trustees of the settlement (but not other liable parties) are discharged from liability for any tax on the event in question six months after its occurrence (and in the case of an excepted settlement any HMRC charge for the tax is extinguished) unless in the meantime HMRC have issued a notice requiring an account of the property concerned.

(f) The trust register

By virtue of The Money-Laundering, Terrorist Financing and Transfer of Funds (Information on the Payer) Regulations 2017 (SI 2017/692) HMRC is obliged to maintain a register of trusts (known as the Trust Registration Service – TRS) and trustees are required to provide information (updated as appropriate) for inclusion on the register. The regulations came into force on 26 June 2017. The register has two functions – to provide and maintain a register of beneficial ownership of certain defined trusts and the means for trustees to register trusts with HMRC in order to obtain a tax reference number and to deliver tax returns.

Under the regulations, 'taxable relevant trusts' must be registered. A relevant trust is an express UK trust or an express non-UK trust. An express trust is one created intentionally by the settlor whether inter vivos or by will (and so a trust created by operation of law, such as a resulting trust or a constructive trust, does not have to be registered). A UK trust is one where all the trustees are UK resident or, in the case of trustees with mixed residence status, where at least one trustee is UK resident and the settlor was resident when the trust was settled or funds added to it. A non-UK trust is not such a trust. All such relevant trusts must however be taxable in order to be registerable – they must have income or assets in the UK on which they are liable to income tax, capital gains tax, inheritance tax, stamp duty land tax (or their Scottish or Welsh equivalents) or stamp duty reserve tax. Hence trusts with wholly non-UK resident trustees only need to register if they have such a UK tax liability.

By virtue of The Money-Laundering and Terrorist Financing (Amendment) (EU Exit) Regulations 2020 (SI 2020/991) which came into effect on 20 October 2020, the requirement to register is extended to all relevant trusts (and not just those with a UK tax liability), unless they are specifically excluded. In this context the definition of a 'relevant trust' under the 2017 regulations is extended. Consequently, as a result of the 2020 regulations, the following trusts are under an obligation to register on the HMRC Trust Register:

- UK and non-UK taxable relevant trusts (as per the original 2017 regulations);
- Type A trusts – non-taxable UK express trusts which are neither specifically excluded nor registered elsewhere in the EEA;
- Type B trusts – non-taxable non-UK express trusts which have at least one UK-resident trustee and which either acquire UK land or property, or enter into business relationship with a UK adviser (including a solicitor, tax adviser or accountant) who is subject to money laundering regulations and which are neither specifically excluded nor registered elsewhere in the EEA; and
- Type C trusts – non-taxable non-UK express trusts where all trustees are non-UK resident and which acquire UK land.

Excluded trusts in the context of Type A trusts are those that are considered low risk for money laundering or terrorist financing purposes or because information is held about them elsewhere. The full list of excluded trusts is set out in Schedule 3A to the 2017 regulations, including:

- trusts which arise in commercial transactions, financial markets and for client monies;
- trusts imposed by legislation (eg under the intestacy rules);
- trusts imposed by court order (eg on divorce or to hold compensation payments);
- pension scheme trusts;
- trusts of insurance policies which pay out on death (provided it is within two years of death), terminal illness, permanent disablement or to meet healthcare costs;
- charitable trusts (both registered and unregistered);
- trusts where the only beneficiaries are disabled persons;
- pilot trusts created before 6 October 2020 with assets of less than £100 (pilot trusts set up on or after 6 October 2020 will therefore have to register);
- trusts having effect on death (a will trust) provided they do not remain in existence for more than two years after the testator's death;
- trusts created by co-ownership of land or other property (where the trustees and beneficiaries are the same persons – but not where they are different persons); and
- trusts which meet certain legislative requirements (including employee benefit trusts, bereaved minors trusts (BMTs) and 18-25 trusts – see **Example C1**).

It will be noted that bare trusts are not excluded trusts and prima facie are registerable (unless they are bank accounts held for children or vulnerable persons). It is HMRC's view that unauthorised unit trusts must be registered if the relevant conditions are met.

The registration requirements can be very complex to apply in practice. It must be noted that trusts can, from time to time, move between being registerable trusts and being excluded trusts. Moreover, the categories of registerable trusts take priority over the excluded list, so that any trust which is excluded may become a registerable trust (for example) if it acquires a UK tax liability (and so needs to acquire a taxpayer reference number) – even if it is just a one-off tax payment. Take for example, a BMT with UK trustees created under a parent's will. It is thus an express trust and so a relevant trust for registration purposes. Although a BMT is on the excluded list, if the trustees, during the minority of the beneficiaries, acquire UK land and incur SDLT, the BMT becomes registerable by reason of having a tax liability. By contrast had the BMT arisen on the parent's intestacy, it arises by operation of law and is an excluded trust; moreover it is not a relevant trust – hence it is not registerable even were the trustees to acquire UK land and incur a UK tax liability. However, in the latter case, if the trust has UK income and the trustees are subject to the self-assessment rules, they will need a taxpayer reference number which can only be obtained if the trust is on the trust register. In this case, however, the reporting obligations under the 2017 regulations will not apply to such a trust.

Taxable trusts created on or after 6 April 2021 must register on or before 1 September 2022 or within 90 days of their creation or within two years after death in the case of a will trust (whichever is the later). The time when taxable trusts created before that date must register is more complex and depends on the type of tax payable and whether the trust has been liable to income tax or capital gains tax before. Where such a trust becomes liable to income tax or capital gains tax for the first time, it must be registered on or before 5 October in the tax year following that in which the trust starts to receive income or makes a capital gain. Where such a trust has been liable to income tax or capital gains tax before, it must have been registered on or before 31 January in the tax year following that in which the trust receives any income or makes a capital gain. Where such a trust is liable to any of the other taxes that make it a taxable trust (eg IHT), it must be registered on or before 31 January in the tax year following that in which the trust has a tax liability. Finally, where such a trust is liable for more than one tax so that both of the above deadlines apply, it must be registered before the earlier of the two deadlines.

Non-taxable trusts created on or before 6 October 2020 must register on or before 1 September 2022 (and this applies even if the trust has come to an end). Non-taxable trusts created after 6 October 2020 must register on or before 1 September 2022 or within 90 days of their creation or within two years after death in the case of a will trust (whichever is the later).

Under the registration regulations taxable and non-taxable trusts are required to provide different types of information. However, both taxable trusts and non-taxable Type A trusts must provide details of its beneficial owners (ie settlor, trustees and beneficiaries) and controlling interests in entities in overseas countries outside the EEA. The practical aspects of trust registration is covered in a two-part article in Taxation dated 22 April 2021 and 6 May 2021 entitled 'What's next for the trust register' by H Thornley. The HMRC has also created a separate manual on trust registration on their website which contains further detailed information on the registration of trusts.

An HMRC summary note on trust registration (including the information that must be provided) may be found at: www.gov.uk/guidance/register-a-trust-as-a-trustee. Once registered a trust is under an obligation to notify HMRC of any changes to the information kept on the trust register or of the coming to an end of the trust. An HMRC summary note on a trust's obligation to maintain the accuracy of the trust register may be found at: www.gov.uk/guidance/manage-your-trusts-registration-service.

Penalties of £5,000 are levied for non-compliance with the registration and register maintenance rules.

Explanatory Notes

Accounts, returns and provision of other information for inheritance tax

(1) An *Account* is a document completed by a transferor (or other person liable for inheritance tax) providing details of a disposition or event to which a liability to inheritance tax may apply.

A *Return* is a document submitted by a person about transactions affecting others.

HMRC have powers to require a person to provide information and documents, although this does not extend to information in respect of which legal professional privilege exits. These powers are set out in FA 2008 Sch 36 (which came into force for the purposes of IHT by virtue of FA 2009 s 96(1) with effect from 1 April 2010) and are discussed in more detail in the companion publication to this work, **Tolley's Taxwise I 2023/24.**

Notice of Determination in the context of inheritance tax

(2) The Notice of Determination by the Board under s 221 dealt with in **part (b)** of the Example may be issued to the transferor, or to any person liable for any of the tax chargeable on the value transferred, or to anyone making a claim in respect of the value transferred.

The notice may specify all or any of the following:

(a) Date of transfer;

(b) Value transferred and value of any property to which the value transferred is wholly or partly attributable;

(c) Transferor;

(d) Tax chargeable and persons liable;

(e) Tax overpaid and date from which interest on overpayment will be added (and rate of interest);

(f) Any other relevant matter (s 221(1) and (2)).

(3) The determination of any fact relating to a transfer is to be in accordance with the account or return submitted if the Board is satisfied that it is correct but otherwise is to be made by the Board to the best of their judgment (s 221(3)).

Appeals against Notices of Determination and Reviews by HMRC in the context of inheritance tax

(4) Once notice of appeal has been given to HMRC within 30 days after service of a Notice of Determination, three possibilities arise (s 223A):

(a) the appellant requires a review by HMRC,

(b) HMRC offer a review, or

(c) the appellant notifies the appeal to the tribunal or (where the issue is the value of land in the UK) to the appropriate tribunal as referred to in **part** (e) of the Example.

Those possibilities are essentially mutually exclusive for the time being, but as will be seen the appellant regains the right to notify the appeal to the tribunal after a review by HMRC. Once a review by HMRC has been offered or required, no further HMRC review can be required or offered.

The tribunal to be notified will in principle be the First-tier Tribunal (Tax Chamber), but that tribunal may transfer to the Upper Tribunal a case that has been categorised as Complex (SI 2009/273 rule 28). However, appeals where the matters to be decided are substantially confined to questions of law may be notified direct to the High Court instead (provided it can at the relevant time still be notified to the tribunal) if either:

(i) it is agreed between the appellant and HMRC that the appeal will be to the High Court, or

(ii) the High Court gives leave on an application by the appellant (s 222(2) and (3)).

If the question to be determined by the tribunal turns on a question as to the value of land (for example, in **part** (b) of the Example, if the value of the shares turned on the value of land owned by the company) the tribunal may refer any question as to the value of land to the 'appropriate tribunal' (see **part** (c) of the Example), rather than the taxpayer being required to make a fresh appeal (s 222(4A)).

1. Review required by appellant

If the appellant requires HMRC to review the case they must within 30 days (or such longer period as is reasonable) notify the appellant of their view of the matter in question; HMRC then have 45 days (or longer as agreed) in which to notify the appellant of the conclusions of the review and their reasoning. If they fail to do so within that period, the review is treated as having upheld HMRC's view of the matter as initially notified in response to the appellant's requirement for review, but HMRC must still notify the appellant of the conclusion that the review is treated as having reached (ss 223B, 223E).

The appellant can then notify the appeal to the First-tier Tribunal within the 'post-review period' (or later if the tribunal gives permission). The post-review period is 30 days starting with the date of the document in which

HMRC give notice of the conclusion of their review, or (if they failed to do so within the time allowed) the period between expiry of HMRC's time limit for the review and 30 days after they notified the appellant of the deemed conclusion (s 223G).

2. Review offered by HMRC

If HMRC offer a review they must also notify the appellant of their view of the matter in question; the appellant then has 30 days in which to accept the offer of review, or to notify the appeal to the tribunal.

If the appellant does accept the offer of review then the review proceeds in the same way as if it had originally been required by the appellant (see **1 above**); the 45 day time limit for HMRC to notify their conclusions starts with the day when they received notification of the appellant's acceptance of the offer of review (s 223G).

If, on the other hand, the appellant fails to accept the offer within the time allowed then HMRC's view as notified is conclusive and the consequences are as if, on the date that they gave notice of that view, the tribunal had determined the appeal in accordance with the terms of HMRC's view (s 223C). The appellant is still able to notify the appeal to the tribunal, but only if the tribunal gives permission, which would be unlikely unless he could show good reason for having failed to accept the offer of review (s 223H).

3. Notification of appeal to the tribunal

As indicated in **part (b)** of the Example, there is no set time limit for notifying the appeal to the tribunal after giving notice of appeal to HMRC within the 30-day period from the Notice of Determination. The right to notify the tribunal is disapplied (temporarily) once HMRC have notified their view of the matter in response to a requirement for review under s 223B, or have offered a review (with their view) under s 223C; notification is then allowed only if permitted by ss 223G, 223H as referred to in **1** and **2 above** (s 223D(5)). The procedure is laid down in SI 2009/273 as amended.

Once the appeal has been notified to the tribunal, the tribunal is to decide the matter in question. It must confirm the determination (if relevant, as varied under s 223E on HMRC's review) unless the tribunal is satisfied that it ought to be varied (or further varied) or quashed (s 224).

(5) An appeal against a decision of the First-tier Tribunal (other than certain excluded decisions of a mainly procedural kind) may be made by either party to the Upper Tribunal, but only on a point of law that arises from that decision, and only with permission (from either such tribunal): Tribunals, Courts and Enforcement Act 2007 s 11. The procedure is laid down in SI 2008/2698 as amended.

A similar right of appeal – again only on a point of law and again only with permission – is available from the Upper Tribunal to the Court of Appeal (in Northern Ireland or England and Wales as the case may be, or in Scotland the Court of Session) under s 13 of the same Act.

Excepted estates for the purposes of inheritance tax

(6) Where an estate is an excepted estate the personal representatives will swear a revised form of oath stating that the gross value of the estate does not exceed the appropriate amount.

In relation to deaths occurring before 1 January 2022 the rules on the description of excepted estates are as follows:

(A) Low value excepted estates: under para 4(2) the conditions are:

(i) the deceased was domiciled in the UK at the date of death;

(ii) the estate consists only of property passing under the deceased's will or intestacy or under a trust, nominated property, or joint property passing by survivorship;

(iii) where any trust assets were held in a single trust in which the deceased had an interest in possession and had a value not exceeding £150,000;

(iv) not more than £100,000 represents the value of property situated outside the UK;

(v) the deceased died without having made any chargeable transfers in the seven years before his death except cash, quoted shares or quoted securities, or land and buildings (and contents), with a total gross value not exceeding £150,000. For the purpose of this test alone:

- business property relief and agricultural property relief are disregarded, and
- in relation to a death on or after 1 March 2011, transfers totalling more than £3,000 in any tax year which are claimed to be exempt transfers by virtue of the normal expenditure out of income exemption must be counted as though they were chargeable transfers (The Inheritance Tax (Delivery of Accounts) (Excepted Estates) (Amendment) Regulations 2011, SI 2011/214 reg 1(2));

(vi) the gross value of the estate did not exceed the general nil-rate band in force at the date of death the gross value of the estate plus transfers within seven years of death plus exempt transfers to spouse/civil partner, charities etc within seven years of death do not exceed the general nil-rate band in force at the date of death (or, for deaths occurring on or after 6 April 2010, double that amount if the further requirements below are satisfied). The residence nil-rate band has no application in the context of the excepted estates regulations.

(B) Exempt excepted estates: under para 4(3) the conditions are:

(i) the deceased was domiciled in the UK at the date of death;

(ii) the conditions set out in A above at (ii) to (v) apply;

(iii) the gross value of chargeable assets of the estate (before deducting liabilities, reliefs or exemptions), when added to the cumulative chargeable gifts made in the seven years before death, does not exceed £1,000,000;

(iv) (in relation to deaths on or after 1 March 2011) the total value transferred on the deceased's death to a spouse, civil partner or charity is greater than nil; and

(v) the net chargeable estate after deduction of spouse/civil partner and charity exemptions together with the total liabilities of the estate does not exceed the general nil-rate band in force at the date of death (or, for deaths occurring on or after 6 April 2010, double that amount if the further requirements below are satisfied). The residence nil-rate band has no application in the context of the excepted estates regulations. For deaths occurring on or after 1 April 2014 the total liabilities of the estate that may be deducted in calculating the net chargeable estate do not include those not discharged after death, those attributable to financing excluded property and those which are prevented from being taken into account by any other provisions (The Inheritance Tax (Delivery of Accounts) (Excepted Estates) (Amendment) Regulations 2014, SI 2014/488 reg 2).

(C) Excepted estates for foreign domiciliaries: under para 4(5) the conditions are:

(i) the deceased was domiciled in the UK at the date of death;

(ii) the estate consists only of cash or quoted shares which pass by will, intestacy or survivorship;

(iii) the estate's gross value does not exceed £150,000.

- the deceased was the spouse or civil partner of another person immediately before the death of that other person (the 'first deceased person');
- the deceased had survived the first deceased person;
- the first deceased person died on or after 13 November 1974 (where he was the spouse of the deceased) or the first deceased person died on or after 5 December 2005 (where he was the civil partner of the deceased);

- a claim is made pursuant to IHTA 1984 s 8A by virtue of which the nil-rate band at the time of the deceased's death is treated as increased by 100% and the claim is made in respect of not more than one first deceased person;
- the first deceased person died domiciled in the UK;
- the value of the first deceased person's estate is attributable wholly to property passing under his will or intestacy or by survivorship in a beneficial joint tenancy;
- of that property not more than £100,000 represented value attributable to property which immediately before the first deceased person's death was situated outside the UK;
- the first deceased person died without having made any chargeable transfers during the period of seven years ending with his death (business property relief and agricultural property relief being ignored in determining whether he made a transfer of value; also, in relation to death on or after 1 March 2011, transfers made less than seven years prior to his death totalling more than £3,000 in any tax year which are claimed to be exempt transfers by virtue of the normal expenditure out of income exemption must be counted as though they were chargeable transfers); and
- the value transferred by any chargeable transfer made on the death of the first deceased person was not reduced by virtue of business property relief or agricultural property relief.

In the context of A(vi) and B(v) above, the general nil-rate band in force at the date of the deceased's death is doubled for deaths occurring on or after 6 April 2010. However, this will be the case only where the following criteria are met:

See The Inheritance Tax (Delivery of Accounts) (Excepted Estates) Regulations 2004, SI 2004/2543 reg 5A as inserted by The Inheritance Tax (Delivery of Accounts) (Excepted Estates) (Amendment) Regulations 2011, SI 2011/214 reg 4.

Persons required to deliver an account for inheritance tax

(7) The provisions requiring those liable to inheritance tax in lifetime to render an account are dealt with in part (d) of the Example.

The personal representatives of a deceased person must deliver an account of all property which formed part of the estate at death unless the estate is an excepted estate. Where there are no personal representatives then:

(a) every person in whom property of the estate vests, or who is beneficially entitled to an interest in possession on or after the deceased's death, and

(b) where property passes to a settlement without an interest in possession, every person for whose benefit any of that property, or income from it, is applied

must deliver an account to the Board specifying the property in which he has an interest.

The account is submitted on HMRC account form IHT400. This is accompanied by a worksheet (IHT400 Calculation). HMRC produce additional materials in the form of IHT400 Notes – Guide to completing your Inheritance Tax account, IHT400 Helpsheet – Working out the interest on Inheritance Tax payments and IHT400 Rates and Tables.

Penalties regarding inheritance tax

(8) The penalty regime is discussed in **Example A7**.

In addition to that commentary it should be noted that for deeds of variation made on or after 1 August 2002 that give rise to an increase in the inheritance tax liability, s 245A has been amended by FA 2002 s 120 to include a penalty where personal representatives fail to send HMRC a copy of the variation and notify the amount of additional tax payable (see **Example B6 explanatory note 5**).

(9) Personal representatives should be aware that HMRC are taking a harsher attitude to the question of penalties where they consider that an HMRC Account containing estimated valuations has been submitted without the personal representatives having made 'the fullest enquiries that are reasonably practicable in the circumstances' as required by s 216(3A). In *Robertson v CIR* (2002), the Revenue (as HMRC was known at the time) sought to impose a penalty of £10,000 on an executor who had submitted an account within six weeks after the testator's death containing estimated figures which were later found to be substantially understated, even though corrective accounts had been submitted less than six months after the death. The Special Commissioners found in favour of the executor, commenting that the Revenue had wholly failed to show that the executor was guilty of negligence. He had acted in accordance with accepted practice in submitting estimated figures and making prompt arrangements for professional valuations. The Revenue were held to have acted wholly unreasonably and the executors were entitled to costs in connection with the hearing. Despite the executor's success in this case, it would be advisable for personal representatives to ensure that they have made all enquiries that are *reasonably practicable* before including estimated figures in HMRC Accounts.

Trusts involving UK land – additional registration requirement

(10) In addition to registering a trust with HMRC in pursuance of the Money Laundering regulations, certain trusts that own UK land may have to observe an additional reporting requirement. The Economic Crime (Transparency and Enforcement) Act 2022 creates the register of overseas entities (ROE) to be maintained by Companies House.

The Act requires non-UK incorporated legal entities (eg a trust which has non-UK incorporated company as one of its trustees) that acquire or sell UK land (or that already own UK land when the legislation comes into force) are required to register and provide information (which must be updated or re-confirmed annually) regarding their own beneficial owners (which may be individuals, companies, governments or other entities). Information must be given only in respect of those persons that, directly or indirectly, own more than 25% of the company's shares or voting rights, or have the right to appoint or remove a majority of the company's board of directors, or have the right to exercise significant control over the company. Registration is also required where a nominee holds land on behalf of the overseas corporate trustee.

Where the UK land is held by a non-UK incorporated company whose shares are owned by a trust, then the trust is the beneficial owner of the corporate entity. In this case, additional specific information on the trust itself must be provided when the company itself registers on the ROE. The additional information includes the identity of the settlor and beneficiaries and the date on which the trust was created.

Overseas entities must take reasonable steps to identify and obtain information about its beneficial owners. This includes giving an information notice to anyone the entity knows or has reason to believe is a beneficial owner of the entity. If the registerable owner is a trustee, the must confirm or correctly of the required information about the trust that is specified in the notice and supply any information that the notice states the entity does not already have.

Unless it is on the ROE, a non-UK company may not have its name registered by the Land Registry as the owner of UK land and so will not be able to sell or buy (or otherwise deal in) UK land. Where a non-UK incorporated company fails to register or provide updated information a criminal offence is committed which may result in penalties and imprisonment of the company's officers. Registered overseas companies (and other entities) will remain on the ROE until they have successfully applied to be removed once they are no longer the owner of UK land.

Further reading

(11) A useful article on accounting for IHT and associated matters may be found in *Taxation* magazine for 6 February 2020, entitled 'A higher burden', authored by Simon and Sharon McKie. An article by Charles Bradley in *Tax Adviser* for June 2022 explores the anomalies that arise in charging penalties in the context to inheritance tax.

(12) An article regarding the registration of employee benefit trusts (EBTs) and employee ownership trust (EOTs) may be found in *Tax Journal* for 4 March 2022, entitled 'HMRC's trust registration services: changes for employee trusts' by Liz Hunter and Graeme Whitfield. An article discussing whether certain types of trust (eg trusts of life policies, pilot trusts) are required to be registered may be found in *Taxation* for 10 March 2022, entitled 'The time is now' by John Woolley. An article discussing the penalties for failing to comply with the

trust registration and register maintenance formalities may be found in *Taxation* for 11 August 2022, entitled 'Trustees' duties' by John Woolley.

Question

A.

In relation to both capital gains tax and inheritance tax, summarise:

(i) the events giving rise to a charge;

(ii) the amount chargeable;

(iii) the rates of tax;

(iv) some common exemptions and reliefs;

(v) whether phasing of disposals is advantageous;

(vi) the advantages/disadvantages of lifetime disposals as compared to a transfer on death;

(vii) the benefits, if any, of an individual emigrating.

B.

Your client, Charles, a wealthy widower, is a director and majority shareholder in an unquoted trading company that was established many years ago.

His wife died suddenly 18 months ago, leaving her estate to Charles; it comprised shares in quoted companies and jewellery worth £175,000, together with life insurance policies, cash, and personal possessions with a combined value of £160,000. The quoted shares and jewellery have increased in value since her death, but the value of the personal possessions is broadly unchanged and the remaining assets remain in cash form.

Charles is aged 62 and is considering retiring within the next year or so. He is also considering disposing of some of his assets, either by sale or possibly by gift, but is undecided whether to dispose of them during his lifetime or by will on his death.

Taxation will be a major factor influencing his decision regarding the disposition of his assets, and he has stated that he wishes to minimise any tax liability arising.

He has estimated his total estate to have a value of approximately £1,180,000, including the assets left to him by his deceased wife, broadly comprised as follows:

His 70% shareholding in the unquoted family trading company, valued at £140,000.

His 18% shareholding in an unquoted company which supplies the family company, valued at £60,000, (the other shares being held by his brothers and sister).

The quoted shares and jewellery from his wife's estate, now worth a total of £225,000.

Other quoted shares valued at £108,000.

His private residence (which has always been in his sole ownership) valued at £495,000 (free of mortgage).

A plot of land on which he and his wife had planned to build a bungalow for their retirement valued at £40,000.

A whole of life insurance policy on his life with a market value of £40,000 and a surrender value of £36,000. He has been paying premiums of £750 per quarter on this policy for the past 14 years and the policy secures a minimum sum assured of £75,000.

Furniture, other jewellery and general personal possessions with a total value of £25,000, the highest value item being valued at £2,500.

Cash at bank, building society and at home – total value £232,000.

Private motor car valued at £9,000.

He has one daughter and two grandsons, one of whom joined him last year in the family company. None of these is a disabled person. He has also developed a considerable interest in Heartbeat (UK) – a registered charity.

Suggest any action that Charles might take, and any disposals he might make which would result in a nil or small tax liability, and which would reduce the tax payable on his eventual death.

Answer

A. Capital gains tax summary

(i) *Chargeable disposals*

The capital gains tax provisions apply to the disposal of chargeable assets during lifetime. No charge is made on death. 'Disposal' includes sales, gifts and loss or destruction of assets; chargeable assets are all forms of property other than those that are specifically exempt. Options, debts, currency other than sterling, and rights are included, but not betting winnings or damages for personal or professional injuries.

(ii) *Calculation of gain or loss*

A chargeable gain (or allowable loss) is calculated by comparing the value on disposal with the sum of the cost price, costs of acquisition and costs of sale. All assets owned on 31 March 1982 are deemed to have had a cost equivalent to their market value at that date, even if that is lower than the amount actually spent to acquire them. All gains are chargeable gains unless they are specifically declared to be exempt.

Treatment of losses

Chargeable gains are reduced by allowable losses of the same year before the annual exemption of the year of disposal is taken into account. The net gain arising is then reduced by allowable losses brought forward (or carried back from the year of death), but not so as to waste the annual exemption of the year of disposal.

(iii) *Rates of tax*

There are four main rates of capital gains tax (CGT) for individuals. In respect of gains arising on the disposal of residential property (whether in the UK or overseas), the rates of CGT are 18% and 28%. In respect of gains arising on the disposal of all other assets, the rates of CGT are 10% and 20%. All UK taxpayers whose Step 3 income equals or exceeds the UK basic rate limit of £37,700 (for 2023/24) will be liable at the 20% or 28% rates (as the case may be) on their chargeable gains. If their Step 3 income is less than the basic rate limit, they will be liable at the 10% or 18% rates (as the case may be) to the extent that their chargeable gains fall within the remainder of the basic rate band and, and at 20% or 28% (as the case may be) on any excess. For Scottish and Welsh taxpayers, the Scottish and Welsh rates and limits that apply to their non-savings non-dividend income have no bearing on the determination of the rates at which they pay capital gains tax on their chargeable gains.

If an individual has gains from both residential property and other property, he may choose which chargeable gains are subject to the appropriate lower rate of CGT, up to the unused amount of his basic rate band. For these purposes, the unused amount of the basic rate band is reduced by the amount of any gains that are taxed at the special CGT rate of 10% under business asset disposal relief or investors' relief. Gains which are not charged at a lower rate are charged at the higher rate appropriate to their nature. This means that any unused basic rate band can be used in the most beneficial way to reduce the amount of CGT charged.

The net chargeable gains for this purpose are the individual's chargeable gains for the year after deducting allowable losses (for the current year and any brought forward amount from earlier years) and the annual exemption. They also include any gains from earlier years in respect of which the charge was deferred, for example gains reinvested in shares under the Enterprise Investment Scheme (EIS), which, subject to conditions, can be deferred until, typically, the EIS shares are disposed of. To the extent that any such deferred gains were realised before the CGT reforms in FA 2008 Sch 1, the computation of those gains as made in the year they were realised is unaffected (so that they retain, where appropriate, the benefit of:

- indexation allowance,

- the 'kink test' for assets held at 31 March 1982 where the acquisition cost and other allowable expenditure incurred before that date exceeded the market value of the asset at that date, and
- halving relief where an asset was acquired before 31 March 1988 from a person who held that asset at 31 March 1982 and where some or all of the latter person's gain was, instead of being taxed on them at the time, deducted from the new owner's acquisition cost otherwise applicable – for example through hold-over relief).

Individuals' gains which qualify for business asset disposal relief (formerly known as entrepreneurs' relief) (see **Tolley's Taxwise I 2023/24**) are taxed instead at 10%, up to a maximum lifetime limit of £10 million (increased to this figure for 2011/12 and later years of assessment (TCGA 1992 s 169N)) but reduced again from 11 March 2020 to £1 million. This limit rose rapidly after business asset disposal relief (entrepreneurs' relief) was introduced with effect from 6 April 2008; it was initially £1 million; for disposals between 6 April 2010 and 22 June 2010 inclusive it was £2 million; for disposals between 23 June 2010 and 5 April 2011 it was £5 million; and for disposals between 6 April 2011 and 10 March 2020. If a disposal in one of those earlier periods which qualified in principle for entrepreneurs' relief gave rise to gains exceeding the limit then applicable, the excess was chargeable at the full rate then applicable and only the amount on which relief was in fact granted is taken into account against the subsequently increased lifetime limit. Individuals' gains which qualify for investors' relief (see **Tolley's Taxwise I 2023/24**) are also taxed instead at the rate of 10%, up to a maximum lifetime limit of £10 million (ss 169VC, 169VH) which limit is separate and distinct from that applicable to business asset disposal relief.

The rate of CGT for personal representatives and trustees is 28% in respect of gains arising on the disposal of residential property (whether sited in the UK or overseas) and 20% otherwise. However, for trustees only, if gains qualify for business asset disposal relief by reference to a beneficiary who has an interest in possession in the trust property (see **Example D3** for more rules applicable to trustees, which are much more restrictive than for individuals) then those gains, up to the applicable limit for the relief as explained in **Example D3**, are liable instead at 10%. Business asset disposal relief and investors' relief is not available to personal representatives. Investors' relief is available to trustees.

(iv) *Exemptions and reliefs*

Exemptions from capital gains tax include:

- A principal private residence (subject to certain conditions);
- Private motor cars (including vintage motor cars);
- Tangible movable assets (chattels) that are wasting assets, including racehorses, but excluding chattels used in a business on which capital allowances have been or could have been claimed;
- Other chattels (including business chattels) if sold for less than £6,000, subject to rules for sets (and with a degree of relief if the consideration exceeds that figure).

Reliefs include:

- Rollover relief enabling gains to be deferred when qualifying business assets are sold and replaced.
- Deferral relief when a gain is reinvested by a cash subscription for unquoted shares in a qualifying trading company under the enterprise investment scheme. The gain is deferred until, typically, the qualifying shares are sold or replaced.
- Gifts holdover relief enabling gains to be regarded as reducing the donee's acquisition cost for capital gains tax, in respect of gifts of business assets including shares in unquoted trading companies, agricultural land, shares giving 5% of the voting rights in a quoted trading company, or gifts which are the subject of an immediate chargeable transfer for inheritance tax (whether or not the inheritance tax computation produces an actual liability, and including occasions of charge that are within the extended meaning of chargeable transfer) or are prevented from being so by specific inheritance tax reliefs such as for bereaved minors' trusts or age 18-to-25 trusts.
- Gifts of assets to charities.

- Gifts of heritage property in relation to which suitable undertakings are given.

(v) *Advantages of phasing disposals*

By disposing of assets over a period of years a number of annual exemptions may be used. Note that any unused annual exemption cannot be carried forward, and unused losses cannot be carried back (except losses of the year of death, which may be carried back against gains in excess of the annual exemption in the three previous years, latest first). But this advantage of phasing disposals does not apply to disposals of chattels to the same person (or to connected persons or persons acting in concert) if they form part of a set.

(vi) *Disposals in lifetime or on death*

On death there is no charge to capital gains tax and there is an automatic uplift to market value at that time for those entitled to the assets, whereas a disposal in lifetime (whether gratuitous or otherwise) may give rise to a charge. If a gain has been rolled over or held over against the cost of qualifying replacement business assets owned by the taxpayer absolutely, the death of the taxpayer means that the gain never gets charged to tax unless the held over gain was claimed on transfer into a qualifying IIP trust or by by way of EIS investment by the trustees of such a trust. By contrast, where holdover relief has been claimed on a gift of an asset, the donee's capital gains tax cost is reduced as indicated in (iv), thus resulting in a potentially higher gain when the donee disposes of the asset at a profit.

The death of the donor following a lifetime gift which is comprises a disposal of an asset for capital gains tax purposes will not cause a revision to the donee's acquisition cost for the asset, however soon after the gift it occurs. However, if the gift itself, and/or the death of the donor within seven years after it, gives rise to a charge to inheritance tax in respect of the gift, then in some (but not all) circumstances the donee will obtain a deduction for that inheritance tax in computing his gain on an eventual disposal of the asset in question. The circumstances in which this deduction will be available are:

(a) Where the gift was an immediately chargeable transfer for inheritance tax (within TCGA 1992 s 260, which expressly excludes potentially chargeable transfers): s 260(7). If that condition is satisfied then the deduction is available (both for the tax initially chargeable and for any additional tax chargeable as a result of the donor's death – s 260(8)), whether or not hold-over relief under s 260(3) is claimed or indeed can be claimed (for example if the donee was non-UK resident at the date of the gift but is nevertheless chargeable to capital gains tax on his eventual disposal of the asset – eg through being UK resident by then, or by virtue of the asset being used by him in the UK for a trade carried on by him through a UK branch or agency). It is not even necessary that the inheritance tax should have been borne by the donee (so that a deduction will be available for inheritance tax paid by the donor). Any such deduction is however limited to the chargeable gain otherwise accruing on the donee's disposal, ie it cannot give rise to an allowable loss.

(b) Where the gift is of a business or agricultural asset on which hold-over relief is claimed and allowed under TCGA 1992 s 165 (extended by Sch 7 Pt 1). This section cannot apply where the gift was an immediately chargeable transfer for inheritance tax (s 165(3)(d)); but it does apply to potentially exempt transfers of such assets – with all necessary adjustments being made to the donee's capital gains tax position if the donor's death (within seven years of the gift) occurs after the donee's initial capital gains tax liability has been established (s 165(10), (11)). Again any deduction cannot give rise to an allowable loss.

It will be seen that a potentially exempt transfer will be outside either of these circumstances if it is not of a business or agricultural asset, or if hold-over relief in respect of such an asset is not, or cannot be, claimed. Where that is the case, the donee will obtain no relief against capital gains tax for any inheritance tax for which he may become liable in the event of the donor's death occurring within seven years after the gift.

(vii) *Effect of emigration*

Capital gains tax is chargeable on worldwide assets of taxpayers who are resident (or before 2013/14 ordinarily resident) in the UK, but subject to the remittance basis where claimed (or if in certain circumstances where no claim is needed) where the taxpayer is domiciled in a country other than the UK.

If a taxpayer ceases permanently to be resident (and before 2013/14 also ordinarily resident) in the UK then, subject to the exception mentioned below for UK-sited residential and non-residential property (and shares in property rich companies), he will not be liable to UK capital gains tax in future tax years unless the assets are situated in the UK and are used in a trade carried on in the UK. A charge can also occur on accrued gains on the export of a UK company or trust. The charge to capital gains tax has, with effect from 6 April 2015, been extended to non-UK resident persons who own and dispose of residential property situated in the UK (extended again to the disposal of all landed property and shares in UK property rich companies from 6 April 2019). For more detail on this see **Tolley's Taxwise I 2023/24.**

A taxpayer can therefore avoid UK capital gains tax by emigration if gains are realised in a tax year after he has become non-UK resident, except in relation to any UK land, shares in property rich companies and assets used in the UK for the purposes of a trade. In certain circumstances split year treatment can apply for an individual who emigrates, such that he is not chargeable in respect of disposals taking place in the remainder of the tax year in which he becomes non-UK resident. If, however, he were to return to the UK and to become resident within five calendar years after the date on which he becomes non-UK resident, gains on assets held on emigration that were realised while he was non-resident would be chargeable in the tax year of return. However, in order for this rule to apply the taxpayer must have been resident in the UK for four of the seven tax years before the year of departure, Any such gains realised in the tax year of departure (or the UK resident part of that year where split year treatment applies) would be taxed as gains of that tax year. The rules also prevent the exploitation of double tax agreements during the period of absence: if a taxpayer is resident in the UK, but under a double tax treaty would be treated as non-resident (such that a gain would be taxed at a low or nil-rate) then UK capital gains tax will be payable overriding the DTA provisions; but if a gain has been charged to tax in another country, and is also charged in the UK on the taxpayer's return within five years then the tax paid overseas is at least deductible from the UK liability.

Inheritance tax summary

The material discussed below is also covered (in more detail) in **Example A1** and **Example A4.**

(i) *Chargeable transfers*

Inheritance tax is chargeable on certain lifetime gifts (principally gifts to relevant property trusts (ie most trusts created inter vivos after 21 March 2006), on wealth at death, on certain transfers out of trust, and in respect of relevant property trusts at ten yearly intervals and on interim distributions of capital. If a taxpayer makes a lifetime gift to an individual (not being his spouse or civil partner), or to a trust that meets the restrictive requirements for creating one of the four types of disabled person's interest (see **Example C3**), then provided the donor survives the gift by seven years or more, it is not liable to inheritance tax. This is known as a potentially exempt transfer. All other lifetime gifts are immediately chargeable transfers, though if the amount of the gift (after any available reliefs or exemptions) falls within the taxpayer's available nil-rate band then no inheritance tax will actually be charged (subject to review if the taxpayer's death occurs within seven years of the gift). Certain gifts are totally exempt from tax (see **(iv) below**).

(ii) *Chargeable amount*

Where a lifetime gift is immediately chargeable, the chargeable amount is the difference between the value of the donor's estate before the transfer and its value after the transfer (the value in each case not necessarily being equal to the property's market value). The same applies to potentially exempt transfers to quantify the amount that is taxed if the donor dies within seven years. If the donor bears the inheritance tax then that tax will reduce the value of the estate after the transfer, increasing the chargeable transfer. This is known as grossing up the gift.

(iii) *Rates of tax*

Any *chargeable* transfers of the last seven years are added together. To that total is added the value of the current chargeable transfer, which is charged to tax as the highest part of the total. For 2023/24 there is no inheritance tax on the first £325,000 of cumulative transfers (the nil-rate band). Lifetime immediately chargeable transfers in excess of £325,000 are taxed at 20%, which is half of the full rate.

The nil-rate band is fixed at £325,000 until 2027/28 inclusive.

Potentially exempt gifts made within seven years before a donor's death become chargeable transfers on his death, with any chargeable transfers within the seven years before the gift also being taken into account in calculating the tax payable. The value taken into account is that at the time of the gift (as reduced for a fall in value where the relief in IHTA 1984 s 131 applies – see **Example A14**), but the rate of tax used is the full rate (currently 40% beyond the nil-rate threshold, the reduced rate of 36% not applying in this context), not the half rate. If the rate (taking account of the nil-rate band) is lower at the date of death than at the date of the gift then the rate at death is used for this purpose. If the gift was made more than three years before death then any tax payable on the gift is reduced by a taper relief, but this affects only the amount of tax not the amount of the gift as taken into account for taxing later chargeable transfers (including that on the death itself).

Where a transfer was chargeable in lifetime, and the donor dies within seven years, tax is recalculated at the full rate (that is 40%, the reduced rate of 36% not applying in this context, and again on the scale in force at the date of death if that is more beneficial than the scale in force at the date of the transfer), taper relief being available as for potentially exempt transfers. The tax payable, if any, is reduced by the tax paid in lifetime; but no repayment is available if the lifetime tax exceeds the tax recalculated at death (as it would, in a simple case, more than five years after the original transfer since taper relief would by then bring the charge below the lifetime rate which is one half of the death rate). The adjusted charge on an immediately chargeable lifetime transfer may be affected if the donor had made earlier potentially exempt transfers which themselves become chargeable because the donor died within seven years of making them.

Tax on the death estate is calculated by adding the estate to chargeable transfers within the seven years before the death and taxing it as the highest part of that total (at the full rate of 40% or the reduced rate of 36% (as the case may be) to the extent that the value of the estate, having taken into account the residence nil-rate band (RNRB) in respect of deaths occurring on or after 6 April 2017, exceeds the nil-rate band available). The RNRB applies where a person dies owning a home that is inherited by one of his direct descendants (as defined). An additional amount (known as a downsizing addition (DA)) may be taken into account in calculating an individual's RNRB. This recognises the fact that individuals who had downsized to a smaller property or who had sold their home when they moved into care might lose some or all of their entitlement to the RNRB. The downsizing provisions provide a way for any RNRB that might otherwise have been lost due to the disposal or downsizing to be reinstated, as long as their other assets are inherited by their direct descendants. (See **Example A2 part b.**)

(iv) *Exemptions and reliefs*

Exemptions include:

- Transfers between spouses and civil partners (but if the transferee is not UK domiciled, this exemption is limited to the amount of the nil-rate band in force when the transfer takes place (currently £325,000 up to and including 2027/28); before 2013/14 the non-domiciled spouse exemption limit was £55,000 – for more information see **Example A5 (c)**)
- Annual exemption for lifetime gifts — £3,000 pa
- Small lifetime gifts to same person — not exceeding £250 pa
- Normal expenditure out of income
- Gifts in consideration of marriage or registration of a civil partnership
  - — £5,000 by a parent
  - — £2,500 by a grandparent/remoter ancestor or a party to the marriage/civil partnership
  - — £1,000 by any other person
- Gifts to UK registered charities, political parties, housing associations, or for national purposes
- Conditional exemption for heritage property
- Gifts made more than seven years before death (see **(i) above**).

Reliefs include:

- Business property relief (relief being at 100% on an interest in a business or unquoted shareholdings; controlling holdings in quoted companies, and certain assets used by a partnership in which the donor is a partner, or a company controlled by him, qualify for 50% relief).
- Agricultural property relief (at 100% for owner-occupied property and property let on leases granted on or after 1 September 1995, and 50% for other let property).
- Quick succession relief, reducing the tax payable where a donee dies within five years after receiving a chargeable transfer on which tax was originally suffered.

It is also possible to use a deed of variation within two years after death to alter the way a deceased person's estate is distributed without this counting as a gift by the original beneficiary (see **Example B6**).

(v) *Advantages of phasing disposals*

Regular gifts could be covered by the exemption for normal expenditure out of income provided they are habitual (eg by payments of regular premiums under an insurance policy), and leave the taxpayer with sufficient income to maintain his normal lifestyle.

Other lifetime gifts to individuals would be potentially exempt in so far as they are not covered by the annual exemption of £3,000. If the previous year's annual exemption was not used, that would also be available to reduce the transfer. The earlier year's annual exemption is only available after that of the current year has been used in full. Any of the previous year's exemption not then utilised will be lost. So phasing disposals can utilise successive years' annual exemptions.

Even though a gift is not covered by a specific exemption, no tax is payable in lifetime or on death to the extent that the gift is covered by the nil-rate band (taking into account gifts made within the previous seven years). So phasing disposals over a period of more than seven years can allow use of a reconstituted nil-rate band after the earlier transfers have fallen out of the inheritance tax accumulation. The residence nil-rate band does not apply to gifts of a home to direct descendants made during lifetime.

(vi) *Disposals in lifetime or on death*

Although the tax payable on gifts made more than three but less than seven years before death may attract taper relief, that is irrelevant unless the cumulative total at the time of the lifetime gift exceeds the nil-rate band applicable at the date of death, since no tax will be payable to which any taper relief can apply.

Because lifetime gifts are accumulated with earlier chargeable transfers (made within seven years before the date of the gift) it is possible for gifts made within seven years before death to increase the overall burden of inheritance tax.

Subject to the above, potentially exempt lifetime gifts are normally advantageous as they are completely exempt after seven years, are not chargeable in any event if covered by the nil-rate band, and if chargeable, possibly attract taper relief. Any part of the nil-rate band used to cover such transfers would, however, reduce the amount available on the death estate.

In the case of assets attracting 100% business property relief it may not be advantageous to make a lifetime transfer. This is because a liability to capital gains tax can arise on the gift. The gain may be held over for capital gains purposes (see **point (iv)** under capital gains tax summary above), but it will reduce the base value to the donee (**point (vi)** of the capital gains tax summary above), whereas on death there is an automatic uplift to market value for capital gains tax purposes without any capital gains tax being payable. There would, however, be no liability to inheritance tax at the time of a lifetime gift because of the 100% relief, nor if the donor died within seven years, provided the gifted business assets were still held by the donee and, in certain cases, still qualified as relevant business property.

In the case of a person's home a lifetime transfer (provided the individual has somewhere else to live, perhaps by renting suitable accommodation) may be advantageous from a capital gains tax perspective on account of any gain being exempt by reason of only or main residence relief (although some of the gain may be taxable if the residence was not occupied by the taxpayer throughout his period of ownership). The donee's base cost will be the market value of the residence at the time of the transfer. There would be no liability to inheritance tax at the time of a lifetime gift provided it qualified as a potentially exempt transfer although a charge could arise if the donor died within seven years of making the gift. No residence nil-rate band would be available in respect of the charge then arising. That being said, part of his estate may be nevertheless be chargeable at 0% in respect of any downsizing amount to which he may be entitled (see **Example A2**).

Donations to a UK registered charity are exempt transfers whether made in lifetime or on death. The advantage perhaps of making a charitable legacy under a will is that, in respect of deaths occurring on or after 6 April 2012, the reduced rate of inheritance tax of 36% may apply in relation to an estate where 10% or more of the net estate (after deducting exemptions, reliefs and the nil-rate band) is left to a UK registered charity.

(vii) *Effect of emigration*

Inheritance tax is chargeable on worldwide assets of a person domiciled in the UK. To emigrate without changing domicile has no effect.

Even if a person presently domiciled in the UK changes his domicile he will still be deemed UK domiciled for at least three calendar years following the change, and thereafter will remain liable to inheritance tax on UK sited property no matter where his domicile is.

See **Example A5(c)** for more information on deemed domicile and elective domicile.

B. Suggested course of action for Charles

The transfer to Charles on his wife's death was exempt because of the spouse exemption. Until October 2007, her nil-rate band would have been wasted (unless she had made chargeable or potentially exempt gifts in the seven years before her death), requiring urgent consideration of a deed of variation in respect of her estate to ensure that only the excess over his wife's available nil-rate band remained in Charles's estate and prospectively liable to inheritance tax on his own death. The advent of the transferable nil-rate band in October 2007 (and the transferable residence nil-rate band which is available from 6 April 2017) (see **Example A3**) has however reduced the importance of ensuring, as a fundamental principle, that the nil-rate band of the first to die is used in all cases.

The following points should be considered in order to improve the present and potential future tax position.

(i) Charles should consider a deed of variation to redirect the appreciating assets (quoted shares and jewellery) left to him by his wife. This will remove £225,000 from Charles's estate while not counting as a gift by Charles, and using only £175,000 of his wife's nil-rate band that could otherwise have been transferred to Charles's estate in the event of his death. The deed could be directly in favour of his daughter, or of the grandchildren; alternatively it could direct the assets in question to a discretionary trust, of which he is a trustee, so that he can still exercise some control over the assets. The settlor of that trust for inheritance tax purposes would be Charles's wife, not Charles himself.

    The deed should also be made effective for capital gains tax, since otherwise it would give rise to a capital gains tax disposal of the assets redirected, with gains realised (subject to the impact of the chattel exemption in relation to the jewellery) of £50,000. If the deed directs the assets into a trust then Charles will be the settlor for both capital gains tax and income tax purposes; so if Charles were thinking of including himself (or any future wife of his) as a beneficiary then he would be charged to income tax on the trust's income (but not on its gains, so long as the trustees were UK resident).

    The deed of variation must be completed within two years after Charles's wife's death, and must contain the necessary statement to the effect that it is intended to operate for both inheritance tax and capital gains tax purposes (see **Example B6**).

(ii) Charles could make transfers of his shareholding in the family trading company in 2023/24, covering any capital gains tax liability with gifts holdover relief. The gifts would initially be potentially exempt transfers covered by 100% business property relief (BPR) for inheritance tax. If Charles died within seven years, then provided the donees had retained the shares given to them (or validly replaced them), BPR of 100% would still be available so long as the company's status and activities still qualified. If Charles does not wish to give all of the shares directly to his family, trusts could be used so long as Charles himself were excluded from benefit so that there was no gift with reservation. Although a gift to a trust would involve an immediately chargeable transfer, the 100% BPR would negate any immediate charge; but there would still be a need for the trustees to retain the shares, and for the company to remain an unquoted trading company, for at least seven years so as to avoid the loss of that relief in the event of Charles's death within that period.

(iii) Charles should without further delay assign the life policy to the trustees of a discretionary trust with a wide and flexible class of beneficiaries sufficient to include anyone whom he might wish to benefit from the policy on his death, but excluding him so that there is no reservation of benefit. Whilst this will give rise to a chargeable transfer so far as his annual exemption is not available, the value transferred by it will be significantly below the policy proceeds that would become payable (and taxable as part of his estate on death) if Charles were to die suddenly shortly afterwards. The value of the policy in Charles's estate before assignment (which would be the measure of the lifetime transfer of value on his divesting himself fully of the policy) is not restricted to the higher of the surrender value and the (actuarial) market value: by virtue of IHTA 1984 s 167 the minimum value to be attributed to a policy in connection with a transfer of value will be the total of the premiums paid under the policy prior to the transfer, less any sums paid under the policy or in consideration for the surrender of any right conferred by it or by any policy for which it has been directly substituted. In the present case this statutory minimum value is £42,000 (14 years' premiums at £750 per quarter), which exceeds both the other figures given and must therefore be used as the basis of the value transferred.

(iv) Further gifts could be made in so far as no material liability to capital gains tax is crystallised (eg cash gifts; chattels worth less than £6,000; possibly the land owned if it has a high base value), or on which gifts holdover relief would be available (eg shares in supplier company or gifts to a trust; although the latter would be chargeable transfers for inheritance tax (whatever the terms of the trust, the gifts could be restricted so that they were covered by available reliefs and the nil-rate band)). As before, Charles and any future wife or civil partner of his should be excluded from benefit under any trust; that is especially important if hold-over relief is sought on the gift into the trust since that is unavailable where the settlor has (or later acquires) an interest under the trust. (However unlikely it might be felt that Charles would acquire a civil partner in future, it is necessary to cover this in the drafting of a tax-effective settlor-exclusion clause.)

(v) Any gifts into trust, or otherwise involving immediately chargeable transfers, should be made before gifts to individuals that will be potentially exempt transfers, because adverse inheritance tax consequences would follow if they were made in the opposite order and Charles's death occurred within the ensuing seven years. This is because the potentially exempt transfers would become chargeable transfers in that event, and would retrospectively increase the settlor's inheritance tax accumulation for the seven years immediately preceding the formation of the trust(s), locking that increased amount into the inheritance tax computations for the trust(s) under the relevant property regime for the whole duration of the trust(s).

(vi) Thereafter annual gifts could be made utilising the capital gains tax annual exemption, currently £6,000 (£3,000 for 2024/25; £12,300 for 2022/23). For inheritance tax, such gifts would be reduced by the £3,000 annual exemption. Gifts could include quoted shares and/or the unquoted shares in the supplier company. The latter would attract 100% business property relief for inheritance tax.

(vii) Care must be taken not to allow the taxation advantages of a gift to outweigh the personal requirements of the taxpayer.

(viii) Any gifts to charity which Charles wishes to make could be made either in lifetime or under his will. If made in lifetime these would reduce Charles's estate without giving rise to a liability either to capital gains tax or inheritance tax, and he can make gift aid payments of any amount to charity and save higher or additional rate income tax on the gross equivalent, providing he makes an appropriate gift aid declaration. He can also obtain higher or additional rate relief for gifts to charities of quoted stocks and shares, shares on the Alternative Investment Market (AIM) and the ISDX-Quoted market, and of UK land and buildings. All such gifts are valued at their open market value plus any incidental costs of making them. If Charles makes a charitable legacy under his will the reduced rate of inheritance tax of 36% may apply in relation to his estate if the legacy amounts to 10% or more of his net estate (after deducting exemptions, reliefs and the nil-rate band).

Explanatory Note

For further notes on liability to inheritance tax see **Examples A1** to **A6**; business property relief see **Example A21**; agricultural property relief see **Example A22** deeds of variation see **Example B6**; domicile see **Example B7**; and the reduced rate of inheritance tax see **Example B12**. Capital gains tax generally is dealt with in detail in the companion book **Tolley's Taxwise I 2023/24**. For a discussion of the inheritance tax and capital gains tax implication of lifetime planning, see an article entitled 'Interaction and potential problems' by Kevin Offer in *Taxation* published on 25 July 2019. For a review of estate planning in general, see an article entitled 'Keep it in the family' by John Woolley in *Taxation* published on 8 July 2021, 'Whose house is it anyway' by Katherine Bullock in *Taxation* published on 9 March 2023, 'Time to reconsider' by Mark Pearce in *Taxation* published on 16 March 2023 and 'A gift for generations' by Andrew Hubbard (featuring Matthew Hutton's book 'Your last gift') in *Taxation* published on 18 May 2023. For a review of the importance of will drafting in the context of estate planning see the article 'Working together' by Julie Bulter and Angela Evans in *Taxation* published on 11 May 2023.

Question

Mr Gregory, a higher rate taxpayer, is a 68-year old widower for whom you act as tax adviser. He came to see you on 31 May 2023 and told you that he had just been informed by his doctor that he had only a few months left to live. He intends that all his wealth should pass to his only son Neil (who will be his sole executor). He has heard that in some circumstances it might be advantageous either to transfer some of his assets immediately to Neil as a gift or alternatively to sell some of his assets and then to transfer the sale proceeds to Neil as a gift.

Mr Gregory is not currently in a position to make cash gifts as he has just drawn out the last of his savings from his bank account. He provides you with the following information concerning his assets:

(i) He owns 2,000 shares in Bingo plc, a quoted company, currently valued at £480. He acquired the shares for £14,350 in December 2002.

(ii) He acquired 20,000 £1 shares at par out of an issued share capital of 200,000 shares in Peck Limited, a retail company, in February 2021. His shares have been valued recently at £1.20 each. The investment qualified for income tax relief at 30% under the enterprise investment scheme.

(iii) He acquired 10,000 £1 shares out of an issued share capital of 10,000,000 shares in Zingo plc, a quoted land dealing company, for £7 each in November 2005. The shares are currently worth £30 per share.

(iv) All tax liabilities have been agreed and paid on the due date up to 5 April 2023. Mr Gregory does not expect to have any income tax liabilities outstanding on his death, as the income he receives between now and then will have suffered tax at source; in fact it is estimated that the income tax computation up to the date of his death will show a repayment due of £1,250.

Other relevant information is as follows:

(v) He had taxable capital gains in the previous four years of assessment as follows:

	2019/20	*2020/21*	*2021/22*	*2022/23*
	£	£	£	£
Net gains	16,200	15,000	Nil	15,025
Less: Annual exemption	(12,000)	(12,300)	Nil	(12,300)
Taxable gains	4,200	3,000	Nil	2,725

(vi) In January 2022 he had made an outright gift of his principal private residence to his son Neil who now resides there and Mr Gregory went to live with his brother. The value of the residence at that time was £250,000 but it has since risen to £400,000. Neil has now suggested that Mr Gregory should come to live with him rent-free. Mr Gregory has refused to go to live with Neil partly on personal grounds, but also because he believes that if he does, problems might arise in connection with inheritance tax; instead, because his health is beginning to fail and his brother cannot provide the increasing physical assistance Mr Gregory needs, he has admitted himself to a care home. The gift of his residence is the only gift which Mr Gregory has made so far.

(vii) His son Neil, who is due to get married shortly, has recently started up in business and has indicated that he will need to convert any assets which he receives from his father into cash by 31 December 2023 at the latest, in order to invest in the business.

(a) Indicate the optimum tax strategy for Mr Gregory regarding lifetime gifts.

(b) Assuming that Mr Gregory had in fact gone to live with Neil in his former private residence, state the inheritance tax consequences which would have arisen.

(c) Assuming that Mr Gregory adopts the strategy suggested under (a) above, calculate the inheritance tax liability arising on the basis that he died on 22 August 2023.

Assume that the rate of interest on tax repayments remains at 4.25%, the rate which has applied since 22 August 2023.

Answer

(a) Tax strategy re lifetime gifts

Disposals of assets in lifetime may attract capital gains tax on their growth in value. Furthermore, if the disposal is a gift, it may be reckonable for inheritance tax.

Mr Gregory is almost certain to die within seven years, and therefore even if a gift was initially a potentially exempt transfer for inheritance tax, it would become chargeable on his death. The taper relief for inheritance tax applicable after three years will almost certainly not be available due to Mr Gregory's shortened life expectancy.

By comparison, assets retained until death obtain a capital gains tax free uplift to probate value, thus avoiding a liability to capital gains tax. A gift in lifetime may therefore attract a liability to both capital gains tax and inheritance tax, whereas the same asset given on death would only be liable to inheritance tax.

Against that double charge, a gift in lifetime attracts any unused inheritance tax annual exemptions or marriage exemption and the value subsequently chargeable on death because the seven-year period has not been survived is the value at the date of the gift. Mr Gregory gave his house to his son in January 2022. The value at that date of £250,000 will be reduced by the annual exemptions for 2021/22 and 2020/21 and will be included in calculating the inheritance tax on Mr Gregory's death at £250,000 – £6,000 = £244,000, not at its current value of £400,000.

As Mr Gregory does not have long to live, the increase in value up to the date of death of any asset given away now is likely to be minimal, but the inheritance tax annual exemptions of 2022/23 and 2023/24 are available. In ordinary circumstances an exemption is available for gifts that are normal expenditure out of income. Although there is no fixed minimum period during which regular gifts have to have been made to constitute 'normal expenditure', it is necessary that a pattern of actual or intended payments has been established (*Bennett & Others v CIR (1994)* (see **explanatory note (1) of Example A1**)). Thus a 'death bed' resolution to make periodic payments for life does not create an exemption for such payments under the normal expenditure out of income provisions.

To create a liability to capital gains tax would not be advisable. If, however, the disposals realised net capital losses, any losses in the tax year of death may be carried back against the capital gains liabilities of the three preceding years, latest first, tax being repayable accordingly. The loss carry-back relief is not wasted against gains already covered by the annual exemption. As Mr Gregory is likely to die before 5 April 2024, immediate crystallisation of losses would be useful. Care must be taken not to give loss-producing assets to connected persons such as Neil; a loss on a disposal to such a person can only be utilised against future gains on disposals to the same person whilst they are still connected, which is very unlikely if death is imminent.

The recommended strategy would be to:

(i) Sell the shares in Bingo plc, realising a capital loss as follows:

	£
Cost of shares December 2002	14,350
Sale proceeds in say July 2023	(480)
Loss on Bingo plc shares	(13,870)

(ii) Relieve the loss on the Bingo plc shares against gains of the three years preceding death (assuming death in 2023/24):

	2022/23	*2021/22*	*2020/21*	
	£	£	£	£
Gains	15,025	Nil	15,300	
Loss re Bingo plc shares	(2,725)		(3,000)	(5,725)
	12,000		12,300	

	2022/23	2021/22	2020/21	
	£	£	£	£
Less: Annual exemption	(12,300)		(12,300)	
	Nil		Nil	
Available loss (as above)				13,870
Unused losses				8,145

The tax saving from carrying back the loss to 2022/23 is £2,725 @ 20% = £545. The due date of payment for the 2022/23 tax is 31 January 2024, so if Mr Gregory died before that date the capital gains tax originally due would not be paid. Otherwise it would be repaid. The repayment due as a result of carrying back the loss to 2020/21 is £3,000 @ 20% = £600.

As far as repayment supplement is concerned, although the *tax saving* is calculated by reference to the tax position of the earlier year, the claim relates to the later year, and repayment supplement is payable only if the repayment is made after 31 January following that later year. Where losses are carried back from the year of death, the deduction is made automatically without the need for a claim (TCGA 1992 s 62(2)). TMA 1970 Sch 1B para 2(7) provides, however, that for repayment supplement purposes the carry-back is treated in the same way as if a claim was required. In this Example, repayment supplement would only be payable if the tax was repaid after 31 January 2025. The tax will almost certainly have been repaid by that date, but if it has not been, repayment supplement will be payable from that date at 4.25% per annum based on the above assumption.

(iii) Make a gift during 2023/24 to Neil of the appropriate number of shares in Zingo plc.

	£
The gain on each Zingo plc share would be:	
Market value	30.00
Less: Cost	(7.00)
Gain per share	23.00

The available capital loss in 2023/24 after carry back against 2022/23 and 2020/21 is £8,145 as indicated in (ii) above, which covers a potential gift of 354 shares (@ £23.00 gain per share). The available exemptions for inheritance tax are:

		£
Annual	2023/24	3,000
	2022/23	3,000
Marriage (on gift to Neil)		5,000
		11,000

This covers a potential gift of 366 shares (@ £30 each).

(Note that the sale or gift of shares in Peck Limited would give rise to a clawback of enterprise investment scheme relief at 30%, since they will not have been held for three years until February 2024).

Mr Gregory should therefore give Neil 366 shares in Zingo plc. By gifting 366 shares instead of 354 (the maximum gift for CGT purposes) the loss to be carried back is restricted by approximately £276 (12 × £23.00), losing the benefit of a CGT refund of £55.20 (£276 @ 20%). This however is better than paying inheritance tax at 40% on £360 (12 shares @ £30), an additional cost of £144.

Making gains in 2023/24 in excess of £8,145 would mean that the losses available to carry back would be reduced to below £5,725 and the capital gains tax repayment for earlier years would be further reduced accordingly. As a result Mr Gregory's annual capital gains tax exemption cannot be used in 2023/24, because to use the annual exemption, gains would need to exceed the losses of £13,870, and no losses would be left to carry back. The executors are unlikely to make losses when they convert assets to cash for Neil because they take the assets at probate value, and even if they did, those losses are not available to carry back against Mr Gregory's gains.

(b) Inheritance tax consequences of Mr Gregory going to live with Neil

Mr Gregory's reason for leaving his brother's house suggests that Mr Gregory's illness is such that he is unable to maintain himself. Provided such an eventuality was not foreseeable in January 2022 (at the time of the original gift of the property), then Mr Gregory could return to his former residence without breaching the gifts with reservation rules or the use of pre-owned asset provisions.

FA 1986 Sch 20 para 6(1)(b) provides such an exemption in relation to gifts of an interest in land when the donor's circumstances change in a way that was unforeseen at the time of the original gift and the benefit provided by the donee to the donor represents reasonable provision for the care and maintenance of an elderly or infirm relative. This provision also applies referentially to prevent a pre-owned asset charge (FA 2004 Sch 15 para 11(5)(d)).

Without such exemption Mr Gregory's return to his former residence would nullify the hoped-for inheritance tax advantages of the original gift and would return the value of the house to his estate at his death. In addition the original gift, which was a potentially exempt transfer, would still be included in the lifetime chargeable gifts if death occurred within seven years after the original gift. However, relief is given to prevent double charging (FA 1986 s 104 and SI 1987/1130). However, were the value of the residence to form part of Mr Gregory's estate at his death by virtue of its being property subject to a reservation, a residence nil-rate band (RNRB) will be available when calculating the inheritance tax payable on his estate. Although the residence will not in fact be inherited by his son Neil on his death (Neil acquired the property under the lifetime gift in January 2022), for the purposes of the RNRB, the residence will be treated as inherited by his son (IHTA 1984 s 8J(6)). (See **Example A2 part b** for a detailed explanation of the RNRB.)

(c) Inheritance tax as a result of Mr Gregory's death on 30 September 2023

				Gross	*Tax (2023/24 scale)*
			£		£
Gifts in lifetime:					
January 2022					
Gift to Neil — house			250,000		
Less: Annual exemptions	2021/22	3,000			
	2020/21	3,000	(6,000)		
Potentially exempt transfer now chargeable				244,000	Nil
July 2023					
Gift to Neil					
366 shares in Zingo plc @ £30 per share			10,980		
Less: Marriage exemption		5,000			
Annual exemptions	2023/24	3,000			
	2022/23	2,980	(10,980)	Nil	Nil
				244,000	Nil

			Gross	Tax (2023/24 scale)
		£	£	£
Mr Gregory's estate at death – 30 September 2023				
Proceeds of sale of Bingo plc shares		480		
Income tax repayment		1,250		
Capital gains tax repayment**		545		
Shares in Zingo plc				
10,000 – 366 = 9,634 @ £30		289,020		
Shares in Peck Limited				
20,000 @ £1.20	24,000			
Less: Business property relief 100%	(24,000)	Nil	291,295	84,118*
			535,295	84,118*

(* 535,295 – 325,000 = £210,295 @ 40%)

Inheritance tax liability on death of Mr Gregory £84,204

** Assuming that the 2022/23 CGT liability of £545 was discharged as a result of the carried-back loss (**see (a)(ii) above**), the repayment will consist of £2,725@ 20% = £545, based on the loss carried back to 2020/21 (£3,000 as in **(a)(ii) above**) less loss used in 2023/24 of £276 as in (iii) = £2,724.

Supplementary note

The general principles of inheritance tax are dealt with in earlier Examples. In particular normal expenditure out of income and the residence nil-rate band is dealt with in **Example A1** and **Example A2** respectively, gifts with reservation in **Example B1**, pre-owned assets in **Example B4**, and double charges relief in **Examples B2** and **B5**. The capital gains tax provisions are outlined in **Example A24**. Capital gains tax is dealt with in detail in the companion to this book, **Tolley's Taxwise I 2023/24**. For a discussion of the inheritance tax and capital gains tax implication of succession planning for a business see an article entitled 'Lifecycle of a business: succession planning' by Helena Luckhurst and Katie Mitchell in *Tax Journal* published on 20 September 2019.

Question

Thomas and Maria have been married for many years. Their daughter, Julia, was born in February 1973 and their son, Edmund, in October 1974. Thomas started in business on his own account in 1970 as a manufacturer of domestic hardware. Their relevant financial history is as follows:

March 1970 — The family home is bought by Maria for £6,000.

May 1987 — Thomas buys 100,000 ordinary shares in Huntingdon Ltd, a trading company that has since become listed on the Stock Exchange.

31 March 1995 — Thomas transfers all his business assets (except vehicles of £30,000 which he retains personally) to a new company, Thomas Ltd, in consideration for ordinary shares valued at £300,000 (Maria holding one share as nominee). Business assets immediately before the transfers were:

	£
Goodwill	110,000
Plant, at cost less depreciation	55,000
Vehicles, at cost less depreciation	30,000
Stock, at cost or lower market value	65,000
Debtors	90,000
Cash	40,000
Creditors	(60,000)
	330,000

Thomas Ltd continues the trade without a break.

November 2005 — Maria gives the family home (then valued at £80,000) in equal shares to Julia and her husband Henry. Maria and Thomas then move to their second home (which had cost £62,000 in 1993, at which time an election had been made for capital gains tax that the original home remained the principal private residence).

February 2006 — Maria places £32,500 cash into trust for Edmund for life, with remainder to Julia or her children (Julia has a son and a daughter). The trustees invest the money in a building society account which pays interest monthly.

May 2019 — Thomas gives 70% of the shares in Thomas Ltd to Edmund.
Company assets, at historical cost, are:

	£
Goodwill on acquisition from Thomas	110,000
Freehold factory bought July 1995	225,000
Shares in 100% subsidiary, allotted May 1997	100,000
Other non-chargeable assets	368,000
	803,000

In May 2019 goodwill is valued at £400,000. The factory is used for the trade (which is to continue) and is worth £600,000. The subsidiary's only assets are a portfolio of investment properties worth £230,000.

October 2019 — Thomas places his holding of shares in Huntingdon plc (then valued at £170,000) into a discretionary trust. The beneficiaries are Julia, Edmund and all their descendants. Thomas' holding was less than 5% and he did not work for the company. The gain arising on the transfer was £85,278.

May 2023 — Edmund dies intestate. He is unmarried and without children. In addition to his shares in Thomas Ltd (whose assets have not changed in value since May 2019) he leaves a house worth £165,000 and other investments of £70,000. Under the rules of intestacy his estate will pass to Thomas and Maria, who apply for letters of administration in January 2024.

All persons mentioned (including the trustees of the trusts referred to) are UK resident.

Shares in Thomas Ltd at May 2019 are to be valued:

(i) as to a 100% holding, on an assets basis;

(ii) as to a 70% holding, on an assets basis discounted by 20%;

(iii) as to a 30% holding, £225,000 for the holding.

Any inheritance tax on lifetime transfers is paid by the donor.

(a) Work out the gain on the gift by Thomas of 70% of his shares in Thomas Ltd taking into account any available CGT reliefs, and comment on the CGT position in relation to other disposals from November 2005 onwards.

(b) Identify and quantify all chargeable and potentially exempt transfers, advising how much inheritance tax is payable on chargeable transfers, when it is payable, and any other factors that may be relevant.

(c) Advise the beneficiaries under Edmund's intestacy of the main planning points that arise on his death.

Answer

(a) Capital gains tax liabilities 6 April 2005 onwards

November 2005	—	Gift of family home by Maria — covered by principal private residence exemption — no chargeable gain.	
February 2006	—	Cash into trust by Maria — no chargeable disposal.	
May 2019	—	Gift by Thomas to Edmund of 70% of shares in Thomas Ltd:	
		Valuation of Thomas Ltd — assets basis	£
		Factory	600,000
		Subsidiary	230,000
		Non-chargeable assets	368,000
		Goodwill	400,000
			1,598,000
		Valuation of gift: 70% × (1,598,000 × 80%)	894,880
		Cost — March 1995 (70% × 300,000)	(210,000)
		Gain	684,880

Holdover relief will be available, for any gain relating to the chargeable business assets – restricted to the fraction:

$$\frac{\text{Chargeable business assets}}{\text{Total chargeable assets}} \text{ ie } \frac{600{,}000 + 400{,}000}{600{,}000 + 400{,}000 + 230{,}000}$$

Available for relief:

$$\frac{1{,}000{,}000}{1{,}230{,}000} \times 684{,}880 = £\,556{,}813$$

	£
Held-over gain	556,813
Gain chargeable before annual exemption (684,880 – 556,813)	£128,067

October 2019 — Gift by Thomas of shares in Huntingdon plc to discretionary trust

The gain of £85,278 can be held over under TCGA 1992 s 260, as the disposition is an immediately chargeable transfer for inheritance tax.

Note The base cost of the 100,000 shares in Huntingdon plc in the trustees' hands is therefore 170,000 – 85,278 = £84,722.

May 2023 — No liability to capital gains tax on death of Edmund.

(b) Inheritance tax

Inheritance tax position of Maria

					£	£
November 2005	—	Gift of house				80,000
		Less:	Annual exemptions	2005/06	3,000	
				2004/05	3,000	(6,000)
		Potentially exempt transfer				74,000

The transfer would only have become chargeable if Maria had died before November 2012 but no tax would have been payable in any event, since the transfer would have been below the nil-rate threshold (although the nil-rate band available against the additional charge on the February 2006 gift and in turn Maria's estate at death would have been correspondingly reduced).

					£	£
February 2006	—	Gift of cash into interest in possession trust				32,500
		Less:	Annual exemptions	2005/06 already used	Nil	
				2004/05 already used	Nil	
		Potentially exempt transfer				32,500

As a potentially exempt transfer, if Maria had died before February 2013, no tax would have arisen on the gift as it would not have exceed the nil-rate band then in force (even if death had occurred before November 2012 and it had been aggregated with the November 2005 potentially exempt transfer that would have become chargeable to inheritance tax). If she had died after February 2013 no tax would be payable on the gift to the interest in possession trust, but it would be aggregated with later gifts and the death estate, thus increasing the inheritance tax payable.

Inheritance tax position of Thomas

May 2019 — Gift of 70% of shares in Thomas Ltd to Edmund.

			£
Valuation of gift:			
Holding before gift — 100% of 1,598,000			1,598,000
Holding after gift — 30% minority			(225,000)
Loss to estate			1,373,000
Less: business property relief			
$100\% \times 1{,}373{,}000 \times \frac{1{,}368{,}000^*}{1{,}598{,}000}$			(1,175,384)
			197,616
(* The investment holding subsidiary is an excepted asset for business property relief)			
Less: Annual exemptions	2019/20	3,000	
	2018/19	3,000	(6,000)
Potentially exempt transfer			191,616

Note — The shares that were returned to Thomas following the death of Edmund would again form part of Thomas' estate. However should he die within seven years of having made the gift, ie before May 2026, relief will be given to prevent double charging. No liability will arise on the potentially exempt transfer itself, since it is below the nil-rate threshold.

October 2019	—	Gift of shares in Huntingdon plc to discretionary trust	
		Value of gift (annual exemptions already used)	£170,000

No inheritance tax is payable at the time of the gift as the cumulative total of gifts immediately liable to inheritance tax is below the 2019/20 nil-rate threshold of £325,000. If Thomas should die before May 2026, the gift would be aggregated with the May 2019 potentially exempt transfer that would then become chargeable and inheritance tax would be payable to the extent that the aggregate amount exceeded the nil-rate threshold at the time of death (prospectively (assuming no change to the nil-rate threshold in 2026/27) 191,616 + 170,000 – 325,000 = £36,616). If he should die after May 2026 but before October 2026 no tax would be payable on the gift to the discretionary trust, but it would be aggregated with later gifts and the death estate, thus increasing the inheritance tax payable.

Inheritance tax position re death of Edmund in May 2023

	£	£
Value of free estate:		
Shares in Thomas Ltd (70% holding) (1,598,000 × 70%, less 20%)	894,880	
Less: Business property relief (100% available as second transfer was on death even though not owned for two years – s 109)		
$100\% \times 894{,}880 \times \frac{1{,}368{,}000^*}{1{,}598{,}000}$	(766,080)	128,800
(* The investment holding subsidiary is an excepted asset)		
House (see **explanatory note 5**)		165,000
Other investments		70,000
		363,800
Settled property — trust of Maria		32,500
		396,300

Inheritance tax payable (396,300 – 325,000) @ 40% = £28,520

	£
Payable by:	
Personal representatives:	
$\frac{363{,}800}{396{,}300} \times 28{,}520 =$	26,181
Trustees:	
$\frac{32{,}500}{396{,}300} \times 28{,}520 =$	2,339
	28,520

Of the total liability, the tax relating to the Thomas Ltd shares can be paid by instalments without interest to the due date and that relating to the house by instalments with interest from 1 December 2023; therefore the amount actually due from the personal representatives on application for probate will be:

Shares

	$\frac{128,800}{363,800} \times 26,181 \times \frac{1}{10}$ =	927	(with interest on balance only if paid late)
House	$\frac{165,000}{363,800} \times 26,181 \times \frac{1}{10}$ =	1,187	(with interest on balance from 1 December 2023)
Other investments	$\frac{70,000}{363,800} \times 26,181$ =	5,038	
		£7,152	

(c) Advice to Thomas and Maria as beneficiaries of the estate of Edmund

The value in Edmund's estate is reverting to yourselves. As the oldest generation, you are likely to die before other members of the family. It may be preferable for Edmund's estate to go to your daughter Julia or to your grandchildren. If this course of action is decided on then it could be achieved by the use of a deed of variation. Such a deed would not save inheritance tax on Edmund's death but might significantly reduce the potential liability on your own deaths. The deed must be executed within two years of Edmund's death (ie by May 2025).

It should be noted that if an instalment option asset (ie either the Thomas Ltd shares or Edmund's house) is sold, the outstanding instalments of inheritance tax become payable immediately.

The funding of the inheritance tax could be achieved by Thomas Ltd purchasing its own shares from the estate. This would qualify for special treatment and HMRC clearance should be obtained for the purchase not to be treated as a distribution by Thomas Ltd.

If no deed of variation occurs then should either of you die within five years after Edmund's death (ie before May 2028) quick succession relief would be available in your estates in respect of the assets inherited from him in so far as they are not exempt from tax on your death (because, for example, the assets are left to a charity or devolve on the surviving spouse). In the same way, should the devolution of Edmund's estate be varied in favour of Julia and she were to die or make a chargeable transfer of her interest in the settled property devolving on her following Edmund's death, before May 2028, quick succession relief would be available by reference to the tax payable on Edmund's death.

Explanatory Notes

Valuation of assets for capital gains tax and inheritance tax

(1) This Example shows the way in which both capital gains tax and inheritance tax may be relevant when gifts are made, and the different rules that apply when dealing with each tax. Note particularly that in valuing a shareholding, the open market value of the holding is taken for capital gains tax (TCGA 1992 s 272), hence the gift of 70% of Thomas's 100% holding in Thomas Ltd to Edmund in May 2019 is discounted by the 20% reduction for a 70% holding, whereas for inheritance tax the 'loss to the donor' principle applies, the shares therefore being taken into account for inheritance tax as a 100% holding, reduced to a minority holding. (IHTM09712 and the following paragraphs of the Inheritance Tax Manual deal with situations where two or more separate assets may be treated as a single unit of property for valuation purposes.) The value of the gift is therefore different for capital gains tax and inheritance tax, ie:

Capital gains tax	£894,880
Inheritance tax	£1,373,000

When considering the capital gains tax acquisition value for those who inherit a deceased's assets, on the other hand, s 274 provides that where the value of an asset comprised in a person's estate has been *ascertained* (whether in any proceedings or otherwise) for the purposes of inheritance tax, that value is taken to be the market value of the asset at the date of death for capital gains tax (overriding the normal 'open market value' provisions in s 62). This enables any higher inheritance tax value to be used in those circumstances, for example where the inheritance tax related property rules apply. This can also be relevant where an unquoted shareholding passes on death to several people – each will take as acquisition value a suitable proportion of the whole, not, merely the value of the holding he inherits in isolation.

Where, however, no tax is due because of reliefs or exemptions, the value of assets will not be *ascertained* for inheritance tax, so their capital gains acquisition value would be the open market value. This would apply, for example, where 100% business property relief is available on family company shares, or where a transfer of such shares is covered by the nil-rate band. It has been suggested that where this would give lower acquisition values, the problem could be overcome by having a minimal amount of 'excepted assets', not qualifying for business property relief, within the company (see **explanatory note 2**), so that a valuation would then be necessary. HMRC have, however, stated that if very little or no tax was at stake, it was unlikely that an ascertained value would be negotiated by Shares Valuation Division (Tax Bulletin April 1995).

In the case of *Stonor & Mills (Dickinson's Executors) v CIR* (2001), no inheritance tax was payable on the estate because of the charities exemption and the operation of the nil-rate band. The executors sold freehold properties from the estate for significantly more than the probate value, resulting in large capital gains. They tried to get the Revenue (as HMRC was then known) to accept the sale values as amended probate values, but the Revenue refused on the grounds that an investigation into values was not necessary since charity relief had been claimed. The executors then made a claim under IHTA 1984, s 191 (land sold within three years after death – see **Example A12 part B**) to substitute the sale proceeds for the probate value, thus increasing the capital gains tax base cost and eliminating the gains. It was held that since no one was liable to pay any tax on the estate no one was entitled to make a s 191 claim; but this argument would not be available to HMRC if some tax, albeit of small amount, were due apart from the intended s 191 claim.

HMRC have reiterated (see IHTM33026) the point that in circumstances where no tax is due on the sold land because the chargeable estate is below the nil-rate threshold, or the land sold is exempt from tax, or the land sold attracts 100% relief, then no claim under s 191 lies. Their argument is that because there is no tax attributable to the value of the land, so there is no person liable to pay the tax in respect of that asset. If there is no liable person then there is no 'appropriate person' within the terms of the section. HMRC acknowledges that even though the tribunal in the *Stonor* case noted that there is nothing specific in the legislation to disallow claims to substitute a higher value, nevertheless it is their opinion that the purpose of s 191 is to provide relief from Inheritance Tax and that if a taxpayer insists that a higher sale value be substituted, the claim will be referred to their technical division.

(2) Capital gains tax holdover relief on gifts under TCGA 1992 s 165 is available (subject to UK residence of the transferee) only on business assets and not on assets held as investments (other than farming land owned by an agricultural landlord, which can qualify for s 165 relief). Gifts relief under s 260 is available on any asset, providing the gift is immediately liable to inheritance tax, hence the relief on the October 2019 gift by Thomas to the discretionary trust.

Transfer of business to company

(3) Thomas will not have been able to roll over the chargeable gains on the transfer of his personal business to Thomas Ltd in 1995 under s 162, since not all of the (non-cash) assets were transferred in consideration for the shares. Hence the value of the shares received, £300,000, is not reduced by roll-over relief.

Interaction of holdover relief and business asset disposal relief

(4) Thomas' disposal of shares in Thomas Ltd would qualify for business asset disposal relief (formerly known as entrepreneurs' relief) as a material disposal of shares in a personal trading company (s 169I). By claiming holdover relief, his business asset disposal relief is effectively forgone on the part of the gain held over and the unrelieved gain is transferred to Edmund. Edmund would not qualify for business asset disposal relief on an eventual disposal unless he were also an employee or officer of the company. In the event, his death results in the elimination of all deferred capital gains under s 62 (assets deemed not to be disposed of on death).

Residence nil rate band

(5) Edmund's estate is not entitled to a residence nil rate band as his house is not directly inherited, it passing on his intestacy to his parents, Thomas and Maria (see **Example A2 part (b), explanatory note 3**).

Cross references

(6) See **Example A6 explanatory note 7** for the position when both capital gains tax and inheritance tax are payable on the same transfer. For detailed notes on business property relief see **Example A21**, on quick succession relief see **Example B3**, on the instalment option see **Example A7** and on deeds of variation in relation to a deceased's estate see **Example B6**. Note in this Example that a variation would not result in additional tax payable on Edmund's estate, since there are no exempt beneficiaries. Had additional tax been payable, the amount would have had to be notified to HMRC Inheritance Tax and a copy of the variation sent, within six months after the deed was effected. Capital gains tax is dealt with comprehensively in the companion to this book **Tolley's Taxwise I 2023/24**.

Question

Mr Shah, a local tax adviser who runs a small practice, has written to you. You met him recently at a business networking event where he had explained that he was in need of advice regarding one of his clients. You agreed to help him and he has sent you further details of the client's position.

The client, Mr Ray, who has lived in the UK all his life, got chatting with a UK investment professional when both were on holiday abroad. He had suggested that Mr Ray could reduce his wealth and save himself inheritance tax by entering into particular arrangements which involve him, by a series of transactions, transferring some of his assets to an overseas discretionary trust in favour of his children. As the arrangements are mainly effected abroad, it was explained to Mr Ray that no disclosure to HMRC of the arrangements would be required.

Although Mr Shah is unsure as to whether the arrangements will be tax effective, he is particularly concerned whether it is correct that the arrangements, should he go ahead with them, do not have to be disclosed to HMRC, and it is on this matter that he has approached you for some general guidance.

(i) In what circumstances do the rules on the disclosure of inheritance tax avoidance schemes apply?

(ii) Who is under a duty to disclose such schemes to HMRC?

(iii) What other duties fall on that person?

(iv) What are the sanctions for failing to carry out the duties identified?

Answer

(i) Application of the DOTAS rules

Introduction

Finance Act 2004 introduced rules regarding the disclosure of tax avoidance schemes (DoTAS). The regime imposes duties on tax advisers and others to disclose to HMRC details of certain tax avoidance schemes. When first introduced the regime did not apply to inheritance tax. With effect from 6 April 2011 however, the rules were extended to apply to inheritance tax to the extent provided for in the Inheritance Tax Avoidance Schemes (Prescribed Descriptions of Arrangements) Regulations 2011, SI 2011/170 reg 1. In broad terms, arrangements that sought to avoid inheritance tax charges arising on transfers of property into trust may have come within the DoTAS regime (see **explanatory note** 8). In 2016 the regime in relation to IHT was extended by the Tax Avoidance Schemes (Prescribed Descriptions of Arrangements) (Amendment) Regulations 2016, SI 2016/99, reg 4 to all inheritance tax avoidance regimes but only where they involved (what are known as) the confidentiality and premium fee hallmarks. If a scheme did not feature either of these hallmarks, it was notifiable only if it fell within the 2011 Regulations. The 2011 (but not the 2016) Regulations have now been revoked and, with effect from 1 April 2018, have been replaced by the Inheritance Tax Avoidance Schemes (Prescribed Descriptions of Arrangements) Regulations 2017, SI 2017/1172. Leaving aside schemes that feature the confidentiality or premium fee hallmarks, the types of inheritance tax avoidance arrangements that must now be disclosed are much wider than were previously notifiable under the 2011 Regulations (limited as they were to schemes involving transfers to trust). HMRC's guidance on DoTAS has been updated for these changes and can be accessed at www.hmrc.gov.uk/aiu/dotas-guidance.pdf.

Scope of the DOTAS regime

The DoTAS regime applies to notifiable arrangements and notifiable proposals (FA 2004 s 306).

Arrangements include any scheme, transaction or series of transactions and notifiable arrangements are those which:

- are set out in regulations issued by the Treasury;
- enable (or might be expected to enable) any person to obtain an advantage in relation to any tax set out in the regulations; and
- are expected to give rise to the obtaining of the tax advantage as their main benefit (or one of their main benefits).

Notifiable proposals are proposals for arrangements which if entered into would be notifiable arrangements. In *HMRC v Hyrax Resourcing and others* [2019] STC UKFTT 175 it was found that a scheme gave rise to a tax advantage because it was intended to avoid or reduce the charge to tax. It held that the natural and ordinary meaning of 'tax advantage' is that it refers to a contrast in tax liability between one position and another that would otherwise have existed.

In relation to inheritance tax (IHT) and leaving aside schemes that feature the confidentiality or premium fee hallmarks, the arrangements which have been set out in regulations as falling within the DoTAS regime are those that an informed observer (having studied the arrangements and having regard to all relevant circumstances) would reasonably conclude meet two conditions – the first relating to certain charges to inheritance tax and the second relating to the nature of the steps involved in the arrangements. The informed observer test is crucial to the application of the rules as this provides the context within which the conditions are to be considered.

An informed observer is regarded as an independent person but one who has all the relevant information about the scheme and has sufficient knowledge to understand both the scheme and the relevant statutory context. He is assumed to have the appropriate knowledge and skillset to reach the conclusions that the rules apply. The 'relevant circumstances' which the informed observer has to take into account include the non-taxable benefits that are expected to arise from the arrangements, the overall effect or consequences of the arrangements, the terms of the documentation and the substance of the arrangements and HMRC's guidance and published statements.

As described in FA 2004 s 318(1) (adapting the definition to apply to inheritance tax (IHT)), an advantage is obtained where there is:

- relief or increased relief from IHT;
- repayment or increased repayment of IHT;
- avoidance or reduction of a charge to IHT;
- avoidance or reduction of an assessment to IHT;
- avoidance of a possible assessment to IHT;
- a deferral of any payment of IHT;
- an advancement of any repayment of IHT;
- avoidance of any obligation to account for IHT.

Without further detailed information, it is not clear whether the rules on the disclosure of tax avoidance schemes apply to the arrangements which have been described to Mr Ray; but Mr Shah will, when he obtains further information, be able to formulate an opinion as to whether the arrangements fall into the DoTAS regime in so far as it applies to IHT.

To assist him in formulating that opinion he should ask himself the following questions:

(i) Do the arrangements (or proposals for arrangements) feature the confidentiality or premium fee hallmarks?

With effect from 23 February 2016 the confidentiality and premium fee hallmarks (which before that time applied to tax avoidance arrangements involving certain taxes other than IHT) were extended to IHT (The Tax Avoidance Schemes (Prescribed Descriptions of Arrangements) (Amendment) Regulations 2016, SI 2016/99, reg 4). So if Mr Ray goes ahead with the arrangements on the basis that he is required to keep them confidential, or where his payment for the work is linked to its success, that will have a bearing on the application of the DoTAS rules to those arrangements.

Any arrangements implemented by Mr Ray are notifiable under the confidentiality hallmark if any element of them (including the way in which they are structured) gives rise to a tax advantage and it might reasonably be expected that the promoter would wish the way in which that element of those arrangements secures, or might secure, a tax advantage to be kept confidential from any other promoter. This is likely to be the case where an element of the arrangements is sufficiently new and innovative that the promoter would want the details to remain secret in order to maintain his competitive advantage and ability to earn fees. Arrangements are also notifiable under the confidentiality hallmark if it might reasonably be expected that the promoter would wish to keep the way in which any element of the arrangements secures or might secure the tax advantage confidential from HMRC and a reason for doing so is to facilitate repeated or continued use of the same element, or substantially the same element, in the future. This is likely to be the case where an element of the arrangements is sufficiently new and innovative that the promoter would want the details to remain secret in order to facilitate repeated or continued use of any element of the arrangements. The rules on the confidentiality hallmark are found in The Tax Avoidance Schemes (Prescribed Descriptions of Arrangements) Regulations 2006, SI 2006/1543, reg 6.

Any arrangements implemented by Mr Ray are notifiable under the premium fee hallmark if it might reasonably be expected that a promoter would be able to obtain a premium fee from a person experienced in receiving services of the type being provided. A premium fee is a fee chargeable by virtue of any element of the arrangements from which the tax advantage expected to be obtained arises and which is to a significant extent attributable to that tax advantage or to any extent contingent upon the obtaining of that tax advantage. The hallmark contains a hypothetical test that does not depend on a premium fee actually being received and considers whether in the absence of the Disclosure of Tax Avoidance Schemes regime a premium fee could be obtained. The question is whether it might reasonably be expected that a promoter could charge a premium fee if he wished to do so. That a promoter does not charge a premium fee is not conclusive, though the hallmark would be met if he does. 'Fees' for these purposes are drawn very widely and include amounts paid directly or indirectly to the promoter. The test must be applied from the perspective of a client who is experienced in receiving tax advice or other services of the type being provided. Where a client regards the advice as valuable and not generally available he would be prepared to pay a premium for it. Equally, by contrast, if similar advice was available elsewhere the client would be unwilling to pay more than a normal fee for it. It is recognised that almost any fee obtained in relation to tax planning can to some extent be said to be attributable to obtaining a tax advantage. So a 'premium fee' for this purpose is a fee that is to a significant extent attributable to the tax advantage or is contingent upon a tax advantage as a matter of law being obtained. The hallmark will not apply to situations where the fee is wholly contingent on factors other than the tax analysis underpinning the scheme being correct (eg the location of the adviser, the urgency of the advice, the size of the transaction, the reputation of the tax adviser etc). The rules on the confidentiality hallmark are found in The Tax Avoidance Schemes (Prescribed Descriptions of Arrangements) Regulations 2006, SI 2006/1543, reg 8.

If the arrangements which Mr Ray proposes to implement do feature the confidentiality or premium fee hallmarks, then Mr Shah must advise that they are notifiable. If they do not, Mr Shah must ask himself the next question.

(ii) If the arrangements do not feature the confidentiality or premium fee hallmarks, are the arrangements (or proposals for arrangements) excepted from disclosure?

Arrangements ('current arrangements') are excepted from disclosure (ie they are not notifiable to HMRC) if they benefit from the 'established practice' exception. This means that the current arrangements must implement a proposal which itself has already been implemented by 'related arrangements' and the current arrangements are substantially the same as those earlier arrangements. Arrangements are related to the current arrangements if they were entered into before 1 April 2018 and, at the time they were entered into, they accorded with established practice of which HMRC has indicated their acceptance (The Inheritance Tax Avoidance Schemes (Prescribed Descriptions of Arrangements) Regulations 2017, SI 2017/1172, reg 5).

There are two elements to identifying an (earlier) related arrangement. First the pre-1 April 2018 arrangement has to accord with established practice and secondly, HMRC must have indicated their acceptance of that established practice. Established practice is demonstrated by reference to published material (eg HMRC manuals, textbooks and journal articles) or by other written evidence of what had become common practice at the time when the (earlier) arrangements were entered into. HMRC's acceptance of established practice may again be shown through published material (eg its internal material) or other means (eg correspondence with the Chartered Institute of Taxation).

Having determined that the current arrangements implement a proposal that had previously been implemented by related arrangements, which proposal was not then notifiable as it pre-dated 1 April 2018, the final criterion for the current arrangements to be within the exception is that they must be substantially the same as the earlier, related arrangements. In order to meet this condition, the current arrangements must be compared with the related arrangements and the current arrangements have to implement the same proposal as was implemented by the related arrangements. Any differences between the two sets of arrangements then have to be evaluated to decide whether they are substantial.

An exception from the requirement to disclose also applied under the 2011 Regulations – the so-called 'grandfathering exception'. It should be noted that with the revocation of the 2011 Regulations the grandfathering exception no longer protects grandfathered schemes (see **explanatory note 8**) from disclosure. What this means is that grandfathered schemes must be subject to scrutiny under the new rules before it is decided that a current arrangement that implements a grandfathered scheme is not notifiable.

What this means for Mr Shah is that the exception will apply in relation to the scheme suggested to Mr Ray if that scheme (or a substantially similar one) had already been implemented (for another person) prior to 1 April 2018, was not notifiable under the earlier disclosure rules, and accorded with pre-1 April 2018 established practice (in the sense described above). The purpose of the exception is to remove from the requirement to notify IHT planning schemes whose workings are well-understood and agreed. In short, the scheme being suggested to Mr Ray will not have to be notified if the scheme has been sold and implemented at least once before 1 April 2018, HMRC has indicated its acceptance that it achieves that well-understood outcome and it is sold and implemented again (ro Mr Ray) without it now being changed.

If the arrangements which Mr Ray proposes to implement do benefit from the 'established practice' exception, Mr Shah may advise that they are not notifiable. If they do not so benefit, Mr Shah must ask himself the next question.

(iii) If the arrangements are not excepted from disclosure under the 'established practice' exception, it must then the asked whether those arrangements (or proposals) meet condition 1.

Condition 1 is met if the main purpose or one of the main purposes of the arrangements is to enable a person to obtain one or more of the following advantages in relation to IHT (the 'tax advantage') —

(a) The avoidance or reduction in a relevant property entry charge. This imports the original 2011 rules.

(b) The avoidance or reduction is a charge to IHT on relevant property at the ten-year anniversary, the exit charge in respect of relevant property or the charge arising in connection with close company transfers.

(c) The avoidance or reduction of a charge to IHT arising in connection with the gift with reservation of benefit rules but only where there is no pre-owned asset income tax charge.

(d) A reduction in the value of property in a person's estate without giving rise to a chargeable transfer or a PET.

If the arrangements which Mr Ray proposes to implement do not satisfy condition 1, Mr Shah may advise that they are not notifiable. If they do, Mr Shah must also ask himself the next question.

(iv) If the arrangements meet condition 1, it must be asked whether they also meet condition 2.

Condition 2 is that the arrangements involve one or more contrived or abnormal steps without which the tax advantage could not be obtained. While condition 1 identifies arrangements that reduce or avoid the listed charges to IHT, the arrangements are only notifiable if they also meet condition 2. There will be many commonly used tax planning arrangements that fall within the charges listed in condition 1 but which do not meet condition 2; consequently the arrangements will not be notifiable. Examples of well-understood planning schemes are set out in **explanatory note 1**.

It is condition 2 which effectively excludes normal and straightforward IHT planning from being notifiable. However IHT planning that requires greater complexity or contrivance to achieve intended tax advantages is more likely to be notifiable. Examples of arrangements that HMRC suggest might be notifiable are set out in **explanatory note 2**.

In considering condition 2, the arrangements themselves must be reviewed to conclude whether they involve one or more contrived or abnormal steps; but then it must also be considered whether those contrived or abnormal steps are necessary to achieve the tax advantage. For example, the use of trusts is not itself contrived or abnormal, so that a gift to a discretionary trust would not of itself satisfy condition 2. If however a more complex trust structure were used (eg for added protection of the trust property), the additional complexity might lead an informed observer to conclude that those additional steps are contrived or abnormal in the sense that it was unusual to go to those lengths and levels of complexity. However, even though the steps are contrived or abnormal, they must still be required to achieve the tax advantage if condition 2 is to be met. The nature of the steps must be considered from the point of view of an informed observer.

If the arrangements which Mr Ray proposes to implement do not satisfy condition 2, Mr Shah may advise that they are not notifiable. If they do, Mr Shah must advise that they are notifiable.

Where doubt exists over whether an arrangement or proposal is notifiable, HMRC may apply to the First-tier Tribunal for an order, in the nature of a declaration, that the proposal or arrangements are notifiable (FA 2004 s 306A). This is likely to be as a precursor to penalty proceedings against the promoter for his having failed to notify HMRC of the arrangements or proposals at the appropriate time (as to which see **parts (ii)** and **(iv)** below).

(ii) Who is under a duty to disclose the arrangements?

Where an arrangement or proposal (collectively called a scheme in the rest of this Example) is notifiable, then the promoter of the scheme is under a duty to supply certain information about it to HMRC within quite short time limits discussed below (FA 2004 s 308(1), (3)).

Who is a promoter?

In accordance with FA 2004 s 307(1), (2), a person is a promoter in relation to a scheme if, in the course of a business involving the provision to other persons (typically clients) of services relating to taxation:

- he is to any extent responsible for the design of the scheme; or
- he is to any extent responsible for organising or managing the implementation of the scheme; or
- he makes the scheme available for implementation by other persons; or
- he makes a firm approach to another person with a view making the scheme available for implementation by that (or any other) person.

In HMRC's opinion a person makes a scheme available for implementation if and when the scheme is fully designed, it is capable of being implemented in practice and the person communicates information about the scheme to clients or potential clients, suggesting that they enter into the scheme (but it does not matter whether full details of the scheme are communicated at that time).

In order to make a firm approach to another person, the following conditions have to be met (see FA 2004 s 307(4A), (4B), (4C), inserted by FA 2010 s 56, Sch 17 para 2 and effective from 1 January 2011 by virtue of the Finance Act 2010 Sch 17 (Appointed Day) Order 2010, SI 2010/3019 art 2):

- the would-be promoter makes a marketing contact with another person (ie he communicates information about the scheme to the other person with a view to him or any other person entering into transactions forming part of the scheme but the information excludes an explanation of the tax advantage to be obtained from using the scheme);
- at the time of making contact the scheme is substantially designed (ie the nature of the transactions to form part of the scheme has been sufficiently developed that it would be reasonable to believe that a person who wishes to obtain the tax advantage communicated might enter into the scheme. HMRC believe that this point in time will normally coincide with the point where a promoter has sufficient confidence in the tax analysis of the scheme to market it);
- the would-be promoter makes the contact with a view to making the scheme available for implementation by the other person (ie the would-be promoter makes the contact so that he can obtain clients who will buy the scheme from him).

If a person fulfils only the first condition above and not the third, whether or not the second condition (which does not necessarily depend on anything done by the person making the marketing contact) is also fulfilled, he will be regarded as an 'introducer' (rather than a promoter) but as introducer he is still under a duty to provide HMRC with information about the promoter (FA 2004 ss 307(1A), 313C). This 'firm approach' test applies with effect from 1 January 2011 as referred to above and is designed to trigger disclosure of a marketed scheme early in the marketing process. Under the rules as they applied before 1 January 2011, a promoter only had to disclose a scheme within five days of its being available for implementation. In order to extend this period artificially, some promoters held back key elements of a scheme when selling it to clients (because it could not then be said to be available for implementation). At a later time the final elements of the scheme were revealed and the scheme implemented immediately on a managed basis for all clients who had signed up to it. Some schemes were thus implemented quickly and widely before HMRC had the chance to block them.

By virtue of the Tax Avoidance Schemes (Promoters and Prescribed Circumstances) Regulations 2004, SI 2004/1865, a person will not, however, be a promoter where:

- he is the employee (including an office holder) of an employer who is a promoter or user of the scheme (reg 3(1));
- he is, in the course of providing tax advice, not responsible for the design of any element of the scheme (including the way in which it is structured) (reg 4(2); HMRC calls this the 'benign test');
- he is to any extent responsible for the design of the scheme but does not provide tax advice in relation to it (reg 4(3); HMRC call this the 'non-advisor test');
- he is not responsible for the design of all the elements of the scheme (including the way in which it is structured) and cannot reasonably be expected to know whether the scheme is notifiable (reg 4(4); HMRC call this the 'ignorance test');
- he is responsible for the organisation or management of the implementation of the scheme but is not connected with the promoter of the scheme (reg 5);
- he is under a duty of confidentiality to his client by reason of legal professional privilege (in Scotland, confidentiality of communications) and that client has not waived his privilege in relation to the scheme (reg 6) (but in this case the user of the scheme will be required to disclose it to HMRC).

In *HMRC v Curzon Capital* [2019] UKFTT 63, the tribunal found that the provider of administration services for the implementation of a scheme was not a promoter in terms of s 307 (because the provider of those services had not made a firm approach to another person with a view making the scheme available for implementation by that (or any other) person). The provider of the administration services in the case was not in a position to make the scheme available for implementation and so was not a promoter. The tribunal observed that s 307(2) requires an assessment of the nature of the overall business through which the services are provided rather than the nature of the specific activities that took place.

FA 2004 s 316C (introduced by FA 2015 Sch 17 para 17) enables HMRC to publish information about promoters and schemes that are notified to it (see below) which have been issued with a scheme reference number (see **part** (iii) below). However, HMRC may only publish the information in respect of schemes whose reference number has been issued on or after 26 March 2015 whose details have not been notified to HMRC under s 308, s 309 or s 310 before that day (FA 2015 Sch 17 para 21). HMRC must inform a promoter before publishing any information which would identify that person as a promoter and not publish any information that will identify scheme users. FA 2004 s 316D (also introduced by FA 2015 Sch 17 para 17) requires HMRC to publish information about court rulings that are relevant to the earlier publication of information about promoters and schemes under s 316C, but only if the ruling is given on or after 26 March 2015.

What is the promoter's duty in relation to notification?

A promoter of a notifiable proposal must within a certain time provide HMRC with certain information relating to the proposal (FA 2004 s 308(1)). A promoter of a notifiable arrangement must within a certain time after he becomes aware of any transaction forming part of the arrangement provide HMRC with certain information relating to the arrangement (unless the arrangement implements a proposal that has already been notified) (FA 2004 s 308(3)).

Where a person is a promoter in relation to two or more schemes which are substantially the same (whether they relate to the same parties or different parties), he does not need to provide information if he has already provided information in relation to any other schemes (FA 2004 s 308(5)). Whether two schemes are substantially the same will depend upon an assessment of the differences between them. In HMRC's view a scheme is no longer substantially the same if the effect of any change would be to make any previous disclosure misleading in relation to a second (or subsequent) client. In general where the tax analysis is substantially the same, HMRC will regard schemes as substantially the same where the only change is a different client. HMRC also state that changes to schemes that deal with changes in the law or accounting treatment or changes in the tax attributes of a scheme will result in schemes being not substantially the same.

A scheme may have more than one person who is a promoter in accordance with the definitions set out above. In such a case, only one promoter has to disclose the scheme and where he has done so, the other co-promoters are discharged from their respective duties of having to make a disclosure (FA 2004 s 308(4)–(4C)).

The information that the promoter must provide in relation to an IHT scheme is set out in the Tax Avoidance Schemes (Information) Regulations 2012 SI 2012/1836 (which consolidate the information regulations made since 2004). It must, under reg 4 (as supplemented by HMRC guidance), be sufficient as might reasonably be expected to enable an Inspector of Taxes to comprehend the manner in which the proposal is intended to operate and must include the following:

- the promoter's name and address;
- signification (effected by ticking the relevant box on the form) that the disclosure is being made under the IHT disclosure rules;
- a summary of the scheme;
- the name of the scheme (if any);
- information in straightforward terms (which may include common technical or legal terms) explaining each element of the scheme (including the way in which it is structured) from which the tax advantage arises (attaching copies of any prospectus or scheme diagrams that might assist in the explanation of the scheme);
- the statutory provisions on which the tax advantage is based.

The promoter must use form AAG1 to notify HMRC of a scheme (a letter or substitute form will not suffice) and it may be accessed from www.hmrc.gov.uk/aiu/index.htm.

In these cases, FA 2004 s 308(2) (as read with reg 5 of the above Information Regulations) provides that the time within which notification must occur is within a period of five working days beginning with the earliest of:

- the date following that on which the promoter first makes a firm approach to another person in relation to a scheme with a view to making the scheme available for implementation by him or others;
- the date following that on which the promoter makes a scheme available for implementation by another person;
- the date following that on which the promoter first becomes aware of the implementation of any transaction forming part of the scheme.

The time limit for notifying HMRC of a scheme will often pass before a client has actually done anything to implement the scheme and will almost always pass before he has fully implemented the scheme. Some schemes which are notified may never be implemented by any client.

In certain cases, HMRC may force a promoter to disclose further information (including documents) about a scheme if they believe he has not provided all of the above information and they have the permission of the First-tier Tribunal (FA 2004 s 308A). The tribunal will give its permission where it is satisfied that HMRC has reasonable grounds for suspecting that the information (or documents) forms part of the information listed above or will support or explain that information.

Where a promoter is ordered by the tribunal to disclose further information about a scheme, he has 10 working days to comply with the tribunal's order starting on the day after that on which the order is made, although HMRC may give him an extension (FA 2004 s 308A(5), (6); Tax Avoidance Schemes (Information) Regulations 2012, SI 2012/1836 reg 5(2)).

FA 2004 s 310A (introduced by FA 2014 s 227) provides, with effect from 17 July 2014, HMRC with additional powers to force a promoter to disclose, in the form and manner specified, further information (including documents) about a scheme within 10 working days of the request for information. Where a promoter fails to comply with the request, HMRC may apply to the First-tier Tribunal for an order requiring the information or documents to be produced (s 310B). Under s 310A HMRC does not need the prior permission of the First-tier Tribunal to request the information or documents.

FA 2004 s 310C (introduced by FA 2015 Sch 17 para 1) requires promoters to notify HMRC within 30 days if the name of a scheme, or the name or address of a promoter, changes after a reference number has been issued under s 311 (see part (iii) below). This duty applies only in respect of reference numbers allocated on or after 26 March 2015 to schemes whose details have not been notified to HMRC under s 308 before that day (FA 2015 Sch 17 para 19). In the case where there is more than one promoter of a scheme, a promoter is only obliged to provide information about changes to a promoter's details that apply specifically to itself and the requirement on another promoter to provide information is satisfied if that information has been provide by another promoter.

If HMRC have reasonable grounds to suspect that a person has been non-compliant in relation to further aspects of the DoTAS regime, they may apply to the First-tier Tribunal for an order authorising them to obtain the further information they seek. These powers relate only to the following:

- 'pre-disclosure' enquiries into non-disclosure of a scheme (seeking information from a would-be promoter or introducer as to why a scheme has not been disclosed) (FA 2004 s 313A);
- orders for supplementary information following on from such pre-disclosure enquiries (FA 2004 s 313B);
- notice requiring a person suspected of being an introducer to provide information leading to the promoter of a scheme or a person with whom he has made a marketing contact (FA 2004 s 313C);
- orders stating that a scheme is disclosable (FA 2004 s 314A).

Persons other than promoters with disclosure duties

In some cases, the duty to disclose a scheme does not fall on its promoter. In this case the duty falls on the user of the scheme and it arises where:

(a) the promoter is resident outside the UK and no promoter is resident in the UK (FA 2004 s 309(1)). The user must disclose the scheme within five working days of entering into it; he must disclose the scheme on form AAG2 (a letter or substitute form will not suffice). He will not, however, have to discharge this duty where a promoter discharges the duty of the client to notify HMRC (FA 2004 s 309(2)).

(b) there is no promoter (ie the scheme is devised in-house within an organisation) (FA 2004 s 310). The user must disclose the scheme within 30 working days of entering into it; he must disclose the scheme on form AAG3 (a letter or substitute form will not suffice).

(c) the promoter is a lawyer and is unable to disclose a scheme because of legal professional privilege (s 314). The user must disclose the scheme within five working days of entering into it; he must disclose the scheme on form AAG2 (a letter or substitute form will not suffice).

FA 2004 s 316B (introduced by FA 2015 Sch 17 para 16 with effect from 26 March 2015) enables persons to voluntarily provide information or documents to HMRC which they suspect may assist HMRC in determining whether there has been a breach of any of the requirements of the DoTAS provisions.

(iii) What other duties fall on the promoter?

Two additional duties fall on a promoter: the duty to notify the client of the scheme reference number (SRN) and the duty to provide HMRC with details of clients to whom they have provided such numbers.

Duty to notify client of scheme reference number

Once a scheme has been notified to HMRC, they may allocate to it an eight-digit reference number. They have 90 days (30 days before 26 March 2015) within which to do this, but the allocation of the number is not an indication that the scheme is tax effective. Where they do so, HMRC are under a duty to notify the promoter of that number (FA 2004 s 311(1)). The promoter who provides services to a person in connection with the scheme has a duty, in turn, to provide that person with the scheme's reference number (SRN) unless HMRC relieve him of that duty (FA 2004 s 312(1)).

Providing the client with the SRN must take place within 30 working days after the later of:

- the date on which the promoter becomes aware of any transaction which forms part of the scheme; and
- the date on which he himself is notified of the SRN by HMRC (FA 2004 s 312(2), (3)).

In accordance with the Tax Avoidance Schemes (Information) Regulations 2012, SI 2012/1836 reg 6, the promoter must supply the client with the following information in order to discharge his duty under section 312:

- the promoter's name and address;
- the name or a brief description of the scheme;
- the SRN;
- the date the SRN was sent by him to the client.

Form AAG6 must be used for this purpose (a letter or substitute form will not suffice) and it may be accessed from www.hmrc.gov.uk/aiu/index.htm.

HMRC advise that, although there is no obligation to do so, promoters may find it convenient to provide the SRN to a client when the scheme is made available to him rather than wait until he has implemented it. If the promoter does this using AAG6, then he does not need to notify the number again when he becomes aware of the client entering into the scheme. Where a promoter has been provided with more than one SRN in relation to a scheme, only one of the numbers has to be disclosed to the client.

Once the notification duties have been discharged, further notification duties then fall on the client. First, he has within 30 days to provide (again using form AAG6) the same information listed above to any other person whom he might reasonably be expected to know is or is likely to be party to the scheme and who might reasonably be expected to gain a tax advantage in relation to any relevant tax because of the scheme (FA 2004 s 312A; Tax Avoidance Schemes (Information) Regulations 2012, SI 2012/1836 reg 6).

Finance Act 2013 s 223 has introduced a further duty on the client to provide information. Where a promoter has notified a client of a scheme reference number, the client must provide the promoter with information relating to the client (FA 2004 s 312B). This further information will enable HMRC to identify the client (especially in cases where the information currently provided does not enable HMRC to identify the client from the information they hold). The content of this further duty is set out in the Tax Avoidance Schemes (Information) Regulations 2012, SI 2012/1836 reg 8A (introduced by the Tax Avoidance Schemes (Information) (Amendment) Regulations 2013 SI 2013/2592 reg 16). The client has to provide the promoter with their unique tax reference number and national insurance number within 10 days of the later of the client receiving the scheme reference number or the date that the client first enters into a transaction forming part of the notifiable arrangements.

Secondly, under FA 2004 s 313(1) and Tax Avoidance Schemes (Information) Regulations 2012, SI 2012/1836 reg 11(2), the client (and any other person who is party to a notifiable scheme) in turn falls under a duty (to be discharged within 12 months from the end of the month in which he first enters into a transaction forming part of the scheme) to provide HMRC with information relating to:

- the SRN reference number;
- the tax year in or the date on which he obtains or expects to obtain the tax advantage under the scheme.

If the client is required to deliver an inheritance tax return (IHT100) to report a lifetime chargeable transfer that forms part of the scheme, then he must discharge the above duty by providing the above information in that return, unless one of the exceptions below applies. He has to record the SRN in box K1 on the return. The return is due 12 months of the end of the month in which the transfer takes place and if this is no later than the date on which the client must report the SRN, then the return may be used by the client as the means of discharging his duty. No other tax return form (eg an income tax return) may be used by the client to disclose the SRN in relation to an IHT tax avoidance scheme (and if it is disclosed on another return, the client has not discharged his duty to notify HMRC).

There are certain exceptions to the client's duty to use form IHT100 as the vehicle for discharging his duty under the DoTAS rules to disclose the SRN:

- if the date for submitting form IHT100 is later than the date by which he must report the SRN;

- if he is late in submitting form IHT100;
- if he has not disclosed the SRN in form IHT 100 which has already been submitted;
- if he needs to disclose more than one SRN (form IHT100 has space for notifying only one SRN); in this case he must however still use form IHT 100 for one of the SRNs.

In such cases the client must disclose the SRN (or those for which there was not space on form IHT100), and certain additional information (see below), on form AAG4(IHT) (a letter or substitute form will not suffice) and it may be accessed from www.hmrc.gov.uk/aiu/index.htm.

That form must also be used if the client is not liable to submit form IHT100 – whether because he has made a chargeable transfer which is an excepted transfer (within the Inheritance Tax (Delivery of Accounts) (Excepted Transfers and Excepted Terminations) Regulations 2008, SI 2008/605), or because any transfer of value he has made is exempt or potentially exempt or a combination of both, or because he has not made a transfer of value at all.

When submitting Form AAG4 (IHT) to HMRC the client must give:

- the SRN;
- his name and address;
- the tax year in which or the date on which he expects to obtain the IHT advantage.

What is noticeable from the form, however, is that there are fields for three items of information not required covered by reg 11(3) of the Information Regulations – the client's (user's) email address, his telephone number (this, but not the email address, is identified as optional), and arguably the IHT reference number (this does not seem to fall within the wording of reg 11(3)(b) viz 'any National Insurance number, tax reference number, PAYE reference number or other **personal** identifier allocated by HMRC to the person to whom the information relates' (emphasis added)).

Duty to notify HMRC of client lists

Where the promoter of a scheme has provided services to a client in connection with the scheme *and* is under a duty to provide the client with the SRN (and the supplementary information as set out above), he must, as from 1 January 2011 and within 30 days after the end of each calendar quarter, provide HMRC with his own name and address and a list of the names and addresses (and on or after 4 November 2013, the tax reference numbers and national insurance numbers) of clients who have implemented a scheme (together with its SRN) in that calendar quarter (identifying the end of the quarter) (s 313ZA; Tax Avoidance Schemes (Information) Regulations 2012, SI 2012/1836 reg 13 as amended by the Tax Avoidance Schemes (Information) (Amendment) Regulations 2013/2592 regs 17–19). The lists apply to schemes disclosed at any time. A promoter is not under a duty to provide nil returns.

The duty to provide client lists for any quarter is triggered by the duty to provide a client with an SRN which in turn happens on the later of the promoter receiving the SRN from HMRC or his becoming aware of any transaction forming part of the scheme (as described above). HMRC are of the opinion that the latter date will most usually trigger the duty to provide client lists. Examples of the application of these rules are in **explanatory note 3**.

Promoters can submit client lists online using the Shared Workspace facility of HMRC's website or using a form which has to be obtained from HMRC (which needs to be contacted in order for the form to be obtained – telephone 020 7438 6733).

The duty to provide client lists also applies to co-promoters whether or not they have made a separate disclosure informing HMRC of the existence of a scheme. In certain cases HMRC may relieve promoters of the duty. HMRC's intentions here are to identify clients that fail to report the SRN to HMRC on their tax returns (or otherwise) and to get an early indication of the extent to which a scheme is being used.

There is an extended deadline for the provision by the promoter of a client's tax reference number and national insurance numbers ('the client's numbers'). As explained above, under s 213B a client has to provide a promoter with his numbers within 10 days of the later of receiving the SRN or the date that the client first enters into a transaction forming part of the tax avoidance arrangements. If these events occur at or near the end of the quarter for which the promoter has to provide client lists, the promoter may not have the information to provide to HMRC.

In such a case the promoter must, within 30 days of the end of the calendar quarter concerned, inform HMRC that one of the following three scenarios applies:

- the client has notified the promoter that he does not have the numbers;
- the client has not complied with his obligation to inform the promoter of the numbers;
- the time limit for the client to provide his numbers has not expired (except in this scenario, notification must be made by the 16th day after the quarter).

Where the time limit for the provision by the client of his numbers has not expired, then the duty to provide the client's numbers to HMRC is extended to 60 days after the end of the calendar quarter concerned (Tax Avoidance Schemes (Information) Regulations 2012, SI 2012/1836 reg 13 as amended by the Tax Avoidance Schemes (Information) (Amendment) Regulations 2013/2592 regs 17–19).

S 313ZB gives HMRC power, in cases where it suspects the client identified on a promoter client list is not the only party to the arrangements (be they users of the scheme or other parties involved in the selling and execution of the scheme), to require the promoter to provide further prescribed information about parties to the arrangements. The content of this further duty is set out in the Tax Avoidance Schemes (Information) Regulations 2004, SI 2004/1864 reg 13A (introduced by the Tax Avoidance Schemes (Information) (Amendment) Regulations 2013 SI 2013/2592 reg 20). If the promoter holds the information, he must, within 10 days of HMRC requiring him to do so, provide the name and address of the other parties to the arrangements, any identification number allocated to them by HMRC and sufficient information as might reasonably be expected to enable HMRC to comprehend the manner in which the parties are involved in the arrangements.

(iv) Sanction for failing to carry out the duties of a promoter

In relation to a promoter, there are two main sets of penalties imposed by TMA 1970 s 98C: disclosure penalties and information penalties. In both cases the initial penalty must be determined by the First-tier Tribunal after a hearing involving both HMRC and the promoter. There is a right of appeal to the Upper Tribunal against any penalty imposed by the Tribunal.

A promoter may be liable to penalties if he fails to comply with his duty (under FA 2004 s 308) to notify HMRC of a scheme (TMA 1970 s 98C(1)(a)(i)). The amount of the initial penalty is up to £600 for each day during the period beginning with the first day after the end of the five-day notification period (as described above) and ending with the earlier of the day on which the penalty is determined by the First-tier Tribunal and the last day before the day on which disclosure is made. In determining the amount of this penalty in any case, the Tribunal must take into account the fees received by the promoter so that the penalty can be set at a level that reflects the economic advantage of not disclosing a scheme. The tribunal has the power to adjust the penalty computed using the daily rate up to a maximum of £1 million if it considers the penalty so set to be an insufficient deterrent in the circumstances. If the failure to notify continues after the above penalty is imposed, the promoter may be liable to further penalties imposed by HMRC up to £600 for each day on which the failure continues after the day on which the initial penalty was imposed.

A promoter may be liable under TMA 1970 s 98C (1)(a)(ii) to an initial penalty (imposed by the First-tier Tribunal) of up to £5,000 if he fails to provide information or updated information (or provides it otherwise than in the prescribed format) as required of him under the DoTAS regime, including failure to notify his client of an SRN and failure to provide client lists to HMRC. HMRC may impose a daily penalty of up to £600 for each day that the failure to provide information continues after the initial penalty has been determined.

The penalties will not be imposed if the promoter has a reasonable excuse for non-compliance (TMA 1970 s 118(2)). HMRC say that what amounts to a reasonable excuse will vary according to the nature of the failure and the type and circumstances of the person involved. They view it as being some exceptional and unforeseeable event beyond the person's control that formed an insurmountable obstacle to timely compliance.

HMRC have indicated that they will select cases for penalty proceedings based on:

- the level and knowledge/experience of the promoter of the DoTAS regime and the tax system generally;
- the promoter's previous behaviour in relation to the DoTAS regime;

- the adequacy of the systems the promoter has in place to ensure compliance with the DoTAS regime;
- the nature of the behaviour that led to the failure (eg was it an isolated error, or was it because of carelessness or a deliberate act);
- whether the promoter altered HMRC to the error of his own volition;
- what the promoter did after the error was discovered to prevent recurrence.

Explanatory Notes

Inheritance tax – examples of arrangements that are not notifiable

(1) The DoTAS rules insofar as they apply to IHT do not, subject to the application of the confidentiality and premium fee hallmarks, catch straightforward inheritance tax planning. HMRC has set out in their guidance the following examples of straightforward planning arrangements (together with explanations as to why conditions 1 and 2 together are not met):

(a) A lifetime gift to a spouse or civil partner

(b) Regular gifts out of income

(c) Transfers of value equal to the available nil-rate band into trust, which may be repeated every seven years

(d) Executing a Will, deed of variation or disclaimer which gives rise to exemption from IHT

(e) Executing a Will that leaves property to an exempt beneficiary such as a spouse or charity

(f) Executing a deed of variation to which IHA 1984 s 142 applies to transfer assets in death to an exempt beneficiary

(g) Disclaiming an entitlement under a Will to which IHTA 1984 s 142 applies where there is an exempt residuary beneficiary

(h) Purchase of shares which will qualify for business property relief after they have been owned for two years

(i) Gift of land where the donor continues to use that land but pays a full consideration for tis use

(j) Gift of an undivided share of property which is subsequently used by both the donor and donee

(k) A non-UK domiciled individual who is not UK resident transfers funds from a sterling-denominated UK bank account in to US dollar-denominated bank account so that the bank account is left out of account under IHTA 1984 s 157

(l) A non-UK domiciled individual transfers non-UK situs property into a trust (from which he can benefit) just before becoming deemed domiciled in the UK

(m) Immediately before a ten year anniversary a distribution is made from a relevant property trust to reduce the charge on the subsequent ten year anniversary

(n) Gift and Loan Trusts/Loan Trusts

Inheritance tax – examples of arrangements that HMRC suggest may be notifiable

(2) The DoTAS rules insofar as they apply to IHT do not, subject to the application of the confidentiality and premium fee hallmarks, catch straightforward inheritance tax planning. HMRC has set out in their guidance the following examples of planning arrangements which may be notifiable (together with explanations as to why conditions 1 and 2 together may be met):

(a) Arrangements to gift shares which qualify for business property relief (BPR) into trust and subsequently sell the shares back to the transferor

(b) Creation of a reversionary lease

(c) Creation of employee benefit trusts (EBTs)

Examples of duty to provide client lists – DoTAS in the context of inheritance tax

(3) The following are examples based on those provided by HMRC as to how the duty to provide client lists operates. References below to a given client 'implementing' a scheme are to a step being taken or a transaction being entered into (whether by the client or otherwise) in implementing the scheme for that client.

Example 1

Promoter P discloses a scheme to HMRC in late April 2023 and HMRC issues an SRN. On 17 May 2023 P becomes aware that client X has implemented the scheme and he issues X with the SRN on 16 June 2023. On 30 June 2023 P becomes aware that client Y has implemented the scheme and issues Y with the SRN on 30 July 2023.

P is required to provide information about clients X and Y in the client list for the period 6 April 2022 to 30 June 2022, due by 30 July 2023.

Example 2

Promoter P discloses a scheme on 22 April 2023. On 29 April 2023 he becomes aware that client X has implemented the scheme. P receives an SRN from HMRC on 2 May 2023. P's duty to notify the client of the SRN is triggered on 2 May 2023.

P is required to provide information about client X to HMRC in the client list for the period 6 April 2023 to 30 June 2023, due by 30 July 2023.

Example 3

Promoter P has disclosed two schemes (A and B) to HMRC each of which has been issued with an SRN. In the period to 30 June 2023, he becomes aware that clients X and Y have implemented scheme A and that clients Y and Z has implemented scheme B.

P will be required to submit two forms by 30 July 2023, one for scheme A (containing information about clients X and Y) and the other for scheme B (containing information about clients Y and Z).

The due dates must be strictly observed and it does not matter that they may fall at the weekend or on a Bank Holiday, Good Friday or Christmas Day.

The DOTAS regime in relation to other taxes and NIC

(4) The application of the DoTAS regime to other taxes and NIC is contained in the companion publication to this work, **Tolley's Taxwise I 2023/24.**

A General Anti-Abuse Rule and its application to inheritance tax

(5) In the government's opinion, the distinction between tax evasion and tax avoidance has become blurred and the fairness of the tax system has been the subject of debate. Against this background Finance Act 2013 Pt 5 enacts rules for the purpose of counteracting tax advantages from tax arrangements that are abusive (collectively known as the anti-abuse rule (GAAR)). The rule, which applies to all tax arrangements entered

into on or after 17 July 2013, aims to set a new standard as to what is, and what is not, acceptable tax planning and it applies in particular for the purposes of inheritance tax. In effect, the GAAR requires a taxpayer to act in accordance with the spirit of tax law and not merely within the letter of the law. The GAAR imposes an overriding statutory limit on the extent to which taxpayers can go in trying to reduce their tax bill, even if they act within the law.

Arrangements are tax arrangements if, having regard to all the circumstances, it would be reasonable to conclude that the obtaining of a tax advantage was the main purpose or one of the main purposes of the arrangements. This is an objective test and involves asking whether a transaction has been reshaped or has been entered into under different terms and conditions in order to change significantly the tax result that would otherwise have arisen.

Arrangements are 'abusive' (and hence the limit of legitimate tax planning is reached) if entering into them or carrying them out cannot reasonably be regarded as a reasonable course of action in relation to the relevant tax provisions ('the double reasonableness test'). This two-stage test asks: (1) can there be a reasonably held view that (2) the arrangements are a reasonable course of action? This double reasonableness test is an objective test. It requires, first, a consideration of whether the tax arrangements are a reasonable course of action. Then secondly it requires a consideration of whether the answer to the first test (ie that the arrangements are reasonable or not) is itself reasonable! This is built into the GAAR to protect taxpayers. Tax arrangements are not within the GAAR just because someone holds the view that arrangements are an unreasonable course of action; that person's view must itself also be reasonable. Just because a view is commonly held does not mean that it a reasonable view.

All circumstances must be taken into account when applying the test and the legislation includes a non-exhaustive list of circumstances which must be considered (eg any abnormal or contrived steps, the policy and principles behind the tax rules in question, and any shortcomings in the law). Tax arrangements may be abusive if they give rise to certain results (such as a tax result which differs from the economic result) but only if it is reasonable to assume that the result was not anticipated when the relevant tax provisions were enacted. On the other hand, arrangements might not be abusive if they accord with established practice and HMRC had indicated its acceptance of that practice at the time the arrangements were entered into.

A clear indication of acceptable tax planning is not readily defined under the GAAR and in practice its application needs to be carefully considered for all but the most straightforward arrangements that seek to obtain a tax saving. Tax advantages arising from abusive tax arrangements are to be counteracted by the making of just and reasonable adjustments, whether in respect of the tax in question or any other tax to which the GAAR applies. The main purpose of counteraction is to deny the tax advantages gained by the arrangements but it may take any form. HMRC must comply with the procedural requirements set out in FA 2013 Schedule 41 before making any such adjustments. In particular HMRC must refer the matter to an independent advisory panel for its view before taking the matter further. Taxpayers themselves are also expected to declare any abusive arrangements they enter into and to self-counteract the tax advantages that flow from them as part of the self-assessment process. The main significance of this is to provide a means for HMRC to impose penalties on the tax owing if counteraction is required. Where a tax arrangement is counteracted, a penalty equal to 60% of the counteracted advantage will be levied.

HMRC has issued guidance on the application of the GAAR (see www.hmrc.gov.uk/avoidance/gaar.htm). Examples relating to inheritance tax may be found in Part VI of Part D of the guidance (see www.hmrc.gov.uk/avoidance/gaar-partd-examples.pdf). The examples are, however, only illustrative and HMRC do not endorse any of them. The examples provide useful guidance on the relevant questions to be addressed and the principles to be applied but it will still be difficult to gauge where some arrangements stand.

An opinion of the GAAR advisory panel states that a scheme using a transfer to an employee benefit trust (EBT) to reduce the value of an individual's estate on death was abusive. Four months before her death, an individual set up a company of which she and another were the only directors. Both funded the company with £700,000 in equity. The company established an EBT and the individual transferred her shares in the company to the EBT. She died two months later. The transfer reduced the value of her estate and a claim was made that the transfer to the EBT was exempt from IHT under IHTA 1984 s 28. Further there would be no ongoing periodic charges within the trust (because it was an EBT). In the panel's opinion, the transfer of the shares to the trust for the benefit of employees at a time when it did not have and did not need any, was contrived and abnormal. If the company had been well established with a long-standing workforce, gifting shares into the trust might have been a legitimate aim of ensuring employees were incentivised to continue the business after the donor's death. However, in the case before the panel, there was no such business or employees and the only persons who could benefit from the trust on the donor's death were her issue. The panel's view was that the transfer of the shares a chargeable lifetime transfer in respect of which a supplementary charge to IHT at 40% arose. Moreover as she was also a beneficiary of a trust, the trust property was potentially subject to tax on her death as a gift with reservation of benefit (see **Example B1**). The panel referred to example D2 from Part D of HMRC's GAAR guidance. Consequently the use of EBTs in deathbed planning is clearly seen as abusive.

A second GAAR opinion in relation to inheritance was delivered in January 2023. It concerned the extraction of profits from an estate, using options, by utilising non-excluded property.

The GAAR sits alongside and where necessary takes priority over all existing tax law. HMRC will usually apply the specific tax rules to a taxpayer's arrangements before considering whether there is any abuse, but they may invoke the GAAR first if they choose to do so. Just because an arrangement is within the particular tax rules concerned does not means it is not abusive under the GAAR and conversely, an arrangement which is not abusive and so is outside the GAAR may still be challenged by HMRC. In particular the GAAR is one strand in HMRC's approach to tackling avoidance and does not displace the DoTAS regime.

The GAAR is discussed further in the companion publication to this work, **Tolley's Taxwise I 2023/24**.

Further general anti-avoidance measures

(6) FA 2014 Part 4 and Part 5 introduce further general anti-avoidance measures concerning, respectively, Follower Notices and Accelerated Payments (Part 4) and High Risk Promoters of Tax Avoidance Schemes (Part 5). Both sets of measures took effect from 21 July 2014.

FA 2014 Part 4 (which applies inter alia to inheritance tax) introduces two new consequences for certain users of tax arrangements. The first is a power for HMRC to issue a 'follower notice' where:

(a) HMRC is enquiring into a taxpayer's tax return or claim, or there is an ongoing appeal reading entries on a return or a claim,

(b) HMRC consider that the tax return or claim was submitted on the basis that the taxpayer could reduce his tax liability (or claim a repayment) as a result of a tax avoidance arrangement, and

(c) HMRC are of the view that the courts have decided in another case that the avoidance arrangement is ineffective. This will be the case where the Supreme Court has ruled on the efficacy of the arrangement, where another court or tribunal has made such a ruling and no appeal has been pursued or permission to pursue and appeal has been refused.

HMRC has 12 months from the date on which the judicial ruling is made or, if later, the day on which the return or claim was received by HMRC to issue a follower notice. The follower notice requires the taxpayer to amend his return to remove the entries relating to the tax avoidance arrangement so that the liability becomes the amount that it would have been if the arrangement had not been used. The amendment must be made within 90 days after the date of the follower notice or 30 days after HMRC issues a determination against representations made following the issue of the follower notice. Representations may be made in writing to HMRC within 90 days of the date of the notice on the grounds that the conditions for issuing the follower notice have not been met, the court's ruling is not relevant to the tax avoidance arrangements in question, or the follower notice was not given by the deadline. The legislation further sets out what happens if a taxpayer elects not to take those steps. HMRC will charge interest from the due date that the tax should have been paid until it is paid. It can also charge tax-geared penalties if notices are not complied with before the deadline. If the taxpayer fails to amend his return following a follower notice then the penalty is between 10% and 50% of the tax that the scheme was aiming to save. The taxpayer has a right of appeal against any penalty charged under these provisions and he has 30 days after the penalty is imposed to exercise his right. These penalties are in addition to the penalties for late filing, failure to notify and/or penalties for the error in the return for the inclusion of the failed tax avoidance arrangement.

The second of the measures contained in FA 2014 Part 4 is a requirement to pay the amount of the asserted tax advantage to HMRC on receipt of an 'accelerated payment notice' so as to deny a taxpayer the cash flow advantage of not having to pay his tax while any enquiry and subsequent tax appeal is unresolved. This notice can be given where the following conditions are met:

(a) HMRC is enquiring into the taxpayer's tax return or claim, or there is an ongoing appeal reading entries on a return or a claim,

(b) the tax return or claim was submitted on the basis that the taxpayer could reduce his tax liability (or claim a repayment) as a result of a tax avoidance arrangement, and

(c) the tax avoidance arrangements are caught by the legislation which will be the case where:

   (i) a follower notice is issued in relation to the tax avoidance arrangement, as described above;

   (ii) the tax arrangements are notifiable under the Disclosure of Tax Avoidance Scheme (DoTAS) rules; or

   (iii) HMRC is taking counteraction under the General Anti-Abuse Rule (GAAR).

The tax payable under an accelerated payment notice must be made within 90 days after the date of the notice or 30 days after HMRC issues a determination against representations made following the issue of the accelerated payment notice. The payment does not have to be made all at once as long as it is paid by the due date. Although there is no right of appeal against an accelerated payment notice, representations may be made in writing to HMRC within 90 days of the date of the notice on the grounds that the conditions for issuing the accelerated payment notice have not been met or the tax specified in the notice is incorrect. The amount payable is the amount relating to the tax advantage that the use of the scheme tries to achieve. HMRC calculates the amount to the best of its information and belief and so may not be the same amount due when the enquiry is completed or appeal is settled. If the amount of tax payable under the accelerated payment notice is more than the amount finally payable, a repayment (together with interest) will be made by HMRC.

HMRC will charge tax-geared penalties if the amount shown in the accelerated payment notice is not paid by the due date. If the amount is not so paid a 5% penalty may be levied; additional levies may be made of 5% of the amount due 5 months after the deadline and a further 5% of the amount due 11 months after the deadline. The taxpayer has a right of appeal against any penalty charged under these provisions and he has 30 days after the penalty is imposed to exercise his right. Penalties will not be charged where the taxpayer has a 'time to pay' arrangement in place before the due date or has a reasonable excuse for non-payment. Interest is not charged on the late payment of the accelerated payment amount itself. However, interest is charged for the late payment of tax. For interest purposes any amount paid under an accelerated payment notice is treated as a payment of tax so that interest will stop accruing on the amount of tax equal to the amount of the accelerated payment from the date it is paid. Interest may also be charged on the late payment of any penalties. HMRC also have considerable powers to collect tax debts including contacting taxpayers for payment, using bailiffs to enforce payment and applying to the courts to wind up companies or declare individuals bankrupt.

Accelerated payment notices are issued on a scheme by scheme basis and so, if a number of schemes are used, accelerated payment notices may not all be issued to a taxpayer at the same time. The notice will cover only the tax advantage relating to the specific avoidance scheme covered by the notice and the amount shown may not be the final liability agreed which may be larger or smaller than the amount of the notice. The notice does not include any interest or penalties and so when an enquiry or appeal is finalised there may be additional amounts to pay.

If a taxpayer receives an accelerated payment notice at the same time as an opportunity is in place to settle his tax liabilities, the amount payable under the notice may not be calculated on the same terms offered in the settlement opportunity. Settlement opportunity calculations may also include interest and penalties. The notice may therefore not be for the same amount as the figure requested in order to settle the matter in full with HMRC.

FA 2014 Part 5 introduces new legislation applying to certain promoters of tax avoidance schemes (PoTAS). This legislation is designed to tackle the particular behaviours which have been identified amongst certain promoters of tax avoidance schemes (eg failure to comply with DOTAS or respond to HMRC information notices) and in doing so improve the transparency of certain promoters with HMRC with appropriate sanctions if the promoter does not want to comply voluntarily. In broad outline, the provisions define promoters of avoidance schemes, identify when they have triggered 'threshold' conditions targeting specified behaviours, and provide for a 'conduct' notice to be applied to these promoters. Those who fail to comply with a conduct notice may be issued with a 'monitoring' notice, which requires pre-approval by a Tribunal. Names of promoters subject to a monitoring notice will be published by HMRC, including details of how the conduct notice was breached, and the promoter will be required to publish its monitored status to clients. These information requirements (which are provided for in The Finance Act 2014 (High Risk Promoters Prescribed Information) Regulations 2015 (SI 2015/549)) apply to monitored promoters, and intermediaries and clients of monitored promoters. In effect promoters will have to tell its clients that they are being monitored so that their customers are aware of the risks of using them. HMRC's guidance on PoTAS was issued on 12 February 2015. It can be accessed at www.gov.uk/government/publications/promoters-of-tax-avoidance-schemes-guidance.

(7) The Serial Tax Avoidance Regime (STAR) (as introduced in Sch 18 FA 2016) applies to anyone who has entered into a tax avoidance arrangement, where the arrangement is defeated and the defeat becomes final after 5 April 2017. The avoidance arrangements concerned are those that are disclosable under the DoTAS rules, where a follower notice has been issued or where there a notice of a decision under the GAAR. 'Defeat' in this context has a wide meaning and includes a scheme defeated by a decision of a court and in the case where a taxpayer reaches settlement with HMRC agreeing to make an amendment to their return or claim or decrease the tax advantage sought by HMRC. For there to be a defeat there must be a final counteraction under the GAAR, of DoTAS arrangements or as a result of a follower notice (where a return or claim is amended to counteract the advantage, the taxpayer agrees to relinquish the tax advantage or the counteraction is final (including settlement with HMRC or a final decision by a tribunal where there is no prospect of appeal).

A defeat will trigger the issue of a warning notice which remains in place for 5 years. Any subsequent defeats will also trigger warning notices extending the warning period. During the notice period the taxpayer must report the use of any tax avoidance schemes. Where there is a subsequent defeat of a scheme a penalty will be charged. The penalty is a percentage of the counteracted advantage. The penalties increase depending on the number of defeats during the notice period (ie 20% for the first defeat, 40% for the second and 60% for the third and subsequent defeats). Where three schemes are defeated within the five-year warning period, HMRC can publicly name the taxpayer as a serial tax avoider, stop the taxpayer claiming or making use of direct tax reliefs for three years where the defeated schemes involved misuse direct tax reliefs.

IHT DoTAS hallmark before 1 April 2018

(8) IHT came within the DoTAS regime from 6 April 2011 (The Inheritance Tax Avoidance Schemes (Prescribed Descriptions of Arrangements) Regulations 2011, SI 2011/170 reg 1). This note deals with that regime which applied until it was replaced on 1 April 2018.

The arrangements which were set out in the regulations as falling within the DoTAS regime were those which resulted in property becoming 'relevant property' where the main benefit of the arrangements was that an advantage was obtained in relation to 'a relevant property entry charge' (that is to say the charge to IHT which arises when an individual in his lifetime makes a transfer of value which results in property being held on trust in circumstances where the property becomes relevant property (The Inheritance Tax Avoidance Schemes (Prescribed Descriptions of Arrangements) Regulations 2011, SI 2011/170 reg 2). For the definition of a 'transfer of value' see Example A1 and for that of 'relevant property' see **Example C10 explanatory note 8.**

Had Mr Shah been considering whether those regulations applied to the arrangements described to Mr Ray, he would asked himself the following questions:

(i) Are there arrangements (or proposals for arrangements) which result in property becoming 'relevant property'?

Where arrangements do not at any stage lead to property becoming relevant property, then the scheme will not need to be disclosed. Property may be settled on trust as part of the arrangements, but it is only where it becomes relevant property that the scheme may require disclosure. The property does not need to become relevant property immediately after it is settled; a scheme may require disclosure if at any point in the arrangements property becomes relevant property. If property becomes relevant property, then the scheme may require disclosure even if the property ceases to be relevant property at a later date. In the context of this Example, the proposed arrangements would involve Mr Ray 'by a series of transactions, transferring some of his assets to an overseas discretionary trust in favour of his children'; this first question appears therefore to require an affirmative answer on the information given.

(ii) If yes, do those arrangements (or proposals) enable a 'relevant property entry charge' advantage to arise?

As described above, although a tax advantage is widely drawn, the scheme would have to be disclosed only if there is a tax advantage in respect of the IHT arising on the settlement of the relevant property trust during the individual's lifetime as a result of his making a transfer of value. If the arrangements achieve only other IHT advantages, then disclosure will not be required under the DoTAS regime in so far as it applies to IHT. Furthermore the trust must be constituted by a 'transfer of value' made by the individual as defined in IHTA 1984 s 3(1) (that is a disposition made by him that results in the diminution in the value of his estate). HMRC give the following examples of where arrangements may have to be disclosed:

- Where there are arrangements which result in property becoming relevant property, there is no transfer of value, but, in the absence of other intervening steps in the arrangements there would have been a transfer of value. Disclosure may be required in this case because (as the guidance puts it) the arrangements have, by definition, resulted in an advantage in respect of the property entry charge.
- Where due to the arrangements the value of the property which becomes relevant property is greater than the loss to the settlor's estate, then disclosure may be required because an advantage may have been obtained in respect of the property entry charge.
- Where the relevant property entry charge is relieved (unless there are no wider arrangements other than a single step claim to relief/exemption or use of the nil-rate band).

The ambit of the relevant property entry charge is discussed further in **explanatory note 1**.

(iii) This is an objective, comparative test (*CIR v Parker* (1966)). It considers the value of the expected tax advantage compared to the value of any other benefits likely to be enjoyed. HMRC have expressed the view that those who plan tax arrangements fully understand the tax advantage which schemes are intended to achieve. They expect it will be obvious to any potential client what the relationship is between the tax advantage and any other benefits of the arrangements they are entering into.

If he had answered yes to all three of these questions, Mr Shah could have been satisfied that the arrangement was a notifiable IHT scheme (unless it was grandfathered – see the next paragraph). If he had answered no to any of these questions then the arrangement would not have been a notifiable IHT scheme (although the disclosure rules for other taxes may still have applied). See **explanatory note 9** for a list of 'schemes' published by HMRC which they accepted were not notifiable, either because they did not fulfil the conditions for disclosure or because of the grandfathering exception below.

There is one circumstance in which, despite having answered each of the above questions affirmatively, an arrangement (or proposal) might yet not have been notifiable and that was where the arrangement (or proposal) was the same (or substantially the same) as arrangements (or proposals) which were implemented before 6 April 2011 (or which were made available for implementation before that date or about which a promoter made a firm approach to another person before that date) (The Inheritance Tax Avoidance Schemes (Prescribed Descriptions of Arrangements) Regulations 2011, SI 2011/170 reg 3). This was known as the grandfathering exception (see **explanatory note 9**). Even if the application of this rule took the arrangements outside the DoTAS regime in so far as it applied to IHT, the disclosure rules for other taxes may still have applied.

It was one of the aims of the extension of the disclosure rules to IHT to restrict disclosure to new schemes. Yet, it was a question of fact whether the arrangements were protected from disclosure under the grandfathering exception. HMRC stated that evidence of grandfathering would have included the existence and substance of the arrangement being clearly described in tax manuals or publications, the production of an affidavit where evidence that the grandfathering rule applies is subject to legal professional privilege and a practitioner's own records as to when they made, or learned that competitors were making, an arrangement available.

HMRC have stated that arrangements that typically would not be excluded from disclosure include those where property becomes relevant property and an advantage is obtained in respect of the IHT property entry charge:

- where the claim that there is no transfer of value relies on a series of transactions where, in the absence of all other intervening steps, there would have been a transfer of value and entry charge;
- where reliefs and exemptions are used in such a way that the arrangements are not covered by the grandfathering exception;
- where an individual makes a potentially exempt transfer to another person and the arrangements are such that the subject-matter of the transfer becomes relevant property (unless, again, the arrangements are covered by the grandfathering exception).

IHT arrangements fell within the ambit of the DoTAS regime if as a result of any element of the arrangements property became relevant property and a main benefit of the arrangements was that an advantage was obtained in relation to a 'relevant property entry charge'. A relevant property entry charge is defined as the charge to inheritance tax which arises on a transfer of value (as defined in IHTA 1984 s 3(1)) made by an individual during his life as a result of which property becomes relevant property (The Inheritance Tax Avoidance Schemes (Prescribed Descriptions of Arrangements) Regulations 2011 SI 2011/170 reg (2), (3)). In s 3(1) a transfer of value is defined as a disposition made by a person as a result of which there is a diminution in the value of his estate (so-called actual transfers of value).

The question that arises is whether the DoTAS regime, in the IHT context, encompasses only actual transfers of value since the regulations mention only s 3(1). Section 3(4) provides that references in the IHTA 1984 to a 'transfer of value made' include references to events on the happening of which tax is chargeable as if a transfer of value had been made (so-called deemed transfers of value). Although the regulations do not specifically mention s 3(4), is its effect imported into the DoTAS regime? On a strict reading of s 3(4), it is only where the phrase 'transfer of value made' is found in the Act that s 3(4) applies; in s 3(1) one finds only the words 'transfer of value' which is in turn defined by reference to a 'disposition made'. On a narrow interpretation it would appear that deemed transfers of value are not within the ambit of the DoTAS rules. On a purposive construction, given that the DoTAS arrangements are part of HMRC's weaponry of protecting the tax base from the effects of avoidance arrangements, there is an argument for a wider interpretation of the regulations so as to say that deemed transfers of value (eg termination of an estate IIP and attribution to participators of a close company's transfer of value) may give rise to a relevant property entry charge as defined. On this wider interpretation, there would be a relevant property entry charge, for example, if an IPDI or a disabled person's interest under a Will trust came to an end and the property concerned became relevant property as a result.

If one takes the narrow view, then there is no other form of transfer of value other than a disposition that results in the diminution of an individual's estate. Since 'disposition' includes a disposition made by associated operations (s 272), it is clear that a (single) transfer of value can be made by two or more operations taken together (s 268(3)). If transfer of value has the s 3(1) meaning then anything amounting to 'wider arrangements' (as referred to in HMRC's examples) which was not also 'associated operations' would seem not capable of giving rise to a transfer of value.

Schemes not within the conditions or within the grandfathering exception — DoTAS in the context of inheritance tax

(9) The following are 'schemes' which, if there are no additional arrangements, HMRC regarded as not falling within the DoTAS regime for IHT (as it applied before 1 April 2018) either because the conditions for the application of the DoTAS regime are not met or because the grandfathering exception applies to the scheme:

- arrangements where property does not become relevant property;

- single-step arrangements that qualify for relief or exemptions;
- the purchase of business assets with a view to transferring them into a relevant property trust after two years;
- the purchase of agricultural assets with a view to transferring them into a relevant property trust after the period that results in the transfer qualifying for agricultural property relief;
- pilot settlements (even though they may lead to tax advantages in respect of the ten-yearly charge or exit charge, as such charges are not covered by the regulations because they are not 'relevant property entry charges');
- discounted gift schemes where the grandfathering exception applies (any further development of such schemes involving relevant property would be disclosable);
- excluded property trusts, disabled trusts, employee benefit trusts and qualifying IIP trusts;
- transfers on death into relevant property trusts;
- changes in distribution of deceased estates;
- transfers of value equal to the value of the nil-rate band every seven years;
- loans into trust;
- insurance policy trusts;
- making a chargeable transfer followed by a potentially exempt transfer;
- transfer of deferred shares into a relevant property trust (unless the transfer is part of arrangements which enable an advantage to be obtained in respect of the relevant property entry charge when disclosure may be required. This will depend on whether it can be shown that the grandfathering exception applies.);
- gifts of items of national importance;
- transfer of pension death benefits into a relevant property trust (unless the transfer is part of arrangements which enable an advantage to be obtained in respect of the relevant property entry charge when disclosure may be required. This will depend on whether it can be shown that the grandfathering exception applies.);
- where property is transferred into a relevant property trust and the settler retains a reversionary interest so long as it can be shown that the grandfathering exception applies;
- dispositions that do not give rise to transfers of value;
- gifts to companies.

The foregoing is just a summary of the headings in the list in HMRC's guidance (see para 13.7 of HMRC's Guidance on the Disclosure of Tax Avoidance Schemes published on 31 January 2014); reference should be made to the guidance as a whole as many of the entries are qualified further. Also HMRC have confirmed that it is not sufficient for an arrangement to have been established practice before 1 April 2018 (even if HMRC had indicated their acceptance of this as for example they had done for reversionary lease schemes in 2010 which were implemented correctly). For the exemption to apply there must be a specific plan or scheme in existence before 1 April 2018 and it must be this same plan or scheme that is being implemented now. A generic idea or scheme containing common features would not be sufficient.

DAC 6

(10) DAC 6 is the sixth version of the EU Directive of Administrative Co-operation and within the EU facilitates the exchange of information between Member states. It includes provision for disclosure regimes. As regards

the UK, DA6 imitates the DOTAS regime and requires certain persons to file information that is within their knowledge, possession or control on reportable cross-border arrangements. Arrangements are reportable where, in addition to meeting other conditions, they exhibit one or more of five hallmarks. The Directive was implemented into UK law by FA 2019, s 84 and the International Tax Enforcement (Disclosable Arrangements) Regulations 2020 (SI 2020/25).

Following the UK's departure from the EU, DAC 6 ceased to apply in the UK, except in respect of reportable arrangements that met the Category D hallmark (which is in two parts). Hallmark D1 (Undermining reporting obligations) seeks to identify arrangements created to circumvent the OECD standard for automatic exchange of financial account information in tax matters (ie the common reporting standard). Hallmark D2 (Obscuring beneficial ownership) seeks to identify and report on offshore structures with little substance, are incorporated or managed in a jurisdiction different from that of the beneficial owner and where the beneficial owners cannot be identified. This hallmark requires a review of all companies that operate in low or zero tax territories where they have failed the local substance rules. Further information about the remnants of DAC 6 and their application in the UK see para 600000 of HMRC's 'International Exchange of Information Manual'.

The continued application of Hallmark 6 within the UK is provided for the UK's free trade agreement with the EU, but its continued operation is for a limited period. It will cease to apply when the UK introduces legislation to implement mandatory reporting under the OECD Mandatory Disclosure rules.

Inheritance Tax — Personal and Estates — Specific Topics

Question

I B Smart is aged 62 and in poor health; his wife is aged 55 and in excellent health. They have two children, John aged 22 who is a director of the family trading company, Smart & Co Ltd, and Jill aged 24, who is married with one child aged six months. The wills of Mr and Mrs Smart each provide for the whole of their estates to be left to the surviving spouse for life and on the death of the survivor to be divided equally between the children.

A few years ago they were worried about their potential inheritance tax liabilities on their deaths. At that time they had not made any chargeable transfers and their estates consisted of:

	I B Smart	*Mrs Smart*
Shares in Smart & Co Ltd	49 shares	49 shares
Freehold offices rented at £10,600 pa to Smart & Co Ltd	£130,000	Nil
Villa in Spain valued at	£176,000	Nil

They also owned as joint tenants the freehold estate in their private residence, valued at £317,000, and had joint accounts at building societies totalling £196,000.

Mr Smart had recently retired from the family company and was drawing a pension of £40,000 pa. This pension would increase by 3% pa and on his death a 2/3rds pension would be payable to Mrs Smart.

The estimated value of the shares in Smart & Co Ltd is:

100% holding	£1,230 per share
98% holding	£1,224 per share
51% holding	£1,200 per share
49% holding	£1,000 per share
2% holding	£100 per share

There are 100 shares in issue.

No dividends have been declared.

At the time when they were considering their inheritance tax position, it was their wish to continue living in their main residence but to spend four weeks per year in Spain. They believed that in order to meet their personal expenditure it would be necessary for them to continue to receive all of the rent on the offices as well as the pension but they were prepared to forgo the rent on the overseas property of £5,000 pa (rent £500 per week in season). They did not wish to give away any cash.

After talking informally to an acquaintance who is a personal finance consultant they attempted to mitigate their liability by Mr Smart giving all of his shares in Smart & Co Ltd to their son John and the holiday home to their daughter Jill, reserving the right to use it rent free when they wished. Both gifts were made on the same day in May 2023. They did not alter their wills.

Nine months after effecting the above transfers Mr and Mrs Smart were, in February 2024, involved in a boating accident in Spain. Mrs Smart died immediately and Mr Smart four weeks later. The gifted assets were still owned by the respective donees.

Assuming that:

(1) all values are unaltered;

(2) the legislation in force in 2023/24 has always had effect; and

(3) the personal representatives of Mr Smart neglect to elect to take advantage of the provisions under IHTA 1984 s 8A and s 8L (transfer of nil-rate band and residence nil-rate band between spouses – see **Example A3**):

(a) Set out the inheritance tax liabilities arising in 2024 on the assumption that Mr Smart had *not* undertaken the gifts in May 2023.

(b) Set out the inheritance tax liabilities which do arise in 2024 following his having effected the gifts in May 2023.

(c) Compute the tax liabilities on the assumption that, instead of effecting the above gifts in May 2023 the following events happened on that date:

(i) Mr Smart gave the Spanish property to Jill. Mr and Mrs Smart undertook to pay open market rent of £500 per week when they visit the Spanish property.

(ii) Mrs Smart gave a 47% interest in Smart & Co Ltd to John.

(iii) The freehold office premises were transferred to Mrs Smart.

(iv) The building society accounts were transferred into Mrs Smart's sole ownership.

(v) Each of their wills was altered to provide that on death a discretionary trust should be created for the benefit of the surviving spouse, children and grandchildren, with specific bequests to the trustees of the business property, shares and residue of the estate (the house passing to the spouse by survivorship).

(d) Compare the tax liabilities in the three situations had the boating accident occurred nine years later rather than nine months, all values and tax rates remaining the same and assuming that no other change in the law occurs. In this case you should also assume that the personal representatives of Mr Smart also neglect to elect to take advantage of the provisions under IHTA 1984 s 8L (transfer of residence nil-rate band between spouses – see **Example A3**) and that in scenario (c) the events happen in May 2032.

Answer

I B Smart — gifts with reservation

(a) *If gifts had not been made*

Death of Mrs Smart in February 2024

		£	£
Estate:			
Shares in Smart & Co Ltd (**explanatory note 3**)			
49 × £1,224		59,976	
Less: 100% business property relief		(59,976)	Nil
½ share of jointly owned assets:			
Freehold house		158,500	
Building society accounts		98,000	256,500
Not chargeable because of spouse/civil partner exemption – no inheritance tax payable			256,500

Death of Mr Smart in March 2024

Estate:			
Freehold house		317,000	
Property in Spain		176,000	
Freehold offices	130,000		
Less: 50% business property relief	(65,000)	65,000	558,000
Shares in Smart & Co Ltd			
98 × £1,224 (one half owned by Mr Smart and one-half life interest from Mrs Smart)		119,952	
Less: 100% business property relief		(119,952)	Nil
Building society accounts			196,000
Estate chargeable to inheritance tax			754,000
Less: residence nil-rate band			(175,000)
Balance of estate chargeable to inheritance tax			579,000
Tax payable (at 2023/24 rates) (579,000 – 325,000 = 254,000 @ 40%)			101,600

(b) *If gifts were made in May 2023*

Death of Mrs Smart in February 2024

Mrs Smart's estate would have been exempt as before – all property was left to Mr Smart for life or absolutely as the surviving joint tenant (but Mrs Smart's shares were valued in their own right as a 49% holding at £1,000 per share since Mr Smart's shares had been given to John and were no longer related property).

Death of Mr Smart in March 2024

(1) *Charging gift with reservation in death estate and ignoring the lifetime gift to Jill*

	£	£
Freehold house	317,000	
Property in Spain (gift with reservation)	176,000	
Freehold offices (no BPR as no control)	130,000	623,000
Shares in Smart & Co Ltd		
49 × £1,000 (life interest from Mrs Smart)	49,000	
Less: 100% business property relief	(49,000)	Nil
Building society accounts		196,000
Estate chargeable to inheritance tax		819,000

Tax on gifts made within seven years before death

Shares to John		
before transfer	$\frac{49}{98} \times (98 \times £1{,}224) =$	59,976
after transfer — no shares held		Nil
		59,976
Less: 100% business property relief		(59,976)
		Nil

The shares still qualify for business property relief at 100% as the donee (John) still owns them on the death of his father. So no amount is chargeable on death in respect of the gift, and no amount cumulates.

Inheritance tax payable on death

	Gross £	*Tax* £
Cumulative transfers within seven years before death	Nil	Nil
Estate on death	819,000	127,600*
Less: residence nil-rate band	(175,000)	
Balance of estate on death	644,000	127,600*
(*644,000 – 325,000 = 319,000 @ 40%)		
Tax payable on estate at death (which is the total tax payable as a result of Mr Smart's death, since no tax was payable on gifts within previous seven years)		£127,600

(2) *Charging lifetime gift to Jill and ignoring the value of the Spanish villa in the death estate*

Death estate as above	819,000
Less: property in Spain	(176,000)
	£643,000

Tax on gifts made within seven years before death

Shares to John as above		Nil
Property in Spain to Jill		176,000
Less: Annual exemptions		
2023/24	3,000	
2022/23	3,000	(6,000)
PETs now chargeable		£170,000

No tax payable on death within seven years since the 2023/24 nil-rate threshold is not exceeded.

Inheritance tax payable on death

	Gross	*Tax*
	£	£
Cumulative transfers within seven years before death	170,000	Nil
Estate on death	643,000	125,200*
Less: residence nil-rate band	(175,000)	
	638,000	125,200*
(*663,000 – 325,000 = 313,000 @ 40%)		
Tax payable on estate at death		125,200
Add tax on gifts within previous seven years		Nil
Total tax payable as a result of Mr Smart's death		£125,200

As the first calculation gives a greater amount of tax than the second, that is taken as the one that determines the tax liabilities. The effect is that all of the tax will be payable out of Mr Smart's estate, and borne equally between John and Jill.

(c) *If alternative events had occurred in May 2023*

Death of Mrs Smart in February 2024

Estate:	£	£
Business property	130,000	
Less: 50% business property relief	(65,000)	65,000
Freehold house – ½	158,500	
Less: Exempt on devolution to spouse	(158,500)	Nil
Shares in Smart & Co Ltd		
2 × £1,200 (related property – 51% holding)	2,400	
Less: 100% business property relief	(2,400)	Nil
Building society accounts		196,000
Chargeable to inheritance tax		261,000

			Gross	Tax
Gifts within seven years before death:			£	£
Shares to John				
before transfer	$\frac{49}{98} \times (98 \times £1{,}224) =$	59,976		
after transfer	$\frac{2}{51} \times (51 \times £1{,}200) =$	(2,400)		
		57,576		
Less: 100% business property relief		(57,576)		
		nil		
Cumulative transfers within seven years before death			Nil	
Estate on death			261,000	Nil
No tax payable since 2023/24 threshold is not exceeded			261,000	Nil

Death of Mr Smart in March 2024

Estate:		
Freehold house		317,000
Shares in Smart & Co Ltd		
49 shares @ £1,000	49,000	
Less: 100% business property relief	(49,000)	Nil
		317,000

				Gross	Tax
Gifts within seven years before death:					£
To Jill					
Spanish property			176,000		
Less: Annual exemptions	2023/24	3,000			
	2022/23	3,000	(6,000)		
Cumulative transfers within seven years before death				170,000	Nil
Estate on death				317,000	Nil
Less: residence nil-rate band				(175,000)	
				312,000	Nil

(*chargeable amount with nil-rate band)

(d) *Comparative tax liabilities if deaths had occurred nine years later*

(a) *If proposed gifts had not been made in May 2023*

There would be no changes to the computation of the tax payable on Mrs Smart's death.

The tax payable on the death of Mr Smart in March 2023 was £101,600.

(b) *If proposed gifts had been made in May 2023*

If the donor survived the gifts (including the lifting of the reservation) by more than seven years, there would be no charge to tax on the gifts and therefore the double charges regulations would not apply. The Spanish property would, however, still be included in Mr Smart's estate, so the position (as in option (1) under the double charges regulations, as illustrated) would be:

	Gross	*Tax*
	£	£
Cumulative transfers within previous seven years	Nil	Nil
Estate on death (including Spanish property)	819,000	
Less: residence nil-rate band	(175,000)	
Chargeable estate on death	644,000	127,600*

* (644,000 – 325,000 = 319,000 @ 40%)

(c) *Revised proposals – alternative gifts made in May 2032*

Mrs Smart – death in February 2032

Cumulative transfers within previous seven years (as before with BPR)	Nil	Nil
Estate on death (within nil-rate band)	261,000	Nil

Mr Smart

Cumulative transfers within previous seven years	170,000	Nil
Estate on death (after residence nil-rate band of £175,000)	142,000	Nil*
*cumulative amount entirely within nil-rate band	312,000	

Explanatory Notes

Effect of different scenarios on inheritance tax liabilities

(1) This Example illustrates that it is possible to increase the liability to inheritance tax by making gifts without considering their tax implications.

The tax liability on the second death if none of the gifts were made would amount to £101,600 (no liability arising on first death).

The making of the first set of gifts led, following the earlier death of Mrs Smart, to the tax liability on the death of Mr Smart being increased by £26,000 to £127,600.

By comparison if the alternative gifts had been made, then, on the first death (Mrs Smart) no tax would be payable and on the second death (Mr Smart) no tax would be payable either. An overall reduction in tax of £101,600 would arise.

If Mr Smart had predeceased his wife in 2023 then the tax liabilities under the proposals at (c) would have become:

Mr Smart

		£	£
Gifts within seven years before death			
— property to Jill (176,000 – 6,000 annual exemptions)			170,000
Estate on death:			
Shares in Smart & Co Ltd			
49 shares @ £1,200 (related property 51%)		58,800	
Less: 100% business property relief		(58,800)	Nil
Freehold house —		158,500	
Exempt since devolving on Mrs Smart		(158,500)	Nil
			170,000

No tax is payable since the nil-rate threshold is not exceeded.

		£	£
Mrs Smart			
Gifts within seven years before death (as before with BPR)			Nil
Estate on death:			
Freehold house		317,000	
Office premises (no BPR, only 2% of shares held)		130,000	
Shares in Smart & Co Ltd			
2 × £100	200		
Less: 100% business property relief	(200)	Nil	
Building society accounts		196,000	643,000
Chargeable estate			643,000
Less: residence nil-rate band			(175,000)
Balance of chargeable estate			468,000
Tax payable (£468,000 – £325,000 = £143,000 @ 40%)			£57,200

Taking both deaths together the total tax payable is £57,200.

Thus the reduction from £101,600 would be £44,400.

In considering how best to mitigate inheritance tax liabilities, it is necessary to remember the continuing need of the parties for the income from the business property, and that the personal residence cannot be transferred (except to each other) whilst the Smarts remain in residence. (If it were transferred to a third party and the Smarts continued to live in the property, the transfer would be a gift with reservation and therefore fails to achieve the intended IHT saving, as well as potentially worsening the CGT position of the donee in due course.) However, the second proposals would mitigate the potential liabilities regardless of who died first. (The transfer of the office premises to Mrs Smart is not caught by the gifts with reservation provisions because of the spouse exemption, see **explanatory note 4** below.) Furthermore after the earlier death of Mr Smart, Mrs Smart could possibly start to make use of the annual exemption by making gifts to her children or grandchildren if her capital was likely to be increased by unspent income.

Transfers to discretionary trust – inheritance tax treatment

(2) The amounts transferred to the discretionary trust on the death of Mrs Smart would be potentially liable to further inheritance tax charges, because although she had made no transfers in the seven years before her death, the initial value of the property comprised in the settlement (being the values *before* business property relief) is above the nil-rate threshold of £325,000, ie:

Business property	130,000
Shares in Smart & Co Ltd	2,400
Building society accounts	196,000
	£328,400

A liability will arise if there are any taxable payments (ie capital distributions) from the settlement within ten years. The rate of tax applicable to such exits would be arrived at as follows:

(328,400 – 325,000) @ 20% = £680, which gives an effective rate on £328,400 of 0.207%. The actual rate would be a time-fraction of 30% of that effective rate, represented by the following formula:

$$30\,\% \times 0.207\,\% \times \frac{X}{40}$$

where X is the number of complete quarters since the creation of the settlement.

A liability at or after ten years would only occur if the assets increased in value to the extent that, after business property relief, their combined values exceeded the nil-rate threshold then in force. For detailed notes on discretionary trusts see **Examples C10 to C14**, particularly **Example C13 explanatory note 5**.

In the event that the property was appointed absolutely to the beneficiaries within two years after death (following the later death of Mr Smart) it will be deemed to have been left to them direct by Mrs Smart under her will (s 144) and therefore no exit charge would arise on the appointment. See **Example C14 explanatory note 5**. For the purposes of capital gains tax, however, the trustees would be treated as making a disposal of the property and would be chargeable to capital gains tax in respect of any gains arising in excess of their annual exemption. Gifts holdover relief under TCGA 1992 s 260 would not be available as there is no charge to inheritance tax on the appointment; relief may be available under s 165 if the property appointed was business property (as defined for the purposes of that section).

Related property: valuations for inheritance tax and capital gains tax

(3) The related property rules (IHTA 1984 s 161) apply to the shares in Smart & Co Ltd and accordingly it is necessary to look at the appropriate proportion of the value of the combined holdings of Mr and Mrs Smart before and after the transfer. Furthermore the entitlement to business property relief depends on the value of all the shares held by Mr and Mrs Smart (but not those held by the trustees of the discretionary settlement). Business property relief is not available on the office premises if the combined holding of shares drops to 50% or below. See **Examples A12, A20** and **A22** for the related property rules and **Example A21** for the rules relating to business property relief.

The related property provisions do not apply in the context of capital gains tax. For capital gains tax purposes, the value of an asset in the hands of a beneficiary is its open market value at the date of death (TCGA 1992 s 62). It is, however, provided by TCGA 1992 s 274 that if the value of an asset has been *ascertained* for inheritance tax, the same value applies for capital gains tax. But if shares qualify for 100% business property relief, or qualify for the spouse exemption, or the value of the chargeable portion of the estate is below the nil-rate threshold, their value will not need to be ascertained for inheritance tax, so that the normal open market value rule will apply for capital gains tax. The beneficiary's acquisition value may thus be lower than the inheritance tax value, since it will be based on the number of shares held by the beneficiary in isolation. See **Example A26 explanatory note 1** for further comments on this point.

Gifts with reservation for inheritance tax

(4) Before 18 March 1986 it was possible to make a gift that was effective for IHT purposes even if the donor continued to receive some benefit from the asset given away. FA 1986 put a stop to this by introducing new rules, similar to those that existed for Estate Duty, designed to make sure that such gifted assets in which a benefit was retained would still be treated as part of the donor's estate for IHT purposes. These are the Gift with Reservation (GWR) rules and they catch any gift of an asset in which the donor retains some form of benefit or enjoyment, or does so subsequently. The effect of the rules is that even though, in reality, the legal and beneficial ownership of the property has been passed to another person it nevertheless is treated as part of his estate on death if the reservation still subsists at that time. For transfers on or after 9 March 1999 separate rules apply to gifts of certain land and gifts of settled property and these are discussed in **explanatory note 5**.

FA 1986 s 102 and Sch 20 provide in respect of gifts on or after 18 March 1986 that if an asset is transferred and

(a) possession and enjoyment of the property is not bona fide assumed by the donee at or before the beginning of the relevant period, (ie the period beginning seven years before the donor's death or, if the gift is made within that seven-year period, the period from the gift to the date of death); or

(b) at any time in the relevant period the property is not enjoyed to the entire exclusion, or virtually to the entire exclusion, of the donor and of any benefit to him by contract or otherwise,

then the asset is subject to a reservation (s 102(1)). This means that the asset transferred is treated as property within the donor's estate at the date of his death (s 102(3)).

So, in order to avoid the operation of the rules, there must be a clear period of seven years before death (or from the date of the gift) in which the donor did not reserve any benefit in the gift property. This means that it is possible for a gift to be subject to the GWR rules at one point in time, but provided the reservation ceases and the donor survives for a further seven years, then the application of the GWR rules falls away.

The GWR also, clearly do not apply where the conditions for their application are not satisfied. This will be the case, firstly, where the possession and enjoyment of the property gift is assumed by the donee. This will occur where the gift of the property is perfected so that the ownership of the property is vested in the donee. Secondly, no GWR arises where the gifted property is enjoyed to the entire exclusion of the donor. Whether or not this condition is met is a matter of fact, but if the donor is so excluded at the date of the gift but later in the relevant period is not so excluded, then the property will be subject to the GWR rules at that later point. Thirdly, no GWR arises where the gift property is enjoyed virtually to the entire exclusion of the donor. This provides scope for the donor to enjoy some limited benefit in the gifted property and for it not to be subject to the GWR rules. The level of *de minimis* benefits that are permitted is not defined in statute but examples are set out by HMRC in Tax Bulletin 9 dated November 1993. They include giving away a house but staying there for not more than two weeks a year in the donee's absence, social visits to the house or visits for babysitting the donee's children, giving away a car and receiving lifts in it less than three times a month and giving away some land and using it for dog-walking. Finally it must be noted that for the rules to apply the benefit enjoyed by the donee must be referable to the property gifted. So, if an individual owns shares in a company which he gives away and the company owns a property in which they live and continues to do so after the gift, there is no reservation of benefit as there is no reservation of benefit in the shares themselves (IHTM14334).

In effect the GWR rules create a fiction for IHT purposes, namely that the donor owns the property subject to a reservation (as it is called – s 102(2)) at his death despite the property being in the ownership of the donee as a matter of property law. The property becomes aggregated with the rest of the donor's estate. It is important not to lose sight of this fiction and the reality. Ownership of the property passes at the date of the inter vivos gift and the donee does not benefit from any capital gains tax uplift on the death of the donor (the property not being property which the donor would have disposed of under his will). Also if the donor and donee die within a short period of each, two charges to IHT arise in relation to the same property (see below). Another consequence of the fiction and the reality is that if a donor reserves a benefit in settled property, the value of the asset remains in the donor's estate but the asset held by the trust may be subject to the IHT charges that apply to settled property that is relevant property (eg where it is held on discretionary trusts).

The liability for the tax arising on property which is subject to a reservation of benefit is primarily that of the donee although the donor's personal representatives have a secondary liability. Where the gift is of illiquid the done will have to use other resources to pay the tax. Where the donee is a beneficiary of the residue of the donor's estate, he may be able to fund the liability from those assets but this will not always be the case.

Some common examples of gifts that are caught by the GWR rules are of a home which the donee leases back to the donor at less than full market rent, of shares on which the donor enjoys the dividends and of books which remain in the donor's library. The creation of a joint bank account is a typical situation that can be caught by the GWR rules (as explained further below). The benefit retained by the donor in the property given away can arise simply as a matter of fact (as illustrated in the foregoing examples) or under a contract. An example of a reservation of benefit under contract is where the donor gives shares to the donee on the basis that the donee will appoint the donor as director of the company after the gift, entitling the donor to remuneration.

The GWR rules apply to gifts to trusts in the same way as they apply to outright gifts. If the donor retains any interest in the property gifted once it is settled property, this will constitute a gift with reservation. Examples of where this will be the case are gifts to trust for the benefit of the donor's children with reversion to the donor if the children die under a specified age, gifts on discretionary trusts where the donor is a member of the class of beneficiaries and gifts on discretionary trusts where the trustees have the power to add the donor to the class of beneficiaries.

The gifts with reservation provisions do not apply by virtue of s 102(5) if or to the extent that the transfer is covered by one of the following inheritance tax exemptions (as to which see **Example A1**):

— transfers between spouses/civil partners (IHTA 1984 s 18) (see * below for further commentary)

— small gifts (s 20)

— gifts in consideration of marriage or civil partnership (s 22)

— gifts to charities (s 23)

— gifts to political parties (s 24)

— gifts to housing associations (s 24A)

— gifts for national purposes etc (s 25)

— maintenance funds for historic buildings (s 27)

— employee trusts (s 28).

It is worth noting that the gift with reservation of benefit rules can still apply to gifts that are exempt under the annual exemption (s 19) and the normal expenditure out of income exemption (s 21) and this is a trap that can easily catch out many donors.

* In order for the spouse protection from the operation of the gift with reservation of benefit rules to apply, the property concerned has to become comprised in the estate of the transferor's spouse. The requirement is clearly satisfied where the spouse becomes the beneficial owner of the property following its transfer. The condition is also satisfied to settled property that is subject to a reservation where, on the death of the settlor, the settlor's spouse becomes beneficially entitled to the property either under the original terms of the settlement or a subsequent appointment made thereunder and prior to the settlor's death. The same applies where the spouse's entitlement on the settlor's death is a QIIP (see **Example C3**). Note that the efficacy of the spouse exemption to keep property outside the gifts with reservation rules was restricted from 20 June 2003 so that a GWR results where property became settled property as a result of a gift (with an interest in possession for the donor's spouse) (FA 1986 s 102(5A)–(5B)). This rule still applies after the changes to the settled property rules made by FA 2006, but will in practice now be of potential application only where a spouse's interest in possession is a disabled person's interest. However, it should be noted that the spouse protection does not apply if the reservation of benefit ceases inter vivos or in the case where the property is held on discretionary trust for a class of beneficiaries which includes the spouse. This is because he rules operate to treat the cessation as a deemed PET by the donor and not by deeming the donee spouse to

become beneficially entitled to the property. Also the spouse protection does not apply (ie gift with reservation rules in respect of gifts between spouses will not be dis-applied) where the donee spouse is not domiciled in the UK for IHT purposes to the extent that the transfer exceeds the amount of the limited spouse exemption (see **Example A5(c)**).

If it can be shown that the property which is subject to a reservation ceases to be so subject prior to his death, then the donor is treated as making a potentially exempt transfer of the property at the time that the reservation ceases (FA 1986 s 102(4)). Such a transfer cannot be reduced by annual exemptions. The donor will need to survive seven years from the date of cessation of benefit in order for the gift to be fully outside his estate for IHT purposes.

The initial gift of the property is still a transfer of value (despite the effect of the gift with reservation rules), and it may be a chargeable lifetime transfer or a potentially exempt transfer (valued after deducting available annual exemptions). If it is potentially exempt then it will not be charged to tax in its own right if the donor survives seven years (but this will not detract from the operation of the gifts with reservation rules). This means that two potentially exempt transfers may exist in relation to the same item of property at any one time. Relief is given in this case under the Double Charges Relief rules (see **Example B2**).

A donee may die shortly after the donor has effected a gift with reservation so that a second charge to IHT arises on the same property; the first charge arises because the property is deemed to be part of the donor's estate and the second charge arises because the property is actually part of the donee's estate. Quick succession relief (QSR) (see **Example B3**) is not available in this case because the QSR rules require that on the death of the donee his estate was increased by the chargeable transfer that occurred on the death of the donor. This is not the case as the property subject to the reservation of benefit was not transferred to the donee on the donor's death but by reason of an earlier inter vivos transfer. In this case there is no provision for relief under the Double Charges relief rule.

These provisions are illustrated in the Example. The proposed gift of the Spanish property to Jill will not remove the property from Mr Smart's chargeable estate for inheritance tax purposes if Mr and Mrs Smart continue to use the property rent free. If, however, the original gift was made nine years before Mr Smart's death as in **part (d)** of the Example, the gift as such would escape tax, but the value of the property would still be brought into his estate if the reservation had not been released at the time of his death. If say he had released the reservation between three and four years before his death he would be treated as making a further potentially exempt transfer to Jill equal to the value of the property at that time (not reduced by any annual exemptions). That transfer would be subject to the additional charge to inheritance tax at the time of his death (subject to taper relief of 80%), but the value of the property would not be added to his estate at his death.

An exception to the gifts with reservation rules is made when either:

(i) full consideration is given for any right of occupation or enjoyment retained or assumed by the donor and the property is land or chattels (Sch 20 para 6(1)(a)), or

(ii) in the case of land, the donor later occupies the property as a result of a change of circumstances that was unforeseen at the time of the original gift and the benefit provided by the donee to the donor represents no more than reasonable provision for the care and maintenance of an elderly or infirm relative (Sch 20 para 6(1)(b)).

Thus the payment by Mr and Mrs Smart of full market rent for their occupation of the Spanish property would be sufficient to nullify the reservation of benefit arising from their use of the property (but if they paid less than a market value rent for their use of the property, a reservation of benefit would still arise in full); the second exception might apply, depending on the circumstances, to any occupation rent free by Mr Smart after the boating accident. However, care must be taken because if after regaining their health the donor continues to occupy the property without paying a market rent, they will no longer be protected from the application of the gift with reservation rules.

It would be easy to assume that giving full consideration in return for retaining benefit would avoid the GWR rules in every case, but this is only the case if the gift is of land or chattels. For the full consideration exclusion to apply it should be an amount agreed under a bargain negotiated at arm's length, the parties should be independently advised and normal commercial criteria in force at the time should be followed (IHTM14341).

Continuing gifts made under the terms of a regular premium insurance policy effected before 18 March 1986 are not caught by the gifts with reservation rules, unless the policy is altered after that date.

Further exclusions apply where the property gifted is excluded property; such property cannot be the subject to the GWR rules (IHTM14310) (see **Example A5**). The GWR rules are also in effect excluded where the gift qualifies for 100% business property relief (see **Example A21**) or agricultural property relief (see **Example A22**). If a reservation of benefit subsists in residential property and the donor dies on or after 6 April 2017, the RNRB will be available of the property was gifted inter vivos to a lineal descendant of the deceased.

There are special rules to provide for the benefits reserved to be followed through when the original property is substituted by replacement property, with appropriate adjustments if the donee provides consideration. So the GWR rules cannot be avoided by the donee substituting the gift property for another or by the donee giving the gifted property to a third party (including his personal representatives on his death). In either case, via tracing rules, the GWR rules will apply to the substituted property (Sch 6 para 2(1)–(3) or the property that has been transferred to the third party (Sch 6 para 2(4)–(7), para 4). Tracing does not apply to gifts of money but the pre-owned assets income tax charge may apply in this case (see **Example B4 part C**).

The Upper Tribunal had decided that the grant (for no consideration) of an under-lease by a head lessor on terms that the latter reserved covenants for the payment to him by the under-lessee of service charges and for repair to the flat by the under-lessee were benefits that resulted in the under-lease being property in which the head lessor enjoyed a reservation of benefit (*Buzzoni v RCC* (2012)). The reservation of the service charge and the other covenants meant, in the opinion of the Upper Tribunal, that the under-lessee as tenant and donee could not enjoy the lease to the entire exclusion of the donor. However, the Court of Appeal unanimously overturned this decision (*Buzzoni v RCC* (2013)). First it was observed that although the benefit of the covenants attached to the head lease, the rights conferred by the covenants were obtained by virtue of the under-lease, the subject of the gift, and not by virtue of the reversion retained by the head-lessor. However, and crucially, despite this, the benefits derived from the under-lease covenants did not affect and made no difference to the under-lessee's enjoyment of the under-lease. The second limb of FA 1986 s 102(1)(b) requires consideration of whether the *donee's* enjoyment of the property gifted is to the exclusion of any benefit to the donor. The focus is not primarily on the question whether the donor has obtained a benefit from the gifted property but whether the donee's enjoyment of that property remains exclusive. The statutory question is whether the donee enjoyed the property to the entire exclusion or virtually to the entire exclusion of any benefit to the donor. If the benefit to the donor does not have any impact on the donee's enjoyment, then the donee's enjoyment *is* to the entire exclusion of any benefit to the donor. To come within the scope of the second limb of the subsection the benefit must consist of some advantage which the donor did not enjoy before he made the gift (as was the case in *Re Nichols* – see below).

In *Buzzoni* the under-lessee was already under obligations, set out in the licence to underlet, to the head lessor. Those obligations precisely matched obligations which they entered into with the head lessor. The obligations did not in any way detract from the enjoyment of the under-lease because the obligations imposed by those covenants did not add to the obligations already imposed by the licence. Even if the head lessor obtained a benefit that she had not previously enjoyed, it was not obtained at the expense of the under-lessee's enjoyment of the under-lease. It neither added to nor subtracted from their enjoyment in the light of the obligations into which they had already entered with the head lessor. Consequently it was concluded that there was no reservation of benefit by the head-lessee in the under-lease.

This contrasts with the position of the taxpayer in *Re Nichols* (1975) where a father conveyed the fee simple in the family home to his son with the benefit to himself of a leaseback of the property in which he continued to live with his wife. The lease contained a full repairing covenant by the donee son. The Court of Appeal held that the right to have the mansion house and outbuildings repaired under that covenant did not exist before, and therefore could not be something simply not given. It was reserved out of the gift, since it was a covenant immediately operative and running with the land. The covenant was not comprised in the leasehold retained. Moreover, in that case the covenant of repair was of benefit to the donor father in occupation. The taxpayer in the *Buzzoni* case did not occupy the flat, and the positive contract of repair was regarded as much if not more of a benefit to the beneficiaries. A gift with reservation was also found to exist in the case of *Earl Grey* (1898) which concerned a reservation of rent.

Buzzoni was considered in the case of *Viscount Hood (Executor of the Estate of Lady Diana Hood) v RCC* [2016] UKFTT 59 but was distinguished so that a gift with reservation was found to exist on the facts of the case. Lady Hood was the lessee of a lease of a property. Later she sub-let the property to her three sons. The sub-lease was made on and subject to the same terms, covenants, provisos and conditions as were contained in the head lease. Lady Hood, as sub-lessor, and her sons, as sub-lessees, respectively covenanted to perform and observe those provisions as if they had been repeated in the sub-lease. Following Lady Hood's death, HMRC issued a determination on the grounds that the creation of the sub-lease was a disposal by way of gift by the deceased of property subject to a reservation of benefit. HMRC contended that the sub-lease could not be said to be property enjoyed to the entire or virtually entire exclusion of 'any benefit' to Lady Hood, as the donor, because she obtained a benefit, namely the sub-lessees' covenants in the sub-lease to observe certain of the provisions of the head lease. It was submitted that Lady Hood was in effect provided with an indemnity from the sub-lessees for the performance of her covenants as lessee under the head lease. Thus the sub-lease constituted property subject to a reservation. The executor appealed contending that the sub-lessees enjoyed the donated property (the sub-leasehold proprietary interest) to the entire or virtually entire exclusion of any benefit to Lady Hood. They argued *inter alia* that the benefit of the sub-lessees' covenants enjoyed by Lady Hood did not 'impact on' or 'trench on', and was not 'at the expense of' the donees' enjoyment of the donated property. The tribunal found for HMRC. Following *Buzzoni* it observed that in construing s 102(1)(b), the focus was not primarily on the question whether the donor had obtained a benefit from the gifted property, but whether the donee's enjoyment of that property remained exclusive. If the benefit to the donor had no impact on, was irrelevant to and made no, or virtually no, difference to the donee's enjoyment, then the donee's enjoyment was to the entire or virtually entire exclusion of any benefit to the donor. It was necessary that the benefit consisted of some advantage which the donor did not enjoy before he made the gift, but that was not in all cases a sufficient condition that excluded the operation of the gift with reservation rules. The question was whether, to the extent that the benefit of the positive covenants in the sub-lease was retained out of the donated property, the enjoyment of the donated property was, prior to the grant of the sub-lease and the giving of the positive covenants, already subject to obligations the performance of which would fulfil those under the positive covenants. The enjoyment of the property should already be subject to obligations which mirrored or duplicated those contained in the positive covenants. On the facts, to the extent that the benefit of the positive covenants in the sub-lease was derived from the donated property in question, the enjoyment of the sub-lessees was not to the exclusion of any benefit to Lady Hood. The benefit of the sub-lessees' covenants enjoyed by Lady Hood impacted on or trenched on the donees' enjoyment of the donated property and the sub-lease created by her was a disposal by way of gift of property subject to a reservation.

A key difference between the *Lady Hood* case and the *Buzzoni* case was that in *Buzzoni* the covenants were given by the sub-leases to the landlord of the lessee and not to the lessee herself. Therefore in *Buzzoni* the taxpayer (the lessee) only received a small, indirect benefit and the value of the covenants she received was regarded as insubstantial. In *Lady Hood* the covenants were made with, and benefited Lady Hood (ie the lessee herself) and so were of too great a value for her to be said to have been excluded from benefit. Another key difference between the two cases was that in *Buzzoni* the sub-sub lessees to whom Lady Hood made her gift were not parties to the head lease and so when they gave covenants to Lady Hood these were benefits derived from the gifted property and not benefits that she already enjoyed before the gift was made. The burden on the donees of the covenants was a condition of the gift and as such could not be treated as something that Lady Hood retained out of her existing rights over the property. The distinction between the two cases is the subject of an article in *Tax Adviser* magazine which may be accessed at www.taxadvisermagazine.com/article/pet-spotting.

The case has gone on appeal both to the Upper Tribunal ([2017] UKUT 276) and the Court of Appeal ([2018] EWCA Civ 2405) but on both occasions that appeal has been dismissed. In the Court of Appeal it was accepted that the sub-lease was enjoyed by the sons 'to the entire exclusion, or virtually the entire exclusion' of their mother in terms of s 102(1)(b), but the key question was whether the sons' enjoyment of the sublease was 'to the exclusion . . . of any benefit [to Lady Hood] by contract or otherwise' (s 102(1)(b) second limb). HMRC contended that this further test was not satisfied because the sons entered into a direct covenant with their mother in the sub-lease to observe and perform the provisions in the head lease as if they had been repeated (subject to any necessary modifications) in the sub-lease. The benefit of that covenant was a benefit by contract to the deceased that had no prior existence before the sub-lease was granted, and which was of substantial value to her. The executors argued that the donated property was the sons' sub-leasehold estate, which from the outset had the sub-tenants' covenants in the sub-lease imprinted on it.

The Court of Appeal stated that the 'property' that the deceased gave to her sons could only be identified as the sub-lease, which had to be regarded as a whole. No sensible distinction could be drawn, at least at a preliminary stage, between the legal estate in land that she created by the sub-demise, on the one hand, and the mutual covenants into which the parties entered in the sub-lease, on the other hand. Both the estate in land and the covenants formed part of a single transaction, and it would be artificial to distinguish between them because neither would have come into existence without the other. The gift made by the deceased was a gift of an interest in land subject to, and with the benefit of, the obligations that the parties agreed to undertake in the sub-lease. However, that identification of the subject matter of the gift was not sufficient to exclude the operation of s 102. The property, ie the sub-lease viewed as a whole, would be property subject to a reservation in the deceased's estate unless it was enjoyed by the donee, that is her sons, to the entire exclusion, or virtually to the entire exclusion, of any benefit to her by contract or otherwise. That condition could not be satisfied when the deceased, as the intermediate or mesne lessor, had the benefit of the positive covenants given by her sons, including the obligation to observe and perform the provisions of the head lease throughout the term of the sub-lease. So in her capacity as the intermediate lessor of the property, Lady Hood had the benefit of the positive covenants given by her sons. This was, in the Court's opinion, a benefit to Lady Hood of real, and more than minimal value; and crucially, the benefit had not prior existence before the grant of the sub-lease. The Court added that the fact that the benefit to the donor was inseparable from the gift itself only went to show the closeness of the connection between the gift and the benefit. *Nichols* [1975] 1 WLR 534 and *Ingram* [2010] 1 AC 293 were authorities for the proposition that if the gift of a leasehold interest is accompanied by positive covenants which confer additional benefits on the donor, there is a gift with reservation of benefit within s 102(1)(b).

Transfers of monies into a joint bank account can often (although not always) be regarded as a gift with reservation of benefit. At one end of the spectrum is a joint account where the deceased retains ownership of the funds and no gift is made until death (*Young v Sealy* (1949)), usually as a convenience for obtaining immediate use of the funds after death. At the other end of the spectrum is a tenancy in common with each joint holder having separate ownership of a separate share in the account. In these cases a gift with reservation of benefit is unlikely to arise. The status of a gift into a joint bank account (whether as one with reservation of benefit or not) depends on the facts of every case, but examples of where there was a reservation of benefit may be found in *Sillars & Anor v IRC* (2004) and *Matthews v RCC* (2012). In the case of *Sillars & Anor* the Special Commissioners held that where a building society account was changed to the name of a mother and two daughters, but the mother was the only person who made transfers into the account and made withdrawals, that the whole of the balance remained in the mother's estate even though one-third of the interest had been declared for income tax on the returns of each of the daughters. This was held to be a gift with reservation, not an account held as tenants in common.

A gift with reservation of benefit may arise where property is settled on discretionary trust. This is best explained through an example. Consider Hardy who settles £500,000 for himself for life, with remainder to his wife. The transfer is a chargeable lifetime transfer and so inheritance tax will be payable at the 20% lifetime rate on the excess over his available nil-rate band. The settlement will be subject to ten-year and exit charges as appropriate.

If Hardy has nothing more than the right to income, there will be no gift with reservation: the 'gift' (as opposed to transfer of value) is merely of the reversionary interest, see *Commissioner of Stamp Duties (NSW) v Perpetual Trustee Co* (1943) and compared IHTM14392. Care would therefore be needed in relation to the pre-owned assets charge, the application of which would depend on the nature of the trust assets; let land would be safest.

However, if there is a power to release capital to Hardy, or he is the object of some other power of appointment, the transfer will be treated as a gift of the whole property and caught by the reservation of benefit rules. Consequently, the trust fund (of whatever value at that time) will be subject to inheritance tax as part of Hardy's estate when he dies. Some relief from the double charge (on creation of the settlement and on death) would be available under the double charges regulations SI 1987/1130 (see **Examples B2 and B5**).

The problem would have been worse had Hardy settled assets which gave rise to a chargeable gain. The transfer would have given rise to a capital gains tax liability with no scope for any holdover relief (because the donee trust was settlor-interested).

(5) The gifts with reservation legislation was amended to counter the decision in *Ingram v CIR* (1999). The House of Lords held that the gift with reservation rules (as set out above) did not apply to Lady Ingram, who

created a rent-free lease for herself of her freehold property and then gave away the freehold. Special rules therefore exist to deal with gifts of land in which the donor retains a benefit. Where land is the subject-matter of the gift, the new rules apply in place of the original GWR rules as described in **explanatory note 4**. However, the effect of both sets of rules is the same.

Under FA 1986 ss 102A, 102B and 102C, gifts of interests in land or shares of interests in land made on or after 9 March 1999 will be treated as gifts with reservation if, in the relevant period as set out above, there is some significant interest, right or arrangement which enables or entitles the donor (or his spouse or civil partner) to occupy the land to a material degree without paying full consideration.

It is notable that occupation of the gifted property by a spouse or civil partner will trigger the gift with reservation rules under these separate provisions for land. This is not so for other gifts under the gift with reservation rules and these are only triggered where the donor retains a benefit. There is therefore a mismatch between the two sets of rules in this sense and something that can catch out donors when making gifts of land.

(6) Those provisions do not apply where the gift is covered by one of the inheritance tax exemptions listed in **explanatory note 4**, nor where exception (i) or (ii) in that note applies. Nor do they apply where, despite some negligible benefit retained, the donor is virtually excluded from any enjoyment of the land, or where the donor cannot occupy or enjoy the land until the interest given away expires (for example when a lease terminates) (s 102A(4)).

In *Buzzoni v RCC* (2011) the First-tier Tribunal commented that the requirement to be 'virtually' excluded from benefit imposed a very high test. To be virtually excluded from benefit meant to be as good as excluded; to be excluded for all practical purposes. An exceedingly remote chance of benefit or where the benefit is real but very slight might mean that a taxpayer is 'virtually' excluded but not otherwise. This is case is discussed in more detail in **explanatory note 4** above.

A further exclusion applies under s 102A(5) which provides that a right or interest will not be significant for the gift with reservation rules applicable to land if it was granted or acquired before the end of seven years ending with the date of the gift. This exclusion provides leeway for reversionary lease schemes to avoid the gift with reservation rules. A reversionary lease is one where, say, a freeholder grants a lease of land to another person in reversion, meaning that the lessee will not be able to take possession of the lease and move into the affected premises until a future time. Such schemes can be effective for inheritance tax purposes to reduce the value of the freeholder's estate as the value of his freehold will reduce over time as the period between the grant of the lease and the time when it falls into possession of the lessee expires. So if the donor grants a reversionary lease of land which he has owned for more than seven years, his continued occupation of the land following the grant of the lease will not result in his having a gift with reservation of benefit in the gifted lease. However, if the donor grants a reversionary lease within seven years of acquiring his freehold interest, s 102A ensures that he has a gift with reservation in the gifted lease (unless the other provisions of that section apply to exclude the application of the gift with reservation of benefit rules, for example because the lessor pays full consideration for the right to continue to occupy the leased premises). It must not be forgotten, however, that a pre-owned assets income tax charge may arise where the gift with reservation rules do not (see IHTM44102).

(7) Where there is a gift of an undivided share of an interest in land, the donor and donee may both occupy the land provided the donor receives no other benefit at the donee's expense in connection with the gift (ie the donee pays no more than his fair share of the outgoings) (FA 1986 s 102B(4)). If the donee pays all of the household's outgoings, the donor would receive a benefit connected with the gift of the donee's interest in the property and a gift with reservation would arise. Moreover, the donee's occupation of the property must be genuine and if the donee were to give up occupation in the future, the gift with reservation of benefit rules will result in the donee's interest in the property falling back into the donor's estate for inheritance tax purposes.

(8) For further comments on gifts with reservation relating to land see **Example B4**. For the interaction of the gifts with reservation provisions and business and agricultural property relief, see **Example A21 explanatory note 7**. For a discussion of the gift with reservation of benefit rules applying the context of the gift of the family home, see an article in *Tax Adviser* magazine entitled 'Gifting the family home' by Meg Saksida which may be accessed at www.taxadvisermagazine.com/edition/5326.

(9) Under FA 1986 s 102ZA the termination of a qualifying IIP during the lifetime of the beneficiary and on or after 22 March 2006 is treated as a gift of the property in which the interest subsists. If the beneficiary continues to benefit from that property, it will then be subject to the gifts with reservation rules.

Pre-owned assets income tax

(10) Since 6 April 2005 where the gifts with reservation provisions do not apply in relation to a transfer of property, a free-standing income tax charge may apply instead where the transferor continues to benefit from the use of the asset that was formerly owned by him. A similar charge will arise in relation to the use of assets at low cost or to the use of assets purchased with funds provided by the user. The charge applies to tangible and intangible assets. For details see **Example B4**.

Inheritance tax relief for double charges

(11) Making a gift with reservation of benefit as outlined in **explanatory notes 4** and **5** is one of the occasions within the inheritance tax legislation where it is possible to get a double charge to tax. There are regulations to eliminate such double charges (SI 1987/1130). The operation of the regulations for gifts with reservation where the original gift was potentially exempt is illustrated in the Example. See **Example B2** for the other occasions when double charges arise and the detailed provisions of the regulations and **Example B4** for their interaction with the pre-owned assets provisions.

Inheritance tax – more than one double charge

(12) When most lifetime transfers were potentially exempt, there were few occasions in practice where the double charges regulations could come into effect. Following FA 2006, many more gifts are not potentially exempt and the occasions on which the double charges regulations will apply have increased. The regulations are very complex, and even so they do not cover the possibility of a single donor being affected by more than one occasion of double charge, such as for example if Mr Smart had made a cash gift to his daughter, in addition to the gift with reservation, and the daughter had then made a loan back to Mr Smart. No guidance has been given on the procedure to be followed in such a case.

Same day transfers for inheritance tax

(13) Where transfers that are or become chargeable transfers are made on the same day, the annual exemption is apportioned between them (IHTA 1984 s 19(3)(b)) even if one of the transfers was chargeable immediately and the other was potentially exempt. For detailed notes on this point, see **Example B5 explanatory note 1.**

Capital gains implications of gifts with reservation

(14) Where there are gifts with reservation of benefit, not only is the inheritance tax chargeable on the higher of the two bases as indicated in the Example, but for capital gains tax the tax-free uplift to market value on death does not apply (the property subject to the gift not being an asset of which the deceased was competent to dispose – TCGA 1992 s 62(1)). Instead the donee's capital gains tax base cost will be the market value of the property at the date of the gift (subject to any available holdover relief claims).

Inheritance tax residence nil-rate band

(15) The RNRB available on Mrs Smart's death is unused because her share of the home passes to her husband by right of survivorship and so it is not closely inherited. An amount of RNRB is available for transfer to Mr Smart's for use on his death, but this depends upon his executors making the requisite claim (which in the context of the Example they have failed to do). Mr Smart's estate benefits from a RNRB as he dies on or after 6 April 2017 owning a home which is closely inherited by passing under a disposition under his will to his son and daughter (his direct descendants). As his estate (before business property relief) does not exceed the taper threshold of £2 million (the estate being valued at £938,952), the amount of the RNRB prima facie available is £175,000 (the default allowance for 2023/24). The actual amount of RNRB used in calculating the inheritance tax arising in respect of Mr Smart's estate is limited to the chargeable value of the proportion of his home that is closely inherited. In this case, the chargeable value of Mr Smart's home is £317,000 and as the whole home is closely inherited this figure acts as the limit on the amount of RNRB available. The limit does not operate in Mr Smart's case and so the amount of the RNRB used in calculating the IHT arising on his estate is £175,000. See **Example A2 part (b)** for a detailed discussion on the RNRB.

(16) In the context of the gifts with reservation regime, where a home forms part of a deceased person's estate immediately before his death as a result of the operation of FA 1986 s 102(3) in relation to a disposal of the property made by the deceased by way of gift during his lifetime, an individual is regarded as inheriting the property if he is the person to whom the disposal was made (IHTA 1984 s 8J(6)).

Further reading

(17) A useful article summarising the law on gifts with reservation of benefit and HMRC's application of the rules to a number of problematic areas entitled 'How to handle the reservation of benefit provisions' by Emma Chamberlain OBE may be found in *Tax Journal* dated 8 May 2020.

Question

(a) Albert, a bachelor aged 70, sold his business for cash in 2007 and subsequently carried out the following:

May 2017	Gave his younger sister Beryl cash of £142,000 (no previous gifts having been made)
June 2017	Created a discretionary trust with cash of £304,500, the trustees paying any tax due. The potential beneficiaries of the trust were his brothers and sisters and their children.

In June 2018 Beryl died. During her lifetime she had made an unsecured interest-free loan of £136,000 to her son's business. On her death she left to Albert the debt due from her son.

In July 2023 Albert died, leaving an estate of £314,000, including the £136,000 debt due from his nephew's business. He had lived in rented accommodation all his life and so did not own a home at the time of his death.

Calculate the tax payable as a result of Albert's death.

(b) In July 2023 Andrew died, aged 87. He had been a widower for many years and had supported his only grandson Barry in his business ventures. In May 2019 Andrew had made a gift of £166,000 to Barry to help launch a new product in his business. Andrew had made no gifts earlier in 2019 or in 2018.

In June 2019 Andrew had created a discretionary trust with cash of £331,000, including as beneficiaries his only daughter Clarice, her children and Barry's children. The trustees paid any tax due.

In June 2020 Andrew was taken ill and had to move into a nursing home. He sold his house and received a loan from Barry of £100,000 to help fund the fees.

In July 2023 the value of Andrew's estate was £50,000, before deducting the debt of £100,000 to Barry.

Calculate the tax payable as a result of Andrew's death.

Answer

Double charges regulations

(a) *Tax payable as a result of Albert's death*

Lifetime gifts

			£	£
May 2017	Gift to Beryl			142,000
Less:	Annual exemptions	2017/18	3,000	
		2016/17	3,000	(6,000)
Potentially exempt transfer				136,000

		Gross	*Tax on 2017/18 scale*
		£	£
June 2017	Gift to discretionary trust	304,500	Nil*
(* the value of the gift falls within the nil-rate band of £325,000)			
Tax payable by trustees			£Nil

On death of Albert — July 2023

(1) *Including loan inherited from Beryl in Albert's estate and ignoring gift to Beryl in May 2017*

		Gross	*Tax on 2023/24 scale*
		£	£
June 2017	Gift to trust (within nil-rate band)	304,500	Nil
July 2023	Estate on death	314,000	117,400*
		618,500	117,400*

(* 618,500 – 325,000 = 293,500 @ 40%)

Tax payable by trust	Nil
Tax payable by estate	117,400
Total tax payable as a result of Albert's death	£117,400

(Note that if Albert had died earlier than June 2023, ie less than five years after Beryl's death, quick succession relief would have been available by reference to the tax paid in Beryl's estate on the £136,000 debt left to him by Beryl — see **Example A22**.)

(2) *Including gift to Beryl in May 2017 and ignoring value of gift back in Albert's estate*

		Gross	Tax on 2023/24 scale
		£	£
May 2017	Gift to Beryl	136,000	Nil
June 2017	Gift to trust	304,500	46,200*
		440,500	
July 2023	Estate at death (excluding £136,000 loan)	178,000	71,200
		618,500	117,400**

(* 440,500 – 325,000 = 115,500 @ 40%)
(** 618,500 – 325,000 = 293,500 @ 40%)

	Gross	Tax on 2023/24 scale
	£	£
Tax payable by Beryl's estate on gift from Albert (within nil-rate band)		Nil
Tax payable by trust		
Tax after taper relief* (46,200 × 20%)		9,240
Tax payable by Albert's estate		71,200
Total tax payable as a result of Albert's death		£80,440

* Gift made more than six but less than seven years before death

As (1) results in a higher amount of tax payable, that calculation is used to calculate the tax liabilities (see **explanatory note 4**).

(b) *Tax payable as a result of Andrew's death*

Lifetime gifts

		£	£
May 2019 — Gift to Barry			166,000
Less: Annual exemptions	2019/20	3,000	
	2018/19	3,000	(6,000)
Potentially exempt transfer			160,000

		Gross	Tax on 2019/20 scale
		£	£
June 2019	Gift to discretionary trust	331,000	1,200*

(* 331,000 – 325,000 = 6,000 @ 20%)

Tax payable by trustees	£1,200

On death of Andrew — July 2023

(1) *Excluding £100,000 of May 2018 gift and not deducting debt in Andrew's death estate*

		Gross	Tax on 2023/24 scale
		£	£
May 2019	Gift to Barry (within nil-rate band)	160,000	
Less:	amount subsequently lent back	(100,000)	
		60,000	
June 2019	Gift to trust	331,000	26,400*
		391,000	
July 2023	Estate at death	50,000	20,000
		441,000	46,400**

(* 391,000 – 325,000 = 66,000 @ 40%)
(** 441,000 – 325,000 = 116,000 @ 40%)

Tax payable by trust			
Tax after taper relief* (26,400 × 60%)		15,840	
Less:	tax already paid at time of gift	(1,200)	14,640
Tax payable by estate			20,000
Total tax payable as a result of Andrew's death			£34,640

*Gift made more than four but less than five years before death

(2) *Charging full gift in May 2019 and allowing debt as a deduction in Andrew's death estate*

		Gross	Tax on 2023/24 scale
		£	£
May 2019	Gift to Barry (within nil-rate band)	160,000	Nil
June 2019	Gift to trust	331,000	66,400*
July 2023	Estate at death (50,000 – 100,000, see **explanatory note 7**)	Nil	Nil
		491,000	66,400

(* 491,000 – 325,000 = 166,000 @ 40%)

Tax payable by trust			
Tax after taper relief* (66,400 × 60%)		39,840	
Less:	tax already paid at time of gift	(1,200)	38,640
Total tax payable as a result of Andrew's death			38,640

*Gift made more than four but less than five years before death

The second calculation results in the higher amount of tax payable; therefore that is the calculation used to compute the tax liability.

Explanatory Notes

Relief for double charges from inheritance tax

(1) There are several occasions within the inheritance tax legislation where a double charge to tax may arise. Double charges occur, inter alia, where there are gifts with reservation, under the pre-owned asset rules, where there are 'mutual transfers' (ie where a gift is made and the donee makes a gift back), and where a gift is made and the donee then lends money to the donor. In the latter case, the debt is disallowed when calculating the donor's estate at death.

On basic principles a debt is only deductible from an estate if:

(i) it is incurred for full consideration (IHTA 1984 s 5(5)) and without a realistically enforceable right of reimbursement, and

(ii) is paid by the executors, and

(iii) it is not connected with any gifts received directly or indirectly by the lender from the deceased. (However this restriction does not apply if it can be shown that the loan was not made out of the property derived from the deceased and was not facilitated by the deceased's gifts.)

When a borrower repays a loan which would otherwise not be a deductible loan, he is treated as making a potentially exempt transfer of the amount repaid at the time of repayment (FA 1986 s 103).

(2) Regulations have been made under the authority of FA 1986 s 104, by SI 1987/1130, SI 2005/724 and SI 2005/3441 to eliminate double charges. In each case two calculations are made, and the calculation that produces the higher amount of tax is the one used to establish the amount of tax payable. If both calculations produce the same amount of tax, the first calculation stipulated in the regulations is treated as producing the higher amount and is thus the calculation used to determine the liability. Whether or not the total amount of tax works out the same, the burden of the tax may fall on different people (see **explanatory note 4** below).

Double charges relief from inheritance tax for gifts with reservation of benefit

(3) A lifetime gift with reservation of benefit may be either potentially exempt (eg the gift of a house to another individual while reserving the right to live in it), or immediately chargeable (eg where a gift is made to a discretionary trust of which the donor is a beneficiary). The method laid down in the 1987 double charges regulations for gifts with reservation (SI 1987/1130 reg 5) is firstly to charge the gift with reservation in the deceased's estate and ignore the lifetime transfer. The second calculation is to charge the lifetime transfer and leave the property in which the reservation subsists out of the deceased's estate. If the gift was a chargeable lifetime transfer on which inheritance tax was payable when it was made, and the first calculation produces the higher figure, the tax payable in lifetime is deducted from the additional tax payable on death in respect of the lifetime transfer.

The rules are illustrated in **Examples B1** and **B5**.

Double charges relief for pre-owned assets income tax

(4) Where a taxpayer has a liability to income tax under the pre-owned assets rules following a transfer of value (see **Example A24** and **Tolley's Taxwise I 2023/24**) and elects to eliminate that liability by deeming the gifts with reservation provisions for inheritance tax to apply to the transfer, then a double charge to inheritance tax could arise. This would occur if the taxpayer died within seven years of the original gift. Tax would arise on the original gift, and also on the property subject to the reservation. As in **explanatory note 3**, two calculations are made. The first is to charge the property in which the deemed reservation subsists as part of the deceased's estate and to ignore the lifetime transfer. The second calculation charges the lifetime gift and excludes the value of the deemed reservation from the deceased's estate. Again the higher tax liability applies.

These provisions (SI 2005/724 reg 6) only apply where both the lifetime gift and the deemed reservation relate to the same individual. Therefore, where in certain schemes, such as 'Eversden', one spouse or civil partner makes the lifetime gift, but the election under the pre-owned asset rules places the property in the estate of the other spouse or civil partner, no double charges relief is available.

(5) A different form of potential double charge is relieved by SI 2005/3441. It deals with one of the means of unscrambling certain types of scheme, known as Double Trust or Home Loan schemes that were attacked by the pre-owned assets legislation. (See the article by Emma Chamberlain on the current position of such schemes in the March 2013 edition of *Tax Adviser*.) Under such a scheme, the taxpayer sold his house to the trustees of an interest in possession trust for himself. As part of the scheme, the purchase price was not paid by the trustees; consequently a debt arose in relation to the monies owed to the taxpayer by the trustees. (The property itself, subject to the debt, would have remained within his estate for inheritance tax purposes, prior to 2006.) He then gave away the benefit of that debt by way of a potentially exempt transfer. The value of his estate, if he survived for seven years thereafter, would include the value of the property reduced by the amount of the debt owed by the trustees; the PET would have become absolutely exempt.

Arrangements of this sort were often found unattractive following the introduction of the pre-owned assets legislation which imposes an income tax charge on the taxpayer (see **Example B4**). As an alternative to making the opt out election referred to in **explanatory note 4**, a taxpayer could unscramble the scheme by placing the debt in the hands of a party who could (without breach of trust) write it off with the result that the amount of the debt no longer reduced the value of the house in the taxpayer's estate. Consequently, if the taxpayer died within seven years of the disposal of the debt and its write off, his estate would be subject to inheritance tax on the value of the house and on the value of the gift of the debt. The tax due is calculated as the greater of the tax on the gift and on the death, and the other occasion of charge is ignored. In this way the potential double charge is avoided.

Double charges relief from inheritance tax for gift and gift back

(6) With regard to a gift and gift back where the first gift was initially potentially exempt but then becomes chargeable, the 1987 regulations (SI 1987/1130 reg 4) provide for the first calculation to include the property given back in the estate of the original donor and ignore the potentially exempt gift, and the second calculation to charge the potentially exempt gift and ignore the value of the property given back in the estate of the original donor.

This is illustrated in **part (a)** of the Example in relation to the gift by Albert to Beryl and her bequest to him of the debt owing from her son. The first calculation showed the higher amount of tax payable, so that calculation was used to calculate the tax liabilities.

Note how the incidence of tax may vary:

	Calculation 1	*Calculation 2*	*Saving/(Loss)*
	£	£	£
Payable by trust	Nil	9,240	9,240
Payable by estate	117,400	71,200	(46,200)

Double charges relief for gift and loan back

(7) Where a gift is made followed by a loan to the donor by the donee, and the donor dies within seven years when the debt he owes is still outstanding, the first calculation under the 1987 regulations (SI 1987/1130 reg 6) is to ignore any deduction for the debt and the amount of the gift equal to the loan. The second calculation is to charge the full amount of the gift and also allow the debt. This is illustrated in **part (b)** of the Example, where the second calculation (charging the full amount of the gift to Barry and allowing the debt to Barry as a deduction in Andrew's estate) showed the higher amount of tax payable and was thus used to calculate the tax liabilities arising. Where the first calculation shows the higher amount, credit may be due for all or part of any tax paid on the gift in lifetime.

(8) In practice, Andrew's estate is insolvent as the debt to Barry exceeds the available assets. This does not prevent a liability to inheritance tax arising on earlier gifts as that charge is made on the donees. The rules relating to gifts followed by subsequent loans back to the donor are designed to prevent avoidance of tax by the making of potentially exempt transfers at a time when death is very unlikely within seven years

(and therefore term assurance is very cheap) followed by a loan of a similar amount thus removing assets from the tax computation whilst retaining effective control of both the capital and the income arising from those assets. If in the Example the first calculation had produced the greater overall tax charge, with part of it due from Andrew's estate, this would have increased the degree of insolvency; it would not have negated the application of FA 1986 s 103 to disallow the debt for inheritance tax purposes.

More than one double charge: relief from inheritance tax

(9) The double charges regulations do not cover the possibility of a single donor being affected by more than one double charge, and no guidance has been given as to the procedure to be followed.

Transfers to trusts and inheritance tax

(10) Where lifetime transfers are made to most trusts (before 22 March 2006, confined primarily to discretionary trusts), tax liabilities may arise within the trust if there are any capital distributions from the trust to beneficiaries. For details see **Examples C10** to **C14**. There will be no such liabilities in this Example, since the transfers in both parts (a) and (b) were of cash and were below the nil-rate threshold at the death of the donor; but a charge could apply at the tenth anniversaries of the settlement of the respective trusts (and on subsequent such anniversaries) depending on the value of the trust investments at those times and the nil-rate band then in force.

Inheritance tax residence nil-rate band and downsizing addition

(11) No RNRB is available in calculating the charge to inheritance tax on his estate when he dies, as Andrew does not own a home at that time. A downsizing addition is not available as he sold his house to move into a nursing home before 8 July 2015. See **Example A2 part (b)** for a detailed discussion on RNRB and downsizing addition.

Question

On 6 April 2017 Basil made gifts to his brothers Simon and Charles of £169,000 each.

Basil died on 26 November 2019 leaving an estate of £200,000.

By his will he provided for a legacy to Charles of £90,000 (free of tax) with the residue to Simon.

On 12 March 2020 Simon died. His estate was valued at £362,000 including the residuary legacy from Basil. He left the whole of his estate to his surviving brother Charles.

Charles died on 10 May 2023 when his estate was worth £482,000. He left the whole of his estate to his cousin.

Compute the tax payable by the personal representatives of each of the brothers on the assumption that none of the brothers had made any lifetime transfers other than those stated.

Answer

Death of Basil — 26 November 2019

Tax on gifts made within seven years before death:

			Gross	Tax on 2019/20 scale
			£	£
6 April 2017	Gift to Simon		169,000	
	Gift to Charles		169,000	
			338,000	
	Less: Annual exemptions			
	2017/18	3,000		
	2016/17	3,000	(6,000)	
PETs now chargeable			332,000	2,800*

(* 332,000 – 325,000 = 7,000 @ 40%)

The £2,800 is not reduced by taper relief since the gifts are within three years before death.

		£
Tax payable —	Simon	1,400
	Charles	1,400
		2,800

Inheritance tax on Basil's Estate

	Gross	Tax
	£	£
Cumulative transfers within seven years before death	332,000	2,800
Estate on death	200,000	80,000
	532,000	82,800*

(* 532,000 – 325,000 = 207,000 @ 40%)

Division of Estate

	£
Pecuniary legacy to Charles free of tax	90,000
Inheritance tax (see **explanatory note 3**)	80,000
Residue to Simon	30,000
	200,000

Death of Simon — 12 March 2020

Inheritance tax on death

		Gross	Tax on 2019/20 scale
		£	£
Cumulative transfers within seven years before death		Nil	Nil
Estate on death		362,000	14,800*
(* 362,000 – 325,000 = 37,000 @ 40%)			

Inheritance tax payable:

		£	£
Due on estate before QSR			14,800
Less: Quick succession relief			
Gift from Basil 6 April 2017 (£169,000 less £3,000 exempt, tax £1,400)			
2 to 3 years before	$60\% \times \frac{166{,}000 - 1{,}400}{166{,}000} \times 1{,}400$	832	
Residuary gift from Basil's estate 26 November 2019 (see **explanatory note 3 and 8**)			
less than 1 year before	$100\% \times \frac{30{,}000}{30{,}000 + 20{,}000} \times 20{,}000$	12,000	(12,832)
Inheritance tax payable by personal representatives of Simon			1,968

The estate passing to Charles is:

	£
Estate	362,000
Less: Inheritance tax	(1,968)
	360,032

Death of Charles — 10 May 2023

Inheritance tax on death

	Gross	Tax on 2023/24 scale
	£	£
Cumulative transfers within seven years before death	Nil	Nil
Estate on death	482,000	62,800*
(* 482,000 – 325,000 = 157,000 @ 40%)		

Inheritance tax payable:

		£	£
Due on estate before QSR			62,800
Less: Quick succession relief			
Gift from Basil 6 April 2017			
Over five years before Charles's death		Nil	
Legacy from Basil's estate 26 November 2019 (see **explanatory note 3 and 8**)			
3 to 4 years before	$40\% \times \frac{90{,}000}{90{,}000 + 60{,}000} \times 60{,}000$	14,400	
Residuary gift from Simon's estate 12 March 2019			
	$40\% \times \frac{362{,}000 - 1{,}968}{362{,}000} \times 1{,}968$	783	(15,183)
3 to 4 years before			
Inheritance tax payable by personal representatives of Charles			47,617

Explanatory Notes

Quick succession relief

(1) Where a person dies shortly after receiving a chargeable transfer on which IHT has been paid, the transfer has increased the estate at death and therefore attracts tax in the deceased's estate, as well as having been taxed at the time of the earlier chargeable transfer. Relief is provided where the *death occurs* within five years after the chargeable transfer is made; the relief is known as quick succession relief (IHTA 1984 s 141). There is no requirement for the recipient to retain the asset obtained by that transfer.

(2) The first step is to calculate the tax payable on the original transfer. A potentially exempt transfer becomes a chargeable transfer on the death of the donor within seven years. Although the tax is calculated using the rates applicable at the time of death, the date of the original transfer is relevant in determining the percentage used in calculating quick succession relief. The part of the transfer covered by the annual (or any other) exemption is not a chargeable transfer and is therefore excluded from the QSR calculation. As the donee is responsible for the tax on a PET, grossing up is not required.

(3) The inheritance tax payable on the death of Basil is a charge on the residue (see **Example A7 explanatory note 10**). Thus the amount receivable by Simon is the net £30,000. The estate rate is 40% so that the figures to use in the calculation of quick succession relief are a gross legacy of £50,000 (£30,000 x 10/6) with tax paid of £20,000. Put another way (in the terms of s 141) the tax of £80,000 on Basil's estate was attributable to the net gifts of £90,000 to Charles and £30,000 to Simon, so the parts of it attributable to those gifts were respectively:

$$80{,}000 \times \frac{90{,}000}{30{,}000 + 90{,}000} = 60{,}000$$

and

$$80{,}000 \times \frac{30{,}000}{30{,}000 + 90{,}000} = 20{,}000$$

(4) The total tax on the deceased's estate is reduced by the quick succession relief. Thus if his estate for inheritance tax includes assets outside his free estate, such as settled property in which he had a qualifying

interest in possession, each fund benefits proportionally from the relief. This typically means a partial loss of relief to the fund which is suffering a second tax charge on the same value. See also **explanatory note** 7 and **Example C4**.

(5) Where death occurs within one year of the transfer the relief is 100% of the *tax paid on the previous transfer*, reduced in the proportion of net value transferred to the deceased over the gross chargeable transfer.

Where the period between transfer and death is over one year, the percentage becomes:

1 to 2 years	80%
2 to 3 years	60%
3 to 4 years	40%
4 to 5 years	20%

Donee dying before donor

(6) If the donee dies before the donor then the original gift will continue to be a potentially exempt transfer at that time. Tax will be charged on the estate of the donee (including the gift) without relief. If the donor subsequently dies within seven years of the original gift then the original gift becomes a chargeable transfer, with the tax payable being a liability of the executors of the donee. The inheritance tax due on the death of the donee then needs to be recomputed, and quick succession relief may become available in the process. See **Example C6** for an illustration of this point.

Quick succession relief on trust property

(7) Quick succession relief is also available where there are successive charges within five years on trust property in which there is a qualifying interest in possession. The rates of relief are the same as those in **explanatory note 5** above, with the percentage relief depending on the period between the successive charges (s 141). For a more complex example of quick succession relief, showing the treatment of settled property and giving further detailed notes, see **Example C4**. That Example also illustrates and explains how quick succession relief operates in the context of an estate qualifying for the lower rate of inheritance tax of 36%.

Alternative calculation of quick succession relief

(8) Depending on the way in which the information is presented, the calculation of quick succession relief may be carried out by using the formula: estate rate of IHT in relation to donor's estate × increase in value of legatee's estate × relevant QSR percentage.

In the Example, the estate rate in relation to Basil's estate is 40% (being 80,000/200,000 × 100% = 40%). The residue of Basil's estate that passes to Simon after tax amounts to £30,000. Hence amount of quick succession relief arising on Simon's death is: 40% × £30,000 × 100% = £12,000. The pecuniary legacy of £90,000 made under Basil's will to Charles is a tax-free gift and the amount of quick succession relief arising on Charles's death is: 40% × £90,000 × 40% = £14,400.

Residence nil-rate band

(9) Charles's whole estate is left to his cousin and so, even if it does include his home, he is not entitled to a residence nil-rate band as the home is not directly inherited (see **Example A2 part (b) explanatory note 3**).

Other double charges reliefs

(10) Quick succession relief applies where as in this Example successive transfers are charged in relation to different donors. There are other occasions under the inheritance tax rules where property can be charged twice in relation to the same donor. Regulations made under the authority of FA 1986 s 104 provide relief against double charges to tax in those circumstances (SI 1987/1130). This will normally be where there are gifts with reservation, pre-owned assets or non-deductible debts (see **Examples B1, B2** and **B4**).

Question

A.

Lucton, a widower aged 80, lives with his unmarried and only daughter Frances at Hayseeds, a bungalow currently valued at £250,000.

His only other asset of significance is £300,000 invested in a building society account.

He has already made a transfer of value of £80,000 in the last but one tax year, £6,000 of which was covered by annual exemptions (for the year of transfer and the previous year) leaving a balance of £74,000 as a potentially exempt transfer.

He is conscious that the value of the bungalow is likely to increase, thus worsening the potential inheritance tax position upon his death, when the bungalow is to devolve upon Frances.

Three schemes have been suggested to him for the mitigation of inheritance tax:

(a) That the bungalow is given to Frances now, but that he continues to live in it with her, since at least this would ensure that whilst the gift less the annual exemption would be a chargeable transfer if he died within seven years, future growth would be in the hands of Frances and not his own.

(b) That the bungalow is sold to Frances for its current market value but that the purchase price would be left on loan to her. Lucton would then waive £3,000 of the loan each year, the waiver being covered by his annual exemption for inheritance tax.

(c) That the bungalow is retained by Lucton and instead £300,000 in cash is given to Frances. As Lucton would then have no liquid assets, Frances would each year lend £20,000 to Lucton to enable him to maintain his present lifestyle.

Discuss whether any of these schemes will be successful in mitigating inheritance tax.

B.

A wealthy client, Mr Douglas, who is *not* a farmer, has been involved in the following transactions during the current tax year. All land has been owned by Mr Douglas for more than ten years.

(a) He divided his land at Ambridge into Upper and Lower Ambridge. He gave Lower Ambridge to his son Kirk and both Mr Douglas and Kirk started to use the two properties in partnership. None of the land is partnership property.

(b) He granted a lease of Green Gables at a nominal rent to his wife and himself as tenants in common; he then gave the freehold reversion to his daughter Anne. Thereafter he occupied Green Gables with his wife.

(c) He granted a landlord's repairing lease of Blackacre at a commercial rent to his wife and himself. He then gave the freehold reversion to Anne.

Explain, with references to statute and case law as appropriate, whether any of these transactions are likely to constitute a gift with reservation for inheritance tax purposes.

C.

Mrs Jones, a wealthy widow, wished to reduce her estate's liability to inheritance tax. In order to do so she gave Catherine, her only daughter, £500,000 in cash in May 2020. Catherine had invested the £500,000 in the stock market, realising those investments for just £420,000 in January 2021 which she used towards the purchase of a property in Cornwall in February 2021 for £700,000. Mrs Jones visited this property with Catherine when it was purchased but did not stay there; however in early 2023 she decided that she would like to live there each summer, and with Catherine's agreement she took up residence on 6 April 2023. For the remainder of the year Mrs Jones continues to live in her London residence. Although Mrs Jones is aged 72 she is in good health and would be expected to live for at least another 15 years. She is a 40% income taxpayer (assume that nothing in this Example pushes her income into the 45% rate bracket). For 2023/24 the annual rental value of the Cornwall property would be £36,000 pa and its open market value on 6 April 2023 is £900,000. Mrs Jones has no legal obligation to contribute towards the costs of that property.

(a) Explain why an income tax charge might arise, and set out how long Mrs Jones could spend at the Cornwall property before a computation needs to be carried out.

(b)

(i) Compute the 2023/24 income tax liability arising for a full year's occupation based upon the above facts,

(ii) set out how long Mrs Jones could occupy the property in the coming years without in fact incurring an income tax charge, and

(iii) state how soon this aspect would need to be reconsidered.

(c) Set out any available election to mitigate that charge (assuming that inheritance tax rates and rules remain unchanged).

Answer

A. Lucton — proposals to mitigate inheritance tax

(a) Gift of property while continuing to live in it

By continuing to live in the bungalow with Frances after the gift, Lucton will be retaining a benefit from the gift (see **Example B1 explanatory notes 5 and 6**).

In order to make an effective transfer it is necessary to show that the subject-matter of the gift is enjoyed to the entire or virtually the entire exclusion of the donor and of any benefit to him by contract or otherwise. The transfer of ownership to Frances, with Lucton continuing to live there, would not, therefore, be a viable way of mitigating the inheritance tax position, since in the case of land or a chattel the actual occupation or possession is only disregarded if it is made for full consideration.

In this case no consideration is proposed. If a full rent was paid by Lucton for his occupation of the bungalow this could give rise to a charge to income tax on Frances (subject to any 'rent a room' relief) and could also affect her capital gains exemption in respect of owner occupation of the bungalow.

Occupation of land is also disregarded where the occupation by the donor results from a change of circumstances arising since the time of the gift, being a change which was unforeseen at that time and was not brought about by the donor to save inheritance tax. Furthermore the occupation must occur at a time when the donor has become unable to maintain himself through old age or infirmity and must represent a reasonable provision by a donee who is a relative for the care and maintenance of the donor. Clearly Lucton would not qualify under this heading as he already occupies the bungalow and will continue to live there.

The original transfer to Frances, less the current and previous years' annual exemptions, will be a potentially exempt transfer, becoming chargeable if Lucton dies within seven years. As a gift with reservation the property will, however, continue to be treated as part of Lucton's estate for the purpose of the inheritance tax charge on his death. The value of the property will only be taken out of Lucton's estate if it ceases to be property subject to a reservation. In that event Lucton would be deemed to make a potentially exempt transfer to Frances equal to the value of the property at that time, in addition to the potentially exempt transfer made when he gave her the property (and without the benefit of any annual exemptions). There are regulations to eliminate any double tax charge (see **Example B2**).

If Lucton made a gift of an *undivided share of the bungalow* to Frances and both she and Lucton continue to live at Hayseeds then the reservation of benefit rules will not apply provided the gift is unconditional and there is no collateral benefit to Lucton (see **Example B1 explanatory note** 7). The payment by Frances of Lucton's share of the running costs (which where appropriate might be proportional to use rather than just to ownership) would be such a benefit. The protection of this provision would however not apply if Frances later ceased to occupy the property, or died.

(b) Sale of property with purchase price left on loan

If the bungalow were sold to Frances at its current market value, the purchase price being left on loan to her and then waived at £3,000 per annum (as to which see **explanatory note** 3), HMRC would probably argue that the associated operations rules should apply. They may also take that view if, instead of waiving parts of the debt, Lucton were to make periodic cash gifts to Frances to use his annual exemptions; but it is less easy to accept that the associated operations rule could apply in that event so long as Frances is not seen to make corresponding repayments of the loan.

If later gifts of either sort are properly treated as associated operations with the sale, the value of the bungalow at the time of the last waiver would have to be ascertained, and any excess of that value over its value at the time of the sale would be treated as a potentially exempt transfer at the time of the last of the waivers.

Thus, the mitigation of the potential inheritance tax liability by disposing of an appreciating asset for its present value in consideration for a non-appreciating loan debtor would be negated. The annual exemptions will, however, have been used against any waivers, avoiding them being wasted if there was no other facility for using them, and effectively limiting the potential chargeable transfer to the increase in value between the time of the last waiver and that of the actual transfer (the amount of the debt not waived at the time of death would itself form part of the estate). However in view of Lucton's age, it is probable that most of the value will fall to be charged to inheritance tax on death.

The fact that interest on the loan was or was not charged does not apparently affect HMRC's attitude.

(c) Cash gift followed by loans back

The gift of £300,000 cash by Lucton to Frances, less the current and previous years' annual exemptions totalling £6,000, would be a potentially exempt transfer provided possession and enjoyment is fully assumed by Frances. This means that there would be no immediate liability to tax. If Lucton died within seven years of his earlier potentially exempt transfer of £74,000, tax would be payable on the gift to Frances, unless the nil-rate threshold had in the meantime increased above £368,000 (ie £294,000 + £74,000). Taper relief would reduce any tax payable if Lucton survived the gift to Frances by three years, and after seven years the gift would cease to be potentially liable to tax.

However, if Lucton retains a benefit by way of contract or otherwise the gift is negated. If the amount repaid to Lucton is by way of loan then this will also affect the position, as any debt incurred after 17 March 1986 that arises from a disposition made by the borrower will not be a deductible debt on death. (But if, as is implied, Lucton uses the £20,000 cash each year to support his lifestyle, he will not have accumulated that money as savings upon which inheritance tax could be levied.) Furthermore any repayment of that debt by Lucton will be a further transfer, albeit potentially exempt.

If the amounts paid to him by Frances after his gift to her could be treated as a disposition made in favour of a dependent relative for his reasonable care and maintenance they would not be a transfer of value by Frances (IHTA 1984 s 11(3)), and may not be regarded by HMRC as a reservation of benefit to Lucton if at the time of the original gift by him there was genuinely no expectation that they would be paid. On the facts given, it might be hard to resist a suggestion of reservation; but if Lucton had limited his cash gift to say £170,000 (retaining £130,000 to cover his expenses over the next few years by which time he would be in his mid/late 80s) it would be harder for HMRC to make that link.

B. Douglas — land transactions

(a) Gift of land subsequently used by partnership of donor and donee

Unless the use of Lower Ambridge by Mr Douglas (through the partnership) is for full consideration then the transfer would appear to be a gift with reservation, as the property is not enjoyed to the entire (or virtually entire) exclusion of the donor (FA 1986 s 102A). If, however, the two properties are of similar value and profit sharing and capital sharing ratios are equal, then full consideration would appear to be given and the gifts with reservation rules and pre-owned asset provisions would not apply (FA 1986 Sch 20 para 6).

All of the relevant circumstances would have to be taken into account to determine full consideration. These would include profit shares, values, actual input to the partnership and any actual rent paid.

(b) Division of asset followed by gift of part

Where a donor splits an asset into parts and then makes a gift of the whole of a part without retaining an interest in that part then the gifts with reservation rules are in principle avoided, though the rules were tightened in 1999 insofar as landed property is concerned. In this Example Mr Douglas has divided Green Gables into a leasehold interest and a freehold reversion and has then given the freehold reversion to his daughter Anne. Mr Douglas and his wife continue to occupy Green Gables under the leasehold interest.

Until FA 1999 this would have been outside the rules for gifts with reservation, although unless the grant of the lease and the subsequent gift of the freehold reversion were independent transactions, HMRC might have sought to use the associated operations rules of IHTA 1984 s 268 to say that the grant of the lease and the gift of the freehold reversion were a single transaction occurring at the time of the gift of the freehold, so that the lease at a nominal rent would be a benefit retained by Mr Douglas. Under FA 1986 s 102A, from 9 March 1999 it is no longer possible to avoid the gifts with reservation rules by taking a leasehold interest and giving away the freehold (see **explanatory note 6**). Mr Douglas's gift of the freehold of Green Gables to Anne will therefore be treated as a gift with reservation.

(c) Grant of lease followed by gift of freehold

In giving away a freehold reversion Douglas must not reserve a benefit in that gift. In the case of *Nichols v CIR* (1975) it was held that where a gift was made of freehold land, subject to an obligation on the donee to grant an immediate lease back and to keep the property in full repair, this amounted to a gift with reservation. But in Mr Douglas' case (i) the lease was created before the gift of the freehold, rather than reserved out of it, and (ii) he is paying a full commercial rent, so it is considered that the daughter's obligation to repair the property would be reflected in the rent and that no benefit would be regarded as having been reserved. FA 1986 s 102A (introduced by FA 1999 as referred to in **(b) above**) does not apply where the donor's right to occupy the land to the exclusion of the donee depends on full consideration.

C. Mrs Jones – pre-owned assets

(a) Attribution of cash gift towards property now occupied

A charge to income tax arises in principle because Mrs Jones has contributed towards a property she now occupies. An absolute gift of cash is not normally subject to the inheritance tax gifts with reservation provisions. However under the pre-owned asset income tax rules a charge will apply where it is reasonable to attribute the gift as a contribution directly or indirectly, towards the acquisition of the property now occupied. This does not apply if the outright gift of money was made at least seven years before the taxpayer first occupied the premises. For Mrs Jones the period is only two years ten months.

Occupation is a very wide term and could even include usage for storage or sole possession of the means of access linked with occasional use of the property. Incidental usage is not considered to be occupation. This could include:

- Stays not exceeding two weeks each year (one month if the owner is present and it is the owner's residence).
- Social visits that do not include overnight stays.
- Domestic visits eg babysitting the owner's children.
- Temporary stays eg for convalescence after medical treatment or to look after the owner whilst they are convalescing.

However if the property is a holiday home which is only used on an occasional basis by the owner then even occasional visits by the donor could be deemed to be occupation.

It would appear that Mrs Jones wishes to use the Cornwall property for a number of weeks each year. Unless she pays full market rent for that occupation (which would be liable to income tax in the hands of her daughter) she will be liable to a pre-owned asset income tax charge. If she keeps her possessions at the property, and even more so if she retains a key to it, for the rest of the year then there is a risk she will be regarded as occupying it for the whole year not just for the weeks she physically spends there; the remainder of this Example assumes that she does not fall foul of this and that we are concerned only with the time she actually spends there.

If her occupation was for less than one month per year no charge would arise provided her daughter lived in the property as her residence and was present; otherwise occupation could cause the charge to occur.

In practice it would be advisable to pay full market rent for limited occupation of holiday accommodation.

(b) Income tax liability on pre-owned asset

(i) 2023/24 with occupation for whole year

To apply the pre-owned assets rules in the case of a property contributed to (rather than disposed of by) the taxpayer, it is necessary to ascertain the part of the property's value, at the valuation date (6 April 2023 on the facts given), that can reasonably be attributed to the consideration provided by the taxpayer.

On the facts, Mrs Jones's contribution to the £700,000 price of the Cornwall property she now occupies was not the full £500,000 original gift but the £420,000 into which it can clearly be traced; so the proportion of the purchase price attributable to her contribution was:

$$\frac{420{,}000}{700{,}000} = 60\%$$

(Equally, if Catherine's investments had gone up rather than down in value this increased value would be taken into account where traceable into the purchase.)

The appropriate rental value for (in effect) the first five tax years in which Mrs Jones occupies the property is thus:

$$£36{,}000 \times \frac{60\,\% \times 900{,}000}{900{,}000} = £\,21{,}600$$

This gives an income tax liability for 2023/24 based on a full tax year of occupation, of:

£21,600 @ 40% = £8,640.

Depending on the level of Mrs Jones's 2023/24 taxable income within the 40% bracket (£37,700 to £150,000), the extra £21,600 of income could in practice lead to a greater increase in her tax liability than the basic £8,640, through loss of part or all of her personal allowance. This would arise if her income before the pre-owned assets charge was between £78,400 and £125,140 (at which latter level the personal allowance would already have been fully extinguished).

(ii) Occupation for only part of tax year

This full-year notional taxable income figure of £21,600 would be scaled down according to the part of the tax year for which Mrs Jones is to be regarded as being in occupation (as to which see **(a) above**). Therefore if her occupation is for no more than 84 days in the tax year (and there were no other pre-owned assets income to take into account), her 2023/24 liability would be nil because the de minimis level of £5,000 of pre-owned assets income is not exceeded:

$$\frac{84}{365} \times £\,21{,}600 = £\,4{,}970$$

Because this de minimis provision creates a full exemption from the pre-owned assets rules, there is in that situation no additional income to be taken into account in connection with the restriction of the personal allowance.

(iii) When must the figures be reappraised?

The valuation date is initially the date when the taxpayer first took up occupation, and 6 April in each subsequent tax year; but the value of the property itself, and its annual rental value, are reassessed not yearly but in five-year cycles. (In consequence the proportion of the value at the valuation date that is attributable to the taxpayer's contribution will also be fixed for five years at a time before it needs to be reappraised; in practice, on any such reappraisal, an adjustment will generally only be made where further money has been spent in the meantime, whether or not contributed to by the taxpayer, which is reflected in the value of the property at the five-year anniversary.)

It therefore follows that Mrs Jones can, on the values stated, be sure of falling within the de minimis exemption if she restricts her occupation to a maximum of 84 days in each tax year until and including 2027/28. The market value and rental value of the property would be reassessed at 6 April 2028, as would the proportion of the value that is attributable to Mrs Jones's contribution(s) – including any further contributions made since the original purchase of the property. (See **explanatory note 11**).

(c) Election to mitigate charge

Mrs Jones could elect by 31 January 2025, by completing form IHT500, that the Cornwall property is not subject to an income tax charge, but instead, for so long as she continues to occupy the property, the chargeable proportion of the property value will be treated as part of her estate at her death. The chargeable proportion will be broadly as in (**b**) **above**, namely such part of the value of the property at the valuation date as can reasonably be attributed to the consideration she provided; but since the valuation date for this purpose is the date of Mrs Jones's death, the proportion will reflect:

(i) any further capital expenditure on the property by Catherine in the meantime, and

(ii) any other contributions made by Mrs Jones (after, as well as before, she went into occupation),

in each case so far as reflected in the value of the property at that time.

If Mrs Jones ceases to occupy the Cornwall property then, as for a gift with reservation, the appropriate proportion of the value of the property (on similar principles but calculated at the date she ceases to occupy) will form part of her cumulative lifetime transfers for inheritance tax, as a deemed potentially exempt transfer, if her death occurs within the following seven years.

If Mrs Jones is unlikely to occupy the property for more than two or three years it would be beneficial to elect for inheritance tax to apply as there is a high probability that she would live more than seven years after vacating the property and therefore no tax charge would arise.

If Mrs Jones intends to remain in residence indefinitely it is possible that even 15 or so years of charge to income tax would be less than the initial inheritance tax saving of £200,000 (£500,000 @ 40%). The actual inheritance tax payable would, of course, be higher if the value of the property increased over that period. For example if on the death of Mrs Jones the Cornwall property was worth £1.8 million(and she had made no further payments reflected in its then value) then the inheritance tax liability on her death in respect of her use of the pre-owned asset might be seen as:

$$1{,}800{,}000 \times \frac{420{,}000}{700{,}000} = \pounds\,1{,}080{,}000 \text{ @ } 40\% = \pounds\,432{,}000$$

However, the comparison of the potential accumulated income tax charge, weighed against the potential eventual inheritance tax saving, would of course need to take account of the fact that revaluations for the pre-owned assets charge, such as for rental value, fall to be made every five years.

(See **explanatory note 13**).

Explanatory Notes

Associated operations for inheritance tax

(1) Where a transfer of value is made by associated operations carried out at different times, it is treated as made at the time of the last of them (IHTA 1984 s 268). For the meaning of 'associated operations' see **Example A20.**

(2) Where any one or more of the earlier operations also constitutes a *transfer of value* made by the same transferor, the value transferred by the earlier operations is treated as reducing the value transferred by all the operations taken together (s 268).

(3) Thus, the annual waivers in **part (b)** of the Example, being themselves *transfers of value*, albeit potentially exempt, reduce the value transferred by taking all the operations together. The fact that the waivers are not chargeable does not alter the fact that they were transfers of value (as distinct from chargeable transfers), a chargeable transfer being a transfer of value other than an exempt transfer (s 2(1)).

Ensuring that gifts are properly made for the purposes of inheritance tax and capital gains tax

(4) Under general law a transaction will amount to an effective gift if either the donor effectively transfers the ownership of an asset to the donee with the intention of making a gift or the donor effectively declares himself

to be a trustee of the asset for the donee (as this results in the donee becoming the beneficial owner of the asset). Care should always be taken to ensure that a gift is effective (ie for the ownership of the property gifted to be transferred to the donee). Whilst title to certain assets passes by delivery (eg a watch) there are legally proper ways of transferring title to other assets, such as company shares by a properly constituted and stamped form of transfer and freehold and leasehold properties by deed (and registration where appropriate). In the case of a taxpayer who is the beneficiary of a trust where he is the beneficial owner of the shares, if he orally instructs those trustees to hold his beneficial ownership for his grandchildren, his attempt to settle his beneficial interest on new trusts will not be effective because the transfer of beneficial ownership can be made only in writing (Law of Property Act 1925 s 53(1)(c); *Grey v IRC* (1960)). An intended but incomplete gift will not therefore be sufficient for tax purposes, although in fact the donee might enjoy the benefit of the gift. If the donor has done all in his power to perfect a gift, an omission by the donee will not make it imperfect for tax purposes (eg if the donor has delivered a properly constituted and stamped share transfer but the donee has failed to have it registered or the company concerned has refused to register it) (*Re Rose* (1952)). A cheque only constitutes a valid gift after it has been cleared by the donor's bank, so that if the donor dies before the cheque has been presented the gift is not complete (*Re Owen* (1949)). Under the rule in *Strong v Bird* (1874) an imperfect gift becomes perfect when the donee subsequently acquires the legal title to the asset, for example, as executor of a deceased donor, the intention to make the gift having remained until death.

As far as loan waivers are concerned, HMRC Inheritance Tax consider that they are not effective for inheritance tax unless the waiver is effected by deed.

Gifts with reservation

(5) FA 1986 ss 102 and 103 introduced anti-avoidance legislation relating to gifts with reservation and debts, applicable to events occurring on or after 18 March 1986. These rules apply where a donor reserves a benefit from a gift or subsequently enjoys the benefit of the gifted property (eg gift of a house that the donor continues to occupy, or a settlement into a discretionary trust where the settlor is also a beneficiary).

Under these rules a gift with reservation is treated in the same way as any other gift at the time it is made, but special rules apply on the death of the donor. If the reservation ceased more than seven years before death then no charge arises on death. If the reservation ceased within seven years before death then the gift is taxed as if it had been made as a potentially exempt transfer at the time it ceased, on the basis of its value at that time (but without the benefit of any annual exemptions), even though the original gift will also be taxed if it was made within seven years before death. There are regulations to eliminate the double charge to tax. For details see **Example B1**.

In addition to the specific rules denying a deduction for debts related to excluded property, foreign currency bank accounts and relievable property (see **Example A12(C)**), debts are not deductible from the estate of a deceased person unless they were incurred for full consideration for the deceased's own use or benefit and were not created out of property derived from the deceased as a transfer of value or part of an associated operation. Again there are regulations to prevent double charges to tax, which are dealt with in **Example B2**.

(6) In relation to gifts of land on or after 9 March 1999, the gifts with reservation rules are extended by FA 1986 ss 102A, 102B and 102C. The background to the legislation is the 1999 House of Lords' decision in *Ingram v CIR* and the effect of old estate duty law on the inheritance tax provisions.

Some of the estate duty cases drew very fine distinctions. In *Chick v Commissioners of Stamp Duties of New South Wales* (1958), a farmer had made a gift of grazing land to his son in 1934 and in 1935 the land was brought into a partnership in which the farmer was a partner. The farmer was deemed to have reserved a benefit in the land because of his partnership interest. The *Chick* case was followed by legislation under which no reservation was assumed if the later benefits were only available because of full consideration provided by the donor. In *Munro v Commissioners of Stamp Duties of New South Wales* (1934), a farmer gave away land but continued as a partner in the family partnership that farmed the land. He was considered not to have given the land itself, but his interest in the land subject to the rights of the partnership, so that no benefit had been retained. The difference between the two cases is that the *Chick* gift was initially unfettered but the farmer later enjoyed a benefit from the gifted property, whereas the *Munro* gift was subject to the partnership interest at the time it was made. It was stated by Lord Simonds in *St Aubyn v AG* (1952) that a donor does not bring himself within the provisions 'by retaining something which he has never given'.

This principle was considered in the case of *Ingram v CIR*, decided by the House of Lords in 1999. Lady Ingram conveyed the freehold of her property to a bare trustee, who then granted a lease to her and conveyed the freehold reversion to a trust for the family. The High Court held that there was no reservation of benefit, although it was also held that someone could not grant a lease to a nominee, since this would amount to contracting with himself. The Court of Appeal held that the lease was a nullity as the interposing of a mere nominee did not alter the fact that Lady Ingram was effectively both landlord and tenant of the property (*Rye v Rye* (1962)). It was also noted that a nominee cannot effectively contract with his principal (following the Scottish case of *Kildrummy (Jersey) Ltd v CIR* (1990)). This was overruled by the House of Lords, where it was held that 'if the benefits which the donor continues to enjoy are by virtue of property which was never comprised in the gift, he has not reserved any benefit out of the property of which he disposed'. The House of Lords unanimously declined to follow *Kildrummy*, stating that 'a trustee in English law is not an agent for his beneficiary'.

This decision has led to the changes in the law referred to above where a gift is made of an interest in land (for details see **Example B1 explanatory notes** 5 to 7).

Pre-owned assets

(7) With effect from 6 April 2006 a free-standing income tax charge applies to the benefit of using an asset that was formerly owned by the taxpayer. A similar charge will apply to the use of assets at low cost or to the use of assets purchased with funds provided by the taxpayer. The charge applies to land and tangible and intangible assets.

(8) The income tax charge does not apply:

(i) To property given away before 18 March 1986 (FA 2004 Sch 15 para 3(2); para 6(2) and para 8(2)).

(ii) If the property was transferred to a spouse/civil partner (or to a former spouse/civil partner under a Court Order) (Sch 15 para 10(1)(c)). This also applies where the property is held in trust and the spouse/civil partner or former spouse/civil partner has an interest in possession (Sch 15 para 10(1)(d)) – there is no requirement that this be a qualifying IIP within IHTA 1984 s 49(1).

(iii) If the property remains within the estate of the former owner under the 'Gift with Reservation' rules (Sch 15 para 11). Note that FA 2006 s 80 amended FA 2004 Sch 15 para 11 with retrospective effect to provide an exception from the exemption provisions in respect of some interests in possession including those which arose before the exception was introduced.

(iv) If the property was sold by the taxpayer at an arm's length price (Sch 15 para 10(1)(a)).

(v) Where a disposition is prevented from being a transfer of value by IHTA 1984 s 17, relating to deeds of variation and certain other post-death rearrangements, as in these circumstances it is ignored for the pre-owned asset rules (Sch 15 para 16). The provision is poorly drafted and would technically not protect, for example, a variation that gave effect to a negotiated compromise of a dispute over the devolution of the deceased's estate.

(vi) To property transferred into a qualifying interest in possession trust for the benefit of the former owner. This is excluded from the income tax charge because the property remains in the estate of the donor for inheritance tax purposes (Sch 15 para 11(1)) (now only applicable where the interest in possession is a disabled person's interest, since any other retained interest in possession is not a qualifying IIP). However the exemption ceases when the interest in possession comes to an end (Sch 15 para 10(2)) although this would now amount to a gift with reservation under FA 1986 s 102ZA.

(vii) Where the gift is of property and the former owner has given part of their interest to someone with whom they share an occupation or the former owner needs to move back into the gifted property following changes in circumstances (Sch 15 para 11(5)(d)). These rules are the same as gift with reservation rules for inheritance tax.

(viii) Where the disposal was an outright gift wholly covered by annual small gifts exemptions, or was for the maintenance of the family (Sch 15 para 10(1)(d), (e)).

(ix) As a result of an outright gift of money made more than seven years before the first date of enjoyment of property/chattels acquired with the funds, as such a gift will be disregarded as consideration (Sch 15 para 10(2)(c)).

(x) The use of a commercial equity release scheme.

(9) The pre-owned asset charge does not apply in any fiscal year:

(a) Where the former owner is not resident in the UK, or

(b) Where the former owner is resident in the UK but domiciled elsewhere for inheritance tax purposes and the property is not UK property, or

(c) Where the former owner was previously domiciled outside the UK for inheritance tax purposes the charge does not apply to property disposed of before becoming domiciled in the UK (Sch 15 para 12).

(10) The income tax charge applies to the use of land or enjoyment of land, chattels and intangible assets (defined as everything other than land or chattels).

For the charge to apply to land:

- the taxpayer must occupy the land (wholly or with others) and
- either the disposal condition or the contribution condition must apply (Sch 15 para 3(1)).

The disposal condition is that at any time after 17 March 1986 the taxpayer owned an interest in the relevant property, or in property the disposal of which has directly or indirectly funded the relevant property, and has disposed of all or part of that interest otherwise than by an excluded transaction (see **explanatory note 8** above).

The contribution condition is that the taxpayer has since 18 March 1986 contributed directly or indirectly to the purchase of the relevant property otherwise than by an excluded transaction (see **explanatory note 8** above).

(11) Different rules apply to quantify the deemed income to be charged, depending on whether the charge arises on land, chattels or intangibles.

Land

The charge for land is calculated by taking the appropriate rental value less any amount that the taxpayer is legally obliged to pay the owner of the relevant land in the period in respect of its occupation. The appropriate rental value is:

$$R \times \frac{DV}{V}$$

where:

R is the rent that might reasonably be expected to be obtained on a year to year letting where tenant pays all rates, charges and council taxes and the landlord bears the cost of repairs, maintenance and insurance.

DV depends on the circumstances:

- if the taxpayer previously owned the property or an interest in it, DV is the value of that interest on the valuation date, or the appropriate proportion of that value if he only disposed of a part of that interest;
- if the taxpayer previously owned a property (or an interest in it) which this property replaced, DV is so much of this property's value on the valuation date as is reasonably attributable to the property or

interest originally disposed of by him, or to the appropriate proportion of that former property if he only disposed of a part of his interest in it;

- if the contribution condition but not the disposal condition applies, DV is so much of this property's value on the valuation date as is reasonably attributable to the consideration provided by the taxpayer.

V is the value of the relevant land at the valuation date.

For example, John gave a property worth £100,000 to his son Peter in 2007. Peter sold the property for £350,000 in 2012 buying a further property for £400,000. John moves into the relevant property in 2023 when it had an annual rental value of £36,000. The contribution that could reasonably be attributed to the gifted property would be:

$$\frac{350{,}000}{400{,}000}$$

(being the proportion of the cost of the relevant property funded by John's gift).

That proportion is then applied to the annual rental value of the property as at the valuation date of £36,000 in order to ascertain the amount of John's deemed income for a full tax year.

$$\frac{350{,}000}{400{,}000} \times 36{,}000 = \text{£}\,31{,}500\ @\ 40\% = \text{£}12{,}600 \text{ patax payable at the } 40\% \text{ rate}$$

Valuation date is set out in SI 2005/724 para 2 being 6 April in the relevant tax year, or if later the first day in the tax year on which enjoyment of the asset occurs.

As brought out in the Example at C, the (market) value of the property and its rental value are effectively set for five years at a time, even though there is technically a valuation date in each separate tax year.

The income tax payable is calculated by adding the appropriate rental value to the taxable income of the donor.

Chattels

In the case of chattels the charge is similar to that for land but with a notional amount of interest (on the value of the chattel at the valuation date), with similar rules to land applying to replacement chattels and cash. The rate of notional interest for this purpose is the official rate for beneficial loans to employees which was reduced to 2.0% (from 2.25%) with effect from 6 April 2021 (see The Taxes (Interest Rate) (Amendment) Regulations 2021 (SI 2021/249) reg 2) and increased to 2.25% with effect from 6 April 2023 (see The Taxes (Interest Rate) (Amendment) Regulations 2023 (SI 2023/216) reg 2).

Intangibles

For intangibles a charge only arises where they are held within a settlement (within the inheritance tax definition) and the settlor retains an interest (within the income tax definition, but unaffected by any interest of the settlor's spouse or civil partner). Again the liability is based upon notional interest, at the same official rate, on the value of the intangibles concerned at the valuation date.

Available reductions or deductions

Where the asset is only enjoyed (or the settlor is only interested) for part of a year the charge is reduced accordingly. As regards land and chattels (but not intangibles) there is no charge if full consideration is paid for use of the asset, and the charge is reduced by payments made under a legal obligation for the use of the asset. For intangibles, a deduction is allowed for income tax or capital gains tax payable by the taxpayer under specified charging provisions which charge the settlor of settled property, so far as the tax is attributable to the property that attracts the pre-owned assets charge.

(12) If the aggregate notional values before contribution do not exceed £5,000 then this is *de minimis* and there is no charge (Sch 15 para 13).

If a charge arises on the enjoyment of land or chattels, but where the pre-owned assets charge also catches intangible property whose value derives (in whole or in part) from the value of the land or chattels, only the higher of the two chargeable amounts applies (Sch 15 para 18).

There are provisions preventing a double charge to income tax under both the employee benefit in kind rules and the pre-owned asset rules – the employment charge takes priority and the deemed employment income is deducted from the pre-owned assets deemed income (Sch 15 para 19).

(13) Where a taxpayer is potentially chargeable to income tax by reference to their enjoyment of any land, or chattels, or intangible property for the first time, then they may make an election. The effect of the election, if made, is that the asset is to be treated as caught by the gifts with reservation rules for inheritance tax and therefore no income tax charge arises. This is a deeming provision, the asset does not actually form part of their estate and therefore there is no uplift in value for capital gains tax when death occurs.

If the taxpayer permanently ceases to have occupation or use and enjoyment of the asset then the same consequence applies as under the gifts with reservation rules, namely that a potentially exempt transfer is deemed to have occurred at the cessation of use. If more than seven years then elapse since last enjoyment of the asset then no inheritance tax charge arises on that property on the taxpayer's death.

The election is required by 31 January following the end of the fiscal year of first use. Schedule 15 para 23(3)(a) expressly permits HMRC to accept late elections. For HMRC's approach see IHTM 44077.

Where the whole of the asset would not be attributed to the donor for pre-owned assets purposes then a similar restriction will apply to the proportion treated as caught by the gifts with reservation rules; ie: the chargeable proportion of asset value is:

$$\text{Value} \times \frac{DV}{V}$$

where DV and V have the meaning set out in **explanatory note 11** above, save that in the context of the election provisions:

- the transactions relevant to the calculation of DV include those after the election takes effect as well as those before it, and

- the valuation date is the date of death (if use continues), or of lifetime cessation of use (or of a beneficial interest in possession in settled property).

(14) The charge is intended to penalise users of inheritance tax avoidance schemes, such as the double trust home loan scheme (the intention of which was to remove the value of the principal private residence from the donors' estate but to enable continued use of the property), or, where the full consideration for the use of the asset is negligible as compared with the open market value of the asset.

(15) However, the charge will also apply to situations where a taxpayer would not expect a charge to arise. For example where a donor gives away assets (eg cash) and then in the future uses property acquired with those assets without paying a full commercial consideration, and does not fall within any of the exceptions for inheritance tax set out at **explanatory note** 4(i) or pre-owned asset exceptions at **explanatory note** 8. Previously if the gift was made at least seven years before the death of the donor there were no tax consequences. Since 2005 an income tax charge may arise.

Example

John gave £300,000 in cash to his daughter, Wendy, on the occasion of her marriage in 2018. She used £200,000 of that gift to buy a picture soon afterwards. On 6 June 2023 Wendy moved to Australia on a temporary contract for three years. She left the picture with John who hung it in his hall. The open market value as at May 2023 is £450,000. Wendy returns in 2026 reclaiming possession of the picture on 6 June 2026. John is still alive in July 2032. Assume an Official Rate of 2.2% throughout, and that John pays tax at 40% in each tax year except 2026/27 when his other income is already sufficient to be liable at 45% (assuming the rate is still in force).

The cash/picture is not caught by the gifts with reservation rules for inheritance tax because Wendy took full bona fide possession and enjoyment of the cash when first gifted in 2018 and the tracing provisions do not apply to cash gifts. Because the gifts with reservation rules do not apply, the picture is not excluded from the pre-owned asset charge. An income tax charge arises in principle because John has the use of property purchased with funds provided by him within the last seven years before his use started.

Two thirds of the cost of the picture was met from John's gift, so (in the absence of other expenditure) that will be the proportion of the picture's value on the valuation date that is reasonably attributable to the consideration provided by John.

The relevant valuation dates are 6 June 2023, 6 April 2024, 6 April 2025 and 6 April 2026, but the value of the picture in all cases is taken at 6 June 2023 since the later dates are all within five years of the first valuation date.

The amount of deemed income for a full tax year can therefore be seen (showing the full statutory fraction) to be:

$$2.2\,\% \times \pounds 450{,}000 \times \frac{\frac{2}{3} \times 450{,}000}{450{,}000} = 2.2\,\% \times \frac{2}{3} \times \pounds 450{,}000 = \pounds 6{,}600$$

John did not have the use of the picture for the whole of 2023/24 or 2026/27, so the amount of deemed income – and his consequent income tax liability – for the four tax years is:

Year	Fraction of year	Deemed income (fraction of £6,000)	Tax liability on deemed income at marginal rate
2023/24	10/12	5,500	£2,200
2024/25	12/12	6,600	£2,640
2025/26	12/12	6,600	£2,640
2026/27	2/12	1,100*	£0*

* Deemed income as calculated is below £5,000 so *de minimis* exemption applies

The income tax charge would be avoided if John elected by 31 January 2027 for the gifts with reservation rules for inheritance tax to apply. As he does live for at least seven years after he ceased to possess the picture in June 2026, no inheritance tax charge would in practice arise.

Alternatively John could pay full rental value for the use of the picture. If he is responsible for insurance this could be very low.

(16) The key traps to be aware of in relation to the pre-owned asset tax (POAT) regime are as follows:

- There are no provisions that ameliorate unexpected changes in circumstances. For example, a father gives his son money to purchase a property jointly for their joint occupation. If the son is posted elsewhere for work and moves out of the property, a POAT charge will arise.

- The de minimis threshold of £5,000 a year is calculated before making any reduction for rental payments made by the taxpayer. Further rental payments must be made pursuant to a legal obligation in order to be deductible; a proper rental agreement is required. Payments made by a taxpayer are deductible only in the year they are made; payments of rent made in advance in relation to later years do not have the effect of avoiding a charge in those later years. Further the payment must be made direct to the owner of the property, not some third party.

- Transfers to a spouse or civil partner are exempt from POAT but not to an unmarried partner. A POAT charge will arise and continue to apply even though they may subsequently marry.

(17) See also the companion book, Tolley's Taxwise I 2023/24, for calculation of the rate of income tax payable by a donor.

Question

Agnes Brown was a wealthy, childless widow who doted on her nephew Simon. Having not made any gifts previously, she decided in 2016 to begin passing on some of her wealth to Simon and on 17 October 2016 she made a gift to him of a number of investments as follows:

(1) 3,000 shares out of her long-standing holding of 16,500 shares in Brown Retailing Ltd, a trading company with an issued share capital of 30,000 shares. The other 13,500 shares are already held by Simon.

(2) 15,000 shares in Landy plc, which were quoted at 180–188p with marked bargains at 180 and 182p.

On 11 November 2018, following the birth of Simon's first child, Agnes settled her remaining shares in Brown Retailing Ltd on discretionary trust, including herself, Simon and his child amongst the class of beneficiaries.

Feeling that perhaps she had favoured Simon to an unfair extent, she gave £100,000 to her niece Pauline on 21 December 2018.

On 10 March 2019 upon the advice of her professional adviser, she excluded herself from all benefit under the discretionary trust by deed of the same date.

An offer of £1m for the whole of the issued share capital of Brown Retailing Ltd was received on 14 November 2021. This was accepted by all shareholders. The trustees reinvested the discretionary trust's proceeds into quoted shares.

Agnes died on 30 September 2023, leaving an estate valued at £700,000 including her home valued at £250,000 and the following assets all held for more than two years:

(i) a 30% holding valued at £50,000 in Blue Ltd, an unquoted investment company;

(ii) a 5% holding valued at £60,000 in Pink plc, a trading company on the Alternative Investment Market;

(iii) a 60% holding valued at £100,000 in Green Ltd, an unquoted investment company; and

(iv) a 40% holding valued at £200,000 in Black Ltd, an unquoted trading company.

Under the terms of her will Agnes added a further £100,000 cash to the discretionary trust. The rest of her estate was divided equally between Simon and Pauline.

On 26 September 2024 the trustees of the discretionary trust appointed £50,000 from the cash received from the executors to Simon on the basis that he was to pay any tax due. At this time the trustees still held the same quoted shares bought in 2021, and no other assets apart from the cash received under Agnes Brown's will.

The value of an ordinary share in Brown Retailing Ltd at the relevant times was as follows:

	17.10.16	*11.11.18*	*10.3.19*
	£	£	£
75–100%	25	42	40
50–74%	20	31	30
25–49%	15	24	23
0–24%	10	16	15

There are no other relevant transfers of shares in Brown Retailing Ltd.

Calculate the inheritance tax payable in respect of the above events.

Answer

Agnes Brown — inheritance tax position in lifetime

	£
17 October 2016	
Gifts to Simon:	
3,000 shares in Brown Retailing Ltd	
16,500 shares at £20 (55% holding)	330,000
13,500 shares at £15 (45% holding)	(202,500)
Loss to estate	127,500
Less: Business property relief 100%	
(see **explanatory note 1**)	(127,500)
Potentially exempt transfer	Nil
15,000 shares in Landy plc @ ½ (180 + 182) = 181p, giving transfer of value of	27,150
Less: Annual exemptions 2016/17 and 2015/16	(6,000)
Potentially exempt transfer	21,150
11 November 2018	
Settlement on discretionary trust	
13,500 shares in Brown Retailing Ltd	
at £24 per share (45% holding)	324,000
Less: Business property relief 100%	
(see **explanatory note 2**)	(324,000)
Transfer of value	Nil
21 December 2018	
Gift to Pauline	100,000
Less: Annual exemptions 2018/19 and 2017/18	(6,000)
Potentially exempt transfer	94,000
10 March 2019	
Release of reservation —	
13,500 shares in Brown Retailing Ltd at	
£23 per share (45% holding)	310,500
Less: 100% business property relief (see **explanatory note 2**)	(310,500)
Potentially exempt transfer	Nil

On death of Agnes Brown — 30 September 2023

(a) Gifts on 17 October 2016

		Gross	*Tax on 2023/24 scale*
		£	£
Transfers within seven years before death:			
Accumulation in seven years before gifts on 17 October 2016		Nil	Nil
Gifts to Simon (see **explanatory note 1**):			
Shares in Brown Retailing Ltd	122,553		
Shares in Landy plc	26,097		
		148,650	Nil

(b) Gift to trust on 11 November 2018

Accumulation in preceding seven years (to calculate additional tax only, cumulative transfers not affected — see **explanatory note 2**):

17 October 2016			
Gifts previously potentially exempt		148,650	Nil
11 November 2018			
Settlement of shares on discretionary trust as above	Nil		
Add business property relief no longer available (see **explanatory note 2**)	324,000		
Less: Annual exemptions 2018/19 and 2017/18	(6,000)	318,000	56,660*
		466,650	56,660*

(* 466,650 – 325,000 = 141,650 @ 40%)

As death takes place between four and five years after the transfer, the tax payable by the trustees is reduced by 40% to £56,660 × 60% = £33,996.

(c) Gift on 21 December 2018

Accumulation in seven years before gift to Pauline on 21 December 2018

17 October 2016	148,650	Nil
11 November 2018 (see above and **explanatory note 2**)	Nil	Nil
21 December 2018		
Gift to Pauline (annual exemptions reallocated to trust as above — see **explanatory note 2**)	100,000	Nil*
	248,650	Nil*

(* 248,650 is within nil-rate band)

(d) Exclusion from benefit – deemed potentially exempt transfer

10 March 2019

Release of reservation — total inheritance tax payable will be the higher of:

(i) Disregarding the original gift and charging the potentially exempt transfer on release, or

(ii) Charging original gift and disregarding subsequent potentially exempt transfer.

(i) *First calculation*

	Gross	Tax on 2023/24 scale
	£	£
Accumulation in seven years before gift on 17 October 2016	Nil	Nil
17 October 2016		
Gift to Simon — as above	148,650	Nil
11 November 2018		
Settlement on discretionary trust — ignored	Nil	Nil
21 December 2018		
Gift to Pauline — as above	100,000	Nil
10 March 2019		
Release of reservation		
Potentially exempt transfer now chargeable		
(business property relief no longer available – see **explanatory note 2**)	310,500	93,660*
	559,150	93,660*

(* 559,150 – 325,000 = 234,150 @ 40%)

As death takes place between four and five years after release of reservation, tax payable by trustees is 60% × £93,660 = £56,196,

(ii) *The second calculation is as already calculated at (b) above, ie cumulative transfers of £466,650 and tax payable of £33,996*

The tax due on death must then be taken into account in both calculations.

(iii) *Tax on death – first calculation*

In the first case, however, the lifetime transfers exceeded the nil-rate band at death, so the tax payable on the death estate would be:

		£	£
30 September 2023 — death of Agnes Brown			
Estate on death			700,000
Less:	Business property relief		
	100% × £60,000 (shares in Pink plc)	60,000	
	100% × £200,000 (shares in Black Ltd)	200,000	(260,000)
			440,000
Tax @ 40%			176,000

(iv) *Tax on death – second calculation*

In the second case the tax would be:

	Gross £	Tax on 2023/24 scale £
30 September 2023 — death of Agnes Brown — accumulation in seven years before death		
17 October 2016	148,650	Nil
11 November 2018 (see above)	Nil	Nil
21 December 2018	100,000	Nil
	248,650	Nil
Estate on death (less business property relief)	440,000	145,460*
	688,650	145,460*

(* 688,650 – 325,000 = 363,650 @ 40%)

Total tax payable on lifetime gifts and death is:

First calculation (i) + (iii) above	(56,196 + 176,000)	£232,196
Second calculation (ii) + (iv) above	(33,996 + 145,460)	£179,456

The first calculation (ignoring the lifetime gift of the Brown Retailing Ltd shares to the discretionary trust and taxing the release of reservation) therefore shows the higher total tax liability, and inheritance tax is therefore payable as follows:

	£
By Agnes Brown on creation of discretionary trust in lifetime	Nil
By Simon ((a) above)	Nil
By Pauline ((c) above)	Nil
By trustees of discretionary trust ((d)(i) above)	56,196
By personal representatives((d)(iii) above)	176,000
((b) above, which is the same as (d)(ii) above, is disregarded under the double charges regulations, as is (d)(iv) above)	
On appointment by discretionary trust to Simon on 26 September 2024 (being within two years of death – s 144 – see explanatory note 6)	Nil

Explanatory Notes

Same day transfers in the context of inheritance tax

(1) Where two or more transfers of value are made on the same day, the annual exemption is apportioned between them (IHTA 1984 s 19(3)(b)). Business property relief is deducted in arriving at the amount of a transfer of value. The treatment of the annual exemption in relation to potentially exempt transfers outlined in **Example A1** makes the calculation of the potentially exempt transfers by Agnes Brown in this Example particularly difficult. The gift of the shares in Brown Retailing Ltd on 17 October 2016 initially qualifies for 100% business property relief (see **Example A21 part A(c)** for rates of business property relief) so that the transfer of value is reduced to nil as shown. On the same day as the gift of the Brown Retailing Ltd shares, Agnes made the gift of the shares in Landy plc, the transfer of value being £27,150, which is not eligible for business property relief. Annual exemptions for 2016/17 and 2015/16 are therefore allocated to the gift of shares in Landy plc.

When Agnes Brown died on 30 September 2023, the shares in Brown Retailing Ltd no longer qualified for business property relief. It is understood to be the view of HMRC that the annual exemption should then be reallocated between the gifts as follows:

$$\text{Brown RetailingLtd Shares}\frac{127,500}{154,650}\times 6,000 \quad £4,947$$

$$\text{Landyplc shares}\frac{27,150}{154,650}\times 6,000 \quad £1,053$$

The revised potentially exempt transfers would then be:

Brown Retailing Ltd shares	127,500 – 4,947	122,553
Landy plc shares	27,150 – 1,053	26,097
		£148,650

Alternatively it could be argued that the original allocation of the annual exemption stands despite the withdrawal of business property relief. The gifts to Simon would then be £127,500 in respect of the shares in Brown Retailing Ltd and £21,150 in respect of the shares in Landy plc. In this instance the tax position is the same in any event, as both gifts were made to Simon and there is no inheritance tax liability. However, if a tax liability arose payable by different persons, this point may be taken. The total gifts to Simon would still amount to £148,650 and this amount is included in subsequent calculations.

Business property relief

(2) For detailed notes on business property relief see **Example A21**. The relief is not available when calculating the tax on a potentially exempt transfer that becomes chargeable as a result of the donor's death within seven years if the relevant conditions are no longer satisfied at that later time (s 113A(1)). Similarly, where business property relief has been given against a transfer that was a chargeable transfer in lifetime, the relief is not available when calculating any additional tax payable as a result of the death of the transferor within seven years unless the conditions for the relief are satisfied at that time (s 113A(2)) (see **Example A21 part a(c)**). Note that the withdrawal of business property relief on a transfer that was a chargeable transfer in lifetime only affects the calculation of any additional tax payable on that transfer. The original chargeable transfer is taken into account in the accumulation for the purpose of working out the position on later transfers and on the death estate.

In this Example the original chargeable transfer to the discretionary trust on 11 November 2018 qualified for 100% relief so it did not increase the cumulative total at that time. The cumulative total taken into account in calculating the tax on the gift to Pauline the following month therefore shows the 11 November transfer at nil. (For a further illustration see **Example A21**.)

The wording of the legislation supports the view that business property relief is effective immediately to the extent that the original transfer is covered by the annual exemption and that only the balance can be affected by the withdrawal of business property relief if the donor dies within seven years. For transfers on or after 28 November 1995, subsection (7A) was introduced into s 113A, which provides that when applying the rules for withdrawing business property relief on transfers within seven years before death, the relief is disregarded in establishing whether there is a potentially exempt or chargeable transfer. The reason for the change is that it had been contended that a transfer that initially qualified for 100% business property relief became a transfer of nil, and was therefore wholly within the £3,000 annual exempt limit, so no chargeable or potentially exempt transfer remained to be reconsidered if the donor died within seven years and no withdrawal of relief could therefore take place. The Revenue (now HMRC) did not agree with this view, and the FA 1996 change was made 'for the removal of any doubt'. A similar change was made to s 124A (in subsection (7A)) in relation to agricultural property relief.

The change is intended only to establish that a transfer exists, and does not seek to quantify the amount of the transfer. It is considered, therefore, that it does not affect the view stated above that if a slice of the original transfer is covered by the annual exemption, the business property relief on that slice cannot later be withdrawn. This is however not relevant where the original transfer qualified for 100% relief, because the annual exemption would not be used against a nil transfer. (See also **Example B7 explanatory note 7**.)

When Agnes Brown excludes herself from benefit under the settlement, thus bringing an end to the reservation of benefit in her lifetime, she is deemed to make a disposition of the settled property by a disposition which is a potentially exempt transfer (FA 1986 s 102(4)). That excludes the application of any annual exemptions otherwise available; but in the Example there would be no need to invoke the annual exemption in any event since the transfer qualifies at this stage for business property relief. By virtue of FA 1986 Sch 20 para 8, business property relief and agricultural property relief are available against the potentially exempt transfer on a reservation coming to an end, or against the charge on death if the reservation continues until death, (in either case the 'material transfer') provided:

- the relief was available to the donor in respect of the property in question against the transfer of value which constituted the disposal by way of gift in relation to which the reservation of benefit arose, and
- the property in question would attract the relief at the date of the material transfer if it were made by the donee rather than by the donor. For the purpose of this test the donor's ownership before the gift, and where relevant for agricultural property relief occupation before the gift, is attributed to the donee (para 8(2)); *but* to determine if shares or securities contributed to control of the company in question, such as to constitute relevant business property falling within IHTA 1984 s 105(1)(b) or (cc), they are treated as though they had been owned by the donor continuously since the date of the gift (para 8(1A)(a)). (This provision also applies, in terms, in relation to s 105(1)(bb), which now refers simply to any unquoted shares in a company but used, before 6 April 1996, to require a minimum 25% holding to obtain relief.)

In the Example the shares in Brown Retailing Limited were still unquoted at the date the reservation of benefit ceased (10 March 2019); and although they had then only been owned by the trustees for a few months, the attribution of Agnes Brown's previous period of ownership to the trustees prevents relief being otherwise denied by the failure of the two-year minimum period of ownership in IHTA 1984 s 106.

Care needs to be taken in relation to the treatment of the annual exemption when business property relief is withdrawn. **Explanatory note 1** deals with the situation where the 100% relief is withdrawn from a transfer that was originally potentially exempt, ie the gift to Simon of shares in Brown Retailing Ltd (with the additional complication that another transfer was made on the same day), and similarly the deemed potentially exempt transfer on release of the reservation. The Example also illustrates the 100% relief being withdrawn from a transfer that would otherwise have been a chargeable transfer, ie the transfer to the discretionary trust on 11 November 2018. The annual exemptions of 2018/19 and 2017/18 were originally given against the 2018/19 gift to Pauline. When the business property relief is withdrawn at Agnes's death, the annual exemptions will be reallocated to the transfer to the discretionary trust, since the trust transfer occurred earlier in the tax year than the transfer to Pauline.

(3) No business property relief is available on Agnes Brown's death in relation to her holdings in:

Blue Ltd — an *investment* company.

Green Ltd — an *investment* company.

Business property relief of 100% is available on the holding in Pink plc as it is a trading company on the Alternative Investment Market (AIM), and on the investment in Black Ltd, an unquoted trading company.

Consequences of reduction in IHT rates

(4) In calculating the tax, or additional tax, due on lifetime transfers as a result of Agnes Brown's death within seven years, the 2023/24 nil-rate band is used here in all cases because it is equal to or larger than (and so the average rate of tax equal or lower) that at the dates of the relevant lifetime transfers: Schedule 2 para 2. It would be different if the scale at the date of death were higher: the tax (or additional tax) would then be calculated using the scale (or nil-rate band) in force at the dates of the respective original transfers.

[NB – Schedule 2 applies where there is a 'reduction of tax', defined as a reduction of tax by the substitution of a new Table in Schedule 1 (Schedule 2 para 1(a)). It is far from clear how this would apply if the new Table was capable of increasing the tax due at some levels of chargeable transfer but reducing it at others, for example if the nil-rate band were increased to £500,000 but the rate of tax applicable above that figure were 50%.]

Double charges relief for inheritance tax

(5) The situations when a double charge to tax occurs and the reliefs under the Inheritance Tax (Double Charges Relief) Regulations 1987 (SI 1987/1130) are dealt with in **Examples B1** and **B2**. The regulations apply to the release of reservation on 10 March 2019 in this Example, when Agnes Brown excludes herself from benefit under the discretionary trust. The release is specifically treated as a potentially exempt transfer by FA 1986 s 102(4), despite the fact that someone else's estate has not been increased, nor has an interest in possession in the trust been created.

In this Example no tax was payable by the trustees of the discretionary settlement in the settlor's lifetime. If any lifetime tax had been payable on such a transfer, then where, as in this Example, the first calculation produced the higher figure, the lifetime tax (up to but not exceeding the part of the death tax payable relating to the transfer) would be deducted from the tax payable by the trustees following Agnes Brown's death (see **Example B2 explanatory note 3**).

Post-death variations of a will for inheritance tax

(6) The assets of the discretionary trust following Agnes Brown's death consist of shares acquired on the takeover of Brown Retailing Ltd in November 2021 and £100,000 added in cash under the terms of Agnes Brown's will. The appointment of £50,000 to Simon on 26 September 2024 is in cash, the shares being retained in full. Accordingly it is a variation of the property settled by will within two years of the date of death and is treated as a disposition at death for inheritance tax and not as a distribution out of the discretionary trust (s 144). Section 144 applies where a distribution is made out of property settled by will within two years after the death and before any interest in possession has subsisted in the property. The distribution is treated as if it had been made under the terms of the will. (See **Example C11 explanatory note 9** where such a distribution is made within the first three months after death.)

(7) Akin to the post-death distribution from property settled by a will within two years of death, is the case where a testator expresses a wish that property bequeathed by his will should be transferred by the legatee to another person and the legatee complies with the wish within the period of two years after the death of the testator. In that case the inheritance tax regime has effect as if the property transferred had been bequeathed by the will to the transferee (s 143) and the transfer of the property made by the legatee is not a transfer of value (s 17(b)).

(8) For detailed notes on post-death variations of a will see **Example B6**.

Residence nil-rate band

(9) Agnes's estate is not entitled to a residence nil-rate band on her death as her home is not directly inherited, her nephew, Simon, not being her descendant (see **Example A2 part (b) explanatory note 3**).

Question

Dr and Mrs Slowe made their wills without professional advice, each leaving the whole of his/her estate to the surviving spouse with the proviso that should the spouse predecease him/her the estate should be divided between their children.

On 31 December 2023 they were involved in a road accident in which Dr Slowe (aged 50) died instantly. Mrs Slowe (aged 51) was seriously injured and died seven days later. They had two children, John (aged 25) and Jill (aged 18).

At death Dr Slowe's interest in the group practice in which he was a partner was valued at £250,000. He also owned assets valued at £50,000, and the family home, valued at £600,000, was in his sole ownership. He had no interest in any settlements nor had he made any lifetime gifts.

Mrs Slowe had assets of her own valued at £75,000 and was the life tenant of the estate of her late father, who died on 20 February 1999, the reversionary interest passing to her children equally. The settlement was valued at £325,000 on 7 January 2024. During her lifetime Mrs Slowe had made chargeable transfers amounting to £85,000 (all less than three years before death).

(a) Compute the inheritance tax payable by reason of the deaths of Dr and Mrs Slowe taking into account any possible transfer of their nil-rate bands.

(b) Consider whether it would be possible to mitigate that liability.

(c) Comment on what the tax position would have been if they had died simultaneously.

(d) Assuming professional advice had been obtained before death so that the wills had included an appropriately worded survivorship clause, recompute the inheritance tax payable consequent upon their deaths.

(e) Prepare a table comparing the tax payable at (a) and (d), and comment on the difference in tax payable at (d) with what would have been payable under (b) and (c).

Answer

(a) Inheritance tax payable on deaths of Dr and Mrs Slowe

Inheritance tax payable on death of Dr Slowe — 31 December 2023

Nil since all property passes to Mrs Slowe (his wife) which is an exempt transfer.

Inheritance tax payable on death of Mrs Slowe — 7 January 2024

		£	£
Free estate			
Family home			600,000
Other assets —	Own	75,000	
	Husband's estate:		
	Assets from partnership	250,000	
	Other assets	50,000	375,000
			975,000
Settled property			
Life interest in estate of late father			325,000
Amount subject to inheritance tax			1,300,000

Inheritance tax accumulation

	Gross	*Tax*
	£	£
Cumulative transfers prior to death	85,000	Nil
Estate	1,300,000	154,000*
Less: residence nil-rate band (see **explanatory note 10**)	(350,000)	
	1,035,000	154,000*

(* 1,035,000 – 650,000 (see **explanatory note 10**) = 385,000 @ 40%)

Estate rate $\frac{154,000}{1,300,000} \times 100 = 11.8462\%$

Inheritance tax payable:		
By personal representatives	975,000 @ 11.8462%	115,500
By trustees of settled property	325,000 @ 11.8462%	38,500
		£154,000

(b) Mitigating Mrs Slowe's inheritance tax liability

The personal representatives of Mrs Slowe could, within two years after Dr Slowe's death, make a written disclaimer of the gift to her under his will (IHTA 1984 s 142). This would result in an intestacy. But because under the intestacy rules a 28-day survivorship period applies to the spouse entitlement, the effect of such a disclaimer would be that Dr Slowe's estate would pass to the children. The same effect would be obtained if, again within two years of Dr

Slowe's death, Mrs Slowe's personal representatives entered into a written variation under s 142 to redirect the assets to the children.

If a deed of variation or disclaimer is executed, it will not be a transfer of value and inheritance tax will be calculated as though the deed displaced the provisions of the will (ie computed as in **part (d)** of the Example) *provided* in the case of a variation (not a disclaimer) that the instrument of variation contains a statement that the variation is intended to have that effect.

Since additional tax would be payable on Dr Slowe's estate, then within six months after the date of such a variation Dr Slowe's personal representatives, together with Mrs Slowe's personal representatives, would have to notify HMRC Inheritance Tax of the amount of extra tax and send a copy of the variation. See **explanatory note 5** for further details.

(c) Simultaneous deaths (commorientes)

Where two or more persons die at the same time or in circumstances where it cannot be known which survived the other(s), it is assumed under the rule of commorientes (as it applies in England and Wales) that the elder died first and accordingly that the younger is deemed to have survived the elder (Law of Property Act 1925 s 184). However, for inheritance tax purposes s 4(2) provides that they shall be assumed to have died at the same instant. (Under Scots Law, where two persons die simultaneously or in circumstances in which it is uncertain who survived whom, each is to be treated as having failed to survive the other for all purposes affecting title or succession to property (Succession (Scotland) Act 2016, s 9)).

Any bequest from one to the other will accordingly be ignored for inheritance tax purposes since neither survived the other. Therefore if Dr and Mrs Slowe had both died at the same time (or if it could not be determined who died first) then for the purposes of general law (ie the actual devolution of the assets) Mrs Slowe (being the elder) would be deemed to have died first, and her estate would pass under her will to her husband. On the death of Dr Slowe his estate (now including his wife's estate) would pass under his will to the children.

For inheritance tax purposes, however, Dr Slowe would be deemed to have died at the same time as Mrs Slowe and his estate for inheritance tax would not include his wife's assets.

Even so (as explained further in **explanatory note 8**), when computing the inheritance tax liability on the estate of Mrs Slowe the assets other than the settled property would in fact pass to Dr Slowe's estate and therefore would be exempt (s 18), whereas the settled property would revert under the terms of the settlement to the children and a liability would arise as follows:

Inheritance tax payable on simultaneous deaths

	£	£
Mrs Slowe (elder)		
Free estate	75,000	
Less: Exempt transfer to Dr Slowe	(75,000)	Nil
Settled property		
Life interest in estate of late father		325,000
Amount subject to inheritance tax		325,000

Inheritance tax accumulation

	Gross	Tax
	£	£
Cumulative transfers prior to death	85,000	Nil
Estate on death	325,000	34,000*
	410,000	34,000*

(* 410,000 – 325,000 = 85,000 @ 40%)

	£
Inheritance tax payable:	
By personal representatives	Nil
By trustees of settled property	34,000

Dr Slowe (younger)	£	£
Family home		600,000
Interest in practice	250,000	
Less: 100% business property relief	(250,000)	Nil
Other assets (excluding Mrs Slowe's assets of £75,000)		50,000
Amount subject to inheritance tax		650,000

Inheritance tax accumulation

	Gross	Tax
	£	£
Cumulative transfers prior to death	Nil	Nil
Estate on death	650,000	Nil*
Less: residence nil-rate band (see **explanatory note 10**)	(350,000)	
Balance of chargeable estate	300,000	
Inheritance tax payable by personal representatives		Nil*
(*chargeable estate within nil-rate band (**explanatory note 10**))		

(d) Survivorship clauses

To prevent devolution and taxation problems relating to deaths at or near the same time, it is common to include a survivorship clause in a will. For example, the bequest to the spouse is made conditional upon that person surviving for a specified period such as thirty days after the first death. Such clauses are effective for inheritance tax purposes provided the specified period does not exceed six months (s 92) and tax is computed as if the dispositions which take effect at the end of the period (or on the earlier death of the contingent legatee) had taken place at the first death. If 30-day survivorship clauses had been included in the wills of Dr and Mrs Slowe (or if Mrs Slowe's personal representatives had disclaimed the inheritance or entered into a variation as indicated in **part (b)** above) the tax position on their deaths would have been as follows:

Inheritance tax payable on death of Dr Slowe — 31 December 2023

		£
Family home		600,000
Interest in practice	250,000	
Less: 100% business property relief	(250,000)	Nil
Other assets		50,000
Estate on death for inheritance tax		650,000

Inheritance tax accumulation

	Gross	Tax
	£	£
Cumulative transfers prior to death	Nil	Nil
Estate on death	650,000	10,000*
Less: residence nil-rate band	(350,000)	
	300,000	

Inheritance tax payable by personal representatives (as in (c))	Nil

*chargeable estate within nil-rate band

Inheritance tax payable on death of Mrs Slowe — 7 January 2024

	£
Free estate	
Assets	75,000
Settled property	
Life interest in estate of late father	325,000
Estate on death	400,000

Inheritance tax accumulation

	Gross	Tax
	£	£
Cumulative transfers prior to death	85,000	Nil
Estate on death	400,000	64,000*
	485,000	64,000*

(* 485,000 – 325,000 (see **explanatory note 10**) = 160,000 @ 40%)

Estate rate

$$\frac{64,000}{400,000} \times 100 = 16.0\%$$

Inheritance tax payable:

		£
By personal representatives	£75,000 @ 16%	12,000
By trustees of settled property	£325,000 @ 16%	52,000
		64,000

(e) Comparison of tax payable

	Under (a) above (without variation)	*With survivorship clause*
	£	£
By personal representatives of Dr Slowe	Nil	Nil
By personal representatives of Mrs Slowe	115,500	12,000
	115,500	12,000
By trustees of settled property	38,500	52,000
	154,000	64,000

Tax of £74,000 would also be payable if a disclaimer or variation as at (b) were executed.

The tax payable in the event of simultaneous deaths (c) is £34,000 (£34,000 + £Nil). The difference of £30,000 compared with the tax payable had the survivorship clause or a variation or disclaimer operated is because Mrs Slowe's own assets of £75,000 are in the event of simultaneous deaths exempt from inheritance tax since under the general law (as it applies in England and Wales) they pass to her (younger) husband even though by s 4(2) they are not then counted as part of his estate for inheritance tax purposes (s 4(2) does not nullify the actual transfer of the assets under the general law and the application of the spouse exemption); whereas they are chargeable in her estate if they pass directly to her children as they would under the survivorship clause or variation/disclaimer, and attract tax at 40% = £30,000 (see **explanatory note** 8).

Explanatory Notes

Inheritance tax on estates of Dr and Mrs Slowe

(1) Because Dr Slowe predeceased his wife the whole of his estate passed to her under the will. This is an exempt transfer and no inheritance tax is payable (s 18). Accordingly when Mrs Slowe died there was no quick succession relief because her estate had not been increased by a chargeable transfer (s 141).

Conversely, Mrs Slowe will benefit from 100% of Dr Slowe's unused nil-rate band and unused residence nil-rate band. This means that if the increase is claimed, her nil-rate band and residence nil-rate band will be increased by £325,000 and £175,000 respectively for 2023/24 – the year of her death (see **explanatory note 10**).

(2) Mrs Slowe's estate includes the value of her husband's share in the professional partnership. As she is not a partner this does not qualify for business property relief. For notes on business property relief see **Example A21**.

(3) The wording of the wills resulted in the second estate being increased in value and attracting a large amount of tax, whilst the first estate lost the benefit of its business property relief because the relievable asset passed to an exempt beneficiary in whose hands it could not attract the relief: neither Mrs Slowe nor Dr Slowe's executors carried on the business. The failure to use Dr Slowe's nil-rate band, which would have been serious before 9 October 2007, is now not a problem provided a claim is made within the time allowed to transfer the benefit of his nil-rate band to his widow's estate. Also, provided a claim is made within the time limit allowed, the benefit of a residence nil-rate band is also transferred to Mrs Slowe. The benefit from the deed of variation would be very substantial because the total inheritance tax payable would be reduced from £154,000 to £64,000, giving an overall saving of £90,000. Such a deed would not have been necessary in the particular circumstances if the wills had contained a survivorship clause. However, if Mrs Slowe had survived longer than the time specified in such a survivorship clause there would still have been a loss of business property relief, and the better approach in Dr Slowe's will would have been to ensure that his interest in his

professional practice should pass to a chargeable beneficiary (which could be a discretionary trust) even if his wife survived him, and not get aggregated with his widow's estate.

Deeds of variation for inheritance tax

(4) In this Example the use of the provisions in s 142 (Alteration of dispositions taking effect on death) would be fairly straightforward and could be used to rewrite the provisions of Dr Slowe's will to advantage. In practice complications can occur if the family cannot agree on a revised disposition of the estate, or if one or more of the original beneficiaries is an infant and therefore does not have the legal capacity to agree to a variation. Court consent would be needed to reduce an infant beneficiary's entitlement.

(5) As indicated in **part (b)** of the Example, a variation of the way in which a deceased's estate is distributed, either under a will or under an intestacy, is effective for inheritance tax provided the instrument of variation includes a statement that it is intended to have that effect, made by those making the variation, and by the personal representatives of the deceased whose estate is subject to the variation if additional tax is payable (s 142(2), (2A)). The personal representatives can only refuse to make the statement if they hold insufficient assets to discharge the additional tax liability (s 142(2A)). If a beneficiary has died before the date of the variation, his personal representatives can act in his stead, but the authority of the beneficiaries of that estate will be needed where the variation reduces the interest of the survivor's estate, and should in practice join in the variation to avoid queries from HMRC over that authority.

In relation to deaths occurring on or after 6 April 2012, if a deed of variation has the effect of creating or increasing a legacy (or of creating or increasing a gift out of the residue of the estate) to a charity (or a registered sports club), then the deed is effective only if it is shown that the charity or club (or the trustees of a charitable trust as the case may be) has been notified of the existence of the deed of variation (s 142(3A), (3B) inserted by FA 2012 Sch 32 para 9). This new rule applies whether or not the redirection of the deceased's property to the charity or club is sufficient for any part of his estate to qualify for the lower rate of inheritance tax (see **Example B12**). This does not impose a requirement for the charity (or club) to be a party to the deed of variation, but evidence must be provided that the charity (or club) is aware of the fact that property is to be redirected to it. HMRC has indicated that copies of an exchange of letters between the parties involved will show that the charity (or club) is aware of the arrangements will be sufficient for this purpose.

Where the effect of a variation is that additional tax is payable, the beneficiaries and the personal representatives of the deceased whose estate is subject to the variation must notify HMRC Inheritance Tax of the amount of extra tax and send a copy of the variation within six months after the date it is made (s 218A). Penalties apply for failure to comply (s 245A(1A)).

Instruments of variation are also effective for capital gains tax purposes provided the instrument contains a statement by those making it that it is intended to have that effect (TCGA 1992 s 62(7)).

Instruments of variation that are drawn up incorrectly may be rectified in certain circumstances. In *Sherdley v Sherdley* [1987] STC 217 the House of Lords stated that a court will make an order for the rectification of a document if it is satisfied of two matters. First it has to be satisfied that the instrument does not give effect to the true agreement or arrangement between the parties, or to the true intention of a grantor or covenantor. Secondly the court has to be satisfied that there is an issue, capable of being contested, between the parties or between a covenantor or a grantor and the person he intended to benefit, it being irrelevant first that rectification of the document is sought or consented to by them all, and second that rectification is desired because it has beneficial fiscal consequences. On the other hand, the court will not order rectification of a document as between the parties or as between a grantor or covenantor and an intended beneficiary, if their rights will be unaffected and if the only effect of the order will be to secure a fiscal benefit. In *Pitt v Holt* [2013] UKSC 26 the Supreme Court reaffirmed the position stating that rectification is strictly limited to some clearly established dispute between the words of a legal document and the intention of the parties to it, the remedy not being concerned with consequences. This case is the leading authority on the recission of a non-voluntary disposition for mistake. The principles established by the case are:

- the donor must have been mistaken (rather than ignorant or inadvertent);
- the mistake must be of a relevant type – a causative mistake – and it applies to a mistake as to tax consequences just as it does to any other form of mistake; and

- the mistake must be sufficiently serious as to render it unjust on the part of the donee to retain the property given to him. The gravity of the mistake is determined by reference to unconscionableness, injustice and unfairness.

Where these tests are met, a court has discretion to whether to not to set aside the disposition.

In *Giles v The Royal National Institute for the Blind* [2014] EWHC 1373 a claim for the rectification of a deed of variation was successful. That case concerned two sisters, Hilda and Ellen. Hilda had pre-deceased Ellen who was a beneficiary of Hilda's will. Like Hilda, Ellen had left some specific legacies and the residue of her estate to four charities. However, the combined effect of the two wills was that the assets that had passed to Ellen under Hilda's will and then to the charities was chargeable to inheritance tax. The personal representative of both estates had entered into a deed of variation to redirect Ellen's entitlement under Hilda's will to the four charities to avoid the inheritance tax. However, the effect of the wording of the deed was defective and a charge to inheritance tax remained in respect of a certain item of property. The personal representative applied for rectification of the deed of variation as the drafting had not produced its intended effect. The claim was successful as they provided proof of the error, the error related to the intended effect of the document (and not its consequences), and furthermore there was an issue in that the four charities had intimated that they had a claim in negligence against the solicitor who had drawn up the deed of variation. The effect of the order of rectification would not be only to secure tax advantages.

In *PM Bullard v WH Bullard & VW Faire* [2017] EWHC 3 it was held that a defective double trust arrangement (which was a popular way to save IHT on the family home before 2003) could be rectified. Such an arrangement involves the transfer of the right to receive the price of the sale of the home to an IIP trust (which transfer would have been a PET under the law as it applied at the time). The IIP trust established by the taxpayer in the case was for the benefit of her two adult and five minor grandchildren. However, the trust concerned was not a true IIP trust as the Trustee Act 1925 s 31 rendered the rights of the minor beneficiaries contingent on their attaining the age 18 (thus suspending the IIP which the settlor intended them to have) The taxpayer sought rectification of the trust deed to oust the operation of s 31 and was successful. Referring to the *Giles* case above, the court granted relief on the four-part test of rectification set out in *Re Butlin's ST* [1976] Ch 251 concluding that:

- the claimant had a clear intention to avoid an immediate IHT charge to which the instrument did not give effect
- there was an actual flaw as to the legal effect of the deed, which resulted in an effect contrary to the claimant's intentions
- the claimant had an active intention to create absolute IIP rights as opposed to not intending the eventual result
- there was an issue capable of being contested: the interests that were intended to be absolute becoming contingent.

The case of *Smith v Stanley* [2019] 2 WLUK 174 involved an application by trustees to set aside a deed of appointment in relation to the beneficiary of a trust that had been established under of a deed of variation of an estate. The deed of appointment was entered into following advice as to its tax consequences. The advice was wrong and so the trustees had entered into the deed mistakenly understanding its true tax effect. The High Court followed the approach in *Pitt* that although there would be an inheritance tax saving, this was not a reason for refusing the relief sought. The judge considered that the mistake involved in the case was sufficiently serious for two reasons. First the amount of IHT payable on account of the transaction mistakenly entered into was considerable and that the consequence of the mistake was that the effect of the deed of variation (described as an unexceptional step of tax mitigation) was negated. He concluded that it would be unconscionable to leave the mistake uncorrected and ordered the deed of appointment to be set aside.

Hartogs v Rothschild Trust (Schweiz) AG [2019] EWHC 1915 is a further example of where the court granted rectification in relation to transactions there were entirely tax driven. The court applied the rule set out in *Pitt* that if the mistake is in relation to the tax consequences of a transaction provided it is sufficiently serious, rectification will be granted even though the arrangements entered into were to achieve a beneficial tax outcome. The schemes in relation to which the mistake arose were non-controversial, plain vanilla, tax mitigation arrangements (namely the settling by a non-UK domiciliary of overseas trusts of overseas property to protect it from exposure to IHT). It was decided that it would be unconscionable for the taxpayer's mistake (as to his domicile when he settled the trust, in respect of which he had received incorrect professional advice) to be left uncorrected and for him to be left with a substantial and immediate tax liability.

By contrast in *Estera Trust (Jersey) v J Singh* [2019] EWHC 2039 the court refused to intervene in structuring a transaction in such a way as to enable one party to pay capital gains tax rather than income tax. As the arrangements were tax avoidance schemes it was reluctant to and did not intervene. Distinguishing the House of Lords case of *Sherdley* (see above), the High Court accepted that although there may be exceptional circumstances where the courts may assist in structuring an arrangement so as to produce a favourable tax outcome, thus was only where HMRC already accepted that the transaction/scheme was effective in avoiding tax. The transaction in the case had not such precedence and so the court concluded that there was no public policy argument to support an award of the type the taxpayer had requested.

In *Ware v Ware* [2021] EWHC 694 the High Court granted rectification of two deeds of appointment made by trustees of two will trusts. Each deed had mistakenly and unnecessarily included provisions terminating the claimant's interest in possessions and appointed new ones in their place. The trustees had intended however only to add additional persons as default beneficiaries of the trust. The deed of appointment gave rise to unintended IHT consequences. In granting rectification, the court held that the evidence clearly showed that the trustees' intention was limited to adding additional beneficiaries of the trust and in order to achieve this it was not necessary to end the life interests (which was never the trustees' intention). The deeds therefore had unintended legal effect and it was for that reason that rectification was granted; the mistake was not merely limited to unintended fiscal consequences.

An article by M Ofili entitled 'Make no mistake' which discusses rectification (and recission) of documents in a tax context may be found in *Taxation* dated 13 January 2022.

(6) The property which may be subject to variation or disclaimer under s 142 includes 'excluded property' (as to which see **Example A5**) but not property in which the deceased had retained a benefit (see **Example B1**) or settled property in which the deceased at the time of his death had a qualifying interest in possession (s 142(5), and see **Example C3**). (Someone who *becomes entitled* to an interest in settled property may disclaim, but not vary, his entitlement under s 93.) Where an asset is held jointly as joint tenants, and one of the joint tenants dies, then even though the survivor acquires the deceased's share automatically, he may use a deed of variation to redirect his entitlement to someone else. Section 142 can also be used in cases of intestacy. The provisions do not, however, apply to any disclaimer or variation which is made for consideration in money or money's worth, other than consideration which takes the form of another interest in the same estate which also qualifies for relief under the same provision (s 142(3)) (the same applies to a disclaimer under s 93). Where a variation results in property being held in trust for not more than two years from the date of death, the disposition at the end of the short-term interest in possession (say) is treated as made by the deceased at the date of death (s 142(4)). This provision prevents a variation being used to obtain the benefit of the surviving spouse exemption by redirecting property left as part of the chargeable estate to the spouse for a period of up to two years after the death and claiming potentially exempt transfer treatment when that interest comes to an end and the property passes to others. Section 142(4) only deals with interests which are provided by the variation (read with the will) to come to an end within that period – if they terminate by death or by some act separate from the variation then the usual consequences would follow and s 142(4) would not apply. Similarly, a fixed-term interest ending more than two years after the death will not be caught by s 142(4), though HMRC will take a careful look at the matter (IHTM35095).

(7) The survivorship clause and a deed of variation affect the devolution of the property itself. The treatment for inheritance tax purposes where there are deaths at the same instant does not, however, affect the provisions of the will, commorientes applying where relevant and thus making a survivorship clause valuable from the devolution point of view, quite apart from it being included for tax purposes.

Commorientes in the context of inheritance tax

(8) The deeming provisions of s 4(2) apply when it is not known which of two or more persons have died first (see **part (c)** of the Example). They do not, however, apply where there is evidence that one died before the other(s) when, in the absence of a survivorship clause or a family deed, the best one can hope for in terms of tax relief is quick succession relief (see **Example B3**). The insertion of a survivorship clause in a will is therefore most important since as indicated earlier a deed of variation is not always practicable; in the will of

the older spouse or civil partner it is good practice to dis-apply the survivorship provision in circumstances such that the commorientes rule would apply, so as to capture the additional saving of inheritance tax highlighted in **parts (c)** and **(e)** of the Example. It should however be borne in mind that, if one spouse has insufficient assets to absorb a single nil-rate band and the other has more than is covered by a single nil-rate band, a survivorship clause does risk losing the benefit of the transferable nil-rate band (see **explanatory note 10** and **Example A3**) if the poorer spouse happens to be the second to die, but without having fulfilled the survivorship condition. This situation can only be rectified by means of a variation in relation to the estate of the (wealthier) spouse who died first.

It is important to appreciate that the deeming provision of s 4(2) applies only for the purposes of s 4(1) (which provides for a deemed transfer of value to occur when a person dies). Section 4(2) does not affect the actual devolution of an estate nor, in the case of commorientes in England and Wales (the position is different in Scotland and Northern Ireland – see IHTM12193 and IHTM12194 respectively), the application of the spouse/civil partner exemption (s 18). Section 18 still applies on the transfer of property on death from the elder to the younger spouse or civil partner. Hence in this example on Mrs Slowe's death s 18 applies. On Dr Slowe's death s 4(2) applies to exclude Mrs Slowe's assets in her free estate from Dr Slowe's death estate for the purposes of the charge arising under s 4(1) on his death; because Mrs and Dr Slowe die at the same time Dr Slowe's own estate only is taxed in connection with his death. The result of this is that Mrs Slowe's free estate escapes inheritance tax on both deaths. So the children, the beneficiaries under Dr Slowe's will, acquire their mother's free estate without it having incurred an inheritance tax charge. The position would have been different if Mrs Slowe had died intestate; her estate would have passed directly to her children and no spouse exemption would have been in point. Similarly, the position is different if Mrs Slowe's will had a survivorship clause as discussed in **parts (D)** and **(E)** of the Example.

Deeds of variation — effect on capital gains tax and income tax

(9) It should be noted that a deed of variation is effective both for inheritance tax and for the 'death' rules (TCGA 1992 s 62) of capital gains tax (provided the variation includes a statement to that effect) and does not give rise to a charge to stamp duty or stamp duty land tax. The inheritance tax effect is valid for all purposes of inheritance tax (s 142). In the case of *Marshall v Kerr* (1995) HL, it was confirmed that the capital gains tax effect was restricted to eliminating a capital gains charge by not treating the redirection of the assets as a disposal by the original beneficiaries, and that it did not affect other capital gains tax provisions (so that if, for example (in the context of the law as it applied at that time), the variation consisted of creating a trust in which the original beneficiary had an interest, the beneficiary would be regarded as a settlor for TCGA 1992 s 77 – see **Example D2 part B**).

It is possible to make a deed of variation effective for capital gains tax and not inheritance tax, or vice versa. If the variation was not effective for inheritance tax, the redirected assets would be treated as being transferred under the normal inheritance tax rules, so that the transfers would be potentially exempt unless they were to a relevant property trust (which in these circumstances will be any trust other than a bare trust or where a disabled person's interest takes effect immediately). Where a trust is created through a deed of variation which is effective for inheritance tax, the settlement is regarded as commencing at the date of death, so that the ten-year anniversaries for a relevant property trust date from that time.

The deed of variation does not affect the income tax position. Any income arising before the variation which is paid out to the original beneficiary is charged to tax on the original beneficiary. Furthermore, if a parent varies in favour of his/her infant child, this constitutes a settlement within the terms of ITTOIA 2005 ss 620, 648 (a so-called 'parental settlement') and any subsequent income arising before the child becomes 18 or marries under that age is chargeable as income of the parent under ITTOIA 2005 ss 629, 631, 632.

TCGA 1992 s 68C (and ITA 2007 ss 472, 473) affects variations of wills or intestacies etc occurring on or after 6 April 2006, irrespective of the date of death of the deceased person in question.

Section 68C applies where a transfer of property following a death is varied in circumstances where TCGA 1992 s 62(6) applies. The main conditions for s 62(6) to apply in respect of a variation are that the variation is made within two years after the deceased person's death, and the instrument of variation contains a statement that the provision is to apply.

Section 68C provides that, in any case where property becomes settled property in consequence of the variation but would not otherwise have become settled property, a person listed below will be treated for

TCGA purposes (except where the context otherwise requires) as having made the settlement and as having provided the property for the purposes of the settlement.

Four categories of person (in all cases referring effectively to the original beneficiary) are identified in this context:

- The first category comprises anyone who, immediately before the variation, was entitled to the property (or to property from which it derives) absolutely as legatee.
- The second category relates to a person who would have become entitled to the property (or to property from which it derives) absolutely as legatee but for the variation.
- The other two categories relate to individuals who would have fallen into either of the first two categories had they not been infants or other persons under a disability.

Section 68C provides for a different result where property which is not settled property immediately before the variation (in practice, because it is still vested in the deceased's personal representatives, in that capacity and not as trustees) would have become comprised in a settlement (whether it is a settlement which arose on the deceased person's death or a pre-existing settlement), but the effect of the variation is that the property, or property derived from it, becomes comprised in a different settlement. In such circumstances, the deceased person (not the original beneficiary making the variation) will be treated for TCGA purposes (except where the context otherwise requires) as having made that other settlement.

Similarly, where, immediately before the variation, property is comprised in a settlement and is property of which the deceased person is a settlor, and the effect of the variation is that the property, or property derived from it, becomes comprised in another settlement the deceased person is to be treated for TCGA purposes as having made that other settlement.

Where the deceased person is treated as having made a settlement, he or she is treated for TCGA purposes as having made the settlement in question immediately before their death. This will not apply in any case where the settlement in question arose on the death of the deceased person.

Transfer of the nil-rate band

(10) Sections 8A to 8C, introduced by FA 2008, allow a claim to be made to transfer any unused IHT nil-rate band on a person's death to the estate of their surviving spouse or civil partner who dies on or after 9 October 2007. This applies where the IHT nil-rate band of the first deceased spouse or civil partner was not fully used in calculating the IHT liability of their estate. When the surviving spouse or civil partner dies, the unused amount may be 'added' (in the way explained in the next paragraph) to their own nil-rate band. A full explanation of the transferable nil-rate band provisions can be found in **Example A3**.

Where a valid claim to transfer unused nil-rate band is made, the nil-rate band that is available when the surviving spouse or civil partner dies will be increased by the proportion of the nil-rate band unused on the first death. For example, if on the first death the chargeable estate is £162,500 and the nil-rate band is £325,000, 50% of the nil-rate band would be unused. If the nil-rate band when the survivor dies is £350,000, then that would be increased by 50% to £525,500.

The amount of the nil-rate band that can be transferred does not depend on the value of the first spouse or civil partner's estate. Whatever proportion of the nil-rate band is unused on the first death is available for transfer to the survivor.

It is important to remember that even if all the assets passing under the will are left to the surviving spouse or civil partner, there may be other components of the aggregate 'estate' on death for IHT purposes (such as assets in trust with a qualifying interest in possession, or gifts to other people made within seven years of death) which involve chargeable transfers. If present, these may use up some or all of the nil-rate band in the normal way, and so reduce the amount of unused nil-rate band that may be available for transfer.

In this case in **part** (a) none of his nil-rate band was utilised on the death of Dr Slowe so 100% of the amount in force at the date of Mrs Slowe's death is available for transfer ie £325,000. The amount to be taken off her estate before the application of IHT is therefore £650,000 (£325,000 × 2).

A claim may also be made to transfer an individual's unused RNRB on his death to his surviving spouse or civil partner. This applies where the individual's default allowance or adjusted allowance (as the case may be) was not fully used on his death (as is the case in **part (a)** in respect if Dr Slowe) (s 8G). A claim is also in point where, when an individual dies, he does not own a home or, if he does, his home is not closely inherited (as is the case in **part (c)** in respect of Mrs Slowe (ss 8F(3), 8G). When, in turn, the surviving spouse or civil partner dies, the brought-forward allowance (as it is called) is added to their default allowance at the date of their death (s 8D(5)(f)) from which their RNRB is calculated (in accordance with the rules set out in **Example A2(b)** and includes DA in appropriate cases). The claim must be made within 24 months from the end of the month in which the surviving spouse or civil partner dies (s 8L). For a detailed explanation of the transfer of the RNRB between spouses and civil partners, see **Example A3 part E**.

In **part (c)** Mrs Slowe dies first but she has used all of her nil-rate band against the life interest trust (even before taking account of her lifetime transfers – her estate is £410,000) and therefore none is available on the subsequent death of Dr Slowe. By contrast her unused RNRB may be claimed by the personal representatives of Dr Slowe. However, if most of the value of the life interest trust had not given rise to a chargeable transfer (eg if all but £12,500 of the trust property had been excluded property by reference to foreign situs and a non-UK domiciled settlor) it appears that a transfer of the unused portion of Mrs Slowe's nil-rate band to Dr Slowe's estate would have been possible even though her free estate does not form part of his taxable estate as a result of the commorientes rules. The effect simply exaggerates the benefits of the latter rules in the rare situation where they apply. The revised calculations would be as follows:

Inheritance tax payable on simultaneous deaths

Mrs Slowe (elder)	£	£
Free estate	75,000	
Less: Exempt transfer to Dr Slowe	(75,000)	Nil
Settled property		
Life interest in estate of late father (non-excluded property)		12,500
Amount subject to inheritance tax		12,500

Inheritance tax accumulation

	Gross	Tax
	£	£
Cumulative transfers prior to death	85,000	Nil
Amount liable on death	12,500	Nil
	97,500*	Nil

*utilising only 30% of Mrs Stowe's nil-rate band – no tax

Dr Slowe (younger)	£	£
Family home		600,000
Interest in practice	250,000	
Less: 100% business property relief	(250,000)	Nil
Other assets (excluding Mrs Slowe's assets of £75,000)		50,000
Amount subject to inheritance tax		650,000

Inheritance tax accumulation

	Gross	*Tax*
	£	£
Cumulative transfers prior to death	Nil	Nil
Estate on death	550,000	Nil*

	Gross	*Tax*
	£	£
Less: residence nil-rate band	(350,000)	
Balance of chargeable estate	200,000	
Inheritance tax payable by personal representatives		Nil*

*subject to claim, nil-rate band increased by 70% unused on Mrs Slowe's death:

£325,000 × 170% = £552,500, which exceeds chargeable estate

In **part (d)** again Dr Slowe dies first but as his estate on death amounts to £650,000 the general nil-rate band will have been fully utilised on his death with no surplus available to Mrs Slowe.

Question

A.

To what extent is domicile relevant for inheritance tax purposes?

Explain the extended meaning given to domicile for the purposes of inheritance tax.

B.

Leonardo, who was born in Italy to Italian parents whose home country is Italy, has lived and worked in the UK since July 2011, but plans to return to Italy following his retirement.

On 31 January 2024 he made a chargeable transfer of £333,000 before deducting exemptions, paying the inheritance tax due himself on the due date, having made no earlier transfers.

His remaining assets, at current values, comprise:

(a) 10,000 £1 shares in Exodus plc (registered in Scotland) quoted on the London Stock Exchange at 134p–140p with recorded bargains at 134, 135 and 136.

(b) 10,000 no par value bearer shares in Canadian Timber Limited. The company register is in Ontario, Canada, and the shares are quoted on the Ontario Stock Exchange at the sterling equivalent of 90–92.

(c) A half share in a painting in the UK which Leonardo and his brother, Vincento, had bought in 1990, each providing one half of the purchase money. Its value is £48,000 but a half share is worth £22,000.

(d) A residential investment property in Pisa, Italy, valued at €200,000.

(e) Three insurance policies with a UK insurance company on his life:

  (i) taken out in 2013; the proceeds of £50,000 will be left to his wife, who will receive nothing else,

  (ii) taken out in 2015 on which he had paid the premiums and under which £15,000 will become payable to his executor,

  (iii) taken out in 2017 in trust for his grand-daughter under which £30,000 becomes payable on his death. Leonardo had paid each annual premium of £600 himself.

(f) Debts owing to him of:

  (i) £1,500 by Michael living in the UK, and,

  (ii) €1,000 by Manolo living in Italy.

(g) Cash held in bank accounts:

  (i) in the UK £4,250,

  (ii) in Italy €3,000.

(h) His gold watch valued at £800 and gold ring valued at £1,450, both held in the UK.

(i) His private dwelling-house in London valued at £370,000 plus furniture valued at £20,000.

(j) His UK trading business which he has run as a sole trader since his arrival in the UK, valued at £160,000.

(k) 25,000 £1 ordinary shares in Whiz Investments plc, an English-registered open-ended investment company (OEIC) quoted on the London Stock Exchange at 720p–730p.

Assume the current rate of exchange to be €1.12 = £1.

All share certificates and house deeds are held by Leonardo's solicitor at his office in Italy.

Leonardo is considering making further gifts during his lifetime as follows:

(i) his Canadian Timber Ltd shares to his niece living in Canada,

(ii) his half share in the painting, and his shares in Whiz Investments plc, to his brother, Angelo, living in London,

(iii) his investment property (in which he had never lived) in Pisa, Italy, to his daughter living in London,

(iv) his gold ring to his grandson, living in London, in consideration of his forthcoming marriage,

(v) his business in the UK to his son, living in London.

(1) Compute the inheritance tax payable by Leonardo following the January 2024 transfer, stating the date it falls due, and the inheritance tax which would be payable if Leonardo were to die unexpectedly within the week following the transfer, not having made any further gifts, his estate (after the deducting the 2013 insurance policy proceeds to his wife) being left to his grandchildren. In the case of tax payable on death, identify the amounts which can be paid by instalments, the period over which instalments are payable, and the extent to which relief from interest is given on tax so payable.

(2) State whether any amounts would become chargeable to inheritance tax if Leonardo, not having died in February 2024, had made the further gifts in (i) to (v) above in March 2024 and whether any additional tax would arise if Leonardo were then to die at any time in the eight years following the making of those gifts (assuming the inheritance tax legislation remains unaltered).

Answer

A. Relevance of domicile for inheritance tax

Domicile is relevant for inheritance tax purposes because, whilst the tax is charged on gratuitous transfers of UK assets regardless of the domicile of the transferor, it is also charged on gratuitous transfers of assets by persons of UK domicile regardless of where the property is situated.

Therefore it is necessary to know the domicile of the transferor when the transfer involves assets situated outside the UK, or units in UK authorised unit trusts or shares in open-ended investment companies (OEICs). The same applies in certain cases to the domicile of the beneficiary of a trust – see **Example A5 part (b)**.

It is important to remember that since domicile is primarily a concept of private international law – to determine the legal system with which a person is most closely connected – a 'country' for this purpose is a separate legal jurisdiction, not necessarily a separate political state. The United States comprises fifty different 'countries'. The point is sometimes of vital importance: residence in one state of the United States when intending to settle permanently in a different state will not give rise to the acquisition of a domicile of choice in either.

For this reason it is technically wrong (though convenient shorthand for tax purposes) to speak of someone being domiciled 'in the UK': the United Kingdom comprises three different countries in this sense: England and Wales; Scotland; and Northern Ireland.

Until the Domicile and Matrimonial Proceedings Act 1973 s 1 came into force, a married woman acquired the domicile of her husband. However, that common law rule ceased to apply with respect to marriages after 31 December 1973. Accordingly in the case of transfers between spouses/civil partners it is necessary to know the domicile of both parties because if the transferor is domiciled in the UK but the transferee is domiciled abroad then the spouse/civil partner exemption is, from 6 April 2013, limited to an amount equal to the nil-rate band then in force (£55,000 before 6 April 2013) (s 18(2), (2A) – see **Example A5 part (c)** for more detailed information). Individuals who are domiciled outside but resident in the UK and who have a UK domiciled spouse or civil partner may, from 6 April 2013, elect to be treated as domiciled in the UK for the purposes of IHT (see **Example A5 part (a)** for more detailed information).

A person's country of domicile is usually the country that he regards as his natural home, and a change of domicile requires a high standard of proof. A domicile of origin is acquired at birth. This may be displaced by the acquisition of a domicile of choice. To do so requires both actual residence in the chosen country and an intention to make that country the person's permanent home; all circumstances of the person's life will be taken into account in deciding his intentions in this context (a conscious statement of intent will of itself usually be of little probative value since it may be self-serving). Positive action will generally be advisable if it is intended to establish a new domicile for tax reasons, eg changing residence, making a new will in the country of choice, obtaining citizenship etc and severing ties with the previous country. However, for inheritance tax purposes retaining overseas electoral voting rights will not be taken into account in determining an individual's domicile (FA 1996 s 200). If the domicile of choice is later abandoned without a new domicile of choice being established then the domicile of origin is revived: a person can never be without a domicile in law. (It is considered that Leonardo would have retained his domicile of origin in this Example, as he was born in Italy to Italian parents and intends to return there on retirement. He also retains a house and a bank account in Italy and keeps his documents with his Italian solicitor.)

The domicile of a settlor of settled property, at the time he settled it, is also relevant for inheritance tax since the settled property will then be excluded property to the extent that it comprises assets situated outside the UK, or units in UK authorised unit trusts or shares in open-ended investment companies.

For inheritance tax purposes domicile has an extended meaning. There is a concept of 'deemed domicile' for inheritance tax which applies throughout the United Kingdom. The deemed domicile rules were amended with effect from 6 April 2017 and they provide that the following persons are treated as domiciled in the UK (IHTA 1984 s 267 as amended):

(i) Persons who on or after 10 December 1974 were, under the general law, domiciled somewhere in the UK at any time within the three years immediately before the transfer (or death).

(ii) Persons who were formerly domiciled residents for the tax year in which the time of transfer or death falls.

(iii) Persons who were resident in the UK on or after 10 December 1974 and for least 15 of the 20 *tax years* preceding the tax year in which they make the transfer (or die) and for at least one of the four tax years ending with the tax year in which they make the transfer (or die). For this purpose residence for any part of a tax year will count.

Under the rules as they applied until 5 April 2017 the following persons were treated as domiciled in the UK (s 267 as it then applied):

(i) Persons who on or after 10 December 1974 were, under the general law, domiciled somewhere in the UK and were so domiciled within the three years preceding the transfer.

(ii) Persons who were resident in the UK on or after 10 December 1974 and in not less than 17 out of the 20 income tax years ending with the tax year of transfer. For this purpose residence for any part of a tax year will count, so a deemed UK domicile under this rule can arise after not much more than 15 years' continuous residence.

In the context of the current second test, an individual is a 'formerly domiciled resident' in relation to a tax year if he was born in the UK, his domicile of origin was in the UK, he was resident in the UK in that tax year and he was resident in the UK for at least one of the two tax years immediately preceding that tax year (s 272). This rule will not apply to an individual who has a UK domicile of origin but who was born abroad.

For more detailed information on the deemed domicile rules see **Example A5 part (a)**.

B. Leonardo — inheritance tax payable

1. *Inheritance tax payable re January 2024 transfer*

Leonardo is domiciled in Italy, therefore property located outside the UK is excluded property. (He was born in Italy and is only in his thirteenth successive (whole or part) tax year of UK residence so is not affected by the deemed domicile rules at this point.) The inheritance tax position on the transfer on 31 January 2024 is as follows:

				Gross £	*Tax (2023/24 scale)* £	*Net* £
31 January 2024						
Gifts within previous seven years				Nil	Nil	Nil
Chargeable lifetime transfer			333,000			
Less: Annual exemptions	2023/24	3,000				
	2022/23	3,000	(6,000)			
Net transfer grossed up*				327,500	500	327,000
				327,500	500	327,000

**Net*		*Gross*
325,000		325,000
2,000	$(\times \frac{100}{80})$	2,500
327,000		327,500

Inheritance tax payable by Leonardo on 31 July 2024 = £500 (being (327,500 – 325,000) @ 20%).

If Leonardo died in February 2024

	Gross	Tax (2023/24 scale)
	£	£
Gifts within seven years before death:		
31 January 2024		
Chargeable transfer	327,500	1,000*
Cumulative transfers in seven years prior to death	327,500	1,000
(* 327,500 – 325,000 = 2,500 @ 40%)		

Inheritance tax payable by donee on 31 January 2024 transfer:

On death	1,000
Less: due from Leonardo (and so his estate) on lifetime transfer	(500)
Due from donee 31 August 2023	£500

Estate for inheritance tax purposes on death would be:

			£
Shares in Exodus plc (UK company, share register in UK)			
10,000 £1 shares @ 135 (midpoint between 134 and 136, being less than 134 + (¼ × (140 – 134) = 135½))			13,500
Canadian Timber Limited shares — excluded property			Nil
Painting held in UK — one half share			22,000
Investment property in Italy — excluded property			Nil
Insurance policies	— 2013		50,000
	— 2015		15,000
Loans	— Michael		1,500
	— Manolo — excluded property		Nil
Cash at bank	— UK		4,250
	— Italy — excluded property		Nil
Possessions	— gold watch		800
	— gold ring		1,450
UK house			370,000
Furniture			20,000
Business		160,000	
Less: 100% business property relief		(160,000)	Nil
Shares in Whiz Investments plc (UK OEIC) – excluded property			Nil
			498,500
Less: Debts — inheritance tax due on chargeable gift made 31 January 2024			(500)
			498,000
Less: Exempt legacy — widow (2013 insurance policy)			(50,000)
Chargeable estate			448,000

Note

The 2017 life policy that was effected in trust for the benefit of Leonardo's grand-daughter does not form part of the estate. The annual premiums do not cumulate, having been exempt as gifts out of income.

As business property is left as part of residue to non-exempt beneficiaries and there is a specific gift to an exempt beneficiary (widow), business property relief will be reduced rateably (s 39A):

			£
Estate before reliefs and exemptions (448,000 + 160,000 + 50,000)			658,000
Less:	Business property relief		(160,000)
			498,000
Less:	Exempt legacy to widow	50,000	
	Restricted by reference to business property relief		
	$160{,}000 \times \dfrac{\text{Exempt estate}(50{,}000)}{\text{Total estate}(658{,}000)}$	(12,158)	(37,842)
Estate chargeable to inheritance tax			460,158
Tax thereon @ 40% (lifetime transfers being above nil threshold)			£184,063
Amount payable by instalments			

$$\text{UK house}\frac{370{,}000}{498{,}000} \times 184{,}063 = £136{,}754$$

Payable by ten equal yearly instalments of £13,675 from 31 August 2024 plus interest on the full outstanding balance.

2. *Inheritance tax position if gifts in (i) to (v) were made in March 2024 and Leonardo died within following eight years*

(i) As the Canadian Timber Ltd shares are situated outside the UK, they are excluded property and not chargeable to UK inheritance tax on transfer.

(ii) The transfer of the half share of the painting to Angelo would be a potentially exempt transfer of £22,000 (no annual exemptions being available since they are already fully used). No inheritance tax would be due provided Leonardo lived for seven years, otherwise the gift would be added to the transfers of £327,500 made within seven years before the date of the gift and inheritance tax would be due based upon the scale and rate of tax applicable at the date of death. The shares in Whiz Investments plc, a UK OEIC, are excluded property and the gift of them would not constitute a transfer of value.

(iii) The transfer of the investment property in Pisa to Leonardo's daughter would be excluded as Leonardo is not domiciled in the UK.

(iv) The gift of the ring valued at £1,450 to Leonardo's grandson, whilst not excluded property (unless situated outside the UK at the time the gift was made, for example handed over when both parties were on holiday in Italy), would be exempt as a gift of not more than £2,500 made by a grandparent in consideration of the grandson's marriage.

(v) The transfer of the business to Leonardo's son would attract 100% business property relief, so that the potentially exempt transfer would be nil (see **explanatory note** 7). The transfer would not be liable to inheritance tax unless Leonardo died within seven years after making the transfer. If death occurred within the seven year period, the entitlement to business property relief would have to be reconsidered at that time. The relief would only continue to be available provided the son continued to satisfy the qualifying conditions up to the date of Leonardo's death (see **Example A21**).

If Leonardo died more than three but less than seven years after giving away the painting or business, any tax payable upon the potentially exempt transfers becoming chargeable would be reduced as follows:

Death more than	3 years but less than	4 years after gift	— 20%
Death more than	4 years but less than	5 years after gift	— 40%
Death more than	5 years but less than	6 years after gift	— 60%
Death more than	6 years but less than	7 years after gift	— 80%

After seven years no liability would arise on death in respect of these gifts.

Explanatory Notes

Situation of property for inheritance tax

(1) The normal common law rules of English law apply to determine where property is situated.

(a) Land is in the country where it is physically situated (but mortgages of land are treated as debts).

(b) Debts are in the country where the debtor resides (including from January 2016 according to HMRC practice as stated in IHTM27279) specialty debts – ie those debts created under a deed; before that date HMRC treated specialty debts as being situated where the deed was physically located (as appears to be correct according to the case law – see *Gurney v Rawlins* (1863); *Commissioner of Stamps v Hope* (1891)).

(c) Shares are located where the share register is kept. (The place where the shares are quoted, if they are, is not relevant.)

(d) Life insurance policies are situated where the proceeds are payable (unless under seal, in which case they are situated where the policy is).

(e) Business property is situated where the business is carried on.

(f) Tangible property (including currency) is wherever it is physically situated.

(g) Bank accounts are situated at the branch at which the deposits are payable (subject to what is said in **explanatory note 5** regarding foreign currency accounts).

(h) HMRC's view is that exchange tokens (cryptoassets) are located where the individual who beneficially owns them is resident. Therefore, even if the exchange tokens of a UK resident are held in a digital wallet outside the UK, they will be subject to IHT on the beneficial owner's death.

Excluded property for inheritance tax

(2) Foreign property in foreign ownership is excluded property for inheritance tax purposes. The property must be situated outside the UK and the person beneficially entitled to it must be non-UK domiciled (s 6(1)). However, with effect from 6 April 2017, this rule does not apply in relation to overseas property comprising certain shares in a close company, certain interests in partnerships and certain loans where the value of the property is attributable to UK residential property. Consequently, the charge to inheritance tax is extended to UK residential property that is held or financially supported by or through overseas structures by trustees or individuals who are domiciled outside the UK. Shares in a close company and an interest in a partnership (provided it is, counted together with the holdings or interests of connected persons, at least a 5% holding or interest) will not be excluded property where the value of the shares or partnership interest is directly or indirectly attributable to UK residential property. In determining the value of the shares or interest that is attributable to a UK residential property, the liabilities of the company or partnership are to be attributed to all the property it holds on a rateable basis. This means that where a company or partnership holds a UK residential property as well as other property, any liabilities of that company or partnership will be attributed

to each property in proportion to its value. The rights of a creditor under a loan are not excluded property where the loan has been used by an individual, partnership or trustees to finance the acquisition (maintenance or enhancement) of UK residential property or the acquisition of shares in or an interest in a close company or partnership and the acquisition (maintenance or enhancement) by that company or partnership of a UK residential property. A loan ceases to be within these exclusionary rules where the UK property interest which the loan financed is disposed of. Where the shares in a company, the interest in a partnership or the creditor rights of a loan (which have been described above) are sold, the proceeds are also not treated as excluded property for a two-year period starting with the date of disposal of the property concerned. Where the proceeds are held in a qualifying foreign currency bank account (see below), likewise the bank account is also not left out of account for IHT purposes for the same two-year period. The proceeds will become excluded property again at the end of this two-year period.

(3) Similarly holdings in authorised unit trusts and OEICs are excluded property where the person beneficially entitled to it is non-UK domiciled (s 6(1A)). 'Authorised unit trust' and 'open-ended investment company' are defined in s 272 by reference to Financial Services and Markets Act 2000 s 243 and s 236 respectively.

(4) The following is also excluded property:

(a) National Savings etc owned by persons domiciled in the Channel Islands or Isle of Man (s 6(3)).

(b) Certain government securities issued as being exempt from tax where they are owned by persons of a description specified in the conditions of issue of the security concerned (s 6(2)) (see **Example A5 part (b)**). The specified conditions prior to FA 1996 required the holder to be neither domiciled nor ordinarily resident in the UK, but the reference to domicile is excluded in current issues. From 17 July 2013 the condition for exemption is no longer based on being not ordinarily resident in the UK but is based on being regarded as not resident in the UK (FA 2013 Sch 46 para 114). Where securities issued before that date are acquired after 5 April 2013, the holder of the securities will benefit from the exemption if he is not resident in the UK (despite the terms of issue of the securities referring to his being not ordinary resident in the UK).

In these two cases domicile has its ordinary meaning and not the extended inheritance tax meaning (s 267(2)).

For further notes on the meaning and treatment of excluded property see **Example A5 part (b)**.

Foreign currency bank accounts for inheritance tax

(5) Where a person who is *neither resident nor domiciled/deemed domiciled* (and before 2013/14 also not ordinarily resident) in the UK dies, any UK sited foreign currency accounts with a bank (as that term is defined in ITA 2007 s 991 (s 157(6)) are left out of account in valuing the estate immediately prior to death. This also applies to such accounts held by trustees of settled property in which the deceased held a beneficial interest in possession unless the settlor was domiciled in the UK at the date of the settlement or the trustees are UK domiciled and resident (and before 2013/14 ordinarily resident) at the time of the beneficiary's death (s 157 (3)). The residence (and before 2013/14 ordinary residence) status of an individual (but not trustees) is determined using the normal income tax rules (s 157(4)(a)). The IHTA 1984 contains its own definition of the residence status of trustees in this context, namely that trustees of a trust are deemed to be not resident and (before 2013/14) not ordinarily resident in the UK unless both the general administration of the trust is ordinarily carried on in the UK and the trustees (or a majority of them) are resident and (before 2013/14) ordinarily resident in the UK (s 157(4)(b)). It should be remembered that s 157 applies only to a death so that lifetime gifts made out of foreign currency bank accounts may give rise to a charge.

Works of art for inheritance tax

(6) Works of art which are physically present in the UK on the death of a foreign owner because they have been brought to the UK solely for public exhibition, cleaning or restoration are not counted as part of his UK estate if normally kept overseas (s 5(1)(b)).

Inheritance tax business property relief

(7) The comment that the potentially exempt transfer (resulting from Leonardo's gift of his UK trading business) would be nil is convenient, if technically inaccurate, shorthand for the purpose of highlighting the need to

reassess the position in the event of Leonardo's death within seven years after the gift of the UK trading business. The true analysis in detail is as follows:

(a) Leonardo's estate after the gift is worth less than it was before the gift (business property relief is not taken into account in determining the value of a person's estate). Therefore he has made a transfer of value – s 3(1). At this stage of the analysis, the value transferred by this transfer of value is the difference between the value of his estate before the gift and its value after the gift; presumptively this will be equal to the value of the business itself (but if the removal of the assets of the business from his estate had an adverse effect on the value of other assets he retained, the reduction might be more.)

(b) By virtue of s 104 the value transferred by that transfer of value is reduced by BPR of, in this Example, 100%, so to nil assuming there are no excepted assets involved (but see **(d) below**).

(c) Any available annual exemption is taken into account before any balance of a transfer of value remains to be categorised as either immediately chargeable or potentially exempt. However, with a value transferred of nil, after business property relief, the annual exemption is untouched by this gift at the date it takes place, and, at this stage of the analysis, the transfer of value has in effect been fully eliminated by the relief.

(d) If Leonardo's death were to occur within the ensuing seven years, account must be taken of s 113A(7A) which provides that business property relief is to be disregarded in determining, for the purpose of s 113A, whether there is a potentially exempt transfer or a chargeable transfer. (See s 124A(7A) which makes similar provision in relation to agricultural property relief.) Thus, the pre-relief diminution in value in Leonardo's estate at **(a) above** is used for this purpose, and since the gift was to an individual it is the potentially exempt transfer aspects of s 113A that fall to be applied (see **Example A21 part A(c)**) – hence the shorthand expression referred to above. If his son does not still own the business at Leonardo's death (or did not own it at his own death, if the son had predeceased Leonardo), inheritance tax on the gift will be charged in the light of Leonardo's death without allowing business property relief; and (the original gift being a potentially exempt transfer for the purpose of s 113A) Leonardo's inheritance tax accumulation for the purpose of the charge on his death (and any intervening transfers of value, had there been any) will also be computed without allowing business property relief on the gift of the business.

In the Example, Leonardo had exhausted his available annual exemptions earlier in the same tax year, against the January 2024 transfer. If the gift of the business had been the *first* of several transfers of value that Leonardo made in the particular tax year, and business property relief had been withdrawn under s 113A on his death within seven years, the available annual exemptions would have had to be re-allocated against this gift – see the final paragraph of **Example B5 explanatory note 2.**

In the perhaps unusual case where the pre-relief diminution in the transferor's estate falls entirely within any available annual exemption, s 113A(7A) will not result in any actual loss of relief even where relief would otherwise be withdrawn apart from this point on the annual exemption.

Example

On 6 April 2023 Stephen gave to Thomas his entire holding of shares in Unquoted Ltd, a trading company. The holding was a small minority holding worth £2,750 and the shares are unquoted. No other shares in the company are comprised in Stephen's estate. Stephen had made a chargeable transfer of £400,000 in 2022/23; on 1 July 2023 he made a cash gift to Vanessa of £3,000. Following an unexpected takeover bid for Unquoted Ltd Thomas sold the shares for £30,000 in June 2024, and Stephen died in December 2024.

Stephen's gift to Thomas, at the time it is made, attracts 100% business property relief so that the value transferred is nil, and therefore makes no impact on Stephen's annual exemption (see **(c)** above) – so that the cash gift to Vanessa uses Stephen's 2023/24 annual exemption. (The 2022/23 exemption is not available for carry-forward, having been used in the process of quantifying the chargeable transfer made that year.)

On Stephen's death, applying s 113A(7A), business property relief is to be disregarded in determining whether there is a potentially exempt transfer or a chargeable transfer; but if the relief is disregarded then the gift of shares would be fully exempt by virtue of Stephen's 2023/24 annual exemption, and so the transfer of value involved is, for s 113A purposes, neither potentially exempt nor chargeable. As a result, neither s 113A(1) nor s 113A(2) falls to be applied, and there is no loss of relief in relation to Stephen's gift to Thomas.

Further, because there is in fact no loss of relief, the value transferred by that gift remains at nil as a result of the relief originally computed, so Stephen's 2023/24 annual exemption remains fully available against the subsequent cash gift to Vanessa. Its impact in precluding a potentially exempt or chargeable transfer for the purpose of s 113A, as in the preceding paragraph, is solely for the purpose of testing whether s 113A as a whole should be applied, and it can only have any wider consequences if s 113A as a whole applies to create a loss of relief and therefore to absorb some or all of the annual exemption in fact.

If by contrast the shares had been worth £3,250 at the date of the gift to Thomas, then on Stephen's death the test under s 113A(7A) would have shown a potentially exempt transfer of £250, thus triggering a loss of relief under s 113A(1). Of the £3,250 reappraised value transferred, £3,000 would be exempt under the annual exemption and £250 would be chargeable, triggering a 40% inheritance tax liability on Thomas in respect of the gift of shares in the sum of £100. In turn, the cash gift to Vanessa made later in the same tax year would no longer benefit from the annual exemption, and Vanessa would have a 40% inheritance tax liability in respect of that gift in the sum of £1,200.

(8) For further examples and notes on the interaction of exempt legacies and business property relief see **Examples A16** and **A18**. For details of business property relief generally, see **Example A21**.

Types of domicile

(9) For detailed notes on the possible types of domicile an individual might have see **Example A5 part (a)**.

Question

David, a bachelor domiciled in England, who had worked a small agricultural holding for many years, died on 1 May 2023 leaving to his nieces and nephews, the following estate in England:

'Freehold agricultural land extending to 30 acres and buildings together valued at £123,500 of which the agricultural value was £92,000.

Farming machinery and stores valued at £24,884.

Timber (growing on separate freehold land) valued at £123,000, being operated on a commercial basis. The land itself was valued at £150,000 but was subject to a mortgage of the same amount, for which the lender held no security other than the land.

Leasehold house (his main residence) valued at £157,500.

Household chattels and car valued at £22,850.

A quoted shareholding valued at £80,822 (being a 20% holding that David had owned for many years).

Bank balance £2,303.'

English debts and funeral expenses (all allowable) totalled £7,233.

In addition David owned the following property in Afaria:

'Freehold house valued at 74,500 fars.

Furniture valued at 28,750 fars.

Bank balance 9,580 fars.'

His gardener was owed wages of 830 fars and these were paid to him after David's death.

He also owned the following property in Nyria:

'Leasehold house valued at 22,450 nyrs.

Furniture valued at 12,250 nyrs.

Bank balance of 3,750 nyrs.'

There were no outstanding liabilities in Nyria.

Death duties abroad, with no interest if paid within six months of death, are calculated on total assets less liabilities at the following flat rates:

Afaria 10%; Nyria 8%.

The UK and Afaria (but not Nyria) have a double taxation agreement.

On 1 May 2023 exchange rates were:

Afaria 1 far = 100/120p; Nyria £1 = 0.48/0.50 nyrs.

On 1 July 2023 the executor obtained probate by presenting a provisional account in which, after appropriate reliefs, realty was included at £75,000, instalment option personalty at £200,000 and non-instalment option personalty at £171,000.

Inheritance tax was not paid on realty or the instalment option personalty.

The timber was sold standing for £127,500, which was received on 1 August 2023, no election having been made for the value at death to be left out of account under IHTA 1984 ss 125 to 130.

On 20 June 2021 David had made a potentially exempt transfer (after exemptions) of £132,000 to his sister, which was his only lifetime transfer.

By his will he left £30,000 to his brother, with the residue to his sister.

On 30 November 2023 the executor presented a corrective account.

Prepare statements showing:

(a) Death duty payable in Afaria and Nyria (assuming the rates of exchange when the duty was paid were unchanged from 1 May 2023).

(b) Any balance of inheritance tax and interest payable in England on 30 November 2023 on the assumption that the minimum amount of inheritance tax was paid at that time, the balance being deferred.

(c) The amount of tax that can be deferred.

Answer

(a) Death duty payable overseas

		Fars		£
Afaria	— House	74,500		74,500
	Furniture	28,750		28,750
	Bank balance	9,580		9,580
		112,830		112,830
	Less: Debts	(830)		(830)
		112,000	@ 1 far = 100p	112,000
	Death duty in Afaria @ 10%	11,200	@ 1 far = 120p	£13,440
		Nyrs		£
Nyria	— Leasehold house	22,450		44,900
	Furniture	12,250		24,500
	Bank balance	3,750		7,500
		38,450	@ £1 = 0.5 nyrs	76,900
	Death duty in Nyria @ 8%	3,076	@ £1 = 0.48 nyrs	£6,408

(b) Computation of inheritance tax due on 30 November 2023 (Death 1 May 2023)

Inheritance tax paid on account 1 July 2023 on non-instalment option personalty of £171,000:

		Gross	Tax
		£	£
Potentially exempt transfers within seven years before death, now chargeable:			
20 June 2021		132,000	Nil
Estate on death per provisional account:			
Realty after reliefs	75,000		
Instalment option personalty after reliefs	200,000		
Non-instalment option personalty after reliefs	171,000	446,000	101,200*
		578,000	101,200*

(* 578,000 – 325,000 = 253,000 @ 40%)

Tax paid 1 July 2023 on £171,000 non-instalment option personalty:

$$\frac{171{,}000}{446{,}000} \times £101{,}200 = £38{,}801$$

Inheritance tax due on 30 November 2023 in respect of corrective account

				Date of death 1 May 2023	
			£	£	£
Freehold agricultural land and buildings				123,500	
Less:	Agricultural property relief	100% × £92,000	92,000		
	Business property relief	100% × £31,500	31,500	(123,500)	
				Nil	
Freehold land less mortgage thereon (£150,000 – £150,000)				Nil	
Freehold house in Afaria				74,500	74,500
Personalty — with instalment option					
Farm machinery and stores			24,884		
Less:	Business property relief — 100%		(24,884)	Nil	
Leasehold house in England				157,500	
Leasehold house in Nyria				44,900	202,400
Personalty — without instalment option					
Timber (sold)			123,000		
Less:	Business property relief — 100%		(123,000)	Nil	
Quoted shares (20% holding)				80,822	
Chattels				22,850	
Bank balance				2,303	
In Afaria	— chattels		28,750		
	bank balance		9,580	38,330	
In Nyria	— chattels		24,500		
	bank balance		7,500	32,000	
				176,305	
Less:	Debts and funeral expenses — UK		7,233		
	Debts in Afaria		830	(8,063)	168,242
Chargeable estate					445,142

	Gross	Tax
	£	£
Inheritance tax accumulation in seven years before death	132,000	Nil
Estate chargeable on death and tax thereon	445,142	100,857*
	577,142	100,857*

(* 577,142 – 325,000 = 252,142 @ 40%)

Estate rate is $\frac{100,857}{445,142} \times 100 = 22.657\%$

Since this average rate clearly exceeds the rates paid overseas, the double taxation relief will be the duty paid overseas.

		£	£	£
Liability on estate			100,857	
Less:	Double tax relief —			
	Afaria	13,440		
	Nyria	6,408	(19,848)	
			81,009	
Less:	Paid on account on 1 July 2023 (see above)		(38,801)	42,208
Less:	Tax deferred (at estate rate of 22.657%)			
	Realty			
	House in Afaria £74,500	16,880		
	Less: Double tax relief:			
	$\frac{74,500}{112,000} \times £13,440$	(8,940)	7,940	
	Instalment option personalty £202,400	45,858		
	Less: Double tax relief on house in Nyria:			
	$\frac{44,900}{76,900} \times £6,408$	(3,741)	42,117	50,057
	Tax repayable to personal representative on non-instalment property			(7,849)
Being:	Tax on non-deferred personalty of £168,242 at estate rate of 22.657%		38,119	
	Less: Double tax relief:			
	Afaria $\frac{37,500}{112,000} \times £13,440$	4,500		
	Nyria $\frac{32,000}{76,900} \times £6,408$	2,667		
			(7,167)	
			30,952	
	Less: Paid on account		(38,801)	
			£(7,849)	
Tax payable by personal representative on deferred property				
	$\frac{1}{10} \times 50,057$			5,006
Total amount repayable 30 November 2023 (no interest due)				(2,843)

(c)

		£
Tax deferred		50,057
Less:	First instalment	(5,006)
Amount deferred as at 30 November 2023		£45,051

Explanatory Notes

Converting values of foreign assets and foreign tax for the purposes of inheritance tax

(1) Foreign assets are valued by using the lower value of the exchange rate quoted, ie the more advantageous to the taxpayer. Where foreign tax is paid it is converted to sterling by using the higher value of the exchange rate on the date of payment (restricted to the amount paid if in sterling).

Agricultural and business property relief

(2)

(a) Agricultural property relief at 100% is available under IHTA 1984 s 116 on the agricultural value of the farm land and buildings. Business property relief at 100% is available under s 104 on the excess over the agricultural value and on the farming machinery and stores.

(b) Business property relief is also available at 100% on the growing timber. An election could have been made under s 125 for the timber (but not the land on which it stands) to be left out of account on David's death, but with business property relief at 100% there is no point in doing so. Had it been left out it would have had to be brought in later at its sale value, and only 50% business property relief would have been available on the subsequent sale (s 127(2)) (see **Example B11 explanatory note 10**).

Business property relief is also available on the land on which the timber stands but it is only given on the value of business assets less liabilities so that the land does not attract the relief in this case because its value is wholly eliminated by the mortgage.

Where the only security for the mortgage is the business land, it is not possible to reduce the business property by business property relief and then deduct the mortgage from other assets.

(c) For detailed notes on agricultural and business property relief and growing timber see **Examples A21** and **B11 part (A)**.

Instalment option for inheritance tax

(3) The option for tax to be paid by ten yearly instalments is available on the following assets in this Example:

Land in the UK and abroad (including leaseholds)

Business and agricultural property

The first instalment is due six months after the end of the month in which the death occurred, ie on 30 November 2023 (s 227(3)).

Inheritance tax: payment of tax and interest on underpaid/overpaid tax

(4) Inheritance tax on death is payable on presentation of the HMRC Account (s 226(2)), ie on 1 July 2023 in this Example, the tax then accounted for being on the provisional amount of £171,000 non-instalment option personalty. The inheritance tax, however, is not due until six months after the end of the month in which the death occurred, ie by 30 November 2023, so the corrective account showing the revised amount payable was submitted in time to stop any interest arising on unpaid tax. In fact the provisional amount paid exceeded the actual liability, so that a refund of £2,843 is due and the question of interest on unpaid tax does not arise.

The amount overpaid on the earlier presentation of the account on 1 July 2023 does not attract an interest supplement. This is not overpaid tax but tax paid in advance of the due date. The amount of £2,843 found to be overpaid at 30 November 2023, on the other hand, will attract interest from that date until it is repaid (the current rate of interest is 4.25% subject to any changes after 22 August 2023).

Interest on unpaid tax on instalment assets is charged only from the date the instalment is payable, except for land which, unless the land is agricultural property or part of an interest in a business, attracts interest on the whole of the tax unpaid.

The first instalment due on 30 November 2023 was paid on time and accordingly no interest was payable thereon.

Interest will therefore arise from 1 December 2023 to the date of payment on the remainder of the tax on the freehold house in Afaria, the English leasehold and the leasehold house in Nyria, whether or not the instalments are paid on time; the present interest rate is 7.75% subject to any changes after 22 August 2023.

In this Example the inheritance tax payable on the estate is less than the amount payable on the provisional account that the personal representatives had submitted. Personal representatives need to be aware that HMRC are taking a harsher attitude to penalties where a provisional account understates the values of the assets – see **Example A23 explanatory note 9.**

Overseas liabilities in the context of inheritance tax

(5) Overseas liabilities are allowable as a deduction from the deceased's estate providing such debts would be allowable if UK debts. Normally the liabilities are deducted primarily from the value of overseas assets with any surplus deductible from UK assets (s 162(5)). If the liability is secured on UK property or is payable in the UK then the debt is deductible from UK property. See **Example A12(c)** for a detailed explanation of the rules on how liabilities are taken into account for the purposes of inheritance tax.

Double tax relief for the purposes of inheritance tax

(6)

(a) Double tax relief is available where the same property is charged to tax both in the UK and overseas. Relief is given under s 158 where the UK has a double tax agreement with the country concerned and otherwise unilaterally under s 159. Where there is a double tax agreement it will usually give greater relief than that available under s 159, but if it does not, the taxpayer is given the benefit of the unilateral relief of s 159.

(b) Section 159 enables the overseas duty paid to be deducted provided that this does not exceed the UK tax on the same property. In determining whether the UK tax is greater than the overseas tax, the average rate of UK tax is taken. This differs from double taxation relief for income tax where the UK tax applicable to overseas income can be taken as the highest rate of UK tax which applies to that taxpayer in that year of assessment.

The UK tax on the overseas property in this Example is clearly greater than the overseas tax on the same property, the UK average rate being 22.657% compared with 10% in Afaria and 8% in Nyria.

(c) Section 159 also gives relief where both the UK and another country impose tax on property situated in a third country, or where property is situated in the UK under UK law and in another country under that country's law. Relief is calculated by the formula:

$$\frac{A}{A+B} \times C$$

where A is the inheritance tax, B is the overseas tax and C is whichever of A and B is smaller.

(d) For a further account of the interaction between Double Taxation and IHT see **Example A5 part (d).**

Double tax relief for the purposes of inheritance tax

(7) David's estate is not entitled to a residence nil-rate band as his home is inherited by his nieces and nephews and so is not directly inherited (see **Example A2 part (b) explanatory note 3**).

Question

A has made cumulative chargeable transfers amounting to £239,000, all in the year ending 5 April 2016 (having utilised his annual exemption in each year before then).

In May 2016 he gave a fine painting that he had owned for the last ten years to his son S. The picture was worth £95,000 in the open market at the time of the gift.

In November 2016 he gave a similar picture, then worth £100,000 in the open market, to his daughter D.

In both cases any liability for capital gains tax did not arise as the requisite undertakings were given by S and D.

On 20 March 2018 S gave his picture, then valued at £117,500, to his wife W, who is an American citizen but who has a domicile of choice in the UK and is resident here. She immediately took it to New York to hang in the family gallery.

A died in December 2020 leaving an estate valued at £400,000 equally to his son S and daughter D. He had lived in rented accommodation all his life and so did not own a home at the time of his death.

An undertaking was given by the daughter that she would keep the picture in the UK; that she would take reasonable steps for its preservation; and that she would allow reasonable access to the public to view it.

On 3 August 2023 D sold her painting at an international auction room for £150,000, out of which the auctioneers took £15,000 in fees, and capital gains tax on the sale amounted to £8,800.

Both pictures were designated by the Treasury as being of national, scientific, historic or artistic interest. Appropriate claims for relief are made in connection with all transfers.

Calculate the inheritance tax payable as a result of these events.

Answer

Inheritance tax

May 2016	Picture to S	95,000
	Less: Annual exemption 2016/17	(3,000)
	Potentially exempt transfer	92,000
November 2016	Picture to D — potentially exempt transfer	100,000

On death of A – December 2020

		Gross £	Tax on 2020/21 scale £
Gifts in lifetime:			
Cumulative transfers (year ended 5 April 2016)		239,000	Nil
May 2016			
Gift of picture to S (potentially exempt transfer now chargeable)		92,000	2,400*
		331,000	2,400*
(* 331,000 – 325,000 = 6,000 @ 40%)			
November 2016			
Potentially exempt transfer of picture to D, now a chargeable transfer	100,000		
Less: Conditional exemption	(100,000)	Nil	
Inheritance tax accumulation at death		331,000	2,400
Estate on death		400,000	160,000
		731,000	162,400**
(** 731,000 – 325,000 = 406,000 @ 40%)			
Tax payable by S (with interest on unpaid tax from 1 July 2021) after taper relief			
60% × £2,400	£1,440		
Tax payable by A's personal representatives (with interest on unpaid tax from 1 July 2021)	£160,000		

Chargeable event — sale of picture by D on 3 August 2023

				Gross	*Tax at half rate 2023/24 scale*
				£	£
A's inheritance tax accumulation as above				731,000	81,200*
(* 731,000 – 325,000 = 406,000 @ 20%)					
Value of picture (sale proceeds)			150,000		
Less:	Fees	15,000			
	Capital gains tax	8,800	(23,800)	126,200	25,240
				857,200	106,440
Tax payable by D (with interest on unpaid tax from 1 March 2023)					£25,240

Explanatory Notes

Inheritance tax: conditional exemption for works of art and other heritage property

(1) Conditional exemption from inheritance tax for works of art and other heritage property is provided in IHTA 1984 ss 30 to 35A. Eligible assets are:

Works of art and other objects or collections or groups of objects that are pre-eminent for their national, scientific, historic or artistic interest

Land of outstanding scenic, historic or scientific interest

Buildings of outstanding historic or architectural interest together with their amenity land and objects historically associated with them.

(2) Transfers are conditionally exempt if designated by the Treasury *following a claim* made within two years of the event (for example following death), provided an appropriate undertaking is given by such person as the Treasury consider appropriate (usually the transferee).

(3) The undertaking depends upon the category of property, but applies until death or disposal and generally requires reasonable public access, preservation and in the case of objects, retention in the UK, until death or further disposition (s 31). Public access cannot be by prior appointment only, and the owner may be required to publicise information about the conditionally exempt asset. In their Trusts and Estates Newsletter dated August 2014, HMRC comments that they have found that the way the access requirements are shown in the undertaking can cause problems in relation to objects. Access requirements may need to be frequently updated unless the objects are on long term loan to a museum or are in a property that is regularly open to the public. The terms of the undertaking usually need to be updated to reflect changes every time they are made. In order to avoid these problems, HMRC comment that they will be using a more generic form of access provision in all current and future cases. Sample clauses are provided in the Newsletter and may be accessed at: www.gov.uk/government/uploads/system/uploads/attachment_data/file/382104/newsletter-0814.pdf

(4) The conditional exemption is not available if the transfer would be exempt anyway by reason of transfers to charities or one's spouse/civil partner (s 30). But on a transfer to a spouse/civil partner of property that is the subject of an earlier conditional exemption, the spouse/civil partner would have to renew the undertaking to retain the conditional exemption (s 32).

Availability of conditional exemption from inheritance tax

(5) Conditional exemption is available upon:

(i) Death.

(ii) Lifetime transfers where transferor and spouse/civil partner have between them been beneficially entitled to the subject matter throughout the preceding six years.

(iii) Lifetime gifts not qualifying under (ii) where the transferor acquired the subject matter on an inheritance tax/capital transfer tax conditionally exempt death transfer (s 30(3)).

Inheritance tax: potentially exempt transfers and conditional exemption

(6) When a potentially exempt transfer of heritage property is made, no claim for conditional exemption may be made until the transferor dies, and a claim will not then be relevant if the transferor has survived the gift by seven years. If he dies within seven years, s 26A provides that the potentially exempt transfer will nonetheless be exempt if the property has in the meantime been sold by private treaty to an approved body (Sch 3) or surrendered to HMRC in satisfaction of tax (s 230). If the property has been sold other than to an approved body, no claim for conditional exemption may be made. The circumstances at the transferor's death will determine whether conditional exemption is available, and if an undertaking is already in force for capital gains tax or for maintenance fund purposes it will be treated as an undertaking under s 30 (s 31(4G)).

In this Example both gifts in 2016 are potentially exempt (after deducting the annual exemption from the earlier gift), so claims for conditional exemption for inheritance tax would not be made at the time of the gifts. In order to avoid capital gains tax arising on the gifts, however, it would have been necessary for A to procure the appropriate undertakings as indicated in note 3 from S and D under the provisions of TCGA 1992 s 258, leading to the gifts being treated on a no gain no loss basis (see **explanatory note 13**).

The removal of the picture to America by S's wife W in 2018 does not affect the status of A's gift as a potentially exempt transfer. See **explanatory note 13** for the capital gains tax consequences of S's gift to W.

On the death of A in December 2020 the potentially exempt transfers become chargeable. S cannot claim conditional exemption (because the conditions are not satisfied at the time of A's death) and tax is payable. (The transfer from S to W was an exempt transfer and therefore did not affect the inheritance tax accumulation of S.) D can claim conditional exemption, thus saving inheritance tax of 40% × £100,000 = £40,000 less taper relief of 40% = £24,000 at that time.

Inheritance tax: chargeable events in the context of conditional exemption

(7) Inheritance tax is payable following a conditionally exempt transfer when a chargeable event occurs.

A 'chargeable event' is:

(i) Material breach of an undertaking.

(ii) Death (when a new conditionally exempt transfer might occur).

(iii) Disposal by sale, gift (when a new conditionally exempt transfer might again occur) or otherwise.

In cases (ii) and (iii), that is death or disposal, a surrender to the Board of HMRC to pay inheritance tax, or a sale by private treaty to an approved body (eg museum) is not a chargeable event (IHTA 1984 s 32). A private treaty sale to an approved body would be below market value, but above the after tax sum that would arise on an open market sale, thus dividing the benefit of the tax saving between the vendor and the approved body.

(8) Inheritance tax is chargeable on the value of the subject matter at the time of the chargeable event. The value is the sale proceeds or market value as appropriate. An unconnected sale will usually fix the value at the sale proceeds (s 33(1)(a) and (3)).

In theory, the lower rate of inheritance tax (ie 36% – see **Example B12**) could apply in relation to a chargeable event if either there was an unutilised charity exemption available when the original tax calculations were made or as a result of changes in the rate of tax (ie by an increase in the amount of the nil-rate band). However, the lower rate of inheritance tax is disregarded in the case of a chargeable event which, therefore, is always charged at the rate of 40% (s 33(2ZA) introduced by FA 2012 Schedule 23 para 4 with effect from 6 April 2012). Therefore, the lower rate of IHT does not apply to any deferred tax charge under s 32 even if the 10% test was satisfied originally.

(9) The tax is calculated according to the inheritance tax accumulation of the 'relevant person' at the date of the chargeable event. The relevant person is the person who made the conditionally exempt transfer of the property. If there have been two or more such transfers, but only one within the last 30 years ending with the event then the relevant person is that last person. Otherwise HMRC may select the accumulation of any transferor out of those making appropriate claims in the last 30 years (s 33(5)).

If the relevant person is alive at the time of the chargeable event (which cannot apply in the case of a potentially exempt transfer, because such a transfer only becomes chargeable, and therefore eligible for conditional exemption, on the donor's death), the half scale rate is used, and the rate is not increased to the full rate even if the donor then dies within seven years of the date of the conditionally exempt transfer. If the relevant person is dead at the time of the chargeable event, the full scale rate is charged if the transfer was made on death, and the half scale rate if it was made in lifetime (s 33(1)(b) and (2)).

(10) When D sold her picture, this was a chargeable event giving rise to a charge under s 32, with inheritance tax payable by her on the net proceeds of sale (s 33(3)). The half scale rate applies as the conditional exemption was given on a lifetime potentially exempt transfer that became chargeable because of the death of A within seven years after the gift. The tax has therefore been calculated by adding the proceeds to A's lifetime and death transfers, but using the half scale rates in force at the date of A's death. If, however, the rates of tax have reduced between death and the date of the chargeable event, the rates that apply are those in force at the time the asset ceases to qualify for exemption (Sch 2 para 5). There appears to be an anomaly here in that the half scale rate can never apply in normal circumstances to a potentially exempt transfer (though the effective charge may be at less than the half scale rate where the potentially exempt transfer was more than five years before death so that taper relief of at least 60% has accrued). It appears therefore that tax could be avoided by claiming conditional exemption on death, even if a chargeable event takes place soon after the claim had been accepted. It may be that such conduct would be attacked by HMRC as a composite transaction under the *Ramsay* doctrine, thus treating the chargeable event as occurring on the death and attracting tax at the full rate.

Inheritance tax: variation of undertakings in the context of conditional exemption

(11) Once given, an undertaking may be varied by agreement between HMRC and the person bound by the undertaking (s 35A). If that person does not agree with a variation proposed by HMRC within six months, and the First-tier Tribunal (Tax Chamber) considers it to be just and reasonable, the tribunal may direct that it should be made, with effect from a date not less than 60 days after the date of the direction.

Due date of payment of inheritance tax on failure of conditional exemption

(12) Where tax becomes payable as a result of the occurrence of a chargeable event, such as the breach of an undertaking as in this Example, the due date is six months after the end of the month in which the event by reason of which it is chargeable occurs (s 226(4)). Interest on overdue tax runs from that due date (s 233(1)(c)).

Capital gains tax and heritage property

(13) As far as capital gains tax is concerned, a gift of heritage property in lifetime that is potentially exempt from inheritance tax does not qualify for the gifts holdover relief under TCGA 1992 s 260. The gain may, however, escape tax in the donor's hands under TCGA 1992 s 258 if the appropriate undertaking described in IHTA 1984 s 31 is given as indicated in **explanatory note 6.** The effect for capital gains tax purposes is that the person making the disposal by way of gift and the person acquiring it are treated as if the asset was acquired from the one making the disposal for a consideration of such an amount as would secure that on the disposal neither a gain nor a loss would accrue to the one making the disposal (TCGA 1992 s 258(4)).

On sale (other than to an approved body) or material breach the asset is treated as sold for its market value and capital gains tax arises (TCGA 1992 s 258(5)). A gift is treated for this purpose as a sale to an individual (triggering the deemed disposal for market value) unless the undertaking under TCGA 1992 s 258 is renewed by the donee. If inheritance tax is chargeable on the same occasion, any capital gains tax payable reduces the value to be included as a chargeable transfer for inheritance tax (TCGA 1992 s 258(8)).

In the Example, A would have needed to submit undertakings by S and D under s 258, establishing no gain no loss treatment for capital gains tax, to avoid an immediate capital gains tax charge on the 2016 gifts. By virtue of ss 258(5), (6) the gift of the picture by S to his wife would give rise to a deemed disposal at market value and be a breach of the undertaking unless the undertaking was renewed by W. TCGA 1992 s 58, which provides for a no gain, no loss treatment for disposals between spouses or civil partners, generally overrides other provisions of TCGA 1992 that specify or fix the amount of the consideration deemed to be given on a disposal or acquisition. However, that does not assist S here because the deemed sale under TCGA 1992 s 258(6) is to 'an individual' without specifying his identity; in other words, the deemed sale is made without reference to the identity of the actual donee. Since the legislation does specify a spouse as the deemed purchaser, s 58 has no application. If W gave the undertaking, it would be breached when she took the asset out of the UK and she would be the one who was deemed to have sold it – and (because it is a breach of undertaking rather than an actual disposal) reacquired it – for market value. Although S also becomes liable to inheritance tax on the 2016 gift of the painting because of his father's death within seven years, he cannot deduct the capital gains tax paid by him (if any) from the inheritance tax value, because the occasion of the inheritance tax charge is the 2016 gift from the father, not the 2018 disposal by S to his wife.

As far as D is concerned, she still held the painting at her father's death and the conditional exemption for inheritance tax will therefore apply, the capital gains tax undertaking being treated as an undertaking under s 30 (see **explanatory note 6**). When she sold the painting, both inheritance tax and capital gains tax are charged on that single occasion, so the capital gains tax may be deducted from the value to be charged to inheritance tax, as shown in the Example.

Inheritance tax residence nil-rate band and conditional exemption

(14) The operation of the RNRB in the context of estates with conditionally exempt property is set out in IHTA 1984 s 8M. Where a deceased estate includes a home that is conditionally exempt and that is closely inherited (see **Example A2 explanatory note (3)**), to the extent that the home is conditionally exempt, it is treated as not closely inherited. This means that the appropriate proportion of the RNRB (see **Example A2 explanatory note (5)**) is available to carry forward (see **Example A3 part E**) and used on the subsequent death of a spouse or civil partner or, if earlier, the calculation of the recapture charge if the conditional exemption ends (such on the sale of the home or the breaking of the relevant undertakings). The rate of charge on those occasions takes into account RNRB not used on the deceased's death by reason of the conditional exemption except to the extent it has already been used in the form of a brought-forward allowance on the death of a surviving spouse or civil partner. If the chargeable even takes place before the death of the surviving spouse or civil partner, the latter's brought-forward allowance is adjusted downwards to take account of the using up of the RNRB in determining the IHT charge on the chargeable event. A downsizing addition is also available in respect of a conditionally exempt home and operates in a similar way. In practice the types of estate which are conditionally exempt and which contain a home that is closely inherited are likely to be too large to admit of the availability of a RNRB so that the above commentary is likely to be of theoretical interest only.

Question

Mackenzie Ltd is a property holding and investment company.

The following is a summary of its balance sheet at 31 December 2023:

Mackenzie Ltd		
Balance sheet as at 31 December 2023		
Freehold Properties		1,720,000
(Market value £3,000,0000)		
Quoted Investments		1,200,000
(Market value £1,250,000)		
Bank Deposit Account	200,000	
Bank Current Account	10,000	210,000
		3,130,000
Less: Loan Accounts:		
Robert Mackenzie	1,200,000	
James Mackenzie	200,000	
Duncan Mackenzie	300,000	1,700,000
Net assets		£1,430,000
Financed by:		
Issued Capital: shares of £1 each		10,000
Reserves		1,420,000
Shareholders' Funds		£1,430,000

The issued capital has since December 1993 been held by:

Robert Mackenzie		4,000
James Mackenzie	) Robert's sons	3,750
Duncan Mackenzie	)	2,250
		10,000

On 11 January 2024 Mrs Newman, Robert Mackenzie's daughter, and her three children returned to this country from overseas. To provide for them, Robert withdrew £400,000 from his loan account with the company, which enabled him on 15 January 2024 to give £437,500 to Mrs Newman. Some of the company's investments were sold to produce sufficient cash to pay the £400,000 to Robert.

A meeting of the members was held on 18 January 2024 at which it was resolved that one of the freehold properties owned by the company and valued at £900,000 should be conveyed to Miss Diana Crawley, a very close friend of Robert's. The house was conveyed to her on 20 January 2024 without payment.

Assuming that Robert had made previous chargeable transfers totalling £330,000 in 2018/19, that James had made a gift of £81,000 to his son on 31 December 2023 and that Duncan had made no gifts other than £200,000 to his wife in December 2019, calculate the inheritance tax payable in connection with the above.

Answer

Mackenzie Ltd — apportionment of transfer of value on 20 January 2024

Transfer of value by close company on 20 January 2024 apportioned amongst participators:

Robert Mackenzie	0.40	×	900,000	=	360,000
James Mackenzie	0.375	×	900,000	=	337,500
Duncan Mackenzie	0.225	×	900,000	=	202,500
					£900,000

Inheritance tax payable:
Robert Mackenzie

Inheritance tax accumulation

				Gross	*Tax on 2023/24* Scale	Net
				£	£	£
Previous transfers within seven years				330,000	1,000*	329,000
(* 330,000 – 325,000 = 5,000 @ 20%)						
15 January 2024						
Gift to daughter			437,500			
Less: Annual exemptions	2023/24	3,000				
	2022/23	3,000	(6,000)			
Potentially exempt transfer			431,500			
20 January 2024						
Apportioned from Mackenzie Ltd (net amount)						360,000
Grossed up				450,000**	90,000	
				780,000	91,000	689,000

** £360,000 is wholly within the tax band of 20% for lifetime gifts.

$$\text{The gross transfer is therefore: } 360{,}000 \times \frac{100}{80} = £450{,}000.$$

James Mackenzie

Inheritance tax accumulation

				Gross	Tax on 2023/24 scale	Net
				£	£	£
Gift to son on 31 December 2023 is a potentially exempt transfer of:						
Gift			81,000			
Less: Annual exemptions	2023/24	3,000				
	2022/23	3,000	(6,000)			
			75,000			
20 January 2024						
Apportioned from Mackenzie Ltd (net amount)						337,500
Grossed up				340,625*	3,125	
				340,625	3,125	337,500

* £337,500 – £325,000 = £12,500 is within tax band of 20% for lifetime gifts.

The gross transfer is therefore:	$12{,}500 \times \frac{100}{80}$		15,625
	325,000	@ nil rate	325,000
	337,500		£340,625

Duncan Mackenzie

Inheritance tax accumulation

				Gross	Tax on 2023/24 scale	Net
				£	£	£
Previous transfer to wife — exempt				Nil	Nil	Nil
20 January 2024						
Apportioned from Mackenzie Ltd (net amount)			202,500			
Less: Annual exemptions	2023/24	3,000				
	2022/23	3,000	(6,000)	196,500*	Nil	196,500
Net gift grossed up				196,500	Nil	196,500

* £196,500 – £325,000 = nil within 20% tax band for lifetime gifts. The transfer is wholly within the nil-rate band.

Inheritance tax payable

	£
On conveyance by company	
Robert Mackenzie	90,000
James Mackenzie	3,125
Duncan Mackenzie	Nil
Payable by Mackenzie Ltd	93,125
By Robert Mackenzie on gift to his daughter	£nil

(£6,000 of transfer covered by annual exemptions, balance of £431,500 potentially exempt transfer)

Explanatory Notes

Apportionment of close company transfers of value for the purposes of inheritance tax

(1) Where a close company makes a transfer of value, the transfer is apportioned amongst the participators and each participator is deemed to have made a net transfer of the amount apportioned to him (IHTA 1984 s 94(1)). HMRC take the view that only actual transfers (as distinct from those apportioned to participators from a close company) can be potentially exempt transfers, so that the apportioned amounts in this Example are immediately reckoned for inheritance tax.

If, however, the estate of a participator increases in consequence of the transfer, that increase is deducted from the amount chargeable on him, because his personal wealth has only decreased by his share of the close company transfer less the consequential increase in his wealth.

(2) The exempt transfer reliefs for small gifts, normal expenditure out of income and marriage gifts are not available, but the annual exemption is (s 94(5)).

(3) The surrender of losses under the corporation tax group relief provisions (CTA 2010 ss 98–110) does not constitute a transfer of value (s 94(3)).

(4) Where an asset is transferred between group companies on a no loss no gain basis under the provisions of TCGA 1992 s 171, the rights of minority participators are not taken into account for the purpose of apportioning transfers of value under IHTA 1984 s 94 provided the transfer has only a small effect on the value of the minority participators' rights (s 97). The provisions of s 97 were extended by FA 2001 s 106 to cover *deemed* intra-group no loss no gain transfers on or after 1 April 2000 under the provisions of TCGA 1992 s 171A. For detailed provisions relating to the tax treatment of groups of companies see the companion book **Tolley's Taxwise I 2023/24.**

Transfers liable to income tax or corporation tax

(5) The apportionment rules do not apply to any part of the transfer that is liable to income tax or corporation tax in the recipient's hands (IHTA 1984 s 94(2)(a)). This will eliminate transfers of assets to participators who are employees and to directors, which would be charged to income tax as employment income under the benefits code (ITEPA 2003 s 203) and also transfers to other participators, because they would be charged as distributions (CTA 2010 s 1064 and ITTOIA 2005 s 383). A transfer by a close company to an Employee Benefit Trust may give rise to a transfer of value (s 13).

Alterations of capital etc of a close company in the context of inheritance tax

(6) Changes in the rights or number of unquoted shares of a close company are treated as if made by a disposal at that time by the participator and are chargeable accordingly (s 98). Such transfers cannot be potentially exempt (s 98(3)).

Effect for inheritance tax of apportionment on participators

(7) The apportioned amounts are included in the inheritance tax accumulations of the participators, unless an individual has not more than 5% of the transfer apportioned to him, in which case although the tax is computed by reference to his inheritance tax accumulation at that time, the transfer is not added to his cumulative total (s 94(4)).

Liability for payment of inheritance tax

(8) The liability to pay the inheritance tax is primarily that of the company, but if the company does not pay by the due date, liability extends to the participators and to the person who received the property transferred, except that a participator to whom not more than 5% of the transfer has been apportioned has no liability (s 202).

Capital gains tax in relation to close companies

(9) Transfers at an undervalue by a close company also have a capital gains tax effect, in that the difference between the price paid (if any) and the market value is apportioned amongst the shareholders and regarded as reducing the capital gains tax base cost of their shares (TCGA 1992 s 125).

(10) The realisation of investments by the company has nothing to do with the inheritance tax position of any of the shareholders. It is just exchanging one asset for another (but it might trigger a charge to corporation tax on a capital gain).

(11) The gift of the property to Miss Crawley by the company is a disposal for capital gains purposes. Since the disposal is not at arm's length the company has a chargeable gain of the difference between the market value of the property and its cost plus indexation allowance to date (TCGA 1992 s 17). However, that tax liability is not taken into account in quantifying the loss to the company's estate resulting from the gift (IHTA 1984 s 5(4)), which equates simply to the market value of the property itself.

Withdrawals from loan account – inheritance tax treatment

(12) The withdrawal by Robert of £400,000 from his loan account with the company does not comprise a transfer of value by him. He has simply put himself in cash funds by exchanging one asset for another.

The conveyance of the property to Miss Crawley would have been better arranged as a withdrawal of Robert's loan account. The personal capital gains effect at **explanatory note 9** would have been avoided, and the gift of the property *by him* to Miss Crawley would have been a potentially exempt transfer. An immediate tax cost of £93,125 would have been avoided and the inheritance tax accumulations of all three shareholders not affected. There would however have been a liability to stamp duty land tax on the transfer, the reduction in Robert's loan account being the chargeable consideration (FA 2003 Sch 4 para 8(1)).

Question

A

In 1997 Mr and Mrs John Webb acquired shares in Pirling Ltd, a small private investment company, of which they have since been directors.

The shares in the company are held as follows:

	Shares held	*% of issued share capital*
Mr Webb	1,201	26.69
Mrs Webb	1,199	26.64
	2,400	53.33
Others (not related persons)	2,100	46.67
	4,500	100.00

Mr and Mrs Webb are each considering transferring out of their respective holdings 350 shares to their adult son David by way of gift. In the event that they proceed, the transfers will be effected on the same day in January 2024, but Mrs Webb will execute her transfer and complete her gift first.

It is expected that HMRC Shares Valuation Division will agree valuations as follows:

53.33% holding	£500 per share
45.55% holding	£315 per share
37.77% holding	£250 per share

Mr Webb's father died in 2016 when his estate comprised a long-standing forestry business the assets of which included standing timber valued at £120,000, which he left to John, and other assets of £431,000 (net of the 100% business property relief on the forestry business and leaving the timber out of account). An election was made to leave the timber out of account and inheritance tax was paid on the £431,000 at the death scale applicable at that time.

Mr Webb now proposes to sell the timber for £220,000 during 2023/24.

He estimates that felling expenses will amount to £24,000 and that the subsequent cost of restoring roads and fences will be £16,000.

The potentially exempt transfers (after exemptions) made up to 5 April 2023 by Mr and Mrs Webb were £356,000 and £171,000 respectively, all made between 6 April 2020 and 5 April 2021.

Assuming the legislation remains unchanged for future years, calculate:

(i) The potential liability to inheritance tax resulting from Mr and Mrs Webb's proposals if one (but not both of them) dies during 2024/25.

(ii) The inheritance tax liability in respect of the disposal of the timber.

B

Mr Rosewell, a UK domiciled individual, owned a set of four Rennie Mackintosh chairs which he wanted to give to his son. Rather than gift them as a set, he gifted them individually to his son in August 2018, 2019, 2020 and 2021 so as to lower the gifted value.

The relevant values were:

Number of chairs	2018 £	2019 £	2020 £	2021 £
Four	40,000	44,000	48,000	52,500
Three	30,000	33,000	36,500	40,000
Two	17,500	19,250	21,000	23,500
One	6,250	6,875	7,500	8,250

In September 2021 Mr Rosewell gifted £335,500 cash into a discretionary trust of which he is a beneficiary. The trustees agreed to pay any tax due, and retained the whole trust fund in cash throughout.

Mr Rosewell's father (a widower) had died in May 2014. In his will he left woodlands including standing timber with a then value of £125,000 to Mr Rosewell. The father's estate was worth £575,000 excluding the timber and the executors elected to exclude the timber from the chargeable estate. In February 2022 Mr Rosewell gifted the woodland to his son, who agreed to pay any tax due. The land was then worth £375,000 and the timber £150,000. The woodland was not run as a business by either Mr Rosewell or his father.

After the transactions detailed above Mr Rosewell's estate was worth £200,000 net of liabilities. Under his will he left half of the estate to his wife and the balance equally between his son and daughter.

Mr Rosewell is concerned about the inheritance tax exposures were he to die, for example, in December 2023. His health has significantly deteriorated in the last few months. He has made no other gifts or transfers apart from those stated above.

Explain the inheritance tax implications of the above transactions if Mr Rosewell were to die on 30 December 2023 (assuming all assets retain their current values, that all trust income has been distributed rather than added to capital, and that the legislation remains unchanged).

Answer

Part A

(i) *Mr and Mrs Webb — Potential liability to inheritance tax on death in 2024/25 in respect of gifts of shares*

Mr Webb

		Gross	Tax on 2024/25 scale
		£	£
Potentially exempt transfers at 5 April 2023 now chargeable		356,000	12,400*
(* 356,000 – 325,000 = 31,000 @ 40%)			
January 2024			
Gift of shares in Pirling Ltd to son (**working note (b)**)	165,565		
Less: annual exemptions 2023/24 and 2022/23	(6,000)		
Potentially exempt transfer now chargeable		159,565	63,826
		515,565	76,226**
(** 515,565 – 325,000 = 190,565 @ 40%)			
Inheritance tax payable:			
By donees of potentially exempt gifts made in 2020/21 (ie more than three years before Mr Webb's death)			
Taper relief of either 20% or 40% would be available depending on the dates of the gifts and the date of Mr Webb's death. If he died less than four years after making the gifts, the amount payable would be 80% × £12,400			£9,920
By David on gift of shares (within three years before death, therefore no taper relief)			£63,826

Mrs Webb

		Gross	Tax on 2024/25 scale
		£	£
Potentially exempt transfers at 5 April 2023 now chargeable		171,000	Nil
January 2024			
Gift of shares in Pirling Ltd to son (**working note (a)**)	332,065		
Less: annual exemptions 2023/24 and 2022/23	(6,000)		
Potentially exempt transfer now chargeable		326,065	68,826*
		497,065	68,826*
(* 497,065 – 325,000 = 172,065 @ 40%)			

Inheritance tax payable:	
No tax is due from the donees of the gifts made in 2020/21 because the amount chargeable is below the nil-rate threshold.	
By David on gift of shares (within three years before death therefore no taper relief)	£68,826

(ii) *Liability to inheritance tax on sale of timber in 2023/24*

			Gross	Tax on 2023/24 scale
			£	£
Father's estate net of BPR at death (excluding timber) (431,000 – 325,000 = 106,000 @ 40%)			431,000	42,400
Sale of timber		220,000		
Less: Expenses				
Felling	24,000			
Restoration*	16,000	(40,000)	180,000	72,000**
			611,000	114,400

The person who is entitled to the sale proceeds, ie Mr Webb, is liable to pay the tax, although the tax is calculated by reference to the father's estate.

* Allowable expenses are expenses of disposal and of replanting. It is considered that the restoration of the roads and fences would form part of the disposal expenses.

** Since the timber constituted 'relevant business property' in Mr Webb's father's estate, the rate at which tax is charged (and so the tax payable) is reduced by 50% (see **explanatory note 10**).

Inheritance tax payable by Mr Webb is therefore £72,000 × 50% = £36,000.

Working Notes

Computation of gifts

(a) *Mrs Webb* (using related property rules)

Value of shares before transfer (53.33% holding)		£
	$\frac{1,199}{2,400} \times (2,400 \text{ @ } £500) =$	599,500
Value of shares after transfer (45.55% holding)		
	$\frac{849}{2,050} \times (2,050 \text{ @ } £315) =$	(267,435)
Reduction in estate		332,065

(b) *Mr Webb* (using related property rules)

Value of shares before transfer (45.55% holding)

$$\frac{1{,}201}{2{,}050} \times (2{,}050\ @\ £315) = 378{,}315$$

Value of shares after transfer (37.77% holding)

$$\frac{851}{1{,}700} \times (1{,}700\ @\ £250) = (212{,}750)$$

Reduction in estate 165,565

Part B

Inheritance tax implications of transactions by Mr Rosewell in the event of his death on 30 December 2023

Position on gifts in lifetime

Gifts of Rennie Mackintosh chairs to son (using associated operations rules for second and subsequent gifts)

			£	£
August 2018	Value of set of four chairs		40,000	
	Value of three chairs		(30,000)	
	Transfer of value		10,000	
	2018/19 annual exemption	3,000		
	2017/18 annual exemption	3,000	(6,000)	
	Potentially exempt transfer			4,000
August 2019	Value of four chairs		44,000	
	Value of two chairs		(19,250)	
	Loss to donor		24,750	
	Less: earlier transfer		(10,000)	
	Transfer of value		14,750	
	2019/20 annual exemption		(3,000)	
	Potentially exempt transfer			11,750
August 2020	Value of four chairs		48,000	
	Value of one chair		(7,500)	
	Loss to donor		40,500	
	Less: earlier transfers (10,000 + 14,750)		(24,750)	
	Transfer of value		15,750	
	2020/21 annual exemption		(3,000)	
	Potentially exempt transfer			12,750
August 2021	Value of four chairs		52,500	
	Less: earlier transfers (10,000 + 14,750 + 15,750)		(40,500)	
	Transfer of value		12,000	

	£	£
2021/22 annual exemption	(3,000)	
Potentially exempt transfer		9,000

Gift with reservation to discretionary trust

		Gross	*Tax (2021/22 scale)*
		£	£
Sept 2021	Settlement on trust	335,500	2,100*
(* 335,500 – 325,000 = 10,500 @ 20%)			

Lifetime inheritance tax payable by trustees £2,100

Gift of woodlands to son

The gift of the woodlands to Mr Rosewell's son in February 2022 would trigger a charge to inheritance tax in respect of the timber in Mr Rosewell's father's estate, based on the value at the date of disposal. Since the father's estate was well in excess of the inheritance tax nil-rate threshold at the time of the gift (2021/22), the tax charge would be £150,000 @ 40% = £60,000, payable by Mr Rosewell six months after the end of the month of disposal, ie by 31 August 2022. The tax would reduce the value of the transfer to the son, as follows:

		£	£
February 2022	Market value of woodlands (375,000 + timber 150,000)	525,000	
	Less: Tax payable re father's estate	(60,000)	
	Potentially exempt transfer		465,000

On Mr Rosewell's death – 30 December 2023

Since Mr Rosewell made both a chargeable transfer and a gift with reservation to the discretionary trust (he being within the class of beneficiaries), the double charges regulations must be used when computing the tax following his death. The first calculation is to charge the gift in the death estate and ignore the transfer to the trust, and the second to charge the gift to the trust and exclude it from the death estate.

First calculation (ignoring gift to trust)

		Gross	*Tax (on 2023/24 scale)*
		£	£
Gifts within seven years before death:			
August 2018	PET re gift of chairs	4,000	Nil
August 2019	PET re gift of chairs	11,750	Nil
August 2020	PET re gift of chairs	12,750	Nil
August 2021	PET re gift of chairs	9,000	Nil
Sept 2021	Gift to trust — ignored	Nil	Nil
Feb 2022	Gift of woodlands	465,000	71,000*
		502,500	71,000*

			Gross	Tax (on 2023/24 scale)
			£	£
(* 502,500 – 325,000 = 177,500 @ 40%)				
Value of estate on death:				
Free estate	200,000			
Less: Spouse exemption	(100,000)	100,000		
Settled property subject to reservation		333,400**	433,400	173,360
			935,900	
Total tax payable				244,360

** Initial value of trust £335,500 less tax of £2,100 paid by trustees out of the amount settled.

Second calculation (excluding value of trust from death estate)

			Gross	Tax (on 2023/24 scale)
			£	£
Gifts within seven years before death:				
August 2018	PET re gift of chairs		4,000	Nil
August 2019	PET re gift of chairs		11,750	Nil
August 2020	PET re gift of chairs		12,750	Nil
August 2021	PET re gift of chairs		9,000	Nil
Sept 2021	Chargeable transfer to discretionary trust		335,500	19,200*
			373,000	19,200*
(* 373,000 – 325,000 = 48,000 @ 40%)				
Feb 2022	Gift of woodlands		465,000	186,000
Value of estate on death		200,000		
Less:	Spouse exemption	(100,000)	100,000	40,000
			938,000	
				245,200
Less:	tax paid in lifetime			(2,100)
Total tax payable				243,100

Since the first calculation shows the higher tax figure (£244,360), that calculation applies. The tax of £2,100 paid by the trustees in lifetime is, however, allowed as a credit against the tax payable in respect of the trust property at death, reducing the total payable to £242,260 (see **explanatory note** 5). Inheritance tax is therefore payable as follows:

By son re woodlands		71,000
By trustees of discretionary trust 333,400 @ 40%	133,360	
Less: paid in lifetime	(2,100)	131,260
By personal representatives		40,000
		242,260

Explanatory Notes

Inheritance tax business property relief on shares

(1) Business property relief is not available in respect of the transfer of shares by Mr and Mrs Webb because they are shares in an investment company. See **Example A21** for detailed notes on business property relief.

Consecutive transfers and their effect on inheritance tax

(2) Care must be taken to calculate the transfers in the correct order. The Example states that Mrs Webb makes her transfer first, thus her accumulation must be used to record the loss in value attributable to the loss of control. Note that although the shares held by Mr Webb also lose value that loss is not due to a transfer of value made by Mr Webb and is therefore not chargeable. HMRC could use the associated operations provisions to counter the loss to the Exchequer but do not normally do so unless the transactions are actually linked or form part of an avoidance package.

For notes on associated operations, see **Examples A20** and **B4.**

Even though the associated operations provisions may not apply, the related property provisions will apply. See notes to **Example A12** for further details.

(3) If Mr Webb were to make his transfer of shares first then the potential liabilities (using related property rules) would become:

Mr Webb

		£
Value of shares before transfer (53.33% holding)	$\frac{1{,}201}{2{,}400} \times (2{,}400 \text{ @ £}500) =$	600,500
Value of shares after transfer (45.55% holding)	$\frac{851}{2{,}050} \times (2{,}050 \text{ @ £}315) =$	(268,065)
Reduction in estate		332,435

Inheritance tax payable on death in 2024/25

		Gross	*Tax on 2023/24 scale*
		£	£
Cumulative chargeable transfers (as before)		356,000	12,400
January 2024			
Gift of shares in Pirling Ltd to son	332,435		
Less: annual exemptions 2023/24 and 2022/23	(6,000)		
Potentially exempt transfer now chargeable		326,435	130,574
		682,435	142,974

(* 682,435 - 325,000 = 357,435 @ 40%)

Mrs Webb

		£
Value of shares before transfer (45.55% holding)		
	$\frac{1,199}{2,050} \times (2,050 \text{ @ } £315)$	377,685
Value of shares after transfer (37.77% holding)		
	$\frac{849}{1,700} \times (1,700 \text{ @ } £250)$	(212,250)
Reduction in estate		165,435

Inheritance tax payable on death in 2024/25

		Gross £	Tax on 2024/25 scale £
Cumulative chargeable transfers (as before)		171,000	Nil
January 2023			
Gift of shares in Pirling Ltd to son	165,435		
Less annual exemptions 2023/24 and 2022/23	(6,000)		
Potentially exempt transfer now chargeable		159,435	2,174
		330,435	2,174

(* 330,435 – 325,000 = 5,435 @ 40%)

A comparison of the potential inheritance tax liabilities in respect of the gifts of shares is:

	Mrs Webb makes first transfer Accumulation	Tax £	*Mr Webb makes first transfer* Accumulation	Tax £
On death in 2024/25 of				
Mr Webb	515,565	63,826	682,435	130,574
Mrs Webb	497,065	68,826	330,435	2,174
		132,652		132,748

This illustrates that the order in which transfers are made may alter not only the potential total liabilities, but also where the burden of the tax falls and the future accumulation for inheritance tax. This will be particularly important not only where there are different beneficiaries but also in the context of future gifts. This point is also illustrated and discussed in Example A8.

Growing timber – inheritance tax treatment

(4) Where an estate *on death* includes growing timber, an election may be made under IHTA 1984 s 125 to leave the timber (but not the land on which it stands) out of account in valuing the estate at death. The election must be made within two years of the date of death and is only available if the deceased either had been beneficially entitled to the land throughout the previous five years, or had become entitled to it without consideration (for example, by gift or inheritance). With effect from 17 July 2014, where a liability has been incurred on or after 6 April 2014 to acquire land or trees or underwood, or to plant the trees or underwood, or to maintain or enhance the value of the trees or underwood, the liability is deductible only to the extent that it reduces the value of the trees or underwood concerned to nil (s 162B(5), (6)). These rules also apply

to occasions when inheritance tax is charged on relevant property trusts (s 162B(9)). (For more detail on the deductibility of liabilities incurred in relation the matters listed above, see **Example A12 part** (c).)

(5) The election may not be made if the woodland is occupied with agricultural land and the occupation is ancillary to that of the agricultural land. In those circumstances, however, agricultural relief would be given if the necessary conditions were fulfilled.

For details of agricultural property relief, see **Example A22.**

(6) Following an election, the subsequent disposal by sale or gift of the timber gives rise to a charge to inheritance tax under s 126 on the sale price less allowable expenses, or if the disposal is for less than full consideration, the market value (s 127(1)). Allowable expenses are the costs of sale and expenses of replanting within three years of disposal, or such longer time as the Board allows (s 130(2)). Where the disposal of the timber is itself a chargeable transfer or, as in **part b** of this Example, a potentially exempt transfer that becomes a chargeable transfer, the tax charged in respect of the original estate as a result of the disposal of the timber also reduces the value transferred, as illustrated for Mr Rosewell (s 129).

(7) The disposal proceeds are treated as value transferred by the deceased at the date of *death*, forming the top slice of the property passing on death and thus attracting the highest rates of tax (s 128). But where there have been reductions in the rates of tax, the death scale current at the time of *disposal* is used (Sch 2 para 4). (Previous transfers by the person making the disposal are immaterial so it does not matter in what order Mr Webb makes his gift of shares and the disposal of timber; nor how long he has owned the timber since his father's death.) The tax is due six months after the end of the month in which the disposal takes place, with interest payable from that date. Section 208 provides that the person entitled to the proceeds of sale (or the person who would be entitled if the disposal were a sale) is liable for the tax.

Where a charge to tax arises following the deferral of inheritance tax owing to a claim for woodlands relief it may theoretically be possible for the lower rate of inheritance tax (ie 36% – see **Example B12**) to apply to it if either there was an unutilised charity exemption available when the original tax calculations were made or as a result of changes in the rate of tax (ie by a subsequent increase in the amount of the nil-rate band). However, the lower rate of inheritance tax is disregarded in the case of a recapture charge which, therefore, is always levied at the rate of 40% and calculated as the top slice of the deceased's estate in the normal way (s 128(2) introduced by FA 2012 Schedule 23 para 6 with effect from 6 April 2012). Therefore, the lower rate of IHT does not apply to any deferred tax charge under s 128 even if the 10% test was satisfied originally.

Instalment option for payment of inheritance tax

(8) If the disposal of the timber is itself a chargeable transfer, or a potentially exempt transfer that becomes chargeable because of the donor's death within seven years (as is the case in **part b** of this Example), the value transferred thereby is reduced by the tax charged under **explanatory note** 7 in arriving at the chargeable transfer (s 129). See **part b** of this Example and **explanatory note 6**. Section 229 provides that a claim may be made for the tax chargeable on such a transfer to be paid by ten equal annual instalments, commencing six months after the end of the month in which the transfer is made. Although this would be possible for a chargeable lifetime transfer, such as to a relevant property trust, it could not apply to a potentially exempt transfer, nor to any additional tax on a chargeable lifetime transfer, because the liability would not exist until after the donor's death. It appears, therefore, that this provision should have been amended to take account of the current treatment of potentially exempt transfers and additional liabilities on chargeable lifetime transfers. It is considered that the instalment option would in practice be available, with the first instalment being due six months after the end of the month in which the donor died. If any instalment is paid late, interest is payable only on the late instalment and not on the full amount outstanding (s 234).

Death before disposal of woodland – effect on inheritance tax

(9) If the person who inherits woodlands on which an election has been made dies before the timber is disposed of, no inheritance tax charge can arise in respect of the earlier death (s 126(1)).

Furthermore, a new election may then be made on the second death.

Inheritance tax business property relief for growing timber

(10) Where woodlands constitute 'relevant business property', ie where they are operated on a commercial basis, they qualify for 100% business property relief. But if an election is made to leave such timber out of account on a death, the net sale proceeds on subsequent sale are reduced by only 50% (s 127(2)). Elections should not therefore be made where the 100% relief is available (although part of the 100% relief may not be effective because of the way the estate devolves – see **Examples A16** and **A18**). Where an election has already been made, as it was (unwisely) in **part a** of this Example, and the timber is subsequently sold, the relief can only be given at the 50% rate, which was not revised when the rates of business property relief were increased in 1992. The availability of the 50% relief depends on the forestry business having been eligible for business property relief (at whatever rate) on the death of Mr Webb's father.

For notes on business property relief see **Example A21**.

Transitional estate duty provisions

(11) Under the transitional provisions that were introduced when estate duty was replaced by capital transfer tax (now inheritance tax), a liability to estate duty will arise on the sale of timber that was left out of account on a pre 13 March 1975 death. But if an inheritance tax transfer of value (other than to a spouse) intervenes (for example, the death of the person beneficially entitled) estate duty will not be chargeable at all and the transfer will be dealt with under the inheritance tax provisions (Sch 7 para 2). Such a transfer is expressly precluded from being a potentially exempt transfer and will therefore be a chargeable transfer unless covered by exemptions (FA 1986 Sch 19 para 46). This provision strictly applies to the whole of any property of which any part, however small, is subject to the deferred estate duty charge. In relation to transfers made before 6 April 2018, by HMRC Concession F15, any part of the property that is not subject to the deferred charge will not be prevented from being a potentially exempt transfer. The concession has been enacted in respect of transfers made on or after 6 April 2018 and the legislation is to the same effect (see FA 1986 Sch 19 para 46 (as amended) (Enactment of Extra-Statutory Concessions Order 2018 (SI 2018/495, arts 2, 3)).

Associated operations for inheritance tax

(12) The attempt by Mr Rosewell to reduce the value of the gift of the chairs by giving them in different tax years is blocked by the associated operations provisions of s 268 (for details see **Examples A20** and **B4**). Spreading the gifts does, however, enable the annual exemptions to be used.

Inheritance tax gifts with reservation and double charges regulations

(13) By including himself as a beneficiary of the discretionary trust, Mr Rosewell has made a gift with reservation. The effect is that the gift to the trust is chargeable when made, but the value of the trust property will still be included in his estate on his death for inheritance tax purposes so long as he is included as a beneficiary. See **Example B5** for an illustration of the deemed potentially exempt transfer if such a reservation in lifetime is released.

(14) In this Example the effect of the gifts with reservation rules is to charge tax twice, and the double charges regulations (SI 1987/1130) give relief for the double charge by providing for tax to be charged at the higher of two calculations, the first being to charge the gift in the death estate and ignore it in lifetime and the second to charge the gift in lifetime and exclude it from the death estate. For the detailed provisions and further illustrations see **Examples B1, B2** and **B5**.

(15) When making the first calculation, in which the gift to the trust in lifetime is ignored and is included in the death estate at its then value, the tax paid on the gift in lifetime is not taken into account as such; but in this Example it was paid by the trustees at the time and therefore reduced the cash retained at Mr Rosewell's death which falls to be included in his estate as property subject to a reservation. If, however, the first calculation proves to give the higher figure of tax payable, the tax paid in lifetime is credited against the tax attributable to the property that is subject to the reservation. Note, however, that this credit is taken into account *after* deciding which of the two calculations shows the higher figure (SI 1987/1130 reg 5(4)). In **part b** of this Example, had the lifetime tax been deducted before making the comparison, the second calculation would have shown the higher tax figure (£241,000 compared with £242,260).

When giving credit for the tax paid in lifetime in the second calculation, that figure will be restricted to the tax payable on death shown in the earlier part of the calculation. That restriction does not apply in this Example.

Capital gains tax implications of gift of chairs

(16) Mr Rosewell's gifts of the chairs to his son also have implications for capital gains tax. There are two separate provisions affecting the capital gains calculations. The first is the connected persons provisions of TCGA 1992 ss 19 and 20. Where assets are disposed of within a period of six years to one or more connected persons (such as Mr Rosewell's son in this Example) and their value taken together is higher than their separate values, the disposal value is taken to be a proportionate part of the aggregate value, and the legislation provides that earlier tax charges should be adjusted appropriately. The second is the chattels exemption of TCGA 1992 s 262, which provides that chattels such as antiques are exempt if sold for £6,000 or less, with marginal relief for proceeds above £6,000. If articles that constitute a set are sold on different occasions to the same person (or connected persons) the transactions are treated as a single transaction for the purpose of the exemption, earlier tax charges similarly being required to be adjusted appropriately. See the companion to this book, **Tolley's Taxwise I 2023/24**, for full details of the capital gains tax provisions.

Question

George Ladymede died on 31 August 2023 owning the following property, his interests in which were valued for inheritance tax purposes as follows:

UK and overseas quoted investments	£50,000
Antique clock	£30,000
Cash on deposit	£220,000
Freehold house in the UK	£600,000
Long lease of a flat in Canada	£80,000

The Canadian flat was owned by George as joint tenants with his civil partner, Bert Lampett. They used it as a holiday home. George and Bert owned the antique clock as tenants in common.

On 31 August 2023, George's outstanding liabilities (all of which are deductible for inheritance tax purposes) were £3,000 and his funeral expenses amounted to £2,000. One of the quoted investments (which was valued at the time of George's death at £5,000) was sold by his executors on 28 September 2023 for £3,000, less expenses of sale of £150 giving net proceeds of £2,850.

By his will George gave the residue of his estate to his nephews and nieces in equal shares absolutely after the payment of pecuniary legacies of £100,000 to his local rugby union club (a registered community amateur sports club) and £10,000 to his local authority.

George had made the following cash gifts during his lifetime:

2011	16	October	Painting to his cousin on the occasion of her marriage	£8,000
2019	9	June	Niece on her 21st birthday	£581,000
2021	2	August	Oxfam, a UK national charity	£40,000

Immediately after making the gift of the painting, George's cousin moved to America in order to develop her career as an academic fine arts historian and asked George to keep hold of the painting. He still had it hanging in his living room when he died at which time it was valued at £10,000.

George's late civil partner, Claude Drysdale, had died on 5 August 2020 and under his will he had settled £50,000 on trust for the benefit of George for life and then to Cynthia Drysdale, his sister, absolutely. The residue of Claude's estate which was valued at £100,000 was left to Cynthia's adult children absolutely. The trustees had invested the £50,000 settled on them and the value of the trust fund in August 2023 was £80,000. George was also the life tenant of a trust settled by his childhood friend during the friend's lifetime in 2022; the remainderman of that trust is Heart UK, a national, registered charity.

You are required to:

(a)

(i) Calculate the inheritance tax payable in respect of George Ladymede's death on the basis that no elections are made under IHTA 1984 Sch 1A to merge the components of his estate or to opt out of the lower rate of inheritance tax; and that the executors of George's estate make an election under IHTA 1984 s 8A to claim the transfer of unused nil-rate band.

(ii) Calculate the inheritance tax payable in respect of George Ladymede's death on the basis that an election is made under IHTA 1984 Sch 1A para 7 by the trustees of Claude Drysdale's trust and the executors of George's estate to merge their components of his estate; and that the executors also make an election under IHTA 1984 s 8A (as above).

(b) Calculate the inheritance tax payable under each alternative in **part (a)** in respect of George Ladymede's estate on the basis that George's gift to his niece in June 2019 was £256,000.

(c) If the donation to the rugby club had been only £85,000, explain the steps that may be taken so that the lower rate of inheritance tax may apply to the general component of George Ladymede's estate, and how having to take these steps may have been obviated. In the context of this discussion assume that George's gift to his niece in June 2019 was the original amount of £581,000.

Answer

Part A(I)

Inheritance tax payable on George Ladymede's death in respect of lifetime gifts – 31 August 2023

				Gross	Tax on 2023/24 scale
			£	£	£
Gifts within seven years before death:					
Accumulation before first such gift				Nil	Nil
Gift to niece – 9 June 2019			581,000		
Less:	Annual exemptions				
	2019/20	3,000			
	2018/19	3,000	(6,000)		
			575,000	575,000	10,000*
				575,000	10,000

(*575,000 – 550,000 = 25,000 @ 40%) (Note)
Tax payable by George's niece after taper relief is £10,000 × 60% = £6,000

The gift of the painting by George on 16 October 2011 is not subject to a charge to tax when George dies as the gift was made more than seven years before his death. However, it is a gift in respect of which a reservation of benefit exists.

The gift of cash to Oxfam, a UK national, registered charity on 2 August 2021 was exempt when made and does not become chargeable on George's death.

Note: As George's executors have made an election under IHTA 1984 s 8A, Claude's unused nil-rate band is transferred to them. In order to work out the amount of the nil-rate band on George's death, the following calculation (as explained fully in **Example A3**) is carried out:

In relation to Claude's death:
M = £325,000
VT = £100,000
As M > VT, there is unused nil-rate band of £225,000 (325,000 – 100,000) on Claude's death.
E = M – VT = £225,000
NRBMD = £325,000
The percentage of the nil-rate band available to transfer to George is:

$$\frac{225,000}{325,000} \times 100\,\% = 69.2308\%$$

When George dies in 2023 the statutory nil-rate band in force is £325,000.
This will be increased by the above percentage to £325,000 + (325,000 × 69.2308%) = £550,000.
So when George dies the nil-rate band that he is entitled to is £550,000.

Estate of George Ladymede deceased

		Date of death 31 August 2023 £	£
Free Estate			
Quoted investments			50,000
Antique clock			30,000
Cash on deposit			220,000
Freehold house in the UK			600,000
Leasehold flat in Canada			80,000
			980,000
Less:	Liabilities	3,000	
	Funeral expenses	2,000	(5,000)
Value on death			975,000
Less:	Loss on sale of quoted shares		
	Probate value	5,000	
	Proceeds (before expenses)	(3,000)	(2,000)
			973,000
Less:	Legacy to rugby club	100,000	
	Legacy to local authority	10,000	
	Civil partner exemption (re flat in Canada)	80,000	(190,000)
Free estate chargeable to inheritance tax on death			783,000
Settled Estate			
IPDI in trust settled by Claude Drysdale			80,000
Property with reservation of benefit			
Painting			10,000
Total value of George's chargeable estate			873,000

The value of the chargeable estate wholly exceeds the amount of the nil-rate band available on George's death. The rates at which tax is payable in respect of the estate is derived from the application of the choice of rate method statement below giving tax payable as follows:

	Gross £		*Tax on 2023/24 scale* £
Free estate	783,000	@ 36%	281,880
Settled estate	80,000	@ 40%	32,000
Property with reservation of benefit	10,000	@ 40%	4,000
Total tax payable in respect of the estate			317,880

The executors of George's estate are liable to pay the tax arising in respect of the free estate (making an election to pay the tax attributable to the freehold house by instalments if they so choose). The trustees of the Drysdale trust are liable to pay the tax arising in respect of the settled estate and George's cousin is liable to pay the tax arising in respect of the painting (ie the property with reservation of benefit) (see **Example A7**).

Choice of rate of inheritance tax – no merger election made

Given that George has made a donation of £100,000 to his local rugby club (which is a registered community amateur sports club) it is necessary to investigate whether inheritance tax is charged at the lower rate.

Five steps (as explained further in **explanatory notes 17–21**) are followed to ascertain this:

- Step 1: Calculate the chargeable amount of each component of the estate (ie the net value of the property comprised in the component after deducting liabilities, reliefs and exemptions applicable to the component); record also the value of any property in which the deceased has a reservation of benefit.

- Step 2: Deduct from the amount of each component determined under Step 1 and the value of any property in which the deceased has a reservation of benefit, the appropriate proportion of the available nil-rate band applicable to each component and such property (ie the amount of nil-rate band left over after allowing for any increase that arises from the transfer of unused nil-rate band under IHTA 1984 s 8A and taking into account any chargeable transfers made during the seven years before death).

- Step 3: Add to the amount of each component determined under Step 2, any charitable donation(s) from which it is paid and restate the chargeable amount of each component of the estate. This amount is the 'baseline amount' of each component. Record again the value (as ascertained under Step 2) of any property in which the deceased has a reservation of benefit.

- Step 4: Perform the 10% test – that is, compare with 10% of the baseline amount for each component, the 'donated amount' (ie the charitable donation) in respect of the component. The donated amount made from a component must be at least 10% of the baseline amount of that component if the 10% test is to be satisfied.

- Step 5: Choose the rate of inheritance tax to be applied to the chargeable amount (ie the Step 2 amount) of each component. If the 10% test is satisfied for a component of the estate, apply the 36% rate of inheritance tax to that component. If not, apply the 40% rate of inheritance tax to that component. The property in which the deceased had a reservation of benefit is also be charged to inheritance tax of 40% (but apply the 36% rate of inheritance tax to such property if an election is properly made under IHTA 1984 Sch 1A para 7 to merge it with one or more components of the estate in respect of which inheritance tax is charged at 36%).

Applying this method statement to George Ladymede's estate:

- Step 1: Calculate the chargeable amount of each component of George's estate and record also the value of any property in which he has a reservation of benefit.

	Property with Reservation of Benefit	*Survivorship Component*	*Settled Property Component*	*General Component*
	£	£	£	£
Painting	10,000			
Leasehold flat		80,000		
Drysdale trust			80,000	
Freehold house				600,000
Quoted investments				50,000
Cash on deposit				220,000
Antique clock				30,000

	Property with Reservation of Benefit	*Survivorship Component*	*Settled Property Component*	*General Component*
Less: civil partner exemption		(80,000)		
Less: liabilities and funeral expenses				(5,000)
Less: loss on sale of quoted shares				(2,000)
Less: legacy to local authority				(10,000)
Less: legacy to rugby club				(100,000)
Value of components	£10,000	Nil	80,000	783,000

- Step 2: Deduct from the amount of each component determined under Step 1 and the value of any property in which the deceased has a reservation of benefit, the appropriate proportion of the available nil-rate band applicable to each component and such property.

  The nil-rate band of £550,000 available on George's death has been fully utilised in computing the tax payable on the lifetime gift (a potentially exempt transfer) to his niece on 9 June 2019 which became chargeable on his death. Hence there is no amount of nil-rate band to apportion in relation to his estate and no amount to deduct under Step 2. The result of Step 2 therefore is the same as Step 1 in this Example.

- Step 3: Add to the amount of each component determined under Step 2, any charitable donation(s) from which it is paid and restate the chargeable amount of each component of the estate. This amount is the 'baseline amount' of each component. Record again the value (as ascertained under Step 2) of any property in which the deceased has a reservation of benefit.

	Property with Reservation of Benefit	*Survivorship Component*	*Settled Property Component*	*General Component*
	£	£	£	£
Value of components after Step 2	10,000	Nil	80,000	783,000
Add: gift to rugby club				100,000
Baseline amount of each component	10,000	Nil	80,000	883,000

- Step 4: Perform the 10% test – that is, compare with 10% of the baseline amount for each component, the 'donated amount' (ie the charitable donation) in respect of the component. The donated amount made from a component must be at least 10% of the baseline amount of that component if the 10% test is to be satisfied.

  In George's case the donated amount is £100,000 and is paid wholly out of the general component of the estate. So the 10% test is applied in relation to that component only. The baseline amount of the general component is £883,000. 10% of the baseline amount is £88,300. The test is whether the donated amount is at least 10% of the baseline amount of the relevant component. Here, as the donated amount of £100,000 is larger than £88,300, the 10% test is met.

- Step 5: As the 10% test is met in relation to the general component, tax is charged on the chargeable amount of the general component of George's estate at 36%. The other components and the property in which George has a reservation of benefit are charged to tax at 40%. In this Example, the total inheritance tax payable in respect of George's estate is £317,880 as per the calculation performed above.

Part A(II)

As in **part a(i)**, the tax arising on George's death in respect of the lifetime gift to his niece is £6,000 and there is no tax on the gift of the painting and the gift to Oxfam. George's estate is also valued in the same way as in **part a(i)**.

The value of the chargeable estate wholly exceeds the amount of the nil-rate band available on George's death. The rates at which tax is payable in respect of the estate is derived from the application of the choice of rate method statement below giving tax payable as follows:

	Gross		Tax on 2023/24 scale
	£		£
Free estate	783,000	@ 36%	281,880
Settled estate	80,000	@ 36%	28,800
Property with reservation of benefit	10,000	@ 40%	4,000
Total tax payable in respect of the estate			314,680

The executors of George's estate are liable to pay the tax arising in respect of the free estate (making an election to pay the tax attributable to the freehold house by instalments if they so choose). The trustees of the Drysdale trust are liable to pay the tax arising in respect of the settled estate and George's cousin is liable to pay the tax arising in respect of the painting (ie the property with reservation of benefit) (see **Example A7**).

By making an election under IHTA 1984 Sch 1A para 7, the trustees of the Drysdale trust have reduced their inheritance tax liability from £32,000 to £28,800 (a saving of £3,200).

Choice of rate of inheritance tax – merger election made

Given that the trustees of the Drysdale trust and the executors of George's estate have made an election under IHTA 1984 Sch 1A para 7, then the general component and the settled property component of the estate is combined into a notional single component and the method statement is applied accordingly.

- Step 1: Calculate the chargeable amount of each component of George's estate and record also the value of any property in which he has a reservation of benefit.

	Property with Reservation of Benefit	*Survivorship Component*	*Notional Component*
	£	£	£
Painting	10,000		
Leasehold flat		80,000	
Drysdale trust			80,000
Freehold house			600,000
Quoted investments			50,000
Cash on deposit			220,000
Antique clock			30,000
Less: civil partner exemption		(80,000)	
Less: liabilities and funeral expenses			(5,000)
Less: loss on sale of shares			(2,000)
Less: legacy to local authority			(10,000)
Less: legacy to rugby club			(100,000)
Value of components	10,000	Nil	863,000

- Step 2: Deduct from the amount of each component determined under Step 1 and the value of any property in which the deceased has a reservation of benefit, the appropriate proportion of the available nil-rate band applicable to each component and such property.

  The nil-rate band of £550,000 available on George's death has been fully utilised in computing the tax payable on the lifetime gift (a potentially exempt transfer) to his niece on 9 June 2019 which became chargeable on his death. Hence there is no amount of nil-rate band to apportion in relation to his estate and no amount to deduct under Step 2. The result of Step 2 therefore is the same as Step 1 in this Example.

- Step 3: Add to the amount of each component determined under Step 2, any charitable donation(s) from which it is paid and restate the chargeable amount of each component of the estate. This amount is the 'baseline amount' of each component. Record again the value (as ascertained under Step 2) of any property in which the deceased has a reservation of benefit.

	Property with Reservation of Benefit	*Survivorship Component*	*Notional Component*
	£	£	£
Value of components after Step 2	10,000	Nil	863,000
Add: gift to rugby club			100,000
Baseline amount of each component	10,000	Nil	963,000

- Step 4: Perform the 10% test – that is, compare with 10% of the baseline amount for each component, the 'donated amount' (ie the charitable donation) in respect of the component. The donated amount made from a component must be at least 10% of the baseline amount of that component if the 10% test is to be satisfied.

  In George's case the donated amount is £100,000 and is paid wholly out of the notional component of the estate. So the 10% test is applied in relation to that component only. The baseline amount of the notional component is £963,000. 10% of the baseline amount is £96,300. The test is whether the donated amount is at least 10% of the baseline amount of the relevant component. Here, as the donated amount of £100,000 is larger than £96,300, the 10% test is met.

- Step 5: As the 10% test is met in relation to the notional component, tax is charged on the chargeable amount of the elements of the notional component of George's estate at 36%. The property in which George has a reservation of benefit is charged to tax at 40%. In this Example, the total inheritance tax payable in respect of George's estate is £314,680 as per the calculation performed above.

Part B(I)

Inheritance tax payable on George's death in respect of lifetime gifts – 31 August 2023

			Gross	Tax on 2023/24 scale
		£	£	£
Gifts within seven years before death:				
Accumulation before first such gift			Nil	Nil
Gift to niece – 2 June 2019		256,000		
Less: Annual exemptions				
2019/20	3,000			
2018/19	3,000	(6,000)		
		250,000	250,000	Nil*
			250,000	Nil

No tax arises as the gift is within the nil-rate band

The gift of the painting on 16 October 2011 is not subject to a charge to tax when George dies as the gift was made more than seven years before his death. However, it is a gift in respect of which a reservation of benefit exists.

The gift of cash to Oxfam, a UK national charity on 2 August 2021 was exempt when made and does not become chargeable on George's death.

Note: As in **part a(i)**, as George's executors have made an election under IHTA 1984 s 8A, Claude's unused nil-rate band is transferred to him. As before George is entitled to a nil-rate band of £550,000 on his death.

Estate of George Ladymede deceased

The deceased estate of George Ladymede is as it is stated in **part a(i)** above. The value of the chargeable estate falls partly (ie as to £300,000) within the nil-rate band available on George's death. That amount is first apportioned across the elements of the estate that are held at more than one title (see **explanatory note 24**).

	Property with Reservation of Benefit	Settled Estate	Free Estate
	£	£	£
Chargeable values	10,000	80,000	783,000
Less: nil-rate band			
10/873 × 300,000	(3,437)		
80/873 × 300,000		(27,491)	
783/873 × 300,000			(269,072)
Taxable amounts	6,563	52,509	513,928

The elements of the estate after the apportionment are charged to tax at the rates derived from the application of the choice of rate method statement below giving tax payable as follows:

The tax payable is:

	Gross		Tax on 2023/24 Scale
	£		£
Free estate	513,928	@ 36%	185,014
Settled estate	52,509	@ 40%	21,003
Property with reservation of benefit	6,563	@ 40%	2,625
Total tax payable in respect of the estate			208,642

The executors of George's estate are liable to pay the tax arising in respect of the free estate (making an election to pay the tax attributable to the freehold house by instalments if they so choose). The trustees of the Drysdale trust are liable to pay the tax arising in respect of the settled estate and George's cousin is liable to pay the tax arising in respect of the painting (ie the property with reservation of benefit) (see **Example A7**).

Choice of rate of inheritance tax – no merger election made

Given that George has made a donation of £100,000 to his local rugby club (which is a registered community amateur sports club) it is necessary to investigate whether inheritance tax is charged at the lower rate. Applying the method statement set out above to George Ladymede's estate:

- Step 1:Calculate the chargeable amount of each component of George's estate and record also the value of any property in which he has a reservation of benefit.

  The calculation is identical to that at Step 1 in **part a(i)** above and is not replicated here except to state the totals of the components and the property in which George has a reservation of benefit:

	Property with Reservation of Benefit	*Survivorship Component*	*Settled Property Component*	*General Component*
	£	£	£	£
Value of components	£10,000	Nil	80,000	783,000

- Step 2: Deduct from the amount of each component determined under Step 1 and the value of any property in which the deceased has a reservation of benefit, the appropriate proportion of the available nil-rate band applicable to each component and such property.

  Of the nil-rate band of £550,000 available on George's death, £250,000 has been utilised in computing the tax payable on the lifetime gift (a potentially exempt transfer) to his niece on 9 June 2019 which became chargeable on his death. Hence the amount of nil-rate band to apportion between the components of his estate is £550,000 – £250,000 = £300,000.

  So the amount of the available nil-rate band that is apportioned to each component and the property in which George has a reservation of benefit is:

  Settled property component: 80,000/873,000 × 300,000 = £27,491

  General component: 783,000/873,000 × 300,000 = £269,072

  Property with reservation of benefit: 10,000/873,000 × 300,000 = £3,437

	Property with Reservation of Benefit	*Survivorship Component*	*Settled Property Component*	*General Component*
	£	£	£	£
Value of components after Step 1	10,000	Nil	80,000	783,000
Less: apportioned nil-rate band	(3,437)	Nil	(27,491)	(269,072)
Value of components after Step 2	6,563	Nil	52,509	513,928

- Step 3: Add to the amount of each component determined under Step 2, any charitable donation(s) from which it is paid and restate the chargeable amount of each component of the estate. This amount is the 'baseline amount' of each component. Record again the value (as ascertained under Step 2) of any property in which the deceased has a reservation of benefit.

	Property with Reservation of Benefit	*Survivorship Component*	*Settled Property Component*	*General Component*
	£	£	£	£
Value of components after Step 2	6,563	Nil	52,509	513,928
Add: gift to rugby club				100,000
Baseline amount of each component	6,563	Nil	52,509	613,928

- Step 4: Perform the 10% test – that is, compare with 10% of the baseline amount for each component, the 'donated amount' (ie the charitable donation) in respect of the component. The donated amount made from a component must be at least 10% of the baseline amount of that component if the 10% test is to be satisfied.

  In George's case the donated amount is £100,000 and is paid wholly out of the general component of the estate. So the 10% test is applied in relation to that component only. The baseline amount of the general component is £613,928. 10% of the baseline amount is £61,392. The test is whether the donated amount is at least 10% of the baseline amount of the relevant component. Here, as the donated amount of £100,000 is larger than £61,392, the 10% test is met.

- Step 5: As the 10% test is met in relation to the general component, tax is charged on the chargeable amount of the general component of George's estate at 36%. The other components and the property in which George has a reservation of benefit are charged to tax at 40%. In this Example, the total inheritance tax payable in respect of George's estate is £208,642 as per the calculation performed above.

Part B(II)

As in **part b(i)**, no tax arises on George's death in respect of his lifetime gifts.

The deceased estate of George Ladymede is as it is stated in **part a(i)** above. The value of the chargeable estate falls partly (ie as to £300,000) within the balance of the nil-rate band available on George's death. That amount is first apportioned across the elements of the estate that are held at more than one title (see **explanatory note 24**).

	Property with Reservation of Benefit	*Settled Estate*	*Free Estate*
	£	£	£
Chargeable values	10,000	80,000	783,000
Less: nil-rate band			
10/873 × 300,000	(3,437)		
80/873 × 300,000		(27,491)	
783/873 × 300,000			(269,072)
Taxable amounts	6,563	52,509	513,928

The elements of the estate after the apportionment are charged to tax at the rates derived from the application of the choice of rate method statement below giving tax payable as follows:

The tax payable is:

	Gross		*Tax on 2023/24 Scale*
	£		£
Free estate	513,928	@ 36%	185,014
Settled estate	52,509	@ 36%	18,903
Property with reservation of benefit	6,563	@ 40%	2,625
Total tax payable in respect of the estate			206,542

The executors of George's estate are liable to pay the tax arising in respect of the free estate (making an election to pay the tax attributable to the freehold house by instalments if they so choose). The trustees of the Drysdale trust are liable to pay the tax arising in respect of the settled estate and George's cousin is liable to pay the tax arising in respect of the painting (ie the property with reservation of benefit) (see **Example A7**).

By making an election under IHTA 1984 Sch 1A para 7, the trustees of the Drysdale trust have reduced their inheritance tax liability from £21,003 to £18,903 (a saving of £2,100).

Choice of rate of inheritance tax – merger election made

Given that the trustees of the Drysdale trust and the executors of George's estate have made an election under IHTA 1984 Sch 1A para 7, then the general component and the settled property component of the estate is combined into a notional single component and the method statement is applied accordingly. (It will be recalled that George's cousin, the beneficial of the property in which he has a reservation of benefit has not joined in this election.)

- Step 1: Calculate the chargeable amount of each component of George's estate and record also the amount of any property in which he has a reservation of benefit.

	Property with Reservation of Benefit	*Survivorship Component*	*Notional Component*
	£	£	£
Painting	10,000		
Leasehold flat		80,000	
Drysdale trust			80,000
Freehold house			600,000
Quoted investments			50,000
Cash on deposit			220,000
Antique clock			30,000
Less: civil partner exemption		(80,000)	
Less: liabilities and funeral expenses			(5,000)
Less: loss on sale of shares			(2,000)
Less: legacy to local authority			(10,000)
Less: legacy to rugby club			(100,000)
Value of components	10,000	Nil	863,000

- Step 2: Deduct from the amount of each component determined under Step 1 and the value of any property in which the deceased has a reservation of benefit, the appropriate proportion of the available nil-rate band applicable to each component and such property.

  Of the nil-rate band of £550,000 available on George's death, £250,000 has been utilised in computing the tax payable on the lifetime gift (a potentially exempt transfer) to his niece on 9 June 2019 which became chargeable on his death. Hence the amount of nil-rate band to apportion between the components of his estate is £550,000 – £250,000 = £300,000.

  So the amount of the available nil-rate band that is apportioned to each component and the property in which George has a reservation of benefit is:

  Notional component: 863,000/873,000 × 300,000 = £296,564

  Property with reservation of benefit: 10,000/873,000 × 300,000 = £3,436

	Property with Reservation of Benefit	*Survivorship Component*	*Notional Component*
	£	£	£
Value of components after Step 1	10,000	Nil	863,000
Less: apportioned nil-rate band	(3,436)	Nil	(296,564)
Value of components after Step 2	6,564	Nil	566,436

- Step 3: Add to the amount of each component determined under Step 2, any charitable donation(s) from which it is (they are) paid and restate the chargeable amount of each component of the estate. This amount is the 'baseline amount' of each component. Record also the value (as ascertained under Step 2) of any property in which the deceased has a reservation of benefit.

	Property with Reservation of Benefit	*Survivorship Component*	*Notional Component*
	£	£	£
Value of components after Step 2	6,564	Nil	566,436
Add: gift to rugby club			100,000
Baseline amount of each component	6,564	Nil	666,436

- Step 4: Perform the 10% test – that is, compare with 10% of the baseline amount for each component, the 'donated amount' (ie the charitable donation) in respect of the component. The donated amount made from a component must be at least 10% of the baseline amount of that component if the 10% test is to be satisfied.

  In George's case the donated amount is £100,000 and is paid wholly out of the notional component of the estate. So the 10% test is applied in relation to that component only. The baseline amount of the notional component is £666,436. 10% of the baseline amount is £66,643. The test is whether the donated amount is at least 10% of the baseline amount of the relevant component. Here, as the donated amount of £100,000 is larger than £66,643, the 10% test is met.

- Step 5: As the 10% test is met in relation to the notional component, tax is charged on the chargeable amount of the elements of the notional component of George's estate at 36%. The property in which George has a reservation of benefit is charged to tax at 40%. In this Example, the total amount of inheritance tax payable in respect of George's estate is £206,542 as per the calculation performed above.

Part C

If the bequest made by George to the rugby club (payable out of his free estate) had been only £85,000, then the 10% test would not have been met in relation to the general component of his estate and none of his estate would have been taxed at 36% but rather at 40%.

As shown in **part a(i)** above, the amount of George's estate before taking into account the legacy to the club is £883,000. If the amount of the legacy is £85,000, the value of his free estate is £798,000. In such a case the baseline of the general component of the estate is £883,000. 10% of the baseline amount is £88,300. The test is whether the donated amount is at least 10% of the baseline amount of the relevant component. Here, as the donated amount of £85,000 it is less than £88,300, the 10% test is not met. Therefore, the free estate is not charged to inheritance tax at the lower rate of 36%. The inheritance tax payable in respect of the free estate is thus £798,000 × 40% = £319,200.

In this case the beneficiaries of George's residuary estate (ie his nephews and nieces) may consider making a deed of variation so as to increase the amount of the legacy to the rugby club. The usual conditions for the making and submission of such a deed of variation must be observed (see **Example B6**). Additionally, however, the beneficiaries must notify the rugby club of the existence of the deed of variation (s 142(3A), (3B)). If they enter into a deed of variation whereby the legacy to the rugby club is increased by £3,300 from £85,000 to £88,300, then the value of George's free estate will be £883,000 – £88,300 = £794,700. In this case the baseline of the general component of the estate is £883,000. 10% of the baseline amount is £88,300. The test is whether the donated amount is at least 10% of the baseline amount of the relevant component. Here, as the donated amount of £88,300 is equal to £88,300, the 10% test is met. Therefore, the free estate is charged to inheritance tax at the lower rate of 36%. The inheritance tax payable in respect of the free estate is thus £794,700 × 36% = £286,092.

The making of the deed of variation increasing the legacy to the rugby club by £3,300 has reduced the amount of inheritance tax payable in respect of George's free estate by £33,108 from £319,200 to £286,092. It is clear that entering into the deed of variation has been worthwhile. The additional inheritance tax saved by the beneficiaries of the residuary estate more than pays for the additional payment to the club.

In order to obviate the need to revise charitable legacies in Wills continually, a clause may be worded so that a specific legacy to charity will always meet the 10% test. The clause drafted by HMRC may be located at IHTM 45008 (see **explanatory note 37**).

Explanatory Notes

Introduction to the lower rate of inheritance tax

(1) FA 2012 s 207 and Sch 32 introduced Sch 1A to IHTA 1984 which provides for a lower rate of inheritance tax (namely 36%) to be charged on a deceased person's estate where 10% or more of his net estate has been left to a charity or a registered community amateur sports club. The new rate takes effect for deaths occurring on or after 6 April 2012 (FA 2012 Sch 32 para 10(1)).

Conditions for the application of the lower rate of inheritance tax

(2) The lower rate may apply where an individual dies owning property within the charge to IHT and all or part of the taxable value of his estate is in excess of his nil-rate band (which excess the legislation refers to as 'TP' (IHTA 1984 Sch 1A para 1)).

(3) In addition to this primary condition, the charitable giving condition has to be met. This will be the case if, for one or more 'components' of the estate (taking each component separately) the 'donated amount' is at least 10% of the 'baseline amount' (Sch 1A para 2(2)). The lower rate applies separately to each component that makes up a deceased estate so that it is possible that one component is charged at 36% whilst others pay tax at 40%.

The components of a deceased estate for the purposes of the lower rate of inheritance tax

(4) Sch 1A para 3(1) provides that for the purposes of applying the lower rate of inheritance tax, a person's estate (as defined in s 5) is divided into three components:

(a) the survivorship component;

(b) the settled property component;

(c) the general component.

Property in which a reservation of benefit subsists is not specifically identified as a component of an estate. However, it is capable of being merged with a component of the estate so that the lower rate may even apply to such property (see **explanatory notes 27–33** below).

(5) The *survivorship component* is defined in Sch 1A para 3(2) as being made up of all the jointly owned assets or common property in the estate that passes by survivorship (or under a special destination in Scotland). It also includes any overseas property that passes under the law of the country in which it is situated that corresponds to survivorship in England and Wales or Northern Ireland, or special destination in Scotland. In this Example, the Canadian flat, but not the antique clock, is the property comprised in the survivorship component of George's estate.

(6) Normally property passing by survivorship may not of itself qualify for the lower rate of tax. This is because the deceased is unable to leave his share of the property to charity if the surviving joint owner is not a charity. In such a case, the property in this component may qualify for the lower rate by way of merger as **part a**(ii) and **part b**(ii) of this Example illustrate. The survivorship component may also so qualify where the surviving joint owner redirects part of their entitlement to charity under a deed of variation (see **explanatory notes 38–43**) or where, if the deceased owned a number of items of joint property with different joint owners, some of which were charities. It must not be forgotten that all the jointly owned assets are taken together to make up the survivorship component and where some of such property passes to charity, the amount so passing may satisfy the 10% test in relation to the baseline amount of the component as a whole.

(7) At IHTM 45004 HMRC state the opinion that where property is held in joint names of the deceased and another person for convenience but the deceased provided all the funds so that the full value of the property is charged to tax at death, the property should still be treated as part of the survivorship component because as a matter of fact the funds pass to the surviving owner.

(8) Sch 1A para 3(3) provides that the *settled property component* of an estate is made up of all the settled property to which the deceased was beneficially entitled immediately before his death by reason of enjoying an interest in possession in the settled property (the interest in possession must be a qualifying interest in possession so that the settled property is treated as part of the deceased person's estate) and charged to inheritance tax as such on his death. This means that the interest in possession must be a qualifying interest in possession (see **Example C3**), namely a pre-budget day 2006 interest, an immediate post-death interest, a transitional serial interest or a disabled person's interest. The settled property component will also include property that devolves under a Settled Land Grant (IHTM 45005 and IHTM 05103). Where the deceased was entitled to more than one qualifying interest in possession, the settled component of his estate is made up of the aggregate of all that settled property.

This component does not include a non-qualifying interest in possession (eg an interest possession in trust property which is not a transitional serial interest to which the deceased became beneficially entitled after 21 March 2006). Neither does such an interest form part of the general component of the deceased person's estate as such an interest is not included in the definition of an estate under s 5. In this Example, George's IPDI comprises the property in his settled property component, but not his interest in the trust settled in 2022 by his childhood friend.

Generally speaking, the deceased cannot alter the destination of settled property and so this component may only qualify for the lower rate of IHT by merger. But if the deceased were the beneficial owner of more than one qualifying IIP and the remainderman of one or more of those estate IIPs is a charity, then this component may qualify for the lower rate if more than 10% of the total value of all of the qualifying IIPs pass to charity. However, it is not possible to vary the destination of trust assets by a deed of variation and so this route to accessing the lower rate of inheritance tax is blocked in relation to this component.

(9) Property in which a reservation of benefit subsists, although treated as part of a deceased estate for inheritance tax purposes, is not a component of an estate for the purposes of applying the lower rate of inheritance tax. This is because the reservation of benefit rules do not apply to gifts to charity (Sch 1A para 3(4)(c)). Such property cannot of itself qualify for the lower rate (the property in law belonging to the person to whom it was given) although it can so qualify by merger with any or all of the other components (see **explanatory notes 27–33**). In **part a(ii)** and **part b(ii)** of the Example, the property in which a reservation of benefit subsists (ie the painting) could be merged with the general and settled property component as 10% of the baseline notional component thereby formed (ie £973,000 and £673,000 respectively) would exceed the donated amount of £100,000 in both cases. For whatever reason, George's cousin has chosen not to avail herself of the election to merge.

(10) The *general component* of an estate is made up of all the property comprised in the estate apart from property comprised in the other components and any property subject to a reservation of benefit (Sch 1A para 3(4)). Generally speaking it will comprise the deceased's free estate, joint property owned by the deceased as a tenant in common, property over which the deceased had a general power of appointment and property subject to a nomination. All property, other than property in the other components of the estate and property in which a reservation of benefit subsists must be added together to establish the value for the general component as a whole for the purposes of applying the rules relation to the lower rate.

(11) The normal inheritance tax rules for establishing the taxable amount of the estate (and hence the components) will apply in determining whether the 10% test is met (subject to two exceptions where grossing up and where 39A apply – see **Example A15, Example A16, Example A17** and **Example A18**) (Sch 1A para 6(3)).

The donated amount for the purposes of the lower rate of inheritance tax

(12) A donated amount exists in relation to a component of an estate. It is the amount of that part of the component in question that is exempt from IHT under s 23 by reason of being paid on an individuals' death to a charity or a registered community amateur sports club (Sch 1A para 4). This could be a legacy of a specific amount or a share of the residue of the estate. It is possible for wills to be drafted in such a way that any charitable legacy to be made actually meets the 10% test (see **explanatory note 37** below). The donated amount for a particular component of the estate is the total value of gifts to charities or registered community amateur sports clubs that are paid form that component and which qualify for exemption as gifts to charity or to registered clubs under s 23(1).

(13) It is important to ensure that the gift is exempt under s 23(1). The lower rate of inheritance tax cannot apply if the gift is exempt under s 24A (Gifts to housing associations) or s 25 (Gifts for national purposes). So, for example, if the deceased makes a gift to one of the national bodies identified in Sch 3, although the gift is exempt from tax under s 25, it does not count as part of the donated amount for the purposes of applying the lower rate of tax. So in this Example, the gift by George to his local authority is not counted as part of the donated amount in relation to the general component of his estate even though, being an exempt transfer, it reduces the value of the general component of his estate.

(14) However, donations to some bodies mentioned in Sch 3 will count towards the donated amount because those bodies are charities by definition (see **explanatory note 15**). The major institutions set up for charitable purposes such as the National Gallery or Tate or to a charitable organisation such as The Arts Fund are likely to be charities in any case within s 23 and so a bequest to them may count as part of the donated amount. However, it would be a matter of fact whether any of the other bodies or a local museum or gallery was a charity.

Charity – meaning for tax purposes

(15) In relation to deaths occurring (and indeed other transfers of value made) on or after 1 April 2012 (see The Finance Act 2010 Sch 6 Part 2 (Commencement) Order 2012 SI 2012/736 art 5) a charity is defined for inheritance tax purposes in FA 2012 Sch 6 para 1(1). (It will be noted that although the definition of a charity takes effect from 1 April 2012, the lower rate of inheritance tax applies only in relation to deaths occurring on or after 6 April 2012.)

FA 2012 sets out a four-stage test to determine if an organisation is eligible for UK charity reliefs and it states that 'charity' means a body of persons or trust that:

(a) is established for charitable purposes only;

(b) meets the jurisdiction condition;

(c) meets the registration condition; and

(d) meets the management condition.

The definition of 'charity' contained in the Charities Act 2011 s 1 is superseded for the purposes of inheritance tax (Charities Act 2011 s 1(2)). (However, the above definition of charity for tax purposes is displaced if any particular provision of IHTA 1984 gives a different definition (FA 2010 Sch 6 para 1(3).)

HMRC may publish the name and address of any body of persons or trust that appears to them to meet, or at any time to have met, the definition of a charity as set out above (FA 2010 Sch 6 para 6). The list would only be a guide as to potential donees and to the bona fides of the charity and omission from the list will not necessarily signify that the organisation is not eligible for inheritance tax charity tax reliefs. Potential donors may check that a charity is recognised by asking for it to confirm that it has an HMRC charity reference number.

Charitable purposes

The term 'charitable purposes' is defined in the Charities Act 2011 s 2 as a purpose which is for the public benefit *and* falls into any of the following descriptions of purposes:

(a) the prevention or relief of poverty;

(b) the advancement of education;

(c) the advancement of religion;

(d) the advancement of health or the saving of lives;

(e) the advancement of citizenship or community development;

(f) the advancement of the arts, culture, heritage or science;

(g) the advancement of amateur sport;

(h) the advancement of human rights, conflict resolution or reconciliation or the promotion of religious or racial harmony or equality and diversity;

(i) the advancement of environmental protection or improvement;

(j) the relief of those in need because of youth, age, ill-health, disability, financial hardship or other disadvantage;

(k) the advancement of animal welfare;

(l) the promotion of efficiency of the armed forces of the Crown, or of the efficiency of the police, fire and rescue services or ambulance services;

(m) any other purpose not within (a) to (l) above but which is recognised as charitable purposes under existing charity law.

This definition of 'charitable purposes' was first set out in the Charities Act 2006 s 2 (replaced with effect from 14 March 2012) by the Charities Act 2011 s 2) and brought into force on 1 April 2008 (Charities Act 2006 (Commencement No.4 Transitional Provisions and Savings) Order 2008, SI 2008/945) and replaces the earlier technical meaning ascribed to them under English law, as set out in the Statute of Elizabeth I (1601) (The Charitable Uses Act 1601), namely:

(a) the relief of poverty;

(b) the advancement of education;

(c) the advancement of religion;

(d) other purposes of a charitable nature beneficial to the community not falling under any of the other heads.

(see *Pemsel v IRC* (1891)).

The Jurisdiction Condition

Under the law as it stood before 1 April 2012 (in so far as it applied to inheritance tax), the body of persons or trust that is established for charitable purposes had to be established in the UK (*The Camille and Henry Dreyfus Foundation Inc v CIR* (1955)). The UK charity might have overseas objectives eg relief of famine in Africa – that was not a problem – but an entity established abroad (eg in Africa) would not have qualified. However, FA 2010 has ameliorated this strict common law rule somewhat. In passing it will be noted that charities established in Jersey (and any of the other Crown Dependencies of Guernsey and the Isle of Man) are in a special position. In (see *Routier and Ano v RCC* [2014] EWHC 3010 relief was denied under the above rule in respect of a gift in 2007 to a charity established in Jersey to build homes for the elderly in Jersey which is not part of the UK. However, this decision was reversed by the Supreme Court ([2019] UKSC 43) on the ground that a refusal to grant relief was an unjustifiable restriction on the EU principle of freedom of movement of capital (which applied to transfers of capital between the UK and Jersey). Hence the taxpayer obtained relief for the gift.

In order to satisfy the definition of 'charity' for inheritance tax purposes, the body of persons or trust concerned has to meet the jurisdiction condition. The condition is met if the body or trust falls to be subject to the control of the High Court in England, the Court of Session in Scotland, the High Court in Northern Ireland, or any other court in the exercise of a corresponding jurisdiction under the law of a EU member state or a territory specified in regulations (currently Iceland and Norway – see The Taxes (Definition of Charity) (Relevant Territories) Regulations 2010, SI 2010/1904, and Lichtenstein – see The Taxes (Definition of Charity) (Relevant Territories) (Amendment) Regulations 2014, SI 2014/1807) (FA 2010 Sch 6 para 2). Thus charities established in the EU, Norway and Iceland are now within the inheritance tax provisions (and contributions to such charities will now attract tax relief under IHTA 1984 s 23).

The Registration Condition

Under the law as it stood before 1 April 2012 (in so far as it applied for inheritance tax purposes), a charity (established in the UK) did not have to be a registered charity – it could have been an unregistered body provided it had charitable purposes. With effect from 1 April 2012, in order for a body of persons or trust to satisfy the definition of 'charity' for tax purposes, it has to meet the registration condition. The purpose of this condition is to ensure that only organisations that comply with their charity obligations in their home country are eligible for UK charity reliefs.

In the case of a body of persons or trust that is a charity within the meaning of the Charities Act 2011, the registration condition is met if the entity has complied with any requirement to be registered in the register of charities kept under Charities Act 2011 s 29 (FA 2010 Sch 6 para 3(1)(a), (2)). In other words, if the law requires a charity to be registered then it must be so registered. See www.gov.uk/how-to-register-your-charity-cc21b on guidance as to how to register a charity.

In the case of any other body of persons or trust (ie a non-English entity), the registration condition is met if the entity has complied with any requirement under the law of a territory outside England and Wales to be registered in a register corresponding to that mentioned above (FA 2010 Sch 6 para 3(1)(b), (3)).

The Management Condition

In order for a body of persons or trust to satisfy the definition of 'charity' for tax purposes, it has to meet the management condition. An entity meets the management condition if its managers are fit and proper persons to be managers of the body or trust (FA 2010 Sch 6 para 4). 'Managers' means the persons (ie individuals and/or companies as the case may be) having the general control and management of the administration of the body or trust. As to when a person is 'fit and proper' is not further defined and so takes its natural meaning. HMRC have published guidance on how this test is to be applied (see www.hmrc.gov.uk/charities/guidance-notes/chapter2/fp-persons-test.htm).

If the management condition is not actually met during any period, it is nevertheless deemed to have been met if HMRC considers that the failure to meet the management conditions has not prejudiced the charitable purposes of the body or trust, or it is just and reasonable in all the circumstances for the condition to be treated as met (FA 2010 Sch 6 para 5). For example, if the manager is not a fit and proper person at any time, HMRC can still deem the management condition to have been met. This may be the case where a charity appoints an ex-offender to a position of trust. If the ex-offender is not involved in the financial administration of the charity, then HMRC may exercise its discretion and deem the management condition to have been met. HMRC will exercise its discretion under this provision to ensure the test does not impose an undue burden on existing charities.

Registered community amateur sports clubs – definition for tax purposes

(16) IHTA 1984 s 23 applies to a registered community amateur sports club as defined in CTA 2010 Pt 13 Chap 9 as amended by FA 2012 s 52 (IHTA 1984 s 23(7)). A club is entitled to be registered as a community amateur sports club if it is, and is required by its constitution to be, a club that:

(a) is open to the whole community;

(b) is organised on an amateur basis; and

(c) has as its main purpose the provision of facilities for, and promotion of participation in, one or more eligible sports. With effect from a date to be specified in regulations, new CTA 2010 s 660A prevents a club from meeting the 'main purpose' test if the number of its members that do not participate in the club's sporting activities exceeds a certain percentage of all the members of the club. This percentage will be specified in regulations made by the Treasury. The Treasury may also make regulations in new s 660A defining when members of the club are to be regarded as participating, or participating occasionally, in the sporting activities of the club, and which activities are to be regarded as 'sporting' (FA 2013 Sch 20 para 5).

In addition the club must meet:

(a) the location condition; and

(b) the management condition,

although these latter two requirements do not have to be reflected in the club's constitution and only have to be met in practice (CTA 2010 s 658).

These conditions are defined further in CTA 2010 ss 659–661C. Eligible sports have been designated under CTA 2010 s 661 by the Relief for Community Amateur Sports Clubs (Designation) Order 2002 (SI 2002/1966). The sport must appear on the list maintained by the National Sports Councils (ie UK Sport, Sport England, Sport Scotland, the Sports Council of Wales and the Sports Council of Northern Ireland) of activities recognised by them. That list includes rugby union.

Finance Act 2013 Sch 40 para 8 provides that the Treasury may specify in regulations a new 'income condition' which a club must meet in order to be a registered club. The new condition may restrict or prohibit the receipt of different types of the income, including income of a specified description which could include, for example, income from non-members. The Community Amateur Sports Clubs Regulations 2015 (SI 2015/725) (which took effect on 1 April 2015) have been enacted as a result.

The baseline amount for the purposes of the lower rate of inheritance tax

(17) The baseline amount exists in relation to a component of an estate. It is the amount calculated in accordance with the steps set out in Sch 1A para 5. These steps are set out in **part a(i)** of the Example and is the amount ascertained at Step 3 of the method statement.

(18) As regards Step 1, the normal inheritance tax rules for establishing the chargeable amount of each components (Sch 1A para 6(3)). Hence deductions are taken for liabilities, reliefs and exemptions applicable to the property comprised in the component; for example, the property in the survivorship component of George's estate is valued at nil as it benefits from the civil partner exemption.

(19) The computation of the appropriate proportion of the available nil-rate band at Step 2 requires careful attention. Schedule 1A para 5 defines the 'appropriate proportion' as a proportion equal to the proportion that the amount determined under Step 1 bears to the value transferred by the *chargeable transfer* as a whole (the *chargeable transfer* itself being the deemed transfer that the deceased person makes on his death (Sch 1A para 10). In other words, the denominator of the fraction used to ascertain the appropriate proportion of the available nil-rate band to be deducted from a component of an estate will include property in which a gift of reservation subsists; the denominator is, in short, the amount of the deceased's net taxable estate. This dilutes the amount of the available nil-rate band that is deducted from a component of an estate and so increases the baseline amount (thus requiring a larger donated amount if the 10% test is to be satisfied). This is illustrated in **part b** of this Example.

(20) It will be observed that, except where an election has been made to merge components of an estate, the result of Step 2 in relation to the survivorship and general components equals the amount of the deceased's free estate and the result of Step 2 in relation to the settled property component coincides with his settled estate (see **part a(i)** and **part b(i)** of the Example). These amounts are then charged to tax at the rate determined after the application of Steps 4 and 5 of the method statement. Where the amounts do not so coincide (see **part a(i)**) and **part b(ii)** of the Example), then additional consideration needs to be given to the quantification of the deceased's free and settled estate before the rate of tax is applied (see **explanatory note 24**).

(21) In Steps 4 and 5 of the method statement the charitable giving condition (see **explanatory note 3**) is applied and the rate of tax is chosen. It will be observed that the condition (which requires a comparison of the donated amount with the baseline amount of a component) can never apply to property in which a reservation of benefit subsists.

The relief – part of estate that qualifies for the lower rate of inheritance tax

(22) Where the conditions for the application of the lower rate of IHT are met, then the IHT charged on the part of the TP (see **explanatory note 2** for definition) that qualifies for the lower rate of tax is charged at the rate of 36%. To the extent that the TP does not qualify for the 36% rate of IHT, it is charged to tax at the rate of 40% (Sch 1A para 2(1)).

(23) The part of the TP that qualifies for the lower rate of tax is all the property in each of the components of the estate where the amount donated to charity is at least 10% of the baseline amount for those components (Sch

1A para 2(5)). So property in the estate is matched to the property comprised in each component and the value of the property so matched (to the extent that the nil-rate band is exceeded) is taxed at the lower rate if the component in which it is comprised so qualified. So it is possible that some property in the estate may be taxed at the rate of 36% whilst other property is charged to tax at the full rate (as indeed this Example illustrates).

(24) However, before the tax is computed thought needs to be given as to how the nil-rate band applies to the estate. Ordinarily, where a single rate of tax applies to all of the property comprised in an estate, the nil-rate band is deducted from the total chargeable amount of the estate and then the tax on the total estate is apportioned to those persons who are liable for the tax on the free, settled and other elements of the estate (see **Example A8**). This straight-forward approach will not be possible where different rates of tax apply to an estate. It is suggested that a practical solution to this problem (although not one contemplated at all by the legislation – the legislation does not order the parts of an estate for the purposes of applying the nil-rate band to those parts) is to apportion the nil-rate band across the property in the estate that is held at different titles and then to apply the appropriate rate of tax to that property. This is the approach taken in **part b** of the Example. Very often the value of part of an estate will coincide with the value of a component of an estate ascertained after the application of Step 2 of the method statement (but this is not necessarily the case) (see **explanatory note 20**).

(25) The lower rate of IHT applies only to the IHT charge that arises on the death estate. As illustrated in respect of the gift to George's niece in **part a** of this Example, it does not apply in relation to the supplementary charge arising in relation to lifetime transfers made by the deceased within the period of seven years before his death. Lifetime transfers to charity (ie Oxfam in this Example) also have no effect in ascertaining whether the lower rate applies to an estate.

(26) An election may be made by the 'appropriate person' in relation to a component of an estate for the lower rate of IHT not to apply to it (even though it might otherwise do so) (Sch 1A para 8). The procedure for making the election is set out in **explanatory note 32** below and the definition of an appropriate person in relation to a component is set out in **explanatory note 31** below.

Election to merge components of an estate in the context of the lower rate of inheritance tax

(27) In **parts a**(ii) and **b**(ii) of this Example, as not all of the donated amount has been 'used' by the general component, the ability to merge other components of the estate with the general component arises. The persons eligible to make a merger election (see **explanatory note 31**) need to test the consequences of an election to merge and be confident that the value of the assets comprised in each component are unlikely to alter significantly before deciding which components to merge – although it is possible to withdraw an election or use a deed of variation to make an additional charitable legacy should the value of assets alter unexpectedly.

(28) Under Sch 1A para 7(1) an election may be made if the donated amount for a component of an estate is at least 10% of the baseline amount of that component (called the 'qualifying component').

(29) The effect of the election is that the qualifying component is merged with one or more other components of the estate (as specified in the election) so that the merged components are then treated as a single deemed or notional component (Sch 1A para 7(3), (5)). The merger can also be effected in relation to property in which a reservation of benefit exists (Sch 1A para 7(4), (5)).

(30) Accordingly, if the donated amount for the notional component is at least 10% of the baseline amount for the notional component, the property in the merged component is charged to tax at 36% (see **parts a**(ii) and **b**(ii) of this Example).

(31) The election has to made by the 'appropriate person' in respect of the qualifying component and each of the other components (or property in which a reservation of benefit subsists) merged with the qualifying component (Sch 1A para 7(6)). In Sch 1A para 7(7) the appropriate persons are defined as follows:

(a) In relation to the survivorship component, all of those to whom the property in that component passes on the deceased's death. If the other joint owner has already died before an election is made, his personal representative can join the election in his place.

(b) In relation to the settled property component, the trustees of all the settled property in that component. If there are many trusts in the settled component this will entail a large number of persons (qua trustees) joining in the election.

(c) In relation to the general component all the personal representatives of the deceased or, if there are none (a rare occurrence where perhaps no grant of representation has been taken out), all those who are liable for the tax in respect of the general component.

(d) In relation to property in which a reservation of benefit exists, all of those in whom such property is vested when the election is to be made.

It is essential that all the correct persons make the election otherwise it will not have been made validly.

(32) The procedure for making an election is set out in Sch 1A para 9. The election has to be made by notice in writing to HMRC within two years after the deceased's death (by 31 August 2024 in this Example). An election may also be withdrawn by notice in writing to HMRC given by all of those entitled to make the election. An election must be withdrawn no later than the end of the period of two years and one month after the deceased's estate (ie effectively within one month of the latest time that an election could have been made (by 30 September 2024 in this Example)). These time limits may be extended by the HMRC by such period as it may allow. If the election for merger (or opt out – see **explanatory note 34** below) is made before the delivery of the IHT400, a separate schedule IHT430 can be used; otherwise there is no specified form for either election.

(33) The merger of components operates only for the purposes of applying the 10% test and does not alter the value of the components concerned. So the stipulated share of, say, the general component of an estate passing to a charity is the amount provided under the Will (or variation of it); one does not revise the share of the estate passing to charity by reference to the merged estate – because that does not reflect what the charity receives or what the Will provides. Similarly, where an election has been made to merge components, the election applies only for the purposes of the 10% test and it does not alter where the liability for IHT falls.

Election to opt out the lower rate of inheritance tax

(34) The lower rate of inheritance tax applies automatically if the 10% test is met. It is possible, however to dis-apply the lower rate. If an election is made under Sch 1A para 8(1) in relation to a component of an estate, then the donated amount for that component is deemed to be less than 10% of the baseline amount for it (whether or not it actually is). In this way, by deeming the charitable donation to have failed the 10% test, the application of the lower rate of inheritance tax is disapplied in relation to the component or components concerned.

(35) The election is to be made by the 'appropriate person' (see **explanatory note 31**) with respect to the component concerned (Sch 1A para 8(2)). The procedure applicable to the opt-out election is as explained in **explanatory note 32** above.

(36) The decision to exercise the opt-out election will probably be based on grounds of cost. There may be cases where the administrative costs, such as valuing assets, outweigh the benefit of the lower rate of tax. For example, if an individual leaves his house to charity under his will, it does not need to be valued because it is exempt from inheritance tax and will not be included in the deceased's estate. However, to work out whether the estate would qualify for the lower rate of tax, the house would have to be professionally valued and the cost of doing so might outweigh the benefits. Where an opt-out election is made, the component concerned is subject to IHT at the 40% rate.

Model clause to ensure application of lower rate of inheritance tax

(37) To avoid the need to revise charitable legacies in Wills continually, a clause may be worded so that a specific legacy to charity will always meet the 10% test. The clause drafted by HMRC, which may be found at IHTM 45008 reads as follows:

'I give to [*name of charity*] such a sum as shall constitute a donated amount equal to 10 (*or larger figure*) per cent of the baseline amount in relation to the [general component] [aggregate of the general, [survivorship], [settled property] components and [reservation of benefit property]] of my estate.

The legacy given by this clause shall in no event:

(i) be less than £nn whether or not the lower rate of tax shall be applicable; and

(ii) exceed £nn (the upper limit) even if in consequence of this restriction in the value of the legacy the lower rate shall not apply. [If this proviso shall apply and in consequence the lower rate of tax shall not be payable, the amount of this legacy shall [be equal to the amount of the upper limit] [be reduced to £nn] [lapse]].'

HMRC regard this as the essential wording to qualify for the lower rate although they do say that the clause may be followed by other administrative provisions. It follows from the wording of the clause that the amount of the legacy may not be known until the value of the estate is ascertained and the amount of charity exemption will change as the value of the estate changes. The clause only fixes the size of the legacy to be paid under the Will. It does not override the requirement for an election to be made to merge components to enable other components of the estate to benefit from the lower rate of tax. The first proviso in the clause ensures that even if the estate is not liable to inheritance tax the legacy is still payable to the charity. The second proviso ensures the charitable legacy does not exceed a fixed amount, even though that may mean that the estate does not qualify for the lower rate.

A model Will clause has also been produced by STEP (see www.step.org/step-model-clause-iht?).

Deed of variation and the lower rate of inheritance tax

(38) Where a deceased individual's Will does not include a charitable legacy that is sufficient for a component of the estate to pass the 10% test (or where there is no charitable legacy at all), it is open to the beneficiaries of the estate to execute a deed of variation to increase (or create) a charitable legacy so that the estate can benefit from the lower rate. The benefit of making a deed of variation in such a case is illustrated in **part C** of this Example.

(39) In fact, where an individual has left 4% or more of his chargeable estate to charity, it would be possible for the beneficiaries to increase this amount to 10% under a deed of variation at no detriment to themselves as the distributable estate would remain the same (or could be higher) whilst the charity benefits from a larger bequest. For example, consider an unmarried person with an estate of £2,000,000 who has made lifetime transfers that use up his nil-rate band. If 4% of his estate is left to charity (with residue to his family), the charity would receive £80,000. The tax payable on the individual's estate would be (2,000,000 – 80,000) × 40% = £768,000 (representing an effective rate of tax of 38%) which means his family would receive £1,152,000 (2,000,000 – 80,000 – 768,000). If they were to effect a deed of variation to increase the charitable legacy to £200,000 (ie 10% of the deceased's estate), the charity would receive £200,000 and the tax payable on the estate would be (2,000,000 – 200,000) × 36% = £648,000 (representing an effective rate of 32%). The family would still receive £1,152,000 (2,000,000 – 200,000 – 648,000).

(40) The usual conditions for the making and submission of such a deed of variation must be observed (see **Example B6**). Additionally the 'appropriate person' has to be notified of the existence of the deed of variation (s 142(3A)). In this context the appropriate person is the charity or registered club to which the property is given or, if the property is to be held on trust for charitable purposes or for the purposes of registered clubs, the trustees in question (s 142(3B)). In other words, where property is redirected to a charity or registered club by means of a deed of variation, the variation is not to be treated as being made by the deceased unless the persons executing the deed show the charity, club or trustees mentioned above have been notified of the deed of variation. This rule applies whether or not the redirection is sufficient for any part of the estate to qualify for the lower rate. This does not impose a requirement for the charity (or club) to be a party to the deed of variation, but evidence must be provided that the charity (or club) is aware of the fact that property is to be redirected to it. HMRC has indicated that copies of an exchange of letters between the parties involved will show that the charity (or club) is aware of the arrangements will be sufficient for this purpose.

(41) The situation dealt with in **part C** of this Example to redirect part of an estate or additional assets to a qualifying charity is a common situation when a deed of variation may be made so that advantage may be taken of the lower rate of inheritance tax. Deeds of variation may be useful in other circumstances so that advantage may be taken of the lower rate of inheritance tax. For example, property passing by survivorship will not normally qualify for the charity exemption at all and will not be entitled to the lower rate of

inheritance tax. However, the surviving joint owner is liable for the tax attributable to the joint property (s 200(1)(c)) and so he may choose to redirect part of his entitlement to charity by a deed of variation in order to benefit from the lower rate.

(42) A deed of variation will not be effective where it merely seeks to sever a joint tenancy. Such a variation does not result in the severed property switching to the general component (and so, perhaps, qualifying for the lower rate of tax). Rather the joint property continues to be included in the survivorship component of the estate for the purposes of the 10% test. Since Sch 1A para 3(2) describes the survivorship component as the property comprised in the deceased estate *immediately before death* liable to pass by survivorship. A deed of variation cannot vary the way in which property was owned before the death of the deceased.

(43) Also if a beneficiary varies his entitlement so that another component will be able to benefit from the lower rate, the provision of s 142(3) will not normally apply as the variation is only bringing about an extra reduction in tax over and above the reduction that would already arise through an increase in the amount qualifying for the charity exemption.

Effect of changes in the value of an estate and the lower rate of inheritance tax

(44) The post-mortem reliefs that apply in respect of property valued under the related property rules (see **Example A12**), shares (see **Example A13**) and land (see **Example A12**) may alter the value of an estate so that it comes to qualify for the lower rate of inheritance tax and this possibility must not be overlooked when taking the benefit of such reliefs. In this Example, the post-mortem relief in respect of the sale of the quoted investment does not alter the value of the general component of George's estate dramatically, but if it did then the above considerations will come into play.

(45) For example, consider Millicent who, having made no lifetime transfers, dies on 2 November 2023 leaving a net estate valued at £655,000 (including a house valued at £450,000) when the IHT400 was delivered. She leaves a legacy of £30,000 to the RSPB. The donated amount is £30,000 and the baseline amount of the general (and only) component of her estate is £655,000 – £325,000 = £330,000, 10% of which is £33,000. It is clear that the 10% test is not met. In the year following her death the house is sold for £410,000 realising a loss of £40,000 and loss on sale relief is claimed by her executors. Millicent's estate is now valued at £615,000 (655,000 – 40,000). The donated amount is still £30,000 but the baseline amount of the general (and only) component of her estate is £615,000 – £325,000 = £290,000, 10% of which is £29,000. It is clear that the 10% test is now met with the result that the lower rate of inheritance tax applies in relation to her estate.

Abatement of a charitable legacy and its effect on the lower rate of inheritance tax

(46) Where there are insufficient assets in a deceased estate to pay all the legacies under the Will, then the legacies abate in accordance with the law on wills. Where this results in a charitable legacy being reduced, it is the reduced amount that is treated as the donated amount for the purposes of applying the 10% test. For example, consider a deceased person who dies owing a net estate of £500,000 and under whose Will there are specific legacies of the same class of £570,000 to his relatives and a charitable legacy of £20,000. Prima facie the lower rate of inheritance tax applies as the baseline amount is £175,000 (500,000 – 325,000) and the charitable bequest exceeds 10% of that amount. However, the legacies exceed the net estate and so they are abated rateably to £483,051 to the relatives and £16,949 to the charity. The donated amount is now £16,949 which is less than £17,500, 10% of the baseline amount and so the lower rate of inheritance tax does not apply to the estate.

Inheritance tax residence nil-rate band and its effect on the lower rate of inheritance tax

(47) In this example, although George died owning a residential property, it was not inherited by his direct descendants and so his RNRB is nil and does not affect the calculation. Had the property been so inherited then a RNRB would be available and would be given effect to in the usual way when calculating the amount of tax payable. However, in the calculation of the choice of rate at Step 2 RNRB is not available and would not be apportioned across the various components of the estate and any property in which the deceased had a reservation of benefit. This is because the legislation refers only to the apportionment across the estate of the general nil-rate band.

Cross references to other Examples on the lower rate of inheritance tax

(48) The introduction of the lower rate of inheritance tax has affected other areas of the inheritance tax regime and the following Examples discuss that impact in the case of the grossing up of free of tax legacies (**Example A15** and **Example A17**), the attribution of value to residuary gifts in cases of business and agricultural property (**Example A16** and **Example A18**), the recapture charge in relation to heritage assets (**Example B9**), the recapture charge in relation to woodlands (**Example B11**) and quick succession relief (**Example C4**).

Question

Prepare a document for a training session setting out the key aspects of the inheritance tax treatment of an individual in relation to his pension schemes.

Answer

Introduction

Schedule IHT409 to Inheritance Tax Account Form IHT400 (Pensions) should be completed if a deceased person received, or had made provision for, a pension or benefit from an employer or under a personal pension policy (including a retirement annuity contract) other than the state pension. Although this account must be made on the death of an individual in calculating the 'estate' charge to IHT, this note also considers the lifetime charge to IHT that can arise in respect of a deceased individuals being a member of a pension fund.

Contributions to pension funds

In general terms lifetime transfers made by an individual that result in a fall in the value of his estate are 'transfers of value' that, unless they are exempt or outside the scope of IHT, give rise to IHT consequences (see **Example A1**) – IHTA 1984, s 3.

Generally speaking, where an individual makes a contribution to their pension fund, they do not make a transfer of value as the rights they acquire in relation to the fund by making the contribution form part of their estate. There is no fall in value of their estate. It will also be noted in this regard that where an individual transfers a fund from one pension scheme to another, there is no transfer in value as the death benefits have no enhanced value so that any loss is negligible.

There are some exceptions, namely where an individual makes a contribution to another individual's pension fund. This is treated as a transfer of value on general principles and is treated in the same way as any other transfer of value (see **Example A1**). The transfer may be exempt if, for example, the individual is able to invoke the normal expenditure out of income exemption (s 21) (see **Example A1 part (c), paragraph (d)**) or the spouse exemption (s 18) (see **Example A1 part (c), paragraph (a)**), where, in the latter case if the transferee pension scheme is for the benefit of the individual's spouse or civil partner.

A transfer of value may arise where, within two years before he died, an individual, whilst in ill-health, makes a nomination, appointment or assignment of death benefits (eg the death benefits that typically form part of a pension fund are payable outside their estate). In this case the loss to the transferor's estate is considerable. HMRC adopts a two-year rule so that it will only investigate cases if death occurs within two years of transfer, provided at the time of transfer, the individual was already in ill health and was aware of it. The same consequence may arise where the individual makes any changes to the benefits he is entitled to under the scheme (in cases where the scheme administrator cannot, by virtue of exercising discretion, override the nomination or appointment). Some examples of changes in benefits that might be made are:

- where, once having reached pensionable age, the deceased whilst in ill health had determined not to take the payment of his pension at that time;
- where having got to pension age and chosen to take income drawdown he decides at a later stage, while in ill health, to reduce the level of income taken. (Income drawdown is the situation where the deceased has reached pension age but has chosen not to buy an annuity that will provide his pension, but instead decides to draw a certain level of income from the retirement fund with a view to buying an annuity at a later date.); or
- having got to pension age and chosen to take phased retirement, he decides at a later date (and whilst in ill health, to reduce the number of segments taken). Phased retirement is the situation where the deceased has divided his pension entitlement into a series of segments and agreed with the pension provider a plan on retirement to take so many segments each year.

Contributions made by an employer to an employee's pension fund are not regarded as transfers of value from the employer's perspective and so are outside the scope of IHT (s 12(2)). This will only be the case however where the contribution is to an employee's registered pension scheme or a qualifying non-UK pension scheme.

Also, certain dispositions are not transfers of value even though the estate of the person making them may fall in value. The types of disposition that fall into this category include a failure during lifetime to exercise rights to drawdown designated funds from a drawdown pension fund or a flexi-access fund so that there are unused funds on death (s 12A). This means that the value of a deceased estate is not reduced by the omission to draw down all the funds.

Where a member of an employer-financed retirement benefits scheme (EFRBS) makes (or is deemed to make) a disposition in connection with the EFRBS, the disposition may constitute a gift with reservation (see **Example B1**), where the class of discretionary beneficiaries includes the member's personal representatives. In these circumstances it is HMRC's view that the scheme member will be its settlor because he has provided funds, either directly or indirectly, and the inclusion of his legal personal representatives amongst the class of beneficiaries is not consistent with his exclusion or virtual exclusion from the potential conferment of substantial benefit on him.

Failure to exercise a right in relation to a pension fund

The failure by an individual to exercise a right is, by virtue of IHTA 1984 s 3(3), treated as a disposition by the individual which could give rise to a lifetime transfer of value by him if there is a consequential fall in the value of his estate (see **Example A1, explanatory note 8**). In relation to a failure by an individual to exercise a pension right in relation to their pensions fund, no disposition is regarded as arising (s 12(2ZA). This is the case in relation to deaths occurring on or after 6 April 2011 and only in relation to the individual's registered pension scheme or a qualifying non-UK pension scheme. An individual fails to exercise pension rights under a pension scheme if he does not become entitled to the whole or any part of e pension or lump sum (or both) under the pension scheme at a time when he was eligible to become so entitled (whether or not be becomes entitled to any other benefits under the scheme) (s 12(2F)). The rules as they applied before 6 April 2011 are discussed in more detail in *Tolley's Estate Planning 2011–12*.

However, this exclusion did not originally apply to persons who elected to draw down all or part of their pensions thereby becoming entitled to those funds. Having become entitled, any failure by them to exercise their rights over the drawdown funds so that they left funds undrawn on their death meant that the rule on failure to exercise a right applied and an IHT charge could arise. This was on the basis that the exclusion in s 12(2ZA) applied only to the member's right to elect to crystallise the pension plan and so draw benefits. It did not apply to the member's rights actually to draw the funds once they had been designated as drawdown funds (although this omission has not been corrected retrospectively (see the next paragraph)). For example, Jessica was aged 70 when she dies on 1 February 2017 holding rights in a pension plan from which she had drawn no benefits. While Jessica had omitted to exercise a right to have crystallised her plan, s 12(2ZA) protected her from an IHT in respect of her failure to exercise her right. By contrast, Alice, aged 75, crystallised her pension plan on 1 August 2015 taking a 25% tax-free lump sum. She designated the remaining fund as a drawdown fund but took no income. She died shortly afterwards on 2 December 2015. The protection of s 12(2ZA) did not apply to Alice as she was already in income drawdown at the time of her death.

From April 2015 changes were introduced to the pension tax rules that allow more people to flexibly access their money purchase pension funds from age 55. Such flexible access arrangements and an increase in drawdown arrangements mean that the IHT charge can apply to more people. FA 2016 s 93 effectively introduces an exemption so that an IHT charge will not arise where a person has failed to exercise their rights to draw designated funds from a drawdown pension fund or a flexi-access drawdown fund during their lifetime and so has left unused funds when they die. The 'exemption' takes effect retrospectively from 6 April 2011 in respect of drawdown pension funds and from 6 April 2015 in respect of flexi-access drawdown funds. This change to the law benefits Alice in the above illustration. See **Example A4 part (a)** for details on dispositions that are not transfers of value which now include pension drawdown funds not used up.

A possible charge to IHT may arise in relation to the failure to exercise a right where the pension fund is not one of those listed in s 12(2ZA), for example an employer-financed retirement benefits scheme (EFRBS). Also, before 6 April 2011 an IHT charge could arise in a scheme member's lifetime under s 3(3) if he did not exercise his right to take pension benefits. The charge applied at the latest time when the right could be exercised, ie immediately before death. For example, if a scheme member did not take his pension when his life expectancy was seriously impaired and this resulted in an enhanced death benefit being paid to his beneficiaries then IHT could apply (see *HMRC v Parry* [2018] STC 2324 and [2020] STC 1836). But IHT was not charged in respect of these enhanced death benefits where the beneficiary was a spouse, civil partner or person who was financially dependent on the scheme member. Nor was IHT applied where a scheme member chose not to exercise a right at a time when this choice did not trigger a charge (for example, choosing not to take a pension when he was in good health) and did not subsequently vary that choice, even when a reduction in his life expectancy would in strictness trigger an IHT charge. In addition, payments arising in these circumstances which are made to charity were also be exempted from IHT.

Possible heads of charge to IHT on death

IHTA 1984 s 151 provides that the value of an interest in an individual's registered pension scheme or a qualifying non-UK pension scheme that comes to an end on his death is excluded from his estate but only if the interest is or is a right to a pension or annuity and is not a benefit provided otherwise than by way of a pension or annuity. Such an interest does not therefore attract an estate charge to inheritance tax.

It will be noted, however, that lump sum death benefits and other scheme benefits do not come within this exclusion. However, such sums will only form part of the deceased's estate where the estate is entitled to them as of right and not where the trustees or administrators of the trust fund have to exercise a discretion to pay the death benefits to the estate and its beneficiaries. This will most typically apply where pension scheme benefits are paid in accordance with a binding instruction by an individual and the scheme provider has not discretion over the payments; the charge arises by reason if it's being a general power exercisable by the deceased (s 5(2)). So if a lump sum becomes payable on the scheme member's death, and if the deceased had not irrevocably alienated his right to the lump sum by writing it under irrevocable trusts, the sum will be due to the estate and will be a chargeable asset of the estate. In the case where the deceased could at his death have signed a 'nomination', ie a general power of appointment under which the trustees would have to pay the lump sum to the beneficiary of the nomination. Had the payment of the proceeds been at the trustees' discretion, even if guided by a letter of wishes, it would not form part of the deceased's estate (*Kempe and Roberts (personal representatives of Lyon, decd) v CIR* [2004] STC (SCD) 467).

The payment of a pension or other benefit will usually cease when the person entitled to it dies. In some cases, however, a pension may be guaranteed for a fixed minimum period, and death within that period will give the estate a right to continue to receive the outstanding payments. That right is an asset of the estate, which must be returned, on Schedule IHT409 (and so may also potentially give rise to an estate charge to IHT). The IHT Guaranteed Annuity Calculator published on HMRC's website shows how such a pension annuity is to be valued. That will not, however, apply where only a small arrear of pension is due from the date of the last monthly payment to the date of death or where payments continue to be made to a surviving spouse or a civil partner.

Certain categories of property are not included in an individual's estate (see **Example A5(b)**). In relation to pensions they are as follows:

(a) Certain pensions payable in respect of colonial service (IHTA 1984, s 153).

(b) Pension payments and gratuities – certain pension payments and gratuities are treated as being paid abroad so that any amounts due in respect of them to the estate of a deceased pensioner who dies whilst domiciled abroad will be excluded property.

Additionally there are special rules about pensions paid to former employees of former colonial governments: on the death of a former employee any pension or gratuity payable under the Government of India Act 1935, s 273, or an equivalent scheme under the Overseas Pensions Act 1973, s 2, is exempt from inheritance tax on the pensioner's death irrespective of his domicile (but the pension is not excluded property as such, so cannot be disposed of in lifetime without inheritance tax consequences). For these rules see IHTA 1982, s 153.

Following the enactment of the Taxation of Pensions Act 2014, in respect of deaths occurring after 5 April 2015, funds in a pension scheme can be passed on to a deceased's beneficiaries outside his estate for inheritance tax purposes, as a pension fund. However, if an individual withdraws his accumulated fund from the pension, it will become part of his estate and subject to inheritance tax as any other property owned directly by him.

Pension trusts

Where property is held in trust, the IHT treatment depends on the type of trust involved (see **Example A1** for a general explanation). A trust based pension scheme that is not a registered pension scheme, or a qualifying non-UK pension scheme will be a relevant property trust and so liable to exit charges and ten year anniversary charges (IHTA 1984 s 58(1)(d)) (see **Example C11**). Typically, therefore, HMRC 'approved' pension funds will not suffer these IHT charges (for example, in relation to the exit charge, a payment of death benefits to beneficiaries) but an employer-financed retirement benefits (EFRBS) scheme will (unless it was established before 6 April 2006 when it will be protected from such charges as a 'sponsored superannuation scheme'.

Explanatory notes

(1) For a general discussion on contributions and benefits in relation to pension funds see **Example A6 Tolley's Taxwise I 2023/24.**

Inheritance Tax — Settled Property

Question

Hartford, who had never married, owned and operated a farm in Cheshire until his death on 31 May 2023.

Hartford had made two lifetime gifts as follows. On 14 October 2008 he gave £112,700 to his sister Providence. On 25 September 2015 he gave £148,500 to his cousin Lansing in consideration of Lansing's marriage, which took place on that date.

The assets owned by Hartford at the time of his death were valued for probate as follows:

	£
Freehold farm in Cheshire (agricultural value £640,000)	780,000
Quoted investments, personal possessions and bank balances	335,500

Debts due at death and funeral expenses (all allowable in calculating inheritance tax) totalled £7,280.

Hartford was also life tenant of a trust of his brother's residuary estate under the brother's will; Hartford's interest had commenced on the death of the brother on 25 November 2018, when the value of the residuary estate was £83,800, out of which (taking account of a separate trust fund in which the brother had had a qualifying life interest for many years) inheritance tax of £18,500 was paid as a result of the brother's death. On 31 May 2023 the trust fund consisted of quoted investments valued at £153,850 (including gross accrued income £3,012) and there was also undistributed income (after income tax) due to Hartford amounting to £3,730.

By his will, which was made in February 2005, Hartford made a specific bequest of £117,000 to a qualifying political party. The farm was left absolutely to his cousin Lansing and the residue was to be held in trust for Sally (born 2004) the infant child of his deceased sister Augusta, on Sally's attaining age 25 with power to accumulate income up to that age. Hartford was Sally's legal guardian at the time of his death.

(a) **State the points relating to taxation that should have been taken into consideration if Hartford had, a year before he died, requested advice on the terms of the trust created by Hartford's will for his sister's infant child.**

(b) **Calculate the inheritance tax payable as a result of Hartford's death, stating the persons responsible for payment of the tax and the amount payable by each.**

(c) **State what difference, if any, it would have made to the calculations in (b) if the gifts to Providence and Lansing had been made one year later, ie 14 October 2009 and 25 September 2016 respectively.**

(d) **State the rate of inheritance tax that will be charged when Sally becomes absolutely entitled to Hartford's residuary estate at age 25, assuming present statutory inheritance tax rates remain unchanged.**

Answer

(a) Hartford – Tax points in relation to the trust for Sally

Hartford's will was drafted before the substantial changes to the inheritance tax treatment of trusts introduced by the Finance Act 2006. When it was prepared the anticipation was that the trust for Sally would qualify as an accumulation and maintenance settlement under IHTA 1984 s 71 as then applicable, and that the trust would carry no inheritance tax implications (so long as the trustees did not carry out depreciatory transactions) when Sally either became entitled to the capital by age 25 or died under that age. If the trust had not deferred Sally's entitlement to income until the same age at which she would receive the capital, she would have become entitled to an interest in possession at age 18 and (under the pre-2006 regime) the fund would have been exposed to inheritance tax in the event of her death between then and age 25.

A trust created by the will of someone who dies on or after 22 March 2006 will be subject to the relevant property regime unless:

(i) it is for the benefit of someone to whom the testator was a parent (or a person in loco parentis), and satisfies the conditions for treatment as either:

(A) a bereaved minor's trust within s 71A; or

(B) an age 18-to-25 trust within s 71D; or

(ii) it confers an interest in possession taking effect immediately on the testator's death (which will be either an immediate post-death interest under s 49A or a disabled person's interest under s 89B(1)(c), depending on whether the beneficiary is a disabled person at the date of the testator's death); or

(iii) the beneficiary is a disabled person and, though not having an interest in possession, the trust meets the conditions for a disabled person's interest under s 89(1) that is treated for inheritance tax purposes as an interest in possession.

Hartford would have been advised that the relevant property regime would be relatively disadvantageous and that, since he is within the extended definition of 'parent' for the purpose of (i) because he is Sally's legal guardian (s 71H), options (i)(A), (i)(B) and (ii) were all open to him for avoiding the relevant property regime. The trust incorporated in the will would in principle be within (i)(B) as an age 18-to-25 trust since Sally is to become entitled to the trust capital by age 25 (and would have been in principle within (i)(A) as a bereaved minor's trust if the will had specified instead that she should receive capital by age 18).

There are several conditions that must be satisfied in either case (which are in practice likely to be met satisfactorily by a trust in the straightforward terms indicated): while Sally is living and under the specified age (25 or 18 as the case may be):

- she must either have an interest in possession in the income, or any of the trust income that is applied is to be applied (except for a de minimis amount) for the benefit of Sally,
- the capital must also not be capable of being applied for the benefit of anyone other than Sally, and
- her entitlement at the specified age must include not just the capital and future income but all undistributed or accumulated income.

The statutory power of advancement, or express powers to similar effect, will not offend these conditions (even if not limited to half the beneficiary's interest as is the statutory power itself).

If the will were, unusually, to confer an interest in possession immediately (as opposed to once Sally has reached majority, given that she is under 18 at Hartford's death), and the above conditions were satisfied, then the inheritance tax effect would differ according to whether her capital entitlement was to arise by age 18 or by age 25. In the former case the trust would be a bereaved minor's trust notwithstanding the interest in possession; in the latter case the interest in possession would be an immediate post-death interest and the trust would not be an age 18-to-25 trust. (On the other hand if it is an age 18-to-25 trust to start with, and an interest in possession were then to arise in Sally's favour on her attaining majority, the trust would remain within the age 18-to-25 trust regime.)

Inheritance tax treatment of bereaved minors' trusts

A bereaved minor's trust benefits from broadly the same inheritance tax privileges as the former accumulation and maintenance trusts: no charge will arise:

(i) on Sally becoming absolutely entitled to the settled property on or before attaining the specified age of 18 years; or

(ii) on Sally's death before her attaining the specified age of 18 years;

(iii) on funds being paid or applied for Sally's advancement or benefit; or

(iv) on the payment of costs or expenses attributable to the trust property.

Inheritance tax treatment of age 18-to-25 trusts

While the beneficiary of an age 18-to-25 trust is still under age 18 the inheritance tax treatment of the trust is essentially the same as with a bereaved minor's trust: none of the events in **(i)** to **(iv) above** will give rise to a charge. Once the beneficiary has reached age 18, the position changes. Payments of costs or expenses are still exempt, but the other three events will give rise to an inheritance tax charge under the special regime in s 71F.

This regime is similar to that which applies to exit charges under the relevant property regime in the first ten years of a trust's existence (see **Example C11 explanatory note 6**). A notional chargeable transfer is supposed, based on the settlor's cumulative total of chargeable transfers in the seven years leading up to the formation of the trust (in this case Hartford's death) and the value of the trust property in the trustees' hands immediately after its formation (plus where relevant the initial value of property in any related settlement (which, in respect of exit charges occurring on or after 18 November 2015, must be property in the related settlement which was itself an 18-25 settlement at the time of its commencement) and of any further property added to the trust after its formation). The effective rate of inheritance tax on that notional transfer is calculated using the lifetime rate (the half scale rate), and the rate that applies to the s 71F charge is the relevant fraction of that effective rate. The relevant fraction is:

$$\frac{3}{10} \times \frac{N}{40}$$

where N is the number of completed quarters since the beneficiary's 18th birthday (or if later 6 April 2008, the date when the age 18-to-25 trust came into effect).

The amount to which this rate is applied is the amount by which the value of the settled property in the age 18-to-25 trust is reduced as a result of the event giving rise to the charge.

Interaction with capital gains tax

On the beneficiary (or someone else on his death under the specified age) becoming absolutely entitled to the trust property under a bereaved minor's trust or an age 18-to-25 trust, such that a deemed disposal for capital gains tax purposes occurs (see **Example D2**), hold-over relief under TCGA 1992 s 260 will be available whether or not the circumstances are such that an inheritance tax charge arises under the special regime in s 71F.

Depreciatory transactions

As with the former accumulation and maintenance trust regime, a charge would arise, under either of the regimes just discussed, if the trustees were to effect a depreciatory transaction, or if something were to happen which took the trust outside the bereaved minor's trust rules (or the age 18-to-25 trust rules, as the case may be) which was not within (i) to (iv) above. (The latter would almost certainly not arise except as a result of a deliberate act, such as an exercise of a power of advancement which deferred the vesting of capital beyond the specified age.) The rate on such a charge – set by s 70(6)–(9) which is applied referentially – does not depend on the value of the property concerned, but purely on the length of time the trust has been within the bereaved minor's trust regime. The rate charged is again reduced if any of the property is, or was, excluded property.

(b) Inheritance tax payable as a result of Hartford's death on 31 May 2023

					£
Estate at death was as follows:					
Freehold farm in Cheshire				780,000	
Less:	agricultural property relief	100% x 640,000	640,000		
	business property relief	100% x 140,000	140,000	(780,000)	Nil
Quoted investments, personal possessions and bank balances					335,500
Accrued income (net) from trust fund (£3,012 x 80%)					2,410
Undistributed income due from trust fund					3,730
					341,640
Less:	debts and funeral expenses				(7,280)
					334,360
Less:	qualifying political party bequest				(117,000)
					217,360
Settled property (153,850 – 2,410)					151,440
					368,800

The only lifetime transfers made by Hartford were the potentially exempt transfer to Providence on 14 October 2008, which became completely exempt on 14 October 2015, and the potentially exempt transfer to Lansing on 25 September 2015, which became completely exempt on 25 September 2022.

The tax payable on the death estate is therefore (see **explanatory note** (3)):

368,800 – 325,000 = 43,800 @ 40%		17,520	
Less: quick succession relief	$20\% \times 18{,}500 \times \frac{65{,}300}{83{,}800}$	(2,883)	£14,637

Payable as to $\frac{217{,}360}{368{,}800} \times 14{,}637 = £8{,}627$ by Hartford's personal representatives

and as to $\frac{151{,}440}{368{,}800} \times 14{,}637 = £6{,}010$ by trustees of settled property

(c)

If the transfers to Providence and Lansing had been made a year later, there would be no difference in relation to the transfer to Providence – the potentially exempt transfer would have become completely exempt on 14 October 2016. The transfer to Lansing would have been within seven years before Hartford's death and would thus become a chargeable transfer. The position would therefore be:

Cumulative transfers at Hartford's death:				*Gross* £	*Tax* £
25 September 2016	Gift to Lansing		148,500		
	Less:	Marriage exemption	(1,000)		
		Annual exemptions			
		2016/17	(3,000)		
		2015/16	(3,000)		
	PET now chargeable			141,500	Nil
Estate at death				368,800	74,120
				510,300	74,120**

(** 510,300 – 325,000 = 185,300 @ 40%)

Tax on estate at death		74,120	
Less: quick succession relief	$20\% \times 18{,}500 \times \frac{65{,}300}{83{,}800}$	(2,883)	£71,237

Payable as to $\frac{217{,}360}{368{,}800} \times 71{,}237 = £41{,}985$ by Hartford's personal representatives

and as to $\frac{151{,}440}{368{,}800} \times 71{,}237 = £29{,}252$ by trustees of settled property

Thus the transfer to Lansing would not itself attract tax, since it was below the nil-rate threshold, and the taper relief of 80% for transfers within six and seven years before death would not therefore be relevant, but the transfer would take up £141,500 of the nil-rate band otherwise available to the death estate. The tax on the death estate would accordingly increase by £141,500 @ 40% = £56,600 (ie 71,237 – 14,637).

(d) Inheritance tax rate on Sally's entitlement at age 25

One feature of the special charging regime for age 18-to-25 trusts under s 71F is that it is possible, right from the outset, to calculate the rate of tax that will be charged when the beneficiary becomes entitled at the specified age, subject only to changes in the statutory scale of rates and to the effect of any later additions to the trust. This is because the only variables (the settlor's cumulative total and the value of the trust property (and of the property in any related settlement) immediately after the trust commences can be quantified from the start. The rate of the charge is unaffected by any changes in value of the trust property – the same rate will apply even if the fund has increased in value tenfold in the meantime.

The initial value of the trust fund for Sally – being Hartford's free estate (other than the farm left to Lansing), net of debts (including inheritance tax borne by the residue of his estate), funeral expenses and the bequests to the political party – was £208,733 (217,360 - £8,627) as in **(b) above.** With this information the rate chargeable under s 71F when Sally becomes absolutely entitled at age 25 (28 quarters after her 18th birthday) is calculated as follows:

(i) Timing of Hartford's lifetime gifts as in main example

	Gross	*Tax on 2023/24 Scale*
Notional chargeable transfer		
Cumulative total (Hartford's cumulative total at death)	Nil	Nil
Value transferred (initial value of trust fund)	217,360	Nil
Total transfers (within nil-rate band)	217,360	Nil

Effective rate on notional transfer $\frac{0}{217,360} = 0\%$

Therefore rate chargeable on entitlement at age 25 = 0%.

Explanatory Notes

Will trusts in the context of inheritance tax

(1) When property is left by a will to a trust the normal rules for settlements apply (see **Examples C3 to C19**). Accordingly if the will conferred an interest in possession (which since 22 March 2006 would be a qualifying IIP as an immediate post-death interest or a disabled person's interest, unless the conditions for bereaved minor's trust status were fulfilled) then the trust fund would be deemed to be part of the estate of the person with that interest, as in the case of Hartford under his brother's will trust in this Example. However, when the beneficiaries are minors it is usual to retain a degree of discretion over the income of the settlement and where that is done then, unless the trust qualifies as a bereaved minor's trust or an age 18-to-25 trust, the rules relating to discretionary settlements apply (see **Example C11**).

Inheritance tax treatment of transfer to Providence

(2) Providence would have no liability as a result of Hartford's death whether her gift had been made on 14 October 2008 or 14 October 2009. As a potentially exempt transfer the gift becomes completely exempt after seven years. In computing the liability on the gift to Lansing, if it had been made on 25 September 2016, only chargeable transfers in the previous seven years would be taken to form the opening figures. The gift to Providence, being potentially exempt, and subsequently completely exempt, is not taken into account.

Inheritance tax residence nil-rate band

(3) Hartford dies owning a freehold farm which presumably includes a farmhouse which is his home. However no RNRB is available in calculating the IHT payable on Hartford's estate because, being left to his cousin, it is not closely inherited (as a cousin is not a lineal descendant of the deceased). Even if the farmhouse had been closely inherited, no RNRB would have been given effect to in the calculation of the IHT arising on Hartford's estate as the chargeable value of the farmhouse would have been nil on account of APR and (probably) BPR. See **Example A2 part (b)** for an explanation of the RNRB.

In the context of the RNRB and Will trusts, a home is 'inherited' by an individual (B) where the home becomes comprised on an individual's (D) death in a bereaved minor's trust within s 71A or an age 18-to-25 trust within s 71D and is held on trusts for the benefit of B (s 8J(4)(b)). A home is similarly inherited where it becomes comprised on the death of D in a trust and B becomes beneficially entitled on D's death to an IIP in the home provided the IIP is an immediate post-death interest under s. 49A or a disabled person's interest under s 89 (s 8J(4)(a)). The home is closely inherited where B is in the qualifying class of individuals set out in s 8K. See **Example A2 explanatory note (3)** for additional information in this regard.

Cross references

(4) For notes on agricultural property relief and business property relief, see **Example A21**; for notes on exemptions, see **Example A1**; and quick succession relief, see **Example B3** and especially **explanatory note 4 to that Example.**

Question

It is September 2023 and Edward (aged 65 and just retired) is considering settling his entire assets worth £728,000 (including a home acquired before 8 July 2015 and now worth £250,000) on his wife Mary for life, then to their only adult son, Brian to be held on trust to pay the income to Brian with power to release capital and with remainders over to charity on Brian's death. Edward will be completely excluded from any interest in the settlement. Brian is not a disabled person.

The settlement may either be made now or included in Edward's will to take effect after his death. In either case any inheritance tax arising will be paid and borne by the trustees of the settlement.

Edward had made a lifetime gift of £306,000 to his brother Jon on 5 September 2022 utilising his unused annual exemptions. He had made no gifts in the year to 5 April 2022, but had used his annual exemptions for years prior to that. Edward died on 12 December 2024.

Assuming that the trust was settled (and that the trustees paid the tax in respect of the funds settled on them), the value of the trust at the date of Mary's death on 3 February 2029 is £900,000 (including the home which is now worth £500,000). Assume that the nil-rate band for 2028/29 is £350,000, the residential enhancement is £175,000 and that Mary left her entire free estate to a housing association.

Indicate the taxation implications of Edward's proposals, and explain the general principles governing the taxation of such settlements.

Answer

The taxation implications of Edward's proposals are as follows:

Inheritance tax

Settlement on spouse during lifetime

The settlement of his assets by Edward on Mary will be a chargeable transfer and subject immediately to IHT unless Mary is a disabled person within IHTA 1984 s 89(4)–(4A), because the life interest falls outside the provisions of s 49(1A).

	Gross	*Tax on 2023/24 scale*
2022/23		
Gift to Jon	306,000	
Less: Annual exemptions 2022/23 and 2021/22	(6,000)	
Potentially exempt transfer	300,000	
2023/24		
Transfer of assets to settlement	728,000	
	(3,000)	
Less: Annual exemption 2023/24	725,000	80,000*

*£725,000 – 325,000 = £400,000 @ 20%

When Edward dies in December 2024 both his gift to Jon in 2022 and to the trust will be charged to inheritance tax at 40% as Edward has not survived the making of the gifts by seven years.

Lifetime settlements made on or after 22 March 2006 are generally subject to the inheritance tax rules which previously applied only to discretionary trusts. Therefore, the assets held by the trustees of an interest in possession settlement will not usually form part of the estate of the life tenant where the settlement was made during lifetime after 21 March 2006. So on Mary's death her life interest will not form part of her estate.

This, however, has its drawbacks. In particular, as seen above the creation of the settlement will represent a chargeable event (previously, lifetime transfers into interest in possession settlements constituted PETs, or were exempt if the interest in possession was in favour of the settlor's spouse or civil partner). Furthermore, the settlement will be subject to the ten-year charge and exit charge rules for relevant property trusts – including exit charges if capital is released to Mary herself.

The following trusts remain outside the rules previously limited to discretionary trusts:

(a) Bare trusts (where the beneficiary continues to be treated as entitled to the assets held under the bare trust; the trust property of a bare trust is not settled property).

(b) Interest in possession trusts where the interest in possession is a qualifying interest in possession (see **Example C3**), namely:

  (i) an immediate post-death interest (IPDI) (see below);

  (ii) a disabled person's interest (broadly an interest in possession for a person incapable of looking after his affairs because of mental disorder, or a person in receipt of attendance allowance, a disability living allowance, personal independence payment, an increased disablement pension, constant attendance allowance, or armed forces independence payment);

(iii) a transitional serial interest (TSI) (see below) (s 49(1A)); or

(iv) where the beneficiary has been beneficially entitled to the interest in possession continuously since before 22 March 2006.

To be a transitional serial interest in a settlement (s 49B–E):

(i) the settlement must have been set up before 22 March 2006; and

(ii) immediately before 22 March 2006, there must have been an individual with a beneficial interest in possession in the settlement;

(iii) that person's interest must have come to an end after 21 March 2006 but before 6 October 2008 or, that person's interest must have come to an end after 21 March 2006 and after 5 October 2008 on his death provided that the person with the current interest in the settlement was the deceased's spouse or civil partner at the time of his death; and

(iv) the person with the current interest in the settlement must have become beneficially entitled to that interest at that time; and

(v) the interest must not be a disabled person's interest or an interest of a bereaved minor (IHTA 1984 s 49B).

The rules for bereaved minors are found in s 71A. They apply only for settlements which:

(a) are set up under the English intestacy rules or by:

(i) a parent (or a person in loco parentis) of the beneficiary in their will;

(ii) the Criminal Injuries Compensation Scheme; or

(iii) the Victims of Overseas Terrorism Compensation Scheme,

(b) give the minor the capital and income of the trust absolutely when the minor reaches the age of 18.

Settlement on spouse on death of settlor

An immediate post-death interest (IPDI) under s 49A arises where an individual becomes beneficially entitled to an interest in possession in settled property provided certain conditions are met:

(a) the interest in settled property arises immediately on the death of the settlor by reason of his will or intestacy;

(b) the person becomes beneficially entitled to an interest in possession on the death of the settlor whether or not he or she died intestate;

(c) the interest in possession is not a disabled person's interest; and

(d) the trust is not a bereaved minor's trust.

If the conditions are met the interest in possession will be a qualifying IIP and the trust property will form part of the beneficiary's estate (s 49) rather than being relevant property.

On Edward's death

Edward's estate is valued at £728,000. The potentially exempt transfer to Jon of £300,000 on 5 September 2022 (above) becomes a chargeable transfer but falls entirely within the nil-rate band of £325,000. Mary's IIP takes effect immediately on his death and is thus an IPDI, with the capital treated as owned by her (or, if she were a disabled person at Edward's death, her IIP would be a disabled person's interest); the residuary estate held on trust for Mary is therefore exempt under s 18. Edward's estate includes a home but it is not closely inherited. Although Brian is Edward's son, there is no disposition of the home to him (and so Brian does not inherit the home – s 8(1)) as the home becomes settled on an IIP trust. Of itself the settlement of the home on trust does not prevent the home from being inherited. However, in order for the home to be inherited it must become comprised in a settlement on Edward's death and Brian (who is not disabled and who is an adult) must become beneficially entitled at the time of Edward's death to an interest in possession in the property which is an immediate post-death interest. As under Edward's will trust, Brian becomes entitled, only on the death of Mary, to a successive interest in possession in the trust it cannot be said that he becomes entitled to an interest in possession on the death of Edward. Hence the amount of the RNRB available for calculating the IHT arising on Edward's death is nil. Nevertheless an amount equal to Edward's default allowance of £175,000 is available for carry forward to Mary (his spouse) (s 8F).

On Mary's death

Mary is treated as beneficially entitled to the underlying settled property by virtue of her IPDI (s 49), and it therefore forms part of her estate for the purpose of the deemed transfer of value on her death under s 4(1). Mary's free estate passes to a housing association and is therefore exempt, so the settled property comprises Mary's only chargeable estate. Edward had used £300,000 of his £325,000 nil-rate band through the gift to Jon, so 7.7% of it is available for transfer to Mary's estate, subject to a claim by her personal representatives or (if they do not claim) by the trustees of Edward's will trust. Mary's nil-rate band of £350,000 is thus increased by that percentage to (£350,000 × 107.7% =) £376,950. See **Example A3**. For the purposes of the RNRB there is an inheritance of a home which immediately before the deceased's death was settled property in which the deceased was beneficially entitled to an interest in possession, provided the beneficiary of the home becomes beneficially entitled to it on the deceased's death (s 8J(5)). Immediately before her death the home was settled property in which Mary was beneficially entitled to an interest in possession. The question is whether Brian now becomes beneficially entitled to the home on Mary's death. Brian's interest in the property arises on account of his enjoying an interest in possession in Edward's will trust following the death of his mother, the preceding life tenant. Consequently he cannot be said to become beneficially entitled to the home on Mary's death; he merely becomes entitled, as successive life tenant under his father's will trust, to an interest in possession in the trust in which the home is settled. Neither can it be argued that Brian becomes beneficially entitled to the property by virtue of the deeming provisions in s 49 as Brian's interest in possession in his father's will trust is neither an immediate post-death interest (as he did not become entitled to his interest in possession in the death of his father) not a transitional serial interest (as the will trust commenced after 21 March 2006). Although Brian is Mary's son, as he cannot be regarded as having inherited the property, the home cannot be regarded as closely inherited. Hence the amount of the RNRB available for calculating the IHT arising on Mary's death is nil (s 8F).

Value of Mary's chargeable estate at 3 February 2029	900,000
Tax due (£900,000 – 376,950) @ 40% =	£209,220

Prior to 22 March 2006 Brian's subsequent interest in possession would also have led to the settled property being comprised in his estate. However, as already intimated, since it is created out of an existing settlement after 5 October 2008 it is neither a TSI nor an IPDI. Whilst the assets remain in trust the relevant property rules will apply (see **Example C11**).

Release of life interest

If, prior to her death, Mary relinquished or assigned her life interest in the settlement in favour of Brian, this would be a deemed transfer of value, against which the annual (and if relevant marriage) exemptions for the year of release and previous year would be available unless otherwise used provided Mary gave the requisite notice to the trustees within six months of the relinquishment or assignment (s 57 and see **Example C6 explanatory note 3**). The treatment of the balance would depend on:

(a) whether Mary's life interest was a qualifying IIP (an IPDI or a disabled person's interest (DPI)) or not (lifetime settlement where Mary was not a disabled person), and

(b) whether or not Brian became absolutely entitled immediately on the release or assignment (which on the facts stated would depend on the trustees exercising their power to release capital before or simultaneously with Mary's release or assignment); if he did not, his interest in possession (unless he was himself a disabled person at the date the property was originally settled so that his interest would be a DPI) would not be a qualifying IIP in any event, and the trust fund would become relevant property if it was not so before.

Brian's interest:	*Absolute entitlement or DPI*	*Continuing IIP other than a DPI*
Mary – qualifying IIP	potentially exempt transfer	immediately chargeable transfer
Mary – non-qualifying IIP	relevant property exit charge	no IHT event – trust property remains relevant property

Additionally, if Mary's life interest was a qualifying IIP,

(i) she would be regarded as making a gift of the underlying trust property for the purpose of the gift with reservation rules (FA 1986 s 102ZA), so that any benefit subsequently enjoyed by her (or any interest retained by her under the terms of the trust) would result in those rules applying to the property and taxing it as part of her estate on her death (or as a failed potentially exempt transfer if the benefit had ended during her lifetime but within seven years before her death); and

(ii) if the trust continued (in the relevant property regime) rather than Brian being absolutely entitled, Mary rather than Edward would be treated as having made the settlement (at the date her qualifying IIP came to an end) for the purpose of the relevant property rules (s 80, see **Example C12 explanatory note 1**); but ten-year anniversaries would nevertheless still occur by reference to the date Edward had made the settlement rather than the date Mary's qualifying IIP came to an end (s 61(2), see **Example C12 explanatory notes 4, 6**).

No question of entitlement to a residence nil-rate band arises in lifetime in relation to a lifetime gift of property.

Assignment to settlor

Edward, if he settled the trust in his lifetime, would have been excluded from benefit by the terms of the settlement, but that would not prevent his becoming a beneficiary if Mary chose to assign her life interest to him. If she did this, the inheritance tax consequences would again depend in part on whether Mary, or for that matter Edward, was a disabled person when the trust was settled. Edward would not become absolutely entitled – he would merely take over Mary's right to income for the rest of her life, after which Brian's interest would take effect as previously. The position can be summarised as follows:

(a) If Edward was not a disabled person when he put the property into the trust:

  (i) If Mary's interest had not been a qualifying IIP, the trust property would already be within the relevant property regime, and it would continue to be so without an IHT charge by reference to the assignment. However, although the gift with reservation rules would not have applied in Edward's case prior to Mary's assignment because he was excluded from benefit, they would apply once he became entitled to Mary's life interest; accordingly, on his death while Mary was still alive the trust property would be taxed as part of his estate on his death (without prejudice to any charge under the relevant property rules (FA 1986 s 102(3)). Alternatively, on the reservation ceasing during his lifetime (eg if he in turn assigned or relinquished the life interest, or if it came to an end through Mary's death while Edward was still living), Edward would be deemed to have made a potentially exempt transfer of the trust property concerned (FA 1986 s 102(4)), which would become chargeable if he were to die within seven years afterwards.

  (ii) If on the other hand Mary's interest had been a disabled person's interest (DPI) then (as with a relinquishment in favour of Brian on a continuing trust, see above) the assignment would give rise to a deemed transfer of value which (apart from annual exemptions so far as made available by her to the trustees by notice as above) would be an immediately chargeable transfer. The property concerned would become relevant property as Edward's interest in possession is taken not be a DPI as above. As a result of amendments to the 'gift with reservation' rules introduced in 2003 to counteract the decision in *IRC v Eversden* [2003] EWCA Civ 668; [2003] STC 822, Edward is not protected from those rules by the fact that the original gift to the trust attracted spouse exemption as a result of Mary's DPI (FA 1986 s 102(5)(a)).

(b) If Edward had been a disabled person when he put the property into the trust, his interest in possession would be a disabled person's interest (s 89B)(1)(c)) and he would therefore be treated as becoming beneficially entitled to the trust property (s 49(1A)(b)). (This would not be so if he were disabled at the date of Mary's assignment but not when he originally formed the trust, since he would not then be within the definition of 'disabled person' in s 89(4), (4A).) In principle Edward would still be subject to the gifts with reservation rules, but this would have no impact because he would already be treated as beneficially entitled to the trust property by reason of his DPI. Accordingly:

(i) If Mary's interest had not been a qualifying IIP, the property would leave the relevant property regime, incurring an exit charge in the process (see **Example C11 explanatory note 4**). On termination of Edward's interest in possession he would make a chargeable transfer (or a potentially exempt transfer if he were still living and Brian became absolutely entitled at that time).

(ii) If Mary's interest had also been a DPI, then her deemed transfer of value on termination of her interest in possession (ss 51, 52, see **Example C3**) would be an exempt transfer under s 18. If, on termination of Edward's interest in possession, the property remained in trust and Brian did not become absolutely entitled, the property would enter the relevant property regime at that time and for the purpose of the relevant property rules the settlement would be treated as commencing only at that time (s 80, see above (but again with ten-year anniversaries being based on the date of the original settlement by Edward, s 61(2)).

No question of entitlement to a residence nil-rate band arises in lifetime in relation to a lifetime gift of property.

The application of the gift with reservation rules in relation to Mary by virtue of FA 1986 s 102ZA, if her life interest was a DPI and so a qualifying IIP, would be the same as if she had released her interest to Brian instead of assigning it to Edward (see above).

Capital Gains Tax

Settlement by will

If Edward waits until his death to make the transfer into the settlement for Mary, there will be no capital gains tax payable because death is not a chargeable occasion for capital gains tax, although the deceased's assets are regarded as acquired at probate value by those on whom they devolve (ie legatees, trustees, or personal representatives as the case may be) (TCGA 1992 s 62). Therefore, on the trust property being released to the trustees by the executors, the trustees would be deemed to acquire the trust property at probate value at the date of Edward's death (TCGA 1992 s 62(4)).

Lifetime settlement

If Edward makes the transfer into the settlement for Mary during his lifetime, then the capital gains tax exemption for absolute transfers between spouses does not apply. Gift relief under TCGA 1992 s 165 or s 260 is not available in respect of disposals of assets to the trustees of a trust in which the settlor has an interest where the disposal is made on or after 10 December 2003 (s 169B–169G). Although Edward himself is excluded from benefit by the terms of the settlement, s 169F provides that any interest of the settlor's spouse is to be treated as the interest of the settlor.

These provisions also claw back or prevent any gifts relief in relation to disposals to trusts which become settlor-interested settlements within a certain time period. This period begins immediately after the disposal and ends immediately before the sixth anniversary of the start of the tax year next following that in which the disposal is made.

As Mary will have a life interest in the new settlement (whatever its treatment for inheritance tax), Edward will be deemed to have an interest in the settlement from the outset and holdover relief will not be available.

Death of life tenant

When a life tenant dies then, provided the life interest was a qualifying IIP including, in relation to deaths of vulnerable beneficiaries occurring on or after 5 December 2014, a deemed IIP ('a deemed DPI'), the trust property is treated as having been disposed of and immediately reacquired at probate value; but, as with the death of someone owning assets absolutely, there is no capital gains tax charge on the trust assets. (If the settlement had been made in lifetime and any gains had been deferred under the holdover provisions of s 165 or s 260 prior to 10 December 2003 – which however is not possible here because of the trust being treated as settlor-interested as referred to above – the deferred gains would become chargeable on the life tenant's death. If any of the property in the trust at that time is qualifying property for holdover relief under s 165, the deferred gains on that property could be the subject of a further claim for holdover relief.)

If therefore Mary's life interest is an IPDI or a DPI (including a deemed DPI), on her death neither the trustees nor Brian will be liable to capital gains tax in respect of the assets in the settlement. Those assets which devolve upon Brian (some may have to be sold in order to pay inheritance tax unless Brian wishes to retain all the assets and fund the tax by other means – perhaps by instalments if the property is instalment option property) will do so for capital gains purposes at their market value at the date of his mother's death, and those retained by the trustees in order to sell them to raise cash for the payment of inheritance tax will also have a base value equivalent to their market value at that time (TCGA 1992 s 73). (If Brian became absolutely entitled at Mary's death then the trustees would hold as bare trustees for Brian from then on and any disposals by them would be attributed to Brian anyway.)

If on the other hand Mary's life interest is not a qualifying IIP (or, as the case may be, not a deemed DPI) – as would be the case if Edward made the settlement in his lifetime and Mary was not a disabled person at the time – then her death would not give rise to any deemed disposal by the trustees unless and until Brian became absolutely entitled.

Release of life interest

If Mary relinquishes her entitlement during her lifetime (whether in favour of Brian or Edward), the position will be the same as on her death with a non-qualifying IIP (or, as the case may be, a non-deemed DPI): unless and until Brian becomes absolutely entitled there will be no deemed disposal by the trustees, but when he does, the trustees will be deemed to make a disposal at that time at the then market value, any gains held over if the settlement was created in lifetime becoming chargeable, and capital gains tax will be payable accordingly (less any annual exemption available to the trustees and subject to any available holdover relief or main residence exemption) (TCGA 1992 s 71).

Trustees' own gains

If, during the continuation of the trust, the trustees themselves realise capital gains on the disposal of trust assets, for example on the switching of investments, then the trustees will be liable to tax on the gains at 20% (or 28% if the gains are in respect of residential property), subject to availability of the annual exemption (TCGA 1992 Sch 1C para 5). The annual exemption for a trust (other than one which fulfils the conditions for a disabled person's trust in TCGA 1992 Sch 1C para 2 – a disabled person being defined in the same was as for inheritance tax purposes (that is in accordance with the meaning in FA 2005 Sch 1A) is half that available to individuals (£3,000 for 2023/24), provided it is the only settlement created by the settlor since 6 June 1978 (see **Example D2 part c**).

Income Tax

Tax liability of settlor and beneficiary

If the settlement is made by Edward in his lifetime, then since Mary is entitled to the income it will be treated as a settlement in which he retains an interest because she is his wife, and all income arising, whether distributed by the trustees or retained by them, will be liable to income tax as part of Edward's net income during his lifetime (ITTOIA 2005 s 624). Had Edward given Mary outright ownership of the property transferred rather than merely a right to income, the settlement rules would not have applied. However, the settlement is not sufficient effectively to transfer income from Edward to Mary for income tax purposes because he is giving her only a right to income and not outright ownership of the assets. Following Edward's death, the income whether distributed or not will be treated as Mary's income while her interest continues. This will also apply if the settlement is made on Edward's death.

Tax liability of trustees

The trustees in each case will have a default basic rate liability (or dividend ordinary rate liability if the income is dividend income) unless the income is mandated direct to Mary in order to save administrative cost and inconvenience. Any liability at the higher or additional rates (or dividend upper or dividend additional rates) will be assessed on Edward, or Mary his widow, as the case may be. Edward would be entitled to recover any tax paid by him from the trustees or from Mary (ITTOIA 2005 s 646).

Before 6 April 2016, where the trust income was either dividend income or had had basic rate tax deducted at source, it was HMRC practice to allow the trustees to omit the income from their tax return (because the income was taxable on the beneficiary whether distributed or not). The same treatment is accorded the trustees where they mandate trust income direct to the beneficiary so that it is taxable directly on the beneficiary (see TSEM 3040 and 3763). Following the abolition of the tax credit (FA 2016 Sch 1 para 1) and the repeal of the duty of banks and building societies to deduct basic rate tax at source from interest (s 39, Sch 6) an additional compliance burden will now fall on the trustees of interest in possession trusts as this practice does not prima facie apply. In their *Trusts and Estates Newsletter* dated April 2016 HMRC acknowledge this problem and have introduced the following interim arrangement. For 2016/17 HMRC will not require fresh self-assessment notification from trustees of both interest in possess and discretionary trusts (or personal representatives dealing with estates in administration) where the only source of income is savings interest and the tax liability is below £100. They have confirmed that the same arrangement will continue to apply for 2017/18 (*HMRC Trusts and Estates Newsletter*: April 2017) and 2018/19 (*HMRC Trusts and Estates Newsletter*: December 2017), 2019/20 and 2020/21 (*HMRC Trusts and Estates Newsletter*: August 2019) and 2021/22 and 2022/23 (*HMRC Trusts and Estates Newsletter*: May 2021). The same treatment will apply in 2023/24 (*HMRC Trusts and Estates Newsletter*: April 2023). From 2024/25 ITA 2007, s 24B (enacted by F(No 2)A 2023 s 29 and Sch 1 para 10) provides that where the net income of trustees is £500 or less, it is treated as being £0 so that effectively they are not charged to income tax.

Computation of the tax charged on Edward, and Mary after his death

Where income is treated as Edward's income, it is charged at the rates of income tax which would have applied in charging it if it had arisen directly to him. The amount on which he is charged to tax cannot be reduced by any trust expenses, since he is only permitted to deduct amounts that would have been deductible if he had received the income directly (ITTOIA 2005 ss 619, 621, 623; see **Tolley's Taxwise I 2023/24**). For a more detailed discussion on income taxed as that of the settler, see **Example F1**.

After Edward's death, Mary is taxed as the beneficiary of an interest in possession trust. Unless the income has been mandated directly to her, the trust expenses will be paid out of the taxed income of the trust, and the balance remaining will be paid to her, the trustees giving her a certificate indicating the amounts of tax deducted at the basic or dividend ordinary rate of tax as the case may be. The tax deducted will count towards the tax payable by her or (except so far as it comprises dividend tax credits, which are not repayable) will be refundable to her if it exceeds her liability.

Question

Explain, with appropriate reference to both statute and case law, what is meant by an 'interest in possession' in settled property, commenting specifically on the impact that powers granted to the trustees may have on the position.

Summarise the ways in which settlements with an 'interest in possession' are treated for inheritance tax purposes and explain the position both before and after the changes made by Finance Act 2006.

Answer

Meaning of 'interest in possession'

The Inheritance Tax Act 1984 (IHTA 1984) uses the term 'interest in possession' but it is not defined in the legislation. The meaning of the expression is essentially one of the general law: it must be an interest in the trust property (ie an entitlement, as distinct from a mere right to be considered as an object of a discretionary power); and the interest must be in possession (as distinct, primarily, from being in reversion such as to come into possession only at some time in the future).

The definition put forward by HMRC, and accepted by the House of Lords in *Pearson and Others v CIR* (1980), is that 'an interest in possession in settled property exists where the person having the interest has an immediate entitlement to any income produced by that property as the income arises; but that a discretion or power, in whatever form, which can be exercised after income arises so as to withhold it from that person negatives the existence of an interest in possession. For this purpose a power to accumulate income is regarded as a power to withhold it, unless any accumulations must be held solely for the person having the interest or his personal representatives.' Thus an interest in possession can be summarised as being a present right of present enjoyment, without any further decision of the trustees being required.

Having the present right of present enjoyment means that the beneficiary must have a right to enjoy the income (if any) of the settlement as it arises. A beneficiary may have an interest in possession in property which produces no income. It is not necessary for the beneficiary to be entitled to the gross income from the settled property: the fact that the trustees may deduct their administrative expenses from the gross income does not defeat a beneficiary's interest in possession. Because of this a beneficiary will still have an interest in possession even if he has to wait until expenses have been deducted before receiving the income.

There have been a number of cases in which the issue has been whether or not an interest in possession was created by reason of provisions allowing a beneficiary to reside in property owned by the trustees. This issue is essentially just one manifestation of the same test, namely a present right of present enjoyment. See for example *IRC v Lloyds Private Banking* (1998), *Woodhall's Executor v IRC* (2000), *Faulkner v IRC* (2001), *Cook and Daw v IRC* (2002), *Oakley and Hutson v IRC* (2005), *Judge v HMRC* (2005) and *Fairbairn's Trustees v HMRC* (2007) and *M Vincent* [2019] UKFTT 657.

An interest in possession will not subsist in settled property if the trustees have powers that affect the net income remaining after payment of administration expenses. Purely administrative powers such as power to pay taxes, to charge fees or pay insurance do not defeat an interest in possession. On the other hand the existence of dispositive powers such power to accumulate income, or a power to pay or apply income to or for the benefit of another beneficiary, will prevent an interest in possession from subsisting in the settled property.

However, it is immaterial whether or not powers exist which could bring an interest in possession to an end; if an interest meets the foregoing characteristics then, while it continues, it is an interest in possession, and the exercise of the powers in question would merely bring the interest to an end, not prevent its existence for the time being.

An interesting case in which it was held that an interest in possession did not exist is *Nicholas John Hall & Christopher Valentine Lopez (as trustees of the Carolina Raboni estate) v HMRC* [2023] UKFTT 32. In that case the deceased owned a house which was left to her nieces and nephews. However, the deceased had granted her friend the right to live rent free in the house for the rest of his life and the property could not be sold without his consent. The deceased's estate did not have enough money to pay her inheritance tax liability and her legatees paid the tax personally as they were unwilling to sell the house to raise the necessary funds (given that their aunt's friend was in occupation of the property). In identifying the nature of the right that the friend enjoyed in relation to the house and in answering the question whether the friend had an interest in possession in the house, the First-tier Tribunal asked what the executors could have done in the circumstances. The residuary beneficiaries could have compelled administration of the estate and HMRC could have compelled them to pay the deceased's tax liability. In order to do so, the only option they had was to sell the house. This meant that the friend enjoyed no interest in possession in the house because, there being a creditor in relation to the estate (ie HMRC), the friend could not enforce a right under the will to live there. He did not have an immediate right to occupy the house.

Inheritance tax treatment of settlements

Where property is held in trust, the inheritance tax treatment of that property depends on the type of trust. IHTA 1984 divides trusts into three categories:

- those where there is an interest in possession that results in the beneficiary being treated as beneficially entitled to the underlying settled property under s 49; as a result the property is within the beneficiary's estate for IHT purposes, and since 22 March 2006 these IIPs are referred to as **'qualifying IIPs'**;
- those where there is no qualifying IIP (and generally no interest in possession at all), but which are given a degree of privileged status (see **Example C10 explanatory note 8**); and
- all other trusts. The property in these (unless excluded property, typically within IHTA 1984 s 48(3), (3A)) will be in the 'relevant property' regime, which since 2006 can be regarded as the mainstream IHT rules for trusts; prior to 2006 the relevant property rules were largely confined to discretionary trusts. Since then many interest in possession trusts will be within the relevant property regime.

Qualifying interests in possession since FA 2006

As a preliminary point, in certain circumstances an interest in possession may be treated as existing for inheritance tax purposes even though none exists within the definition explored above. The treatment of such trusts for income tax and capital gains tax will follow the nature of the trust itself: there is no actual interest in possession and the deeming is solely for inheritance tax purposes; but it will of course be the inheritance tax treatment which affects the availability of capital gains tax holdover relief under TCGA 1992, s 260 if an asset leaves the settlement. Examples include the tenant's interest under a lease for life granted otherwise than for full consideration (s 43(3)); a discretionary trust of income that arises on forfeiture of a protected life interest under Trustee Act 1925 s 33; or a disabled person's trust under s 89(2) or s 89A. However these deemed interests in possession will only be qualifying IIPs if they fall into one or other of the four categories listed below.

Since 22 March 2006 the four cases where an interest in possession will be within s 49, such as to be a qualifying IIP, are as follows, provided in all cases the interest in possession is not in favour of a bereaved minor in circumstances where the trust falls within the rules for bereaved minors' trusts in s 71A (see below):

(a) *Pre-2006 interests* (a non-statutory term): Where the beneficiary has been entitled to the IIP since before 22 March 2006.

(b) *Transitional serial interests*: Where the beneficiary became, on or after 22 March 2006, beneficially entitled to the IIP in immediate succession to:

  (i) the qualifying IIP of a beneficiary who had been beneficially entitled to that IIP since before 22 March 2006, and where the succession (in lifetime or on death) took place before 6 October 2008 (s 49C);

  (ii) the qualifying IIP of the beneficiary's spouse or civil partner who had been beneficially entitled to that IIP since before 22 March 2006, and where the succession took place on the death of the spouse/civil partner (s 49D); or

  (iii) one of a succession of qualifying IIPs, going back to before 22 March 2006, in a contract of life insurance held in the trust immediately before that date, so long as each succession (other than the first within (i) above) took place on the death of the beneficiary with the previous estate IIP (s 49E).

(c) *Immediate post-death interests*: Where the settlement was effected by will or under the law relating to intestacy and the beneficiary became beneficially entitled to the IIP on the death in question (s 49A).

(d) *Disabled person's interests*: These are of four related types:

  (i) Where the beneficiary was a disabled person (within the definition in s 89(4)–(4A)) which incorporates the standard definition of a disabled person for tax purposes in FA 2005 Sch 1A – broadly, an individual incapable of looking after his affairs because of mental disorder, or one in receipt of attendance allowance, the care component of disability living allowance at the middle or highest rates (and from 6 April 2014 (by virtue of FA 2014 s 284(2)(a)), the mobility component at the higher rate of disability living allowance), the daily living component of personal independence payment (and from 6 April 2014 (by virtue of FA 2014 s 284(2)(b)), the mobility component of personal independence payment), increased disablement pension, constant attendance allowance or armed forces independence payment) at the date the property in question was originally settled, and either:

- has a deemed interest in possession within s 89(2) (which requires that, during his lifetime, there is no actual interest in possession and that, if any of the trust property or income arising from it is applied for his benefit (s 89(1)); or
- became beneficially entitled to his (actual) interest in possession on or after 22 March 2006 if the trusts on which the settled property is held provide that, if any of the trust property is applied during the disabled person's lifetime it is applied for his benefit (s 89B(1)(c)); or

(ii) where (on or after 22 March 2006) the beneficiary makes the settlement for his own benefit and he satisfies HMRC that, at that time, he has a condition which makes it reasonable to expect that he will as a result become a disabled person within the definition just mentioned, and either

- the beneficiary-settlor has a deemed interest in possession within s 89A (the conditions of which are similar to s 89(2)) but so that *any* application of trust property or any income arising from it during his lifetime must be for his benefit, and with the additional requirement that, if the settlement is capable of being brought to an end during his lifetime, then as a result either he will be absolutely entitled or another disabled person's interest within (i) above will subsist (s 89A(1), (2), (3)), or
- the beneficiary-settlor has an (actual) interest in possession on or after 22 March 2006 and *any* application of trust property during his lifetime must be for his benefit (s 89B(1)(d)).

In the case of trusts within s 89, s 89A, s 89B(1)(c) and s 89B(1)(d), they are not to be regarded as failing to satisfy the conditions described above only if the trustees have the powers of advancement conferred by the Trustee Act s 32 (or have powers to like effect) or have powers that enable them to apply otherwise than for the benefit of the person who is disabled or is expected to become disabled amounts (whether consisting of income or capital, or both) not exceeding the lower of £3,000 and 3% of the value of the settled property during the period in question (s 89(3), (3A), s 89A(6A), (6B) and s 89C(1), (2)).

The rules described above reflect the amendments made to the legislation by FA 2013 Sch 42 paras 6, 7 and 10. The new rules in s 89 and s 89A have effect in relation to property transferred into trust on or after 8 April 2013 (FA 2013 Sch 42 para 9(1)). Transitional provisions ensure that IHTA 1984 s 89 and s 89A continue to apply to property transferred on or after 8 April 2013 to 'grandfathered trusts', namely trusts that were created before that date and which have remained unchanged since that date, or that arise after that date under a will or codicil executed before 8 April 2013 which have remained unchanged since that date or that arise under a will created after 7 April 2013 that contains the same terms in relation to the trust as a will executed by the same settlor before that date (FA 2013 Sch 42 paras 9(2), 20). The new rules in s 89D(1)(c) and s 89D(1)(d) have effect in relation to property transferred into trust on or after 17 July 2013 (FA 2013 Sch 42 para 10(3)). Transitional provisions ensure that those sections continue to apply to property transferred on or after 17 July 2013 to 'grandfathered trusts' (defined as above but in relation to 17 July 2013 rather than 8 April 2013) (FA 2013 Sch 42 para 10(4), (5)).

With effect from 9 December 2009 a fifth category was added, namely:

(e) *Purchased IIPs*: Where the beneficiary became entitled to the IIP on or after 9 December 2009, at a time when he was domiciled in the UK, and did so under an arm's length transaction within s 10 (s 5(1B)).

If an interest in possession is a disabled person's interest then it cannot also be an immediate post-death interest or a transitional serial interest, even if it would otherwise meet the requirements for those respective categories.

The rules for bereaved minors' trusts are found in s 71A and, if applicable, take priority over those for qualifying IIPs (though an IIP in favour of a minor will be unusual). They apply only where the settlement in question:

(1) was set up for the benefit of a beneficiary under age 18 at least one of whose parents has died (note the extended meaning of 'parent' in s 71H which includes step-parents and those with parental responsibilities):

- by a parent of the beneficiary in their will;

- by the English intestacy rules on the death of the beneficiary's parent or remoter ancestor. (Before 1 February 2012, this could only arise in the case of remoter ancestors if the intervening generation(s) had already died. With effect from 1 February 2012, under the Estates of Deceased Persons (Forfeiture Rule and the Law of Succession) Act 2011, an individual may, in certain circumstances, inherit on the intestacy of a remoter ancestor where the intervening generation(s) have not died.);
- under the Criminal Injuries Compensation Scheme; or
- under the Victims of Overseas Terrorism Compensation Scheme,

(2) ring-fences the whole of the capital and income (except for a small annual amount not exceeding the lower of £3,000 and 3% of the value of the settled property during the period in question) for the benefit of the beneficiary during his minority, and

(3) gives the beneficiary the capital and income of the trust absolutely when he reaches the age of 18.

Inheritance tax treatment of trusts with a qualifying interest in possession

Where s 49 does apply, the value of the settled property in which the qualifying IIP subsists forms part of the estate of that person for IHT purposes.

There are two consequences:

(a) Distributions of capital to the beneficiary with the qualifying IIP do not attract an inheritance tax charge, unlike the position with relevant property trusts. The supporting capital was previously part of the taxpayer's estate in the form of trust property and is now part of his estate in the form of free estate.

(b) On the beneficiary's death the settled property is aggregated with his free estate and tax is charged on the entirety. If the qualifying IIP comes to an end in any other way, or is disposed of by the beneficiary in his lifetime, this involves a deemed transfer of value by the beneficiary, with effects on his inheritance tax accumulation as if he had made the gift out of his free capital.

Since 22 March 2006, such a transfer in the beneficiary's lifetime is a PET (or exempt, if in favour of his spouse/civil partner) only if:

- another individual becomes absolutely entitled,
- a disabled person's interest arises,
- a transitional serial interest arises (which is not possible after 5 October 2008 for lifetime transfers), or
- the qualifying IIP was an immediate post-death interest (not a disabled person's interest) and the property becomes held for a minor child of the deceased settlor under a bereaved minor's trust (s 3A(1A)).

In other cases where the trust continues (other than for wholly charitable purposes), the termination of the qualifying IIP will involve an immediately chargeable transfer and the property will no longer form part of the beneficiary's estate; but if the beneficiary remains interested it will be caught by the gifts with reservation rules at his death or when the reservation ceases.

Although the tax liability in respect of the settled property will usually be imposed on the trustees rather than on the beneficiary with the qualifying IIP, the effect of this treatment is to increase the rate of tax on any subsequent chargeable transfer by the beneficiary or, in the case of a liability on death, to increase the estate rate and therefore the tax payable on the beneficiary's free estate at death by reason of the aggregation of the free estate and the settled property.

Inheritance tax treatment of relevant property trusts (with or without an interest in possession)

The relevant property rules can be briefly summarised as follows (see further **Examples C10 to C13**):

(a) On the tenth anniversary of the creation of the settlement it is subject to a ten-year charge (s 64).

The charge, on the value of the relevant property after deducting any business property relief or agricultural property relief, is 30% of the tax (calculated at the rate of 20%) that would be payable on a notional chargeable transfer (see **(c)(i) below**); for many years it has been impossible therefore for the resultant rate to exceed 6%, but this would be affected if, for example, the scale of rates on death were to change to include a rate higher than 40%.

A further such charge will occur every ten years thereafter.

(b) There is also an exit charge when property in such a settlement ceases to be relevant property (either because the property leaves the settlement or for any other reason, for example the property becoming subject to a qualifying IIP – now in practice confined to a disabled person's interest) (s 65).

The charge in this event is at a proportion of the rate used on the last ten-year anniversary (that proportion being based on the number of complete quarter-years (fortieths) that have elapsed since that last ten-year anniversary). This will be suitably adjusted if further property has been settled since the ten-year anniversary, or if property which was not relevant property at that time has become relevant property since then (s 69).

If there has not yet been a ten-year anniversary, the rate to which the X fortieths fraction is applied is again worked out by reference to a notional chargeable transfer, different to that used for the ten-yearly charge (see **(c)(ii) below**) (s 68).

(c) The rate scale used when working out the tax on these notional chargeable transfers is what could be called the scale for lifetime chargeable transfers, ie one half of the normal (death) scale applicable at the date of charge. The trust has its own inheritance tax accumulation, based primarily on that of the settlor when he put property into the trust (although in certain circumstances this can be replaced with a later cumulative total if greater).

(i) In respect of ten-year anniversaries falling on or after 18 November 2015 the notional chargeable transfer used to work out the tax on a ten-yearly charge (which is then used in relation to subsequent exit charges) in respect of the settlement under consideration ('the primary settlement') is, under s 66(4), generally the value of the relevant property itself, plus any relevant property in related settlements (those made on the same date), the value of any same-day additions to the primary settlement (as defined in s 62A), and certain aggregable same-day additions to non-related settlements, In the case of settlements other than the primary settlement, the value used is that immediately after the property in question was settled (historic amount), whereas the relevant property in the primary settlement is valued at the date of the ten-yearly charge (current amount). Same-day additions are valued as set out in s 62A(2). The IHT accumulation to be used will be that of the settlor in the seven years before he made the trust (or if greater, the cumulative total in the seven years before he later added property to the trust), but will include also the amount on which exit charges (**(b) above**) have been imposed in the ten years leading up to the ten-yearly charge.

In respect of ten-year anniversaries falling before 18 November 2015 the calculation of the notional chargeable transfer used to work out the tax on a ten-yearly charge (which is then used in relation to subsequent exit charges) is generally a transfer of the relevant property itself, plus other property in the trust that has never yet been relevant property, and any property in related settlements (those made on the same date). In the latter two cases the value used is that immediately after the property in question was settled (historic amount), whereas the relevant property is valued at the date of the ten-yearly charge (current amount). The IHT accumulation to be used will be that of the settlor in the seven years before he made the trust (or if greater, the cumulative total in the seven years before he later added property to the trust), but will include also the amount on which exit charges (**(b) above**) have been imposed in the ten years leading up to the ten-yearly charge.

If the settlement was made before the introduction of capital transfer tax on 27 March 1974, the only components of the notional transfer are the value of the relevant property at the date of the ten-yearly charge, and the amount subjected to exit charges in the preceding ten years.

(ii) In respect of an exit charge occurring on or after 18 November 2015 and before any ten-year anniversary has occurred, the notional chargeable transfer used to work out the tax is based on the value of the relevant trust property (and of relevant property in any related settlement) immediately after it was settled (without the benefit, for this purpose, of any reliefs) and other property added later, using the settlor's IHT accumulation in the preceding seven years (s 68(5)).

In respect of an exit charge occurring before 18 November 2015 and before any ten-year anniversary occurred, the notional chargeable transfer used to work out the tax was based on the value of the trust property (and of that in any related settlement) immediately after it was settled (without the benefit, for this purpose, of any reliefs) and other property added later, using the settlor's IHT accumulation in the preceding seven years.

Explanatory Notes

Inheritance tax privileged trusts with a non-qualifying interest in possession

(1) It is technically possible for an interest in possession to subsist in favour of the beneficiary of either of the two forms of privileged trusts for younger beneficiaries introduced by FA 2006:

(a) a bereaved minor's trust, subsisting under the will or intestacy of the beneficiary's deceased parent where the child is still under age 18 and will become absolutely entitled to capital by age 18 (s 71A);

(b) an age 18-to-25 trust where the beneficiary is still under age 25 and will become absolutely entitled to capital by age 25 (s 71D). Such a trust may subsist either under the will of the beneficiary's deceased parent, or in favour of a beneficiary under a pre-2006 trust which until 5 April 2008 was within the former regime for accumulation and maintenance trusts in s 71.

It will be rare for an interest in possession to subsist while the beneficiary is under age 18, because Trustee Act 1925 s 31 has the effect of precluding an interest in possession pending attainment of that age (*Stanley v IRC* (1944)). Deliberate drafting to exclude the effects of that section would be needed. But if the beneficiary does have an interest in possession during his minority then it shares some limited characteristics with a qualifying IIP (but specifically without bringing the trust property within the beneficiary's estate) and could on that account be termed a 'privileged minor's IIP':

- distributions of capital for the beneficiary's benefit, or such that he becomes absolutely entitled not later than age 18, will not attract an inheritance tax charge (ss 71B(2)(a), (c), 71E(2)(a), (d)) – though this is of course the case whether or not he has an interest in possession;

- a capital gains tax uplift in base value applies on the beneficiary's death under age 18 (TCGA 1992 ss 72(1A), (1B), 73(2A)).

Once the beneficiary has passed age 18 without having become absolutely entitled (under an age 18-to-25 trust) – whether or not he attains an interest in possession at that point – both these advantages evaporate, though the trust remains outside the relevant property regime and the rate of tax on his absolute entitlement or death may well be more favourable.

Creation of interest in possession settlement: inheritance tax and capital gains tax consequences

(2) Until 2006 the lifetime formation of an interest in possession trust for an individual – though triggering a chargeable disposal of the assets in question for capital gains tax purposes (see **Example D2 explanatory note** 4) – would not involve an immediate chargeable transfer:

- either it was neutral if in favour of the settlor himself,

- or it was an exempt transfer if in favour of the settlor's spouse or civil partner, or to the extent that it was covered by annual or marriage gift exemptions or the normal income expenditure exemption,

- or it was a potentially exempt transfer if in favour of any other individual – so that (apart from the gift with reservation rules) an actual charge to inheritance tax would be escaped if the settlor survived for seven years, and even if he failed to do so the value transferred would be fixed at the date of the transfer even if the trust property had increased in value by the time the settlor died.

Since 22 March 2006, the transfer of assets to either sort of trust (even if for the benefit of the settlor or his spouse or civil partner) will constitute an immediately chargeable transfer for inheritance tax (save where covered by the annual or normal income expenditure exemptions), and the trust will be within the relevant property regime, with the sole exception of a transfer to a trust conferring a disabled person's interest. Care is needed in cases where the trust is for the settlor's benefit: see the Example in **explanatory note** 4 below.

The transfer will still involve a disposal for capital gains tax purposes; but because it is immediately chargeable – provided the trustees are UK resident, and subject to the important exception of settlor-interested trusts (TCGA 1992 s 169B–169C) – holdover relief will be available under TCGA 1992 s 260 so that an immediate capital gains tax charge need not be incurred.

Furthermore, if a UK resident beneficiary later becomes absolutely entitled to the same asset under the relevant property trust (or a non UK resident beneficiary becomes so entitled where the asset concerned is UK residential property (extended from 6 April 2019 to all landed property and shares in companies and interest in partnerships and trusts deriving 75% of their value from land) within the scope of NRCGT), holdover relief should again be available to allow him to take over the trustees' base value which in turn would have been based on that of the settlor. Holdover relief will also be available in the case of a settlor-interested trust where a UK resident beneficiary becomes absolutely entitled to an asset under a relevant property trust. (See however the warning about entitlements within three months after commencement of the settlement, or after a ten-year anniversary, in **Example D2 explanatory note 6**.)

Interest in possession settlements in the context of the inheritance tax residence nil-rate band

(3) In the context of the RNRB, a home is 'inherited' by an individual (B) where the home becomes comprised on an individual's (D) death in a trust and B becomes beneficially entitled on D's death to an IIP in the home provided the IIP is an immediate post-death interest under s 49A or a disabled person's interest under s 89 (s 8J(4)(a)). The home is closely inherited where B is in the qualifying class of individuals set out in s 8K. Where immediately before D's death, a home is settled property in which D was beneficially entitled to an interest in possession (which by necessary implication means that D must have enjoyed a qualifying interest in possession in the trust property), B inherits the home if B becomes beneficially entitled to it on D's death (s 8J(5)). Reading the provisions of s 8J(5) in the context of 8J(4)(a), this means the home must pass into B's ownership absolutely. Again, the home is closely inherited where B is in the qualifying class of individuals set out in s 8K. See **Example A2 explanatory note (3)** for additional information in this regard.

Discretionary or relevant property trusts

(4) Detailed notes on the tax treatment of relevant property trusts are given in **Examples C10 to C14**.

Question

A.

Robin died on 31 January 2006 and the inheritance tax on his estate was payable out of residue at an estate rate of 25%.

His will provided for the following (separate from the gift of residue):

(1) A bequest to his married daughter Merle of 25,000 shares of £1 each in Fieldfare plc, quoted on the Stock Exchange at 398–406p.

(2) The creation of a settlement, the assets of which amounted to £30,000, under which the income was payable to Merle for life, then to Merle's daughter Jenny for life, with remainder to Merle's son Martin. None of the assets of the settlement was residential property.

On 1 November 2015 Merle gave Jenny 12,500 of the shares in Fieldfare plc that she had inherited from her father. The shares were quoted on that day at 272–276p. She had made previous potentially exempt transfers amounting to £299,000 (after exemptions), all on 1 January 2010.

Merle and Jenny were involved in an accident and as a result Merle died on 20 January 2016, leaving her free estate to her son Martin. Jenny survived the accident but was left mentally disabled on account of the severe head injuries that she had sustained. She eventually died on 31 August 2023, having made no lifetime transfers, and leaving her estate (which included no residential property) to her brother Martin. Jenny had been born on 19 January 1991.

Their respective estates were valued for probate as follows:

	Merle	*Jenny*
	20.1.16	*31.8.23*
	£	£
12,500 shares each in Fieldfare plc	36,750	38,000
Other assets (net of liabilities)	24,025	276,250
Settled fund (net of liabilities)	32,000	22,750

(a) Compute the inheritance tax payable on the death of Merle on 20 January 2016.

(b) Without performing any computations, explain the basis on which inheritance tax will be charged on the death of Jenny on 31 August 2023.

B.

On the assumption that Jenny is Merle's civil partner (rather than her daughter) and that Martin is Jenny's brother (but not the son of Merle), calculate the inheritance tax arising on Jenny's death on 31 August 2023.

C.

Lavinia died on 14 November 2023 owning property valued at £450,000. She had lived in rented accommodation all her life and so did not own a home at the time of her death. Under her will a UK national, registered charity was to benefit from a pecuniary legacy of £75,000. In addition to the property she alone owned, her estate included property valued for inheritance tax purposes at £750,000 which she owned beneficially as joint tenants and a qualifying IIP in trust property valued at £1,875,000. In computing the amount of tax payable on her death, it is ascertained that her estate was entitled to quick succession relief in the sum of £120,000.

Calculate the tax payable as a result of Lavinia's death on the assumption that she made no lifetime transfers and identify who pays the tax and the amount payable by each of them.

Answer

A.

(a) Inheritance tax payable on death of Merle (20 January 2016)

				Gross £	Tax on 2015/16 scale £
Gifts within seven years before death:					
1 January 2010				299,000	Nil
1 November 2015					
Gift to Jenny 12,500 shares @ 273			34,125		
Less: Annual exemptions	2015/16	3,000			
	2014/15	3,000	(6,000)		
Potentially exempt transfer now chargeable				28,125	850*
Cumulative transfers in seven years prior to death				327,125	850*

(* 327,125 – 325,000 = 2,125 @ 40%)

Estate of Merle deceased

	Date of death 20 January 2016 £
Free estate:	
12,500 shares in Fieldfare plc	36,750
Other assets (net of liabilities)	24,025
	60,775
Settled property (Robin's will trust) (net of liabilities)	32,000
Chargeable to inheritance tax on death	92,775

		Tax on 2015/16 scale £
Cumulative transfers in seven years prior to death	327,125	850
Chargeable estate on death	92,775	37,110*
	419,900	37,960

(* £92,775 @ 40% = £37,110)

Inheritance tax payable:

On gifts within seven years before death			
	Payable by transferees of gifts in 2009/10 (previously potentially exempt transfers)		Nil
	Payable by Jenny re gift of shares on 1 November 2015, previously potentially exempt		£850
On estate at death as computed			37,110
Less:	Quick succession relief re gift of shares from Robin (see **explanatory notes 5 and 6**)		
	$20\% \text{ of } \left(\frac{100{,}000}{133{,}333} \times 33{,}333\right)$	5,000	
	Quick succession relief re settled property (see **explanatory notes 5 and 7**)		
	$20\% \text{ of } \left(\frac{30{,}000}{40{,}000} \times 10{,}000\right)$	1,500	(6,500)
Inheritance tax payable on Merle's estate			£30,610

Payable by executors:

$$\frac{60{,}775}{92{,}775} \times 30{,}610 \qquad £20{,}052$$

Payable by trustees of settled property:

$$\frac{32{,}000}{92{,}775} \times 30{,}610 \qquad £10{,}558$$

(b) Inheritance tax payable on death of Jenny (31 August 2023)

Robin's death occurred before 22 March 2006 and so Merle's life interest under his will in the fund of £30,000 is an interest that arose before 22 March 2006 and as such it is a qualifying IIP. However, Jenny's successor life interest in the fund is not a qualifying IIP. It does not qualify as a transitional serial interest because Jenny did not succeed to it until after 5 October 2008 (IHTA 1984 s 49C(3)) (see **explanatory note 8**).

Even though Jenny was mentally disabled when she succeeded to the interest in possession and for the whole time she was entitled to it between Merle's death and her own, Jenny's interest in possession is also not a disabled person's interest. She can only be a 'disabled person' within the definition in s 89(4), (4A) if her disability existed at the time the property was transferred into the settlement, ie in this case on Robin's death on 31 January 2006.

The settled property will therefore not form part of Jenny's estate on her death on 31 August 2023; without it, her estate of £314,250 is below the 2023/24 nil-rate band of £325,000, and thus no inheritance tax is due on it even before invoking quick succession relief in respect of Merle's gift of shares.

Instead, despite Jenny's interest in possession, the settled fund will have been within the relevant property regime in the period between Merle's and Jenny's deaths. An exit charge arises under s 65 on Martin becoming absolutely entitled when Jenny dies, and this is after the first ten-year anniversary (following Merle's death on 20 January 2016) which occurred on 31 January 2016. The rate of tax applicable when Martin becomes absolutely entitled to the trust property is that which applied at that previous ten-year anniversary. Assuming that Robin's will did not create any other settlements, the rate of tax under s 66 at the ten-year anniversary will be established by reference to:

- the effective rate on a notional transfer, at the 20% lifetime rate, of the value of the trust property on 30 January 2016 by a transferor with Robin's inheritance tax accumulation immediately before his death;
- multiplied by thirty fortieths (thirty completed quarters expired between 31 January 2016 and 31 August 2023).

However, the calculation has the benefit of the 2023/24 nil-rate band of £325,000. Robin's inheritance tax accumulation immediately before his death must have been less than £295,000 (£325,000 nil-rate band less £30,000 initial value), since the estate rate at his death (with net assets in his estate after tax in excess of a minimum of £130,000) was well below 40% with the 2005/06 nil-rate band being £275,000. Accordingly, whether a charge arises on 31 August 2023 when Martin becomes absolutely entitled to trust property depends upon the value of the property on 30 January 2016. From the values of the settled property given on 20 January 2016 and 31 August 2023 this appears to be in the range £32,000 to £22,750 so that any exit charge will be very small indeed.

Because Jenny's life interest was not a qualifying IIP, there is no exemption from capital gains tax on any unrealised gains within the trust fund on Martin's becoming absolutely entitled on her death. Even if no inheritance tax is actually charged in respect of the relevant property exit charge, that does not stop it from being a chargeable transfer for inheritance tax, so if Martin is UK resident (unless the asset is UK residential property in which case his residence is immaterial) it is open to him and the trustees to claim holdover relief under TCGA 1992 s 260.

B.

Inheritance tax payable on death of Jenny (31 August 2023)

If Jenny were the civil partner of Merle, then her life interest under Robin's will in the fund of £30,000 is a qualifying IIP. Jenny's successor life interest in the fund is a qualifying IIP because, being a life interest that succeeds a pre-22 March 2006 qualifying IIP enjoyed by her civil partner, it qualifies as a transitional serial interest. This is so despite Jenny not succeeding to Merle's qualifying IIP until after 5 October 2008 – the limitation date not applying in a case where the successor life interest arises on the death of a spouse or civil partner (IHTA 1984 s 49D) (see **explanatory note 9**).

Estate of Jenny deceased

	Date of death 31 August 2023
	£
Free estate:	
12,500 shares in Fieldfare plc	38,000
Other assets (net of liabilities)	276,250
	314,250
Settled property (Robin's will trust) (net of liabilities)	22,750
	£337,000

Inheritance tax payable:

	£
Tax payable on Jenny's estate is (337,000 – 325,000) = 12,000 @ 40%	4,800

Payable by executors:

$$\frac{314,250}{337,000} \times 4,800$$ £4,476

Payable by trustees of settled property:

$$\frac{22,750}{337,000} \times 4,800$$ £324

C. Death of Lavinia — 14 November 2023

Inheritance tax on death

	Gross £	*Tax on 2023/24 scale* £
Cumulative transfers within seven years before death	Nil	Nil
Estate on death (after legacy to charity)	3,000,000	1,056,625*
(* See choice of rate workings below)		

Inheritance tax payable:

		£	£
Due on estate before QSR (see choice of rate workings)			
General component		120,375	
Survivorship component		267,500	
Settled property component		668,750	
			1,056,625
Less:	Quick succession relief (see QSR workings below)		
	General component	13,671	
	Survivorship component	30,380	
	Settled property component	75,949	(120,000)
Tax payable on Lavinia's death			£936,625

The tax due of £936,625 is payable by as follows:

By the personal representatives:	(120,375 – 13,671) =	£106,704
By the surviving joint tenant:	(267,500 – 30,380) =	£237,120
By the trustees of settlement:	(668,750 – 75,949) =	£592,801
		£936,625

Choice of rate workings – Lavinia's estate

Given that Lavinia has left a pecuniary legacy to a UK national, registered charity it is necessary to investigate whether inheritance tax is charged at the lower rate.

Five steps are followed to ascertain this:

Step 1: Calculate the chargeable amount of each component of Lavinia's (ie the gross value of the property comprised in the component after deducting liabilities, reliefs and exemptions).

	Survivor-ship component	*Settled property component*	*General component*
	£	£	£
Value of components after Step 1	750,000	1,875,000	375,000

Step 2: Deduct from the amount of each component determined under Step 1, the appropriate proportion of the available nil-rate band applicable to each component (ie the amount of nil-rate band left over after allowing for any increase that arises from the transfer of unused nil-rate band under IHTA 1984 s 8A and taking into account any chargeable transfers made during the seven years before death). Lavinia's available nil-rate band is £325,000 and it is allocated between the components as follows:

Survivorship component: 750,000/3,000,000 × 325,000 = £81,250

Settled property component: 1,875,000/3,000,000 × 325,000 = £203,125

General component: 375,000/3,000,000 × 325,000 = £40,625

	Survivor-ship component	*Settled property component*	*General component*
	£	£	£
Value of components after Step 1	750,000	1,875,000	375,000
Less: apportioned nil-rate band	(81,250)	(203,125)	(40,625)
Value of components after Step 2	668,750	1,671,875	334,375

Step 3: Add to the amount of each component determined under Step 2, any charitable donation(s) from which it is (they are) paid and restate the chargeable amount of each component of the estate. This amount is the 'baseline amount' of each component.

	Survivor-ship component	*Settled property component*	*General component*
	£	£	£
Value of components after Step 2	668,750	1,671,875	334,375
Add: gift to charity			75,000
Baseline amount of each component	668,750	1,671,875	409,375

Step 4: Perform the 10% test – that is, compare with 10% of the baseline amount for each component, the 'donated amount' (ie the charitable donation) in respect of the component. The donated amount made from a component must be at least 10% of the baseline amount of that component if the 10% test is to be satisfied.

In Lavinia's case the donated amount is £75,000 and is paid wholly out of the general component of the estate. So the 10% test is applied in relation to that component only. The baseline amount of the general component is

£409,375 and 10% of the baseline amount is £40,375. The test is whether the donated amount is at least 10% of the relevant component. Here, as the donated amount of £75,000 is larger than £40,375, the 10% test is met.

Step 5: As the 10% test is met in relation to the general component, tax is charged on the chargeable amount of the general component of Lavinia's estate at 36% (which in this case equates to the amount ascertained after Step 2 above). The property comprised in the other components of Lavinia's estate is charged to tax at 40%.

	Gross		*Tax on 2023/24 scale*
	£		£
General component of the estate	334,375	@ 36%	120,375
Survivorship component	668,750	@ 40%	267,500
Settled property component	1,671,875	@ 40%	668,750
Total tax payable in respect of the estate			1,056,625

QSR workings in respect of Lavinia's estate

Where an estate contains more than one component and not all of the components qualify for the lower rate (but at least one of them does), any QSR must be apportioned between them under IHTA 1984 s 141A. Under this section QSR is so apportioned by reference to the tax payable in respect of each component. The QSR available in Lavinia's case is 120,000 and is divided as follows:

General component: 120,375/1,056,625 × 120,000 = £13,671

Survivorship component: 267,500/1,056,625 × 120,000 = £30,380

Settled property component: 668,750/1,056,625 × 120,000 = £75,949

Explanatory Notes

Inheritance tax quick succession relief

(1) Under the provisions of IHTA 1984 s 141, quick succession relief applies where the value of a person's chargeable estate for inheritance tax purposes was increased by a chargeable transfer made not more than five years before

(a) his death, or

(b) a lifetime charge on settled property in which the deemed transferor had a qualifying interest in possession (where the earlier transfer was or included the making of the settlement or was made after the making of the settlement). The terms of this limb of s 141 are such that it can only refer to a qualifying IIP (as defined in **Example C3**), even though no express restriction was introduced by FA 2006.

The rates of quick succession relief are as follows:

Period between earlier and later transfers	*Percentage relief*
1 year or less	100%
1+ to 2 years	80%
2+ to 3 years	60%
3+ to 4 years	40%

Period between earlier and later transfers	*Percentage relief*
4+ to 5 years	20%

The percentage relief is calculated on the part of the tax paid on the previous transfer that the net value then transferred bears to the gross chargeable transfer at that time, or, in the terms of s 141 itself, 'a percentage of the tax charged on so much of the value transferred by the first transfer as is attributable to the increase [in the recipient's estate]': some of the tax charged on that gross value transferred is attributable to the tax itself.

Where the later transfer is made on death, whether it relates to free estate or settled property, the quick succession relief reduces the total tax chargeable because of the death, as shown in **part (a)** of the Example, so that the apportionment of the tax payable between free estate and settled property is of the tax as reduced by quick succession relief. This is the effect of s 141(3) which strictly provides that quick succession relief is apportioned between the free estate and the settled estate by reference to the capital values of each.

Inheritance tax – quick succession relief and successive transfers

(2) Where an individual who has a qualifying IIP in settled property transfers parts of his interest therein at different times and more than one later transfer occurs within five years of his acquisition of the life interest, then quick succession relief is available on the second and subsequent transfers within the five years, but only to the extent of any tax not used up on the earlier transfers. In this connection a transfer uses up the full amount of tax paid on the earlier transfer of which the tax relievable on the later transfer is a percentage (s 141(4), (5)).

For example:

A grants a life interest to B by will trust. Within two years B releases part of his interest to a discretionary trust (C), then in the fifth year after A's death B releases the remainder of his interest to a second discretionary trust (D).

The proportion of tax on A's transfer relevant to the increase in B's estate is say £25,000. Transfer of part interest within two years to C trust attracts tax of say £8,000 and transfer of remainder to D trust within five years tax of say £7,000.

The quick succession relief available on the transfer to the C trust is 80% × £25,000 so the amount of £8,000 is fully covered by quick succession relief, representing £10,000 of the original £25,000 (£8,000 = 80% × £10,000) leaving £15,000 still available. The transfer to the D trust attracts quick succession relief of 20% of £15,000 = £3,000 to set against the tax payable of £7,000.

Valuation of quoted securities for inheritance tax

(3) Quoted securities are valued one quarter up from the lower of the two quoted prices. Thus on Robin's death a quotation of 398–406p per share becomes 400p (398 +(406 – 398)/4).

Inheritance tax quick succession relief: gift by Merle to Jenny of inherited shares

(4) Quick succession relief was not available on Merle's gift of the Fieldfare plc shares to Jenny despite Merle having acquired the shares by a chargeable transfer on death less than five years earlier, because it only applies where the *later transfer* is on death or termination of an estate IIP in settled property.

Inheritance tax quick succession relief: position on death of Merle

(5) As Merle's death occurred more than four years but within five years after Robin's death, quick succession relief is available at 20%. The quick succession relief applies both on the shares transferred to her and on the life interest in the settled fund that passes to Jenny on Merle's death.

(6) The value of the shares transferred to Merle on Robin's death was:

25,000 shares in Fieldfare plc @ 400p (see **explanatory note 3**)	100,000
Tax thereon (25% of gross = 25/75 of net)	33,333
Gross transfer	£133,333

(7) The value of the assets transferred to the settled fund on Robin's death was:

Assets	30,000
Tax thereon (25% of gross = 25/75 of net)	10,000
Gross transfer	£40,000

Position on death of Jenny: status of IIP for inheritance tax

(8) In **part A** of the Example Jenny's interest in Robin's will trust would have been a transitional serial interest, and therefore a qualifying IIP (see further **Example 4C3**), if (under s 49C):

(i) the settlement was set up before 22 March 2006 (on Robin's death on 31 January 2006); and

(ii) immediately before 22 March 2006, there was an individual (Merle) with a beneficial interest in possession in the settlement; and

(iii) that person's interest must have come to an end after 21 March 2006 but before 6 October 2008; and

(iv) Jenny became beneficially entitled to that interest at that time; and

(v) the interest is not a disabled person's interest (see **part A(b)** of the Example); and

(vi) Jenny is not a minor and therefore the trust for her cannot be subject to the rules for bereaved minors' trusts in s 71A.

The condition in (iii) is not satisfied as Merle's interest in possession (which arose on Robin's death and hence before 22 March 2006) came to an end on Merle's death on 20 January 2016 (which is after 5 October 2008). Consequently, Jenny is not treated as beneficially entitled to the assets in the fund at her death.

(9) In **part B** of the Example Jenny's interest in Robin's will trust is a transitional serial interest, and therefore a qualifying IIP (see further **Example C3**), because (under s 49D):

(i) the settlement was set up before 22 March 2006 (on Robin's death on 31 January 2006); and

(ii) immediately before 22 March 2006, there was an individual (Merle) with a beneficial interest in possession in the settlement; and

(iii) that person's interest must have come to an end after 21 March 2006 and after 5 October 2008 on his death (which it did on Merle's death on 20 January 2016); and

(iv) that person (ie the person who died) was the spouse or civil partner of the person (Jenny) who succeeded to the beneficial interest in possession; and

(v) Jenny became beneficially entitled to that interest at the time of Merle's death; and

(vi) the interest is not a disabled person's interest (see **part A(b)** of the Example); and

(vii) Jenny is not a minor and therefore the trust for her cannot be subject to the rules for bereaved minors' trusts in s 71A.

(10) In **part B** of the Example, on Jenny's death no additional tax arises in relation to the gift by Merle of the shares in Fieldfare plc on 1 November 2015 as they were transferred by one civil partner to another and so were exempt from inheritance tax.

(11) In both **part A** and **part B** of the Example, Jenny's death does not occur within five years after that of Robin and so quick succession relief is not in point. Had it done so, although the same fund is charged on both deaths, Jenny's estate was not increased by Robin's chargeable transfer and so quick succession relief is not applicable on Jenny's death by reference to Robin's chargeable transfer in any event.

(12) For more details regarding the inheritance tax regime for relevant property trusts touched on in **part A(b)** of the Example see **Examples C10** to **C13**.

Quick succession relief in the context of the lower rate of inheritance tax

(13) Quick succession relief reduces the tax chargeable on the value transferred on death (ie the value of a deceased person's estate). Where no charitable legacy is provided for in the deceased's will, quick succession relief is apportioned between the components of the estate by reference to the capital values of the components (s 141) – see **part A(a)** of this Example and the apportionment of quick succession relief in respect of Merle's estate.

In a case where a charitable legacy is provided for in the deceased's will, this method of apportionment will also be employed where:

(i) his estate comprises only one component which qualifies for the lower rate of inheritance tax, or

(ii) his estate comprises more than one component and all the components qualify for the lower rate of inheritance tax.

However, where the estate contains more than one component and not all of the components qualify for the lower rate of inheritance tax but at least one of them does so qualify, then the method of apportioning quick succession relief to be employed between the components is that provided for in s 141A (introduced by FA 2013 Sch 23 para 7). Under this method, as illustrated in **part C** of this Example, quick succession relief is apportioned by reference to the tax payable by each component and not its capital value (s 141A(3), (4)). Where one or more components of an estate are merged pursuant to elections made under Sch 1A para 7 the apportionment under s 141A(3) is carried out by reference to the single notional component thereby created (and not the individual components forming part of the deemed single component) (s 141A(5)). For a detailed explanation of the merger of components of an estate see **Example B12**.

The reason for the introduction of this modified method of apportionment is that quick succession relief operates so as to reduce the tax chargeable on the value of the aggregate estate. Where the lower rate of inheritance tax applies, the total tax chargeable will be lower than at the full rate. If quick succession relief continued to be apportioned by reference to the capital value of the components of the estate, the component qualifying for the lower rate of inheritance tax (the general component in **part C** of this Example) would be entitled to quick succession relief as if it bore tax at the full rate (ie as if it were bearing an equal proportion of the overall tax – which, of course it is not if it is paying tax at the lower rate). By apportioning the quick succession relief by reference to the tax due on each component (and not its capital value), the result is the relief reflects the fact that the component qualifying for the lower rate of inheritance tax is bearing a smaller proportion of the overall tax liability.

Question

Mr Maxford died on 7 January 2024. He was UK domiciled. The following information is held:

(1) He had previously owned a 14% shareholding (70,000 shares) in Maxford plc, an unquoted trading company, for many years.

(2) In February 2014 he gifted 30,000 of the Maxford plc shares to trustees of a discretionary trust for his adult children.

(3) In May 2018 he gifted 20,000 of the Maxford plc shares to a trust in which his daughter has a life interest. (He was excluded from benefit under both trusts and the trustees retained the shares.)

(4) The agreed share values at the time of both gifts were:

Shareholding	*Per share value* £
11% to 15%	10.00
5% to 10%	5.00
Below 5%	3.00

In February 2020 Maxford plc was listed on the Alternative Investment Market. All donees had retained their shares.

(5) In 2003 he had inherited a 51% shareholding in Minota plc, a company whose shares are listed on the London Stock Exchange. In July 2020 he gifted a 10% shareholding then worth £680,000 to his daughter and she held them at his death when they were worth £200,000.

(6) No other transfers had been made. Donees agreed to pay any tax due in respect of transfers to them.

His estate at death comprised:

(i) His house worth £800,000.

(ii) A life interest in his uncle's estate which had commenced on his uncle's death in June 2019. The uncle's estate at his death was worth £235,000 on which inheritance tax of £27,500 was suffered. On Mr Maxford's death his daughter became entitled to the capital, which was then worth £300,000.

(iii) 20,000 shares in Maxford plc valued at £10 per share.

(iv) Holdings of quoted shares as follows:

Number / %	*Company*	*Value at death* £
7,000	Green plc	107,000
3,500	Blue plc	42,000
6,000	Red plc	8,000
41%	Minota plc	850,000

In the six months following death the following share sales occurred:

Shares sold	*Company*	*Gross proceeds*
		£
6,000	Green plc	84,000
2,000	Blue plc	35,000
600	Red plc	950

In his will, Mr Maxford left his Maxford plc shares to his daughter. His house was left equally to his widow and daughter, subject to his widow having full use and enjoyment of the house for her lifetime or for so long as she wished. The balance of his estate went to his son.

(a) Calculate the inheritance tax payable as a result of the death of Mr Maxford.

(b) Calculate the allocation of any tax due between the free estate and settled property.

Answer

(a) Inheritance tax payable as a result of death of Mr Maxford

Position on gifts in lifetime

		Gross £
February 2014	Gift of 30,000 Maxford plc shares to discretionary trust –	
	Value of 70,000 shares @ £10	700,000
	Value of 40,000 shares @ £5	(200,000)
	Loss to estate	500,000
	Less: business property relief	(500,000)
	Chargeable transfer	Nil
May 2018	Gift of 20,000 Maxford plc shares to life interest trust –	
	Value of 40,000 shares @ £5	200,000
	Value of 20,000 shares @ £3	(60,000)
	Loss to estate	140,000
	Less: 100% business property relief	(140,000)
	Chargeable transfer	Nil
July 2020	Gift of 10% holding of Minota plc shares to daughter	680,000
	Less: 50% business property relief	(340,000)
		340,000
	Less: Annual exemptions 2020/21 and 2019/20	(6,000)
	Potentially exempt transfer	334,000

On Mr Maxford's death 7 January 2024

Lifetime transfers in seven years before death

No additional tax is payable on the February 2014 gift, since this was more than seven years before Mr Maxford's death. (It is, however, included in the inheritance tax accumulation until February 2021, with the capacity to affect the July 2020 gift accordingly if there had been some restriction on the business property relief through the presence of excepted assets within the company.)

Business property relief remains available on the other gifts providing the transferees have retained what they were given (or have replaced it with other qualifying property) and the property still qualifies as relevant business property. A listing on the Alternative Investment Market does not affect the status of unquoted shares, so that the May 2018 gift to the life interest trust will still retain entitlement to the 100% relief. The position on the July 2020 gift of Minota plc shares to the daughter is as follows:

C5.4 TAX ON DEATH — BUSINESS PROPERTY RELIEF, SETTLED PROPERTY, QUICK SUCCESSION RELIEF

	Gross	*Tax on 2023/24 scale*
	£	£
Cumulative transfers in previous seven years	Nil	Nil
July 2020 PET now chargeable	334,000	3,600*
	334,000	3,600*

(* 334,000 – 325,000 = 9,000 @ 40%)

As the Minota plc shares have fallen in value at the date of death, the daughter may claim under IHTA 1984 s 131 to have the tax on her gift recomputed as follows:

Value of gift as above		334,000
Value on death	200,000	
Less: 50% business property relief	(100,000)	
Annual exemptions	(6,000)	(94,000)
Reduce transfer by		240,000

This reduces the tax due to nil. The amount included in the inheritance tax accumulation, however, remains at £334,000.

Estate at death

		£	£
House		800,000	
Less: Spouse exemption (see **explanatory note 4**)		(800,000)	Nil
20,000 shares in Maxford plc @ £10		200,000	
Less: 100% business property relief		(200,000)	Nil
Quoted shares (see **explanatory note 5**):			
Green plc	7,000 shares	107,000	
Blue plc	3,500 shares	42,000	
Red plc	6,000 shares	8,000	
Minota plc	41% (see **explanatory note 2**)	850,000	1,007,000
Free estate			1,007,000
Settled property – immediate post-death interest in uncle's estate			300,000
			1,307,000

Inheritance tax thereon:		
Cumulative transfers in previous seven years	334,000	3,600
Estate at death	1,307,000	552,800*
	1,641,000	526,400

(* 1,641,000 – 325,000 = 1,316,000 @ 40%)

Tax on estate	522,800
Less: Quick succession relief re uncle's estate (4 to 5 years) $20\% \times \frac{207,500}{235,000} \times 27,500$	(4,856)
	517,944

(b) Allocation of tax between free estate and settled property

	£
Tax on estate as above	517,944

$$\text{Estate rate} = \frac{517{,}944}{1{,}307{,}000} \times 100 = 39.628\%$$

Tax on free estate 1,007,000 @ 39.628%	399,054
(payable by personal representatives, reducing son's residue accordingly)	
Tax on settled property 300,000 @ 39.628%	118,890
(payable by trustees, reducing daughter's entitlement accordingly)	
	517,944

Explanatory Notes

Inheritance tax business property relief

(1) Business property relief for unquoted shares in a trading company has been at 100% since 6 April 1996.

Thus the Maxford plc shares retained by Mr Maxford until his death qualify for 100% business property relief in the death estate. Since they were left as a specific gift to his daughter, there is no restriction of the exempt legacy of the house to the spouse by reference to the business property relief (see **Example A16** for further details).

(2) Since 10 March 1992 quoted shares in a trading company have qualified for business property relief of 50% if they give the transferor control immediately before the transfer, hence the relief in respect of the gift of the Minota plc shares to the daughter. There is no relief in the death estate on the Minota plc shares retained by Mr Maxford, since he no longer had a controlling holding; but the fact that the daughter's holding is not a controlling holding in its own right does not cause a loss of relief when computing the tax on death (IHTA 1984 s 113A(3)(b), (4)(a)).

Fall in value of gift for the purposes of inheritance tax

(3) The claim for tax to be computed on the value of a gift at death where that is lower than the value at the time of the gift does not affect the cumulative transfers figure for the purpose of later transfers, so the amount included in lifetime transfers remains at £334,000. For detailed notes on such claims see **Example A14**.

Legacy of house to spouse and daughter: interest in possession for inheritance tax and residence nil-rate band

(4) The stipulation in Mr Maxford's will that his spouse was entitled to full use of the property created a life interest in the daughter's share of the property (*IRC v Lloyds Private Banking* (1998)). Mrs Maxford therefore owns half the property outright and has a life interest in the other half which, being an immediate post-death interest, is a qualifying interest in possession. In both cases the spouse exemption applies. For detailed notes on interests in possession and property see **Example C3**.

Consequently there was no disposition of the daughter's share of the house to her (s 8J(2)) and neither was the daughter the person who became beneficially entitled to the interest in possession on her father's death (s 8J(4)(a)). Consequently there was no inheritance by a lineal descendant of Mr Maxford's house. As the house is not closely inherited, the tax on Mr Maxford's estate is computed without the benefit of a residence nil-rate band. However, an amount of £175,000 is carried forward to his wife and whether a residence nil-rate band is available on her death will be addressed at that time. This is likely to be the case if the house is retained until her mother's death as the daughter will then take her share of the house (at least) on her mother's death (s 8J(5)). See **Example A2 part (B)** for a full discussion of the residence nil-rate band and **Example A3 part C** for a discussion of the transfer of the residence nil-rate band to a surviving spouse.

Sale of quoted shares at a loss within twelve months after death (ss 178–189)

(5) Although 6,000 of the Green plc shares were sold at a loss within twelve months after death, no relief may be claimed, since the overall result of the sales was a profit as follows:

			Death value	*Realised value*
			£	£
Green plc	6,000 shares	6,000/7,000 × 107,000	91,714	84,000
Blue plc	2,000 shares	2,000/3,500 × 42,000	24,000	35,000
Red plc	600 shares	600/6,000 × 8,000	800	950
			116,514	119,950

For detailed notes on claims for a loss on quoted shares see **Example A10**.

Question

A.

(a) Brian is the life tenant of a settlement created before 22 March 2006, comprising quoted securities. On 30 September 2008, when the fund was valued at £169,000, he released his life tenancy for the benefit of the succeeding life tenant, Carol.

Brian had made a previous transfer in the form of a gift to his brother on 26 May 2008 of £186,000.

After relinquishing his interest in the settlement he made a gift of £60,000 to a friend on 8 June 2020.

On 12 April 2023 Brian died leaving free estate of £469,000 to his brother.

Calculate the inheritance tax payable.

(b) Carol, who succeeded to the life tenancy from Brian in (a) above, was killed in a road accident on 1 May 2019, having made no previous transfers.

The settlement was then valued at £175,000. On the death of Carol the property passed to her son David (aged 35), the remainderman, absolutely.

Carol left free estate of £172,000, which passed to David under the intestacy rules.

Calculate the inheritance tax position on her death.

B.

Antony and Benjamin each have a life interest in half of a trust fund, with remainder to Denis, the assets of the whole fund consisting entirely of a loan of £120,000 to a close company, repayable at seven days' notice.

On 30 June 2016 Antony sold his interest to Clive for its full market value of £20,000.

Before Antony sold his interest to Clive he had made a chargeable transfer of £294,000 to a discretionary trust in August 2010, but had not made any later transfers of value.

Antony died on 31 May 2023 leaving an estate of £448,000.

Benjamin died on 30 December 2023. Before his death he had made potentially exempt transfers (after exemptions) in the previous seven years amounting to £226,000 and his estate was valued at £100,000, excluding his interest in the trust.

Sufficient of the loan was repaid for the trustees of each fund to meet their inheritance tax liabilities on each occasion, and from the first such occasion the trustees therefore maintained separate accounts for each fund. Antony, Benjamin, Clive and Denis are not related to each other.

Compute the inheritance tax payable by the trustees of each fund by reference to the above events.

Where relevant, proper notice was given to the trustees of availability of exemptions within the appropriate time limit for both **part A** and **part B** of the Example.

Answer

A.

(a) Brian

Inheritance tax accumulation

26 May 2008			
Gift to brother			186,000
Less: Annual exemptions	2008/09	3,000	
	2007/08	3,000	(6,000)
Potentially exempt transfer			£180,000
30 September 2008			
Release of life tenancy – potentially exempt transfer			169,000
8 June 2020			
Gift to friend			60,000
Less: Annual exemption 2020/21			(3,000)
Less: Annual exemption 2019/20			(3,000)
Potentially exempt transfer			£54,000

Death of Brian — 12 April 2023

Inheritance tax payable on gifts within seven years before death

	Gross	*Tax (on 2023/24 scale)*
	£	£
8 June 2020		
Gift to friend	54,000	Nil
Cumulative chargeable transfers at death	54,000	Nil
Free estate on death	469,000	79,200*
	523,000	79,200*

*(523,000 – 325,000) = 198,000 @ 40%

Inheritance tax payable

	£	*By*
On free estate	79,200	personal representatives

(b)

Estate of Carol — Inheritance tax position as at date of death 1 May 2019

		£
Free estate		172,000
Settled property		175,000
		347,000
Inheritance tax on 2019/20 death scale (no previous transfers)		8,800*
(* 347,000 – 325,000 = 22,000 @ 40%)		
Payable by:		
Personal representatives	$\frac{172,000}{347,000} \times 8,800 =$	4,362
Trustees of settlement	$\frac{175,000}{347,000} \times 8,800 =$	4,438
		8,800

B. Antony

Inheritance Tax Accumulation

Cumulative transfers to date				294,000
30 June 2016				
Sale of life interest in trust				
Value transferred (share of trust fund)			60,000	
Less: Proceeds of sale			(20,000)	
			40,000	
Less: Annual exemptions	2016/17	3,000		
	2015/16	3,000	(6,000)	
Chargeable transfer				£34,000
(Tax arising on transfer: 328,000 – 325,000 = 3,000 @ 20% = 600)				

31 May 2023 — Death of Antony

	Gross £	Tax (on 2023/24 scale) £
Tax payable by trustees on chargeable transfer 30 June 2016:		
Cumulative transfers within seven years before 30 June 2016 –		
Chargeable transfer in August 2010	294,000	Nil

		Gross	Tax (on 2023/24 scale)
		£	£
Chargeable transfer 30 June 2016		34,000	1,200*
		328,000	1,200*
(* 328,000 – 325,000 = 3,000 @ 40%)			
Tax payable by personal representatives on estate at death:			
Cumulative transfers within seven years before 31 May 2023		34,000	Nil
Estate on death		448,000	62,800*
		482,000	62,800*
(* 482,000 – 325,000 = 157,000 @ 40%)			
Inheritance tax payable:			
	By trustees (six to seven years before death)		
	1,200 subject to taper relief at 20%		£240
	Less: tax paid in respect of lifetime transfer		(£600)
	payable		Nil
	By personal representatives		£62,800

Benjamin — Date of death 30 December 2023

Inheritance Tax Accumulation

		Gross	Tax (on 2023/24 scale)
		£	£
Potentially exempt transfers within seven years before death, now chargeable		226,000	Nil
Value chargeable on death:			
Free estate	100,000		
Settled property	60,000	160,000	24,400*
		386,000	24,400*
(* 386,000 – 325,000 = 61,000 @ 40%)			

Tax payable:

By personal representatives

$$\frac{100,000}{160,000} \times £24,400 = \quad 15,250$$

By trustees

$$\frac{60,000}{160,000} \times £24,400 = \quad 9,150$$

£24,400

Summary of inheritance tax payable by trustees

		£
By trustees of Antony's trust fund		
On sale of Antony's life interest to Clive 30 June 2016	Chargeable lifetime transfer	£600
On Antony's death 31 May 2023:		
Re potentially exempt transfer 30 June 2016		Nil
By trustees of Benjamin's trust fund		
On Benjamin's death 30 December 2023		9,150

Explanatory Notes

Inheritance tax: termination of a qualifying interest in possession

(1) Where a person, before 22 March 2006, had an interest in possession in the whole or any part of a settlement, the appropriate part of the capital of the trust fund continues to be treated for inheritance tax purposes as belonging to that person absolutely (IHTA 1984 s 49(1)). (An interest in possession broadly means an entitlement as of right to *income* from a settlement. For further notes on this point, and the other cases of qualifying IIPs where the same treatment applies after 21 March 2006, see **Example C3**.)

Carol acquired her interest after 21 March 2006; but she took it, before 6 October 2008, in succession to Brian who had been entitled to it since before 22 March 2006 and Carol's interest is therefore a transitional serial interest (TSI) under s 49C. (This would not be affected by the fact that the succession took place by purchase rather than without consideration.) Carol's interest is accordingly a qualifying IIP and she is treated as beneficially entitled to the assets on her death in 2019.

If the person with a qualifying IIP dies (s 4(1)) or his interest terminates under the terms of the trust, or he disposes of the interest by releasing or assigning it (s 52), there will be a potential charge to inheritance tax. It would be unfair for the person in possession of the interest to have to pay any inheritance tax arising as that person has no control over the assets of the settlement. Any tax is therefore payable by the trustees (s 201(1)). If the transfer is, or becomes, a chargeable transfer, however, the value transferred is added to the inheritance tax accumulation of the person with the interest in possession (s 52), and the tax is calculated as though the transfer had been made by that person.

After the transfer/termination the trust assets are no longer included in the estate of the transferor, but instead in that of the transferee (provided he became absolutely entitled or has a qualifying IIP). If, however, the transferor dies within seven years after the date of transfer, the potentially exempt transfer rules apply in the normal way and tax on the potentially exempt transfer is chargeable on the normal scale, any tax arising being payable by the trustees.

(2) The termination of a qualifying interest in possession during the lifetime of the person beneficially entitled to that interest is treated under s 52(1) as a transfer of value equal to the value of the property in which the interest in possession subsisted. The estate of the transferor immediately before the transfer is deemed to include the whole of the property in which he had an interest in possession and therefore the reduction in value of the estate as a result of the assignment is the full value of the property in which he had an interest in possession less any amount received as consideration for the assignment (s 52(2)). Where consideration is received, exemption cannot be claimed as a commercial transaction because s 52(1) and (2) expressly provide for tax to be payable. The easiest way to look at it is that whilst the life tenant's IHT estate has been depleted by the underlying value of the trust fund which it is deemed to contain, it has at the same time increased by the proceeds received, so that the transfer of value is the difference between the two.

Trusts created after 21 March 2006 will generally be relevant property trusts for inheritance tax purposes, meaning that the termination of an interest in possession in trust property is irrelevant unless it results in property leaving the trust (in which case there will be an exit charge). The situation is different where there is a qualifying interest in possession. The termination of such an interest in possession during the lifetime of the life tenant in a case where an individual becomes absolutely entitled to the trust property will be a potentially exempt transfer by the life tenant. There will, however, generally be a chargeable lifetime transfer where the settlement continues.

Termination of a qualifying IIP: availability of IHT exemptions

(3) For events after 21 March 2006, if the termination of a qualifying IIP occurs during the person's lifetime and

(i) another individual becomes absolutely entitled,

(ii) a disabled person's interest arises,

(iii) (not later than 5 October 2008) a TSI arises, or

(iv) the qualifying IIP was an immediate post-death interest (not a disabled person's interest) and the property becomes held for a minor child of the deceased settlor under a bereaved minor's trust

(and the individual becoming entitled in (i)–(iii) is not the spouse or civil partner or the person whose interest terminates, such as to attract spouse exemption) then the transfer is a potentially exempt transfer and will only become a chargeable transfer should the former life tenant die within seven years. The transfer is, however, a *deemed* transfer of value and accordingly the small gifts exemption and exemption for normal expenditure out of income do not apply (ss 20(3), 21(5)).

On the other hand the annual and marriage gifts exemptions are expressly made available provided the transferor gives the trustees of the settlement a notice informing them of the availability of the exemptions, within six months after the date of *termination* (s 57). Both the annual and marriage exemptions would be taken into account in arriving at the potentially exempt transfer (ss 51(2), 57). Other exemptions are also available (see **explanatory note 5**).

Notice is required within that six-month period even though the transfer is a potentially exempt transfer and the exemption may never have to be used against the trust fund if the former life tenant survives (and would thus be wasted if the life tenant made subsequent transfers of value from his free estate in the same tax year). It is therefore not always obvious that it would be in the life tenant's best interests to make his exemptions available to the trustees, unless the six-month period lasts beyond the end of the current tax year and he can judge the position with full knowledge of how matters have evolved.

As to the form of any notice, the HMRC Inheritance Tax Manual (IHTM 16083) states merely that the notice should be given 'in writing'. The notice is not to be sent to HMRC but should be retained by the trustees in case HMRC subsequently require evidence of the allocation of the exemptions (in the event of the death of the transferor within seven years).

(4) Even though any tax that may arise on the termination of the life interest is payable by the trustees and not by the transferor, his accumulation is increased by the amount of the transfer if it becomes a chargeable transfer, thus increasing his and his estate's tax liability on any later transfers. Brian in **part A**, and Antony and Clive in **part B**, of the Example would therefore at least want to consider surrendering their annual exemptions to the trustees for use against the transfers if they had made no other transfers against which the exemptions could be utilised.

(5) If the termination of a qualifying IIP occurs on the death of the person entitled to it, the value of the assets in the settlement is added to the free estate and tax calculated on the aggregate. The trustees are then liable to pay a proportionate part of the total inheritance tax payable.

For both lifetime and death terminations the exemptions for transfers to spouse/civil partner (if entitled absolutely or to another qualifying IIP), charities or political parties are available.

If on the other hand the interest in possession that comes to an end, or is disposed of, is not a qualifying IIP, the death of the life tenant will not give rise to any inheritance tax consequence in his estate as the trust fund would not be deemed to form part of the life tenant's estate.

Release of Brian's life interest; inheritance tax treatment

(6) On the release of Brian's pre-2006 life interest in **part A** of the Example there is a transfer of value based on the underlying assets in the settlement. Since Brian is entitled to the whole of the income of the trust, the whole capital value of the fund is deemed to be transferred. Because another interest in possession for an individual (Carol) follows on from Brian's pre-2006 interest, and the release took place before 6 October 2008 when the transitional period came to an end, Carol's interest in possession qualifies as a TSI under s 49C and is therefore a qualifying IIP. For this reason the transfer is at that point potentially exempt (after deducting annual exemptions, following due notice by Brian to the trustees of their availability).

On the death of Brian his accumulation is recomputed for the seven years prior to death, with any potentially exempt transfers made in that period now being treated as chargeable transfers. The rates used for the re-computation are those applicable at his death on 12 April 2023. In the case of transfers occurring more than three years before death, taper relief reduces the tax on those particular transfers without affecting the overall computation.

Death of Carol and subsequent death of Brian

(7) In the absence of a disclaimer removing the settled property from Carol's estate at her death, tax of £4,362 is payable by her personal representatives on her free estate by 30 November 2019, six months after the end of the month of her death, or earlier application for letters of administration.

Disclaiming interest in a settlement; inheritance tax treatment

(8) A person who becomes entitled to an interest under a settlement (any type of interest, not just a life interest) may as a matter of the general law disclaim (refuse to accept) his entitlement so long as he has done nothing to accept it. A disclaimer must be of the whole interest and not just part of it. Merely obtaining information about it does not amount to acceptance. The ability to disclaim passes to that person's personal representatives in the event of its still subsisting (through non-acceptance) at his death.

Provided such a disclaimer is not made for money or money's worth, the person is treated for inheritance tax purposes as never having become entitled to the interest (s 93). Once benefits have been accepted, any purported disclaimer would not operate as a disclaimer under the general law, and could therefore not benefit from the rule in s 93. The normal tax consequences would therefore follow in relation to the succession to the interest; furthermore it would be necessary to establish whether the purported disclaimer had no legal effect at all (in which case the person who made it would remain entitled to the benefit of the interest), or whether as a matter of interpretation it operated as a lifetime gift to the next beneficiary in line, with tax consequences accordingly.

There is no parallel to IHTA 1984 s 93 in the capital gains tax legislation although there is provision for disclaimers in TCGA 1992 s 62(6).

Trustees' retaining funds to meet potential inheritance tax liabilities

(9) Trustees of settlements may have a potential tax liability for seven years after a release of a qualifying IIP. Accordingly funds must be retained for that period to meet those liabilities.

(10) In **part B** of the Example, there are two inheritance tax consequences when Antony dies in 2023:

(a) the June 2016 chargeable lifetime transfer (by Antony in favour of Clive) is charged again to tax. Although it was the only chargeable transfer within the seven years before Antony's death, so that it is within his nil-rate band for the purpose of calculating the tax on his estate, it nevertheless incurs a liability on the trust fund because it was itself made within seven years after the earlier transfer to the discretionary trust in August 2010. This demonstrates that lifetime gifts which constitute immediately chargeable, as distinct from potentially exempt, transfers may remain relevant to the calculation of inheritance tax due by reason of the death for up to practically 14 years after they were made.

(b) Clive's interest in the trust is not a qualifying IIP (as it arises after 5 October 2008). Its duration was only ever for the balance of Antony's lifetime – if Antony had outlived Clive then the IIP would have continued in favour of Clive's estate. In both cases the property in which Clive's IIP subsists is taxed under the relevant property regime and it terminates when the trust fund passes to the remainderman, Denis. This does not result in any IHT consequence for Clive.

On the death of Benjamin his interest in possession, dating from before 22 March 2006 and therefore a qualifying IIP, is chargeable in the normal way, that is by aggregation with his free estate, and the tax on the total is apportioned rateably to the various parts of his estate.

Reversion to settlor or spouse/civil partner: inheritance tax treatment

(11) If a qualifying IIP comes to an end during the settlor's lifetime, and the settled property reverts to the settlor, tax is not chargeable (s 53(3)). Furthermore tax is not chargeable if the settlor's spouse/civil partner (or widow/widower or surviving civil partner if settlor had died less than two years earlier) becomes beneficially entitled to the property and is domiciled in the UK (s 53(4)).

In either case the entitlement must be absolute if it is to benefit from this exemption; this may involve less favourable capital gains tax implications if the assets have grown in value, see **Example D2 part A(b)**. The exemption does not however apply if the settlor or spouse/civil partner acquired the reversionary interest for a consideration in money or money's worth (s 53(5)); but the inapplicability of the inheritance tax exemption will not affect the operation of the capital gains tax rules.

Question

(a) Fred, who had been entitled to an annuity under a fund settled by his aunt's will on her death in 1994, died on 31 August 2023. The amount of the annuity was £5,000. The value of the fund as a whole on that date was £500,000 and it produces an average annual income yield of 5%. Assume the current yield shown in the FTSE Actuaries Index for British Government Stocks (Irredeemables) was 2.5%.

Calculate the value of the annuity fund for inheritance tax purposes on the death of Fred.

(b) Jim, the life tenant of a settled fund, also died on 31 August 2023. His life tenancy, to which he had become entitled in 2005, was subject to an annuity of £5,000 in favour of Gordon. The value of the fund as a whole was £500,000 on that date and the annual income yield was 6%. Assume the current actual dividend yield of the FTSE Actuaries All Share Index was 3%.

Calculate the value of the fund underlying the life tenancy for inheritance tax purposes on the death of Jim.

Answer

(a) Fred died — 31 August 2023

Value of Annuity Fund

		£
Without IHTA 1984 s 50(3) Annuity £5,000 Income of fund (£500,000 × 5%) £25,000 Share of capital attributable to Fred		
	$\frac{5,000}{25,000} \times 500,000$	100,000
With s 50(3) Annuity £5,000 Notional income of fund (£500,000 × 2.5%) £12,500 Minimum share of capital attributable to Fred		
	$\frac{5,000}{12,500} \times 500,000$	200,000
Value for inheritance tax of Fred's annuity fund		£200,000

(b) Jim died — 31 August 2023

Value of part remaining after an annuity

		£
Without s 50(3): Annuity £5,000 Income of fund (£500,000 × 6%) £30,000 Share of capital attributable to Jim (ie after annuity of £5,000)		
	$\left(\frac{30,000 - 5,000}{30,000}\right) \times 500,000$	416,667
Value of the annuity fund (500,000 – 416,667)		£83,333
With s 50(3) Annuity £5,000 Notional income of fund (£500,000 × 3%) £15,000		
Value of fund		500,000

Less: Maximum value of annuity fund		
	$\frac{5,000}{15,000} \times 500,000$	(166,667)
Minimum value of part remaining		333,333
Value for inheritance tax of fund underlying Jim's life tenancy		£416,667

Explanatory Notes

(1) A person who has a qualifying interest in possession (including an annuity) in settled property is treated for the purposes of inheritance tax as owning the underlying settled property absolutely. A qualifying interest in possession is such an interest acquired before 22 March 2006 or is one of the following (s 49(1), (1A)):

- an immediate post-death interest (s 49A);
- a disabled person's interest (s 89–89B); or
- a transitional serial interest (s 49B–49E);
- an interest in possession that was purchased at arm's length by its owner after 8 December 2009 when he was domiciled in the UK (s 5(1B)).

For full details of those additional categories – see **Example C3.**

(2) Where one beneficiary of a settlement is entitled to a fixed amount of income and another to the remainder of the income, then to arrive at their respective shares of the trust fund the fund is divided in proportion to their shares of income (s 50(1)). The income arising over the previous twelve months is usually used for this purpose.

(3) However, if only one of the interests in the settlement is to be valued for the purpose of calculating a chargeable transfer, s 50(3) contains anti-avoidance provisions to prevent loss of tax to HMRC where the yield of the fund may have been arranged to reduce the taxable amount.

The anti-avoidance provisions *do not apply* where chargeable transfers of *both* of the interests are made *at the same time*, since the whole of the supporting capital will in those circumstances be caught in any event.

(4) The value of the annuity fund becomes:

(a) In the case of a transfer of the annuity – not *less* than its capital value using the current yield on the FTSE Actuaries Index for British Government Stocks (Irredeemables).

(b) In the case of a transfer of the remainder – not *more* than its capital value using the current actual dividend yield on the FTSE Actuaries All Share Index.

The use of these particular indices is prescribed by SI 2000/174, effective from 18 February 2000. The actual figures are obtainable from the *Financial Times*.

(5) The value of Fred's annuity fund included in his estate is therefore the higher of £25,000 (arrived at using the actual income yield of the fund) and £200,000 (arrived at using the notional income yield of 2.5% being the yield on British Government Irredeemable Stocks).

In arriving at the value of the property supporting Jim's life tenancy, the value of the annuity fund using the actual income yield is 1/6th of £500,000 = £83,333. Since this is less than the maximum permitted value of £166,667 using the All-Share Index, the anti-avoidance provision in s 50(3) does not apply in valuing Jim's interest for inheritance tax purposes on his death.

(6) The formula for the determination of the capital value of an annuity can give rise to inequitable results where the settled property consists of real or leasehold property – depending on whether death is immediately before or after new rents are received. Before 6 April 2015, extra-statutory concession F11 (Property chargeable on the ceasing of an annuity) allowed this imbalance to be addressed. It stated that where an annuity was charged wholly or in part on real or leasehold property, and HMRC were satisfied that a capital valuation of the property at the date of death (or alienation of the interest) restricted to its existing use, reflected an anticipated increase in rents obtainable for that use after that date, appropriate relief would be given in calculating the proportion of the property on which tax was chargeable. The government withdrew this concession on 6 April 2015 citing it as obsolete (see HMRC document entitled 'Extra-Statutory Concessions' dated 6 April 2015).

Question

Amelia Dobbin, a widow, died on 15 July 2023.

Her first husband, George Sedley, who died in 1971, had by his will left the residue of his estate (which did not include a residential property) to Amelia absolutely. In 1973 she made a settlement of this inherited property under which she took a life interest with remainder to her son Paul.

At her death the settled fund consisted of investments valued at £249,000.

Her second husband, William Dobbin, who died in July 1974, settled the residue of his estate on Amelia for life with the remainder to Rebecca, his daughter by a previous marriage. Amelia never married again following the death of William.

This settled fund on Amelia's death was valued at £300,000 including a home valued at £200,000 which she continued to occupy for the rest of her life.

Amelia had made two transfers of value prior to her death.

On 1 January 2012 she transferred assets to Rebecca's husband, the value of the transfer being £70,900. On 10 June 2021 she gave £172,000 to her son Paul.

For many years up to the date of her death Amelia had owned, and farmed as sole trader, 200 acres of agricultural land (which is included in the balance sheet of the farming business), the open market value of which at her death is £400,000 and the agricultural value £300,000. The other assets of the farming business are valued at £96,000. There is no farmhouse on the land.

Amelia's free estate at death, apart from the farm land and other business assets, consisted of £40,000 Crawley Corporation 6% Stock 2024, quoted at 92–94 ex div (interest paid 15 February and 15 August), furniture and effects valued at £13,500, net income due to her from the settlements £4,320 and a bank balance of £8,590.

Her personal liabilities and funeral expenses amounted to £4,370 all of which were paid by her executors after her death.

By her will she left £50,000 to a registered charity, £2,000 to a major British political party, and the residue to a close friend.

(a) Prepare a statement of the amount on which inheritance tax is chargeable on Amelia's death.

(b) Compute the inheritance tax payable, stating by whom it will be borne.

Assume that there was no transferable nil-rate band available on the death of George Sedley and that William Dobbin left an estate in excess of £30,000.

Answer

Amelia Dobbin deceased

(a) *Calculation of amount on which inheritance tax is chargeable on death — 15 July 2023*

Free estate					
Agricultural and business property					
Farm land – open market value	400,000				
Less: Agricultural property relief – 100% of agricultural value	(300,000)				
Leaving non-agricultural value of farm land	100,000				
Other farm business assets	96,000	196,000			
Less: Business property relief 100%		(196,000)	Nil		
Other assets					
£40,000 Crawley Corporation 6% stock @ 92½% ex div		37,000			
Interest due (half year)	1,200				
Less: Income tax @ 20%	(240)	960	37,960		
Furniture and effects			13,500		
Income due from settlements			4,320		
Bank balance			8,590		
				64,370	
Less Funeral expenses and liabilities paid after death				(4,370)	60,000
Less: Exempt legacies:					
Charity				50,000	
Political party				2,000	
				52,000	
Giving a deduction (after apportionment of agricultural and business property relief – explanatory note 3) of					
$£52{,}000 \times \frac{60{,}000\text{(free estate after APR / BPR)}}{556{,}000\text{(free estate before APR / BPR)}}$					(5,612)
Net value of free estate chargeable to inheritance tax on Amelia's death					54,388

Settled property

1973 Settlement by Amelia on herself for life		
Investments	249,000	
1974 Surviving spouse settlement (William Dobbin Will Trust)		
Transitional exemption (see **explanatory note 4**)	Nil	249,000
Total estate chargeable to inheritance tax on Amelia's death		303,388

(b) *Inheritance tax payable at death — 15 July 2023*

On potentially exempt transfers within seven years before death (ie 16 July 2016 to 15 July 2023):

				Gross £	*Tax* £
10 June 2021					
Gift to son			172,000		
Less: Annual exemptions	2021/22	3,000			
	2020/21	3,000	(6,000)		
Potentially exempt transfer now chargeable				166,000	Nil
				166,000	Nil

On estate at death:

	Gross £	*Tax (on 2023/24 scale* £
Inheritance tax accumulation within seven years before death as above	166,000	Nil
Chargeable assets at death and tax thereon	303,388	57,755*
	469,388	57,755*

(* 469,388 – 325,000 = 144,388 @ 40%)

The inheritance tax of £57,755 is borne as follows:

By personal representatives

Value of free estate (as reduced by APR and BPR)	60,000	
Less: Exempt transfers (as reduced by APR and BPR)	(5,612)	
	£54,388	

$$£57,755 \times \frac{54,388}{303,388} = \qquad 10,354$$

By trustees of 1973 settlement

Value of settled property £249,000

$$£57,755 \times \frac{249,000}{303,388} = \qquad 47,401$$

£57,755

Explanatory Notes

Valuation of quoted securities for inheritance tax

(1) Quoted securities are valued at a quarter-up from the lower of the quoted prices (or halfway between the highest and lowest bargains marked if less), any accrued income therefore being included in the quotation. If quoted ex-interest, the whole of the forthcoming income (net of basic rate income tax) must be added to the resultant valuation, since the whole of that income would have been forthcoming had a sale been made at the point of death, not just the part accrued on a day to day basis up to the date of death. The quarter-up rule which is derived from TCGA 1992 s 272(3) as that section applied before 6 April 2015, is applied, as a matter of practice, for IHT valuation purposes (see IHTM18093). The Market value of Shares, Securities and Strips Regulations 2015 (SI 2015/616) which amended the valuation basis for capital gains tax purposes does not apply for the purposes of inheritance tax.

Inheritance tax – agricultural and business property relief

(2) For detailed notes on business property relief and agricultural property relief see **Example A21** and **Example A22** respectively.

(3) The free estate is reduced by the exempt legacies to the charity and political party. Such legacies are completely exempt (IHTA 1984 ss 23, 24). However unless agricultural and business property is left as a specific legacy rather than as part of the residue of the estate, the benefit of agricultural property and business property relief is allocated over the exempt and chargeable free estate, thus effectively diluting the value of those reliefs where there are exempt legacies (s 39A, and see **Examples A16** and **A18**).

For detailed notes on the charity and political party exemptions see **Example A1**.

Estate duty — surviving spouse exemption

(4) Where one party to a marriage died before 13 November 1974 and the other dies after 12 March 1975 (the date on which estate duty was abolished and capital transfer tax/inheritance tax commenced to be chargeable on death) any property which would have been exempt from estate duty under the 'surviving spouse' exemption of FA 1894 s 5(2) is left out of account for inheritance tax (Sch 6 para 2).

The estate duty exemption applied only to property in which the surviving spouse had a limited interest (eg for life or widowhood) and of which she/he was at no time competent to dispose; the exemption did not apply to property that passed absolutely. The property comprised in the settlement established by Amelia's second husband (William) on his death in July 1974 is therefore left out of account for inheritance tax under this transitional provision. No question of the availability of a residence nil-rate band in respect of the home comprised in the settlement can therefore arise as Amelia's estate did not include a home when she died. As she is not survived by a spouse no question as to a carry-forward amount of residence nil-rate band arises either.

(5) Although Amelia at her death only had a life interest in the 1973 settlement comprising the assets from her first husband's (George's) estate, she did at one time (between 1971 and 1973) have an absolute interest in those assets, having herself created the settlement in her own favour. The transitional relief at **explanatory note 4** does not therefore apply.

Until the major changes in FA 2006, a settlement upon oneself (a so-called 'self-interested settlement') with remainder to specified persons was a useful way of determining in one's lifetime the destination of specified property upon death. For further notes on this point see **Example F5 explanatory note 8.**

The assets comprised in the settlement itself remained in the settlor's estate for inheritance tax purposes through the interest in possession rules, so there would not be even a potentially exempt transfer when such a settlement was made, no transfer of value having taken place.

The settled fund remained chargeable to inheritance tax on the death of the settlor, so no tax was avoided, but the lifetime settlement determined the devolution on death, thus safeguarding against any possible family problems arising, say, from remarriage or other doubts within a family.

Since 22 March 2006 the making of any settlement in the settlor's lifetime, even in the settlor's own favour, entails an immediately chargeable transfer (with a lifetime charge to inheritance tax to the extent that the settlor's nil-rate band is exceeded, and with potential effects on the settlor's death up to 14 years later, see **Example C6 explanatory note 12**(a)), unless the settlement confers a disabled person's interest on the settlor or some other person; for what is meant by a disabled person's interest see **Example C3**.

Inheritance tax – transfer of nil-rate band

(6) For an account of the provisions relating to the transfer of the nil-rate band from one deceased spouse/civil partner to their widow/widower/surviving partner see **Example A3**. In summary, anyone who dies after 8 October 2007 who has previously been in a marriage or civil partnership, where the marriage or civil partnership came to an end on the death of the other spouse or civil partner, may make use of any nil-rate band which was not used on the death of the predeceasing spouse or civil partner, irrespective of when the predeceasing spouse or civil partner died. Where the first spouse dies before 25 July 1986, ie the date when IHT replaced capital transfer tax, it is still possible to claim transfer of nil-rate band which was not used on their death. However, the unlimited exemption for gifts to a UK-domiciled surviving spouse taking effect on death only came into force from 13 November 1974. Between 22 March 1972 and 12 November 1974 the estate duty exemption for a gift to a surviving spouse was limited to £15,000. The nil-rate band was also £15,000. William Dobbin died between those dates but left an estate in excess of £30,000. There can therefore be no transfer of nil-rate band to Amelia. Before 22 March 1972 there was no spouse exemption from estate duty. George Sedley died before that date, hence the assumption in the question that there is no transferable nil-rate band as a result of his death.

Inheritance tax – potentially exempt transfers

(7) Amelia made potentially exempt transfers on 1 January 2012 and 10 June 2021. The earlier transfer became completely exempt on 1 January 2018. The second transfer became a chargeable transfer by reason of her death on 15 July 2023, but since it is below the nil-rate threshold no tax is payable on it (and taper relief is not therefore relevant). It does, however, reduce the nil-rate band available against the death estate.

Question

Richard died in 2005 and left his estate consisting of marketable securities in trust for his brother Alan for life and thereafter absolutely to Alan's son, Lawrie.

Lawrie died on 1 June 2023. His estate, including his interest in expectancy on the death of Alan, was left under his will to his only daughter Gladys (who is not a disabled person) for life and thereafter to his nephew John absolutely.

Lawrie's estate comprised:

'Personal assets £460,000 including a home valued at £175,000 unencumbered by any mortgage

Interest expectant on the death of Alan valued at £32,000.'

His funeral expenses amounted to £1,700 and his debts, including £100 owed to his turf accountant, amounted to £3,400. All of his debts were paid after his death by his executors. He had made no lifetime transfers.

Alan died on 31 December 2023, the value of the settled property in Richard's Will Trust on that date amounting to £55,000. Alan's personal estate (which did not include any residential property) was valued at £233,000. He had made one previous transfer on 6 October 2020, being a gift to Lawrie of quoted shares then valued at £143,000.

Calculate the inheritance tax payable on the above events.

Answer

Inheritance tax computation on death of Lawrie (1 June 2023)

Value of estate for inheritance tax

			£
Free estate			460,000
Reversionary interest:			
Interest in expectancy on death of Alan – excluded property, therefore			Nil
			460,000
Less: Funeral expenses paid		1,700	
Debts paid	3,400		
Less: amount paid to Turf accountant	(100)	3,300	(5,000)
Chargeable to inheritance tax			430,000
Less: residence nil-rate band			(175,000)
Balance of estate chargeable to inheritance tax			255,000
Inheritance tax on 2023/24 scale (255,000 – 325,000 = Nil @ 40%)			Nil

Inheritance tax computation on death of Alan (31 December 2023)

Inheritance tax accumulation

				Gross £	*Tax* £
6 October 2020					
Shares transferred			143,000		
Less: Annual exemptions	2020/21	3,000			
	2019/20	3,000	(6,000)	137,000*	Nil
Estate at death:					
Free estate			233,000		
Settled property – Richard's settlement			55,000	288,000	40,000**
				425,000	40,000**

* This will have been a potentially exempt transfer when it was made, but becomes a chargeable transfer since death occurred within seven years. No tax is payable, however, because it is below the nil rate band.
(** 425,000 – 325,000 = 100,000 @ 40%)

Tax of £40,000 on estate is payable as follows:

By trustees of Richard's Will Trust

$$\frac{55,000}{288,000} \times £40,000 \qquad 7,639$$

By personal representatives $\frac{233,000}{288,000} \times £40,000$ 32,361

£40,000

Explanatory Notes

Inheritance tax treatment of reversionary interests

(1) A reversionary interest in settled property is excluded property whether it is transferred in lifetime or on death, unless it was acquired for a consideration (as illustrated in the case of Executors of the estate of *Linington v HMRC* [2023] UKFTT 89), or unless it is one to which the settlor or his spouse/civil partner has at any time been beneficially entitled (or for interests acquired before 10 March 1981, is presently beneficially entitled) (IHTA 1984 s 48). Accordingly the value of the reversion in this Example is excluded from Lawrie's estate for inheritance tax purposes.

For detailed notes on excluded property see **Example A5**.

(2) The reason for excluding reversionary interests from a person's estate for inheritance tax purposes was that the capital value of the settlement (as distinct from the value of the right to receive the income for the time being) is included in the estate of the person presently entitled to receive the income for interests in possession created before 22 March 2006 (a qualifying IIP) and for some interests in possession created on or after that date.

For other interests in possession created inter vivos on or after 22 March 2006, the settlement is subject to a separate charging regime based upon the value of the trust property and, therefore, it is still appropriate to exclude reversionary interests from tax on a general basis.

Inheritance tax – quick succession relief

(3) The settled property does not give rise to quick succession relief on the death of Alan since it was *not* chargeable on the death of Lawrie (see **Examples C4 and C6**).

The settlement made by Richard granted a life interest to Alan and a reversion to Lawrie.

That made by Lawrie (of *inter alia* his reversionary interest) granted a life interest to Gladys with reversion to John.

The fund left by Richard therefore devolves as follows:

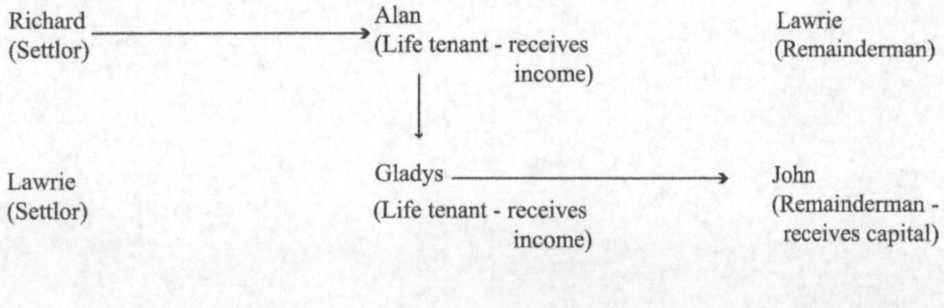

Lawrie therefore never had an interest in possession in the income of the settlement made by Richard and was therefore not chargeable to inheritance tax on the transfer of the reversion on his death. This passed as part of his estate from which Gladys is to enjoy the income for her life, and will not be chargeable to inheritance tax until Gladys' interest in the fund ceases (ordinarily upon her death). On Alan's death on 31 December 2023, however, the trust fund under Richard's Will is reduced by inheritance tax of £7,639, reducing the value that passes into Lawrie's Will Trust from which Gladys is to enjoy the income. It does not reduce the amount charged to inheritance tax on Lawrie's death, because the reversionary interest was excluded property and therefore not charged to tax in the first place.

Inheritance tax – treatment of debts in deceased's estate

(4) Debts may be deducted from the chargeable estate if they are:

(i) Reasonable funeral expenses, including the cost of a tombstone (s 172).

(ii) Liabilities imposed by law or incurred for a consideration in money or money's worth (including income and other taxes) (s 5(3), (5)).

(iii) Liabilities for inheritance tax providing they are paid from the estate (ss 5(4) and 174(2)).

A debt may not be deducted, however, to the extent that the creditor has received gifts from the deceased (FA 1986 s 103). For details see **Example B2.**

The amount due to the turf accountant is not incurred for consideration in money or money's worth and cannot therefore be deducted in arriving at the chargeable estate of Lawrie.

With effect from 17 July 2013 (when FA 2013 received Royal Assent), additional rules apply to deal with the repayment of liabilities after death. First, in arriving at the value of a deceased estate, a deduction for a liability will only be allowable to the extent that the liability has been repaid on or after death out of the assets in the estate, provided the deduction is not disallowed by some other rule (s 175A(1)). Secondly, if a liability has not been so paid after the deceased's death, it may still be deductible in computing the value of his estate but only where it is shown that there is a real commercial reason for not repaying the liability and leaving part of it unpaid is not part of arrangements to obtain a tax advantage (s 175A(2)). In the context of this second rule, a real commercial reason is one where it is shown that the liability is to a person at arm's length (or that an arm's length creditor would not require the liability to be repaid) (s 175A(3)), and tax advantage includes income tax, capital gains tax and inheritance tax (s 175A(5)). For more detail on the treatment of liabilities in the context of inheritance tax, see **Example A12 part C.**

Inheritance tax – residential nil-rate band

(5) Lawrie's estate benefits from a RNRB as he dies after 6 April 2017 owning a home which is closely inherited by passing under his will to a settlement in which his daughter (his direct descendant) immediately became entitled to an interest in possession and that interest is an immediate post-death interest (IHTA 1984 s 8J(4), s 49). As his estate does not exceed the taper threshold of £2 million, the amount of the RNRB prima facie available is £175,000 (the default allowance for 2023/24). The actual amount of RNRB used in calculating the inheritance tax arising in respect of Lawrie's estate is limited to the chargeable value of the proportion of his home that is closely inherited. In this case, the chargeable value of Lawrie's home is its unencumbered value of £175,000 and as the whole home is closely inherited this figure acts as the limit on the amount of RNRB available. The limit does not operate in Lawrie's case and so the amount of the RNRB used in calculating the IHT arising on his estate is £175,000. See **Example A2 part (b)** for a detailed discussion on the RNRB.

Question

The trustees of a discretionary settlement made by Harold on 1 November 1973 made the following appointments under powers given to them in the settlement, the cumulative transfers made by the trustees in the ten years prior to 1 November 2003 being £210,000.

(i)	1 July 2006	£40,000	cash to Andrew absolutely
(ii)	1 April 2013	£60,000	cash to Harold's wife Mary
(iii)	1 August 2023	£92,800	quoted securities to Brian absolutely

Harold, the trustees and the beneficiaries are all domiciled and resident in the United Kingdom. One other trust made by Harold on 5 May 1978 (also with UK resident trustees) is still in existence throughout 2023/24.

The appointments all provide that any tax payable is to be borne by the recipient beneficiaries.

(a) Calculate the inheritance tax payable (if any) as a result of each of the above appointments and also the amount payable on the 2003 and 2013 ten-year anniversaries.

The value of relevant property on 31 October 2003 was £162,000 and on 31 October 2013, £302,000 (excluding the £25,000 addition referred to in (b) below). There was unaccumulated income in the trust of £10,000.

The chargeable gain accruing to the trustees as a result of the appointment to Brian on 1 August 2023 was £12,825, and they made no other disposals for capital gains tax during 2023/24.

(b) If Harold added £25,000 to the original settlement on 1 November 2009 (at which time his gross chargeable transfers for the seven years to that date amounted to £240,000 including the £25,000 then transferred) calculate the revised tax liabilities assuming that the value of relevant property at 31 October 2013 was £338,000, including the addition to the settlement which was valued at £36,000 on that date.

The payment of £60,000 to Mary on 1 April 2013, and the appointment of quoted securities to Brian on 1 August 2023, can both be shown to be wholly derived from the funds in Harold's original settlement.

(c) How would your answer to (b) differ if the addition of £25,000 on 1 November 2009 had been made not by Harold but by Mary (with the same record of previous transfers)?

Answer

(a) Inheritance tax position of settlement made 1 November 1973

	Gross £	Tax £
1 November 2003		
Ten-yearly charge (see **explanatory notes 3 and 4**):		
Distributions in previous ten years (ie amounts subject to exit charges)	210,000	Nil
Value of relevant property on 31 October 2003	162,000	23,400*
	372,000	23,400*

Actual rate is 30% of effective rate

$$\frac{23,400}{162,000} \times 30\ \% = 4.333\%$$

Tax payable by trustees is £162,000 × 4.333% = £7,020

* Tax is calculated on 2003/04 scale (372,000 – 255,000 = 117,000 @ 20%)

1 July 2006

Exit charge – on distribution to Andrew

Amount chargeable = £40,000

Actual rate at previous ten-year anniversary recomputed for change of rates

2006/07 scale 372,000 – 285,000 = 87,000 @ 20% = £17,400

Actual rate is 30% of effective rate

$$\frac{17,400}{162,000} \times 30\ \% = 3.222\%$$

Number of complete quarters between 1 November 2003 and 30 June 2006 = 10

Tax payable by trustees and deducted from distribution to Andrew

$$£40,000 \times 3.222\ \% \times \frac{10}{40}$$ £322

1 April 2013

Exit charge – on distribution to Mary

Amount chargeable = £60,000

Actual rate at previous ten-year anniversary recomputed for change of rates

2012/13 scale 372,000 – 325,000 = 47,000 @ 20% = £9,400

Actual rate is 30% of effective rate

$$\frac{9,400}{162,000} \times 30\ \% = 1.741\%$$

Number of complete quarters between 1 November 2003 and 31 March 2013 = 37

Tax payable by trustees and deducted from distribution to Mary

		Gross £	Tax £
	$£60,000 \times 1.741\,\% \times \frac{37}{40}$		£864
1 November 2013			
	Ten-yearly charge		
	Distributions in previous ten years (ie between 1 November 2003 and 31 October 2013)	100,000	Nil
	Value of relevant property on 31 October 2013	302,000	15,400**
		402,000	15,400**
	(** 402,000 – 325,000 = 77,000 @ 20%)		
	Actual rate is 30% of effective rate		
	$\frac{15,400}{302,000} \times 30\,\% = 1.529\%$		
	Tax payable by trustees is £302,000 × 1.529% =		4,618
1 August 2023			
(i)	Capital gains tax deemed disposal on appointment to Brian		
	Trust annual exemption of £3,000 shared with one other trust		
	Chargeable gain accruing to trustees	12,825	
	Annual exemption for this settlement: half of £3,000	(1,500)	
	Gain chargeable to tax	£11,325	
	Capital gains tax payable by trustees (to be borne by Brian) @ 20%	£2,265	
(ii)	Inheritance tax exit charge – on distribution to Brian		
	Total value		92,800
	Less: Capital gains tax borne by Brian		(2,265)
	Amount chargeable		£90,535
	No change in actual rate applying at previous ten-year anniversary		
	2023/24 scale 402,000 – 325,000 = 77,000 @ 20%	£15,400	
	Actual rate is 30% of effective rate		
	$\frac{15,400}{302,000} \times 30\,\% = 1.529\%$		
	Number of complete quarters between 1 November 2013 and 1 August 2023 = 39		
	Inheritance tax payable by trustees (to be borne by Brian)		
	$£90,535 \times 1.529\,\% \times \frac{35}{40} =$		£1,350
	Summary:		
	Capital gains tax		2,265
	Inheritance tax		1,350
	Total tax to be paid by Brian, or raised from securities before distribution		£3,615

(b) Additions to existing settlement by Harold

	£	£
1 November 2009		
Recalculation of amount charged at previous (2003) ten-year anniversary because of addition to property in the settlement:		
Distributions in ten years to 31 October 2003		210,000
Value of relevant property at 31 October 2003	162,000	
Value of property added 1 November 2009	25,000	187,000
		397,000

1 April 2013

Exit charge – on distribution to Mary

Amount chargeable = £60,000

Revised rate at previous ten-year anniversary following addition to settlement, using 2012/13 scale:

397,000 – 325,000 = 72,000 @ 20% = £14,400

Actual rate is 30% of effective rate

$$\frac{14{,}400}{187{,}000} \times 30\ \% = 2.310\%$$

Number of complete quarters between 1 November 2003 and 31 March 2013 = 37

Tax payable by trustees and deducted from distribution to Mary

$$£60{,}000 \times 2.310\ \% \times \frac{37}{40} \qquad £1{,}282$$

		Gross £	Tax £
1 November 2013			
Ten-yearly charge (see **explanatory note** 7)			
Distributions in previous ten years subject to an exit charge		100,000	Nil
Chargeable transfers made by Harold in seven years preceding addition to settlement (240,000 – 25,000)		215,000	
Deemed accumulation for notional transfer		315,000	
Value of relevant property on 31 October 2013:			
Derived from original fund	302,000		
Derived from addition	36,000	338,000	
		653,000	65,600*

(* 653,000 – 325,000 = 328,000 @ 20% = £65,600)

Actual rate is 30% of effective rate

$$\frac{65{,}600}{338{,}000} \times 30\ \% = 5.822\%$$

proportionately reduced where relevant property added in previous ten years.

Tax payable by trustees:

On relevant property held for preceding ten years

£302,000 @ 5.822%	17,582

On relevant property added 1 November 2009		
$£36,000 \times 5.822\,\% \times \frac{16}{40}$		838
		£18,420

1 August 2023

		Gross £	Tax £
(i)	Capital gains tax on appointment to Brian as before		2,265
(ii)	Inheritance tax exit charge — on distribution to Brian		
	Amount chargeable after CGT deduction as before	90,535	
	Actual rate at previous ten-year anniversary recomputed for change of rates using 2023/24 scale		
	Distributions in previous ten years subject to an exit charge	100,000	
	Chargeable transfers made by Harold in seven years preceding addition to settlement (240,000 – 25,000)	215,000	
	Deemed accumulation for notional transfer	315,000	Nil*
	Value of relevant property on 31 October 2013	338,000	65,600†
	(no distinction between original and added property)	653,000	65,600†
	(* within 2023/24 nil-rate band £325,000)		
	(† 653,000 – 325,000 = 328,000 @ 20% = £65,600)		
	Actual rate is 30% of effective rate		
	$\frac{65{,}600}{338{,}000} \times 30\,\% = 5.822\,\%$		
	Number of complete quarters between 1 November 2013 and 1 August 2023 = 39		
	Inheritance tax payable by trustees (to be borne by Brian)		
	$£90{,}535 \times 5.822\,\% \times \frac{39}{40}$		£5,139
	Summary:		
	Capital gains tax		2,265
	Inheritance tax		5,139
	Total tax to be paid by Brian, or raised from securities before distribution		£7,404

(c) Addition to existing settlement by Mary

The result of the addition being made by someone other than the original settlor is that there are now two people who are settlors in relation to the settlement. IHTA 1984 s 44(2) provides that in such a case 'and if the circumstances so require [Part 3 of the IHTA 1984 (except for s 48(4)–(6) dealing with FOTRA securities as excluded property)] shall have effect in relation to [the settlement] as if the settled property were comprised in separate settlements'. HMRC equate 'if the circumstances so require' to 'in a straightforward case' (IHTM42553).

So the addition (and the property derived from it) would be treated as the making of a separate settlement by Mary. That separate settlement would first have property comprised in it on 1 November 2009, which is therefore its commencement date; and so its first ten-year anniversary will fall on 1 November 2019. The inheritance tax accumulation attributed to the notional chargeable transfer used to work out the rate then applicable will include Mary's chargeable transfers in the seven years prior to (but not including) the date of the addition (£215,000 in the Example, ie £240,000 less the £25,000 addition itself); distributions from the property derived from Harold's 1973 settlement will not be counted for that purpose as they will only affect the deemed separate settlement made by him.

Therefore on the basis that the appointments on 1 April 2013 and 1 August 2023 can both be shown to have been wholly derived from the original settlement, the inheritance tax exit charges on each of them will be as in **part** (**a**) above. Correspondingly the ten-year charge on 1 November 2013 would be worked out, only on the original property, in the same way as in **part** (**a**). The trust treated as settled by Mary is subject to its first ten-year anniversary charge on 1 November 2019.

The other point to note in relation to the addition by Mary is that she is evidently a beneficiary of the settlement since she received a distribution on 1 April 2013. Therefore, the settled property from time to time representing her addition will be within the gifts with reservation rules so far as she is concerned. This does not preclude the levying of inheritance tax charges under the relevant property regime in the usual way; but it will mean that on Mary's death the property in question will be subject to inheritance tax by aggregation with her estate. (Alternatively if she ceases to be a beneficiary, or to the extent that distributions are made from this fund to other beneficiaries, the reservation will cease and Mary will be treated as having made a potentially exempt transfer at that time.)

Explanatory Notes

Charging relevant property trusts to inheritance tax

(1) Until 2006 the relevant property regime (and its equivalent in the early days of capital transfer tax) was essentially for trusts (other than those for which specially privileged treatment was thought appropriate) whose charging regime could not rationally be linked to the lifetime of a beneficiary. Primarily this meant discretionary and accumulation trusts. For all interest in possession trusts the underlying capital was treated as part of the beneficiary's estate and taxed on his death, in the same way as had been the case in the days of estate duty before capital transfer tax was introduced.

The Finance Act 2006 changed that focus, and the relevant property regime became the primary inheritance tax regime for settled property. The cases where a new interest in possession would be within the old regime were severely limited (to immediate post-death interests and disabled person's interests); but transitional provisions for beneficiaries whose interests in possession date from before 22 March 2006, and for those who succeeded to those interests before 6 October 2008 (or, in a limited number of cases, later than that) will ensure that there are plenty of 'qualifying interests in possession' in existence for many years to come.

See **Example C3** for an explanation of what interests in possession can be classified as qualifying IIPs, and of how the settled property is taxed when a qualifying IIP subsists or comes to an end.

The relevant property regime is centred on the imposition of a tax charge every ten years at 30% of the lifetime rate (approximating broadly to a charge at the full lifetime rate once in a generation) based on certain assumptions in respect of ten-year anniversaries occurring on or after 18 November 2015. These assumptions (in the form of a 'notional chargeable transfer' used to compute the rate) take account not only of the relevant property in the trust itself but also of the relevant property in any trusts made on the same date (related trusts), additions made on the same day of property to non-related trusts containing relevant property (same-day additions) and non-relevant trusts to which there has been an aggregable same-day addition; and crucially (for settlements made, or property added, on or after 27 March 1974 when capital transfer tax was announced) the settlor's inheritance tax accumulation in the seven years prior to his putting property into the trust (or the highest such accumulation if he contributes property on different dates) is permanently attached to the settlement for this purpose. (See **explanatory notes 3** and **7**, and **Example C11** for trusts made after 26 March 1974.)

The ten-yearly charge is supplemented by a proportional, or 'exit', charge when property leaves the relevant property regime (**explanatory notes 5** and **6**), subject to some exceptions (see **explanatory note 10**).

Unlike the regime for qualifying IIPs, the relevant property regime does not involve the settled property being deemed to be comprised in anyone's estate (though where something turns on ownership, for example business property relief or agricultural property relief, the owners are the trustees). Therefore the trustees cannot make transfers of value or chargeable transfers. Any occasion on which tax is charged under the relevant property regime (or the subsidiary regimes for certain 'privileged' types of trust, also in Chapter 3 of Part 3) nevertheless is treated as a chargeable transfer for the purpose of any other references to chargeable transfers in the IHTA 1984 (s 2(3)).

Pre-27 March 1974 settlements under the inheritance tax relevant property regime

(2) The basic rules of the relevant property regime are somewhat modified in relation to a settlement that was created before 27 March 1974. Except where property is added to the trust on or after that date, the trust's inheritance tax accumulation will not include any element by reference to the settlor's position; furthermore the only property which counts towards the notional transfer which determines the rate is relevant property within the same trust.

Inheritance tax ten-yearly charge

(3) On the tenth anniversary of the creation of the settlement and every subsequent tenth anniversary (but not before 1 April 1983) a charge to inheritance tax arises. This is known as the principal or 'ten-yearly' charge (s 64).

The charge is made on any *relevant property* (see **explanatory note 8**) held in the trust immediately before the ten-year anniversary. See **explanatory note 9** about reducing the tax on relevant property that has not been relevant property throughout the ten-year period. (See **Example A4(A)** for an explanation of the rules on how property is valued.)

The rate of tax is determined by reference to a notional transfer of the relevant property made immediately before the ten-year anniversary, where the notional transferor had previously made chargeable transfers of a specified amount (see **explanatory note 4**), and *one half* the normal death scale rate in force at the date of the charge is used to arrive at the tax on the notional transfer. There is no grossing up (s 64). The rate of tax charged on the relevant property in the trust is 30% of the effective rate of tax on the notional transfer. With the current half scale rate of 20% this gives a maximum charging rate of 6% (see **explanatory note 11** about business or agricultural property relief and the instalment option).

The rules for arriving at both the notional transfer itself and the previous transfers are different for pre-27 March 1974 trusts and trusts made on or after that date. For the detailed rules relating to post-26 March 1974 trusts see **Example C11**.

Cumulative transfers at ten-year anniversary

(4) For pre-27 March 1974 trusts, the inheritance tax accumulation at the anniversary date will normally only show transfers occurring during the preceding ten years. Those transfers will comprise:

(a) the amounts on which exit charges have been made under s 65 (see **explanatory notes 5** and **6**), and

(b) at the first ten-year anniversary only, distribution payments (as defined under the old rules) up to 8 March 1982 (the equivalent during that time of the relevant property exit charge). This cannot be relevant for a ten-year anniversary charge occurring on or after 1 April 1993.

Thus, in the Example, the charge in 2013 uses the exit charges of the preceding ten years:

	£
1 July 2006	40,000
1 April 2013	60,000
	100,000

These previous transfers are cumulated with the relevant property in the trust at the ten-year anniversary to compute the tax at one half normal rates on the notional transfer and arrive at the effective rate. The tax charge on the relevant property is then at 30% of the effective rate (s 66). In each case the tax is calculated at the rates in force at the date of the charge.

Special rules apply when property has been added to the settlement, or has become relevant property (for example on the termination of a prior qualifying IIP as in **Example C4 part B**), during the ten-year period. These are detailed in **explanatory note 7**.

Inheritance tax exit charges

(5) In addition to the ten-yearly charge (**explanatory notes 3** and **4**) a charge to inheritance tax arises when property in a settlement ceases to be relevant property (s 65). This charge is known as the exit charge. If the tax is payable out of the relevant property remaining in the trust, the distribution is grossed up using the rate of tax payable on the distribution (ie after reducing it under **explanatory note 6** below, if appropriate, according to the complete quarters since the last ten-year anniversary) (s 65(2)). (For an illustration of grossing up see **Example C11**.) The method of computing exit charges occurring after the first post-31 March 1983 ten-year anniversary of the settlement is the same for both pre-27 March 1974 settlements and settlements made on or after that date. (Different rules apply to exit charges before the first ten-year anniversary, but that is not now relevant to settlements made before 27 March 1974. See **Example C11 explanatory note 5**.)

(6) The charge on distributions after the first ten-year anniversary is found by using the rate of tax computed at the previous ten-year anniversary (but where the scale of rates has been reduced the rate deemed to have applied at that anniversary is re-calculated using the revised scales (Sch 2 para 3), as shown in **Example C11** (where the same rule applies to relevant property settlements made after 26 March 1974)). The exit charge rate is arrived at by applying to that previous rate the fraction x/40 where x is the number of complete quarters in the period since the previous ten-year anniversary (s 69). If, therefore, the distribution occurs on the anniversary, or within three months thereafter, no exit charge is payable. The charge is levied on the difference between the value of relevant property before the distribution and its value thereafter. Thus the 'loss to the donor' principle applies to discretionary settlements. The maximum rate for an exit charge is 5.85%, ie 6% (maximum rate at previous ten-year anniversary) × 39/40.

Special rules apply where property has been added to a settlement since the date of the last ten-year charge (see **explanatory note 7**).

Added property: effect on inheritance tax charges

(7) Where property has been added to a pre-27 March 1974 settlement after 8 March 1982 as a result of a chargeable transfer by the settlor, then on the occasion of the following ten-year anniversary the inheritance tax accumulation is deemed to commence with the distributions subject to an exit charge in the previous ten years, plus the aggregate of the values transferred by the settlor in the seven years preceding the date of the addition to the settlement disregarding transfers made on that day. Where two or more additions have been made then the higher of the two (or more) possible figures will be used (s 67(4)). Thus a modest addition to an existing settlement can give rise to a substantial increase in the tax payable. In the Example the ten-yearly charge on 1 November 2013 would increase from £4,618 to £18,420 if £25,000 was added to the settlement on 1 November 2009.

This rule is not triggered if the transfer of value resulting from the addition is wholly an exempt transfer – ie covered in full by the annual exemption (s 19) or, perhaps more significantly, by the exemption for normal expenditure out of income (s 21). In relation to ten year anniversaries falling on or after 6 April 2014, the rule is also not triggered in relation to deemed relevant property (that is the income of the trust that arose more than 5 years before the ten year anniversary, which, when it arose, no person was beneficially entitled to an interest in possession (neither a qualifying or a non-qualifying interest) in the underlying property and which has not been formally accumulated by the trustees) (s 66(2A) as read with s 64(1A) and FA 2014 Sch 21 para 4(3)) (see **explanatory notes 8** and **9** for a further explanation of this point).

Although the total value of relevant property added in the previous ten years is chargeable to tax and is added to the accumulation to arrive at the rate of tax, the rate of tax chargeable on that added property is reduced by one-fortieth for each complete quarter before the date that the property became relevant property. In the Example the property was added after six years (24 quarters) and therefore tax was payable on the added property of £36,000 @ 5.822% × 16/40 = £838; being a charge for the last four of the ten years (16 quarters) (s 66(2)).

In addition to affecting the subsequent ten-year charge the addition will also increase the exit charge on any distribution occurring after its settlement. This is because it is necessary both for pre- and post-27 March

1974 settlements to recompute the tax rate on the previous ten-year anniversary by including in the calculation the value of property added subsequently as though it were relevant property at that time (s 69(2), (3)). This is illustrated by the difference in rates in **part (b)** of the Example in relation to the distribution on 1 April 2013 to Mary where the tax increased from £966 to £1,282.

If the £60,000 paid in **part (b)** to Mary on 1 April 2013 had come partly from the original settlement and partly from the added property then two separate computations would be required. The fraction applicable to the added property will not take into account the complete quarters (since the date of the previous anniversary) occurring before the day that the property was added (ss 68(3), 69(4)).

Thus, assuming that £54,000 came from the original settlement and £6,000 from the added property, the computation would be:

	£
1 April 2013	
Exit charge – on distribution to Mary	
Original property = £54,000	
Revised rate at previous ten-year anniversary 2.310%	
Number of complete quarters = 37	
Tax payable:	
$£54{,}000 \times 2.310\,\% \times \frac{37}{40}$	1,154
Property added on 1 November 2009 – £6,000	
Complete quarters 1 November 2003 to 1 November 2009 = 24	
Appropriate fraction is $\frac{37-24}{40} = \frac{13}{40}$	
Tax payable:	
$£6{,}000 \times 2.310\,\% \times \frac{13}{40}$	45
	£1,199

Where there is no indication as to whether a distribution is paid out of the original property or added property, it is treated as coming out of each proportionately.

Property will be deemed to have been added if the settlor makes any chargeable transfer which results in the value of the property in the settlement increasing, unless:

- the addition was merely of value, without adding to the settled property as such, and
- it can be shown that the transfer was not primarily intended to increase the value of the settlement, and
- the actual increase was not more than 5% of the pre-addition value (s 67(2)).

Meaning of 'relevant property' for inheritance tax

(8) If an interest in possession subsists in settled property, the property will not be relevant property if the interest in possession is a qualifying IIP (see **Example C3**), or in certain circumstances if it is owned by a company whose business consists wholly or mainly of acquiring interests in settled property. The company must have bought the interest for full value from a beneficiary in whose hands it was a qualifying IIP (s 59).

In all other cases the settled property will be subject to the relevant property regime unless it falls within one of the following special exceptions:

(i) Charitable trusts (whether temporary or permanent).

(ii) Property held on the terms of one of the restrictive types of trust for children and young people applicable since FA 2006, namely:

- bereaved minor's trusts;
- age 18-to-25 trusts; or
- accumulation and maintenance trusts (see **Example C15**) set up before 22 March 2006 (and still remaining within the more circumscribed conditions that have applied for such trusts since 6 April 2008).

(iii) Maintenance funds for historic buildings, etc.

(iv) Pension funds.

(v) Employee and newspaper trusts (unless there is an interest possession that is not an estate IIP and which, if owned by a company whose business consists wholly or mainly of acquiring interests in settled property, was not an estate IIP in the hands of the beneficiary from whom the company bought it for full value).

(vi) Trade or professional compensation funds.

(vii) Protective trusts where the discretionary trust was triggered by a forfeiture before 12 April 1978.

(viii) Privileged trusts for disabled persons where funds were settled before 10 March 1981.

(ix) Excluded property.

It has been held in *Gilchrist (as trustee of the JP Gilchrist 1993 Settlement) v HMRC* that scrip dividends received by a discretionary trust are capital of the settlement and so do form part of the trust's relevant property (and hence are subject to a ten year anniversary charge). Although ITTOIA 2005 s 410 operates so as to give rise to notional or fictional trust income (notwithstanding the terms of the settlement) for the purposes of (what is now) ITA 2007 s 479 in the hands of the trustees (so that the fictional trust income is subjected to the dividend trust rate of income tax), the Upper Tribunal held that the deeming effect of ITTOIA 2005 s 410 is limited to income tax; scrip dividends are not deemed to be income for general trust purposes or for the purposes of taxes other than income tax. In *Gilchrist*, the Upper Tribunal did not follow *Pierce v Wood* (2009) (which held to the contrary) finding that the case was wrongly decided. In *Seddon v HMRC* [2015] FTT 539, where the issue before the Tribunal was whether a scrip dividend was in principle income or capital, it followed the decision in *Gilchrist* and held that the scrip dividend formed part of the capital of the trust in question on the basis that it was bound to follow the later of two conflicting first instance authorities where the later authority fully considered earlier authorities (which the Upper Tribunal in *Gilchrist* had done).

Other trust property which is not subject to the relevant property regime includes:

(a) Equitable Life 'authorised payments' are disregarded in determining the value of relevant property immediately before a ten-year anniversary (The Taxation of Equitable Life (Payments) Order 2011 SI 2011/1502 art 5).

(b) HMRC Statement of Practice 8/86 made on 10 November 1986 sets out HMRC's practice concerning the inheritance tax treatment of the income of relevant property trusts prior to 6 April 2014. By virtue of the statement HMRC take the view that undistributed and unaccumulated income should not be treated as a taxable trust asset; and for the purposes of determining the rate of charge on accumulated income, the income should be treated as becoming a taxable asset of the trust on the date the accumulation is made. In this Example, the £10,000 of unaccumulated trust income is therefore not treated as part of the trust's relevant property when calculation the ten-year anniversary charge in 2013.

In relation to ten-year anniversaries falling on or after 6 April 2014, however, this practice has now changed. FA 2014 Sch 21 para 4 introduced new rules in relation to unaccumulated income and the ten-year anniversary charge. By virtue of IHTA 1984 s 64(1A) property held by the trustees of a settlement immediately before a ten-year anniversary is regarded as relevant property (ie it is deemed relevant property) comprised in a settlement at that time if:

- it is income of the settlement;
- it arose before the start of the five years ending immediately before the ten-year anniversary;
- it arose (directly or indirectly) from property comprised in the settlement, that when the settlement arose was relevant property; and
- when it arose, no person was beneficially entitled to an interest in possession (both qualifying and non-qualifying interests) in the property from which the income arose.

In other words, unaccumulated income can only be deemed to be relevant property if it derives from relevant property and arises more than five years before the ten-year anniversary in question. So, for example, if a ten-year anniversary of a discretionary trust falls on 15 August 2023, it is only the trust's unaccumulated income arising before 15 August 2018 that comes within the scope of this rule. The rule can therefore be seen to have retroactive effect.

HMRC's Trusts and Estates Newsletter of August 2014 comments that it is not necessary, for this purposes, for trustees to keep highly detailed records of movements on the income account. Unless a specific part of income has been distributed, HMRC will assume that income is distributed on a 'first in, first out' basis so that to arrive at any balance that should be treated as relevant property, trustees may take the balance on the income account immediately before the ten year charge arises and deduct from it the income that has arisen during the preceding five years. Any remaining balance should then be treated as relevant property. Where trust accounts are not made up to the anniversary of the trust, HMRC will generally be content to follow the trustees' reasonable approach to allocating income to the five year period immediately before the ten year charge.

In relation to ten-year anniversaries falling before 22 July 2020 (the day on which the Finance Act 2020 was passed), unaccumulated income of settlements made by persons not domiciled in the UK is not deemed relevant property (ie it is itself excluded property) if it arose from relevant property that at the ten-year anniversary is situated outside the UK or is represented by a holding in an authorised unit trust (AUT) or an open-ended investment company (OEIC) (s 64(1B)). In relation to ten-year anniversaries falling on or after 22 July 2020, unaccumulated income arising from property situated outside the UK or represented by a holding in an AUT or OEIC is not treated as deemed relevant property (ie it is itself excluded property) only where the settlor of the settled property was not domiciled in the UK at the time the property originally *became comprised* in the settlement (whenever that might have been) (s 64(1B)). For this purpose, the income generated from property representing previous accumulations of income is treated as having become comprised in the settlement at the same time as the capital (producing the earlier accumulation) became comprised in the settlement (s 64(1BA)). In other words, unaccumulated income arising from accumulated income is treated in the same way as the original property giving rise to the accumulated income.

Unaccumulated income that is invested abroad or in an AUT or OEIC cannot however be treated as excluded property while the settlor is deemed domiciled in the UK as a formerly domiciled resident (see **Example A5 part (b)**(ii)).

Also excluded as deemed relevant property is income which arose from relevant property but which is reinvested in exempt gilts which would (if properly treated as accumulated income) be excluded property. Exempt gilts will only be excluded property where all the beneficiaries who could ever become entitled to capital or income from the settled property meet the conditions on which the gilt is issued (which on and after 6 April 2013 means that the persons must not be resident in the UK) (s 64(1C)).

(9) If property in a settlement has not been relevant property throughout the whole of a given ten-year period then the charge on that property will not take into account the complete quarters (since the date of the previous ten-year anniversary) occurring before the day that the property became relevant property (s 69(4), applying s 68(3)). See **Example C4 part B** and **Example C12** for an illustration of this point.

In relation to ten-year anniversaries falling on or after 6 April 2014, the above added property rule is not triggered in relation to deemed relevant property (ie unaccumulated trust income as defined in **explanatory note** 8 above) (s 66(2A) as read with s 64(1A) and FA 2014 Sch 21 para 4(3)).

Capital gains tax and inheritance tax relevant property exit charges

(10) Under s 165(2), if a beneficiary becomes absolutely entitled to settled property by virtue of the event which gives rise to an inheritance tax charge under Part 3 Chapter 3 (which includes relevant property exit charges), then the amount of the capital gains tax is deductible from the amount otherwise chargeable to inheritance tax, provided the capital gains tax is borne by the beneficiary – as is the case in the Example for the appointment to Brian.

A similar rule applies in relation to an individual's chargeable transfer if the capital gains tax is borne by the donee. If on the other hand the tax in such a case is borne by the transferor, it is not taken into account as an additional loss to his estate (s 5(4)).

For the rates of capital gains tax for disposals during 2023/24 see **Example F6 explanatory note 14**, and for the division of the trust annual exemption between different trusts made by the same settlor see **Example F6 explanatory note 15**.

Conversion of relevant property into non-relevant property: effect on inheritance tax

(11) An exit charge can (and in certain cases does) arise if trustees convert relevant property into property that is not relevant property. Such a charge is prevented in most instances, however, by specific provisions. Thus there is no exit charge when property ceases to be relevant property because it is transferred to an employee trust (subject to detailed conditions – see s 75), or becomes held for charitable purposes without limit of time, or becomes the property of a national body such as a museum or the National Trust, or a political party or a non-profit making body (s 76). This is subject to the proviso that the property does not cease to be used for the purposes of the body concerned.

An important exemption from the exit charge is available in the case of a settlement made by a settlor who was not domiciled, or deemed domiciled, in the UK at the time. In such a case property situated outside the UK is excluded property. Since excluded property is not relevant property (see **explanatory note 8(ix)**), an exit charge would otherwise arise if trustees of such a trust moved trust property out of the UK (physically as with chattels, or by exchanging a UK asset for a non-UK one). Section 65(7) provides exemption in such a case. In relation to exit charges arising on or after 22 July 2020 (the date on which the Finance Act 2020 was passed), the exemption applies in relation to property situated outside the UK only where the settlor was not domiciled in the UK at the time the property originally became comprised in the settlement (rather than when the settlement was made) (FA 2020 s 73(6)).

Unfortunately, possibly by oversight, a corresponding exemption from an exit charge was not enacted in relation to a holding in an AUT or OEIC (when they were added to the categories of excluded property where non-UK domiciled persons are concerned (IHTA 1984 s 48(3A) added by FA 2003)). This anomaly has now been addressed by FA 2013 s 173 which introduces IHTA 1984 s 65(7A). No exit charge will arise where the trustees of a discretionary trust switch UK assets held in a trust made by a non-UK domiciled individual to investments in AUTs and OEICs. This change has retrospective effect from 16 October 2002 so that no tax will have arisen in those trusts which already held AUTs or OEICs when the changes introduced by FA 2003 came into effect and neither will any tax have arisen in those trusts where UK assets were invested in OEICs and AUTs since the coming into effect of FA 2003. However, in relation to exit charges arising on or after 22 July 2020, the exemption applies in relation to property comprising holdings in an AUT or OEIC only where the settlor was not domiciled in the UK at the time the property originally became comprised in the settlement (rather than when the settlement was made) (FA 2020 s 73(6)).

Although an exit charge does not arise when a distribution for charitable purposes is made from a temporary charitable trust (ie where the income, and perhaps the capital, is for the time being applicable solely for charitable purposes but the trust will convert, or is capable of being converted, for other purposes at some time in the future), a special charge is made under s 70 on the cessation of the trust or on a non-privileged distribution. This is calculated by reference to the time that the property has been so held (but not before 13 March 1975) and is the sum of:

- 0.25% for each of the first forty quarters;
- 0.20% for each of the next forty quarters;
- 0.15% for each of the next forty quarters;
- 0.10% for each of the next forty quarters;
- 0.05% for each of the next forty quarters.

Thus the maximum rate of 30% cannot apply until 2025.

If the trust pays the tax then the amount must be grossed up.

Instalment option: payment of inheritance tax

(12) It should be noted that where inheritance tax is payable on property eligible for the instalment option, that option is available to trustees of a settlement, provided that the property remains in the settlement (s 227(1)(c)). For details of property eligible see **Example A7** at **explanatory note** 7. If the property is business or agricultural property qualifying for 50% relief, the 6% maximum rate of charge for discretionary trusts is effectively 3% on that property, and when paid by instalments over ten years this becomes 0.3% a year.

Question

Nicholas Carraway, whose gross chargeable transfers in the preceding seven years totalled £197,000 and who had no available annual exemptions, settled a sum of £100,000 on 6 April 1995 in a discretionary trust, personally paying the inheritance tax chargeable on the scale at that time.

On 21 September 1997 the trustees made a distribution of £4,000 to A, subject to payment of tax out of that amount.

On 1 April 2002 the trustees made a distribution of £6,000 to B, subject to payment of tax out of that amount.

The market value of the trust fund on 5 April 2005 was £161,000.

On 27 May 2009 the trustees made a distribution of £20,000 to C, paying the tax out of the remainder of the settled fund.

The market value of the trust fund on 5 April 2015 was £300,000.

On 10 October 2023 the trustees terminated the trust and made a final distribution of £330,000 to D, subject to payment of tax out of that amount.

Compute the inheritance tax payable on each chargeable occasion.

Answer

Tax position of settlement (settlor having paid the tax on the settlement)

Initial value of settlement = £100,000

Inheritance tax – effective rate (originally calculated using 1995/96 scale but revised using 1997/98 scale to calculate tax on distribution 21 September 1997):

	Gross £	*Tax* £
Settlor's previous transfers within seven years before commencement of settlement	197,000	Nil
Initial value of settlement	100,000	16,400*
	297,000	16,400*

(* 297,000 – 215,000 = 82,000 @ 20%)

Actual rate is 30% of effective rate

$$\frac{16,400}{100,000} \times 30\% = 4.92\%$$

21 September 1997

Exit charge on distribution to A

Amount chargeable = £4,000

Actual rate applicable at formation of settlement (revised using 1997/98 lifetime scale as above) – 4.92%

Number of complete quarters between 6 April 1995 and 21 September 1997 = 9

Tax payable by trustees and deducted from distribution to A

$$4,000 \times 4.92\,\% \times \frac{9}{40}$$ £44

1 April 2002

Exit charge on distribution to B

Amount chargeable – £6,000

Actual rate applicable at formation of settlement (revised using 2001/02 lifetime scale):

297,000 – 242,000 = 55,000 @ 20% = £11,000

Actual rate is 30% of effective rate

$$\frac{11,000}{100,000} \times 30\% = 0.288\%$$

Number of complete quarters between 6 April 1995 and 31 March 2002 = 27

Tax payable by trustees and deducted from distribution to B

$$£6,000 \times 3.3\% \times \frac{27}{40} =$$ £133

	Gross £	Tax using 2005/06 scale £
6 April 2005		
Ten-yearly charge (using one half of death rate at 6 April 2005)		
Settlor's previous transfers within seven years before commencement of settlement	197,000	
Distributions subject to exit charges in previous ten years (£4,000 + £6,000)	10,000	
	207,000	Nil
Value of relevant property – 5 April 2005	161,000	18,600**
	368,000	18,600**

(** 368,000 – 275,000 = 93,000 @ 20%))

Actual rate is 30% of effective rate

$$\frac{18,600}{161,000} \times 30\% = 3.466\%$$

Tax payable by trustees is £161,000 × 3.466% = £5,580

27 May 2009

Exit charge on distribution to C

Actual rate at previous ten-year anniversary (revised using 2009/10 lifetime scale):

368,000 – 325,000 = 43,000 @ 20% = £8,600

Actual rate is 30% of effective rate

$$\frac{8,600}{161,000} \times 30\% = 1.602\%$$

Number of complete quarters between 6 April 2005 and 26 May 2009 = 16

Rate of exit charge applicable

$$1.602\% \times \frac{16}{40} = 0.641\%$$

Distribution (net) – £20,000

$$\text{Gross equivalent thereof } £20,000 \times \frac{100}{99.359} = £20,129$$

Exit charge payable by trustees £20,129 × 0.641% = £129

(*not* deducted from £20,000 distribution to C)

	Gross £	Tax using 2005/06 scale £
6 April 2015		
Ten-yearly charge (using one half of death rate at 6 April 2015)		
Settlor's previous transfers within seven years before commencement of settlement	197,000	
Distributions in preceding ten years subject to an exit charge	20,129	
	217,129	Nil
Value of relevant property – 5 April 2013	300,000	38,426†
	517,129	38,426†

(† 517,129– 325,000 = 192,129 @ 20%)

Actual rate is 30% of effective rate

$$\frac{38,426}{300,000} \times 30\% = 3.843\%$$

Tax payable by trustees is £300,000 × 3.843% = £11,529 £11,529

10 October 2023

Exit charge on distribution to D

Amount chargeable – £330,000

Effective rate, and actual rate, at previous ten-year anniversary are not revised since 2023/24 lifetime scale is unchanged

Number of complete quarters between 6 April 2015 and 9 October 2023 = 34

Tax payable by trustees and deducted from final distribution

$$£330,000 \times 3.843\% \times \frac{34}{40}$$ £10,780

Explanatory Notes

Inheritance tax ten-yearly charge on post-26 March 1974 relevant property settlements

(1) The rules relating to settlements containing *relevant property* have changed very little since the scheme was enacted with effect from 9 March 1982. (The pre-1982 rules were capable of giving rise to charges on what were known as *distribution payments*, the then equivalent of the exit charges described in **explanatory note 4**, and also, if the trustees were not UK resident, to annual charges in effect on account of the next ten-yearly charge – as to which see **explanatory note** 3.) There is essentially a single regime covering relevant property in general, but there are some variants in the case of pre-27 March 1974 settlements and these are dealt with in **Example C10.**

Until 22 March 2006 when the classification of trusts was substantially altered by FA 2006, relevant property was broadly confined to discretionary trusts. Since that date (apart from certain transitional rules) it will include many trusts with an interest in possession, and most trusts which, apart from the rule change, would have enjoyed privileged treatment as accumulation and maintenance trusts. Relevant property is defined in detail in **Example C10 explanatory note** 8. The concept of deemed relevant property arising by reference to a trust's unaccumulated income (effective for ten-year anniversaries falling on or after 6 April 2014) is also explained in that explanatory note.

(2) A charge arises under the post-1982 legislation on each tenth anniversary of the settlement (the first ten-year anniversary of a settlement in existence when the new rules were introduced could not fall before 1 April 1983). This charge is applied to the *relevant property* held in the trust at the anniversary date, without grossing up (IHTA 1984 s 64).

For post-26 March 1974 settlements the ten-yearly charge is arrived at as follows (s 66):

(a) The settlement is deemed to make a notional transfer immediately before the ten-year anniversary comprising:

(i) the value of the relevant property in this settlement immediately before the ten-year anniversary, ie its value on the day before the anniversary;

(ii) in respect of ten-yearly charges arising before 18 November 2015, the value, immediately after it became comprised in the settlement, of any property which was not then relevant property and has not subsequently become relevant property whilst remaining comprised in the settlement (eg where part of the settled property has always been subject to a qualifying interest in possession);

(iii) the value of the property in any related settlement at the time the related settlement commenced (s 66). A related settlement is a settlement made by the same settlor and commencing on the same day (excluding settlements in which all the property is held without time limit for charitable purposes) (s 62). It is immaterial whether the making of that settlement involved a chargeable transfer or an exempt transfer or even (if it created a qualifying IIP for the settlor) no transfer of value at all.

(iv) in respect of ten-yearly charges arising on or after 18 November 2015, the value of any same-day additions. If the settlor of more than one qualifying settlement (which are not related settlements – ie they were made on different days, not on the same day) makes a transfer(s) of value on a single day under which the value of the property comprised in more than one of those settlements is increased, whether or not the amount of property in them is added to, in relation to each of those settlements the increases in value in the other settlement(s) is a same-day addition (ss 62A, 62B, 62C). (See **Example C12** for a further discussion on same-day additions.); and

(v) in respect of ten-yearly charges arising on or after 18 November 2015, the value immediately after another settlement commenced of the relevant property then comprised in that other settlement but only where an increase in the value of the property comprised in that other settlement is represented by the value of a same-day addition aggregated under (iv) above and that other settlement is not a related settlement.

With effect from 18 November 2015, it is now possible to ignore non-relevant property in the same settlement, a related settlement and a settlement on which same-day additions are made.

(b) The notional transfer in (**a**) is added to the notional previous transfers to arrive at the effective rate of tax on the notional transfer in (**a**)(i).

The notional previous transfers are:

(i) Any chargeable transfers made by the settlor in the seven years prior to the creation of the settlement (excluding transfers made on the day the settlement commenced), except where (e) below applies. (It should be noted that if any potentially exempt transfers made before the transfer into settlement become chargeable because of the donor's death within seven years, this will affect the cumulative total of chargeable transfers. This could happen before or after the date of the ten-year charge, and if it was after, the ten-year charge would have to be recomputed accordingly.)

(ii) Any amounts on which exit charges have been levied under s 65 within the previous ten years (see **explanatory note 4**).

(iii) In the case of the first ten-year anniversary if it occurred before 9 March 1992, any distribution payments (see **explanatory note 1** above) made under the old rules before 9 March 1982 but within the ten years before the anniversary.

To compute the tax charge on the notional transfer the lifetime rate – ie one half of the death rate – of tax is used.

(c) Having arrived at the effective rate of tax on the notional transfer, take 30% of that effective rate to arrive at the actual rate applicable to the ten-yearly charge. (However, if or to the extent that the chargeable relevant property that is not deemed relevant property had not been relevant property throughout the ten-year period, the rate on such property is further reduced by $^{1}/_{40}$th for each complete quarter that had elapsed in the ten-year period before the property became relevant property. Deemed relevant property is charged to tax at the full rate.) At current rates this gives a maximum charging rate of 6%.

(d) Apply the *rate* arrived at in **explanatory note (c)** above to the taxable value of the *relevant property* in the trust at the ten-year anniversary, ie to the property at **explanatory note (a)(i)** above. In arriving at the taxable value, agricultural or business property reliefs are deducted where applicable in the usual way; if any taxable value attributable to such property remains after applying the relief (eg if it qualifies for only 50% relief, and/or relief is restricted by reference to any non-agricultural value or excepted assets), payment of the tax referable to it can be spread over ten years free of interest if the instalment option is available – see **Example A6 explanatory note 7**. Note that the effect of including **explanatory note (a)(ii)** to (v) in the notional transfer is to give a higher total for the *notional* transfer, and thus possibly a higher tax *rate*, but the charge is levied on the relevant property **(a)**(i) only.

(e) In the same way as for pre-27 March 1974 settlements, where property has been added to the settlement within the previous ten years and at least part of the addition comprised a chargeable transfer (as to which see further **Example C10 explanatory note 7**), then although the charge on that property is proportionately reduced as indicated in (c) above, the settlor's previous cumulative transfers at **explanatory note (b)(i)** become the chargeable transfers made by him in the seven years preceding the addition to the settlement, if that gives a higher total. Where more than one addition has taken place then either the commencement date or any one of the addition dates is used, whichever gives the highest cumulative total for the previous seven years (s 67).

Where the total used is at one of the addition dates then it is possible that this total will include earlier transfers to the settlement. This would result in a transfer being included twice, eg if the addition was made less than seven years after the commencement of the settlement, the settlor's seven year cumulative total at the date of the addition will include the original chargeable transfer on the creation of the settlement, and (unless it has been the subject of an exit charge, as to which see the next paragraph below) that property will also form part of the relevant property in the settlement (ie included at **explanatory note (a)**(i) above). In such circumstances the seven year cumulative total is reduced by the net amount put into the settlement.

Similarly that seven year cumulative total may include the value of property which has ceased to be relevant property at the date of the ten-year charge and has been the subject of an exit charge under s 65 (ie included at **explanatory note (b)**(ii) above). Then the seven year cumulative total is reduced by the value attributable to the property subject to that exit charge (s 67(3)(b), (5)).

A double counting relief also applies where property has been the subject of an exit charge but has since become relevant property again. (This will be very uncommon since the changes made by FA 2006, but before 22 March 2006 a typical example would have been on the creation of an interest in possession within the last ten years which had subsequently ended.) The value of such property would thus appear both as relevant property (under **explanatory note (a)**(i) above) and also as property on which an exit charge had been levied in the last ten years (under **explanatory note (b)**(ii) above). In such circumstances the latter amount is reduced by the smaller of:

- the value at the time of the exit charge; or
- the value on the day before the ten-year anniversary (s 67(6)).

These rules do not apply to a trust's unaccumulated income that is deemed to be relevant property by virtue of s 64(1A). This is because such income cannot be regarded as comprised in a chargeable transfer made by the settlor as a result of which the value of the trust property was increased (s 67(1)).

(f) Where the trust property includes a residential property, no residence nil-rate band is available in calculating any inheritance tax due.

(3) Under the pre-9 March 1982 rules, a proportional periodic charge was payable annually where trustees were not resident in the UK but this charge was abolished when the rules were changed. Any unused tax credit arising from the payment of such annual charges is available against *any* payments under the revised rules, ie both ten-yearly charges and exit charges (s 85).

Exit charges

(4) A further charge to inheritance tax arises when property in a settlement ceases to be relevant property (or if the trustees make a disposition which devalues the relevant property in the settlement). This is known as the 'exit charge' (s 65). No exit charge arises, however, if such an event occurs within the first three months after a ten-year anniversary, or within the first three months after the settlement is made (s 65(4)). Neither does an exit charge arise in respect of the payment of costs and expenses of the trustees or a payment to a beneficiary which is income in his hands (s 65(5)).

An exit charge does not arise where settled property ceases to be relevant property by reason only of becoming excluded property because it ceases to be situated in the UK or a trust comes to own units in an AUT or shares in an OEIC (in both cases, in respect of exit charges occurring before the date on which FA 2020 was passed, where the settlor of the trust was not domiciled in the UK at the time the trust was made) (s 65(7), (7A)). In respect of exit charges occurring on or after the date on which FA 2020 was passed, an exit charge does not arise in these cases only where the settlor of the property concerned was not domiciled in the UK at the time the property originally became comprised in the settlement (rather than when the settlement was made) (FA 2020, s 73(6)). Both exemptions includes the case where, on or after 6 April 2017, property becomes excluded property by reason of the settlor ceasing to be resident in the UK after a period of being deemed domiciled in the UK by virtue of being a formerly resident individual (s 67(7B)). It also includes the case where, on or after 6 April 2017, shares in an overseas close company or interest in a partnership that holds UK residential property, or the proceeds of sale of such property, becomes excluded property (s 67(7C), (7D)) (see **Example A5 part 4(b)(i) and (ii)**).

Where an exit charge occurs after there has been a ten-year anniversary of the settlement, its rate is linked to that which applied on the ten-year anniversary (or would have applied but for any later changes in the amount (rather than value) of property that is relevant property, and but for any fractional reduction that applied at the ten-year anniversary because the property had not been relevant property throughout the preceding ten years): see **explanatory note 5**.

If there has not yet been a ten-year anniversary, that approach cannot be used and a different formula has to be employed to produce the 'linked' rate: see **explanatory note 6**.

In either case, the full rate so ascertained is then reduced by applying the fraction of $^x/_{40}$ where x is the number of *complete* quarters in the period since the preceding ten-year anniversary (or since the settlement was formed) (ss 69(4), 68(2)).

If the property was not relevant property throughout the period since the preceding ten-year anniversary, or since the settlement commenced, the rate of tax on that property is reduced by deducting, from what would otherwise be x in the $^x/_{40}$ fraction, the number of complete quarters that had expired before it became relevant property. In such a case x in the $^x/_{40}$ fraction can never be less than 1 (ss 69(4), 68(3)).

The value transferred on an exit charge is the difference between the value of relevant property before the distribution and its value after the distribution. Thus the 'loss to the donor' principle applies, and grossing up is necessary if the tax is not to be borne out of the fund that ceases to be relevant property (see **explanatory note 6**). The rate used for grossing up is the actual rate found under the relevant formula, taking account therefore of the appropriate reduction using the $^x/_{40}$ fraction. Where the property that ceases to be trust property is a residential property, no residence nil-rate band is available in calculating any inheritance tax due.

Exit charge after a ten-year anniversary has occurred

(5) For both pre- and post-27 March 1974 settlements where a ten-year anniversary has already occurred (even if there was no relevant property at that date), the exit charge is calculated (using the time-fraction referred to in **explanatory note 4**) by reference to the rate of tax computed at the previous ten-year anniversary, recalculated (if lower) using one half of the death scale in force at the date of the distribution (s 69(1), (4)).

In respect of exit charges occurring before 18 November 2015, when property has been added to a settlement, or has become relevant property, since the date of the last ten-year charge, it is necessary (for this purpose alone) to recompute the ten-yearly charge as if that property had been relevant property at the date of the ten-yearly charge, but taken at its value when it in fact became relevant property (s 69(2), (3)).

In respect of exit charges occurring on or after 18 November 2015, it is necessary (for this purpose alone) to recompute the ten-yearly charge as if property in the following categories (whether or not it has remained comprised in the settlement) had been relevant property comprised in the settlement at the date of the ten-yearly charge and any same-day addition made on or after the most recent ten-year anniversary had been made immediately before that anniversary (s 69(2A)), The categories of property, as set out in s 69(2) (as amended by F(No 2)A 2015 Sch 1 para 5(3)), are:

(i) relevant property has been added to a settlement at any time in the period beginning with the most recent ten-year anniversary and ending immediately before the date on which the exit charge arises;

(ii) in respect of the same period, property which was not relevant property at the time it was added has subsequently become relevant property; and

(iii) property which was comprised in the settlement immediately before the most recent ten-year anniversary was not then relevant property has since (in the period referred to in (i) above, become relevant property.

In the case of property in category (i) above, the value to be attributed to it is its value immediately after it became comprised in the settlement; in the case of categories (ii) and (iii) the value to be attributed to the property is its value when it became (or last became) relevant property (s 69(3) (as amended by F(No 2)A 2015 Sch 1 para 5(4)). Where the property that ceases to be trust property is a residential property, no residence nil-rate band is available in calculating any inheritance tax due.

For further details see **Example C10** at **explanatory note 7**.

Exit charge before first ten-year anniversary

(6) Where an exit charge arises before the first ten-year anniversary then for post-26 March 1974 settlements the rate to which the time-fraction in **explanatory note 4** is applied is 30% of the effective rate (s 68(2)).

In respect of exit charges arising before 18 November 2015, this effective rate is found by applying the lifetime rates (ie one half of the death rates) of inheritance tax then applicable to a notional chargeable transfer which is the sum of:

(a) the value of all the property in the settlement immediately after the settlement commenced, whether it is relevant property or not, plus

(b) the value of the property in any related settlement immediately after it commenced, plus

(c) the value of any added property at the time of its addition to the settlement (this includes accumulated income that has been treated as an accretion to capital, the date of addition being the date that the accumulation was so treated),

based on assumed previous chargeable transfers equal to any chargeable transfers made by the settlor in the seven years prior to the day on which the settlement was created. Note that the value of property immediately after the settlement in question commenced, in each of cases (a) to (c) above, is not necessarily the same as the value transferred by the settlor in contributing it to the settlement: in particular no deduction can be made in this context for business property relief or agricultural property relief.

In respect of exit charges arising on or after 18 November 2015, this effective rate is found by applying the lifetime rates (ie one half of the death rates) of inheritance tax then applicable to a notional chargeable transfer which is the sum of:

(a) the value of only the relevant property in the settlement immediately after the settlement commenced, plus

(b) the value of only the relevant property in any related settlement immediately after it commenced, plus

(c) the value of any added property at the time of its addition to the settlement which was relevant property at that time (whether or not it has remained relevant property comprised in the settlement) (this includes accumulated income that has been treated as an accretion to capital, the date of addition being the date that the accumulation was so treated), plus

(d) the value, at the time it became (or last became) relevant property, of property which was comprised in the settlement immediately after it commenced and was not then relevant property but which has since (and before the occasion of the exit charge), become relevant property, or of property which since the settlement's commencement has been added to the settlement and which was not relevant property at the time of its addition but has since (and before the occasion of the exit charge) became so, in both cases whether or not the property has remained relevant property comprised in the settlement, plus

(e) the value of any same-day additions (as defined in **explanatory note 2(a)(iv)** above), plus

(f) the value immediately after another settlement commenced of the relevant property then comprised in that other settlement but only where an increase in the value of the property comprised in that other settlement is represented by the value of a same-day addition aggregated under (e) above and that other settlement is not a related settlement.

again based on assumed previous chargeable transfers equal to any chargeable transfers made by the settlor in the seven years prior to the day on which the settlement was created. Note that the value of property immediately after the settlement in question commenced, in each of cases (a) to (f) above, is not necessarily the same as the value transferred by the settlor in contributing it to the settlement: in particular no deduction can be made in this context for business property relief or agricultural property relief.

Various problems arise in respect of a settlor's premature death within seven years of making a settlement. These include:

(i) additional tax being due through recomputation at death rates of the tax due on the original transfer to settlement, and

(ii) a failed PET made by the settlor prior to the formation of the settlement, which would both

- add to the settlor's inheritance tax accumulation which affects the settlement for as long as it comprises relevant property and
- increase the tax on the transfer which created the settlement.

The problems can be illustrated in this brief example:

A always used up his annual exemption by a gift of £3,000 to his nephew on 20 April each year.

On 10 May 2016 A gave his daughter £65,000

On 12 June 2017 he gave his son £100,000

On 1 September 2017, he set up a discretionary settlement with funds of £361,000, paying the tax due himself.

A died on 1 May 2023.

Original IHT position on gift to discretionary trust:

Gifts to son and daughter – PETs

Set up of discretionary trust – This is a chargeable transfer of £361,000. A has a nil cumulative total and the nil-rate band for 2017/18 was £325,000. The excess of £36,000 is grossed up (using the lifetime rate) as tax is paid by the settlor (36,000 × 100/80 = 45,000).

Chargeable transfer (gross)	£370,000
Tax paid by settlor (370,000 – 325,000 = 45,000 @ 20%)	£9,000

Reappraisal on subsequent death of Mr A (1 May 2023), using 2023/24 rates

Failed PETs to son and daughter

Transfers of £100,000 to his son and £65,000 to his daughter are within Mr A's nil-rate band so no further tax is payable. The cumulative total of transfers is however now increased to £165,000.

Transfer to discretionary trust

	£
Chargeable transfer to trust	370,000
Cumulative transfers	165,000
	535,000
Tax on death scale (535,000 – 325,000 = 210,000 @ 40%)	84,000
Tax payable after taper relief @ 60% (five to six years)	50,400
Less: paid in 2017/18	(9,000)
Additional tax payable by trustees	41,400

If the settlor's death occurs before a distribution out of the trust, the charge on the distribution is calculated accordingly. If the settlor dies after the distribution is made the exit charge may be increased and additional tax will then be payable. This is because, as above, any failed PETs on death will increase the amount of the settlor's previous transfers in the seven years before the commencement of the settlement. If aware of earlier PETs, therefore, well-advised trustees will make a suitable retention from any property distributed within the first seven years; but often they may be unaware of the settlor's earlier transfers and therefore – although in reality the trustees may need to consider relying on indemnities – the counsel of perfection would be to assume provisionally that no nil-rate band is available until the settlor has survived a full seven years from the making of the settlement.

The effect of the settlor's death on occasions of charge is considered in more detail in **Example C13**.

If a gift into settlement was free from IHT because of the availability of BPR or APR, and the property involved is subsequently disposed of by the trustees within seven years after it was settled, the trustees should prudently consider replacing it with other agricultural or business property so as to shelter any charge within IHTA 1984 ss 113B and 124B in the event of the settlor failing to survive the seven year period.

Grossing up

(7) If the exit charge is to be borne out of the fund that incurs the exit charge then no grossing up is necessary (s 65(2)(a)). The trustees, not the beneficiary in the case of a distribution, are liable for the tax, and so will deduct it from the distribution.

However, if the tax is to be paid out of the relevant property retained in the settlement then the chargeable amount must be grossed up (s 65(2)(b)). In the Example the distributions to A, B and D did not require any grossing up as the tax was to be borne by, and so deducted from, the distribution. C, however, was to receive £20,000 on a net basis, after payment of tax. The fund of relevant property has therefore been reduced by £20,000 plus the tax thereon £129, a total transfer of £20,129.

This is calculated by using the formula of:

$$\text{Net transfer} \times \frac{100}{(100 - \text{rate of tax})} = \text{gross transfer}$$

In this Example the rate of tax is 0.641% and therefore the calculation is:

$$£20,000 \times \frac{100}{(100 - 0.641)} = £20,129$$

Tax planning

(8) Although the treatment of discretionary trusts is complex, they have a useful role to play in tax planning.

If a settlor has not made any chargeable transfers, he can presently transfer assets to the value of £325,000 into a discretionary trust every seven years without either incurring inheritance tax or (provided the trust is not settlor-interested and the trustees are UK resident) incurring any immediate charge to capital gains tax (since the holdover relief in TCGA 1992 s 260 is available on *chargeable* transfers, whether any inheritance tax is payable on those transfers or not). Any transfers out of the trust in the first ten years will then not attract inheritance tax because the initial value of the trust property (**explanatory note 6(a)** above) is within the nil-rate band (subject to what is said below about business and agricultural property).

Care needs to be taken, however, if the settlor has already made potentially exempt transfers, because a liability on the transfer to the trust could then arise if he died within seven years, and also on distributions out of the trust. The rule of thumb must be to make chargeable transfers into a relevant property trust *before*, rather than after, any potentially exempt transfers.

Furthermore, now that all lifetime transfers into trust are subject to the relevant property regime (except where a disabled person's interest arises, see **Example C3**) it will be possible in many cases for trusts to maintain the flexibility of discretionary trusts rather than be constrained by the use of interest in possession settlements (or, before 6 April 2008, accumulation and maintenance trusts). Before the changes made to the tax treatment of dividend income from 6 April 2016, the above advantage of creating a discretionary trusts had to be weighed against the disadvantage which would have arisen where the trust would have had significant dividend income that was planned to be distributed rather than accumulated and capitalised. In such a case it would still have been preferred to create an interest in possession, even though for inheritance tax purposes this would not have been a qualifying IIP, because of the income tax considerations discussed in **Example F7 explanatory note 9** but this consideration has now fallen away following those changes to the tax treatment of dividend income.

If the property transferred into trust qualifies for 100% or 50% business or agricultural relief, this increases the amount that can be transferred without tax being payable, subject to what is said above about potentially exempt transfers. Distributions of the business or agricultural property out of the trust will also qualify for the appropriate rate of relief provided the trustees have by then fulfilled the required period of ownership or occupation. However, if a distribution is of unrelieved property (or the rate of relief is less than 100%) then the rate of tax on an exit charge within the first ten years will not be guaranteed (subject to changed legislation) to be nil even where the transfer into the trust was within the nil-rate band, because the whole of the value of the business or agricultural property is taken into account in calculating the initial value of the settlement (see **explanatory note 5(a)** above). Any exit charges on distributions within the first *ten* years are based on the full unrelieved value of the property when settled; in other words the availability of APR/BPR is ignored unless the asset distributed qualifies for such relief in its own right. (The same point applies where the transfer into the trust was partly covered by annual exemptions in addition to the maximum available nil-rate band.) For further details see **Example C13** at **explanatory note 5**.

(9) The changes made to the legislation in respect of exit and ten-yearly charges arising on or after 18 November 2015 (as described above) have negated the tax efficiency of having created pilot trusts – that is trusts created by the same settlor on different days (so as not to be related settlements) using nominal amounts and to which, on a later date (typically the death of the settlor) additional sums would simultaneously be added. Since such trusts were not related settlements, the rate of tax applicable to each in relation to subsequent exit and ten-yearly charges was calculated without having to aggregate the value of the property in each of them when computing the notional chargeable transfers upon which the rate of tax is based. This in effect gave each separate trust its own nil-rate band and reduced considerably the amount of tax arising on each chargeable occasion. See **Example C12** for a numerical example of the issue.

Spouse as discretionary beneficiary under a trust created by will

(10) It is possible to include a surviving spouse/civil partner as one of the discretionary beneficiaries, thus ensuring that property is not left directly to the surviving spouse/civil partner to swell that spouse's/civil partner's own estate. Prior to the introduction in 2007 of a transferable nil-rate band between spouses and civil partners (see **Example A3**), this was a common ploy, in the will of the first of a couple to die, in order to reduce inheritance tax on the second death.

In many cases it is no longer considered necessary to make use of a discretionary trust in the will of the first spouse to die because this will not result in any tax saving on the death of the survivor. The following examples illustrate the point.

Example A – Use of discretionary will trusts prior to transferable nil-rate band

Mr and Mrs Forster have estates in their sole names of £301,000 and £282,000 respectively. In addition they own a freehold house as joint tenants valued at £400,000. Their wills each leave all of their estate to the other (or to their only child in the case of the second spouse to die). They have not made any lifetime gifts. If both had died before 9 October 2007 their potential liability to inheritance tax (at 2007/08 rates) would have been:

		£
On first death:		
	Inter-spouse transfer – exempt	Nil
On second death:		
	Estate of Mr Forster	301,000
	Estate of Mrs Forster	282,000
	House	400,000
		983,000

Tax thereon (983,000 – 300,000 = 683,000 @ 40%) = £273,200

If, however, their wills had provided for an amount equal to the nil-rate band for inheritance tax to devolve upon a discretionary settlement, from which the surviving spouse, child and, say, grandchildren could benefit, with the residue of the estate devolving on the spouse, then the nil-rate band of the spouse dying first would be utilised, viz:

		£
On first death (say Mr Forster)		
	Free assets	301,000
	Pecuniary legacy to discretionary trust	300,000
	Residue to spouse	1,000
	½ share of house (passes to spouse by survivorship)	200,000
	Exempt transfer	201,000
Value of Estate		
	Own assets	301,000
	½ share of house	200,000
		501,000
	Less: exempt transfer	(201,000)
	Chargeable estate	300,000
	Covered by nil-rate band.	
On Mrs Forster's death		
	Own assets	282,000
	Residue from husband's estate	1,000
	House	400,000

On first death (say Mr Forster)	£
	683,000

Tax thereon (683,000 – 300,000 = 383,000 @ 40%) = £153,200

Thus taking both deaths together the discretionary trust would at the time of the second death (before 9 October 2007) save inheritance tax equal to the value of the nil-rate band on the first death (£300,000 @ 40% = £120,000). Provided the value in the discretionary trust does not increase faster than the rate of increase of the nil-rate band, no further tax will be payable on capital distributions from the trust. The surviving spouse would be able to have use of the income (and capital) of the trust with the agreement of the trustees (but distributions must not be made within first three months – see **explanatory note 11** below). The non-dividend income and the dividend income of the trust would be subject to income tax in the trustees' hands at 45% and 38.1 (37.5% in 2015/16) respectively (apart from the first slice income of £1,000), but this will be recoverable to the extent that it exceeds the beneficiary's personal tax liability if the income is distributed (see **Example F6** for further details, and **Example F7 part (2)** and **explanatory note 9** for certain complications with distributions of dividend income).

Example B – Use of discretionary will trusts after transferable nil-rate band

Assume the same facts as in **Example A** but the survivor (Mrs Forster) dies between 9 October 2007 and 5 April 2008. The potential inheritance tax liability without the use of a discretionary trust (still using 2007/08 rates) is:

		£
On first death:		
	Inter-spouse transfer – exempt	Nil
On second death:		
	Estate of Mr Forster	301,000
	Estate of Mrs Forster	282,000
	House	400,000
		983,000
Tax thereon (983,000 – 600,000* = 383,000 @ 40%) = £153,200		

* Mr Forster has not used his nil-rate band at all so Mrs Forster's nil-rate band is augmented by 100% and she therefore has £600,000 rather than £300,000 available.

If Mr and Mrs Forster's wills had provided for an amount equal to the nil-rate band to devolve upon a discretionary settlement, from which the surviving spouse, child and, say, grandchildren could benefit, with the residue of the estate devolving on the spouse, then the nil-rate band of the spouse dying first would be utilised, so the survivor's nil-rate band is not increased at all. Thus, the second calculation produces the same result (inheritance tax of £153,200 is payable on Mrs Forster's death) and there is no advantage in making use of the discretionary trust.

If Mrs Forster had died *after* 5 April 2008, the statutory nil-rate band at her death would have increased from £300,000 and so the potential nil-rate band on her death, with the benefit of a 100% transfer, would therefore be more than this £600,000. If the value of the property in the discretionary trust under Mr Forster's will had not increased, therefore, the trust would have resulted in a smaller overall value falling within the combined nil-rate bands, and therefore a higher overall inheritance tax charge, than if Mrs Forster had inherited outright or the trust had conferred a qualifying IIP on her instead. Where such trusts are used it is possible to unravel them within two years of the first death (see **explanatory note 11** below).

However, there are still circumstances where a discretionary will trust may have a role to play, for instance:

- to hold property whose value is thought likely to escalate after the first death at a greater rate than (double) the expected growth in the statutory general nil-rate band which is fixed at £325,000 until 5 April 2026 or the residence nil-rate band whose maximum basic amount has been £175,000 since 6 April 2020; or
- to hold property which will attract agricultural or business property relief on the first death, but is unlikely to do so on the survivor's death (whether because the property will have been sold by then or

because the business was dependent on a professional qualification of the first to die and cannot be carried on by the survivor); or

- to receive agricultural or business property, with the benefit of APR or BPR, which the trustees might consider selling to the surviving spouse in the hope that she may fulfil the relevant period of ownership or occupation thereafter and thus obtain double relief for the family at the end of the day.

In general terms there may be little point in having in place simple wills whereby assets devolve outright to family members if those assets then become exposed to risk, including an increase in the tax payable on a second death. Suitable trust arrangements provide flexibility in enhancing the prospects for both wealth preservation (such as protection against care fees, divorce, second marriages, incapacity and the like) as well as securing considerable tax savings. The latter point is well illustrated in the article in *Taxation* magazine entitled 'Flexible Friends' which can be accessed at www.taxation.co.uk/Articles/2017/04/18/336285/flexible-will-trusts-iht-planning

In some cases it is therefore felt better to continue to draft wills to include a discretionary trust of the nil-rate band, and/or of relievable property, leaving open the option of unravelling the trust (or converting it to interest in possession form for the survivor) within two years after the first death if the circumstances at that time are not such that a continuing discretionary trust is felt to be beneficial.

Distribution, or restructuring, within two years after death

(11) If a relevant property trust is created by will, distributions out of it within two years after the death are treated as having been made under the will (s 144) rather than being treated as amounts on which an exit charge is payable. This is a very useful provision enabling maximum flexibility to be built into a will so that the estate may be distributed taking into account the situation at the time of the death, rather than having to review the will regularly to ensure that its provisions are still appropriate. In respect of deaths occurring on or after 10 December 2014, this backdating effect for distributions applies throughout the two-year period following the death. This is the result of F(No 2)A 2015 s 14 which addressed an anomaly in s 144 (known as the 'Frankland trap' (as explained below in **explanatory note 13**) which denied the backdating effect for distributions made within the first three months after death (or, in a case where the will leaves property to the trustees of an existing pilot discretionary trust, within three months after a ten-year anniversary of that trust that happens to fall within two years after the settlor's death – the commencement of the settlement in that case will be when property was first put into the pilot trust), because exit charges do not apply to such distributions (see **explanatory note 4**).

(12) Where distributions of assets from a discretionary trust within two years after death are treated as made at death as indicated in **explanatory note 11** above, the capital gains tax position must be considered if the assets are liable to that tax and have increased in value since death. The capital gains tax gifts holdover relief of TCGA 1992 s 260 only applies if the distribution is chargeable to inheritance tax (see **Example D2 explanatory note 3**), which it is not where IHTA 1984 s 144 applies. Capital gains tax cannot therefore be held over unless the assets qualify for business gifts holdover relief under TCGA 1992 s 165 (as to which see **Example D2 part A(d)**). See **Example D2 explanatory note 5** for a way in which, with forethought on the part of the executors, a capital gains tax charge on the distribution may be avoided.

Historical development of s 144

(13) To be within the provisions of s 144 as it stood before FA 2006, a distribution had to in principle be one on which tax would otherwise be chargeable (though the rule also extended and still extends to distributions to employee trusts, charities or political parties, or maintenance funds for historic buildings, so long as these would incur a charge apart from the exemptions in s 75, s 76 or Sch 4 para 16(1) respectively). It must have not therefore occurred within the first three months after death (or, in a case where the will leaves property to the trustees of an existing pilot discretionary trust, within three months after a ten-year anniversary of that trust that happened to fall within two years after the settlor's death – the commencement of the settlement in that case will have been when property was first put into the pilot trust), because exit charges did not apply to such distributions (see **explanatory note 4**). In the case of *Frankland v CIR* (1997), within three months after the creation of a discretionary trust by will, the trust property was transferred to a trust in which the surviving spouse had a life interest. The intention was to avoid the inheritance tax on the death estate through the substitution of an exempt spouse transfer for the taxable transfer to the discretionary trust. It was held that s 144 did not apply (and so spouse relief did not become available retrospectively) because there would have been no exit charge on the transfer to the life interest trust (s 65(4), **explanatory note 4** above). This trap

(known as the 'Frankland trap') affected distributions to charities as well as outright distributions to a surviving spouse; the position for appointments of a life interest changed in part following the reforms in FA 2006 (but the trap still applied in the case of a disabled person's interest), see **explanatory note 14.**

(14) Section 144 was amended by FA 2006 to ensure that the backdating effect of the provision extended to the appointment of an interest in possession out of a relevant property trust established by the will (and indeed this is still the position). Except where the beneficiary was a disabled person at the death, so that the IIP would be a disabled person's interest, such an appointment within the two-year period did and still will give rise to an immediate post-death interest notwithstanding the requirement of s 49A that the interest should have taken effect immediately on the death (so that, apart from the new s 144(4)–(6), the property affected would not have ceased to be relevant property and would therefore not have triggered the backdating provision). The same provisions dealt and still deals with appointments on terms that meet the requirements for a bereaved minor's trust (s 71A) or an age 18-to-25 trust (s 71D), though it is arguable that the requirement of those sections (that the trusts should have been 'established by the will') would anyway have been fulfilled as a matter of interpretation, reading the appointment with the original terms of the will. Because the mechanism of the new provision does not depend on an event that would otherwise give rise to an exit charge, the three-month trap evident in the *Frankland* case (**explanatory note 13** above) did not apply in these cases, though it was unfortunately left to catch the unwary where property left the relevant property regime within the three-month period. Thus, if backdating under s 144 was to apply:

(a) three months had to have elapsed from the death (or ten-year anniversary) in the case of appointments or distributions to the deceased's surviving spouse or civil partner absolutely, or to a charity, or the creation of a disabled person's interest; but

(b) there was (as is still the case) no need to wait for the three month period to expire if the appointment or distribution creates an interest in possession for someone who definitely was not a disabled person at the deceased's death within the definition in s 89(4)–(6), or trusts that meet the requirement for a bereaved minor's trust or an 18-to-25 trust.

Question

A.

On 6 June 2013 H, who had made no previous transfers of value, settled £80,000 on discretionary trust (the terms of which satisfied the requirements of IHTA 1984 s 89A(1)(c) (Self-settlement by person expected to fall within the definition of 'disabled person'), with remainder to his wife, W, for life, with remainder on her death on discretionary trusts for the benefit of their children and grandchildren. On that date his wife, W, and one of their children, William, were disabled persons within the meaning of FA 2005 Sch 1A, and had been so for some time. At the time of the settlement HMRC accepted that a medical condition from which H was then suffering was such that it was reasonable to expect that he would become a disabled person as so defined.

H died on 5 May 2014 when his own assets were valued at £90,000.

His cumulative chargeable transfers at that date were £95,000.

By his will he left all his property to his children equally.

His wife, W, died on 4 October 2014 leaving assets valued at £196,000.

By her will she settled £50,000 cash on discretionary charitable trusts without limit of time, and the residue on discretionary trusts for her brother and his children.

She had made chargeable transfers of value totalling £129,750, all less than seven years before her death.

The settled fund under H's settlement was valued at £110,000 at W's death.

On 8 February 2015 the trustees of H's settlement appointed £30,000 gross to the eldest child, William, for life with remainder to his children who attained 18 or being daughters sooner married, but if William died without living issue, the appointed sum was to revert to the main trust fund. On that date William was still a disabled person as defined for the purposes of inheritance tax.

On 10 October 2020 William and his wife (who had no children) were killed in a car accident.

After payment of expenses in connection with his death, the fund appointed to William, which then fell back into the main fund of the settlement created on 6 June 2013, was valued at only £24,000. William's estate as a whole was insufficient to give rise to an inheritance tax charge on his death.

The rest of the property in that settlement was valued at that date at £96,000.

The recombined settlement may be taken to have the following values:

As at 5 June 2023	£113,640
As at 4 May 2024	£125,410
As at 3 October 2024	£157,624

(a) Calculate the inheritance tax payable in connection with the appointment on 8 February 2015 and on the first ten-year anniversary.

(b) To what extent would the answer differ if William had not been a disabled person (for the purposes of inheritance tax) on 6 June 2013 when H settled the trust but had become such a person by 8 February 2015 when the trustees of H's trust made the £30,000 appointment to him for life?

(So far as future events are concerned assume that the law set out in IHTA 1984 as amended does not change.)

B.

On 1 May 2013, at a time when he had made no earlier gifts, Sam settled £20 on discretionary trust (Trust A) for the benefit is his minor children. On 2 May 2013 he settled £20 on a second discretionary trust (Trust B) also for the benefit of his minor children. No further transfers were made by Sam and no property was added to either trust prior to his death on 3 May 2023 when, under the terms of a codicil (executed on 3 May 2013) to his Will which had been written in 2011, the proceeds of two life assurance policies totalling £650,000 are to be paid equally into each trust. The values of the funds in the trusts have not altered between Sam's death and May 2033.

(a) Calculate the inheritance tax payable on the ten year anniversaries of both trusts falling in 2033 on the assumption that the nil-rate band is of the same amount was it was on Sam's death.

(b) Explain to what extent the answer would differ Sam had died on 3 September 2016.

Answer

A.

(a) *Inheritance tax on 8 February 2015 appointment and on first ten-year anniversary*

6 June 2013	–	H settles £80,000 on discretionary trust for himself expecting to become a disabled person
	–	No IHT payable as no loss to his estate as H is deemed to have a qualifying IIP in the fund
5 May 2014	–	H dies, settlement passes to spouse for life – exempt transfer as the property passes onto an interest in possession trust for his wife who is a disabled person as defined for the purposes of inheritance tax (which being a qualifying IIP is treated as a transfer to W herself)
4 October 2014	–	W dies and, for the purpose of the relevant property rules, becomes the deemed settlor, at this date, of the trust made in fact by H on 6 June 2013

Tax position of deemed settlor W at date of her death, 4 October 2014

		Gross £	*Tax on 2014/15 scale* £
Cumulative transfers in seven years to date of death		129,750	Nil
Free estate on death	196,000		
Less: Charitable settlement (exempt)	(50,000)		
	146,000		
Interest in possession in husband's 2013 settlement	110,000	256,000	24,300*
		385,750	24,300*

(* 385,750 – 325,000 = 60,750 @ 40%)

IHT payable: £

By personal representatives $\frac{146,000}{256,000} \times £24,300 =$ 13,859

By trustees of settlement $\frac{110,000}{256,000} \times £24,300 =$ 10,441

24,300

Initial value of relevant property in related settlement (W's will trust)

Free estate	196,000
Less: to charitable trusts	(50,000)
	146,000

Less:	IHT payable by personal representatives	(13,859)
		£132,141

Initial value of relevant property in discretionary settlement (ie value at time it was deemed to commence)

	Value of fund in which W had an interest in possession at her death	110,000
Less:	IHT payable by trustees	(10,441)
		£99,559

8 February 2015 – Exit charge on creation of life interest for William

		Gross £	*Tax on 2014/15 scale* £
Settlor's 7-year cumulative total at time settlement deemed to commence		129,750	Nil
Notional transfer			
Initial value of settlement	99,559		
Initial value of related settlement	132,141		
Initial value of added property	Nil	231,700	7,290*
		361,450	7,290*

(* 361,450 – 325,000 = 36,450 @ 20%)

Actual rate is 30% of effective rate

$$\frac{7,290}{231,700} \times 30\% = 0.944\%$$

Quarters since settlement deemed to commence

4 October 2014 to 8 February 2015 = 1 quarter

Tax payable:

$$0.944\% \times \frac{1}{40} \times 30,000 = £7$$

6 June 2023 ten-year charge

	Original settlement	*Property reverting to settlement*	
Values (net of IHT on his death) on William's fund reverting to settlement	96,000	24,000	120,000
	80%	20%	100%
Same proportions of value immediately before ten-year anniversary	90,912	22,728	113,640
Date property last became relevant property	4 October 2014	10 October 2020	

Complete quarters since 6 June 2013 until property last became relevant property		5	29

		£
Assumed cumulative total:		
Settlor's 7-year cumulative total at time settlement deemed to commence		129,750
Property subject to exit charges in last 10 years		30,000
		159,750
Less:	Amount included in that cumulative total (exit charge) and also reflected in value of relevant property at ten-year anniversary	(22,728)
		137,022
Assumed transfer at 10-year anniversary:		
Relevant property at 5 June 2023		113,640
Initial value of relevant property in related settlement		132,141
		245,781

	Gross £	*Tax on 2023/24 scale* £
Assumed cumulative total	137,022	Nil
Assumed transfer at 10-year anniversary	245,781	11,561
	382,803	11,561*

(* 382,803 – 325,000 = 57,803 @ 20%)

Actual rate is 30% of effective rate

$$\frac{11,561}{245,781} \times 30\% = 1.411\%$$

		Original settlement	*Property reverting to original settlement*
Quarters excluded from appropriate fraction (above)		5	29
Quarters counted for appropriate fraction (balance of 40)		35	11
Tax payable:			£
Original settlement	1.411% × 35/40 ×	90,912	1,122
Returned property	1.411% × 11/40 ×	22,728	88
Value of settlement, and total tax, at 10-year anniversary		£113,640	1,210

(b) *Differences if William becomes a disabled person between 6 June 2013 and 8 February 2015*

W is still treated as the deemed settlor of the 2013 settlement for the purpose of the relevant property rules, and therefore her own will trust remains relevant as a related settlement. However, there is a major difference in relation to the appointment of the life interest to William, which in this instance has no inheritance tax consequences (see **explanatory note 3**).

Since the appointed fund remains relevant property as a result, there is no need to apportion the fund between the appointed fund and the main fund for the purpose of calculating the ten-year charge at 6 June 2023: the whole trust fund was relevant property (despite William's life interest as a disabled person in the appointed fund) at all times after W's death on 4 October 2014. The computation is therefore less complex, as follows:

Initial value of relevant property in related settlement (W's will trust)

Free estate		196,000
Less:	to charitable trusts	(50,000)
		146,000
Less:	IHT payable by personal representatives	(13,859)
		£132,141

6 June 2023 ten-year charge

Value of whole fund immediately before ten-year anniversary	113,640	
Date property last became relevant property 4 October 2014		
Complete quarters since 6.6.2013 until property last became relevant property	5	
Assumed cumulative total:		£
Settlor's 7-year cumulative total at time settlement deemed to commence		129,750
Property subject to exit charges in last 10 years		Nil
		129,750
Assumed transfer at 10-year anniversary:		
Relevant property at 5 June 2023		113,640
Initial value of relevant property in related settlement		132,141
		245,781

	Gross	*Tax on 2023/24 scale*
	£	£
Assumed cumulative total	129,750	Nil
Assumed transfer at 10-year anniversary	245,781	10,106*
	375,531	10,106*

(* 375,531 – 325,000 = 50,531 @ 20%)

Actual rate is 30% of effective rate $\frac{10,106}{245,781} \times 30\% = 1.234\%$

Quarters excluded from appropriate fraction (above)	5
Quarters counted for appropriate fraction (balance of 40)	35

Tax payable at ten-year anniversary: $1.234\% \times \frac{35}{40} \times 113{,}640 =$ £1,227

B

(a) *Ten year charges in 2033*

1 May 2033 ten-year charge for Trust A

	£
Assumed cumulative total:	
Settlor's 7-year cumulative total at time settlement commenced	Nil
Property subject to exit charges in last 10 years	Nil
	Nil
Assumed transfer at 10-year anniversary:	
Value of relevant property at 1 May 2033	325,020
Value of same-day addition (see **explanatory note 10**)	325,000
	650,020

	Gross £	*Tax on 2033/34 scale* £
Assumed cumulative total	Nil	Nil
Assumed transfer at 10-year anniversary	650,020	65,004*
	650,020	65,004*

(* 650,020 – 325,000 = 325,020 @ 20%)

Actual rate is 30% of effective rate $\frac{65,004}{650,020} \times 30\% = 3\%$

Tax payable at ten-year anniversary: 3 % × 325,020= 9,751

2 May 2033 ten-year charge for Trust B

	£
Assumed cumulative total:	
Settlor's 7-year cumulative total at time settlement commenced	Nil
Property subject to exit charges in last 10 years	Nil
	Nil
Assumed transfer at 10-year anniversary:	
Value of relevant property at 1 May 2033	325,020
Value of same-day addition (see **explanatory note 10**)	325,000
	650,020

Assumed cumulative total:

	Gross	Tax on 2033/34 scale
	£	£
Assumed cumulative total	Nil	Nil
Assumed transfer at 10-year anniversary	650,020	65,004*
	650,020	65,004*

(* 650,020 – 325,000 = 325,020 @ 20%)

Actual rate is 30% of effective rate $\frac{65,004}{650,020} \times 30\% = 3\%$

Tax payable at ten-year anniversary: 3 % × 325,020= 9,751

The total tax paid by both trusts on the occasion of the twentieth anniversaries of their creation is £19,502. This is the same amount as if the proceeds from the life assurance policy had been settled on one of the trusts only.

(b) *Death of Sam on 3 September 2016*

If Sam had died on 3 September 2016, the two trusts would have been protected settlements so that the settlements of the sums on his death are not treated as same day additions (see **explanatory note 11(c)**). Consequently, in calculating the rate of tax applicable to each settlement, the elements taken into account in the computation of the notional transfer are limited to the value of the relevant property in the trust at the time of the ten-year anniversary. In the Example that would be £325,020 which after deduction of the nil-rate band would result in an approximate 0% effective rate of tax arising which, in turn, means that no tax liability arises in 2033. This illustrates the (historic) tax efficiency achieved in creating pilot trusts (see **explanatory note 10**). However, as shown in **part B(a)**, this is no longer the case on or after 18 November 2015 when legislation came into force to reform the inheritance tax treatment of relevant property trusts where there is now the requirement to take into account the value of same-day transfers in computing the rate of tax applicable on a ten year anniversary The protected nature of the trusts in **part B(b)** of the Example is part of the transitional provisions introduced as part of the reform. As a result of the reform, taxpayers should review their Wills and ensure that they are amended to take into account the new rules.

Explanatory Notes

Settlement on self: inheritance tax consequences

(1) A transfer of value normally occurs when a person transfers property to a settlement.

Prior to 22 March 2006, if the settlor retained an interest in possession in the property in the settlement then there was no loss to his estate and therefore no transfer of value. Since that date, that treatment can only apply if the settlor's interest is a disabled person's interest (as to which see **Example C3**). In the **part A** of the Example H enjoys a contingent interest in the discretionary trust settled by himself in expectation that he may become a disabled person (as defined); H is treated as beneficially entitled to an interest in possession in the settled property (IHTA 1984 s 89A(4) and that interest is a disabled person's interest (s 89B(1)(b) and so a qualifying interest in possession (s 49). Hence H makes no transfer of value when he creates the trust.

In all other cases there will be a transfer of value even where the settlor has an immediate interest in possession; moreover, the settled property will always be relevant property, and the transfer of value (beyond the annual exemption or normal income expenditure exemption) will always be a chargeable transfer, unless a disabled person's interest is conferred on some other party. (In that case, if the other party is the settlor's spouse or civil partner, the spouse exemption will apply, otherwise it will be a potentially exempt transfer.)

Where the settlor or his spouse does have a qualifying interest in possession at the outset (much less common from 22 March 2006 for the reason stated), if the property subsequently becomes held on discretionary trusts, or (subject to the possibility of a transitional serial interest up to 5 October 2008) an interest in possession arises in favour of anyone other than the settlor or his spouse, then for the purpose of the relevant property rules the settlor or spouse (whoever last had the interest in possession) is deemed to have created a separate settlement at that time (unless the original settlement was made before 27 March 1974) (s 80).

Accordingly, for the purpose of the relevant property rules, the discretionary settlement in the Example is not deemed to be made until W dies, since until then H, and then W, had successive qualifying IIPs.

Inheritance tax treatment of related settlements

(2) Any other settlements created at the time of W's death would normally be related settlements (s 62(1)).

However the charitable trust is not regarded as related as the assets are held for charitable purposes without limit of time (s 62(2)) – see **Example C11 explanatory note 2(a)(iii)**.

Furthermore the transfer to the charitable trust is an exempt transfer (s 23) thus reducing the estate chargeable on W's death.

The inheritance tax payable on W's death in respect of the settlement is met by the trustees, thus reducing the initial value of the discretionary settlement deemed to be made by her from £110,000 to £99,559.

Exit charges for inheritance tax

(3) In **part A(a)** of the Example the interest in possession appointed to William was a qualifying IIP because it was a disabled person's interest and William was a disabled person at the time the trust was originally settled on 6 June 2013 (see **Example C3**). The appointment therefore resulted in the appointed fund ceasing to be relevant property, which is the primary event giving rise to an exit charge under the relevant property regime (see **Example C11 explanatory note 4**).

In **part A(b)** of the Example the appointment to William took place after 22 March 2006, and the life interest appointed to him (from a discretionary trust) could therefore only be a qualifying IIP if William had been a disabled person (at the date the trust property was in fact transferred into settlement, namely in 2013) (s 89(4)) (see **Example C3**). As this was not the case, the appointed property therefore remains relevant property, and there is no exit charge or other inheritance tax event at that time.

(4) The effective rate of tax on an exit charge depends upon whether the event giving rise to it occurs before the first ten-year anniversary (s 68) or after that date (s 69).

Although the settlement was deemed to be created by the death of W, the anniversary date is fixed by s 61 as being the tenth anniversary of the date when the original settlement commenced (s 61(2)).

(5) For the purpose of computing the assumed cumulative total and notional transfer, the date of the deemed creation of the settlement applies and accordingly the settlement commences with W's seven-year cumulative total immediately prior to her death, the settlement created by her will becoming a related settlement.

(6) Although the cycle of ten-year anniversaries runs from the date of the actual original settlement (**explanatory note 4** above), the quarters that are counted towards the appropriate fraction, to determine the rate on the exit charge, start from the commencement of the settlement, which is W's death (4 October 2014 as explained in **explanatory note 1** (s 68(2)).

Inheritance tax ten-yearly charge

(7) On the tenth anniversary of the original settlement (6 June 2023) a ten-yearly charge arises under s 64 even though only approximately eight years and seven months have elapsed since the settlement was deemed to commence on W's death.

As the property subject to the exit charge (appointment of life interest to William) is also included in the value of relevant property (because of the death of William and his wife and the consequent reversion of the property to the discretionary settlement), the assumed cumulative total is reduced in **part A(a)** of the Example by the lower of:

(a) the amount subject to the exit charge of £30,000; or

(b) the proportionate value at the ten-year anniversary of the property which has reverted (s 67(6), (7) as applied by s 66(5)).

At the time the property reverted to the settlement it was valued at £24,000 and the other property in the settlement at £96,000. Accordingly 20% (£24,000 out of £120,000) of the value at 6 June 2023 (£113,640), or £22,728, derives from the fund that had been appointed to William and subsequently reverted.

In **part A(b)** of the Example this reduction does not arise because there was no exit charge on the appointment of William's life interest.

(8) In **part A** of the Example the ten-year anniversary of the settlement originally created by H occurs after 17 November 2015, the date on which changes were made as regards the inclusion of property in a related settlement in the computation of the ten-year charge were made by FA 2017 Sch 1 para 3. For ten-year charges occurring before that date, *all* property in a related settlement is considered in calculating the charge; after that date only *relevant* property in such a settlement is counted. On the facts of the Example, the property in the related settlement is relevant property so that there would be no change (in principle) to the calculation shown had the ten-year anniversary occurred before that date.

(9) The charge at the ten-year anniversary is reduced by the number of complete quarters prior to the appropriate date. Again the appropriate fractions in **part A(a)** of the Example reflect the fact that part of the property only became relevant property on 4 October 2014, and part last reverted to the settlement on 10 October 2020 (s 66(2)). In **part A(b)** of the Example the whole trust fund has been relevant property since W's death on 4 October 2014 – William's life interest was not a qualifying interest in possession and the appointed fund remained relevant property like the continuing discretionary fund.

(10) Historically multiple trusts have been used to secure the benefit of a number of nil-rate bands without having to wait seven years between the creation of settlements. This use of so-called 'pilot trusts' entailed a settlor setting up a series of settlements on different days (so that they were not created on the same day so as to be related settlements). Subsequently property was added (typically on the settlor's death) to each trust on the same day. Since only related trusts were (historically) cumulated in determining the rate of tax applicable on exit and ten-yearly charges, this resulted in each trust having its own nil-rate band, the funds added to each of the other settlements being disregarded when arriving at the rate of IHT applicable. HMRC's legal challenge against such planning failed (*Rysaffe Trustee Co (CI) v IRC* (2003)). This planning has now been blocked with the use of the concept of a 'same-day addition' as illustrated in **part B** of the Example.

The ten-yearly charges arising in 2033 in respect of Sam's trust fall on or after 18 November 2015 when legislation came into force to reform the inheritance tax treatment of relevant property trusts. Part of that reform adds the requirement to take into account the value of same-day transfers in computing the rate of tax applicable. The rules in this regard apply to exit and ten-year charges arising on or after 18 November 2015 in respect of relevant property trusts created on or after 10 December 2014 and relevant property trusts created before that day where the trust is not a protected settlement (see **explanatory note 11(c)**).

A same-day addition occurs in relation to a settlement if, as provided in s 62A(1), the following conditions are met:

(a) there is a transfer of value by a person as a result of which the value of the property in a settlement ('Settlement A') increases;

(b) as a result of another transfer of value (or indeed the same transfer) made by that person on the same day, the value of the property in another settlement ('Settlement B') increases;

(c) that person is the settlor of both Settlement A and Settlement B;

(d) at any point in time between the commencement of Settlement A or Settlement B as appropriate and ending with the transfer of value concerned all or any part of the property comprised in Settlement A was relevant property; and

(e) at that point, or at any other point in the above period, all or any of the property in Settlement B was relevant property.

Hence the same-day addition rules also do not, in terms, catch additions made on different days if those additions have no taxable value. For example where multiple trusts are created on different days and subsequently there is added to them property qualifying for 100% business property relief (see **Example A21**) or 100% agricultural property relief (see **Example A22**), each trust will in effect continue to enjoy its own nil-rate band (as described above and as illustrated in **part B(b)** of the example). The same result will arise in relation to an asset with no initial value (eg a term life assurance policy with no surrender value parts of which can be settled in separate trusts created on different days). Neither do the same-day addition rules apply where either Settlement A or Settlement B is a trust in which there is no relevant property (as may be the case where, say, Settlement A was settled in lifetime on interest in possession trusts for disabled persons or Settlement A was created under a will and is an immediate post-death interest. In both cases the Settlement A is a qualifying IIP and so not a relevant property trust (see **Example C3**). In such cases Settlement A would not be taken into account in applying the same-day addition rules.).

The value of a same-day addition is the increase in value of the property in Settlement B as a result of the transfer of value by the person (in this case £325,000) (s 62A(2)).

The transfers of value in relation to Settlement A or Settlement B on the creation of the settlement can be a same-day addition but not if settlements A and B are related settlements (ie settlements created by the same settlor on the same day) (s 62A(4)). What is important for the operation of the above conditions is that the value of the property in the respective settlements increases and it is immaterial whether the amount of property comprised in them is increased as a result of the person's transfer of value (s 62A(5)). So there can be a same-day addition where there is an increase in the value of property comprised in a settlement without an increase in the amount of property in the settlement.

Same-day additions primarily occur on the death of a person in relation to the deemed transfer of value (of his estate) that he is deemed to make at that time under s 4. However, same-day additions may occur in lifetime but only if both of the following two conditions are met (s 62B(2));

(a) the increase in value of the property in Settlement A as a result of the transfer of value by the person exceeds £5,000, or where there are two or more transfers on the same day, the increase in value of the property in Settlement A as a result of all such transfers exceeds £5,000 (ie this is an anti-fragmentation rule to prevent individuals avoiding the same addition rules by transferring amounts in excess of £5,000 to Settlement A in multiples of £5,000) (s 62B(3)), and

(b) the increase in value of the property in Settlement B as a result of the transfer of value by the person exceeds £5,000, or where there are two or more transfers on the same day, the increase in value of the property in Settlement B as a result of all such transfers exceeds £5,000 (s 62B(4)).

(11) Certain transfers of value are not regarded as same-day additions. A same-day addition cannot occur:

(a) in respect of the creation of settlements where the settlements are related (ie settlements made on the same day by the same settlor). At the heart of the concept of a same-day addition are transfers of value in respect of settlements made by the same settlor but on different days (s 62A(4)); or

(b) if all the property comprised in Settlement A or Settlement B after the respective transfers of value in respect of those settlements is held for charitable purposes without limit of time (s 62B(1)(a),(b)); or

(c) if either or each of Settlement A and Settlement B is a protected settlement (s 62B(1)(c)). A protected settlement is a settlement that commenced before 10 December 2014 where (s 62C(1)):

(i) there have been no transfers of value by the settlor on or after 10 December 2014 as a result of which the value of the settled property increased (ie no additions have been made by the settlor after that date. It will be noted that there are no exceptions to this prohibition, not even for small amounts. The addition, for example, of a small sum to fund the trustees' legal expenses would abrogate the protected settlement status of the trust concerned, as would an addition which is exempt from IHT, such as the transfer of a sum under £3,000) (s 62(2)),or

(ii) there has been a transfer of value by the settlor on or after 10 December 2014 as a result of which the value of the settled property increased but that transfer occurred on the death of the settlor before 6 April 2017 and the reason the value of the property in the settlement increased was because of a disposition under the settlor's will that had remained substantially unchanged since immediately before 10 December 2014 (ie the only addition has been made under a will executed before 10 December 2014 where the settlor dies before 6 April 2017) (s 62C(3),(4)); or

(d) if either or each of the transfers of value in respect of Settlement A and Settlement B results from the payment of a premium under a life insurance contact which provides for premiums to be paid at regular intervals of one year or less throughout the contract term, of is made to fund such a payment (s 62B(1)(d)); or

(e) in respect of a transfer of value made during the settlor's lifetime provided the increase in value as regards the property in both settlements is less than the de minimis amount set out above (s 62B(2)).

(12) The use of pilot trusts or multiple trusts was, before the introduction of the same-day addition rules, a common device to minimise inheritance tax in relation to exit and ten-year anniversary charges. The question of whether such trusts are still worthwhile is discussed in a series of articles entitled 'Multiple Trusts' written by Emma Chamberlain and published in the *Tax Adviser* magazine dated February 2022 and March 2022.

(13) See Examples C10, C11 and C13 for further details of relevant property trusts.

Question

On 6 June 2013 Smith retired from the family farming partnership which had commenced 20 years earlier when he had taken his brother and their respective sons into partnership.

His cumulative chargeable transfers at that date were £242,352 arising out of transfers of value made in December 2006, and he had not yet made any potentially exempt transfers.

At the time of his retirement he transferred the freehold interest in one of his farms, valued at £100,000, which had been leased for the last 18 years to a non-family tenant farmer, to the trustees of a discretionary settlement (the B Trust) which he created at the same time. The trust was in favour of the children of his brother, who had recently been killed in a farming accident for which Smith felt some moral responsibility. Smith agreed to pay any inheritance tax due.

On the same date he settled £100,000 of the cash due to him from the partnership on a second discretionary settlement in favour of his own children (the C Trust).

The trustees of this settlement paid any inheritance tax due.

On 5 May 2014 Smith added £24,000 in cash to the B Trust (on which the trustees paid the inheritance tax due).

On 6 May 2014 Smith gave his own children £245,000 in cash.

On 1 January 2015 the trustees of the B Trust appointed £18,000 to the late brother's eldest son (on which the son paid the tax).

On 9 September 2016 when the B Trust consisted of the farm and 12,000 £1 shares in ABC plc, Smith added a further 120,000 £1 shares in ABC plc to that trust and paid the inheritance tax himself.

On 2 February 2019 the trustees of the B Trust appointed 66,000 shares in ABC plc to the eldest daughter absolutely (on which the daughter paid the tax).

The assets in the B Trust were:

	Market value of farm	*Shares in ABC plc at value for inheritance tax*
9 September 2016	£200,000	140p each
2 February 2019	£210,000	150p each
5 June 2023	£300,000	200p each
6 June 2023	£300,000	201¾p each

The B Trust had £6,000 of income arising from the trust property in 2022 that the trustees had not accumulated.

Calculate the inheritance tax payable by the trustees in connection with the two appointments from the B Trust and on the first ten-year anniversary of that trust.

Ignore capital gains tax and assume that Smith the settlor is still living and that the position regarding occupation of the farm has remained unchanged throughout.

Answer

6 June 2013 – formation of B and C Trusts

Tax position of settlor — Smith

				Gross	Tax (on 2013/14 scale)	Net
Inheritance tax accumulation						
6 June 2013				£	£	£
Cumulative transfers to date (December 2006)				242,352	Nil	242,352
B Trust – Farm			100,000			
Less: Agricultural property relief 50% (see **explanatory note** 5)			(50,000)			
			50,000			
Less: Annual exemptions	2013/14	3,000				
	2012/13	3,000				
		6,000				
			(2,000)**			
Net transfer, grossed up (see **explanatory note** 4)			48,000		4,957	
C Trust – Cash			100,000			
Less: Annual exemptions 2013/14 and 2012/13			(4,000)**			
Gross transfer			96,000		9,913***	
Total transfer on 6 June 2013			144,000	144,000		
				386,352	14,870*	371,482

(* 386,352 – 312,000 = 74,352 @ 20%)
(** Apportionment of annual exemptions — see **explanatory note 1**)
(*** Apportionment of tax – see **explanatory note 1**)

	B Trust	C Trust	Total
Total value transferred by transfers of value	50,000	100,000	150,000
Percentage of total value transferred	33.33%	66.67%	100%
Exemptions as above, apportioned	2,000	4,000	6,000
Tax as above, apportioned	4,957	9,913	14,870

Tax position of settlements:

Initial value of B Trust (settlor pays tax)	£100,000
Initial value of C Trust (a related settlement) – £100,000 less tax £9,913	£90,087

5 May 2014 — Property added to B Trust

Tax position of settlor — Smith

				Gross	Tax (2014/15 scale)
Inheritance tax accumulation				£	£
Cumulative transfers in last seven years (see **explanatory note 9**(i))				148,957	Nil
Added property			24,000		
Less: Annual exemptions	2014/15	3,000			
	2013/14	Nil**	(3,000)	21,000	Nil*
				169,957	Nil*
(* within nil-rate band of £325,000)					
Initial value of added property =	£24,000				
(** 2013/14 exemption already used on 6 June 2013)					

Tax position of B Trust

1 January 2015

Exit charge on distribution to late brother's eldest son (Note – as farm is not sold the distribution must come from property added on 5 May 2014 and the tax calculation is affected accordingly)

		Gross	Tax (2014/15 scale)
		£	£
Settlor's seven-year cumulative total at time settlement commenced (IHTA 1984 s 68(4)(b)) – see **explanatory note 9**		242,352	Nil
Notional transfer (s 68(4)(a) and (5))			
Initial value of settlement (B Trust)	100,000		
Initial value of related settlement (C Trust)	90,087		
Initial value of added property (to B Trust)	24,000	214,087	26,287
		456,439	26,287*

(* 456,439 – 325,000 = 131,439 @ 20%)

Effective rate:

$$\frac{26,287}{214,085} \times 100\,\% = 12.279\%$$

Appropriate fraction (s 68(3)):

Complete quarters since settlement commenced

6 June 2013 to 1 January 2015	6 quarters
Less: Complete quarters before property added	
6 June 2013 to 5 May 2014	3 quarters
	3 fortieths

Tax payable on cash distribution to son:		
Value distributed	18,000	
Tax	$18{,}000 \times 12.279\,\% \times 30\,\% \times \frac{3}{40}$	£50

9 September 2016 — further added property

Tax position of settlor — Smith

				Gross	Tax (2016/17 scale)	Net
				£	£	£
Cumulative transfers in last seven years — see **explanatory note 9(ii)**			Nil	169,957	Nil	169,957
Added property 120,000 shares @ 140p			168,000			
Less: Annual exemptions	2016/17	3,000				
	2015/16	3,000	(6,000)			
Net transfer						162,000
Grossed up*				163,739	1,739	
				333,696	1,739	331,957
* Cumulative net transfers		331,957				
Nil-rate band		325,000				
Excess grossed up at 20%		6,957	$\times \frac{100}{80} =$	8,696	1,739	

Initial value of added property – £168,000 (tax paid by settlor)

Tax position of B Trust

2 February 2019

Exit charge on distribution to eldest daughter (Shares deemed to have been appropriated pro-rata out of property added on 5 May 2014 and 9 September 2016, since the farm is still owned)

		Gross	Tax (2018/19 scale)
		£	£
Assumed Transfer:			
Settlor's seven-year cumulative total at time settlement commenced (see **explanatory note 9**)		242,352	Nil
Notional transfer			
At 1 January 2015 (above)	214,087		
Initial value of further property added 9 September 2016	168,000	382,087	59,887
		624,439	59,887*

(* 624,439 – 325,000 = 299,439 @ 20%)

Effective rate: $\frac{59,887}{382,085} \times 100\,\% = 15.674\%$

Actual rate before appropriate fraction is 30% of effective rate, ie 30% × 15.674% = 4.702%

Appropriate fraction:		
Quarters since settlement commenced		
6 June 2013 to 2 February 2019	22	22
Less: Complete quarters before first addition (as above)	3	
Less: Complete quarters before second addition		
6 June 2013 to 9 September 2016		13
	19	9

Tax payable on distribution of 66,000 ABC plc shares at £1.50 to daughter

Value distributed £99,000:

re 2014 addition (12,000 shares)

$$4.702\,\% \times \frac{19}{40} \times £\,99{,}000 \times \frac{12{,}000}{132{,}000} = 201$$

re 2016 addition (120,000 shares)

$$4.702\,\% \times \frac{9}{40} \times £\,99{,}000 \times \frac{120{,}000}{132{,}000} = 952$$

£1,153

6 June 2023 – B Trust ten-year charge (see explanatory notes 8, 9 and 10)

		Gross	Tax (2023/24 scale)
		£	£
Assumed cumulative total:			
Settlor's seven-year cumulative total at time settlement commenced (see **explanatory notes 9 and 10**)		242,352	
Exit charges in previous 10 years			
1 January 2015	18,000		
2 February 2019	99,000	117,000	
		359,352	6,870

Assumed transfer:

Relevant property – value as at 5 June 2023 (excluding the un-accumulated income of 2022)

Farm	300,000		
Less: Agricultural property relief 50%	(150,000)		
	150,000		
66,000 shares in ABC plc @ 200p	132,000		
	282,000		
Initial value of related settlement	90,087	372,087	74,417
		731,439	81,287**

(* 359,352 – 325,000 = 34,352 @ 20%)
(** 731,439 – 325,000 = 406,439 @ 20%)

Effective rate $\frac{74{,}417}{372{,}085} \times 100\,\% = 20\%$

(Note that with the present single rate structure the effective rate will always be 20% if the assumed cumulative total exceeds the nil-rate threshold, and in that event the subsequent calculations are not necessary. It is still, however, necessary to value the respective parts of the settled fund if it has not all been settled for the full ten years.)

Appropriate fraction

	Complete quarters before fund became relevant property	*Resulting numerator*	*Shares*	*Value for IHT*
Farm – settled for full ten years	0	40		150,000
Shares – 6/66 added 5 May 2014	3	37	6,000	12,000
Shares – 60/66 added 9 September 2016	13	27	60,000	120,000

Farm – no reduction (settled for full ten years)

Shares – 6/66 added 5 May 2014 = three quarters reduction giving 37/40

Shares – 60/66 added 9 September 2016 = 13 quarters reduction giving 27/40

IHT payable:

Farm – original fund	$20\,\% \times 30\,\% \times \frac{40}{40} \times £\,150{,}000 =$	9,000
6,000 shares – first addition	$20\,\% \times 30\,\% \times \frac{37}{40} \times £\,132{,}000 \times \frac{6{,}000}{66{,}000} =$	666
60,000 shares – second addition	$20\,\% \times 30\,\% \times \frac{27}{40} \times £132{,}000 \times \frac{60{,}000}{66{,}000} =$	4,860
		£14,526

Explanatory Notes

Same day transfers and their effect on the calculation of inheritance tax

(1) Where two transfers are made on the same day, the annual exemptions are divided between the transfers proportionally to the value transferred, even if one of the transfers was a potentially exempt transfer (s 19(3)(a)). In this Example both transfers are immediately chargeable.

The transfer to the B Trust is added to the inheritance tax accumulation before the gift to the trustees of the C Trust because the tax on the former gift is to be met by Smith (and so is grossed up – by taking this transfer first, grossing up occurs at the lowest rate possible – which is 0% in this Example) , whereas the trustees of the C Trust are to meet the tax due on that later transfer and the total tax on both gifts would be higher if they were included the other way round. IHTA 1984 s 266(1) allows transfers made on the same day to be dealt with in the order which results in the lowest value chargeable.

Section 266(2) then provides that once the value of each same-day transfer has been established, the chargeable value of each is ascertained (in this Example this entails the deduction of the annual exemption available). The chargeable values of all the same-day transfers are then added together and tax is calculated on that basis (ie as if all the transfers were one chargeable transfer). The effective rate of inheritance tax may then be calculated (by taking the total tax payable and dividing it by the total value of the chargeable transfers) and in turn the actual tax payable on each transfer may then be ascertained. In this Example the tax payable on the deemed single chargeable transfer of £144,000 is £14,870. The effective rate of tax is therefore £14,870/£144,000 × 100% = 10.3285%. The tax payable on the transfer to the B Trust is therefore £48,000 × 10.3285% = £4,957 and that payable on the transfer to the C Trust is £96,000 × 10.3285% = £9,913.

Related settlement for inheritance tax

(2) Because the C Trust is made on the same day as the B Trust they are related settlements to each other (s 62).

Although the amount settled by Smith in the C Trust was £100,000, inheritance tax of £9,913 was payable by the trustees, giving an initial value of £90,087 applicable to that related settlement. The amount settled is relevant property.

(3) The tax on the B Trust is paid by Smith (the settlor) and therefore its initial value remains at £100,000. The amount settled is relevant property.

(4) The chargeable transfer of £48,000 so far as grossing up is required falls within the nil-rate band on the scale applicable in 2013/14. The tax attributable to the transfer under s 266(2) is £4,957 and this is payable by Smith. The value of the chargeable transfer made by him for cumulation purposes is therefore £48,000 + £4,957 = £52,957.

Inheritance tax exit charge – identification of property when property has been added

(5) The rate of tax payable on the exit charges depends on whether the property leaving the settlement came from the original settlement (or property held at the previous ten-year anniversary) or property added, because of the differing periods for which the respective funds have been relevant property.

In this Example the original settlement of the B Trust was a farm which is still owned throughout the period under consideration, so therefore the distributions must always be from the added property.

Note however that where property has qualified for annual exemptions and/or business or agricultural relief in calculating the tax due on its transfer into the settlement, this is not taken into account in calculating the initial value of the settlement, so any exit charges on distributions within the first ten years are based on the full value of the property when settled, as shown in the Example in relation to the exit charge on 1 January 2015 (s 68). If the distribution itself consists of qualifying business or agricultural property, the relief is available in arriving at the value of the distribution (providing the trustees satisfy the conditions for relief). When calculating the ten-yearly charge, business or agricultural property relief is taken into account in arriving at the value of the trust property, as shown in the Example in the calculation on 6 June 2023 (s 66) and this in turn affects the exit charge applied to capital distributions made in the following ten years.

The rate of agricultural property relief on the transfer of the farm to the settlement in 2013 was 50% for tenanted agricultural property rather than 100% for owner occupied property etc, because the tenancy had been granted before 1 September 1995 (see **Example A22**). Where rates of relief increase after a settlement, the increased rate may be taken into account in computing any *additional* liability to inheritance tax resulting from a death within seven years where the date of death is *after* the date of increase. However the increased rate is *not* applied to calculations of the accumulated transfers brought forward where the original chargeable transfer was before the date of increase even if that amount is used to calculate liabilities after that date.

Agricultural property relief will be available to the trustees in respect of the ten-year charge on 6 June 2023, since they have owned the farm for more than seven years, but again only at 50% as the lease was granted prior to 1 September 1995 and vacant possession is not available within twelve months.

Inheritance tax exit charge – rate of tax when property has been added

(6) The effective rate of tax on an exit depends upon whether the distribution occurs before the first ten-year anniversary (in which case s 68 applies) or after the first ten years (then s 69 applies) (see **Example C11 explanatory notes 4 to 6**).

In this Example both exit charges are before the first ten-year anniversary, so the effective rate is calculated by adding a notional transfer to the settlor's seven-year cumulative total at the time the settlement commenced.

The notional transfer is the sum of the initial values of the original settlement, related settlements and added property (including accumulated income treated as an accretion to capital) but ignoring the availability of agricultural property relief. For exits occurring on or after 18 November 2015, the property in each case must be relevant property.

The effective rate is reduced to an appropriate fraction comprising the number of complete quarters (ie three-month periods) from the date the settlement commenced to the date of the charge, divided by 40.

However when the property leaving the settlement is not part of the original settlement then the numerator is reduced by the number of complete quarters from the date of settlement to the date the property is added.

The tax payable on the distribution is then 30% of the appropriate fraction of the effective rate.

(7) On the occasion of the second distribution it should be noted that the rate must be recomputed using the inheritance tax rates then applicable (if lower) and, because further property has been added, the notional transfer has been increased.

Provisions to avoid double counting on a ten-year inheritance tax charge where property has been added to a settlement

(8) Where property has been added to the settlement after 8 March 1982 when the law relating to relevant property trusts altered (strictly because 'the settlor has made a chargeable transfer as a result of which the value of the property comprised in the settlement was increased') the rules in s 67 apply when calculating the tax charge on the ten-year anniversary.

The 'assumed cumulative total' to be used includes whichever is highest of

- the settlor's seven-year cumulative total as at the date the settlement commenced, and
- his seven-year cumulative total at the time of each respective addition, reduced when appropriate as explained below.

If no reductions were made this procedure might result in double counting, eg if the addition is made less than seven years after the commencement of the settlement, the settlor's seven-year cumulative total at the date of the addition will include the sum originally settled as well as earlier additions which (unless the property has been the subject of an exit charge) form part or all of the relevant property in the settlement now subject to the ten-year charge. It will also reflect the initial value of any related settlement.

In such circumstances the seven-year cumulation is reduced by so much as is attributable to property whose value is taken into account in the 'assumed transfer' (s 67(5)(a)).

Similarly the seven-year cumulative total at the time of an addition may reflect the value of property which has ceased to be relevant property at the date of the ten-year charge and has been the subject of an exit charge in the previous ten years. Once again the seven-year cumulation is reduced by the amount attributable to the property in respect of which the exit charge was made (s 67(5)(b)).

Double counting relief also applies where property has been the subject of an exit charge on the creation of a qualifying interest in possession within the last ten years, but has since become relevant property again. Its value would appear both as relevant property and as property on which an exit charge had been levied in the last ten years. In such circumstances, the latter amount is reduced by the smaller of the value at the time of the exit charge and the value at the time of the ten-year charge, as illustrated in **Example C12** (s 67(6)).

(9)

(i) In the Example Smith's seven-year cumulative total at the time of the first addition (5 May 2014), and the available reduction in calculating the effective rate on the ten-year charge on the B Trust, is:

		Cumulative Total	*Available Reduction*
		£	£
(a)	his seven-year cumulation prior to the creation of the B Trust — December 2006 – now spent because more than seven years before addition	Nil	Nil
(b)	relating to the creation of the B Trust (see **explanatory note 4**)	52,957	52,957
(c)	by reference to the creation of the related settlement (C Trust). Of this sum £9,913 was used by the trustees to pay the tax so that only £90,087 is attributable to the initial value of the related settlement in the 'assumed transfer'	96,000	90,085
		148,957	143,044

(ii) Smith's seven-year cumulative total at the time of the second addition (9 September 2016), and the available reduction in calculating the effective rate on the ten-year charge on the B Trust, is:

		Cumulative Total	*Available Reduction*
		£	£
(a)	his seven-year cumulation prior to the creation of the B Trust (spent, see **(i)(a) above**)	Nil	Nil
(b)	relating to the creation of the B Trust, as in (i)(b) **above**	52,957	52,957
(c)	by reference to the creation of the related settlement (C Trust), as in (i)(c) **above**	96,000	90,087
(d)	by reference to the first addition of £24,000. The chargeable £21,000 (after annual exemptions) is therefore attributable to relevant property in the settlement at the time of the ten-year charge or to property that is the subject of the exit charge on 1 January 2015	21,000	21,000
(e)	Gift to children – potentially exempt	Nil	Nil
		169,957	164,044

In both cases transfers on the same date as the addition (ie including the addition itself) are excluded from the cumulative total, though the net addition may feature in the notional transfer itself.

(iii) The assumed cumulative total is therefore the highest of:

		£	£
(a)	Settlor's seven-year cumulative total prior to the creation of the settlement		242,352
(b)	Settlor's seven-year cumulative total on first addition (see (i) **above**)	148,957	
	Less: Available reduction	(143,043)	5,914
(c)	Settlor's 7-year cumulative total on second addition (see (ii) **above**)	169,957	
	Less: Available reduction	(164,042)	5,915

Accordingly the cumulative total on creation of the settlement ((iii)(a) **above**) is used.

Effect of settlor's death

(10) Note that if Smith had died before 6 May 2021 then the potentially exempt gift of £245,000 to his children on 6 May 2014 would have become chargeable. This would alter the calculation of liability at the time of the second addition (even though death occurred after the tax had been agreed). The seven-year cumulative total at the date of the second addition would then be:

	Cumulative Total	*Available Reduction*
	£	£
As 9(ii) (a) to (d) above	169,957	164,042
(e) Gift to children – now chargeable	245,000	Nil
	414,957	164,044

The assumed cumulative total would therefore now be the highest of:

		£	£
(a)	Settlor's seven-year cumulative total prior to the creation of the B Trust (2013)		242,352
(b)	Settlor's seven-year cumulative total on first addition to the B Trust (2015)	148,957	
	Less: Available reduction	(143,044)	5,913
(c)	Settlor's seven-year cumulative total on second addition to the B Trust (2016)	414,957	
	Less: Available reduction	(164,044)	250,913

This would revise the inheritance tax liability on 2 February 2019, but not the ten-year anniversary on 6 June 2023 as the effective rate of tax was already at the maximum amount of 20%, as follows:

Exit charge 2 February 2019

	Gross	Tax (2018/19 scale)
	£	£
Assumed transfer:		
Settlor's cumulative total as above	250,913	Nil
Notional transfer (see above under 'Tax position of B Trust')	382,087	61,600
	633,000	61,600*

(* 633,000 – 325,000 = 308,000 @ 20%)
Actual rate is 30% of the effective rate

$$\frac{61,600}{382,085} \times 30\,\% = 4.837$$

Tax payable:

re 2014 addition (12,000 shares)

$$4.837\,\% \times \frac{19}{40} \times £\,99,000 \times \frac{12,000}{132,000} = 207$$

re 2016 addition (120,000 shares)

$$4.837\,\% \times \frac{9}{40} \times £\,99,000 \times \frac{120,000}{132,000} = 979$$

£1,186 (previously £1,153)

6 June 2023 – ten-year charge

	Gross	Tax (on 2023/24 scale)
	£	£
Settlor's cumulative total as above	250,913	Nil
Exit charges in previous 10 years (see above at **51.5**)	117,000	
	367,913	8,583*
Assumed transfer (see above at **51.5**)	372,087	74,417
	740,000	83,000**

(* 367,913 – 325,000 = 42,913 @ 20%)
(** 740,000 – 325,000 = 415,000 @ 20%)

$$\frac{74,417}{372,085} \times 100\,\% = 20\%$$

		Gross	Tax (on 2023/24 scale)
		£	£
IHT payable:			
Farm – original fund	20% × 30% × £150,000	9,000	
6,000 shares – 1st addition	$20\% \times 30\% \times \frac{37}{40} \times £132{,}000 \times \frac{6{,}000}{66{,}000}$	666	
60,000 shares – 2nd addition	$20\% \times 30\% \times \frac{27}{40} \times £132{,}000 \times \frac{60{,}000}{66{,}000}$	4,860	
		£14,526	(previously £14,526)

(11) The relevant value of the property comprised in the settlement is its value on the day preceding the tenth anniversary – in this case 5 June 2023 (s 64). The £6,000 of income arising from the trust property in 2022 that the trustees had not accumulated is not deemed relevant property of the trust as the income arose less than five years before the ten-year anniversary (s 64(1A)).

Associated operations

(12) If two or more settlements of an identical or substantially similar nature were set up over a short term, HMRC Capital Taxes originally took the view that the associated operations provisions of s 268 (as to which see **Example A20**) would apply. This would have resulted in the settlements being treated as a single settlement set up at the time of the last settlement, with only one nil-rate band. In the case of *Rysaffe Trustee Co (CI) Ltd v IRC* (2002), however, the High Court held that as a matter of general law the creation of five identical settlements must be treated as five separate settlements, not one. It was up to the settlor to determine if he wished to create more than one settlement and the associated operations provisions of s 268 could not apply.

(13) For further notes on discretionary trusts see **Examples C10, C11** and **C12.**

Question

A has a protected life interest within Trustee Act 1925 s 33(1) in a trust fund created before 22 March 2006 by his uncle; after A's death the trust fund is to pass to A's cousin's son (the uncle's grandson) absolutely. On 1 July 2018 A purported to assign that life interest to his brother. The trustees pointed out that the attempted alienation was ineffective and brought the protected life interest to an end, substituting for it a statutory discretionary trust of income under which the beneficiaries were A, his wife and their children.

A also has a life interest under the will of his father who died on 1 April 2019; on A's death this fund is to pass to A's son, S, absolutely.

On 1 May 2022 A sold this life interest to a Reversionary Interest Society for £200,000 – the full market value of the interest. The assets of the trust fund were worth £564,000 at that time.

He did not advise the trustees of the fund of the availability of his annual inheritance tax exemptions.

On 21 April 2023 A, who was fit and well, transferred his flat (held on a recently granted 99-year lease), then valued at £200,000 on a vacant possession basis, to his daughter D, reserving to himself a lease of the property at a peppercorn rent for 85 years determinable by one month's notice given by the landlord at any time after his death. Until he acquired the flat under the 99-year lease, A had never owned a home of his own, having lived in rented accommodation all his life. Following the transfer of the flat to her (subject to the 85-year lease to her father) D never occupied the flat as her home as she owned her own house. The value of the lease in A's hands at that time was £80,000, and the value of the flat in D's hands subject to the lease was £100,000. The flat could be let in the open market for £500 per month.

On 1 May 2023, A was killed in a car accident. His other assets totalled £30,000 net – he had spent the money received from the Reversionary Interest Society.

His uncle's discretionary, formerly protective, trust fund was then valued at £305,000.

By his will, A created a discretionary trust of the whole of his free estate in favour of his children. On 12 March 2025 the trustees appointed a sum of £10,000, free of tax, to S absolutely.

The only previous transfer which either A or his daughter had made before the events described was a gift of £108,000 (after annual exemptions) that A made in July 2010.

(i) Assuming that A's transfer of the flat to his daughter (subject to the reserved lease) was for no consideration:

- (a) Calculate the inheritance tax payable as a result of these transactions and consequent upon A's death.
- (b) Calculate the rate at which inheritance tax will be payable on future appointments out of the discretionary trust created by A's will.
- (c) Calculate the inheritance tax consequences, if any, if A's daughter D gives the necessary one month's notice under the terms of the lease to terminate it with effect from 1 January 2024, at which date the vacant possession value of the flat is £215,000.
- (d) State (without calculation) the inheritance tax consequences if D decided not to give such notice but then died unexpectedly on 31 March 2024.

(ii) How would your answers to (i)(a)–(d) **above** differ if, instead of transferring the flat for no consideration, A had sold it to his daughter (still subject to the reserved lease on the same terms) for £170,000 which was, under the contract, to be paid by her on 1 July 2023 (with the outstanding price being charged on the flat in A's favour in the meantime since the transfer still took place on 21 April 2023)?

Ignore any capital gains tax implications.

Answer

(i) Flat transferred for no consideration

(i)(a) Inheritance tax on transactions and death

A — lifetime transactions

			Gross £	Tax on 2022/23 scale £
1 July 2018				
Forfeiture of protected life interest – No transfer of value – A's interest in possession deemed to continue (IHTA 1984 s 88(2))				
1 May 2022				
Cumulative chargeable transfers within previous seven years (ie since 2 May 2015)			Nil	Nil
Sale of life interest under father's will trust				
Value of trust fund		564,000		
Less: Amount received		(200,000)		
Chargeable transfer			364,000	7,800*
			364,000	7,800*
(* 364,000 – 325,000 = 39,000 @ 20%)				
21 April 2023				
Transfer of flat to daughter				
Market value with vacant possession		200,000		
Less: Value retained through lease 'for life'		(80,000)		
Loss to A's estate		120,000		
Less: Annual exemptions				
	2023/24 3,000			
	2022/23 3,000	(6,000)		
Potentially exempt transfer (see **explanatory notes 3 and 4**)		114,000		

D — lifetime transaction

Receipt of flat subject to reserved lease 'for life'	
Consideration given by D	Nil
Value of flat in D's hands subject to lease	100,000
Increase in value of D's estate	100,000

Deemed grant of lease 'for life' worth £80,000 to A is thus for more than full consideration, so no deemed settlement and no transfer of value by D (see **explanatory note 4**).

Death of A — 1 May 2023

	£	£
Free estate		
Lease 'for life', see **explanatory notes 3, 4 and 6**	500	
Net other assets	30,000	30,500
Property subject to reservation		
Flat		200,000
Settled property		
Deemed life interest in protective trust		305,000
Total estate on death		535,500

Inheritance tax due on death

Date of death 1 May 2023

Value of flat, which is property subject to a reservation, contributed to lifetime gifts and is also taxed on death. Therefore, under the double charges regulations, take whichever is higher of:

- tax disregarding the potentially exempt transfer and taxing the reservation of benefit, and
- tax disregarding the reservation of benefit and taxing the potentially exempt transfer.

In the first calculation the value caught as a gift with reservation must be reduced by the residual value of the lease, which forms part of A's estate in any event.

		Gross	*Tax on 2023/24 scale*
First calculation: disregard PET, charge reservation			
		£	£
On gifts within seven years before death			
Transfers within seven years before 1 May 2023 (ie on and after 2 May 2016)		Nil	Nil
1 May 2022 – sale of life interest		364,000	15,600*
		364,000	15,600*
(* 364,000 – 325,000 = 39,000 @ 40%)			
On estate at death			
Estate as above	535,500		
Less: Residual value of lease	(500)		
		535,000	214,000
		899,000	229,600**
(** 899,000 – 325,000 = 574,000 @ 40%) – see **explanatory note 6** as regards non-availability of RNRB			

		Gross	Tax on 2023/24 scale
Second calculation: disregard reservation, charge PET		£	£
On gifts within seven years before death			
Transfers within seven years before 1 May 2023			
(ie on and after 2 May 2016)		Nil	Nil
1 May 2022 – sale of life interest		364,000	15,600*
21 April 2023 – transfer of flat – PET now chargeable		114,000	45,600
		478,000	61,200**

(* 364,000 – 325,000 = 39,000 @ 40%)
(** 478,000 – 325,000 = 153,000 @ 40%)

On estate at death			
Estate as above	535,500		
Less: Property subject to reservation	(200,000)		
		335,500	134,200
		813,500	195,400***

(*** 813,500 – 325,000 = 488,500 @ 40%) – see **explanatory note 6** as regards non-availability of RNRB

First calculation produces higher charge, so tax payable is:			£
By trustees of father's will trust		15,600	
Less: paid on original transfer		(7,800)	7,800
By personal representatives but recoverable from daughter D:	$\frac{199{,}500^{*}}{535{,}000} \times 214{,}000 =$		79,800
By personal representatives from free estate:	$\frac{30{,}500^{**}}{535{,}000} \times 214{,}000 =$		12,200
By trustees of protective trust	$\frac{305{,}000}{535{,}000} \times 214{,}000 =$		122,000

(* £200,000 - £500 – see **explanatory note 6**)

(** £30,000 + £500 – see **explanatory note 6**)

Termination of life interest owned by Reversionary Interest Society

1 May 2023 – A's death brings the interest to an end and his son S becomes absolutely entitled. Apart from the additional tax arising from A's death within seven years after selling the interest (above), no further inheritance tax charge arises. The trust property was not in an individual's estate immediately before A's death, nor was it relevant property – see **explanatory note 2.**

Appointment of £10,000 by the trustees of A's will to S

12 March 2025 – Appointment is within two years after the death and is deemed to have been made by A under his will (s 144). No further tax is payable. In particular, no adjustment is made to the tax arising on A's estate on accounting of any downsizing addition as A never owned a home on 8 July 2015 which had been subsequently sold or downsized from and hence no entitlement to downsizing addition ever arose (see **Example A2 part (b)** for details on residence nil-rate band (RNRB) and downsizing addition).

(i)(b) Discretionary trust created by A's will

		£
A's free estate		30,500
Less:	appointment to son	(10,000)
		20,500
Less:	tax payable by executors	(12,200)
Net value received by discretionary settlement created by the will		8,300

Rate of tax on distributions before the first ten-year anniversary on 1 May 2033

Distributions made before 1 May 2025 will (like the appointment on 12 March 2025) be treated for inheritance tax purposes as having been made on A's death without having entered the settlement (s 144, see **explanatory note 8**).

A's seven-year cumulative total at *commencement of settlement* (ignoring transfers of value made on that day, that is the transfer of value deemed to have been made on A's death), was £364,000 (using the operative, first, calculation in (i)(a) above, see **explanatory note 9**). The position of the settlement subject to s 144 is therefore as follows:

	£
Cumulative total of settlor	364,000
Net value received as above	8,300
	372,300

As the cumulative total in respect of the notional transfer in s 68 exceeds the nil-rate threshold, the 'effective' rate of tax on the notional transfer is 20%, so that the rate of tax on distributions made after the second anniversary of A's death but before the first ten-year anniversary is N/40ths of 6% (30% × 20%), 'N' being the number of complete quarters since 1 May 2023.

If tax rates generally have been reduced when the distribution occurs, the 'effective rate' is recalculated using the new reduced rates.

Rate of tax at ten-year anniversaries

This is 30% of the 'effective rate' found by assuming a transfer of value equal to the value of the trust fund immediately before the ten-year anniversary (ie on 30 April 2033, 30 April 2043 and so on), made by a transferor whose cumulative total is deemed to be £364,000 (the settlor's cumulative total disregarding the gift of the flat as in the operative, first, calculation above, see **explanatory note 9**) *plus* the amounts taxed on exit from the discretionary trust in the preceding ten years, using one half the death scale current at the date of the ten-year anniversary.

The value charged to tax is the value of the 'relevant property' in the settlement immediately before the anniversary on the appropriate 30 April. 'Relevant property' in this context is discussed in detail in **Example C10**.

Rate of tax between ten-year anniversaries

This is the 'appropriate fraction' (ie (X–Y)/40 – where 'X' is the number of completed quarters since the last ten-year anniversary and 'Y' is the number of those quarters completed before the property became relevant property, or 0 if it was relevant property throughout) of the rate charged on the last ten-year anniversary.

If the tax rates have been reduced since the last ten-year anniversary, the current lower rates are substituted.

(i)(c) Inheritance tax position on termination of lease 'for life'

The lease 'for life' had (apart from the impact of the gifts with reservation rules) already lost practically all its value in A's estate (see **explanatory note 3**) as a consequence of A's death itself – not as a result of any disposition made by A, or any failure by him to exercise a right, so there is no transfer of value by him. The giving, and subsequent expiry, of D's notice as the landlord have no effects for inheritance tax so far as D is concerned.

(i)(d) If D had died without terminating the lease

In real terms, practically the whole value of the flat became referable to D's interest, as a result of her being entitled to terminate the lease by just one month's notice at any time after A's death. That right, exercisable by the landlord, continues in favour of her estate following her death and therefore the failure to give notice during her lifetime neither caused a loss of value to her own estate nor any increase in the value of anyone else's estate. Thus that failure did not cause a deemed disposition under s 3(3), and the full value of D's interest is taxable as part of her estate on her death. No question of any entitlement to a residence nil-rate band (RNRB) arises on D's death as D had never occupied the flat as her home (see **Example A2 part (b)** for a detailed discussion of the RNRB).

None of this is affected by the application of the gifts with reservation rules as regards the position of A's estate on his death, which have no bearing on the position of other parties.

(ii) Flat sold for £170,000

(ii)(a) Inheritance tax on transactions and death

A — lifetime transactions

			Gross	Tax on 2023/24 scale
			£	£
1 July 2018				
Forfeiture of protected life interest – No transfer of value as above				
1 May 2022				
Sale of life interest under father's will trust – chargeable transfer as above			364,000	7,800
21 April 2023				
Sale of flat to daughter				
Market value with vacant possession			200,000	
Less: Amount receivable on sale			(170,000)	
			30,000	
Less: Value retained through lease 'for life' (excluded from A's estate, see **explanatory note 5 para (ii)**)			Nil	
Loss to A's estate			30,000	
Less: Annual exemptions				
	2023/24	3,000		
	2022/23	3,000	(6,000)	
Potentially exempt transfer (see **explanatory note 5**)			24,000	

D — lifetime transaction

21 April 2023			
Purchase of flat subject to reserved lease 'for life'			
Amount payable for flat			170,000
Less: Value of reversion on lease 'for life' (see **explanatory note 5 para (a)**): $\frac{200,000 - 170,000}{80,000} \times 200,000 = *$			(75,000)
Loss to D's estate			95,000
Less: Annual exemptions	2023/24	3,000	
	2022/23	3,000	(6,000)
Chargeable transfer – see **explanatory note 5 para (iv)**			89,000

No previous transfers so nil tax

Deemed grant of lease 'for life' is for less than full consideration, so lease 'for life' is a deemed settlement and the flat is settled property (s 43(3))

$$(*\frac{\text{Consideration received for grant of lease}}{\text{Arm's length consideration for grant of lease}} \times \text{Vacant possession value of flat})$$

Death of A — 1 May 2023

	£	£
Free estate		
Amount due from D re flat sale	170,000	
Lease 'for life' – not part of A's estate for inheritance tax purposes (see **explanatory notes 3, 5 and 6**)	Nil	
Net other assets	30,000	200,000
Settled property		
Deemed life interest in protective trust		305,000
Total estate on death		505,000

Inheritance tax due on death

Date of death 1 May 2023

	Gross	*Tax on 2023/24 scale*
	£	£
On gifts within seven years before death		
Transfers within seven years before 1 May 2023		
(ie on and after 2 May 2016)	Nil	Nil
1 May 2022 – sale of life interest	364,000	15,600*
21 April 2023 – transfer of flat — PET now chargeable	24,000	9,600
	388,000	25,200**

(* 364,000 – 325,000 = 39,000 @ 40%)

(** 388,000 – 325,000 = 63,000 @ 40%)

On estate at death

(Nil-rate band already exceeded by lifetime transfers; see **explanatory note 6** as regards non-availability of RNRB)

£505,000 @ 40%		202,000
Tax payable		£
By trustees of father's will trust	15,600	
Less: paid on original transfer	(7,800)	7,800
By daughter D		9,600
By personal representatives: $\frac{200,000}{505,000} \times 202,000 =$		80,000
By trustees of protective trust $\frac{305,000}{505,000} \times 202,000 =$		122,000

Termination of life interest owned by Reversionary Interest Society

1 May 2023 – No inheritance tax consequence, as above.

Appointment of £10,000 by the trustees of A's will to S

12 March 2025 – Appointed interest deemed to take effect on death, no inheritance tax charge, as above.

(ii)(b) Discretionary trust created by A's will

	£
A's free estate	200,000
Less: appointment to son	(10,000)
	190,000
Less: tax payable by executors	(80,000)
Net amount received by discretionary settlement created by the will	110,000

Rate of tax on distributions before the first ten-year anniversary on 1 May 2033

Inheritance tax implications are as in **part** (i) above but with changed values (subject to s 144) as follows:

	£
Cumulative total of settlor (see **explanatory note 9**)	388,000
Net amount received as above	110,000
	498,000

As in **part** (i) the rate of tax on distributions made after the second anniversary of A's death but before the first ten-year anniversary is N/40ths of 6% (30% × 20%), 'N' being the number of complete quarters since 1 May 2023. If tax rates generally have been reduced when the distribution occurs, the 'effective rate' is recalculated using the new reduced rates.

Rate of tax at ten-year anniversaries

Implications are as in **part** (i) above, but the settlor's cumulative total used in the computation is now £388,000 (see **explanatory note 9**).

Rate of tax between ten-year anniversaries

Implications are as in **part** (i) above.

(ii)(c) Inheritance tax on termination of lease 'for life'

The lease for 85 years determinable after A's death continues after A's death until brought to an end, by expiry of D's notice. In the meantime A's personal representatives (and the discretionary trust under A's will) have a continuing interest in possession in the deemed settlement constituted by the lease 'for life' (s 43(3)). This is still a non-qualifying interest in possession and the settled property – the flat itself, as a whole – remains relevant property.

On expiry of D's notice, on 1 January 2024, the lease (deemed settlement) comes to an end and D becomes absolutely entitled to the flat free from the lease. This gives rise to an exit charge under the relevant property rules, since the flat has ceased to be relevant property (s 65).

The settlor of the deemed settlement was the daughter, as it was she who paid more than the value of the flat subject to the reserved lease. The settlement had commenced on 21 April 2023 so the exit charge occurs before any ten-year anniversary; two complete quarters had elapsed between then and the exit charge on 1 January 2024. The position of the settlement is:

	£
Seven-year cumulative total of settlor immediately before settlement commenced	Nil
Initial value of settled property under deemed settlement:	
Value of flat free of lease	200,000
Notional transfer – within 2023/24 nil-rate band, so effective rate 0%	200,000

Thus there is no inheritance tax to pay by way of exit charge. If the daughter had given the notice soon after A's death so that it expired before 21 July 2023, no exit charge event would have occurred in the first place (s 65(4)), but this makes no practical difference in the circumstances.

(ii)(d) If D had died without terminating the lease

The value of the daughter's reversionary interest is a fixed proportion of the unencumbered value of the flat from time to time, for as long as the deemed settlement under s 43(3) continues; on the facts that proportion here is 37.5% (see **explanatory note 5 para** (a)). Its value is included in the daughter's estate because it is not excluded property (s 48(1)(c)), and will be taxed as part of her free estate on her death accordingly, subject to any spouse exemption etc.

Insofar as the daughter paid too much for the flat subject to the lease 'for life', she can be seen to have made a gift of the excess of £50,000 (£170,000 cash plus £80,000 lease less £200,000 vacant possession value). The gift was not in fact into a settlement (the deemed settlement is of the flat as a whole, not of the lease, and the excess in reality took the form of cash rather than the lease; the cash is not represented by the flat even if unsettled cash gifts were subject to the tracing rules for the gifts with reservation provisions); so the flat is not caught by the gifts with reservation rules so as to be charged on the daughter's death.

For the eleven months since A's death and before her own, the daughter could have brought the lease to an end by one month's notice given at any time, but she decided not to do so. Had she done so at least a month before her death, the settlement would have come to an end on expiry of the notice (see (ii)(c) above) and the whole unencumbered value of the flat would then have been in her estate at her death. HMRC may therefore seek to pursue a claim that the daughter's estate should be taxed as though she had made a transfer of value equal to the difference between vacant possession value and the statutory value of her reversionary interest, by virtue of s 3(3); after all, the daughter's decision not to give notice, after considering the matter, shows that the failure to exercise that right to give notice was deliberate and not inadvertent.

It is thought that such a claim could be resisted for a combination of two reasons:

(a) A deemed disposition under s 3(3) occurs, if at all, at the latest time the person could have exercised a right in question. The daughter's mere decision not to exercise it did not amount to abandonment of the right, and so she could have changed her mind at any time and given notice right up to the moment she died. Any such notice would not have expired, and brought to an end the lease 'for life' and so the deemed settlement, until a month after her death. The settlement would therefore still have been in existence at her death, and her interest would still have been the reversionary interest.

(b) Section 3(3) applies if the failure to exercise the right in question results in the person's estate being diminished, and that of another person (or of settled property not subject to an estate IIP) being increased. The artificially fixed proportions of value attributed to the reversionary interest and the interest in possession (see **explanatory note** 5) mean that, while the settlement continued as above, the failure to give notice did not result in the daughter's estate being worth any less at her death (or before); merely in its not *increasing* when the notice expired a month after the death.

However, it is not impossible that the lease could be held to cease to be a lease 'for life', as defined, instantly upon the giving of notice to terminate it, since at that point its expiry date becomes fixed without reference to any death. In that event the deemed settlement would terminate at the moment of service of notice; as a result, by giving the notice in her lifetime D could have secured that the value of her estate at her death included the full value of the flat, not merely the artificial value attributed to her reversionary interest under the deemed settlement. Even then it is not entirely clear that the 'missing' value could be taxed on D's death through the failed PET resulting from a deemed disposition under s 3(3): as just mentioned, for such a deemed disposition to be found, the failure to give notice must have resulted in the estate of another person (or of settled property not subject to a qualifying IIP) being increased, and for HMRC's argument to succeed it would be necessary to read 'increased' as meaning in the circumstances 'greater than it would have been at D's death had the notice been given', as opposed to 'greater than it was immediately before the giving of the notice'. The latter is perhaps the more natural meaning of 'increased', but the former may perhaps be justifiable on a purposive construction.

Explanatory Notes

(1) *1 July 2018 – purported assignment to brother of protected life interest – inheritance tax treatment*

When A's life interest comes to an end there is no transfer of value because A is deemed to retain his interest in possession (s 88(2)). Where the protected life interest with Trustees Act 1925 s 33(1) was created before 22 March 2006 and the purported assignment of the interest occurs on or after 22 March 2006, the interest in possession that the beneficiary is deemed to retain for the purposes of inheritance tax is deemed to have arisen before 22 March 2006 (IHTA 1984 s 88(3)) and is therefore a qualifying IIP. Where the protected life interest with Trustees Act 1925 s 33(1) was created on or after 22 March 2006 and the interest if the beneficiary is an immediate post-death interest, a disabled person's interest or a transitional serial interest and a purported assignment of the interest occurs, the interest in possession that the beneficiary had before the purported assignment is deemed to continue uninterrupted for the purposes of inheritance tax after the purported assignment (IHTA 1984 s 88(4), (5)). Where the protected life interest with Trustees Act 1925 s 33(1) was created on or after 22 March 2006 and the interest if the beneficiary is neither an immediate post-death interest, nor a disabled person's interest nor a transitional serial interest, the interest in possession is not deemed to continue and a statutory discretionary trust supervenes in accordance with Trustees Act s 33 (IHTA 1984 s 88(6).

(2) *1 May 2022 – sale of life interest – inheritance tax treatment*

A's life interest under his father's will is an immediate post-death interest, and therefore a qualifying interest in possession even after the FA 2006 changes (see **Example C3**).

Although the sale by A of his life interest to the Reversionary Interest Society is a commercial transaction for full value, s 10 does not prevent its giving rise to a transfer of value because s 52(2) expressly provides that a transfer of value arises with an allowance for the sale price received, ie a lifetime transfer of £564,000 (the value of the assets comprising the trust fund) less the £200,000 received = £364,000.

The transfer is not a potentially exempt transfer because the interest does not become comprised in the estate of another individual, nor is another individual's estate increased as a result of the transfer, and it therefore falls outside s 3A.

Section 57 allows the annual and marriage exemptions to be applied to events on the happening of which tax is chargeable under s 52 (ie the coming to an end during lifetime of estate interests in possession in settled property) provided the transferor (the person with the estate interest in possession which came to an end) gives the trustees a formal notice within six months of the transfer, telling them of the availability of the exemption and the extent to which he is making it available.

As no such notice has been given, the exemptions are not available to the trustees.

At first sight the assigned life interest in the hands of the Reversionary Interest Society is not a qualifying IIP because it is not beneficially owned by an individual. However it is a qualifying IIP within s 59 because it was a qualifying IIP in the hands of the person from whom the Society acquired it, and it was acquired for full value by a company whose business consisted wholly or mainly of acquiring interests in settled property. The qualifying interest in possession prevents the property in A's father's will trust from being relevant property, and so there is no inheritance tax charge when the settlement comes to an end on A's death.

(3) *Leases 'for life' generally for inheritance tax*

For the purposes of inheritance tax a lease for life, or for a period ascertainable only by reference to a death (eg 'until one month after the death of X'), or which is terminable on or at a date ascertainable only by reference to a death (such as the lease in the Example or a lease of property in England and Wales that is purportedly granted for life, whether that of the tenant or of one or more other people), is deemed to be a settlement of the property leased, unless the lease was granted for full consideration in money or money's worth – s 43(3). (In England and Wales a lease that is purportedly granted for life, or determinable with life or marriage, takes effect as a lease for 90 years determinable by at least one month's notice given after the death (or marriage) of the person in question (unless the lease was granted for no rent and no premium): Law of Property Act 1925 s 149(6). Section 43(3) applies whatever the location of the property.) For the purpose of this Example all such cases are referred to compendiously as leases 'for life'.

Where (as in the Example and where Law of Property Act 1925 s 149(6) applies) a lease 'for life' can be terminated only by notice after the relevant death, it will inevitably remain in existence for a time after the death, at least for the period of notice plus whatever delay there is between the death and the service of the notice (if indeed the landlord does serve notice, which it would plainly be in his interest to do). As a matter of property law the lease during that period forms part of the lessee's estate and therefore vests in his personal representatives.

Where deemed settlement treatment under s 43(3) applies:

(a) The settled property under the deemed settlement is the whole (unencumbered) property. The leasehold interest (which entitles the lessee to occupy or otherwise enjoy the property) is an interest in possession in that settled property, and the superior interest (typically the freehold, but in this Example the 99-year head-lease) is a reversionary interest in it. Artificial valuation rules apply for inheritance tax purposes to the interests of landlord and lessee in such a case – see **explanatory note 6**. Where the lease 'for life' is granted by a lifetime transaction after 21 March 2006, the deemed settlement will inevitably be within the relevant property regime (with the property and the lease excluded from the estate of the lessee accordingly, see **explanatory note 6**), unless at the time of its grant the lessee is a disabled person within s 89(4)–(6) such as to make the deemed interest in possession (the lease) a disabled person's interest.

(b) It is not clear at what point the deemed settlement will come to an end. There seem to be as many as three possibilities:

(i) that the deemed settlement will continue for as long as the lease remains in existence (ie, in the Example, until the expiry of the 85-year term or of a notice, given after A's death, to terminate it sooner);

(ii) that the lease 'for life' ceases to be within the description in s 43(3), and so ceases to be a deemed settlement, either:

- immediately the lessee's death has occurred (on the basis that it then becomes terminable at any time, not by reference to a future death); or
- immediately a notice is served to terminate it on expiry of the notice (on the basis that it then becomes a lease that will terminate at an identified calendar date that is ascertainable without reference to any death).

It is thought that the better view is in line with (i) above, on the basis that fewest anomalies in the inheritance tax treatment would follow from this analysis.

But where there is no deemed settlement then normal inheritance tax principles will apply and the leasehold and reversionary interests will be included in the estates of the lessee and the landlord respectively at their ordinary market values.

(4) *21 April 2023 – Lease 'for life' – no settlement for inheritance tax*

In **part** (i) of the Example, where A's flat is transferred for no other consideration but reserving a lease 'for life' to him, the transferor, this does not in terms fit the terms of the statutory exclusion from s 43(3) namely that the lease was 'granted' for full consideration. However HMRC will treat the lease for this purpose as though it had been granted by D, the transferee, in return for (and, logically, immediately after) the transfer of the unencumbered 99-year headlease; that consideration will thus be more than full consideration received by D, and there is no deemed settlement.

On the contrary, it is A as transferor whose estate has been depleted as a result of the transaction. The resultant transfer of value is a potentially exempt transfer since it results in the flat (subject to the retained lease 'for life') being comprised in D's estate. But it is also a gift, and is caught as a gift with reservation; this has no inheritance tax consequences during A's lifetime, but will affect the tax on his death (see **explanatory note 6** below).

(5) *21 April 2023 – Lease 'for life' – deemed settlement for inheritance tax*

In **part** (ii) of the Example, D undertakes to pay A cash for the transfer of the flat as well. It is assumed that the principle outlined in the previous paragraph will still be applied; on that basis, it appears that D could be treated as having granted the lease 'for life' (worth £80,000 on a full consideration basis) in return for £30,000 (being the difference between the £200,000 vacant possession value of the flat and the £170,000 cash sum that she has undertaken to pay). Therefore the lease 'for life' can be seen to have been 'granted' by her for less than full consideration, and s 43(3) will give rise to a deemed settlement accordingly.

In place of normal valuation principles applying to the two parties' interests in the settled property (the flat), the proportions of the property's value from time to time ('V') that are to be attributed to them are fixed, for as long as the deemed settlement subsists, by reference to the relationship between the consideration given for the lease when it was granted ('X') and the consideration which would have been given for it at that time between unconnected parties ('Y'). Of these figures, only V varies with time; the fractions of V attributed to:

(a) the landlord's (reversionary) interest (which is not excluded property – s 48(1)(c)) is X/Y (s 170), which in **part** (ii) of the Example is 30,000/80,000 or 37.5%, and

(b) the lessee's interest is the entire balance, or (Y – X)/Y (s 50(6)), which in the Example is (80,000 – 30,000)/80,000 or 62.5%.

This latter rule, in s 50(6), is predicated on the lessee's interest being a qualifying IIP, as all interests in possession owned by individuals were before 2006. However, in **part** (ii) of the **Example** A became beneficially entitled to his interest in possession after 22 March 2006; because he was not a disabled person at the time, his interest in possession is not a qualifying IIP, and so s 50(6) seems to be irrelevant in such a case. Some aspects of the treatment of deemed settlements arising from s 43(3) were less than clear even before the FA 2006 changes; leases 'for life' were not addressed in those changes and the position since then is if anything more confusing, but it would appear that:

(i) The flat as a whole comprises the settled property which is therefore relevant property.

(ii) Because A's interest is an interest in possession but not a qualifying IIP, no property or value enters A's estate on the lease being created; the interest in possession (the lease 'for life') itself is not part of his estate (s 5(1), (1A)); this has the result that the value of the lease he in fact retains cannot (unlike the cash consideration) be deducted from the value of the flat that he transfers to D, and there is thus a loss of £30,000 (£200,000 – £170,000) to A's estate as a result of the transaction.

(iii) That exclusion from A's estate does not prevent the real value of the lease from being taken into account as consideration given by D for the transfer of the flat to her, as above – even though this produces the apparently illogical result that both parties have made transfers of value in the course of the same transaction.

(iv) A further result of the exclusion of the leasehold interest (interest in possession) from A's estate is that D's transfer of value cannot be a potentially exempt transfer (neither A's estate nor the value of it is increased); it is therefore an immediately chargeable transfer except so far as covered by annual exemptions.

Although A has made a transfer of value because of the artificial exclusion of the lease 'for life' from his estate (which is a potentially exempt transfer because property became comprised in D's estate in consequence), he has not made a gift; on the contrary D has, in terms of real values, made a gift to him. Accordingly he cannot be caught by the gift with reservation rules; but because A is still in occupation of the flat despite having made a disposal of it, the pre-owned assets income tax rules are potentially in point for him. However, his disposal (taking account of the reserved lease, which is 'a right expressly reserved by him over the property') was for more, not less, consideration than he would have been paid in a transaction between unconnected parties (ie for £170,000 cash owed + £80,000 value of the lease = £250,000, as compared with the £200,000 open market value of the flat), and the sale is thus an excluded transaction for the purpose of those rules, within FA 2004 Sch 15 para 10(1)(a). (Alternatively it could be argued that the sale could not be an excluded transaction because it was a one-sided deal, even though it favoured A rather than prejudicing him; but in that case it would appear to be a non-exempt sale within para 4(4) of the same Schedule, producing a negative 'appropriate proportion' and a nil income tax charge.)

(6) *1 May 2023 – inheritance tax position on A's death*

On A's death the tax on transfers of value made within the last seven years is recalculated using the full-scale rates in force at the date of death and by accumulation with transfers within the seven years preceding each gift.

The difference between the tax calculated on this basis and the tax originally calculated using the lifetime rates in force at the time of the transfer is due from the trustee of A's father's will trust (IHTA 1984 s 201).

The lease for 85 years determinable after A's death continues after A's death in his personal representatives' hands (see **explanatory note** 3 above), as an asset of the discretionary trust under A's will. However, A's death now means that the lease can be terminated by the landlord at one month's notice at any time, and the lease will, in the real world, become almost valueless as a result of the death. Correspondingly, A's death means that the value of the flat in the landlord's (D's) hands increases suddenly to practically vacant possession value, since vacant possession can now be recovered by giving just one month's notice at any time. The inheritance tax implications of these changes depend on whether or not the lease is deemed to be a settlement by virtue of s 43(3) (see **explanatory notes** 4 and 5 above):

- Where it is not a deemed settlement (see **explanatory note** 4), this change in the value of the asset in A's estate will be taken into account under s 171 for the purpose of quantifying his taxable estate on his death (before applying the gifts with reservation rules, see below). In **part** (i) of the Example this reduced value is assumed for illustration to equate to one month's rental value (the minimum time for which the lease in these changed circumstances permits its owner to continue in occupation).

  Because the flat is caught by the gifts with reservation rules in **part** (ii) of the Example (see **explanatory note** 4), A's estate on his death will include its value so far as not comprised in his estate in any event: FA 1986 s 102(3). The residual value of the lease 'for life' (above) is in A's estate without the gifts with reservation rules, so these rules add back the balance of the £200,000 open market value. Since A had made a potentially exempt transfer shortly beforehand whose value was referable to the value of the flat, this in turn brings into play the double charges regulations (SI 1987/1130 reg 5); for further details see **Examples B2, B3** and **B8**.

Although D was the beneficial owner of the 85-year lease of the flat (which was his home) on his death, there is no entitlement to a residence nil-rate band in calculating the tax on his estate as the flat is, by being settled on discretionary trust, not closely inherited (see **Example A2 explanatory note 3**).

- Where it is deemed to be a settlement under IHTA 1984 s 43(3), as in **part** (ii) of the Example, the real-world change of value is overridden by the artificial statutory valuation rules for inheritance tax purposes which apply in consequence; but in any case A's interest in possession in the deemed settled property is not a qualifying IIP so neither the settled property (the flat) nor the interest in possession itself (the lease) forms part of his estate for inheritance tax purposes immediately before his death (see **explanatory note 5**, especially point (ii)). As D was not the beneficial owner of the 85-year lease of the flat on his death, there is no entitlement to a residence nil-rate band in calculating the tax on his estate (see **Example A2 part (b)**).

A's chargeable estate on death includes the value of the property in the protective trust in which his life interest is deemed to continue (see **explanatory note 1**). In **part (ii)** of the Example it also includes the sum of £170,000 due to him from his daughter, but (as just noted) not the interest in possession under the deemed settlement arising from the lease 'for life'.

As regards the apportionment of liability for the tax payable on A's death in **part (i)(a)** of the Example, A's personal representatives are liable for the tax not only on A's free estate but also on the flat so far as caught by the gifts with reservation rules (s 200(1)(a)); but the tax chargeable by reason of the gifts with reservation rules is not part of the general testamentary and administration expenses of A's estate, because the flat does not vest in the personal representatives on A's death (s 211(1)). As a result, the personal representatives are entitled to be repaid the latter tax by D as the person in whom the flat is vested (s 211(2)). £500 out of the £200,000 open market value of the flat is comprised in A's free estate (and does vest in the personal representatives), in the form of the value of the lease 'for life', so that £500 is added to the £30,000 of net other assets in establishing the amount which the personal representatives must discharge from A's estate. The proportion of the overall tax that is attributable to the gifts with reservation rules is calculated by reference to the value of the flat so far as not included in A's estate under general principles – viz £200,000 – £500 = £199,500.

(7) *Capital gains tax position on A's death*

When A's cousin's son becomes absolutely entitled to the assets in A's uncle's trust on A's death, the deemed disposal of the trust assets under TCGA 1992 s 71 will give rise to chargeable gains in the trustees' hands in the usual way, subject to the possibility of hold-over relief under TCGA 1992 s 260 if the nephew is UK resident. Although A's interest in possession (before the purported assignment) is deemed to continue until his death for inheritance tax, despite the forfeiture of the protected life interest, that treatment does not apply for capital gains tax purposes and the trust is discretionary at A's death.

The same applies in relation to the assets to which A's son becomes absolutely entitled on A's death under A's father's will trust – even though that occurs on the termination of an actual life interest – because the life interest was not then owned by the person whose death brought it to an end but rather by the Reversionary Interest Society.

There are no capital gains tax implications of the deemed settlement in relation to the lease 'for life'. That deeming is solely for inheritance tax purposes, and the capital gains tax treatment of the flat and the interests in it follows the factual position. There is therefore no disposal by D (whether personally or in her capacity as a trustee of the deemed settlement) on A's death, or on the giving or expiry of the notice to terminate the lease: she acquired the 99-year leasehold interest at the outset, and the terminability, or actual termination, of the lease 'for life' following A's death does not alter what she owns. D's base cost in **part** (ii) of the Example will not be the whole £170,000 she paid, but will be restricted by TCGA 1992 s 18 (or, in **part** (i) of the Example, increased) to the market value of what she acquired from her father namely the property subject to the lease. As seen in **explanatory note 5**, she overpaid by £50,000 in **part** (ii) of the Example, suggesting that her base cost might therefore be £120,000; but there is a loss of marriage value through separating the two interests and the flat subject to the lease is said to be worth just £100,000 in D's hands; since A will have qualified for main residence relief on his disposal, it is foreseeable that HMRC may seek to argue that A's disposal value, and so D's base cost, is restricted to that £100,000.

In A's hands the lease loses most of its value on his death because it becomes terminable by the landlord on one month's notice; but this loss on one of the assets of which he was competent to dispose is not an allowable loss, any more than a gain arising on his death would have been a chargeable gain (and in any case the lease will have been a wasting asset, once A's life expectancy was below 50 years).

(8) *12 March 2025 – distribution within two years after death – inheritance tax treatment*

Example B6 illustrates how IHTA 1984 s 142 allows beneficiaries within two years after a death to vary the dispositions of the deceased's estate without that variation being itself a transfer of value, and for the tax payable in connection with the death to be calculated as though the variation had been made by the deceased himself.

Similarly, s 144 provides that distributions made within two years after death, out of property settled by the deceased's will in which there has been no qualifying IIP, are treated as having been made at the time of the death and are not therefore subject to an exit charge. (See **Example C11 explanatory notes 10** and **12** for the position on transfers within the first three months, which may not benefit from that basic rule for deaths that occurred before 10 December 2015, and **explanatory note 11** for the interaction of s 144 with capital gains tax.)

The £10,000 appointed by the trustees of A's will to A's son is therefore deemed for the purposes of inheritance tax to have been given to him by his father A under his will with effect from A's death, and does not give rise to any exit charge under the relevant property rules.

(9) See **Example C11** for the rules for calculating the rate at which inheritance tax will be payable on appointments after the first ten-year anniversary out of the discretionary trust created by A's will.

In relation to the rate applicable before the first ten-year anniversary, or on ten-year anniversaries, **parts (i)(b)** and **(ii)(b)** of the Example illustrate the rules described in **Example C11** subject to one point of detail, which differs as between **part** (i) and **part** (ii). It relates to the treatment of the value transferred by A in the transfer of value comprising the transfer of the flat to D, which, although potentially exempt at the time, became a chargeable transfer as a result of A's death within seven years.

- In **part (i)** of the Example, that transfer constitutes a gift with reservation (A gave away the flat worth £200,000 and retained just the lease 'for life' worth £80,000), and the result of applying the double charges regulations on A's death is that the calculation which disregards that transfer of the flat produces the higher tax charge. Apart from those rules, the settlor's cumulative total immediately before the commencement of the discretionary trust under A's will would have been £478,000 (£364,000 from the sale of his life interest plus £114,000 from the transfer of the flat). But the double charges regulations (SI 1987/1130 reg 5(4)(b)) also have the result that, because the tax on A's death is calculated ignoring the transfer of the flat, the value transferred by that transfer is to be treated as reduced to nil for inheritance tax purposes so that the figure to be used in the relevant property calculations is £364,000. (This reduction to nil is subject to one exception not relevant to this Example, relating to lifetime transfers which were immediately chargeable, rather than potentially exempt as in the Example; if an exit charge or ten-yearly charge arises under the relevant property rules in relation to a settlement while the settlor is still living, the settlor's factual cumulative total resulting from the lifetime chargeable transfer is to be used, and not retrospectively revisited as a result of applying the double charges regulations on his death, but for charges arising after his death the rule applies as outlined above.)
- In **part (ii)** of the Example the fact that A makes a transfer of value at all on selling the flat to D (and reserving the lease 'for life') results purely from the artificial exclusion of the lease from his estate by virtue of s 5(1)(b), (1A). The transaction is not (even in part) a gift by A, and accordingly is not subject to the rules for gifts with reservation. Accordingly there is nothing to exclude from A's cumulative total of lifetime transfers the £24,000 potentially exempt (and now chargeable) transfer of the flat, so that the settlor's cumulative total used for relevant property computations in relation to the discretionary trust under A's will, including as before the £364,000 sale of his life interest, is £388,000.

Question

A.

Explain the differing inheritance tax (IHT) treatment of property settled by Will for the benefit of young children of whom the testator was a 'parent' within IHTA 1984 s 71H if:

(i) the children will take capital at age 18;

(ii) the children will take capital at age 25 with no income entitlement before that except at the discretion of the trustees;

(iii) the children will take income entitlements at age 18 and capital at age 25; and

(iv) the children will take income entitlements at age 25 but the capital will remain settled for the time being thereafter.

B.

You have received an enquiry from a wealthy client. He intends to transfer £375,000 into a settlement for his young children and for the next generation on their deaths. He seeks your advice as to the type of trust that should be settled. He is of the opinion that it is highly irresponsible for any parent to let an 18-year-old receive substantial capital and neither is he entirely happy about his children receiving their entitlement at 25.

He has asked you to suggest what strategy he should consider in settling the trust and to set out what reporting requirements and other on-going tax-related responsibilities your advice would entail.

You are required to draft paragraphs for a letter to be sent to your client in response to his enquiry. Assume that you are writing in August 2023.

C.

Another of your clients of more modest means wants to know whether there would be any tax advantages if he and his wife transferred funds to their children. The children are aged 15, 12 and 10.

Prepare notes on the points to be made to this client.

D.

Family investment companies may be used as an alternative to trusts for the purposes of estate planning.

Prepare brief notes on family investment companies.

Answer

A.

A(i) Capital at age 18

If the Will of a deceased parent of a child aged under 18 provides that the child will become entitled to the capital, together with any income and accumulated income, of his share of property settled by the Will no later than age 18, and certain further conditions (below) are satisfied, then the child's share will be within the regime for bereaved minors' trusts in IHTA 1984 s 71A. Thus if the testator leaves several children all under 18, and the conditions are satisfied in relation to all of them, the whole trust fund will be within that regime.

The further conditions, set out in s 71A(3)(b) and (c), are essentially that, so long as the child in question is living and under age 18, no application of any of the settled property or its income may be made for the benefit of any beneficiary other than the particular child. The condition as to income is not infringed if the particular child 'is entitled to all the income (if there is any) arising from any of the settled property' (s 71A(3)(c)(i)) – put more shortly, that means that he has an interest in possession (IIP) (see **Example C3**, and see further below).

In relation to property transferred into trust on or after 8 April 2013 (FA 2013 Sch 43 para 9(1)), where the trustees have powers that enable them to apply amounts (whether consisting of income or capital, or both) not exceeding the annual limit other than for the benefit of the bereaved minor, the trust does not thereby cease to qualify as a bereaved minors trust within s 71A (s 71(4)(za)).The prescribed annual limit is defined in s 71A(4A) as the lower of £3,000 or 3% of the value of the trust fund during the tax year in question.

The existence (as opposed to exercise) of certain powers of advancement (to pay or apply capital for the advancement or benefit of the beneficiary), whether they are, or are to like effect as, the statutory powers applicable in England and Wales or Northern Ireland, will also not prevent the condition as to capital entitlement from being satisfied even though they are wide enough in their application to permit property to be applied in ways that do not themselves fulfil the requirements of s 71A: see s 71A(4)(a)–(e), and see in more detail **Example C16 explanatory note 9**.

If the trust meets the requirements of s 71A then, although as a seemingly primary rule an IHT charge will arise under s 71B(1) on property ceasing to fulfil the s 71A qualifying conditions (or on the trustees entering into a depreciatory transaction), this charge is negated by s 71B(2) in all the 'usual' circumstances of a 'policy-compliant exit', namely:

- on the beneficiary becoming entitled to capital at or before age 18;
- on any application of capital for his benefit before that age; or
- on the beneficiary dying under age 18 (however the property in question then devolves).

Tax is also not charged where an amount is paid or applied otherwise than for the benefit of a bereaved minor where the above exemptions (and those in s 70(3), (4)) do not apply (s 71A(2A)). However, the negation of the charge is limited to the lower of the amount so paid or applied and the annual limit (s 71A(2B)).

An IIP for a beneficiary under age 18 would in practice be unusual – so far as English law at least is concerned, it would have to be the result of deliberate drafting to negate the effect of Trustee Act 1925 s 31, see *Stanley v IRC* (1944) and **Example C3 explanatory note 1**. Where one does exist, it will not be a qualifying IIP (see **Example C3**), but will not negate the IHT exemptions under s 71A just described. Furthermore, if an IIP in favour of the testator's minor child comes into force on the testator's death and the conditions for a bereaved minor's trust are fulfilled, the IIP will not be an immediate post-death interest (IPDI); rather the bereaved minor's trust regime takes priority in such a case (with more favourable results, than for an IPDI (a qualifying IIP), if the beneficiary's death were to occur under age 18).

A(ii) Capital at age 25 with no income entitlement meanwhile

In this instance the share of each beneficiary will meet the qualifying conditions for an age 18-to-25 trust under s 71D, provided equivalent further conditions to those for bereaved minors' trusts are fulfilled (see above, but in this case the requirements apply so long as the beneficiary is living and under age 25, not merely until he is 18). Again, the mere existence of powers of advancement or powers to pay or apply the income and/or capital of the trust not exceeding the annual limit for persons other than the bereaved minor will not prevent these conditions from being fulfilled; and again it is not inconsistent with age 18-to-25 trust status for an IIP to subsist so long as the other conditions are fulfilled. Until 5 April 2015, extra-statutory concession F8 Accumulation and maintenance settlements (which historically applied to old-style accumulation and maintenance trusts under s 71) continued to be relevant for the interpretation of s 71D and provided that the conditions of that section were regarded as being met even if no age was specified in the trust instrument, provided that it was clear that a beneficiary would in fact become entitled to the settled property by the age 25. The concession has now been recorded as obsolete in the list of HMRC extra statutory concessions published on 6 April 2015.

The IHT treatment of an age 18-to-25 trust has some features in common with that of a bereaved minor's trust in the sense that its privileges revolve around the three events listed in **part A(i)** above which attract exemption under that regime. The age 18-to-25 trust regime, like that for bereaved minors' trusts, provides for an exit charge on property ceasing to be held on terms which fulfil the conditions for the regime to apply (and on depreciatory transactions by the trustees), under s 71E(1); but if any of the three events just referred to occurs not later than the 18th birthday of the beneficiary of an age 18-to-25 trust, exemption is given from that exit charge (s 71E(2)). Exemption also applies, by s 71E(2)(c), if the reason for the property leaving the age 18-to-25 trust regime is that it becomes subject to the bereaved minor's trust regime (essentially if the qualifying age for entitlement to capital is reduced to 18 from whichever age, not exceeding 25, had been specified previously). Tax is also not charged where an amount is paid or applied otherwise than for the benefit of a bereaved minor where the above exemptions do not apply; again the negation of the charge is limited to the lower of the amount so paid or applied and the annual limit (s 71E(4A)).

If, however, one of those three events occurs after the relevant beneficiary has attained age 18, exemption from the exit charge does not apply, but instead a less harsh rate of charge applies (under s 71F) than if the charge arose in other circumstances (when the calculation of the charge is at what might be called a 'time-based flat rate', irrespective of the value of the property concerned, under s 71G – see **Example C16 explanatory note 3**). The calculation under s 71F is practically indistinguishable from the calculation of a relevant property exit charge before the first ten-year anniversary, under s 68, with two important exceptions that combine to make this regime significantly more favourable overall than the relevant property regime:

- the s 71F rate applies however long has elapsed since the commencement of the settlement at the testator's death (which could be around 25 years in the case of a child of the testator recently born, or still *in utero*, at that time), with no ten-year charges applying in the meantime; and
- the quarters that are counted towards the time-fraction (by which the effective rate on the notional chargeable transfer is multiplied) are reckoned only from the 18th birthday of the beneficiary in question (or if later from 6 April 2008 when the property entered the age 18-to-25 trust regime), not from commencement of the settlement as under s 68.

The notional transfer used to calculate the 'settlement rate' (the effective rate on that notional transfer) for the purpose of the s 71F charge uses the cumulative total of chargeable transfers by the testator in the seven years before his death, and the amount of the transfer itself is made up of three elements:

(i) the initial value (in the trustees' hands immediately after the death) of the property comprised in the settlement in which the exit charge arises (*whether or not* that property is or has been within the age 18-to-25 trust regime, or even is still comprised in the settlement);

(ii) the initial value of the property in any related settlement(s), which, in respect of charges arising on or after 18 November 2015, is taken into account only if it itself is property held on trusts to which the age 18-to-25 trust regime applies; and

(iii) the initial value of any property which became comprised in the (same) settlement after the settlement commenced and before the date of the exit charge (whether or not it has remained comprised in the settlement up to that date). (Seemingly the only way in which this category could be relevant to a Will trust, bearing in mind that property added by a third party would be treated as comprised in a separate settlement by s 44(2), is if property from a related settlement (made or deemed to be made (see s 80) by the testator at the same time, ie at the date of his death) were later transferred into the age 18-to-25 trust – there does not appear to be any mechanism to counter the double-counting that would be involved in this situation, but it is a situation that will be rare at the best of times, and easily avoided in any case.)

These values are all unrelated to the current value of the property within the age 18-to-25 trust regime (or otherwise still comprised in the settlement). It therefore follows that it is possible to calculate with certainty, as soon as IHT values at the testator's death have been established and subject only to the effect of future changes in IHT rates generally, the 'settlement rate' as defined in s 71F, to which the 'relevant fraction' (30% of the familiar time-fraction) would in future be applied in working out the amount of tax payable on a beneficiary's 25th birthday or earlier vesting, distribution or death. On the 25th birthday of a beneficiary who was under age 18 at the death, and for whom therefore the maximum possible relevant fraction will apply if no capital is applied for his benefit before age 25, it will be seen that the relevant fraction cannot exceed 28/40ths (seven years = 28 quarters between his 18th and 25th birthdays).

A(iii) Income entitlements at age 18 with capital at age 25

The position in this case is identical to that in **part A(ii)** above. The fact that beneficiaries take IIPs at age 18 is not inconsistent with the continuance of the age 18-to-25 trust regime; see one of the alternative conditions relating to income, in s 71D(6)(c)(i), namely that, so long as the beneficiary in question is living and under the age of 25, he must be 'entitled to all the income (if there is any) arising from any of the settled property'.

A(iv) Income entitlements at age 25 with capital remaining settled thereafter

Whilst a trust of this sort may have been common in Wills made before the 2006 Budget on 22 March 2006, because it would have qualified as an accumulation and maintenance trust under s 71 as applicable before that date (see **Example C16 explanatory notes 1–3**), if a testator dies on or after that date with a Will in this form the property in question will be subject to the relevant property regime (though with the possibility, within the flexibility conferred by the terms of the trust, of restructuring onto an alternative basis with backdated effect under s 144, whether as a bereaved minor's trust under s 71A, an age 18-to-25 trust under s 71D, or as an IPDI under s 49A).

For details of the IHT charges arising under the relevant property regime, see **Example C11**.

B. Other settlements for minors

If you wish to make a lifetime gift to your children you have broadly two options. First, you can make an outright gift (to a bare trust on behalf of your children). This means that they can insist on receiving the capital as soon as they are 18. Such a gift would constitute a potentially exempt transfer and will escape inheritance tax altogether provided you live for seven years after the gift. In view of your understandable objections to giving 18-year olds substantial sums of money, I would not recommend that you followed this option. However, you should note that it is the most inheritance tax-friendly solution (though any income generated is treated as yours at the same time as it arises to the bare trustees; it does not have to be paid to the child or applied for his benefit).

Alternatively, you can settle the funds into a trust. Since 22 March 2006, the inheritance tax treatment has been the same for both interest in possession trusts (essentially those where the beneficiaries have a right to receive the income from a fixed interest in the trust) and discretionary trusts (those where the trustees have a lot more freedom about paying income and capital to the beneficiaries). In the circumstances I would suggest that you consider using a discretionary trust as that gives you the greatest flexibility in the future – there is no requirement to distribute income or capital by any given age. As regards income tax, the income generated while the children are still under 18 and unmarried could not be distributed for their benefit without its being taxed as if it were yours at the time of the distribution. It would also be necessary to provide that you and any putative wife (or for that matter civil partner) of yours are excluded from all possibility of benefiting from the trust.

If you proceed, inheritance tax will be payable at 20% from the funds entering the trust, except so far as covered by your annual exemption. However, on the basis that you have made no chargeable transfers to date, the first £6,000 will be covered by your annual exemption for this year and for last year, and the next £325,000 by the nil-rate band. Please note that the enhancement mentioned above in respect of the transferable nil-rate band does not apply to lifetime gifts.

Therefore, assuming for the sake of illustration that you were to gift £375,000, and to specify that any tax was to be borne by the trust, the trustees would be required to pay inheritance tax of £8,800 ((£375,000 – £6,000) – £325,000 @ 20%). If instead you chose to pay the tax yourself, the tax charge would be calculated on a 'grossing-up' basis and would work out at £11,000 ((£369,000 + £11,000) – £325,000 @ 20%).

This tax will be payable (assuming you make the gift before the end of September 2023) by 30 April 2024 If you make the gift after the end of September 2023 and before 6 April 2024, the tax will be payable six months after the end of the month in which you make the gift.

Further tax will be payable out of the trust fund should you die within seven years of making the gift. This will be payable six months after the end of the month in which you die.

If the tax is not paid on the due date, interest is charged at the rate in force at that time.

In both cases (the immediate lifetime charge, and the further tax on death), there is technically a 12-month period allowed for filing a return (plus the remainder of the month current at the date of the event in question); but because interest starts to run well before the end of that time limit it is unwise to leave submitting the return until the end of the 12 months, at least without having reviewed the figures carefully and put money down with HMRC against the tax liability that is expected.

The maximum lump sum you can give without triggering any immediate inheritance tax charge is £331,000 (the current nil-rate band of £325,000 plus the two unused annual exemptions totalling £6,000). The trust will incur inheritance tax charges in the future under two headings:

- on every tenth anniversary of its formation. Currently the maximum possible rate on each ten-year anniversary is 6%, though in practice the rate is likely to work out substantially lower than that unless the value of the trust has grown enormously in the meantime, since the trustees would be able to take advantage of the fact that you had not made any use of your nil-rate band prior to forming the trust.

- on any capital released from the trust. In the first ten years, based on an initial gift into trust of £366,200 (£375,000 less tax due thereon met by the trust as calculated above based on current legislation) the rate applicable would be a maximum of 0.658% in the final three months of the ten-year period and proportionally reduced depending on the time elapsed since formation of the trust (ie (£366,200 – £325,000) × (30% × 20%) × 39/40). (Technically the formula takes a starting-point of (in this example) a 0.675% rate reduced to a fraction of itself, n/40, where n is the number of complete quarters since the formation of the trust, with therefore a maximum of 39/40ths in the final quarter of the ten-year period.) After the first ten-year anniversary, the rate would be based on the rate used at the immediately preceding ten-year anniversary, again scaled down by reference to the number of quarter-years elapsed since that ten-year anniversary.

I think you will agree that this regime for discretionary trusts is not a particular disincentive to setting one up. I should also draw your attention to a further valuable exemption which you could use to top up the initial capital amount that you put into such a trust. This arises because, as I understand it, your relatively frugal lifestyle means that you have a substantial amount of spare income each year. So long as you lay down a pattern to this effect (which need not be tied to a fixed monetary sum – it could be done by way of a formula if that were easy enough to test and administer), so that the gifts can be shown to be part of your 'normal expenditure', you can give away as much as you choose of your excess income each year, without this counting as a taxable gift by you even if you failed to survive it by the seven year period I have mentioned above.

This 'normal expenditure' exemption would not be available to the trust and thus additions to the trust by way of regular gifts out of income would have an impact on the rate of inheritance tax payable by the trustees on distributions and ten-year anniversary charges – I could let you have an illustration if you wished – but the facility for removing value from your own taxable estate without a charge at that time, even if at some point you find you are terminally ill, is a very valuable planning tool. The main rider is that HRMC will look very carefully at such gifts after your death, and you would need to set up a very disciplined record-keeping system to enable your personal representatives, when the time comes, to justify the claim that the gifts were all fully exempt.

Initial and ongoing reporting requirements:

1. In relation to yourself

(i) In principle you must file an inheritance tax return within 12 months after making the initial gift to the trustees, as above. However, if you limit the size of the gift to what is covered by your annual exemptions and statutory nil-rate band (or to 80% of the nil-rate band if the gift is made in the form of anything other than cash or quoted shares or securities), you are only required to file such a return in your lifetime if HMRC notify you to that effect. Your personal representatives would need, in the return for your estate, to disclose the gift in any case if you died within seven years afterwards, and the trustees as donees would in that case need to file a return of the gift as well.

(ii) So long as you are confident, with good reason, that subsequent gifts to the trust out of your income each year met the criteria for exemption, you would not be obliged to submit any inheritance tax return in respect of them. In the event of your death, however, your personal representatives will be required to disclose such gifts made within the seven years prior to your death so that HMRC can test the claim that they are exempt; if they were to succeed in overturning the claim for any such gifts within the last seven years, it is quite possible that they would seek to extend the enquiry to examine gifts before that time for which the same exemption was claimed, since if they were successful in such an attack this would mean that the gifts in question would have been taxable lifetime gifts. For this reason my recommendation above as to record-keeping must extend to preserving all the records in question – however long the period before your death that they cover – until the inheritance tax position of your estate has been completely finalised.

(iii) In addition to that, you will need to include in your tax return for the year ended 5 April 2024 full details of any chargeable assets disposed of in order to raise the funds for (or transferred in kind to) the settlement, so that any chargeable gains arising may be calculated. If there are any such gains beyond your annual exemption of £12,300, and any available losses in the present or earlier tax years, the capital gains tax rate applicable will be 20% (28% in respect of residential and non-residential property and shares which derive at least 75% of their value from land) to the extent that the gains plus your income exceed the basic rate limit for income tax.

(iv) Income arising under the settlement will not affect you in so far as it is accumulated for the benefit of your children; but if, while the children are under 18 years of age and unmarried, the trustees make any payment for their maintenance, education or benefit the amount so paid will, as I have mentioned, be regarded as your income for tax purposes, and will consequently need to be included in your personal income tax return; this applies as much to capital payments as to income, except that in the case of capital the amount is limited to the income that arose (or later arises) while they are still unmarried minors. You would be entitled to recover any tax paid by you under these provisions from the trustees or from the children who receive the income. However, the majority of the trust's income (beyond the first £1,000) will be taxed in the trustees' hands at the highest rates that could apply to your own personal income, and conceivably your own liability on the amount in question may be less than what the trustees had paid; in that event, if you obtained a tax repayment, you would be bound to pay it over to the trustees rather than retaining it for yourself. I should also mention that in the past, to the extent that the trust's income consisted of dividend income arising before 2016/17, there was an increased income tax cost of making income payments compared with dividend income received directly. (See generally **points 2(ii)** and **2(iii) below**.)

(v) Equivalent reporting responsibilities will apply if you make any additions to the settlement in future years that are not fully covered by exemptions.

2. In relation to the trustees

(i) The trustees should inform HMRC that the settlement has been created and obtain a reference number (a unique taxpayer reference) for the settlement. There is now an online system (the Trusts Registration Service) in respect of the registration of trusts (which generates the unique taxpayer reference). It must be used by trustees (and their agents) to register and update records and it replaces the paper 41G(Trust) form (which has not been accepted since the end of April 2017) and the ad hoc process for trustees to notify changes in their circumstances. This will affect trustees who register new trusts with HMRC and existing trustees who need to update their details. Trustees will need to update the Trusts Register each year that the trust generates a UK tax consequence. Also trustees must ensure and confirm the Trusts Register is accurate and up to date, guaranteeing their obligations under the Fourth Money Laundering Directive are complied with. This includes those trusts that have already registered using the 41G(Trust) form. In their *Trusts and Estates Newsletter* of April 2017 HMRC have confirmed that registration does not apply to trusts that have closed where the trustees have received a letter from HMRC stating that they have updated their records to show that the trust has ended.

(ii) Income tax return forms must be prepared and submitted by the trustees for each year ended 5 April. The forms give details of the income of the trust, the trustees' expenses and outgoings, disposals and deemed disposals for capital gains tax purposes, details of any distributions made to the children and may include the calculation of the self-assessed tax liability. The income of a discretionary settlement is chargeable at the trust rate – currently 39.35% for dividends and 45% for other income, except that the first £1,000 of income, plus the amount used for expenses, is charged at 8.75% for dividends and 20% for other income. If a time came when the children were given a right to the income arising for the time being, the charge on the trustees would be restricted to 7.5% on dividend income and 20% on other income, though the children (so long as they were no longer minors, or were married though under 18) would have credit for tax borne by the trustees and would either have additional tax to pay, or would obtain a tax refund according to their personal circumstances.

(iii) If the trustees distribute any funds for the maintenance or education of one or more of the children when they are still under 18 and unmarried then, as stated above, any past or future trust income (up to a maximum of the amount distributed) will be treated as your income for tax purposes. Even so, the amount of any such income will be declared in the trust tax return and will be included in calculating the income liable at the 38.1% and 45% rates. The trustees will deduct tax at 45% from the payments. Once the children have married or reached age 18, distributions (or income entitlements, if conferred by the trustees) will no longer give rise to liability (or a right to refund) on your part as described in **point 1(iv)** above; instead the children would include income distributions (or entitlements as the case may be) on their own tax returns, with credit for the tax paid by the trustees; this would effectively be the same as in **2(ii) above**, but using the higher amounts of tax at the trust level while the trust remains discretionary.

(iv) The capital gains of the discretionary settlement will be chargeable at 20% (28% in respect of residential and non-residential property and shares which derive at least 75% of their value from land) after the deduction of allowable losses and of the annual exemption (£3,000 for 2023/24, reduced if you have created more than one settlement after 6 June 1978 that is still in existence during the relevant tax year). If assets are distributed in kind, the trustees will be treated as disposing of them at that time for capital gains tax purposes; but if the recipient beneficiary is UK resident then the trustees and the beneficiary can instead secure that the beneficiary takes over their base cost through a claim for hold-over relief – with an unfortunate technical exception in a case where the distribution occurs either within three months after the trust is made or after one of the ten-yearly inheritance tax charges mentioned in **2(v) below**. In a case where the UK residential property is distributed, then hold-over relief is available regardless of the residence status of the recipient beneficiary.

(v) Inheritance tax returns will need to be filed by the trustees in relation to the ten-yearly and interim distribution charges that I have referred to, within six months from the end of the month in which the chargeable event occurs, except that this is not obligatory unless and until specifically required by HMRC in cases where the amount used to calculate the rate of tax is no more than 80% of the statutory nil-rate band for the time being (assuming that no other settlements are created on the same day).

3. In relation to your children

(i) The children have no reporting responsibility until they reach age 18 (or, theoretically, marry under that age).

(ii) When income is distributed to your children, this will be shown on their tax returns (which you will complete whilst they are minors). This reporting obligation arises even where the income is taxed as though it were yours (**point 1(iv)** above), but in that case they will have no liability.

I shall be happy to discuss any of the above points with you in more detail if you wish, and to assist in the completion of relevant forms.

(An interesting article entitled 'Providing by Will – Choosing the right sort of trust' by Emma Chamberlain may be found in the September 2022 edition of the *Tax Adviser* magazine.)

C. Transferring funds to infant children

(1) Where funds are transferred to children under 18, there is little opportunity to obtain any income tax advantages. The funds transfer would be treated for income tax as a settlement. Unless it is covered by one of the exceptions listed below, settlement income that is paid to or would otherwise be treated as the income of a child of the settlor who is under 18 is treated as the parent's income and not the child's (ITTOIA 2005 s 629). Before 27 February 2023 (when The Marriage and Civil Partnership (Minimum Age) Act 2022 came into force), the additional requirement was that the child of the settlor had to be under 18 and unmarried (or not in a civil partnership). Since the coming into force of the Act, 16 and 17 year olds are no longer allowed to marry (or enter into a civil partnership), even with parental consent. A settlement includes 'any disposition, trust, covenant, agreement, arrangement or transfer of assets' (s 620).

(2) The inclusion of income that would otherwise be treated as income of the child extends the charge to income arising within a 'bare trust', under which the child has an absolute right to the property and income, but the trustees (who could be the parents) are the legal owners, effectively holding as the child's nominee. The income arising to a bare trust created on or after 9 March 1999 is treated as that of the parent-transferor as it arises to the bare trustees; it does not have to be paid to the child or applied for his benefit. Bare trusts used to escape this income tax treatment before 9 March 1999, though they have (to some) the disadvantage that the child cannot be prevented from obtaining legal ownership of the funds at age 18.

(3) Each parent may, however, give each such child a capital sum from which not more than £100 gross income arises each year, without falling foul of that rule. If income exceeds the limit the whole amount is taxable (s 629(3)).

(4) The changed rules for bare trusts (**point 2** above) do not alter the capital gains treatment, which treats gains arising as the child's gains against which the annual exemption (currently £6,000 for 2023/24) is available, the rates of tax on any gains beyond his exemption being 10% (18% in respect of residential property and non-residential property and shares which derive at least 75% of their value from land) to the extent that the child's income has not used up his basic rate band for income tax, and 20% (28% in respect of residential property and non-residential property and shares which derive at least 75% of their value from land) above that level. Funds could therefore be invested for the child purely for capital growth, with no income arising. This does not, however, give the former benefits of being able to use the child's personal allowance and lower tax rates against income.

(5) Other possibilities, which also do not make use of the children's allowances and lower tax rates, are as follows:

   (a) Friendly society policies (with premiums up to £25 per month or a single annual premium of £270 – but see **explanatory note 20(b)**).

   (b) Contributions of up to £2,880 net per child into a personal pension plan. The basic rate tax relief of 20% is added to the amount invested in the plan, so that for a contribution of £2,880 the plan investment would be £3,600.

   (c) Junior ISAs (JISAs) for children under 18 (see **explanatory note 19**). When a parent contributes to a JISA on behalf of their child, the funds are not considered to be settlement income from the parent (see paragraph 18.1.7 of the ISA guidance notes: www.hmrc.gov.uk/isa/isa-guidance-notes.pdf).

(6) Where a child aged 16 or 17 opens a cash individual savings account (ie an adult ISA) with funds provided by the parents then this will be treated as a settlement and the income arising will be taxable on the parent until the child's 18th birthday or earlier marriage if before 22 February 2023 (subject to the de minimis amount of £100), even though income within an ISA is normally tax free. But the tax freedom of an ISA will then continue for the child's benefit once he/she has reached age 18 or married (see **explanatory note 19**).

D. Family investment companies

It is common for family members to pass assets (eg investments) down the generations. Family investment companies (FICs) are an alternative to the more traditional family discretionary trust, as a means of passing family wealth down to children and remoter generations while allowing the older members to maintain control over the assets. Once a FIC has been fully set up, its shareholders will, typically, be different generations of a family. By not using a trust, exit and ten-year anniversary charges are immediately avoided.

A FIC is typically formed by parents providing funds for investment through interest-free loans or by subscribing for preference shares (or a combination of both). Neither of these arrangements is regarded as a chargeable event for IHT purposes and using cash generated by the company's investments. the money transferred by either means can be extracted tax-free from the FIC at a later date. Subscribing for shares in a company does not give rise to stamp duty or capital gains tax liabilities.

The parents, who will be directors of the FIC (typically with control over investment decisions as to capital appreciation and income), will also typically subscribe for two further classes of shares in the company:

- voting shares which will give them control of the FIC as shareholders and directors; and
- non-voting shares which are gifted to the children (preferably before significant value accrues on those shares).

The gift of the non-voting shares will not be subject to IHT, provided that the parents survive this event by seven years, and capital gains tax is unlikely to arise as any gain on disposal is likely to be minimal. Furthermore, any subsequent growth in value following an outright gift of the shares will normally fall outside the parents' estates (although care is needed to ensure that the gifts with reservation IHT anti-avoidance provisions do not apply to treat the shares as remaining in the parents' estates). At the time the shares are gifted the parents may make interest free loans to the company; such loans are also unlikely to trigger the gift with reservation of benefit rules in relation to the gifted shares (as there is a benefit to the donee rather than a benefit reserved by the donor). If the company's shares are spread (say, 25% each) between each parent and adult child, the value of the separate shareholdings are likely to be subject to discounts (eg to reflect non-controlling interests in the company), and so may further reduce IHT exposure in the parents' estates. The shares in the FIC are unlikely however to attract any IHT reliefs dues to its investment activities.

Once the company is set up, the company will typically acquire investment assets. The parents who set up the company may themselves sell assets to the company for their market value but capital gains tax and stamp duty or stamp duty land tax liabilities could arise. Where residential property is acquired by a company, it will be liable to stamp duty land tax at the additional 3% surcharge rates.

Dividends paid by the FIC will come from the non-voting shares. Assuming that the children are adults, any amount in excess of the younger individual's combined personal and dividend tax allowances (£13,570 for 2023/24) will be taxed at 8.75% if it falls into the basic rate band and at 33.75% if it reaches the higher rate bracket.

One important feature is that the FIC will pay corporation tax on its profits (including capital gains) at 25%. The 19% small profits rate, which applies to companies with profits of £50,000 or less from then onwards, is unlikely to be relevant for FICs because the lower rate is not available for close investment-holding companies.

Other tax-related considerations for FICs are:

- Capital gains realised by an FIC are currently chargeable at 25%. For the time being, this is higher than the main rate of CGT for individuals (20%). Where assets have been held since before 1 January 2018, an indexation allowance can reduce the FIC's gain. If an FIC is disposing of all or part of a holding of at least 10% in a trading company, the substantial shareholding exemption should be available.
- Dividends received by an FIC (including from overseas) are likely to be exempt from corporation tax.

Dividends from abroad may be subject to a withholding tax. Withholding tax is offset against the UK corporation tax on the corresponding income. However, if the income is exempt from tax, any withholding tax will not be repaid by HMRC and so will represent a real cost to the FIC.

A FIC can claim a corporation tax deduction for interest paid on loans taken out against the value of its investments where the loans have been used for the purposes of the company's business (eg in order to acquire new shares or to manage the operation). Annual loan interest deductions may be restricted where the total interest payable exceeds £2,000,000. By contrast, individuals are not permitted to claim tax relief on the interest on loans to acquire a share portfolio.

Expenses incurred by the FIC in managing its investments and running the business will be eligible for corporation tax relief. This will include investment managers' fees and remuneration paid to employees or directors and contributions to pension funds. The company can set off these expenses against its taxable income and gains – any unrelieved amount can be carried forward and deducted from the FIC's future taxable profits. Tax relief for such expenses is not available to individual investors.

On the liquidation of an FIC, CGT will be charged at 20% on any capital distributions (subject to the application of the anti-avoidance provisions in s 396B ITTOIA 2005).

Explanatory Notes

Bereaved minors' trusts and age 18-to-25 trusts: meaning of 'parent'

(1) For the purposes of ss 71A to 71G 'parent' is not limited to a person who is a parent of the child in question as a matter of general family law (including where relevant the family law of other jurisdictions in cases where the private international law of one of the jurisdictions of the UK requires reference to such law); by virtue of s 71H the word includes a step-parent, and in addition a person is to be treated as the parent of another individual if, immediately before he died, that person had parental responsibility (or in Scotland parental responsibilities) for the individual under the law of England and Wales, Scotland or Northern Ireland.

Bereaved minors' trusts and age 18-to-25 trusts: class gifts and variable shares

(2) The application of the age 18-to-25 trust regime and the bereaved minor's trust regime to trusts in favour of a class of beneficiaries under the relevant age for the time being was unclear at the time of the enactment of FA 2006. Following an exchange of correspondence between the Chartered Institute of Taxation (CIoT), the Society of Trust and Estate Practitioners (STEP) and HMRC an agreed guidance note relating to ss 71A, 71D and accumulation and maintenance trusts was published. This may now be found at IHTM42816. All potential beneficiaries must be living at the date a trust enters the age 18-to-25 trust or bereaved minors' trust regime – ie the class of beneficiaries must be closed. Trusts where the trustees have power to vary the shares in which beneficiaries will take at the stated age, while they are still under that age, are acceptable provided that the share of a beneficiary who has reached the stated age must not be capable of increase or decrease. Further, if a trust currently has three beneficiaries and such a power is exercised revocably so as to allocate the fund equally between two of them, the trust will leave the regime in question, and become relevant property, unless the third beneficiary is permanently excluded and the retained flexibility is purely between the two. By contrast, if the revocable allocation were as to 48% each for beneficiaries A and B, and 2% for beneficiary C, future adjustments (while all three are under the relevant age) could be on any basis between A, B and C since C has retained at least some share within the relevant regime throughout.

Property entering the age 18-to-25 trust or bereaved minors' trust regimes from other regimes; inheritance tax treatment

(3) It is possible for property to enter the bereaved minor's trust regime or the age 18-to-25 trust regime on the termination of an IPDI or a disabled person's interest, since neither regime requires that the trusts in question should take effect immediately on the testator's death. The typical situation would be where the testator's surviving spouse or civil partner takes a life interest in priority to the trust for the testator's children, and then dies or surrenders his/her interest (other than by deed of variation) before the children have attained the qualifying age to become absolutely entitled; but the same principle would apply even if the spouse exemption were not available on the testator's death because the life interest was granted to some other party. If the IIP in question comes to an end in the lifetime of its beneficiary, this would involve an immediately chargeable transfer if the property then entered the age 18-to-25 trust regime, but a potentially exempt transfer (s 3A(3B)) if it entered the bereaved minor's trust regime.

Doubts have been expressed as to whether property can move from the relevant property regime into either the bereaved minor's trust regime or the age 18-to-25 trust regime. Such a situation can arise in the case of a discretionary will trust where appointments are made for the benefit of a deceased settlor's children within two years of his death. Section 144 which provides for distributions from a discretionary will trust within two years of the individual's death to be treated as made under his Will contains specific reference to s 71A (bereaved minors trusts) and s 71D (age 18-25 trusts). HMRC's interpretation of the law is that such trusts can therefore arise by virtue of the reading back effect of s 144. They are of the opinion that s 144(3)(c)(ii), (6)(b) operates to treat s 71A and s 71D trusts as capable of being created under the deceased's Will (see IHTM35182). See **Example C11** for more information about discretionary will trusts.

Additions to a testamentary age 18-to-25 trust: inheritance tax treatment

(4) For further commentary on the 'policy-compliant' exit charge under s 71F (ie the more favourable rate that applies in circumstances to which the policy of the age 18-to-25 trust regime is directed) see **Example C16 explanatory notes 7, 8**. In practice, not least having regard to s 44(2) which will (if it makes any difference) result in property added by a different settlor being treated for IHT purposes as comprised in a separate settlement, it is as good as impossible to conceive of a situation where property not originally comprised in the settlement might be added to it (**Example C16 explanatory note 7(c)**) where the age 18-to-25 trust is established under the Criminal Injuries Compensation Scheme, the Victims of Overseas Terrorism Compensation Scheme or under the Will of the beneficiary's parent who by definition is now deceased. That category could easily be relevant, however, where property has entered the age 18-to-25 trust regime on transition from a former accumulation and maintenance trust (see **Example C16**) since there could have been many additions to the settlement in question before the FA 2006 changes took effect.

Favourable CGT treatment up to age 18 of bereaved minors' trusts and age 18-to-20 trusts

(5) When the beneficiary of a bereaved minor's trust or an age 18-to-25 trust becomes absolutely entitled to capital not later than age 18, a claim to hold-over relief for capital gains tax (CGT) purposes is available by virtue of TCGA 1992 s 260(2)(da), (db), subject to the usual requirement that the beneficiary must be UK resident.

Another respect in which favourable CGT treatment is available, for both a bereaved minor's trusts and age 18-to-25 trusts, is that in the event of the beneficiary dying under age 18 and (unusually) having an IIP within either regime immediately before his death, a tax-free revaluation of the assets concerned for CGT purposes will take place even though the IIP in either such case is a non-qualifying IIP (TCGA 1992 ss 72(1A), (1B), 73(2A)). Tax planning will usually be furthest from trustees' minds in the event of a child under 18 having a life-threatening illness or injury, but if he is the beneficiary of a trust in either category and is expected not to survive then consideration might be given to creating an IIP in his favour if the fund in question has significant unrealised gains, so as to secure this tax-free uplift in base cost in the event of his death.

Inheritance tax: 2–year time limit for post-death restructuring

(6) In relation to the time limit for restructuring a Will trust to take advantage of backdating for IHT purposes under s 144, the time limit 'within the period of two years after the death' would expire at the end of the second anniversary, as HMRC accept in the Inheritance Tax Manual in relation to the identical requirement for deeds of variation, see IHTM35024; so appointments that take effect on the second anniversary will attract backdating treatment.

A further source for age 18-to-25 trusts and bereaved minors' trusts?

(7) Bereaved minor's trust or age 18-to-25 trust status can also arise for a trust established under the terms of the Victims of Overseas Terrorism Compensation Scheme, for which legislation was put in place by the Crime and Security Act 2010. The scheme became active on 16 April 2012 and applies to incidents that have occurred on and after 1 January 2002. Victims who are injured in such an overseas terrorist act which has also been designated by the Foreign Secretary, who have an ongoing disability as a result of their injuries, and are British, EU, EEA or Swiss citizens who have been resident in the UK for three years immediately prior to the designated terrorist act (or are members of the Armed Forces or an accompanying dependant of a member of the Armed Forces) may be eligible, on making a claim within six months of 16 April 2012 (or the date of the incident if later), for a payment under the scheme. Persons bereaved as a result of a designated terrorist act will not, however, be eligible for a payment as will victims who have recovered from their injuries.

Income tax treatment of payments re settlor's infant, unmarried children

(8) The income of discretionary and accumulation settlements is essentially charged at the dividend trust rate, currently 39.35%if it is dividend or similar income (see **Example F1** for details) and at the rate applicable to trusts, currently 45% if it is non-dividend income.

However, under ITA 2007 s 491 the first slice of trustees' income otherwise within the charge to these special trust tax rates will instead be charged at the income tax rate appropriate to the type of income. Therefore, if payments are received net of basic rate tax (for example, patent royalties or yearly interest) up to the limit of this first slice income, then the trustees will have no further tax to pay.

The first slice for this purpose is basically £1,000, subject to restriction where more than one trust made by the same settlor is in existence for the time being (see **Example F6 explanatory note 1**). It is calculated *net* of trust management expenses, so where relevant it will be calculated net of other deductions taken at Step 2 of the income tax computation as well.

Although the trust management expenses are for other purposes deducted from the trust income taxed at the lowest rate first, the reverse order will apply to first-slice income, namely the basic rate at 20% first, followed by dividends at 8.75%.

See **Examples F1, F6** and **F7** for further details on the lower rates for first-slice income, the interaction of first-slice income with trust expenses, and the additional liabilities to which it can give rise where amounts are distributed.

Although any payment made by the trustees of a discretionary trust for the maintenance or education of a child of the settlor who is under 18 and unmarried is deemed to be the settlor's income, it is not so treated *before* the payment is made. The trustees are therefore liable to tax at the 39.35% and 45% rates as the case may be, and any payments for the children are grossed up at that rate (ITA 2007 ss 493–498). (See **Example F1** under heading *Income taxed* as income of settlor for the effect of the treatment of dividend income on the overall tax charge where dividend income is paid to minor children via a discretionary trust.)

Notification of liability to income tax for trusts

(9) Since the trustees are chargeable to income tax on the trust income that arises, they must notify HMRC that they are so liable within six months after the end of the first relevant tax year. This is the same requirement as that of an individual taxpayer and carries a penalty of up to 100% of the tax due in the event of failure to notify (TMA 1970 s 7).

Person becoming absolutely entitled as against the trustees: gifts holdover relief in the context of capital gains tax

(10) When a person becomes absolutely entitled to trust assets as against the trustees, other than on the death of a beneficiary with an interest in possession that was a qualifying IIP for inheritance tax purposes (see **Example C3**), the assets are deemed to have been disposed of by the trustees at market value for capital gains tax purposes. Any capital gain arising may be held over (subject to the recipient's UK residence) under the provisions of TCGA 1992 s 260, unless the person becoming entitled on the death was the spouse or civil partner of the deceased beneficiary such as to attract the inheritance tax spouse exemption on the death, because s 260(2)(a) specifically allows a gain to be held over on a disposal which is a chargeable transfer for inheritance tax purposes. (This includes exit charges under the relevant property regime – hence the technical exception referred to in **part B** of the Example, **point 2(iv)**, because an exit charge in those circumstances is disapplied by IHTA 1984 s 65(4); there would however still be the possibility of holding over the gain if the assets in question qualified as business assets, or were such as to attract agricultural property relief for inheritance tax, by virtue of TCGA 1992 s 165 and Sch 7.)

Inheritance tax: accumulation and maintenance type settlements

(11) No new accumulation and maintenance settlements can be established after 21 March 2006. Those already in existence continued within the same regime until 5 April 2008, after which time that particular regime would only continue if the capital was (or had become) payable to the beneficiaries when they reach the age of 18, and (if the beneficiaries were not grandchildren of a common grandparent) the trust had not been in that regime for more than 25 years.

If an accumulation and maintenance settlement ceases to qualify within those narrower rules, because of the 25-year rule, the trustees are liable to an inheritance tax charge at (in practice) a fixed rate of 21%. Thereafter it would be within the relevant property regime and the normal ten-yearly and exit charges would apply.

(12) Settlements which ceased to be A & M settlements on 6 April 2008 simply because of the requirement to pay capital by the age of 18 did not incur an inheritance tax charge on that event; and so long as the trust provided for the capital to be distributed no later than age 25 they moved at that time into the age 18-to-25 trust regime. This is in some respects similar to the relevant property regime during the first ten years of a trust's existence, but in other respects more beneficial (no periodic charge, and no charge while the beneficiary is under age 18; the quarters for the n/40 fraction are only counted from a beneficiary's 18th birthday). See further **Example C16.**

Inheritance tax reporting by personal representatives of potentially exempt transfers that become chargeable

(13) Potentially exempt transfers that become chargeable because of the death of the donor within seven years must be included in the account delivered by the personal representatives, along with details of the deceased's estate (IHTA 1984 s 216). Section 216 also requires potentially exempt transfers to be reported by the donee, the donee being primarily liable for payment of the tax.

The tax treatment of bare trusts

(14) Bare trusts used to provide a simple way of enabling children's personal allowances and lower tax rates to be used against funds from the parent, so long as the income merely accumulated for the children's benefit without actually being paid to them. The parents could act as trustees and there thus need be no administration costs.

As mentioned in **part C point 2** of the Example, the earlier income tax advantages of bare trusts by parents in favour of their children under 18 were negated with effect from 9 March 1999 (FA 1999 s 64). The parental settlement rules apply to the income arising under a bare trust settled by a child's parent on or after 9 March 1999 whether the income is paid to the child or not. However the advantages continue for bare trusts created by parents before that date provided no funds are added (see ITTOIA 2005 Sch 2 para 133). Where funds are added to a pre-9 March 1999 bare trust, the parental settlement rules apply only to the income arising from the added funds. Except for dividend credits, the tax deducted at source from the accumulated income may in such a case be reclaimed to the extent that it exceeds the child's liability.

The revised rules do not prevent tax-efficient bare trusts being created by a parent's will, or by other relatives. It is not, however, possible for a parent to circumvent the rules by creating a bare trust for a relative's or friend's children and for the relative/friend to do the same for his children by way of a reciprocal arrangement (ITTOIA 2005 s 620).

(15) Property held on a bare trust is in the legal ownership of the trustees and must remain in their ownership if and so long as the beneficiary is a minor (since a minor cannot give a valid receipt). As and when the beneficiary is over 18 he may call for the legal ownership to be transferred to him at any time.

Under self-assessment, trustees are not required to complete tax returns in respect of bare trusts (although they may send a return of *income*, but not capital gains, if they wish – see **Example F6 explanatory note 10**), and the child must show the income and gains in his own return.

(16) Because the property is held for the beneficiary absolutely, it is not settled property for capital gains tax (TCGA 1992 s 60), and any gains are taxable on the beneficiary, so that the full annual exemption of £6,000 in 2023/24 (£12,300 for 2022/23) is available unless used against other gains.

(17) There is now an equivalent to TCGA 1992 s 60 in the income tax legislation in the shape of ITA 2007 s 466. The trustee is effectively only a nominee, so the provisions of ITA 2007 s 479 charging tax at the dividend trust rate of 39.35% where a company purchases the trustees' shares (see **Example F8 explanatory note 4**) do not apply.

(18) For inheritance tax, too, the property is not settled property since it is held for the beneficiary absolutely; any accumulations of income while he is under 18 belong to him nevertheless (and to his estate, at whatever age he dies). A transfer to a bare trust is therefore a potentially exempt transfer, so that tax will not be payable providing the donor survives the transfer by seven years.

Inheritance tax residence nil-rate band

(19) In the context of the residence nil-rate band (RNRB) and tax planning with trusts for minors, a home is 'inherited' by an individual (B) where the home becomes comprised on an individual's (D) death in a bereaved minor's trust within s 71A or an age 18-to-25 trust within s 71D and is held on trusts for the benefit of B (s 8J(4)(b)). A home is similarly inherited where it becomes comprised on the death of D in a trust and B becomes beneficially entitled on D's death to an IIP in the home provided the IIP is an immediate post-death interest under s. 49A or a disabled person's interest under s 89 (s 8J(4)(a)). The home is closely inherited where B is in the qualifying class of individuals set out in s 8K. See **Example A2 explanatory note** (3) for additional information in this regard. It will be noted that a home is not regarded as inherited where it is settled on a discretionary trust. An outright gift of a home to a bare trust is inherited by the beneficiary of such a trust (s 8J(1)) and where that beneficiary is the lineal descendant of the deceased (as defined), the home will be regarded as closely inherited for the purposes of the RNRB.

Other tax-efficient ways of benefiting children

(20) In addition to creating bare trusts that do not produce income but offer capital growth, parents may use funds for the benefit of their children without being caught by the income tax parental settlement rules as follows, as indicated in the Example at **part C point 5**:

(a) It was possible to purchase National Savings and Investments Children's Bonds for children under 16 (maximum holding per child £3,000 in latest issue plus holdings in earlier issues) but from 30 September 2017 they are no longer on sale (Issue 37 being the final issue which may be held to maturity when it can be reinvested or encashed). Interest on the bonds is tax-free. They run for five years at a time, so a bond that was bought just before the child's 16th birthday would mature just before the child's 21st birthday.

(b) Premiums of up to £270 in any 12-month period (or £300 if premiums are payable more frequently than annually, for instance quarterly or monthly) for each child may be paid on a qualifying friendly society policy. The proceeds of the policy are tax-free and the society does not pay tax on its income and gains in respect of such policies.

(c) Personal pension contributions of up to £2,880 net, £3,600 gross, per child may be paid each year. The child may not, however, draw any benefits from a pension plan until pension age is reached (currently age 55).

(d) Junior ISAs may be set up for children who do not have a Child Trust Fund account or, from 6 April 2015, for children whose Child Trust Fund is transferred to a Junior ISA. They are tax-free savings accounts for children under the age of 18. The Junior ISA annual contribution limit for 2023/24 is £9,000 (£9,000 in 2022/23) and this may be kept on deposit and invested in stocks and shares. Any money placed into a Junior ISA will not be able to be accessed until the child turns 18 years old. At this point, the Junior ISA will become a full ISA and the adult limit of £20,000 (2023/24 and 2022/23) will apply. From 2015/16 an additional ISA allowance is available for spouses or civil partners following the death of an ISA saver on or after 3 December 2014, equal to the value of that deceased saver's ISA holdings at the date of their death. As a result, the surviving spouse or civil partner has this additional allowance as well as their own ISA subscription limit in the year of death of their late spouse or civil partner. From 6 April 2016 there is the facility to offer a flexible account whereby withdrawals during the year may be replaced without the replacement counting towards the subscription limit.

These tax-efficient payments do not, however, give any opportunity for using the child's personal allowance and lower rates of tax.

Family investment companies

(21) For further information on corporation tax and the tax treatment of companies in general, see the companion volume, **Tolley's Taxwise I 2023/24**. Detailed case studies on the use of family investment companies in inheritance tax planning may be found in the following articles: 'Meet the Masons' by Victoria Christopher in *Taxation* dated 12 September 2019 and 'In Trusted Company' by Stephen Haggett in *Taxation* dated 30 July 2020. A comparison between the use of trusts and FICs in estate planning is discussed in an

article entitled 'Keeping your Options Open' by Sam Hart and Craig in *Taxation* dated 17 June 2021. Also see the chapter on family investment companies in the 2023/24 edition of **Tolley Tax Planning.**

Question

A.

On 8 July 2005 George, who had made no previous chargeable transfers, settled £210,000 in an accumulation and maintenance trust for his three grandchildren Henry, Isobel and Jessica. (If any further grandchildren were born thereafter they would not share in the trust fund.) Under the terms set out in the trust deed the named beneficiaries were to take capital at age 25 in equal shares (and would not take interests in possession before then). The trustees were given power to pay or apply up to the whole of a beneficiary's presumptive share of capital for his advancement or benefit. The grandchildren's dates of birth were:

Henry	—	10 November 1980
Isobel	—	7 February 1990
Jessica	—	10 April 1992

During 2012 the trustees became very concerned at the company that Isobel was keeping, and at her apparent financial imprudence. These concerns did not diminish during the following years, and as Isobel's 25th birthday was approaching they exercised their power of advancement on 30 January 2015 by directing that Isobel's share of the trust fund should be applied for her benefit by being retained in trust instead of vesting in her absolutely at age 25; that the income arising from it once she reached that age should be held on protective trusts for Isobel's benefit during her lifetime (with power for the trustees to pay or apply capital for her benefit at their discretion); and that on Isobel's death the capital should be held for the benefit of her children if any at age 25 or, if she had no children, should be held absolutely for Henry and Jessica in equal shares.

On 31 October 2023 Isobel was found dead of a drug overdose at the age of 31. She had no children.

At all times since the sale of the company the trust fund has been held in cash and quoted investments, save so far as distributed to beneficiaries becoming absolutely entitled. All three grandchildren are UK resident. Values on the following dates were as follows (all relevant liabilities – other, where relevant, than any IHT which has not yet fallen due for payment – having been discharged by these respective dates):

10 November 2005	£810,000	(all three shares combined)
30 January 2015	£560,000	(Isobel's and Jessica's shares combined; Henry's share had been fully distributed following his attaining age 25)
7 February 2015	£564,000	(Isobel's and Jessica's shares combined – the trustees had not yet completed their intended appropriation of assets between the two)
7 July 2015	£290,000	(Isobel's appropriated share)
7 July 2015	£295,000	(Jessica's appropriated share)
10 April 2017	£310,000	(Jessica's appropriated share)
31 October 2023	£315,000	(Isobel's appropriated share)

Explain the inheritance tax position resulting from each of the above events and where necessary calculate any inheritance tax charges arising. Comment on the capital gains tax position on each occasion, but assume that any capital gains tax charges are held over where possible.

B.

How would your answer differ if the trust had provided for the grandchildren to become entitled to capital at age 35, with income entitlements vesting at age 25, but in fact the trustees had exercised their power of advancement on Jessica's 25th birthday to make both her and Henry absolutely entitled forthwith (with Isobel's fund being dealt with exactly as in A above)?

Answer

A. – Vesting age for capital 25

George's settlement was made before the formation of new accumulation and maintenance trusts within IHTA 1984 s 71 was prohibited by FA 2006, and met the requirements of that section for accumulation and maintenance trust status (see **explanatory notes 1, 2**).

Henry's 25th birthday occurred on 10 November 2005 and he thereby became absolutely entitled to his one-third share of the trust capital, worth £270,000 (plus any income accumulated from his share). The property concerned thereby ceased to be settled property, becoming instead comprised in Henry's estate, and by the same token ceased to be within s 71; but an exit charge on the latter circumstance under s 71(3) was precluded by s 71(4)(a). Henry's absolute entitlement involved a deemed disposal by the trustees of the one-third of the trust assets that vest in him, under TCGA 1992 s 71. Because the fund was within IHTA 1984 s 71 up to the moment of Henry's absolute entitlement, hold-over relief could be claimed under TCGA 1992 s 260(2)(d), based on the fact that IHTA 1984 s 71(4) precludes an IHT exit charge.

At the end of the transitional period for phasing out all but the simplest of accumulation and maintenance trusts, on 6 April 2008, George's settlement left the accumulation and maintenance trust regime and passed into that for age 18-to-25 trusts (see **explanatory note 4(b)**), without an exit charge under s 71(3) because of FA 2006 Sch 20 para 2(5). (This event had no CGT consequences.)

However, when the trustees exercised their power of advancement on 30 January 2015 so as to resettle Isobel's share (including accumulated income) on terms that no longer met the s 71D requirements for age 18-to-25 trust status, that share incurred an IHT exit charge on that date under s 71E (property ceasing to be property to which s 71D applies, where the beneficiary has already attained age 18) and entered the relevant property regime. Because the event causing the property to leave the age 18-to-25 trust regime is the application of the property for Isobel's benefit (see **explanatory note 9**), the rate of tax used to compute the exit charge is established under s 71F (see s 71F(1), (2)(c) and **explanatory notes 7, 8**). Any tax chargeable on this event would implicitly have to be met from Isobel's share, not from Jessica's share which comprised the remainder of the settled property, so grossing up would not apply to establish the amount chargeable. (See **(i) below**.)

The CGT position on the advancement for Isobel's benefit would depend on whether or not the exercise of the power of advancement gave rise to entirely new and independent trusts or whether the property remained comprised in the same settlement albeit on varied terms (as to which see **explanatory note 10**). However, even if the answer on the facts was in the former sense, giving rise to a deemed disposal and reacquisition by the trustees, any gain could be held over by virtue of TCGA 1992 s 260(2)(a) because one and the same disposition by the trustees is a chargeable transfer (within the extended meaning of that term under IHTA 1984 s 2(3)).

Isobel's 25th birthday occurred on 7 February 2015, and in accordance with the terms of the resettlement she became entitled to a protected life interest in her share of the trust fund. That is an interest in possession, but it does not fall within any of the four types of qualifying IIP; the share remains within the relevant property regime and Isobel's 25th birthday has no impact for IHT purposes. There is no CGT consequence.

8 July 2015 was the tenth anniversary of the formation of the trust – a 'ten-year anniversary'. Unlike Jessica's share which remained within the age 18-to-25 trust regime, Isobel's share by then was subject to the relevant property regime, and so incurred a ten-year charge under that regime. Any IHT due in respect of the age 18-to-25 trust exit charge on 30 January 2015 became payable on 31 July 2015, so assuming that the trustees would have left it until close to that date to have made the payment, the amount of that charge would have been deductible from the value of Isobel's share for the purpose of the relevant property ten-year charge. (See **(ii) below**.) The ten-year anniversary is not relevant for CGT purposes. As the ten-year anniversary occurred before 18 November 2015, the initial value at the time of its settlement of non-relevant property that has always remained, whilst settled, non-relevant property is included in the computation of the notional transfer that feeds into the calculation of the effective rate. In respect of ten-year anniversaries occurring on or after 18 November 2015 that element of the calculation is no longer relevant having been repealed by F(No 2) A 2015 Sch 1 para 3(2)(a).

Jessica in turn attained age 25 on 10 April 2017, and like Henry before her she became absolutely entitled to her share of the trust fund (including any accumulated income). That share ceased to be settled property and therefore also ceased to meet the requirements for the age 18-to-25 trust regime under IHTA 1984 s 71D. Like Isobel's share on the exercise of the trustees' power of advancement (but unlike Henry's share before the FA 2006 changes), Jessica's share incurred an exit charge under s 71E on leaving that regime, also computed in accordance with s 71F. (See **(iii) below.**) As in Henry's case, Jessica's absolute entitlement gave rise to a deemed disposal and reacquisition by the trustees, but one which qualified for hold-over relief – this time by virtue of TCGA 1992 s 260(2)(a) because of being a 'chargeable transfer' for IHT purposes (within the extended meaning of that expression).

Isobel's death on 31 October 2023, without children, results in Henry and Jessica becoming absolutely entitled to Isobel's share, which therefore ceases to be settled property and, in the process, also to be relevant property. As such Isobel's share incurs an exit charge under the relevant property regime under IHTA 1984 s 65. As this exit charge occurs after the first ten-year anniversary of the settlement, the tax is computed in accordance with s 69. (See **(iv) below.**) As before, the absolute entitlement of Henry and Jessica gives rise to a deemed disposal and reacquisition by the trustees, with hold-over relief being available by virtue of TCGA 1992 s 260(2)(a) as when Jessica reached age 25. Even if Isobel had done nothing to incur a forfeiture of her protected life interest (such as attempting to assign her right to income, or becoming bankrupt), so that she still had an IIP (as opposed to a deemed IIP for IHT purposes) at her death, it was not a qualifying IIP and therefore any gain accruing to the trustees on that deemed disposal remains a chargeable gain. The tax-free revaluation for CGT purposes on the death of a life tenant under TCGA 1992 s 72(1)(a) only applies where the IIP was a qualifying IIP.

The IHT charges on these various events are calculated as follows.

(i) 30 January 2015 — age 18-to-25 trust exit charge on Isobel's share

Chargeable amount (s 71F(4))		
Amount by which value of s 71D property is less immediately after chargeable event		£280,000
Relevant Fraction (s 71F(5), (6))		
Numerator of time element of Relevant Fraction: number of complete quarters in period to 29 January 2015 elapsed since Isobel's share entered s 71D regime: 6 April 2008 to 5 January 2015	27	quarters
Relevant fraction is three tenths of time element		
Settlement Rate (s 71F(7)–(9))		
	Gross	*Tax on 2014/15 scale*
	£	£
Settlor's seven-year cumulative total at commencement of settlement (8 July 2005)	Nil	Nil
Notional transfer (no additions or related settlement)		
Initial value of property in George's settlement at 8 July 2005	210,000	Nil*
	210,000	Nil*
(* Below £325,000 nil-rate band)		
Effective rate, and so settlement rate, is therefore	0.000%	
Tax payable (s 71F(3))		
Chargeable amount × Relevant Fraction × Settlement rate		
Tax payable is:	$280{,}000 \times (\frac{27}{40} \times \frac{3}{10}) \times 0.000\,\% =$	£ Nil

(ii) 8 July 2015 — relevant property ten-year charge on Isobel's share

Chargeable amount (s 64(1))

Relevant property at ten-year anniversary – Isobel's share				£290,000
Effective rate on notional transfer (s 66(3)–(5))				
			Gross	*Tax on 2015/16 scale*
			£	£
Settlor's seven-year cumulative total at commencement of settlement (8 July 2005)			Nil	Nil
Notional transfer (no related settlement)				
Chargeable amount as above		290,000		
Less: unpaid IHT re 30 January 2015 charge on Isobel's share		0		
Initial value of other property in settlement:				
Whole trust fund at 8 July 2005	210,000			
Less: Isobel's share (1/3rd)	(70,000)	140,000	430,000	21,000*
			430,000	21,000*

(*430,000 – 325,000 = 105,000 @ 20%)

Actual full rate is three tenths of effective rate: $\frac{21{,}000}{430{,}000} \times \frac{3}{10} =$ 1.465%

Appropriate fraction (s 66(2))

Number of complete quarters elapsed since commencement of the settlement before Isobel's share became relevant property on 30 January 2015:
8 July 2005 to 7 January 2015 — 38 fortieths

Tax payable is: $1.465\,\% \times \frac{40-38}{40} \times 290{,}000 =$ £212

(iii) 10 April 2017 — age 18-to-25 trust exit charge on Jessica's share

Chargeable amount (s 71F(4))

Amount by which value of s 71D property is less immediately after chargeable event — £310,000

Relevant Fraction (s 71F(5), (6))

Numerator of time element of Relevant Fraction: number of complete quarters elapsed in period to 9 April 2017 since Jessica's share entered s 71D regime:
6 April 2008 to 5 April 2017 — 36 quarters

Relevant fraction is three tenths of time element

Settlement Rate (s 71F(7)–(9))

Same calculation as in (i) **above** (notional transfer £210,000, nil cumulative total), but using 2017/18 scale (nil-rate band £325,000): effective rate is still — 0.000%

Tax payable (s 71F(3))

Chargeable amount × Relevant Fraction × Settlement rate

Tax payable is: $310{,}000 \times (\frac{36}{40} \times \frac{3}{10}) \times 0.000\,\% =$ £Nil

(iv) 31 October 2023 — relevant property exit charge on Isobel's share

Chargeable amount (s 65(2))		
Amount by which value of relevant property is less immediately after chargeable event		£315,000
Rate applicable (s 69(1)–(2))		
Rate applicable, before appropriate fraction, is rate charged at preceding ten-year anniversary but disregarding time-fraction under s 66(2)		
No property added to settlement, and no increase in relevant property, since ten-year charge, so no need to recalculate under s 69(2)		
Scale of rates (nil-rate band) unchanged since ten-year charge in 2015/16, so no need to recalculate under Sch 2 para 3		
Therefore full rate before appropriate fraction is	1.465%	
Appropriate fraction (s 69(4))		
Number of complete quarters in period to 30 October 2023 elapsed since ten-year anniversary: 8 July 2015 to 7 October 2023	33	fortieths
Tax payable is:	$1.465\ \% \times \frac{33}{40} \times 315{,}000 =$	£3,784

B. – Vesting age for capital 35

If the vesting age for capital entitlements had been specified in George's settlement as 35 rather than 25 (with income entitlements vesting at age 25), the settlement would still have qualified as an accumulation and maintenance trust prior to 2006, because the key requirement was the vesting of at least an IIP by age 25.

On Henry's 25th birthday on 10 November 2005 he became entitled to an IIP and s 71 accordingly ceased to apply to his share of the fund. As in **part A**, an exit charge under s 71(3) was prevented by s 71(4)(a). The assets in Henry's share of the fund remained settled property for CGT purposes and there was no deemed disposal accordingly. Henry's IIP is a qualifying IIP, as all were prior to 22 March 2006, and remained so after that date since he had become beneficially entitled to it before then.

The terms of the trust in relation to Isobel's and Jessica's shares, as at the end of the transitional period on 6 April 2008, were not such as to satisfy the requirements of s 71D as an age 18-to-25 trust (because capital would not vest absolutely by age 25), so at that time both shares passed into the relevant property regime, again without an exit charge under s 71(3). This event was of no significance for CGT purposes.

The exercise of the trustees' power of advancement for Isobel's benefit on 30 January 2015 had no implications for IHT purposes; in contrast to **part A**, the property was already relevant property, and remained so after as before. For CGT purposes the issue as to whether or not the property passed into a separate trust (see **explanatory note 10**), and thus became the subject of a deemed disposal and reacquisition by the trustees under TCGA 1992 s 71, becomes much more important as a result: if there was such a deemed disposal, hold-over relief under s 260 would not be available in respect of it because there is no associated event for IHT purposes.

The position on Isobel's 25th birthday on 7 February 2015 is the same as in **part A**, with no implications for either IHT or CGT.

The ten-year charge under the relevant property regime, on 8 July 2015, now affects both Isobel's and Jessica's shares (see (i) below) – again with no CGT implications. Again, as the ten-year anniversary occurred before 18 November 2015, the initial value at the time of its settlement of non-relevant property that has always remained, whilst settled, non-relevant property is included in the computation of the notional transfer that feeds into the calculation of the effective rate. In respect of ten-year anniversaries occurring on or after 18 November 2015 that element of the calculation is no longer relevant having been repealed by F(No 2) A 2015 Sch 1 para 3(2)(a).

When the trustees exercise their discretion on Jessica's 25th birthday, on 10 April 2017, to make both her and Henry absolutely entitled to their respective shares of the trust fund, Jessica's share incurs a relevant property exit charge under IHTA 1984 s 65 (see **(ii) below**), but Henry receives his share without IHT charge because he already had a qualifying IIP (s 53(2)). Both shares are the subject of a deemed disposal and reacquisition by the trustees for CGT purposes; in Jessica's case, because of the associated chargeable transfer for IHT purposes, hold-over relief is available by virtue of TCGA 1992 s 260(2)(a), but in Henry's case there is no associated IHT event and therefore CGT will be chargeable.

Finally, on Isobel's death there is an IHT relevant property exit charge on her share of the fund in the same way as in **part A** (see **(iii) below**), with CGT hold-over relief being available in the same way.

The IHT calculations under this scenario are as follows:

(i) 8 July 2015 — relevant property ten-year charge on Isobel's and Jessica's shares

Chargeable amount (s 64(1))

Relevant property at ten-year anniversary:	
Isobel's share	290,000
Jessica's share	295,000
	585,000

Effective rate on notional transfer (s 66(3)–(5))

			Gross	*Tax on 2015/16 scale*
			£	£
Settlor's seven-year cumulative total at commencement of settlement (8 July 2005)			Nil	Nil
Notional transfer (no related settlement)				
Chargeable amount as above		585,000		
Initial value of other property in settlement:				
Whole trust fund at 8 July 2005	210,000			
Less: Isobel's and Jessica's shares (2/3rds)	(140,000)	70,000	655,000	66,000*
			655,000	66,000*
(*655,000 – 325,000 = 330,000 @ 20%)				
Actual full rate is three tenths of effective rate:	$\frac{66,000}{655,000} \times \frac{3}{10} =$		3.023%	

Appropriate fraction (s 66(2))

Number of complete quarters elapsed since commencement of the settlement before Isobel's and Jessica's shares became relevant property on 6 April 2008: 8 July 2005 to 7 January 2008	10	quarters
	$3.023\% \times \frac{40-10}{40} = 2.267\%$	
Therefore applicable rate is		

Tax payable

On Isobel's share	£290,000 @2.267% =	6,574
On Jessica's share	£295,000 @ 2.267% =	6,688
		£13,262

(ii) 10 April 2017 — relevant property exit charge on Jessica's share

Chargeable amount (s 65(2))		
Amount by which value of relevant property is less immediately after chargeable event		£310,000
Rate applicable (s 69(1)–(2))		
Rate applicable, before appropriate fraction, is rate charged at preceding ten-year anniversary but disregarding time-fraction under s 66(2)		
No property added to settlement, and no increase in relevant property, since ten-year charge, so no need to recalculate under s 69(2)		
Scale of rates (nil-rate band) unchanged since ten-year charge in 2015/16, so no need to recalculate under Sch 2 para 3		
Therefore full rate before appropriate fraction is	3.023%	
Appropriate fraction (s 69(4))		
Number of complete quarters in period to 9 April 2017 elapsed since ten-year anniversary: 8 July 2015 to 7 April 2017	7	fortieths
Tax payable is:	$3.023\,\% \times \frac{7}{40} \times 310{,}000 =$	£1,640

(iii) 31 October 2023 — relevant property exit charge on Isobel's share

Chargeable amount (s 65(2))		
Amount by which value of relevant property is less immediately after chargeable event		£315,000
Rate applicable (s 69(1)–(2))		
Rate applicable, before appropriate fraction, is rate charged at preceding ten-year anniversary but disregarding time-fraction under s 66(2)		
No property added to settlement, and no increase in relevant property, since ten-year charge, so no need to recalculate under s 69(2)		
Scale of rates (nil-rate band) unchanged since ten-year charge in 2015/16, so no need to recalculate under Sch 2 para 3		
Full rate before appropriate fraction as in (ii) above	3.023%	
Appropriate fraction (s 69(4))		
Number of complete quarters in period to 30 October 2023 elapsed since ten-year anniversary: 8 July 2015 to 7 October 2023	33	fortieths
Tax payable is:	$3.023\,\% \times \frac{33}{40} \times 315{,}000 =$	£7,856

Comparative summary of IHT charges

	Part A – vesting age 25				*Part B – vesting age 35*			
Share of:	*Henry*	*Isobel*	*Jessica*	*Total*	*Henry*	*Isobel*	*Jessica*	*Total*
Henry's 25th birthday	Nil			Nil	Nil			Nil
Advancement for Isobel (A(i))		Nil		Nil		Nil		Nil
Isobel's 25th birthday		Nil		Nil		Nil		Nil
Ten-year anniversary (A(ii), B(i))		212		212		6,574	6,688	13,262
Jessica's 25th birthday (A(iii), B(ii))			Nil	Nil		Nil	1,640	1,640

	Part A – vesting age 25				Part B – vesting age 35			
Share of:	*Henry*	*Isobel*	*Jessica*	*Total*	*Henry*	*Isobel*	*Jessica*	*Total*
Isobel's death (A(iv), B(iii))		3,784		3,784		7,856		7,856
Totals	Nil	3,996	Nil	3,996	Nil	14,430	8,328	22,758

The two most significant factors leading to the lower charges in **part A** are:

- the fact that two shares of the trust fund, instead of one, are within the relevant property regime in **part B** and so subject to the ten-year charge as well as exit charges, and
- the fact that the relevant property regime uses current values (of the part of the fund comprising relevant property – and before 18 November 2015 initial value for property in the same settlement that has never been relevant property) in the notional transfer for both ten-year charges and exit charges; whereas the age 18-to-25 trust exit charges use only the initial value (of the whole trust fund), see **explanatory note 7, 8**.

Explanatory Notes

The former accumulation and maintenance trust regime for inheritance tax

(1) To qualify as an accumulation and maintenance trust before the FA 2006 changes took effect on 22 March 2006, the terms of a trust had, by IHTA 1984 s 71(1), to be such that:

(a) one or more beneficiaries would, on or before attaining a specified age not exceeding 25, become beneficially entitled to the trust property or to an interest in possession in it; and

(b) no interest in possession subsisted in the trust property, and income from it was to be accumulated so far as not applied for the maintenance, education or benefit of a beneficiary (still aged under 25).

It was implicit that there must have been at least one beneficiary within the eligible class living at the date the trust entered the accumulation and maintenance trust regime, though if the death of a member of the class left the class temporarily depopulated but capable of being repopulated through the birth of further members, and the other conditions continued to be fulfilled (effectively allowing no other option in the meantime than the accumulation of income arising), then the trust could generally remain within s 71 for the time being.

If those conditions were met, then no IHT charges would arise while the property remained within the accumulation and maintenance trust regime, or if it left that regime either through a beneficiary's share vesting as mentioned (absolutely or for an IIP) or through the death of a beneficiary while vesting by the specified age would still have been possible (s 71(4)). Because of the first limb of s 71(1)(b) (above), requiring that no interest in possession must subsist, it is clear that property left the accumulation and maintenance trust regime the moment an IIP arose in respect of it.

(2) In *Inglewood v IRC* (1982) the Court of Appeal held that the certainty required by the condition in s 71(1)(a) (above) was not infringed by the existence of the statutory power of advancement in Trustee Act 1925 s 32, even though this power is wide enough to allow an effective resettlement of the property concerned (*Pilkington v IRC* (1962, HL)). The statutory power permits advancements only up to one half of the presumptive or vested share of the beneficiary advanced, but in practice HMRC have regarded this principle as applying where the statutory power is (as it commonly is) extended to apply to the whole of that share, and as extending to powers to similar effect to the statutory power (again up the whole of the relevant share). (See further **explanatory note 9** below.)

(3) Unless the class of beneficiaries was limited to grandchildren of a common grandparent (and children of such a grandchild who died before qualifying for his entitlement), there was a 25-year maximum period for which the trust could remain within the accumulation and maintenance trust regime, and at the end of those 25 years any part of the fund in which IIPs had not yet vested would leave that regime and pass into the relevant property regime. In that event (and in any other situation in which property left the accumulation and

maintenance trust regime, apart from those expressly protected by s 71(4), or if property within that regime was devalued by a disposition made by the trustees) an exit charge arose under s 71(3), which was computed according to the length of time for which the property in question had been within the accumulation and maintenance trust regime at a rate found (without any reference to the value involved) by adding together the following percentages (s 70(6), applied by s 71(5)):

- 0.25% for each of the first forty complete successive quarters in the relevant period,
- 0.20% for each of the next forty,
- 0.15% for each of the next forty,
- 0.10% for each of the next forty, and
- 0.05% for each of the next forty.

This formula appears in the section dealing with temporary charitable trusts, and applies to various other time-based flat rate exit charges for 'special' trusts (see now s 71(5) (pre-2006 accumulation and maintenance trusts retaining that status after 5 April 2008), s 71B(3) (bereaved minors' trusts), s 71G (age 18-to-25 trusts where the exit charge does not attract the 'favoured' rate in s 71F), s 72(5) (employee and newspaper trusts), s 73(3) (protective trusts following a forfeiture of the protected life interest where that occurred before 12 April 1978), s 74(3) (disabled persons' trusts formed before 10 March 1981), and (setting out the scale expressly rather than referentially) s 79(6) (disposals or breach of undertakings in relation to heritage property in relevant property trusts) and Sch 4 para 13 (heritage property maintenance funds)). It is apparent that the maximum rate to which the formula can give rise, after 50 years within the particular regime, is 21%.

The impact of the FA 2006 reforms on accumulation and maintenance trusts for inheritance tax

(4) With effect from 22 March 2006 no property could become newly held on accumulation and maintenance trusts, whether by original settlement or otherwise, and once property passed out of that regime it could not re-enter it. Moreover, unless by the end of a transitional period (5 April 2008) such a trust provided for absolute entitlement (and not merely an interest in possession) to arise by age 18, any property which at that date remained within the accumulation and maintenance trust regime would lose that status at that date, albeit without thereby incurring an exit charge under s 71(3): see FA 2006 Sch 20 para 2(5). If the property remained settled property on leaving the accumulation and maintenance trust regime, there were three possibilities:

(a) In theory, if an IIP or deemed IIP arose which met the requirements for a disabled person's interest (see **Example C3**) then that IIP would be a qualifying IIP. This however would be very rare since it would depend on the beneficiary in question having fulfilled the conditions for treatment as a disabled person, not at the date the IIP or deemed IIP arose but at the date the property in question had originally been put into trust.

(b) If the terms of the trust were such as to ensure that beneficiaries must become absolutely entitled by age 25 (and requirements were met in relation to the possible application of trust income in the meantime which are generally somewhat more stringent than under s 71, but in one way less stringent since they allow of a beneficiary being entitled to an IIP – see generally s 71D(6)), then the trust would pass into the age 18-to-25 trust regime under ss 71D–71G (see below). Section 71D(7) makes express provision comparable to the effect of the *Inglewood* decision (**explanatory note 2** above, and see **explanatory note 9** below).

(c) But in any other case the property would pass into the relevant property regime with effect from 6 April 2008. This would also be the case where, within the transitional period, a beneficiary became entitled to an IIP (including a protected life interest) pursuant to the terms of a pre-2006 accumulation and maintenance trust (unless the terms of the trust were within (b) above). In this case the relevant property regime would apply from the date when the IIP arose.

(5) The government's basic position in 2006 was that any exemption from the relevant property regime should be limited to cases where the beneficiary was under 18, had lost a parent (and with two minor exceptions the trust arose under the parent's will or intestacy), and was guaranteed to become entitled to the capital no later than age 18 – requirements that form the basis of the bereaved minor's trust regime under s 71A. They made

great play of this being a recently-introduced requirement for a vulnerable beneficiary election where the beneficiary is not disabled (see **Example F4 explanatory note 8** and **Examples C1** and **C2**).

The age 18-to-25 trust regime represented a concession designed to allow some relief from the full rigour of the relevant property regime while nevertheless imposing some IHT price for the ability to postpone the vesting of capital beyond age 18 – though to no later than age 25. An age 18-to-25 trust can be created only in the same circumstances as a bereaved minor's trust; but the second concession allowed by the government in 2006 was that a former accumulation and maintenance trust whose terms (as opposed to means of establishment) met the requirements for an age 18-to-25 trust by the date when accumulation and maintenance trusts generally were to be phased out could attract the same treatment as such a trust that was established on the death of the beneficiary's parent.

Whereas it was possible under the accumulation and maintenance trust regime to provide for a class of beneficiaries into which further members might be born after the trust was established (typically before the first member of the class reached the qualifying age for an interest in possession), the qualifying conditions for the age 18-to-25 trust regime are such that all potential beneficiaries must be living at the date the trust enters that regime. In the Example George's settlement was restricted to his three named grandchildren from the outset, so no steps were needed to exclude future-born grandchildren prior to the end of the transitional period on 6 April 2008. For age 18-to-25 trusts benefiting a class of beneficiaries see further **Example C17 explanatory note 2.**

(6) The IHT price exacted for this concession is an exit charge that arises on property leaving an age 18-to-25 trust, except where it vests absolutely (or is applied for benefit of a beneficiary) by, or he dies under, age 18 (see s 71E(1), (2)). (Such vesting or application would typically be in exercise of a discretion since otherwise the trust, if arising on a parent's death, would generally be a bereaved minor's trust; or, if continuing from a former accumulation and maintenance trust but securing capital entitlement as of right by age 18, would remain within the newly-restricted accumulation and maintenance trust rules of s 71 as amended.) So long as the beneficiary is not older than his 25th birthday and the circumstances in which the exit charge arises mirror those that would qualify for exemption if the beneficiary had not passed his 18th birthday (see above) – what might be termed 'policy-compliant' or 'favoured' circumstances, ie those at which the creation of the age 18-to-25 trust regime was targeted – the rate at which the exit charge is levied is derived from the formula in s 71F; otherwise the harsher regime of s 71G (the 'time-based flat rate' described in **explanatory note 3** above) applies, as indeed it does for bereaved minors' trusts as well.

The age 18-to-25 trust 'policy-compliant' exit charge for inheritance tax

(7) The calculation of tax under s 71F is in substance identical to the charge that applies under the relevant property regime before the first ten-year anniversary of the settlement (s 68), but counting quarters towards the time-fraction from no earlier than the relevant beneficiary's 18th birthday or 6 April 2008 if later, not from the commencement of the settlement. (For one unusual facet of the different time-counting between the two provisions see **Example C17 explanatory note 12.**) Additionally, property within the age 18-to-25 trust regime does not suffer an IHT charge if a ten-year anniversary of the settlement occurs in the meantime.

In particular, the elements which go to make up the value transferred by the notional chargeable transfer used to establish the 'settlement rate' defined in s 71F(7)–(9) comprise:

(a) the initial value (in the trustees' hands immediately after settlement) of the property comprised in the settlement in which the exit charge arises (*whether or not* that property is or has been within the age 18-to-25 trust regime, or even is still comprised in the settlement),

(b) the initial value of the property in any related settlement(s), and

(c) the initial value of any property which became comprised in the (same) settlement after the settlement commenced and before the date of the exit charge (whether or not it has remained comprised in the settlement up to that date).

It should be remembered that the 'initial value' in this context is the value of the property in question in the hands of the trustees in question. Accordingly it is immaterial whether or not the transfer of the property to the trustees had qualified for business property relief (as the family company shares would have done in the

Example) or agricultural property relief. Similarly, the parcel of shares in the trustees' hands immediately after its transfer to them will be valued in its own right, without being aggregated with any other holdings of the transferor or for that matter of the trustees.

(8) It is noteworthy that, in the context of a former accumulation and maintenance trust that converted to an age 18-to-25 trust at the end of the transitional period on 6 April 2008, these rules apply irrespective of how long or short a time the settlement has been in existence. Some such settlements may well have been in existence for decades beforehand, some (often as discretionary trusts before conversion to accumulation and maintenance trust status) even from before the introduction of capital transfer tax in 1974 (though this latter feature is not recognised within the drafting of s 71F, which contains no provisions equivalent to s 68(6)).

It can be seen that the values set out in points (a)–(c) of **explanatory note 7** above are all unrelated to the current value of the property within the age 18-to-25 trust regime (or otherwise still comprised in the settlement); and in the case of an older settlement they will be very much historic values. It follows that, even before an existing accumulation and maintenance trust passed into the age 18-to-25 trust regime at the end of the transitional period, it would have been possible to establish with certainty (subject only to the effect of future changes in IHT rates generally) the 'settlement rate' to which the s 71F 'relevant fraction' (three tenths of the familiar time-fraction) would in future be applied in working out the amount of tax payable on a beneficiary's 25th birthday or earlier vesting, distribution or death.

Put another way – as demonstrated in the Example – if the *original* value of the property settled into this settlement and any related settlements, taken together with the settlor's 7-year cumulative total of transfers when he made the settlement, was less than the *current* nil-rate band for the time being, the rate of 'policy-compliant' exit charge under s 71E will always be 0% (unless the overall IHT rate-structure is radically revised so as to tax amounts lower than that).

Settled advances: effect for inheritance tax

(9) As already noted, despite the considerable width of such powers as demonstrated in such cases as *Pilkington v IRC* (1962, HL), *Re Clore's Settlement Trusts* (1966) and *Re Hampden's Settlement Trusts* (1977), the mere *existence* of powers to pay or apply trust property for the advancement or benefit of a beneficiary (whether the statutory power in Trustee Act 1925 s 32 or its Northern Ireland equivalent or a power to like effect, and whether or not extending to the whole of the beneficiary's presumptive or vested share) will not prevent the trust's terms from complying with the requirement of the age 18-to-25 trust regime that the beneficiary will become entitled to the capital by age 25 (s 71D(6)). The same applies to the bereaved minor's trust regime (s 71A(4)), and applied in practice to accumulation and maintenance trusts (*Inglewood v IRC*, **explanatory note 2** above).

However, any *exercise* of such a power must be recognised within the IHT regime according to its trust law effects. Often its effect is simply to create an immediate absolute entitlement, but equally 'settled advances', such as in relation to Isobel's share in the Example, are far from uncommon. If the trust terms applying as a result of the exercise of the power do not fit within the scope of the IHT regime applicable immediately beforehand then the property will leave that regime, and in that case an exit charge under that regime will arise unless a specific exemption is in point.

In the case of an age 18-to-25 trust or a bereaved minor's trust, such an exemption is conferred, inter alia, if property is paid or applied for the advancement or benefit of the relevant (living) beneficiary on or before his attainment of age 18 (ss 71E(2)(d), 71B(2)(c)). So long as the terms of exercise of the power are genuinely considered by the trustees to be for the advancement or benefit of the beneficiary concerned and that view is objectively tenable (ie not one which no reasonable body of trustees could have arrived at), and so long as what is done under the power is otherwise permissible under trust law (contrast *Pilkington v IRC* where the particular advancement proposed would have infringed the rule against perpetuities), the exercise of the power will be valid and it is considered that HMRC will not be in a position to contend that it was not for that beneficiary's benefit (but see further below). Accordingly a resettlement of the sort made for Isobel would attract the exemption just mentioned if the beneficiary advanced is under age 18; or, within an age 18-to-25 trust, it would attract the 'policy-compliant' rate of exit charge, under s 71F (see **explanatory note 6** above) even though it results in a position that does not comply with the policy of s 71D.

Section 3 of the CIoT/STEP Agreed Guidance (see **Example C17 explanatory note 2**) records that the exit charge, in the case of a settled advance, would be 'computed according to the provisions in s 71F, assuming the proper exercise of the power causes property to be "paid or applied for the advancement or benefit of B"; otherwise, the computation would be under s 71G'. However, if it was otherwise, then the exercise of the power would almost certainly be void, so if HMRC pressed ahead with a determination of a charge based on s 71G the trustees ought to succeed on any appeal, either by reducing the charge to the s 71F level or by having it discharged altogether because the settled advance was not valid. There is nevertheless a potential question as to how far determination of this latter issue lies within the jurisdiction of the Tribunal between the trustees and HMRC, and an application to the court between the trustees and the beneficiaries might be needed in order to establish the validity of the exercise (within the terms of the power namely for the benefit of the stated beneficiary) one way or the other.

CGT and transfers to separate settlements

(10) The question whether an advancement or appointment under powers conferred by a settlement results in the transfer of the affected assets to the trustees of a separate settlement is at root one of trust law not tax law. As a result of decided cases such as *Hart v Briscoe* (1978), *Hoare Trustees v Gardner* (1978), *Roome v Edwards* (1981) and *Bond v Pickford* (1983), the answer will partly be dictated by whether the power is of sufficient width to allow such a transfer in the first place (if it is not then the property cannot have passed into a separate settlement). If on the other hand the power is of sufficient width (as is undoubtedly the case with powers of advancement on the lines of Trustee Act 1925 s 32, see **explanatory note 9** above), that does not force one to the conclusion that its exercise necessarily involves such a transfer; the answer will turn on the actual terms in which the power is exercised. If the newly appointed trusts do not exhaust the beneficial interests this will usually be indicative that no separate settlement has been created; but even if they do, that is only one factor to be taken into account, and the conclusion on this issue is frequently influenced by the detailed drafting of the document in question.

If the property is found to have passed from one settlement to another as a matter of general trust law, then this will be the case for CGT purposes as well. Whether or not the persons who are the trustees of the settled property are the same after the exercise as before (an issue which is not determinative of the trust law question), the trustees of the separate settlement will be regarded as having become absolutely entitled to the assets concerned as against the trustees of the original settlement, within the meaning of TCGA 1992 s 60(2) (and see also TCGA 1992 s 69(1) as to the separate deemed personality of trustees of separate settlements), thus triggering a deemed disposal and reacquisition under TCGA 1992 s 71.

CGT hold-over relief: deduction for IHT

(11) Where hold-over relief is claimed on the basis that the CGT disposal is a chargeable transfer for IHT purposes, any IHT attributable to the value of the asset disposed of will be allowed as a deduction against any eventual disposal of the asset by the transferee, though not so as to create a loss: TCGA 1992 s 260(7). See in more detail **Example A24(vi)**.

Miscellaneous

(12) For further instances of IHT calculations under the age 18-to-25 trust regime see **Examples C17, C19**. For protective trusts see **Example D2 explanatory note 1**.

Question

The executors and trustees of Alex's Will approach you in mid-November 2023 for advice in relation to the IHT treatment of an appointment they propose to make under his Will. They outline the following facts:

(A) Sadly Alex, while away from home on business within the UK, was caught in the cross-fire of a gangland shooting, and killed, late on 19 April 2022.

(B) Soon after his marriage to Brenda, in 2020, Alex had made a fully discretionary Will trust, asking his trustees in a letter of wishes to ensure that Brenda was generously provided for in the event of his death, but without placing significant funds under her control. He went on to explain that he was concerned that outright provision for her would be unwise in view of her known history of mental instability and financial improvidence.

(C) Brenda was seven months pregnant at the time Alex was killed; though in good health generally, she went into premature labour early the following day as a result of shock at the news, giving birth to twins who are both now fit and healthy. Brenda however became seriously depressed in the aftermath, and spent ten months in a psychiatric hospital; she is now coping better, but is still somewhat fragile.

(D) Around the time that Brenda had moved in with Alex in August 2018, he had discovered that she had accumulated serious credit card and other debts, and Alex had paid off her creditors in the sum of £46,000. Apart from modest charitable donations he had made no other gifts within the last seven years of his life, or otherwise relevant for IHT purposes.

(E) Alex's estate at his death amounted to £2.8 million net, of which £800,000 comprised Alex's apartment and £750,000 comprised shares in two rapidly-growing trading companies in which Alex had invested a total of £400,000 in 2018: C Ltd whose shares are unquoted, and D Ltd whose shares are traded on the Alternative Investment Market.

(F) A defined benefits lump sum death benefit of £300,000 became payable on Alex's death under his employers' pension and life assurance scheme (PLAS), which the scheme administrators, after representations from the executors had settled for Brenda's benefit on 2 September 2022, about three months after she had been admitted to hospital. (The PLAS, since 2010, a registered pension scheme, had been established by Alex's employers under a trust deed as a personal pension scheme on 1 April 2010, shortly after Alex started working for them, and Alex was a contributing member of the scheme from the time it was set up.) The terms of this trust (Brenda's Lump Sum Trust) are modelled on IHTA 1984 s 89(1), with the capital passing for the twins' benefit on Brenda's death or the twins' 21st birthday if later.

(G) A lump sum of £240,000 became payable for the benefit of the twins under the Criminal Injuries Compensation Scheme (CICS) by virtue of Alex's death, and under the terms of the scheme was placed in trust for the twins absolutely at age 21, or for Brenda if neither of the twins reaches age 21 (the Twins' CICS Trust).

(H) All the IHT due on Alex's death has been paid and the administration of his estate has just been completed by assent into the names of the trustees. Taking account of the realisation of some assets at a profit, and the payment of administration expenses, the assets now in the trustees' hands comprise:

   (i) the shares in C Ltd and D Ltd with a present combined value of £900,000;

   (ii) Alex's apartment, occupied by Brenda and the twins, still worth £800,000; and

   (iii) cash (net of provision for income tax and capital gains tax due in respect of the administration period) of £690,000.

(I) The trustees propose to leave the shares in C Ltd and D Ltd unappointed in the discretionary trust for the time being (the Discretionary Fund, which is to bear any IHT on those shares though the trustees do not anticipate any), and to appoint the other net assets as follows:

   (i) £525,000 cash (on a net basis) (the Children's Fund) in trust for the twins at age 25, and

(ii) the apartment and the remaining £165,000 cash (Brenda's Fund) in a protected life interest trust for Brenda and thereafter to be added to the Children's Fund. The trustees confirm that Brenda has not done anything hitherto which would have triggered a forfeiture of a protected life interest if she had been given one by the Will.

Advise the trustees on the following points (assuming no changes in legislation in the meantime other than as to the nil-rate band and the rate of IHT on death chargeable in excess of it, as to which see the table below):

(1) The alternative effects for IHT purposes (with computations) in relation to Alex's estate if the appointment is expressed as:

(a) £525,000 cash to the Children's Fund, and the apartment and everything else other than the C Ltd and D Ltd shares to Brenda's Fund; or

(b) the apartment and £165,000 cash to Brenda's Fund, and everything else other than the C Ltd and D Ltd shares to the Children's Fund.

(2) The IHT status of:

(a) Brenda's Lump Sum Trust, and

(b) the Twins' CICS Trust,

and the rate of IHT that will be chargeable on the Twins' CICS Trust when the twins become absolutely entitled at age 21 in April 2043.

(3) Giving alternative answers according to the structure of the appointment in **1(a)** or **1(b) above**, calculate the IHT that will be charged in respect of the Children's Fund on the twins' becoming absolutely entitled at age 25 in April 2047 (with no earlier distributions of capital), if the Children's Fund has by then grown to £1,800,000 (assume that no capital gains tax becomes payable on that occasion because all unrealised gains are held over). For this purpose assume that Brenda is still living at that time.

(4) How would your answers to **3 above** differ, and what additional IHT charges would arise, if in the meantime:

(i) Shortly before the flotation on the London Stock Exchange of both C Ltd and D Ltd (still trading companies), the trustees had on 28 August 2042 appointed irrevocably that the Discretionary Fund should be added to the Children's Fund. Assume for this purpose that the shares in the two companies were worth a total of £3 million at the date of that appointment and in the preceding April, and that the assets representing them (after discharging intermediate liabilities including capital gains tax arising on the flotation, and after subsequent further gains) had recovered to £2.9 million in April 2047.

Or:

(ii) Brenda had attempted in 2032 to raise money by selling her right to income from Brenda's Fund (thereby incurring a forfeiture of her protected life interest), and had subsequently died on 14 January 2038 (having made no relevant lifetime transfers), so that Brenda's Fund accrued then to the Children's Fund. Assume for this purpose that, net of the IHT charge arising on Brenda's death,

- Brenda's Fund was worth £2,100,000 when she died and £2,375,000 on 20 April 2047;
- Brenda's free estate (which did not contain any home), which became held for the twins' benefit under the intestacy rules of the Administration of Estates Act 1925, was worth £20,000 when she died and £22,000 on 20 April 2040; and
- the trust fund of Brenda's Lump Sum Trust was worth £750,000 when Brenda died, £800,000 on 31 March 2040 and £900,000 on 20 April 2043.

The IHT scales to be assumed are as follows:

Tax year	*Nil-rate band*	*Rate on death above nil-rate band of which the lifetime rate is one-half thereof*
2018/19	£325,000	40%
2022/23	£325,000	40%
2039/40	£550,000	48%
2042/43	£575,000	50%
2043/44	£575,000	50%
2047/48	£500,000	35%

Answer

Immediately before his death on 19 April 2022, Alex was married to Brenda; following his death Brenda gave birth to twins on 20 April 2022.

The trusts that have been established as a result of Alex's death are shown in the following diagram:

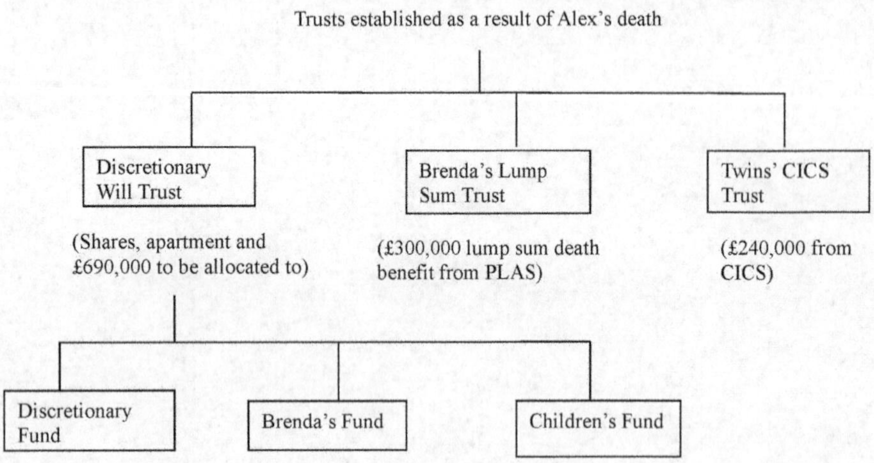

1 Discretionary Will trust: proposed appointment

The proposal for an appointment is made about five months before the second anniversary of Alex's death, so provided the appointment is made on or before that anniversary the dispositions resulting from it will be treated for IHT purposes as though they had applied immediately on Alex's death (s 144). Accordingly the Children's Fund will be regarded as fulfilling, from the date of death, the requirements for an age 18-to-25 trust, and Brenda's Fund as conferring on Brenda an IPDI. Because of this backdating, assets passing into Brenda's Fund will retrospectively attract the spouse exemption on Alex's death, giving rise to an appropriate partial refund of the IHT previously paid by the executors.

The proposed appointment described by the trustees, in paragraph (I) of the facts, would on the face of it deal only with the net assets presently in the trustees' hands, which of course are after having deducted the IHT paid by the executors on Alex's estate. It is reasonably clear that the only assets intended to remain held on discretionary trusts are the shares in C Ltd and D Ltd; but the formulation of the appointment needs to be such as to make it clear whether the calculation of the revised IHT liability of the estate should proceed:

- on the footing that the £525,000 cash allocation to the Children's Fund is in the nature of a pecuniary legacy – with Brenda's Fund then being in the nature of a residuary gift such as to include the IHT refund; or
- on the footing that the only assets to pass to Brenda's Fund are the apartment and the £165,000 cash, with the Children's Fund then being the effective residuary gift and taking the benefit of the IHT refund as well as the £525,000 cash.

The difference between these two alternatives will be in the application of IHTA 1984 ss 36–42 dealing with the allocation of exemptions between specific gifts and residuary gifts, as demonstrated below. If the gift to Brenda's Fund is to be framed as the residuary gift, the non-exempt specific gifts will need to be grossed up under s 38 to the extent that they do not bear their own tax (which would be the case for the Children's Fund as the £525,000 is to be appointed 'on a net basis').

In both cases account must be taken of the payments totalling £46,000 by Alex in or about August 2018 to Brenda's creditors to clear her debts (see **explanatory note 1**). The position in this respect is:

August 2018 – lifetime transfer			
Payments to Brenda's creditors			46,000
Less: Annual exemptions	2018/19	3,000	
	2017/18	3,000	(6,000)
Chargeable or potentially exempt transfer (see **explanatory note 2**) – within nil-rate band			40,000

The position on Alex's death, under the two alternative structures for the appointment outlined, is as follows.

1(a) *£525,000 cash to the Children's Fund, everything else except shares to Brenda's Fund*

19 April 2022 – Death of Alex		*Gross*	*Tax on 2022/23 scale*	*Net*
		£	£	£
Chargeable transfers within seven years before death		40,000	Nil	40,000
Chargeable estate at death (residue exempt):				
C Ltd/D Ltd shares (subject to tax) to Discretionary Fund	750,000			
Less: business property relief (**explanatory note 3**)	(750,000)	Nil	Nil	Nil
Net cash legacy to Children's Fund, grossed up (**explanatory note 4**)		685,000	160,000*	525,000
		725,000	160,000*	565,000
(* 725,000 – 325,000 = £400,000 @ 40%)				

No residence nil-rate band is available because Alex's home is settled on Brenda's fund and is not therefore inherited by the twins.

1(b) *Apartment and £165,000 cash to Brenda's Fund, everything else except shares to the Children's Fund*

19 April 2022 – Death of Alex			*Gross*	*Tax on 2022/23 scale*
			£	£
Chargeable transfers within seven years before death			40,000	Nil
Estate at death:				
C Ltd/D Ltd shares	750,000			
Apartment	800,000			
Other assets	1,250,000			
		2,800,000		
Less: Business property relief on shares		(750,000)		
Less: Spouse exemption on:				
Apartment	800,000			
Cash legacy	165,000			
		(965,000)		
			1,085,000	320,000*
			1,125,000	320,000*

(* 1,125,000 – 325,000 = £800,000 @ 40%)

No residence nil-rate band is available because Alex's home is settled on Brenda's fund and is not therefore inherited by the twins

Resultant division of the gross estate at death

	Scenario (a)	*Scenario (b)*	*Difference*
	£	£	£
Discretionary Fund	750,000	750,000	0
Brenda's Fund	1,365,000	965,000	(400,000)
Children's Fund	525,000	765,000	240,000
HMRC – tax	160,000	320,000	160,000
	2,800,000	2,800,000	0

2 IHT status of externally-funded trusts

2(a) *Brenda's Lump Sum Trust*

Brenda was in a psychiatric hospital suffering from severe depression when the trust was formed to receive the £300,000 from the PLAS; and she remained in hospital for a further seven months afterwards, so it is reasonable to conclude that, at the date of formation of Brenda's Lump Sum Trust and transfer of the £300,000 into it, she was incapable of administering her property or managing her affairs, and that the reason for this incapacity was mental disorder within the meaning of the Mental Health Act 1983. It would be wise for the trustees to obtain written evidence of the position in this respect for future reference.

As such, Brenda will have been a disabled person in relation to Brenda's Lump Sum Trust under the definition in s 89(4), (4A) as read with FA 2005 Sch 1A, which depends entirely on the status of the beneficiary 'when the property was transferred into settlement'. Brenda will therefore have a deemed IIP under s 89(2), which is a disabled person's interest under s 89B(1)(a) and therefore a qualifying IIP under s 49(1), (1A)(b). Accordingly the property comprised in this trust fund from time to time will be regarded as comprised in Brenda's estate for IHT purposes, so if the trustees wish to apply any capital for her benefit at any point this will have no IHT implications.

On the other hand, on her death the trust fund will be aggregated with the remainder of her estate and exposed to an IHT charge accordingly. If the twins are still aged under 21 at Brenda's death then the net property in Brenda's Lump Sum Trust would become relevant property at that time, with the prospect of an exit charge under the relevant property regime when the twins then become absolutely entitled at age 21.

The PLAS was itself constituted as a trust, and accordingly the funding of Brenda's Lump Sum Trust would have involved the transfer of the £300,000 from the one settlement to the other. Section 81 provides that where property passes from one settlement into another without another person having become beneficially entitled to it in the meantime then the property is treated as remaining comprised in the first settlement. However, that treatment is only for the purpose of Part 3 Chapter 3, and s 89 is in Part 3 Chapter 4 so unaffected by that rule. (If the rule had extended to s 89 then Brenda would seemingly only have counted as a disabled person if she had fulfilled the qualifying conditions for that status at the date the property in question was transferred into the PLAS in the first place, but fortunately that issue does not arise.) Section 81 may however be relevant if the twins do not become absolutely entitled immediately on Brenda's death (through being still aged under 21, see above), since the relevant property rules *are* comprised in Part 3 Chapter 3; see further **part 4(ii)**.

The transfer from the PLAS itself would not have involved IHT implications since the property in a registered pension scheme is not relevant property (s 58(1)(d)), and equally is not the subject of a qualifying IIP or within the scope of any of the other 'special trust' regimes for IHT purposes. Where property in such a scheme is applied to pay lump sum death benefits under FA 2004 s 168 in respect of a member, it remains treated for this purpose as comprised in the registered pension scheme, and therefore is not relevant property, until it is so applied (IHTA 1984 s 58(2A)(a)). A defined benefits lump sum death benefit must, by FA 2004 Sch 29 para 13 be paid within two years after the date on which the scheme administrator first knew of the member's death (or, if earlier, could reasonably have been expected to know of it), so the period for which the property can remain treated as non-relevant property under this provision is necessarily limited to, in practice in most cases, little more than two years. This two-year rule applies however only to lump sums paid before 6 April 2016 and has been repealed from that date (F(No 2)A 2015 s 21(9)).

2(b) *The Twins' CICS Trust*

The terms of this trust meet the requirements for an age 18-to-25 trust within s 71D, whether or not those terms negate Trustee Act 1925 s 31 under which the twins would become entitled to IIPs from age 18 (see generally **Example C15 part A(ii), (iii)**). Being established under the Will of the beneficiaries' parent is only one method by which a trust whose terms meet those requirements will fall within s 71D: trusts established under the CICS will also qualify (as will trusts which meet the necessary requirements and which on 5 April 2008 were within the accumulation and maintenance trust regime of s 71, see **Example C16**).

As referred to in **Example C15 part A(ii)**, once the initial value of the settled property (and of the property in any related settlement which, in respect of exit charge arising on or after 18 November 2018, is itself an 18-25 trust within s 71D) is known, and assuming:

- that the structure of the legislation remains unchanged, and
- that there are no additions to the trust (see **Example C15 explanatory note 4**),

the only future factor that will have any bearing on the IHT rate chargeable on any age 18-to-25 trust exit charge is future changes in IHT rates. The values that are used to determine the settlement rate are on that basis purely the initial values of the property in the settlement in question and in any related settlements, which are ascertainable as soon as the property has been put into trust.

In the case of the Twins' CICS Trust there is no related settlement and the initial value of the trust property is the £240,000 CICS award that was placed into the trust. That is well below the nil-rate band of £575,000 assumed to be in force in 2043/44 when the twins will become absolutely entitled at age 21, so the 'settlement rate' under s 71E(7) – and with it therefore the rate of tax chargeable on the exit charge at that time – would be 0%, whatever the then value of the settled property.

3 IHT charge on the Children's Fund on the twins' 25th birthday

Applying the same analysis as in **Example C15 part A(ii)** and **part 2(b)** above (and taking account of **Example C15 explanatory note 4**), once the IHT values on Alex's death are known (having regard to the backdating effect of s 144 on the trustees' proposed appointment), that will give all necessary details of the notional transfer used to calculate the 'settlement rate' under s 71E(7)–(9) for any future exit charge on the Children's Fund. The values used for that purpose in the circumstances are purely the initial values (immediately after Alex's death) of the property settled by Alex's Will other than Brenda's Fund (which, by reason of being subject to an IPDI, counts for these purposes as not entering any settlement on Alex's death – see s 80 and **explanatory note 7**). As the twins' 25th birthday occurs after 17 November 2015, this is so however only where the Children's Fund and the Discretionary Fund are treated as a single settlement, not where they are treated as two related settlements as the discretionary fund was not an 18-25 trust within s 71D at its commencement; the calculations below treat them as two parts of a single settlement since that is how they were in fact constituted as a matter of trust law under the Will, and the trustees will be concerned to ensure, for CGT reasons, that the appointment of the Children's Fund (and Brenda's Fund) does not give rise to their passing into a separate settlement for trust law purposes from the retained shares (see **Example C16 explanatory note 10**).

Thus, with an assumption as to IHT rates in 2047/48 when the twins' 25th birthday occurs, the rate applicable can be confidently predicted as below: it will not vary according to the value of the property in the Children's Fund at the time, but using the assumed value of £1.8 million (net of CGT) the tax itself can also be predicted as follows.

3(a) *Children's Fund originally appointed as just £525,000 cash*

20 April 2047 — age 18-to-25 trust exit charge on the Children's Fund

Chargeable amount (s 71F(4))

Amount by which value of s 71D property is less immediately after chargeable event — £1,800,000

Relevant Fraction (s 71F(5), (6))

Numerator of time element of Relevant Fraction: number of complete quarters in period to 19 April 2047 elapsed since Children's Fund entered s 71D regime: 20 April 2040 to 19 April 2047 — 28 quarters

Relevant fraction is three tenths of time element

Settlement Rate (s 71F(7)–(9))

		Gross £	Tax on 2047/48 scale £
Settlor's 7-year cumulative total at commencement of settlement (19 April 2022)		40,000	Nil
Notional transfer (no additions or related settlement)			
Initial value of property in Alex's Will Trust at 19 April 2022:			
Children's Fund	525,000		
Brenda's Fund (explanatory note 7)	0		
Discretionary Fund	750,000	1,275,000	142,625*
		1,315,000	142,625*

(* 1,315,000 – 500,000 = £815,000 @ ½ × 35%)

Effective rate, and so settlement rate, is therefore:

$$\frac{142,625}{1,275,000} = 11.186\%$$

Tax payable (s 71F(3))

Chargeable amount × Relevant Fraction × Settlement rate

$$1,800,000 \times (\frac{28}{40} \times \frac{3}{10}) \times 11.186\% =$$ £42,283

Tax payable is:

3(b) *Children's Fund originally appointed as everything else except Brenda's Fund and the shares*

20 April 2047 — age 18-to-25 trust exit charge on the Children's Fund

Chargeable amount (s 71F(4))

Amount by which value of s 71D property is less immediately after chargeable event — £1,800,000

Relevant Fraction (s 71F(5), (6))

Numerator of time element of Relevant Fraction: number of complete quarters in period to 19 April 2047 elapsed since Children's Fund entered s 71D regime: 20 April 2040 to 19 April 2047 — 28 quarters

Relevant fraction is three tenths of time element

Settlement Rate (s 71F(7)–(9))

		Gross £	Tax on 2047/48 scale £
Settlor's 7-year cumulative total at commencement of settlement (19 April 2022)		40,000	Nil
Notional transfer (no additions or related settlement)			
Initial value of property in Alex's Will Trust at 19 April 2022:			
Children's Fund	765,000		
Brenda's Fund (**explanatory note 14**)	0		
Discretionary Fund	750,000	1,515,000	184,625*
		1,555,000	184,625*

(* 1,555,000 – 500,000 = £1,055,000 @ ½ × 35%)

Effective rate, and so settlement rate, is therefore:

$$\frac{184,625}{1,515,000} = 12.186\%$$

Tax payable (s 71F(3))

Chargeable amount × Relevant Fraction × Settlement rate

Tax payable is:

$$1,800,000 \times (\frac{28}{40} \times \frac{3}{10}) \times 12.186\% = \quad £46,063$$

The reason for the lower settlement rate in scenario (a) is simply the smaller Children's Fund in that scenario (see the comparative table in **part 1** above), which sets the value transferred by the notional chargeable transfer under s 71E(7).

4 Alternative scenarios for part 3 above

4(i) *If the Discretionary Fund had been added to the Children's Fund on 28 August 2042*

The shares in C Ltd and D Ltd were relevant property from Alex's death until the appointment of the Discretionary Fund as an addition to the Children's Fund on 28 August 2042. On the basis that the trusts which then become applicable were 'established under the Will' in terms of s 71D(2)(a) (see **Example C15 explanatory note 3**), the property in the Discretionary Fund would then have become subject to the age 18-to-25 trust regime, and thereby ceased to be relevant property, with an exit charge under the relevant property regime accordingly.

(Doubts have been expressed as to whether property can move from the relevant property regime into either the bereaved minor's trust regime or the age 18-to-25 trust regime. Such a situation can arise in the case of a discretionary will trust where appointments are made for the benefit of a deceased settlor's children within two years of his death. Section 144 which provides for distributions from a discretionary will trust within two years of the individual's death to be treated as made under his Will contains specific reference to s 71A (bereaved minors trusts) and s 71D (age 18-25 trusts). HMRC's interpretation of the law is that such trusts can therefore arise by virtue of the reading back effect of s 144. They are of the opinion that s 144(3)(c)(ii), (6)(b) operates to treat s 71A and s 71D trusts as capable of being created under the deceased's Will (see IHTM35182). For the implications if this were the wrong view, see **explanatory note 6.**)

Additionally, two ten-year anniversaries of the settlement have occurred in the meantime, on 19 April 2032 and 19 April 2042, and the Discretionary Fund will have been subject to ten-year charges on those occasions.

However, on the basis that the shares in both C Ltd and D Ltd remained either completely unquoted, or merely listed on the Alternative Investment Market, up to the London Stock Exchange flotation shortly after the 28 August 2042 appointment, and (as stated) that both were still trading companies, then (subject to the impact of any excepted assets within s 112 on the respective share values) the value subject to both the ten-year charges in April 2032 and April 2042, and the exit charge on 28 August 2042, would be reduced to nil by 100% business property relief. Accordingly no IHT would have been payable on any of those three occasions.

The exit charge under the age 18-to-25 trust regime on the twins' 25th birthday would on this basis be calculated as follows:

4(i)(a) Children's Fund originally appointed as just £525,000 cash

	Original Children's Fund	Former Discretionary Fund	Total value
20 April 2047 — age 18-to-25 trust exit charge on the Children's Fund			
Chargeable amount (s 71F(4))			
Amount by which value of s 71D property is less immediately after chargeable event	£1,800,000	£2,900,000	£4,700,000
Relevant Fraction (s 71F(5), (6))			
(Calculated separately for original Children's Fund and former Discretionary Fund)			
Numerator of time element of Relevant Fraction: Number of complete quarters in period to 19 April 2047 elapsed since twins' 18th birthday or (if later) property entered s 71D regime (see **Example C15 explanatory note 12**):			
Original Children's Fund: 20 April 2040 to 19 April 2047	28		fortieths
Former Discretionary Fund: 28 August 2042 to 27 February 2047		18	fortieths
Relevant fraction is three tenths of time element			
Settlement Rate (s 71F(7)–(9))			
As in **part 3(a)**	$\frac{142,625}{1,275,000} = 11.186\%$		
Tax payable (s 71F(3))			
(Calculated separately for original Children's Fund and former Discretionary Fund)			
Chargeable amount × Relevant fraction × Settlement rate			
On original Children's Fund	$1,800,000 \times \frac{28}{40} \times \frac{3}{10} \times 11.186\ \% =$		£42,283
On former Discretionary Fund	$2,900,000 \times \frac{18}{40} \times \frac{3}{10} \times 11.186\ \% =$		£43,793
Total tax chargeable			£86,076

4(i)(b) Children's Fund originally appointed as everything else except Brenda's Fund and the shares

20 April 2047 — age 18-to-25 trust exit charge on the Children's Fund

	Original Children's Fund	*Former Discretionary Fund*	*Total value*
Chargeable amount (s 71F(4))			
Amount by which value of s 71D property is less immediately after chargeable event	£1,800,000	£2,900,000	£4,700,000
Relevant Fraction (s 71F(5), (6))			
Numerator of time element of Relevant Fraction as in 4(a) above	28	18	fortieths
Relevant fraction is three tenths of time element			
Settlement Rate (s 71F(7)–(9))			
As in part 3(b)	$\frac{184{,}625}{1{,}515{,}000} = 12.186\%$		
Tax payable (s 71F(3))			
(Calculated separately for original Children's Fund and former Discretionary Fund)			
Chargeable amount × Relevant fraction × Settlement rate			
On original Children's Fund	$1{,}800{,}000 \times \frac{28}{40} \times \frac{3}{10} \times 12.186\,\% =$		£46,063
On former Discretionary Fund	$2{,}900{,}000 \times \frac{18}{40} \times \frac{3}{10} \times 12.186\,\% =$		£47,708
Total tax chargeable			£93,771

4(ii) *If Brenda's Fund had accrued to the Children's Fund on her death in 2038*

4(ii)(a) Brenda's Fund and Brenda's free estate

Brenda's protected life interest in Brenda's Fund was an IPDI, having been appointed within two years after Alex's death, with backdated effect for IHT purposes by virtue of s 144 (see **part 1** above). Accordingly, the forfeiture resulting from a purported assignment of the right to income (rendered ineffective by Trustee Act 1925 s 33 which brings the income entitlement to an end and substitutes a discretionary trust of income – see **Example D2 explanatory note 1**) is disregarded under s 88: Brenda is deemed for IHT purposes to continue to be entitled to the same IIP (the IPDI) that she had before the forfeiture, without interruption. Therefore the property in Brenda's Fund was still comprised in Brenda's estate for IHT purposes at her death, and charged to IHT accordingly. The charge on her death extended to Brenda's Lump Sum Trust, as well as Brenda's free estate, all of which would have been aggregated to calculate the charge which has already been deducted in arriving at the values given in the question.

When, under the terms of the trustees' appointment which established it, Brenda's Fund became held on the same terms as the Children's Fund on her death on 14 January 2038, the property in question entered the age 18-to-25 trust regime. At that date the twins were still aged 15. An exit charge under that regime will arise when they become absolutely entitled at age 25. However, the property formerly comprised in Brenda's Fund (unlike the former Discretionary Fund in **part 4(i)** above, and not following the general trust law) will not form part of the same settlement for the purposes of the age 18-to-25 trust rules as the Children's Fund, but rather it will count as a separate, deemed, settlement made by Brenda herself on her death, by virtue of s 80 (see **explanatory note 7**).

The age 18-to-25 trust exit charge at the twins' 25th birthday on 20 April 2047 will therefore, in relation to the property derived from Brenda's Fund, be calculated in respect of this deemed settlement. Because it is not a calculation in relation to Alex's Will trust, the way in which the initial appointment under Alex's Will had been structured – affecting the initial value of the two other funds established as a result of that appointment – has no bearing on the calculation relating to the deemed settlement.

Brenda's free estate became held on the statutory trusts for the twins' benefit on her intestacy. The statutory trusts (see **Example A19 explanatory note 6**) provide for the twins to become absolutely entitled at age 18; the property is settled property in the meantime but is the subject of a bereaved minors' trust (s 71A(1)(a)), so there will be no IHT charge on their becoming entitled to capital from it at age 18 on 20 April 2040, or on its being applied for their benefit before that age. However, because Brenda is the settlor of this trust taking effect on her death, it is a related settlement in relation to the deemed settlement of Brenda's Fund, However, this will not be taken into account in calculating the settlement rate for the purpose of the age 18-to-25 trust exit charge on the deemed settlement referred to above as it is not a related settlement that is an 18–25 trust under s 17D; rather it is a bereaved minor's trust under s 71A. From 18 November 2015, 18-25 settlements can only be related with other 18-to-25 settlements and not simply all other trusts created on the same day. The calculations for the latter are therefore as follows:

20 April 2047 — age 18-to-25 trust exit charge on Brenda's Fund

Chargeable amount (s 71F(4))

Amount by which value of s 71D property is less immediately after chargeable event		£2,375,000
Relevant Fraction (s 71F(5), (6))		
Numerator of time element of Relevant Fraction: number of complete quarters in period to 19 April 2047 elapsed since Children's Fund entered s 71D regime: 20 April 2040 to 19 April 2047	28	fortieths
Relevant fraction is three tenths of time element		

Settlement Rate (s 71F(7)–(9))	*Gross* £	*Tax on 2047/48 scale* £
Settlor's seven-year cumulative total at commencement of deemed settlement (14 January 2038)	Nil	Nil
Notional transfer (no additions)		
Initial value of property in deemed settlement		
Brenda's Fund	2,100,000	
	2,100,000	280,000*
(* 2,100,000 – 500,000 = 1,620,000 @ ½ × 35%)		
	$\frac{280,000}{2,100,000} = 13.333\%$	
Effective rate, and so settlement rate, is therefore:		

Tax payable (s 71F(3))

Chargeable amount × Relevant Fraction × Settlement rate

Tax payable is $2,375,000 \times (\frac{28}{40} \times \frac{3}{10}) \times 13.333\ \% =$ £66,498

See **explanatory (9)** as to why no residence nil-rate band is available in the above computation.

4(ii)(b) Brenda's Lump Sum Trust

Brenda's Lump Sum Trust became relevant property on her death: although the twins are due to become absolutely entitled at age 21, the trust does not arise in any way that can fall within s 71D as an age 18-to-25 trust. Its funds derive from the PLAS and, as noted in **part 2(b)** above, s 81 will have been in point when the lump sum death benefit was paid across into Brenda's Lump Sum Trust, deeming the property comprised in the latter to have remained comprised in the former for the purpose of Part 3 Chapter 3 (including the relevant property rules).

A ten-year anniversary of the PLAS (and so affecting Brenda's Lump Sum Trust) occurred on 1 April 2040, giving rise to a ten-year charge in relation to the latter trust (though calculated by reference to the former) on that date. There is also a relevant property exit charge on 20 April 2043 when the twins become absolutely entitled under the terms of this trust at age 21. These charges are calculated as follows:

1 April 2040 — relevant property ten-year charge – Pension & Life Assurance Scheme

Chargeable amount (s 64(1))

Relevant property at ten-year anniversary:		
Brenda's Lump Sum Trust at 31 March 2040		800,000
Effective rate on notional transfer (s 66(3)–(5))	Gross	*Tax on 2039/40 scale*
	£	£
Settlor's seven-year cumulative total at commencement of settlement (1 April 2010)	Nil	Nil
Notional transfer (no addition or related settlement)		
Chargeable amount as above	800,000	60,000*
	800,000	60,000*

(* 800,000 – 550,000 = 250,000 @ ½ × 48%)

Actual full rate is three tenths of effective rate:

$$\frac{60,000}{800,000} \times \frac{3}{10} = 2.250\%$$

Number of complete quarters elapsed since preceding ten-year anniversary before the fund became relevant property on Brenda's death on 14 January 2038:

1 April 2030 to 31 December 2037 — 31 quarters

Tax payable:

$$2.250\% \times \frac{40 - 31}{40} \times 800,000 = \quad £4,050$$

20 April 2043 — relevant property exit charge = Pension & Life Assurance Scheme

Preliminary: Recalculation of rate for ten-year charge with new IHT scale to establish whether there has been a 'reduction in tax'

Chargeable amount (s 64(1)) as above		800,000
Effective rate on notional transfer (s 66(3)–(5))	*Gross*	*Tax on 2043/44 scale*
	£	£
Settlor's seven-year cumulative total at commencement of settlement (1 April 2010)	Nil	Nil
Notional transfer (no addition or related settlement)		
Chargeable amount as above	800,000	56,250*
	800,000	56,250*

(* 800,000 – 575,000 = 225,000 @ ½ × 50%)

Actual full rate is three tenths of effective rate ((40 – 31) / 40 fraction used at ten-year anniversary under s 66(2) is disregarded by s 69(1), (2))	$\frac{56,250}{800,000} \times \frac{3}{10} = 2.109\%$

Calculation of exit charge

Chargeable amount (s 65(2))

Amount by which value of relevant property is less immediately after chargeable event:			
Brenda's Lump Sum Trust			900,000
Rate applicable (s 69(1)–(2))			
Lower effective rate on ten-year charge calculations is produced by recalculation			
Therefore full rate before appropriate fraction is		2.109%	
Appropriate fraction (s 69(4))			
Number of complete quarters in period to 19 April 2043 elapsed since ten-year anniversary: 1 April 2040 to 31 March 2043		12	fortieths
Tax payable:	$2.109\% \times \frac{12}{40} \times 900,000 =$		£5,694

Explanatory Notes

Status of Alex's lifetime transfer for inheritance tax

(1) Brenda and Alex were not married at the time Alex paid off Brenda's debts in August 2018, and spouse exemption was therefore not available against Alex's transfer of value (ie the disposition by him as a result of which his estate was £46,000 less than previously); this is not affected by their subsequent marriage. To the extent not covered by his available annual exemptions, therefore, the transfer would have been an immediately chargeable transfer unless it could be shown to be a potentially exempt transfer (see explanatory note 2). In the circumstances that Alex had made no previous chargeable transfers and the amount in this case was well within his nil-rate band, it is not necessary to investigate or form a view one way or the other, or to allocate the transfer between the two categories: his death occurred within the ensuing seven years, and the transfer absorbs the same amount of Alex's nil-rate band at death either way.

(2) To have been a potentially exempt transfer (so far as in excess of Alex's available annual exemptions) to any extent, the transfer of value made by paying off Brenda's debts must have been a 'gift to another individual' within the definition in s 3A(2), which applies:

(a) to the extent that the value transferred is attributable to property which, by virtue of the transfer, becomes comprised in the estate of that other individual, or

(b) so far as that value is not attributable to property which becomes comprised in the estate of another person, to the extent that, by virtue of the transfer, the estate of that other individual is increased.

Clearly the money used to pay off Brenda's debts, by direct payment to her creditors, did not (as money) become comprised in Brenda's estate; if PET status were therefore to apply it must be by virtue of s 3A(2)(b). The reality however is that Brenda's position before the debts were paid off would almost certainly have been insolvent, with liabilities exceeding assets. It is not thought that her estate for IHT purposes can be described as having a negative value: in practice, whenever liabilities exceed assets, the value is zero (so that excess liabilities in a person's free estate cannot be deducted against a different fund which counts as part of his estate, for example a trust fund in which he had an estate IIP). Alex's transfer would therefore have been an immediately chargeable transfer except so far as Brenda had assets of her own which gave rise to a positive value for her net estate once the liabilities had been paid off (so that there was an increase from nil – to this extent the payment would have met the terms of s 3A(2)(b) and would have been potentially exempt rather than immediately chargeable).

This issue can be avoided, if foreseen and if the debtor is trusted, by paying the money to the debtor and allowing them to pay off the debts, since then the money clearly would become comprised in the debtor's estate (albeit only temporarily) and so qualify as a 'gift to an individual' as defined.

Inheritance tax business property relief and unquoted shares

(3) The shares in both C Ltd and D Ltd count as unquoted shares for business property relief purposes: quotation on the Alternative Investment Market is not quotation on a recognised stock exchange. (For further notes on business property relief see **Example A21.**)

Specific gift with exempt residue: grossing up for inheritance tax

(4) As a result of Alex's death within seven years, the lifetime transfer is now a chargeable transfer irrespective of the issue discussed in explanatory note 2, and absorbs £40,000 of Alex's nil-rate band leaving £285,000 available against the £525,000 net legacy to the Children's Fund in part 1(a) of the Example. The remaining £240,000 of the net legacy must be grossed up at the 40% rate of tax (see **Example A15**) as follows:

$$240,000 \times \frac{100}{60} = £400,000$$

Dates from which quarters are counted: inheritance tax exit charges

(5) The main difference between the age 18-to-25 trust 'policy-compliant' exit charge under s 71F on the one hand, and the relevant property exit charge that applies before the first ten-year anniversary under s 68 on the other, is the counting of quarters towards the 'relevant fraction' (s 71F(5), (6)) or the appropriate fraction (s 68(2), (3)): see **Example C16 explanatory note 7**. The calculations in **part 4(i)** of the Example highlight an apparent peculiarity of the s 71F approach in cases where some of the property within the age 18-to-25 trust regime under a single settlement (and subject to the exit charge) has been subject to that regime for longer than other property – and in particular where the property which entered the regime later did so at a time when the beneficiary in question had already reached age 18.

The counting of quarters towards the numerator of the 'relevant fraction' under s 71F starts from the 18th birthday of the beneficiary in question or, if later, from the day on which the property in question entered the age 18-to-25 trust regime (s 71F(5)(a)); thus 6 April 2010 in this Example. (Quarters throughout which the property in question was excluded property are then excluded under s 71F(6), as to which see **Example C19 parts B and C.**) The result, as shown in the Example, is that 'complete successive quarters' may have to be counted from different dates in relation to different property that is subject to the exit charge.

By contrast, s 68(3) (and, referentially, s 69 after a ten-year anniversary – s 69(4)) deals with a similar situation under the relevant property regime rather differently. The quarters in that case are all counted from the commencement of the settlement (or the last ten-year anniversary for s 69 purposes); but in the case of any property that has not been relevant property for the whole of the intervening period, complete quarters which had already expired before the property in question became (or last became) relevant property are deducted from the basic total (see **Example C12 explanatory note 4** and **Example C11**). Thus the quarters are all counted from the same date.

What if property cannot move from the relevant property regime to the age 18-to-25 trust regime for inheritance tax?

(6) The answer to **part 4(i)** of the Example works on the basis that the Discretionary Fund does enter the age 18-to-25 trust regime, and thereby ceases to be relevant property, on being appointed as an addition to the Children's Fund on 28 August 2042 (see the discussion in **Example C15 explanatory note 3**). If this were wrong, there would be no exit charge at that time by virtue of that appointment (on a zero value by virtue of business property relief), but instead on the twins becoming in April 2047 absolutely entitled to the Children's Fund (which by then includes the Discretionary Fund in **part 4(i)**), there would be a relevant

property exit charge at that time on the £2.9 million value of the property derived from the shares in C Ltd and D Limited. (The age 18-to-25 trust exit charge would be correspondingly limited to the property representing the original Children's Fund, calculated as in **part 3** above.)

Paradoxically, in the particular circumstances this relevant property exit charge would work out more favourably than the age 18-to-25 trust exit charge so far as referable to the assets derived from the Discretionary Fund as shown in **part 4**(i) (see the comparative summary below, where the reason for this paradox is explained). The relevant property calculations, for each of scenarios (a) and (b) in **part 1**, would be as shown below. Because the nil-rate band has in the meantime decreased but the rate of tax applicable in excess of it has also decreased, it is not possible to ascertain whether the rate scale in force at the date of the exit charge amounts to 'tax [being] reduced' within s 9 (such as to result in the rate of the ten-year charge being recomputed using the later scale under Sch 2 para 3), without in both cases first computing the rate of tax applicable on the ten-year charge (which in fact applied to a nil value transferred after business property relief) on *both* the original 2042/43 rate scale *and* the 2047/48 rate scale. Either way the full rate arrived at under s 66(1) is not reduced by a time fraction under s 66(2), because the Discretionary Fund had been relevant property throughout the preceding ten-year period.

The amount subject to the ten-year charge does not need to be recalculated for the purpose of ascertaining the rate to be used for the exit charge, under s 69(2A), because no property has been added to the settlement or become relevant property in the period since the ten-year anniversary, even though the relevant property has in the meantime lost the benefit of business property relief.

CALCULATIONS IF THE DISCRETIONARY FUND REMAINS RELEVANT PROPERTY UNTIL 2047:

(A) Children's Fund originally appointed as just £525,000 cash

19 APRIL 2042 — RATE OF TEN-YEAR CHARGE ON THE DISCRETIONARY FUND

(i) Original rate calculation		
Chargeable amount (s 64(1))		
Relevant property at ten-year anniversary		
Shares in C Ltd and D Ltd		3,000,000
Less 100% business property relief		(3,000,000)
		Nil
Effective rate on notional transfer (s 66(3)–(5))	*Gross* £	*Tax on 2042/43 scale* £
Settlor's seven-year cumulative total at commencement of settlement (19 April 2022)	40,000	Nil
Notional transfer (no related settlement)		
Chargeable amount as above	Nil	Nil
	40,000	Nil*
(* below nil-rate band £575,000)		
Actual full rate is three tenths of effective rate: 0%		
(ii) Recalculation using rates at date of exit charge		
Chargeable amount (s 64(1))		
Relevant property at ten-year anniversary, as above		Nil

Effective rate on notional transfer (s 66(3)–(5))	*Gross* £	*Tax on 2047/48 scale* £
Settlor's seven year cumulative total at commencement of settlement (19 April 2022)	40,000	Nil
Notional transfer (no related settlement)		
Chargeable amount as above	Nil	Nil
	40,000	Nil*

(* Less than nil-rate band of 500,000)

Actual full rate is three tenths of effective rate: ie 0%

20 APRIL 2047 — RELEVANT PROPERTY EXIT CHARGE ON THE DISCRETIONARY FUND (NOW WITHIN THE CHILDREN'S FUND)

The full rate ascertained from (i) is the same (ie there has not been a 'reduction in tax' in the meantime) and therefore the original rate calculation is used.

Chargeable amount (s 65(2))

Amount by which value of relevant property is less immediately after chargeable event:	2,900,000

Rate applicable (s 69(1)–(2))

Lower effective rate on ten-year charge calculations is produced by original calculation

Therefore full rate before appropriate fraction is	0%

Appropriate fraction (s 69(4))

Number of complete quarters in period to 19 April 2047 elapsed since ten-year anniversary: 19 April 2042 to 18 April 2047	20	fortieths

Tax payable: $0\% \times \frac{20}{40} \times 2,900,000 =$ £ Nil

(B) Children's Fund originally appointed as everything else except Brenda's Fund and the shares

19 APRIL 2042 — RATE OF TEN-YEAR CHARGE ON THE DISCRETIONARY FUND

(i) Original rate calculation

Chargeable amount (s 64(1))

Relevant property at ten-year anniversary, as above	Nil

Effective rate on notional transfer (s 66(3)–(5))	*Gross* £	*Tax on 2042/43 scale* £
Settlor's seven year cumulative total at commencement of settlement (19 April 2022)	40,000	Nil
Notional transfer (no related settlement)		
Chargeable amount as above	Nil	
Initial value of other relevant property in settlement:		

Brenda's Fund (**explanatory note 7**)	Nil	Nil*
	40,000	Nil*

(* Less than nil-rate band of 575,000)

Actual full rate is three tenths of effective rate: ie 0%

(ii) Recalculation using rates at date of exit charge

Chargeable amount (s 64(1))

Relevant property at ten-year anniversary, as above — Nil

Effective rate on notional transfer (s 66(3)–(5))	*Gross* £	*Tax on 2047/48 scale* £
Settlor's seven-year cumulative total at commencement of settlement (19 April 2022)	40,000	Nil
Notional transfer (no related settlement)		
Chargeable amount as above	Nil	Nil
	40,000	Nil*

(* Less than nil-rate band of 500,000)

Actual full rate is three tenths of effective rate: ie 0%

20 APRIL 2047 — RELEVANT PROPERTY EXIT CHARGE ON THE DISCRETIONARY FUND (NOW WITHIN THE CHILDREN'S FUND)

Again the full rate ascertained from (i) is the same (ie there has not been a 'reduction in tax' in the meantime) and therefore the original rate calculation is used.

Chargeable amount (s 65(2))

Amount by which value of relevant property is less immediately after chargeable event: — 2,900,000

Rate applicable (s 69(1)–(2))

Actual full rate is three tenths of effective rate: ie 0%

Appropriate fraction (s 69(4))

Number of complete quarters in period to 19 April 2047 elapsed since ten-year anniversary: 19 April 2042 to 18 April 2047 — 20 fortieths

Tax payable: $0\% \times \frac{20}{40} \times 2,900,000 =$ £Nil

COMPARATIVE SUMMARY (PART 4(I))

	age 18-to-25 trust exit charge (part 4(i))	*relevant property exit charge (above variant)*
(a) Children's Fund originally appointed as pecuniary legacy	43,793	Nil
(b) Children's Fund originally appointed as residuary gift	47,708	Nil

The tax referable to the former Discretionary Fund, on the twins becoming absolutely entitled to it at age 25 following its appointment into the Children's Fund in 2043, works out less, on these particular facts, under the relevant property regime than under the age 18-to-25 trust regime. But this is not a typical result, and usually the age

18-to-25 trust exit charge can be expected to be significantly more lenient – see for example the comparative summary at the end of **Example C16**.

The reason for the reverse result on the particular facts of **part 4(i)** is the fact that the value taken into account for the property in the Discretionary Fund (as part of the notional chargeable transfer) is not its *true* current value at the date of the most recent ten-year anniversary, but rather its discounted value – the full value has in practice been eliminated, on the facts, by 100% business property relief. In addition, following the changes made by F(No 2)A 2015, the notional chargeable transfer no longer includes the initial value of other non-relevant property in the settlement. As a result, under the relevant property rules, the notional chargeable transfer used to compute the rate that applied (to a zero chargeable amount) on that ten-year anniversary – and which is then used again, multiplied by the appropriate fraction, for the exit charge under s 69 – is nil; whereas under the age 18-to-25 trust rules of s 71F the initial values used to set the settlement rate are those of both the Children's Fund (Brenda's Fund being ignored because of the effect of s 80, see explanatory note 7) and the Discretionary Fund.

Initial IPDI of settlor's spouse: creation of trusts for inheritance tax

(7) Section 80 (see **Example C12 explanatory note 1**) applies where either the settlor, or the settlor's spouse or civil partner (which include surviving spouse or surviving civil partner), is beneficially entitled to a qualifying IIP in property immediately after that property becomes comprised in the settlement (the true settlement). For the purpose of Part 3 Chapter 3 (ss 58–85), the property is treated as not having become comprised in the true settlement on that occasion. Instead, if the property continues to be settled property when none of those persons is beneficially entitled to a qualifying IIP, it is treated as becoming at that time comprised in a separate settlement (the deemed settlement) made by whichever of them ceased (or last ceased) to be beneficially entitled to a qualifying IIP in it.

This applies to Brenda in relation to Brenda's Fund under Alex's Will Trust, and accordingly:

- Brenda's Fund is not regarded as comprised in a settlement made by Alex for the purpose of age 18-to-25 trust or relevant property calculations affecting the Children's Fund or the Discretionary Fund – whether the same settlement as those funds (viz Alex's Will Trust, the true settlement), or a related settlement); and
- a deemed settlement is accordingly regarded as having been made by Brenda on her death in **part 4(ii)**.

As such, the trust of Brenda's free estate for the twins under the intestacy rules – of which she is the actual settlor, and which also obviously took effect on her death – will be a related settlement to the deemed settlement of Brenda's Fund in **part 4(ii)**, since both (for the purpose of Part 3 Chapter 3) commenced at Brenda's death (see ss 60, 62).

Brenda's Lump Sum Trust on the other hand will not be a related settlement with either of those trusts, even though (as with Brenda's Fund) Brenda had a qualifying IIP (in this case a disabled person's interest) which came to an end on her death and the property remained settled property pending the twins becoming absolutely entitled at age 21. Alex was not an actual settlor of Brenda's Lump Sum Trust, so s 80 cannot apply to treat Brenda instead as settling that trust on her death when her qualifying IIP comes to an end. Even if it were correct (see **explanatory note 15**) that Alex falls to be treated as a settlor in relation to the PLAS (so far as concerns benefits in relation to his membership of the scheme), through having been a contributory member of the PLAS, neither he nor Brenda had an IIP in the property concerned immediately after it became comprised in the PLAS, so s 80 cannot apply by that means either.

Transfers from pension funds to private trusts: identity of settlor for inheritance tax

(8) Where relevant property derived from a pension or similar trust is treated as remaining comprised in that trust by virtue of s 81, following payment of a lump sum on the death of a member, it may be relevant to establish whether the member should be treated as having become a settlor of the property in question at the time he became a contributing member of the scheme (as may have been the case for the purpose of the trust law rule against perpetuities before the Perpetuities and Accumulations Act 2009 came into force – see the Law Commission Report LawCom 251 para 3.53). If that were the case his seven-year IHT cumulative total of chargeable transfers at that time would seemingly be relevant to the calculation of relevant property charges (it can generally be assumed that any contributions by him to the scheme will always be exempt transfers under the normal income expenditure exemption (s 21), so there would be no reassessment of his

lifetime cumulative total under s 67 on any relevant property ten-year charge). The facts of the Example assume, however, that Alex had made no lifetime transfers that would be relevant for this purpose, even if he were to be regarded as a settlor in this way.

There is also the question of the commencement date of the settlement which will determine the cycle of ten-year anniversaries; again the facts of the Example make it unnecessary to reach a view as to whether Alex is a settlor, since he was a member of the PLAS from the moment that it was constituted on 1 April 2010. Where s 81 applies to a transfer from one settlement to another, the transferee settlement (here Brenda's Lump Sum Trust) is subject to the same cycle of ten-year anniversaries as the transferor settlement (here the PLAS).

For further commentary on s 81, including as to certain practical issues affecting the trustees of the different settlements involved, see **Example C18**.

Inheritance tax residence nil-rate band

(9) In the context of the Example, under his Will, Alex's home became comprised in a life interest trust (that is an IPDI) for the benefit of his wife Brenda on his death. In **part 4(ii)** of the Example it is postulated that on her death in 2038 the home becomes comprised in the existing 18-to-25 trust also established under Alex's Will. The question that arises is whether the home may be regarded as closely inherited on Breda's death so that a residence nil-rate band is used in computing the inheritance tax arising at that time. It is considered that the answer to this question is no. Property that becomes comprised in an 18-to-25 settlement is regarded as inherited where it becomes comprised in such a settlement 'on' the death of the deceased (s 8J(4)(b)). This provision is not met for two reasons. First the property does not become comprised in a settlement on Brenda's death; it is already settled property. Secondly, even if this view is incorrect, s 8J(4) operates only where the deceased owned the property itself before his death (which Brenda did not). That s 8J(4) operates in this way follows from the provision of s 8J(5) which deal with the case where immediately before the deceased's death the property was already settled property. If s 8J(4) could be said to apply to already settled property then s 8J(5) would be otiose. S 8J(5) provides that where, immediately before the deceased's death, the property was settled property in which the deceased was beneficially entitled to an interest in possession, a person inherits the property if the person becomes beneficially entitled to it on D's death. Although Brenda was beneficially entitled to an interest in possession in the home by reason of her IPDI, the twins did not become beneficially entitled to it on her death as it remained subject to the trusts of the 18-to-25 settlement. Even if at the time of their mother's death the twins had turned 18 so that they started to enjoy an interest in possession in the 18-to-25 trust, that interest in possession does not give them a beneficial interest in the property (if that were enough to satisfy s 8J(5) for tax purposes) as such an interest is not a qualifying interest under s 49.

Question

A.

Alan, a widower, died domiciled in the UK on 15 June 1976 leaving his whole estate (worth £282,000 after tax) to his daughter Barbara for life, with remainder to Barbara's daughters Clare, Diana and Emily in equal shares absolutely. He had made lifetime gifts to the three granddaughters of £3,000 each on 20 December 1975, but no other gifts falling to be taken into account for capital transfer tax purposes.

Clare settled her reversionary interest in a discretionary trust of which she was a beneficiary on 1 November 1980. Diana did likewise on 3 February 1989, and Emily did the same on 20 March 1989. (All three discretionary settlements are separate from each other; none of the granddaughters had made any previous chargeable transfers.)

Barbara died on 22 May 1999 without having made any lifetime transfers relevant for IHT purposes. At that time the trust fund under Alan's Will comprised a relatively small minority holding worth £120,000 of shares in Fixit Ltd, a trading company whose shares were quoted on the Alternative Investment Market, which the trustees had bought in August 1997; and other assets worth £871,000 net of liabilities. The Fixit shares and other assets were each divided and distributed in equal shares to the trustees of the granddaughters' respective settlements. Barbara left her entire free estate to her husband absolutely.

On 9 December 2000 the trustees of Diana's settlement appointed £250,000 of quoted investments and cash (net of any tax chargeable on this appointment) on to accumulation and maintenance trusts in favour of Diana's recently-born first child and any further children born before the first of them reaches age 25; those who reach age 25 will take life interests at that point with remainders to the next generation. No change has since been made to the terms of this accumulation and maintenance trust.

Based on the values of the trust property set out in the table below, calculate any tax charges that have arisen under the inheritance tax relevant property regime in relation to any of the settlements before 5 April 2024. Fixit Ltd has continued to trade throughout, and in August 2005 its shares became quoted on the London Stock Exchange. The values of the shares, and of the remaining assets of each of the three settlements so far as held on discretionary trusts, on the following dates were as follows:

	Fixit shares (one-third of original parcel)	*Clare's settlement other assets*	*Diana's settlement (discretionary fund) other assets*	*Emily's settlement other assets*
31 October 2000	£50,000	£300,000	£300,000	£300,000
14 June 2006	£115,000	£390,000	£270,000	£380,000
2 February 2009	£85,000	£365,000	£255,000	£375,000
19 March 2009	£110,000	£380,000	£265,000	£385,000
31 October 2010	£140,000	£425,000	£295,000	£410,000
14 June 2016	£160,000	£450,000	£310,000	£430,000
2 February 2019	£190,000	£500,000	£400,000	£400,000
19 March 2019	£190,000	£500,000	£400,000	£400,000
31 October 2020	£220,000	£530,000	£425,000	£430,000

B.

How would your answer differ if Barbara had been Alan's wife (and had remarried after Alan's death) and Clare, Diana and Emily had been their daughters?

Answer

A.

The first ten-year anniversaries of Clare's, Diana's and Emily's settlements occurred on 1 November 1990, 3 February 1999 and 20 March 1999 respectively. Barbara's life interest was still continuing at those dates, so the property in the three settlements still consisted purely of the reversionary interests that had been settled originally. As such the settlements contained no relevant property at those respective dates (see IHTA 1984 s 48(1)), so no ten-year charges arose.

Similarly, ten-year anniversaries of Alan's Will trust occurred on 15 June 1986 and 15 June 1996, but because Barbara had a qualifying IIP in the whole of the trust fund at those times there was no relevant property in the trust (see s 58(1)) and therefore no ten-year charge on either occasion.

On Barbara's death on 22 May 1999, the value of the property passing into the three reversionary settlements is calculated as follows:

A.1 Death of Barbara (22 May 1999)		*Gross*	*Tax on 1999/2000 scale*
		£	£
Chargeable transfers within seven years before death		Nil	Nil
Estate at death:			
Free estate – wholly covered by spouse exemption		Nil	Nil
Alan's Will trust:			
Fixit Ltd shares	120,000		
Other assets (net)	871,000		
	991,000		
Less: Business property relief on shares	(120,000)	871,000	256,000*
		871,000	256,000*

(* 871,000 – 231,000 = 640,000 @ 40%)

Resultant division of the gross estate at death	*Fixit Ltd shares***	*Other assets*
	£	£
Clare's settlement	40,000	205,000
Diana's settlement	40,000	205,000
Emily's settlement	40,000	205,000
HMRC – tax		256,000
Total	120,000	871,000

(** exact fraction of value of entire holding, see **explanatory note 10**)

Clare's settlement suffers a relevant property ten-year charge on 1 November 2000, calculated as follows:

A.2 Clare's Settlement — 1 November 2000 — relevant property ten-year charge

Chargeable amount (s 64(1))

Relevant property at ten-year anniversary:	
Fixit Ltd shares at 31 October 2000	50,000
Less: 100% business property relief	(50,000)
Other assets at 31 October 2000	300,000
	300,000

Effective rate on notional transfer (s 66(3)–(5))

	Gross £	*Tax on 2000/01 scale* £
Settlor's seven-year cumulative total at commencement of settlement (1 November 1980)	Nil	Nil
Notional transfer (no addition or related settlement)		
Chargeable amount as above	300,000	13,200*
	300,000	13,200*

(* 300,000 – 234,000 = 66,000 @ 20%)

Actual full rate is three tenths of effective rate:

$$\frac{13{,}200}{300{,}000} \times \frac{3}{10} = 1.320\%$$

Number of complete quarters elapsed since preceding ten-year anniversary before the fund became relevant property on Barbara's death on 22 May 1999:

1 November 1990 to 30 April 1999 = 34 quarters

Tax payable:

$$1.320\ \% \times \frac{40-34}{40} \times 300{,}000 = £594$$

The appointment from Diana's settlement onto accumulation and maintenance trusts on 9 December 2000 (grossed up at the rate that applies to the exit charge) incurs a relevant property exit charge, calculated as though the property that had passed into both Diana's and Emily's settlements were still comprised in Alan's Will trust (see **explanatory note 3(a)**) as follows (see also **explanatory notes 9 and 10**):

A.3 Alan's Will Trust (re Diana's Settlement) — relevant property exit charge on 9 December 2000

Lifetime transfers by Alan		£	£
20 December 1975 – Gifts to granddaughters – 3 at £3,000			9,000
Less: annual exemptions	1975/76	1,000	
	1974/75	1,000	(2,000)
			7,000

15 June 1996 — recalculated rate of (notional) ten-year charge on Alan's Will Trust

Chargeable amount (s 64(1))

Assumed relevant property at ten-year anniversary (see **explanatory note 10**):	£	£	£
Fixit Ltd shares at 22 May 1999:			
Diana's settlement	40,000		
Emily's settlement	40,000	80,000	
Less: 100% business property relief		(80,000)	Nil
Other assets at 22 May 1999:			
Diana's settlement		205,000	
Emily's settlement		205,000	410,000
			410,000

Effective rate on notional transfer (s 66(3)–(5))			*Gross*	*Tax on 2000/01 scale*
			£	£
Settlor's seven-year cumulative total at commencement of settlement (15 June 1976)			7,000	Nil
Notional transfer (no related settlement)				
Chargeable amount as above		410,000		
Initial value of other property in settlement:				
Whole trust fund (Barbara's IIP)	282,000			
Exclude two thirds to prevent double-counting (see **explanatory note 9**)	(188,000)	94,000	504,000	55,400*
			511,000	55,400*

(* 511,000 – 234,000 = 277,000 @ 20%)

Actual full rate is three tenths of effective rate:

$$\frac{55{,}400}{504{,}000} \times \frac{3}{10} = 3.298\%$$

9 December 2000 — relevant property exit charge on Alan's Will trust

Appropriate fraction (s 69(4))

Number of complete quarters in period to 8 December 2000 elapsed since ten-year anniversary: 15 June 1996 to 14 September 2000	17	quarters
Less: Number of complete quarters in period to 8 December 2000 elapsed before Diana's and Emily's shares became relevant property on Barbara's death on 22 May 1999: 15 June 1996 to 14 March 1999	(11)	quarters
Numerator of appropriate fraction	6	fortieths

Rate applicable (s 69(1)–(2))

Full rate before appropriate fraction derived from recalculated (notional) ten-year charge calculation as above — 3.298%

$$3.298\,\% \times \frac{6}{40} = 0.495\%$$

Rate applicable to exit charge

Chargeable amount (s 65(2)(b)) and tax payable	*Gross*	*Tax at calculated rate applicable*	*Net*
Amount by which value of relevant property is less immediately after chargeable event, grossed up:			
Property appointed onto accumulation and maintenance trusts	£251,243*	£1,243	£250,000

$$*250{,}000 \times \frac{100}{100 - 0.495\%}$$

A relevant property ten-year charge arises in respect of Diana's and Emily's settlements (combined, as if the property were still comprised in Alan's Will trust) on 15 June 2006, calculated as follows:

A.4 Alan's Will Trust (re Diana's and Emily's Settlements) — 15 June 2006 — relevant property ten-year charge

Chargeable amount (s 64(1))	
Relevant property at ten-year anniversary:	
Fixit Ltd shares at 14 June 2006 (now quoted)	
Diana's settlement	115,000
Emily's settlement	115,000
Other assets at 14 June 2006	
Diana's settlement	270,000
Emily's settlement	380,000
	880,000

Effective rate on notional transfer (s 66(3)–(5))

		Gross £	Tax on 2005/06 scale £
Notional cumulation:			
Settlor's seven-year cumulative total at commencement of settlement (15 June 1976)	7,000		Nil
Exit charges within preceding ten years (appointment in Diana's settlement)	251,243	258,243	
Notional transfer (no addition or related settlement)			
Chargeable amount as above		880,000	170,649*
		1,138,243	170,649*

(* 1,138,243 – 285,000 = 853,243 @ 20%)

Actual full rate is three tenths of effective rate:

$$\frac{170{,}649}{880{,}000} \times \frac{3}{10} = 5.818\%$$

Number of complete quarters elapsed since preceding ten-year anniversary before the fund became relevant property on Barbara's death on 22 May 1999 (s 66(2)):

15 June 1996 to 14 March 1999 = 11 quarters

Tax payable: $5.818\,\% \times \frac{40-11}{40} \times 880{,}000 =$ £37,119

On 6 April 2008 the property in the accumulation and maintenance trust fund of Diana's settlement became relevant property since (following the changes made by FA 2006) the terms of the trust qualify neither for continuing accumulation and maintenance trust status nor for age 18-to-25 trust status, because capital does not vest by age 25. However no exit charge under s 71(3) arises in consequence: FA 2006 Sch 20 para 2(5).

Clare's settlement suffers a further relevant property ten-year charge on 1 November 2010, calculated as follows:

A.5 Clare's Settlement — 1 November 2010 — relevant property ten-year charge

Chargeable amount (s 64(1))	
Relevant property at ten-year anniversary:	
Fixit Ltd shares at 31 October 2010 (now quoted)	140,000
Other assets at 31 October 2010	425,000
	565,000

Effective rate on notional transfer (s 66(3)–(5))

	Gross	Tax on 2010/11 scale
	£	£
Settlor's seven-year cumulative total at commencement of settlement (1 November 1980)	Nil	Nil
Notional transfer (no addition or related settlement)		
Chargeable amount as above	565,000	48,000*
	565,000	48,000*

(* 565,000 – 325,000 = 240,000 @ 20%)

Actual full rate is three tenths of effective rate:

$$\frac{48,000}{565,000} \times \frac{3}{10} = 2.549\%$$

Fund had been relevant property throughout the ten years since preceding ten-year anniversary: no reduction of full rate

Tax payable: $2.549\,\% \times 565,000 =$ £14,401

A relevant property ten-year charge arises in respect of Diana's and Emily's settlements (combined, as if the property were still comprised in Alan's Will trust) on 15 June 2016, calculated as follows:

A.6 Alan's Will Trust (re Diana's and Emily's Settlements) — 15 June 2016 — relevant property ten-year charge

Chargeable amount (s 64(1))	
Relevant property at ten-year anniversary:	
Fixit Ltd shares at 14 June 2016 (now quoted)	
Diana's settlement	160,000
Emily's settlement	160,000
Other assets at 14 June 2016	
Diana's settlement	310,000
Emily's settlement	430,000
	1,060,000

Effective rate on notional transfer (s 66(3)–(5))

	Gross	*Tax on 2016/17 scale*
	£	£
Notional cumulation:		
Settlor's seven-year cumulative total at commencement of settlement (15 June 1976)	7,000	Nil
Notional transfer (no addition or related settlement)		
Chargeable amount as above	1,060,000	148,400*
	1,067,000	148,400*

(* 1,067,000 – 325,000 = 742,000 @ 20%)

Actual full rate is three tenths of effective rate:

$$\frac{148,400}{1,060,000} \times \frac{3}{10} = 4.2\%$$

Tax payable: $4.2\% \times £1,060,000 =$ £44,520

Clare's settlement suffers a further relevant property ten-year charge on 1 November 2020, calculated as follows:

A.7 Clare's Settlement — 1 November 2020 — relevant property ten-year charge

Chargeable amount (s 64(1))

	£
Relevant property at ten-year anniversary:	
Fixit Ltd shares at 31 October 2020	220,000
Other assets at 31 October 2020	530,000
	750,000

Effective rate on notional transfer (s 66(3)–(5))

	Gross	*Tax on 2020/21 scale*
	£	£
Settlor's seven-year cumulative total at commencement of settlement (1 November 1980)	Nil	Nil
Notional transfer (no addition or related settlement)		
Chargeable amount as above	750,000	85,000
	750,000	85,000

(* 750,000 – 325,000 = 425,000 @ 20%)

Actual full rate is three tenths of effective rate:

$$\frac{85,000}{750,000} \times \frac{3}{10} = 3/4\%$$

Fund had been relevant property throughout the ten years since preceding ten-year anniversary: no reduction of full rate

Tax payable: $3/4\% \times £750,000 =$ £25,000

B.

The position up to and including the ten-year anniversary of Clare's settlement on 1 November 2000 is unchanged from **part A.** Thereafter the exit charge and ten-year charges affecting Diana's and Emily's settlements are computed individually in relation to those settlements, without reference to the position of Alan's Will trust (which had in fact come to an end and been wound up): see **explanatory note 3(b)**. The revised calculations for those charges are set out below. The position in 2008 in relation to the accumulation and maintenance fund appointed under Diana's settlement, and the ten-year charges arising in 2010 and 2020 in relation to Clare's settlement, are unchanged from **part A**.

B.1 Diana's Settlement — relevant property exit charge on 9 December 2000

3 February 1999 — recalculated rate of (notional) ten-year charge on Alan's Will Trust

Chargeable amount (s 64(1))

Assumed relevant property at ten-year anniversary (see **explanatory note 10**):	£	£
Fixit Ltd shares at 22 May 1999 (1/3 x 120,000):	40,000	
Less: 100% business property relief	(40,000)	Nil
Other assets at 22 May 1999 (1/3 x (871,000 – 256,000)):		205,000

Effective rate on notional transfer (s 66(3)–(5))

	Gross	*Tax on 2000/01 scale*
	£	£
Settlor's seven-year cumulative total at commencement of settlement (3 February 1989)	Nil	Nil
Notional transfer (no related settlement and no other property in settlement) (see **explanatory note 10**)		
Chargeable amount as above	205,000	Nil*

* (205,000 – 234,000) = Nil @ 20%

Actual full rate is three tenths of effective rate:

$$\frac{0}{205{,}000} \times \frac{3}{10} = 0\ \%$$

9 December 2000 — relevant property exit charge on Diana's settlement

Appropriate fraction (s 69(4))

Number of complete quarters in period to 8 December 2000 elapsed since ten-year anniversary: 3 February 1999 to 2 November 2000	7	quarters
Less: Number of complete quarters in period to 8 December 2000 elapsed before Diana's and Emily's shares became relevant property on Barbara's death on 22 May 1999: 3 February 1999 to 22 May 1999	(1)	quarter
Numerator of appropriate fraction	6	fortieths

Rate applicable (s 69(1)–(2))

Full rate before appropriate fraction derived from recalculated (notional) ten-year charge calculation as above	0.00%
Rate applicable to exit charge	$0\ \% \times \frac{6}{40} = 0\%$

Chargeable amount (s 65(2)(b)) and tax payable	*Gross*	*Tax at calculated rate applicable*	*Net*
Amount by which value of relevant property is less immediately after chargeable event, grossed up:			
Property appointed onto accumulation and maintenance trusts	£250,000*	£Nil	£250,000
(* Grossing up at 0% equates to a gross chargeable value 250,000)			

B.2 Diana's Settlement — 3 February 2009 — relevant property ten-year charge

Chargeable amount (s 64(1))

Relevant property at ten-year anniversary:	
Fixit Ltd shares at 2 February 2009 (now quoted)	85,000
Other assets at 2 February 2009	255,000
	340,000

Effective rate on notional transfer (s 66(3)–(5))

		Gross £	*Tax on 2008/09 scale* £
Notional cumulation:			
Settlor's seven-year cumulative total at commencement of settlement (3 February 1989)	Nil		
Exit charges within preceding ten years	250,000	250,000	
Notional transfer (no addition or related settlement)			
Chargeable amount as above		340,000	55,600*
		590,000	55,600*

(* 590,000 – 312,000 = 278,000 @ 20%)

Actual full rate is three tenths of effective rate:

$$\frac{55{,}600}{340{,}000} \times \frac{3}{10} = 4.906\%$$

Number of complete quarters elapsed since preceding ten-year anniversary before the fund became relevant property on Barbara's death on 22 May 1999:

3 February 1999 to 22 May 1999 = 1 quarter

Tax payable: $4.906\,\% \times \frac{40-1}{40} \times 340{,}000 =$ £16,263

B.3 Emily's Settlement — 20 March 2009 — relevant property ten-year charge

Chargeable amount (s 64(1))

Relevant property at ten-year anniversary:	
Fixit Ltd shares at 19 March 2009 (now quoted)	110,000
Other assets at 19 March 2009	385,000
	495,000

Effective rate on notional transfer (s 66(3)–(5))

	Gross	Tax on 2008/09 scale
	£	£
Notional cumulation:		
Settlor's seven-year cumulative total at commencement of settlement (20 March 1989)	Nil	
Exit charges within preceding ten years	Nil	Nil
Notional transfer (no addition or related settlement)		
Chargeable amount as above	495,000	36,600*
	495,000	36,600*

(* 495,000 – 312,000 = 183,000 @ 20%)

Actual full rate is three tenths of effective rate:

$$\frac{36,600}{495,000} \times \frac{3}{10} = 2.218\%$$

Number of complete quarters elapsed since preceding ten-year anniversary before the fund became relevant property on Barbara's death on 22 May 1999:

20 March 1999 to 22 March 1999 =	0 quarters
Tax payable: $2.218\ \% \times \frac{40-0}{40} \times 495,000 =$	£10,979
	£16,263

B.4 Diana's and Emily's Settlements — 3 February 2019 and 20 March 2019 respectively — relevant property ten-year charges

The value of the property in both settlements is the same and so the same amount is charged to tax on the respective ten-year anniversaries as follows:

Chargeable amount (s 64(1))

Relevant property at ten-year anniversary:	
Fixit Ltd shares at 19 March 2019	190,000
Other assets at 19 March 2019	400,000
	590,000

Effective rate on notional transfer (s 66(3)–(5))

		Gross	Tax on 2018/19 scale
		£	£
Notional cumulation:			
Settlor's seven-year cumulative total at commencement of settlement (20 March 1989)	Nil		
Exit charges within preceding ten years	Nil	Nil	
Notional transfer (no addition or related settlement)			
Chargeable amount as above		590,000	53,000*
		590,000	53,000*

(* 590,000 – 325,000 = 265,000 @ 20%)

Actual full rate is three tenths of effective rate:

$$\frac{53,000}{590,000} \times \frac{3}{10} = 2.695\%$$

Tax Payable	£590,000 x 2.695% =	£15,900

Explanatory Notes

Inheritance tax treatment of granddaughters' reversionary interests

(1) A reversionary interest – a future interest under a settlement whether vested or contingent, see IHTA 1984 s 47 – is excluded property, apart from certain exceptions not relevant to the Example (s 48(1), see **Example A5(a)(iv)** and **Example A5 explanatory note 1**). Excluded property is not relevant property (s 58(1)(f)).

The interests of Alan's granddaughters under his Will, assigned to the trustees of their respective settlements, were (so long as Barbara's life interest continued) absolute interests in remainder, not dependent on the granddaughters fulfilling any qualifying condition such as surviving Barbara or reaching some stated age, and were thus vested rather than contingent interests. On Barbara's death these interests came into possession, and thereby ceased to be reversionary interests. They were now therefore (absolute) interests in possession, but the trustees of the granddaughters' settlements were not beneficially entitled to them. The property subsequently transferred to those trustees from Alan's Will Trust replaced these absolute IIPs; but the property held by the trustees was relevant property from the time of Barbara's death since excluded property status ceased then with the reversionary status of the interests.

(2) Each of the granddaughters is a beneficiary of her own discretionary settlement; but in Clare's case the gifts with reservation rules do not apply because she set up the settlement before 18 March 1986. While Diana's and Emily's settlements, made on 3 February 1989 and 20 March 1989 respectively, are still in existence and they are still beneficiaries of them, the settled property for the time being is property subject to a reservation within FA 1986 s 102; if they die while that remains the case, or within seven years after it ceased to be the case, the trust property will be taken into account for the purpose of the IHT charge on their estates (and may give rise to a liability of the settlement trustees as the persons in whom the property is vested, at least by way of a liability to reimburse Diana's and Emily's personal representatives under s 211(3)); but that does not alter the fact that, after Barbara's death, the property in Diana's and Emily's settlements are within the relevant property regime and subject to IHT charges under that regime; no credit is given for such charges against any charge by virtue of the gifts with reservation rules, though the value of the property subject to a reservation would clearly be reduced by any relevant property charges that had arisen in the meantime.

Identity of the settlor for the purposes of the inheritance tax relevant property rules

(3) Settlor is widely defined (in reasonably familiar terms) by s 44. Where this definition results in more than one person being a settlor 'and the circumstances so require', Pt 3 (the settled property rules) applies as if the settled property [derived from each] were comprised in separate settlements (s 44(2)).

There are however two rules under which property comprised in one settlement as a matter of trust law may be deemed to be comprised in a different settlement, possibly with a different settlor, for the purpose of the IHT rules relating to settlements without a qualifying IIP in Pt 3 Ch 3 (ie not confined to the relevant property rules but including for example the rules for age 18-to-25 trusts in s 71F); but this deeming treatment is not applicable for more general IHT purposes beyond these rules, even for the other settled property chapters of Pt 3 (and see **explanatory note 14**).

(a) If property moves from one settlement direct to another, without a person becoming beneficially entitled to the property itself in between, it is treated as staying in the transferor settlement (s 81).

This rule is modified in relation to transfers that took place before 10 December 1981 but after 26 March 1974, or where a reversion to a qualifying IIP was settled before 10 December 1981. In such a case the property is only deemed to have stayed in the same settlement if the switch took place by the same disposition.

In **part A** of the Example the transfers from Alan's Will trust to the three granddaughters' settlements took place following Barbara's death in May 1999, and so after 10 December 1981; none of them is therefore protected by the first part of the modification just referred to. In the case of Clare's settlement, but not those of Diana or Emily, the settlement of the reversionary interest took effect before 10 December 1981. Therefore, for the purpose of the relevant property and other rules in Pt 3 Ch 3, the property in fact transferred to Diana's and Emily's settlements is treated, by virtue of s 81, as remaining comprised in Alan's Will trust; but the property transferred to Clare's settlement is unaffected by s 81 and the relevant property rules apply to that settlement on its own.

(b) An initial qualifying IIP of the settlor or the settlor's spouse/civil partner will result in the settlement being treated as not being made until neither of them has a qualifying IIP, and as made by the one who last had the qualifying IIP (s 80). (Where the settlement was actually made on or after 22 March 2006, this can apply only to immediate post-death interests and disabled person's interests.) For further discussion of this rule see **Example B17 explanatory note 14**, and for an example of the implications see **Example B17 part B.4(ii)**.

This is the position in **part B** of the Example: Barbara's life interest was a qualifying IIP, and whereas in **part A** Barbara was Alan's daughter, in **part B** she was his wife. Accordingly, for the purpose of the relevant property rules there was by virtue of s 80 no settlement until that life interest came to an end on Barbara's death.

Of course, at that same point in time as a factual matter the entire trust fund of Alan's Will trust ceased to be settled property under that trust because the three reversionary interests vested absolutely in possession, bringing the trust to an end. There is thus a question as to how s 80 and s 81 should interact.

(i) One approach might be to hold that a deemed settlement by Barbara should be regarded as having come into existence, momentarily, under s 80 before the property passed into the three reversionary settlements – so that s 81 would then operate on the property ceasing to be comprised in that deemed settlement when it in fact passes into the daughters' settlements.

(ii) The opposite approach would be to regard the words 'becomes held on trusts under which neither of [the settlor or his spouse/civil partner] is beneficially entitled to an interest in possession', in the second half of s 80(1), as referring solely to trusts whereby the property would remain settled property under the (actual) settlement, ie, in the Example, under Alan's Will trust. On this view, whilst the first half of s 80(1) would still apply (treating Alan's Will trust as not being a settlement for the relevant property rules while Barbara's IIP continued), the second half would not operate to give rise to a deemed settlement because no property became 'held on trusts' of that description.

It is thought that (ii) represents the better view, and this is the basis on which **part B** of the Example proceeds. The main reasons for this conclusion are:

- that (i) involves giving wider effect to artificial statutory deeming provisions than their clear purpose requires (see *Marshall v Kerr* (1995) or *Russell v IRC* (1988)) – it would superimpose a second deeming (continuance under s 81) onto an initial deeming (the momentary deemed settlement under s 80); and
- that if (i) were correct it would (and in startling contrast to the basic position under s 81 in **part A** of the Example), result in Clare's settlement, as well as those of Diana and Emily, being caught up in the effects of the statutory deeming because the protective terms of s 81(3) could not be fulfilled on the 'momentary settlement by Barbara' analysis: this 'momentary settlement' would be 'the first settlement' to which it was attempted to apply s 81(1), and the reversionary interest that was settled before 10 December 1981 was not 'expectant on the termination of a qualifying interest in possession subsisting under the first settlement' so interpreted.

Ascertaining the ten-year anniversary date of settlements for the purposes of inheritance tax

(4) The cycle of ten-year charges usually starts from the 'commencement of the settlement' (s 61(1)) – which of course requires as a first step clarification of what is the settlement for the purpose of these rules, see above.

The commencement of the settlement is the date on which the settlement first had property comprised in it: s 48A. That is not necessarily the date written at the top of the trust deed, though it frequently will be unless the position is complicated by ss 80 or 81 (above). So a settlement of a token cash sum, to which a substantial addition is later made, will commence at the date when the cash sum was received by the trustees. (This is the principle behind the use in certain contexts of 'pilot settlements', established initially with a modest cash sum and envisaging substantial later funding into two or more such trusts with, therefore, separate commencement dates such as not to be related settlements; two main contexts are when funding lifetime pilot trusts on the settlor's death, or when dividing a gift (eg of shares) between several trusts as was explored in *Rysaffe Trustee Co (CI) Ltd v IRC* (2003). However, the use of pilot trusts as a planning mechanism has been negated by the changes made by F(No 2) A 2015 Sch 1 para 2 which requires, in respect of ten-year charges arising on or after 18 November 2015, the counting of 'same-day additions' in working out the notional transfer by reference to which the rate of tax applying at a ten-year anniversary is calculated. See **Example C12 part B** for a discussion of same-day additions.)

(5) Where property has moved from one settlement to another and s 81 applies (see **explanatory note 3(a)** above), the basic rule still applies, so that it will be the commencement date of the *transferor* settlement which determines the cycle of ten-year charges. (It is not impossible that s 81 could operate in relation to two successive transfers – from settlement A to settlement B, and then some years later from settlement B to settlement C – and in that case it would be the commencement date of settlement A which set the cycle of ten-year anniversaries for both settlement B and settlement C.)

Accordingly in **part A** of the Example the ten-year anniversaries of Diana's and Emily's settlements on 3 February 2009 and 20 March 2009 respectively do not give rise to any charge under the relevant property regime since those settlements contain no property other than what was (in reality, but not for relevant property purposes) transferred from Alan's Will trust following Barbara's death. If Diana or Emily had settled additional property apart from the reversionary interests, that property would have been the subject of ten-year charges on those respective dates; as demonstrated in the Example, both of them suffer a ten-year charge on the property derived by each from Alan's Will trust on 14 June 2006 and 14 June 2016 (the 30th and 40th anniversaries of Alan's death), computed as though the property in each case remained comprised in Alan's Will trust.

(6) There is however an exception to the basic rule in s 61(1), relating to the provisions of s 80 regarding initial qualifying IIPs of the settlor or the settlor's spouse/civil partner (**explanatory note 3(b)** above). Here, even though the property is treated as not becoming comprised in the settlement for Pt 3 Ch 3 purposes until the initial qualifying IIP (or successive IIPs, if all in favour of those persons) has ended, the ten-year charge cycle will start from the commencement of the actual settlement conferring the initial qualifying IIP (the 'true settlement' to use the terminology in **Example B17 explanatory note 14**), see s 61(2).

Accumulation and maintenance trust appointment under Diana's settlement – inheritance tax treatment

(7) The appointment on to accumulation and maintenance trusts in December 2000 involved the property concerned ceasing to be relevant property (see s 58(1)(b)), which gave rise to an exit charge under s 65. In **part A** this is calculated in relation to Alan's Will trust by virtue of s 81 as above. The appointment was on a net basis so, in ascertaining the amount to be charged to tax on that occasion it is necessary to gross up the £250,000 appointed fund at the rate applicable to the exit charge.

The exit charge arises after the first ten-year anniversary of Alan's Will trust (in fact, after the second, in June 1996), so it is calculated under s 69. The basic rule of s 69 is to use the rate that applied to the preceding ten-year charge (updated for any subsequent reduction of IHT rates by virtue of Sch 2 para 3). Since there was in fact no ten-year charge because there was no relevant property at the ten-year anniversary (due to Barbara's qualifying IIP), that might without more suggest a rate of 0%; but in fact it is necessary to take account of s 69(2) (and s 69(2A) in respect of exit charges occurring on or after 18 November 2015) which applies where, on or after the most recent ten-year anniversary, property has become comprised in the settlement (not relevant here) or property which was comprised in the settlement immediately before the ten-year anniversary, but was not relevant property at that time, has become relevant property (which is the case with the property that in reality passed into both Diana's and Emily's settlements on Barbara's death, though treated for Pt 3 Ch 3 purposes as still comprised in Alan's Will trust). Where this is the case, the preceding ten-year charge has to be recalculated, for the purpose of establishing the rate applicable under s 69, on the assumption that the property that thus changed its status (from non-relevant to relevant property) had been relevant property at the ten-year anniversary, but valued at the date when it in fact became relevant property (here the date of Barbara's death, see s 69(3)).

The same provision applies in **part B** of the Example to require recalculation of the (otherwise non-existent) ten-year charge, to include the value of property which had since become relevant property; but in this case, having regard to the conclusion in **explanatory note 3(b)** above regarding the interaction (or otherwise) between ss 80, 81, the question is confined to Diana's settlement on its own (where the non-relevant property at the preceding ten-year anniversary was the reversionary interest ie excluded property), and the date is different because, with s 81 not applying, the cycle of ten-year charges runs from the date Diana's settlement in fact first had property (the reversionary interest) comprised in it, namely 3 February 1989 so that the recalculation is in respect of the ten-year anniversary on 3 February 1999. Nevertheless the rate scale to be used is the one in force at the date of the exit charge (9 December 2000), since this scale was more lenient than the one in force in February 1999 (Sch 2 para 3).

There is a second aspect to the fact that property in the settlement had become relevant property since the preceding ten-year anniversary. This relates to the calculation of the appropriate fraction under s 69(4). This applies referentially s 68(3), which provides for quarters to be excluded from the numerator of the fraction if they had fully expired before the property became (or last became) relevant property.

(8) For the treatment of accumulation and maintenance trusts from 6 April 2008, following expiry of the transitional period provided under FA 2006, see **Example C16**.

In the present Example the former accumulation and maintenance trust fund will be aggregated with the remainder of the property in Diana's settlement for the purpose of the next ten-year charge (15 June 2026 in **part A**, 3 February 2019 in **part B**). That fund will therefore at first sight feature twice in the notional chargeable transfer used to calculate that ten-year charge (**explanatory note 9** below): both in the amount being subjected to the ten-year charge at that time (see para (a) of that note), and in the prior cumulative total under para (ii) of that note. In these circumstances s 67(6), applied by s 66(5), applies to prevent double-counting; for an instance of this see **Example C12(a)**.

Notional chargeable transfer for calculating the rate of the inheritance tax ten-year charge

(9) The principles for calculating a relevant property ten-year charge, under s 66, are explained in **Example C11 explanatory note 2**. The components of the notional chargeable transfer used for that purpose (in so far as a ten-year anniversary occurring before 18 November 2015) can be summarised as being:

Value transferred:

(a) relevant property being subjected to the ten-year charge, valued immediately before the ten-year anniversary; plus

(b) other property in the same settlement which was not relevant property when it became comprised in the settlement and has not subsequently become relevant property while remaining comprised in the settlement, valued immediately after it became comprised in the settlement; plus

(c) property comprised in a related settlement immediately after it commenced, valued at that time.

Prior cumulative total:

(i) chargeable transfers made by the settlor in the seven years ending on the day the settlement commenced, excluding transfers made on that day or before 27 March 1974; plus

(ii) amounts on which relevant property exit charges have been levied in the preceding ten-year period (ie since the commencement of the settlement or the preceding ten-year anniversary).

In respect of ten year charges arising on or after 18 November 2015, component (b) above is no longer taken into account, in component (c) only the relevant property comprised in a related settlement is counted and additional components in respect of same day additions are included.

In **part A** of the Example, the relevant property in Diana's and Emily's settlements, which features in component (a) of the value transferred, was in fact comprised in the deemed settlement (Alan's Will trust) immediately after it commenced, and was not relevant property at that time because it was subject to Barbara's qualifying IIP. However, it is prevented from being double-counted, through inclusion in component (b), because that component excludes property which has since become relevant property. (It is immaterial whether or not it remained relevant property having once become relevant property; so the fund appointed on to accumulation and maintenance trusts in December 2000, which shares the same history, does not re-enter the computation under this heading on leaving the relevant property regime.) The property which ultimately passed into Clare's settlement, however, is counted within component (b).

As to component (i) of the prior cumulative total, when Alan died, the legislation provided for cumulation of chargeable transfers throughout a donor's lifetime, but starting only from the introduction of capital transfer tax on 27 March 1974; and all transfers of value that were not exempt were chargeable transfers (potentially exempt transfers did not exist before 1986). However, for the purpose of the relevant property rules under s 66(5)(a) (ten-year charges) and s 68(4)(b) (exit charges before the first ten-year anniversary) the relevant period is restricted to seven years in any case, excluding transfers before that date. The annual exemption at that time was £1,000 (with a transitional extension to include transfers before 6 April 1976 which would have attracted the small gifts exemption for estate duty purposes – not relevant in the Example). The settlor's cumulative total is permanently built in to relevant property computations relating to his settlement – **part A** illustrates that, subject to the exclusion of transfers made before 27 March 1974 it does not matter how long ago the chargeable transfers took place, so long as they were within seven years before the commencement of the settlement or (if s 67(1), (2) apply, see **Example C10 explanatory note 7 and Example C11 explanatory note 2**(e)) before the settlor added property to the trust.

(10) In **part A** of the Example, the exit charge on the appointment of accumulation and maintenance trusts in Diana's settlement – treated as part of Alan's Will trust as explained in **explanatory note 3**(a) – is calculated under s 69, the basic rule in which is to use the rate of tax (before any discount by the appropriate fraction under s 66(2)) which applied at the preceding ten-year anniversary. But the relevant property which, at the date of the exit charge, is treated as comprised in Alan's Will trust (being the property which in fact was comprised in both Diana's and Emily's settlements) was not relevant property at the preceding ten-year anniversary of Alan's Will trust, so the rate of ten-year charge must be recalculated as though that property had been relevant property at the date of the ten-year charge (s 69(2)). However, the valuation date at which to include it is in these circumstances not the ten-year anniversary but rather when it became (or last became) relevant property, which in the Example was immediately after Barbara's death on 22 May 1999 (s 69(3)). Any quarters (since the last ten-year anniversary) which had fully expired before the property in question became (or last became) relevant property are then excluded from the number of quarters otherwise used to calculate the appropriate fraction for the purpose of the exit charge (s 69(4), applying s 68(3)).

Because the Fixit Ltd shares in Alan's Will Trust constitute a relatively small minority holding and are quoted on the Alternative Investment Market, the values of smaller parcels than the whole immediately after Barbara's death are taken in the Example to be equal to an exact corresponding fraction of the value of the whole parcel held by the trustees of Alan's Will.

When calculating the equivalent exit charge in **part B** of the Example, there is no property in Diana's settlement which was not, and has never become, relevant property, such as to form component (b) in the value transferred under the recalculated notional ten-year charge; all the settled property was originally excluded property (the reversionary interest), which was not then relevant property, but the whole trust fund became relevant property when that interest came into possession on Barbara's death.

Inheritance tax excluded property where deeming provisions apply

(11) Where property is in fact comprised in one settlement, but is deemed by s 80 or s 81 to be comprised in a different settlement, then certain tests in connection with the excluded property rules are tightened up as a precaution against avoidance. (Again these provisions operate only for the purposes only of Pt 3 Ch 3, but in this instance not including ss 78, 79 dealing with heritage property.) In particular:

(a) The usual rule for settled property situated outside the UK is that it is excluded property if the settlor was not domiciled (or deemed domiciled) anywhere in the UK at the time the settlement was made (s 48(3)). Before 22 July 2020 (the date on which the Finance Act 2020 was passed), if however s 81 applied so as to deem the property to be comprised in a different settlement (the deemed settlement – namely the transferor settlement, out of which the property in question passed into a separate settlement) from the one it is actually comprised in (the true settlement), then by virtue of s 82(1), (3) excluded property status applies only if both the settlor of the true settlement and the settlor of the deemed settlement were not UK domiciled (or deemed domiciled) at the time the true settlement in question was made. This means that where a settlor established two trusts before becoming UK domiciled, the trustees were able to transfer property between the two trusts after he had become UK domiciled without jeopardising the excluded property of the transferred property (deemed still to be in the transferred settlement). On or after 22 July 2020, non-UK property transferred to another trust will be excluded property only if the settlor of the deemed settlement remains non-UK domiciled immediately before the transfer or has died before the transfer. Where the settlor has become domiciled in the UK at the time of the transfer and is still alive at that time, the property (now comprised in the true settlement) will no longer be regarded as excluded property in relation to the deemed settlement (s 82A). This means that where the settlor of the settlements has become UK domiciled by the time the property is transferred, the property loses its excluded property status (unless the settlor has died).

Section 80 applies where a settlor or his spouse have a QIIP immediately after a settlement comes into existence. In the case of s 80 the deemed settlement will be the one that is deemed to be made by the settlor or his spouse or civil partner when the last successive qualifying IIP of any of those persons came to an end. Before 22 July 2020, non-UK property in such a settlement was excluded property provided the settlor was non-UK domiciled when the trust was first established and the settlor or his spouse or civil partner was non-UK domiciled at the time the QIIP ceased. In other words the excluded property status of the settlement would be re-tested on the death of the settlor or his spouse when the last of them died and so depended on that person's domicile at the time of his death (s 82 prior to its amendment by FA 2020 s 74(3)). On or after 22 July 2020, in addition to re-testing the domicile of the last person to lose their QIIP, the domicile of the settlor of the QIIP trust must also be re-tested at the same time. In other words property that becomes comprised in the deemed settlement will be regarded as excluded property only if the settlor of the QIIP trust was not domiciled in the UK at the time that trust (ie the real trust) was settled and that he was not a formerly domiciled resident for the tax year (s 81B).

Curiously there is no equivalent rule in s 81B, s 82 or s 82A in relation to holdings in authorised unit trusts (AUTs), or shares in open-ended investment companies (OEICs), which attract excluded property status under s 48(3A) if the settlor was neither domiciled nor deemed domiciled in the UK when the settlement was made.

(b) The usual rule for FOTRA securities which are comprised in a settlement, and in which no qualifying IIP subsists, is that they will be excluded property if the relevant qualifying condition (not being resident, or in the case of certain older securities being not ordinarily resident or not domiciled, in the UK) is fulfilled in relation to all known persons for whose benefit the settled property or income from it has been or might be applied (s 48(4)(b), see **Example C19 explanatory note 8**). If however the circumstances are such that s 81 applies (though in this case the circumstances are spelt out afresh rather than referentially to s 81), then by virtue of s 48(5), (6) excluded property status will only apply to such securities if the above test is fulfilled in relation to both the transferor settlement and the transferee settlement.

This rule is, in terms, of no application in a situation where s 80 applies to treat the securities as being comprised in a deemed settlement made by the last IIP beneficiary mentioned in that section. But s 80 applies only for the purpose of Pt 3 Ch 3, and s 48(4) is not included in that Chapter. Therefore, for the purpose of s 48(4) the FOTRA securities will be comprised at all times in the original (true) settlement, and it will be the known beneficiaries of that settlement (which will include the erstwhile holder(s) of the qualifying IIP which caused s 80 to apply) whose ordinarily resident (and possibly domicile) status must be examined for the purpose of the test under s 48(4)(b). So no additional provision is needed to bring such IIP beneficiaries within the scope of the provision.

(c) If relevant property is invested into FOTRA securities and thereby becomes excluded property under the rule in s 48(4)(b) (see **(b) above**), this would ordinarily give rise to an exit charge under the relevant property regime. In general, s 65(8) provides an exemption from the exit charge in these circumstances provided that the settlor was neither domiciled nor deemed domiciled in the UK when the property became comprised in the settlement. If however, in relation to events occurring before 22 July 2020 (when the Finance Act 2020 was passed), s 80 or s 81 applied as referred to in (a) above, then by virtue of s 82(2), (3) the s 65(8) exemption applies only if both the settlor of the true settlement and the settlor of the deemed settlement were not UK domiciled (or deemed domiciled) at the time the settlement in question was made. In relation to events occurring on or after 22 July 2020, then by virtue of s 81B(3) and s 82A(3), the s 65(8) exemption applies by testing only the common law domicile of the settlor concerned.

Practical inheritance tax issues following a transfer between settlements

(12) Where property in more than one actual trust is deemed to be comprised in a single settlement (which may or may not be one of those concerned, and may or may not still be current as a trust in its own right), this can easily lead to difficulties of information as between the different sets of (actual) trustees, particularly if one or more of them are determined to be secretive or un-co-operative; it may even lead to a need for property in each trust to be valued on a different basis from that which would apply taking the property on its own. Where, for example, two sets of trustees both hold shareholdings in a private company, it will be the aggregate holding that falls to be valued for this purpose. The trustees of each actual settlement will therefore need to maintain contact and provide each other with information as to the status and value of property in their trust – or else they will have to rely on such information being accurately collected and collated by HMRC; HMRC are unlikely to release more than the barest details to one or other set of trustees on grounds of taxpayer confidentiality.

(13) As a matter of inheritance tax computation where s 81 applies, there is a single computation by reference to the original settlement (Alan's Will trust in **part A** of the Example), and the resultant liability will be attributed to the settlements in which the relevant property is actually comprised in proportion to the value of each settlement's property that is being subjected to the charge. As seen in **part A**, the rate applicable on the ten-year charge may be influenced by appointments or distributions made by the trustees of just one of the actual settlements involved (here Diana's settlement). The result might be seen as Diana's settlement taking the benefit of the deemed settlement's nil-rate band in priority to the ten-year charge calculation that affects both her and Emily's settlements (but predominantly Emily's, in terms of remaining value at the date of the ten-year charge). There is no mechanism for adjustment of the ten-year charge between the two settlements to compensate for this, and if the trustees of Diana's settlement were to agree to bear a greater proportion of the ten-yearly charge to that which emerges from the basic computation they might be exposed to criticism from the beneficiaries of that settlement.

(14) It may at first sight be unclear exactly who should be regarded as the trustees in given circumstances for the purposes of liability for the tax under s 201(1), and liability to deliver accounts under s 216(1)(c).

It was seen in **part A** of the Example that the property in Diana's and Emily's settlements is treated by s 81 as remaining in Alan's Will trust for the purposes of Pt 3 Ch 3, and thus for the purpose of the exit charge on 9 December 2000 and the ten-year charge on 15 June 2006. This might be thought to point to the trustees of Alan's Will trust as the persons on whom the primary liability for the tax, and for delivering accounts, would fall, even though it is the trustees of the two transferee settlements who hold the property giving rise to the charge (and even though Alan's Will trust, in the circumstances of the Example, will have been fully wound up).

However, the deeming treatment under s 81 is confined to Pt 3 Ch 3, and the provisions as to liability for tax, and delivery of accounts etc, are contained in Pt 7 and Pt 8 respectively. There is nothing to prevent the references in those provisions to 'the trustees of the settlement' from relating purely to the trustees of the settlement(s) in which the property in question is actually comprised (as opposed to being deemed to be comprised for the purpose of Pt 3 Ch 3, which is concerned essentially just with computational issues (and dates on which computations hinge). It is thought that this interpretation, which has the merit of practicality (though still subject to the issues noted in **explanatory note 12** above), would be accepted by HMRC.

Question

A.

On 4 August 2005 Vikram, domiciled in India, settled £10 million (take from an account held with his bank in India) on a discretionary settlement managed and invested outside the UK and with non-UK-resident trustees. He had never owned any assets situated in the UK (other than personal effects and spending money on his business visits to the UK, none of which he gave away).

On 6 June 2012 the trustees bought a flat in a university town in the UK to accommodate Vikram's son Akhil during his forthcoming studies. It was bought with the proceeds of sale of an asset that was purchased for £100,000 when the settlement was originally made.

On 3 August 2015 the value of the flat, still owned by the trustees, was £325,000. Vikram, who visited the UK for two or three days every month on business, approached you in August 2015 for confirmation as to the trustees' position, having heard from an acquaintance about ten-yearly inheritance tax (IHT) charges on discretionary trusts. He told you he understood the inheritance tax threshold was £325,000 and that the tax only extended to assets within the UK and so he assumed there was no problem for the trust. In answer to a question from you he told you that the rest of the trust fund, which had all remained invested outside the UK from the outset, was worth £14.5 million; of that amount £10 million comprised unquoted shares in the call centre outsourcing company that Vikram runs in Bangalore, which the trustees had subscribed for when Vikram set the company up in November 2005.

(i) Set out the advice that you would have given Vikram in 2015 on the trustees' IHT obligations, and his own position in that regard.

(ii) Would there have been any way in which the position of Vikram's settlement could have been improved by any earlier action taken by the trustees?

(iii) How would your advice to Vikram in relation to the trustees' IHT obligations change if the trust had been settled eight years later in 2013 so that its ten year anniversary would have occurred on 4 August 2023? In this case assume that the trustees purchased the flat on 6 June 2020.

(iv) Explain the effect of the decision of the High Court in *Barclays Wealth Trustees (Jersey) Ltd & Michael Dreeland v RCC* [2018] STC 2465 as to the nature of the property that trustees of excluded property trusts may subsequently acquire after the creation of the trust. What is the effect on this decision of the provisions in Finance Act 2020?

(v) Explain briefly the rules regarding excluded property in the context of a settlement.

B.

Sheila and Ricky, an unmarried Australian couple, had been living in London for ten years on account of Ricky's job when Sheila died unexpectedly on 25 June 2012. Under her Will Sheila left a legacy of £500,000 in trust for their son Shane, to which he was to become absolutely entitled at age 25 but with income to be accumulated in the meantime except so far as the trustees chose to release it to him; and the rest of her estate to Ricky absolutely.

Sheila's estate at her death comprised the house in which they were living in London, valued at £850,000 but subject to a mortgage in favour of the Jersey branch of the Aussie Bank for £800,000; personal effects and cash within the UK worth a total of £135,000; and a portfolio of non-UK investments and cash, managed by the Aussie Bank in Jersey, worth £1.8 million. In May 2008 Sheila had bought a vintage sports car at auction in London for £66,000 and given it to Ricky for his 50th birthday, but had made no other relevant gifts.

Sheila's executors appropriated £500,000 of the Jersey portfolio to Shane's settled legacy soon after Sheila's death. In 2018 Shane started a university course in Sheffield and at his request the trustees on 18 September 2018 purchased a house there for him and his girlfriend to live in. The house cost £200,000, and the remainder of the trust fund was worth £400,000 at that time.

Ricky and Sheila had both anticipated returning to Australia on Ricky's retirement, and Ricky in fact took early retirement in 2021 after Shane had graduated, and did return to live in Australia soon afterwards.

Shane found a job in Sheffield on graduating and was still living in the house when he reached age 25 on 28 February 2024. The house was worth £260,000 at that time and the rest of the trust fund, still invested abroad, was valued at £525,000. The Jersey trustees ask your advice as to whether they have any liability for UK IHT in relation to the house before they transfer it and the remainder of the Jersey portfolio into Shane's name. (They ask you not to concern yourself with income tax or capital gains tax since they are sufficiently familiar with the rules and will be able to supply Shane with the relevant details, from the records they have kept throughout, for inclusion in his 2023/24 UK tax return.) Advise the trustees, and calculate any IHT that may be due.

C.

Dawn died on 13 January 2014 leaving a life interest in her house (worth £650,000) to her friend Yvette (with whom she had been living since 2006), and her residuary estate of £1.5 million (net of the IHT on Dawn's death) in trust for Dawn's only son Gordon. Gordon, who was born on 25 April 1999, was also to receive the house on Yvette's death, on the same terms as the residuary estate, namely that he was to take capital at age 25, with a right to income from age 18; if he were to die under 25, the fund would go to Dawn's brother Ed who had emigrated to New South Wales many years before. Dawn had made a potentially exempt transfer of £81,000 (after available annual exemptions) to Ed four years previously, which became a chargeable transfer as a result of her untimely death.

Gordon went to study economics at university in Los Angeles in August 2019 when he was 20, and had already become severely disillusioned with the British political system. He did not visit the UK again until a short break over Easter in 2023, during which he informed Yvette that he would never be returning to the UK but was now settling permanently in California.

On 17 June 2023 the UK-resident trustees of Dawn's Will, noting that Gordon has not been resident in the UK for several years and is unlikely to return, invest all but £100,000 cash of the trust fund into FOTRA securities – rendering the greatest part of the fund excluded property within s 48(4)(b) because the only possible beneficiaries (Gordon and Ed) are both now resident (and almost certainly domiciled too, so far as relevant) outside the UK.

(i) Advise the trustees as to the inheritance tax implications for them of Gordon's 25th birthday on 25 April 2024, when the value of the FOTRA securities is £1.45 million and the £100,000 not so invested is still held in cash and worth £100,000.

(ii) How would your answer differ if Gordon's birthday had been on 25 March 1998, Dawn's Will had provided for Gordon to become entitled to capital at age 30 rather than age 25, the trustees had nevertheless distributed the whole fund to Gordon on his 25th birthday in the exercise of their discretion but that all other events had occurred on the dates stated and that values remain unchanged? Assume that the trustees pay any tax owed by them on time.

Answer

A.(i)

The ten-year IHT charge that arose on 4 August 2015 was computed as follows.

4 August 2015 — ten-year charge on Vikram's settlement

			Gross £	*Tax on 2015/16 scale* £
Settlor's seven-year cumulative total at commencement of settlement (4 August 2005)			Nil	Nil
Notional transfer (no related settlement), see explanatory note 1:				
Relevant property at ten-year anniversary – flat		325,000		
Initial value of other property in settlement:				
Whole initial trust fund	10,000,000			
Less: Cash used to buy flat	(100,000)			
		9,900,000	10,225,000	1,980,000*
			10,225,000	1,980,000*

(*10,225,000 – 325,000 = 990,000 @ 20%)

Actual full rate is three tenths of effective rate:

$$\frac{1,980,000}{10,225,000} \times 30\ \% = 5.809\%$$

Number of complete quarters elapsed since commencement of the settlement before the flat became relevant property on 6 June 2012:

4 August 2005 to 4 May 2012 = 27 quarters

Tax payable: $5.809\ \% \times \frac{(40-27)}{40} \times 325{,}000 =$ £6,136

The trustees were liable for this amount of tax, which fell due for payment on 28 February 2017, that is six months after the end of the month in which the ten-year anniversary occurred (IHTA 1984 s 226(3C)) and would have attracted interest (at 3% the rate in force until 21 August 2018 when it was increased to 3.25%) on any amount paid late (s 233). Because the tax was attributable to the value of land, it could have in theory been discharged, at the option of the trustees, by ten equal yearly instalments, the first being payable on the due date for tax as above (s 227); but because the tax for the time being unpaid would have continued to attract interest at the rate from time to time applicable (payable as an addition to each annual instalment, s 227(3)) and the trustees would have had the resources to discharge the tax in full at the time it fell due, it would have been unattractive to exercise the instalment option in such a case. The tax and interest while unpaid is a charge on the flat under s 237.

The trustees had (and, if undischarged, will continue to have) an obligation to submit an account in form IHT100 (with event form IHT100d) specifying the property to the value of which the tax is attributable (s 216(1)(c), (4)), and the value of that property. That was prima facie limited to the flat. As noted, however, the initial value of the trust fund, so far as not presently represented by the flat, was also relevant to the calculation of the rate of tax chargeable on the value of the flat, and the account, and this was part of the information that was called for in the event form IHT100d. This obligation is backed by penalty provisions for failure to deliver an account (or failure, or worse, to take reasonable care in its completion).

Since the trustees are not UK resident, Vikram, as settlor of the trust, would also concurrently be liable for the tax chargeable (s 201(1)(d)). He was not personally obliged to submit an IHT account, though.

A.(ii)

The initial value of the settled property which was not relevant property at the date of a ten-year charge in 2015 was only taken into account if it 'was not then [immediately after it became comprised in the settlement] relevant property and has not subsequently become relevant property while remaining comprised in the settlement' (s 66(4)(b)). Therefore it would have been possible to rid the settlement permanently of this 'initial value' factor by bringing the whole of the non-UK property into the UK at some point during the first ten years of the trust's existence, so long as it has been re-exported (reinvested abroad) before the date of the ten-year charge and before an event that would otherwise trigger an exit charge.

In the case of Vikram's settlement, this would have been difficult after the trustees had invested into Vikram's company, but could easily have been accomplished in the first few months of the settlement's existence if the trustees had transferred the cash into a UK bank account in their names and then subsequently transferred it back abroad.

Although the transfer abroad would involve the property in question ceasing to be relevant property, by becoming excluded property under s 48(3), that is expressly exempted from the exit charge otherwise applicable by s 65(7). If that had been done in **part A(i)**, the value transferred by the notional chargeable transfer on the ten-year charge would indeed have been restricted to the current value of the flat, and the rate of IHT payable on the flat would then have been genuinely 0% as Vikram had supposed when seeking advice.

A.(iii)

If Vikram had settled the discretionary trust eight years later, the ten-year IHT charge would then arise on 4 August 2023, this is after 17 November 2015 when legislation had come into force to reform the inheritance tax treatment of relevant property trusts. Part of that reform removes the requirement to take into account the value of trust property that has never become relevant property. On this basis the computation of the ten year charge to be levied on the discretionary trust settled by Vikram in 2013 would be as follows.

4 August 2023 — ten-year charge on Vikram's settlement

		Gross	*Tax on 2023/24 scale*
		£	£
Settlor's seven-year cumulative total at commencement of settlement (4 August 2013)		Nil	Nil
Notional transfer (no related settlement), see **explanatory note 1:**			
Relevant property at ten-year anniversary – flat	325,000		
	325,000		Nil*

(*325,000 – 325,000 = Nil @ 20%)

Actual full rate is three tenths of effective rate:

$$\frac{0}{325{,}000} \times 30\,\% = 0\%$$

Number of complete quarters elapsed since commencement of the settlement before the flat became relevant property on 6 June 2020:

		Gross	Tax on 2023/24 scale
		£	£
4 August 2013 to 4 May 2020 = 27 quarters			
Tax payable:	$0\ \% \times \frac{(40-27)}{40} \times 325{,}000 =$		£Nil

The trustees would not be liable for any tax on the 10-year anniversary so that Vikram's understanding that, in the context of an excluded property trust with no related settlement and in respect of which there is no same-day addition, is correct in that the tax extends only to assets within the UK. The trustees have no obligation to submit an account in form IHT100.

A.(iv)

The advice set out in **part** A(ii) above is, following the changes made on 18 November 2015 to reform the inheritance tax treatment of relevant property trusts, now of historic interest. However, it does, subject to the changes effected by FA 2020 (see below), contain a fundamental point of ongoing significance that if any of the property in an excluded property trust after it is constituted becomes situated in the UK, that property will not be protected from the application of exit and ten-yearly charges as it will then be the relevant property of the trust. A way in which such UK sited property can be protected from such a charge is, before the occasion on which the charge arises, for it to be converted back into non-UK sited property so that it takes on again its character as excluded property. The efficacy of this simple strategy is given added strength from the decision, on appeal, in the case of *Barclays Wealth Trustees (Jersey) Ltd & Michael Dreeland v RCC* [2017] STC 2465.

In that case a settlor created a Jersey resident discretionary trust ('the Jersey Trust') at a time when he was not domiciled in the UK and settled non-UK sited property on it. Subsequently the settlor created a UK resident discretionary trust ('the UK Trust') at a time when he had become deemed UK domiciled. Some of the property in the 'Jersey Trust' was then transferred to the UK trust and converted to UK sited property. Later, just before the ten year anniversary of the Jersey Trust, that property was transferred back to the Jersey Trust and converted to non-UK sited property. The non-UK sited property was still held by the Jersey Trust on the ten year anniversary date.

When the settlor created the Jersey Trust it was, under s 48(3), an excluded property trust being a non-UK resident trust created by a non-UK domiciled settlor and on which was settled non-UK sited property. The property would have been exempt from the 10-year charge had it stayed there. The UK Trust was not an excluded property trust being as it was settled by a UK domiciled individual. When the property of the Jersey Trust was transferred to the UK Trust it lost its excluded property status. When it was transferred back to the Jersey Trust and converted to non-UK sited property, the taxpayer claimed that the property re-acquired its exclude property status and so was not chargeable to IHT at the time of the Jersey Trust's ten year anniversary. HMRC disagreed and the case came before the High Court which found for HMRC. However, on appeal the Court of Appeal reversed the decision of the High Court, preferring the taxpayer's arguments.

The basis on which the taxpayer argued that the property had re-acquired its excluded property status was by reference to a complex set of statutory provisions. Despite the actual transfer of the property to the UK Trust, s 81 deems the property to remain settled in the Jersey Trust. In spite of that, s 82 deems that property to lose its excluded property status because the UK Trust was settled by a UK domiciled individual. (The property deemed to remain in the Jersey Trust under s 81 would not have lost its excluded property status had the UK Trust been settled by a non-UK domiciled person.) This was the position of the property at the time of the ten year anniversary of the Jersey Trust. Nevertheless the taxpayer argued that as the property had, prior to the trust's ten year anniversary, become non-UK sited while being comprised in the Jersey Trust it reacquired its nature as excluded property being non-UK sited property held on a trust created by a non-UK domiciled settlor. In other words reliance was placed on the terms of s 48(3) to negate the effect of s 82.

HMRC took a different approach and argued on the basis of s 43 which defines a settlement and a settlor. They concentrated on the event of the transfer back to the Jersey Trust and argued that it constituted a disposition whereby the property was held on the Jersey Trust so that, in accordance with the definition of a settlement in s 43(2), that was an act that created a settlement. At that date the settlor was domiciled in the UK and so the transferred property comprised in the act of settlement was not excluded property under s 48(3). HMRC's case involved identifying the transfer of the property back by the UK Trust as being a disposition which gave rise to a settlement of the property which is subject to it. The property is settled and it then takes its place in the overall settlement (that is the Jersey Trust).

Whilst not adopting wholesale the arguments of HMRC, the High Court preferred their argument. The Court of Appeal was not so convinced and adopted the arguments of the taxpayer. It held that the Jersey Trust was a single trust for IHT purposes constituted by a number of separate dispositions of property. IHTA 1984, s 48(3) required one to look at a single settlement as it was constituted from time to time, whether by one or a series of transfers into the settlement and provided that any foreign property comprised in it was excluded property unless the settlor was UK domiciled when the settlement was made. That time was to be determined in accordance with the usual principles of trust law and would normally be the occasion on which the settlor first executed a trust instrument and constituted the trust by providing property to the trustee. When property was transferred from the Jersey trust to the UK trust, s 81 was engaged which deemed the property to have remained in the Jersey trust. When the property was subsequently transferred back to the Jersey trust, the force of the deeming in s 81 became spent. But since the property of the Jersey trust was deemed to have remained in that trust throughout, it was not consistent with that deeming to argue that the property was at the same time the subject of a disposition into that trust. If the property had never left the Jersey trust it would never have been anything other than excluded property. There was no mischief which required the language of the Act to be interpreted so as to produce the opposite conclusion merely because there was an intermediate transfer of the property between the two settlements.

The court did however leave open the situation where a non-UK domiciled person settles an excluded property trust, later acquires a UK domicile and then makes further transfers of overseas property into that settlement. It refused to express an opinion whether the same outcome would apply in such circumstances.

The matter is, of course, a lot simpler where only a single trust is concerned (as in the case of Vikram's trust). The simple expedient of altering the situs of trust property is an effective way of sheltering the property in an excluded property trust, notwithstanding the domiciliary status of the settlor of the excluded property trust may be altered at the time the situs of the settled property is altered.

Finance Act 2020 (FA 2020) has introduced provisions to reverse the decision in the *Dreeland* case. Section 73 has altered the time at which the excluded property status of settled property is tested. The decision was based on the wording of IHTA 1984 s 48(3) as it stood before the enactment of FA 2020 on 22 July 2020, namely that the status of the property was tested at the time the settlement was made. Now, on or after 22 July 2020, the status of the property is tested at the time it became comprised in the settlement (and IHTA 1984 s 48(3) has been amended accordingly). Consequently, non-UK property added to a trust will be excluded property only if the settlor was non-UK domiciled when the property was settled. So if a settlor, after becoming UK domiciled, adds property to a trust made at a time when he was not UK domiciled, that property is not excluded property (although any existing excluded property in the settlement is not tainted and will remain excluded property). However, there are no rules determining how any tracing exercise is to be done when the original and added property have become intermingled. The changes to IHTA 1984 s 48(3) take effect from 22 July 2020 (the day on which FA 2020 was passed) but are made retrospective so that even if a settlor added property to a trust before that day (when he had become UK domiciled), the property so added will not be excluded property (FA 2020 s 73(11)). In the context of the observation made in the first paragraph above, this means that trustees will be able to convert UK sited property back into non-UK sited property (so that it takes on again its character as excluded property) only where at the time of the conversion the settlor of the trust is still non-UK domiciled. This is the position in which the trustees of Vikram's trust find themselves; however, had Vikram become UK domiciled when the trustees converted the property, the property would not have regained its excluded property status.

Like changes are made in relation to the status of the property of a trust comprising a holding in an authorised unit trust (AUT) or open-ended investment company (OEIC) (by virtue of IHTA 1984 s 48(3A)). The changes made by FA 2020 apply also in relation to an individual who is a formerly domiciled resident (s 48(3E)) and clarify that income arising from settled property which is accumulated so that it becomes trust property takes its nature from the property from which it was derived (IHTA 1984 s 48(3F)). So, if on or after 22 July (when FA 2020 was enacted), income deriving from settled property that is accumulated is treated as becoming comprised in the settlement at the time the property itself became comprised in the settlement and itself becomes excluded nor non-excluded property as the case may be.

The effect of s 81, as relied upon the court, has been grandfathered so that it applies only to transfers between trusts that occurred before 22 July 2020 (the day on which FA 2020 was passed) (FA 2020 s 74). The changes that affect s 81 are described in **Example C18 explanatory note 11.**

A.(v)

Prior to the 22 July 2020 (the date of enactment of Finance Act 2020), settled property situated outside the UK where the settlor was domiciled outside the UK at the time the settlement was made is excluded property (s 48(3)). However, from 6 April 2017 this rule is subject to exceptions as follows. Where the settlor of property comprised in a settlement is not domiciled in the UK at the time the settlement was made, the property is not excluded property at any time in a tax year if the settlor was a formerly domiciled resident in that year (s 48(3B)). An individual is a 'formerly domiciled resident' in relation to a tax year if he was born in the UK, his domicile of origin was in the UK, he was resident in the UK in that tax year and he was resident in the UK for at least one of the two tax years immediately preceding that tax year (s 272). This means that settled property loses its excluded property status in a tax year where the individual is resident in that tax year provided he has the status of being a 'formerly domiciled resident' in the year in which he is so resident (s 48(3E)). FA 2020, s 73 has effected changes to IHTA 1984 s 48(3) and s 48(3E) so that the status of property as excluded property is tested at the time the property becomes comprised in the settlement (rather than when the settlement is made). The changes are described in **part A(iv)** of this Example and are retrospective in their application.

Settled property will also not be excluded property (from 6 April 2017) where it comprises certain shares in a close company, certain interests in partnerships and certain loans and the value of the property is attributable to UK residential property (s 48(3) rider). Consequently the charge to inheritance tax is extended to UK residential property that is held or financially supported by or through overseas structures by trustees or individuals who are domiciled outside the UK. Shares in a close company and an interest in a partnership (provided it is at least a 5% holding or interest) will not be excluded property where the value of the shares or partnership interest is directly attributable to UK residential property. In determining the value of the shares or interest that is attributable to a UK residential property, the liabilities of the company or partnership are to be attributed to all the property it holds on a rateable basis. This means that where a company or partnership holds a UK residential property as well as other property, any liabilities of that company or partnership will be attributed to each property in proportion to its value. The rights of a creditor under a loan are not excluded property where the loan has been used by an individual, partnership or trustees to finance the acquisition (maintenance or enhancement) of UK residential property or the acquisition of shares in or an interest in a close company or partnership and the acquisition (maintenance or enhancement) by that company or partnership of a UK residential property. A loan ceases to be within these exclusionary rules where the UK property interest which the loan financed is disposed of. Where the shares in a company, the interest in a partnership or the creditor rights of a loan (which have been described above) are sold, the proceeds are also not treated as excluded property for a two-year period starting with the date of disposal of the property concerned. These rules are contained in Sch A1 and are discussed in further detail in **Example A5 part d(i) and (ii)**.

B.

The trust for Shane created on 25 June 2012 under Shelia's Will was an age 18-to-25 trust within s 71D. Shane became entitled to an interest in possession on his 18th birthday on 28 February 2017, but this is not a qualifying IIP and the settled property remained subject to the age 18-to-25 trust provisions until Shane became absolutely entitled on his 25th birthday on 28 February 2024. At that time, the whole of the trust property ceases to be settled property to which s 71D applies, and an IHT exit charge therefore arises under s 71E(1)(a). This is calculated in accordance with s 71F since the circumstances are within s 71F(2)(a). The trustees are liable for this charge, for which they will need to retain adequate funds before distributing the balance to Shane. The charge is calculated as follows:

28 February 2024 — age 18-to-25 trust exit charge on Sheila's Will Trust

	Sheffield house	*Jersey portfolio*	*Total value*
Calculation of chargeable amount (s 71F(4))			
Amount by which value of s 71D property is less immediately after chargeable event	£260,000	£525,000	£785,000

	Sheffield house	*Jersey portfolio*	*Total value*
Calculation of Relevant Fraction (s 71F(5), (6))			
(Calculated separately for Sheffield house and remainder of trust fund)			
Value at date of divergent treatment (purchase of Sheffield house)	£200,000	£400,000	£600,000
Number of complete quarters in period to 27 February 2024 elapsed since Shane turned 18 on 28 February 2017: 28 February 2017 to 28 February 2024	28	28	quarters
Less: Number of complete quarters in that period throughout which settled property in question was excluded property:			
Sheffield house: never non-excluded property	0		quarters
Jersey portfolio: 28 February 2017 to 28 February 2024		(28)	quarters
Numerator of time element of Relevant Fraction	28	0	fortieths
Relevant fraction is three tenths of time element			

Calculation of Settlement Rate (s 71F(7)–(9))

				Gross £	Tax on 2023/24 scale £
Settlor's seven-year cumulative total at commencement of settlement (25 June 2012):					
May 2008 — gift of vintage sports car			66,000		
Less: annual exemptions	2008/09	3,000			
	2007/08	3,000	(6,000)	60,000	Nil
Notional transfer (no related settlement and no later addition to trust)					
Value of settled property immediately after settlement commenced				500,000	47,000*
				560,000	47,000*

(*560,000 – 325,000 = 235,000 @ 20%)

Settlement rate is effective rate: $\frac{47,000}{500,000} \times 100 =$ 9.400%

Tax payable (s 71F(3))

(Calculated separately for Sheffield house and remainder of trust fund — s 71F(6))

Chargeable amount × Relevant Fraction × Settlement rate

On portion of trust fund represented by Sheffield house at date of charge	$260,000 \times (\frac{27}{40} \times \frac{3}{10}) \times 9.4\,\% =$	£5,132
On portion of trust fund represented by Jersey portfolio at date of charge	$525,000 \times (\frac{0}{40} \times \frac{3}{10}) \times 9.400\,\% =$	£Nil
Total tax payable		£5,132

C.(i)

The trust for Gordon under Dawn's Will was an age 18-to-25 trust within s 71D. Gordon became entitled to an interest in possession on his 18th birthday on 25 April 2017, but this is not a qualifying IIP and the settled property remained subject to the age 18-to-25 trust provisions until Gordon became absolutely entitled on his 25th birthday on 25 April 2024. At that time, the whole of the trust property ceases to be settled property to which s 71D applies, and an IHT exit charge therefore arises under s 71E(1)(a). This is calculated in accordance with s 71F since the circumstances are within s 71F(2)(a). The trustees are liable for this charge, for which they will need to retain adequate funds before distributing the balance to Gordon.

The fact that the whole of the trust property on 25 April 2023 was excluded property (see **explanatory note 8**) is no protection against that exit charge, given that excluded property status has not prevailed at all times since Gordon's 18th birthday; in this respect the rules for age 18-to-25 trusts are different from those that concern relevant property, since excluded property cannot be relevant property and is therefore not subject to an exit charge (see **explanatory note 1**). (However see **part C(ii)** para (a), and the slight variant in **explanatory note 3**, for another consideration in such cases.)

The exit charge is calculated as follows:

25 April 2024 — age 18-to-25 trust exit charge on Dawn's Will Trust residuary fund

Calculation of chargeable amount (s 71F(4))

Amount by which value of s 71D property is less immediately after chargeable event:	
Cash	100,000
FOTRA securities	1,450,000
	£1,550,000

Calculation of Relevant Fraction (s 71F(5), (6))

	Cash	FOTRA securities	
Number of complete quarters in period to 24 April 2024 elapsed since Gordon's 18th birthday: 25 April 2017 to 24 April 2024	28	28	quarters
		(3)	
Less: Number of complete quarters in that period throughout which settled property in question was excluded property:		25	
Cash: 25 April 2017 to 24 April 2024	0		quarters
FOTRA securities: 25 July 2023 to 24 April 2024			quarters
Numerator of time element of Relevant Fraction	28		fortieths
Relevant fraction is three tenths of time element			

Calculation of Settlement Rate (s 71F(7)–(9))

		Gross £	Tax on 2024/25 scale £
Settlor's seven-year cumulative total at commencement of settlement (13 January 2014):			
May 2010 – Gift to Ed after annual exemptions		75,000	Nil
Notional transfer (no later addition to trust)			
Value of settled property immediately after settlement commenced:			
Residuary estate net of IHT	1,500,000		
House (life interest to Yvette) (see **explanatory note 7**)	650,000	2,150,000	380,000*
		2,225,000	380,000*

(*2,225,000 – 325,000 = 1,900,000 @ 20%)

$$\frac{380,000}{2,150,000} \times 100 = 17.674\%$$

Settlement rate is effective rate

Tax payable (s 71F(3))

Chargeable amount × Relevant Fraction × Settlement rate

On portion of trust fund retained in cash at date of charge	$100,000 \times (\frac{28}{40} \times \frac{3}{10}) \times 17.674\% =$	£3,712
On portion of trust fund represented by FOTRA securities at date of charge	$1,450,000 \times (\frac{25}{40} \times \frac{3}{10}) \times 17.674\% =$	£48,051
Total tax payable		£51,763

C.(ii)

The significant difference from **part C(i)** is the fact that the trust, in this variant, provided for Gordon's capital entitlement to arise later than the age of 25 which is one of the core requirements for an age 18-to-25 trust. Accordingly the trust will have entered the relevant property regime on 13 January 2014.

Three events subsequent to that date are significant under the relevant property regime:

(a) The purchase of the FOTRA securities by the trustees on 17 June 2023. As explained in **explanatory note 8** the property concerned thereby became excluded property; since excluded property is not relevant property (s 58(1)(f)), the FOTRA securities ceased to be relevant property, which is the basic trigger for an exit charge under s 65(1). Section 65(8) provides a limited exemption from this exit charge where the reason for the property ceasing to be relevant property is where it is invested into FOTRA securities and thereby becomes excluded property by virtue of s 48(4)(b); but that exemption is of no avail in respect of Dawn's Will Trust because it only applies if the settlor of the trust was not domiciled in the UK when the settlement was made (or after 22 July 2020 (ie the date of enactment of FA 2020), but with retrospective effect, when the property became comprised in the settlement). The charge arises before the first ten-year anniversary of the settlement and is therefore calculated under s 68. The amount subject to the charge has to be grossed up because the charge is based on the loss of value to the relevant property in the trust and the liability for tax arising from the charge is also taken into account in determining the value of the relevant property that remains.

(b) 13 January 2024 is the first ten-year anniversary of the settlement, being the tenth anniversary of Dawn's death. As such, a ten-year charge arises. The FOTRA securities are not relevant property and so are not subject to the charge, though the cash is; but the exit charge incurred when the money invested into FOTRA securities left the relevant property regime is part of the IHT accumulation used to calculate the effective rate of tax on the notional transfer under s 66.

(c) The distribution to Gordon on his 25th birthday, making him absolutely entitled at that time (five years sooner than would have been the case apart from the exercise of the trustees' discretion), would ordinarily give rise to an exit charge on the remaining cash as it ceases to be relevant property at that time. However, Gordon's 25th birthday on 25 March 2024 falls within three months after the ten-year anniversary of the settlement on 13 January 2024, and as a result s 65(4) negates the exit charge that would otherwise have arisen. The absolute entitlement to the FOTRA securities has no IHT consequences so far as the trustees are concerned.

The calculations in relation to events (a) and (b) above are as follows:

17 June 2023 — relevant property exit charge on Dawn's Will Trust residuary fund

Calculation of effective rate on notional transfer (s 68(4), (5))

		Gross	Tax on 2023/24 scale
		£	£
Settlor's seven-year cumulative total at commencement of settlement (13 January 2014):			
May 2010 – Gift to Ed after annual exemptions		75,000	Nil
Notional transfer (no later addition to trust)			
Value of settled property immediately after settlement commenced:			
Residuary estate net of IHT	1,500,000		
House (life interest to Yvette) (see **explanatory note 7**)	650,000	2,150,000	380,000*
		2,225,000	380,000

(* 2,225,000 – 325,000 = 1,900,000 @ 20%)

Effective rate $\frac{380,000}{2,150,000} = 17.674\%$

Calculation of appropriate fraction (s 68(2), (3))

Number of complete quarters in period to 16 June 2023 elapsed since commencement of settlement: 13 January 2014 to 12 April 2023	37	quarters
	37	fortieths

Appropriate fraction is three tenths of time element

Rate chargeable on exit charge (s 68(1))

Appropriate fraction of effective rate $(\frac{37}{40} \times \frac{3}{10}) \times 17.674\% = 4.905\%$

Amount on which tax is charged (s 65(2))

Amount by which value of relevant property is less immediately after chargeable event

		Gross	Tax on 2022/23 scale	Net
		£	£	£
Net transfer, grossed up (s 65(2)(b)):				
Value of FOTRA securities becoming excluded property	1,450,000	1,524,791*	74,791**	1,450,000

$(*\frac{1,450,000}{100\% - 4.905\%})$

(** 1,524,791 @ 4.905%)

Tax charged £74,791

13 January 2024 — ten-year charge on Dawn's Will Trust residuary fund

Amount on which tax is charged (s 64(1))			
Value of relevant property immediately before ten-year anniversary:			
Cash (see **explanatory note 9**)			100,000
Calculation of effective rate on notional transfer (s 66(3)–(5))			
Inheritance tax accumulation (s 66(5))			
Settlor's seven-year cumulative total at commencement of settlement (13 January 2014):			
May 2010 – Gift to Ed after annual exemptions		75,000	
Cumulative relevant property exit charges in preceding 10 years		1,524,791	
		1,599,791	254,958*
(* 1,599,791 – 325,000 = 1,274,791 @ 20%)			
Notional transfer (s 66(4))			
Amount subject to ten-year charge			
Residuary estate	100,000		
House (life interest to Yvette) (see **explanatory note** 7)	650,000	750,000	150,000**
		2,349,791	404,958
(** 2,349,791 – 325,000 = 2,024,791 @ 20%)			

Effective rate (above nil-rate band) $\frac{150,000}{750,000} = 20.000\%$

Applicable rate before time-fraction is three tenths of that rate 6.000%

Tax charged $100,000 \times 6.000\ \% =$ £6,000

Explanatory Notes

The influence of excluded property on the rate of IHT under the relevant property regime

(1) It is tempting for the trustees of a non-domiciled settlor's discretionary settlement, who have always invested abroad, to think that they can safely afford to hold UK-located property up to the level of the current IHT nil-rate band, even at the time a ten-year charge is due, on the basis that the UK property would be the only property subject to the charge on that occasion. Whilst the last proposition, in terms, is indeed correct, it is not true that it is just the UK property which serves to set the rate of tax. Discounting for the moment same-day additions and their effect (as to which see **Example C12**), under s 66(4) the value transferred by the notional chargeable transfer that is used for that purpose comprises three (or on or after 18 November 2015, two) elements:

(a) the value on which the ten-year charge is imposed;

(b) in respect of ten year charges arising before 18 November 2015, 'the value immediately after it became comprised in the settlement [initial value] of any property which was not then relevant property and has not subsequently become relevant property while remaining comprised in the settlement'; and

(c) the initial value of the property (related property only on or after 18 November 2015) comprised in any related settlement immediately after it commenced.

It is (b) above which brought in the rest of the trust fund in **part A(i)** of the Example, at its initial value, giving rise to a near-maximum 'effective rate' of tax on the notional transfer despite the absence of any previous chargeable transfers by settlor. The initial value of trust assets for this purpose is unaffected by any business property relief or agricultural property relief that might otherwise be in point (eg in relation to the transfer of the assets in question to the trustees), since the initial value is simply the value of the assets in question in the trustees' hands, not the value transferred by any transfer of value.

It is always necessary in any event to check that the settlor has not made other chargeable transfers (of UK-situated assets, having regard to his foreign domicile) in the seven years leading up to the formation of, or any addition to the settlement – see s 67, **Example C10 explanatory note 7** and **Example C11 explanatory note 2(e)**.

In **part A(i)** the actual rate chargeable is reduced by reason of the flat not having been relevant property throughout the ten-year period since formation of the settlement, under s 66(2). However, if a UK asset has been held continuously since soon after the start of the ten-year period, the reduction in the full rate otherwise applicable, on account of the time-fraction in that subsection, will not be great.

The problem just alluded to has been greatly reduced by the reform brought about with effect from 18 November 2015 as element (b) above has been repealed and element (c) is limited to relevant property in a related settlement. With effect from 18 November 2015, it is now possible to ignore non-relevant property in the same settlement, a related settlement and a settlement on which same-day additions are made. The effect of the reform is, in the context of the Example, illustrated in **part A(iii)**.

(2) The fact that the unquoted shares in the outsourcing company would attract 100% business property relief, if they were themselves subject to an IHT charge within the trust, is of no assistance to the trustees in respect of the calculation of the ten-year charge. The shares are excluded property in any event, and so not relevant property; so business property relief on them cannot reduce the amount being charged to IHT. By contrast, if the company in question had been a UK company and the shares UK-situated assets, the shares would have been relevant property and thus within point (a) rather than (b) in **explanatory note 1** above; their value for the purpose of establishing the amount on which the ten-year charge is levied would then have been reduced by business property relief, as they had been owned by the trustees for more than two years, and it is that reduced amount which would have entered into the value transferred by the notional chargeable transfer.

(3) If trustees transfer part of the trust fund into the UK, with a view to restoring excluded property status soon afterwards as in **part A(ii)** of the Example, they may do this (provided Vikram is still non-UK domiciled) by changing its location to non-UK property or invest part of the money into UK authorised unit trusts (AUTs) or open-ended investment companies (OEICs) (both of which since 16 October 2002 also attract excluded property status when held in a settlement made by a non-UK domiciled settlor, see s 48(3A)). (A warning used to be sounded against trustees investing in AUTs and OEICs, but this is, following the enactment of FA 2013 s 173, no longer a problem (see **explanatory note (11)** of **Example C10** for more details)). The excluded property status of the trust fund cannot however be restored where the settlor has become UK domiciled at the time the trustees re-acquire the non-UK sited property or the units in the AUT or the OEIC.

Interests in possession under age 18-to-25 trusts for the purposes of inheritance tax

(4) If Sheila's Will in **part B** had provided (expressly, or through the operation of a statutory provision such as Trustee Act 1925 s 31 in England and Wales) for Shane to become entitled to the income of the trust fund from age 18, pending his absolute entitlement to capital if he attained 25, in principle that would still leave the trust governed by the IHT provisions for age 18-to-25 trusts in s 71D. An IIP can subsist under the age 18-to-25 trust rules, although such an IIP is not a qualifying IIP (see **Example C3 explanatory note 1**).

However, in the case of a death on or after 22 March 2006, an IIP that arises within two years after the death, provided no qualifying IIP has in fact subsisted in the meantime in the property settled by the Will, will be treated under s 144(3), (4) as though it had subsisted from the death and will therefore be an immediate post-death interest. Thus if on the face of the Will a trust will fall within s 71D and the beneficiary will obtain an IIP at age 18, a beneficiary aged between 16 and 18 at the date of death will, from age 18, have an IPDI and s 71D will in his case be regarded as having not applied in the meantime. This is essentially the same backdating effect as if the Will had provided for a fully discretionary trust which had been appointed onto IIP terms within the two years after the testator's death (see **Example C14 explanatory note 8**).

Inheritance tax treatment of excluded property in age 18-to-25 trusts

(5) In most contexts, if property is excluded property at the time an IHT charge would otherwise arise, then it is not subject to the charge. That is true, in particular, of the relevant property exit charge under s 65(1): if excluded property leaves the trust, it is not relevant property (s 58(1)(f)), and so no charge can arise on its 'ceasing' to be relevant property.

The exit charge on age 18-to-25 trusts under s 71E, in circumstances falling within s 71F(2) where the beneficiary is aged over 18 (which might be regarded as events within the policy of s 71D as a 'favoured' regime – see **Examples C16** (particularly **explanatory notes 7, 8**) and **C17** (particularly **explanatory note 12**)) is modelled very closely on the relevant property exit charge during the first ten years of a settlement's existence (as to which see **Example C11 explanatory note 6**). It might therefore be expected that excluded property leaving an age 18-to-25 trust in these 'favoured' circumstances would be exempt from the exit charge otherwise applicable.

However, that is not the approach taken by s 71F. Instead, the fact that the property in question is excluded property goes only to a potential reduction of the fraction that would otherwise be the 'relevant fraction'. Under s 71F(6), where the amount on which the exit charge is being levied is attributable to property that was excluded property at any time during the period between the beneficiary's 18th birthday and the date of the exit charge, then any quarter throughout which the property was excluded property is disregarded in establishing the relevant fraction.

This approach reflects what has always been the case in relation to exit charges under the various 'special trust' regimes under or referential to s 70(7) (which includes the harsher formula under s 71G for the s 71E exit charge on age 18-to-25 trusts where the circumstances are outside the 'favoured' policy for such trusts); but it nevertheless provides a curious contrast with the relevant property exit charge on which the s 71F exit charge was so closely based. Whilst age 18-to-25 trusts may not feature very often in the planning armoury of non-domiciled settlors, the approach taken in s 71F(6) will restrict the scope for securing full exemption on the beneficiary becoming absolutely entitled, except where the property concerned remains excluded property throughout the time between the 18th and 25th birthdays of the beneficiary concerned.

Inheritance tax treatment of excluded property in Sheila's estate

(6) In **part B** of the Example no spouse exemption is available on Sheila's death since she is unmarried; but it is clear that she is not domiciled in the UK (and she has not lived in the UK for long enough to have a UK deemed domicile under s 267), so since the mortgage liability reduces the value of the house (s 162(4)) only £185,000 of Sheila's estate (£135,000 of personal effects and cash, plus (£850,000 – £800,000) in respect of the house) is included in the chargeable transfer on her death. (The remainder of Sheila's estate, comprising the Jersey portfolio, is excluded property and so outside her estate for IHT purposes on death, see s 5(1)(b).) That £185,000 chargeable transfer, even after taking account of the £60,000 (after annual exemptions) lifetime gift to Ricky just over four years before Sheila's death, fell wholly within the nil-rate band of £325,000 applicable at Sheila's death in 2012/13. For notes on domicile and its significance for IHT purposes see **Examples A5(c)** and **B7**.

Separate IIP funds settled at the same time as an age 18-to-25 trust – inheritance tax treatment

(7) In **part C(i)** of the Example the house left in trust for Yvette is subject to an IIP in her favour, but is nevertheless counted (at its value immediately after Dawn's death) towards the value transferred by the notional transfer used to calculate the Settlement rate for the purpose of s 71F. In respect of a charge arising on or after 18 November, this is so only where the house and the residuary estate are regarded as comprised in a single settlement with two sub-funds (s 71F(9)(a)). It is not the case where two separate (but inevitably related, because both commenced on Dawn's death) settlements arise as related settlements are taken into account only where they themselves are in the 18–25 trust regime (s 71F(9)(b)) and here the trust created for Yvette is a qualifying IIP trust being a trust in which an immediate post death interest subsists (s 49A). The answer in the Example is prepared on the basis that a single settlement was created on Dawn's death.

This mirrors the position after 17 November 2015 in relation to relevant property trusts, where under both s 66(4)(c), for ten-year charges, and s 68(5)(a), (b), for exit charges before the first ten-year anniversary, other relevant property in a related settlement, both count towards the notional chargeable transfer. (See **part C(ii)** of the Example for an illustration of this – the calculation of the effective rate under s 68(4), (5) is almost identical to that under s 71F(7)–(9).) The exception to this, on a ten-yearly charge, is where property comprised in the same settlement was initially, or has subsequently become, relevant property; but this exception merely proves the rule, since in that case it will either still be relevant property and counted towards the notional transfer under s 66(4)(a) or (apart from the exemption under s 65(7) on becoming foreign-situated excluded property, see **part A(ii)** of the Example and **explanatory note 3**) will have given rise to an exit charge which then cumulates towards the next ten-year charge under s 66(5)(b).

If Dawn and Yvette had been civil partners at the time of Dawn's death, then Gordon would have benefited in two ways: first, property subject to Yvette's IIP would have attracted exemption on Dawn's death, reducing the IHT charge at that time which was payable out of the residuary estate (though by the same token increasing the initial value of the residuary fund for the purpose of calculating the Settlement rate); and secondly the IIP fund would no longer have counted towards establishing the Settlement rate because, as a result of s 80, that fund would have been treated for the purpose of IHTA 1984 Pt 3 Ch 3 (which includes the provisions for age 18-to-25 trusts) as not having become comprised in a settlement at Dawn's death (see **Example C17 explanatory note 14**). (Had Yvette later died at a time when Gordon had not yet become absolutely entitled in remainder then the house would be treated as settled by Yvette at that time, again as a result of s 80.)

FOTRA securities as excluded property for inheritance tax

(8) FOTRA [free of tax to residents abroad] securities are excluded property when in the beneficial ownership of a person of a description specified in the conditions of issue (see item (vii) in the list at **Example A5(a)**). For securities issued on or after 30 April 1996 and before 17 July 2013 (no relevant securities being extant before 30 April 1996), the condition is not being ordinarily resident in the UK and for securities issued on or after 17 July 2013 the condition is not being resident in the UK. Where, on or after 6 April 2013 a person becomes the beneficial owner of a security issued before 17 July 2013, if obtaining the exemption is conditional on being not ordinarily resident in the UK, the statutory rule conferring the exemption has effect as if obtaining the exemption were conditional instead on being not resident in the UK (FA 2013 Sch 46 para 114). In other words, for securities acquired before 6 April 2013, the exemption will continue to be based on an individual being not ordinarily resident.

This treatment of FOTRA securities is mirrored for settled property in two alternative ways: under s 48(4) they are excluded property if:

(a) a person of the relevant description is entitled to a qualifying IIP in them; or

(b) where no qualifying interest in possession subsists in them, all known persons for whose benefit the settled property or income from it has been or might be applied, or who are or might become beneficially entitled to or to an interest in possession in it, are persons of the relevant description.

The domicile of the settlor in these cases is for most purposes immaterial, in contrast to the position for property situated overseas and for AUTs and OEICs (see **explanatory note 3** above); but, historically, as in **part C(ii)** of the Example, it is of crucial significance in determining under s 65(8) whether or not a relevant property exit charge arises on property in a relevant property trust becoming excluded property by virtue of s 48(4)(b) (see **Example C18 explanatory note 11(c)**).

The reference in s 48(4)(b) to 'the settled property' is taken to be to the fund held on separate trusts, from the outset, in which the FOTRA securities are comprised; in **part C** of the Example it would be confined to the residuary estate and would not include the house in which Yvette has a qualifying IIP (because it meets the conditions for an immediate post-death interest). (The decision at first instance in *Minden Trust (Cayman) Ltd v IRC* (1984) that 'the settled property' in this context means the whole of the property comprised in the settlement, not merely the exempt gilts and the property representing or represented by them, is thought to be distinguishable in that the circumstances there involved property that had been derived from an earlier, continuing, settlement with a wider range of beneficiaries, whereas in the Example (even if the house is correctly regarded as part of the same settlement rather than a separate, related, settlement) there have never been, nor will be under the terms of the trust, any possible beneficiaries of the residuary fund other than Gordon and Ed. On appeal in the *Minden Trust* case the Court of Appeal expressed no opinion on this issue, having decided the case in favour of the trustees on other grounds since overtaken by what is now s 48(5), see below.) On this basis the fact that neither Gordon nor Ed is resident in the UK in June 2023 (in the context of the facts in **part C(i)**) or at any material time thereafter causes the FOTRA securities purchased by the trustees at that time to be excluded property from that time onward until the settlement comes to an end on Gordon's becoming absolutely entitled the following year.

If property passes from one settlement to another without any person becoming absolutely entitled to it (and not merely to an IIP in it), then s 48(4)(b) will only be satisfied in relation to the property comprised in the transferee settlement if its conditions are also satisfied in relation to the property comprised in the transferor settlement: s 48(5). This anti-avoidance rule (introduced in response to the sort of arrangements carried out in the *Minden Trust* case in early 1978) does not apply where the transfer between settlements occurred before 20 April 1978, and applies in somewhat modified form if the transfer took place after 19 April 1978 but before 10 December 1981. Furthermore, by s 48(6) it does not apply if the transfer takes place as a result of the vesting of a reversionary interest expectant on the termination of a qualifying IIP, and the reversionary interest was settled on the trusts of the transferee settlement before 10 December 1981. (These rules in s 48(5), (6) echo similar rules applicable to the excluded property status of property situated outside the UK under s 82 (as it applied before 22 July 2020 when FA 2020 came into effect), see **Example C18 explanatory note 11(b)**.)

Miscellaneous points

(9) In **part C(ii)** the tax due in respect of the exit charge arising on 17 June 2023 falls due for payment on 31 December 2023, so that, in terms of the assumption stated in the Example, at the time of the ten-year anniversary charge that liability has been discharged.

(10) For penalties in connection with IHT accounts see **Example A7(c)**. For further notes on ten-year charges and exit charges in relation to relevant property trusts see **Examples C10–C13**. For modifications to excluded property rules in cases where property is deemed for certain purposes to be comprised in a different settlement from the one in which it is actually comprised, see **Example C18 explanatory note 11**. For capital gains tax in relation to non-UK resident trusts see **Example D4**.

(11) The inheritance tax settled property provisions relating to excluded property were altered with effect from 21 March 2012 with the introduction of IHTA 1984 ss 74A and 74B (FA 2012 s 210). Where an individual, domiciled in the UK, acquires an interest in settled excluded property which, as result of tax avoidance arrangements concerned with that acquisition, gives rise to a reduction in the value of that individual's estate, the property will cease to be excluded property and a charge to inheritance tax will arise in respect of the reduction. The charge will largely replicate the tax treatment that a UK-domiciled individual would incur if the assets within the offshore trusts, which are excluded property and which otherwise would be ignored for inheritance tax purposes, had instead been transferred by him to a UK relevant property trust. The assets settled in the offshore trust, upon ceasing to be treated as excluded property, will become subject to the relevant property regime with its attendant charges on exits and ten year anniversaries.

Capital Gains Tax for Trustees and Personal Representatives

Question

A.

John Bird died on 30 September 2021. By his will he left one half of his estate to his wife (aged 65) and one half to his son (aged 42). His executors, Mrs Bird and her son Rupert, obtained probate on 1 April 2022. There was no inheritance tax payable. The estate, which was valued at £500,500 (gross), included the following assets:

Asset	*Probate value* £
950 shares of £1 each in Bird Enterprises Ltd, a trading company (the other 50 shares being owned by Mrs Bird, who was a director working part-time and had subscribed for the shares at par in February 2001). Rupert was an employee in the company.	235,000
10,000 shares in Computer Games plc, a quoted company	17,500
3,600 shares in Midwest Bank plc held in an ISA following the flotation of the former building society	10,200

Mrs Bird and her son decided to sell Bird Enterprises Ltd because without its founder, Mr Bird, they were too dependent on the skills of individual employees. Although a number of outside offers were made in the meantime, on 31 March 2024 they (ie the executors together with Mrs Bird personally) accepted a bid of £350,000 from the management for the whole of the company.

The Midwest Bank received a takeover offer of £2.50 per share from a High Street bank on 3 April 2023 which Mrs Bird and her son accepted.

On 10 February 2024 Micro plc made a cash offer of £3.30 per share or 4% Redeemable Loan Stock to the same value in any proportions for each share in Computer Games plc (the loan stock is within the definition of qualifying corporate bonds (QCB)).

The administration of the estate was completed 1 April 2024.

Neither Mrs Bird nor her son will have any further capital disposals in 2023/24.

(a) State the capital gains tax payable for 2023/24 if all of the above transactions are undertaken by Mrs Bird and her son as executors (and they accept cash for the Computer Games shares).

(b) Set out alternative suggestions which would have mitigated the tax payable.

B.

Write a brief set of notes on the availability of principal private residence relief, gifts holdover relief, investors' relief and business asset disposal relief (formerly known as entrepreneurs' relief) to the UK resident personal representatives of a deceased estate. Include a note on their capital gains tax treatment if they own plant and machinery and their ability to make a negligible value claim.

Answer

A. The executors of John Bird – tax computations

(a) *Capital gains tax payable for 2023/24*

Estate of John Bird deceased

	£	£	£
Bird Enterprises Ltd — sale proceeds 950 shares March 2024		332,500	
Probate value September 2021	235,000		
Costs of title 0.8%	1,880	(236,880)	95,620
Midwest Bank plc —			
Sale proceeds April 2024 3,600 shares @ £2.50		9,000	
Probate value	10,200		
Costs of title 0.8%	82	(10,282)	(1,282)
Computer Games plc —			
Sale proceeds February 2023 10,000 shares @ £3.30		33,000	
Probate value	17,500		
Costs of title 0.8%	140	(17,640)	15,360
			109,698
Annual exemption			(6,000)
Chargeable gains for the year			103,698
Capital gains tax payable by executors @ 20% (see **Example A24 a (iii)**)			£20,740

Mrs Bird

Bird Enterprises Ltd —			
Sale proceeds 50 shares March 2024		17,500	
Cost		(50)	
		17,450	
Annual exemption		(6,000)	
Qualifying chargeable gains for the year		11,450	
Capital gains tax payable by Mrs Bird @ 10% on £11,450 (see **explanatory note 10** re: business asset disposal relief)			1,145
Total capital gains tax payable by executors and Mrs Bird (£20,740 + £1,145)			£21,885

(b) *Ways of mitigating tax payable*

The overall tax payable could be mitigated as follows:

Transferring shares in Bird Enterprises Ltd to beneficiaries before sale

If Mrs Bird and her son as executors had transferred, or at least appropriated, the shares to themselves as individual beneficiaries prior to the sale, they would be deemed to have taken the shares at the date of death (without any corresponding disposal by them in their capacity as personal representatives) (TCGA 1992 s 62(4)). This would then have enabled both of them to benefit from business asset disposal relief on the sale, in respect of all the shares sold (see **explanatory note 10**). Their revised personal capital gains tax position for 2023/24 (subject to any losses arising to them as individuals) would be:

Mrs Bird

	£	£	£
Bird Enterprises Ltd —			
Sale proceeds 525 shares March 2024 (166,250 + 17,500)		183,750	
Cost of 50 shares in February 2001	50		
Probate value of 475 shares September 2021	117,500	(117,550)	
			66,200
Annual exemption			(6,000)
Qualifying chargeable gains for the year			60,200
Capital gains tax payable by Mrs Bird @ 10% on £60,200			
			£6,020

Rupert Bird

Bird Enterprises Ltd —			
Sale proceeds 475 shares March 2024 (£332,500/2)		166,250	
Probate value September 2021		(117,500)	48,750
Annual exemption			(6,000)
Qualifying chargeable gains for the year			42,750
Capital gains tax payable by Rupert @ 10% on £42,750			£4,275

The transfer of shares to Mrs Bird and Rupert would, however, be treated as a distribution of the estate's income equal to the lower of the value of the shares transferred and the amount of the estate's income to which they are entitled and would therefore trigger a charge to higher rate tax in their hands. Since the administration was completed within the same tax year (April 2024) as the transfer (March 2024), however, this is irrelevant, since the income would already have been distributed.

Shares in Computer Games plc

The executors could transfer the whole of the shares to themselves as beneficiaries, enabling the beneficiaries to take loan stock, or they could take loan stock themselves as executors and pass it on to themselves as beneficiaries, thus deferring the capital gain. On 3 April 2023, however, they had incurred a loss on the disposal of the Midwest Bank plc shares. To use that loss and also their annual exemption, the executors could take the cash offer on 4,741 Computer Games plc shares and loan stock in respect of 5,259 shares, giving the estate a capital gains tax liability of:

	£	£
Sale proceeds 4,741 shares @ £3.30	15,645	
Proportion of probate value: $\frac{4,741}{10,000} \times 17,640$	(8,363)	7,282
Loss on Midwest Bank plc shares as in (a) above		(1,282)
		6,000
Annual exemption		(6,000)
Chargeable gains		Nil

See **explanatory note 4.**

This enables both the executor's annual exemption and the loss on the Midwest Bank shares to be substantially fully utilised. (Losses incurred by executors can only be offset against a gain accruing to them as executors in the same or a future year and cannot be transferred to beneficiaries. A similar tax saving could have been achieved if the Midwest Bank shares had been transferred to the beneficiaries before the Bank was taken over, so that the loss would arise to Mrs Bird and Rupert. The Computer Games plc shares on which the cash offer was taken could then be reduced so as to realise gains of approximately £6,000 as before.)

Effect of above suggestions

As a result of the above, the capital gains tax payable for 2023/24 would be reduced from £20,740 to £10,295 (6,020 + 4,275), ie by £10,445. Mrs Bird and Rupert would, however, each have redeemable loan stock in Micro plc with accrued gains of:

	£
5,259 shares @ £3.30	17,355
Proportion of probate value $\frac{5,259}{10,000} \times 17,500 =$	(9,203)
Accrued gain	8,152

* See **explanatory note 4.**

Even so, if the loan stock was redeemed over a number of years in which the beneficiary had few other gains, the accrued gain would be covered by the annual exemptions of the years of disposal.

B. UK resident personal representatives – capital gains tax reliefs

(a) *Private residence exemption*

Where following a death, the deceased's private residence is to be sold by his personal representatives, a chargeable gain may arise between death and sale by reason of the appreciation in value of the home. Under s 225A, on their making a claim, the private residence exemption is available to the personal representatives if the property has, both before and after the death, been used as the main residence of individuals who are entitled to 75% or more of the sale proceeds either absolutely or for life. So two conditions have to be met if personal representatives are to be entitled to PPR relief.

First, immediately before and immediately after the deceased's death, the dwelling-house must have been the only or main residence (PPR) of one or more individuals (s 225A(2)). The sub-section does not identify who these individuals are; it will be seen that they need to be the legatees or heirs of the deceased. Since the dwelling-house has to be the PPR of the 'individual' immediately after the deceased's death, the term 'individual' cannot refer to the deceased himself.

The second condition (as set out in s 225A(3)) is that:

(a) the individual or one of the individuals has an entitlement as legatee of the deceased person to (or to an interest in possession in) the whole or any part of the net proceeds of disposal, or two or more of those individuals have such an entitlement (known as a relevant entitlement), and

(b) the relevant entitlement accounts for, or the relevant entitlements together account for, 75% or more of the net proceeds of disposal.

It is clear that the second condition itself comprises two parts. First, dealing with the case where only one individual satisfies the first condition, the individual occupying the dwelling as his main residence at the time of the deceased's death (and immediately after it) must be a legatee to the deceased. This means he must be a person entitled to take under the deceased's will or intestacy. But what must he be a legatee of? The legislation is a little cryptic here – it says that the individual must be entitled to the net proceeds of 'disposal', which means (employing the definition in s 225A(4)(a)) the net proceeds of the disposal of 'the asset' realised by the *personal representatives*. The use of the definite article in this definition indicates that the individual must be a legatee to the proceeds of sale realised on the disposal of the dwelling-house itself. But the proceeds do not have to pass into the absolute ownership of the individual; it is sufficient if they pass into a trust in which the individual has an interest in possession in respect of those proceeds. In short, therefore, the individual mentioned in condition one must occupy the dwelling as his home and be entitled to the (net) proceeds realised by the *personal representatives* when they come to sell that dwelling house.

In the case where there are two or more individuals who occupied the dwelling-house as their PPR, only one of them has to have a relevant entitlement as explained above; but the condition is still met if two or more of them have relevant entitlements. It seems that not all the occupants of the PPR have to be legatees to the (net) proceeds of disposal when the *personal representatives* come to the sell, provided at least one of them is.

The entitlement as legatee must be to the 'net proceeds' of the disposal. Section 225A(4) *d*efines these as the proceeds of the disposal of the dwelling-house realised by the *personal representatives* less incidental costs allowable as a deduction under s 38(1)(c) in computing the gain accruing to the*m* on that disposal (assuming that none of the proceeds is required to meet the liabilities of the deceased person's estate, including any liability to IHT). So it could be that the individuals concerned actually get to receive none or only a proportion of the proceeds of the *personal representatives'* disposal of the dwelling because those proceeds have to be used by them to pay the deceased's debts, but that does not affect the fulfilment of the first limb of the second condition. The fact that the legislation refers to 'proceeds of disposal' rather than the 'consideration from the disposal' seems to indicate that the *personal representatives* must have sold the dwelling-house in order for the condition to be satisfied, although it would seem an arm's length sale is not necessary.

The second limb of the second condition provides that it is necessary that the individual concerned is entitled to at least 75% of the (net) proceeds of disposal realised by the personal representatives on their disposal of the dwelling-house. Where more than one person has a relevant entitlement, then their entitlements together must account for at least 75% of the (net) proceeds. So, in order for this limb of the condition to be satisfied, one first has to ascertain the net proceeds (ie after incidental costs of sale) and then be able to allocate at least 75% of that net amount to the legatees together who have relevant entitlements.

Where an election has to be made to determine which of two dwelling-houses is a PPR in respect of a legatee, the notice under s 222(5)(a) is to be a joint notice between the personal representatives and the individual(s) entitled to occupy the dwelling-house (see condition one below) (s 225A(5)(b)).

Examples

Henry died in 2023 and in his Will he left his home equally to his two cousins, Richard and William. Richard and William had lived with Henry for some years prior to his death. In 2023 Henry's personal representatives sold the home. They are able to make a claim for PPR relief in respect of any gain accruing to them. Richard and William had occupied the home as their PPR immediately before and after Henry's death, and together they are entitled to 100% of the net proceeds of the personal representatives' sale of the home.

Edward died in 2023 and in his Will he left his home equally to his three cousins, John, Michael and Alexandra. Michael and Alexandra had lived with Edward for some years prior to his death. John lived in his own home. In 2024 Edward's personal representatives sold the home. They are unable to make a claim for PPR relief in respect of any gain accruing to them. Although Michael and Alexandra had occupied the home as their PPR immediately before and after Henry's death, together they are entitled only to 66.7% of the net proceeds of the personal representatives' sale of the home.

For detailed notes on the computational aspects of the private residence exemption see **Example M4** in the companion to this book, **Tolley's Taxwise I 2023/24.**

(b) *Gifts holdover relief*

Personal representatives do not qualify for gifts holdover relief under s 165 or s 260, but trustees do. Where the residue of the estate is left on trust, the personal representatives should ensure that assets on which gifts holdover relief is to be claimed have been formally appropriated to the trustees before being gifted to the trust beneficiaries. The trustees are then treated as acquiring the assets at the date of death. The Finance Act 2006 changes to IHT for trusts also impinge on the CGT holdover provisions (as set out in **explanatory note** (8)).

(c) *Business asset disposal relief and investors' relief*

Business asset disposal relief (formerly known and entrepreneurs' relief) and investors' relief is not available in respect of disposals made by personal representatives.

(d) *Exemption from capital gains tax for plant*

Section s 44(1) defines plant as a wasting asset with the result that any gain arising on the disposal of plant which is tangible moveable property is not chargeable to capital gains tax (s 45(1)). In *HMRC v The executors of Lord Howard of Henderskelfe* (2014) the executors of Lord Howard had sold a painting 17 years after his death realising a substantial gain. The deceased, and following his death the executors, had permitted the painting to be used by the company that ran the trade of opening his house to the public. The painting was displayed in that part of the house that was open to the public. The executors argued that the gain arising on the sale of the painting was not chargeable to tax as being plant that was tangible moveable property and was exempt under s 45. HMRC contended that even if the painting was plant in the hands of the company, it was not plant in the hands of the executors as they were not carrying on the trade that engaged its use; when they sold the picture, they were not, therefore, selling any plant.

The Court of Appeal found for the executors. It held that although only items used in a trade, profession or vocation could constitute 'plant' within the meaning of s 44(1)(c), and therefore the plant had to have been in the possession of the trader whose business it was, nothing could be derived from s 44 to suggest a legislative intention that the only disposal of plant to which the s 45(1) exemption could be claimed to apply was a disposal by the trader who had used the plant. Moreover, s 45(1) plainly included no express limitation of its application to disposals of plant by the trader as opposed, for example, to disposals by the lessor or licensor of the plant. The focus was not on the identity of the disponor but on the subject matter of the disposal, namely tangible movable property which was a wasting asset. If the property was plant, it was such an asset. The wording of s 45(1) showed that the exemption was not intended to be confined, in the case of the disposal of plant, to a disposal by the trader. The language of s 45(2) showed that in the case of disposals of plant, the draftsman had in mind that the disponor might be someone other than the trader but that such disponor could still enjoy the exemption.

The court also rejected arguments to the effect that the painting was not actually plant. There was nothing in s 44 to suggest that 'plant' was an asset with a limited life that wasted away with use. What was 'plant' was not identified by the predictable life of a chattel. It was identified by whether or not the chattel passed the test set out in *Yarmouth v France* (1887); and an item was capable of doing so whatever its predicted life. Once an item qualified as 'plant' it was in every case deemed by s 44(1)(c) to be a wasting asset.

The perceived tax advantage achieved in that case has been negated as the case has been overruled with effect from 6 April 2015 by an amendment to s 45 introduced by FA 2015 s 40. The amendment (effected by the introduction of TCGA 1992 s 45(3A),(3B)) ensures that the exemption applies to assets used as plant in a business only where the asset has been used by a disponor as plant for the purposes of his own business. Consequently personal representatives now benefit from the exemption from plant and machinery only if they themselves carry on a trade.

(e) *Negligible value claims*

Trustees, as the owners of an asset, may make a negligible value claim if the asset has become of negligible value whilst owned by them (ss 24(1A), 24(1B)). Where a claim is made, they are treated as having sold and immediately reacquired the asset at the time of the claim for a consideration of an amount equal to the value specified in the claim (s 24(2)(a)). This is likely to result in their realising an allowable loss for capital gains tax purposes. The trustees can, if they so choose, be treated as making the allowable loss at any time in the two-year period preceding the start of the tax year in which the claim is made provided they owned the asset at the earlier time and the asset had become of negligible value at that earlier time (s 24(2)(b)).

In *HMRC v Drown & Leadley (as executors of J J Leadley)* (2017) the question arose whether the executors of a deceased person could make a negligible value claim on behalf of the deceased in respect of shares that had become of negligible before his death but in respect of which the deceased had not himself made a claim. The Upper Tribunal held that a claim could not be so made by the executors on the basis that the shares had become of negligible value before they were owned by them as executors. The possibility of a negligible value claim in respect of the shares had died with the deceased. There was no provision in the legislation that a claim could be treated as made at a time other than that at which it was submitted. The purpose and wording of s 24 suggested that the taxpayer had still to own the asset at the point that a negligible vale claim was submitted in respect of it. A deceased person and his personal representatives could not be equated. The Taxation of Chargeable Gains Act 1992 treated the two as distinct and provided for personal representatives to be deemed to acquire the assets of a deceased person on his death for a consideration equal to their market value (albeit without a corresponding disposal) (s 62). The beginning of the personal representatives' ownership period was determined as a matter of law and fact in accordance with the Act and one cannot merge the distinct personalities of the deceased and his personal representatives.

Similar arguments may be made in relation to claims to loss relief in respect of loans to traders; s 253(3) requires the person who made the qualifying loan to make a claim that it has become irrecoverable (and hence to have realised a allowable loss in respect of the principal that cannot be repaid). Personal representatives cannot make such a claim in respect of a loan made by the deceased.

Explanatory Notes

Capital gains tax treatment of personal representatives

(1) On death the deceased's assets are acquired by the personal representatives at market value (TCGA 1992 s 62(1)(a)), but there is no deemed disposal by the deceased and no capital gains tax is payable as a result of the death (s 62(1)(b)).

(2) The personal representatives – the executors in this Example – are treated as a separate single and continuing body of persons (s 62(3)). All their dealings as personal representatives are completely separate from their dealings as individuals. Capital gains and losses are accordingly computed and assessed on them as personal representatives. Under self-assessment any tax due on capital gains is payable on 31 January following the end of the tax year. The rate of tax on personal representatives' gains is, with effect from 6 April 2016, 28% in respect of disposals of residential property and 20% in respect of disposals of other property (s 1H(5)(6)). Prior to 6 April 2016 a single rate of capital gains tax of 28% applied to personal representatives' gains. See **Example A24 a(iii)**.

(3) The personal representatives are entitled to an annual exemption of the same amount as an individual for the tax year of death and the following two tax years (s 1K(7)). If the administration of the estate has not been completed in that time there is no annual exemption for later years and any gains arising are chargeable at the 20% and 28% rates as the case may be.

Probate valuation costs for the purposes of capital gains tax

(4) When computing the gain or loss on sales of assets by the personal representatives, the cost of acquiring the assets can be increased by the costs incurred in valuing them for probate (*CIR v Richards' Executors* (1971)).

SP2/04 sets out the scale of expenses allowable under s 38(1)(b) for the costs of establishing title in computing the gains or losses of personal representatives on the sale of assets comprised in a deceased person's estate.

	Gross value of estate	*Allowable expenditure*
A	Not exceeding £50,000	1.8% of the probate value of the assets sold by the personal representatives.
B	Over £50,000 but not exceeding £90,000	A fixed amount of £900, to be divided between all of the assets of the estate in proportion to the probate values and allowed in those proportions on assets sold by the personal representatives.
C	Over £90,000 but not exceeding £400,000	1% of the probate value of the assets sold.
D	Over £400,000 but not exceeding £500,000	A fixed amount of £4,000, to be divided as at **B above**.
E	Over £500,000 but not exceeding £1,000,000	0.8% of the probate value of the assets sold.
F	Over £1,000,000 but not exceeding £5,000,000	A fixed amount of £8,000, to be divided as at **B above**.
G	Over £5,000,000	0.16% of the probate value of the assets sold, subject to a maximum of £10,000.

The scale has effect where the death in question occurred on or after 6 April 2004.

A deduction for probate valuation costs only applies where the sale is by the personal representatives and not where the sale is by the beneficiaries themselves. It should, however, be noted that the actual costs, if any, of the *beneficiary* relating to the acquisition of the asset are deductible (s 64(1)(a)), and also any costs of the personal representatives *in transferring* assets to them (s 64(1)(b)). As Mrs Bird and Rupert have undertaken the transactions themselves it is unlikely there are any such costs.

HMRC have agreed (see SP 2/04) the following scale of allowable expenditure under ss 38 and 64(1) for expenses incurred after 6 April 2004 by corporate trustees in the administration of estates and trusts. HMRC will accept computations based either on this scale or on the actual allowable expenditure incurred (but not both).

The scale is as follows:

Transfers of assets to beneficiaries etc

(i) *Publicly-marketed shares and securities*

(A) One beneficiary – £25 per holding transferred.

(B) Two or more beneficiaries between whom a holding must be divided – as **(A) above** to be divided in equal shares between the beneficiaries.

(ii) Other shares and securities – as **(i) above** with the addition of any exceptional expenditure.

(iii) Other assets – as **(i) above** with the addition of any exceptional expenditure.

For the purpose of this statement of practice, shares and securities are regarded as marketed to the general public if buying and selling prices for them are regularly published in the financial pages of a national or regional newspaper, magazine, or other journal.

Actual disposals and acquisitions

(i) Publicly-marketed shares and securities – the investment fee as charged by the trustees.

(ii) Other shares and securities – as **(i) above**, plus actual valuation costs.

(iii) Other assets – the investment fee as charged by the trustees, subject to a maximum of £75, plus actual valuation costs.

Where a comprehensive annual management fee is charged, covering both the cost of administering the trust and the expenses of actual disposals and acquisitions, the investment fee for the purposes of (i), (ii) and (iii) **above** will be taken to be £0.25 per £100 on the sale or purchase moneys.

Deemed disposals by trustees

(i) Publicly-marketed shares and securities – £8 per holding disposed of.

(ii) Other shares and securities – actual valuation costs.

(iii) Other assets – actual valuation costs.

Valuation for capital gains tax where no inheritance tax payable

(5) Where no inheritance tax is payable on death, the values included in the application for probate will not be binding on HMRC for capital gains tax unless specifically agreed with them (see **Example A26 explanatory note 1**). The personal representatives may therefore wish to file form CG34 after the sale of shares in Bird Enterprises Ltd to agree the acquisition cost and gain prior to the submission of the self-assessment return. It must be noted that the CG34 procedure cannot be used in advance of a sale.

The CG34 process involves the completion of form CG34 and its submission to HMRC before the taxpayer files a return but after the disposal has taken place. The details of the transaction and the requisite valuation must be set out on the form. It is necessary to specify the date in respect of which the valuation is required and the taxpayer must put forward their view of the relevant value. The asset must be described in sufficient detail for HMRC to identify it. The calculation of the gain which uses the valuation must also be submitted with the firm as must an estimate of the tax payable. If any reliefs (eg business asset disposal relief) are relied upon they too must be set out. Where unquoted shares in private companies are involved, three years' accounts up to the valuation date must also be supplied. For land, copies of leases must be supplied together with a plan if the land has not been developed.

Where form CG43 has been submitted and full disclosure (free from material error) made, any value agreed by HMRC is binding on them in computing any tax due on the gain. HMRC require three months to check a valuation included in form CG43 and so the form must be submitted more than three months before the filing date of a return (otherwise it will not be processed and the CG43 procedure is automatically terminated).

Shares held by a personal representative in an ISA

(6) Although the shares in Midwest Bank plc were held in an ISA and were not therefore liable to capital gains tax in John Bird's hands, that treatment ceases on death on or before 6 April 2018. The shares are held by personal representatives as a normal chargeable asset. Therefore the loss between death and disposal is available for relief (a gain would have similarly been a chargeable gain).

Disposal of assets by the personal representatives or the beneficiaries of a deceased estate: considerations to be taken into account on deciding appropriate course of action

(7) The executors must carefully consider the taxation implications of selling assets themselves or transferring them to the beneficiaries. These include:

Sale by executors

Capital gains tax rate is 28% in respect of the disposal of residential and non-residential property (between 6 April 2016 and before 5 April 2019 on residential property only) and 20% otherwise.

Annual exemption is available in year of death and two following years only.

Base costs of assets include costs of the estate (SP 2/04, and see **explanatory note 4**).

Losses are only available against gains of the estate.

Sale by beneficiaries

Capital gains tax rate is 18% (in respect of the disposal of residential and non-residential property (between 6 April 2016 and before 5 April 2019 on residential property only)) and 10% otherwise so far as chargeable gains plus taxable income do not exceed the basic rate limit, or 28% (in respect of the disposal of residential property) and 20% otherwise as to any excess of chargeable gains. The appropriate rate will be 10% if business asset disposal relief or investors' relief applies.

Each beneficiary has his own annual exemption.

Acquisition value is probate value (subject to what is said in **Example A26 explanatory note 1**).

Acquisition date is date of death.

Personal losses may be offset against gains on assets acquired; losses on assets acquired may be offset against personal gains.

The distribution of a capital asset triggers an income tax charge in the hands of the beneficiary to the value of any undistributed income arising in the estate (see **Example E1 explanatory note 2**).

Furthermore, the tax may be borne by different beneficiaries. In this Example the cash to be distributed following a sale by the executors in respect of the three shareholdings held in the estate would be:

		£
Sale proceeds:	Bird Enterprises Ltd	332,500
	Computer Games plc	33,000
	Midwest Bank plc	9,000
		374,500
Less: Capital gains tax		(20,740)
Divided equally		353,760

Thus one can compare the impact of the tax liabilities with and without the mitigation proposals in (b) as follows:

	without mitigation		*with mitigation*	
	Mrs Bird	*Rupert*	*Mrs Bird*	*Rupert*
	£	£	£	£
Re Bird Enterprises Ltd	1,145	0	6,020	4,275
Re estate	10,370	10,370	0	0
	11,515	10,370	5,390	3,645
Deduct liability with mitigation	(6,020)	(4,275)		
Tax saved through mitigation steps	5,495	6,095		

Thus both beneficiaries would have achieved a saving if they as executors had arranged for the disposal of Bird Enterprises to be made by them personally rather than as executors, but Rupert's saving would have been larger compared with Mrs Bird's.

The main reason for the savings is because the beneficiaries personally can both (in this Example) benefit from business asset disposal relief which is not available to the executors. The reason Rupert's saving is larger than Mrs Bird's is that, although two whole annual exemptions are utilised in both scenarios, the mitigation scenario allows each beneficiary to take the benefit of one whole exemption, whereas, without the mitigation steps, Mrs Bird uses her own exemption to the full and the benefit of the executors' exemption is split equally between her and Rupert as beneficiaries.

Gifts holdover relief for personal representatives and trustees

(8) As stated in the Example, personal representatives do not qualify for gifts holdover relief under TCGA 1992 s 165 or s 260, but trustees do. Where the residue of the estate is left on trust, the personal representatives should ensure that assets on which gifts holdover relief is to be claimed have been formally appropriated to the trustees before being gifted. The trustees are then treated as acquiring the assets at the date of death.

The Finance Act 2006 changes to IHT for trusts also impinge on the CGT holdover provisions in so far that:

- transfers into and out of trusts that now come within the 'relevant property' rules will in principle be automatically eligible for hold-over relief under TCGA 1992 s 260(2)(a), but there are nevertheless certain exceptions to this in relation to property coming out of a relevant property trust, namely:

  (i) where the distribution is made in the three month window after a ten-year anniversary or the commencement of the settlement, because an IHT exit charge is specifically disapplied on that occasion by IHTA 1984 s 65(4) – see **Example D2 explanatory note 6;**

  (ii) where the settlement was created by will and the distribution is made within two years after the testator's death, because the absolute entitlement will then be treated for IHT purposes, by IHTA 1984 s 144, as having arisen on the death so that no IHT charge under the relevant property regime arises – see **Example C11 explanatory note 11;** or

  (iii) insofar as the property coming out of trust is excluded property (see **Example A4 part (b)**), since that is not relevant property and is therefore not the subject of an exit charge under the relevant property regime – see **Example C10 explanatory note 8** and **Example D2 explanatory note 4;**

- hold-over relief under TCGA 1992 s 260(2)(d)–(db) is available where the distribution is exempted from an IHT charge under the special IHT rules for trusts for minor children referred to in **Example C3 explanatory note 1;**

- the special rules in TCGA 1992 ss 72, 73 relating to the death of a person entitled to an interest in possession are restricted to assets that are subject to a qualifying IIP in the sense explained in **Example C3.**

Business asset disposal relief and investors' relief for personal representatives and trustees

(9) For a description of business asset disposal relief under TCGA 1992 ss 169H–169S, and its limited application to trustees, see **Example D3**. The relief is not available against disposals by personal representatives.

In this case, if the mitigation proposals at (**b**) are implemented, Mrs Bird and Rupert are director and employee respectively and have shareholdings in excess of 5% (presumably carrying equivalent rights to distributable profits and assets on a winding up) making Bird Enterprises Limited their 'personal company' in each case. In Mrs Bird's case she has actually owned 5% for over two years; in Rupert's case, because his acquisition is treated as having taken place at his father's death, he is treated as having owned the shares he inherits for over two years. Business asset disposal' relief therefore applies to the gains on the disposal of Bird Enterprises Ltd shares by each of them.

(10) Personal representatives do not qualify for investors' relief.

The charge to capital gains tax on non-UK resident persons

(11) The charge to capital gains tax has been extended by FA 2015 to non-resident persons (including personal representatives) in relation to the disposal of UK residential property and the private residence exemption has been modified in respect of non-resident persons. FA 2020 extends the charge to capital gains to non-resident persons (including personal representative) in relation to the disposal of UK non-residential property and shares in property-rich companies (ie those that derive at least 75% of their value from UK land). For details of this aspect of the charge to capital gains tax see the companion to this book, **Tolley's Taxwise I 2023/24.**

Personal representatives are subject to the special 'report and pay' compliance rules (effective from 6 April 2020) that are applicable in relation to the disposal of UK residential property. See **Example F6 explanatory note 16** for more detail on these rules.

Question

A.

The termination of a life interest in settled property can occur in various circumstances, including:

(a) where, on the death of the life tenant, the settlement (or a part) comes to an end and the trust property passes to the remainderman (not being the settlor),

(b) as in (a) but the property passes to the original settlor,

(c) where, on the life tenant's death, there is a successive life tenancy such that the trust continues, and

(d) where the interest ceases otherwise than on the death of the life tenant.

State the capital gains tax situation of the trustees in each of the events (a) to (d) above, giving appropriate statutory references. Explain also the position of a beneficiary who disposes of his interest.

B.

Where capital gains tax is payable by trustees, state the position regarding the capital gains tax rate and the annual exemption, and indicate the position if the settlor has retained an interest in the settlement.

Answer

In this Example the term 'privileged IIP' will be used to include both a qualifying IIP and a 'privileged minor's IIP' (a non-statutory term explained in **Example C3**). In particular, in relation to deaths occurring on or after 5 December 2013, the term is extended to encompass deemed interests in possession in disabled person's trusts (FA 2014 s 56) so that the same capital gains tax treatment now applies to property within a disabled person's trust where the disabled beneficiary has no interest in possession in the trust property as is available where the disabled beneficiary does have an interest in possession.

A. Termination of life interests in settled property – capital gains tax treatment

(a) *Where the settlement or part thereof comes to an end on the death of the life tenant and the trust property passes to the remainderman (not being the settlor)*

The settled property to which someone becomes absolutely entitled (whether in his own right or as trustee of a separate settlement) is deemed to be disposed of at market value and immediately reacquired by the trustees; but where that occurs on the death of a beneficiary who had a privileged IIP no chargeable gain (or allowable loss) arises on the disposal except as indicated below (TCGA 1992 ss 71–73). In other words there is an adjustment to the base cost of the settled property and the trustees then hold that property as bare trustees for the person entitled thereto.

Where the asset disposed of, or part thereof, was the subject of a claim for gifts holdover relief under s 165 or s 260 when the trustees acquired it, then if a chargeable gain arises on the deemed disposal of the asset, the gain is restricted to the amount of the held-over gain (s 74). If a loss arises on the deemed disposal of such an asset, the loss so arising is an allowable loss.

Where the life interest did not extend to the whole of the settled property to which someone became entitled on the life tenant's death, then there is no exemption from the capital gains charge on the deemed disposal, but any gain arising is reduced by a proportion representing the life tenant's interest (s 73(2)).

If the interest in possession of the life tenant was not a privileged IIP, then any gain or loss on a s 71 deemed disposal will be a chargeable gain or allowable loss, treated in the same way as in **part (d)** below.

(b) *As in (a) but the property passes to the original settlor*

If the original settlor becomes absolutely entitled on the death of the life tenant, and the life tenant's interest was a privileged IIP, then there is a deemed disposal and reacquisition of the settled property as in (**a**) above, but the consideration is deemed to be such that no gain or loss accrues to the trustees, rather than being at market value. In other words, the settlor acquires the property at its base cost at the time he made the settlement. Where the deemed disposal is of an asset held by the trustees at 31 March 1982, then the original settlor is also deemed to have held the assets on that date. Therefore on a subsequent disposal by the original settlor his base cost will be the asset's market value as at 31 March 1982 even though the asset was actually owned by the trustees, not by the settlor, on that date.

As in (**a**), if the interest in possession was not a privileged IIP this rule does not apply, and any gain or loss will be treated in the usual way as per (**d**) below.

(c) *Where, on the life tenant's death, there is a successive life tenancy*

If the life tenant's interest was a privileged IIP, then the consequences are similar to those in (**a**) above. The settled property is deemed to be disposed of at market value and immediately reacquired by the trustees, but no chargeable gain arises on the disposal (s 72), other than any gain held over under the gifts holdover provisions (s 74) or enterprise investment scheme deferral relief provisions (see **explanatory note** 7).

If the life tenant's interest was not a privileged IIP, there is no deemed disposal on the life tenant's death unless the trust comes to an end as in (**a**) above. The base value of the trust assets in the trustees' hands remains unchanged.

(d) *Where the life interest ceases otherwise than on the death of the life tenant*

Whether the life interest is a privileged IIP or not, such a termination has no capital gains tax effect if the property remains in trust, and the capital gains tax base value of the property remains the same. If, however, a beneficiary (whether the life tenant or someone else, which would include the trustees of a separate settlement where relevant), become absolutely entitled to any property against the trustees at that time, there is a deemed disposal at market value, and deemed reacquisition as bare trustees for the beneficiary, and the trustees are chargeable to capital gains tax accordingly (s 71).

However, if the beneficiary is UK resident (or non-resident but the trust asset is residential or non-residential property or shares in companies deriving at least 75% of their value from UK land (before 6 April 2019 residential property only) subject to CGT under the NRCGT provisions – see explanatory note 5), a claim may be made by the trustees and beneficiary jointly for any gain to be held over under one of two provisions of TCGA 1992:

(i) under s 260 if the deemed disposal entails a chargeable transfer for inheritance tax or would entail an inheritance tax charge but for one of a specified range of reliefs (notably in connection with accumulation and maintenance trusts (if any still exist), bereaved minor's trusts and age 18-to-25 trusts); or

(ii) under s 165 and Sch 7 if the property consists of any of the following:

- Assets used in a business by the trustees or the life tenant.
- Unquoted shares in a trading company.
- Shares in a trading company in which the trustees hold 25% or more of the voting rights.
- Property that would qualify for agricultural property relief (Sch 7 paras 1–3).

Where a beneficiary becomes absolutely entitled subs 71(2)–(2D) provide:

(i) Losses on actual disposals by the trustees before the beneficiary becomes absolutely entitled cannot be transferred to the beneficiary. Such losses will remain losses of the trustees, for which relief may be obtained within the trust according to the normal rules.

(ii) Losses arising on the deemed market value transfer to the beneficiary that the trustees cannot use against gains arising at the time of the transfer of the property or earlier in the same tax year will be treated as made by the beneficiary who has become absolutely entitled to the asset, but the loss will be ring-fenced in the beneficiary's hands: he will be able to use the loss only to reduce a gain on the disposal of the particular asset, or in the case of land, an asset derived from the land. See **explanatory note 3** for more information regarding the use of losses by trustees and beneficiaries on the deemed market value transfers to beneficiaries.

Disposal by beneficiary of his interest in a trust

If someone with an interest in a settlement (either a life interest or a reversionary interest) disposes of his interest, the disposal is not subject to capital gains tax unless the interest had been acquired for money or money's worth by him or by a predecessor in title of his (s 76(1)). This exemption does not, however, apply (even if the interest disposed of was not acquired for money or money's worth) to:

(1) disposals which take place at a time when the trustees are not resident in the UK (s 85). In such a case some relief is available where the trust became non-resident after 18 March 1991 (triggering a deemed disposal of the assets by the trustees at that time) and the beneficiary's interest was acquired before the change of residence; the beneficiary's base value for his interest under the trust is in effect updated to the date of the change in residence (s 85(2)–(9)).

(2) disposals of an interest in a trust whose trustees have at any time been not resident in the UK (s 76(1A), (1B)).

On a person becoming absolutely entitled to the assets of the settlement, he is deemed to have disposed of his interest for the then market value of the assets (s 76(2)) – alongside the deemed disposal by the trustees of the assets to which he becomes entitled, and reacquisition as bare trustees for that beneficiary. The beneficiary's deemed disposal will not result in a chargeable gain – even if it would otherwise be caught by one of the exclusions at **1** and **2** above – unless the interest had previously changed hands for money or money's worth; in such a case s 76(2) in effect ensures a charge on the beneficiary in respect of the gain in the value of his (or his predecessor in title's) investment in the interest.

Special rules apply where there is a disposal for actual consideration (other than in the form of another interest under the same settlement, unless that other interest had previously changed hands for actual consideration) of an interest under a trust that is settlor-interested at the date of the disposal, or has been so at any time in the preceding two tax years. If the trust is UK resident in the tax year of disposal, and the settlor is or has been resident in the UK in the current year or in any of the previous five tax years (or ordinarily resident in any of those years if they fall before 2013/14), then the beneficiary's disposal of his interest will trigger a deemed disposal and reacquisition of the trust assets by the trustees at market value (or of a relevant part or fund of them if the interest does not extend to the whole). It is irrelevant whether the person disposing of the interest in the trust is not UK resident; any tax is payable by the trustees, but they are given a statutory right to recover it from the beneficiary who made the disposal (s 76A and Sch 4A). However, provision is made by paragraph 10 of that Schedule to prevent double-counting as between the beneficiary's disposal of his interest and the trustees' deemed disposal, the general effect of which is to preserve the charge on the higher of the two net gains or to allow the smaller of the two allowable losses.

B. Capital gains tax rate etc

Charging trust gains to tax

Subject to what follows, UK resident trustees are chargeable to tax on their chargeable gains less allowable losses as for individuals. In the main, reliefs available to individuals such as private residence relief and business assets roll-over relief are also available to trustees; but as regards private residence relief it is important to remember that it will be unavailable to trustees (except in a heritage property maintenance fund trust) for the period falling after 9 March 2003 if the base value of the property in question is to any extent reduced (directly or indirectly) as a result of a claim for gifts holdover relief under s 260, whether that claim was made before or after the disposal on which private residence relief would otherwise be available (s 226A).

There are anti-avoidance provisions in s 79A that prevent losses arising on trustees' disposals being set against gains they make on assets that had been transferred to the trust if the transferor or someone connected with him had bought an interest in the trust and had claimed gifts holdover relief on the transferred assets.

The capital gains tax rate for trusts for disposals occurring on or after 6 April 2016 is 28% in respect of the disposal of residential property (wherever situated) and 20% otherwise, which also applies to personal representatives of a deceased's estate (s 1H(5)(6)). The capital gains rate for trusts for disposals occurring before 6 April 2016 is a single rate 28%.

Trusts in which settlor retains an interest

The former capital gains tax equivalent to the income tax provisions for taxing the settlor on income of a settlor-interested trust, in ss 77–79, was abolished for UK trusts by FA 2008 with effect from 6 April 2008, though in the case of non-UK resident (or dual resident) trusts a similar (and more wide-ranging) regime applies under s 86 and Sch 5 (see **Example D4 explanatory note 5**).

To complement the rule in s 169B that denies gift relief under the provisions of s 165 or s 260 in respect of disposals of assets by a settlor to the trustees of a trust in which he has an interest, the trustees holding assets that were the subject of a gifts holdover relief claim on the transfer to the trustees will face a clawback charge under s 169C if the trust becomes settlor-interested (whether by reference to the original settlor or another person (such as his spouse)) within a certain time period. This period begins immediately after the disposal to the trustees that benefited from gift relief and ends at the end of the sixth tax year thereafter. This does not apply if the terms of the trust meet the 'disabled beneficiary' conditions, in favour of a disabled settlor, or in the case of a heritage property maintenance fund trust. The conditions are similar to, but not identical to, those described in the next section relating to the annual exemption available to a disabled person's trust.

Capital gains tax annual exemption

Where tax is chargeable in the name of the trustees on a held-over gain, or under the provisions in **part A (d)** above, or on disposals of trust assets by the trustees, the trustees can claim an annual exemption equal to half the amount exempt for an individual, ie £3,000 for 2023/24 (£6,150 in 2022/23).

If, however, the same person is the settlor in relation to more than one trust created after 6 June 1978 (with certain exceptions including charitable trusts), the exemption of £3,000 is divided between those trusts, with a minimum exempt slice for each trust of £600 (Sch 1C paras 5(2), 6(3)). This rule applies to settlements arising under a will or intestacy as well as those created in lifetime. (For more details see **Example F6 explanatory note 15**.)

If the trust is a trust for a disabled person, the full annual exemption of £6,000 is available, reduced pro rata if there is more than one disabled trust established by the same settlor after 9 March 1981, with again a minimum exempt amount for each trust of £600 (Sch 1C paras 2(1), 6(2)). Where there was more than one settlor of the disabled person's trust in question, the pro rata division uses whichever settlor produces the maximum reduction in the trustees' annual exempt amount, but again only taking account of other disabled person's trusts made by each of them (Sch 1C para 6(6)).

Finance Act 2013 introduced provisions to harmonise the definition of trusts for disabled persons and other vulnerable persons. Whereas previously, in relation to the capital gains annual exemption, trusts had to provide that at least half of the trust fund had to be used for the benefit of the disabled person and that no income was to be applied except for his benefit, new trusts must now secure that:

(a) no capital distribution (unless it does not exceed a prescribed annual amount) can be made other than for the benefit of the disabled person, and

(b) the disabled person must be entitled to all of the income arising from the trust fund, or that no income of the trust in excess of a prescribed annual limit may be applied for the benefit of any other person (Sch 1C para 3).

The rule allows a small sum (whether consisting of income or capital, or both) not exceeding 'the annual limit' (currently defined in Sch 1C para 3(4)(a),(5) as the lower of £3,000 or 3% of the value of the trust fund during the tax year in question), to be applied otherwise than for the benefit of the disabled person.

The possibility of breach of those conditions by means of an exercise of the statutory power of advancement can be disregarded so long as the power is not actually exercised in an offending way.

Finance Act 2013 also introduced a uniform definition of a disabled person for all tax purposes (see FA 2005 Sch1A). It includes those who by reason of mental disorder are incapable of managing their affairs; and those in receipt of one of a number of welfare payments. See **Example F4** for a fuller discussion of the definition.

The introduction of these rules does not affect the application of the rules on the exempt amount to certain 'grandfathered' trusts. They are trusts created before 8 April 2013 and which have remained unchanged since that date and trusts that arise on or after 8 April 2013 under the will (or codicil) of a testator executed before 8 April 2013 that has not been altered in so far as it relates to the trust (or if the will was executed on or after 8 April 2013 it replicates the terms of a will (in so far as it relates to the trust) executed before that date) continue to be entitled to an annual exemption (FA 2013 Sch 44 paras 13(7), 20)).

Explanatory Notes

Types of trust and their CGT treatment

(1) The main types of trust are bare trusts, trusts with an interest in possession (IIP), and discretionary trusts. (It should be noted that a 'relevant property trust' is an IHT concept that encompasses a number of types of trust and is not a type of trust in its own right.)

Where someone is a bare trustee this means that the beneficiary is absolutely entitled to the trust property as against the trustee. The capital gains tax (CGT) treatment is therefore to look through the trust and to deem the trustee's acts as being those of the beneficiary (TCGA 1992 s 60); and equally for inheritance tax (IHT) the trust property is not settled property but property to which the beneficiary is beneficially entitled in his own right (and thus part of his estate). For further details see **Example C15**.

As seen in **part A** of the Example, the CGT treatment of life interest trusts is dependent on the IHT categorisation of the IIP, as to which see further **Example C3** (TCGA 1992 ss 72, 73).

Most interest in possession trusts are life interest trusts, but sometimes an interest may cease earlier, for example if a widow remarries. (An annuity is another form of interest in possession, and there are detailed rules for both IHT and CGT purposes to identify the extent of the settled property that is to be treated as underlying the annuity: see IHTA 1984 s 50(2)–(4), TCGA 1992 s 72(3)–(5).)

A protected life interest (where the life interest is automatically replaced by a discretionary trust of income in the event of the life tenant's bankruptcy, attempted assignment of his interest or related events – see Trustee Act 1925 s 33) is an interest in possession while the life interest has not been 'forfeited' in that way, and its tax treatment is no different from other interests in possession. If and when a forfeiture occurs, the trust switches to the income tax and CGT rules for discretionary trusts, following the trust law treatment; but for IHT, if the IIP was a privileged IIP in the first place, the forfeiture will be disregarded and it will remain a privileged IIP (IHTA 1984 s 88).

(2) Trustees are treated for CGT purposes as a single deemed person distinct from those who may from time to time occupy the position of trustee, and, if that deemed person is UK resident, gains arising on the disposal of trust assets are assessable on the trustees (other than bare trustees, as indicated in **explanatory note 1** above) (TCGA 1992 s 69, which also sets out the rules for determining the residence status of the deemed person).

Creation of settlement – capital gains tax treatment

(3) When a settlement is created the settlor is deemed to have disposed of the entire property transferred to the settlement at its market value, even if he retains an interest as beneficiary or is a trustee under the settlement, and he is therefore chargeable to capital gains tax accordingly (subject to any available reliefs and exemptions) (TCGA 1992 s 70).

If the assets transferred are business assets (as defined by TCGA 1992 s 165) or the transfer is *immediately chargeable* to inheritance tax (whether or not there is any actual inheritance tax payable (TCGA 1992 s 260)) then provided the trustees are UK resident the settlor can avoid incurring a personal CGT liability on the gain by making an election to hold it over so that it reduces the trustees' base acquisition cost, and unlike other gifts relief elections the donees do not have to join in the election. For gifts into settlement on or after 10 December 2003 this facility is not available if the settlor retains an interest or the trust becomes settlor-interested within six years (ss 169B, 169C). For nearly all lifetime transfers into family trusts since 2006, gifts holdover relief will be available under s 260: apart from special cases such as heritage maintenance fund trusts and employee trusts, and even where the trust is primarily for the settlor's own benefit, the only cases where the transfer will not be immediately chargeable to IHT, but only *potentially exempt*, will be where the transfer is to a bare trust for the benefit of an individual or the trust confers a disabled person's interest at the outset.

In the case of a privileged IIP trust, the held-over gains crystallise when the beneficiary dies, as indicated in **part A** of the Example. In a relevant property trust, the held-over gains are similarly triggered when assets are transferred to beneficiaries (see **explanatory note 6**). In both cases this will be subject to any further holdover relief claim that the circumstances may allow.

If the settlor's disposal gives rise to losses rather than gains, then under the 'connected persons' rules, the losses can only be set against gains on other disposals to the trustees. These rules will also apply as between the trustees and any beneficiaries with whom they are connected; but note that (except in relation to companies of which they collectively exercise control) trustees are not connected with the settlor's spouse and relatives after the settlor's death. Even if the trustees and beneficiaries *are* connected, this does not prevent the trustees' losses arising from the disposal to the beneficiaries being transferred to the beneficiaries to the limited extent allowed by TCGA 1992 s 71(2)–(2D), as indicated in **part A (d)** of the Example.

Where the trustees realise a loss on the deemed market value transfer to a beneficiary, they are required to use that loss first against so-called 'pre-entitlement gains', that is gains made on such deemed market value transfers to the beneficiary and gains made on actual disposals in that part of the tax year that falls before the deemed transfer in respect of which the loss arose. Only the balance of the loss may be transferred to the beneficiary.

For example, assume that a beneficiary becomes absolutely entitled to the whole of the settled property of a trust which comprises asset A on which a gain of £4,000 arises, asset B on which a loss of £5,000 arises and cash of £25,000 being the proceeds of an earlier asset disposal. The loss on asset B will be first set against the gain on asset A, and the balance of the loss of £1,000 will be passed to the beneficiary. This can only be set against a gain realised by the beneficiary on the disposal of asset B.

Also consider Greenacres which is held in trust for Andrew. It cost the trustees £300,000 but is now worth only £200,000. Greenacres is appointed to Andrew. Some years later he sells it for £280,000; in the same year he makes gains from the disposal of other assets of £25,000. Andrew's gain on the disposal of Greenacres of £80,000 can be offset by the loss of £100,000 inherited from the trustees. The balance of the loss of £20,000 cannot, however, be set against his other gain of £25,000 in respect of which (subject to the annual exemption) he must pay capital gains tax.

Emigration of trustees – capital gains tax consequences

(4) Emigrating trustees are charged not only on gains held over at the time the funds were settled but on the whole of any increase in value of the trust assets up to the time of emigration (TCGA 1992 s 80). If the emigration occurs solely as a result of the death of a UK resident trustee and the trustees become UK resident again within six months thereafter, the deemed disposal on emigration is disapplied, except in relation to assets that were disposed of by the trustees between the death and the re-immigration of the trust, or where a gain on their disposal would be protected from UK CGT by a double tax agreement. There is a similar rule for trusts which become UK resident solely by reason of the death of a non-UK resident trustee and which re-emigrate within six months: the emigration charge in such a case is limited to assets that were acquired in the UK-resident period with the benefit of hold-over relief (TCGA 1992 s 81). For detailed notes on non-resident trusts see **Example D4**.

In the case of *Trustees of the P Panayi Accumulation & Maintenance Settlements v HMRC* (Case C646/15), the Court of Justice of the European Union has held, in a preliminary ruling, that the exit charge arising under TCGA 1992, s 80 is, because it cannot be deferred, contrary to the freedom of establishment principle enshrined in the EU Treaties.

HMRC unsuccessfully sought to argue that the treaty freedoms did not apply to trusts. The CJEU noted that the freedom of establishment given by Art 49 was a very broad concept and applies to 'companies or firms constituted under civil or commercial law, including co-operative societies, and other legal persons governed by public or private law, save for those which are non-profit-making'. The court held that the activity of the trustees in relation to the trust property and the management of its assets were inextricably linked to the trust. Therefore, the trust and its trustees constituted an indivisible whole. A trust should be considered an entity which, under national law, has rights and obligations that enable it to act as such within the legal order concerned. It followed that an entity such as a trust that possesses rights and obligations which enable it to act in its own right and that carries on an economic activity may rely on freedom of establishment.

In the light of this case new legislation has been introduced (see TMA 1970, s 59BB, Sch 3ZAA) to provide for CGT exit charge payment plans. The legislation applies to gains arising on or after 6 April 2019. It enables trusts that cease to be UK resident and become resident in the EEA to defer, in certain cases, payment of the CGT that may arise on that occasion. The trustees can defer payment by entering into a CGT exit charge payment plan (ECPP) provided they are able to demonstrate that when they ceased to be UK resident they had a right of freedom of establishment, the assets subject to charge have been used for an economically significant economic activity in the UK and that immediately after becoming non-UK resident they became resident elsewhere in the EEA and use the assets for an economically significant activity carried on there (Sch 3ZAA para 3).

The ECPP may apply to all the tax arising on emigration or just part of it. The amount of tax that is deferred under the ECPP is payable in six equal instalments, the first being due on the day the full amount would have been due without entering into the ECPP (Sch 3ZAA paras 4 and 5).

An application by trustees to enter into an ECPP is made to HMRC by the date on which the tax deferred would ordinarily be payable. The trustees must undertake to pay the deferred tax and interest due on it in accordance with the plan. An ECPP will be void if all material facts are not disclosed to HMRC or where the deferral of tax payments is the main purpose of arrangements that include the change of residence. The ECPP must include details of residency and the amount of tax being deferred (Sch 3ZAA para 6 and 7).

Once an ECPP has been entered into, HMRC will expect payment of the tax only in accordance with the plan. Whilst the plan is in place the ordinary penalty provisions are overridden and will only be activated of the taxpayer fails to make payment under its terms. However, interest is still due on the amount of tax deferred and interest must be paid on each instalment of tax as it is paid. The trustees are free to pay any outstanding balance, with interest, before the end of the ECPP period. Should the trustees become bankrupt or resident (including treaty resident) in a country outside the EEA, the full outstanding balance is due on the date the next instalment would have been due (Sch 3ZAA para 8).

Persons becoming absolutely entitled to trust property – capital gains tax consequences

(5) TCGA 1992 s 71 applies not only when a beneficiary under a privileged IIP trust becomes absolutely entitled as against the trustees, as outlined in **part A(d)** of the Example, but also where a beneficiary of a relevant property trust becomes so entitled. The trustees are deemed to have disposed of the assets to the beneficiary at market value at that time and are chargeable to capital gains tax accordingly.

The gifts holdover relief provisions of ss 165 and 260 outlined in **explanatory note 3** are, however, available if the conditions are satisfied and the beneficiary is UK resident (although being non-UK resident is not a bar to gifts holdover relief where the asset disposed of is UK residential property – s 261ZA). A distribution from a relevant property trust will be a chargeable event for inheritance tax, triggering an exit charge under IHTA 1984 s 65 and thus satisfying the s 260 requirement, unless (s 65(4)) it takes place within three months after the creation of the settlement or within three months after a ten-year anniversary or is chargeable as the income of the beneficiary.

Where a discretionary trust is created by will, distributions to beneficiaries within the two years after the death (but not within the first three months) are treated as if made under the will for inheritance tax purposes (IHTA 1984 s 144 – see **Example C11 explanatory notes 10** and **12**). For capital gains tax purposes, however, if such a distribution was of chargeable assets that had grown in value since the date of death, the trustees would be liable to tax on the gain arising under TCGA 1992 s 71 (subject to any available annual exemption), unless the business gifts holdover relief of s 165 was available. Relief under s 260 would not be available because the distribution would not be a chargeable event for inheritance tax. One way of avoiding a capital gains tax charge in these circumstances would be for the trustees to appoint assets to a beneficiary *before* the assets were appropriated to the trustees by the personal representatives. The trustees would then be bare trustees (as to which see **explanatory note 1**), and as and when the assets were appropriated to them by the personal representatives, their acquisition would be deemed to be that of the beneficiary, who would thus take over the personal representatives' acquisition cost.

Alternatively the trustees could vary the original disposition of the property by means of a deed of variation executed under TCGA 1992 s 62(6). After the assets have vested in them but within two years of the death, the trustees may, by means of the deed of variation, cause the property to be treated as acquired by the beneficiary directly under the deceased's will. The beneficiary would then take the assets as legatee at the personal representatives' acquisition cost. The usual purpose of a deed of variation is to re-direct assets for IHT purposes under IHTA 1984 s 142 but this is precluded by the use of a discretionary will trust under s 144 (s 142(4)). However, it is possible to make the election under TCGA 1992 s 62(7) independently of any election under IHTA 1984 s 142 or the application of IHTA 1984 s 144. For a more detailed treatment of deeds of variation generally, see **Example B6**.

Creation of life interest out of discretionary trust – capital gains tax consequences

(6) On any restructuring of the terms of a trust – for example if property is held under a discretionary trust and a life interest is created in the property – it has to be established whether a separate settlement has been created or whether the original settlement continues (*Roome v Edwards* (1981) and *Bond v Pickford* (1983)). If the original settlement is treated as continuing, the restructuring will have no immediate capital gains consequences.

If the restructuring was held to involve the relevant assets passing into a separate settlement, this would be an occasion of charge under TCGA 1992 s 71, since another 'person', ie the trustees of the new settlement, would become entitled to the trust property as against the trustees of the original settlement. In most cases nowadays the restructuring would not result in an exit charge for inheritance tax under IHTA 1984 s 65 (see **explanatory note 6** above), such as to permit a claim to holdover relief under TCGA 1992 s 260; a trust that is once within the relevant property rules will only cease to be so if a disabled person's interest is created. If on the other hand a qualifying IIP existed before the restructuring, the restructuring may well give rise to a deemed transfer of value by the beneficiary with that IIP, which would now with very few exceptions be a chargeable transfer on entry into the relevant property regime such as to attract holdover relief subject to the trustees being UK resident.

Enterprise investment scheme deferral relief for trustees

(7) If trustees reinvest gains by making a cash subscription for enterprise investment scheme (EIS) shares, they may claim deferral relief under the provisions of TCGA 1992 s 150C and Sch 5B (but not EIS income tax relief or capital gains exemption) (Sch 5B para 17). This applies to interest in possession trusts (except where the IIP is for a fixed term) in which any of the beneficiaries is an individual or a charity, and to discretionary trusts in which all beneficiaries are individuals or charities.

Seed Enterprise Investment Scheme re-investment relief and Social Enterprise re-investment relief are not available to trustees.

Capital gains tax anti-avoidance provisions — apportionment of gains of non-resident companies to trustees

(8) There are provisions in TCGA 1992 s 3 to attribute gains in a non-resident company to UK resident participators if the company would have been a close company if UK resident. For gains realised after 20 March 2000, where the UK participators are trustees, the gains cannot be prevented from being so attributed by reason of the provisions of a double tax agreement (TCGA 1992 s 79B). For further details of the provisions of TCGA 1992 s 3 see **Example D4 explanatory note 17**.

The charge to capital gains tax on non-UK resident persons

(9) The charge to capital gains tax has been extended by FA 2015 to non-resident persons (including personal representatives) in relation to the disposal of residential property and the private residence exemption has been modified in respect of non-resident persons. FA 2019 extends the charge to capital gains to non-resident persons in relation to the disposal of UK non-residential property and shares in property-rich companies (ie those that derive at least 75% of their value from UK land). For details of this aspect of the charge to capital gains tax see the 2023/24 edition of **Tolley's Taxwise I.**

Individuals, personal representatives and trustees are subject to the special 'report and pay' compliance rules (effective from 6 April 2020) that are applicable in relation to the disposal of UK residential property. See **Example F6 explanatory note 16** for more detail on these rules.

Question

A.

Describe the operation of business asset disposal relief (formerly known as entrepreneurs' relief) for trustees, contrasting this with the scope of the relief as it applies to individuals.

B.

Belvoir Ltd is an unquoted trading company whose shares (which carry voting rights, rights to distributable profits and assets on a winding up) are owned as follows:

Robert Fairfax	6%
Thomas Fairfax	6%
Florence Fairfax	10%
Fairfax Family Trust	78%

Robert and Thomas (who are brothers) are the directors of the company and have been so since Malcolm, their father died in 1984. Florence, their mother, is still alive. Robert, Thomas, and Florence are the life tenants of the Fairfax Family Trust each having an interest in possession in the trust assets. A fourth beneficiary of the trust is Mary (Florence's daughter) who owns no shares in Belvoir Ltd and who is studying for a fine arts degree. She too is a life tenant of the trust. Florence and her three children enjoy the income from the trust in equal shares; the trustees have not appropriated any of the trust property into separate funds. The trustees of the Fairfax Family Trust have owned their shares since 1984 when Malcolm Fairfax died; the shares were settled under the terms of his will.

On 10 May 2023 the shareholders of the company were made an exceptionally attractive offer for their shares which they accepted. The following gains arose to the shareholders:

Robert and Thomas Fairfax	£3m each
Florence Fairfax	£5m
Fairfax Family Trust	£39m

Thomas made a gain of £50,000 qualifying for entrepreneurs' relief (as it was then called) in 2019 in respect of which he made a claim.

Calculate (with explanations) the amount of capital gains tax payable by the trustees in 2023/24 assuming that the disposal of the shares in Belvoir Ltd is their only disposal in that year. You should assume that Thomas does not make a claim for business asset disposal relief by 31 January 2025 in respect of his £3 million gain, but that he does enter into a joint claim for the relief with the trustees in October 2024. You should also assume that Robert will enter into a joint claim with the trustees only if his personal gains benefit from business asset disposal relief to the fullest extent possible.

C.

Describe in brief the operation of investors' relief in so far as it applies to trustees.

Answer

A.

The rules for business asset disposal relief (BADR) (known before 6 April 2020 as entrepreneurs' relief) are set out in TCGA 1992 ss 169H–169S (inserted by FA 2008). The relief is available to individuals and trustees of a settlement, but not to personal representatives of a deceased person's estate.

The circumstances in which BADR relief is available to trustees are very much more circumscribed than those applicable to individuals. To explain this it will be convenient to summarise first the rules for individuals in outline (a more detailed explanation can be found in the companion book, **Tolley's Taxwise I 2023/24**).

Outline of business asset disposal relief as applicable to individuals

For individuals the relief is available with effect from 6 April 2008 (subject to certain conditions, to an overall lifetime limit of £1 of gains arising in respect of disposals occurring on or after 11 March 2020 (£10 million of gains for disposals before that date), and to the making of a claim) if the individual disposes of (or, in the case of (ii)–(iv), of an interest in):

(i) the whole or part of a trading business carried on by him alone or in partnership (s 169I);

(ii) assets in use for the purposes of a such business when he ceased to carry it on (s 169I);

(iii) shares in a trading company where he is a director or employee of that company (or of another company in the same group) and holds at least 5% of the ordinary share capital and 5% of the voting rights (and for disposals on or after 29 October 2018, at least 5% of the distributable profits and assets on a winding up) (s 169I); or

(iv) assets in use for the purpose of a business of which (or part of which) the individual makes a qualifying disposal as partner within (i), or the business of a company of whose shares he makes a qualifying disposal within (iii), where his disposal of such assets is made as part of his withdrawal from participation (as defined) in the business in question (s 169K).

The conditions include a two-year minimum period of ownership (one year for disposals before 6 April 2019), use or status as employee or director, which runs up to the date of the disposal or, where the business in question has ceased to be carried on, up to the date of its cessation. Additional rules applicable to disposals occurring on or after 6 April 2019 provide entitlement to BADR for individuals whose shareholding is diluted below the 5% qualifying threshold as a result of a new share issue in respect of gains arising on the shares held up to that time.

If a transaction in relation to shares or securities would otherwise not constitute a disposal as a result of ('paper for paper') relief for corporate reorganisations (ss 127–130), or would involve the deferral of a gain until disposal of a qualifying corporate bond (s 116), it is possible to elect out of those rules in order to claim BADR on disposals comprised in the current transaction (ss 169Q–169R). A current charge at 10% may be thought preferable to a deferred charge at 20% (which applies to gains made by an individual on or after 6 April 2016 where his income is charged at the higher rate or dividend upper rate). The relief is also available, on a transitional basis, in certain circumstances where gains that have been deferred from disposals made on or before 5 April 2008 (under the rules for the enterprise investment scheme or for venture capital trusts, or into a qualifying corporate bond under s 116) become chargeable after that date (FA 2008 Sch 3 paras 7–8).

Relief in the case of (i), (ii) and (iv) above is confined to the disposal of relevant business assets, which excludes shares and securities and any other assets which are held as investments (s 169L).

Where the relief is allowed, the rate of capital gains tax on the gains to which it applies is 10% in place of the usual 10% and 20% BADR rates that would otherwise apply. In determining at what rate(s) an individual should be charged to CGT on any other gains, gains qualifying for BADR are set against any unused basic rate band before non-qualifying gains, with the result that those non-qualifying gains will typically be liable at the 20% non-BADR rate without the benefit of the 10% non-BADR rate. See **Example A23**(a)(iii) for further commentary on the capital gains tax treatment of individuals.

Business asset disposal relief for trustees

Trustees are not able to claim BADR in connection with their own participation in a business on behalf of the trust, but only by reference to participation in the business by a 'qualifying beneficiary': that is, an individual who has an interest in possession (otherwise than for a fixed term) in the whole of the settled property or the part of it which consists of or includes the settlement business assets disposed of by the trustees. (The inheritance tax status of the interest in possession is not relevant in this context, but it must be an actual interest in possession (see **Example C3**), not something which for inheritance tax purposes is a deemed, but not actual, interest in possession.) It follows that in the case of a discretionary trust, or where in some other way the trustees have power or are obliged to accumulate all the trust's income or have discretion as to the distribution of that income, they cannot benefit from BADR when realising a gain on the disposal of trust assets, because there is in such a case no interest in possession and so no possibility of a qualifying beneficiary.

There must be a 'disposal of trust business assets', as restrictively defined in s 169J: the disposal by the trustees must be of:

(a) shares or securities of a company where the qualifying beneficiary is a director or employee of that company (or of another company in the same group) and holds (in his own right and additionally to the trustees' holding) at least 5% of the ordinary share capital and 5% of the voting rights (and for disposals on or after 29 October 2018, at least 5% of the distributable profits and assets on a winding up or at least 5% of the proceeds of a sale) in his own right; holdings by the trustees will not count towards these thresholds; or

(b) assets used or previously (up to cessation) used for the purpose of a business carried on by the qualifying beneficiary (alone or in partnership) so long as the qualifying beneficiary ceases to carry on the business on the date of the trustees' disposal or within three years before that. (His ceasing to be a member of the partnership carrying on the business will count as cessation of the business by him for this purpose.)

In both cases a two-year minimum period of ownership (one year in respect of disposals occurring before 6 April 2019), use, employment or directorship (as relevant) applies as for individuals:

- in the case of (a) the qualifying beneficiary must have fulfilled all the conditions there referred to for a continuous period of at least two years (one year in respect of disposals occurring before 6 April 2019) ending not earlier than three years before the date of the trustees' disposal; and
- in the case of (b) the business must have been carried on by the qualifying beneficiary for a continuous period of at least two years (one year in respect of disposals occurring before 6 April 2019) ending not earlier than three years before the date of the trustees' disposal.

In 2021 the Upper Tribunal, in *CRC v The Quentin Skinner 2005 Settlement L and Ors* [2021] STC 412 held that the individual must also be a qualifying beneficiary throughout the two-year (or one-year) minimum period of ownership. It reversed the decision of the First-tier Tribunal holding that the tribunal erred in law to hold that the qualifying beneficiary only had to hold an interest in possession under the trust at the time of the trustees' disposal of the trust business assets. The Tribunal explained that Parliament had provided for a relief to be available to the trustees, and, in so doing, had provided for the amount of the gain arising to the trustees to be set against the qualifying beneficiary's BADR limit (now of £1 million). That amounted to an effective transfer of a part of the qualifying beneficiary's lifetime allowance to the trustees. Parliament intended that 'transfer' to be premised on the existence of an enduring link between the qualifying beneficiary's business and the interest in possession in the trust enjoyed by the qualifying beneficiary. Such a link was provided only if there was a requirement in TCGA 1992 s 169J for the beneficiary to be a qualifying beneficiary throughout the two-year (or one-year) period mentioned in TCGA 1992 s 169J(4).

The decision of the Upper Tribunal has in turn been reversed by the Court of Appeal in *CRC v The Quentin Skinner 2005 Settlement L and Ors* [2022] STC 1795. The court held that both the logical structure and the drafting technique of s 169J pointed strongly towards a reading that an individual who was a qualifying beneficiary at the date of disposal, by virtue of satisfying the definition in s 169J(3), did not also need to satisfy the requirements of that definition throughout the period of one year (now two years) during which the 'relevant condition' in s 169J(4) or s 169J(5) had to be met if there was to be a disposal of trust business assets that qualified for BADR. The structure of the section required the reader to consider in turn whether the three ingredients of a disposal of trust business assets were present. The court concluded, having regard to that structure and the clear language of the provision, that where the disposal was of shares, the company had to be the qualifying beneficiary's personal company, it had to be either a trading company or the holding company of a trading group, and the qualifying beneficiary had to be an officer or employee of the specified description throughout the one-year (now two-year) period. It would be wholly foreign to that carefully delineated statutory scheme if the reader then had to extract from s 169J(4) and s 169J(5) a further condition, nowhere expressly articulated and conspicuously absent from s 169J(3) (which defined a qualifying beneficiary) itself, to the effect that the qualifying beneficiary's interest in possession had to subsist not only on the date of disposal, but also throughout the one-year (now two-year) period when the 'relevant condition' was met. If that had indeed been the statutory intention, it would have been expected that the additional requirement would have been expressly included in the definition of a qualifying beneficiary.

A claim for BADR in respect of a disposal by trustees must, to be valid, be made jointly by the trustees and the qualifying beneficiary. The deadline for claims is the first anniversary of 31 January following the end of the tax year in which the qualifying business disposal is made (corresponding to the last date on which a taxpayer can amend his self-assessment return in normal course). HMRC confirm in their Capital Gains Tax Manual at CG63970 that 'A claim to [Business Asset Disposal Relief] is not irrevocable, it may be amended or revoked within the time limit and the provision for self assessment and stand alone claims may extend the time limit for amendment, particularly when an enquiry is opened'.

If, on the same day, there is both a disposal of trust business assets in respect of which an individual is the qualifying beneficiary and a qualifying business disposal by the individual, s 169N(8) applies as if the disposal of trust business assets were later.

For trustees, the £1 million lifetime limit (10 million in respect of disposals before 11 March 2020) is that of the qualifying beneficiary in question, and if, on the same day, there is both a disposal of trust business assets in respect of which an individual is the qualifying beneficiary and a qualifying business disposal by the qualifying beneficiary in his individual capacity, so that if the combined gains exceed the qualifying beneficiary's lifetime limit then the beneficiary will take the benefit of BADR in priority to the trustees (s 169N(8)).

In cases where there is more than one beneficiary with, at the material time, an interest in possession in the settled property or the part comprising the settlement business assets, the proportion of the trustees' gain that would otherwise qualify for BADR is restricted by s 169O to the fraction B/A where:

B is the qualifying beneficiary's income interest in the part of the settled property which comprises the settlement business assets disposed of (restricted, if he has more than one interest in possession, to the interest by virtue of which he is the qualifying beneficiary), and

A is the total of the income interests of all the beneficiaries with interests in possession in that part of the settled property.

For this purpose the 'material time' is the end of the latest period of two years (one year in respect of disposals occurring before 6 April 2019), ending not earlier than three years before the date of the trustees' disposal, throughout which:

- in the case of (a) above the beneficiary was an officer or employee of a relevant company and held at least 5% of the ordinary share capital and voting rights (and for disposals on or after 29 October 2018, at least 5% of the distributable profits and assets on a winding up), or
- in the case of (b) above the business was carried on by the qualifying beneficiary.

B.

Entitlement of the trustees to business asset disposal relief

First the trustees need to establish whether they are entitled to BADR at all. They are indeed so entitled because

- They dispose of settlement business assets being the shares of Belvoir Ltd (s 169J(1)(a), (2)(a)).
- There is an individual who is a qualifying beneficiary (s 169J(1)(b)); in fact there are two qualifying beneficiaries being Thomas and Robert being individuals who have, under the trust, an interest in possession in the settled property (s 169J(3)). In *CRC v The Quentin Skinner 2005 Settlement L and Ors* [2022] STC

1795, it was held that there was no qualifying time period during which and individual had to be a beneficiary, provided he was a qualifying beneficiary on the date of the trustees' disposal. The qualifying time period during which the company had to be the personal company of the beneficiary (as provided in s 169J(4)) was not impliedly imported into the rule in s 169J(3).

- Throughout a period of two years since 11 May 2018 (the earliest date on which a continuous period of two years could have started which ends not earlier than three years before the date of the trustees' disposal on 10 May 2023) the company has been the personal company of the beneficiaries (ie they own 5% or more of the ordinary share capital of the company and thereby 5% or more of the voting rights, and of the rights to distributable profits and assets on a winding up or of the rights to proceeds of a putative sale of the shares) and they have been officers of the company (s 169J(4)). Voting rights do not actually need to be exercised, but they must be capable of being exercised (*Hepworth (Inspector of Taxes) v Smith* 54 TC 369).

Amount of the trustees' gain potentially qualifying for business asset disposal relief

Of the gain of £39 million realised by the trustees, only one half of it is potentially eligible for BADR. This means that at least £19.5 million of their gain is immediately taxable at 20%.

The reason for this is that Florence and Mary are not qualifying beneficiaries for the purpose of BADR insofar as it applies to trustees. Although both of them have an interest in possession in the trust, Florence, although a shareholder in Belvoir Ltd, does not work for the company, and Mary owns none of the shares. As such only the 'relevant proportion' of the trustees' gain potentially attracts BADR (s 169O(1)(a), (2)) and that proportion is ascertained by reference to how much of the total trust's income arises to qualifying beneficiaries. Here 50% of the trust's income arises to qualifying beneficiaries, and so only 50% of the trustees' gain potentially attracts BADR (s 169O(4)). The balance of the trustees' gain remains a chargeable gain (s 169O(3)).

The proportion is ascertained at the 'material time' which, in this case where the trust assets are shares in a qualifying company, is the end of the latest period of two years ending within the period of three years before the date of the disposal throughout which the conditions in the third bullet point above are met. The three-year period before the date of disposal runs from 11 May 2020 to 10 May 2023. The latest two-year period (within this period) during which those conditions are met runs from 11 May 2021 to 10 May 2023. The final day of the two-year period is 10 May 2023 and it is on that date that the proportion must be ascertained. See **explanatory note 3** as well.

The claims to business asset disposal relief by the trustees

BADR is to be given only on the making of a claim (s 169M(1)), and in the case of a disposal of trust business assets the claim must be made jointly by the trustees and the qualifying beneficiary (s 169M(2)(a)). Consequently, the trustees must enter into separate joint claims with Robert and Thomas respectively if the trustees' gains are to benefit from BADR. These claims will be separate from any claims which Robert or Thomas make of their own accord in respect of disposals of assets owned by them absolutely.

Amount of the trustees' gain qualifying for business asset disposal relief

The amount of gain arising to the trustees that qualifies for BADR depends upon whether BADR has been claimed and allowed in respect of any previous disposals of assets that qualify for BADR. There are such earlier relevant qualifying business disposals in the following cases (see s 169N(7)):

- where the disposal is made by an individual, the previous qualifying disposals are those made by the individual and those made by trustees in respect of which the individual was a qualifying beneficiary as defined above;

- where the disposal is made by trustees, the previous qualifying disposals are those made by the trustees in respect of which the individual was a qualifying beneficiary as defined above and those made by the individual himself.

The effect of this rule is that claims made to BADR by an individual whether by himself or jointly with trustees, count towards using up the lifetime amount of BADR to which he is entitled (namely £10m from 6 April 2011 to 10 March 2020, and £1m from 11 March 2020). If the individual decides to join in a claim for relief by the trustees he must in effect share his lifetime limit for BADR with the trustees of the trust of which he is a qualifying beneficiary; but he has no obligation to join in such a claim.

In this Example, Thomas made a claim in 2019 for entrepreneurs' relief (as it was then called) of £50,000. This means that in 2023/24 only £950,000 of his lifetime limit of qualifying gains remains. As Thomas makes no personal claim in 2023 for BADR in respect of the gain of £3m arising to him personally on the sale of the shares in Belvoir Ltd, Thomas and the trustees can jointly claim that £950,000 of the trustees' gain qualifies for BADR relief.

Robert, on the other hand, has, in 2023, previously used none of this lifetime limit of qualifying gains and so he may claim BADR (both alone and jointly with the trustees) of up to £1m. However, Robert's attitude is that he will only enter into a joint claim with the trustees in respect of their gains to an extent that will ensure that his own personal gains will attract as much relief as possible. Robert has realised a gain of £3m in respect of the disposal of his shares in Belvoir Ltd in 2023 and so will not enter into a joint claim for BADR with the trustee, so that the trustees' gains of £9.75m referable to his status as a qualifying beneficiary will attract the full 20% rate of capital gains tax applicable to the non-residential property gains of trustees.

Capital gains tax payable by trustees

	£	£
Gain arising on the disposal of shares in Belvoir Ltd		39,000,000
Less: amount qualifying for BADR	950,000	(950,000)
		38,050,000
Less: annual exemption		(3,000)
Chargeable gains not qualifying for BADR		38,047,000
Chargeable gains qualifying for BADR	950,000	
Capital gains tax payable by trustees @ 20%		£7,609,400
Capital gains tax payable by trustees @ 10%	£95,000	

The total capital gains tax payable by the trustees in 2023/24 is thus £7,704,400

C.

The rules for investors' relief are set out in TCGA 1992 ss 169VA–169VR (inserted by FA 2016, s 86 and Sch 14). The relief, which is separate from business asset disposal relief, is available to individuals (for which see the companion book, **Tolley's Taxwise I 2023/24** and an article by Giles and Handley entitled 'Investors' Relief' published in *Tax Journal* dated 12 March 2021) and trustees of a settlement, but not to personal representatives of a deceased person's estate. The relief comes in the form of a lower rate of capital gains tax of 10% in respect of a lifetime limit of £10m of qualifying gains, ie those arising on the disposal of shares in an unlisted trading company or the holding company of a trading group (no minimum holding is required) which have been subscribed for by the investor on or after 17 March 2017. The shares must be ordinary shares, subscribed for and fully paid in cash at arms' length for genuine commercial reasons and not part of a scheme or arrangement the main purpose or one of the main purposes of which was the avoidance of tax. The shares cannot be listed on any recognised stock exchange although for this purpose shares listed on AIM are regarded as unlisted.

The circumstances in which investors' relief is available to trustees are very much more circumscribed than those applicable to individuals. As is the case for BADR, trustees are not able to claim investors' relief in connection with a disposal of shares in their own right, but only by reference to an 'eligible beneficiary' (s 169VH).

An individual is an eligible beneficiary in respect of a disposal of qualifying shares if:

(a) immediately before the disposal he had under the settlement an interest in possession (otherwise than for a fixed term) in the whole of the settled property or the part of it which consists of or includes qualifying shares,

(b) he had such an interest throughout the period of three years ending with the date of the disposal,

(c) at no time in that period was he a relevant employee in respect of the company that issued the shares, and

(d) he has by the time of the claim elected to be treated as an eligible beneficiary in respect of the disposal. The individual so elects if he tells the trustees (by whatever means) that he wishes to be so treated. An election may be withdrawn by the individual at any time until the claim is made.

The inheritance tax status of the interest in possession is not relevant in this context, but it must be an actual interest in possession (see **Example C3**), not something which for inheritance tax purposes is a deemed, but not actual, interest in possession. It follows that in the case of a discretionary trust, or where in some other way the trustees have power or are obliged to accumulate all the trust's income or have discretion as to the distribution of that income, they cannot benefit from investors' relief when realising a gain on the disposal of trust qualifying shares, because there is in such a case no interest in possession and so no possibility of an eligible beneficiary.

A claim for investors' relief in respect of a disposal by trustees must, to be valid, be made jointly by the trustees and the eligible beneficiary. The deadline for claims is the first anniversary of 31 January following the end of the tax year in which the share disposal is made (corresponding to the last date on which a taxpayer can amend his self-assessment return in normal course) (s 169VM). As is the case for BADR, a claim to investors' relief is revocable, it may be amended or revoked within the time limit and the provision for self-assessment and stand-alone claims may extend the time limit for amendment, particularly when an enquiry is opened.

In cases where there is more than one eligible beneficiary with an interest in possession in the settled property or the part comprising the settlement's qualifying shares, their respective share of the gain arising to the trustees is ascertained under s 169VI as the trustees' gain multiplied by the fraction X/Y where:

X is the income interest of the eligible beneficiary concerned immediately before the disposal in the part of the settled property which comprises the qualifying shares disposed of, and

Y is the total of the income interests of all the eligible beneficiaries with interests in possession in that part of the settled property.

For trustees, the £10 million lifetime limit for investors' relief is that of the eligible beneficiary in question, and must be restricted by total amount of any gains that, in relation to earlier disposals made by the individual concerned were charged at the investors' relief rate of 10% combined with the total amount of any trust gains that, on any previous trust disposal in respect of which the individual was an eligible beneficiary, were charged at the investors' relief rate of 10% (s 169VL). This means that should an eligible beneficiary have exhausted his own lifetime limit, then in respect of that portion of the trustees' gain that exceeds £10m, no investors' relief is available.

Explanatory Notes

(1) Before 23 June 2010 when the pre-6 April 2016 single trustees' rate of 28% was introduced, the mechanics of entrepreneurs' relief (as it was then known) were different, involving the reduction of the relevant chargeable gains by 4/9ths (producing the same result when the reduced figure was then taxed at 18%), but it was still the unreduced gains figure which counted towards the lifetime limit of relief.

(2) That lifetime limit was originally £1 million when entrepreneurs' relief (as it was then known) was introduced with effect from 6 April 2008. It rose to £2 million on 6 April 2010 and to £5 million on 23 June 2010. The limit was again increased with effect from 6 April 2011, to £10 million by FA 2011 s 9 before reducing to £1 million for disposals occurring on or after 11 March 2020 (FA 2020, Sch 3, para 2).

(3) A further example of the 'material time' is as follows (and is based in the example given at CG64140). The trustees make a disposal of shares on 31 March 2020 upon which a gain arises and against which a claim for entrepreneurs' relief (as it was then known) is made. The period of three years up to the date of that disposal begins on 1 April 2017. The company in which the shares are sold ceased to trade on 31 December 2019 and so it ceased at that time to be a qualifying company for the purposes of entrepreneurs' relief. The material time would be at the end of the one-year period 1 January 2019 to 31 December 2019 (ie 31 December 2019).

(4) The same apportionment rule applies under s 169O(1)(b) where there are at least two beneficiaries of a trust, one of whom has an interest in possession in a part of the settled property and that part consists of or includes the shares or assets disposed of that qualify for BADR relief. For example, Chris owns 20% of the shares in an unquoted trading company of which he is a director. The rest of the shares are owned by a trust, 75% of the income of which arises to Chris by reason of his interest in possession in the trust property. The rest (25%)

of the income of the trust falls to the trustees to accumulate or distribute according to their absolute discretion to a class of beneficiaries which includes Chris. If the shares of the company are sold only 60% (ie 75% of the trustees' holding of 80%) of any gain arising potentially qualifies for BADR. Although Chris is a member of the discretionary class of beneficiaries, this additional interest in the trust is ignored when the proportion of the trustees' gain potentially qualifying for BADR is ascertained (s 169O(5)).

Question

A.

In May 1988, at a time when he was UK resident, Stephen Jones set up a discretionary trust for the benefit of his four cousins – this was the only trust that he had created. The trustees paid inheritance tax of £44,000 on the chargeable transfer of £330,000 and the capital gains of £110,000 arising on the transfer of the assets were held over. Stephen acted as trustee, together with his solicitor and a close friend.

In February 1989 Stephen emigrated (permanently) and the administration of the trust was transferred to new trustees all of whom were and are resident outside the UK. Had the trust's assets been disposed of at that time capital gains of £155,000 would have arisen (including the gain held over).

The beneficiaries, Matthew, Mark, Mary and Matilda were all minors at the date of the settlement, and have been resident (and prior to 6 April 2013 ordinarily resident) in the UK at all times. However, although all the children were born in the UK and Mark, Mary and Matilda have a UK domicile, Matthew's domicile of origin was in Massachusetts, USA, and this remains unchanged to date.

The trustees subsequently undertook the following transactions:

June 1997	Disposal of a freehold office property for £360,980 (net of costs). The property was part of the original trust fund and had been subject to holdover relief when it was settled. It had cost Stephen Jones £50,000 in early March 1982 and was worth £100,000 in May 1988.
September 1997	Disposal of quoted shares in Jonah plc for £25,000. These shares had been acquired by the trustees in March 1990 for £9,650.
May 1998	Purchase of warehouse property in England for £150,000.
June 1998	Sale of UK residential investment property for £200,000. This property had been bought by the trustees in December 1988 for £62,034 including costs.
July 2023	Sale of non-residential property assets not qualifying for business asset disposal relief for £244,652 realising a gain of £111,400. The assets had originally been settled by Stephen but had not been subject to a holdover claim at that time.

In addition to distributing all income year by year, the trustees made capital distributions out of the settlement as follows:

	Matthew	*Mark*	*Mary*	*Matilda*
	£	£	£	£
May 1996	Nil	Nil	60,000	20,000
December 1997	90,000	60,000	Nil	70,000
May 1999	6,000	6,000	6,000	Nil
August 2023	40,000	40,000	40,000	45,000

The re-referenced retail prices index for the dates given was:

March 1982	79.44
May 1988	106.20
December 1988	110.30
February 1989	111.82
March 1990	121.40
June 1997	157.50
September 1997	159.30
April 1998	162.60

Calculate the capital gains chargeable on the trustees and the beneficiaries in respect of the above transactions, stating if any supplementary charge will apply.

For ease of reference, the capital gains tax annual exemption for individuals is as follows:

1997/98	£6,500
1998/99	£6,800
1999/2000	£7,100
2000/01	£7,200
2001/02	£7,500
2002/03	£7,700
2003/04	£7,900
2004/05	£8,200
2005/06	£8,500
2006/07	£8,800
2007/08	£9,200
2008/09	£9,600
2009/10	£10,100
2010/11	£10,100
2011/12	£10,600
2012/13	£10,600
2013/14	£10,900
2014/15	£11,000
2015/16	£11,100
2016/17	£11,100
2017/18	£11,300
2018/19	£11,700
2019/20	£12,000
2020/21	£12,300
2021/22	£12,300
2022/23	£12,300
2023/24	£6,000

The annual exemption for discretionary trusts is half the above amounts (except where several trusts have been made by the same settlor after 6 June 1978 – see **Example F6 explanatory note 15**). The rate of capital gains tax payable by such trusts was 34% for 1997/98 to 2003/04; 40% from 2004/05 to 2007/08; 18% from 2008/09 to 2009/10, and for gains in 2010/11 arising before 23 June 2010; and 28% for gains arising in 2010/11 on or after 23 June 2010 and for all later tax years until 5 April 2016. From 6 April 2016 capital gains tax is charged at 28% on residential property gains and 20% otherwise.

B.

Set out the capital gains that would have been chargeable on the trustees and beneficiaries in respect of the settlement in A if the trustees had remained UK resident despite Stephen Jones alone having emigrated in 1989.

C.

Set out the capital gains that would have been chargeable on the trustees and settlor on the assumption that the settlement was on Stephen Jones for life and then to his four cousins at age 60 (with a right to income in the meantime after cessation of Stephen Jones's life interest). Assume also that Stephen did not emigrate in 1989, but rather: the administration of the trust was transferred to non-resident trustees in February 1989, the capital payments up to May 1998 were all made to Stephen Jones, on 1 December 1998 Stephen Jones excluded himself from any further benefit under the trust by releasing his life interest in favour of his cousins, and finally the capital payments in May 1999 and August 2023 were made to the cousins.

Answer

A. Overseas trusts – capital gains tax treatment – pre-1991 trust

Capital gains on creation of settlement

When a settlement is created, the settlor is deemed to have disposed of the entire property in the settlement at its market value, even if he retains an interest as beneficiary or is a trustee of the settlement, and he is therefore chargeable to capital gains tax accordingly (subject to available reliefs and exemptions) (TCGA 1992 s 70).

When the assets transferred are business assets (s 165) or the transfer is immediately chargeable to inheritance tax (s 260), then provided the settlement is a UK resident settlement (see s 166) and (from 10 December 2003 onwards) it is not a settlor-interested settlement (within the broad definition of that term employed by s 169B), the settlor can avoid being liable for tax on the gains at that time by making an election to hold over the gains so that they in turn reduce the trustees' base acquisition costs. For disposals prior to 19 March 1989 holdover relief was given under FA 1980 s 79 and covered all assets, although no relief was then available on a subsequent disposal of the asset by the donee for any inheritance tax paid on the settlement of the asset.

Since Stephen Jones had created a UK resident discretionary trust, the transfer of assets to the trust was chargeable to inheritance tax. If he had retained an interest in the trust, the trust income would be chargeable to income tax on him (see **Example F5**) and this treatment would also have applied to any capital gains realised by the trustees while Stephen Jones was UK resident (even while the trust was also UK resident) for tax years up to and including 2007/08. (Since 2008/09 gains made by settlor interested trusts are charged on the trustees.) For capital gains following the emigration of the trust see **part C**.

The gains arising on the creation of the settlement were held over under FA 1980 s 79.

Capital gain on emigration of Stephen Jones

The emigration of Stephen Jones in February 1989 did not create or crystallise a liability for capital gains tax on any gains held over, or on any increase in the value of the assets between the date they were settled and the date of emigration.

Export of trust prior to 19 March 1991

When non-resident trustees were appointed in in February 1989, the gains of £110,000 held over on the creation of the trust became chargeable but the accrued gains of £45,000 on the trust's assets were not chargeable as they were not realised (TCGA 1992 s 168) (see **explanatory note 9** for emigration of a trust on or after 19 March 1991). The liability for the capital gains tax on the held-over gains was that of the trustees, although if the amount had not been paid within twelve months from the due date (1 December 1990) HMRC would have a claim to recover the tax from Stephen Jones.

Subsequent disposals

Although the non-residents trustees, are not chargeable to UK capital gains tax, the capital gains on disposals by the trustees must still be calculated in the same manner and on the same basis as if they were UK resident (it sometimes happens that such calculations are only commissioned after many years when a distribution to a UK resident beneficiary has been made or is in prospect). The gains are then attributed to beneficiaries by reference to any capital sums they have received from the trust in that or any earlier year, except to the extent that those capital sums have already been matched with earlier capital gains. Before 6 April 2018 capital payments made to all beneficiaries (regardless of their residence) were matched with trust gains. However, subject to certain exceptions, with effect from 6 April 2018 no account is taken of capital payments made to beneficiaries who have been non-UK resident throughout the tax year concerned (s 87D). This means that trust gains cannot, from that date, be attributed to non-UK resident beneficiaries (who are exempt from capital gains tax in respect the attributed gains). Where gains are attributed to beneficiaries (whether before or on or after 6 April 2018), they cannot exceed the actual capital sums received, and are chargeable on the beneficiaries in the year of attribution. Only beneficiaries who are resident (or, prior to 6 April 2013, ordinarily resident) in the UK (regardless of their domicile since 6 April 2008) are immediately assessed to capital gains tax on gains attributed to them (s 87) (although this observation is less meaningful in respect of gains attributed to beneficiaries on or after 6 April 2018 when gains are attributed only to UK resident beneficiaries). The normal annual exemption for capital gains tax is available to the UK resident beneficiaries on the attributed amounts, and is applied against the gains attributed to them in priority to their own gains. The attributed gains did not, however, attract taper relief in the beneficiaries' hands while that relief applied (that is in relation to gains realised before 6 April 2008), since where applicable the gains would have been reduced by any available taper relief when they arose in the trust. It is not possible to offset a beneficiary's own capital losses against attributed gains (s 1E(4)) (but whilst taper relief was in force (1998/99 to 2007/08 inclusive) a settlor's own capital losses could be set against gains attributed to him under s 86, but only after they had so far as possible been set against his own gains; that restriction was removed with the abolition of taper relief with effect from 6 April 2008.) See **explanatory notes 5, 10 and 11** in respect of the attribution of gains to resident settlors and also **explanatory note 17** regarding the anti-avoidance provisions applicable from 21 March 2000.

The position in respect of the non-resident trust is as follows:

Gains

	£	£
1997/98		
Sale proceeds freehold office property June 1997		360,980
Less: Market value May 1988	100,000	
Indexation allowance $\left(\frac{157.5 - 106.2}{106.2}\right) = .483$	48,300	
		(148,300)
Gain		212,680
Sale proceeds Jonah plc shares September 1997		25,000
Less: Cost March 1990	9,650	
Indexation allowance $\left(\frac{159.3 - 121.4}{121.4}\right) = .312$	3,010	
		(12,660)
Gain		12,340
Total gains for 1997/98 (212,680 + 12,340) =		£225,020
1998/99	£	£
Sale proceeds UK property June 1998		200,000
Less: Cost December 1988	62,034	
Indexation allowance to April 1998 $\left(\frac{162.6 - 110.3}{110.3}\right) = .474$	29,404	
		(91,438)
Total gains for 1998/99		108,562

	£
2023/24	
Gain on disposal of assets July 2023	111,400
Total gains for 2023/24	111,400

Attribution of gains

	Matthew £	*Mark* £	*Mary* £	*Matilda* £	*Total* £
1997/98					
Capital payments received to date	Nil	Nil	60,000	20,000	80,000
Capital payments received in year	90,000	60,000	Nil	70,000	220,000
	90,000	60,000	60,000	90,000	300,000
Trust gains of year attributed to each beneficiary (90:60:60:90)	67,506	45,004	45,004	67,506	225,020
Excess capital payments received to date	22,494	14,996	14,996	22,494	74,980
1998/99					
Unmatched capital payments b/fwd	22,494	14,996	14,996	22,494	74,980
Trust gains of year attributed to each beneficiary (restricted to actual payments to date)	22,494	14,996	14,996	22,494	74,980
Trust gains of 1998/99					108,562
Gains attributed as shown					(74,980)
Unmatched trust gains of 1998/99					33,582
1999/2000					
Capital payments received in year	6,000	6,000	6,000	Nil	(18,000)
Trust gains attributed to each beneficiary (restricted to actual payments)	6,000	6,000	6,000	Nil	18,000
Unmatched trust gains of 1998/99					33,582
Matched with capital payments received in 1999/2000					18,000
Balance of unmatched trust gains of 1998/99					15,582
2023/24					
Capital payments received in year	40,000	40,000	40,000	45,000	165,000
Trust gains of 2023/24 attributed to each beneficiary (40:40:40:45)	27,006	27,006	27,006	30,382	111,400
Trust gains of 1998/99 attributed to each beneficiary (40:40:40:45)	3,778	3,777	3,777	4,250	15,582
Total trust attributed gains	30,784	30,783	30,783	34,632	126,982
Excess capital payments c/fwd	9,216	9,217	9,217	10,368	38,018

The attributed gains will be chargeable on the beneficiaries (except Matthew, who is not UK domiciled, in respect of gains which arose prior to 6 April 2008,) in the year of attribution, eg Mark will be chargeable on £45,004 in 1997/98, £14,996 in 1998/99, £6,000 in 1999/2000, and £30,783 (27,006 + 3,777) in 2023/24, less his annual exemption in each case unless otherwise used.

In Matthew's case the £27,006 matched against current year's gains in 2023/24 is chargeable except so far as Matthew is a remittance basis user (so that he would not have any annual exemption) and does not remit the capital payment into the UK. He is not charged on his share (ie £3,778) of the unallocated gain brought forward from before 2008/09 (FA 2007 Sch 7 para 124(2)) nor on the earlier attributed gains totalling £96,000 (1997/98 – £67,506; 1998/99 – £22,494; 1999/00 – £6,000).

In 2023/24 the capital gains tax payable by the beneficiaries other than Matthew on their shares of the unallocated gain of £15,582 brought forward from 1998/99 is increased by a supplementary charge, because the gain arose in 1998/99, and was not distributed in that year, or the following year (1999/2000). The charge is calculated by reference to a chargeable period that runs from 1 December in the tax year following that in which the gain was made to 30 November in the tax year following that in which the capital payment was made (although the period cannot start earlier than six years before that 30 November date). The chargeable period therefore runs from 1 December 2001 to 30 November 2023 = 22 years limited to six years (maximum period). The amount of the supplement added to the capital gains tax payable is equal to the amount that would be yielded if the tax carried interest at the rate of 10% per annum for the chargeable period. Hence the capital gains tax payable by each beneficiary other than Matthew is increased by 60% (see **explanatory note 14**).

For example assume Matilda has no gains in her own right in the year 2023/24, and that her income for that year (net of her personal allowance) falls £5,000 short of the basic rate limit. Her liability will be:

Total attributed gains	34,632			
Less Annual exemption	(6,000)			
Capital gains tax chargeable on	28,632			
Tax payable @ 10% on	5,000	=	500	
Tax payable @ 20% on balance	23,632	=	4,726	5,226
Of which proportion relating to 1998/99 is 4,250/34,632 x 5,226		=	£641	
Supplementary charge re 1998/99	£641 @ 60%	=		385
Total tax payable				£5,611

(to be shown in box 9 on the capital gains summary sheet SA108 of the self-assessment tax return).

By comparison, if in 2023/24 Mary has capital gains of £7,100 in her own right (none of which relates to the disposal of residential property) and has income (net of her personal allowance) that already exceeds the basic rate limit, her liability will be:

Total attributed gains	30,783			
Less annual exemption (see **explanatory note 8**)	(6,000)			
	24,783			
Own gains	7,100			
Capital gains tax chargeable on	31,883			
Tax payable on personal gains @ 20%	7,100	=	1,420	
Tax relating to gains attributed in respect of capital payment @ 20%	24,783	=	4,957	6,377
Of which proportion relating to 1998/99 is 3,777/30,783 × £4,957		=	608	
Supplementary charge in respect of 1998/99 gains	£608 @ 60%	=		365
Total tax payable				£6,742

B. Position if trust had remained UK resident after Stephen Jones emigrated

If the trustees had remained UK resident after February 1989, the gain of £110,000 held over when the trust was created would not have become chargeable until the trust assets in question were disposed of. The revised capital gains on the trustees' disposals would be chargeable on them in the tax year in which the disposals took place. The trust would have an annual exemption of one-half of the exemption for individuals and tax would be payable on the remaining gains at the rate applicable to trusts (later 'trust rate') from time to time prior to 6 April 2008 and at the non-residential property rate of 20% for the 2023/24 gain (28% in the period 6 April 2008 to 5 April 2016). There would be no relief by reference to the non-domiciled beneficiary, Matthew. The position would therefore be as follows:

		£	£
1997/98			
Sale proceeds freehold office property June 1997			360,980
Market value May 1988		100,000	
Less held-over gain:			
Market value on transfer to trust	100,000		
Less: Cost March 1982	(50,000)		
Indexation allowance $(\frac{106.2 - 79.44}{79.44}) = .337$	(16,850)		
Settlor's gain	33,150		
Gain halved and held over (settlor acquired asset before 31 March 1982)	16,575	(16,575)	
		83,425	
Indexation allowance: £83,425 × 0.483 as in A		40,294	(123,719)
Gain			237,261
Gain on Jonah plc shares acquired by trustees in March 1990 (as in A)			12,340
Total gains			249,601
Less: annual exemption (½ × 6,500)			(3,250)
Gains (chargeable at 34%)			246,351
1998/99			
Gain on sale of UK property bought by trustees in December 1998 (as in A)			108,562
Less: annual exemption (½ × 6,800)			(3,400)
Gains (chargeable at 34%)			105,162
2023/24			
Gain on sale of assets in July 2023 as in A			111,400
Less: annual exemption (½ × 6,000)			(3,000)
Gains chargeable at 20%			108,400

C. Position if Stephen Jones had been life tenant and had remained UK resident but the trust had emigrated

The creation of a life interest settlement on Stephen Jones in May 1988 would have given rise to a chargeable gain which could have been held over under FA 1980 s 79 as before (see answer to **part a** above). The held-over gain would then have been chargeable on the trustees, but with Stephen Jones as settlor being concurrently liable if the trustees failed to pay the tax, on the export of the trust in February 1989 as in A above.

The subsequent disposals by the trust would be treated as in A, ie there would be capital gains tax computations as though the trustees were still resident in the UK. Since the trust emigrated before 19 March 1991, the provisions of TCGA 1992 s 86 charging a settlor who retains an interest in a trust on gains arising on or after 17 March 1998 would not have applied before 1999/2000 (see below). Gains arising before 17 March 1998 would have been chargeable on Stephen Jones when capital payments were made to him, with a supplementary charge payable if the payments had not been distributed in the tax year in which the gain arose or the following tax year (as in A above).

By virtue of FA 1998 s 132 gains arising on or after 17 March 1998 in a pre-19 March 1991 settlement whose trustees are not UK resident became chargeable on the settlor if he or his immediate family (or companies they control) can benefit under the settlement. Gains arising between 17 March 1998 and 5 April 1999 were not so charged until 6 April 1999 to allow settlors time to reorganise their affairs. Stephen Jones did this in December 1998 by releasing his life interest in favour of his cousins (though the release would not have achieved exemption from the s 86 charge if any persons in his immediate family had been eligible beneficiaries – see **explanatory note 10**). The release would have been a potentially exempt transfer for inheritance tax since the cousins became entitled to interests in possession on the release of a prior life interest before 22 March 2006 (see **Examples C3 and C6**).

The gains attributable to Stephen Jones would have been as follows (before his personal annual exemption or any personal losses prior to 6 April 1998):

	£
1997/98	
Capital payments in 1996/97	80,000
Capital payments in 1998/99	220,000
	300,000
Trust gains attributed to Stephen Jones (actual)	(225,020)
Excess capital payments to date	74,980
1998/99	
Trust gains of the year	108,562
Gains attributed to Stephen Jones – excess capital payments to date	(74,980)
Unattributed trust gains of 1998/99 c/fwd	33,582

As Stephen Jones ceased to be a beneficiary of the trust on 1 December 1998, the unattributed 1998/99 trust gains of £33,582 could not be attributed to him, but would be attributed to the four cousins, together with subsequent gains, as and when capital payments were made to them. The first capital payment was made in 1999/2000 and would have been treated as in **part A** of the Example.

Explanatory Notes

Capital gains tax legislation relating to offshore trusts; the residence of trustees

(1) The capital gains tax charges relating to offshore trusts are complex and contain many points of difficulty. As illustrated by the Example, trusts which have been in existence for many years have had to contend with several major changes in the law. The following notes outline some of the key dates and changes which have an ongoing effect on current tax liabilities. Because of the way gains arising to a non-resident trust can be carried forward and matched with payments to beneficiaries many years later, it is necessary to keep abreast of the changes in the calculation of capital gains throughout the life of the trust.

Until the introduction of FA 2006, there were different rules determining the residence status of trustees for income and capital gains tax. These were harmonised by that Act so that with effect from 6 April 2007 trustees are treated as resident (and, before 6 April 2013, ordinarily resident) in the UK if either:

(a) all the trustees are resident in the UK; or

(b)

(i) at least one trustee is resident in the UK, and

(ii) a settlor in relation to the settlement was resident, ordinarily resident or domiciled in the UK when the settlement is made (ITA 2007 s 475, TCGA 1992 s 69).

An additional rule introduced in the process was that, for the purpose of the above test, a trustee who is not resident in the UK is to be treated as so resident at any time when he acts as trustee in the course of a business which he carries on in the UK through a branch, agency or permanent establishment here. This rule is far from easy to apply in practice because of the uncertainties surrounding the concept (for corporate trustees) of a permanent establishment. HMRC's guidance on the matter can be found at www.hmrc.gov.uk/cnr/nr_trusts.htm.

The statutory residence test for individuals (SRT) (which applies from 6 April 2013 by FA 2013 Sch 45) has amended the above definition slightly to reflect the split year treatment where an individual is a trustee during the overseas part of the tax year. However, it should be noted that the split year rules do not apply to trustees except in these circumstances. The new rule provides that an individual who is a UK resident trustee is to be treated as not UK resident (unless he carries on business through a branch or agency) if he becomes or ceases to be a trustee in the tax year, the year is a split year as regards the individual and in that year the only period when the individual is a trustee falls wholly within the overseas part of the year (ie that part of the year during which he is treated as not UK resident) (ITA 2007 s 475(7)–(9); TCGA 1992 s 69(2DA), (2DB)).

Otherwise the SRT does not amend the above rules determining the residence of trustees. The SRT may, however, affect the residence status of individuals who are trustees and of settlors and so, in this indirect way, it should be appreciated that the residence of existing trusts may also be affected. For more detail on the SRT see the companion volume **Tolley's Taxwise I 2023/24**.

Effect for capital gains tax of emigration of trust on trustees

(2) If an election to hold over a settlor's gains had been made under TCGA 1992 s 165 or s 260 (or previously under FA 1980 s 79), the held-over gain crystallised if the trustees emigrated before 19 March 1991. The amount chargeable was the gain originally held over (s 168).

For trusts emigrating on or after 19 March 1991, the emigrating trustees are charged not only on gains held over at the time the funds were settled but on the whole of any increase in value of the trust assets up to the time of emigration (see **explanatory note 9**). Since 19 March 1991 s 168 has accordingly no longer applied where a trust becomes non-resident, and now relates only to the emigration of donees who are individuals.

(3) Where a held-over gain has been charged under s 168 as a result of the emigration of the donee, the base cost at which the donee is deemed to have acquired the asset is its full value at the time of the gift, so that the trustees in the Example will have been treated as having acquired the trust assets at their value on the creation of the settlement. Where that was before 31 March 1982, HMRC apparently took the view that a general rebasing election could only be made by the trustees, even though any charge to capital gains tax would be made on the beneficiaries; but the point is no longer relevant after 5 April 2008 since the 31 March 1982 value will be taken as the acquisition cost in all such cases after that even if it is lower than the true original acquisition cost.

(4) Where a held-over gain was triggered on or after 6 April 1988 but before 6 April 2008 and was wholly or partly attributable to a disposal before 6 April 1988 of an asset acquired before 31 March 1982, only half of the held-over gain was charged to tax (Sch 4 para 4). This halving relief is illustrated in **part B** of the Example.

Attribution of gains of offshore trusts to settlor or beneficiaries

(5) If the settlor who is both resident and domiciled in the UK retains an interest in the trust, gains are charged on him as and when they arise under the provisions of s 86 if the settlement becomes non-resident on or after 19 March 1991, or if funds are added to the trust or the beneficiaries of the trust are varied on or after that date, and in any event from 6 April 1999 in respect of gains arising on or after 17 March 1998 (see **explanatory notes 10** and **11**). Gains taxed on the settlor are not charged on the beneficiaries (s 87(4)(b)).

From 6 April 2017, an individual will be deemed to be domiciled in the UK in a given tax year where he is resident in the UK in that year and he was born in the UK with a UK domicile of origin (ITA 2007 s 835B(3)). Also an individual who has been resident in the UK for 15 out of the 20 tax years preceding a given tax year will be deemed to be domiciled in the UK in that tax year (ITA 2007 s 835B(4)). Gains of offshore trusts are not to be attributed to a settlor where he becomes deemed domiciled in the UK under the 15-year residence rule. TCGA 1992, Sch 5 para 5A provides that s 86 does not apply in a tax year if the following conditions are met:

(a) the tax year is 2017/18 or a later year

(b) the settlor was not domiciled (or deemed domiciled) in the UK when the settlement was created

(c) in the tax year concerned the settlor is neither domiciled nor deemed domiciled in the UK under the rule applicable to individuals who were born in the UK, and

(d) where the settlor is domiciled or deemed domiciled in the UK, he (or the trustees of another settlement of which he is the settlor or a beneficiary) had not provided any property or income directly or indirectly (including the additional of value to property comprised in the settlement) for the purposes of the settlement at any time in the period beginning on 6 April 2017 (or the creation of the settlement, if later) and the end of the tax year concerned. However, when applying this condition the following property or income which is provided for the purposes of the settlement is ignored:

a. property or income provided on arm's length terms

b. property or income provided without any intention by the person providing it to confer a gratuitous benefit on any person

c. a loan made to the trustees of the settlement on arm's length terms as defined (unless a relevant event occurs when the principal of the loan will, on the happening of that event, be treated as having been provided for the purposes of the settlement. A relevant event occurs where interest payable under the loan is capitalised, the trustees otherwise fail to pay the interest in accordance with the terms of the loan or the terms of the loan are varied so that they cease to be arm's length terms)

d. any interest paid to the trustees of the settlement under a loan made by them on arm's length terms

e. repayment of a loan made by the trustees of the settlement

f. where the settlement's expenses relating to administration or taxation for the year concerned exceed its income for that year, any property or income provided to meet that excess.

As and when chargeable gains are made that are not taxed on the settlor under s 86, they are attributed to the beneficiaries and charged to tax, but only to the extent that beneficiaries have received capital payments of an equivalent amount, either in the year in which the gains are made or in an earlier year (for this purpose 'the beneficiaries' could include the settlor if not chargeable under s 86) and, with effect from 6 April 2018, only where the beneficiaries are resident throughout the tax year concerned (s 87D). (See **explanatory note 17** for anti-avoidance provisions to counter schemes to avoid the charge on the beneficiaries.) The gains that are attributed to the beneficiaries are the gains arising to the offshore trustees calculated on the basis that they are resident in the UK; any NRCGT gains (using that acronym as a convenient label to describe the UK gains (and losses) of non-UK resident persons that are charged under s 1A(3) to capital gains tax (itself also referred to as NRCGT for convenience) made by the offshore trustees on the disposal after 5 April 2015 of UK residential property are however not so attributed to the beneficiaries as they will already have been taxed on the trustees themselves as NRCGT gains (s 87(5A)). (With effect from 6 April 2019, the charge to NRCGT is extended to disposals of all land in the UK and to shares that derive at least 75% of their value from UK land.) To the extent that the gain is not treated as a NRCGT gain then it will not be so attributed to the trustees. For example, in computing a gain under the default method, the post- April 2015 gain is subject to NRCGT but the pre-April 2015 gain is not. Only the post-April 2015 amount would be attributed to the beneficiary. Any gains that have not been attributed in this way are carried forward and attributed as and when capital payments are made, as in 1999/2000 and 2023/24 in **part A** of the Example. The capital payments carried forward at the end of 1997/98 represented amounts that the beneficiaries had already received in respect of which no chargeable gains had arisen. When chargeable gains next arose in 1998/99 they were attributed to the beneficiaries because of the excess capital payments at 5 April 1998.

Section 87 charges beneficiaries to tax on gains made by a non-resident trust to the extent that they receive capital payments from the trust. (There are equivalent charging provisions in s 89 for trusts which are UK resident but had been offshore at some time since 10 March 1981, and in Sch 4C where property has been transferred between settlements in circumstances that attract a deemed disposal under Sch 4B which was targeted at schemes known as flip-flop schemes.) Before FA 1998 the s 87 regime applied where the trustees were neither resident nor ordinarily resident at any time in the tax year, if at any time in that year or at the time when he made the settlement the settlor was domiciled and either resident or ordinarily resident in the

UK. In respect of gains realised and capital payments made on or after 17 March 1998, the conditions relating to the settlor's residence and domicile no longer apply (FA 1998 s 130). Both before and after 17 March 1998, however, a beneficiary is not charged unless he is resident (or before 6 April 2013 ordinarily resident) in the UK; and (until the FA 2008 amendments summarised below), he was also not charged unless he was domiciled in the UK at some time in the year in which the gains were attributed to him (TCGA 1992 ss 1A(1), 87(7)). Note that where the income tax provisions of ITA 2007 ss 727, 731 apply (transfer of assets abroad – liability of non-transferors on benefits received), any distributions or benefits are treated as being made first from accumulated income before being treated as capital payments under TCGA 1992 s 87. In this Example all income has been distributed year by year in addition to the capital payments made.

Prior to FA 2008, non-UK domiciled individuals were exempt from both the settlor charge under s 86 and the beneficiary charge in s 87, whether or not they were UK resident.

The exemption from the settlor charge for non-UK domiciled settlors of non-UK resident trusts has remained unaltered (and indeed this exemption remains a central feature of the s 86 regime with the protection afforded, on terms, to overseas trusts whose settlors become deemed domiciled in the UK under the 15-year residence test). However, FA 2008 made changes to the beneficiary charge. As from 6 April 2008, the beneficiary charge in TCGA 1992 s 87 applies to all UK resident beneficiaries (regardless of their domicile). In other words the s 87 regime was extended to resident and non-domiciled individuals. However, such persons to whom trust gains are attributed are subject to the remittance basis. Such persons may claim the remittance basis under ITA 2007 s 809B or are entitled to it under ITA 2007 s 809D. There are complex transitional rules in this regard where gains or capital payments occurred before 6 April 2008.

Also under FA 2008, non-resident trustees were given an option to rebase trust assets to their market values as at 6 April 2008 so that trust gains accruing, but not realised, prior to 6 April 2008 cannot be chargeable if attributed to non-UK domiciled beneficiaries because of being matched with capital payments made to them on or after 6 April 2008. This option is open only to the trustees, and neither settlors nor beneficiaries have the right to make the election in respect of it. This rebasing, if the trustees elect for it, has no effect on the computation of trust gains for the purpose of attribution to beneficiaries who are UK domiciled as well as UK resident.

As a result of the changes:

- Trust gains arising after 5 April 2008 that are matched with capital payments made after 5 April 2008 to non-UK domiciled beneficiaries are generally chargeable to tax.

- The remittance basis applies if the non-UK domiciled beneficiary is a remittance basis user in the year when trust gains are treated as accruing to him. This is so whether the trust gains accrue on UK or non-UK assets. A capital gain so attributed is treated as remitted if the distributed property is received in or brought to the UK. Benefits in kind will be treated as remitted if enjoyed or used in the UK.

Unmatched trust gains brought forward from 2007/08 are not taxed on a non-UK domiciled beneficiary unless (as previously) he is both resident and domiciled in the UK when those gains are treated as accruing to him. Capital payments to non-UK domiciled beneficiaries made prior to 12 March 2008 can be matched with 5 April 2008 trust gains, but only to the extent that:

- there are no capital payments made after 5 April 2008 to which the post 5 April 2008 gains can be attributed first; and

- there are no pre-April 2008 gains accruing by virtue of the rebasing election.

Capital payments made to UK resident but non-UK domiciled beneficiaries between 12 March and 5 April 2008 which are not matched with pre-6 April 2008 trust gains are left out of account in 2008/09 and subsequent years for the purposes of applying TCGA 1992 s 87 – in other words, as a measure to prevent forestalling of the FA 2008 changes, they cannot be used (as they would have been before 12 March 2008, and are again after 5 April 2008) to 'frank' post-5 April 2008 trust gains so as to prevent those gains giving rise to tax charges on beneficiaries who are both resident and domiciled in the UK (FA 2008 Sch 7 para 125).

If the trustees have made a rebasing election, the pre-6 April 2008 element of any gain treated as accruing to the beneficiary is matched with any surplus capital payments made between 12 March and 5 April 2008.

Trust gains brought forward from 2007/08 and treated under section TCGA 1992 s 87(4) as accruing to non-UK domiciled beneficiaries by virtue of capital payments made on or after 6 April 2008 are not taxed unless the beneficiary has in the meantime become both resident and domiciled in the UK. Although the capital payment is received after 5 April 2008, if it is matched to trust gains realised prior to 6 April 2008 or to the pre-6 April 2008 element of any gain on a rebasing election, it is not necessary in this case for the non-UK domiciled beneficiary to be a remittance basis user.

The option to elect for rebasing to the market value as at 6 April 2008, given to trusts which were non-UK resident on 6 April 2008, applies to all assets held by the trust both directly and by its underlying companies. The effect, if the election is made, is that the pre-6 April 2008 element of any trust gains treated as accruing to non-UK domiciled beneficiaries after that date will not be taxed. The election must be made no later than 31 January following the first tax year (starting with 2008/09) in which either a UK resident beneficiary receives a capital payment or the trustees transfer any property to another settlement such that TCGA 1992 s 90 applies.

Any supplementary charge under s 91 for remittance basis users will be calculated based on the year in which the capital payment is made by the trustees, not the year in which it is remitted to the UK by the non-UK domiciled beneficiary. (See **explanatory notes 14** and **15** for a discussion of the supplementary charge.)

A general matching rule was introduced, in s 87A, to the effect that a last in, first out rule is used to match any trust gains with capital payments made on or after 6 April 2008. This applies to all beneficiaries, not just non-UK domiciled beneficiaries, and applies in place of the original first in, first out rule in computing the supplementary charge.

With effect from 6 April 2013 a beneficiary in respect of whom a tax year is a split year (under the SRT) will be taxable under s 87 only on a proportion of any gain attributed to him by reason of a capital payment attributable to the UK part of the year, calculated on a time basis (s 87(7)).

Finance Act 2018 substantially amended the operation of the beneficiary charge under s 87. As already explained above, with effect from 6 April 2018, capital payments made to beneficiaries who are non-UK resident throughout the tax year concerned are ignored in the application of the matching and attribution rules in s 87 and s 87A. This means that accumulated trust gains may no longer be 'washed out' (ie treated as not taxable because they are attributed to non-UK resident beneficiaries). However, this rule is itself dis-applied where capital payments are made to temporary non-resident beneficiaries (for whom the payment is treated as being received in the period when they return to the UK) (s 87E). The dis-application also applies in the tax year in which the settlement ceases to exist when capital payments made to non-UK resident beneficiaries are taken into account so that trust gains may be attributed to them (s 87F). Special rules apply where a UK-resident beneficiary receives a payment in one tax year but emigrates in a later year before the payment is matched with trust gains; s 87 is to be applied without taking into account the unmatched portion of the payment (s 87N). However, where the beneficiary is a temporary non-resident, s 87 is to be applied as if the unmatched payment were received on the beneficiary's return to the UK (s 87P).

Where the beneficiary in receipt of the capital payment is a close member of the settlor's family at the time of receipt and in a tax year when the settlor is UK resident, then the capital payment is treated as received by the settlor so that the gains otherwise attributed to the beneficiaries are treated as accruing to the settlor (s 87G). In this case payments made to all such beneficiaries (whether UK resident or not) are taken into account. Where tax becomes chargeable on the settlor, the settlor may recover the amount from the beneficiary actually in receipt of the capital payment and require HMRC to confirm the amount. A beneficiary is a close family member of the settlor where the settlor is alive and they are the settlor's spouse or civil partner (or a cohabitant of the settlor with whom they living as if they were their spouse or civil partner), or a minor child of either the settlor, spouse, civil partner or relevant cohabitant (s 87H).

Further rules apply where the trustees of an offshore trust make a capital payment to a non-UK resident beneficiary (or a UK resident beneficiary that is a remittance basis user) and there is an arrangement for that person to pass the payment (whether directly or indirectly) on to a UK resident person within three years, the UK resident who ultimately receives the payment is treated as receiving the capital payment from the trustees (s 87J). In this case (and subject to the computational rules specified) the amount treated as received by the UK resident person is matched with the trust's gains so that those gains are attributed to and taxable on them (s 87K). Where the payment so received is received by a close member of the settlor's family, then the settlor is treated as receiving the payment and is taxed accordingly but has the right to recovery of the tax paid from the actual recipient of the payment (s 87L).

(6) It should be noted that the gains attributed to a beneficiary in a year can exceed the capital payments received in that year because of amounts received in prior years (but not before 10 March 1981) (s 87(4), (5), (10)). Therefore Mary, who does not receive any capital payments in 1997/98, has a liability in that year on gains of £45,004, since she had received capital payments in excess of that amount in earlier years. On the other hand, a charge to tax may occur in a year in which no gains are made by the trustees, because capital payments are made when there are unallocated trust gains brought forward. In 1999/2000 there are no gains but Mark and Mary are charged on brought forward gains because of the capital payments received. Furthermore, if those unallocated gains brought forward were realised in an earlier year than the immediately previous year, a supplementary charge is payable, as shown (see **explanatory note 14**).

(7) Prior to 2008/09 Matthew was not charged on the gains attributed to him as, although he is resident and ordinarily resident in the UK, he is not UK domiciled. The attribution nevertheless removed the gains from the record so far as the other beneficiaries were concerned. From 2008/09 onwards Matthew will in principle be charged to capital gains tax to the extent that post 6 April 2008 gains are matched with a post 6 April 2008 capital payment to him; but if he has the benefit of the remittance basis (with a claim where required) under ITA 2007 ss 809B–809E (with the loss of his annual exemption if the remittance basis is available only by virtue of a claim under s 809B) then he is charged only when he remits the capital payment into the UK.

(8) By virtue of TCGA 1992 s 1F where a person's chargeable gains are taxable at different rates, his annual exemption (and any allowable losses (other than NRCGT losses which may only be set against NRCGT gains)) may be deducted from those gains in whatever way is most beneficial. This will usually mean deducting them from the gains that are liable at 20% or 28% (for residential property gains and NRCGT gains) where the taxpayer has part of his basic rate band unused so that some gains are chargeable only at 10% or 18% (for residential property gains and NRCGT gains). The benefit is that much greater in this example to the extent that part of the attributed gain liable at 10% or 20% is also exposed to the supplementary charge. The attributed gains of offshore trusts are amounts that are deemed to accrue to an individual and they are not the actual gains of the trustees themselves (s 86(4), s 87(2)). Consequently such attributed gains are taxed only at the 10% and 20% rates (for attributions made on and after 6 April 2016); none can be taxed at the rates (18% and 28%) applicable to residential property gains. See **Example A24 (a)(iii)** for an explanation of the capital gains tax treatment of individuals.

Emigration of trust on or after 19 March 1991 – capital gains tax treatment

(9) In **part A** of the Example the trust became non-resident in February 1989 and the gains held over on creation of the settlement became chargeable at that time, but not accrued gains on the trust's assets, as they had not been realised. If trustees of a settlement become non-resident on or after 19 March 1991, then they are deemed to have disposed of and immediately reacquired the settled property at market value on the day they become non-resident, so that not only any held-over gains but also accrued gains become chargeable at that time (s 80). Section 168 imposing a separate charge on held-over gains, as illustrated in **part A**, therefore no longer applies where trustees become non-resident on or after 19 March 1991 (see **explanatory notes 2–3**).

The deemed disposal under s 80(2) does not apply to trading assets of a permanent establishment which remain within the charge to UK capital gains tax under s 10 despite the owner's non-resident status. Rollover relief on replacement of business assets under ss 152–156 cannot be claimed if the new assets are acquired after the trust becomes non-resident and are outside the UK tax charge. These provisions also apply to dual resident trusts that are exempt from UK tax on gains because of a double tax treaty.

The deemed disposal under s 80(2) is also dis-applied (subject to revenue protection exceptions in the case of assets disposed of during the period of non-residence, and assets protected by double taxation arrangements) if the trust becomes non-resident solely by reason of the death of a trustee and the trust is repatriated within six months thereafter; but since 6 April 2007 this would only be relevant in the case of settlements whose settlor had no UK residence or domicile connections at the time he made the settlement (see **explanatory note (1)**).

On the emigration of a trust, beneficiaries would normally be treated as having acquired their interests in the trust at the market value at the date of the trust's emigration, as a counterpart to the deemed disposal at trust level under s 80. However, where a trust becomes non-resident on or after 21 March 2000, this uplift to market value does not apply where the trust has a stockpile of gains at the date of emigration that have not been attributed to beneficiaries (s 85).

In the case of Trustees of the *P Panayi Accumulation & Maintenance Settlements v HMRC* (Case C-646/15), the Court of Justice of the European Union has held, in a preliminary ruling, that the exit charge arising under TCGA 1992, s 80 is, because it cannot be deferred, contrary to the freedom of establishment principle enshrined in the EU Treaties.

HMRC unsuccessfully sought to argue that the treaty freedoms did not apply to trusts. The CJEU noted that the freedom of establishment given by Art 49 was a very broad concept and applies to 'companies or firms constituted under civil or commercial law, including co-operative societies, and other legal persons governed by public or private law, save for those which are non-profit-making'. The court held that the activity of the trustees in relation to the trust property and the management of its assets were inextricably linked to the trust. Therefore, the trust and its trustees constituted an indivisible whole. A trust should be considered an entity which, under national law, has rights and obligations that enable it to act as such within the legal order concerned. It followed that an entity such as a trust that possesses rights and obligations which enable it to act in its own right and that carries on an economic activity may rely on freedom of establishment.

In the light of this case new legislation has been introduced (see TMA 1970, s 59BB, Sch 3ZAA) to provide for CGT exit charge payment plans. The legislation applies to gains arising on or after 6 April 2019. It enables trusts that cease to be UK resident and become resident in the EEA to defer, in certain cases, payment of the CGT that may arise on that occasion. The trustees can defer payment by entering into a CGT exit charge payment plan (ECPP) provided they are able to demonstrate that when they ceased to be UK resident they had a right of freedom of establishment, the assets subject to charge have been used for an economically significant economic activity in the UK and that immediately after becoming non-UK resident they became resident elsewhere in the EEA and use the assets for an economically significant activity carried on there (Sch 3ZAA para 3).

The ECPP may apply to all the tax arising on emigration or just part of it. The amount of tax that is deferred under the ECPP is payable in six equal instalments, the first being due on the day the full amount would have been due without entering into the ECPP (Sch 3ZAA paras 4 and 5).

An application by trustees to enter into an ECPP is made to HMRC by the date on which the tax deferred would ordinarily be payable. The trustees must undertake to pay the deferred tax and interest due on it in accordance with the plan. An ECPP will be void if all material facts are not disclosed to HMRC or where the deferral of tax payments is the main purpose of arrangements that include the change of residence. The ECPP must include details of residency and the amount of tax being deferred (Sch 3ZAA para 6 and 7).

Once an ECPP has been entered into, HMRC will expect payment of the tax only in accordance with the plan. Whilst the plan is in place the ordinary penalty provisions are overridden and will only be activated of the taxpayer fails to make payment under its terms. However, interest is still due on the amount of tax deferred and interest must be paid on each instalment of tax as it is paid. The trustees are free to pay any outstanding balance, with interest, before the end of the ECPP period. Should the trustees become bankrupt or resident (including treaty resident) in a country outside the EEA, the full outstanding balance is due on the date the next instalment would have been due (Sch 3ZAA para 8).

Trusts in which the settlor retains an interest – capital gains tax treatment

(10) Where a settlement with non-resident trustees is made on or after 19 March 1991, or becomes non-resident on or after that date, and the settlor is resident (or before 6 April 2013 ordinarily resident) and domiciled in the UK (or from 6 April 2017, deemed domiciled in the UK where the protection described in explanatory note 5 above is not available), and any of a list of defined persons can benefit from the settlement, then the gains of the settlement are attributed to the settlor (s 86). The gains that are attributed to the settlor are the gains arising to the offshore trustees calculated on the basis that they are resident in the UK; any NRCGT gains made by the offshore trustees on the disposal after 5 April 2015 of UK residential property (and after 5 April 2019, of all land in the UK and shares that derive at least 75% of their value from UK land) are however not so charged on the settlor as they will already have been taxed on the trustees themselves (s 86(4ZA)). To the extent that the gain is not treated as a NRCGT gain then it will not be so attributed to

the trustees. For example, in computing a gain under the default method in respect of residential property, the post- April 2015 gains is subject to NRCGT but the pre-April 2015 gain is not. Only the post-April 2015 amount would be attributed to the settlor.

The list of defined persons comprises the settlor and his spouse/civil partner, children, children's spouses/civil partners, any company controlled by one or more of those persons, and any associated company. For settlements with non-resident trustees made on or after 17 March 1998, grandchildren and their spouses (and, since 5 December 2005, their civil partners) are added to the list of defined persons for s 86 purposes (FA 1998 s 131). This also applies to pre-17 March 1998 trusts if, on or after that date, they become non-resident or funds are added or grandchildren become beneficiaries (or a grandchild who was already a beneficiary enjoys a benefit for the first time on or after that date that he would not have been able to enjoy under the terms of the settlement as it stood at that date) (FA 1998 Sch 22).

Before FA 2008 a trust's gains were reduced by taper relief before being attributed to a settlor and the settlor could not use his personal losses to reduce the gains. The abolition of taper relief with effect from 6 April 2008 simplifies this calculation.

The settlor can recover the tax he has paid from the trustees without that amount being treated as the receipt of a capital payment or any other benefit that would have tax consequences. For this purpose he may require HMRC to issue him with a certificate of the tax paid (TCGA 1992 Sch 5 para 6). There is no provision for the settlor to obtain payment from the trustees before he has paid the tax, even though the disposal proceeds relating to the gains will be in the trust. HMRC take a strict view on this point, but (at least where large amounts are at stake) will co-operate to provide a certificate rapidly so as to enable a quick reimbursement. If the settlor fails to take all reasonable steps to recover the tax, then that amount will be considered to be an addition to the settlement unless the trust is unable to remit the amount because of local restrictions. (It may also constitute an addition to the settlement, and a chargeable transfer, for inheritance tax purposes.)

The provisions of s 86 do not apply in a tax year in which the settlor dies, nor in which the last of those individuals who cause him to have an interest dies, or, where the interest is that of a spouse/civil partner, they cease to be married/the civil partnership is dissolved.

With effect from 6 April 2013 a settlor in respect of whom a tax year is a split year (under the SRT) will be taxable under s 86 only on gains which arise in the UK part of the tax year (s 86(4) as amended by FA 2013 Sch 45 para 100).

(11) Before FA 1998 a non-resident trust made before 19 March 1991 was only subject to the provisions of TCGA 1992 s 86 outlined in **explanatory note 10** if funds were added or the beneficiaries were varied to include any of the defined persons.

With effect from 6 April 1999, gains of pre-19 March 1991 non-resident trusts are no longer excluded from the provisions of TCGA 1992 s 86 (Sch 5). Unremitted gains of the period 17 March 1998 to 5 April 1999 were deemed to arise on 6 April 1999, thus bringing them within the provisions. The charge was delayed to enable trusts to reorganise their affairs, for example by excluding the range of defined persons as beneficiaries, or by becoming resident or by winding up the trust. There are, however, anti-avoidance provisions in FA 1989 Sch 23 to prevent exploitation of the transitional period.

The revised provisions do not apply to 'protected settlements', ie where the beneficiaries are confined to:

(i) children of the settlor or his spouse/civil partner who are under 18;

(ii) unborn children of the settlor or his spouse/civil partner;

(iii) future spouses/civil partners of the settlor or his children;

(iv) persons outside the defined categories (eg cousins, as in **part A** of the Example).

This protection ceases, however, when the child reaches age 18. Furthermore, distributions to grandchildren are caught as a result of FA 1998 s 131 (see **explanatory note 10**). The Revenue (now HMRC), however, stated that the existence of grandchildren (of whatever age) as beneficiaries of a pre-19 March 1991 settlement at 6 April 1999 will not cause the settlement to fall outside the 'protected' category (Tax Bulletin December 1998).

(12) Where capital payments are made on or after 6 April 1999 to beneficiaries of pre-19 March 1991 trusts in which the settlor has an interest, they will be matched with any unallocated gains that arose before 17 March 1998, and only when all such unallocated gains have been matched with capital payments will capital payments to beneficiaries be regarded as having been already charged on the settlor. Before 6 April 2008 this matching was on a first in, first out basis (attracting the supplementary charge if appropriate – see **explanatory note 14**); since that date, as indicated in **explanatory note 5**, matching is on a last in, first out basis so that the incidence of the supplementary charge may be deferred (but potentially at the cost of more years' worth of supplementary charge when it does apply).

Settlor who is temporarily non-resident – capital gains tax treatment

(13) To be liable to UK capital gains tax under TCGA 1992 s 86 the settlor must be UK resident (or before 2013/14 ordinarily resident) and UK domiciled in the tax year that gains arise. Under ss 10A, 10AA and 86A, however, a UK domiciled settlor can also be liable if after becoming non-resident he returns to the UK having been away for fewer than five complete years (ie he has been temporarily non-resident as defined in FA 2013 Sch 45 para 110). The charge, on gains arising or attributed to him in the period of absence, is made in the tax year of return to the UK, but it is reduced by any gains that have been charged on UK resident beneficiaries during his period of non-residence.

Capital gains tax supplementary charge

(14) Before FA 1991 there was no financial cost to deferring payment of capital gains tax on gains realised by offshore trusts through not distributing the gains. Where such gains are assessable on beneficiaries for 1992/93 onwards, the tax payable is increased by a supplementary charge (TCGA 1992 ss 91–97). The charge runs from 1 December in the tax year following that in which the trustees' gains arose to 30 November in the tax year after that in which the gain is attributed to the beneficiary as a result of a capital payment being received (any capital payments being regarded as applying to the most recent unallocated gains first). If the period would otherwise exceed six years, however, it starts on 1 December six years before the 30 November charging date (s 92(4)(5)). The supplementary charge does not apply where gains are matched with capital payments in the same or following tax year. Gains made before 6 April 1990 were treated as made in 1990/91. Trustees could 'distribute' such gains before 6 April 1992 without any supplementary charge on the beneficiary. The charge is at an annual rate of 10% of the tax on the capital payment, giving an overall maximum possible effective tax rate (for gains attributed by reference to capital payments received after 22 June 2010 and before 6 April 2016) of 60% of 28% = 16.8%, in addition to the capital gains tax of 28% already payable ie a total charge of 44.8%. In respect of gains attributed by reference to capital payments received after 5 April 2016, the effect rate is 60% of 20% = 12% which in addition to the capital gains tax of 20% already payable gives a total charge of 32%.

In **part A** of the example, the 1997/98 capital gain is more than matched by capital payments made in or before that year, so that the whole gain is apportioned to beneficiaries in that year. The 1998/99 gain of £108,562 is distributed as to £74,980 in that year and £18,000 in 1999/2000, but £15,582 remains unallocated until 2023/24, so that the supplementary charge arises on that part of the 2023/24 assessable gains which derives from that brought-forward balance.

(15) Prior to 6 April 2008 careful planning of capital payments could, in some cases, reduce the overall amount of supplementary charge payable. Say, for example, an overseas trust had two beneficiaries, one liable to capital gains tax at 20% and the other at 40%, and the trustees were to make a capital payment which would partly relate to gains of a year to which the supplementary charge would apply and partly to a later year for which the supplementary charge was not relevant. If a capital payment was made to the lower taxed beneficiary first, this would relate to earlier gains before later gains, so that any part of the payment that attracted the supplementary charge would suffer the additional charge on a 20% tax bill. A payment in a subsequent year could then be made to the higher taxed beneficiary out of gains not liable to the supplementary charge. This ceased to be the case when the 18% flat rate of capital gains tax was introduced in 2008/09, but may again be the case (to a lesser degree) since an individual's liability to the higher 28% rate depends on his total income and gains being above the basic rate limit for income tax. The same point applies following the reduction, from 6 April 2016, of the rates of capital gains tax to 10% and 20% respectively. Similar planning points could apply where there is a non-UK domiciled beneficiary like Matthew in this example who is subject to the remittance basis and does not remit his capital payment, or where, although UK domiciled, a beneficiary is not resident or ordinarily resident in the UK.

Capital gains tax – capital contributions and treatment of interest-free loans and other trust assets

(16) Many non-resident trustees have made payments to beneficiaries by way of loan (often interest-free), rather than outright distributions constituting capital payments to which gains would be apportioned. Such a loan was considered in a criminal case in relation to a confiscation of property order (*R v Harvey* (1998)). The loan was secured by way of a charge on the offender's property. The loan was disregarded, because it was stated to be in reality a gift and that the charge was unlikely to be enforced. The Revenue (as HMRC was then known) took a similar view for tax purposes in relation to offshore trusts, and succeeded in the cases of *Billingham v Cooper* and *Edwards v Fisher*, heard by the Court of Appeal in 2001. In both cases overseas trustees had made interest-free loans, repayable on demand, to UK resident (settlor) beneficiaries of pre-March 1991 trusts. Although the Revenue conceded that such loans had little initial benefit, they contended that the continuation of the loans, through the failure of the trustees to call them in when repayable on demand, meant that benefit was provided on a continuing basis. The Court of Appeal agreed, stating that in giving effect to the purpose of ss 87 and 97, it needed to be considered what benefit a beneficiary actually received, so that the 'loan' payments to beneficiaries were within the capital payments and supplementary charges rules. Similar principles are applied to occupation or use of trust assets in kind for less than commercial consideration (eg rent-free occupation of property).

From 6 April 2017, F(No 2)A 2017, Sch 9 para 1 provides for the value of benefits conferred by a capital payment by way of loan or by way of making movable property or land available. New sections 97A to 97C are inserted into TCGA 1992. As regards a capital payment made by way of loan, the value of the capital payment for any year is the excess of the official rate of interest on the loan over the amount of interest actually payable (s 97A). As regards a capital payment made available by way of making movable property available, the value of the capital payment is, in broad terms, the capital cost of the property multiplied by the official rate of interest (time-apportioned if necessary for the part of the year during which the property was made available) less any amount paid for the use of the property (s 97B). As regards a capital payment made available by way of making land available, the value of the capital payment is, in broad terms, the rental value of the land (as defined) for the period of the tax year during which the land is made available less any amount paid for the use of the land (s 97C).

Apportionment of gains of non-resident companies

(17) A chargeable gain that arises in a non-resident company which would be a close company if resident in the UK is apportioned between its participators. In so far as a participator (alone or with his associates) has at least 25% (10% prior to 6 April 2012 and 5% prior to 7 March 2001) of the gain apportioned to him, and is resident (or before 2013/14 ordinarily resident) in the UK, he is chargeable to capital gains tax on the apportioned amount (subject to the protection afforded by the remittance basis for participators who are not UK-domiciled (s 3D)). These provisions apply to UK resident trustees as well as to individuals (see **Example D2 explanatory note 8** for special anti-avoidance provisions for trustees). Although chargeable to capital gains tax, the gain is computed using corporation tax rules, with indexation allowance (but not taper relief, prior to its abolition) applying (see **Tolley's Taxwise I 2023/24, Example L3** for details).

Such gains may also be apportioned to non-resident trustees (s 3(2)(b)), and may in turn be chargeable on the settlor or beneficiaries under the provisions considered in **explanatory notes 5** and **6** above. The computation of the gain may be affected by a rebasing election made by the trustees under FA 2008 Sch 7 para 126 (see **explanatory note 5** of the Example).

These provisions do not apply to gains on the disposal of an asset (including from 6 April 2012 furnished holiday accommodation) used for the purposes of a trade carried on by the non-resident company wholly outside the UK, or to trading currency. FA 2013 s 62 introduces two further exceptions – first to assets used solely for the purposes of 'economically significant activities' carried on by the company wholly or mainly outside the UK, and secondly, a motive defence is introduced.

If the gain is distributed within four years of the date the gain is realised or, if earlier, three years after the end of the accounting period in which the gain is realised, then the capital gains tax on the apportioned amount can be offset against the income tax on the distribution (or capital gains tax if a capital distribution) that is payable by the participator to whom it was apportioned. (This rule does not protect gains that are apportioned to non-UK resident trustees but attributed to the settlor or beneficiaries under the provisions discussed in **explanatory notes 5** and **6** above.) If not so relieved, the tax is treated as an expense for capital gains tax in computing any subsequent gain on the disposal of the participator's interest in the company (TCGA 1992 s 3C(4)).

Income Tax and Estates

Question

Y, who had retired many years previously, died on 5 April 2022. By his Will he left £5,000 and his shares in Bonanza plc to his daughter D. Y's Will stipulates that interest is not payable by his executor in respect of the £5,000 left to D. The residue of Y's estate was left to trustees for his son X, for life, and thereafter to X's children.

The administration of the estate was completed by Y's solicitor (whom he had appointed as his personal representative) on 5 April 2024.

During the period of administration a dividend of £1,800 was received from Bonanza plc in December 2023. The company had paid no dividends in 2022/23. Otherwise the estate income consisted only of interest received from Y's National Savings investments, his ISAs and funds held on the solicitor's general client account, as follows:

		Residuary income	
	Interest	*Payments to X*	*made on*
	£	£	
2022/23	2,200	1,600	3 March 2023
2023/24	3,600	2,400	20 June 2024

From the interest received in 2023/24, the solicitor paid £640 to Z in May 2024 in settlement of a personal liability due by X to Z, a third party. The amount was paid from the estate income as X was experiencing temporary cash flow difficulties at the time. The solicitor made an assent of the shares in Bonanza plc to D in January 2024.

(a) Indicate the tax liability of the personal representatives in relation to the estate income and state what their responsibilities are for reporting the income.

(b) Explain the income tax treatment of D in 2023/24 in respect of the dividend received by the executor.

(c) Calculate for 2022/23 and 2023/24 the amounts of estate income to be included in X's taxable income.

(d) State whether the estate income that would have been included in X's taxable income would have been different had he been absolutely entitled to the residue (as compared with his limited (life) interest) and the personal representatives had transferred Y's flat worth £185,000 to X at the same time as paying him the £1,600 on 3 March 2023.

Answer

(a) Personal representatives — income tax liability and self-assessment

Tax rates (ITA 2007 ss 11, 14)

Personal representatives are liable to tax either at the default basic rate of 20% (called simply the basic rate before 6 April 2018) or the dividend ordinary rate of 8.75% (7.5% before 2022/23) on any chargeable income (see **explanatory note 13**). They are not liable to tax at the higher or additional rates of tax, do not benefit from the savings nil rate or the starting rate for savings or the dividend nil rate, and are not entitled to a personal allowance. The income of Y's residuary estate consists of interest received and, in 2023/24, a dividend. Following the abolition of dividend tax credits from 6 April 2016 (FA 2016 Sch 1 para 1) the amount of tax which is payable by them arises both in respect of the dividends and the interest is therefore 8.75% and 20% of the respective amounts received as follows:

2022/23 £2,200 @ 20% = £440

2023/24 (£1,800 @ 8.75%) + (£3,600 @ 20%) = £877.50

Reporting requirements

Personal representatives have a duty to report to HMRC any untaxed income received during the period of administration and any capital gains which have arisen in that period on the sale of property forming part of the deceased estate. In accordance with the general rule under TMA 1970 s 7(3), there is no requirement for the personal representatives to notify chargeability where the only income received has been taxed at source or, before 6 April 2016, has a dividend tax credit attributed to it.

Formally, untaxed estate income and capital gains are to be reported under self-assessment on the Trust and Estate Tax Return (SA900) (see **Example E2**). However, for straightforward estates, where the tax liability is small HMRC adopt informal procedures to settle the tax affairs of the personal representative. HMRC's approach to dealing with the income tax and capital gains tax reporting requirements for deceased estates is set out in the Trusts, Settlements and Estates Manual from TSEM 7200 (in particular TSEM 7413 and 7414).

The informal procedures require the personal representatives to provide HMRC with a written summary of income and gains and a computation of the estate's tax liability. The whole period of administration can be reported together and, if the administration has ceased, it is not necessary to wait until after the end of the tax year. This procedure excludes most deceased estates from the self-assessment system, which has many advantages. There is no requirement to set up a new taxpayer record or to complete a tax return. Additionally the time limits, interest and penalties of the self-assessment system do not apply. The standard criteria (see TSEM 7376) for adopting informal procedures are as follows:

(a) The total tax liability of the estate, both income tax and capital gains tax, for the whole period of administration, must not exceed £10,000.

(b) The value of the estate is £2.5 million or less.

(c) The proceeds of assets sold by the personal representatives in any one tax year are not more than £250,000 for deaths before 6 April 2016 and not more than £500,000 for death on or after 6 April 2016.

The process is also described in HMRC's *Trusts and Estates* newsletters dated June 2015, December 2015 and again in August 2018. If HMRC does not agree that informal procedures are appropriate (ie the estate is a complex estate), they will issue a Trust and Estate Tax Return (see **Example E2**).

In their *Trusts and Estates Newsletter* for August 2018, HMRC has confirmed that should an estate be reported as informal at the end of the administration period and then subsequently a criterion for a complex estate is triggered (eg previously unknown assets are discovered), the estate should be registered with HMRC and a self-assessment tax return (SA 900) requested. Such returns will then be required for each year of the administration period to declare all the income and capital gains information. Any payment previously made using the informal route will be transferred and used against the total tax now due and included in the self-assessment statement of account. The estate is registered using the online trust registration service.

(b) Income tax treatment of D in 2023/24

D is entitled, under Y's Will, to a pecuniary legacy of £5,000 and a specific legacy of Y's shares in Bonanza plc. Once the shares have been appropriated by the executor and assented to by him, D, the specific legatee, is treated as owning them from the date of the deceased's death under the doctrine of relating back. A specific legacy carries with it all the income accruing from its subject matter after testator's death. Hence the net income arising from the shares (ie after executor's expenses, if any) runs with the specific legacy with the result that she is entitled to the dividend of £1,800 paid by Bonanza plc in December 2023. D will treat as her dividend income for 2023/24 an amount of £1,800 and she will be credited with the tax paid by the executors of £157.50 (£1,800 × 8.75%). Although the dividend is received by the executor of Y's estate and prima facie taxable on him (see **explanatory note 9**), in practice it is likely that it will be taxed only on the daughter, D.

D is also entitled to a pecuniary legacy of £5,000. Normally a pecuniary legacy carries interest per annum payable on each anniversary of the deceased's death (starting from the first anniversary) at a rate linked to the Bank of England base rate. In this Example, Y's Will provides that the legacy is not to carry interest. Hence D does not receive (and hence is not taxable in 2023/24 on) any interest in respect of her legacy of £5,000.

The rate of interest on pecuniary legacies has changed frequently in the recent past and at the time of writing stands at 3.375% (from 13 June 2023). Before that the rate of interest was 3.188% (21 April 2023 to 12 June 2023), 3% (13 February 2023 to 20 April 2023), 2.625% (16 January 2023 to 12 February 2023), 2.25% (18 November 2022 to 15 January 2023), 1.688% (25 October 2022 to 17 November 2022), 1.313% (2 September 2022 to 24 October 2022), 1.25% (5 July 2022 to 1 September 2022), 0.323% (29 April 2022 to 4 July 2022) and 0.05% (1 June 2020 to 28 April 20222).

(c) Estate income to be included in taxable income of life tenant, X

Where a person has a life (or other limited) interest under a will trust, the amounts to be included in his statutory income during the period of administration are the grossed-up equivalents of the net income payments actually made to him in the tax year (ITTOIA 2005 ss 649–663). The amount of the grossing addition depends on the rate of tax on the underlying income – see (a) above.

Thus the amount to be included in the statutory income of X in 2022/23 is £1,600 × 100/80 = £2,000.

Upon the completion of the administration, any amounts due to the life tenant which remain unpaid are deemed to be paid as income of the tax year in which the administration is *completed* (ITTOIA 2005 ss 649, 654).

Since the administration is completed in 2023/24, X will be deemed to have received the balance due to him in that tax year, ie £3,040 × 100/80 = £3,800. The balance of interest due to him comprises both the £2,400 paid to him direct and the £640 paid to Z by the executor on his behalf in May 2024.

(d) Effect on X's estate income if he had had an absolute interest in residue

Where a person has an absolute interest in the residue of an estate, the payments that will lead to an amount being included in his statutory income during the period of administration are not restricted to income payments made to him; capital payments (including the transfer of assets or the release of debts, ITTOIA 2005 s 681) will be taken into account as well. The amount of such payments is matched against the relevant share of residuary income net of income tax at the applicable rate (according to the type of income). However, the maximum amount that can be included is the 'assumed income entitlement' to date; that is, the total amount taxable in any year cannot exceed the aggregate amount of the residuary income attributable to the person's interest in residue, less amounts taxed in previous tax years (ITTOIA 2005 ss 660, 665–668). The amount so reached is then suitably grossed up if the estate is a UK estate (ITTOIA 2005 s 656).

Upon the completion of the administration, any amounts not paid, up to the 'assumed income entitlement', are deemed to be paid to the beneficiary immediately before completion.

Thus the transfer of Y's flat to X on 3 March 2023 (in addition to the payment of £1,600 to him) will lead to the whole residuary income of £1,760 net (£2,200 gross less tax of £440), being treated as X's income for 2022/23. On completion of the administration in 2023/24 the balance of residuary income – equating to the amount for 2023/24, viz £2,880 net (£3,600 gross less tax of £720) – will be treated as income of X for 2022/23.

Explanatory Notes

Self-assessment position of personal representatives

(1) If all the estate income is taxed income and there are no capital gains, then in most cases a tax return is not required. If a tax return has been issued, it should be submitted but no amounts have to be entered on the return and only the information section needs to be completed (see **Example E2** re Mrs Daley).

The personal representatives supply beneficiaries with form R185 (Estate Income) showing income payments split according to whether the underlying income was taxed at the default basic or dividend ordinary rate of tax and whether the tax is repayable or non-repayable (see **explanatory note 9**).

Personal representatives: Individual Savings Accounts and Solicitors' General Accounts

(2) Only an individual receives interest and dividends tax free from an ISA. Interest and dividends from a deceased's ISA arising to his personal representatives are counted as their taxable income. Before 6 April 2017, interest received in respect of client monies held on a solicitor's general account was received gross. For deaths on or after 6 April 2019, ISA interest/dividend income received on the deceased ISA account is exempt in the hands of the PRs until the earlier of the end of the period of administration, the date the ISA is closed and the third anniversary of the date of death.

Income of specific, general and statutory legatees

(3) As explained in part (b) of the Example, a specific legacy carries with it all the income accruing from its subject matter after the testator's death. A specific legatee is entitled to the net income arising from the property comprised in his specific legacy (unless the Will provides otherwise) from the date of the death of the deceased until the legacy is appropriated to him. Any expenses incurred by the executors and relating to the property comprised in the specific legacy reduce the amount of income to which the legatee is entitled. When the property comprised in his legacy is vested in him by the appropriation, the income which arose from the property in the administration period is also then paid out to the legatee. However, in accordance with the doctrine of relating back, the income is deemed to have arisen to him from the date of the deceased's death. In other words the effect of the assent is to pass to the beneficiary the income payable on the asset since the date of death. It is taxed on him as his income since the time of the deceased's death (*IRC v Hawley* 13 TC 327). This means that the income derives from the asset(s) themselves and so the legatee will have income from the various sources of income comprised in the legacy. The income will also have been taxed in the hands of the PRs and so when the income (and the legacy) is paid to the beneficiary, the PRs will pay the net income net of tax at the default basic or savings rate and will provide the legatee with a Form R185 as proof of his entitlement to the tax credit. This requires the income tax of earlier years to be revisited; although (in accordance with the idea of self-assessment) any additional tax is likely only to be payable on the due dates as they relate to the year of the appropriation. A general legacy carries interest.

A general legacy carries interest from the time at which it is payable. The rate of interest (as set out in **part (b)** of the Example) is that applied to funds in court is 0.1% (from 6 June 2016) (0.3% from 1 July 2009 to 5 June 2016) (unless the testator directs otherwise) and the interest is simple interest. The time from which the interest runs is the time specified in the testator's Will (eg 'immediately after my death') and, in the absence of such a direction, from one year after the testator's death (the so-called executor's year). The rule applies to all general legacies and not only those of money. There are a number of exceptions to the general rule so that, in those cases, interest runs from the date of the testator's death (eg a legacy to a creditor of the testator in satisfaction of the debt, a legacy charged on real property, a legacy to the testator's infant child and statutory legacies). The legacy carries interest from that time until the legacy is actually paid. The charge to tax on the legatee arises when he receives the interest (which is the usual basis of assessment under ITTOIA 2005 Pt 4 Chap 2). There is no doctrine of relating back in such a case. If the legatee refuses to accept the legacy then no charge to tax can arise on him provided the legacy itself has not been set aside for (and so vested in) the legatee (*Dewar v IRC* 19 TC 561; *Spens v IRC* [1970] 3 All ER 295). Before 6 April 2016, the interest was paid gross without deduction of tax at source to UK resident beneficiaries and so no Form R185 was issued.

A statutory legatee is a person which is identified in the Administration of Estates Act 1925 as entitled to a sum of money on the intestacy of the deceased (see **explanatory note 6** of **Example A19**). Statutory legacies carry interest (at the rates set out in the **part (b)** of the Example) from the date of death to the date of the payment of the legacy. The interest is paid without deduction of tax at source by the PRs and the beneficiary is taxed on the interest on a receipts basis (which is the usual basis of assessment under ITTOIA 2005 Pt 4 Chap 2). The interest is paid by the PRs out of the income of the estate or out of capital if there is insufficient income. To the extent that the interest on a statutory legacy is paid out of capital, basic rate tax must be deducted at source in accordance with the rules relating to annual payments (*Trustees of will of Brodie v IRC* (1933)).

Income of beneficiaries of residue of a deceased estate

(4) As to what is treated as the income of the beneficiaries of residue depends on the nature of their interest in the residue. A person has an absolute interest in the whole or part of the residue of an estate if the capital of the residue or that part is properly payable to the person, or, it would be so payable if the residue had been ascertained (ITTOIA 2005 s 650(1)). A person has a limited interest in the whole or part of the residue of an estate during any period if the person does not have an absolute interest in it and the income from it would be properly payable to the person if the residue had been ascertained at the beginning of that period (ITTOIA 2005 s 650(2)).

All payments made to a beneficiary with a limited interest (usually a life interest) in residue will be income. For a beneficiary with an absolute interest, payments must be treated as being liable to income tax in the hands of the beneficiary, up to the gross equivalent of the amount of income received by the estate. In the legislation references to amounts paid include assets transferred to beneficiaries, or debts set off or released, the amount for such items being their value at the relevant date (ITTOIA 2005 s 681).

Where assets have been transferred to beneficiaries with absolute interests in residue during the administration period, therefore, the gross equivalent of their value must be taken into account as a distribution of estate income even though the distribution was of capital, so particular care must be taken in calculating the amount to be shown on forms R185 (Estate Income). See **Example D1** for the capital gains implications of transferring assets to a beneficiary during the administration period.

The beneficiaries of residue are treated as being in receipt of a single source of income known as 'estate income' (ITTOIA 2005 s 649). Except to the extent that the estate income of such a beneficiary derives from the dividend income of the estate, and, from 6 April 2023, from the savings income of the estate, estate income is, by nature, non-savings income (not being listed as a type of savings income in ITA 2007, s 18). To the extent that the estate income of a beneficiary derives from the dividend income of the estate, its nature is preserved in the hands of the beneficiary by virtue of ITTOIA 2005, s 680A. This means that such income, together with the other dividend income of the beneficiary (as defined in ITA 2007, s 19), will benefit from his dividend nil rate (the dividend allowance) and the other rates of income tax applicable to dividend income. From 6 April 2023 (following the enactment of F(No 2)A 2023 s 29 and Sch 2), to the extent that the estate income of a beneficiary derives from the savings income of the estate, its nature is preserved in the hands of the beneficiary by virtue of ITTOIA 2005, s 680B. This means that such income, together with the other savings income of the beneficiary (as defined in ITA 2007, s 18), will benefit from his savings nil rate (the savings allowance) and the other rates of income tax applicable to savings income. Estate income deriving from the non-savings, non-dividend income of the estate (and before 6 April 2023) estate income deriving from the savings income of the estate will be treated as non-savings, non-dividend income of the beneficiary. None of the income so deriving will be taxed by the individual at the savings rates of income tax, in particular the savings nil rate (savings allowance) or the starting rate for savings.

Beneficiaries of a deceased estate with an absolute interest in residue

(5) For someone with an absolute interest in the residue of an estate, if the amounts to be deducted from the income of the estate exceed the income in any year, the excess is carried forward and deducted from future income in computing the residuary income of the estate and thus the beneficiary's assumed income entitlement (ss 666(2), (6)).

(6) If, when the administration is completed, it is found that the total residuary income of the estate is less than the amounts paid to someone with an absolute interest (for example, because large bills are paid in the later stages of the administration), then the amount included in the statutory income of the person concerned is reduced to the actual residuary income. This is done by reducing the income of the tax year in which the administration is completed, then, if necessary, the previous year, and so on (s 668).

Identification of income received by beneficiaries of residue of a deceased estate

(7) 'Just and reasonable' apportionments of income bearing tax at different rates are to be made between beneficiaries with interests in residue. After making any such apportionments, payments to beneficiaries are regarded as being out of brought forward and current income charged at the highest rate (ie the basic rate (or default basic rate as the case may be)) in priority to income charged at the lowest rate (ie dividends charged at the dividend ordinary rate of 8.75% (7.5% for 2021/22)) (ss 670, 679).

The rate of tax used for grossing up the different categories of income received by the personal representatives, in order to ascertain a beneficiary's taxable estate income, is known as the 'applicable rate' (ss 663, 670, 679).

Deceased estates: the applicable rate

(8) Amounts (called basic amounts) paid from estates in administration to beneficiaries are deemed (after being grossed up by reference to the *applicable rate*) to be their income of the tax year in which they are paid (ss 649, 656). The applicable rate used in the grossing up of a basic amount is linked to the rates in force for the year in which the payments are, from 6 April 2023, received by the personal representatives rather than by reference to the rate at the time the income becomes payable to the beneficiaries. Payments made to beneficiaries in a tax year are deemed to be made from the income of the estate in a certain order (namely, starting with the income bearing tax at the highest rate to income bearing tax at the lowest rate) (s 679) and to the extent that a payment is matched with that income, the applicable rate in relation to the payment is the rate of tax applicable to that income (s 663). Any stock dividends or amounts relating to the release of a close company loan which are included in the aggregate income of the estate are treated as bearing income tax at 0% (s 680). In their *Trusts and Estates Newsletter* of December 2016, HMRC confirmed that where dividends are received in the estate before 6 April 2016 but the income is not paid over to the beneficiary until after that date, then they will carry a non-payable tax credit of 7.5%.

Personal representatives: forms R185

(9) Personal representatives supply beneficiaries with an income certificate form R185 (Estate Income) showing the amounts paid as income and tax deducted (or treated as deducted), split between dividend income (dividend ordinary rate) and other income (with tax at the basic rates). The beneficiaries include the information from the R185 in the trusts etc pages in their personal returns.

The tax on some of the income may be shown as non-repayable (ITTOIA 2005 s 680). Non-repayable tax at the 20% rate arises on life policy gains. Other non-repayable tax as provided in that section includes tax credits on dividends paid or payable before 6 April 2016 for which the applicable rate is the former dividend ordinary rate of 7.5%.

This also applies to beneficiaries with only a limited interest in residue.

Completion of administration of a deceased estate

(10) When the administration of the estate is complete, the personal representatives will have assigned the interest in the assets to the trustees of the life interest trust (or be treated as having done so), who take those assets for capital gains tax purposes at the personal representatives' acquisition value – which for assets held by the deceased at his death will be their value at the date of death. This will normally be the probate value as used for inheritance tax purposes; but where a probate value was not *ascertained* for inheritance tax (because no inheritance tax was payable) the capital gains 'open market value' rule applies (see **Example A26 explanatory note 1**). In this latter case the acquisition cost for capital gains tax may be calculated on a different basis from the value used (but not 'ascertained') for inheritance tax purposes, for example where the related property rule (IHTA 1984 s 161) applies for inheritance tax.

Once the interest in the assets has been assigned to the trustees, the trustees are responsible for making the relevant income tax self-assessment returns, paying any tax due and providing beneficiaries as relevant with details of income returnable by them using forms R185 (Trust Income). The beneficiary is then liable to tax on the amount shown on the R185. See **Examples F1–F9** for the income tax treatment of trusts, and in particular **Example F2** for the income tax position of a life interest will trust.

Enterprise investment scheme etc and venture capital trusts: death of investor

(11) Where someone has invested under the enterprise investment scheme, seed enterprise investment scheme, social enterprise investment scheme or venture capital trust scheme, their death does not trigger the withdrawal of the income tax relief on the shares in question, nor will it cause deferred gains to become chargeable. The personal representatives would be liable to capital gains tax on sale of the shares, the acquisition cost being the market value at the date of death.

Personal representatives: the Scottish rates of income tax

(12) The Scotland Act 2012 (which amended the Scotland Act 1998 to this effect) devolved power on the Scottish Parliament to set Scottish rates of income tax for Scottish taxpayers. The 1998 Act was further amended by the Scotland Act 2016 in this regard. The power to make such rates was implemented with effect from 6 April 2017 (The Scotland Act 2016 (Commencement No 2) Regulations 2016 (SI 2016/161)).

The Scottish rates of income tax, namely the Scottish starter rate, Scottish basic rate, the Scottish intermediate rate, the Scottish higher rate and the Scottish top rate, set at 19%, 20%, 21%, 42% (41% in 2022/23 and 47% (46% in 2022/23) respectively, are charged on the non-savings non-dividend income of Scottish taxpayers (as defined in the Scotland Act 1998 s 80D). Deceased estates are not generally affected by the Scottish rates of income tax. Income arising to personal representatives will not be chargeable at the Scottish rates, which applies only to individuals.

However, individuals who are Scottish taxpayers and who receive non-savings non-dividend income from a deceased estate will be charged to income tax on that income at the prevailing Scottish rates.

The Government of Wales Act 2006 has devolved property on the National Assembly for Wales to set Welsh rates for Welsh taxpayers (s 110). The rates are ascertained in accordance with ITA 2007 s 6B(1) whereby the (main) basic, higher and additional rates are reduced by 10% and then the corresponding Welsh rates are added to that amount. The Welsh Rate Resolution of the National Assembly for Wales for 2021/22, 2022/23, 2023/24 and 2024/25 sets the corresponding Welsh rates at 10%. Consequently, for both years the Welsh rates of income tax are the Welsh basic rate (20%), Welsh higher rate (40%) and Welsh additional rate (45%). Deceased estates are not generally affected by the Welsh rates of income tax. Income arising to personal representatives will not be chargeable at the Welsh rates, which applies only to individuals.

However, individuals who are Welsh taxpayers and who receive non-savings non-dividend income from a deceased estate will be charged to income tax on that income at the prevailing Welsh rates.

Rates of income tax applicable to personal representatives

(13) Prior to 6 April 2016, personal representatives paid income tax at the basic rate and the dividend ordinary rate. To accommodate the devolution of powers to Scotland (and later Wales) to set the rates of income tax for Scottish taxpayers, the rates of income tax levied on non-individuals such as trustees and personal representatives are re-named. With effect from 6 April 2017 personal representatives pay tax at the 'default basic rate' (ITA 2007 ss 9A and 11) and the dividend ordinary rate (s 9A). The default basic rate has been set at 20% for 2023/24 (the same as for 2022/23) (Finance Act (No 2) Act 2023 s 3).

Further example: taxation of income in an administration period

(14) For a more complex example of the taxation of income arising to personal representatives in an administration period and the taxation of the estate income of beneficiaries with limited or absolute interests in residue, see **Example F2**.

Question

Mr and Mrs Daley were killed in a road accident on 18 August 2023. Under their wills each appointed their son Arthur as executor. They had each left their entire estate to the other, subject to a 30-day survivorship clause. As default beneficiaries, Mr Daley left his used car business to his son together with one half of residue, the other half being divided between various charities. Mrs Daley, who only had building society investments worth £50,000, named her son as the only beneficiary in default of her husband.

Mr Daley's estate is expected to be valued for probate at:

		£	£
Used car business			900,000
Private residence			440,000
Quoted securities			8,900
National Savings Certificates			41,600
ISA at Midnorth Building Society			10,100
Government securities (interest paid gross)			26,800
Life policies			82,500
Pension policies			104,200
Bank accounts			1,400
Premium bonds			20,000
			1,635,500
Less:	Mortgage	125,000	
	Other debts, funeral expenses	10,500	(135,500)
			1,500,000

Because of business property relief, exemption for charities, the nil-rate band and the residence nil-rate band, no inheritance tax will be payable. Arthur, as executor, will convert all his father's assets (including the business) to cash, and pay the liabilities and legacies. He will use a current account with his bank, and will invest surplus funds on the money market. A premium bond prize of £100,000 was received after his father's death. Arthur anticipates completing the administration of the estate by the end of 2024.

Arthur will also obtain probate on his mother's estate, and will cash in the investments and pay all debts and legacies by March 2024.

Arthur has contacted your firm for advice as to his obligations as executor under self-assessment. Set out the taxation points to be considered from death to the completion of the administration of the estate for both Mr and Mrs Daley.

Answer

Tax liabilities of Mr Daley deceased — executor's obligations

Arthur should notify HMRC as soon as possible after his father's death. As his father's death has occurred after 13 October 2014 he no longer uses form R27 but contacts HMRC direct. HMRC will then send Arthur a self-assessment return. As a self-employed person, Mr Daley will have been within the self-assessment criteria, so Arthur will need to complete a tax return for the period 6 April to 18 August 2023. Arthur, in his capacity as executor, will be responsible for the payment of tax due.

Before 14 October 2014 executors were sent form R27 for completion. The purpose of the form was to enable the executors to finalise the deceased's tax affairs up to the date of death and to claim any repayment due. The form asked for details of the deceased, his financial circumstances before death, and the value of the estate. HMRC did not require copies of the grant of probate or the will, unless they specifically asked for them. Where the deceased taxpayer's circumstances were relatively straightforward, form R27 was used as a substitute tax return to report the income to date of death and claim any repayment due. More complex situations required a self-assessment tax return to be completed and submitted (in addition to the form R27). After 13 October 2014, the R27 was withdrawn and has been replaced with an automated process for PAYE information and a more tailored service (which includes letters that match the individual's circumstances) for self-assessment taxpayers. The reasons for the change in procedure is explained in detailed in HMRC's *Trusts and Estates Newsletter* dated June 2015 and is further addressed in HMRC's *Trusts and Estates Newsletter* dated December 2015.

Cessation of used car business

The death of Mr Daley will denote a cessation of the business for income tax purposes. Ideally accounts should be drawn up to the date of death and submitted with the final self-assessment return, otherwise the profits covering the date of death must be apportioned.

2022/23 tax return

If the 2022/23 tax return of Mr Daley had not been filed before his death, Arthur as executor is responsible for filing it by 31 October 2023 if filing a paper return or 31 January 2024 for a return filed online. See **explanatory note 4.** He is also responsible for paying the outstanding tax for 2022/23 by that latter date. Interest will be charged on tax paid late, although by FA 2009 Sch 53 Pt 2 para 12, interest on tax falling due after death will not start to run until 30 days after the grant of probate.

If the tax is not paid by 28 February 2024 (ie 28 days after the due date), a surcharge of 5% is payable. This increases to 10% if the tax is still unpaid by 31 July. Interest is also payable on any surcharge not paid within 30 days. If there was a reasonable excuse for non-payment throughout the period of default, HMRC (or the First-tier Tribunal) may set aside the surcharge. Inability to pay is not in itself a reasonable excuse; but it is thought that HMRC should accept that lack of access to estate funds pending the grant of probate is a reasonable excuse.

Under TMA 1970 s 9A(2) the enquiry window for income tax self-assessment tax returns will close one year after delivery of the return. For example, if the 2022/23 return was received by HMRC on 31 August 2023, HMRC will have until 31 August 2024 to enquire into the form.

If deliberate errors, whether concealed or not concealed, are discovered, HMRC can issue an assessment for years ending not earlier than six years before death (ie for 2014/15 onwards) and such assessments must be issued not later than four years following the end of the tax year in which the death occurred, ie in the case of Mr Daley's estate not later than 5 April 2027 (TMA 1970 s 40). Normally penalties may be charged where there are deliberate errors. However, HMRC acknowledge that, under the Human Rights legislation, it is not possible to impose tax geared penalties on personal representatives in respect of tax evasion by the deceased where evidence of this comes to light after the taxpayer's death; as a result, their Special Civil Investigations Guidance states at SCIG 05250 'Civil evasion penalties must not be imposed in these circumstances and therefore an investigation under the terms of the Civil Investigation of Fraud Code 9 procedure is not appropriate. An alternative method of investigation should be considered to establish and assess any tax arrears and interest'. (Note however that this is then qualified in relation to cases where the deceased was involved in evasion by a company or partnership, or where a disclosure of irregularities had been made by the taxpayer before his death.) See **Example A7(c)** for more detail on the FA 2008 legislation on penalties.

2023/24 tax return

Following Mr Daley's death in August 2023, HMRC will, on request, issue a tax return for 2023/24 before the end of that tax year (and also before the end of the tax year in which the administration of the estate will be completed). When returns have been submitted HMRC can be asked to give early confirmation if they do not intend to enquire into the return.

Because of Mr Daley's death it will be appropriate for Arthur to apply to HMRC to reduce the payment on account due on 31 January 2024 in respect of 2023/24. The application should be made on the return, or on form SA 303.

Any tax due for the year of death (or earlier years) will be a liability of the estate.

Tax position on investments

The ISA investment retains its tax exemption until death. For deaths on or after 6 April 2018, ISA interest and dividend income received in respect of the deceased's account is exempt in the hands of the personal representatives until the earlier of the date on which the administration of the estate ends, the date the ISA is closed and the third anniversary of the death. Thereafter the normal income and capital gains tax rules apply. An insurance policy will pay out on death and consequently the personal representatives will need to claim the death benefit. Before the claim is accepted by the insurer there are no income tax or capital gains tax implications but any interest paid as a result of late settlement of the claim will be taxable and paid net of tax under ITA s 874 (which imposes a duty to deduct income tax from yearly interest).

The premium bond continues to be tax-exempt, including the prize received. The amount received will be added to the residue of the estate and be distributed accordingly as capital.

Under ITA 2007 s 636(2), if Arthur as personal representative transfers securities to a beneficiary in the interest period in which Mr Daley died, neither Arthur nor the legatee are treated as making or receiving payments. Therefore, in these circumstances no accrued income profit or accrued income loss can arise. However, the exemption for unrealised interest received after a transfer under ITA 2007 s 681 may still be available to the legatee, because s 636(2) does not go so far as to deem a transfer not to have been made, merely to prevent deemed payments from having taken place.

Interest on investments and dividends on shares are taxable when received. They are *not* apportioned for income tax over the period to which they relate. For probate and inheritance tax purposes, however, dividends receivable after death on ex dividend shares (exclusive of the tax credits in the case of dividends receivable before 6 April 2016) and amounts of interest accrued to the date of death on securities (less basic rate tax in the case of interest received before 6 April 2016) are included in the value of the estate. ITA 2007 s 640 introduces rules for small holdings of securities and excludes interest on securities that form part of a deceased person's estate, unless the nominal value of securities held by the personal representatives as such exceeds £5,000 on any day:

(a) in the tax year in which the interest period ends; or

(b) in the previous tax year.

In relation to a transfer with unrealised interest of securities that form part of a deceased person's estate, the deceased's personal representatives are an excluded transferor or excluded transferee unless the nominal value of securities held by the deceased's personal representatives as such exceeds £5,000 on any day:

(a) in the tax year in which the settlement day falls; or

(b) in the previous tax year.

Where there is a transfer of variable rate securities that form part of a deceased person's estate, the deceased's personal representatives are an excluded transferor unless the nominal value of securities held by the deceased's personal representatives as such exceeds £5,000 on any day in the relevant tax year or the previous tax year (see **Example F2**).

Relief is given where an absolute beneficiary is liable to higher rate tax and the estate paid inheritance tax on net accrued income (see **Example F2 explanatory note 4**).

Tax liabilities of Arthur as executor of Mr Daley's estate

Arthur will need to register the estate using the trust and estate online register and will receive a trust and estate self-assessment return (form SA 900) for the period 19 August 2023 to 5 April 2024, and in due course for the period 6 April 2024 to the date of completion of the administration of the estate. The deadline for filing the first of those returns (see **explanatory note 4**) is 31 October 2024 if the return is filed on paper, or 31 January 2025 if it is filed online; but if Arthur wishes HMRC to compute the tax liabilities then he should note that they will only guarantee to do so in time for the due date for payment of the tax (31 January) if the return is filed by 31 October (even if filed online).

Personal representatives are not entitled to personal allowances and are charged tax on the estate income at the dividend ordinary rate on dividends, and at the default basic rate on all other income. Any net capital gains arising on the disposal of assets in excess of probate values are liable to tax at 28% (for gains realised before 6 April 2016 and gains in respect of residential property realised on or after that date) and 20% otherwise, after deducting an annual exemption (£6,000 for 2023/24) in the tax year of death and the next two tax years. After that, the personal representatives are not entitled to a capital gains annual exemption.

Used car business

The actual basis of assessment will apply, ie:

2023/24	19 August 2023 to 5 April 2024
2024/25	6 April 2024 to date of sale

Supplementary pages will be required to be completed. If only one set of accounts is prepared details will be shown on the first return, with the profits for the period after 5 April 2024 deducted. On the second return the box indicating that all details have been shown on the previous return will be ticked. The profits (after capital allowances) will be shown with the exclusion of the amount assessed in the earlier year. There is no liability for Class 4 national insurance contributions.

Investment income

Investment income must be declared and tax paid at the default basic rate (although before 6 April 2016 this applied only to investment income received gross). This will include interest on bank and building society accounts, government securities, and on overseas investments. Interest is also paid gross on all quoted eurobonds, now defined as interest-bearing securities issued by a company (or building society) and listed on a recognised stock exchange (ITA 2007 s 882). Certain payments of yearly interest will have had tax deducted at source (ITA 2007 s 874). The trust and estate tax return includes a provision for personal representatives to omit the details of taxed income from the return unless there are losses or reliefs to set against it to generate a refund. Any profit arising under the accrued income scheme on a sale by the executor will also be taxed at the basic rate of 20%. Where there is any accrued income loss, relief is given by deducting it from the gross income received, thus reducing the amount chargeable at 20%.

Payment of tax

If the net income tax payable for 2023/24 exceeds £1,000, or 20% of the total income tax liability for the year (including tax deducted at source), then payments on account will be required for 2024/25.

Capital gains tax is not included in calculating payments on account. The 2023/24 income tax and capital gains tax (in respect of the disposal of assets other than UK residential property) will be due on 31 January 2025. As the administration of the estate is likely to be almost complete at that time it should be possible accurately to determine the actual liability for 2024/25. Unless covered by the de minimis limits, one half of that liability (excluding capital gains tax), or one half of the 2023/24 net tax liability if less, will be due on 31 January 2025. The second instalment will be due on 31 July 2025 and the balance, together with any capital gains tax in respect of the above assets, on 31 January 2025.

Arthur as executor may prefer to pay the whole amount at an early date in order to complete the administration of the estate.

The same provisions as to interest on overdue tax and surcharges apply as stated above in relation to the tax position of Mr Daley deceased.

Tax liabilities in relation to Mrs Daley

Tax position of Mrs Daley deceased

Arthur has similar obligations as stated above in respect of his mother's estate. Since her only assets are building society accounts, however, it is likely that her affairs will be dealt with under the bereavement service described above. Income arising on the investments is likely to fall within Mrs Daley's personal allowance.

Tax position in relation to Mrs Daley's estate

Formally, untaxed estate income and capital gains are to be reported under self-assessment on the Trust and Estate Tax Return (SA900). However, for straightforward estates, where the tax liability is small HMRC adopt informal procedures to settle the tax affairs of the personal representative (see **Example E1**). No tax return is therefore likely to be required.

If HMRC do issue a notice to file a tax return, Arthur will not be able to tick the second box in Step 1 on the trust and estate tax return SA900 obviating the need to report the income of his mother's estate on the return as not all the following points apply:

- All the income arose in the UK
- He does not wish to claim reliefs
- No annual payments have been made out of capital
- All income has had tax deducted before it was received (or is UK dividends with tax credit)
- There are no chargeable disposals
- There are no accrued income profits or losses, no income from deeply discounted securities, gilt strips, company share buy-backs, offshore income gains or gains on life insurance policies etc
- No capital payments or benefits have been received from a non-resident, dual resident or immigrating trust.

Arthur will not therefore be able simply to go straight to Question 19 in the return to give his, or his adviser's, telephone number and sign the declaration at Question 22. When the administration of the estate is complete the date of completion is shown at Question 21.2. Arthur will therefore have to complete Question 9 and 17 before proceeding to Question 19. It is however likely that only one return, at most, will be required in relation to Mrs Daley's estate. This represents an additional compliance burden for Arthur as compared with the position he would have been in had his mother died three years earlier. If that had been the case his late mother's interest would have been received under deduction of income tax at the basic rate so that Arthur would have had no untaxed income to report and Arthur would have been able to tick the second box in Step 1 of the SA900 and then proceed direct or Questions 19 and 22. In their *Trusts and Estates Newsletter* dated April 2016 HMRC acknowledge this problem and have introduced the following interim arrangement. For 2016/17 HMRC did not require notification from trustees or personal representatives dealing with estates in administration where the only source of income was savings interest and the tax liability was below £100. In their *Trusts and Estates Newsletter* dated April 2017 HMRC confirmed that this interim arrangement also applied in 2017/18. In their *Trusts and Estates Newsletter* dated December 2017 HMRC confirmed once again that this interim arrangement will also apply in 2018/19. In their *Trusts and Estates Newsletter* dated August 2019 the arrangement was extended to apply in 2019/20 and 2020/21, and has been further extended by the Trusts and Estates Newsletter dated May 2021 to apply in 2021/22 and 2022/23. It has been confirmed by HMRC that the same treatment will apply in 2023/24 (see the *Trusts and Estates Newsletter* dated May 2023). From 2024/25 ITA 2007, s 24B (enacted by F(No 2)A 2023 s 29 and Sch 1 para 10) provides that where the net income of personal representatives is £500 or less, it is treated as being £0 so that effectively they are not charged to income tax. Where the net income of personal representatives is treated as being £0, that income will not be charged to tax when it is received as estate income by a legatee.

Explanatory Notes

(1) Where HMRC enquire into a return, they will issue a closure notice stating their conclusions and showing the revisions to the self-assessment and the additional tax due (TMA 1970 s 28A). The personal representatives then have 30 days in which to appeal in writing against conclusions stated or amendments made by the closure notice, giving the grounds of appeal (TMA 1970 ss 31, 31A).

(2) The personal representatives may give HMRC notice of an amendment to the self-assessment return (within the permitted twelve months after the filing date for the return) whilst an enquiry is in progress. The amendment will not restrict the scope of the enquiry but may be taken into account in the enquiry. If it affects the tax payable, it will not take effect unless and until it is incorporated into the s 28A closure notice (see **explanatory note 1** above) (TMA 1970 s 9B).

(3) Questions relating to the subject matter of an enquiry may be referred to the First-tier Tribunal (Tax Chamber) for their determination while the enquiry is in progress on a joint written application by the personal representatives and HMRC. Either party may withdraw from the referral process provided they give notice before the first hearing of the matter by the Tribunal. The determination will be binding on both parties as if it were a decision on a preliminary issue under appeal (TMA 1970 ss 28ZA–28ZE (and ss 31A–31D for companies), and s 47C).

Filing dates for paper and online self-assessment returns

Paper substitutes for Self-Assessment (SA) returns

(4) Computer generated substitute versions of the SA Return are no longer approved or accepted for:

- SA Individual Returns – (SA100 series)
- SA Trust and Estate Returns – (SA900 series)

For the time being, HMRC will continue to accept approved substitutes for the remaining SA returns (including those for trustees of registered pension schemes) and for all other forms they currently approve substitutes for.

SA filing dates

Anyone who is required to file a self-assessment tax return has:

- until 31 October to do so, if they choose to send a paper return; or
- until the following 31 January if they file online.

This allows an additional three months for online filing compared with paper.

The filing obligation is satisfied by the first return received by HMRC and this also triggers any late filing penalty. So if, for example, a paper 2022/23 return is filed after 31 October 2023, it is not then possible to avoid a late filing penalty by filing the return online, even before the deadline for online returns.

In the event that there are problems with HMRC systems close to the filing deadline, taxpayers will not be penalised for late submission of a return due to such problems provided that they, or their agent, file within a reasonable period once the service is restored.

If a notice is given after 31 July the return must be submitted during the period of three months beginning with the date of the notice (for paper returns) or on or before 31 January (for online returns).

If a notice is given after 31 October the return (whether paper return or electronic) must be submitted within three months from the date of the notice.

For detailed notes on the self-assessment provisions see the companion to this book, **Tolley's Taxwise I 2023/24.**

Filing dates for paper and online self-assessment returns

Paper substitutes for Self-Assessment (SA) returns

(5) Computer generated substitute versions of the SA Return are no longer approved or accepted for:

- SA Individual Returns – (SA100 series)
- SA Trust and Estate Returns – (SA900 series)

For the time being, HMRC will continue to accept approved substitutes for the remaining SA returns (including those for trustees of registered pension schemes) and for all other forms they currently approve substitutes for.

SA filing dates

Anyone who is required to file a self-assessment tax return has:

- until 31 October to do so, if they choose to send a paper return; or
- until the following 31 January if they file online.

This allows an additional three months for online filing compared with paper.

The filing obligation is satisfied by the first return received by HMRC and this also triggers any late filing penalty. So if, for example, a paper 2022/23 return is filed after 31 October 2023, it is not then possible to avoid a late filing penalty by filing the return online, even before the deadline for online returns.

In the event that there are problems with HMRC systems close to the filing deadline, taxpayers will not be penalised for late submission of a return due to such problems provided that they, or their agent, file within a reasonable period once the service is restored.

If a notice is given after 31 July the return must be submitted during the period of three months beginning with the date of the notice (for paper returns) or on or before 31 January (for online returns).

If a notice is given after 31 October the return (whether paper return or electronic) must be submitted within three months from the date of the notice.

For detailed notes on the self-assessment provisions see the companion to this book, **Tolley's Taxwise I 2023/24.**

Capital gains tax: 'report and pay' obligations on the disposal of UK residential property

(6) The capital gains (and allowable losses) of personal representatives (and indeed trustees) must be reported on their self-assessment tax returns for a tax year. With effect from 6 April 2021, however, additional and separate compliance obligations (the so-called 'report and pay' requirements) arise for both UK and non-UK resident personal representatives (and indeed individuals and trustees) in respect of their disposals of UK residential property (FA 2019, Sch 2). See **Example F6 explanatory note 16** for a more detailed discussion of the 'report and pay' requirements.

Income Tax and Trusts

Question

Outline the provisions determining the rates of tax applicable to trust income and the way in which the tax payable is accounted for.

Answer

Rates of tax on trust income: basic rules

The trustees of a trust are together treated as if they were a single person (distinct from the persons who are the trustees of the trust from time to time) (ITA 2007 s 474(1)).

Prior to 6 April 2017, the income of a person (who is not an individual) is charged to tax at the basic rate of 20%, unless other rates of income tax are imposed by other provisions of the Income Tax Acts (ss 6, 11). This will be the case where the person's income is 'dividend income'; dividend income (inclusive of a notional tax credit where appropriate for dividend income arising before 6 April 2016) is charged to tax at the dividend ordinary rate of 7.5% (10% in 2015/16) (ss 6, 8, 14). From 6 April 2022 the dividend ordinary rate is increased to 8.75% (FA 2022 s 4). Dividend income includes dividends and other distributions from both UK resident and non-UK resident companies, stock and scrip dividends from UK resident companies and income deemed to arise on the release of a loan to a participator in a close company (s 19).

As from 6 April 2017, following the implementation of the powers that have been devolved to the Scottish Parliament to set the Scottish rates of income tax (see **Example E1 at explanatory note 13**), the income of a person (who is not an individual) is charged to tax at the default basic rate of 20% (ss 6, 6C, 11) and, where the person's income is dividend income (as defined above), at the dividend ordinary rate of 7.5% (ss 6, 8, 14). From 6 April 2022 the dividend ordinary rate is increased to 8.75% (FA 2022 s 4). This scheme for identifying income charged at particular rates is summarised in s 9A.

Consequently, as a basic rule, the income of the trustees of a trust is, for 2017/18 and later tax years, charged to income tax at the default basic rate and the dividend ordinary rate according to its type. In their capacity as such, trustees are not liable to pay income tax at the higher rate, the additional rate, the savings nil rate, the starting rate for savings, the dividend nil rate, the dividend upper rate and the dividend additional rate (which, looking at it in a different way, means that trustees have no so-called 'savings allowance' or 'dividend allowance' which are available only to individuals). None of the Scottish or Welsh rates of income tax apply to trustees; the Scottish and Welsh rates apply only to individuals (and then only to their non-savings and non-dividend income). The income on which the trustees are taxable is determined using the principles applicable to each type of income; but the aggregate of their income is not reduced by personal allowances.

However, this basic rule is set aside in a number of cases. Certain trust income is taxed (ultimately) as the income of the settlor (at his marginal rate of tax). Certain other trust income (called trust rate income) is charged at the trust rate, or, in the case of dividend income, the dividend trust rate (collectively called the trust tax rates). This is the case primarily for accumulation and discretionary trusts.

From 6 April 2016 to 5 April 2022 the dividend trust rate was 38.1% and the trust rate was 45%. From 6 April 2022, the dividend trust rate stands at 39.35% and the trust rate stands at 45% (s 9 as amended by FA 2022 s 4). (In 2015/16 the respective rates were 37.5% and 45%.) For more detailed information see **Examples F6** and **F7**.

Trust income taxed at the trust tax rates

In the case of trusts where the trustees have a power to accumulate income, or where they have a discretion as to whether or not the income is paid to or for the benefit of beneficiaries (or to which beneficiaries it is paid), the trustees are in principle charged to tax at the trust rate of 45% except in relation to their dividend income which is charged at the dividend trust rate of 39.35% (ss 9, 11, 14, 479). This rule alters the basic rule described above in relation to such trusts.

Yet even for such trusts, the income out of which trust management expenses (properly allocable to income) are defrayed, and, subject to anti-fragmentation rules, the first £1,000 of trust rate income (first slice income) is not charged at the trust tax rates, but is instead charged at the default basic or dividend ordinary rate according to the type of income against which the expenses or first slice income is matched (ss 484(4), 491(3)).

If the trustees of accumulation and discretionary trusts make discretionary payments to beneficiaries which constitute income in the beneficiaries' hands, those payments are deemed to have been made net of 45% income tax which the Trustees must account for. In that regard they can treat as tax already paid in calculating how much of the tax at 45% has already been paid by them an amount equal to the total of the tax charged at the default basic and dividend ordinary rates. This was not always the case for tax years before 2016/17 (where the notional tax credit on a dividend could not be so counted) and so in earlier years the tax burden on such payments was significantly increased. For the detailed provisions of the tax arising on discretionary payments see **Example F7**.

Treatment of trustees' expenses and first slice income

Any expenses incurred in connection with a particular type of trust income (for example rental income) are deducted (in accordance with the rules of tax law) in arriving at the assessable income from that source, but there is no relief for general trust management expenses.

However, the income out of which such general trust management expenses are defrayed is not taxed at the trust tax rates but at the default basic rate and dividend ordinary rate as the case may be. Such expenses are regarded as matched first to the trust's dividend income and then to its other income (ss 484(2), 486 – see **Example F7** at **explanatory note 2** for details of the treatment of expenses when the trust tax rates apply).

The first slice income of a trust is matched to trust income *net* of trust management expenses (s 484(3)) and presumably it will also be so ascertained after a trust's other Step 2 deductions (see **explanatory note 1**) have been taken into account (eg annuities paid by the trustees). Although trust management expenses are matched to the trust's dividend income first, the first slice income is matched in the opposite order – default basic rate income at 20% first, followed by dividend income at 8.75% (7.5% in 2021/22). See **Example F6 explanatory note 1** for more detail.

Purchase by company of own shares and other capital receipts

Section 481 provides for the trust tax rates to apply to other amounts which, though not income for trust law purposes, are regarded as the income of the trustees for income tax purposes. This rule applies to interest in possession trusts as well as accumulation and discretionary trusts, but not to unit trusts, charitable trusts, pension funds or where the income is treated as belonging to the settlor or any other person (s 481).

The section applies in particular where a company redeems, repays or purchases its own shares from the trustees of a trust (s 482 Type 1). A payment to the trustees in these circumstances (which is not treated as an exempt distribution under CTA 2010 s 1033) is treated as trust income liable to tax at the dividend trust rate of 39.35% (38.1% in 2021/22) on the amount of the payment (ITA 2007 ss 481(2), (3)). It also applies where trustees are deemed to be in receipt of rental income on the grant of a short lease (s 482 Type 5) and accrued income profits (s 482 Type 2). In this case the deemed income is charged at the trust rate of 45% (ss 481(2), (4)). See **Example F7 explanatory note 6** and **Example F8** respectively for more detail.

Income not taxed at the trust tax rates

Where someone has an interest in possession in a trust fund, or part thereof, or is entitled to an annuity from the fund, that person cannot avoid liability at the higher rate of tax simply because the trustees do not pay out all of the trust income to which that person is entitled. That income is in any event included in his statutory income, by reference, in the first instance, to the statement of trust income and form R185 (Trust Income) (see **explanatory note 2**), and he will be a creditor of the trust for any balance of income due to him. Liability at the trust tax rates does not apply to trust income to which someone is entitled in equity as against the trustees as of right under the terms of the trust (as opposed to pursuant to an exercise of discretion by the trustees).

It will be noted that the trust tax rates do still apply where income is treated for tax purposes as that of the settlor *before* it is distributed (eg where the settlor has settled funds and he and/or his wife are beneficiaries of the trust) and where income is paid from a parental settlement to the minor, unmarried children of the settlor (even though, in both cases, such income is treated as the settlor's under ITTOIA 2005 s 619 (see below) (s 646(8)).

Income of charitable trusts and income from property held for certain occupational and personal pension funds is also excluded from being charged to tax at the trust tax rates (s 479(3)).

Income taxed as income of settlor

Income is taxed as the settlor's income in two main circumstances – first where he retains an interest in a settlement under ITTOIA 2005 ss 623–628 (a settlor-interested trust) and secondly where he has settled property for the benefit of his unmarried, minor children under ITTOIA 2005 ss 629–632 (a parental settlement). A settlor retains an interest in a trust where the income in the trust arises during his lifetime from property (including the income itself and other related property) which, in any circumstances, is or may become payable to or applicable for the benefit of the settlor or his spouse or civil partner (ss 624, 625). Whereas the income of a settlor-interested trust and a parental settlement that is a bare trust created on or after 9 March 1999 or an interest in possession settlement is treated as that of the settlor as soon as it arises, income arising under any other type of parental settlement (generally speaking discretionary or accumulation settlements and bare trusts created before 9 March 1999 to which no property has subsequently been added) is treated as that of the settlor only to the extent that, during the life of the settlor, it is paid to or for the benefit of an unmarried, minor child of the settlor and the amount so paid or applied is £100 or more (s 629(1), (3)). In both of the above cases, income that is treated as arising to the settlor is regarded as the highest part of his income (s 619A) (other than employment income lump sum termination payments under ITEPA 2003 s 403 and life policy gains under ITTOIA 2005 s 465) (ITA 2007 s 1012). The settlor can recover from the trustees or from the person who received the income any tax paid by him on the income that is deemed to be his under the above provisions (ITTOIA 2005 s 646). The settlor is also obliged to return to the trustees any tax repayment he receives in relation to the trust income (s 646).

Where income is taxed as the settlor's income, the charge on him under ITTOIA 2005 s 619 on dividend income is at the dividend nil, ordinary, upper or additional rates as the case may be, and any other income is charged at the basic, upper or additional rates (or their Scottish equivalents) and the various savings rates as the case may be (s 619(2)). In other words, the settlor is treated for tax purposes as if the income had arisen directly to him, with no deduction for management expenses incurred by the trustees.

Where income is treated as the settlor's under the above rules, the question that arises is how the trustees of the trusts concerned are taxed. The answer is that the charge to tax on the trustees is not excluded merely on account of these rules, the trustees being the persons by whom the income is received in the first place (ITTOIA 2005 s 646(8)). This means that, in the case of a discretionary or accumulation trust, for example, the trustees are charged at the trust tax rates of 45% and 39.35% (38.1% in 2021/22) on the income arising in the trust (as described earlier in this note).

This clearly results in the income being charged to tax twice: once in the hands of the trustees and again in the hands of the settlor. There is also the potential under first principles for the income to be taxed a third time when distributed to the beneficiaries of a settlor-interest trust or parental settlement. There are a number of rules in place to prevent the income being taxed more than once. Although tax is first collected from the trustees, an adjustment mechanism ensures that the same income is not taxed twice and that the settlor neither gains nor suffers a loss.

The tax treatment of settlor interested and parental settlements is discussed in more detail in **Example F5**.

Income certificates to beneficiaries (forms R185 (Trust Income))

At the end of each tax year the trustees give income beneficiaries a certificate of their entitlement to/receipt of trust income (form R185 (Trust Income)). It records the income tax paid thereon by the trustees. The income shown on the form will be included in the net income of the beneficiary, whose unused personal allowances will be available to give an income tax repayment, and upon whom any higher (or additional) rate or dividend upper (or additional) rate tax will be charged. The trustees' certificate will show the rates at which tax has been paid. For trusts liable to tax at the trust tax rates, the tax rate shown will be 45% (irrespective of the source of the underlying income). For other trusts the rates shown will be 20% on non-dividend income and 8.75% (7.5% in 2021/22) on dividend income (as described above). Tax credits (in respect of gains from non-qualifying life assurance policies, contracts for life annuities and capital redemption policies) will be shown as non-repayable.

Filing dates for self-assessment returns

Trustees are obliged to make an annual return of trust income and capital gains and to include in that return a self-assessment (SA) of the amounts of tax payable (TMA 1970 ss 8A, 9).

Paper substitutes for SA returns

Computer generated substitute versions of the SA return are no longer approved or accepted for:

- SA Individual Returns – (SA100 series).
- SA Trust and Estate Returns – (SA900 series).

For the time being, HMRC will continue to accept approved substitutes for the remaining SA returns (including those for trustees of registered pension schemes) and for all other forms they currently approve substitutes for.

SA return filing dates

Under TMA 1970 s 8A(1B) anyone who is required to file a self-assessment tax return for a tax year has:

- until 31 October in the following tax year to do so, if they choose to send a paper return; or
- until the following 31 January in the following tax year if they file online.

This allows an additional three months for online filing compared with paper.

The filing obligation is satisfied by the first return received by HMRC and this also triggers any late filing penalty. So if, for example, a paper 2023/24 return is filed after 31 October 2024, it is not then possible to avoid a late filing penalty by filing the return online, even before the deadline for online returns.

In addition, in certain other cases, HMRC will allow extra time beyond the statutory deadline of 31 October – until 31 January – for paper filing without incurring a penalty. These include:

- trustees of registered pension schemes; and
- SA taxpayers for whom facilities to file online are not yet available (see below).

In the event that there are problems with HMRC systems close to the filing deadline, taxpayers will not be penalised for late submission of a return due to such problems provided that they, or their agent, file within a reasonable period once the service is restored.

If a notice is given after 31 July the return must be submitted during the period of three months beginning with the date of the notice (for paper returns) or on or before 31 January (for online returns) (TMA 1970 s 8A(1D)).

If a notice is given after 31 October the return (whether paper return or electronic) must be submitted within three months from the date of the notice (TMA 1970 s 8A(1E)).

Tax payment dates

All sources of income, and also any capital gains, are dealt with under self-assessment, and trustees make payments on account of income tax (not capital gains tax) in the same way as individuals.

The tax payment dates are:

31 January in the tax year	1st payment on account, being one half of the total tax payable for the previous tax year (including the tax at the rate applicable to trusts or dividend trust rate where appropriate but excluding capital gains tax), as reduced by any tax deducted at source
31 July after end of tax year	2nd payment on account (same amount as 1st payment)
31 January after end of tax year	Full liability for year (including capital gains tax) less payments on account and tax deducted at source

For a detailed illustration and the additional compliance rules that must be observed by trustees in relation to capital gains tax when they dispose of UK residential property, see **Example F6**.

Explanatory Notes

(1) In order to work out their liability to income tax, the trustees must follow the seven-step method statement in ITA 2007 s 23. Under Step 1 they identify the amounts of income on which they are charged to tax for the

tax year; the sum of those amounts is their 'total income'. From that total (or from the components of income that make up that total, as the case may be) they deduct, at Step 2, the reliefs set out in s 24(1)(b) to which they may be entitled (see s 24(2)).

(2) At the end of each tax year the trustees give income beneficiaries a certificate of their entitlement to/receipt of trust income (form R185 (Trust Income)). It records the income tax paid thereon by the trustees. The income shown on the form will be included in the net income of the beneficiary. It is considered that ultimately the true income tax position of the beneficiary in relation to the trust's income will be ascertained by reference to the trustees' own self-assessment. Any error by them in reflecting their income and tax figures in the R185 (Trust Income) form may lead to the beneficiary being pardoned (in penalty terms) for the consequential error in his own return if the figures are credible by comparison to what he knows he has received or is entitled to, but he won't be let off the income tax (and interest) implications of the true figures.

Income tax treatment of bare trusts

(3) Bare trusts used to provide a simple way of enabling children's personal allowances and lower tax rates to be used against funds from the parent, so long as the income merely accumulated for the children's benefit without actually being paid to them. The parents could act as trustees and there thus need be no administration costs.

As mentioned in **part C point 2** of **Example C1**, the earlier income tax advantages of bare trusts by parents in favour of their children under 18 were negated with effect from 9 March 1999 (FA 1999 s 64). The parental settlement rules apply to the income arising under a bare trust settled by a child's parent on or after 9 March 1999 whether the income is paid to the child or not. However, the advantages continue for bare trusts created by parents before that date provided no funds are added (see ITTOIA 2005 Sch 2 para 133). Where funds are added to a pre-9 March 1999 bare trust, the parental settlement rules apply only to the income arising from the added funds. Except for tax credits, the tax deducted at source from the accumulated income may in such a case be reclaimed to the extent that it exceeds the child's liability.

The revised rules do not prevent tax-efficient bare trusts being created by a parent's will, or by other relatives. It is not, however, possible for a parent to circumvent the rules by creating a bare trust for a relative's or friend's children and for the relative/friend to do the same for his children by way of a reciprocal arrangement (ITTOIA 2005 s 620).

Income tax treatment of trusts: the Scottish rates of income tax

(4) The Scotland Act 2012 (which amended the Scotland Act 1998 to this effect) devolved power on the Scottish Parliament to set Scottish rates of income tax for Scottish taxpayers. The 1998 Act was further amended by the Scotland Act 2016 in this regard. The power to make such rates was implemented with effect from 6 April 2017 (The Scotland Act 2016 (Commencement No 2) Regulations 2016, (SI 2016/161)).

The Scottish rates of income tax, namely the Scottish basic rate, the Scottish higher rate and the Scottish additional rate, set at 20%, 40% and 45% respectively for 2017/18, are charged on the non-savings income of Scottish taxpayers (as defined in the Scotland Act 1998 s 80D). In 2017/18 the basic rate limit for such income was set at £31,500. In 2018/19 the Scottish rate bands and the rates of income tax were altered further and were as follows in respect of an individual's non-savings non-dividend income:

Name	*Rate*	*Band*
Starter rate	19%	£0–£2,000
Basic rate	20%	£2,001–£12,150
Intermediate rate	21%	£12,151–£31,580
Higher rate	41%	£31,581–£150,000
Top rate	46%	£150,001 and above

In 2019/20 the Scottish rate bands and the rates of income tax were as follows in respect of an individual's non-savings non-dividend income:

Name	*Rate*	*Band*
Starter rate	19%	£0–£2,049
Basic rate	20%	£2,050–£12,444
Intermediate rate	21%	£12,445–£30,930
Higher rate	41%	£30,931–£150,000
Top rate	46%	£150,001 and above

In 2020/21 the Scottish rate bands and the rates of income tax were as follows in respect of an individual's non-savings non-dividend income:

Name	*Rate*	*Band*
Starter rate	19%	£0–£2,085
Basic rate	20%	£2,086–£12,658
Intermediate rate	21%	£12,659–£30,930
Higher rate	41%	£30,931–£150,000
Top rate	46%	£150,001 and above

In 2021/22 the Scottish rate bands and the rates of income tax are as follows in respect of an individual's non-savings non-dividend income:

Name	*Rate*	*Band*
Starter rate	19%	£0–£2,097
Basic rate	20%	£2,098–£12,726
Intermediate rate	21%	£12,727–£31,092
Higher rate	41%	£31,093–£150,000
Top rate	46%	£150,001 and above

In 2022/23 the Scottish rate bands and the rates of income tax are as follows in respect of an individual's non-savings non-dividend income:

Name	*Rate*	*Band*
Starter rate	19%	£0–£2,162
Basic rate	20%	£2,163–£13,118
Intermediate rate	21%	£13,119–£31,092
Higher rate	41%	£31,093–£150,000
Top rate	46%	£150,001 and above

In 2023/24 the Scottish rate bands and the rates of income tax are as follows in respect of an individual's non-savings non-dividend income:

Name	*Rate*	*Band*
Starter rate	19%	£0–£2,162
Basic rate	20%	£2,163–£13,118
Intermediate rate	21%	£13,119–£31,092
Higher rate	42%	£31,093–£150,000
Top rate	47%	£150,001 and above

As the Scottish rate of income tax will be charged only on the non-savings, non-dividend income of Scottish taxpayers who are individuals, trusts are not generally affected by the Scottish rates of income tax. However, individuals who are Scottish taxpayers and who receive non-savings income from a trust will be charged to income tax on that income at the prevailing Scottish rates. Consequently, for beneficiaries of trusts who are Scottish taxpayers, the position will be as follows:

(a) In the case of a *bare trust*, income is treated as arising direct to the beneficiary and as a result those taxpayers who are Scottish taxpayers would include this income in so far as it is non-savings, non-dividend income as part of their total income in the normal way and this would be liable to the Scottish rates of income tax.

(b) In the case of a *discretionary and accumulation trust*, income is distributed to beneficiaries and is received net of tax at the trust rates. Income payments from discretionary trusts derive from the trust and will be liable at the Scottish rates when paid to Scottish beneficiaries.

(c) As regards *interest in possession trusts*, Scottish taxpayers will pay tax at the Scottish rates on the income of the trust in so far as it is non-savings, non-dividend income.

(d) In the case of *settlor interested trusts*, the settlor will be liable at his marginal rate although he will receive a tax credit for the tax paid by the trustees. Income in the hands of the trustees will continue to be charged at their marginal rate and so, if the settlor is a Scottish taxpayer, this income will be chargeable at the Scottish rates in so far as it is non-savings, non-dividend income.

Income tax treatment of trusts: the Welsh rates of income tax

(5) The Government of Wales Act 2006 has devolved property on the National Assembly for Wales to set Welsh rates for Welsh taxpayers (s 110). The rates are ascertained in accordance with ITA 2007 s 6B(1) whereby the (main) basic, higher and additional rates are reduced by 10% and then the corresponding Welsh rates are added to that amount. The Welsh Rate Resolution of the National Assembly for Wales for 2019/20, 2020/21, 2021/22, 2022/23 and 2023/24 sets the corresponding Welsh rates at 10%. Consequently, for all of those years the Welsh rates of income tax are the Welsh basic rate (20%), Welsh higher rate (40%) and Welsh additional rate (45%). These rates apply only to non-savings non-dividend (NSND) income of a Welsh taxpayer. Welsh income tax remains part of the existing UK income tax system and is not a devolved tax.

Prospective amendments

(6) With effect from 6 April 2024, F(No 2)A 2023, s 29 and Sch 2 para 13 will abolish the rules applicable to accumulation or discretionary trusts on their first slice income. Also with effect from that date, new ITA 2007, s 24B is enacted (see F(No 2)A 2023 s 29 and Sch 1 para 10) and it provides that where the net income of a trust is £500 or less, it is treated as being £0 so that effectively the trust is not charged to income tax. The £500 de minimis amount is reduced if, subject to certain exceptions, a settlor of that trust has made other trusts. The reduction is based on similar rules that currently apply to a trust's first slice income.

Question

T, a widower, who had been in business as a sole trader for many years, died on 6 April 2023.

By his will S, his accountant, was appointed executor and trustee and the whole estate was left in trust for his son, U, for life, with remainder to his grandchildren on U's death.

The will did not bar the application of the Apportionment Act 1870, and empowered S to continue T's business so that it could be sold as a going concern.

By the will, S is allowed a fixed annual sum of £1,500 for his services as executor and trustee.

T's income-producing assets apart from the business consisted of:

£20,000 listed 10% loan stock in X plc – interest receivable 31 July and 31 January. Interest was received on the due dates and S apportioned it between capital and income under the Apportionment Act 1870.

Building society deposit – interest receivable 30 June and 31 December. Interest of £200 was received in June and £80 in December 2023. S apportioned the June interest between capital and income under the Apportionment Act 1870.

Property let unfurnished producing rental income during 2023/24 of £1,130 with allowable expenses (none being interest payments) of £430. At 5 April 2023, there were unutilised losses arising from this property of £100.

The business accounts were made up to 5 April each year. Accounts were produced for the two years to 5 April 2023 and 2024 showing tax adjusted profits of £17,200 and £16,420 respectively.

The deceased had a mortgage of £16,000 on his home, provided by a relative. The interest paid by S for the period from 6 April 2023 until December 2023, when the property was sold, was £900.

T, until his death, had been the life tenant of the W settled fund, the sole asset of which was an investment of £40,000 listed 8% debenture stock in Z plc. The due dates for receipt of the interest were 6 April and 6 October. The W trustees normally paid the income to T shortly after it was received, and paid to S, on 31 July 2023, the income due until T's death.

A loan (not by way of overdraft) was taken out by S to enable inheritance tax to be paid on the estate's non-instalment property. The loan interest charged for 2023/24 was £500.

Certain administration expenses were paid on 31 March 2024. These were allocated as to £500 for capital and £1,195 for income. On that date S was paid the annual sum of £1,500 due to him.

(a)

- (i) Prepare a statement showing the income tax payable by the trust for 2023/24 and the amount of income of the trust to which U is entitled for 2023/24, both together with supporting notes explaining your treatment of each of the items mentioned above.
- (ii) In preparing the statement under (a)(i) show clearly the computation required by s 2 of the Apportionment Act 1870.

(b) Show the entries on the R185 (Trust Income) to be given to U for 2023/24.

(c) Explain whether any degree of double taxation has occurred in respect of the trust established under T's will, and if so what, if any, relief in relation to that double taxation is available.

(d) Would your answer to (c) be any different if U had been absolutely entitled to T's residuary estate instead of just having a life interest? Illustrate your answer on the basis that T's taxable estate was £500,000 and the IHT paid in respect of it was £75,000.

Answer

(a)(i) Statement of trust income 2023/24

Often it will be necessary for the executors to administer the estate of a deceased person and then, pursuant to the terms of his Will, to transfer their responsibilities to the trustees of a life interest settlement in respect of the residue of the estate. In this Example the trustees and personal representatives are the same persons. Furthermore the whole of the estate is left in trust to the son of the deceased. In practice in these circumstances, it is usual to treat all of the income as belonging to the trustees from the date of death and to allow the expenses of administration etc against that income. More correctly the executor should issue a form R185 (Estate Income) and complete a self-assessment return for the period of administration of the estate and then do the same as trustee, ie issue form R185 (Trust Income) and complete a further self-assessment return for the remaining part of the same tax year. The answer that follows is based on the practice referred to above, rather than the strict position as explained.

Refer to note			£	£	*Tax* £
	Non-savings income				
1	Trading profit		16,420		
2	Unfurnished lettings		700	17,120	
	Savings income				
3	£20,000 10% loan stock, X plc		2,000		
4	Life tenancy W fund		0		
5	Building society interest		280	2,280	
				19,400	
	Less: Step 2 deduction (ITA 2007, ss 23, 24):				
6	Executor's remuneration (annuity)		1,500		
7	Loan interest re payment of IHT		500	(2,000)	
	Total taxable income of trust			17,400	
	Tax thereon:				
	Non-dividend income	17,400 @ 20%	3,480		
6	*Add*: Tax deducted from executor's remuneration (annuity) (1,500 @ 20%)		300		
	Total tax due		3,780		3,780
	of which tax payable by self-assessment is (see **explanatory note** 8)				3,724
	Income of trust after tax			13,620	
	Less: trust expenses:				
8	Mortgage interest		900		
9	Administration expenses		1,195	(2,095)	
	Net income of trust			11,525	
	Less: apportioned to capital per (b)			(367)	
	Net income available for income beneficiary (U)			11,158	
	Comprising:				
	Income net of tax		13,620		
	Less: apportioned to capital		(367)		

10	*Less*: Used to pay trust expenses (part)	(2,095)	
		11,158	11,158
	Gross equivalent is 11,158 × 100/80 =		13,948

(a)(ii) Computation of income apportioned to capital

Refer to note		£
3	£20,000 10% loan stock X plc 1 February 2023 to 6 April 2023 (64/181 × £1,000)	354
5	Building society interest received 1 January 2023 to 6 April 2023 $\frac{95}{181}$ × *£200*	105
		459
	Less: Income tax @ 20%	(92)
	Net income apportioned to capital	367

Notes relating to statement of trust income

(1) The death of T constitutes a cessation of his sole trade for tax purposes. The trustees are regarded as commencing the business from that date. The first year of charge is 2023/24. Tax will be charged on the profit from 7 April 2023 to 5 April 2024. (Trustees are not liable to Class 4 National Insurance contributions – Social Security Contributions and Benefits Act 1992 Sch 2 para 5.)

(2) The income from lettings is:

Rent income in 2023/24	1,130
Less: allowable expenses	(430)
	£700

The unutilised losses of T personally are not available for carry forward against the income of the will trust. (As to the computation of rental profits in respect of interest, see **Example F7 explanatory note 11**.)

(3) Despite the income from the 10% loan stock having to be allocated to the capital of the estate in so far as the proportion up to the date of death of T is concerned (under Apportionment Act 1870 s 2), the entire income *received* after death has to be included for *income tax purposes* as that of the will trust. The trustees pay the tax on the interest and then apportion the net income between the capital and income funds of the trust for trust law purposes (see **explanatory note (1)** for further detail).

(4) Although the income from the W settlement is received by T's trustees after the date of T's death, the income arose on 6 April when T was still alive. As life tenant of the W fund T was entitled to the income as it arose whilst he was alive. After his death, the income is due to the remainderman or successive life tenant of that settled fund in accordance with its terms. Therefore the income from T's life tenancy forms no part of the income of his executors and ultimately of U's trust. The income which arose before T's death belongs to and is taxable on T personally (in this Example the interest arising on 6 April 2023 only). As such, when it is received by his executor, it forms part of the capital of T's estate. If interest had been payable on different dates – for example 6 June and 6 December – so that the interest period straddled the date of T's death, the interest that would have been paid on 6 June 2023 would have been paid to the trustees of the W settled fund.

The question whether that amount of interest would be apportioned (under the Apportionment Act 1870 s 2) between T (up to the date of his death) and the succeeding beneficiary of the W fund (from T's death) would depend on the terms of the W trust and whether it excludes apportionment under that Act. No information is given on this but it would not, in any case, affect the income or the income tax of T's executors and ultimately U's trust in the Example.

(5) Building society interest will partly have to be allocated to capital of the estate under the Apportionment Act 1870 s 2, but since it is *received* after death it is for *income tax purposes* regarded wholly as income of the will trust. The trustees pay the tax on the interest and then apportion the net income between the capital and income funds of the trust for trust law purposes. The building society interest is treated in the same way as the interest arising on the loan stock of X plc in **note** (3) above.

(6) The £1,500 pa payable to S as executor is regarded as an annual payment, from which income tax at the basic rate must be deducted when making the payment (ITA 2007 ss 449, 901). See **explanatory note 6** for the way in which the tax is accounted for.

Had the will contained a professional executor's charging clause, the amount paid to S would be an administration expense, payable out of the net income.

(7) The interest paid on the loan to pay inheritance tax is allowable in calculating the trust's income liable to income tax (ITA 2007 s 383).

(8) The mortgage interest paid is a trust expense payable out of taxed income.

(9) Administration expenses likewise have to be paid out of taxed income.

(10) Trust expenses are the expenses of administration and as such are regarded as paid out of income which has already suffered tax. They must be distinguished from expenses relating to a particular source, like those of the trade and of the lettings in this case which are allowable in computing the income from that particular source.

Trust expenses are treated as being set against income in the following order (ITA 2007 s 486):

(i) Dividend income (as defined), dividends received by non-UK resident persons in respect of which tax is treated as paid (ITTOIA 2005 s 399), scrip dividends (ITTOIA 2005 s 411), and close company loans written off or released (ITTOIA 2005 s 416). Prior to its repeal on 6 April 2016, the list also included bonus issues of redeemable securities (ITTOIA 2005 s 400(4),(5)) (see FA 2016 Sch 1 para 1).

(ii) Taxed dividends from abroad.

(iii) Non-savings and savings income other than that in (i) and (ii).

The set-off order is in fact the most beneficial, in that it maximises the amount of tax paid by the trust that may be passed on to beneficiaries.

(b) Form R185 (Trust Income) to be given to U for 2023/24

Although for income tax purposes, any income received after death is treated as income of the estate and charged on the trustees, as stated in **notes** 3, 4 and 5 to the computation in **part** (a), any part of that income that has been apportioned to trust capital is not available to the life tenant and is excluded from his income. Hence, the form R185 (Trust Income) to be given to U for 2023/24 therefore excludes the net amount of £1,652 apportioned to capital. The form (based on the computation in **part** (a)) is therefore as follows (although strictly the gross income amounts are not included on the form – they are shown here for ease of identification only):

	Gross	Tax	Net
	£	£	£
Savings income (2,280 – 459)	1,812	362	1,450
Non-savings income	12,133	2,425	9,708
Total	13,945	2,787	11,158

(c) Double taxation – T's Will trust: beneficiary with limited interest

In order to discuss whether double taxation has occurred in respect of the trust established under T's Will (and consequently whether any relief is available), it is necessary to understand the sense in which double taxation can be said to arise. Certain income-bearing assets of an estate are valued for inheritance tax purposes by reference to the income that is in the process of arising (ie accruing) at the date of a deceased's death. The value of the asset (as augmented by the income so accruing) is charged to inheritance tax. When that income is later recognised for income tax purposes (for example when it is received by the executors of the estate and provided it is received as part of the residuary income of the estate), it is charged to income tax. In other words, income which was accrued up to the date of an individual's death but which was received after death forms part of the capital of the deceased's estate and is charged to inheritance tax. The income, when received, will also form part of the residuary income of the estate's personal representatives on which income tax is charged. In this sense, therefore, there is a degree of double taxation of the estate's (and hence ultimately the trust's) income. For example, if the deceased died owning a gilt-edged security at the date of his death, the value of that security as included in his estate for inheritance tax purposes will, in part, be attributable to accrued interest. When the interest is actually paid to the executors after the deceased's death, it will be charged to income tax in their hands. Effectively, the amount of accrued interest has suffered tax twice.

The same principle applies to other income paid after the date of an individual's death but which arose in whole or in part before his death. For example, interest-earning bank accounts are valued for inheritance tax purposes with interest accrued to the date of death. Also the value of a dividend declared before death but payable after death will attract inheritance tax and, following receipt, will form part of the residuary income on which income tax is charged.

Double taxation potentially arises therefore in the sense that an amount (equal to the amount of income accruing to the date of death) is subject to both inheritance tax (as part of the deceased estate's capital) and income tax (as part of the estate's income). However, whether the same person actually suffers a double tax charge on that amount is a different matter and that question is addressed next.

The starting point in finding an answer to the question whether the same person suffers a double tax charge on the same amount starts with a reminder that the estate's residuary income ultimately feeds through to the estate's residuary beneficiaries. The estate income that is treated under ITTOIA 2005 Pt 6 Chap 5 as arising to those beneficiaries depends on the nature of their interest in the residue of the estate and that in turn determines whether they actually suffer both a charge to inheritance tax and income tax in respect of the same amount.

If the residuary beneficiary has a limited interest in the residue of the estate (ie only the income of the residue of the estate is properly payable to him), then he bears tax only on the residuary income of the estate (and not on any inheritance tax charged on the capital of the estate). Hence he does not (and never can) actually experience double taxation in the sense currently being described and so the issue of relief for double taxation does not arise. So in the case of a life interest such as U's in the Example, he personally will not suffer any form of double taxation because his interest is limited to the estate's income. The other part of the duplicated charge is borne by those whose interest is in the estate's capital, that is to say the grandchildren in this Example. So although there is a double charge to tax on the same amount – that is both inheritance tax and income tax – the two charges are borne by different beneficiaries – the life tenant in respect of income tax and the remaindermen in respect of inheritance tax. Hence in such a case the same person does not suffer a charge to both taxes in respect of the same amount. In these circumstances, where the interest of the income beneficiary is limited to income, and the estate capital is reserved for a different beneficiary, no relief is available to either the estate or the beneficiaries for the double charge because the issue of relief cannot arise where different persons suffer charges to different taxes albeit in respect of the same amount.

However, if the residuary beneficiary has an absolute interest in the residue of the estate (ie the capital of the residue of the estate is properly payable to him) then he may experience double taxation in respect of the same amount. Such a beneficiary certainly will bear the inheritance tax arising in respect of the estate; whether he also bears income tax on the residuary income of the estate depends upon the extent of his interest (and that too (obviously) of the residuary beneficiary with a limited interest in the residue). If the interest of the residuary beneficiary with a limited interest in the residue extends to the whole of the residue (ie he is entitled to all the income arising in respect of the residuary estate) then the residuary beneficiary with an absolute interest in the residue will not count any income arising to the executors. However, if the interest of the residuary beneficiary with a limited interest in the residue extends to part only of the residue (ie he is entitled to only some of the income arising in respect of the residuary estate) then the residuary beneficiary with an absolute interest in the residue will count as part of his estate income an amount that is related to the balance of the income of arising to the executors (on which he will bear income tax) as well as the capital of the residue itself (on which he bears inheritance tax). If this is the case, only then will the residuary beneficiary with an absolute interest in the residue be entitled to relief for the double charge to tax that he experiences (and this is explained further in **part (d)** of the Example below; see also **explanatory note 9** and **Example E1**).

Now in this Example, U has a limited interest in the whole of the residue of T's deceased estate. Hence the grandchildren will not count as part of their absolute interest in the residue any income arising to the executors. Hence they do not experience double taxation and the question of relief does not arise. As already explained U does not suffer double taxation either. Hence in the context of this Example, there is no double taxation in the sense in which that term is used in this context.

(d) Double taxation – U as beneficiary with absolute interest

By contrast, if U had been a beneficiary with an absolute interest in the residue of his late father's estate (and so absolutely entitled to the trust property), he would have suffered both income tax on the estate's income and inheritance tax on the estate's capital. However, if U were a higher or additional rate taxpayer, an element of tax relief would have been available in respect of the charge to income tax.

Where accrued income would be reflected in the value of T's estate and charged to inheritance tax, and would also be charged as income after his death, U, as absolute beneficiary, may have been able to claim to reduce the income for higher rate or additional rate (and dividend upper rate or dividend additional rate) purposes (but not for basic or dividend ordinary rate tax purposes) by the inheritance tax charged on the grossed-up amount of the accrued income (ITTOIA 2005 s 669). This alleviates the problem of double taxation described in **part (c)** above.

The relief is computed by multiplying the amount of the accrued income by the average rate of inheritance tax on T's estate.

This amount is then deducted in computing U's estate income in determining the amount of income to be taxed at higher rates.

For a more detailed explanation see **explanatory note 9** and **Example E1**.

Estate taxable	£500,000
Inheritance tax paid	£75,000
Average rate	15%
Income accrued before death (equal to amount in (a)(ii))	367
IHT attributed @15%	55
Gross up at 20%	£14
	£69
Tax credit	£14

Deduct from R185 (Trust Income) figures to give

	Gross	Tax	Net
Savings income	1,822	362	1,450
Less: s 669 relief	(69)	(14)	(55)
	1,753	348	1,395

This will need to be shown on the trust tax return – stating that s 669 relief of £56 (net) has been claimed.

Explanatory Notes

Apportionment of income on death

(1) The Apportionment Act 1870 s 2 lays down the statutory rule of time apportionment for all rents, annuities, dividends and other periodical payments (eg interest) in the nature of income. Its effect is that a beneficiary of the income (whether of a trust, of a deceased estate or otherwise of income-producing assets) is entitled only to the proportion of income that is in the process of arising during his period of entitlement to the income. This means that a computation has to be performed to work out how much income is attributable to such a beneficiary and the computation is performed on the assumption that the income accrued at a constant rate over time. Outgoings must similarly be apportioned (*Re Joel* (1967)).

So in this Example, the Apportionment Act 1870 requires income relating to the period before T's death to be allocated to him and taken into his estate. Also, where a deceased individual was the life tenant of a trust, or where his Will created a new interest in possession trust, the provisions of the Apportionment Act 1870 (and related case law) required that income for the period over which it is earned (or is in the process of arising) must be time-apportioned so as to ascertain the amount that is attributable to the part of the period falling before the individual's death, and that which is attributable to the part of the period following his death. For example, a dividend relating to a company's accounting period ending 31 December 2023 might be paid on 30 April 2024. If the life tenant of a trust entitled to the dividend died on 30 November 2023, the Apportionment Act 1870 requires that 11/12 of the dividend received on 30 April 2024 be allocated to the life tenant. In the case of rent or of interest on loan stock that accrues between two interest payment dates, the position is more straightforward because the period to which it relates immediately precedes the payment date. If the life tenant dies on 31 January and on 31 March the trustees receive rent for the quarter then ending, A's estate will be entitled to one-third of the rent. Nevertheless, the calculations required are time consuming and often result in insignificant adjustments.

As a result, most modern and competently drafted wills or trust deeds specifically exclude the application of all apportionments. The statutory rule in Apportionment Act 1870 s 2 has now been abolished by the Trusts (Capital and Income) Act 2013 s 1 which dis-applies the apportionment rule for trusts settled on or after 1 October 2013 (s 5(3) as read with The Trusts (Capital and Income) Act 2013 (Commencement No 1) Order 2013 SI 2013/676 art 4) (subject to any contrary intention expressed in the trust instrument (s 1(4)). If the Apportionment Act 1870 does not apply in any case, then taking the example of the dividend above, the full dividend belongs to whoever is entitled to it when it is paid on 30 April 2024; in other words the person entitled to income takes the whole amount of it when it arises (ie when it is payable or paid) rather than just the balance of the amount after apportionment.

The Apportionment Act 1870 and the Trusts (Capital and Income) Act 2013 (and the disapplication of either of them) concern the allocation of income between income and capital beneficiaries. They have no application to the computation of inheritance tax on capital, which, according to inheritance tax valuation rules, must reflect accrued income. Neither do they have any application as regards income tax which is charged when income is payable or paid (ie when it arises) and not as it accrues (ie is in the process of arising) from day to day (see below).

(2) For *income tax purposes*, the general income tax rules govern how different types of income are taxed. They determine when income arises (in the sense of being recognised for tax purposes – usually on a receipts basis or an accruals basis) and the person to whom the income so arises. Those rules are as follows:

Dividends

Dividends are taxable when they are due and payable (ITTOIA 2005 s 384). An interim dividend is due and payable and so taxable when it is paid. A final dividend is taxable when it is declared in general meeting (unless the general meeting further resolves that the dividend be due only when it is paid) (*Potel v CIR*). So ordinarily, a final dividend declared before a person's death will be taxable on the deceased.

Interest

Interest is taxable when received (s 370; *Dewar and Leigh v IRC*).

Rents

Rents are recognised in accordance with generally accepted accounting practice (s 275). They are accrued on a day to day basis and the amount earned must be apportioned to the periods before and after death.

Trading profits

There is a deemed cessation of trade when a trader dies, even where the trade is continued by his personal representatives. Profits computed under generally accepted accounting practice (s 25) are apportioned to the basis periods before and after death to reflect the deemed cessation and commencement (s 203).

Pensions, annuities

These are again accrued on a day-to-day basis and the amount receivable must be apportioned to the periods before and after death (ITEPA 2003 s 571). Entitlement to such payments usually ceases on death. If so, any amounts received after death are taxable as part of the deceased's income (s 13). In the case of guaranteed annuities and pensions which continue to be paid for a period after death, they are taxable as estate income.

Salaries

Employment earnings are taxable on a receipts basis (s 18). Amounts received after death, perhaps in relation to commission or bonus, are taxable as estate income (s 13).

Income of life tenant during administration of estate

(3) Where a person has a life interest in the residue of an estate, the amounts to be included in his statutory income during the period of administration are the grossed up equivalents of the actual income payments made to him (see **Example E1** for further details). Where part of the income has been apportioned to trust capital under the provisions of the Apportionment Act 1870, the amounts actually paid to the life tenant will be less than the net income of the trust, as shown in **part** (**b**) of the Example.

Income of beneficiary with absolute interest during administration of estate

(4) Where a person has an absolute interest in the residue of an estate (ie a right to capital as well as to income) again the amounts included in total income during the administration period will be the grossed up equivalent of the actual payments made to him (see **Example E1**).

If interest is paid on overdue inheritance tax, it is not an allowable deduction for someone with an absolute interest (IHTA 1984 s 233(3)). (For someone with a life interest, his income is the gross equivalent of the amounts actually paid to him, so that interest on overdue tax is effectively allowed for higher rate purposes.)

Nature of payments from estate to beneficiaries

(5) Payments from the estate to beneficiaries are treated as made first from income taxed at the 20% default basic rate, then savings income (excluding dividends) taxed at the 20% default basic rate, then dividend income taxed at 8.75% (ITTOIA 2005 s 679).

The different types of income (net of expenses) and the tax deducted therefrom are shown separately on forms R185 (Trust Income).

Executor's remuneration

(6) In order to work out their liability to income tax, the executors must follow the seven-step method statement in ITA 2007 s 23. Under Step 1 they identify the amounts of income on which they are charged to tax for the tax year; the sum of those amounts is their 'total income'. From that total (or from the components of income that make up that total, as the case may be) they deduct, at Step 2, the reliefs set out in s 24(1)(b) to which they may be entitled (see s 24(2)). The executor's remuneration of £1,500 represents an annual payment (often called an annuity), which is a Step 2 deduction for income tax purposes and reduces the trust's income for tax purposes. Tax relief has, however, already been retained out of the payment at 20%. In order to ensure that the tax retained is balanced by an equivalent amount of tax payable (so that the trust suffers no tax on that slice of its income), the trust's income is first reduced by the annuity, and tax is calculated on the resulting trust income at the appropriate rates. The tax payable is then increased by basic rate tax on the amount of the annuity. For an illustration of the treatment where annuities exceed the trust income see **Example F3 part b.**

Self-assessment payments on account limits

(7) Payments on account for a tax year are not required from trustees where:

- the net tax payable by them in the preceding tax year (ie the tax payable by them that was not deducted at source) is less than £1,000, or
- at least 80% of the total tax due for the preceding year (ie including any tax deducted at source) was collected at source.

(TMA 1970 s 59A(1) and Income Tax (Payments on Account) Regulations 1996, SI 1996/1654 (as amended by SI 2008/838)).

Self-assessment by trustees and personal representatives

(8) The self-assessment provisions apply to trustees and personal representatives in the same way as for individuals. Payments on account are due on 31 January in the tax year and 31 July following, each equal to half of the total income tax payable (net of tax deducted at source) for the previous tax year (unless it was below the de minimis thresholds). A balancing payment is then due on the following 31 January (which will include any capital gains tax payable). At the same time the first payment on account for the next year is due.

Payments on account will not be made for the tax year in which a trust commences (here 2023/24), since no tax was payable for the previous year. In this Example therefore all the tax payable by self-assessment, amounting to £3,780, will be due for payment on 31 January 2025. Note that this tax figure is made up of the tax of £3,024 on the non-savings income (net of Step 2 deductions) plus the tax of £456 on the savings income of £2,280 plus the tax of £300 deducted at source from the executor's remuneration.

The first payment on account for 2024/25 will also be due on 31 January 2025. Since there is no capital gains tax in the tax figure of £3,780, the first payment on account for 2024/25 will be half of that figure, ie £1,890. The total amount payable by the trustees on 31 January 2025 is therefore £5,670.

ITA 2007 s 882 now provides that tax is not deducted from payments of interest on quoted eurobonds, which are defined as interest-bearing securities issued by a company and listed on a recognised stock exchange.

For further notes on self-assessment see **Examples F2, F5, F6** and **F7.**

Relief for inheritance tax attributable to income accrued at death (ITTOIA 2005 s 669)

(9) Income that accrued during the lifetime of the deceased but was paid after death is reflected under inheritance tax rules as part of the value of the estate of the deceased person (D). The same income is treated as part of the net statutory income of the estate and therefore enters into the computation of residuary income.

Where this happens, a residuary beneficiary with an absolute interest in the residue who is liable to tax at the higher or additional rate (and dividend upper rate or dividend additional rate) of income tax may claim a deduction from the residuary income of an amount equal to the inheritance tax applicable to the accrued income (ITTOIA 2005 s 669).

A reduction is made in the residuary income of D's estate for that tax year in ascertaining the extra liability, if any, of a person with an absolute interest in the whole or part of the residue of D's estate or any other estate to which that residuary income is relevant.

Instructions for working out the deduction are set out in the legislation as follows:

A beneficiary's extra liability is the amount by which the beneficiary's liability to income tax exceeds the amount it would be if:

(a) income charged at the additional rate or the higher rate were charged at the basic rate and

(b) income charged at the dividend additional rate or the dividend upper rate were charged at the dividend ordinary rate.

The amount of the reduction under subsection (2) is calculated as follows:

Step 1

Calculate the net pre-death income by subtracting from the pre-death income any liabilities which have been taken account both:

(a) in determining the value of D's estate for the purposes of inheritance tax, and

(b) in calculating the residuary income of D's estate for the tax year.

Step 2

Calculate the inheritance tax attributable to net pre-death income by multiplying the inheritance tax to be charged by:

$$\frac{NPDI}{VE}$$

where:

NPDI is the net pre-death income, and

VE is the value of D's estate.

Step 3

Gross up the inheritance tax attributable to net pre-death income by reference to the basic rate for the tax year.

The amount of pre-death income taken into account in determining the value of D's estate is taken to be the actual amount of income accruing before D's death, less income tax at the basic rate for the tax year in which D died.

In the Example itself the income from the W fund would have been treated as accrued income in T's estate and included in the amount chargeable to inheritance tax. However, relief under s 669 does not apply to this income because it is not included in the residuary income of the estate (as explained in **note 4** to the income computation).

The question of double taxation in the context of estate taxation

(10) The issue of the double taxation of the residuary legatees of a deceased estate has been fully discussed in part (c) of the Example. There is another more subtle sense in which double taxation may be said to arise and that

is because of the application of the Apportionment Act 1870 (although this is not the conventional sense in which double taxation is understood in the context of a deceased estate and which finds relief under ITTOIA 2005 s 669; in the conventional sense double taxation arises not on account of the application of the Apportionment Act 1870 but because of the way in which property is valued for the purposes of inheritance tax). The application of the Apportionment Act 1870 in this Example is illustrated in **part (a)(ii)** above (and see **Explanatory Note 1**). The full amount of income arising in respect of the income-producing assets in T's estate is received after T's death by the executors of his estate and is charged to income tax on them. Some of the income so arising – that is the income arising on the X plc loan stock and the building society interest – is, after income tax has been paid or accounted for by them in respect of it, then apportioned by them under that Act to the capital of T's deceased estate. The net amount of that income accruing before his death (ie the amount which is apportioned) becomes part of the capital of T's deceased estate and is then charged to inheritance tax. In this Example, as the grandchildren are the residuary beneficiaries of the capital of T's estate (U having an interest only in its income), it is they who bear the inheritance tax so charged – IHTA 1984 s 211 – and hence it is they who experience a degree of double taxation. What has been added to the capital of the estate in respect of income is a net amount after income tax has been paid and the net income so added to the estate is then charged to inheritance tax. So in this sense the grandchildren may be said to suffer a double charge to both inheritance tax and income tax, but no relief is available to them.

Question

A.

Herbie Fritter (who is not a Scottish or Welsh taxpayer) is the life tenant of a trust fund set up by his grandfather.

The trust income in 2023/24 consisted of taxed interest on £190,000 3% Treasury Stock which had been held for many years. None of the Stock had been acquired before 1999 however.

Trust expenses amounted to £320.

Herbie is a widower aged 70, whose only other income in 2023/24 is a retirement pension of £7,570.

(a) Prepare a statement showing the trust income and show the details to be stated on the income certificate given to Herbie.

(b) Compute Herbie's income tax repayment for 2023/24.

B.

Assume the same facts as above except that Herbie is an annuitant (rather than a life tenant of a trust) entitled to an annuity from the trust amounting to £6,030 per annum gross.

The trustees paid the full annuity in 2023/24, being authorised to use capital to make up the deficiency.

(a) Show the position of the trustees and the figures on the R185 (Trust Income) certificate to be given to Herbie.

(b) Compute Herbie's income tax repayment for 2023/24.

Answer

A. Herbie Fritter — Trust Income

(a) *Statement of trust income 2023/24*

	Net £	*Tax* £	*Gross* £
3% Treasury Stock interest (3% × £190,000 × 80%)	4,560	1,140	5,700
Trust expenses paid therefrom	320		
Regarded as net amount with tax deduction of		80	
and a gross equivalent of			400
Net amount, tax thereon and gross equivalent remaining	4,240	1,060	5,300

Certificate by trustees to Herbie (R185 (Trust Income))

Gross	*Tax*	*Net*
£5,300	£1,060	£4,240

Strictly the Form R185 does not include the gross income amounts but they are shown here for ease of identification.

A.

(b) *Herbie's income tax repayment claim 2023/24*

	£	*Tax* £
Retirement pension	7,570	
Savings income from trust	5,300	1,060
	12,870	
Less: Personal allowance	(12,570)	
Taxable income	300	
Tax payable @ 0% starting rate for savings (see **explanatory note** 5)		Nil
Repayment due		1,060

B. Tax payable by trustees under ITA 2007 s 963

(a) *Statement of trust income 2023/24*

	Net £	*Tax* £	*Gross* £
Trust income after expenses as before	4,240	1,060	5,300
Annuity to Herbie	4,824	1,206	6,030

	Net	Tax	Gross
	£	£	£
Further tax to be paid by trustees		2,266	

The annuity is income in Herbie's hands, even though part of it was paid out of capital. Having accounted for tax at 20% on the full amount of the payment, the trustees will give Herbie the appropriate certificate on form R185 (Trust Income) as follows:

Gross	Tax	Net
£6,030	£1,206	£4,824

B.

(b) *Herbie's income tax repayment claim 2023/24*

			Tax
		£	£
Retirement pension		7,570	
Annuity		6,030	1,206
		13,600	
Less: Personal allowance		(12,570)	
Taxable income		1,030	
Tax payable	@ 20% on £1,030 (see **explanatory note 5**)		206
Repayment due			1,000

Explanatory Notes

Trustees' paying expenses out of capital

(1) Had the trustees been empowered to pay the expenses from capital, their gross income of £5,700 would have been intact (ITA 2007 s 500(2), (3)). In **part a** of the Example, Herbie would have received £4,560 net, the gross equivalent of which would have been the full £5,700 received by the trustees.

If Herbie were liable to tax at 40% or 45%, his higher or additional rate liability would be increased if the trust expenses were paid out of the trust capital.

Payment of annuities

(2) Annuities reduce the payer's income for tax purposes (the payer being the trust in **part b** of the Example). It is, however, provided by ITA 2007 s 901 that tax must be deducted from annuities at the basic rate. The tax relief is normally given by allowing the payer to retain the tax deducted, but an equivalent amount of the payer's income must be taxed at the *basic rate*. The net result is that no tax is suffered on that part of the payer's income. If there is insufficient income to cover the annuity, tax must be accounted for at the basic rate on the excess under ITA 2007 s 963, and no tax relief is available on the payment, since it is made out of trust capital.

Assessments under ITA 2007 s 963

(3) Where tax is payable under ITA 2007 s 963 as indicated in **explanatory note 2** above, HMRC issue assessments outside the self-assessment system for the amount due. Interest on such assessments runs from 31 January following the end of the tax year to which the assessment relates, regardless of when the assessment is issued.

Interest on government stocks

(4) From 6 April 1998, interest on all government stocks is paid gross where the stocks are acquired on or after that date, unless the holders apply to receive the interest net (ITA 2007 s 892). Trustees who already held such stocks at that date are treated as having *opted* for net payment, but they may apply for the gross payment rules to apply. If such an application has been made, the interest received would normally be taken into account in calculating the half-yearly payments on account under self-assessment unless it is covered by the de minimis limit of £1,000 so that half-yearly payments would not be required. See **Example F6** for detailed notes on the treatment of trusts under self-assessment.

Tax on savings and dividend income – non-Scottish and non-Welsh taxpayers

(5) In the case of an individual who is not a Scottish or a Welsh taxpayer, tax is chargeable on an individual's taxable income in excess of his personal allowance (and any other deductions such as blind person's allowance or allowable expenses) (ie his Step 3 income), up to the basic rate limit of £37,700 at the basic rate or savings basic rate of 20% (as the case may be), except so far as his Step 3 non-savings non-dividend income is less than the starting rate limit for savings income of £5,000 (ITA 2007 ss 10, 11D, 12, 16). If taxable Step 3 non-savings non-dividend income (eg earnings, pensions, rents etc) is less than £5,000 then the amount of an individual's savings income up to that amount will be taxed at the starting rate for savings of 0%. Any savings income in excess of the £5,000 limit and up to an amount equal to his savings allowance will be taxed at the savings nil rate of 0%. Any additional amount of savings income is then taxed at the savings basic rate of 20%. If taxable Step 3 non-savings non dividend income is more than this limit, then the 0% starting rate for savings will not be applicable and savings income will be taxed at the interest nil rate of 0% (in respect of the amount of an individual's savings income as is equal to his savings allowance) and in full at the basic savings rate of 20% (in respect of savings income exceeding that amount).

Savings income is defined in ITA 2007 s 18. The most common type is interest, but it also includes profits from deeply discounted securities, accrued income profits, taxable life assurance gains of individuals and personal representatives, and certain purchased life annuity payments. The definition does not include other annuities, such as Herbie's in **part b** of the Example, which is taxable as an annual payment under ITTOIA 2005 ss 683–686.

From 6 April 2016, an individual's savings allowance is one of the three amounts:

(a) £1,000 (provided none of his taxable income is charged to tax at the higher rate or dividend upper rate before taking into account the effect of the savings nil rate or the dividend nil rate (ITA 2007 s 12B(4)),

(b) £500 (provided none of his taxable income is charged to tax at the additional rate or dividend additional rate before taking into account the effect of the savings nil rate or the dividend nil rate (s 12B(3),(8)(b)), and

(c) £0 otherwise (s 12B(2),(8)(a)).

What this means is that if an individual has total income, including some savings income, of between £12,570 and £17,570 the 0% starting rate for savings will apply to their savings income.

However, if the personal allowance has been utilised against non-savings income (as explained above), but the remaining non-savings income is less than £5,000, the balance of the £5,000 starting rate band for savings income can be used to tax savings income at the 0% starting rate for savings. The savings nil rate of 0% will then apply to part of the rest of his savings income. Only the balance of savings income remaining (ie an amount in excess of the savings allowance) is then chargeable at the savings basic rate of 20%.

For example, consider Keith aged 60 who is not a Scottish taxpayer and who has taxable employment and pension income of £13,130 and savings interest of £1,000. Keith's tax free personal allowance for 2023/24 is £12,570 so he only has tax to pay on £560 (£13,130 – £12,570) on his non-savings income. This means that he has used up £560 of the £5,000 starting rate band of 0% for savings income, leaving £4,440 available so that his savings income of £1,000 will be taxed at 0%.

However, if Keith's non-savings income amounted to £25,000 (before personal allowance), none of the starting rate band will be available as his taxable non-savings income is more than his personal allowance of £12,570 plus the savings rate starting limit of £5,000. However, as his savings allowance is £1,000 all of his savings income of £1,000 will still be taxed at 0% (being the savings nil rate). Had his savings income been in excess of £1,000 then the balance of that income would have been taxed in full at 20% savings basic rate.

Apart from dividends which are dealt with below, taxable income over £37,700 up to the higher rate limit of £125,140, is taxed at the 40% higher rate and the 40% savings higher rate (as the case may be) (although an amount of savings income up to the savings allowance will be taxed at the savings nil rate of 0%). Beyond the higher rate limit, the applicable rates of income tax are the 45% additional rate or the 45% savings additional rate (as the case may be) (the savings allowance in such a case being nil).

Dividends (including non-interest distributions from authorised unit trusts) form the highest tranche of income of all individuals and so are taxed at the dividend rate that corresponds to the highest appropriate band of income:

(a) Dividends below the basic rate limit of £37,700 are taxed at the dividend ordinary rate of 8.75% (7.5% in 2021/22).

(b) Dividends between the basic rate limit and the higher rate limit are taxed at the dividend higher rate of 33.75% (32.5% in 2021/22).

(c) Dividends in excess of the higher rate limit are taxed at the dividend additional rate of 39.35% (38.1% in 2021/22).

However, those rates are disapplied in relation to an amount of dividends equal to the dividend allowance and an individual's dividend income (as defined in s 19) equal to that amount is taxed in accordance with the rules in s 13A(2). The effect of that subsection is that where the taxable dividend income is less than or equal to £1,000 (£2,000 for 2022/23), the dividend nil rate of 0% will apply to all of the dividend income. Where the taxable dividend income is above £1,000, the lowest part of the dividend income is taxed at the dividend nil rate of 0% and any excess is taxed at the rate that would apply to that amount if the dividend did not exist. For example, if an individual has taxable non-savings income (after personal allowance) of £37,200 and £12,000 of taxable dividend income, the first £500 of dividend income (up to the basic rate limit of £37,700) which would otherwise be taxed at the dividend ordinary rate is taxed at the dividend nil rate, the next £500 of dividend income (up to the so-called dividend allowance) which would otherwise be taxed at the dividend upper rate is taxed at the dividend nil rate of 0% and the balance of the dividend income of £11,000 is taxed at the dividend upper rate of 33.75%.

Tax on savings and dividend income – Scottish taxpayers

(6) In the case of an individual who is a Scottish taxpayer, tax is chargeable on an individual's taxable income in excess of his personal allowance (and any other deductions such as blind person's allowance or allowable expenses) (ie his Step 3 income). In the case of his non-savings non-dividend income (eg earnings, pensions, rents etc), tax is charged as follows in 2023/24:

Name	*Rate*	*Band*
Starter rate	19%	£0–£2,162
Basic rate	20%	£2,163–£13,118
Intermediate rate	21%	£13,119–£31,092
Higher rate	42%	£31,093–£125,140
Top rate	47%	£125,141 and above

The savings and dividend income of a Scottish taxpayer is charged as if he were a non-Scottish taxpayer. In relation to the savings income of a Scottish taxpayer, tax is charged up to the UK basic rate limit of £37,700 at the savings basic rate of 20%, except so far as his Step 3 income other than dividend and savings income is less than the starting rate limit for savings income of £5,000 (ITA 2007 ss 10, 11D, 12, 16). If taxable Step 3 non-savings non-dividend income is less than £5,000 then the amount of an individual's savings income up to that amount will be taxed at the starting rate for savings of 0%. Any savings income in excess of the £5,000 limit and up to an amount equal to his savings allowance will be taxed at the savings nil rate of 0%. Any additional amount of savings income up the basic rate limit of £37,700 is then taxed at the savings basic rate of 20%. If taxable Step 3 non-savings income is more than the starting rate limit for savings income, then the 0% starting rate for savings will not be applicable and savings income will be taxed at the interest nil rate of 0% (in respect of the amount of an individual's savings income as is equal to his savings allowance) and in full at the basic savings rate of 20% (in respect of savings income exceeding that amount).

Savings income is defined in ITA 2007 s 18. The most common type is interest, but it also includes profits from deeply discounted securities, accrued income profits, taxable life assurance gains of individuals and personal representatives, and certain purchased life annuity payments. The definition does not include other annuities, such as Herbie's in part b of the Example, which is taxable as an annual payment under ITTOIA 2005 ss 683–686.

From 6 April 2016, an individual's savings allowance is one of the three amounts:

(a) £1,000 (provided none of his taxable income is charged to tax at the higher rate or dividend upper rate ignoring the fact that he is a Scottish or Welsh taxpayer and before taking into account the effect of the savings nil rate or the dividend nil rate (ITA 2007 s 12B(4)),

(b) £500 (provided none of his taxable income is charged to tax at the additional rate or dividend additional rate again ignoring the fact that he is a Scottish or Welsh taxpayer and before taking into account the effect of the savings nil rate or the dividend nil rate (s 12B(3),(8)(b)), and

(c) £0 otherwise (s 12B(2),(8)(a)).

What this means is that if an individual has total income, including some savings income, of between £12,570 and £17,570 the 0% starting rate for savings will apply to their savings income.

However, if the personal allowance has been utilised against non-savings income (as explained above), but the remaining non-savings income is less than £5,000, the balance of the £5,000 starting rate band for savings income can be used to tax savings income at the 0% starting rate for savings. The savings nil rate of 0% will then apply to part of the rest of his savings income. Only the balance of savings income remaining (ie an amount in excess of the savings allowance) is then chargeable at the savings basic rate of 20%.

For example, consider Malcolm aged 60 who is a Scottish taxpayer and who has taxable employment and pension income of £13,130 and savings interest of £1,000. Keith's tax free personal allowance for 2023/24 is £12,570 so he only has tax to pay on £560 (£13,130 – £12,570) on his non-savings income at the Scottish starter rate of 19%. This means that he has used up £560 of the £5,000 starting rate band of 0% for savings income, leaving £4,440 available so that his savings income of £1,000 will be taxed at 0%.

However, if Malcolm's non-savings income amounted to £25,000 (before personal allowance), none of the starting rate band will be available as his taxable non-savings income is more than his personal allowance of £12,570 plus the savings rate starting limit of £5,000. However, as his savings allowance is £1,000 all of his savings income of £1,000 will still be taxed at 0% (being the savings nil rate). Had his savings income been in excess of £1,000 then the balance of that income would have been taxed in full at 20% savings basic rate.

Taxable savings income over £37,700 up to the higher rate limit of £125,140, is taxed at the 40% savings higher rate (although an amount of savings income up to the savings allowance will be taxed at the savings nil rate of 0%. Beyond the higher rate limit, the rates of income tax applicable to savings income is the 45% savings additional rate (the savings allowance in such a case being nil).

Dividends (including non-interest distributions from authorised unit trusts) form the highest tranche of income and so are taxed at the dividend rate that corresponds to the highest appropriate band of income:

(a) Dividends below the basic rate limit of £37,700 are taxed at the dividend ordinary rate of 8.75% (7.5% in 2021/22).

(b) Dividends between the basic rate limit and the higher rate limit are taxed at the dividend higher rate of 33.75% (32.5% in 2021/22).

(c) Dividends in excess of the higher rate limit are taxed at the dividend additional rate of 39.35% (38.1% in 2021/22).

However, those rates are disapplied in relation to an amount of dividends equal to the dividend allowance and an individual's dividend income (as defined in s 19) equal to that amount is taxed in accordance with the rules in s 13A(2). The effect of that subsection is that where the taxable dividend income is less than or equal to £1,000 (£2,000 for 2022/23), the dividend nil rate of 0% will apply to all of the dividend income. Where the taxable dividend income is above £2,000, the lowest part of the dividend income is taxed at the dividend nil rate of 0% and any excess is taxed at the rate that would apply to that amount if the dividend did not exist. For example, if an individual has taxable non-savings income (after personal allowance) of £37,200 and £12,000 of taxable dividend income, the first £500 of dividend income (up to the basic rate limit of £37,700) which would otherwise be taxed at the dividend ordinary rate is taxed at the dividend nil rate, the next £500 of dividend income (up to the so-called dividend allowance) which would otherwise be taxed at the dividend upper rate is taxed at the dividend nil rate of 0% and the balance of the dividend income of £11,000 is taxed at the dividend upper rate of 33.75%.

Tax on savings and dividend income – Welsh taxpayers

(4) In the case of an individual who is a Welsh taxpayer, tax is chargeable on an individual's taxable income in excess of his personal allowance (and any other deductions such as blind person's allowance or allowable expenses) (ie his Step 3 income). In the case of his non-savings non-dividend income (eg earnings, pensions, rents etc), tax is charged as follows:

Name	*Rate*	*Band*
Welsh basic rate	20%	£0–£37,700
Welsh higher rate	40%	£37,501–£125,140
Welsh additional rate	45%	£125,141 and above

The savings and dividend income of a Welsh taxpayer is charged as if he were a non-Welsh taxpayer and the above discussion in **explanatory note 6** in this respect in relation to a Scottish taxpayer applies in the same way to a Welsh taxpayer as it does to a Scottish taxpayer (with appropriate adaptations).

Loss of personal allowances for higher earners

(5) The basic personal allowance for income tax is gradually reduced to nil for individuals with adjusted net incomes above £100,000, on a basis of a £1 reduction for each additional £2 of income (ITA 2007 s 35). (The effect of this is a marginal tax rate of 60% for income between £100,000 and £125,140 in 2023/24.) For more detail on income tax see the companion to this book **Tolley's Taxwise I 2023/24**.

Question

A and his wife B died in a car crash on 6 April 2022, being survived by their four children C, D, E and F.

The children's dates of birth are:

C	20 January 2001
D	6 October 2005
E	11 November 2006
F	23 May 2007

By their wills, in addition to bequests to more distant relatives and friends and gifts of their residuary estates to charities, A and B created the following separate trusts for their children. Neither of them had made any other trusts in their lifetimes. None of the children is a Scottish taxpayer.

Under A's will

For C, an annuity of £1,500 to be paid out of the income from 20,000 £1 shares in X plc. It is stipulated that if the income of any year is insufficient to meet the annuity in full, capital is to be used to make good the deficiency. Because of falling profits, X plc was only able to pay a 4% dividend during 2023/24.

For D, 10,000 shares in Y plc if he attains 25 years of age. By Trustee Act 1925 s 31, the income may, at the discretion of the trustees, be applied for D's maintenance while he is under 18; once D attains 18 years of age the income has to be paid to him. The dividends received from Y plc shares in 2023/24 totalled £1,778, of which £1,278 was in the period to 6 October 2023 and £500 after that date. Maintenance paid to D between 6 April and 5 October 2023 was £319. £290 was paid to D in February 2024.

Under B's will

For E, an absolutely vested interest in 10,000 8% preference shares of £1 each in Z plc. The capital cannot be paid to E until the child's 18th birthday, but power is given for payments to be made for E's maintenance out of income. Any income not distributed will be accumulated until E becomes 18. £700 was paid to E during 2023/24.

For F, Rannoch House if he attains 18 years of age. The house is let at an annual rent of £8,660 from 6 April 2023 but was empty in the period from B's death on 6 April 2022 until 5 April 2023 for major renovation work so no rents were received in this period. Consequently no election for the special income tax treatment for trust with vulnerable beneficiary was made for 2022/23 but the trustees wish to consider making such an election for 2023/24.

No maintenance was paid to F during 2023/24 as he has a part-time job from which he earns £4,120 a year with no tax deducted. He has no other income.

By 5 April 2023 the estate had been administered and the funds to satisfy the bequests to C, D and E had been set aside.

(a) Calculate the income tax payable by the trustees of each of the above funds for 2023/24 and state the deadline for any vulnerable person's election in relation to the F Trust.

(b) State the amounts which will be treated as taxable income of each beneficiary for 2023/24.

Ignore the Apportionment Act 1870, which was excluded by both A's and B's wills.

Answer

(a) Income tax payable by trustees for 2023/24

C Trust:

		Gross	Tax
		£	£
Dividends (20,000 × 4% = 800)		800	Nil
Less: Step 2 deduction (ITA 2007 ss 23 – 24) Annuity (part)		(800)	Nil
Taxable income		Nil	Nil
Tax on trust income		Nil	Nil
Tax on annuity	800 @ 20%		160
Total tax payable by trustees under self-assessment (see ITA 2007 s 964) (due 31 January 2025)			160
Tax payable by trustees under ITA 2007 s 963 assessment re annual payment made out of capital (see **explanatory note 1**):			
Balance of annuity of (1,500 – 800)	700 @ 20%		140

Form R185 (Trust Income) to the annuitant will show:

	Gross	Tax	Net
	£	£	£
Annuity	1,500	300	1,200

Strictly the Form R185 does not include the gross income figures but they are shown here for ease of identification.

D Trust:

The trustees are liable to tax in respect of dividend income at the dividend trust rate of 39.35% until the beneficiary has an absolute interest in the income (6 October 2023). From that date the trust becomes an interest in possession trust for income tax purposes so that the dividend income received will be subject to the dividend rate of 8.75% (see **explanatory note 3** for the inheritance tax position) until D becomes entitled to the capital at age 25 (6 October 2030). The position is therefore as follows.

Dividend income (6 April 2023 to 5 October 2023)	1,278			
Tax payable at dividend ordinary rate (first slice income)	500* @ 8.75% =			44
* see **explanatory note 2**				
Tax payable at dividend trust rate	778 @ 39.35% =			306
Tax payable by trustees on trust income (to tax pool) (44 + 306) = £350				
	Net	*Tax*	*Gross*	
Distribution made pre-6 October 2022	319	261	580	
Less: tax in tax pool as above		(306)		
Further tax due from the trustees under ITA 2007 s 496		Nil		Nil
Total tax payable by trustees under self-assessment (due 31 January 2025)				350

As the trust income has not been mandated to the beneficiary, the trustees are also liable for the tax due on the dividend received after 5 October 2023 and so their tax bill will increase by £44 (£500 @ 8.75%).

E Trust:

Dividend income received

10,000 × £1 × 8% = £800.

Tax at the dividend trust rate does not apply as E has an absolute right to the income.

The tax liability on the dividend income is at 8.75% and is £70. The (bare) trustees will have to send in a tax return form SA 900. However, they may tick the box at Step 1 on page 2 of the return and choose to make no income entries. The due date for submitting the return is 31 January 2025. Although there is no need for bare trustees to make a tax return, they do have the right to complete the tax return and account for any basic or ordinary dividend rate tax due on income, provided this is acceptable to all beneficiaries.

The property is not settled property for the purposes of inheritance tax.

F Trust:

Because, under the will of a deceased parent of his, F will become absolutely entitled to all of the trust assets on reaching 18 and only he can benefit from the income in the meantime, the F Trust is a qualifying trust for a 'relevant minor' (FA 2005 ss 23(7), 397) and a vulnerable person election can be made in relation to it (FA 2005 s 24). This will entitle the trustees to claim special treatment for income tax (and for capital gains tax were that applicable to the trust) (FA 2005 Part 2 Chapter 4). The income tax liability would then be calculated by reducing the normal trust tax payable (referred to in FA 2005 s 27 as TQTI) by the excess of that figure over the extra amount of tax the vulnerable beneficiary would pay (FA 2005 s 28 Vulnerable Person's Liability (VQTI)) on the assumption that the trust income is the highest part of his or her income and disregarding any relief given by way of a reduction of income tax.

The vulnerable person election must be made jointly by the trustees and F (no doubt acting through his legal guardian) (FA 2005 s 37), and if it is to have effect from 6 April 2023 the deadline for making it is 31 January 2025.

The calculation of the trustees' income tax liability, as set out in FA 2005 ss 26–28 is:

Steps	
TLV2	Compute F's liability to income tax on the basis that any income distributed to him by the trustees is disregarded and that any reliefs given by way of an income tax deduction are also ignored for this purpose.
TLV1	This is the tax due computed on the same assumptions as for TLV2 but assuming further that the trust income relating to the vulnerable beneficiary was in fact charged on F as the highest part of his income.
VQTI	VQTI = TLV1 – TLV2
TQTI	This is the tax due on the trustees without reference to the vulnerable person rules.
The relief	The trustees' income tax liability is reduced by TQTI – VQTI. The trustees' reduced liability is thus VQTI.

F Trust: calculation of vulnerable person relief – 2023/24

TLV2 F's income ignoring the trust income is his wages of £4,120 which is within his personal allowance – no tax is payable on this.

		£
	Earnings	4,120
	Less: Personal allowance (restricted)	(4,120)
	Taxable income	0
		£
TLV1	Earnings	4,120
	Trust income (rental business profit (assumes no expenses))	8,660
		12,780
		£
	Income including trust (TLV1)	12,710
	Less: Personal allowance	(12,570)
	Taxable income	£210

Tax payable thereon

	£		£
	210	@ 20%	42

VQTI TLV1 minus TLV2 equals VQTI (42 – 0 = 42)

So VQTI is £42

TQTI Tax on trustees (assumes no management expenses for purpose of this Example)

	£		£
First slice income	1,000*	@ 20%	200
Trust rate	7,660	@ 45%	3,447
	8,660		3,647

* The amount of first slice income is £1,000 because the other trust made by B, the E Trust, being a bare trust, does not comprise settled property (ITA 2007 s 466(3)(c)). So B has created only one settlement for the purpose of ITA 2007 s 492.

The relief Trustees' income tax liability reduced by TQTI – VQTI

	£
TQTI	3,647
Less: the relief (3,647 – 42)	(3,605)
Revised liability	42

Note that the above circuitous calculation, as prescribed by the legislation, simply results in a tax liability for the trustees matching that which the beneficiary would have had if the trust income had belonged to him.

(b) Amounts treated as taxable income of the beneficiaries for 2023/24

C	Annuity	£1,500	Tax deducted	£300
D	Discretionary trust income to 5 October 2023			
	£319 × 100/55	£580	Tax deducted	£261
	Income of trust from 6 October 2023			
	— Dividends	£500	Tax deducted	£44
		£1,080		
E	Dividend income vested (that is, an absolute entitlement to it whether or not distributed)	£800	Tax deducted	£70
F	Nil			

In all cases the beneficiary's income is less than the amount of the personal allowance. Unless their personal allowances are covered by other income, C will be able to reclaim all of the tax deducted of £305 and D will be able to reclaim the tax of £298 deducted from the trust distribution and his post 5 October 2023 income entitlement.

F neither receives nor is entitled to any income from the F Trust so has no liability on it. The calculations in relation to the vulnerable person's election determine the (reduced) liability of the trustees and do not give rise to a liability for the vulnerable person himself.

Explanatory Notes

Payment of annuities by trustees: income tax treatment

(1) Where an annuity is payable, tax must be deducted at the basic rate, and tax must be accounted for at that rate on an equivalent amount of income. The effect is to cause tax to be charged on the dividend income of the C trust at 20% rather than the dividend rate of 8.75%. ITA 2007 s 963 provides that tax also has to be paid at the basic rate on the part of the annuity paid out of the capital of the trust.

The fact that the trust's dividend income is effectively taxed at 20% will not disadvantage C. He will be entitled to a credit for, and potential repayment of, the full amount of tax deducted at source from the annuity when it is paid.

For a further illustration of the treatment of an annuity see **Example F3 part b.**

Income tax of trustees: contingent interest of beneficiary

(2) At present D only becomes entitled to the trust capital (the shares in Y plc) if he attains the age of 25; but see **Example F4.2(a)** as to the income arising. Until age 18 the trustees have the power to accumulate income and therefore the dividend income of £1,278 received by the trust before D's 18th birthday on 6 October 2023 is chargeable to tax at the dividend ordinary rate (8.75%) on first slice income and at the dividend trust rate (39.35%) as to the balance (ie a total of £350). As and when payments are made to D during that time they are net of tax at 45% and the tax may be reclaimed by D if appropriate, as indicated in the Example. The trustees must, however, account for the 45% tax deducted from the payments but they can treat as tax already paid by them all the tax charged at the dividend rate (39.35%) on their dividend income when calculating how much tax they must pay; as shown in the Example the amount of tax credited to the tax pool is £350. Given the differential in rates however they could not have paid an actual distribution of more than £703 (equating to £1,278 gross), to D before 6 October 2023, ie:

	£	Available income £
Trust income		
Dividend	1,278	1,278
Tax due and payable	350	(350)
If distribution restricted to £1,278 gross		
Tax at 45% on £1,278	575	
Less: already paid	(350)	
Further tax payable	225	(225)
Net income available for distribution		703

For a more detailed illustration of these provisions see **Example F7.**

The first slice income of the trustees is restricted to £500 because there are two separate current trusts under A's will: ITA 2007 s 492.

From his 18th birthday D is entitled to the income arising after that time whether it is actually distributed or not. However, as the dividend income is not mandated to him, the trustees are liable to account for the tax thereon (which is charged at the lower dividend rate of 8.75%). The amount of £290 paid to him after his 18th birthday in the tax year is irrelevant, since he is entitled to the full dividend received in that period (subject only to trust management expenses) and will eventually receive the rest. In particular the payment cannot be a discretionary distribution of pre-18th birthday income because any balance of undistributed income fell to be capitalised on his attaining age 18 under Trustee Act 1925 s 31(2).

Income tax treatment of trustees: absolute interest of beneficiary – bare trust

(3) Although E is under 18, he has a vested interest in the preference shares in Z plc. The property in the trust is not regarded as settled property because it is held for E who would be absolutely entitled to the property were he not a minor (ie the only bar to his calling on the trustees to transfer ownership of the property to him is his minority) (ITA 2007 s 466(2), (3)).

Contrast the interest of E (vested) with that of D (contingent). Although E cannot personally have the shares in Z plc until he is 18, or even the income for his personal unrestricted use, the shares belong to him. If he dies the asset (and any accumulated income) will form part of his estate. The income from the shares forms part of his statutory income. By comparison D's interest in the shares of Y plc is conditional upon his living to age 25. If he dies then the asset will fall into residue of A's estate and pass to charity. D has no right to the income until he is 18 (other than at the discretion of the trustees). Thereafter he has an absolute right to income which is taxed in his name. Only after the contingency has been eliminated (ie on attaining age 25) will the shares vest in D. There is a considerable body of case law on the question of whether an interest under a will is vested or contingent, and it involves a detailed knowledge of the general law of trusts, which is outside the scope of this book.

Income tax: trust with vulnerable beneficiary

(4) The trust tax rates were originally raised in FA 2004 from 34% to 40%, with effect for the tax year 2004/05, as a tax avoidance deterrent. To prevent tax changes having an adverse effect on trusts with vulnerable beneficiaries, particularly trusts for disabled people and for children with a deceased parent, FA 2005 Chapter 4 (ss 23–45) brought in provisions to protect such individuals. These provisions are all the more helpful now that the rate which was increased to 50% for 2011/12 and 2012/13 was subsequently reduced to 45% for 2013/14 and later years of assessment (at which it still stands).

Income tax: trust with vulnerable beneficiary – vulnerable person election

(5) Trustees holding settled property on qualifying trusts for the benefit of a vulnerable person may make an election, jointly with the vulnerable beneficiary which will allow the trustees then to make a claim year by year for the special tax treatment provided by FA 2005 Chapter 4 to apply for that year. Such an election is irrevocable, and will apply from its effective date until any of the following occurs:

(a) the beneficiary ceases to be a vulnerable person,

(b) the trusts cease to be qualifying trusts, or

(c) the trusts are terminated.

The election must state the date from which it is to be valid and must be made no later than 12 months after 31 January following the tax year in which that date falls.

If one of those events occurs, the trustees have 90 days from the time they become aware of its occurrence to notify HMRC (s 37).

Although the election itself is irrevocable, a claim to the special tax treatment can be made, or not made, by the trustees on a year by year basis while the election remains in force (s 24). The claim, if made, covers both income tax and capital gains tax – it cannot be made for one without the other.

Income tax: trust with vulnerable beneficiary – vulnerable persons

(6) There are two categories of vulnerable person (s 23(7)):

(a) A disabled person, defined as a person with a mental disability who is incapable of administering his property or managing his affairs, or, a person in receipt of any of a number of specified welfare benefits. These are: attendance allowance; the care component of disability living allowance at the middle or highest rates (and from 6 April 2014 (by virtue of FA 2014 s 284(2)(a)), the mobility component at the higher rate of disability living allowance); the daily living component of personal independence payment (and from 6 April 2014 (by virtue of FA 2014 s 284(2)(b)), the mobility component of personal independence payment); increased disablement pension; constant attendance allowance; and armed forces independence payment. Also included are those who would be so entitled to receive attendance allowance, disability living allowance and personal independent payment allowance were it not for their being resident outside the UK or in a care home, hospital or prison (FA 2005 s 38, Sch1A as inserted by FA 2013 Sch 44 para 19).

(b) A relevant minor, being a child aged under 18 at least one of whose parents has died (s 39).

Income tax: trust with vulnerable beneficiary – qualifying trust — disabled persons

(7) To be a qualifying trust for a vulnerable disabled person, the terms of the trust must secure that, during his lifetime or until the trust terminates,

(a) no capital distribution (unless it does not exceed a prescribed annual amount) can be made other than for the benefit of the disabled person, and

(b) that person must be entitled to all of the income arising from the trust fund, or no income of the trust (unless it does not exceed a prescribed annual amount) may be applied for the benefit of any other person (s 34).

The prescribed annual amount is introduced by FA 2013 and takes effect for 2013/14 and later tax years. It is defined in FA 2005 s 34(3B). The rule allows a small sum (whether consisting of income or capital, or both) not exceeding the 'annual limit' (currently the lower of £3,000 or 3% of the value of the trust fund during the tax year in question), to be applied otherwise than for the benefit of the disabled person. If the trust is settlor interested the trust will not qualify for income treat as a trust with a vulnerable beneficiary.

Income tax: trust with vulnerable beneficiary – qualifying trust — relevant minors

(8) A trust is a qualifying trust for a relevant minor if it is:

(a) a statutory trust for a minor under the intestacy rules of England and Wales (Administration of Estates Act 1925 ss 46, 47(1)), or

(b) a trust which:

(i) secures that the relevant minor will become absolutely entitled to both capital and income (including accumulations) not later than age 18, and that no income or capital in excess of a prescribed annual limit (as defined above) can be distributed or applied before that time other than for the benefit of the relevant minor, and

(ii) was established either under the will of a deceased parent of the relevant minor, or under the Criminal Injuries Compensation Scheme or the Victims of Overseas Terrorism Compensation Scheme (s 35).

It must therefore be noted that any trusts established by parents, by will or intestacy, for their minor children, where the children do not become entitled to the settled property until an age over 18 (eg age 18–25 trusts or accumulation and maintenance trusts in the extended form they often took before FA 2006) will not qualify. Hence the D Trust in the Example does not qualify but the F Trust does.

A trust for a disabled person or a relevant minor will not fail the vulnerable beneficiary conditions by reason of the trustees having the powers of advancement conferred by Trustee Act 1925 s 32 or having powers to like effect as those so conferred.

Income tax: trust with vulnerable beneficiary – qualifying trust – part qualification

(9) References to qualifying trusts include trusts where only part of an asset is held on qualifying trusts provided that part, and any income arising from it, can be identified (s 36).

In such cases, or generally where the trustees' total income includes income which is not qualifying trust income, only the relevant proportion of management expenses will be allowed against the qualifying trust income when calculating TQTI. The management expenses are to be apportioned for this purpose by reference to the amount of qualifying trust income as a proportion of the total income of the trustees (s 27(2)).

Income tax: trust with vulnerable beneficiary – part years

(10) Where the trust only qualifies for part of a tax year then income and expenses are related to the qualifying and non-qualifying periods based upon when income arises (s 29).

Income tax: trust with vulnerable beneficiary – special tax treatment

(11) FA 2005 ss 25–29 as amended sets out the special tax treatment rules so far as income tax is concerned. The mechanics of working out the reduction in the trustees' tax liability, with a UK resident beneficiary, are set out in detail for the F Trust in **part** (a) of the Example, but basically the trustees will be able to take account of the vulnerable beneficiary's personal allowance and income tax bands to reduce the amount of income tax payable.

For income tax purposes, the trustees therefore include in their return the tax that would normally be due by them, and then calculate what the tax would be if the income had arisen directly to F, taking into account his other income, gains and allowances. The difference is claimed as a deduction.

Capital gains tax: trust with vulnerable beneficiary – special tax treatment

(12) The special tax treatment for capital gains tax is restricted to cases where the trustees are resident (and before 6 April 2013 ordinarily resident) in the UK the relevant tax year, or are resident in the UK during any part of the tax year (s 30(1)(c)). It also does not apply in the tax year of the death of the vulnerable beneficiary (s 30).

Subject to that, relief in respect of capital gains accruing to the trustees is, since FA 2008, computed in a very similar way to the income tax relief illustrated in **part** (a) of the Example for the F Trust, the effect of which is to reduce the trustees' liability to that which would have been the vulnerable person's liability if the trustees' gains had accrued to him direct. In more detail, the steps for a UK resident vulnerable beneficiary are:

TLVB The vulnerable person's capital gains tax liability for the year apart from this relief.

TLVA	What TLVB would be if the qualifying trusts gains accrued direct to the vulnerable person instead of to the trustees, without any deduction for allowable losses. (It appears that this applies to allowable losses whether of the trustees or of the vulnerable person; this may influence whether the trustees wish to make a claim for a year in which significant losses have been realised, bearing in mind that the claim cannot be made for income tax without also operating for capital gains tax.)
VQTG	TLVA minus TLVB.
TQTG	The trustees' liability on the qualifying trusts gains apart from this relief.
The relief	The trustees' capital gains tax liability is reduced by TQTG – VQTG, so that the effective reduced liability equals VQTG.

The trustees' notional liability (TQTG) is calculated at 20% (28% on gains in respect of residential property), but the vulnerable person's notional liability (TLVA) is calculated at the rate of 10% (18% on gains in respect of residential property) to the extent that taxable gains fall below the basic rate limit (£37,700 in 2023/24). As for general capital gains tax purposes, allowable losses (where taken into account, see TLVA above) and annual exempt amounts can be allocated in the most beneficial way (TCGA 1992 ss 1E(1), 1K(5)).

Income tax and capital gains tax: trust with vulnerable beneficiary – non-UK resident vulnerable persons

(13) Where the beneficiary is not resident in the UK during the tax year, and not resident in the UK during any part of it, the calculations for TVL1, TVL2, TLVA and TLVB are to be carried out on the assumption that he is resident and domiciled in the UK throughout the relevant tax year. Certain additional assumptions are made in calculating TLVA and TLVB for the capital gains tax relief, essentially to secure that overseas losses of the vulnerable person which would be disallowed on grounds of his actual non-UK residence are nevertheless allowed in calculating his liability excluding the qualifying trust gains (FA 2005 ss 28(4), 32, 41(2) and Sch 1).

Self-assessment

(14) See **Example F6** for further details on the way in which income is shown in the self-assessment tax return of the individual.

Inheritance tax: testamentary trusts for children

(15) See **Examples C15, C16** and **C17** for details of the inheritance tax treatment of testamentary trusts for children.

The charge to capital gains tax on non-resident persons

(16) The charge to capital gains tax has been extended by FA 2015 to non-resident persons (including personal representatives) in relation to the disposal of residential property and the private residence exemption has been modified in respect of non-resident persons. FA 2019 extended this charge to all UK property and shares in property-rich companies (which are companies deriving at least 75% of their value from UK land). Hence non-resident persons are liable to capital gains tax on the direct and indirect disposal of UK residential and non-residential property (TCGA 1992, s 1C and Sch 1A, 1B, 4AA). For details of this aspect of the charge to capital gains tax see the companion to this book, **Tolley's Taxwise I 2023/24**.

Question

Garth, a bachelor aged 45 who is not a Scottish or Welsh taxpayer, was injured in a road accident some years ago and the Court awarded the sum of £500,000 compensation to be paid to him.

Garth created a settlement of part of this sum under which he was himself to receive the income for life, the capital upon his death being divisible amongst certain relatives.

The trust income for the year ended 5 April 2024 comprised:

	£
Building society interest	1,600
Interest from government stocks	660
National Savings Bank interest (Direct Saver account)	76
Rents receivable	6,739
Dividends from UK companies (amounts received)	2,000

An amount of £329 was spent on repairs to and the maintenance of the rented property during the year and the premium for insuring it was £205. There was a loss brought forward of £205 on the rented property. Trust expenses allocable to income amounted to £450.

In 2023/24 Garth's only personal income, other than non-taxable social security allowances, consisted of interest on National Savings Bank income bonds of £6,720.

(a) Prepare a statement showing the trust income for 2023/24.

(b) Compute Garth's personal tax position for 2023/24.

Answer

Garth — Trust Income

(a) *Garth's Trustees — Statement of Trust Income 2023/24*

			Gross	*Tax*
		£	£	£
Rent receivable		6,739		
Less: Expenses		(534)		
Loss brought forward		(205)	6,000	
Building society interest		1,600		
Government stocks interest		660		
NSB interest		76	2,336	
Dividends			2,000	
Total income of trust			10,336	
Tax thereon:				
Non-dividend income	8,336 @ 20%	1,667		
Dividend income	2,000 @ 8.75%	175	1,842	1,842
	10,336			
of which tax payable by self-assessment is				1,842
Net income of trust treated as Garth's income			8,494	

(b) *Garth — Income tax liability 2023/24*

					Tax
				£	£
NSB interest				6,720	Nil
Trust dividend income				2,000	175
Trust interest income				2,336	467
Trust rental income				6,000	1,200
				17,056	1,842
Less: Personal allowance (see **explanatory note 13**)				(12,570)	
				4,486	
Tax thereon:					
Dividend income	1,000	@ 0%	0		
	1,000	@ 8.75%	88		
Other income (at starting rate for savings)	2,486	@ 0%	0		
			0		
Tax repayment:					
Total tax deducted at source					1,842
Less: tax liability					(88)
Repayment due					1,754

Explanatory Notes

Settlor-interested trusts

(1) A settlement may be made by a settlor on himself for a number of reasons. In this Example Garth may well have made the settlement so that trustees can administer his assets on his behalf whilst he is suffering from a mental or physical disability. Other reasons for such settlements would include:

(a) A couple with no children, but each having relatives, want to ensure that each set of relatives obtains the appropriate share of their respective estates (rather than the whole devolving upon the relatives of the spouse/civil partner who died last as could occur on intestacy).

(b) To provide certainty for the next generation(s) by creating a settlement under which each of the respective spouse/civil partner would receive the income during their lifetime, their children having the knowledge that the destination of the capital could not be altered by such events as the remarriage of a widow/widower.

(c) A couple with children from different relationships who wish to ensure that their own offspring obtain the appropriate share of their respective estates (removing the possibility that the destination of the capital could be altered after their own deaths, whilst providing income for their co-habitant in the meantime).

Income tax treatment: settlement in which settlor retains an interest and parental settlements

(2) As explained in **Example F1**, income is taxed as the settlor's income in two circumstances – first where he retains an interest in a settlement ITTOIA 2005 ss 623–628 (a settlor-interested trust) and secondly where, having settled property for the benefit of his unmarried, minor children, trust income is paid to or for their benefit ss 629–632 (a parental settlement unless the parental settlement is a bare trust created on or after 9 March 1999 or an interest in possession settlement in which cases the income of the settlement is treated as that of the settlor when it arises). A settlor retains an interest in a trust where the income in the trust arises during his lifetime from property (including the income itself and other related property) which, in any circumstances, is or may become payable to or applicable for the benefit of the settlor or his spouse or civil partner (ss 624, 625).

In this Example, the trust is a settlor-interested trust and Garth is therefore assessable on the trust income; he is so assessable as the income arises and it does not matter whether it is paid to him or not (s 619(2)). Since Garth is treated for tax purposes as if the income had arisen directly to him, no relief is available for the trust expenses of £450 (s 624(1A)). This contrasts with the position of the life tenant in **Example F3** (where the trust is not a settlor-interested trust); in that example the life tenant gets relief for the trust expenses as the income that arises to him is the net income of the trust. In this Example, the trustees of the settlor-interested trust are also taxed on the income because it arises to them (s 646(8)), the tax they pay can be used by Garth against his own tax liability (see **Example F3**). For further notes on settlements in which the settlor retains an interest, see **Example C2**.

(3) Similarly, where a settlor retains an interest in a discretionary or accumulation settlement, there is a potential double charge to tax on the same income: once in the hands of the trustees and again in the hands of the settlor. There are provisions, however, which prevent this from happening. The tax paid by the trustees is simply credited to the settlor; that tax is not also credited to the trustees' tax pool because the income being treated as the income of the settlor does not result from a discretionary payment being made to him (ITA 2007 s 493(1), (2)). Should the settlor subsequently receive a discretionary payment from the trustees, then it is not a taxable receipt from his perspective and it is not deemed to carry a 45% tax credit (ITTOIA 2005 s 685A(5)). Where a settlor-interested trust is not resident in the UK and is in receipt of dividend income, then the trustees are treated as having paid at the dividend ordinary rate on that income (ITTOIA 2005 s 399). This deemed tax credit may not however be passed on the settlor.

See **explanatory note 11** for the practical consequences of the rules explained in this note.

There is also the potential under first principles, for the income to be taxed a third time when distributed to the beneficiaries of a settlor-interest trust or parental settlement (see **explanatory note 5** below).

(4) So where the settlor retains an interest in a discretionary or accumulation trust, the income of the trust is treated as the settlor's and taxed accordingly. The settlor is taxed on all of the income arising and not just on the income distributed to him. The settlor is entitled to recover from the trustees the amount of any extra tax he needs to pay as a result of the application of this rule (although the importance of this has waned as the rates of income tax for trustees have increased). For this purpose, the settlor may ask HMRC to provide him with a certificate specifying the amount of the income on which the settlor has so paid tax and the amount of tax paid (s 646(2)).

Where the settlor is entitled to a repayment of income tax, because, for example, he is liable to income tax at a rate that is lower than that of the trustees as is often the case (or has a lower net tax liability by reason of the trust tax credit), he is obliged to pay over the amount refunded/offset to the trustees (s 646 (5)). The settlor is able to obtain a certificate from HMRC specifying that he has obtained a tax refund and the amount of the refund which is then conclusive evidence of the matter (s 646(6A), (6B)).

(5) In some cases, the settlor may not be a beneficiary of the settlor-interested trust – it could, for example be his spouse or civil partner. If such a beneficiary has an interest in possession, then he is not taxed on the income of the trust at all (because the income is treated as that of the settlor alone and he is taxed on it (s 624(1)). The effect of this section is that the income is not counted as the life tenant's for income tax purposes.

If the settlor-interested trust is a discretionary or accumulation trust, and a discretionary payment is made to a beneficiary who is not the settlor, the amount received forms part of the beneficiary's taxable income. The beneficiary is charged to tax on receipt of the payment (s 685) which is treated as a gross amount that carries a non-refundable tax credit of 45% (s 685A). The section applies only to the proportion of the discretionary 'annual payment' corresponding to the proportion of the trustees' income (of current and previous years of assessment) that has been charged to income tax under s 619 in the hands of the settlor as a result of the settlement being a settlor-interested trust (s 685A(1), (2)). The sum received by the beneficiary is not grossed up and the beneficiary does not receive a form R185 (Trust Income) (s 685A(6)).

The tax which the beneficiary is treated as having paid is not repayable, and cannot be used to reduce or offset his tax liability on other income. To prevent unintended changes in the beneficiary's liability on his other income (since the sum received, not being savings or dividend income, will otherwise be charged before savings and/or dividend income), such a payment from the trust is treated as the highest part of his income (s 685A(4), (5A)).

As already explained in **explanatory note 3**, where the beneficiary who receives such a discretionary payment is the settlor then the annual payment is not a taxable receipt in his hands, nor does it carry the trust rate credit that applies for other beneficiaries of a settlor-interested discretionary trust (s 685A(5)).

See **explanatory note 11** for the practical consequences of the rules explained in this note.

(6) It is not only because a trust is settlor-interested that its income may be treated as that of the settlor. Except in the case of bare trusts created on or after 9 March 1999 and interest in possession settlements, the income of parental settlements (other than those mentioned next) is also treated as the income of the settlor if and when it is paid to or for the benefit of an unmarried minor child of the settlor, unless it is less than £100 in amount in the tax year in question. If the parental settlement is a bare trust created on or after 9 March 1999 or an interest in possession settlement, the income of the settlement is treated as that of the settlor when it arises whether the income is paid to the child or not. This rule applies also to income arising from property added after 8 March 1999 to bare trusts created before 9 March 1999 (see **explanatory note 3 in Example F1**). Where the child has an interest in possession in the trust property, then he is not taxed on the income at all (because the income is treated as that of the settlor alone and he is taxed on it – s 629(1)). Any tax paid by the trustees on the income may be used by the settlor against his own tax liability.

If the parental settlement is a discretionary or accumulation trust or a bare trust created before 9 March 1999 (except in relation to income arising from property added to such a trust after 8 March 1999), the settlor is not taxed on the income as it arises but only when it is paid to or for the benefit of an unmarried minor child. The trust income is taxed at the trust rates and the tax paid by the trustees on the trust income as it arises is credited to their tax pool in the usual way (ITA 2007 s 493(1), (3)). If a distribution takes place, either from income of the current year or from accumulated, undistributed income of earlier years (in the latter case what is trust capital is deemed to be a payment of income but only to the extent that there is underlying (undistributed) income against which to match the distribution (ITTOIA 2005 s 631)), it is grossed up under ITA 2007 s 494(1)–(2) and tax within the pool can be used against the charge that arises on the trustees under s 496.

When income is paid to the child, he is deemed to receive a non-repayable additional rate tax credit under ITTOIA 2005 s 685A as explained in **explanatory note 5** above. However, the settlor gets the benefit of the tax credit attaching to the payment he is treated as receiving (ITA 2007 s 494(3), (4)) and he may set it against his income.

In other words, when any distribution is made, its source will be the trust. It will be an annual payment and it will not, for example, be dividend income. The distribution will be made net of 45% tax. Apart from any tax paid at the dividend ordinary rate on trust dividend income used to defray trust management expenses, the trustees will be able to include the amount paid by them in accounting for that tax – see **Example F7**). This will therefore result in a higher tax charge where a dividend is paid to an infant child via a discretionary trust as compared with a direct settlement by the parent on the child.

Consider, for 2023/24, a dividend of £200 received by a discretionary parental settlement which is paid to the child (and assume that there are no trusts expenses). The net distribution to the child would be 55% of £200 = £110 (tax £90). If the settlor (as an additional rate taxpayer who had already used his so called dividend allowance) had made a gift of shares to bare trustees for the child and the company later declared a dividend of £200 (because bare trusts are within the parental settlement rules) the dividend is taxable on the parent and not on the child and the tax liability on the gross dividend would be only £79, ie:

Gross income	200.00
Tax @ 39.35%	(79.00)
Net receipt	£121.00

(7) Special provisions apply for capital gains tax where a settlor retains an interest in a non-resident settlement — see **Example D4** for details. Capital gains of a settlor-interested trust are however not taxed on the settlor if the trustees are UK resident.

Income tax: gifts to charity by trustees of settlor-interested and parental settlements

(8) Where a UK resident settlor-interested trust or parental settlement gives money to a charity, the amount taxable on the settlor is reduced by the amount (plus tax) given to the charity (ITTOIA 2005 ss 628, 630).

This means that the income given to the charity will be net of tax at the relevant rate applicable to the trustees, ie 45% for discretionary or accumulation trusts and the basic or dividend ordinary rates for interest in possession trusts. Where the trust's income exceeds the amount given to the charity, the amount given to the charity is treated as made rateably out of the trust's different sources of income (unless the trust stipulates that the charity should receive certain sources of income). Trust management expenses are similarly allocated between income that goes to the charity and the remainder of the trust income.

The rate of tax recoverable by the charity depends on the tax payable by the trust. Say, in 2023/24, a trust gives a charity £500 out of the trustees' bank interest. If the trust is a discretionary trust with income (after management expenses) of £10,000, the distribution would be net of 45% tax, so that the tax thereon would be (500 × 45/55 =) £409. The charity would receive £500 from the trustees plus a tax refund of £409, making £909 in all. If the trust is an interest in possession trust, the tax on the distribution of £500 would be (500 × 20/80 =) £125. The charity would receive £500 from the trustees plus a tax refund of £125, making a total of £625.

(9) For the purpose of the anti-avoidance provisions relating to settlor-interested trusts and parental settlements, an interest free or low interest rate loan is an 'arrangement' that, if made with any element of bounty, is within the definition of settlement, so that income from the investment of such a loan is capable of being treated as the settlor's income. The protection of ITTOIA 2005 ss 628, 630 (see **explanatory note 8** above) applies where the loan is made to a charity.

Self-assessment: trustees of settlor-interested and parental settlements

(10) See **Example F6 explanatory note** 7 for the entries on self-assessment returns in relation to trusts in which the settlor retains an interest. HMRC Helpsheet 270 contains detailed information on how to decide whether an interest has been retained; it also deals with parental settlements on minor children (as to which see **Example C15**). Where gifts or loans are made to charity as outlined in explanatory **notes 8** and **9** above, the income does not have to be included in the settlor's self-assessment return.

Income tax: practical consequences of settlor-interested settlements

(11) If the trust is a discretionary or accumulation trust, the trustees must pay tax on their income (in excess of the first slice of income of up to £1,000) at the trust rate of 45%, or at the dividend trust rate of 39.35%. The settlor receives a corresponding tax credit, and since the additional rate of 45% is only applicable to individuals whose income exceeds £150,000 it will often now be the case that the settlor is entitled to a refund of part of the tax suffered by the trustees. If the trust confers an interest in possession then the trustees remain liable only at the basic rate, so the chance of the settlor having additional tax to pay as a result of the income being deemed to be his is greater.

The settlor's right to repayment from the trustees of additional tax for which he found himself liable under these provisions is, from 2010/11, matched by an obligation on him to pass on to the trustees any tax refund that he obtains through being liable at a lower rate than those applicable to the trustees (ITTOIA 2005 s 646(4), (5)). The settlor is able to obtain a certificate from HMRC specifying that he has obtained a tax refund and the amount of the refund which is then conclusive evidence of the matter (s 646(6A), (6B)).

Trustees

Trustees must include all of the trust income on the trust and estate return (SA900). As well as ticking box 8.12 and the box at Q13A to report that the trust is settlor-interested, they also need in the case of a discretionary or accumulation trust to tick box 8.16.

Where discretionary income payments are made to the settlor, they do not form part of his income (ITTOIA 2005 s 685A(5)) and do not need to be disclosed on the SA900. Where they are made to some beneficiary other than the settlor, s 685A takes them outside the usual tax pool arrangements (see **explanatory note** 5 above), and the tax credit they carry is not repayable. So trustees do not need to gross up the payments or account for additional tax to cover the credit. Such payments should therefore not be shown under Q14 in the SA900 – they should be reported instead in the 'Additional information' box 21.9.

Where the settlement is partly settlor-interested and partly not, it is necessary to allocate discretionary payments between the settlor-interested part and the non-settlor-interested part. Rather than try to match them to the underlying income from which they were paid, ITTOIA 2005 s 685A(2) provides for a statutory apportionment. The amount of the discretionary payments from the settlor-interested part is the same proportion of the total discretionary payments as the proportion of total income that is chargeable on the settlor.

So, for example, if the settlor's interest extends only to 30% of the trust fund and the trustees' total income is £5,000, £1,500 is chargeable on the settlor; if the trustees make discretionary payments to other beneficiaries of £2,000, then the entry in box 21.9 of form SA900 (additional information) is:

2,000 × (1,500/5000) = 600

The difference (2,000 – 600 = 1,400) goes in Q14 as normal.

Settlor

The SA107 (supplementary pages for trusts etc) has a separate section for settlor income (boxes 7 to 15). Only the net amount of taxed payments is to be included; there are separate boxes for savings, dividend and other income, in each case where taxed in the trustees' hands at the basic or trust rates or their dividend equivalents, as well as for income where no tax has been suffered/deducted.

Beneficiaries other than the settlor

As seen in **explanatory note 5**, in the hands of a beneficiary other than the settlor the tax credit of 45% attaching to discretionary payments from a settlor-interested settlement is not repayable and is dealt with outside the trustees' tax pool. Instead, tax treated as having been deducted is notional tax, which is ring-fenced – it cannot be set sideways against any other income of the beneficiary, and cannot be repaid. Whereas discretionary receipts dealt with through the tax pool system are to be shown on a net basis in box 1 on the SA107, those from a settlor-interested trust are shown on a gross basis in box 2. The beneficiaries return the actual amount they receive – there is no grossing up. So whatever a beneficiary's marginal rate, the notional tax covers his liability on that income – if he is anything other than an additional rate taxpayer, part of the notional tax will appear to be lost. To avoid pushing other income into a higher tax bracket s 685A (5A) makes it clear that the payment is to be treated as the highest part of the beneficiary's income (except for the purposes of calculating top slicing relief in respect of non-qualifying life insurance gains under ss 535–537). Including such payments in the beneficiary's income (which, by HMRC practice, it was not before 2006) is capable of leading to the restriction or loss of his personal allowance if it takes his total income over £100,000.

Interest on government stocks for income tax

(12) For 2015/16 and earlier years of assessment trustees could make an election to receive interest on the government stocks gross (see **Example F3 explanatory note 4** for details). With effect from 6 April 2016 interest is payable gross in any event; tax will not be payable on the 2023/24 interest until 31 January 2025, but the tax would be included in payments on account for later years, unless covered by the de minimis limit of £1,000 (see **Example F3 explanatory note 5**).

Garth's income tax computation: non-Scottish taxpayer

(13) Garth's personal allowance is deducted in the order and from the types of his income that will result in the greatest reduction in his liability to income tax (ITA 2007 s 25(2)). In order, therefore, to decide how best to use Garth's personal allowance in 2023/24, it is necessary to know how his income for that year will be charged to income tax.

Garth's non-dividend income (which is clearly less than the basic rate limit of £37,700) is charged to income tax at the basic rate (of 20%) except to the extent that it is charged at the starting rate for savings (of 0%) (s 10(2)) subject where applicable, to the savings nil rate (of 0%) which is charged in respect of so much of his savings income up to £1,000 (the amount of his savings allowance being as he is only a basic rate taxpayer) (ss 10(4), 12A). Income tax is charged at the starting rate for savings on so much of Garth's income up to the starting rate limit for savings (£5,000 in 2023/24) as is savings income (eg interest) (ss 12(1), 18). In order to ascertain the extent to which Garth's income up to the starting rate limit for savings consists of savings income (and where applicable, the extent to which Garth's income above the starting rate limit for savings consists of savings income), the rules set down in s 16 are applied:

(i) if Garth has savings income but no dividend income, the savings income is treated as the highest part of his total income (s 16(3));

(ii) if Garth has both savings income and dividend income the savings income and the dividend income together are treated as the highest part of his total income and the dividend income is treated as the higher part of that part of his total income (s 16(5)).

Garth has savings income (ie interest), non-savings income (ie rental income) and dividend income. As the savings and dividend income is treated as the highest part of his income (with dividend income as the higher of the two), the starting rate for savings would apply only to the extent that his non-savings income is less than £5,000. Were his non-savings income to exceed £5,000, the total of his non-savings income and savings income (to the extent that his savings income exceeds his savings allowance of £1,000, Garth having no income taxable at the higher rate or dividend upper rate (s 12B(4)) would be taxed at the basic rate of 20%. His dividend income is prima facie taxed at the dividend ordinary rate of 8.75% (the non-savings and savings income being, in total, less than the basic rate limit of £37,700). However, that rate is disapplied and £1,000 of the dividend income is taxed at the dividend nil rate of 0%with the balance being taxed at 8.7% (s 13A).

Consequently, the question is whether Garth's non-savings income (ie his rental income) is less than £5,000 because, if it is, his savings income will be taxed (in part) at 0%. There is no doubt that this is the case here because Garth's personal allowance will first be used to shelter his non-savings (ie his rental) income as this results in the greatest reduction in his income tax liability (s 25(2)). In fact all of his rental income may be so sheltered as it amounts to £6,000 which is less than his personal allowance of £12,570. The balance of his personal allowance (£6,570) is set against his savings income (ie his interest income) as it would be taxed at 20% to the extent that it exceeds the starting rate limit for savings. By allocating Garth's personal allowance in this way his taxable income comprises savings income of £2,486 (ie £9,056 – £6,570) and dividend income of £2,000. Consequently, all of his savings income is taxed at 0%. In relation to his dividend income, £1,000 is taxed at 0% and the other £1,000 is taxed at 8.75%.

For a further example concerning the application of these rules see **Example F3** (with particular reference to **explanatory note 5**).

Question

The Colenso Trust was created by Charles in 1996. Under the terms of the trust deed the trustees have discretionary power to pay income to any of the named beneficiaries and to accumulate any income that is not so applied.

Charles has created seven other settlements (Trusts T to Z) at different times before and after the Colenso Trust; except as stated below, all of them were made since 6 June 1978, and continued in existence throughout 2023/24:

- Trust T, under which Charles has a vested remainder interest, has had UK resident trustees at all material times;
- Trust U was wound up in 2008 after the FA 2006 changes to inheritance tax;
- Trust V was made offshore in 1974 but the trustees have been UK resident continuously since 1997 and the trust fund is now held and administered for exclusively charitable purposes;
- Trust W (with UK trustees) came to an end when the life tenant died on 30 September 2023;
- Trust X (with non-UK trustees) holds nothing but a continuing life assurance policy on Charles's life, and thus produces no income or chargeable gains;
- Trust Y (with UK trustees) was formed on 10 March 2024 when Charles took out a new life assurance policy on his life written in trust on a contingent basis; and
- Trust Z has UK trustees and the primary beneficiary is a disabled person, with a vulnerable person election in force (see **Example 67 explanatory note 4**).

The income and expenses of the trustees of the Colenso Trust for the year ended 5 April 2024 were as follows:

Income

	£
Dividends from UK companies	2,800
Rent of property let unfurnished	2,850
Interest on National Savings Direct Saver account	465

Expenses

Property expenses	— ground rent	34
	— repairs	646
Accountancy fees		604

The income tax liability of the trust for 2022/23 amounted to £1,696, of which tax credits covered £546. In addition the trustees had made payments on account of £486 on each of 31 January 2023 and 31 July 2023.

The trustees had a tax pool brought forward at 6 April 2023 of £326, and no brought forward allowable losses. During the year the trustees made sales of quoted shares showing the following results after deducting base values and expenses of sale:

- 4 May 2023 – gain £700
- 18 May 2023 – loss £1,500
- 25 August 2023 – gain £2,000

- 19 November 2023 – gain £2,358
- 10 January 2024 – loss £200.

One of the beneficiaries of the trust is Clery, a widower who was born in 1933. He is not a Scottish or Welsh taxpayer.

The trustees paid £4,200 to Clery in 2023/24 which was treated as his income.

His other income for that year was a state pension of £6,820 and income from purchased life annuities totalling £20,000 gross, of which the capital content was £15,000.

(a) Prepare a statement of income and gains for the Colenso Trust for 2023/24.

(b) Compute the tax pool to carry forward to 2024/25 or s 496 tax payable.

(c) Show the tax payable by the trustees under self-assessment.

(d) Calculate Clery's repayment of income tax for 2023/24.

Answer

The Colenso Trust

(a) *Statement of trust income and gains 2023/24*

Income tax liability for 2023/24:

				Gross	*Tax*
			£	£	£
Rent receivable			2,850		
Less: expenses			(680)	2,170	
Savings income					
NSB interest				465	
Dividends				2,800	Nil
Total income of trust				5,435	Nil
Tax thereon:					
On amount equal to grossed up trust expenses (paid out of dividend income and not chargeable at dividend trust rate) (604 × 100/91.25) =	662	@ 8.75%	58		
On balance of dividends at dividend trust rate (2,800 – 662)	2,138	@ 39.35%	841		
On first slice income (see **explanatory note 1**)	200	@ 20%	40		
On remaining income at trust rate	2,435	@ 45%	1,096		
	5,435		2,035		2,035
Of which tax payable by self-assessment is					2,003
Used to pay trust expenses			604	(2,639)	
Net income of trust				2,796	

Capital gains tax liability for 2023/24:

		Tax	
	£	£	
Chargeable gains	5,058		
Less: Allowable losses	(1,700)		
	3,385		
Less: Annual exemption	(750)		(see **explanatory note 15**)
	2,635		
Liable @ 20%		527	

(b) *Tax pool and position under ITA 2007 ss 496–498*

		£
Unutilised tax brought forward at 6 April 2023		326
Tax already accounted for by trustees at:		
Basic rate on first slice income	40	
Trust rate	1,096	
Dividend trust rate (2,138 @ 39.35%)	841	
		1,977
		2,303
Less: Tax on payments made to Clery treated as his income: $4,200 \times \frac{45}{55}$		(3,436)
Tax payable under s 496		1,133
Tax pool exhausted so amount to carry forward to 2024/25		£0

(c) *Tax payable by trustees under self-assessment (POA — payment on account)*

				Tax payable	*Re 2023/24*
		£	£	£	£
31.1.23	1st POA 2022/23			486	
31.7.23	2nd POA 2022/23			486	
31.1.24	Balancing payment 2022/23:				
	Tax due (1,696 – tax credits 546)	1,150			
	Less POAs	(972)	178		
	1st POA 2023/24 (½ × 1,150)		575	753	575
31.7.24	2nd POA 2022/23			575	575
31.1.25	Balancing payment 2023/24:				
	Income tax as in (a)	2,035			
	s 496 liability as in (b)	1,133			
	Capital gains tax as in (a)	527			
	Total liability	3,695			
	Tax due	3,695			
	Less: POAs	(1,150)	2,545		2,545
	1st POA 2024/25 ½ × (3,695 – CGT 527)		1,584	4,129	
	Total tax paid directly for 2023/24				3,695
31.7.25	2nd POA 2024/25			1,584	

(d) *Clery's income tax repayment claim 2023/24*

				Tax
			£	£
Trust income $£4{,}200 \times \frac{100}{55}$			7,636	3,436
State pension			6,820	
Purchased life annuities (income element)			5,000	1,000
Net income			19,456	4,436
Less: personal allowance			(12,570)	
Taxable income			6,886	
Tax payable thereon:				
On trust income and state pension (basic rate)	1,886	@ 20%	377	(377)
On purchase life annuity (starting rate for savings)	3,114	@ 0%	Nil	
On purchased life annuity (savings nil rate)	1,000	@ 0%	Nil	
On purchased life annuity (basic rate)	886	@ 20%	177	(177)
Repayment due				3,812

Explanatory Notes

Income tax rates applicable to accumulation and discretionary trusts

(1) In 2023/24, the income of an accumulation and discretionary trust is liable to tax at the dividend trust rate of 39.35% (39.35% in 2022/23) if it is dividend income and at the trust rate of 45% in respect of other income (ITA 2007 s 9) (see **Example F1** for details).

Under ITA 2007 s 491, the trust's first slice income of £1,000 will not be charged at the trust tax rates, but will instead be charged at the income tax rate appropriate to the type of income against which it is matched (see below).

However, that £1,000 amount of first slice income is restricted by ITA 2007 s 492 where a settlor has made more than one settlement that is in existence at any time during the tax year in question. The £1,000 is replaced by an amount obtained by dividing £1,000 by the number of settlements made by the same settlor, or by £200 if there are more than five other current settlements such that the quotient would be less than £200. For this purpose a settlement will be counted even if:

- its period of existence during the tax year in question does not overlap with that of the subject settlement or of another settlement made by the same settlor (ie where one or more settlements are made or terminated during the tax year);
- its trustees are not UK resident;
- it is not a discretionary or accumulation trust;
- it does not have any income in the tax year;
- a vulnerable person election is in force in respect of it;
- it is a settlor-interested trust; or even

- (anomalously since the trust tax rates do not apply to charitable trusts) it subsists for charitable purposes only. HMRC have at least stated that 'Ordinary donations to third party charities would not be counted as separate settlements when considering the amount of [first slice income]' (see TSEM3016a).

On this basis all of Charles's other settlements in the Example (including Trust V which is resident overseas), except for Trust U which had come to an end before 2023/24, are taken into account for working out the amount of first slice income of the Colenso Trust. Division of the basic amount of £1,000 by seven (six other trusts plus the Colenso Trust) produces a figure below £200 and so the Colenso Trust's first slice income is £200.

ITA 2007 s 492 also sets out the position where there is more than one settlor of a settlement, and in such circumstances the amount of first slice income is the amount obtained in relation to the settlor who had made the largest number of current settlements.

HMRC have confirmed that first slice income is matched to trust income *net* of trust management expenses which is in accordance with s 484(3) (see TSEM3016a).

Although the management expenses are matched with trust income taxed at the lowest rate first, the first slice income is matched in the opposite order – default basic rate income at 20% first, followed by dividends at 8.75% (8.75% in 2022/23).

Apart from the amount of first slice income explained above, trustees are liable to tax at the trust rate or dividend trust rate as the case may be if:

(a) the trust's income is to be accumulated or payable at their discretion, and

(b) it exceeds the trust expenses paid out of income, grossed up at the appropriate rate of tax. The expenses are treated as being defrayed first out of dividends and other UK dividend income (as defined in s 19), then out of dividends from abroad, then out of savings income, then out of non-savings income (see ITA 2007 s 486 and **Example F2 explanatory note 10**). The grossing up rate for the expenses is 8.75% (dividend ordinary rate) for dividend income and 20% (default basic rate) for non-dividend income. The expenses are not allowable deductions for basic or for dividend ordinary rate tax, so tax is charged on an equivalent amount of income at the appropriate rate (8.75% in this Example).

(2) See **Example F7** for an illustration of a trust liable at the trust tax rates where there is a non-UK resident beneficiary.

(3) In this Example, it may be possible to agree that some of the accountancy fees relate to the property income, rather than treating them as general trust expenses, thereby reducing the assessable income and the overall tax liability of the trust.

Self-assessment returns: trustees

(4) The HMRC Trusts, Settlements and Estates Manual states in paragraph TSEM1405 that the trustees of a new trust that does not have any income or gains do not have to notify HMRC of the existence of the trust (though this does not affect the trust from being taken into account for the restriction of the amount of first slice income for other settlements as set out in **explanatory note 1** above). Existing trusts which do not have any income or gains may ask HMRC to close the trust's record. The trustees are, of course, obliged to notify HMRC by 5 October following the relevant tax year, in the same way as individuals, if they do have income and/or gains chargeable to tax (TMA 1970 s 7).

(5) Where a self-assessment return is required, all types of trusts and estates complete the same return (SA 900).

Filing dates for paper and online self-assessment returns: trustees

(6) Trustees are obliged to make an annual return of trust income and capital gains and to include in that return a self-assessment (SA) of the amounts of tax payable (TMA 1970 ss 8A, 9).

Paper substitutes for SA returns

Computer generated substitute versions of the SA return are no longer to be approved or accepted for:

SA Individual Returns – (SA100 series) (but see below as to limited cases where online filing is not yet possible);

SA Trust Returns – (SA900 series).

For the time being, HMRC will continue to accept approved substitutes for the remaining SA Returns (including those for trustees of registered pension schemes) and for all other forms they currently approve substitutes for.

SA filing dates

Anyone who is required to file a self-assessment tax return will have:

- until 31 October to do so, if they choose to send a paper return; or
- until the following 31 January if they file online.

This allows an additional three months for online filing compared with paper.

The filing obligation is satisfied by the first return received by HMRC and this also triggers any late filing penalty. So if, for example, a paper 2023/24 return is filed after 31 October 2024, it is not then possible to avoid a late filing penalty by filing the return online.

In addition, in certain other cases, HMRC will allow extra time beyond the statutory deadline of 31 October – until 31 January – for paper filing without incurring a penalty. These include:

- Trustees of Registered Pension Schemes; and
- Certain categories of SA taxpayers for whom facilities to file online are not yet available.

In the event that there are problems with HMRC systems close to the filing deadline, taxpayers will not be penalised for late submission of a return due to such problems provided that they, or their agent, file within a reasonable period once the service is restored.

If a notice is given after 31 July the return must be submitted during the period of three months beginning with the date of the notice (for paper returns) or on or before 31 January (for online returns) (TMA 1970 s 8A(1D)).

If a notice is given after 31 October the return (whether paper return or electronic) must be submitted within three months from the date of the notice (TMA 1970 s 8A(1E)).

Interest in possession trusts are not required to show any *taxed* income in the return, except where the income has not been mandated to the beneficiaries and there are accrued income losses to be set against the interest (or the trustees are claiming the losses against general income). (Accrued income profits are untaxed income and must be shown.) The trustees must include the interest in their return if its exclusion would make them liable to make payments on account which would not be due if it were included. Also in relation to any interest excluded from their return, the trustees will still, however, need to know the overall tax position in order to be able to ascertain the income payable to the life tenant to be shown on form R185 (Trust Income) (see **explanatory note** 8). The returns for discretionary trusts show both taxed and untaxed income and the amount of the unused tax pool (if any) brought forward from the previous year. For both types of trust, supplementary pages have to be completed where income arises from a trade, partnership, land and property or from abroad, or where there are capital gains, or where the trust is non-resident or dual resident.

(7) To minimise administration burdens, HMRC have a scheme under which trustees responsible for at least 50 trusts dealt with in a single tax office may receive a single notice calling for trust returns and may make a single declaration when submitting a batch of returns. Trustees wishing to operate the scheme must make a

written application. More information can be found in the HMRC Trusts, Settlements and Estates Manual at TSEM 3052.

Self-assessment payments on account limits: trustees

(8) Payments on account for a tax year are not required from trustees where:

- the net tax payable by them in the preceding tax year (ie the tax payable by them that was not deducted at source) is less than £1,000, or
- at least 80% of the total tax due for the preceding year (ie including any tax deducted at source) was collected at source.

(TMA 1970 s 59A(1) and Income Tax (Payments on Account) Regulations 1996 SI 1996/1654 (as amended by SI 2008/838)).

Forms R185 (Trust Income) and beneficiaries' own tax returns

(9) It is advisable for trustees to compute the overall tax position of the trust as quickly as possible after 5 April each year to comply with their responsibilities under self-assessment.

Where a beneficiary is absolutely entitled to the income it will be essential to do so, in order that the R185 (Trust Income) may be completed and forwarded to the beneficiary in plenty of time for him to complete his own self-assessment return or to claim a repayment as the case may be (especially as the beneficiary may plan to submit his tax return on paper, with therefore three months shorter time limit than the trustees face if filing online – see **explanatory note 6** above). For such beneficiaries, if all the income is taxed at source and there are no expenses, it is usual to mandate the income directly to the beneficiary and to include the income in the beneficiary's return as if it were his own income. In the case of a bare trust, ie where the beneficiary has an absolute right to both income and capital, all of the trust income is deemed to be that of the beneficiary and entered as such on the beneficiary's tax return. Trustees of bare trusts are not required to send trust returns but may, if they wish, send a trust return of the trust income, but not capital gains. This does not affect the beneficiary's liability to make his own returns.

Income paid out to discretionary beneficiaries of trusts

(10) Under ITA 2007 s 496, trustees are required to account for tax at the 45% trust rate on income paid out in exercise of their discretion to beneficiaries, and the beneficiaries will be given form R185 (Trust Income) showing the income as non-savings income with tax deducted at 45% (s 495). The tax suffered is available for repayment, as illustrated in the Example. (Different rules apply if the trust is settlor-interested, see **Example F5 explanatory note 9**.)

Tax has to be accounted for under s 496 only where trustees make a discretionary payment which is income in the hands of the beneficiary (s 493(2)) or where the payment is treated under ITTOIA 2005 as the income of the settlor of a parental settlement. A charge may arise under s 496 even where the payment is made out of the capital of the trust. For example where trustees are empowered to make payments to bring a beneficiary's income up to a certain level, such payments will be income whether paid out of current or accumulated income or capital (but see **Example F3 explanatory note 2** as to annuities paid wholly or partly out of trust capital) (see *Stevenson v Wishart* (1987) and *Cunard's Trustees v CIR* (1945)).

The tax to be accounted for by the trustees on a payment to a beneficiary is met first from the 'tax pool' which comprises the following categories of tax paid by the trustees:

(i) any pool of unused tax brought forward at the start of the tax year in question (see **explanatory note 11**);

(ii) tax paid on all first slice income of £1,000 (or a lower amount as in **explanatory note 1**) of trust income;

(iii) the excess of the tax paid at the trust rate on gains on non-qualifying life assurance policies, contracts for life annuities and capital redemption policies over the default basic rate;

(iv) tax paid on all other income liable at the trust rate or trust ordinary rate, including tax deducted at source;

but *not* by any tax on income that has been used to defray trust expenses (see **explanatory note 1(b)**) (s 498). To the extent that the tax pool is insufficient to meet the tax due from the trustees under s 496, they must pay the balance under self-assessment.

(11) If a beneficiary of a discretionary trust has not received a form R185 (Trust Income), he should gross up the income received for tax deducted at 45%. If there is any doubt that part of the payment received is not income, or as to whether it was paid from a settlor-interested trust (see **Example F5 explanatory note 4**), the amount should be shown on his personal return as a provisional figure with a tick in box 20 and the reason for the figure being provisional should be shown in the additional information box at 19. The beneficiary should not delay submitting his return because of the failure of the trustees to provide a form R185 (Trust Income).

Sections 497–498 tax pool: accumulation and discretionary trusts

(12) In many instances, the pool of tax calculated under ss 497–498 will exceed the amount that is due on a discretionary payment, so no amount will be payable by the trustees on that payment. Furthermore tax could be paid on income that is used to cover expenses (see **Example F7**). From 6 April 1999 to 5 April 2016, none of the tax credits on dividends were included in the tax pool. The payments out of income will still have repayable tax of 45% deducted. (Previous trust rates were 34% prior to 5 April 2004; 40% from then until 5 April 2010; and 50% from then until 6 April 2013.) Except to the extent that there is an unused pool of tax brought forward, this will restrict the maximum payment out of dividend income to 55% of the net dividend; otherwise a s 496 liability of 45% of the net dividend will arise (see **Example F4 explanatory note 2** and **Example F7 explanatory note 9** for illustrations).

Note that tax credits on any pre-6 April 1999 dividends were included in the tax pool, and, insofar as they have not been used, those credits remain available to cover s 496 tax on discretionary payments after 5 April 1999.

(13) The s 496 tax payable is added to the tax due under self-assessment and is accounted for in the balancing payment. It also counts in the calculation of the payments on account for the following year. Thus it can increase the tax payable on 31 January following the end of the tax year to 150% of the s 496 liability.

The trustees may not intend to make distributions to beneficiaries in the following tax year and may be tempted to apply to reduce the payments on account by the amount of the s 496 tax. Payments on account are, however, compared with the actual tax due for the subsequent year, and if the reduced payment is below the actual liability for that year, interest is payable on the difference (restricted to the amount of the reduction). It does not matter that the claim to reduce the payments on account was in respect of s 496 tax and the additional liability arises because of an increase in tax because of increased income, tax rate increases, reduced expenses or for any other reason.

Capital gains tax: UK-resident trustees

(14) A trust with UK resident trustees is liable to capital gains tax on the trustees' chargeable gains less allowable losses (including those brought forward from earlier years so far as required to reduce the total gains to the level of the available annual exempt amount), and less the annual exemption itself (as to which see **explanatory note 15** below).

The rate at which that net amount is charged is 28% on gains arising in respect of residential property and 20% otherwise. It is provided that allowable losses, and the annual exempt amount, may be set against gains in the way that is most beneficial to the taxpayer (TCGA 1992 s 1F).

The amount due is payable on 31 January following the tax year, but is not included in the calculation of payments on account for the following year, nor is it available for inclusion in the tax pool for calculating trustees' s 496 liability. With effect from 6 April 2020, trustees that dispose of UK residential property must make a return of that disposal within 60 days of completion of the transaction (increased from 30 days in relation to disposals that have a completion date on or after 27 October 2021 (FA 2022 s 23)) and also pay the capital gains tax due in respect of that disposal by that date (FA 2019 Sch 2) – see **explanatory note 16.**

(15) The basic annual exempt amount for a trust is one half of that applicable to an individual (half of £6,000 for 2023/24 = £3,000) (TCGA 1992, Sch 1C para 5). However, in the same way as the £1,000 first slice income of a discretionary or accumulation trust is reduced (see **explanatory note 1** above), this basic trust exemption is reduced where the settlor has created other trusts which still continue; but the rules for this reduction are different in the capital gains tax context.

If the subject settlement has UK resident trustees, any other trust made by the same settlor must be counted in any tax year (whether or not it is settlor-interested) if:

- both it and the subject settlement were made after 6 June 1978 (in whatever order);
- it is not a disabled person's trust;
- its trustees were UK resident at some point during the tax year;
- it existed at some point during the tax year; and
- some at least of its settled property is held other than for charitable purposes or for the purposes of a registered pension scheme or certain other related types of pension scheme.

A bare trust (which includes a trust that has come to an end through absolute entitlement to its property) is not settled property (TCGA 1992 s 60), and the trust is therefore not a 'settlement'. It will be disregarded in restricting the trustees' annual exemption if it has been a bare trust throughout the tax year concerned.

If there are any trusts meeting the above criteria as well as the subject settlement, the basic annual exempt amount (half that of an individual) is divided between them equally (irrespective of whether they have any chargeable gains in that tax year), subject to a minimum annual exemption equal to one-tenth of the amount available to individuals, ie £600 for 2023/24 (TCGA 1992 Sch 1C para 6(3)).

In this Example Trusts T, W and Y, as well as the Colenso Trust, meet those criteria, so each has an annual exemption for 2023/24 of one quarter of the basic £3,000 trust exemption, ie £750. As to the others:

- Trust U is not counted because it had been wound up before 2023/24.
- Trust V is not counted both because it was made before 1978 and because its property is held for exclusively charitable purposes.
- Trust X is **not** counted because its trustees were not UK resident at any time during 2023/24.
- Trust Z is not counted as it is a trust for a disabled person (TCGA 1992 Sch 1C para 5(1)).

If there is more than one settlor of the subject trust, dilution will occur by reference to whichever of those settlors made the largest number of other trusts meeting the criteria described, subject again to the minimum exemption (for 2023/24) of £600.

The annual exemption available in respect of Trust Z which is for a disabled person is prima facie equal to the annual exemption available to an individual (£6,000 in 2023/24) (TCGA Sch 1C para 2(1)). However as that trust is one a group of qualifying UK trusts the annual exemption is reduced to the greater of one-tenth of the prima facie amount (ie £600) and the amount found by dividing the prima facie amount by the number of trusts in the group (ie £6,000/5 = £1,200) (TCGA 1992 Sch 1C para 6(2)).

Capital gains tax: 'report and pay' obligations on the disposal of UK residential property

(16) The capital gains (and allowable losses) of trustees (and indeed personal representatives) must be reported on their self-assessment tax returns for a tax year (see **explanatory note 6**). With effect from 6 April 2020, however, additional and separate compliance obligations (the so-called 'report and pay' requirements) arise for both UK and non-UK resident trustees (and indeed individuals and personal representatives for that matter) in respect of their disposals of UK residential property (FA 2019, Sch 2). These obligations are in addition to the requirement to report relevant disposals on the normal self-assessment return, not instead of so reporting the disposals.

Residential property includes properties suitable for use as dwellings or those in the process of being built or adapted for such use. Gardens, grounds (without limit on size) and outbuildings count as part of the whole of the residential property if intended to be used with the dwelling. Boarding school, barracks used by members of the armed forces and residential property used by children, older people and those with disabilities or in need of medical or rehabilitative care are not regarded as being residential property for this purpose.

From 6 April 2020 a return (called a 'UK land return' in this note) must be filed and an amount of capital gains tax must be paid on account within 30 days of the completion of a disposal of UK residential land occurring on or after 6 April 2020 (Sch 2 para 3) (increased to 60 days in relation to disposals that have a completion date on or after 27 October 2021 (FA 2022 s 23)). If the completion fulfils a contract entered into before 6 April 2020, however, no UK land return is required. No UK land return is required however where its filing date falls after the main self-assessment tax return has been or is due to be submitted (Sch 2 para 5). Where a property comprises both residential and commercial parts, the gain arising must be apportioned of a just and reasonable basis. Only the residential element will be subject to the report and pay requirements. A separate return must be filed for each UK residential property disposal. If two disposals occur on the same day, a single return may be filed.

As regards both UK resident and non-UK resident trustees, a UK land return will need to be filed where a disposal of UK residential property gives rise to a chargeable gain or an allowable loss (Sch 2 para 4). However, as regards UK resident trustees only, there is no requirement to file a return where a loss is made on disposal, or where a gain is fully covered by a relief (such as the only or main residence relief), the annual exemption and/or carried-forward losses. If two or more disposals take place in a tax year, the annual exempt amount will be set against the disposals in chronological order (it now being more beneficial to use the annual exemption in relation to residential property disposals rather than disposals of other assets). The joint owners of jointly owned property will need to observe the report and pay compliance formalities according to their individual circumstances. Consequently, a disposal of property with multiple owners may give rise to a significant overall gain, but there would be no requirement to report the gain if, when apportioned to each owner, it is covered by their annual exempt amount for example.

Non-UK resident trustees have to file a return even though they may have no tax liability (and failure to do so may give rise to late filing penalties). Further in relation to non-UK resident trustees, their obligation to report and pay arises in respect of the disposal of any UK land or shares in a property-rich company (and any comments in this note made by reference to residential property apply to this wider category of assets as appropriate).

Trustees must make reasonable estimates of the tax payable on the disposal as if the tax year ended on the date of disposal (Sch 2 para 7). In practice this will no doubt be the norm where formal valuations are required in relation to the property. Where reasonable estimates have been used to calculate the payment on account, any understatement of the liability will lead to interest and possible penalties of the return contains a careless error.

Gains on other assets are ignored in calculating the payment on account of capital gains tax in respect of the disposal of residential property. Where an estimate changes, a further return may be filed correcting the estimate and a repayment of tax may be generated if appropriate (Sch 2 para 15). Where a UK land return is submitted, there is no separate requirement for the trustees to notify HMRC of their chargeability (Sch 2 para 18).

Realised capital losses that have been reported (and are hence allowable losses), whether on UK residential land, or any other assets, which are carried forward from an earlier tax year or realised in the tax year before the disposal of the UK residential property (even though they have not yet been reported), may be taken into account when computing the capital gains tax payment on account. However, a loss arising later in the same tax year on an asset (other than residential property) may only be taken into account in the self-assessment and does not affect the tax payable on an earlier land transfer. Such a loss may however, be taken into account when calculating the amount of tax payable in respect of a disposal of residential land later in the tax year. A loss arising on the disposal of UK residential property later in the tax year may be taken into account in relation to the tax payable on an earlier disposal (and will result in a repayment of the tax paid on that earlier disposal together with repayment supplement). However, the later disposal will have to be reported in order for it to be an allowable loss (see below). If trustees know that they will dispose of both landed and non-landed assets in the same tax year, then consideration may be given to ensure that the disposals take place in the most advantageous order.

In computing the tax payable under the report and pay regime, claims and elections (eg principal private residence relief, etc) may be taken into account if it is reasonable to suppose that these will be made or given (Sch 2 para 14). The claim or election must still be formally made in accordance with the rules governing it (eg in the self-assessment return). The conditions for the relief being claimed must be satisfied at the time the payment on account of capital gains tax is required. If they are not an amendment to the land return may be made when the conditions for the relief are met.

In relation to multiple disposals of residential property in a tax year, the amount of capital gains tax due in each disposal after the first is calculated taking into account the tax paid previously.

No UK land return need be filed where a disposal of UK residential property gives rise to a loss. However, if a return would have been acquired had a gain arisen, the trustees may make a return and claim a repayment of any capital gains tax already paid by them in respect of an earlier disposal of UK land in the tax year (Sch 2 para 9).

If events that occurred before the UK land return were not reflected in the calculation of the gain and the taxpayer did not need to make a self-assessment return, amendments may be made to the land return up to the anniversary of the 31 January following the end of the year in which the gain was made. Once a taxpayer files a self-assessment return, not further amendments may be made to the land return. Corrections to the relevant calculations are made through the self-assessment return.

Broadly speaking, a UK land return will be subject to the same provisions as reqards amendments, enquiries and determinations as applies to a self-assessment return (Sch 2 paras 19–22). An amendment to a land return may be made up to the earlier of the filing date of the trustees' tax return and the date it is filed. If no tax return is due to be filed, amendments may be made to a UK land return up to one year after 31 January following the tax year. However, an amendment is permitted only so far as the return could, when delivered, have included the amendment by reference to things already done (eg to substitute a formal value for an estimate used when first submitting the return). Subsequent changes in circumstances are not valid grounds for amending a UK land return and nay repayment of tax occasioned thereby cannot be obtained until the self-assessment return for the year is itself filed.

Special rules apply where the disposal of UK residential land is subject to an option. The grant of the option is itself a disposal. On the subsequent exercise of the option, the grant and exercise is treated as a single disposal (s 144). Nevertheless a UK land return is required on the grant of the option (Sch 2 para 13).

The penalty regime applicable to a UK land return is the same as that for self-assessment returns but without the £10 daily penalties. Hence there is a £100 initial penalty for late filing, a further penalty if the return is six months late and a further penalty if the return is 12 months late.

A useful article on the report and pay requirements is 'Remember the deadline' by J Marks published in *Taxation* dated 3 December 2020.

Clery's income

(17) The rule established in the case of *Drummond* (1915) is that in the case of a discretionary or accumulation trust, in contrast to the position of a beneficiary of an interest in possession trust, the source of a beneficiary's income is the trustees themselves. The distinction is important, as the accurate identification of the source of income is crucial in choosing the correct rate of income tax for the beneficiary. As such the payment received by a discretionary beneficiary is an annual payment in accordance with the definition of that term as set out in *IRC v Whitworth Park Coal Co Ltd* (1959)) (as confirmed in *RCC v Hargreaves Landsdown Asset Management Ltd* [2019] STC 1745). A payment is an annual payment if it has the following attributes:

- First it is made under a binding legal obligation: once the trustees have exercised their discretion they are bound by the trust deed to make the payment and can be forced (in law) by the beneficiaries to make the payment. The beneficiaries are, after the exercise by the trustees of their discretion, entitled to the payments by virtue of the gift made by the settlor. By contrast gifts – mere voluntary, unenforceable payments, however regular in amount – are not income for tax purposes and neither are they money to which the recipient is entitled before it actually reaches him.

- Secondly, the payment must possess the quality of recurrence which it may do even though the amount may be variable or the payments contingent (*Moss' Empires Ltd v IRC* (1937)).
- Thirdly, the payment must be pure income profit in the hands of the payee (ie the amount received by the beneficiary is the amount taxed – there are no expenses that the beneficiary incurs which might reduce the amount on which he is taxable).
- Finally, the payment must belong to the payee and must be part of the payee's income.

Being an annual payment, a charge to tax arises in respect of it under Chapter 7 Part 5 ITTOIA 2005 (ITTOIA 2005 s 683). This means that the beneficiary cannot use his savings allowance or dividend allowance in working out his income tax liability in respect of the income, the income being neither savings nor dividend income (even though the trustees themselves may receive savings and dividend income). See **Example F3, explanatory note 5.**

Question

A trust was established on 6 April 2002. The trust deed stipulates that after paying an annuity of £6,500 per annum to the settlor's sister, the remaining income of each year is to be distributed or accumulated as the trustees deem fit.

The assets placed into the trust consisted of certain properties let unfurnished on landlord's repairing short leases, and cash. The latter was placed on bank deposit and used to fund investments in government securities and quoted shares. None of the properties qualifies as a furnished holiday letting for tax purposes.

At 6 April 2022 the pool of unutilised tax brought forward under ITA 2007 ss 496–498 was £3,750.

The receipts and payments of the trust for 2022/23 and 2023/24 were as follows:

	2022/23	*2023/24*
	£	£
Receipts		
Rents receivable	11,200	11,137
Premium received on granting of 21 year lease	Nil	10,000
Interest on £10,000 9% Government Stock (gross amount)	900	900
Bank interest received	1,400	1,500
Dividends from quoted UK companies (see below)	3,200	2,762
Payments		
Trustees' expenses properly chargeable to income	416	463
Trustees' expenses re investment advice	Nil	100
Loan interest (see below)	200	733
Repairs to the let properties	100	400
Annuity to settlor's sister (gross amount)	6,500	6,500
Discretionary payments of cash from the trust income:		
to A, who is resident in the UK	3,366	Nil
to B, who is not resident in the UK	Nil	3,700

The loan was obtained to finance an extension to one of the let properties. Interest on the 9% Government Stock is exempt from tax in the hands of a non-resident. The trustees' expenses for investment advice have been charged to income by authority of the trust deed.

The amount of income tax paid on account for 2022/23 equalled the liability for 2021/22 of £4,208.

Calculate:

(1) The income of the trust for 2022/23 and 2023/24, showing any liability in respect of income chargeable at special trust rates under ITA 2007 s 479, and the due dates of payment of tax.

(2) The income available for distribution to discretionary beneficiaries for 2022/23 and 2023/24 (individually).

(3) The trust's position under ITA 2007 ss 496–498 at the end of 2023/24 in relation to the discretionary payments made.

(4) Any income tax that may be reclaimable by the non-UK resident beneficiary in respect of the discretionary payment made to him.

Note:

Ignore capital gains tax, and interest on tax or tax refunds.

Answer

(1) Statement of trust income

2022/23

			Gross	Tax
			£	£
Property income (see **explanatory note 6**)			11,100	
Savings income				
Interest on Government Stock			900	
Bank interest			1,400	
Dividends			3,200	
			16,600	
Less: Step 2 deduction (annuity)			(6,500)	
Net total income of trust			10,100	
Tax thereon:				
On amount equal to grossed up trust expenses, excluding those for investment advice (416 × 100/91.25)	456	@ 8.75%		40
On £1,000 of first slice income under ITA 2007 s 491 (20% on property income)	1,000	@ 20%		200
On dividend income not used for expenses, at dividend trust rate (3,200 – 456) (see **explanatory note 2**)	2,744	@ 39.35%		1,080
On balance at trust rate	5,900	@ 45%		2,655
	10,100			
Tax deducted from annuity	6,500	@ 20%		1,300
Less: reduction re property loan interest 200 @ 20% (see **explanatory note 6**)				(40)
Total income tax due				5,235
Of which tax payable by self-assessment is				5,235

Amounts of income tax payable by trustees direct to HMRC under self-assessment for 2022/23 and payments on account for 2023/24 are as follows:

	£	£
31 January 2023:		
½ × 4,208		2,104
31 July 2023:		
½ × 4,208		2,104
31 January 2024:		
Total income tax payable for 2022/23	5,235	
Less: Payments on account	(4,208)	
	1,027	1,027
		5,235
First payment on account for 2023/24 (½ × 5,235)	2,618	
Total amount payable (1,027 + 2,618)	3,645	
31 July 2024:		
Second payment on account for 2023/24 (see **explanatory note 6**)	2,617	

2023/24

			Gross £	*Tax* £
Property income (see **explanatory note 6**)			16,737	
Savings income				
Interest on Government Stock			900	
Bank interest			1,500	
Dividends			2,762	
			21,899	
Less: Step 2 deduction (annuity)			(6,500)	
Net total income of trust			15,399	
Tax thereon:				
On amount equal to grossed up trust expenses, excluding those for investment advice (463 × 100/91.25)	507	@ 8.75%		44
On lease premium (see **explanatory note 6**)	6,000	@ 45%		2,700
On £1,000 of first slice income under ITA 2007 s 491 (20% on property income)	1,000	@ 20%		200
On dividend income not used for expenses, at dividend trust rate (2,762 – 507) (see **explanatory note 2**)	2,255	@ 39.35%		887
On balance at trust rate	5,637	@ 45%		2,537
	15,399			
Tax deducted from annuity	6,500	@ 20%		1,300
Less: reduction re property loan interest 733 @ 20% (see **explanatory note 6**)				(147)
Total income tax due and payable by self-assessment				7,521

Amounts of income tax payable by trustees direct to HMRC under self-assessment for 2023/24 and payments on account for 2024/25 are as follows:

	£	£
31 January 2024:		
As above ½ × 5,235		2,618
31 July 2024:		
½ × 5,235		2,617
31 January 2025:		
Total income tax payable for 2023/24	7,521	
Less: Payments on account	5,235	
	2,286	2,286
		7,521
First payment on account for 2024/25 (½ × 7,521) (see **explanatory note 13**)	3,760	
Total amount payable (2,286 + 3,760)	6,046	

31 July 2025:	
Second payment on account for 2024/25 (see **explanatory notes 6 and 13**)	3,761

(2) Income available for distribution to discretionary beneficiaries

			2022/23		2023/24
			£		£
Trust income (excluding lease premium) after annuity and expenses			9,644*		8,892**
Less:	Tax on first slice income (20%) under ITA 2007 s 491	200		200	
	Tax at trust rate per part (1)	2,655		2,537	
	Tax at dividend trust rate per part (1)	1,081		887	
	Trustees' expenses for investment advice (see **explanatory note 7**)	Nil		100	
	Trustees' expenses re interest on loan not deductible in computing profits	200	(5,135)	733	(4,457)
Add: Tax reduction re property loan interest			40		147
Available for beneficiaries			5,549		4,582
Amount actually distributed was			(3,366)		(3,700)
Leaving undistributed income of			£2,183		£882

*£10,100 total income net of annuity as at part (1), less expenses £456 (grossed up for consistency, ie 416 × 100/91.25).

**£15,399 total income net of annuity as at part (1), less lease premium (capital) £6,000 and expenses £507 (gross equivalent as before).

Note that in so far as the amount shown as available to the beneficiaries includes dividend income, it cannot all be distributed without the trustees incurring a further tax liability, except to the extent that there is unutilised tax brought forward in the tax pool (see **explanatory note 9**).

(3) Trust's position under ITA 2007 ss 496–498 at end of 2023/24 in relation to the discretionary payments made

			2022/23		2022/23
			£		£
Tax at 45% on amounts paid at trustees' discretion to beneficiaries:					
	$£3,366 \times \frac{45}{55}$		2,754		
Tax at 45% on amounts paid at trustees' discretion to beneficiaries:					
	$£3,700 \times \frac{45}{55}$				3,027
Less:	Tax already accounted for by trustees:				
	On first slice income charged at the basic rate	200		200	
on trust income chargeable under ITA 2007 s 479 –					
at trust rate 45%		2,655		2,537	
at dividend trust rate (2022/23) (2,744 @ 39.35%)		1,080			

		2022/23 £		2022/23 £
at dividend trust rate (2023/24) (2,255 @ 39.35%)			887	
Unutilised tax in pool b/f	3,750		4,931	
	7,685		8,555	
Utilised	(2,754)	(2,754)	(3,027)	(3,027)
Unutilised tax in pool c/f	4,931		5,528*	
Amount due from trustees under ITA 2007 ss 496		Nil		Nil

* The amount of £5,528 carried forward represents tax paid at the basic rate on first slice income, at the trust rate, and the dividend trust rate, and it can be used to cover tax at 45% on the gross equivalent of future income distributions.

(4) Tax reclaimable by non-resident beneficiary (see explanatory note 10)

2022/23	No distribution to B – no repayment.
2023/24	Distribution of £3,700 to B (who is not resident in UK) comes from trust income that includes £900 from Government Stock that is exempt from tax in B's hands.

The part of the total tax of £3,027 paid on the discretionary payment of trust income in 2023/24 that represents the interest on the Government Stock is therefore repayable, thus:

$$3{,}027 \times \frac{900}{15{,}899} = 171$$

the denominator of £15,899 being the trust's taxable income of £21,899 before the payment of the annuity, less the lease premium of £6,000 which is a capital receipt.

Explanatory Notes

Income tax: trusts liable to the trust rate and dividend trust rate (trust tax rates)

(1) A trust that can accumulate income, or pay income to the beneficiaries at the discretion of the trustees, is, generally speaking, liable to tax on non-dividend income at the rate applicable to trusts (45% for 2013/14 and later years), and at the dividend trust rate (37.5% for 2013/14 to 2015/16 and 38.1% for 2016/17 to 2021/22 and 39.35% for 2022/23 and later years) on 'dividend income', eg UK dividend income (as defined) and foreign dividends (ITA 2007 ss 19, 479). The trust does not pay income tax at the dividend nil-rate and so is not entitled to the so-called dividend allowance. For 2015/16 and earlier years, in the case of UK dividends, most foreign dividends, and other income carrying a non-repayable tax credit of 10%, the trustees have to pay the balance (27.5%) of the tax credit inclusive amount. The tax liability on foreign dividends will be subject to a claim for double tax relief where foreign tax has been paid. See **Example F1** for details of income carrying non-repayable tax credits and for details of amounts that are not chargeable at the trust rate.

In this Example, the amounts excluded from the charge under s 479 are the lease premium (see **explanatory note 6**) and the annuity to the settlor's sister. The trustees nevertheless have to account for tax on the lease premium at the trust rate of 45% (ss 481–482); on the annuity they must account for tax at the basic rate (s 963). (See **Example F3 explanatory note 2** for annuities.) Under self-assessment, tax is not charged separately for each source of income, and the tax under s 479 is accounted for as part of the trust's overall tax liability.

Income tax: amounts on which trust tax rates are charged

(2) The liability under s 479 applies to the *income* of the trust after deducting any excluded amounts per **explanatory note 1** and allowing for the trustees' first slice income and expenses of managing the trust. Trust expenses are regarded as being met first from income taxed at the dividend trust rate, then other savings income, then non-savings income, grossed up appropriately.

Trust expenses are treated as being set against income in the following order (ITA 2007 s 486):

(i) Dividend income (as defined), dividends received by non-UK resident persons in respect of which tax is treated as paid (ITTOIA 2005 s 399), scrip dividends (ITTOIA 2005 s 411), and close company loans written off or released (ITTOIA 2005 s 416). Prior to its repeal on 6 April 2016, the list also included bonus issues of redeemable securities (ITTOIA 2005 s 400(4), (5)) (see FA 2016 Sch 1 para 1).

(ii) Taxed dividends from abroad.

(iii) Non-savings and savings income other than that in (i) and (ii).

The set-off order is in fact the most beneficial, in that it maximises the amount of tax paid by the trust that may be passed on to beneficiaries.

The trust expenses which are subject to this rule are those which are properly chargeable to income ignoring any express terms of the trust deed (ITA 2007 s 484(5)). This means the rule applies only to expenses properly chargeable to income as a matter of trust law. Expenses properly chargeable against the capital of the trust which are paid out of income under the authority of the trust deed must not be taken into account.

How is the nature of trust management expenses determined? In *Carver v Duncan* (1985) it was held that expenditure incurred for the benefit of the whole estate was properly payable out of capital and not income. In *RCC v Trustees of the Peter Clay Discretionary Trust* (2009), the Court of Appeal defined such expenses as including those incurred in order to confer benefit on both the beneficiaries entitled to income and those entitled to capital when the trust is wound up. In other words, only those expenses incurred exclusively for the benefit of the beneficiaries entitled to income are properly chargeable against the trust's income. In practice, where an expense is capable of being apportioned between income and capital, then the amount attributable to income may be taken into account under s 484 (eg where an identifiable part of the expense is for work carried out for the benefit if the income beneficiaries alone). This practice was condoned in the *Peter Clay* case. HMRC Helpsheet 392 gives examples of expenses properly chargeable to income and those that are capable of being apportioned. For example, if professional fees incurred by trustees for accountancy services can be apportioned between fees attributable to dealing with the trust income and those attributable to dealing with capital, the fees charged by the executive trustee for dealing with those services should also be apportioned.

The income that is excluded from the ambit of ITA 2007 s 479 is an amount equal to the gross equivalent of the expenses. The reason this is done is to ensure that the income which is then charged at the basic or dividend ordinary rates is sufficient to meet both the expenses themselves and the tax thereon (*CIR v Lord Hamilton of Dalzell* (1926)).

Income tax: non-resident discretionary trusts and non-resident life tenants

(3) Where a discretionary trust has income that is not chargeable to UK income tax, because the trust is not resident in the UK (or deemed to be not resident under a double tax treaty), the trust management expenses must be apportioned between the taxable and non-taxable income of that year, and only the proportion applicable to taxable income is allowable in computing the tax under s 479 (s 487).

Similar provisions disallow a proportion of trust expenses in computing the income of a non-resident beneficiary with a life interest (s 501).

Non-UK resident trustees' income of the types listed in s 813 (which includes their UK savings and investment income), although strictly taxable income, would in practice escape being charged to tax because s 811 broadly limits the charge to the tax, if any, deducted at source. Any such income from which tax is *not* deducted is treated by s 487(5), (6) as non-taxable income for the purposes of s 487(1)–(4).

Interest on government stocks: accumulation and discretionary trusts

(4) If the trustees had so elected, the interest on the Government Stock in the Example received before 6 April 2016 would have been paid gross. Interest on Government Stock is paid gross in any event with effect from 6 April 2016. There is a cash flow advantage of receiving gross interest, because payments on account are made half-yearly on 31 January in the tax year and 31 July following, with a later balancing payment (or repayment), on the next following 31 January. See **Example F3 explanatory note 4** for the rules for paying gross interest on *all* government stocks.

Bank and building society interest: accumulation and discretionary trusts

(5) Tax is deducted from both building society interest and bank interest paid before 6 April 2016 to trustees of discretionary trusts, provided in the case of bank interest on deposits made before 6 April 1996 that the trustees or HMRC have notified the bank since that date that the income is income of a discretionary trust (Sch 2 para 154(1), (2), (3)). From 6 April 2016 interest on building society and bank accounts is paid gross.

Lease premiums and interest deductions for rental income: accumulation and discretionary trusts

(6) **Lease premiums**

In relation to the let property, although the lease premium is a capital amount, it is chargeable in part to income tax under ITTOIA 2005 s 277. However, the tax payable is debited to capital in the trust accounts (as any capital gains tax would have been if the premium had given rise to a capital gain); thus the tax reduces the amount of the credit to capital.

Therefore the taxable property income is:

			2022/23		*2023/24*
			£		£
Rents receivable			11,200		11,137
Premium for 21-year lease				10,000	
Property business receipt: $10{,}000 \times \frac{(50-(21-1))}{50} = 10{,}000 \times \frac{30}{50}$				(6,000)	6,000
Balance – consideration for part disposal for capital gains tax				4,000	
			11,200		17,137
Less: Expenses	– Repairs	100		400	
	– Loan interest*	Nil	(100)	Nil	(400)
			11,100		16,737

(*see explanation below)

The lease premium is a capital receipt of the trust and so is not subject to tax under ITA 2007 s 479 (see **explanatory note 1**). However, it is listed as a Type 5 amount in s 482 and so is subject to the trust rate (s 481(4)).

Since the lease premium is a non-recurring item, the trustees might think it appropriate to apply to reduce the payments on account for 2024/25. If, however, the final liability proves to be higher than the payments on account actually made (up to the total of the payments due without a claim, ie £7,521), interest would be charged on the shortfall from the half-yearly payment dates, the rate of interest at the time of writing being 7.75% per annum (which it has been since 22 August 2023).

If the payments on account had exceeded the liability for 2023/24, interest at the appropriate rate (4.25% per annum from 22 August 2023) would be paid on the overpayment from the respective dates that the half-yearly instalments were paid to the date the repayment order was issued. There should therefore be a non-taxable credit to income in the trust accounts, equal to the interest that would have been received, the credit to capital for the lease premium being reduced accordingly (in addition to being reduced by the income tax on the premium plus capital gains tax, if any).

Deduction for interest on residential property related loan

With effect from 6 April 2017 F(No 2)A 2015 s 24 introduces a restriction on the deductibility of interest paid on a loan taken out by a taxpayer for use in his property. The rules are found in ITTOIA 2005 ss 272A–272B and ss 274A–274B. The full amount of interest will no longer be deductible in computing the rental profits but part will instead be given effect to as a reduction in his tax liability. The reduction will be limited to 20% of the interest payable. For 2020/21 and later tax years, no interest will be deductible in computing rental profits and the entire amount will be given as a basic rate tax deduction.

For 2017/18, 2018/19 and 2019/20 the change will be phased in. In 2017/18 75% of the interest will be deductible from rental income and 25% given as a basic rate tax reduction; in 2018/19 50% of the interest will be deductible from rental income and 50% given as a basic rate tax reduction; and in 2019/20 25% of the interest will be deductible from rental income and 75% given as a basic rate tax reduction. Therefore in the Example, for 2022/23 and 20223/24 there are no deductions and the reductions are £200 × 20% = £40 and £733 × 20% = £147 respectively. The amounts given as a tax reduction may be limited by other factors.

As regards trustees, only trustees of accumulation and discretionary trusts are entitled to the tax reduction (ITTOIA 2005, ss 247B and 247C). Somewhat oddly the tax reduction will not be available to the trustees of interest in possession trusts. This will result in their paying more income tax than the beneficiary of the trust, but the latter should be able to obtain a repayment in relation to the net income of the trust income to which they are, of right, entitled and in respect of which they are taxed in their own right.

Costs of investment advice: accumulation and discretionary trusts

(7) The cost of investment advice is of a capital nature and is not to be excluded from the income charged to tax under ITA 2007 s 479 notwithstanding the authority of the trust deed to charge it to income (*Carver v Duncan and Bosanquet v Allen* (1985)) (see **explanatory note 2** above). Nonetheless, because the trust deed authorises the expenses to be charged to income, the amount available for distribution to income beneficiaries is reduced accordingly.

Income tax: income payments to discretionary beneficiaries

(8) Any income payment made to a beneficiary of a discretionary trust, other than to the settlor of a settlor-interested trust (ITTOIA 2005 s 685A(5)) is treated for income tax as being amounts paid net of tax, at 45% for 2014/15 and later years. The tax credit in the beneficiary's hands must be covered by tax paid by the trustees as recorded in the tax pool under ITA 2007 ss 496–498. If the tax credit is not so covered, there is a shortfall and the trustees will have an additional income tax liability in respect of the payment made to the beneficiary. The additional liability does not increase the tax credits recorded in the tax pool which will have a nil balance at the start of the next tax year. See **Example F6 explanatory note 10** (and **Example F7 explanatory note 4** for the position regarding settlor-interested trusts).

As the amount of the tax credit on a discretionary payment to a beneficiary will not always be covered by tax paid by the trustees, they will not be able to distribute the full amount of the trust's available net income without incurring an additional income tax liability under s 496. Tax paid on a premium received on the grant of a short lease will not be credited to the tax pool. Where a trust has dividend income, the tax on that income which is recorded in the tax pool under ss 496–498 will be lower than the tax credited to the beneficiary because;

(a) in respect of dividends received before 6 April 2016 the notional dividend tax credit of 10% is not recorded in the tax pool as it is non-repayable, and

(b) the dividend trust rate of tax is lower than the trust rate which is used to frank the distributions.

(9) The maximum distribution that can be made out of dividend income, without creating an income tax liability is determined by the trust rate of tax because that is the rate applied to the distribution. Therefore, the maximum distribution is 55% for 2013/14 and later years.

The effect on the amount available for beneficiaries in **part (2)** of the Example is as follows:

	2022/23	2023/24
	£	£
Gross dividend income		
(net of trust expenses)		
(3,200 – 456)	2,744	
(2,762 – 507)		2,255
Less: Tax paid at 8.75%	(240)	(197)
Tax credit exclusive amounts	2,504	2,058
55% thereof	1,377	1,132
Amount shown as available for beneficiaries per part (2)	5,549	4,582
Dividend income included therein as above	2,744	2,255
Less:		
Tax at dividend trust rate of 39.35%	(1,080)	(887)
	1,664	1,368
Actual amount available as above	1,377	1,132
Further reduction required (see below)	287	236
Reducing amount available for distribution	5,262	4,346

The further reduction required represents the difference between the dividend ordinary rate and the rate of tax actually paid on the net dividend income:

		2022/23		2023/24
		£		£
Rate of tax credit on distribution		45%		45%
Rate of tax on net dividend	$\frac{1,080-240}{2,504}$ =	33.55%	$\frac{887-197}{2,058}$ =	33.53%
Difference		11.45%		11.47%
	11.45% × 2,504	= 287	11.47% × 2,058	= 236

Higher distributions could be made to the extent that the tax was covered by the tax pool brought forward from year to year. The tax pool will not be fully utilised where the trustees have distributed less than the maximum amount possible in earlier years.

In addition, tax credits on pre 6-April 1999 dividends were repayable and were thus included in the tax pool. If those dividends had not been distributed before 6 April 1999, the credits will be available to cover tax on a post 5 April 1999 distribution.

FOTRA securities: income tax treatment of accumulation and discretionary trusts

(10) Government securities held by someone who is not resident in the UK are free of UK tax, such securities being referred to as FOTRA securities (ITTOIA 2005 ss 713–716 and ITTOIA 2005 ss 153, 713). If a discretionary trust holds such securities and makes distributions to beneficiaries who are not resident in the UK, then under Concession B18, a repayment claim may be made based upon the proportion of exempt income over total income (before Step 2 deductions) of tax credits attributed to distributions. Under the concession, the distribution is treated as made rateably out of income on a last in first out basis. Relief is available for payments out of income arising not earlier than six years before the end of the tax year of payment, provided the trustees have filed tax returns and paid all tax, interest, surcharges and penalties due. Although the concession states that claims must be made within five years from 31 January following the relevant tax year,

in line with the reduction in time limits, it is prudent to make the claim within four years of the end of the tax year concerned, in accordance with the current statutory time limits for other types of repayment claim.

The claim by B in relation to the distribution of £3,700 to him in 2023/24 will be regarded as relating wholly to the 2023/24 trust income, since that income exceeds the amount of the distribution.

The tax accounted for by the trustees for 2023/24 on the distribution of £3,700 is £3,027 per **part** (3) of the Example. The repayment available to B is the proportion of that amount that the £900 interest on the Government Stock bears to the 2023/24 total income before the annuity payment which is (21,899 – 6,000 =) £15,899 (the lease premium not being taken into account since it is a capital receipt). This amounts to £171 as shown in **part** (4) of the Example.

Income tax: anti-avoidance provisions re payments made by discretionary trusts to companies

(11) To prevent companies circumventing the rules by routing dividends through discretionary trusts and thus receiving the income not in the form of dividends but as annual payments from which income tax had been deducted, CTA 2010 s 610 provides that payments made to a *company* by a discretionary trust are not liable to corporation tax in the receiving company's hands, but the income tax deducted from the payments by the trustees is not repayable. This does not apply if the recipient company is a charity, heritage body or a scientific research association, and it only applies to a non-resident company if the payments would otherwise be chargeable to corporation tax as income of a UK permanent establishment. It is not common for companies to receive payments from discretionary trusts, but these provisions are aimed at preventing possible abuse.

Self-assessment payments on account limits: trustees

(12) Payments on account for a tax year are not required from trustees where:

- the net tax payable by them in the preceding tax year (ie the tax payable by them that was not deducted at source) is less than £1,000, or
- at least 80% of the total tax due for the preceding year (ie including any tax deducted at source) was collected at source.

(TMA 1970 s 59A(1) and Income Tax (Payments on Account) Regulations 1996, SI 1996/1654 (as amended by SI 2008/838)).

Question

A.

Mrs Spencer, who was born on 3 April 1949, has a life interest in income under a will trust established by her late husband who died on 30 May 2021.

The trust fund consists of loan stocks and similar securities having a nominal value of £50,000, the interest on which is received gross. In addition a small building society deposit account is held on which interest was received.

During the year to 5 April 2024 the trustees had the following transactions:

(i) On 16 December 2023 contracted to purchase £69,780 nominal of 7% Treasury Stock for settlement on 17 December 2023. The interest payment dates of this stock are 22 May and 22 November.

(ii) On 5 May 2023 contracted to sell £2,059 nominal National Midland 9% Unsecured Loan Stock for settlement on 6 May 2023. The interest payment dates of this stock are 30 June and 31 December.

During the year to 5 April 2024 the trustees received the following income (no expenses being incurred):

	£
Building society interest received	500
Gross income from securities	5,000

Mrs Spencer's only other income for 2023/24 comes from state and occupational pensions totalling £24,820 gross less tax deducted of £2,300.

(a) Compute the accrued income profits or losses on the will trust and state how they will be dealt with.

(b) Compute the income tax payable by or repayable to Mrs Spencer for 2023/24.

B.

Outline the tax position for trusts in relation to:

(a) Scrip dividends.

(b) Demergers.

Answer

A. Mrs Spencer – accrued income scheme

(a) *Accrued income profits or losses for will trust*

Purchase of Treasury Stock

This is a transfer of the Treasury Stock with accrued interest to the trustees and they acquire the right to receive the full amount of the interest payable on 22 May 2024. The accrued interest will be taxable on the seller at that time. The accrued interest is calculated as follows:

Interest accrued to date of settlement	23.11.23 to 17.12.23	=	25 days
Accrued (7% ×£69,780) $\times \frac{1}{2} =$ £2,442 $\times \frac{25}{181}$		=	£337

The trustees as purchasers treat this as an accrued income loss and are entitled to relief by deducting it from the interest they receive, as they are treated as paying it to the seller.

Sale of National Midland Stock

This is a transfer of the stock with accrued interest by the trustees and they will not be entitled to the interest payable on 30 June 2023. This accrued interest will be taxable on the trustees at that time however. The accrued interest is calculated as follows:

Interest accrued to date of settlement	1.1.23 to 6.5.23	=	127 days
Accrued (9% ×£2,059) $\times \frac{1}{2} =$ £93 $\times \frac{127}{182}$		=	£64

The trustees as sellers treat this as an accrued income profit and are liable to be charged on this amount when the buyer receives the next interest payment, as they are treated as receiving it from the buyer.

Taxation treatment

As already intimated, accrued income profits and losses are taken into account in the tax year in which the next interest payment date falls after the settlement date. Accrued income profits are taxed on the trustees at (in principle) the trust rate (see **explanatory note 1**) (ITA 2007 s 481 Type 2). Accrued income is not taxed on Mrs Spencer as life tenant because although it is taxed on the trustees as income it actually represents an accretion to trust capital. Accrued income losses are relieved by reducing the assessable interest received by the trustees. Profits and losses are not netted off unless they relate to the purchase and sale of the same security and its purchase and the sale both take place in the period between two interest payment dates.

The first receipt of interest on the 7% Treasury Stock will be in May 2024. From that interest, the accrued income loss of £337 will be deducted, the balance being taxable as trust income of 2024/25. If the stock is sold by the trustees before May 2024 then the accrued income loss will be deducted from the accrued income profit they would realise on its sale.

The next interest payment date on the National Midland Stock following its sale was June 2023; so the £64 is taxed in 2023/24 and in principle is liable to tax at the rate applicable to trusts of 45%. But since the trustees have no other trust rate income it counts as first slice income of the trustees and will in fact be charged at the basic rate by virtue of ITA 2007 s 491. Accordingly the liability will be £64 @ 20%.

As both stocks are exempt from capital gains tax (being qualifying gilt-edged securities and corporate bonds respectively – TCGA 1992 s 115) no related adjustments for that tax are required.

(b) *Income tax payable by or repayable to Mrs Spencer for 2023/24*

				Tax paid
			£	£
Pension income			24,820	2,300
Will trust (savings income):				
Securities		5,000		
Building society interest		500	5,500	
Total income			30,320	2,300
Less: Personal allowance			(12,570)	
			17,750	
Tax thereon:	12,250 @ 20% basic rate	2,450		
	1,000 @ 0% savings nil rate	0		
	4,500 @ 20% basic rate	900		3,350
Tax payable				1,050

B.

(a) *Scrip dividends*

Where a UK resident company offers scrip shares as an alternative to a cash dividend, certain shareholders taking the scrip option are treated as having stock dividend income equal to the cash equivalent on the share capital issued (ITTOIA 2005 s 411). This means the amount of the cash dividend they would otherwise have received (s 412(1). However, if that amount differs by more than 15% from the market value of the shares issued, the deemed income is the market value of those shares on the first day of dealing (ss 412(2), (3), (4)). For scrip dividends received before 6 April 2016 the notional income is deemed to be net of the dividend ordinary rate of tax of 10% and is grossed up accordingly (s 411(2)). The grossing addition represents a notional tax credit, which is not repayable to non-taxpayers. Following the abolition of tax credits by FA 2016 Sch 1 para 1, for scrip dividends received after 5 April 2016 the notional income is the amount of taxable income.

This treatment applies where an *individual* is beneficially entitled to the *shares*, or where the shares are received by personal representatives or by trustees for whom a cash dividend would be liable at the 'dividend trust rate' under ITA 2007 s 479.

Where the shares give rise to deemed income in this way, the cash equivalent of the share capital issued, (before grossing up in cases before 2016/17), is treated as the capital gains cost of the scrip shares. Such scrip dividend shares are treated as a separate free-standing acquisition and not as part of the existing share capital under the reorganisation rules (TCGA 1992 s 142); but this does not prevent them from being added to the pool of such shares under TCGA 1992 s 104 if forming part of the trust capital.

(i) Life interest trusts

As far as life interest trusts are concerned, the trustees must decide whether, in the light of trust and general law and the terms of the particular trust deed, the shares are received as capital or income.

HMRC's Statement of Practice (SP 4/94) gives their view of the position. They will not seek to challenge the view taken by the trustees (provided the facts support that view) if they have treated the scrip shares either as belonging to the life tenant, or as belonging to trust capital, or as being part of trust capital, but with the life tenant being compensated for the loss of the cash dividend he would have had.

If life tenant is treated as beneficially entitled to the shares

If the life tenant is treated as beneficially entitled to the shares, the trustees would be regarded as holding the shares as bare trustees (except in Scotland, where different rules apply). Any transfer to the beneficiary would therefore be disregarded. For income tax purposes the life tenant would have notional income equal to the cash equivalent of the share capital issued. For capital gains tax, the shares would not form part of the trust holding and the life tenant would be regarded as having purchased the shares separately for that cash equivalent. Any sale of the scrip shares by the trustees would be regarded as a sale by the life tenant, so if the shares were sold at the time of issue under the terms of a cash offer from a broker, same day identification rule (s 105) would apply and there would in fact be an allowable loss because the amount paid by the broker would be less than the issue price of the shares.

If shares are treated as belonging to trust capital

If the trustees treat the shares as belonging to trust capital, there are no income tax implications and the shares are treated as normal scrip shares for capital gains tax and added to the trust's existing holding at a *nil cost*. The trust's position when the shares are disposed of will depend on whether they have exemptions etc available to cover the potential gain. The tax liability (at present tax rates) could be nil or 20% (28% before 2016/17).

If shares are treated as belonging to trust capital with cash payment to life tenant

If the trustees treat the shares as capital but make a cash payment to the life tenant to compensate him for not getting the dividend, the treatment of the shares in the trustees' hands is the same as in the previous paragraph. The cash payment to the life tenant is not, however, an income dividend but a payment out of trust capital, so that income tax must be deducted at source at 20%. There may still be a problem with how much cash to pay, because if the life tenant is a basic rate taxpayer, the tax rate on actual dividends is only 8.75% (7.5% before 2022/23). The trustees must account for the tax on the payment under ITA 2007 s 963 (see **Example F3 part B**), and will show the payment separately on the form R185 (Trust Income) issued to the life tenant who will be taxed on the amount received as an annual payment under ITTOIA 2005 s 683.

If shares are treated as belonging to capital and immediately sold

The shares acquired pursuant to the scrip dividend, form part of the trustees' TCGA 1992 s 104 holding. (FA 2008 s 8 and Sch 2 simplified the rules for pooling of shares.)

The changes mean that in identifying securities disposed of after 5 April 2008, all identical securities owned by the trustees in their capacity as trustees of the particular trust are treated as part of a single pool (a *section 104 holding*), and the allowable expenditure in respect of that holding will be the sum of:

- the market value at 31 March 1982 of all securities in the section 104 holding that were held at that date; and
- the actual cost or CGT acquisition value of all securities in the section 104 holding acquired from April 1982 onwards. (In the case of scrip shares they are acquired at nil cost as above, so no addition will be made to the base cost of the section 104 holding.)

(ii) Discretionary and accumulation trusts

The treatment of scrip dividends received by discretionary and accumulation trusts is not clear. As indicated in the second paragraph of this section, such trusts are treated as receiving notional income if a cash dividend would have been income to which ITA 2007 s 479 applies, the notional income being regarded as accompanied by a notional tax credit at 10% of the tax credit inclusive amount if arising before 2016/17 (ITTOIA 2005 ss 409–414). If, however, the scrip dividend is required under the terms of the trust to be treated as trust capital, there is an argument that it cannot be charged to the dividend trust rate under ITA 2007 s 479 (but that even so, since the scrip shares are within ITTOIA 2005 ss 409–414, they would be treated as a free-standing acquisition for capital gains tax with a base cost equal to the cash equivalent of the shares issued). HMRC do not share this view (so that before 2016/17, HMRC consider that the trustees are liable to tax at the excess of the dividend trust rate of 37.5% over the dividend ordinary rate, on the amount of the scrip dividend, so that a further 27.5% tax is payable). Only the tax actually paid is taken into account when calculating how much tax is payable by the trustees under ITA 2007 ss 496–498 (the tax pool rules) on distributions to beneficiaries (see **Examples F1** and **F7** for further details). The shares have a base cost for capital gains tax equal to the cash equivalent of the shares issued (on which income tax will have been paid), and are added to the section 104 holding in which the source shares are contained unless a disposal is matched with some other shares according to the rules of TCGA 1992 ss 105 and 106A (acquisitions on the same day and within the next 30 days).

In the case of *Howell v Trippier* (2004) (reported as *Red Discretionary Trustees v HMIT* at Special Commissioners level), a discretionary trust received a stock dividend. The trustees elected to receive dividends consisting of further shares in the relevant company. The market value of the stock dividends represented taxable income – the trust return was submitted on the basis that the stock dividend was taxable at the dividend ordinary rate but the Inland Revenue (as HMRC was then known) amended the return to increase income tax payable to the dividend trust rate. The Court of Appeal dismissed the trustees' appeal and confirmed that the dividends were taxable at the dividend trust rate. It was held that in respect of scrip dividends the effect of (what is now) ITTOIA 2005 s 410 is to give rise to notional or fictional trust income (notwithstanding the terms of the settlement) for the purposes of (what is now) ITA 2007 s 479 in the hands of the trustees so that the fictional trust income is subjected to the dividend trust rate of income tax. However, the deeming effect of ITTOIA 20015 s 410 is limited to income tax; scrip dividends are not deemed to be income for general trust purposes or for the purposes of taxes other than income tax (*Gilchrist (as trustee of the JP Gilchrist 1993 Settlement v HMRC* (2015) followed in *Seddon v HMRC* [2015] FTT 539).

(b) *Demergers*

Demergers treated as exempt distributions

There is specific legislation in relation to demergers in CTA 2010 Part 23 Ch 5 (ss 1073–1099). The legislation prevents some of the tax problems that a demerger would otherwise cause. Provided the relevant conditions are satisfied, a demerger may be classed as an 'exempt distribution', and in that event the distribution is not treated as income in the hands of the shareholders. For capital gains tax it is treated either as a reorganisation under TCGA 1992 ss 126–131 (by s 192) or a reconstruction under TCGA 1992 ss 136 and 139, depending on the type of demerger, and there is therefore neither chargeable gain nor allowable loss.

Demerger distributions treated as capital

Demergers may either be direct demergers, where a company distributes shares in one or more 75% subsidiaries direct to its shareholders, or indirect demergers, where a company transfers either a trade or shares in its 75% subsidiaries to another company and that other company makes an issue of shares to the transferor company's shareholders.

In the past, case law (*Bouch v Sproule* (1887) and *Sinclair v Lee (1998)*) developed a distinction between the two types of demerger for the purposes of deciding whether a distribution should be treated as capital or income. The general practice was that a distribution of shares in a direct demerger was a receipt of income, whereas in an indirect demerger, the shares would be an addition to capital.

On 31 January 2013, the Trusts (Capital and Income) Act 2013 (TCIA 2013) (which does not extend to Scotland) received the Royal Assent. Under TCIA 2013 s 2 (which takes effect on 1 October 2013 (Trusts (Capital and Income) Act 2013 (Commencement No 1) Order 2013, SI 2013/676) tax-exempt corporate distributions arising from a demerger are treated as capital of a trust in all cases (unless the provisions of the trust provide otherwise). This rule applies to all trusts whether created or arising before or after 1 October 2013 (s 2(6)). TCIA 2013 s 3 gives the trustees an express power to compensate an income beneficiary out of capital if satisfied that, but for the distribution, there would have been a receipt from the company that would have been a receipt of income for the purposes of the trust. This power is not limited to beneficiaries with an interest in possession but may include discretionary beneficiaries for whom it is customary to receive a discretionary payment of income from the trust.

If a distribution of shares is used to compensate an income beneficiary for the income he would have otherwise received, it is nevertheless treated as a receipt of capital in his hands (TCIA 2013, s 3(2)) with the following tax consequences:

Discretionary trusts

The trustees are not liable to income tax or capital gains tax on demerger distributions. They acquire the shares at their market value at the time of the distribution (TCGA 1992 s 17(1)(a)) and are added to the trustees' s 104 holding. If shares are then distributed to beneficiaries, the distribution is treated for capital gains tax as a disposal of a proportionate part of the holding at market value, the cost for that part of the holding being allowed against the deemed proceeds.

Life interest trusts

The following relates to the treatment of English life interest trusts. (Different rules apply in Scotland.)

The shares belong to the life tenant directly, so they do not form part of the trust's holding, the capital gains tax cost of which is unaffected. The life tenant is treated for capital gains tax purposes as acquiring the shares at market value at the date of the demerger (the distribution being by way of distribution from an company and so other than at arm's length – TCGA 1992 s 17(1)(a)), even though there would have been no reduction of the trustees' allowable cost. (If the trustees retained the shares, there would be a disposal of them by the life tenant to the trustees, and unless he was paid their cash value, he would be the settlor of the shares into the trust.)

Explanatory Notes

Accrued income scheme for trusts

(1) The accrued income scheme provisions are in ITA 2007 Pt 12 (ss 616–681).

The accrued income scheme causes particular difficulties in relation to trusts. The scheme treats amounts that are capital sums under the general (and trust) law as being income for tax purposes and tax is charged (or refunded) accordingly.

The fact that the sums are to be accumulated as part of capital, rather than being income of a beneficiary, is, however, recognised by ITA 2007 s 482, which provides that the trustees are taxed in respect of accrued income profits as Type 2 income at the rate applicable to trusts, ie 45%. However ITA 2007 s 491 provides that such deemed income is chargeable at, in effect, the basic rate if it counts as first slice income. Mrs Spencer's trust is only liable to tax at the trust tax rates on accrued income of £64; as this is less than £200 it is certain that the whole will be chargeable at the basic rate (ie 20%). (Even if Mr Spencer had made many other trusts that were still current, so that the full amount of first slice income of £1,000 fell to be shared between them, it cannot be reduced below £200 for each trust, see ITA 2007 s 492 and **Example F6 explanatory note 1**.)

These rules can lead to an anomaly. The trustees could receive relief at the basic rate for accrued income losses (which is set against the interest they receive) but be liable at the trust rate on an amount of accrued income profit which is in excess of their first slice income and have to pay tax at 45% on the excess.

Because the accrued income profits represent capital sums, they do not form part of a beneficiary's income and are not shown on form R185 (Trust Income).

The trustees then have the problem of how to deal with accrued income profits and losses in the trust accounts. The Accounting Recommendations of the Institute of Chartered Accountants state that where a life tenant may be interested in such accruals, consideration should be given to accounting for the interest and the associated tax on an accruals basis when the securities are purchased and sold. The alternative view, which the authors prefer, is that the accruals treatment should not apply to accrued income profits, and that the tax on accrued income profits should be debited to the capital account of the trust in the year of the liability, as it would have been if it had been capital gains tax. This is also the view of the author of the Society of Trust and Estate Practitioners' (STEP's) Accounting Guidelines, see Appendix 4 to that publication.

There is also doubt as to the treatment of relief for accrued income losses. The relief reduces the trustees' income for tax purposes as shown in **part A**(a) above, and the beneficiary's income for tax purposes is similarly reduced, so that in 2024/25 Mrs Spencer's interest from the 7% Treasury Stock shown on form R185 (Trust Income) will be the gross interest of (7% × £69,780 =) £4,885, reduced by £337, giving taxable income of £4,548. Tax thereon amounts to £910 compared with tax on £4,885 of £977. The reduction of £337 at 20% = £67 in the tax payable will have been reflected in the amount payable by the trustees under self-assessment. If tax had been deducted at source from the interest, the trustees would have a tax refund of £67. The question then is how much should the trustees actually pay to Mrs Spencer. HMRC have stated that this is a matter for the trustees in accordance with the general law, and whatever is paid will not affect the tax treatment. There are several possibilities:

(a) Taxable income £4,548 less tax £910 = £3,638.

(b) Actual gross income £4,885 less tax thereon £977 = £3,908.

(c) As (b) plus tax reduction of £67 = £3,975.

The trustees have actually received net income of £3,908 and have had a tax reduction of £67, and some people therefore favour paying the beneficiary £3,975 as in (c). Before the introduction of the accrued income scheme, however, the part of the purchase price representing accrued interest, ie £337, would have been part of the capital cost of the security. The authors take the view that the logical approach is to regard that treatment as unchanged for trust accounting purposes, and to treat the £67 as a reduction in the cost and to pay to the beneficiary what would previously have been paid, ie £3,908. Thus both accrued income profits and accrued income losses would be dealt with through the trust capital account. This again appears to be the approach followed in the STEP Accounting Guidelines.

Scope of accrued income provisions

(2) The accrued income provisions apply to 'transfers'. This means 'transfer by way of sale, exchange, gift or otherwise' (ITA 2007 s 620(1)(2)), and would include a settlement of securities by an individual, and a transfer of securities to beneficiaries on termination of a trust, as well as the trustees buying and selling the trust securities. The provisions do not apply where securities become vested in an individual's personal representatives on his death (ITA 2007 s 620(1)(2)). Nor do they apply if the personal representatives transfer the securities to a legatee or other person entitled on an intestacy in the interest period in which the individual died (ITA 2007 s 636) (but the exemption for unrealised interest received after a transfer under ITA 2007 s 681 may still be available to the legatee, because s 636(2) does not go so far as to deem a transfer not to have been made, merely to prevent deemed payments from having taken place). There is no exemption for a transfer in a later interest period.

Scrip dividends and demergers for trusts

(3) The problems of trustees who receive scrip dividends or shares on a demerger are outlined in **part B** of the Example. HMRC have given detailed comments on their views, but there are many grey areas which it would be difficult to resolve, even with amended legislation, because of the mismatch between trust law and tax law.

As far as scrip dividends are concerned, where the shares are worth the same as the cash dividend, the simple way to avoid problems is to take the cash. The enhanced scrip dividends which were offered by listed companies a few years ago were worth half as much again as the cash dividend, and there was the option of obtaining the extra cash by selling immediately, thus giving rise to the particular problems mentioned in the Example. Such offers have not been made recently, although enhanced scrip offers may arise in other circumstances.

Purchase by company of own shares etc for trusts

(4) Where a company redeems, repays or purchases its own shares from the trustees of a settlement, the excess of the amount paid over the original issue price is treated as if it were an income distribution, and the trustees are liable to tax at the dividend trust rate of 39.35% (38.1% in 2021/22) (ITA 2007 ss 481–482). This does not apply where the trust income is treated as belonging to the settlor, or where the trust is a unit trust, charitable trust, or pension trust (or presumably where the trust is a bare trust – see **Example C15 explanatory note 8**), but it applies to all other trusts, including interest in possession trusts.

If the purchase is by an unquoted trading company in order to benefit its trade, and specified conditions are satisfied, the purchase is treated as a chargeable disposal for capital gains tax rather than as an income distribution (CTA 2010 ss 1033–1048).

Cross references

(5) See **Example F3 explanatory note 4** for the provisions that apply for receiving interest gross on government stocks, **Example F2 explanatory note 7** for the provisions that apply for receiving interest gross on listed company securities and **Example F6** for the self-assessment provisions in relation to trusts.

Question

You were contacted in May 2023 by the trustees of the Green grandchildren's trust, a trust with UK based trustees and so resident in the UK.

The following details are known:

(1) The trust's main asset is a 27% holding of ordinary shares in Green plc, an unquoted UK trading company. The shareholding was acquired by gift in January 1994 from the settlor. The shares were worth £850,000 at that time and a gain of £650,000 was held over. The settlor had acquired the shares in 1974. This shareholding is now worth about £2 million. It is anticipated that the company may be floated on the London Stock Exchange in the next year or so, in which case the shares could increase in value to over £5 million.

(2) The trust's main source of income is dividends from its shareholding in Green plc. Normally about half the dividend is distributed to the beneficiaries.

(3) The trust was created as an accumulation and maintenance trust which provides for a grandchild of the settlor to receive a life interest at age 25 with capital distributions subject to trustees' discretion. No alteration was made to the trust before 6 April 2008.

(4) There are currently eight grandchildren with age ranges 23 to 45. It is unlikely that any further beneficiaries will come into existence, and the trustees have established eight accounts (with equal numbers of shares) within the trust for administration purposes. Only two of the beneficiaries work for Green plc. The trustees are under pressure to wind up the trust and distribute to the beneficiaries. The trustees have already resolved in principle to distribute fully all retained income within the trust.

(5) The trust had a brought forward tax credit pool for ICTA 1988 s 687 (now ITA 2007 s 497) purposes of £650,000 at 6 April 1999, being mainly tax at the trust rate on dividends.

One of the trustees died recently, and the proposed replacement trustee, who has seen a taxation memorandum placed with the trust deeds by the settlor at the outset, has requested a meeting with the trustees' advisers to review the position generally and to understand how the various changes in income tax, capital gains tax and inheritance tax have affected the trust, and in particular the question whether to retain income and/or capital in the fund or distribute.

Draft technical notes for the meeting with the trustees.

Answer

Technical notes for meeting with trustees of the Green grandchildren's trust

When income is relevant to a grandchild's tax position

(1) Each grandchild, upon reaching the age of 25, has had a life interest in his share of the trust fund, which means that he is entitled to the relevant share of income whether it is distributed or not. Before reaching age 25, he is taxable only on income distributed to him or for his maintenance (the trustees having the power to accumulate income.) So each is currently subject to the usual tax treatment of an individual, including being entitled to the usual personal allowance – £12,570 for 2023/24.

This treatment of distributions applied even during the minority of a grandchild, because the trust was made by the beneficiaries' grandparent; had the trust been made by a parent of the beneficiaries, distributions for the benefit of a beneficiary under age 18 (and unmarried) would have been treated as income of the parent-settlor, not of the beneficiary, up to the amount of income received by the trustees.

When tracing the tax changes over the life of the trust, the starting point is to consider the income – here dividends – in the hands of the trustees to whom it arises, and only then see the effect of this on the beneficiary's position so far as he is liable to tax.

Tax treatment of dividends before 6 April 1999

(2) Before 6 April 1999 dividends carried a repayable tax credit of 25% of the cash dividend (20% of the tax credit inclusive amount), so that a cash dividend of £80 represented a dividend of £100 with a credit of £20, which was repayable to a non-taxpayer. Trust expenses were deducted from net trust income to give the amount available for distribution to beneficiaries.

Beyond that the trustees had no liability on dividends arising from the share of a grandchild with a life interest had there been one (ie a grandchild over 25) because the income would have been his whether distributed or not (see **point 1** above). If the grandchild's personal allowance covered his income, he could have therefore claimed repayment of the dividend credit. If the grandchild was a basic rate taxpayer no further tax was payable. A higher rate taxpayer had to pay a further 20% of the tax credit inclusive amount (25% of the cash dividend).

Where the dividend income was subject to accumulation, or was payable only at the trustees' discretion, it was taxable at the 34% rate applicable to trusts (as it was then known). Any amounts of income distributed to or for the benefit of a grandchild were treated as net amounts from which tax at 34% had been deducted. Grandchildren not liable to tax would recover the whole of the 34% tax, basic rate taxpayers would recover the difference and higher rate taxpayers would pay an extra 6%.

Tax treatment of dividends from 6 April 1999 to 5 April 2004

(3) From 6 April 1999 dividend credits were reduced to 1/9th of the cash amount (10% of the tax credit inclusive figure) – this rule applied up to and including 5 April 2016 when it was abolished (FA 2016 Sch 1 para 1). Trust expenses are deducted from dividend income in priority to other sources of trust income. The dividend tax credits were not repayable. Thus a dividend of £80 carried a non-repayable credit of £8.89.

Grandchildren with a life interest (the first 25th birthday appears to have been in 2003 or thereabouts) were accordingly no longer able to recover the tax credits even if the total was within their personal allowance. Those liable at the basic rate still had no further tax to pay and those with income above the basic rate threshold were liable at the excess of the Sch F (later dividend) upper rate of 32.5% – or 22.5% over the tax credit rate of 10%. Their net position at the end of the day was broadly unchanged by this new system from what it had been before 6 April 1999.

(4) As far as dividends subject to accumulation (or distributable at discretion) were concerned, they became chargeable from 6 April 1999 at a special Sch F (later dividend) trust rate of 25%. The trustees, similarly, were left with broadly the same net of tax income as previously prior to any distributions, ie:

	Pre-6 April 1999	*6 April 1999 to 5 April 2004*
	£	£
Dividend received	80.00	80.00
Tax credit	20.00	8.89
Trust income	100.00	88.89
Less: tax at 37.5%/38.1%/39.35%	(34.00)	(22.22)
Net of tax income	66.00	66.67

However, the fact that the dividend tax credit became non-repayable had an impact on the amount that could be distributed to beneficiaries without leaving the trustees with an additional liability – see **point 6** below – a problem which was only magnified by subsequent increases in the dividend trust rate (see **point 5** below).

Tax treatment of dividends from 6 April 2004 to 5 April 2016

(5) From 6 April 2004 the dividend trust rate for income subject to accumulation or to discretionary distribution was increased from 25% to 32.5%; from 6 April 2010 this was further increased to 42.5%; from 6 April 2013 to 5 April 2016 it was reduced to 37.5%. However, in 2005/06 the concept of a trust's first slice income was introduced in relation to the first £500 of trust income (rising to £1,000 from 2006/07) which would otherwise be chargeable to tax at the trust rate or the dividend trust rate trusts. Such income is instead chargeable to income tax at the basic rate or the dividend ordinary rate, depending on the nature of the income. Therefore, the first £500 or £1,000 of income held on discretionary or accumulation trusts will be charged at these rates.

	Pre-6 April 2004 as above	*2004/05 to 2009/10 inclusive*	*2010/11 to 2012/13 inclusive*	*2013/2014 to 2015/16 inclusive*
	£	£	£	£
Dividend received	80.00	80.00	80.00	80.00
Tax credit	8.89	8.89	8.89	8.89
Trust income	88.89	88.89	88.89	88.89
Less: tax at 25%/32.5%/42.5%/37.5%	(22.22)	(28.89)	(37.78)	(33.33)
Net of tax income	66.67	60.00	51.11	55.56

Grandchildren with a life interest continued to receive dividends with a non-repayable tax credit of 10% and, if higher rate taxpayers, to be liable to the dividend upper rate of 32.5% (less tax credit of 10%). This remained the case from 6 April 2010 to 5 April 2013 except that if their total income was in excess of £150,000 so that they became additional rate taxpayers, the dividend additional rate of 42.5% applied above that threshold (dividends being the top slice of income). From 6 April 2013 to 5 April 2016, the dividend additional rate was reduced to 37.5% (FA 2012 s 1(3), (6)).

Effect on income available for distribution until 5 April 2016

(6) Distributions out of the trust to grandchildren under 25 were for 2013/14 until 2015/16 made net of 45% tax (34% from 1999/2000 to 2003/04 inclusive, 40% from 2004/05 to 2009/10 inclusive, 50% for 2010/11 to 2012/13 inclusive), and taxed as income of the grandchildren as previously. Since 6 April 1999, however, the trustees could not treat dividend credits as tax already paid in calculating how much of the tax on a distribution had already been accounted for, since they could only include as a credit in the tax pool the excess

of tax at the dividend trust rate over the 10% tax credit rate. Between 6 April 2003 and 5 April 2016 this would be 37.5% – 10% = 27.5%. The effect was that (before taking account of first slice income) the maximum distribution out of dividend income was 55% of the tax credit *exclusive* amount. The following table illustrates the position for all years from 1999/2000 to 2015/16:

	1999/2000 to 2003/04 inclusive	*2004/05 to 2009/10 inclusive*	*2010/11 to 2012/13 inclusive*	*2013/14 to 2015/16 inclusive*
	£	£	£	£
Tax credit exclusive dividend income (net of trust expenses), say	1,800	1,800	1,800	1,800
Tax credit (1/9)	200	200	200	200
Trust gross income	2,000	2,000	2,000	2,000
Less: tax on dividend income (25%/32.5%/42.5/37.5%)	(500)	(650)	(850)	(750)
Net income	1,500	1,350	1,150	1,250
Maximum gross payment to beneficiaries:				
Tax credit *exclusive* dividend	1,800	1,800	1,800	1,800
Less: tax thereon @ 34%/40%/50%/45%	(612)	(720)	(900)	(810)
Distributable amount	1,188	1,080	900	990
Tax to be paid by trustees:				
Tax on gross income	500	650	850	750
Less: covered by tax credits	(200)	(200)	(200)	(200)
Payable by trustees on income	300	450	650	550
Tax on distributions	(612)	(720)	(900)	(810)
Further tax due from trustees	312	270	250	260

Although the trustees received £1,800 as income it was not possible to distribute that amount because of the tax due on income. In fact it was not normally possible to distribute all of the net income because of the additional tax due from the trustees on distribution, except so far as that amount could be covered by amounts brought forward within the tax pool. The effect was increased further to the extent that the dividends fell within the trustees' £1,000 first slice income (see **explanatory note 1**): the 45% liability in 2015/16 on distributions would thus have incurred an additional £350 of tax on that £1,000, which would apart from that have suffered only the 10% dividend ordinary rate.

Because the non-repayable tax credit had already been taken into account in working out the tax payable by the trustees on distributions, the whole of the tax deducted from the distributions may have been repaid to non-taxpaying beneficiaries. Thus if the full amount distributable in the above Example had in fact been distributed to a beneficiary in whose hands it fell within his personal allowance, the amount he could recover would bring his total receipt back to the full £1,800 net dividend received by the trustees as follows:

	1999/2000 to 2003/04 inclusive	*2004/05 to 2009/10 inclusive*	*2010/11 to 2012/13 inclusive*	*2013/14 to 2015/16 inclusive*
	£	£	£	£
Maximum amount distributable, and distributed, by trustees as above	1,188	1,080	900	990
Tax on distribution as above, recoverable by beneficiary	612	720	900	810

	1999/2000 to 2003/04 inclusive	*2004/05 to 2009/10 inclu-sive*	*2010/11 to 2012/13 inclusive*	*2013/14 to 2015/16 inclusive*
	£	£	£	£
Gross income of beneficiary	1,800	1,800	1,800	1,800

Tax treatment of dividends from 6 April 2016

(7) With effect from 6 April 2016 tax credits have been abolished (FA 2016 Sch 1 para 1). In the period from 6 April 2016 to 5 April 2022 the dividend ordinary rate was reduced to 7.5% and the dividend trust rate is set at 38.1% (FA 2016 s 5(3)). From 6 April 2022 the dividend ordinary rate has been increased to 8.75% and the dividend trust rate to 39.35% (FA 2022 s 4). Since 6 April 2016, the tax paid by the trust on its dividend income, being the actual payment of a sum of money, may be treated as tax already paid in calculating how much of the tax on a distribution has already been accounted for. Otherwise the tax treatment of trusts has not altered from what it was immediately before 6 April 2016 (apart from changing the name of the basic rate to the default basic rate from 6 April 2017). The changes in the dividend rates means that trustees are left with slightly less net of tax income as previously prior to any distributions, ie:

	2015/16	*2016/17 to 2021/22 (inclusive)*	*2022/23 and later years*
	£	£	£
Dividend received	80.00	80.00	80.00
Tax credit	8.89	Nil	Nil
Trust income	88.89	80.00	80.00
Less: tax on dividend income (37.5%/38.1%/39.35%)	(33.33)	(30.48)	(31.48)
Net of tax income	55.56	49.52	48.52

It is still the case that accumulation and discretionary trusts that receive dividend income cannot distribute that income in full without leaving the trustees with an additional tax liability – albeit a lower liability in 2016/17 and later years as compared with 2015/16; although the tax actually paid by the trustees at the dividend trust rate is wholly credited to the trust pool, the rate of tax that has to be accounted for by them on a distribution (45%) is still higher than the tax they have paid on dividend income (38.1% or 39.35% as the case may be). The maximum distribution of dividend income is still 55% of the dividend received. The following table illustrates the comparative position for 2015/16, 2016/17 to 2021/22 (inclusive) and 2022/23 and later years:

	2015/16	*2016/17 to 2021/22 (inclusive)*	*2022/23 and later years*
	£	£	£
Actual dividend income (net of trust expenses), say	1,800	1,800	1,800
Tax credit (1/9)	200	Nil	Nil
Trust gross income	(2,000)	(1,800)	(1,800)
Less: tax on dividend income (37.5%/38.1%)	(750)	(686)	(708)
Net income	1,250	1,114	1,092
Maximum gross payment to beneficiaries:			
Actual dividend	1,800	1,800	1,800
Less: tax thereon @ 45%	(810)	(810)	(810)
Distributable amount	990	990	990

	2015/16	*2016/17 to 2021/22 (inclusive)*	*2022/23 and later years*
	£	£	£
Tax to be paid by trustees:			
Tax on income (inclusive of tax credit for 2015/16)	750	686	708
Less: covered by tax credits	(200)	(Nil)	(Nil)
Payable by trustees on income	550	686	708
Tax on distributions	(810)	(810)	(810)
Further tax due from trustees	260	124	102

Although the trustees received £1,800 as income it is not possible to distribute that amount because of the tax due on income. In fact it is still not normally possible to distribute all of the net income because of the additional tax due from the trustees on distribution, except so far as that amount could be covered by amounts brought forward within the tax pool.

The whole of the tax deducted from the distributions may be repaid to non-taxpaying beneficiaries. Thus if the full amount distributable in the above Example has in fact been distributed to a beneficiary in whose hands it falls within his personal allowance, the amount he can recover would bring his total receipt back to the full £1,800 dividend received by the trustees as follows:

	2015/16	*2016/17 and later years*
	£	£
Maximum amount distributable, and distributed, by trustees as above	990	990
Tax on distribution as above, recoverable by beneficiary	810	810
Gross income of beneficiary	1,800	1,800

Tax pool brought forward

(8) The provisions in **point 6** from 6 April 1999 onwards may not apply where there is a tax pool brought forward (£650,000 at 6 April 1999 in the case of the Green grandchildren's trust, although this will have been increased by tax paid at the dividend trust rate (formerly Sch F trust rate) on dividends received after that date as indicated in **point 6**). The whole of the brought forward figure, which largely represents dividend tax credits, was fully available to cover the tax on distributions to the beneficiaries. However, on the basis that roughly half of the dividends received each year has been distributed to beneficiaries, the pre-April 1999 tax pool will have been significantly absorbed by the additional tax chargeable on distributions compared to accumulated income. The precise position can only be ascertained from a detailed year by year review since then. However, to the extent that a balance does still remain in the tax pool, it can be used to cover the 'further tax due from the trustees' identified in **point** 7, thus allowing the distribution of a greater amount of current or accumulated income. If a balance still remains in the tax pool when the last grandchild attains age 25, it becomes blocked and can no longer be used.

Although making an income distribution would use some of the residual tax pool brought forward, the benefit would depend on the tax position of the beneficiaries, since if the distribution was chargeable in 2016/17 and later years to higher rate tax in the hands of the grandchild, only a modest amount of tax would be repayable to them (the trustees' 45% liability less the beneficiary's 40% liability) – or nil in the unlikely event that the grandchild already had income in excess of £150,000 so that the whole of the distribution was liable in his hands at the 45% additional rate.

To the extent that trust income has been definitely accumulated so as to form part of the trust capital, it can no longer (as a matter of trust law) be distributed as income; thus, any distribution would be under a power to distribute capital. Its tax treatment in the hands of the beneficiary depends on how it is categorised (whether as income or capital) in his hands (see **Example F6 explanatory note 10**). If it is categorised as capital, inheritance tax rather than income tax would apply to the trustees and no part of the income tax previously suffered could be recovered; nor, on the other hand, would any higher rate income tax be payable.

Capital gains if trust wound up

(9) The Green plc shareholding is currently worth around £2 million, and may increase to over £5 million if the company is floated on the Stock Exchange. Its base cost for capital gains tax in 1994 was £200,000 (850,000 less held-over gain of 650,000), so that there will be a substantial capital gain on disposal which will be taxed at a flat rate of 20% unless it is possible to attract business asset disposal relief (former known as entrepreneurs' relief) in respect of some part of the gain.

(10) For a disposal to qualify for business asset disposal relief in respect of shares or securities held by trustees, a qualifying beneficiary – ie one who has an interest in possession in the assets disposed of, otherwise than for a fixed period (so in the present case limited to grandchildren over age 25) – must have been an officer or employee of the company throughout a period of two years (one year for disposals before 6 April 2019) ending not more than three years before the disposal and the company must have been both a trading company (or the holding company of a trading group) and the beneficiary's 'personal company' (with at least 5% of the ordinary share capital, of the voting rights, and (for disposals after 28 October 2018) with at least 5% of distributable profits and assets on a winding or with at least 5% of the proceeds on disposal) for a corresponding period (TCGA 1992 s 169J). The voting rights do not actually need to be exercised, but they must be capable of being exercised *(Hepworth (Inspect of taxes) v Smith* 45 TC 369).

In the case of the Green grandchildren's settlement, only two of the beneficiaries work for the company, and even if both of them have life interests their respective funds comprise less than 3.4% of the issued shares. Even if their respective funds were of more than 5%, however, life interest shares do not count towards making the company a beneficiary's personal company in any case; so unless one or other of those beneficiaries holds 5% of the company in his own right no business asset disposal relief will be available on a disposal of any part of the trustees' shareholding (TCGA 1992 s 169S(3)). On that basis the whole of the trustees' gain, on the deemed disposal that would result from a terminating the trust in respect of any of the shares, will be taxed at the 20% rate.

(11) As explained in **point 12** below, any distribution of capital, except in the case of the grandchild(ren) who had already attained age 25 by 22 March 2006, would now incur an inheritance tax charge (even if this is at 0% on the figures eg as a result of business property relief), subject to one exception not relevant until early 2023 (see below). Holdover relief under TCGA 1992 s 260 could therefore be claimed in respect of the trustees' gains on those younger grandchildren's shares of the trust, so that the beneficiaries' acquisition costs would be reduced accordingly, provided the grandchildren are UK resident. As regards the proportion held for the benefit of any grandchild(ren) who were already 25 by 22 March 2006 (see **point 12(a)** below), holdover relief could similarly be claimed under TCGA 1992, s 165 and Sch 7 (Relief for gifts of business assets) provided the shares remained unquoted, or the trustees retained 25% or more of the voting rights; for this purpose the whole holding of the trustees can be counted, not merely the part in which life interests had vested before 22 March 2006.

Inheritance tax rules for Accumulation and Maintenance Settlements post-FA 2006

(12) The inheritance tax treatment of the Green grandchildren's trust varies as between the shares of any grandchild(ren) who had already attained age 25 by 22 March 2006, and the remainder.

(a) Any grandchild whose life interest had already vested (at age 25) by that date has a qualifying interest in possession which results in the relevant portion of the trust fund being treated for inheritance tax as if he was the absolute owner of it. To this extent, the winding up of the trust – resulting in the grandchild(ren) concerned becoming absolutely entitled to the fund in which they currently have an interest in possession – would entail no inheritance tax charge.

(b) As regards the remaining shares the trust was still within the privileged rules for A&M settlements at 22 March 2006, when the inheritance tax rules for trusts were substantially altered. Interests in possession arising (on 25th birthdays) on or after that date are not qualifying interests in possession – neither the underlying capital nor the interest in possession itself counts as part of the beneficiary's estate for inheritance tax purposes – except to the extent (most unlikely in the circumstances) that the beneficiary in question met the definition in IHTA 1984 s 89 of a disabled person – not at the date his interest in possession arose, but at the date the shares were originally put into trust. Instead, the relevant share of the fund is within the relevant property regime from the date the interest in possession arose, or from 6 April 2008 if the interest in possession arose after that date (see (c) below).

(c) However, a further feature of the 2006 changes was that A&M settlements in existence before 22 March 2006 lost their privileged status as such (to the extent that it had not already ceased on interests in possession arising) at the end of a transitional period on 6 April 2008.

(i) To the extent that the trust provided by then for beneficiaries to become absolutely entitled to capital at age 25 instead of merely receiving life interests at that age, the trust became an age 18-to-25 trust within IHTA 1984 s 71D, with a more beneficial charging regime than that applicable under the relevant property regime (though in principle a charge, at a more lenient rate, would still be incurred when the beneficiary became absolutely entitled at 25). This was not the case in relation to the Green grandchildren's trust.

(ii) Apart from that the trust became subject to the relevant property regime from 6 April 2008, to the extent that it had not already entered that regime when beneficiaries became entitled to interests in possession on or after 22 March 2006.

To the extent that the relevant property regime applies by virtue of **(b)** or **(c)** above, the settlement is now subject to the exit and ten-yearly charges regime. The cycle of ten-year anniversaries will be based on the date the trust was established in January 1994 rather than the date the trust property became 'relevant property' in April 2008 (or earlier 25th birthdays since 22 March 2006); a ten-yearly charge will thus have arisen in January 2014 in relation to that portion of the trust fund in which the grandchildren's life interests had not vested before 22 March 2006, though the rate of tax on such charge will not have been that large since at least 17 quarter-years since the preceding ten-year anniversary (January 2004) had been completed before the property in question entered the relevant property regime.

An exit charge is not imposed in the three months following a ten-year anniversary (the next of which will not occur until January 2024); through a quirk of the legislation, this will prevent a claim for capital gains tax holdover relief under TCGA 1992 s 260 in respect of distributions made in that three-month period, though relief under TCGA 1992 s 165 and Sch 7 would still be available if the relevant conditions were satisfied at that time (see **point 11** above).

Explanatory Notes

Treatment of dividend income in discretionary trusts

(1) The basic income tax treatment of discretionary trusts is that in respect of income which the trustees have the power to accumulate, or which may be distributed at their discretion, the trustees are liable to tax under ITA 2007 ss 479–481 at the dividend trust rate of 39.35% (38.1% in 2021/22) on dividend income and at the 'trust rate' of 45% on other income. The tax suffered by the trustees forms a tax pool (ITA 2007 ss 493–498), which while it lasts is available to cover the tax on any distributions to the beneficiaries. Since 6 April 1999 not all of the tax charged to the trustees on grossed-up dividends goes into the tax pool, hence the reduced level of possible distribution as indicated in the Example; although the calculation is differently expressed in the legislation, the blocked amount was until 5 April 2016 10% of the grossed-up amount of the dividend, equating to the non-repayable tax credit on the dividend. From 6 April 2016 none of the tax paid on dividend income is blocked and will therefore be credited to the tax pool.

Under ITA 2007 s 491, however, the first £1,000 of income (or less if there is more than one trust current with the same settlor), known as first slice income, is not charged at the trust tax rates, but will instead be charged at the basic rate (default basic rate from 2017/18) or dividend ordinary rate (according to the type of income that comprises the first slice). Therefore, if prior to 6 April 2016 payments were received net of tax (for example, building society interest) and the gross amount did not exceed £1,000, then the trustees would have had no further tax to pay. This is no longer the case since basic rate tax at source is no longer deducted at source from building society and bank accounts (FA 2016 s 39, Sch 6) and the notional tax credit on dividends has been abolished (FA 2016 Sch 1 para 1).

The £1,000 amount set out in ITA 2007 s 491 applies to trust income *net* of trust management expenses (s 484(3)) and other Step 2 deductions from income if there are any.

Although the management expenses are matched with the trust income taxed at the lowest rate first, the income of the trust which is treated as first slice income is regarded as comprising income taxed at the default basic rate of 20% first, followed by dividends at 8.75%.

See **Examples F1**, **F6** and **F7** for the details of this provision including the basis for reducing the £1,000 amount if the settlor has more than one trust still current. The rules on first slice income have applied since 6 April 2005, though its level in 2005/06 was £500 (without reduction provisions). As explained in **Examples F1** the first slice income rule will be abolished with effect from 6 April 2024.

(2) In this Example, once a grandchild reaches age 25 and becomes entitled to a life interest in the trust, his share of the trust income is taxable on him, whether it is received or retained within the trust. If there is unutilised tax within the tax pool under ITA 2007 s 497 when the last grandchild reaches age 25, the unused amount will be wasted, although this would not be a disadvantage to the extent that capital distributions were then made to grandchildren who would be liable to higher rate tax on income distributions. The inheritance tax charge on capital distributions would be at a relatively modest rate even if the shares held by the trustees were by then quoted shares, but would still represent an incentive to have utilised the tax pool in full in distributions to grandchildren who were not higher-rate taxpayers before it became unavailable.

Capital gains tax holdover relief and business asset disposal relief

(3) There are two holdover reliefs available for capital gains tax, the business assets holdover relief of TCGA 1992 s 165 (see **Example D2 part a(d)** for the definition of business assets for this purpose) and the holdover relief of TCGA 1992 s 260 for gifts on which inheritance tax is chargeable – which includes a charge which works out at £0, but not an occasion where an exit charge is prevented by IHTA 1984, s 65(4) relating to distributions within three months after a ten-year anniversary (see **Example C1 explanatory note 3**). No inheritance tax charge arises if the beneficiary who becomes absolutely entitled had a qualifying interest in possession immediately beforehand – which would be the case for those beneficiaries who had reached age 25 before 22 March 2006; but so long as the shares remain unquoted, or the trustees retain 25% of the voting rights, the Green plc shares will be business assets for TCGA 1992 s 165 and attract hold-over relief under that provision instead.

(4) Business asset disposal relief for trustees is examined more fully in **Example D3**.

Wills

Question

Harry and Katie have lived together for over thirty years but despite Harry's many proposals, they had not married. Their only child, Chester, was born on 1 March 2006.

Accepting that he and Katie would probably not marry and prompted by the recent unexpected death of a work colleague, Harry decided he ought to make a Will. He wrote out the terms, which provided for his entire estate to pass to Katie, on a single sheet of notepaper and signed it 'Pops', which was the family name by which both Katie and Chester referred to him, before asking Chester to sign the Will as witness. Harry then phoned his neighbour, Marcy, and asked her to come over and sign the Will as the second witness. When she arrived Chester, with Harry still present, showed her the Will and pointed to his signature stating '*I have already done my bit*'. Harry confirmed that it was his Will and asked Marcy to sign it which she did using the pen Chester passed to her. The Will was dated January 2022.

Following a health scare which caused her to reappraise her position, Katie agreed to formalise their relationship and they married in July 2022. At the wedding reception, Harry produced the Will which he had carried with him in his wallet since its signing in January 2022 and altered it to make a cash gift to Chester writing at the bottom of the page '*At last Katie is Harry's wife*'. This was witnessed by two wedding guests who, at Harry's request, added their signatures to the Will.

Harry died in car crash in August 2023 leaving an estate of £2 million.

You are required to advise Katie and Chester of the validity of the Will and whether they are entitled to benefit under it.

Answer

(1) The validity of a Will is governed by the Wills Act 1837, s 9 which requires that each of the following conditions must be satisfied in relation to the making of a Will:

(a) It must be made in writing and signed by the Testator or by some other person in his presence and by his direction; and

(b) It must appear that the testator intended by his signature to give effect to the Will; and

(c) The signature must be made or acknowledged by the testator in the presence of two or more witnesses present at the same time; and

(d) Each witness must either –

(i) Attest and sign the will; or

(ii) Acknowledge his signature,

in the presence of the testator (but not necessarily in the presence of any other witness) but no form of attestation shall be necessary.

(2) The above conditions must each be considered in relation to Harry's Will and only if all are satisfied will the Will be regarded as valid:

Condition (a)

The Will was in writing – the informal nature of the document (being a piece of notepaper) is irrelevant. This requirement is satisfied.

Condition (b)

Prima facie this requirement would appear not to be satisfied as the Will was not signed formally by Harry using his legal name but rather by using his family name of 'Pops'. However, the Courts give a wide interpretation to this requirement and consider it satisfied if the 'mark' applied was so intended to signal the testator's approval (*Re Cook* (1960)).

Both Katie and Chester referred to and identified with Harry as 'Pops' and so provided the use of the term was indeed intended to represent Harry's signature, it will be accepted as such.

The facts here indicate that Harry intended his signature as 'Pops' to give effect to the Will and so the requirement is satisfied.

Condition (c)

By showing the Will to Chester, Harry is deemed to have acknowledged his signature. The witnesses must be mentally able and physically present during acknowledgement and they must see or have had the opportunity of seeing the testator's signature (*Daintree v Butcher* (1888)). Initially the acknowledgement was invalid as it was carried out in front of only one witness (Chester). However, Harry did state in front of both Chester and Marcy and at the same time that the document was his Will. This requirement would, therefore, appear to be satisfied.

Condition (d)

Chester signed the Will before the second witness arrived but Chester acknowledged his signature in Marcy's presence, after which Marcy appended her signature to the Will. This may be sufficient to satisfy the requirements.

However, there may be an argument that the Will is invalid on the grounds that conditions (c) and (d) were not followed in strict chronological order (*Couser v Couser* (1996)) since Chester acknowledged his signature to Harry before Harry acknowledged his signature to both Chester and Marcy.

In passing it may be noted that conditions (c) and (d) are relaxed in respect of Wills made between 31 January 2020 and 31 January 2024 to accommodate the restrictions on in-person contact during the COVID-19 pandemic (see www.gov.uk/guidance/guidance-on-making-wills-using-video-conferencing).

(3) On the assumption that s 9 has been complied with so that the Will is valid, it is then necessary to consider whether Chester, (who, being 15, and a minor when he witnessed the Will) was a capable witness.

The law does not stipulate a minimum age for a person to be witness; all that is required is that a witness should be aware of his actions and the effect of the Will. The witness should see and be conscious of the act done and be able to prove it by his own evidence (*Hudson v Parker* (1944)).

It is considered that this requirement was met so that, despite his age, Chester will be regarded as a capable witness.

(4) Harry's Will is, by virtue of s 18(1), automatically revoked by his marriage in July 2020 to Katie. However, Harry made an amendment to that Will at the wedding reception and that in turn was validly executed by virtue of s 21 which states:

> 'No obliteration, interlineation or other alteration made in any will after the execution thereof shall be valid or have any effect, except so far as the words or effect of the will before such alteration shall not be apparent, unless such alteration shall be executed in like manner as hereinbefore is required for the execution of the will; but the will, with such alteration as part thereof, shall be deemed to be duly executed if the signature of the testator and the subscription of the witnesses be made in the margin or on some other part of the will opposite or near to such alteration, or at the foot or end of or opposite to a memorandum referring to such alteration, and written at the end of some other part of the will.'

(5) However, perhaps a better and more logical interpretation of the events is that Harry had attempted to revive the January 2022 Will at the reception by the re-execution of the Will revoked on his marriage to Katie. The end result is that the Will is deemed to have been made at the time of the revival in accordance with s 34 which states:

> ' . . . every will re-executed or republished, or revived by any codicil, shall for the purposes of the Act be deemed to have been made at the time at which the same shall be so re-executed, republished, or revived . . . '

Accordingly, Katie will be able to inherit Harry's estate under his Will.

(6) Considering Chester's position, he was made a beneficiary under the revived Will; he was not a beneficiary under the original Will which he witnessed and which had been revoked by Harry's marriage. Consequently, s 15, which otherwise renders a gift to a witness null and void, does not apply in this circumstance.

Therefore, Chester will be able to inherit Harry's estate under the terms of the codicil to the Will.

Question

Susan, a widow, died in a car accident in August 2023. By her Will, which she made in 2006, she made the following legacies:

(1) £100,000 3% Treasury Stock 2027 to the churchwardens of St James, the local parish church.

(2) '*My 10,000 ordinary shares in Widget plc*' to her godson Peter.

(3) '*My 5,000 shares in Ferrets plc*' to her friend, Gladys.

(4) Her home '*Greenacres*' to her daughter Josephine.

The residue of her estate was left under her Will to her son Leon.

Susan's Executors establish the following:

- Susan did not own any Treasury Stock at her death.
- Susan sold her shareholding of 10,000 shares in Widget plc in 2022 but then repurchased 6,000 shares some six months later.
- Ferrrets plc was the subject of a takeover in January 2023 and in place of the original shareholding Susan received 2,000 shares in Whippets plc and cash of £8,000.
- Josephine had died in May 2020. She was survived by her husband, Tim and son Lucas. Tim who inherited all of Josephine's estate died in June 2022 and his son, Lucas died in the same car accident as his grandmother, Susan, in August 2023.
- Four weeks before her death, Susan has exchanged contracts to sell 'Greenacres' for £2.5 million but the contract had not completed at the time of her death.
- A week before her death, Susan executed a codicil by which she gave a legacy of £15,000 to her goddaughter Cerys but made no other changes to her Will.

Advise the Executors on the devolution of Susan's estate, explaining how the doctrines of ademption and lapse apply in the circumstances described.

Answer

(1) Ademption is a common law doctrine applicable in the law of wills to determine what happens when property bequeathed under a will is no longer in the testator's estate at the time of the testator's death.

If the intended recipient of a legacy in a will dies before the testator, the gift may lapse. This means that the gift is void and the property which is the subject-matter of the intended gift becomes part of the residue of the deceased's estate.

(2) The non-residual legacies will be treated in the following ways:

3% Treasury Stock 2027

This is not a specific legacy a Susan did not own any such Stock. Rather it forms the subject-matter of a general legacy and the executors are required actually to purchase the Stock for the churchwardens (*Bothamley v Sherson* (1875)).

It should be noted that the doctrine of ademption which applies only to specific legacies naturally influences the court to lean towards classifying a legacy as a general legacy in cases of doubt (*Re O'Connor* (1948)).

'My 10,000 ordinary shares in Widget plc'

Ademption applies only to a specific legacy which is generally defined as one where the subject matter can be clearly identified so as to distinguish it from the remainder of the estate; this is illustrated in this example by the use of the term 'my'. Although a Will speaks from the date of death, the subject-matter of a specific legacy is construed as referring to property that is in the testator's ownership at the date the Will is drawn up.

The gift to Peter is a specific legacy denoted by the use of 'my' in Susan's description of the property comprising the legacy. However, at the date of her death she does not own the 10,000 shares held by her when she executed her Will. Rather, having sold all of the shares originally owned, she now owns 6,000 shares albeit in the same company and of the same class. Although the shares can still be identified by name and are of the same type and class in the same company, they are not the exact same shareholding that was held at the time the Will was drawn up. Rather they represent a replacement of part of the original holding (*Re Gibson* (1866)).

The non-existence of the actual subject-matter of the specific legacy at date of death causes the legacy to adeem with the result the intended gift to the beneficiary (Peter) fails. He receives nothing and neither is he entitled to any compensation for the ademption of the legacy.

'My 5,000 shareholding in Ferrets plc'

The gift to Gladys is again a specific legacy. However, the stated shareholding in Ferrets plc was not that comprised in Susan's estate on her death. Rather at the date of her death the original shareholding has been replaced with another, the shares in Whippet plc – a replacement shareholding. The question that arises is whether the replacement shareholding, albeit having been compulsorily acquired under the terms of the takeover, save the specific legacy gift from ademption?

Where there has been a change in name and form only which leaves the actual asset itself fundamentally unaltered, ie where a company converts its stock to shares (*Oakes v Oakes* (1852)) there is no ademption. In this case, however, there was far more than a mere change of name and form; the Whippet plc shares are new shares in a different company accompanied by a cash distribution representing part of the value of the original holding in Ferrets plc (*Re Slater* (1907)).

The non-existence of the actual subject-matter of the specific legacy at date of death causes the legacy to adeem with the result the intended gift to the beneficiary (Gladys) fails. She receives nothing and neither is she entitled to any compensation for the ademption of the legacy.

Her home 'Greenacres'

Under Susan's Will the property, a specific legacy, was left to Josephine but as at the date of Susan's death the property is under contract for sale and the executors are bound to carry the sale through to completion. Prima facie the property would be treated as no longer comprised in Susan's estate at the date of her death and under the general rule of ademption the gift would fail.

However, Susan executed a codicil after entering into the contract for the sale of 'Greenacres' and this act is treated as a re-publication of the Will. Even though the codicil made no mention of or reference to the potential property sale, it is considered that the re-publication does provide sufficient ground to permit the £2.5 million sale proceeds to pass to Josephine in place of the original property. However, where a contract of sale is followed by a codicil which operates to re-publish the Will then there is a presumption that the testator intended the specific legatee to have either the property or the proceeds of its sale (*Re Calow* (1982)).

Having established that the sale proceeds do not adeem, the question that now arises is whether in fact those proceeds do pass otherwise than as part of the residue of Susan's estate given that Josephine predeceased Susan. Under the general rule, a gift to a beneficiary who predeceases the testator automatically lapses (*Elliott v Davenport* (1705)) and the re-publication of Susan's Will as described above would not on its own prevent this lapse (*Re Wood's Will* (1861)). However, the lapse may be saved by operation of Wills Act 1837, s 33 which states:

> '(1) Where –
> (a) a will contains a devise or bequest to child or remoter descendant of the testator; and
> (b) the intended beneficiary dies before the testator leaving issue; and
> (c) issue of the intended beneficiary are living at the testator's death,
>
> unless a contrary intention appears by the will, the devise or bequest shall take effect as a devise or bequest to the issue living at the testator's death . . . '

In this case, Josephine (Susan's child) died in 2020 and so predeceased Susan. However, at the time of Josephine's death she had a son, Lucas and so left issue as required by s 33(1)(b). The question however is whether, under s 33(c), Lucas, the issue of the intended beneficiary (Josephine) was living at the time of Susan's death. Lucas died in the same car crash and at the same time as Susan and so prima facie it would seem that this condition is not satisfied since Lucas (the issue of the intended beneficiary) did not outlive Susan (the testator). However, the issue is resolved by operation of the '*commorientes*' rule.

Where two or more persons die in circumstances where it is uncertain which of them survived the others the order of their deaths is determined by reference to the Law of Property Act 1925, s 84 (the '*commorientes*' rule). This rule provides that, the order of their deaths will be presumed to have occurred in the order of seniority (age) for all purposes affecting title to property.

By virtue of this rule, therefore, Susan, as the elder person, is presumed to have died before Lucas. Consequently Wills Act 1837, s 33(c) is met and, accordingly, the proceeds from the sale of '*Greenacres*' will pass to Lucas' estate and devolve under his Will.

If, it were shown that Susan had survived Lucas and has, say, died later that same day, s 33 would not apply and consequently the gift to Josephine would lapse and the £2.5 million proceed would fall into the residue of her estate and pass to Leon.

(3) The residue of Susan's estate (which will now include the shares in Widgets plc and ferrets plc, pass to Leon.

Question

A.

Elissa died in August 2023. She had made a Will without professional help. It contained the following three clauses:

(i) My house 'Farthings' to my relations.

(ii) £200,000 to my good friend Jenny Brown of Whitehill

(iii) The residue of my estate on trust for my sister Agatha for life and then for such of my nieces and nephews as attain 21 equally.

Elissa was a friend of both Jenny Brown who lived at Blackhill and Joan Brown, her sister, who lived at Whitehill.

At the time of her death, Elissa was survived by:

- Her sister Agatha.
- Three nieces (Belinda, Carol and Dora) all under age 18 and the daughters of her deceased sister Eva.
- A stepson, Francis who had a son, Gareth aged 21.

Agatha immediately disclaimed her interest under the Will.

Identify the issues that arise in respect of the interpretation of the terms of Elissa's Will and comment in detail on how those issues are likely to be resolved.

Answer

(1) **My house 'Farthings' to my relations**

The issues that arise in relation to this clause are as follows:

- Is there sufficient certainty with regard to the description of the beneficiary class?
- Does it create a trust or constitute an outright gift?
- Are there any practical problems that arise in giving effect to the gift?

On the assumption that Elissa did indeed have a house of that name at the time of her death, the property may pass to the named beneficiaries but the real issue is whether the term 'relations' is sufficiently precise so as to define the beneficiary class. As regarded a trust, a trust is validly established if, inter alia, there is a certainty of objects (ie beneficiaries) and this rule applies equally to gifts made under a Will. However, in relation to a Will, the rule is somewhat modified (*McPhail v Doulton* (1971)) so that it is necessary only to identify whether a person is or is not within the class of beneficiaries (conceptual certainty) rather than to establish all the potential beneficiaries that form the class (evidential certainty).

Accordingly, '*Farthings*' will be held on trust for sale under the Law of Property Act 1925, s 34 for the benefit of Elissa's relations as joint tenants.

Even so, in order for the clause to be valid, it is necessary that it passes the practical test of '*administrative workability*' as discussed in *McPhail v Doulton* (1971). In the light of this, it may be readily apparent that the class of beneficiaries is potentially too wide as to enable the clause to be practically operative.

Accordingly, the likelihood is that the gift will almost certainly fail.

(2) **£200,000 to my good friend Jenny Brown of Whitehill**

The issues that arise in relation to this clause are as follows:

- Is there any ambiguity as regards the bequest?
- If so how can it be resolved?
- Are there any ways in which any ambiguity may be resolved?

It is a fundamental rule of the interpretation of a Will that where the language used is clear and unequivocal there can be no conjecture or debate as to the intended meaning of the Wlil. Only in cases where interpretation is in doubt are the courts prepared to permit the admission of extrinsic evidence so as to giving meaning to a clause (*Careless v Careless* (1816)).

In this case it is unclear which of the Brown sisters, Elissa intended to benefit. The clause of Elissa's Will refers to Jenny Brown of Whitehill, yet it is Joan Brown who lives at Whitehill, Jenny living at Blackhill. The clause is therefore ambiguous.

In order to resolve the problem, a court may be persuaded to consider extrinsic evidence.

Alternatively, assistance may be provided under the rule in *Falsa Demonsta* which provides that an incorrect description of a gift may be ignored so as to enable the gift to be correctly given effect to (*Re Price* (1932)). In this instance, the word '*Jenny*' could be set aside so that the clause would then read '*Brown of Whitehill*' and evidence used to identify the beneficiary 'Brown' as Joan. However, it must be understood that access to this rule is limited; rather it can be used only where there is certainty as to which part of the description of a gift is incorrect. If this cannot be determined then this rule cannot be employed.

(3) **The residue of my estate on trust for my sister Agatha for life and then for such of my nieces and nephews as attain 21 equally**

1. What is meant by the term residue?

There is no ambiguity in what is meant by the term 'residue'. It means all of the assets of Elissa's estate that are not otherwise the subject of specific or general legacies.

2. What is the nature of that gift of residue?

The gift creates an interest in possession trust (which, for tax purposes will be a qualifying interest in possession known as an immediate post death Interest (IPDI)) in favour of Agatha for life with gifts over in remainder for Elissa's nieces and nephews who attain the age of 21 years. This constitutes a class gift in remainder as the beneficiaries (Elissa's nieces and nephews) are united by a common blood tie (*Kingsbury v Walter* (1901)).

3. When does the class close?

Generally speaking, under the rule in *Andrews v Partington* (1791), a class of beneficiaries closes when the first member of the class (Elissa's nieces and nephews) attains the relevant age. However, where there is an intermediate life interest (here in favour of Agatha) the rule in *Re Emmet's Estate* (1880) applies and postpones vesting until the later of the death of the life tenant or when the first of the remaindermen reaches age 21.

In this case, it is most likely that the class of remaindermen will not close until Agatha's death on the basis all beneficiaries will have turned 21 by that time. This will result in the inclusion as remaindemen of all Elissa's nephews and nieces born after her death who are alive at the date the class closes and who go on to satisfy the contingency by attaining age 21.

4. Does the gift in remainder create a joint tenancy or tenancy in common?

In the absence of words to the contrary, the gift will create a joint tenancy but on satisfaction of the contingency a beneficiary may convert their inherited share to a tenancy in common by severing the joint tenancy.

5. Is Elissa's stepson's son, Gareth, within the beneficiary class?

On a strict interpretation of the clause, Gareth is not within the beneficiary class since there is no direct blood tie between Elissa and Gareth and Gareth is not Elissa's nephew. That having said, it may be possible to argue that the term '*nephew*' was used by Elissa in a wider sense as a general description of certain persons (akin to a friend of the family being referred to as '*Uncle*') but on the facts there is no evidence to support such an argument. Furthermore, there is no obvious indication of ambiguity (*Gilmour v MacPhillamy* (1930)).

Accordingly, Gareth will not be within the defined class of beneficiaries and may not benefit under Elissa's Will.

6. What is the effect of Agatha's disclaimer?

It might be thought that the act of disclaimer has the immediate effect of advancing the interest of the vesting of the gift in remainder but this is not the case. Whilst this was suggested in the case of *Re Davies* (1957), the later cases of *Re Harker* (1969) and *Re Kebty-Fletcher* (1969) indicate that the class gift remains open until the death of Agatha, the life tenant. In other words the consequences of her disclaimer are ignored.

Accordingly, Agatha's disclaimer has no effect. This in turn means that any nieces and nephews of Elissa during born after her death but during Agatha's lifetime would form part of the class of remaindermen and so potentially benefit under Elissa's Will.

INDEX

References are to page numbers.

E

Tolley's

Taxwise Part II

Tolley's Taxwise is published as a two-volume set. These highly practical tax books offer expert guidance on how to approach real-life computations by providing all the relevant points from current legislation, case law and other official material. Both volumes include numerous worked examples with detailed explanatory notes enabling both tax practitioners and students to gain a thorough understanding of the relevant law and practice.

Tolley's Taxwise I and II are written by tax experts who are renowned not only for their technical skills but also for their ability to explain complex issues in simple terms. As tax practitioners and lecturers in taxation, the authors draw on their extensive knowledge of the UK tax system to include the most relevant worked examples with clear and detailed explanatory notes.

Their unique skills are combined here with the UK's leading tax publisher to provide you with all the information you need in the most accessible format.

Taxwise II 2023-24 is required reading for tax practitioners and students sitting professional tax examinations. This volume covers Inheritance Tax and Taxation of Trusts and Estates. The 2023-24 edition has been fully updated to reflect the latest changes.

What the press say about Tolley's Taxwise:

"...could hardly be bettered in its wide range of practical examples. Solutions are clearly laid out and amply explained." Journal of the Law Society of Scotland

"...it is hard to see how any serious student could do without this valuable book. The explanatory notes are far more comprehensive than could reasonably be expected and for general practitioners these explanatory notes themselves are well worth the price of the book." Tax Adviser

ISBN 978-0-7545-5912-2

9 780754 559122

Tolley® Tax intelligence from LexisNexis®

Lexis House, 30 Farringdon Street, London EC4A 4HH | 0330 161 1234